Handbook of Post-Western Sociology: From East Asia to Europe

Post-Western Social Sciences and Global Knowledge

Series Editor

Laurence Roulleau-Berger (CNRS/ENS *de Lyon*)

Editorial Board

Chang Kuyng-Sup (*Seoul National University*)
Han Sang-Jin (*Seoul National University*)
Svetla Koleva (*Institute for the Study of Societies and Knowledge, Sofia*)
T.N. Madan (*University of Delhi*)
Nira Wickramasinghe (*Leiden University*)
Shujiro Yasawa (*Seijo University*)
Toshio Sugiman (*Kyoto University*)
Qu Jingdong (*Peking University*)
Xie Lizhong (*Peking University*)

VOLUME 5

The titles published in this series are listed at *brill.com/psgk*

Handbook of Post-Western Sociology: From East Asia to Europe

Edited by

Laurence Roulleau-Berger
Li Peilin
Kim Seung Kuk
Yazawa Shujiro

BRILL

LEIDEN | BOSTON

Cover illustration: "Constellations" painting by Frances Berger, 2022. Courtesy of the artist.

The Library of Congress Cataloging-in-Publication Data is available online at https://catalog.loc.gov

Typeface for the Latin, Greek, and Cyrillic scripts: "Brill". See and download: brill.com/brill-typeface.

ISSN 2352-5827
ISBN 978-90-04-52931-1 (hardback)
ISBN 978-90-04-52932-8 (e-book)

Copyright 2022 by Laurence Roulleau-Berger, Li Peilin, Kim Seung Kuk and Yazawa Shujiro. Published by Koninklijke Brill NV, Leiden, The Netherlands.
Koninklijke Brill NV incorporates the imprints Brill, Brill Nijhoff, Brill Hotei, Brill Schöningh, Brill Fink, Brill mentis, Vandenhoeck & Ruprecht, Böhlau, V&R unipress and Wageningen Academic.
Koninklijke Brill NV reserves the right to protect this publication against unauthorized use. Requests for re-use and/or translations must be addressed to Koninklijke Brill NV via brill.com or copyright.com.

This book is printed on acid-free paper and produced in a sustainable manner.

Contents

Preface   XIII
Acknowledgments   XX
List of Figures and Tables   XXI
Notes on Contributors   XXV

Introduction: Post-Western Sociology   1
  Laurence Roulleau-Berger

PART 1
Post-Western Social Sciences: From East Asia to Europe

SECTION 1
Toward Post-Western Social Sciences

1   Toward Post-Western Sociology   21
    Laurence Roulleau-Berger

2   The Emergence and Characteristics of Chinese Sociology   48
    Li Peilin

3   What Are Post-Western Sociologies?   61
    Xie Lızhong

4   The Oneness Logic: Toward an East Asian General Theory   90
    Kim Seung Kuk

5   To Create a Post-Western Sociology: A Brief Sketch of Japanese Sociology   124
    Yazawa Shujiro

SECTION 2
Non-hegemonic Traditions and Pluralism in Asian Social Sciences

6   Chinese Sociology: Traditions and Dialogues – Localized Knowledge Production as Post-Western Sociology   143
    Li Youmei

7   Development of Sociological Thought in the Early Modern Period of Japan   157
    Yama Yoshiyuki

8   Sociological Sinicization: A Chinese Effort in Post-Western Sociology   171
    Zhou Xiaohong and Feng Zhuqin

9   Proposing a Global Sociology Based on Japanese Theories   198
    Shoji Kōkichi

10 De-Westernization or Re-Easternization: Towards Post-Western Conceptualization and Theorization in the Sociology of Korea   218
    Lim Hyun-Chin

11 Cosmopolitan Sociology: A Significant Step But Not the Final Task for Post-Western Sociology   233
    Kim Mun Cho

SECTION 3
Heritages and "Re-Asiatization" of Social Sciences

12 Chinese Economic Sociology: From the Perspective of Post-Western Sociology   251
    Yang Dian

13 Thirty Years of Labor Sociology in China   274
    Shen Yuan

14 Voice of the Dead: Hibakusha Collective Memory against the Western Ethos   292
    Nomiya Daishiro

CONTENTS

15   COVID-19 and Hegemonic Modernity: Post-Western Sociological
     Imaginations   306
       Han Sang-Jin

16   Wanderers and the Settled: Perspectives of Kunio Yanagita and Kazuko
     Tsurumi on Social Change   326
       Okumura Takashi

SECTION 4
Epistemic Autonomies and Located Knowledge

17   Case Studies towards the Analysis of Total Social Construction   349
       Qu Jingdong

18   Risk Governance, Publicness, and the Quality of the Social   374
       Yee Jaeyeol

19   The Korean Wave as a Glocal Cultural Phenomenon: Addressing the
     New Trends in Korean Studies   398
       Jang Wonho

20   Development of Critical Theory Based on the Analysis of Literary Works
     on Tenderness: Habermas's Thesis and Akira Kurihara's Work   413
       Deguchi Takeshi

21   From Social Equilibrium to Self-Production of Society: The Transition of
     China's Sociological Recognition on China's Society   429
       Sun Feiyu

22   Sociology without Society: The Dreyfus Affair, the Taigyaku Affair,
     and the Sociology of Life   447
       Kikutani Kazuhiro

23   Weber "Fever" in China (1980–2020): Scholarly Communication and
     Discipline Construction   464
       He Rong

PART 2
Translation and Ecologies of Knowledge: Dialogues East–West

SECTION 5
Globalization and Social Classes

24   Wealthization and Housing Wealth Inequality in China   487
       Li Chunling

25   Squeezing the Western Middle Class: Precarization, Uncertainty and Tensions of Median Socioeconomic Groups in the Global North   495
       Louis Chauvel

26   A New Approach to Social Inequality: Inequality of Income and Wealth   510
       Shin Kwang-Yeong

27   Globalization and Social Inequality in the Context of Japan   530
       Sato Yoshimichi

SECTION 6
Youth and Education

28   Educational Expansion and Its Impacts on Youth in Transitional China   545
       Wu Yuxiao

29   Exploring Educational Institutions' Major Roles and Norms to Understand Their Effects: The Example of France   559
       Agnès van Zanten

30   Youth and Transition from School to Work in Japan   569
       Asano Tomohiko

31   Education as an Institution and a Practice: Issues and Perspectives in Korean Sociology   580
       Kim Byoung-Kwan

SECTION 7
State and Governance

32 Urban Renewal, Urban Restructuring: The City as Inescapable Western Representation   597
    Agnès Deboulet

33 State and Society in Urban Renewal and Social Governance   605
    Shi Yunqing

34 The State, Civil Society, and Citizens through Local Governance in Japan   616
    Yamamoto Hidehiro

SECTION 8
Ethnicity and Space

35 The Border of Ethnicity Worlds   629
    Ahmed Boubeker

36 Ethnicity, Space, and Boundary-Making among the Hui in Nanjing   641
    Fan Ke

37 Considering Super-diversity in Immigration: Post-Western Sociology and the Japanese Case   664
    Tarumoto Hideki

38 Spatial Confinement of Migrant Workers in Korea   677
    Choi Jongryul

SECTION 9
Social Movements and Collective Action

39 Contributions of Japanese Environmental Sociology in Non-Western Contexts   691
    Hasegawa Koichi

40 Social Movements and Collective Action   710
   Lilian Mathieu

41 State's Temperament and the Control of Collective Action in Contemporary China   719
   Feng Shizheng

SECTION 10
Gender and Inequalities

42 Gender and Inequalities in France   731
   Christine Détrez

43 Changing Gender Dynamics and Family Reinstitutionalization in Contemporary China   741
   Ji Yingchun

44 Revisiting Comparative Frameworks and Gender Inequality in Japan   752
   Nemoto Kumiko

45 Two Contradictory Trends in Korea in the COVID-19 Era: "Condensed Radicalization of Individualization" and "Community Orientation"   761
   Shim Young-Hee

SECTION 11
Environment and Mistrust Crisis

46 How Ecological Civilization Contributes to Post-Western Sociology   779
   Wang Xiaoyi and Anier

47 The Post-Western Anthropocene   786
   Paul Jobin

48 East Asian Compressed Ecological Modernization: Modus of Developmental State and Technological Response to the Environmental Crisis   799
   Satoh Keiichi

49 The Legacy of the Developmental State and the Rise of Fragmented Green Growth   812
    Hong Deokhwa and Ku Dowan

SECTION 12
Individuation, Self, and Emotions

50 Management, Experience, and Performance: Emotional Regimes in Contemporary Society   823
    Cheng Boqing and Wang Jiahui

51 The Individual and Society: The End of an Alliance and the Burden of Emotions   840
    François Dubet

52 From the Deepest Dimension to Society   848
    Yazawa Shujiro

53 Emotions of Fear, Anger, and Disgust in Contemporary Korean Society   859
    Kim Wang-Bae

SECTION 13
Cities, Migration, and Work

54 Beyond "Post-Western" Urban Studies   883
    Machimura Takashi

55 Sociology of Migration and Post-Western Knowledge   893
    Laurence Roulleau-Berger

56 Social Integration of China's Floating Population   907
    Wang Chunguang and Lu Wen

SECTION 14
Global Health and New Future

57 Global Health Challenges and a New Future   921
    Zhao Yandong and Hong Yanbi

58 East–West Dialogue for Global Health Care Challenges in the Era of
    COVID-19 and Beyond   928
    Hosoda Miwako

59 Expanding Epidemic Preparedness to Include Population Memory:
    A Key for Better Epidemic Management   937
    Frédéric Le Marcis

60 South Korea Has Controlled the COVID-19 Outbreak But Failed to
    Prepare Accountable Hospitals and Doctors   956
    Cho Byong-Hee

Conclusion   978
    Laurence Roulleau-Berger, Li Peilin, Kim Seung Kuk and Yazawa Shujiro

Postface   995
    Sari Hanafi

Index   999

Preface

1 The Proposal and Development of Post-Western Sociology (*by* Li Peilin)

Post-Western sociology was proposed nearly a decade ago. In 2006 when I served as the Director of the Institute of Sociology, Chinese Academy of Social Sciences (CASS), my friend, Professor Laurence Roulleau-Berger, Research Director at National Centre for Scientific Research of France (CNRS), École Normale Supérieure of Lyon, as a visiting professor, visited me in Beijing. In 2012, we decided to establish an International Associated Laboratory (LIA)[1] "Post-Western Sociology in Europe and in China" jointly established by the French National Center for Scientific Research (CNRS), the École Normale Supérieure (ENS) of Lyon and the Chinese Academy of Social Sciences (CASS). Professor Laurence Roulleau-Berger put forward the concept of "post-Western sociology" when we discussed the name of the laboratory. To be honest, I was astonished because "post-Western sociology" was excitative. However, I was also afraid that the concept could be interpreted as opposed to Western sociology and like "postmodernism" and "post-structuralism", it might imply subversion and deconstruction. Professor Laurence Roulleau-Berger insisted, saying that it was the inevitable future of international sociology, and her French colleagues were convinced that this was a creative and potential research field. On the 9th and 10th of November in 2013, CASS, CNRS and ENS jointly held a first opening international conference in Beijing, followed by a second conference in Lyon in January 2014 focused on "Traditions and controversies in trajectories of sociology in Europe and in China". As such, the LIA *Post-Western Sociology and Fieldwork in China and France* was created. Chinese partners included the Department of Sociology of Beijing University, the School of Social and Behavioral Sciences of Nanjing University, and the School of Sociology and Political Science of Shanghai University from China and several French universities.

It was not a coincidence for Professor Laurence Roulleau-Berger to suggest post-Western sociology. Although being interested in non-Western and oriental sociology, especially Chinese sociology, she is first a sociologist and not a

---

1 The LIA is now called the International Advanced Laboratory (IAL) ENS Lyon-Chinese Academy of Social Sciences, *Post-Western Sociology in Europe and in China* since 2021 January the 1st. Professor Li Peilin, Director of the Academic Division of Law, Social and Political Studies of CASS (Peking) and Professor Laurence Roulleau-Berger, Research Director at CNRS are the IAL's co-directors.

traditional sinologist. In 2006, she came to the Institute of Sociology, where I worked, for research as a visiting professor for one year. We quickly became friends, perhaps because I obtained my doctorate in France and began our partnership that lasted over ten years. Professor Laurence Roulleau-Berger is a rarely seen French scholar who lives for work. For more than a decade, we held many international conferences in France and China and co-edited works in English, French, and Chinese, including *La nouvelle Sociologie Chinoise* (CNRS Editions, 2008), *European and Chinese Sociologies: A new dialogue* (Brill, 2012), *China's Internal and International Migration* (Routledge, 2013), and *Ecological Risks and Disasters—New Experience in China and Europe* (Routledge, 2016). Among them, *La Nouvelle Sociologie Chinoise* exerted a strong influence on French sociologists, since Chinese sociology today had never been introduced so comprehensively before, and many people did not even know it existed. Professor Michel Wieviorka, former President of International Sociological Association (ISA), wrote in the conclusion of this book, "Chinese sociology is developings well and is both dynamic and 'global' in the meaning of word: it is rooted in the study of problems in its own society, but also integrated into high-level global discussions" (Roulleau-Berger, Li, Guo and Liu 2008: 489).

Concerning the study of Post-Western sociology, Professor Laurence Roulleau-Berger, invited by Professor Michel Wieviorka, Editor-in-Chief of *Socio*, offered nine articles on post-Western social sciences for the fifth issue of *Socio* in 2015. Out of the nine articles, she wrote "Post-Western Sociology—From China to Europe" and I wrote "Oriental Modernization and China Experience". In 2017, Professor Xie Lizhong from Beijing University and Professor Laurence Roulleau-Berger co-edited *The Fabric of Sociological Knowledge: The Exploration of Post-Western Sociology* (Peking University Press, 2017) in Chinese. In 2018, she invited me to co-edit *Post-Western Sociology—From China to Europe* (Routledge, 2018), writing the introduction entitled *Doing Post-Western Sociology* and one chapter *Post-Western Sociology and Global Revolution*.

Two years later in 2020, Professor Laurence Roulleau-Berger suggested that I work with her to edit the *Handbook of Post-Western Sociology*, saying that it had been included in Brill's publishing plan.

Yet, we wished to deepen our understanding of post-Western theory and invited Professor Kim Seung Kuk from South Korea and Professor Yazawa Shujiro from Japan to join us. Sociologists from these two countries and China had established a stable network over the past two decades with the aim to develop East Asian sociology, which is consistent with the orientation of post-Western sociology. We invited around 60 sociologists from France, China, South Korea, and Japan to work on this book.

What I want to point out is that although representing a new trend in the development of international sociology under the background of globalization, post-Western sociology cannot be regarded as a systematic theory composed of basic assumptions, core concepts, and analytical logic. Therefore, in *Handbook of Post-Western Sociology*, we included different understanding of post-Western sociology. In my view, post-Western sociology has several meanings. First, in non-Western countries, especially developing countries, sociology was introduced from Western countries. In a sense, Western sociology is equivalent to classical and mainstream sociology, so it is easy to use their sociological theories to explain the diverse development experience of various countries, but the aim of post-Western sociology is to reshape contemporary sociology based on the new development experience of different countries. Second, post-Western sociology is for innovation, development, and reconstruction, instead of rejection, subversion, confrontation, and deconstruction. Third, post-Western sociology is an open, inclusive, and future-oriented academic system. It will incorporate new research findings based on fresh development experience, to shape a new sociology, which can include a wider range of international experience, especially development experience from non-Western countries.

2 Toward Non-hegemonic Sociology and Post-Western Theory (*by Laurence Roulleau-Berger*)

For several centuries, the history of the West has been synonymous with the history of the world. The global economy of knowledge is structured around epistemic and hegemonic inequalities and domination. For over two decades, social sciences conceived in Western worlds have lost their hegemony. This historical moment in global thought called into question the conditions of production of universalist and tautological narratives. We are witnessing a "global turning point", distinct from previous turning points, that emerges as a *watershed moment* in the history of social sciences. Western cultural and social hegemonies in practice did not promote the recognition of non-Western social sciences. There was a type of epistemological, ethical and political indecency in Western worlds that ignored non-hegemonic social sciences. As such, the majority of intellectuals in the Western world are unfamiliar with sociologists in Asia, Chinese, Japanese and Korean scholars in particular. They are unaware that prior to 1949, social sciences and sociology in China were established disciplines and that the study of society has been practiced in China for as long as it has in the West, and that the reinvention of sociology in 1978 represents a landmark event in the history of humanities and social sciences.

In 2002, I started conducting research programs in China by adopting a multi-situated sociological stance between Europe and China, creating a transnational theoretical and empirical space. In 2006, when I was visiting professor at the Institute of Sociology, Chinese Academy of Social Sciences (CASS) in Beijing headed by Professor Li Peilin, who became in 2013 vice-President of the CASS, I realized the scope of what we did not but should know about Chinese sociology; it was therefore clear that we needed to reconsider the hegemony of Western social sciences from a Chinese perspective. First of all, it seemed essential to discover the new Chinese sociology recreated since 1979. To this end, as mentioned by Professor Li Peilin, he, Guo Yuhua, Liu Shiding and myself co-edited *La nouvelle sociologie chinoise*, published in 2008 by the CNRS Publishers.

From 2006 onwards with Professor Li Peilin, sociologists from the CASS, the Beijing University (Beijing), the Tsinghua University (Peking) and the Renmin University of China (Beijing) we started drawing the outlines of a dialogic space between Chinese and European sociology. This collaboration was structured around reflecting on the de-Westernization of social sciences in order to progress beyond the East/West dichotomies and binary thought. In 2012, I came to speak of post-Western sociology to pursue our shared reflection on non-hegemonic sociology. My friend Professor Li Peilin and I had many intense and rich discussions. And when I suggested the name Post-Western Sociology for this collaboration as a process of circulation and co-production of knowledge between European and Chinese sociologies (Roulleau-Berger 2016), Professor Li Peilin would have preferred another name, as "post" is a fashionable prefix, and Post-Western Sociology could be interpreted as being opposed to Western sociology. I did agree. Later in 2013, following fruitful discussions with our Chinese colleagues Xie Lizhong, He Rong, Li Youmei, Liu Neng, Liu Yuzhao, Shen Yuan, Sun Feiyu, Qu Jingdong, Yang Yiyin … and French colleagues Ahmed Boubeker, Agnès Deboulet, Christine Détrez, Michel Kokoreff, Michel Lallement, Danilo Martuccelli, Paula Vasquez† … we concluded that we could not find a better concept at this stage.

Consequently, in last fifteen years, we have organized many conferences and workshops and have published several books; some of which have already been mentioned by Professor Li Peilin. We developed increasingly transversal Sino-French perspectives on different topics in the several books mentioned above. In 2014, Liu Shiding and I had already co-edited *Sociologies économiques française et chinoise : regards croisés*. We carried out a cross-sectional study on internal and international migration in China and France through various research programs in order to enable Chinese and Western sociologists to better understand and practice the concept of Post-Western sociology. In addition, Professor Liu Yuzhao and I co-edited *Sociology of Migration and Post-Western Theory*, ENS Publishers, 2021.

All scholars involved agreed that Post-Western sociology should not be confused with non-Western, de-Western, and anti-Western sociology. Professor Xie Lizhong put forward "Post-Western Sociologies", referring to several sociological systems constructed by Western and non-Western sociologists. We, the Chinese and French scholars, also shared fieldwork experiences in China and France, made it crystal clear in each step how Post-Western Sociology was different from Post-Colonial sociology, international sociology, and global sociology. It is meant to open an epistemological and multi-situated space where the circulation of concepts and theories prevents dichotomies between Western and non-Western knowledge. We decided to establish a scientific program for the co-production of Post-Western sociology in order to open an "equal" dialogue on shared theories and theories situated in China and Europe. We started organizing how to define the meaning of Post-Western Sociology. In recent years, we have invited international sociologists with a wealth of experience studying non-hegemonic sociologies to join us, including Professors Yazawa Shujiro, Nomiya Daishiro and Yama Yoshiyuki from Japan; Professor Kim Seung-Kuk, Chang Kyung-Sup, Han Sang-Jin and Shim Young-Hee from South Korea; and Professor Svetla Koleva from Bulgaria.

The CNRS Institute for Humanities and Social Sciences and the École Normale Supérieure of Lyon strongly supported this LIA, convinced that it would have an international impact. The CNRS and the ENS of Lyon played a key role in opening a space for scientific collaboration with the Chinese Academy of Social Sciences, the Universities of Beijing, Shanghai and Nanjing with the creation of the LIA in 2013. We created an epistemological and multi-situated space where the circulation of concepts and theories prevents dichotomies between Western and non-Western knowledge.

Few sociologists endeavor to decenter their gaze to look over the other side of the knowledge boundaries. The release of Edward Saïd's work *Orientalism, the East created by the West* represented a milestone in the history of postcolonial thought. Orientalism had meant the implementation of systems that trapped, captured, oriented gestures, discourses and points of view by seizing "inert" knowledge and incorporate and enclose it in subfields. Post-colonial discourse was based on the idea of provincializing Europe with Chakrabarty and considering the "subaltern histories" with Spivak according to their own value, it had played a crucial role these past 30 years in the challenging Western hegemonies. A growing consensus then emerged around the idea of the crisis of Western civilization.

Post-Western sociology is based on a political ecology of sociological knowledge where diverse knowledges can enter into an articulated dialogue in emancipatory cosmovisions and practices. It is based on the location of common and situated theories between the diversity of "Westernized West", "non-Westernized West", "Easternized East", "Westernized re-oriented East" in order to go beyond hegemonic social sciences and produce post-Western thought. From this ecology of knowledge we can observe, on one hand, the multiplication of epistemic autonomies vis-à-vis Western hegemonies, and, on another hand, epistemic assemblages between European and Asian sociologies. So we can open a Post-Western Space in a creolization process where "Western" and "non-Western" knowledges do interact.

This Handbook is a part of an intense and successful scientific cooperation between Chinese, French, Japanese and Korean sociologists.

References

Li, Peilin, and Roulleau-Berger, Laurence, eds. 2013. *China's internal and international migration*. London and New York: Routledge.

Li, Peilin, and Roulleau-Berger, Laurence, eds. 2016. *Ecological risks and disasters—New experience in China and Europe*. London and New York: Routledge.

Liu Shiding; Roulleau-Berger, Laurence; and Zhang Wenhong, eds. 2020. *The expansion of Economic Sociology. Towards a More Inclusive Practice*. Peking: Social Sciences Academic Press.

Roulleau-Berger, Laurence, dir. 2015. "Inventer les sciences sociales post-occidentales : de l'Asie à l'Europe". *Socio*, n°5.

Roulleau-Berger, Laurence. 2016. *Post-Western Sociology. From China to Europe*. Leiden and Boston: Brill Publishers.

Roulleau-Berger, Laurence, ed. 2021. "Post-Western Sociology". *The Journal of Chinese Sociology* (July 2021), Springer.

Roulleau-Berger, Laurence, and Li, Peilin, eds. 2012. *European and Chinese sociologies: A new dialogue*. Leiden and Boston: Brill Publishers.

Roulleau-Berger, Laurence, and Li, Peilin, eds. 2018. *Post-western sociology—From China to Europe*. London and New York: Routledge.

Roulleau-Berger, Laurence; Li, Peilin; Guo Yuhua; and Liu Shiding, eds. 2008. *La nouvelle sociologie chinoise*. Paris: CNRS Editions.

Roulleau-Berger, Laurence, and Liu Neng, dir. 2017. "*Compressed modernity* et temporalités dans la Chine contemporaine". *Temporalités* n°26, n°2.

Roulleau-Berger, Laurence, and Liu Shiding. 2014. *Sociologies économiques française et chinoise : regards croisés*. Lyon: ENS Editions.

Roulleau-Berger, Laurence, and Liu Yuzhao. 2021. *Sociology of Migration and Post-Western Theory*. Lyon: ENS Publishers.

Xie, Lizhong, and Roulleau-Berger, Laurence, eds. 2017. *Construction of sociological knowledge: An exploration of post Western Sociology* (in Chinese). Beijing: Press of Peking University.

Acknowledgments

We would like to thank very much Meredith McGroarty for her excellent and highly professional editing work.

We would like to thank very much the CNRS Research Center Triangle UMR 5206, École Normale Supérieure of Lyon, for its financial support in the realization of this Handbook.

We are very grateful to Pierre Manoury, PhD Student, Triangle, for his contribution to the editorial work.

Figures and Tables

Figures

4.1	One-three differentiation (三數分化)	99
4.2	One-two differentiation	101
10.1	The historical development of Korean sociology	222
15.1	Global average of evaluation of COVID-19 performance by each city's citizens (June 2020)	317
15.2	The United States' image as assessed by the global average of each city's citizens (June 2020)	317
15.3	The United States' image as assessed by the global average of each city's citizens (September 2020)	317
15.4	The United States' image as assessed by the global average of each city's citizens (September 2021)	318
15.5	The state image of the United States and China by global citizens (June 2020)	319
15.6	The state image of the United States and China by global citizens (September 2020)	319
15.7	The state image of the United States and China by global citizens (September 2021)	319
15.8	Index of the civilizational axis moving to East Asia (September 2021)	323
18.1	Four components of publicness and pursuing values	380
18.2	Typology of a social system	390
18.3	Types of publicness and risk governance	393
19.1	The process of glocal culture development	400
24.1	Rapid growth of family housing wealth in urban China (1988–2019). Data source: The Chinese Household Income Project (CHIP) and Chinese Social Survey (CSS)	488
24.2	Trends of income and housing wealth Gini coefficient in China (1981–2017). Source: The data of Income Gini coefficients are from the National Bureau of Statistics of China. The data of housing wealth Gini coefficients are from the Chinese Household Income Project (CHIP) and Chinese Social Survey (CSS)	489
24.3	Source of housing property in different years (%). Data source: The Chinese Household Income Project (CHIP) and Chinese Social Survey (CSS)	491
24.4	A new social stratification created by wealthization	492

25.1 Population shares in poverty (lightest grey, incomes below 50% of the median), in affluence (darkest fray, incomes above 150% of the median), and in the middle class (medium grey, neither in poverty nor affluence) based on equivalized disposable income circa 1985 and 2020   497
25.2 The "Bourdieusian diamond" in twenty-first century Western societies   498
26.1 Distribution of earnings and housing ownership, 2017   519
26.2 Joint distribution of income and wealth in 2017   519
26.3 Debt by income decile   524
27.1 Temporal change in income inequality by county   531
27.2 Relationship between global forces, local institutions, and social stratification and mobility   532
27.3 Temporal change in non-regular employment rate by gender   534
27.4 Temporal change in non-regular employment rate by firm size   537
28.1 Gross enrollment rate and enrollment size of higher education in China, 1990–2019   546
28.2 Enrollment size of higher education in different types of degree in China, 1990–2019   547
28.3 Gender disparities in educational attainment in China by cohort   548
28.4 Urban–rural divide in educational attainment in China by cohort   550
28.5 Disparities in educational attainment in China by parents' education and occupation   550
28.6 Predicted effects of fathers' ISEI and parents' education on children's probabilities of entering college in 1996, 2006, and 2015   551
28.7 Proportions of "never married" among Chinese youth (aged 18–35) for years between 2003 and 2015, by gender   554
28.8 Average age of first marriage for Chinese youth (aged 18–35) for years between 2003 and 2015, by gender   555
28.9 Rates of labor force participation for Chinese youth (aged 18–35) for years between 2003 and 2015, by gender   556
37.1 Foreign population in Japan (thousands)   667
37.2 Foreign schoolchildren needing Japanese instruction   668
37.3 Foreign workers by residential status   670
45.1 Degree of individualization by city   766
45.2 Degree of community orientation (total, male, female), 2021   769
45.3 Comparison of individualization index and community orientation, 2021   770
45.4 Ideal and expected number of children and the difference by city   772
50.1 The figure of the relationship among three emotional regimes   832
54.1 Urban population at mid-year, 1950–2050, by world region and Asian subregion (thousands)   886

58.1   Ministry of Health, Labor and Welfare's poster calling for prevention of the spread of the new coronavirus infection (April 2020)   933
58.2   The main gate of Zojoji Temple in Minato Ward, Tokyo   934
58.3   *Gosyuin* at Kokuryo Shrine in Chofu City, Tokyo   934
59.1   Gender-starred age pyramid, sub-Saharan Africa, 2019   938
59.2   Mortality, fatality, PCR test: Guinea, Burkina Faso, Sierra Leone (December to July 2020)   943
59.3   Incidence, number of reported deaths: Guinea, Sierra Leone, Burkina Faso (December to July 2020)   943

Tables

4.1   Differentiation of the Oneness and Constitution of the Oneness Logic   100
4.2   Ontological Level   106
4.3   Hybridization   108
4.4   Solipsist and spiritual individualism: One Mind   110
4.5   The middle way for love: a normative theory of action   113
15.1   The following statements describe how COVID-19 is changing the world. How strongly do you agree or disagree with each statement?   321
15.2   The following survey items are concerned with a comparative assessment of the United States and China with regard to COVID-19 health governance. On a scale from 1 to 10, please identify the point you feel most closely matches your opinion   321
15.3   Aspects of global change from the COVID-19 pandemic (September 2020)   322
18.1   Comparison of K type and W type   387
19.1   The number of YouTube views of the top K-Pop groups from October 2020 to October 2021   402
19.2   Idol groups outside of Korea inspired by K-Pop   402
26.1   Measurement of income inequality and wealth inequality, 2017   517
26.2   Descriptive summary of major variables ($N = 18{,}497$)   520
26.3   Household income inequality decomposed through multivariate variables (%)   523
26.4   Wealth inequality decomposed through multivariate variables (%)   525
29.1   Main features of people-changing and people-processing organizations according to Hasenfeld (1972)   560
29.2   Distinctive features of contest and sponsorship according to Turner (1960)   561
37.1   Foreign population in Japan by countries of origin (thousands)   667

37.2	Types of diversity and beyond	673
39.1	Contents of the Japanese environmental textbook	693
39.2	Contents of the US environmental textbook	693
41.1	The use of "mass incident" in 1994	722
45.1	Degree of individualization by three questions on marriage, children, and divorce: based on answers to the question "How strongly do you agree or disagree with the following statements?" 2021	764
45.2	Individualization score in terms of marriage, children, and divorce in Seoul, 2012	765
45.3	The following questions are related to the value of family, children, and work. To what extent do you agree or disagree about the following statements? (mean score by city) 2021	767
45.4	Mean score of community orientation, 2021	769
45.5	Comparison of individualization index and the degree of community orientation of some East Asian and Southeast Asian cities, 2021	770
45.6	Expected and ideal number of children of women by marital status	771
48.1	Greenhouse gas emissions and economic indicators in East Asia (2018)	802
48.2	Total energy supply in West and East countries	804

Notes on Contributors

Anier

is Lecturer at China University of Political Science and Law, postdoc of Institute of Sociology at Chinese Academy of Social Sciences. Her research interest covers economic anthropology, the transformation of nomadism and the reform of grassland property right. Her main publications include "Revisiting Grassland Contracting Policy: A Discussion of Demsetz's Theory of Land Property Right", *Social Sciences in Yunnan*, vol. 233, no. 1 (2020); and "Rethinking about the Mobility: A Review of the End of Nomadism?" *Inner Mongolia Social Sciences*, vol. 40, no. 2 (2019).

Asano Tomohiko

is Professor of Education Department at Tokyo Gakugei University in Tokyo, Japan. His research interest is the process of communication and identity construction of young people. His representative works are: "Multiple Selves of University Students and its Determinants", *Bulletin of Tokyo Gakugei University. Humanities and Social Sciences*, vol. 73 (in Japanese, 2022); "Are digital natives polarizing?" in Daisuke Tsuji, ed., *Net society and Democracy* (in Japanese, Keiso Shobo, 2021); "Otaku culture and gender", *Bulletin of Tokyo Gakugei University. Humanities and Social Sciences*, vol. 72 (in Japanese, 2021); "Agency and rights in youth (Japan)", *Bloomsbury Education and Childhood Studies* (2021).

Ahmed Boubeker

is Professor of sociology and deputy director of "Centre Max Weber" laboratory at Lyon University. His research interests are sociology of migrations, ethnicity, and postcolonial studies. His representative works are: *De Tokyo à Kinshasa. Postmodernité et postcolonialisme* (Editions L'harmattan, 2021); *Les Plissures du social. Des circonstances de l'ethnicité dans une société fragmentée* (Presses Universitaires de Lorraine, 2016); *Les non lieux des immigrations en Lorraine. Mémoire et invisibilité sociale* (Presses Universitaires de Lorraine, 2016); *Les mondes de l'ethnicité* (Balland, 2003); and *Familles de l'intégration* (Stock, 1999).

Louis Chauvel

is Professor of Sociology and Population Studies (University of Luxembourg), Head of the Institute for Research on Socio-Economic Inequality (IRSEI) (2012–today). He had been General Secretary of the European sociological association and member of the Executive Committee of the international sociological association. His main research interests are the dynamics of inequality, social generations and birth cohorts, social and public health and population dynamics (health, wellbeing, suicide, etc.), middle class stability, social policy sustainability, and income/wealth imbalances. His work has been published in journals like *European Sociological Review*, *Social Forces*, *Higher Education*, etc., and he published three books on generations and middle classes: *Destin des générations* (PUF, 1998); *Classes moyennes à la dérive* (Seuil, 2006); and *La spirale du déclassement* (Seuil, 2016).

Cheng Boqing
is Professor and Dean of School of Social and Behavioral Sciences at Nanjing University. His main research fields are theoretical sociology, social governance, sociology of emotions, and history of sociology. He has published such books as *Georg Simmel: The Diagnosis of Modernity* (Hangzhou University Press, 1999); *Out of Modernity: The Reorientation of Contemporary Western Sociological Theory* (Social Sciences Academic Press, 2006); *Emotion, Narrative and Rhetoric: Explorations in Social Theory* (China Social Sciences Press, 2012). His representative papers include "Passion and Society: An Exposition of Marx's Sociology of Emotions", *Sociological Studies*, no. 4 (2017); "Sociological Analysis of contemporary emotional system", *Social Sciences in China*, no. 5 (2017); and "Self, Intermediary, and Society—The Internet as an Emotional machine", *Fujian Tribune*, no. 10 (2021).

Cho Byong-Hee
received a doctorate in sociology from University of Wisconsin-Madison. He served as a professor at Graduate School of Public Health, Seoul National University, and is now an Emeritus professor. He has mainly written papers on medical power and physician behaviors. Recently, he wrote a paper titled "The change of Korean doctor's professionalism and their dominance over health care system" in 2019. Another concern is overcoming the medicalized society. In this regard, he edited a book *Beyond a Sick Society-Developing a Concept of Social Welling* in 2018. Another paper deals with social conflicts over AIDS, titled "Why are Korean protestant churches hostile to homosexuality and AIDS?" in 2018. The most recent co-authored paper is about COVID-19, titled "Effects of pride in K-quarantine on COVID-19 preventive behaviors" in 2021.

Choi Jongryul
is Professor of Sociology, Director of the Center for Migration and Multiculture at Keimyung University, Daegu, South Korea, and President of The Korean Association for Cultural Sociology. He works in the areas of cultural sociology, social/cultural theory, and qualitative methodology. He is the author of

Daughter, Don't Live Like Me* (2021), *The Sociology of Performance: How Does Korean Society Reflect on Itself?* (2019), *The Sociology of Bokagwang: The Cries of Korean Local Youth* (2018), *The Uses of Multiculturalism: A Cultural Sociological Perspective* (2016), *The Strangers of Globalization: Sexuality, Labor, and Deterritorialization* (2013), and *The Cultural Turn in Sociology: Classical Sociology, Revitalized from Science to Aesthetics* (2009).

Agnès Deboulet
is Professor at the University Paris 8 and member of the LAVUE/CNRS. She is currently director of the Cedej in Cairo. As a sociologist and planner, she has been working in several large metropolis on know-how and competencies of ordinary residents facing uncertainties of large scale mega projects. Her recent interest focus on firced displacements in the cities and evictions. Her last publications: "La rénovation urbaine, entre délogement et relogement. Les effets sociaux de l'éviction", with C. Lafaye, in *L'année sociologique*, n°69 (2018); "La mécanique de rue : vertus cachées d'une économie populaire dénigrée", with A. Ndiaye and K. Mamou, in *Métropolitiques* (2019)*; Vulnérabilités résidentielles*, with F. Bouillon, P. Dietrich-Ragon, and Y. Fijalkow (dir.) (2021); *Sociétés urbaines au risque de la métropole* (2022); "Faire face au renouvellement urbain. Retour sur dix ans de recherche coopérative dans le centre-ville de Marseille", with I. Berry-Chikhaoui, P. Lacoste, and K. Mamou, in *Métropolitiques* (2021).

Deguchi Takeshi
is Professor of Sociology at the University of Tokyo. His current research includes Critical Theory of the Frankfurt School and its development in Japan. He is also revisiting the heritage of Japanese critical sociology in terms of "galapagosized sociology" and is using it to propound an analysis of the uniqueness and generality of Japanese culture and society. His recent main works in English are: "Critical Theory and its development in post-war Japanese sociology", in A. Elliot, A. Sawai, and M. Katagiri, eds., *Routledge Companion to Companion to Contemporary Japanese social theory* (2012); "Beyond Shame and Guilt Culture to Globalized Solidarity", *Theory* (Autumn/Winter, 2014); and "Sociology of Japanese Literature after the Great East Japan Earthquake: Analyzing the disaster's underrepresented impacts", in Anthony Elliott and Eric L. Hsu, eds., *The Consequences of Global Disasters* (New York: Routledge, 2016).

Christine Détrez
is Professor of sociology at ENS de Lyon and director of Centre Max Weber. Her research interests are Gender Studies, Sociology of cultural practices, and sociology of emotions. Her representative works are: *Femmes du Maghreb, une

écriture à soi (Paris: La Dispute, 2012); *Sociologie de la culture* (Paris: Armand Colin, coll. Cursus, 2014), *Quel genre?* (Paris: Thierry Magnier, 2015); *Les femmes peuvent-elles être de grands hommes?* (Paris: Belin, 2016); and *Nos mères. Huguette, Christiane et tant d'autres, une histoire de l'émancipation féminine* (with Karine Bastide) (Paris: La Découverte, 2020). She is also novelist, her last novels is *Pour te ressembler* (Paris: Denoël, 2021).

François Dubet

is Sociologist, Emeritus Professor at the University of Bordeaux, Director of Studies at École des Hautes Études en Sciences sociales. His research interests are social movements, education, inequalities and sociological theory. Last publications: *Tous inégaux, tous différents* (Paris: Seuil, 2022); *L'école peut-elle sauver la démocratie?* (with M. Duru-Bellat) (Paris: Seuil, 2020); *Le temps des passions tristes* (Paris: Seuil, 2019); *Ce qui nous unit. Discriminations, égalité, reconnaissance* (Paris: Seuil, 2016); and *La préférence pour l'inégalité* (Paris: Seuil, 2014).

Fan Ke

is Professor of Anthropology of School of Social and Behavioral Sciences at Nanjing University. He received his PhD in anthropology from the University of Washington. His research interests include ethnicity and nationalism, globalization, anthropological and social theory, and sociocultural change of Muslim communities in south China. His recent publications are: *What is Anthropology* (2021); *Understanding Ethnic Identification in Comparative Perspective* (2019); "History, Practice, Limitations, and Prospects: Anthropology in China", *Virtual Brazilian Anthropology* (2022, forthcoming); "Paradigm Chang in Chinese Ethnology and Fredrik Barth's Influence", in Keping Wu and Roberta P. Weller, eds., *It Happens Among People—Resonances and Extensions of the Work of Fredrik Barth* (New York and London: Berghahn Books, 2019, pp. 268–299), and "On the contemporary cultural change: some considerations", *Ethno-National Studies* (2022, forthcoming).

Feng Shizheng

is professor and dean of School of Sociology and Population Studies at Renmin University of China. His research areas include political sociology, historical sociology, organizations, social inequality, state making and social governance, social transformation and political order. He published articles in *Sociological Studies* (China), *Chinese Review of Sociology*, *Chinese Journal of Sociology*, *Journal of Asian Studies* (US), and books such as *Social Governance and Political Order in Contemporary China* (Renmin University of China Press, 2013), *Social Movement Studies in the West* (Renmin University of China Press,

2013), and *Chinese New Blueprint in Social Governance* (Renmin University of China Press, 2018).

Feng Zhuqin
is postdoctoral researcher of Department of Sociology, the School of Social and Behavioral Sciences at Nanjing University. Her main research areas are social capital, *guanxi*, and migration. She has published several articles in the *Journal of Sociology, International Journal of Sociology* and *Social Policy*. She is researching the project of the international migrant social networks in China.

Han Sang-Jin
is Professor Emeritus at Seoul National University (SNU) and lecturer at Columbia University in New York, Peking University in Beijing, École des Hautes Études en Sciences Sociales in Paris, University of Buenos Aires in Argentina, and University of Kyoto in Japan as Visiting Professor. He obtained BA and MA from SNU and PhD from Southern Illinois University, USA. He served as Chairman of the Presidential Committee on Policy Planning during Kim Dae-jung administration and President of the Academy of Korean Studies. He is the author of *Habermas and the Korean Debate* (1998), *Divided Nations and Transitional Justice* (2012), *Beyond Risk Society* (2017), *Asian Tradition and Cosmopolitan Politics* (2018), and *Confucianism and Reflexive Modernity* (2020). As the founder of Joongmin Foundation and EARN (Europe-Asia Research Network), he has been active in promoting research cooperation among East Asian scholars and between the Western and Asian countries.

Sari Hanafi
is currently a Professor of Sociology, Director of Center for Arab and Middle Eastern Studies and Chair of the Islamic Studies program at the American University of Beirut. He is the President of the International Sociological Association. He is as well editor of *Idafat: the Arab Journal of Sociology*. He is the author of numerous journal articles and book chapters on the sociology of religion; connection of moral philosophy to the social sciences; the sociology of (forced) migration applied to the Palestinian refugees; politics of scientific research. Among his recent co-authored books are *The Oxford Handbook of the Sociology of the Middle East* (with A. Salvatore and K. Obuse) and *Knowledge Production in the Arab World: The Impossible Promise* (with R. Arvanitis) and *The Rupture between the Religious and Social Sciences* (Forthcoming in Oxford University Press). In 2019, he was awarded an Honorary Doctorate of the National University of San Marcos and in 2022 he became lifetime corresponding fellow of the British Academy (https://sites.aub.edu.lb/sarihanafi/).

Hasegawa Koichi
is Specially Appointed Professor at Shokei Gakuin University and Professor Emeritus at Tohoku University. He received his PhD from the University of Tokyo. His research interests are environmental sociology, civil society, social movements and social change. His representative works are: *Constructing Civil Society in Japan: Voices of Environmental Movements* (Trans Pacific Press, 2004); *Beyond Fukushima: Toward a Post-Nuclear Society* (Trans Pacific Press, 2015); *Climate Change Governance in Asia* (co-editor; Routledge, 2020); "Japanese Environmental Sociology: Focus and Issues in Three Stages of Development", *International Sociology Reviews* vol. 36, no. 2 (2021), and *Air Pollution Governance in East Asia* (co-editor; Routledge, 2022).

He Rong
is Professor of Sociology of Institute of Sociology at Chinese Academy of Social Sciences, and coordinator of LIA CNRS-CASS since 2014. Her research has two main focuses and has published two books on each, one is *Max Weber's sociology from the perspective of the interaction of economics and sociology* (2009), the other is *The sociological study on Chinese religion* (2015). Among other publications since 2020: "Explore the Alternative Modes of City Economies: Based on a Case Study of Luoyang" (2020), "Images of China: A Further Study by Going Deeper into the Text and Evidence of Max Weber's Confucianism and Taoism" (2020), "Toward an Inclusive Sociology of Religion: Reflections Based on Simmel's Theory of Religion" (2021), and "Weber Coming to China (1920–2020): Reconstruction of Contemporary Intellectuals in a Century of Academic History" (2022).

Hong Deokhwa
is teaching sociology at Chungbuk National University, and his research focuses on energy transition, climate justice, and degrowth. He has authored *The Sociotechnical Regime of Nuclear Power in Korea: The Co-production of Technologies, Institutions, and Social Movements*, and co-authored books, including *Commons Perspectives in South Korea: Context, Fields, and Alternatives*, and *Energy Transition in Korean Peninsula*. His articles published in journals to date include "Critical Issues of Energy Democracy and the Possibility of Energy Commons", "Northeast Asian Supergrid and the Pathway of Energy Transition in Korea", and "Exploring Transition Pathways: Analyzing the Issue between Ecological Modernization, Degrowth, and Eco-socialism".

Hong Yanbi
is Professor of Department of Sociology at Southeast University (China). His research interests include social stratification and mobility, health inequality,

and sociology of education. His recent publications include: "Childhood Health and Social Class Reproduction in China", *Journal of Chinese Sociology* (2021); "Self-selection or Situational Stratification? A Quasi-experimental Study of Health Inequality", *Sociological Studies* (2022); and "Resource Redistribution and Health Inequality in Post-Disaster Recovery: On Three Surveys of Wenchuan Earthquake Recovery (2008–2011)", *Chinese Journal of Sociology* (2019). He is now working on projects concerning the long-term effects of birth weight on individuals' educational performance, cognitive ability development and adulthood health.

Hosoda Miwako

has got his PhD in Sociology from the University of Tokyo, he is professor of Seisa University. After working as a research fellow at the Japan Society for the Promotion of Science, she studied at Columbia University Mailman School of Public Health and Harvard T.H. Chan School of Public Health. Upon returning to Japan, she joined Seisa University in 2012 and served as vice president from 2013 to 2020. Dr. Hosoda was elected as president of the International Sociological Association, Research Committee of Sociology of Health (2018–2023), and Asia Pacific Sociological Association (2017–2020). Her recent publications include: "The Role of Health Support Workers in the Aging Crisis" in M. Saks, ed., *Support Workers and the Health Professions* (Policy Press, 2000, pp. 205–223); and "Qualitative Data Analysis and Health Research" in M. Saks, ed., *Researching Health: Qualitative, Quantitative and Mixed Methods* (Sage, 2019, pp. 203–224).

Jang Wonho

is Professor at the Department of Urban Sociology, University of Seoul. He received his PhD in sociology from University of Chicago. His research area includes urban politics, urban culture, and comparative studies of the pop culture in the global world focusing on the Korean Wave (*Hallyu*). Currently, he is conducting research about glocal culture and social empathy. He is author of *Hallyu and the Transformation of Asian Pop Culture* (in Korean) and *Empathy for Growing Happiness* (in Korean). He has published many papers on pop culture and social empathy, including "Identification, Confucianism, and Intersubjectivity: Issues Related with Social Empathy in East Asia" and "Webtoon as a New Korean Wave in the Process of Glocalization".

Ji Yingchun

is Professor of sociology of School of Sociology and Political Science at Shanghai University. Her research interests include family sociology, gender studies, demographic transition, and modernity in China and to an extent in East

Asia. Her recent publications include: "Understanding Chinese fertility from a gender and development perspective", *Social Sciences in China* (2018); "Mosaic Familism: Daughters providing for parents and the reinstitutionalization of Chinese families", *Twenty-First Century Bi-Monthly* (2020); "Young women's fertility intentions and the emerging bilateral family system under China's two-child family planning policy", *The China Review* (2020); and "A tale of three cities: Distinct marriage strategies among Chinese lesbians", *Journal of Gender Studies* (2021).

Paul Jobin
is Associate Research Fellow at the Institute of Sociology, Academia Sinica, Taiwan. His PhD dissertation on Minamata disease and other industrial diseases in Japan received the Shibusawa-Claudel Prize. His research since then has focused on issues of environmental justice in Japan and Taiwan and has been published in journals such as *Environmental Sociology*; *East Asian Science, Technology and Society* (EASTS); *The Asia-Pacific Journal*; *China Perspectives*; *Politique internationale*; *Ebisu*; *Monde Chinois*; *Travailler*; and *Politix*. Among his recent publications is a co-edited volume on *Environmental Movements and Politics in the Asian Anthropocene* (Singapore: ISEAS).

Kikutani Kazuhiro
is Professor of sociology of the Graduate School of Social Sciences at Hitotsubashi University. His research interests are the History of "the Social" and Sociological Theories. His representative works are: *Naissance of "the Society": History of Social Thoughts from Tocqueville via Durkheim to Bergson* (Kodansha, 2011); *A Nation Without "Society (Conviviality)": Dreyfus Affair and Taigyaku Affair, and Kafu's Grief* (Kodansha, 2015); "Du Fondement Humain et Transcendant de la Démocratie Moderne chez Tocqueville et Bergson", *Considérations inactuelles: Bergson et la philosophie française du XIXe siècle* (OLMS-Weidmann, 2017); Japanese Translation of Émile Durkheim's *Les Règles de la Méthode Sociologique* (Kodansha, 2018); and "Social Facts", *Fundamentals of Sociology: Durkheimian Issues* (Gakubunsha, 2021).

Kim Byoung-Kwan
is Professor of sociology and International Development at Ajou University, South Korea. Educated at the Seoul National University and Harvard University, he teaches and researches social change, social policy, and international development. He has published books and articles on social changes in Korea. His works include Social Structure in Korea, Industrialization and Occupational Mobility in Korea, and Social Justice and Education in Korea.

Kim Mun Cho
is Professor Emeritus of Korea University, Seoul, South Korea. He was professor of sociology at Korea University from 1982 to 2015. He served as President of Korean Society of Social Theory, Korean Association of Science and Technology Studies, Korean Sociological Association and Korean Association of East Asian Sociology. He was appointed as Chair professor of Kangwon National University in 2018. His research activities concentrated on social theory, cultural studies, work and occupations, information society, social studies of science and technology. His academic work has resulted in about 160 refereed papers and 45 books including *Science and Technology and the Future of Korea*; *Class Disparity in Korea*; *The Coming of Convergence Civilization*; *IT and the Shaping of New Social Order* (English), and *Logics and Strategies of Social Integration in Korea*.

Kim Seung Kuk
is Professor Emeritus of Pusan National University and guest professor of Jilin University (~2025) studied sociology at Seoul National University (BA and MA) and Indiana University (PhD). He visited Glasgow University as British Council Fellow (1988) and Essex University as Korea Research Foundation Fellow (1998). He served as the President of Korean Association of Ocean Sociology, East Asian Sociological Association, Korean Sociological Association, and Korean Society for Social Theory. His recent works include: *Toward an Ocean of Hybridisation* (2022), *Solipsist and Spiritualist Individualism* (2018), *The Rise of Hybrid Society and Its Friends* (2015), and *A Quest for East Asian Sociologies* (2014). He won the Korean Academy of Sciences Award (2017) and the Book of Peace by the Institute for Peace and Unification Studies, Seoul National University (2016).

Kim Wang-Bae
is a Professor of Sociology Department, Yonsei University in Seoul, South Korea. He has the career of working for Sociology Department at the University of Chicago as a full time faculty, visiting assistant professor, with lecturing the courses: the Political Economy of East Asia, Urban Space and Social Theory, Contemporary Korean Society, etc. He published several books in Korean: *Reproduction of Labor and Class in Industrial Society* (2001), *Urban, Space and Life World* (2018, second edition) and *Emotion and Society* (2019). Recently he has struggled with the topics about the human right and environment, emotion and non-human being's right. Especially he has made an effort of constructing "the earth jurisprudence and law", actively carrying out the co-representative position of People for Earth.

Ku Dowan
is the director of the Environment and Society Research Institute in Korea. He served as a research fellow of the Korea Environment Institute, an advisor to the Korean Minister for Environment, and a president of the Korean Association for Environmental Sociology. He received his MA and PhD in Sociology from Seoul National University. His main research areas include, but are not limited to, the history of the environmental movement and building ecological democracy. He has published books such as *The sociology of Korean environmental movement*; *People who are searching for alternatives in community*; and *Ecological Democracy*. Additionally, he has co-edited books including *Climate change governance in Asia* and *Air pollution governance in East Asia*.

Frédéric Le Marcis
is Professor of social anthropology at the Ecole Normale Superieure de Lyon (UMR 5206 Triangle), and is currently a visiting research director at the French National Research Institute for Sustainable Development, IRD (UMI 233 TransVIHMI, INSERM U 1175, University of Montpellier). His work questions the logic and experiences of Global Health and risk management through empirical approaches such as epidemics and prisons, studied mainly in West Africa. He co-directed with Marie Morelle the research program ECOPPAF (Economics of punishment and prison in Africa). They recently edited together with Julia Hornberger *Confinement, Punishment and Prisons in Africa*, London: Routledge, 2021, ISBN 9780367444082, 264pp.

Li Chunling
is Professor of Sociology and the Head of the Department of Youth Studies and Education of Institute of sociology at the Chinese Academy of Social Sciences (CASS), and the Director of department of sociology at University of CASS. Her primary research interests are inequality and social stratification, as well as sociology of education and youth studies. She is the author of a dozen books and edited volumes and over one hundred articles and chapters on these issues. Her recent publications include *China's Youth: Increasing Diversity amid Persistent Inequality* (Brookings, 2021); *Towards Inclusive and Equitable Quality Education: Progress and Challenge* (Social Sciences Academic Press, 2017); "A History of Chinese Research on Social Stratification and Mobility: 1949–2019", *Sociological Studies* (2019).

Li Peilin
is Chair Professor of sociology at University of Chinese Academy of Social Sciences, Academic member and director of law, social and political division

of CASS, He received his PhD from University of Paris I (Pantheon-Sorbonne) in 1987. His main research areas focus on social transformation and economic sociology. He has founded Chinese general social survey" (CSS), one of largest national sociological survey since 2006. His publications in English include: *Social transformation and Chinese Experience* (Routledge, 2017); *Urban Village Renovation: The Stories of Yangcheng Village* (Springer, 2020), and *Handbook of Social Stratification in the BRIC Countries* (co-editor; World Scientific, 2013). His latest article in Chinese is "Chinese-style Modernization and New Development Sociology", *Social Sciences in China*, n°12 (2021).

Li Youmei

PhD in Sociology from Sciences Po (France), is Chair professor of sociology at Shanghai University, Editor-in-Chief of *Society*, Director of the Editorial Board of *Chinese Journal of Sociology* and Director of the Research Center of Fei Xiaotong Academic Thought. She was the President of Chinese Sociological Association (2017–2020) and her main research fields are organizational sociology and the transformation practice of social governance in China. She presided over many important research projects such as the Key Project of The National Social Science Fund of China "Research on Theoretical Paradigm Innovation of Contemporary Chinese Transitional Sociology". Her latest publications include *Sociology of Organizations and Strategy Analysis* (SDX Joint Publishing Company, 2019) and *Decoding the Conceptual Logic of Social Construction* (Shanghai People's Publishing House, 2021).

Lim Hyun-Chin

is Professor Emeritus of Sociology and Director of Civil Society Programs, Asia Center, at Seoul National University. He is also an elected member of the National Academy of Sciences, Republic of Korea. Currently, he serves as President of East Asian Sociological Association. He received his BA and MA in Sociology from Seoul National University, and his PhD in Sociology from Harvard University. He was previously the dean of Faculty of Liberal Education, the dean of the College of Social Sciences, and the founding director of Asia Center, all at Seoul National University. His books include *Mobile Asia*; *Global Capitalism and Culture in East Asia*; *Capitalism and Capitalisms in Asia*; and *Asia on Rise: Civilizational Turn*.

Lu Wen

is Lecturer of Wenzhou University and PhD in sociology graduated from the University of Chinese Academy of Social Sciences. His major research is rural sociology. He published several articles in CSSCI journals such as *Education*

Research Monthly, and a book in Chinese: *Homecoming and Surpassing: A Study of the Social Role of Returned Migrant Workers*, co-authored with others.

Machimura Takashi

is Professor of sociology at Tokyo Keizai University, Faculty of Communications Studies, and Emeritus Professor of Hitotsubashi University. His current research themes include global city, urban social movement, mega-events, and infrastructure studies. His publications include "A Search for New Urban Narratives in the Era of Globalization: The Case of Urban Sociology in Japan" (*International Sociology*, Vol. 36, no. 2, 2021), "Gentrification without Gentry in a Declining Global City?: Vertical Expansion of Tokyo and Its Urban Meaning" (*International Journal of Japanese Sociology*, Vol. 30, 2021), "Symbolic Use of Globalization in Urban Politics in Tokyo" (*International Journal of Urban and Regional Research*, vol. 22, no. 2, 1998), and, in Japanese, *Back to Voices of the City: Tokyo from the Perspective of Urban Studies* (Yuhikaku, 2020).

Lilian Mathieu

is Senior Researcher at the French National Center for Scientific Research (CNRS, Centre Max Weber, ENS de Lyon). His research mainly focus on social movements, arts and authoritarian regimes. His recent publications include: "Art and social movements" in Hanspeter Kriesi, Holly McCammon, David A. Snow, and Sarah Soule, eds., *Wiley-Blackwell Companion to Social Movements* (2018); "The space of social movements", *Social Movement Studies* 20(2) (2021); *Dynamiques des tournants autoritaires* (edited with Maya Collombon) (Le Croquant, 2021); and *Columbo: Class Struggle on TV Tonight* (Brill, 2022).

Nemoto Kumiko

is a professor of management in School of Business Administration at Senshu University in Tokyo, Japan. She completed her PhD in sociology at the University of Texas at Austin. Nemoto is the author of *Too Few Women at the Top: The Persistence of Inequality in Japan* (Cornell University Press, 2016). Recent publications include "Global Production, Local Racialized Masculinities: Profit Pressure and Risk-Taking Acts in a Japanese Auto-Parts Company in the United States", *Men and Masculinities* (2018); "The Origins and Transformations of Conservative Gender Regimes in Germany and Japan", *Social Politics* (with Karen Shire); and "Economic Shifts, Consumption of Sex, and Compensatory Masculinity in Japan", *Unmasking Masculinities: Men and Society* (2018).

Nomiya Daishiro

is Professor of sociology at Chuo University, Tokyo, Japan. Received PhD in Sociology from the University of North Carolina at Chapel Hill, USA. Has published and contributed to numerous books and articles in the field of social movements and globalization, including *Global Modernity from Coloniality to Pandemic: A Cross-disciplinary Perspective* (2022), *Summit Protest: Social Movements in the Age of Globalization* (2016), "Knowledge toward Society: Theory and Method in Modern Society" (2005), and *Social Movements and Culture* (2002). Currently Vice-president of the East Asian Sociological Association, and the Japanese Association of Human Resource Development. Also, Head of the Future Sociology Division of the Sociology Committee in the Academy of Science Japan.

Okumura Takashi

is Professor of sociology at Kwansei Gakuin University. He received his PhD from the University of Tokyo in 2003. His research interests are sociological theory, sociology of self and others, and sociology of culture. In recent years he has been researching the work of Japanese sociologists in the postwar period. His publications include: *Anti-Communication* (Kobundo, 2013); *A History of Sociology 1: Discovering Enigmas of Society* (Yuhikaku, 2014); *Keiichi Sakuta vs. Munesuke Mita* (editor; Kobundo, 2016); *Reversal and Remnants: Sociologists as "Others to Society"* (Kobundo, 2018); and *Politics of Mercy: Who Forgives Whom in Mozart's Operas* (Iwanami Shoten, 2022).

Qu Jingdong

is Professor of Department of Sociology and Executive Deputy Director of Institute of Humanities and Social Sciences at Peking University. His research areas are theoretical sociology, social governance, social theory, sociology of history. His main works include: *Absence and Break: A Sociological Study on Anomie* (Shanghai People Publishing House, 1999); *Freedom and Education: On Philosophy of Education of John Locke and Jean Jarques Rousseau* (SDX Joint Publishing Company, 2012); "From total dominance to technical governance: an analysis on thirty years during reform period", *Social Sciences in China*, no. 6 (2009); "The Project System: A new form of State Governance", *Social Sciences in China*, no. 5 (2012); and "After Sacred Society: To Commemorating 100th Anniversary of Émile Durkheim's Death", *Chinese Journal of Sociology*, no. 4 (2017).

Laurence Roulleau-Berger

is Research Director at French National Center for Scientific Research at Triangle, ENS of Lyon. In 1982 she received her PhD and in 2001 her PhD Supervisor in sociology. She has led numerous research programs in Europe and in China in urban sociology, economic sociology, and sociology of migration over thirty years. Since 2006, she is involved in a epistemological way on the fabric of post-Western sociology paradigm. She has published numerous books, articles and chapters, among the most recent: *Post-Western Revolution in Sociology. From China to Europe* (2016); *Work and Migration. Chinese Youth in Shanghai and Paris*, with Yan Jun (2017); *The Fabric of Sociological Knowledge*, co-ed. with Xie Lizhong (2017) (in Chinese); *Post-Western Sociology. From China to Europe*, co-ed. with Li Peilin (2018); *Young Chinese Migrants, Compressed Individual and Global Condition* (2021); and *Sociology of Migration and Post-Western Theory*, co-ed. with Liu Yuzhao (2022).

Sato Yoshimichi
is Professor of sociology of the Faculty of Humanities at Kyoto University of Advance Science and the Graduate School of Arts and Letters at Tohoku University. His research interests are Social Inequality, Social Capital, and Social Change. His representative works in English are: "Does agent-based modeling flourish in sociology? Mind the gap between social theory and agent-based models", in K. Endo et al., eds., *Reconstruction of the Public Sphere in the Socially Mediated Age* (Singapore: Springer, 2017); "Institutions and Actors in the Creation of Social Inequality", in D. Chiavacci and C. Hommerich, eds., *Social Inequality in Post-Growth Japan: Transformation during Economic and Demographic Stagnation* (Routledge, 2016); and "Inequality in Educational Returns in Japan", in F. Bernardi and G. Ballarino, eds., *Education, Occupation and Social Origin: A Comparative Analysis of the Transmission of Socio-Economic Inequalities* (Edward Elgar, 2016).

Satoh Keiichi
is an Assistant Professor of Sociology at the Hitotsubashi University, Japan, and Editorial board of the *Japanese Journal of Sociology*. His research focuses on climate change, social movements, and social capital to which he applies political process theory, sociological theory, and social network analysis. His latest publications include: "Organizational roles and network effects on ideational influence in science-policy interface", *Social Networks* (early view); "The advocacy coalition index", *Policy Studies Journal* (early view); and "Connections result in a general upsurge of protests", *Social Movement Studies* 21(1–2) (2022). He is involved in an international project comparing climate change policy networks (COMPON Project).

Shen Yuan
is Professor of sociology and the former director of Department of Sociology at Tsinghua University, and an adjunct professor of the Department of Sociology at Zhejiang University. He received his PhD from the Graduate School of the Chinese Academy of Social Sciences. His research interests include labor

sociology and economic sociology. His publications include "Social Transition and the remaking of working class", *Sociological Studies*, n°4 (2006); *Market, Class and State* (Social Sciences Academic Press, 2007); and "Strong and Weak Interventions: Two Pathways for Sociological Intervention", *Current Sociology*, vol. 56, n°3 (2008). His publications in recent years are a series of survey reports: *Survey Report on Truck Drivers in China* (4 volumes; Social Sciences Academic Press, 2018, 2019, 2020, 2021).

Shi Yunqing

is Associate Professor of sociology at Institute of sociology of Chinese Academy of Social Sciences. She received her PhD from the Graduate School of Chinese Academy of Social Sciences in 2012. Her research focuses on urban studies, family and parenting studies. Her recent publications include: *Becoming Citizens in China: State and Individual in Inner City Renewal and Urban Social Movements* (Brill, 2022, forthcoming); "One Ruler Measures to the End: Rule Hardening in Grassroots Governance", *Chinese Journal of Sociology*, vol. 7, no. 1 (2021); and "Individualization in China under Compressed and Contradictory Modernity", *Temporalités*, no. 26 (2017).

Shim Young-Hee

is a Professor Emeritus and a sociologist at the Law School, Hanyang University, Seoul, Korea. She had her PhD from Southern Illinois University, USA, and researched at Bielefeld University, Germany and Columbia University, USA. She has also taught at Peking University, China and Kyoto University, Japan. She served as a President of Korean Association of Women's Studies and a Co-Representative of Women Making Peace, a Korea-based NGO. Her publications include: "East Asian Patterns of Individualization and Its Consequences for Neighborhood Community Reconstruction", *Korea Journal* (2018); "Two Dimensions of Family Risk in East Asia", *Development and Society* (2014); "Family-Oriented Individualization and Second Modernity", *Soziale Welt* (2010); *World at Risk and the Future of the Family* (2010); *Gender Politics and Women's Policy in Korea* (2006); and *Sexual Violence and Feminism in Korea* (2004).

Shin Kwang-Yeong

is CAU Fellow at Chung-Ang University in Seoul, Korea. He has been working on inequality, the politics of production and welfare from a comparative perspective. He is the author of "Work in global capitalism", in *The Routledge Handbook of Transformative Global Studies*, ed. by S.A. Hamedi-Hosseini, J. Goodman, S.C. Motta, and B.K. Gills (2021); "Work in the Post-COVID-19 pandemic: the case of South Korea", *Globalizations* (2021); and *Precarious Asia:*

Global Capitalism and Work in Japan, South Korea, and Indonesia (co-authored with A.L. Kalleberg and K. Hewison) (Stanford University Press, 2021).

Shoji Kōkichi
is Professor Emeritus at the University of Tokyo. Former Chief Professor of Sociology, the University of Tokyo and Former Chief Professor of Global Citizenship Studies, Seisen University, Tokyo. His main research interests are Sociological Theory, History of Sociology and Theory of Globalization and Global Society. His representative works are: "Sociology for Global Citizens: A Preliminary Approach", *Bulletin of Seisen University, Research Institute for Cultural Science* (2010); *Messages to the World: from Japanese Sociological and Social Welfare Studies Societies* (ed.; Japan Consortium for Sociological Studies, 2014); *Toward a Sociology of the 21st Century Social Change* and *Toward a Sociology of Sovereign People and Their Historical Awareness* (both in Japanese, ed.; Shin'yosha, 2020); and *Toward a Sociology of the Post-corona Age* (in Japanese, ed.; Shin'yosha, 2022).

Sun Feiyu
is Associate Professor of Sociology at the department of sociology and Vice Dean of Yuanpei College of Peking University. He received his Bachelor and Master degree in Peking University and his PhD degree in York University of Canada. His research areas are mostly on social theory, especially classical psychoanalysis and phenomenological social theory. He publishes in both English and (mostly) in Chinese. His books include: *Social Suffering and Political: Suku in Modern China* (World Scientific, 2013), *Methodology and Life World* (SDX Joint Publishing Company, 2018), and *From Seele to Mind: A Sociological Study of Classical Psychoanalysis* (SDX Joint Publishing Company, 2022). He also does empirical studies on China's society and his recent interests focuses on liberal arts education and social mentality among college students, such as anxiety, depression and narcissism.

Tarumoto Hideki
is Professor of sociology at the Faculty of Letters, Arts and Sciences, Waseda University, Japan. His research interests are citizenship and migration, comparative analysis of immigration policies in European and East Asian countries. His representative works include: "Immigrant Acceptance in an Ethnic Country: The Foreign Labor Policies of Japan", in John Stone et al., eds., *The Wiley Blackwell Companion to Race, Ethnicity, and Nationalism* (John Wiley & Sons, 2020); "Why Restrictive Refugee Policy Can Be Retained? A Japanese Case" *Migration and Development* 8(1) (2019); and "The Limits of Local Citizenship in

Japan", in Thomas Lacroix and Amandine Desille, eds., *International Migrations and Local Governance: A Global Perspective* (Palgrave Macmillan, 2018).

Agnès van Zanten
is a Senior Research Professor working for the Centre National de la Recherche Scientifique (CNRS) at the Observatoire Sociologique du Changement (OSC) of Sciences Po, Paris. She is interested in class-based educational inequalities, elite education, transition to higher education, positive discrimination and widening participation in higher education and educational markets and policies. Her most recent books and edited collections in French and English are *Sociologie de l'école*, sixth edition (with M. Duru-Bellat, G. Farges, and A. Colin, 2022, in press); *Elites in education. Four volumes* (Routledge, 2018); and *Elites, privilege and excellence: the national and global redefinition of educational advantage* (with S.J. Ball and B. Darchy-Koechlin, Routledge, 2015).

Wang Chunguang
is Professor of sociology of Institute of Sociology at Chinese Academy of Social Sciences. His research interests include rural sociology, social policy, social mobility, and international migrants. His recent publications include "The Social and Cultural Subjectivity in the Social Development in China", *Journal of Chinese Social Science* (2019); "The Sociological Discourse on the Co-development of the Rural Modernization and Agricultural Modernization in China", *Sociological Research* (2021); and several books such as *The Reconstruction of the Migrant's Social Space* (Social sciences academic press, 2017). He is now working on project about the relationships between the universal basic income and work attitude in rural China.

Wang Jiahui
is PhD student of sociology, School of Social and Behavioral Sciences at Nanjing University. He graduated from MSc in Social and Public Communication at The London School of Economics and Political Science. His main research interests are social emotions, social governance, and sociological theories.

Wang Xiaoyi
is Professor of sociology at University of Chinese Academy of Social Sciences, research fellow of Institute of Sociology at Chinese Academy of Social Sciences. He is devoted to long-term studies of rural environment. His publications surrounding the topics of climate change, environmental protection and anti-poverty include *Pastoral Communities Under Environmental Pressure* (Social Sciences Academic Press, 2009); *Climate Change and Social Adaptability:*

Study on Pastoral Area of Inner Mongolia (Social Sciences Academic Press, 2014); and *Ecological Migration and Precision Poverty Alleviation: Practice and Experience of Ningxia* (Social Sciences Academic Press, 2017).

Wu Yuxiao
is Professor of sociology of the Department of Sociology at Nanjing University, China. His research interests include social stratification and mobility, sociology of education, gender and family, and youth development. His recent publications include "Private Supplementary Education and Chinese Adolescents' Development: The Moderating Effects of Family Socioeconomic Status", *Journal of Community Psychology* (2021); "Living with Grandparents: Multigenerational Families and the Academic Performance of Grandchildren in China", *Chinese Journal of Sociology* (2021); and "China's Changing Family Structure and Adolescent Development", *Social Sciences in China* (2019). He is now working on projects concerning trends of women's labor force participation and gender role attitudes in China.

Xie Lizhong
is Professor of sociology and the former director of the Department of Sociology at Peking University. His research interests are Sociological Theory, Social development, Modernization and Postmodernization. His representative works are: *An Introduction to the Changes of the Contemporary Society in China* (Hebei University Press, 2000); *Social Theory: Reflection and Reconstruction* (Peking University Press, 2006); *Towards a Pluralistic Discourse Analysis: The Implications of Postmodernism theory for Sociology* (China Renmin University Press, 2009); *The Discursive Construction of Social Reality: Analyzing the New Deal for Example* (Peking University Press, 2012); and *Pluralistic Discourse Analysis: A new model for social analysis* (Peking University Press, 2019).

Yama Yoshiyuki
is Professor of sociology and the Director of Institute of Disaster Area Revitalization, Regrowth and Governance at Kwansei Gakuin University, and he is also adjunct Professor at the Disaster Prevention Research Institute of Kyoto University. His research interests are Sociological Theory, Sociology of disaster, and Community based disaster risk management. His representative works are: *Thought Struggle of Edo* (Kadokawa, 2019) and *Remembrance society* (Shin'yosha, 2009). His latest article is "Sociology of ritual and narrative as post-Western sociology: from the perspective of Confucianism and Nativism in the Edo period of Japan", *The Journal of Chinese Sociology* (2021).

Yamamoto Hidehiro
is Associate Professor in the Faculty of Humanities and Social Sciences at the University of Tsukuba. He received his PhD in Literature at Tohoku University in 2003. His research field focus on political sociology, civil society, local governance, and political inequality. His main works includes *Comparative Urban Governance and Civil Society in Contemporary Japan* (editor; Bokutakusha, 2021, in Japanese); "Interest Group Politics and Its Transformation in Japan: An Approach Informed by Longitudinal Survey Data", *Asian Survey* (2021); *Aftermath: Fukushima and the 3.11 Earthquake* (contributor; Trans Pacific Press, 2017); *Neighborhood Associations and Local Governance in Japan* (Routledge, 2014); and *The Sage Handbook of Modern Japanese Studies* (contributor; Routledge, 2014).

Yang Dian
is Professor and the deputy director of Institute of Sociology at Chinese Academy of Social Sciences. He received his PhD degree in Sociology from Harvard University, and was a visiting scholar at European Commission in 2014. His main research areas are in the fields of economic sociology and the sociology of development, and he has published many articles in top journals such as *Social Sciences in China*. His recent publications include: *The Reconstruction of Corporations: Financial Market and the Modern Transformation of Chinese Enterprises* (Social Sciences Academic Press, 2018); "The Rise of Financial Capitalism and Its Impacts: A Sociological Analysis of the New Form of Capitalism", *Social Sciences in China* (2020); and "Sociological Studies on Finance: Key Issues and Analytical Framework", *Chinese Review of Financial Studies* (2021).

Yazawa Shujiro
is Emeritus Professor of Hitotsubashi University and Seijo University, Tokyo. He was ex-president of Japan Sociological Society. He is a President of East Asian Sociological Association. His research interest is Theory, History of Sociology and Social Movement. Among his main publications are: *A Quest for East Asian Sociologies* (co-edited with Seung Kuk Kim and Peilin Li) (Seoul University Press, 2014); *Theories about and Strategies against Hegemonic Social Science: Beyond the Social Sciences* (co-edited with Michael Kuhn) (Stuttgart: IbidemVerlag, 2015); *The Frontier of Reflexive Sociology* (in Japanese, ed.; Toshindo, 2017); "From Cultural Contradiction of Capitalism to Planetary Society: The End of Modernity, Individuality and Beyond" in Carmen Schmidt and Ralf Kleinfeld, eds., *The Crisis of Democracy?* (Cambridge Scholars Publishing,

2019, pp. 55–74); and "The Indigenization of American Sociology and Universalization of Japanese Sociology", *Journal of History of Sociology* 34(1) (2021).

Yee Jaeyeol
is a Professor of sociology at Seoul National University. He has devoted to the research for solving structural problems in Korean society, and finds the answer in the quality of the society. He has authored *Economic Sociology* (1996) and *Would You Live in Korea If You Are Born Again* (2019). He also co-authored many books including *Are you a middle class?* (2014); *Social Economy and Social Value* (2016); *Social Science Replies to Sewol Ferry Disaster* (2017); *Beyond Suffering Society* (2018); and *Social Value and Social Innovation* (2018).

Zhao Yandong
is Professor of sociology of School of sociology and population studies at Renmin University of China. His research interests include sociology of science, sociological study of disasters and risks, sociology of education, social stratification and mobility, etc. He is experienced in organizing large scale social surveys. His recent publications include: "Long-term effects of housing damage on survivors' health in rural China: Evidence from a survey 10 Years after the 2008 Wenchuan earthquake", *Social Science & Medicine* 270 (2021); "Public Trust in Scientists during Risk Event and its Influencing Factors", *China Soft Science*, no. 7 (2021); and "Close the gender gap in Chinese science", *Nature* 557 (2018).

Zhou Xiaohong
is Professor of the Department of Sociology, the School of Social and Behavioral Sciences at Nanjing University, China. His main research areas include sociological theory, social psychology and Modern Chinese studies. His representative works include: *Tradition and Change: Social Mentality of Peasants in China's Jiangsu and Zhejiang Provinces and Its Evolution Since Modern Times* (SDX Joint Publishing Company, 1998); *Chinese Studies from the Perspective of Globalization* (Paths International, 2016); *Inner Experience of the Chinese People Globalization, Social Transformation, and the Evolution of Social Mentality* (Chief Editor; Springer, 2017); *Culture Reverse (I): The Past and Present of Intergenerational Revolution* (Routledge, 2020); and *Culture Reverse (II): The Multidimensional Motivation and Social Impact of Intergenerational Revolution* (Routledge, 2020).

INTRODUCTION

Post-Western Sociology

Laurence Roulleau-Berger

Although the social sciences were born in Europe for the most part, for almost 20 years now, the Western world has lost its hegemony over the production of their paradigms (Wieviorka 2007), organized around two master narratives: the superiority of Western civilization (through progress and reason) and the belief in the continuous growth of capitalism. Hegemonic thought in the history of social science was generated through a process of "epistemic injustice" (Bhargava 2013). Some Western scholars supported the hypothesis of the marginalization of Eurocentrism and the weakening of European traditions in science. While scientific thought has been constructed as an element of Western societies, this phase in global sociological reasoning has challenged the conditions for creating universalizing and tautological accounts in Western social sciences.

Postcolonial studies were a major step forward in the production of sociological knowledge by displacing Eurocentrism, deconstructing binaries, and creating a narrative to include the multiplicity of world views in the social sciences; this in turn gave rise to Subaltern Studies through epistemologies from the "third-space" (Patel 2003). For over three decades, hegemonic Western thought has been subjected to critical reviews in Asia, Africa, Latin America, and the Arab world by intellectuals responding to Eurocentric fundamentalism (Hanafi 2020). Western hegemonies also received criticism from non-Western and Westernized intellectuals living and working in the heart of the West. A considerable portion of postcolonial critique came from universities in the North. The "Westernization" and "de-Westernization" of knowledge have often gone hand in hand in showing that weapons against Western domination were manufactured in the Western empire (Brisson 2018). The political decline of colonial empires failed to recognize knowledge developed outside the "imperial" borders. According to Raewyn Connell (2007), the sociological canon was essentially formulated in the United States, where social science was viewed through an imperialist lens in the second half of the 20th century. The institutional and academic dependency of certain researchers in the global South on Western social sciences encouraged the replication of theories conceived in the United States, Great Britain, France, and Germany. These mimetic processes have stymied reinterpretations, reformulations, and the production of knowledge in other societies, most notably in Asia.

Numerous avenues are leading to emancipation from Westernisms. For example, *Western Westernisms* are based on the awareness and use of non-hegemonic theories while keeping in mind that they cannot become hegemonic. Or, *Reimagined Westernisms* are produced by integrating fragments of non-hegemonic thinking while retaining epistemic frameworks derived from hegemonic frameworks. Alternatively, *Eastern Westernisms* are based on the coproduction of hybrid thinking by means of strong emancipation from the processes of epistemic colonialization.

To open a Post-Western Space means taking into account the "cosmopolitan turn in social science"—as Beck and Grande argued (2010)—where sociological cosmopolitanisms may be defined by radical openness and inclusiveness and where a plurality of narratives can exist. Westernisms form graduated, plastic, and moving hierarchies that rapidly become elusive. Therefore, it is vital to undo both Westernisms and Easternisms in order to reveal transnational spaces that bring into the light of day a tissue of knowledge that is still partially concealed and even—in some cases—invisible.

Post-Western sociology proceeds from de-centerings and the renewal of universalisms originating in different Eastern and Western spaces. Post-Western sociology is, above all, relational, dialogue-based, and multisituated. This positioning goes beyond postcolonial studies, which could be understood as reinforcing hegemonic positions by means of a strong assertion of critical postures visible in the work of certain intellectuals from the Anglo-Saxon academic world. In post-Western sociology, a strong awareness of hegemonism serves to reveal transnational knowledge spaces in which the diversity of situated knowledge and shared or joint knowledge is rendered visible (Roulleau-Berger 2016; Roulleau-Berger and Li 2018; Xie and Roulleau-Berger 2017).

In this edition, we offer a glimpse beyond the "East" and the "West" by opening the horizons to a wealth of self-directed narratives by societies worldwide, thus laying the foundations for a post-Western space. This is a place where "Western" and "non-Western" sociologies can intersect and interact, forming shared divergent understandings of myriad *ethnoscapes* since for more than 15 years we have produced a *post-Western sociology* to enable a dialogue—on a level footing—on common concepts and concepts situated in European, Chinese, Japanese, and Korean theories, to consider the modes of creation of continuities and discontinuities, the conjunctions and disjunctions between knowledge spaces situated in different social contexts, to work on the gaps between them.

This handbook is divided into two parts:
- Part 1: Post-Western Social Sciences: From East Asia to Europe.
- Part 2: Translation and Ecologies of Knowledge: Dialogues East–West.

In Part 1 from the production of epistemologies of the "Souths" and the re-Easternization of the Westernized East we will introduce the idea of the demultiplication, the complexification and the hierarchization of new epistemic autonomies vis-à-vis Western hegemonies in sociology, and the new epistemic assemblages between European and Asian sociologies (Roulleau-Berger 2016; Roulleau-Berger and Li Peilin 2018; Xie Lizhong and Roulleau-Berger 2017). In fact, epistemic autonomies become plural and diversify, even hierarchize among themselves, without this dynamic of recomposition of the geographies of knowledge in the social sciences being really perceived on the side of the Western worlds. The question of Western hegemonies continues to arise through the process of the recognition, visibility, and legitimacy of this plurality of epistemic autonomies. Then, we identify some transnational theory, theoretical discontinuities and continuities, and located and common knowledge in Western and non-Western contexts.

Part 1, *Post-Western Social Sciences: From Asia to Europe*, will be organized around four sections that reflect different dimensions of the post-Western theory:
- Section 1: Toward Post-Western Social Sciences
- Section 2: Non-hegemonic Traditions and Pluralism in Asian Social Sciences
- Section 3: Heritages and "Re-Asiatization" of Social Sciences
- Section 4: Epistemic Autonomies and Located Knowledge

In Section 1 we will give different definitions of post-Western sociology. Laurence Roulleau-Berger (Chapter 1) explains how a Post-Western Sociology enables a dialogue—held on an equal footing—on European and Asian theories. From an ecology of knowledge we can observe, on one hand, the multiplication of epistemic autonomies vis-à-vis Western hegemonies, and, on the other hand, epistemic assemblages between European and Asian sociologies to coproduce a post-Western space in a cross-pollination process. Then, starting from the origin issue of Chinese sociology, Li Peilin (Chapter 2) discusses the formation of Chinese sociological characteristics, and holds that the growth of sociology with different characteristics in different countries is the basis for the formation of global sociology as a post-Western sociology. The new debates mean that sociologists in non-Western countries are consciously thinking about how global sociology, as a post-Western sociology, has been formed. Xie Lizhong (Chapter 3) will demonstrate, due to the diversity of discourse systems, that "post-Western sociology" will constitute many systems of sociological knowledge that are derived from many discursive sources, including Western discourse systems and non-Western discourse systems; so, "post-Westernization" tries hard to avoid that extreme "Western/non-Western" dichotomy and conveys a tendency to produce the continuity, consistency, and commonality while maintaining those differences. Therefore, it should be a non-hegemonic world of sociological knowledge. Kim Seung Kuk (Chapter 4) will attempt to propose a preliminary approach to constructing an East Asian theory to build a post-Western sociology, employing the concept of hybridization as a key to connect East Asian theoretical perspectives with Western perspectives. Theories of solipsist and spiritualist individualism and middle way for love are also introduced as a uniquely East Asian type of theoretical orientation. East Asian theoretical perspective is an effort to recognize and reinvent both the connectivity and compatibility with a Western perspective. Yazawa Shujiro (Chapter 5) analyzes historical and social contexts, and meanings of post-Western sociology in Japan. The knowledge space is constructed by historical and social background, intellectual contexts, relationship with different knowledge spaces, interests, theoretical attitudes, and theory itself. But the best product of Japanese sociology is post-Western sociology. Japanese sociology is important as a bridge between Eastern and Western sociology.

In Section 2 we draw the theoretical continuities and discontinuities between Western and non-Western sociologies, and we will introduce traditions and controversies.

For Li Youmei (Chapter 6) Chinese sociology has not been able to systematically reflect on its own localized knowledge production process. Therefore, the reconstruction of Chinese sociological knowledge still has a long way to go. This article attempts to reflect on the knowledge production path of Professor Fei Xiaotong, one of the most outstanding sociologists regarding his contribution to the production of localized knowledge of Chinese sociology, to investigate how Chinese sociology will make its own contribution to the "post-Western sociology". Yama Yoshiyuki (Chapter 7) examines the history of Japanese thought, especially the new type of Confucianism and Nativism (Kokugaku) in the Edo period, in comparison with Western sociology. He contributes to reevaluating sociology in the non-Western world by understanding sociology as not limited to Western sociology, and designing the hybrid sociology that integrates Western sociology and non-Western sociology based on these achievements. Zhou Xiaohong and Feng Zhuqin (Chapter 8) shows how in the establishment of Chinese sociology in the early 20th century, the sinicization or indigenization of its disciplinary system began to receive great attention from academia. The author believes that the profound and extensive social transformation in contemporary China not only puts forward the historical mission of sociological indigenization, but also provides a realistic possibility for the accomplishment of this mission and the advancement towards global Chinese sociology. Shoji Kōkichi (Chapter 9), focusing on developing Yoshida's and Mita's theories, is proposing a theory of global sociology that can be used by any sociologist of any country to analyze one's own society in the world society backed up by the global ecology. Sociology is a program science to disclose programs that construct societies and their global nexus taking root in the earth's ecological system. Sociology can propose to reform programs by rejecting bad selections and inserting new ones to make societies better. In his contribution Lim Hyun-Chin (Chapter 10) attempts to examine the major challenges and responses Korean sociology has faced in an era of globalization. Korean sociology has long suffered from lacking its own identity. This lack of identity has inevitably resulted from the development process influenced by Western sociological tradition. Korean sociology is a mixture of American, Japanese, German, English, and even French sociological orientation. Therefore, it is critical for Korean sociology to develop its own concepts and theories. Kim Mun Cho (Chapter 11) considers the cosmopolitan turn in sociology must be a significant movement that enables the recognition of the intellectual limitations of conventional Western sociology. Given the current meta-dynamic of convergence, however, the march to "post-Western sociology" should be continued to the point where all of the boundaries besides the continental divide of the East and the West are to be implored as well. It means an alternative sociological imagination coinciding with the coming age of the convergence civilization.

In Section 3 we will see how post-Western sociology is also organized around common heritages, circulation, and hybridizations of sociological knowledge. Yang Dian (Chapter 12) will explain how Western social sciences have dominated modern social sciences for centuries; however, from the point view of the sociology of knowledge, Western social sciences are just "local knowledge" produced from the experiences of Western countries. The different modernization patterns of China and other non-Western countries call for the development of post-Western sociology, which is more inclusive and scientific, and has stronger explanatory power. Shen Yuan (Chapter 13) tries to sort out the clues of the development of labor sociology on the Chinese mainland during the past 30 years. The last decade of the 20th century may be termed as the first period of the development of contemporary Chinese labor sociology. In the first decade of the 21st century Chinese sociologists tried to classify labor research into theoretical frameworks, especially American sociology. The second decade of 21st century was characterized by the research of exploration of new labor groups and some new visions of theories. Han Sang-Jin (Chapter 15) argues that post-Western sociology calls for a normative vision against the hegemonic modernity built into the Western sociology. He demonstrates how the United States' hegemonic power has been threatened by the analysis of global survey data. He concludes that we should extend post-Western sociological imaginations to conceptualize the possibilities of a non-hegemonic global sociology that we can create and share. Okumura Takashi (Chapter 16) explores the discussions of Yanagita and Tsurumi on the modernizing process of Japan, focusing on the dynamic relationship between wanderers and settlers. Kazuko Tsurumi (1918–2006), a sociologist educated at Princeton under Marion Levy, took Yanagita's (1875–1962) ideas of "wanderers and settlers" seriously, and adapted them to analyze the relationship between *jigoro* (settlers or insiders) and *nagare* (wanderers or outsiders) in Minamata areas damaged by serious industrial pollution causing Minamata disease in 1970s. For Nomiya Daishiro (Chapter 14), away from the Western ethos, a "*hibakusha*" collective memory represented a significant turning-point in the post-war history of two atomic bomb-laden cities, Hiroshima and Nagasaki; it makes a counterargument against the Western modernity and capitalism. So we are invited to come back to a fundamental theoretical question: what constitutes the Western world?

In Section 4 we will see how the epistemic autonomies and local knowledge are constructed in a process of Easternization of the Westernized East which looks like a kind of matrix of epistemic autonomies today in non-Western countries from Asia.

Qu Jingdong (Chapter 17) introduces the post-Western sociological imagination from Chinese experiences. Case study is an irreplaceable sociological strategy for research on social construction. It aims to make a long chain of interpretations from a typical case to the construction of the whole society. Case study is not only influenced by the policies made by central or local governments at different levels, but also located in grassroots customs and mores at the bottom. Sun Feiyu (Chapter 21), in a very close Fei Xiaotong's perspective on "cultural self-consciousness" is contributing to the construction of the theory on the subjectivity in China's sociology. With Yang he raised the concept of social ground, which refers to these "unchanged/stable subjects" in the history of Chinese society. In a non-Western approach the studies of social self-production in China and the social ground are part of efforts of sociological work on cultural consciousness in China. Yee Jaeyeol (Chapter 18) introduces located knowledge with a new theory of publicness in the context of the COVID-19 pandemic. Disaster provides an opportunity to observe the hidden weaknesses of a society. Traditionally, West and East have been regarded as opposites in all three dimensions, and Western ideals, such as democracy and the market, have been regarded as superior models to social issues modernities.

In a framework based on the concepts of the community and the individual an alternative epistemic perspective is used: publicness as a measure of *the social*, combining the degree of public interest, fairness, civic participation, and transparency. Jang Wonho (Chapter 19) purposes a local theory on glocal culture in demonstrating that the Korean Wave is an exemplary of glocal culture, in which the global culture, mixed with Korean culture, has produced a creolized culture that can be consumed transnationally. The glocalizing dynamics of the Korean Wave can be seen in the creation of transnational cultural communities sharing cultural identities based on the Korean Wave and developing a sense of mutual understanding. Hallyu is not really about Koreanness or Asianness, but instead entails the global cultural values of female universalism and gender fluidity. Deguchi Takeshi (Chapter 20) reconsiders the "colonization of the lifeworld" reconsidered from the perspective of "Galapagosized" sociology in Japan. He shed light on one of the influential critical sociologists in Japan, Akira Kurihara, and his theory of *yasashisa no sonzai-shomei* (identity of tenderness) to elucidate contradictions in the reproduction process of personal identity and society at large—namely, how this dysfunction of identity formation generates the mentality of tenderness, which is opposed to values of productivism. In his article Kikutani Kazuhiro (Chapter 22) illustrates the essential difference in the notion of society between France and Japan by comparing two epoch-making affairs of false charges, one of which, referred to as the Dreyfus Affair, occurred in France, and the other, called the Taigyaku Affair, occurred in Japan. He intends to propose a new way of understanding "the social" that surmounts the distinction that lies between Western and Eastern recognition of society. For He Rong (Chapter 23), after an absence of half a century, Max Weber stepped back into the Chinese academic community during the 1980s. Three main themes are of importance: the motivation and values behind contemporary economic endeavors in comparison with the Protestant Ethic; economic strategy as a way of state-building; and the world's vision of China since *Confucianism and Taoism*. Classical paradigms offered by Max Weber could be further developed in combination with Chinese experience. A post-Western sociology should be local and down-to-earth as well as global with open views.

Part 2, *Translation and Ecologies of Knowledge: Dialogues East–West*, will be organized around 10 sections that show how to produce non-hegemonic and post-Western knowledge.

– Section 5: Globalization and Social Classes
– Section 6: Youth and Education
– Section 7: State and Governance
– Section 8: Ethnicity and Space

- Section 9: Social Movements and Collective Action
- Section 10: Gender and Inequalities
- Section 11: Environment and Mistrust Crisis
- Section 12: Individuation, Self, and Emotions
- Section 13: Cities, Migration, and Work
- Section 14: Global Health and New Future

In the post-Western sociology doing with or doing together still looks to be central in the fabric of sociological knowledge in taking account of the alternative political economy of knowledge. In post-Western sociology we will be considering both the local and transnational dimensions of academic research in different fields as part of our attempt to analyze the effects of societal context on the production of theoretical methodologies based on local research situations. However, we will also be analyzing transnational flows between the various contexts of knowledge linked to research methodologies and considering both the processes involved in the production of sociological knowledge and cultural variations in research practices. Theories, knowledge, and methods cannot circulate until these equivalences have been established and appear to be relatively stable, and a framework based on common conventions and norms governing academic research have been put in place. Practices give rise, in these very different contexts, to sociological knowledge obtained in response to questions that are similar but "situated" in sociologists' own societal experiences; we will be posing questions about the universal value of sociological knowledge.

In order to move forward in the production of the paradigm of post-Western sociology, we have shared common and local knowledge by producing cross-sociological perspectives on common topics, by working together in the fields in Europe and Asia, by comparing our ways of conducting quantitative and qualitative research in different research programs. We will analyze how research practices and sociological knowledge are constructed by looking at different and similar forms of experience in Chinese, Japanese, Korean, and European research fields. Crossed views are produced by European and Asian sociologists, allowing us to highlight important differences in the conditions of production of sociological knowledge and to explore their relations with the paradigms developed in Europe and in Asia.

In Section 5 on *Globalization and Social Classes*, Li Chunling (Chapter 24) introduces an important change in the social stratification of China that has occurred over the past 20 years, with the rapid expansion of the middle class that is changing the social structure of China, from a pyramid-shaped structure to an olive-shaped one. Western sociologists' theories about the middle class, such as arguments from C. Wright Mills, Seymour Martin Lipset, or Samuel

Huntington, encounter many problems when they are applied to the definition and analysis of the Chinese middle class. In a very close perspective Louis Chauvel (Chapter 25) is proposing a sociology of social stratification, "occupational classes" based on jobs worked that must be understood within a context of wealth-based domination. Over the last three decades, the wealth-to-income ratio (WIR) in many Western countries, particularly those in Europe and North America, increased by a factor of two. This represents a defining empirical trend: a rewealthization (from the French repatrimonialisation)—or the comeback of (inherited) wealth primacy since the mid-1990s. Shin Kwang-Yeong (Chapter 26) explores how class relations are related to income inequality and wealth inequality in South Korea. There are competing arguments concerning the effect of class on income and wealth inequality. One is the weakening thesis in which the effect of class on income and wealth inequality has been diminishing due to the employment system's flexibility. Another is the opposite thesis, which accentuated the polarization of income and wealth due to the differential return rate to capital and labor for the last decades. For Sato Yoshimichi (Chapter 27) globalization does not directly affect social inequality in each country. Globalization is said to increase the flexibility of labor markets. However, regular workers at the core of the labor markets in Japan are still enjoying a high level of job security because they are protected by strong employment legislation. Thus, globalization has increased inequality not only between social classes but also between regular and non-regular workers in Japan, and it has transformed gender relationships in labor markets.

In Section 6 on *Youth and Education*, Wu Yuxiao (Chapter 28) introduces educational expansion and its impacts on Chinese youth in post-reform China. The past four decades since the market reform have witnessed the tremendous achievement of China's educational development. The rapid educational expansion is accompanied by a widening class gap and urban–rural gap in higher education. The increasing class-based inequality in educational opportunities may lead to furious competition in educational attainment and labor market outcomes among Chinese youth. Agnès van Zanten (Chapter 29) is reviewing Western research on the sociology of education, mostly conducted in the United States, the United Kingdom and France. She first analyzes how lower-class and upper-class students' identities are both reinforced and transformed by the different curricular contents, pedagogy, and evaluation processes to which they are subjected, and how educational institutions characterized by high concentrations of either lower-class or upper-class students channel them through different mechanisms. Asano Tomohiko (Chapter 30) provides an overview of the historical landscape of youth in Japan as well as sociology of youth and education. In the 1960s the Japanese system of transition was established through the period of postwar high economic development. In the late 1970s and through the 1980s, the transition system worked well, and in the early 1990s the "bubble economy" ended and Japan went into a long period of recession. This brought the old topics like labor, class, and inequality to the center of youth studies, focusing on the transformation of the transition system. Kim Byoung-Kwan (Chapter 31) is reviewing some of the accomplishments of Korean sociology of education in recent decades in demonstrating Korean sociology as a whole has long passed the earlier phase where the de facto role of most sociologists was to "import" the concepts, theories, and methodologies from the main, in this case "Western", sociology to apply them in Korean contexts. As long as sociology keeps distancing itself from exclusive and hegemonic practices, it gives us a chance to make a more meaningful contribution to the betterment of social and human beings.

In the Section 7 on *State and Governance*, Agnès Deboulet (Chapter 32) builds a parallel between two case studies in France and in Egypt to underline the persistent presence of a Western paradigm within urban planning practice. In both cases, a post-Western analysis invites us to draw some parallels in situations often deemed as very different because of the nature of the state, the construction of citizenship, and furthermore the complete alterity that is attributed to "South" planning by contrast with planning in the North. Shi Yunqing (Chapter 33) is introducing a theory on the state and the individual in urban renewal and social governance during the social transition in China. The production of citizens and society in the Chinese model has been developed in two processes; the first one started from the society and tried to appeal for legitimacy from the state, while the second one originated from the state and tried to call for an echo from society. In these processes of Chinese society production, located knowledge from the post-Western sociology perspective could be produced. Yamamoto Hidehiro (Chapter 34) is analyzing the development of local governance in Japan and the relationships between the state, civil society, and individuals. The State has withdrawn from the social sphere, and instead various stakeholders, such as businesses, civil society organizations, and local communities, are involved in public services and local management. Japanese civil society organizations have been under strong administrative control, which has prevented them from fully advocating for and making demands on the government.

In the Section 8 on *Ethnicity and Space*, for Ahmed Boubeker (Chapter 35) the interactionist approach of ethnicity has its roots in Western sociology and galvanized academic research in the English-speaking world. In contrast, the concept of ethnicity in France still comes into conflict with a tradition that views it either as an ideological weapon to revive racial theories, or a localized concept in the context of relations between groups in the United States. Here is introduced a reflection on the notion of worlds of ethnicity articulating a view of social worlds specific to the symbolic interactionism of different regimes of historicity. In a close perspective Fan Ke (Chapter 36) is defining ethnicity as a social and political phenomenon, or a subjectively social action, concerning boundaries. Accordingly, in recent years, together with nationalism, ethnicity is suggested to be a phenomenon of intersubjectivity. This is true if one has thought about the emergence of ethnicity as a consequence of interactions among the state and its policy toward cultural or ethnic diversities, local elites, neighboring groups of ethnicities, the mobility of people, and even the impacts of globalization, among many other things. For Tarumoto Hideki (Chapter 37), East Asia might not have a position at the core or the periphery but rather in the semi-periphery of the world system of academic knowledge production. East Asian sociologies might suffer from epistemic injustice such that their capacities to develop their own frameworks are discouraged. East Asian academics can examine and overturn Western theoretical assumptions with reference to East Asian theories and/or empirical cases, for example in examining a Western theoretical concept in migration studies, that is, *super-diversity*. For Choi Jongryul (Chapter 38), in South Korea, migrant workers are not considered as future citizens or long-term residents; they are not considered as fellow humans who can construct a cosmopolitan society together. A grotesque mixture of racialism and modernism is underpinning Korea's imaginary of the social, the question of ethnicity is a very important scientific and political issue. Even though various disciplines are actively discussing multiculturalism, the fundamental reflection on the frame of the nation-state does not seem to be sufficient.

In Section 9 on *Social Movements and Collective Action*, Hasegawa Koichi (Chapter 39) discusses the historical outline of social movements, especially environmental movements, focusing on four major topics in four stages of the movements: (1) political movements of class struggle centered around labor movements by the Socialist and Communist party in 1945–1965; (2) citizens' movements and residents' movements in 1965–1975; (3) the end of the conservative-progressive ideological framework, especially in 1989; and (4) the collapse of the Japanese-style system: institutionalized movements and diversifying activities, including environmental NGOs and other NPOs. For Lilian Mathieu (Chapter 40) the Western sociology of contentious movements has developed decisively during the 1960s and 1970s with the emergence of a wide range of mobilizations among students, feminists, pacifists, gay men and lesbians, ecologists, etc. However, two analytical traditions have developed to study them. One was initiated by the work of Mancur Olson, who has focused on the resources, organizations, cognitive frames, and opportunities afforded to protesters. Then, mainly represented in France by Alain Touraine, the so-called new social movements approach was really influent the criticized by Bourdieusian sociologists. For Feng Shizheng (Chapter 41), in contemporary China, the presumed collective action and social movements tend to be labeled by the official as a "group event". The author traces the historical change of the state's conception of "group event" from 1949 to show that whereas China's regime has transitioned from an ideocracy to a technocracy, the state's conception of social conflicts is undergoing a reverse change from technical to political. This chapter offers a post-Western sociological perspective by highlighting a crucial element understudied in Eurocentric tradition: state-targeting social movements in interaction with the technocratization of a post-revolutionary regime.

In Section 10 on *Gender and Inequalities*, Christine Détrez (Chapter 42) demonstrates sociologists took up the notion in a constructivist perspective: genders are constructed, and they designate the place and expectations that each society assigns to individuals, according to whether they are men or women. These places, on the other hand, are hierarchical, and gender is a system of classification and power. The last few years have seen the emergence of a new research perspective, based on questions of identity and the fluidity of gender, inspired by Queer Studies from Judith Butler. Ji Yingchun (Chapter 43) is introducing the process of theorizing the above dynamics concerning gender, family, and modernity in contemporary China. The above localized theorizing and conceptualization regarding the separation of the two-spheres public/private, mosaic gender ideology, mosaic familism, and mosaic modernity are directly based on Chinese people's daily practices. This pluralistic and dynamic process of knowledge production and reproduction vividly embodies the essence of post-Western sociology. Nemoto Kumiko (Chapter 44) reviews the historical and contemporary roles of the state and the market economy in upholding or transforming gender inequality in the areas of work and family as well as in reaction to the feminist movement; she focuses on institutional obstacles to gender equality in Japan and China. Here the purpose is not to categorize China as fitting into one of the various theoretical models but to highlight the status of gender equality in Japan and China in the areas of work, family, markets, and the feminist movement, in comparison to that of other Western countries. Shim Young-Hee (Chapter 45) is dealing with gender relations in the family in Korean society, focusing on the individualization and community issues in the situation of deepened inequality since the COVID-19 pandemic, to conclude that there coexist two contradictory trends in Korea: one is what she calls the "condensed radicalization of individualization", a Western trend, and the other is "community orientation", an Eastern trend. This coexistence indicates a post-Western tendency in the sense that it goes beyond the "East" and the "West".

In the Section 11 on *Environment and Mistrust Crisis*, Wang Xiaoyi and Anier (Chapter 46) demonstrate how in China, as well as in other industrial societies, food safety became a serious problem for most consumers. Food production has taken place far away from consumers, which brought about mistrust regarding the food production. Consumers do not trust the food, and the movement of new agriculture, including urban agriculture, CSAs, and organic farming, is emerging for analysis. The main concepts in the paper are industrialized agriculture, mistrust, and food safety. For Paul Jobin (Chapter 47) an overwhelming proportion of authors who discuss the Anthropocene, both advocates and opponents of the notion, are from Western Europe, North America, and Australia. For some authors, the anthropos of the Anthropocene discourse is another version of the capitalist white male who finds in this narrative a renewed way to impose his neo-colonial domination. Departing from the domination of Western paradigms in the Anthropocene literature, a few Asian scholars have therefore deemed it necessary to redefine the concept from the angle of postcolonial criticism. Satoh Keiichi (Chapter 48) considers ecological modernization theory (EMT) one of the major environmental theories/discourses among scholars and policymakers. EMT draws its perspective mainly from the Western countries that experienced the set of the characteristics of late modernity, such as post-industrialization and severe environmental degradation. By contrast, the East Asian countries generally have experienced the modernization and the second modernization that have resulted in East Asia's unique response to the environmental crisis. The East Asian response to environmental risk is based on the modern, authoritarian, and technological perspective and not from the reflexive modernity. Hong Deokhwa and Ku Dowan (Chapter 49) are revealing the characteristics of Korean environmental sociology by reviewing major studies in Korean environmental sociology. Korean environmental sociology can contribute to broadening the understanding of the relationship between ecological transition, environmental movement, state, and democracy. Through the development path of the Korea's environmental movement, it is also possible to trace another historical path of environmentalism in social conditions different from those of Western environmentalism or environmentalism of the poor.

In Section 12 on *Individuation, Self, and Emotions*, Cheng Boqing and Wang Jiahui (Chapter 50) are producing the theory of emotional regimes in referring to individual feelings, social structure, and emotions. With the structural changes happening in contemporary Chinese society, three emotional regimes have emerged correspondingly, that is, the managerial regime in the field of work, the experiential regime in consumption, and the performative regime in social interaction. There are tensions and overlaps between the three regimes, which gives rise to a variety of complex situations. This theory of emotional regimes provides sociological insights for understanding contemporary social issues. François Dubet (Chapter 51) has produced the sociology of experience; through the lens of individuals' experiences, his goal is to develop a sociology of the "nature" of inequalities through a two-pronged approach. First, by trying to understand how individuals' subjectivities and emotions are the product of a "system". Second, by identifying how they simultaneously distance themselves from, cultivate, and struggle against the same system. The sociology of experience aims to be a general sociological theory applied to specific subjects, in an effort to stem the endless division in sociology between different paradigms, subjects, and studies. Yazawa Shujiro (Chapter 52) analyzes why the issue of emotion and self has become one of the most fundamental and important issues in Japanese sociology. The autonomous individual is no longer the Subject of the society; the Subject must be made out of the subjective as the collective. The cognitive framework and interpersonal relations are a battleground of deciding characteristics of the society. The author introduces several Japanese theories on the relationships between emotion and the creative subject. Kim Wang-Bae (Chapter 53) attempts to touch on the social conflicts in contemporary Korean society as have occurred in the forms of "emotionalized selves". The social conflicts intermingled with emotions such as fear, anger, and hatred (or disgust) have been emotionalized social conflict. The author shows how the emotions of fear, hatred, and anger are constructed and mixed into the emotionalized subjects. Those emotional energies have mobilized the radically polarized social conflicts. Bourdieu's conceptualization of *habitus* is reinterpreted in the context of emotions.

In Section 13 on *Cities, Migration, and Work*, for Machimura Takashi (Chapter 54) in the intensification of hyper-urbanization, circulations, and migrations in Asia and Africa, it is becoming more and more difficult to distinguish between those who migrate and those who settle. Cities are beginning to have the characteristics of a "dull place" that remains rugged in a "smooth space". How do we capture the process of restructuring cities, labor, and mobility, starting from the difference between the West and the non-West, and then beyond that? With the expansion of cyberspace represented by the Internet, the life of urban citizens has changed significantly, so how should the experience of Asia be incorporated into migration and urban studies that have been developed based on the experience of Europe and the United States for a long time? Laurence Roulleau-Berger (Chapter 55) invited us to recognize that the migration issue for European and Chinese sociologists is a major scientific issue. The process of urban and economic integration is often related to the question of migration, but the assimilation's theory appears to be limited to explain the migratory circulations the process of globalization "from above" and "from below". She is using the concepts of structural processes, individuation, subjectivation, agency, and capabilities to understand the migratory experience. Social and economic inequalities appeared *multisited* in migratory careers, revealing the differentiation and cosmopolitization of migratory biographies around strong injunctions to self-government. In a close perspective for Wang Chunguang and Lu Wen (Chapter 56) the social integration of immigrants has always been a classic problem in sociology. In the late 1990s and early 2000s, there have been many studies and debates in academia and policy around the problem of rural migrants. Compared with immigrants from other countries, especially developed countries, the rural migrants in China, known as "rural–urban migration", have met with some different fusion. In a word, the citizenization and social integration of rural migrants is constantly evolving and expanding.

In Section 14 on *Global Health and New Future*, Hosoda Miwako (Chapter 58) analyzes how people deal with health and illness, focusing on the differences and similarities between the East and the West, including Japan. The medical community, public health community, and others are advocating measures to eliminate health disparities from an institutional perspective based on Western medicine, and to consider the Eastern culture of "living together" with nature, including people; this concept of "living together" is called *kyosei* in Japanese. It is hoped that the dialogue between the East and the West toward a society where we can live together will continue. Zhao Yandong and Hong Yanbi (Chapter 57) show theories in the sociology of health are mainly based on the experiences of Western developed countries, which should be complemented by more studies on the traditions and patterns of non-Western countries. In the context of infectious diseases, like SARS in 2003 and COVID-19 in 2020, the Chinese experience encouraged reflection on the traditional theories of sociology of health based on Western experience, and to explore the possibility of constructing a post-Western theory of sociology of health in the future. For Frédéric Le Marcis (Chapter 59) the COVID-19 pandemic and its aftermath in terms of global vaccine policies provides an opportunity to question the hegemonic logic of global health. While the continents of Asia, Europe, and the Americas have been severely impacted by the epidemic, Africa, which is much less affected, seems to be following suit, despite a very different epidemiological situation. Local arguments are most often either ignored or silenced by local mediators of the global health hegemonic discourse due to international diplomatic–scientific stakes that are difficult to negotiate. By analyzing these descriptions, critical anthropology thus helps to shed light on what really matters to populations. Cho Byong-Hee (Chapter 60) demonstrates that since the outbreak of COVID-19, people around the world have been fearing death and experiencing hardships. The author will focus on the deep-seated marketization of Korean health care and the doctors trying to maintain their vested interests. As COVID-19 had a severe impact on economic, social, and psychological aspects, the global community began to reflect on the crisis of human civilization and the disturbed ecosystem, which is believed to have caused it, and raised concerns that returning to the pre-pandemic lifestyle is not possible.

Bibliography

Beck, U., and E. Grande. 2010. "Varieties of Second Modernity: The Cosmopolitan Turn in Social and Political Theory and Research". *The British Journal of Sociology* 61 (3): 409–444.

Bhargava, R. 2013. "Pour en finir avec l'injustice épistémique du colonialism". *Socio* 1: 41–77.

Brisson, T. 2018. *Décentrer l'Occident*. Paris: La Découverte.

Connell, R. 2007. *Southern Theory*. Cambridge: Polity Press.

Hanafi, S., and C.C. Yi. 2020. Introduction. In *Sociologies in dialogue*, edited by S. Hanafi and C.C. Yi, pp. 1–13. London: Sage.

Patel, S. 2003. "Beyond Binaries: A Case for Self-Reflexive Sociologies". *Current Sociology* 51: 7–26.

Roulleau-Berger, Laurence. 2016. *Post-Western Sociology. From China to Europe*. Leiden and Boston: Brill Publishers.

Roulleau-Berger, Laurence, and Li Peilin, eds. 2018. *Post-Western Sociology—From China to Europe*. London and New York: Routledge.

Xie, Lizhong, and Laurence Roulleau-Berger, eds. 2017. *Construction of Sociological Knowledge: An Exploration of Post-Western Sociology* (in Chinese). Beijing: Press of Peking University.

PART 1

*Post-Western Social Sciences:
From East Asia to Europe*

∴

SECTION 1

Toward Post-Western Social Sciences

CHAPTER 1

Toward Post-Western Sociology

Laurence Roulleau-Berger

The social sciences and particularly sociology have long been almost entirely monopolized by Western cultures. Western hegemonies received criticism from non-Western and Westernized intellectuals living and working in the heart of the West. The "Westernization" and "de-Westernization" of knowledge have often gone hand in hand in showing that weapons against Western domination were manufactured in the Western empire (Brisson 2018). The political decline of colonial empires failed to recognize knowledge developed outside the "imperial" borders. In East Asia, Korea and Japan were undergoing partial and gradual Westernization processes for several decades. We offer a glimpse beyond the "East" and the "West" by opening the horizons to a wealth of self-directed narratives by societies worldwide, thus laying the foundations for a post-Western space. From the production of an epistemology shared with European and Chinese sociologists for 15 years, more recently with Japanese and Korean sociologists, a *post-Western sociology* enables a dialogue—held on an equal footing—on European and Asian theories, to consider the continuities and discontinuities, the conjunctions and disjunctions between knowledge spaces situated in different social contexts. From this ecology of knowledge we can observe, on the one hand, the multiplication of epistemic autonomies vis-à-vis Western hegemonies, and, on another hand, epistemic assemblages between European and Asian sociologies. This groundbreaking contribution is to coproduce a post-Western space in a cross-pollination process where "Western" and "non-Western" knowledges do interact, articulated through cosmovisions, as well as to coproduce transnational fieldwork practices.

1 Where Are the *Wests*?

While scientific thought has been constructed as an element of Western societies, this phase in global sociological reasoning has challenged the conditions for creating universalizing and tautological accounts in Western social sciences. There is also a plurality of Easternisms and semi-Easternisms situated in different epistemic spaces and ordered into hierarchies according to differentiated political, historical, and civilizational contexts. Westernisms form graduated, plastic, and moving hierarchies that rapidly become elusive. According to Raewyn Connell (2019), the academic canon was essentially formulated in the United States, where social science was viewed through an imperialist lens in the second half of the 20th century. The institutional and academic dependency of certain researchers in the global South on Western social sciences encouraged the replication of theories conceived in the United States, Great Britain, France, and Germany. These mimetic processes have stymied reinterpretations, reformulations, and the production of knowledge in other societies, most notably in Asia.

The debate of post-colonial, decolonized, or non-hegemonic sociology has been very active for the last decade in the "West" (Go 2013; Reuter and Villa 2015) and in the East for 30 years (Kim, Li and Yasawa 2014). According to Raewyn Connell (2019) we are invited to think sociologically on a world scale and to be inscribed in a global economy of knowledge, formed in the context of empire and the global Metropole. If the theory of the coloniality of power and knowledge from Quijano (2000) is fundamental to make visible a diversity of local spaces of knowledge outside the Metropole, a multiplicity and a hierarchy of peripheries and semi-peripheries still do exist and the conditions to access them, in each place, must be renegotiated. In 2014, Kim Seung Kuk wrote, "the decline of the West is becoming a reality in which the rise of East Asia becomes a new reality". For 30 years Chinese, Korean, and Japanese sociologists have established epistemic networks in order to produce sociological theories emancipated from hegemonic Western paradigms.

Hegemonies are produced by complex processes, never static and constantly reconfigured; today, *reimagined Westernisms* are produced by integrating fragments of non-hegemonic thinking while retaining epistemic frameworks derived from hegemonic frameworks. In this global turn some scholars are reimagining a new West. A new Eurocentric standpoint appears with new bifurcations. For example, Jobin, Ho and Hsin-Huang (2021) are advocating for an understanding of the Anthropocene theory beyond its current Western focus; for them, in other words, the theory of the Anthropocene discourse is another version of the capitalist white male who finds in this narrative a renewed way to impose his neo-colonial domination (Simangan 2020; Simpson 2020), and so he advocates for a post-Western repolitization of the Anthropocene. We have noticed in China, for example, the theory of Anthropocene is not used by sociologists. We can consider new Eurocentric standpoints and new bifurcations that involve epistemic lines between the Wests and the rest of the world have emerged (Alatas 2003) and refer to a relational position with global hierarchies forged from imperial relations (Go 2016).

The question is why and how are *reimagined Wests* reforming? Does the COVID-19 context influence this process? As a result of the circulation and globalization of knowledge, new hierarchies have emerged, giving rise in turn to new competitive environments in which innovative knowledge is being produced. Anyway, we can consider what Connell (2007) called a "mosaic" theory of multiple knowledge, then remember all social knowledge is situated and that there is no truly "universal" sociology (Go 2016) in order to reveal transnational spaces that bring into the light of day a tissue of knowledge that is still partially concealed, and even in some cases invisible.

2   Towards a Non-Western Centric Sociology

After the theory of the provincialization of Europe by Dipesh Chakrabarty (2000), various theories have been advanced: Arif Dirlik (2007) proposed the theory of global modernity, Ulrich Beck (2006) introduced the theory of cosmopolitanism, and Shmuel N. Eisenstadt (2000) produced the theory of multiple modernities using a comparative civilizational perspective to describe the plural forms of modernities in diverse historical and structural contexts. Also, Göran Therborn (2003) has demonstrated how such contexts are *entangled* with each other in various ways. However, following in the footsteps of Shmuel N. Eisenstadt and Göran Therborn (2003), Ulrich Beck and Edgar Grande (2010) have studied the varieties of modernity and non-modernity and considered not only how they coexist and challenge each other but also how they are embedded.

More recently, we must consider the construction of *non-Western Wests* by certain Western scholars in the social sciences (Bhambra 2014; Brandel, Das and Randeria 2018; Dufoix 2013; Koleva 2018; Roulleau-Berger 2011, 2016; Santos 2014). Epistemologies of the South have been produced by social scientists based in the global South and the global North to recognize an epistemic, cultural diversity. Epistemic injustice also invites us to consider an epistemology of non-visible knowledge. This requires "a decolonial break" from Eurocentric epistemologies to include a plurality of knowledge spaces (Savransky 2017). Boaventura De Sousa Santos (2014) proposed the development of an *Epistemology of the South* that concerns the production of ecologies of knowledge anchored in the experiences of resistance in the anti-imperial South. He invites us to move from an *epistemology of blindness* to *an epistemology of seeing* based on the creation of solidarity as a form of knowledge and the mutual recognition of the Other as equal. Thus, a definition is required of an anti-imperial South space that embodies a plurality of epistemological Souths structured around counterknowledge born out of struggle (Bhambra and Santos 2017). Bhambra (2014) proposed *connected sociologies* in arguing for recognizing historical connections generated by scientific hegemonies, colonialism, dispossession, and appropriation; so, she purposed that we perform a double displacement—empires of domination or conquest and colonialism—to "decolonise" the concepts they have bequeathed to us (Bhambra and Holmwood 2021). At the University of Cambridge Ali Mehghi (2021) considers sociology did not "become" colonized, it was always colonial to begin with.

In 2011, I published in French the book *Dewesternization of Sociology: Europe in the Mirror of China*; the first title was "Decolonizing the Sociology", but the publisher preferred "Dewesternization of Sociology". In this book I showed that there has been a kind of ethical and political epistemic indecency in the Western worlds to ignore non-hegemonic social sciences. I proposed to think less about the plurality of the "provinces of knowledge" than about the continuities and discontinuities, the arrangements and disjunctions between places of knowledge located in different parts of the world that are likely to allow transnational spaces to form. As global entanglement and interconnectedness are the conditions required to understand the assemblages and dis-assemblages between Western and non-Western societies (Hanafi and Yi 2020; Roulleau-Berger and Li 2012), we can take into account new forms of methodological cosmopolitanisms. We have introduced post-Western sociology in a context of a variety of *compressed modernities* (Chang 2010, 2017). The question is to understand how the conjunctions and disjunctions between different regimes of compressed modernities are creating new conditions to produce sociological knowledge.

Sari Hanafi (2021) and Chin-Chun Yi very recently also focused on how different national and regional sociologies can circulate, exchange, co-construct, and enter into dialogue and controversy to stress global recognition beyond the dominant West; if they are discussing the power structure in knowledge production, they do introduce the concept of domination, not through the former problematic on the relation between the centers and the peripheries but around concepts such as multicultural sociology, postcolonial global sociology, cosmopolitanism, and multiple modernities. Sari Hanafi also argued that the postcolonial approach is not sufficient to create new conditions for sociologies to be in dialogue; he considers that it should be supplemented a "post-authoritarian approach", which means the impact of local authoritarianism in the Arab world. In Latin America Anibal Quijano (a Peruvian sociologist), Walter Mignolo (an Argentinian sociologist), and Enrique Dussel (an Argentinian philosopher) are the first to theorize the concept of coloniality; Walter Mignolo introduced the concept of coloniality of knowledge. In the sociology of BRICS with the process of the internationalization of Brazilian sociology a new dialogue was opened with China that started in 2004 with the Chinese Academy of Social Sciences (CASS) and the University of Peking. Then, sociologists from Brazil, Russia, India and China (BRICS) produced the *Handbook on Social Stratification in the BRIC Countries*, including changes of social stratification, the working class, peasants, the middle class, and income inequality. Then, in 2018 *The Handbook of the Sociology of Youth in BRICS Countries* included the history of concepts into research on youth; identity and generation; family, marriage, and sexuality; and education and employment. And Brazilian, Chinese, Indian, and Russian sociologists have defined sociology in the BRICS to produce an understanding of similar and dissimilar social and economic processes in each context through a comparative approach. BRICS sociology should contribute to making sociology a much more international discipline (Dwyer and Martins 2020). In the sociology of BRICS new East–South assemblages have been established outside the North–East connections.

Some scholars open their theoretical spaces in Western countries, separate from Western hegemonic knowledge and breaking the dichotomy between the North and the South, between the West and the non-West, and between modernity and tradition. Thus, in the sense of Lisa Tilley (2017), any decolonial knowledge production must involve consideration of a political economy of knowledge based on a plurality of societal narratives and epistemologies. If there is a diversity of Westernisms and semi-Westernisms, social scientists in Central Europe (Blagojevic 2010) do reject being classified as proponents of exotic Eastern theories and believe that theories should be evaluated on the basis of their heuristic value and not the location of their emergence (Wessely 2020). In Eastern and Central Europe, Svetla Koleva (2018, 2021) has developed non-hegemonic sociology in reestablishing continuities with the past of the discipline, and she argues the view of existing unity in the totalitarian experiences of Eastern European sociologies.

In Latin America Roberto Briceno-Leon (2020) is speaking about a Mestizo (metis) sociology as a result of four traditions: (1) the philosophical sociology of lawyers; (2) the scientific sociology and modernization; (3) the mestizo sociology of dependency (cf. theory dependency); (4) the rejection of miscegenation via Marxist theory. The diversity of contemporary sociology is structured around four tendencies: the miscegenation between sociology and politics, the adoption of multiple influences in a pluri-paradigmatic perspective, inductive sociology by combining qualitative and quantitative methods (survey and life stories), and finally contributing to a "public sociology"—in the sense of Michael Burawoy—in giving political meaning to sociology. But for Roberto Briceno-Leon there is a risk, such as falling into the temptation of global centrism.

So, we are invited to think sociologically on a world scale and to be inscribed in a global economy of knowledge; it means sharing our diverse theoretical and empirical perspectives among sociologists with publics across the world, elaborate assemblages and connections between different local knowledges in a decolonized world's perspective. A non-Western sociology is quite different from global sociology in the sense of Dennis S. Erasga (2020) being emancipated from the issue of "modernocentrism which denies non-Western practices and experience of their inherent value as cultural facticity or ushers a form of palliative indigenization where unbidden respect for local realities is afforded".

Together with Chinese sociologists we have proposed the development of cross-cultural perspectives on sociological knowledge and theoretical methodology in Europe and Asia and the production of a common conceptual and methodological space within which dialogue and intellectual innovation can take place (Roulleau-Berger and Li 2012, 2018; Xie and Roulleau-Berger 2017) in a new dialogue and mutual learning.

3 From the "Re-Easternization of the Westernized East"

In East Asia, the creation of the East Asian Sociologists Network (EASN) in 1992 by Chinese, Japanese, and Korean sociologists to produce connected sociologies represented a major challenge (Kim, Li and Yazawa 2014). Then the East Asian Sociological Association in 2002 started to promote academic exchanges in East Asia and held international conferences several times in Japan and Korea. The 2nd Congress of the East Asian Sociological Association at Pukyong National University, Busan, South Korea, was held on October 29–30, 2021, on *Social Transformation in Asia: Before and After Covid 19*.

Since 1979, diverse Chinese sociology theories have been developed from different perspectives, attesting to a real internationalization of the discipline and the solidification of new boundaries. Chinese sociology gained epistemic autonomy before 1949 and since 1979 outside the dichotomy between the "West" and the "non-West", the colonist and the colonized, outside post-colonial sociology (He Yijin 2018a, 2018b). Sociology in China has been reconstructed since the end of the 1970s around the increasing importance attached to the effects of Chinese civilization, both past and present, and the idea of producing paradigms free of any form of cultural hegemony (Li, Li and Ma 2008; Roulleau-Berger et al. 2008). Therefore, contemporary Chinese sociologies appear to stand within a mosaic of constructivisms against backgrounds of historical or civilizational contexts (Li and Qu 2011; Xie 2012a, 2012b). Chinese sociologists agree with the idea that Western sociologies should not be considered antagonistic to Chinese sociology. Western and Chinese sociologies are not analyzed in a mutually exclusionary relationship. Li Peilin and Wei Jianwen (2018) considered "post-Western sociology" as neither a weapon to deconstruct the hegemony of Western discourse in the post-colonialist discourse nor the further "ideologicalization" in the concept of "East". Instead, they attempt to construct a sociological knowledge system beyond the binary opposition of the West and the non-West.

Then, starting in 2000, the major wave of the sinicization of sociology defined itself in contrast with hegemonic Western thought and indigenization in the international academic environment. In Chinese sociology, we can consider a historic epistemic autonomy refers to the re-establishment of continuities with epistemic frameworks constructed before 1949 and then forgotten. In Europe, most intellectuals ignore renowned pre-1949 Chinese sociology. In *A History of Sociology in China in the First Half of the Twentieth Century*, Li Peilin and Qu Jingdong (2011, 2016) demonstrated how Chinese sociology flourished in a context of intellectual blossoming comparable to that of the spring and autumn periods and to that of the warring states (Qu 2017a).

From a perspective of an alternative epistemic autonomy, He Yijin (2018a, 2018b) considered whether the tense relationship between the West and postcolonial sociology could be found in the Chinese context and whether Chinese sociology has produced historical materialism as its own counterpart. He Yijin analyzed how the sinicization of sociology has been proposed by native scholars to indigenize Western sociology and how Chinese interpretations of Western sociology have been changed.

The issue of epistemic autonomy vis-à-vis Western sociology was first raised in the 1930s by Sun Benwen (Wen and Wang 2012). In 2019, the publication of two articles, written by Xie Yu (2018) and Zhou Xiaohong (2020), sparked controversy and stirred a passionate debate in Chinese sociology. Indeed, this allowed for the questioning of American hegemony, which imposes standards of international scientific legitimacy, such as the necessity to publish in the *American Journal of Sociology* as a supra-norm of scientific recognition. According to Xie Yu, who considers the indigenization of sociology a non-issue, Zhou Xiaohong (2020) defines the indigenization of sociology as the involving issue of a Western hegemonic power in the output of the discipline and as taking differentiated shapes in different historical periods. Chinese sociologists agree with the idea that Western sociologies should not be considered antagonistic to Chinese sociology. Unlike postcolonial studies, which invite a de-Westernization of colonial knowledge, Western sociologies and Chinese sociology are not analyzed in a mutually exclusionary relationship. Then, starting from the year 2000, the main wave of the sinicization of sociology defined itself in contrast with hegemonic Western thought and excessive indigenization to find a strong place in the international academic environment. For instance, Liu Neng and Wu Su (2019) argue that social and cultural practices in China are in part universal, and they refuse the idea of an exaggeration of the Chinese exception. Xie Lizhong (2021) presents a similar perspective by classifying the indigenous sociologies developed in a non-Western country like China into four possible types: "object-transformed indigenization", "supplemented-modified-renewed indigenization", "theoretical substitution indigenization", and "theoretical-methodical substitution indigenization".

In South Korea, Shin Kwang-Yeong (2013) identified three modes of hegemonic social sciences constructed in a double indigenization of social sciences: the development of paradigms in the West; the dominance of located concepts and theories associated with institutional power; and the contested hegemony that refers to unavailable alternative theories. Kim Seung Kuk (2014) spoke of an "East Asian Community (EAC)" and introduced the idea of the invention of an "East Asianism" to propose the orientalization of an East Asia Westernized from hybridizations of "Western" and "non-Western" knowledge, and to move towards a cosmopolitan society by constructing transnational regional identities. For him we were rapidly entering into the world of hybridization which has proliferated over time and space. Kim Seung-Kuk, to break the continuing myth of Orientalism in the name of liberating Easternization or East Asianism, considered, on the one hand, one round of hybridization through the Easternization of a Westernized East Asia, and, on another hand, a second round of hybridization between an emerging non-Western West and an Easternizing East Asia. In opening a dialogue with Bhabha about cultural hybridization, with Antonio Negri about politico-economic hybridization, with Jan Nederveen Pieterse about social hybridization, and with Hwa Yol Jung about transversality and hybridization, he defined East Asian hybrid cultural forms in a cosmopolitan way. Han Sang-Jin (2019) introduced the notion of paradoxical modernity in linking Confucianism as an Asian tradition and reflexive modernity, which came from Europe, particularly from Beck's theory; he demonstrated that reflexive modernity and reflexivity in East Asia differ from the paradigm focused on the global South and a de-colonial or postcolonial way out of their colonial experiences. In a perspective of a theory for reflexive modernity in a cosmopolitan way Han Sang-Jin opened a dialogue with Ulrich Beck on "how to live in a global risk society", with Scott Lash on "reflexive sociology to aesthetic reflexivity", and with Anthony Giddens on "from tradition to reflexive modernization".

For Yazawa Shujiro (2014), Western sociology was diffused in Japan in the context of a process of cultural translation adapted to the Japanese academic field. Until the 1960s, in the context of the development of capitalism, Japanese sociologists were subjected to the influence of American positivism, then to the thinking of Parsons and Marx. This author then explained that after 1980, a postmodern Japanese sociology was developed, with the reappearance of forgotten prewar authors, such as Takada Yasuma and Suzuki Kensuke, and an indigenous sociological theory began to form. For Nomiya Daishiro (2019), if Japanese sociology started from the importation of Western sociology, the incorporation of varied sociological tradition has laid the foundation for the development of Japanese sociology; now, she is providing from sociological imaginations and empirical knowledge multiple perspectives on a global scale.

From a perspective of hybridization Yama Yoshiyuki combines the Western sociological theory of ritual by Durkheim, the Japanese Confucianist theory of ritual by Ogyu Sorai (1666–1728), and the narrative theory of Motoori Norinaga "knowing an empathy toward things" to produce a non-Western hybrid or sociology of narration and narrative. Japanese sociologists, such as Keiichi Sakuta, Akira Kurihara, and Kenji Munesuke Mita, also have developed their own concepts to elucidate the structural and cultural features of Japanese society that cannot be explained by Western traditional sociological theory.

After the Fukushima disaster, Saburo Horikawa (2012) proposed theoretical answers by re-interrogating the notion of "damage" by dealing with its subjective dimension and by inviting the development of a theory of the commons; Torigoe Hiroyuki (2014) developed the theory of life environmentalism by focusing on the existence, the experience, and the ways of life of individuals in communities and common spaces. We can see how the Fukushima disaster has produced new areas of situated knowledge and forms of epistemic autonomy.

The global economy of knowledge is structured around epistemic inequalities, hegemonies, and dominations. A clear division of scientific practices has developed within academic "peripheries", "semi-peripheries", and "cores". Based on the production of an epistemology shared with European, Chinese, Japanese, and Korean sociologists, I am proposing a post-Western sociology to describe an ecology of knowledge and enable a dialogue between *the Western-West*, *the non-Western-West*, *the semi-Western West*, *the Western East*, *the Eastern East*, and *the re-Easternized East* situated on an epistemological continuum. For 20 years Chinese, Korean, and Japanese sociologists have already established epistemic networks in order to produce sociological theories that are far from hegemonic Western paradigms. We have proposed the development of cross-cultural perspectives on sociological knowledge and theoretical methodology in Europe and Asia, and the production of a common conceptual and methodological space within which dialogue and intellectual innovation can take place.

4   The Fabric of Post-Western Sociology

From the epistemology of the Souths and the "re-easternisation of the westernised East" (Kim 2014), we have already introduced the idea of the multiplication, complexification, and hierarchization of new epistemic autonomies vis-à-vis Western hegemonies in sociology, and new epistemic assemblages between European and Asian sociologies (Roulleau-Berger 2016, 2021; Roulleau-Berger and Li 2018). So, on an epistemological continuum, located knowledges coexist in *the Western-Wests*, *non Western-Wests*, *semi Western-Wests*, *Eastern-Easts*, and *non Eastern-Easts*; and the challenge for post-Western sociology is to establish a real dialogue between them through discursive pluralism (2020). However, to progress toward global critical sociology, we have opened trans-epistemic spaces for active dialogue between Western and non-Western sociologies (Roulleau-Berger and Li 2012).

Post-Western sociology refuses term-for-term structural comparisons and favors intersecting viewpoints concerning registers of understanding, agreement, and disagreement as well as the scientific practices. Post-Western sociology can also be defined as global critical sociology. In post-Western sociology, we are producing an ecology of knowledge in which diverse forms of knowledge may interact, articulated through cosmovisions of the world and civilizations, as well as emancipatory and creative practices (Pleyers 2011). This paradigm is developing in a continuum of assemblages, tensions, and the cross-pollination of different segments from this ecology of knowledge. Sociological practices are viewed as relationships of equivalence in the post-Western space. While the processes of cross-pollination and hybridization are particularly manifest in non-Western sociologies, Western sociologies are only slowly integrating situated knowledge produced by other intellectual, scientific, and cultural traditions.

Post-Western sociology does not use the differences but the gaps/intervals between the perspectives, practices, and concepts of Chinese/Asian and European sociologies to coproduce new knowledge, which is the starting point of the construction process of post-Western sociology. Thus, it precedes the conception of theoretical and methodological combinations and assemblages. International sociology and global sociology do not imply this erasing of epistemological boundaries: this is precisely where the distinctions among post-Western sociology, international sociology, and global sociology lie (Li and Roulleau-Berger 2018).

Drawing on European and Asian experiences, we analyzed how a post-Western space has come into being in which sociological knowledge is produced that is both specific and shared and in which theoretical methodologies are gathered based on very different histories and traditions. We have reconstructed the trajectories of given sociological knowledge in Asia and Europe, identify some loci of controversy in the production of knowledge linked to methodological theory, and used controversy as an instrument to analyze the boundaries between conceptual spaces and methods deployed. It means examining those forms of knowledge that appear to be specific; those that seem to be the product of reappropriation, reinterpretation, borrowing, and creolization; and those that seem to be produced in areas of non-translatability, that is, in spaces in which research practices and sociological knowledge in Europe and Asia do not correspond with each other.

In order to understand the evolution of sociology towards Post-Western Sociology, I propose proceeding with four stages.

First, we discussed the some heritages of Western sociology and their forms of appropriation, transformation, and reconfiguration in Asia, for example, the theories of Durkheim, Weber and Bourdieu.

Second, we investigated and defined what makes epistemic autonomy in niches of knowledge—where located knowledge is produced—in different sociologies, and we analyzed how they multiply, diversify, and hierarchize.

Third, we analyzed the circulations and assemblages in transnational spaces of knowledge between Europe and Asia; this will make it possible to show the junctions, the tensions, the (in)compatibilities between acquired knowledge, knowledge produced locally, and knowledge implemented in different contexts. The reconfiguration of global scientific fields produces accelerated transformations. The need to grasp them quickly makes this project so timely and urgent.

Finally, we carried out a multisituated sociology of the fieldwork practices adopted by Asian and European sociologists in order to understand where sociologists' practices might intersect with, shun, or enrich each other in their particular research settings (Roulleau-Berger and Liu 2021). In post-Western sociology undertaking fieldwork together still appears to be central in the fabrication of sociological knowledge by taking into account alternative political economies of knowledge in an *anti-piratic way* (Tilley 2017). In accordance with

Vincenzo Cicchelli (2018), *cosmopolitan imagination* is necessary to develop sociological studies of cosmopolitanism in different fields. Post-Western methodology leads to a multisituated sociology, co-undertaking fieldwork in a plurality of spaces, situations, contexts, and temporalities. This signifies the implementation of contextualized tools to account for assemblies and disjunctions between the narratives of societies. In this instance, here, a post-Western methodology is federated around dynamic and non-hierarchical combinations of societal contexts, structural processes, individual and collective actions, and situational orders. The post-Western conceptual space is relayed by a methodological space in which sociologists access the plurality of the narratives of society and the multivocality or polyphony. In the fabric of post-Western sociology I am calling attention to the simultaneity of different forms of spaces of epistemic autonomy and theoretical pollination in the copresence of differently situated sociologies. Although the processes of cross-pollination and hybridization are particularly manifest in non-Western sociologies, Western sociologies are only slowly integrating situated knowledge produced by other intellectual, scientific, and cultural traditions.

In the post-Western sociology Xie Lizhong (2020) integrated his theory of discursive pluralism, distinct from geographic pluralism, to describe Western and non-Western societies beyond epistemic borders linked to indigenous sociological theories. He considers geographic pluralism to favor the indigenization of sociological thought by producing a discourse in a specific time and space.

5   Western Heritages from Yesterday and Today

Post-Western sociology contains different modes of appropriation and reading the classical authors like Durkheim, Weber, Marx, Foucault, but also the contemporary and major figures like Bourdieu. The idea of confronting our way in understanding these Western heritages in China is a key to entering into the post-Western space.

5.1   *Durkheim's Theory in China*
Durkheim's theory was introduced very early in China (Roulleau-Berger and Liu 2012). Today, intellectual legacies and specific theoretical approaches are still intertwined in Chinese sociology. Durkheim's theories were developed for the first time in 1949. They were taken up twice after 1979, and they have since been revised, for example, by Wu Chun, Li Fangying, Wang Hejian, Chen Tao,

Qu Jingdong, and Zhao Liwei. Durkheim's religion plays a central role in the construction of the social bond in modern Western societies, which makes it possible to understand how individuals share a collective consciousness that creates the feeling of belonging to a moral community. Li Fangying (2006) considered Durkheim to force too much the relation between socialization and religion, between social solidarity and religion, and not think enough about the relationship between religion and social conflict. Wang Hejian (2005) proposed revisiting Durkheim by taking an interest in producing moral goods in the modern Chinese economy. From the perspective of economic sociology, this involves linking economic morality and the social structure, based on an analysis of professional relationships. Chen Tao (2013) was also interested in the contractual society described by Durkheim where morality is generated by communal life and where the autonomy and freedom of individuals, constrained to social facts, are based on the respect of social rules to produce a "normal" society. For Qu Jingdong (2017b), in Durkheim's perspective, collective life transcends individual existence. If studying the moral and social order requires starting from the production of norms in everyday life, the relationship between society and state cannot be thought of as antagonistic but rather as a continuum in which the ethics of professional groups and civic morality link individuals to the state. Last, for Zhao Liwei (2014), Durkheim's theory of suicide appears to be a major contribution that remains very important to understanding modern societies. In this sense, one could say that Durkheim's study of suicide as a general social fact explains the modern human condition.

5.2 Weber's Theory in China

Weber's theory also had a very strong influence in China. His books on China, *Confucianism and Taoism* and *The Religion of China*, occupied a prominent position in Weber's research system. First, Weber's China studies were regarded as Eurocentric and hegemonic studies. According to He Rong (2020), Weber's theoretical ambition was to understand the various types of rationalism in the world's civilization systems, indicating that the world's civilization systems are a rational regulatory system of equality, juxtaposition, and coexistence. She asserted that Max Weber overcame the cleavages between Western and non-Western civilizations. His research on China is part of the grand system of the economic ethics of the world's religions. It is by no means a single process with the West as the only model and teleological orientation; however, it should follow the inherent logic of each civilization system and have its own characteristics. It can be said that this research strategy of his method avoids Eurocentrism. For He Rong, *Confucianism and Taoism* is not only a study of the spiritual temperament of Confucian rationalism, that is, in a dialogue with Protestant ethics, but more than half of the work is devoted to the topic of sociology.

5.3 Bourdieu's Theory in China

Bourdieu's work only began to be known in China in the 1990s; *la Distinction* and *la Noblesse d'Etat* would be translated; in 1996, *Libre-Echange* would be published; then in 1997 the interviews with Loïc Wacquant, *Invitation to reflexive sociology*; in 2000, *Sur la télévision*; in 2011, *Les règles de l'art*; in 2006 *Homo Academicus* was translated (Sapiro 2020). The field theory would be widely mobilized in China, the theory of social reproduction was widely cited in sociological works for about 15 years. Li Lulu (2008) described the double social reproduction process arising out of power instituted by the State and institutions on the one hand, and the imposition of a social and symbolic domination by dominant groups that produce the interiorization of social relationships of domination on the other. This theory echoes Pierre Bourdieu's theory of genetic structuralism; however, the forms of reproduction and social domination are still situated in a socialist context in which instituted power and symbolic domination are constructed from cultural, social, institutional, and political orders linked to the history of Chinese society. Li Lulu explicitly refers to Pierre Bourdieu and poses the hypothesis of the universality of social reproduction processes in which the form varies according to societal contexts.

In a very closed perspective, Li Chunling (2012) shows how social mobility pathways were to diversify from 1979 and the structural barriers to mobility were redefined. She also showed how economic capital played a crucial role in social mobility prior to 1949 but became a negative factor between 1949 and 1980. She explained the paradox of the reforms after 1979, which have increased the opportunities for mobility and at the same time made the boundaries between social groups clearer, for example, elites maintained their position. This approach to social mobility in China also demonstrated how volumes of economic, social, and cultural capital, their structure, and the evolution over time of these properties define what Pierre Bourdieu called "a three-dimensional space" (1979), except that one must also take into consideration the global volume of political capital that combines with resources and powers linked to the very decisive political position in China.

If Western heritages are still quite influential in sociologies from Asia, we cannot consider Eastern heritages to have been mobilized in European sociologies. In China, Korea, and Japan, Confucianism is a common heritage and is revisited in different ways. In Korean sociology, Confucian heritage and

Western sociology are combined; however, in Chinese and Japanese sociology, Confucian heritage is embedded in the Chinese or Japanese traditions. But in Western sociologies Confucian heritage has not been imported.

6   Epistemic Autonomy and Located Knowledge

In post-Western sociology we have identified spaces of epistemic autonomy in European and Asian sociologies in order to circumscribe the located knowledge in each context and open new dialogues between them. In Chinese sociology, we can select the concepts of *guanxi* and "mosaic familialism", and in French sociology we will introduce the concept of public space.

The term *guanxi circle* is really important in Chinese culture and in social sciences. Yang Yiyin (2008, 2012) considers *guanxi* not to be the relationship between two individuals, two groups, or an individual and a group; rather, it indicates a sort of coloration and penetration of social relationship by a Chinese cultural hue. So, she distinguished three levels to define what makes *guanxi*: interpersonal relations, intergroup relations, and group-individual relations. Interdependent self-construal and interdependent self-construal are two typical self-construals. Yang Yiyin introduces *guanxi* as the prescriptivity of interpersonal rules in interpersonal connection and defines it as a subcultural genre of interdependent self but not an exclusive product of Chinese society; it originates from the Chinese traditional mourning dressing system of the Nine Clan and Five Clothing system. The "We" is produced on the one hand by the *guanxi* that draw the particular boundaries of "I"; or, more precisely, what Fei Xiaotong (1992) called the *chaxu geju*, and on the other hand through categories, identifications, and social memberships. "Guanxinization" is the establishment process of the typical "self" and the "we" in Chinese traditional society. "Ziji ren" serves one form of interpersonal relationship among Chinese people. Yang Yiyin has considered

> in the Western culture, the construction of group-individual *guanxi* by the self-construal of independent self tends to be realized through categorization. While in Chinese traditional culture, it is easier to be realized by guanxization in terms of group-individual guanxi by the self-construal of interdependent self.

The We is the result of the relations between guanxinization, categorization, and embedding; *guanxi* today are evaluating in "mixed self" or "polyself". Whereas in Western theories, the *me*, the *I*, and the *Others* are seen as quite distinct moments in a quite discontinuous process of the *self*, in Chinese thinking, these separate steps are not so clearly delineated, as the process itself is much more continuous.

According to Zhang Jingting and Jia Chao (2021) Chinese culture has always attached great importance to emotion; traditional Chinese rule was highly dependent on notions of human kindness and compassion. These authors have distinguished emotional patterns in Chinese history into the traditional structure of feeling, the revolutionary structure of feeling, and the consumerist structure of feeling. Cheng Boqing (2012, 2013) first produced a theory focused on social interaction and *guanxis*, then promoted the sociology of emotions in China. He considered that we have to come back to the *self* and especially to the *Confucian self* and to take account in the transformation of the *modern self*. For Cheng Boqing the way of thinking of the Subject was inscribed in a new Confucianism and Foucault's theory—it means to articulate the *ethical self*: it means the requirements, emotions, and limits in our relationship to Others, *the aesthetical self*; it means affections and feelings, and the *transcendental self*.

In a closed perspective the Confucian patriarchal tradition and the socialist heritage have played a fundamental role in the production of the Chinese experience. During the Mao era, Chinese families sought economic stability, security, and social protection above all. The 1978 reforms deeply revolutionized family structures in Chinese society. The changes brought about by a growing GDP, mass education, and the decline of patriarchy destabilized traditional societal structures in China, particularly in rural areas. During the socialist period, individuals who were excluded from the patriarchal family were more or less forgotten in a dominant collectivism, instead of being integrated in a strong welfare state (Ji Yingchun 2017). With the reinstitutionalization of gender inequalities and of family as an institution, in a context of commodification and privatization in the labor markets, Ji Yingchun (2020) conceptualized the very located concept of *mosaic familialism*, which contains elements of Confucian patriarchal tradition, of socialist heritage and of a compressed modernity, and which is characterized by situations of great social and economic uncertainty for individuals and by new dynamics in family relations.

In French sociology, the issue of democracy and forms of collective action in the public space appears to be highly situated. The question of the voiceless, of the "sans"; is recurrent in public debate; it is central with the urban riots (Kokoreff and Lapeyronnie 2014) that mobilize some of the children of postcolonial immigration and it has been further amplified with the mobilizations of asylum seekers and refugees, and the construction of new situated citizenships (Neveu 2014) from below. In a context of the overexposure of weakened, discriminated, and fragile individuals, the voices of weak actors are raised in the public space. In European democracies, the public space also becomes a place of struggle against social fears and of conquest through mobilizations, demonstrations, rallies, and the staging of collectives of the voiceless. Urban revolts remind us that subaltern minorities can become active, can express a capacity of mobilization, revealing forgotten places of speech. They reveal processes of invisibility of the "forgotten of the democracy" in the modes of social, economic, moral, and political organization.

The definition of what makes located knowledge is really complex because of a plastic and dynamic process, so we have to redefine located knowledge at each new step in the fabric of the post-Western sociology. Moreover, it is impossible to produce a creolized knowledge without knowing how, where, and when located knowledge is produced.

7   Sociologies in Dialogue and Post-Western Assemblages

Based on various research programs in France and China, we have shown in a constructed dialogue how "Western" and "non-Western" theories meet, how shared sociological knowledge and situated knowledge cohabit and become embedded. From the intersecting perspectives of European and Chinese researchers, we have constructed theoretical assemblages between Chinese and European sociology which open up a transnational space for the production of a process of the pollination of knowledge.

7.1   *Inequalities and Social Mobility*

Over the past decade, China's economic and social development has entered a new phase, with a series of historical transitions and new characteristics of the stages, including the continuous and profound changes in the structure of social classes, which have a wide impact on the economy and society (Li and Cui 2020). Instead, as Li Chunling (2019) aptly demonstrated, it accentuated the phenomenon in which intragenerational social inequalities are reproduced between young skilled people and the new generation of young low-skilled migrants. In China, the last 10 years have been marked by increased competition, the devaluation of academic achievement, and a simultaneous and continuous rise in youth's social aspirations. This phenomenon of *structural disqualification* (Bourdieu 1978) impacts low-skilled migrants in China above all. The *widespread and systemic downward social mobility* (Chauvel 2016; Li 2019) has affected the young graduates.

The most profound change has occurred within the workforce, namely the rapid increase in the proportion of "white collars" while the proportion of "blue collars" (industrial workers) has declined. Second, the two main groups of the middle class, the "new middle class" and the "old middle class" are both growing rapidly, with the proportion of the "new middle class" growing which is primarily made up of professionals and technicians. A new urban *underclass* has been formed with the second generation of young, less-qualified migrants. A new process of marginalization and social segregation is produced within Chinese cities linked to forms of unemployment, emerging precariat, and systems of structural disqualification which target young people, especially young migrants.

In France, in Western Europe, the increase in inequalities between the "working rich" (Godechot 2007) and the "working poor" has worsened in a context of *middle-class squeeze*, where the disappearance of intermediate jobs largely affects the working classes and the lower fraction of the middle classes (Duvoux 2017). As in China, the development of self-employed status, for example with auto-entrepreneurs, particularly in digital work, is contributing to an increase in inequalities "from below" linked to the institutionalization of precariat and the development of unemployment. A new European urban underclass is living in segregated working-class suburbs. New migrants, asylum seekers, and refugees are joining them and forming a *global underclass*.

Approaches in terms of social polarization and social reproduction are widely mobilized in the French and Chinese sociologies of social classes. This reflects the *continuous continuities* between the French and Chinese sociological approaches.

7.2   *Ethnicity, Space, and Religion*

In Chinese sociology, just as in European sociology, the deconstruction of the ethnic entity should take societal and historical contexts into account, such as colonialism and nationalism, which produce classifications and fixed moral and social borders. This signifies the deconstruction of ethnic categorizations and classifications in a constructivist approach, interethnic relationships according to Fredrik Barth, as well as ethnic boundaries, globalized religions, and transnational spaces. In China, the term "ethnic group" is a foreign concept. Before the 1960s, studies of ethnic groups were rare in the Chinese social sciences. Since the 1970s, the theory of ethnic boundaries conceived by Fredrik Barth has had broad repercussions in Chinese academic circles and has been widely cited. Thus, *continuous continuities* have been produced around the theory of ethnic boundaries between Western European and Chinese sociologies.

In France, according to Jean-Louis Amselle (1990), ethnicity was a fiction or an illusion produced under the influence of imposed identities in a colonial situation. The public affirmation of ethnicity and tensions between history and memory was also founded by the struggles of postcolonial migrants (Boubeker 2003); the children of postcolonial immigration cling to their cultural and religious traditions, especially Islamic ones.

In Chinese sociology and anthropology, for Fan Ke (2017) the notions of ethnic group and ethnic boundary have brought an entirely new paradigm, and many things people used to take for granted have now begun to receive serious scrutiny. As a result of Barth's work, many scholars have had second thoughts on how people were categorized in the ethnic identification campaign and how this categorization has changed ethnic configurations in China; more importantly, many scholars are questioning how national, ethnic, or any other kind of collective identities has been constructed and reconstructed. In this constructivist approach, for example, Fan Ke (2017) conducted an in-depth field study of the two main Hui groups in the Quanzhou region: the Ding clan and the Guo clan; he described the process of localizing Islam through the activities of the Hui clan and the reappearance of Islamic culture. Mi Shoujiang (2010) also developed the concept of "urban Islamic cultural ecology".

Following in the footsteps of French scholars, Chinese scholars have come to adhere to a constructivist approach to ethnicity (Fan 2017). They conceptualize the dynamic relationships between ethnicity and cultural identity to study ethnic interactions, the relationships between ethnic groups, and the state and the moral boundaries of ethnic groups (He 2017). Nevertheless, the question of ethnicity and religion could be formulated differently in French and Chinese sociologies. For example, situated concepts can be found in Chinese studies, such as the process of "localizing" Islam or even "urban Islamic cultural ecology" (Mi 2010), showing the broad difference between the weakening of urban traditional Muslim communities and rural Muslim communities. So, we also can identify *continuous discontinuities* between Western European and Chinese sociologies

7.3 *Compressed Individual and Global Condition*

In creating theoretical conjunctions between European, American, Chinese, and located knowledge in a post-Western and cross-pollination perspective I have combined different concepts: the concept of *compressed modernity* from Chang Kyung-Sup, and that of *compressibility* from Shi Yunqing (2018); the concept of emotional capitalism from Eva Illouz and Arlie Hochschild; the concepts of individuation in the sense of Yan Yunxiang (2010) and subjectivation in the sense of Paul Ricoeur (2004); and the concept of globalization (Sassen 2007). In China the effects of collisions between temporalities, spaces, and situations specific to *multi-compressed modernity* (Chang 2010, 2017) produce bifurcations, unpredictability, and reversibility in individual and collective biographies. Constant clashes occur between spaces, temporalities, and situations, simultaneously giving rise to a growing number of zones of uncertainty. Each time Chinese youth migrate, a new biographical crossroads appears with a vast number of possible choices, fuelling further uncertainty.

The individual must undergo a series of identity changes due to spatial and professional mobility and changes in *floating work*, thus becoming increasingly multi-compressed. The Chinese migrant reveals the effects of collisions intrinsic to compressed modernity which manufacture what I have called a *compressed individual* who features as "a hero" (Roulleau-Berger 2021b) equipped with strong emotional capacities and forced into a cycle of self-improvement. If emotional capitalism is a culture where emotional and economic practices and discourses influence each other and where feelings and emotions become commodities (Illouz and Hochschild 2006), we can say that an "emotional socialism" exists in China. The *compressed individual* has internalized the injunction to invent a narrative of self-performance, giving rise to young Chinese entrepreneurs and executives in both China and abroad.

8   Conclusion

If the pandemic has favored a process of closing certain social, moral, physical, and political boundaries, it also produces new boundaries of knowledge and new spaces for dialogue. To create dialogues between European, Chinese, Japanese, and Korean sociologies in different fields is a way to open spaces for multiple knowledges to flourish toward a post-COVID "democratic sociology" (Connell 2019) by producing a polyphonic economy of knowledge. *Post-Western sociology* has become a simultaneously local and global critical conception challenging the established boundaries of some scientific territories. It also means taking into consideration new forms of academic competition and hegemony. In the new post-COVID geography of non-hegemonic conceptions we simultaneously analyze the delocalized and relocalized epistemologies of *the Western-Wests, non Western-Wests, semi Western-Wests, Eastern-Easts, non-Eastern-Easts*, the demultiplication of epistemic injustices and autonomies, and new assemblages of local knowledge. We hope the pandemic will not prevent us from coproducing creolized *knowledge* by using a cosmopolitan sociological imagination to create a new future of social sciences.

Bibliography

Alatas, Syed Hussein. 1974. "The Captive Mind and Creative Development". *International Social Science Journal* 24 (4): 691–700.

Alatas, Syed Farid. 2003. Academic Dependency and the Global Division of Labour in the Social Sciences, *Current Sociology* 51 (6): 599–613.

Amselle, J.L. 1990. *Logiques métisses: anthropologie de l'identité en Afrique et ailleurs*. Paris: Payot.
Appaduraï, A. 1996. *Modernity At Large: Cultural Dimensions of Globalization*. Minneapolis, MN: University of Minnesota Press.
Beck, U. 2006. *Qu'est-ce que le cosmopolitisme*. Paris: Aubier.
Beck, U., and E. Grande. 2010. "Varieties of Second Modernity: The Cosmopolitan Turn in Social and Political Theory and Research". *The British Journal of Sociology* 61 (3): 409–444.
Bhambra, G.K. 2014. *Connected Sociologies*. London and New York: Bloomsbury.
Bhambra, G.K. de Sousa Santos. 2017. "Introduction: Global Challenges for Sociology". *Sociology* 51 (1): 3–10.
Bhambra, G.K., and J. Holmwood. 2021. *Colonialism and Modern Social Theory*. Cambridge: Polity Press.
Blagojevic, M. 2010. "The Catch 22 Syndrome of Social Scientists in the Semiperiphery: Exploratory Sociological Observations". *Sociologica* 52 (4): 337–358.
Boubeker, A. 2003. *Les mondes de l'ethnicité: la communauté d'expérience des héritiers de l'immigration maghrébine*. Paris: Balland.
Bourdieu, P. 1978. "Classement, déclassement, reclassement". *Actes de la recherche en sciences sociales* 24: 2–22.
Bourdieu, P. 1979. *La distinction. Critique sociale du jugement* (*Distinction. A social critique of the judgement of taste*). Paris: Les Éditions de Minuit.
Bourdieu, P. 1993. *La misère du monde* [World's misery]. Paris: Seuil.
Brandel, A., V. Das, and S. Randeria. 2018. "Locations and Locutions: Unravelling the Concept of World Anthropology". In *Post-Western Sociology—From China to Europe*, edited by L. Roulleau-Berger and Li Peilin. London and New York: Routledge.
Briceno-Leon, R. 2020. "The Mestizo Sociology in Latin America". In *Sociologies in dialogue*, edited by S. Hanafi and C.C. Yi, pp. 98–114. Sage: London.
Brisson, T. 2018. *Décentrer l'Occident*. Paris: La Découverte.
Chakrabarty, D. 2000. *Provincializing Europe: Postcolonial Thought and Historical Difference*. Princeton, NJ: Princeton University Press.
Chang, Kyung-Sup. 2010. "The Second Modern Condition? Compressed Modernity as Internalized Reflexive Cosmopolitization". *The British Journal of Sociology* 61 (3): 444–465.
Chang, Kyung-Sup. 2017a. "Compressed Modernity in South Korea: Constitutive Dimensions, Manifesting Units, and Historical Conditions". In *The Routledge Handbook of Korean Culture and Society*, edited by Y. Kim, pp. 75–92. New York, NY: Routledge.
Chang, Kyung-Sup. 2017b. "China as a Complex Risk Society". *Temporalités* [En ligne] 26. DOI: https://doi.org/10.4000/temporalites.3810.
Chen, Tao. 2013. "Artificial Society or Natural Society Durkheim's Critique of Social Contract Theory". *Sociological Studies* 3: 47–75.

Chen, Tao, and Xie Jiabiao. 2016. "The Mixed Resistance: Analysis of Environmental Struggle by Peasants". *Sociological Studies* 3: 25–46.
Cheng, Boqing. 2012. *Emotion, Narrative and Rhetoric—Exploration of Social Theory*. Beijing: China Social Sciences Press.
Cheng, Boqing. 2013. "The Sociological Meaning of Emotion". *Shandong Social Sciences* 211 (3): 42–48.
Cicchelli, V. 2018. *Plural and Shared: The Sociology of a Cosmopolitan World*. Boston and Leiden: Brill Publishers.
Connell, R. 2007. *Southern Theory*. Cambridge: Polity Press.
Connell, Raewyn. 2019. *The Good University*. London: Zed Books.
Dirlik, A. 2007. *Global Modernity: Modernity in the Age of Global Capitalism*. Paradigm Publishers.
Dufoix, S. 2013. "Les naissances académiques du global" [Global's academic births]. In *Le tournant global des sciences sociales*, edited by A. Caillé and S. Dufoix, pp. 27–44. Paris: La Découverte.
Duvoux, N. 2017. *Les inégalités sociales*. Paris: PUF.
Dwyer, T., and C.B. Martins. 2020. "The Brazilian Sociological Society and Recent Reflections on the Internationalization of Sociology". In *Sociologies in Dialogue*, edited by S. Hanafi and C.C. Yi, pp. 81–98. London: Sage.
Eisenstadt, S. 2000. *Multiple Modernities*. New Brunswick: Transaction Publishers.
Erasga, S.D. 2020. "Project Filipinong Sosyolohiya: a Nativist Sociology Converses with the Global Sociology". In *Sociologies in Dialogue*, edited by S. Hanafi and C.C. Yi, pp. 81–98. London: Sage.
Fan, Ke. 2017. "Barth's Ethnic Boundary and the Understanding of Frontier in Chinese Context". *Academic Monthly* 49 (7): 99–110.
Fei, Xiaotong. 1992. *From the Soil: The Foundation of Chinese Society*. Berkeley: University of California Press.
Go, J. 2013. "Sociology's Imperial Unconscious: The Emergence of American Sociology in the Context of Empire". In *Sociology and Empire*, edited by G. Steinmetz, pp. 83–105. Durham, NC: Duke University Press.
Go, J. 2016. *Postcolonial Thought and Social Theory*. Oxford: Oxford University Press.
Godechot, O. 2007. *Working rich. Salaires, bonus et appropriation du profit dans l'industrie financière*. Paris: La Découverte.
Han, Sang-Jin. 2019. *Confucianism and Reflexive Modernity: Bringing Community back to Human Rights in the Age of Global Risk Society*. Leiden and Boston: Brill Publishers.
Han, S.-J., and Y.-H. Shim. 2010. "Redefining second modernity for East Asia: a critical assessment". *The British Journal of Sociology* 61 (3): 465–488.
Hanafi, S. 2020. "Post-colonialism vs Post-authoritarianism: The Arab World and Latin America in Comparative Perspective". In *Sociologies in Dialogue*, edited by S. Hanafi and C.C. Yi, pp. 161–177. London: Sage.

Hanafi, S., and C.C. Yi. 2020. "Introduction". In *Sociologies in Dialogue*, edited by S. Hanafi and C.C. Yi, pp. 1–13. London: Sage.

He, Hu. 2017. "On the Construction of Ethnic Groups and Cultural Identity". *Journal of Dalian University for Nationalities* 19 (4): 239–299.

He, Rong. 2020. "Max Weber's View on China: An Investigation Based on Research Position and Text Source". *New Perspectives on World Literature*: 49–59.

He, Yijin. 2018a. "An Alternative Autonomy: The Self-adaptations of Chinese Sociology in the 1950s". In *Post-Western Sociology: From China to Europe*, edited by L. Roulleau-Berger and Peilin Li. Oxford and New York: Routledge.

He, Yijin. 2018b. "Variations of the Other: The Context and Fluctuations of Sinicizing Sociology in China". *Sociological Review of China* 6 (6): 84–95.

Horikawa, S. 2012. "Kankyō shakai-gaku ni totte 'higai' to wa nani ka—posuto 3. 11 No kankyō shakai-gaku o kangaeru tame no ichi sozai to shite" [What is "damage" for environmental sociology? A material for reflection on post-11/03 environmental sociology]. *Journal of Environmental Sociology* 18: 5–26.

Hochschild, A., and E. Illouz. 2006. *Les sentiments du capitalism*. Paris: Seuil.

Ji, Yingchun. 2017. "A Mosaic Temporality: New Dynamics of the Gender and Marriage System in Contemporary Urban China". *Temporalités. Revue de sciences sociales et humaines* (26). DOI: doi.org/10.4000/temporalites.3773.

Ji, Yingchun. 2020. "Masaike Jiating Zhuyi: Cong Never Yanglao Kan Jiating Zhidu Bianqian" [Mosaic Familism: Daughters Providing for Parents and the Reinstitutionalization of Chinese Families]. *Ershiyi Shiji Shuangyuekan* [Twenty-First Century Bi-Monthly] 180 (4): 77–79.

Jobin, Paul, Ming-sho Ho, and Michael Hsiao Hsin-Huang. 2021. *Environmental Movements and Politics of the Asian Anthropocene*. Singapore: ISEAS.

Kim, Seung Kuk, Peilin Li, and Shujiro Yasawa, eds. 2014. *A Quest of East Asian Sociologies*, pp. 313–328. Seoul: Seoul National University Press.

Kim, Seung Kuk. 2014. "East Asian Community as Hybridization: A Quest for East Asianism". In *A Quest for East Asian Sociologies*, edited by Seung Kuk Kim, Peilin Li, and Shujiro Yasawa. Seoul: Seoul University Press.

Kokoreff, M. and D. Lapeyronnie. 2013. *Refaire la cité. L'avenir des banlieues*. Paris: Ed. Seuil.

Koleva, S. 2018. *Totalitarian Experience and Knowledge Production Sociology in Central and Eastern Europe 1945–1989*. Leiden and Boston: Brill Publishers.

Koleva, S. 2021. "Doing Post-Western Sociology in Central and Eastern Europe Before and After the Great Change: Some Epistemological Questions". *The Journal of Chinese Sociology* 8 (10).

Kuhn, M. 2021. *The Social Science of the Citizen Society*. Vol. 1: *Critique of the Globalization and Decolonization of the Social Sciences*. Stuttgart: Ibidem Verlag.

Kwang-Yeong, S. 2013. "The Emergence of Hegemonic Social Sciences and Strategies of Non (Counter) Hegemonic Social Sciences". In *Theories About Strategies Against Hegemonic Social Sciences*, edited by M. Kuhn and S. Yasawa, pp. 77–94. Tokyo: Seijo University.

Li Chunling. 2012. "Social Mobility and Social Class in China: A Comparative Study of Intragenerational Mobility Models Before and After The Economic Reforms". In *European and Chinese Sociologies. A New Dialogue*, edited by L. Roulleau-Berger and Peilin Li, pp. 117–127. Leiden and Boston: Brill Publishers.

Li Chunling. 2019. "Gaige kaifang de haizimen: zhongguo xinsheng dai yu zhongguo fazhan xin shidai" [The new generation and new period of development]. *Shehuixue Yanjiu* 3: 1–24.

Li, Lulu. 2008. "Transition and Social Stratification in Chinese Cities". In *La Nouvelle Sociologie chinoise* [New Chinese sociology], edited by L. Roulleau-Berger, Yuhua Guo, Peilin Li, and Shiding Liu, pp. 119–145. Paris: Editions du CNRS.

Li, Peilin. 2012. "Chinese Society and the China Experience". In *Chinese Society—Change and Transformation*, edited by Peilin Li. London and New York: Routledge.

Li, Peilin. 2015. "La modernisation orientale et l'expérience chinoise". *Socio* 5: 25–45.

Li, Peilin, and Yan Cui. 2020. "Wo guo 2008–2019 nianjian shehui jieceng jiegou de bianhua jiqi jingjishehui yingxiang" [The Changes in Social Stratum Structure From 2008 to 2019 in China and the Economic and Social Impact]. *Jiangsu shehui kexue* [Jiangsu Social Sciences] 4: 51–60.

Li, Peilin, and Wei Li. 2013. "The Work Situation and Social Attitudes of Migrant Workers in China under the Crisis". In *China's Internal and International Migration*, edited by Peilin Li and L. Roulleau-Berger, pp. 3–26. Oxford and New York: Routledge.

Li, Peilin, and Jingdong Qu. 2011. *History of Sociology in China in the First Half of the Twentieth Century*. Beijing: Social Sciences Academic Press.

Li, Peilin, and Jingdong Qu. 2016. *La sociologie chinoise avant la Révolution*. Paris: Editions FMSH.

Li Peilin, Qiang Li, and Rong Ma. 2008. *Shehuixue he zhongguo shehui* [Sociology and Chinese Society]. Beijing: Shehui kexue wenxian chubanshe.

Li, Peilin, and L. Roulleau-Berger, eds. 2013. *China's internal and International Migration*. London and New York: Routledge Publishers.

Liu, Neng, and Wu Su. 2019. "On the Indigenization of Sociology as an Academic Movement". *Journal of University of Jinan* 29 (1): 5–16.

Lian, Si. 2009. *Ants*. Cuilin: Guangxi Normal University Press.

Liu, Wenbin, and Yalin Wang. 2017. "The Re-understanding of Connotation of Sociological Indigenization in China". *Journal of Social Sciences* 19 (1): 50–59.

Meghji, A. 2021. *Decolonizing Sociology*. Cambridge: Polity Press.

Mi, Shoujiang. 2010. "The Process of Urbanization of Islam in China and Its Development Trend". *The Religious Cultures in the World*, n°1: 56–60.

Neveu, C. 2014. *Disputing Citizenship*, with J. Clarke, K. Coll, and E. Dagnino. London: Policy Press.

Nomiya, D. 2019. "A Short History of Japanese Sociology: Its Historical Legacies and Future Dreams". *Economic and Social Changes: Facts, Trends, Forecast* 12 (5): 155–157.

Patel, S. 2010. "At Crossroads. Sociology in India". In *The ISA Handbook of Diverse Sociological Tradition*, edited by S. Patel. London: Sage Publishers.

Pleyers, G. 2011. *Alter-Globalization*. Cambridge: Polity Press.

Qu, Jingdong. 2017a. "Back to Historical Views, Reconstructing the Sociological Imagination: The New Tradition of Classical and Historical Studies in the Modern Chinese Transformation". *Chinese Journal of Sociology* 3: 135–166.

Qu, Jingdong. 2017b. "After Sacred Society: To Commemorating 100th Anniversary of Emile Durkheim's Death". *Chinese Journal of Sociology* 4: 1–32.

Quijano, A. 2000. "Coloniality of Power and Eurocentrism in Latin America". *International Sociology* 15 (2): 215–232.

Reuter, J., and P.I. Villa. 2015. *Postkoloniale Soziologie. Empirische Befunde, theoretische Anschlüsse, politische Intervention*. Bielefeld: Transcript Verlag.

Ricoeur, P. 2004. *Trajectories of recognition*. Paris: Stock.

Roulleau-Berger, L. 2008. "Pluralité et identité de la sociologie chinoise". In *La nouvelle sociologie chinoise*, edited by L. Roulleau-Berger, Yuhua Guo, Peilin Li, and Shiding Liu. Paris: CNRS Publishers.

Roulleau-Berger, L. 2011. *Dewesternization of sociology. Europe in China's looking glass*. La Tour d'Aigues: Editions de L'aube. Translated into Chinese by Social Sciences Academic Press, 2014.

Roulleau-Berger, L. 2021a. "The Fabric of Post-Western Sociology: Ecologies of Knowledge Beyond the 'East' and the 'West'". *The Journal of Chinese Sociology* 8 (10): 2–28.

Roulleau-Berger, L. 2021b. *Young Chinese Migrants. Compressed Individual and Global Condition*. Leiden and Boston: Brill Publishers.

Roulleau-Berger, L. 2016. *Post-Western Revolution in Sociology. From China to Europe*. Boston and Leiden: Brill Publishers.

Roulleau-Berger, L., and Li Peilin, eds. 2012. *European and Chinese Sociologies. A New Dialogue*. Boston and Leiden: Brill Publishers.

Roulleau-Berger, L., and Li Peilin, eds. 2018. *Post-Western Sociology. From China to Europe*. Leiden: Brill Publishers.

Roulleau-Berger, L., Guo Yuhua, Li Peilin, and Liu Shiding, eds. 2008. *La nouvelle sociologie chinoise*. Paris: CNRS Publishers.

Roulleau-Berger, L., and Liu Yuzhao. 2021. *Sociology of Migration and Post-Western Theory*. Lyon: ENS Publishers.

Roulleau-Berger, L., and Liu Zhengai. 2012. "Durkheim's Religion's Theory and Chinese Sociology". *Archives de Sciences Sociales des religions* 159: 135–151.

Santos, B.S. 2014. *Epistemologies of the South: Justice Against Epistemicide*. New York, NY: Routledge.

Santos, B.S., and G.K. Bhambra. 2017. "Introduction: Global Challenges for Sociology". *Sociology* 51 (1): 3–10.

Sapiro, G. 2020. "Chine". In *Dictionnaire International Bourdieu*. Paris: CNRS Editions.

Sassen, S. 2007. *A Sociology of Globalization*. New York, NY: W.W. Norton & Company.

Savransky, M. 2017. "A Decolonial Imagination: Sociology, Anthropology and the Politics of Reality". *Sociology* 51 (1): 91–110.

Shi, Yunqing. 2018. "Individualization in China Under Compressed and Contradictory Modernity". *Temporalités* 26. DOI: https://doi.org/10.4000/temporalites.3853.

Simangan, D. 2020. "Where Is the Asia Pacific in Mainstream International Relations Scholarship on the Anthropocene?" *The Pacific Review* 34 (5): 724–746.

Simpson, Michael. 2020. "The Anthropocene as Colonial Discourse". *Environment and Planning D: Society and Space* 38 (1): 53–71.

Therborn, Göran. 2003. "Entangled Modernities". *European Journal of Social Theory* 6 (3): 293–305.

Tilley, L. 2017. "Resisting Piratic Method by Doing Research Otherwise". *Sociology* 51 (1): 27–42.

Torigoe, H. 2014. "Life Environmentalism: A Model Developed Under Environmental Degradation" [The environmentalism of life: a model developed in the face of environmental degradation]. *International Journal of Japanese Sociology* 23 (1): 21–31.

Wang, Hejian. 2005. "Visit Durkheim Again. The Social Construction of Morality in Modern Economy". *Sociological Studies* 1: 149–247.

Wen, Jun, and Wang Yan. 2012. "Sun Benwen and Sinicization of Sociology". *Journal of Social Sciences* 14 (5): 37–43.

Wessely, A. 2020. "A Missed Cognitive Chance For Social Knowledge". In *Sociologies in Dialogue*, edited by S. Hanafi and C.C. Yi, pp. 65–79. London: Sage.

Wieviorka, M. 2007. *Les sciences sociales en mutation* [Social sciences in mutation]. Auxerre: Editions Sciences humaines.

Xie, Lizhong. 2012a. *Postsociology*. Beijing: Social Sciences Academic Press.

Xie, Lizhong. 2012b. *The Discursive Construction of Social Reality: Analyzing the New Deal for Example*. Beijing: Peking University Press.

Xie, Lizhong. 2020. "Indigenization, Internationalization, Construction of Academic Sociology and Chinese Singularity. From Geographic Pluralism to Discourse Pluralism". *Sociological Research* 35 (1): 1–15.

Xie, Lizhong. 2021. "Post-Western Sociologies: What and Why?" *The Journal of Chinese Sociology* 8 (5): 2–25.

Xie, Lizhong, and L. Roulleau-Berger, eds. 2017. *The Fabric of Sociological Knowledge*. Beijing: Peking University Press.

Xie, Yu. 2018. "Going Beyond the Misunderstandings in the Discussion of the Indigenization of Chinese Sociology". *Sociological Research* 2: 1–13.

Yama, Y. 2021. "Sociology of Ritual and Narrative as Post-Western Sociology: From the Perspective of Confucianism and Nativism in the Edo Period of Japan". *The Journal of Chinese Sociology* 8 (10).

Yang, Yiyin, and Zhang, Shuguang. 2012. "Zai shengren shehui zhong jianwei shuren guanxi: dui daxue tongxianghui de shehui xinlixue fenxi" [Looking for Familiar Faces in a Sea of Strangers: A Social Psychological Analysis of Hometown Associations on College Campus]. *Shehui* [Society] 6: 158–181.

Yang, Yiyin. 2008. "Relation et identité. Approche du processus psychosocial de la formation du 'nous' chez les Chinois" [Relation and identity. An approach to the psychological process of formation of the "we" for Chinese people]. In *La nouvelle sociologie chinoise* [New Chinese Sociology], edited by L. Roulleau-Berger, Yuhua Guo, Peilin Li, and Shiding Liu, pp. 451–481. Paris: Editions du CNRS.

Yasawa, S. 2014. "Civilizational Encounter, Cultural Translation and Social Reflexivity: a note on History of Sociology in Japan". In *A quest of East Asian Sociologies*, edited by Seung Kuk Kim, Peilin Li, and Shujiro Yasawa, pp. 131–167. Seoul: Seoul National University Press.

Yasawa, S. 2019. "Toward a Non-hegemonic Social Science". Seminar. *Toward a non-hegemonic World Sociology*. Saint-Emilion (France), 25–27 June 2019.

Yatabe, K. 2015. "Le dépassement de la modernité japonaise". *Socio* 5: 115–138.

Zhai, Xuewei. 2020. "On the Construction of Confucian Social Theory—Dual Generation and Its Propositions". *Sociological Studies* 35 (1): 56–80.

Zhao, Liwei. 2014. "Suicide and the Situation of Modern People Durkheim's 'Suicide Typology' and Its Human Foundation". *The Journal of Chinese Sociology* 34 (6): 114–139.

Zhou, Xiaohong. 2020. "The Indigenization of Sociology: Narrow or Broad? Pseudo-problem or true reality? A Discussion with Professor Xie Yu and Professor Zhai Xuewei". *Sociological Studies* 1: 16–36.

CHAPTER 2

The Emergence and Characteristics of Chinese Sociology

Li Peilin

Today, economic globalization and cultural diversity seem to be common trends that run parallel to each other. With economic development, academia in non-Western countries has intensified "root-seeking" movements about their own knowledge systems, trying to find their "egos" in history. In China, the famous sociologist Fei Xiaotong calls this post-Western effort a "cultural self-consciousness" in pursuit of "harmony in diversity" and "a united world" (Fei and Zhang 2009).

1 Chinese Indigenous Knowledge and Western Influence

In the West, sociology is generally considered as being put forward by August Comte in France; however, in China, the emergence of sociology is still a problematic and controversial issue. To clarify this issue, it is first necessary to distinguish social thought from sociological thought. The disciplinization of academic thought should be regarded as a modern phenomenon, the result of the delicacy of social labor division in academic research. The wise men and saints of the ancient times and classical antiquity are basically encyclopedic figures that can be found in both Eastern and Western countries.

Chinese social thought can be traced back to the ancient philosophers. But when did Chinese sociological thought emerge? And when was the disciplinization of Chinese sociology complete? Who is the Chinese Comte? Who is the Chinese Emil Durkheim? Would the process of disciplinization of Chinese academic thought have followed its actual trajectory without the introduction of Western academic thought and the exchange, conflict, and collision between Chinese and Western cultures?

During the classical antiquity of China, there was actually a spirit of seeking a unified law of cause and effect to explain all things, and one of the achievements was the theory of Yin and Yang and the 5 elements. But this theory was so prematurely refined that it became a supreme control doctrine and interdicted other thoughts. Moreover, this spirit, which was compatible with the integrated system of knowledge, never went beyond the times in its long development to evolve and transform to seek a unified law of cause and effect in specific disciplines. Molecular biology was not developed from the *Compendium of Materia Medica* (1578), nor were modern physics and chemistry developed from *The Exploitation of the Works of Nature* (1637). The social thought in Chinese history is profound, systematic, and brilliant, but Chinese sociology and sociological thought are the products of the eastward spread of Western culture and cultural integration.

Why does the author say that Chinese sociological thought is a product of cultural integration as well as the eastward spread of Western culture? Because in China during the late 19th and early 20th century, the Enlightenment ideological trend toward empirical evidence coincided with the empirical characteristics of sociology. In 1923, Liang Qichao suggested in his lecture "300 Years of Chinese Academic History" that Chinese academic thought toward pragmatism could be traced back even further. He saw the academic ideological trend of the last 300 years as a reaction against the Taoist tradition of the last 600 years. "The main academic ideological trend in this era was to be tired of subjective meditation but favor objective investigation" (Liang 1985: 91). Many scholars summarize the academic ideological trend in China from the 16th century to the 1840s as "the ideological trend of pragmatism" or "the ideological trend of Ming-Qing Realist Learning" (Chen, Xin and Ge 1989).

The process of cultural integration as well as the eastward spread of Western culture was by no means a poetic and romantic cultural tour, but rather a self-conscious process of enlightenment and self-improvement under Western aggression and humiliation. Liang Qichao, in his article "On Chinese Progress over the Last Fifty Years", published in 1922 for the 50th anniversary of the *Shun Pao*, summarized this process as being three periods in China's enlightenment and academic progress. In the first period, the country "felt the inadequacy of the materials" and began the movement of Westernization after the Second Opium War; in the second period, the country "felt the inadequacy of the system" and began "Constitutional Reform and Modernization" after the disastrous defeat of the First Sino-Japanese War; and in the third period, the country "felt the inadequacy of the culture ultimately". According to Liang Qichao, it can be said that the seeds of the third period were sown by the second period. In the second period, "the most valuable academic production should be Yan Fu's translations, which briefly introduced to the nation the main ideological trend in the 19th century, but unfortunately most of the countrymen could not appreciate it" (Liang [1929] 1989, *On Chinese Progress over the*

Last Fifty Years). Therefore, the so-called "eastward spread of Western culture" was only the inevitable result of the "eastward spread of Western materials" and the "system", and the three periods were a unified process in line with the logic of cause and effect.

As most Chinese scholars know, sociology was originally called "The Academic Thought of Gregariousness" in China, which was marked by Yan Fu's Chinese translation in 1897. He translated *The Study of Sociology*, written by the British sociologist Herbert Spencer in 1873, as "群学肄言" [Study on The Academic Thought of Gregariousness]. The question is, was the name of the discipline "The Academic Thought of Gregariousness" invented by Yan Fu on the basis of his ancient literary skills and his translation standards according to faithfulness, expressiveness, and elegance (信达雅)? Or did such a discipline already exist in China at that time and Yan Fu just used it for convenience when translating? If the concept of "The Academic Thought of Gregariousness" already existed in China at that time, was it consistent with Spencer's interpretation of "sociology"? If there was no such study field as "The Academic Thought of Gregariousness" in China before Yan Fu translated Spencer's work, why did Yan Fu choose "The Academic Thought of Gregariousness (群学)" instead of "sociology (社会学)", which was a translation already available in Japan? Obviously, Yan Fu had already known that the Japanese translated society as "society (社会)" at that time, because he often used the concept of "society" while explaining "The Academic Thought of Gregariousness".

In fact, there was no such specialized study field as "The Academic Thought of Gregariousness" in China before Yan Fu, and no one had ever used this concept. In other words, there was the idea of "Gregariousness (群)" (sort of social thought) but not "The Academic Thought of Gregariousness (群学)" (sort of sociological thought) in China before Yan Fu's introduction of "The Academic Thought of Gregariousness". Yan Fu understood this very well. In a letter to Liang Qichao in 1902, Yan Fu recounted his achievements and hardships during translation, pointing out that for economics, "there existed the theory in China, but its academic thought was absent", and so did "The Academic Thought of Gregariousness" (Yan 1996: 525).

Yan Fu was the first person in China to use the term "The Academic Thought of Gregariousness". The time was probably in 1894. Why did Yan Fu not use the Japanese academic term "sociology" for a discipline that "did not exist" in China? According to Benjamin Schwartz, an American sinologist who studied Yan Fu, Yan Fu objected to the Japanese translation of "society (社会)"

as "society", preferring instead the traditional concept of "Gregariousness" because he believed that the meaning of "Gregariousness" was closer to the concept of "society" as a social group rather than as a social structure. Yan Fu's translation was to "maximize the use of ancient Chinese philosophical metaphors to express Western concepts, but ironically, most of the new words he created were gradually eliminated in the competition with those created by the Japanese" (Schwartz [1964] 1995: 88). However, Yan Fu's translation "The Academic Thought of Gregariousness" is clearly not motivated only by his preference for traditional concepts and ancient Chinese philosophical metaphors. Yan Fu's understanding of "Gregariousness" was, of course, foremost influenced by the ideas of the ancient Chinese philosopher Xunzi. He quoted Xunzi's words several times in explaining the concept of "The Academic Thought of Gregariousness". For example, he stated in *On the Origin of Strength* that "Xunzi said, 'The difference between human beings and animals is that human is gregarious'" (Yan [1895] 1996).

In his *Postscripts of Study on The Academic Thought of Gregariousness* Yan Fu expounded, "Xunzi said, 'The people have traditionally been known to be gregarious'" (Yan [1897] 1996: 127). Xunzi's concept of "Gregariousness" is closer to the meaning of society, which is the reason Yan Fu quoted it. More importantly, Yan Fu's translation at that time had strong practical and urgent overtones. He was in pursuit of enriching the country and strengthening the people, and the ideas of "Enriching the State", "Strengthening the State", "Monarchical System", "Discourse on Ritual Principles", "A Debate on Military Affairs", and "Codes of Monarchs" in Xunzi fit Yan Fu's ideological orientation precisely. In particular, the idea of "strengthening the state by gregariousness" in *Xunzi and Monarchical System* is mostly consistent with Yan Fu's thought about enriching the state and the "sublime words with deep meaning" he read from Spencer's works. For example, Xunzi pointed out in *Monarchical System* that "human is gregarious" because humans can create "hierarchy" according to their social status. The reason for the ability to "behave" in "hierarchy" is that there is "morality", which is the norm to maintain social order. "Morality" and "hierarchy" are necessary factors for a strong and powerful state (Xunzi 1979: 127).

The emergence of sociology in China is naturally the result of the eastward spread of Western culture and the collision and integration of Chinese and foreign cultures. Once sociology was introduced and produced, it was completely incorporated into the Chinese cultural discourse system and conceptual system. But as a new seed, sociology has also changed the Chinese discourse system and conceptual system.

2 The Ideological System of the Academic Thought of Gregariousness: Yan Fu and Liang Qichao

Yan Fu and Liang Qichao are the two scholars who have contributed the most to the emergence of Chinese sociology ("The Academic Thought of Gregariousness"). They both transformed Western sociology with their indigenous knowledge systems, thus imprinting Chinese sociology with Chinese culture.

Yan Fu always said that he found the ideas in Spencer's sociological works "coincided" with the traditional Chinese Confucian culture of investigating the nature of things, pursuing knowledge, cultivating one's moral character, managing one's household, administering state affairs, and bringing peace to the nation. From the perspective of contemporary research, Spencer's theory of the evolution of the social organism is an ideological system completely different from traditional Chinese Confucianism, and they even fundamentally conflict with each other in many ways. What is it in Spencer's work that Yan Fu perceives as a "coincidence"?

The Western works translated by Yan Fu were mainly on sociology, economics, law, and political science that were pragmatic, and less so those on humanities, such as philosophy, because these pragmatic works satisfied contemporary Chinese scholars' preference for practical doctrines for reformation. Spencer and Comte boasted their own sociology was the sum of all social sciences and revealed the fundamental laws of social development. But in Yan Fu's view, the idea of "cultivating one's moral character, managing one's household, administering state affairs and bringing peace to the nation" in *The Great Learning* also represented the views of Chinese Confucian scholars on the fundamental laws of life and social development. Moreover, Spencer believed that human society, like biological evolution, should obey the unified law of "natural selection", which apparently seemed to be consistent with the traditional Chinese theory that man is an integral part of nature. Finally, Spencer's doctrine of organismic evolution was seductive to reformists like Yan Fu, who longed for a rich and strong China, and the social and economic prosperity in England at that time undoubtedly made that doctrine more mythical. Around 1873, when Spencer wrote *The Study of Sociology*, Britain was already the center of the world economy, and the foreign trade of Britain at that time exceeded the sum of France, Germany, and Italy, and was almost four times that of the United States. Britain controlled the seas, and its naval monopoly was undisputed at that time. While the countries on the European continent were caught in the whirlpool of wars and revolutions, Britain was the only country to enjoy peace and tranquility at home. Yan Fu, who had studied at the Royal Naval College, naturally associated such economic progress in Britain with his ideas. The reason his translations, such as the *Evolution and Ethics*, made a sensation in China at that time was closely related to the desire of the Chinese intelligentsia for a rich and powerful nation.

English translations of Comte's writing were available before Yan Fu translated Spencer's work, but Yan Fu was seemingly not interested in Comte's ideas. He found in Spencer's writings a subtlety of meaning that fit with indigenous Chinese knowledge. So, Yan Fu's preference for Spencer was mainly due to the fundamental differences between Spencer and Comte on the question of the origin of the laws of social development. Comte deduced the stages of human social evolution from the law of development of human intelligence, while Spencer deduced the evolution of human social organisms from the law of development of biological evolution—although they were both labeled as "representatives of positivism", their starting points were completely different. Spencer said of such divergence,

> Comte aims at a complete answer to the progress of the concept of human while I aim at a comprehensive answer to the progress of the external world; Comte considers that there is a necessary and real succession among various ideas while I consider that it is among various things; Comte wishes to clarify the origin of natural knowledge while I want to clarify the composition of the various phenomena of nature; he studies the subjective while I explore the objective.
> SPENCER 1904: 570

Spencer's position is obviously closer to the ideological trend of Chinese academics in the late Qing Dynasty towards practicality out of reaction to Song-Ming Neo-Confucianism, and also satisfies the convention of the people who advocate the "Constitutional Reform and Modernization" from the Chinese theory that man is an integral part of nature and an early expression of the distinctive idea in Chinese ethical philosophy that form and function are not separated, in order to reform and establish the customary practice of theory. In particular, Spencer's social evolutionary theory of "survival of the fittest" was like a sweet shower after a long drought to those advocating the "Constitutional Reform and Modernization" pursuing a rich and powerful nation.

Such a preference for Spencer might even have led to a certain misreading of Spencer's ideas. For one of Spencer's key ideas, that is, the idea about the transformation of social structure from a military to an industrial society, Yan Fu, out of his passion for seeking a rich and powerful nation and concern for military and economic power, did not emphasize the fundamental difference between the military stages and the industrial stages in Spencer's theory, and sometimes even equated the two, because he believed that industrial wealth and military strength were identical; another example of a similar misinterpretation is that Yan Fu misinterpreted "laissez-faire individualism" in the 19th century Britain which was representative in Spencer's writings as collectivism emphasizing the power of the state and society as a whole (Schwartz 1995: 52–53, 72).

It was through Yan Fu's introduction of Spencer's theory that Liang Qichao initially understood and absorbed Western sociological ideas and established his own theory about "The Academic Thought of Gregariousness". However, his idea of building the possibility of social integration on collectivist morality seemed closer to the ideas of Comte, whom he did not know much about at that time, while it ran contrary to Spencer's laissez-faire ideology.

In Liang Qichao's view, the intrinsic meaning of "survival of the fittest" being explored in Chinese culture is "sageliness within and kingliness without", which is the supreme purpose of learning in China. He said:

> The supreme purpose of learning can be concluded with the concept of "sageliness within and kingliness without" in *Zhuangzi*. The concept of "sageliness within" refers to enhancing self-cultivation to the limit; while the concept of "kingliness without" is to promote the skills of dealing with people to the limit. And the order has been clearly stated in *The Great Learning*. The methods of "investigating the nature of things, pursuing knowledge, acting in good faith, rectifies one's mind, cultivating one's moral character" in *The Great Learning* are the practices of self-cultivation and "sageliness within"; while the methods of "managing one's household, administering state affairs and bringing peace to the nation" are the practices of dealing with people and "kingliness without".
>
> LIANG [1927] 1985, *Confucian Philosophy*

Therefore, in Liang Qichao's view, sociology mainly studies the academic thought of "kingliness without", i.e., the methods of "managing one's household, administering state affairs and bringing peace to the nation", which is the primary issue prior to politics and economics in "kingliness without".

Compared with Yan Fu's theory, "The Academic Thought of Gregariousness" of Liang Qichao is more integrated into the local knowledge system of Chinese culture. On the one hand, Liang Qichao realized the importance of "gregariousness" and believed it is the group protection method that adapts to the principle of "survival of the fittest"; on the other hand, he distinguished the difference between "formal gregariousness" and "substantial gregariousness" and believed the former is impossible while the latter should be established based on the altruistic "collective morals". The spirit of "individual subordinates to collectives, small collectives subordinate to big collectives, fairness and selflessness, and selfless dedication" has become the primary moral spirit advocated by future reformers and revolutionaries when launching and organizing the public, and Liang Qichao was obviously one of the initiators who took such a spirit as the doctrine of "The Academic Thought of Gregariousness".

Based on the theory of natural evolution and human transformation, Liang Qichao and Yan Fu put forward "The Academic Thought of Gregariousness", which is an ideological system composed of a series of concepts, such as "group-centered", "group protection", "gregariousness", "group perfection", "group morals", "group art", and "group governance". Its core is the group-centered doctrine of "group-centered, change for use", and its backbone is the social integration ideology based on the principle of "gregariousness".

The inference from natural evolution to human transformation is the theoretical foundation of scholars during Chinese constitutional reform and modernization, and also the foundation of "The Academic Thought of Gregariousness" of Liang Qichao and Yan Fu. Liang Qichao clearly pointed out in the author's preface of his famous *General Discussion on Reform*, published in 1896, "What is the necessity of reform? Everything is changing. Change is the trend throughout the history" (Liang [1929] 1989, *Author's Preface of General Discussion on Reform*).

In the time of Liang Qichao, a few scholars standing at the academic forefront began to own a comprehensive and profound understanding of Western academic thought, among whom Liang Qichao was an outstanding member. The reformist scholars were selective in developing Western academic thought, in which the awareness of enriching and strengthening the country played a very important role. Liang Qichao's strong thoughts of "privileging country and group over society and individual" had a material impact on his academic thought, became the political theme of his "The Academic Thought of Gregariousness" and Group Theory, and foreshadowed his future conservatism in politics.

3 Characteristics of Chinese Sociology

The introduction and emergence of sociology in China changed Chinese scholars' research methods. Chinese scholars were awakened to the truth that learning (especially on explaining specific social phenomena and solving specific social problems) can be carried out during the observation of daily life. The application of social investigation methods of sociology in China has further strengthened the practice orientation of Chinese academics. The orientation of "towards life and practice" generated from the introduction and emergence of sociology in China at the end of the 19th century and the beginning of the 20th century, as well as scholars' strong sense of the mission of enriching and strengthening the country formed under the situation of foreign aggression and domestic problems, constituted the tradition of Chinese sociology to intervene and interfere in life, and encouraged a large number of scholars to engage in grassroots life. At the same time, it also constituted a distinctive feature of Chinese sociology: focusing on the differences between the East and the West and the orientation of solving social problems.

Liang Qichao was an early (1906) scholar who put forward the fundamental differences between the East and the West. He put forward that such differences were to prove that the economic society in Europe and the United States was "trapped in a predicament where an urgent revolution is needed", while the economic society in China could only "follow the rules of evolution instead of dangerous and inapplicable revolution" (Li and Wu 1984: 502–503).

In 1915, when Chen Duxiu was about to become a professor of philosophy at Peking University, he published the article "Fundamental Difference in Thought between Eastern and Western Nations" in *The New Youth*, the magazine he founded. In the article, he proposed several suggestions. First, Western nations are war-centered, while Eastern nations are peace-centered. Second, Western nations are individual-centered, while Eastern nations are family-centered. Third, Western nations are centered on laws and benefits, while Eastern nations are centered on relations and mere formalities (Chen 1915). The Eastern nation described by Chen Duxiu is clearly China, and he made his orientation of praising the nationality of the West while denouncing the inferiority of Chinese nation very clear in his statement, suggesting the Chinese patriarchal system has ruined the independent personality of individuals, hindered the free will of individuals, and deprived individuals of the right of legal equality. Therefore, the individual-centered doctrine must be adopted to change the family-centered doctrine in China.

Liang Shuming was probably one of the Chinese scholars who made the most effort to study cultural differences between the East and the West, and he published his book *Eastern and Western Culture and Philosophy* in 1920–1921. Liang Shuming believed that China is an "ethics-centered society", and the patriarchal society in China is a "family-centered society", while "Western modern society is an individual-centered society—especially the United Kingdom and the United States; and society centered on the recent Western trend—especially the Soviet Union", "groups and individuals are two different parties in the West, while the status of family is very low". However, Chinese people have promoted family relations from the middle, and the two parties (neither of which is owned by the other party) of individuals and groups have been integrated in the ethical organization society. Secondly, the West "was religion-oriented in the middle ancient society, and is law-oriented in the modern society", while Chinese society "replaces religions with morals and laws with etiquette". Third, China is a "society with career difference", while the West is a "society with opposite classes". In Western society, "the aristocratic landlords were opposed to the serf class in the middle ancient society, while the capitalists are opposed to the working class in the modern society". Finally, Chinese society had only periodic disorders but without revolution, while Western society had both industrial and social revolutions. Liang Shuming stressed the particularity of Chinese culture and society to explain the inferiority of Chinese nationality, and the transformation of such inferiority should start from "rural self-governance" instead of following the path of Western capitalism (Liang 1990: 1–305).

In 1947, after the field community investigation, Fei Xiaotong started his theoretical analysis of the characteristics of rural China with comparative approach. In his view, the basic structure of Chinese rural society was a "differential pattern" formed by "a network of private connections", while the modern Western society was a "group pattern", "in which connection between individuals relies on a common frame; and everyone has to enter the frame before getting associated with each other". He also believed that Chinese rural society was an etiquette society, while modern Western society was a law-based society; Chinese rural society was a relation-based society, in which blood relationship was the foundation of the status society, while the modern Western society was a geographical society, in which geography was the foundation of the contractual society; "the transition from relation-based integration to geographical integration is a change in the nature of society and also a great change in social history" (Fei 1985: 29, 48–49, 77). When discussing the differences between Chinese rural society and Western modern society, Fei Xiaotong sometimes considered them as two different cultures, but more often he was directly affected by Western modernization theory (especially Ferdinand Tönnies' theory of structural differences between community and society), and he regarded such differences to be phased differences between traditional society and modern society.

Unlike the emerging process of sociology in Western developed countries, the time when Chinese sociology was introduced was the most poverty-stricken and bullying era in Chinese history. At that time, the general consciousness of Chinese intellectuals was to save the country. As a symbol of the emergence of sociology in modern China, during Yan Fu's translation of Spencer's *The Study of Sociology* to *Study on the Academic Thought of Gregariousness*, he did not use direct translation. It is easier for audiences to understand the deep meaning in the sublime words if people read the *Study on the Academic Thought of Gregariousness* together with Yan Fu's *On the Origin of Strength*. In the *Academic Essentials of the Qing Dynasty*, Liang Qichao suggested that Yan Fu was the first Chinese person to disseminate modern Western thought. More importantly, the sociological thought of Yan Fu played an important role in the formation of the ideological system and collective consciousness of enlightenment, country-saving, disorder-settlement, and country-strengthening in Chinese academia during this special period.

About 80 years ago, during the toughest time of China's Anti-Japanese War, in the preface of his doctoral thesis (English edition) *Peasant Life in China*, in 1939, Fei Xiaotong wrote a paragraph conveying a strong sense of mission and consciousness of problems as a Chinese intellectual. He wrote:

> It will be a long and hard struggle, and we are prepared for the worst, even for situations worse than the bombs and poisonous gas of Japan, yet I am firmly confident that, regardless of past errors and present misfortunes, Chinese people, through their perseverance, will once again stand as a great nation in the world, and this book is not a record of a lost history, but a preface of a new world history written with the blood of millions of people.
>
>   FEI [1939] 2007: 16

After China's reform and opening-up in the early 1980s, Chinese sociology has been restored and reconstructed after nearly 30 years of interruption, and the orientation to problems is still its most distinctive feature. Those starting from the research of "small towns", together with other major projects that have been studied by Chinese sociology since then, or those important research outcomes marked with sociological symbols, are almost all related to the major development issues in China and have distinct problem orientation characteristics.

In other words, Chinese sociology has been making efforts with regard to indigenization since its emergence. In the study of Chinese sociology, there have always been tensions between indigenization and internationalization, and there have been some fierce academic debates in this regard. In fact, the two are not completely mutually exclusive. Sociologies in different countries vary a lot, with different characteristics, which constitute international sociology as a whole.

Therefore, we advocate a "post-Western sociology", which is a new international sociology against the background of globalization. This is not to construct a set of sociological ideology beyond Western sociology, but to emphasize that non-Western sociology is also an important part of the new international sociology. Future development of the new international sociology does not only bring the expansion of Western sociology to non-Western countries, but also constructs a new open sociological knowledge system that conforms to diverse developmental experience based on the developmental practices of different countries.

References

Aron, Raymond. 1967. *Les Étapes de la pensée sociologique*. Paris: Gallimard.
Aron, Raymond. 1988. *Main Currents in Sociological Thought.* Translated by Ge Zhiqiang, et al. Shanghai: Shanghai Translation Publishing House.
Chen, Duxiu. 1915. *Fundamental Difference in Thought between Eastern and Western Nations, The New Youth No. 4, Vol. 1.* Quoted from *Century Archives* (1895–1995). Beijing: China Archives Press, 1995.
Chen, Guying, Xin Guanjie, and Ge Rongjin, eds. 1989. *A History of the Thought-tide of Ming-Qing Realist Learning*. 3 vols. Jinan: Qilu Press.
Comte, A. 1907. *Cours de Philosophie Positive*. Vol. 1. Paris: Schleicher Freres.
Coser, Lewis A. (1977) 1990. *Masters of Sociological Thought.* Translated by Shi Ren. Beijing: China Social Science Press.
Fei, Xiaotong. 1985. *Earthbound China*. Beijing: Joint Publishing.
Fei, Xiaotong. (1939) 2007. *Peasant Life in China*. Shanghai: Shanghai People's Press.
Fei, Zonghui, and Zhang Ronghua, eds. 2009. *Fei Xiaotong and Cultural Consciousness*. Hohhot: Inner Mongolia People's Publishing House.
Ge, Maochun, and Jiang Jun, eds. 1984. *Selected Philosophical Thoughts of Liang Qichao*. Beijing: Peking University Press.
Huang, Mingtong, and Wu Xizhao, eds. 1988. *Review of Kang Youwei's Manuscripts*. Guangzhou: Sun Yat-Sen University Press.
Jiang, Fangzhen. (1921) 1985. Introduction to *The Academic Introduction of the Qing Dynasty*. In *Liang Qichao's Comments on the History of Learning of the Qing Dynasty in Two Types*. Shanghai: Fudan University Press.
Kang, Youwei. 1981. *Collection of Kang Youwei's Political Thesis*. Vol. 1. Beijing: Zhonghua Book Company.
Kang, Youwei. 1988. *Changxing Learning Record, Guilin Question Answering, Wanmu Caotang Sayings*. Beijing: Zhonghua Book Company.

Kang, Youwei. 1990. *The Self-Compiled Chronicle of Kang Nanhai (Plus Two Additions)*, collated by Lou Yulie. Beijing: Zhonghua Book Company.

Li, Huaxing, and Wu Jiaxun, eds. 1984. *Selected Works of Liang Qichao*. Shanghai: Shanghai People's Publishing House.

Liang, Qichao. (1927) 1985. "Confucian Philosophy". In *Collection of Ice Drinking Rooms*. Vol. 103. Beijing: Zhonghua Book Company.

Liang, Qichao. 1985. "300 Years of Chinese Academic History". In *Liang Qichao's Comments on the History of Learning of the Qing Dynasty in Two Types*. Shanghai: Fudan University Press.

Liang, Qichao. (1929) 1989. Author preface to *On Groups*. In *Collection of Ice Drinking Rooms Anthology*. Vol. 2 (2). Beijing: Zhonghua Book Company.

Liang, Qichao. (1929) 1989. Author preface to *General Discussion on Reform*. In *Collection of Ice Drinking Rooms Anthology*. Vol. 1 (1). Beijing: Zhonghua Book Company.

Liang, Qichao. (1929) 1989. "General Discussion on Reform". In *Collection of Ice Drinking Rooms Anthology*. Vol. 1 (1). Beijing: Zhonghua Book Company.

Liang, Qichao. (1929) 1989. "On Chinese Progress Over the Last Fifty Years". In *Collection of Ice Drinking Rooms Anthology*. Vol. 39 (14). Beijing: Zhonghua Book Company.

Liang Shuming. (1949) 1990. "Essentials of Chinese Culture". In *Complete Works of Liang Shuming*. Vol. 3. Jinan: Shandong People's Publishing House.

Schwartz, Benjamin I. (1964) 1995. *In Search of Wealth and Power: Yen Fu and the West*. Translated by Ye Fengmei. Nanjing: Jiangsu People's Publishing House.

Spencer, H. 1904. *An Autobiography*. Vol. 2. New York: Appleton.

Wang, Shi. 1982. "Yan Fu and Yan Fu's Translation Works". In *Comments on Yan Fu and Yan Fu's Masterpieces*, compiled by the editorial department of the Commercial Press. Beijing: The Commercial Press.

Wang, Shi, ed., 1986. *Collected Works of Yan Fu*. Vols. 4 and 5. Beijing: Zhonghua Book Company.

Xunzi. 1979. "Xunzi and Monarchical System". In *New Notes on Xunzi*. Beijing: Zhonghua Book Company.

Yan, Fu. (1897) 1996. "Study on the Academic Thought of Gregariousness". In *Selected Works of Yan Fu*, compiled by Lu Yunkun. Shanghai: Shanghai Far East Publishers.

Yan, Fu. 1996. "A Letter to Liang Qichao". In *Selected Works of Yan Fu*, compiled by Lu Yunkun. Shanghai: Shanghai Far East Publishers.

Yan, Fu. (1895) 1996. "On the Origin of Strength". In *Selected Works of Yan Fu*, compiled by Lu Yunkun. Shanghai: Shanghai Far East Publishers.

CHAPTER 3

What Are Post-Western Sociologies?

Xie Lizhong

Due to the work of some sociologists from French, Chinese and other countries, especially the work of Roulleau-Berger, Peilin Li and Xie (Roulleau-Berger 2011, 2015, 2016; Xie and Roulleau-Berger 2017; Roulleau-Berger and Li 2018; Xie 2021), the phrase of "post-Western sociologies" is spreading to a larger scope and is attracting more and more people's attention. However, people may still be a little confused about the meaning of the phrase "post-Western sociologies". As one of the scholars who invented and proposed the phrase of "Post-Western Sociologies" together with Roulleau-Berger and Li, I will try to state my understanding of the connotation and meaning of this phrase in this article, expect to consult with colleagues.

1 What Are "Post-Western Sociologies"?

What are "post-Western sociologies"? In order to understand this phrase, we need make a briefly discuss to the meaning of its two components, "post" and "western sociologies".

Just as the name implies, "post-Western sociologies" are the sociologies formed and developed in the "post" era of the so-called "Western sociologies". In my paper *Post-Sociologies*, according to my explanation of this word, the prefix "post-" means that, first, even though it is not completely opposite to what makes it "post", it is still quite different; second, although it is quite different from what makes it "post", its ultimate form is still not completed and hence difficult to define. Therefore, we cannot give it a fixed name, but vaguely name it as "post-xx" instead, for instance, "post-structuralism", "post-modernism", "post-industry society", "post-modern society", "post-capitalism", "post-planned economy", and so on.

Similarly, "post-Western sociologies" mean that, first, they are quite different from what we called "Western sociologies"; second, their forms are not yet completed and fixed. Therefore, they have to be understood by the difference from the things that makes them "post"-"Western sociologies" (Xie Lizhong 2012: 1–2). Moreover, this also means that, similar to what we do when we understand the word "post-sociologies", in order to understand the true meaning of "post-Western sociologies", we need to understand the things that makes them "post", which are "Western sociologies".

What are "Western sociologies", then? Technically, "Western sociologies" is a concept without an accurate definition. As a Weberian ideal type, "Western sociologies" can be generally defined as such: they refer to those sociological systems that are constructed and developed by Western sociologists, take the social life experience of Western people as material, are under the guidance and constraints of traditional Western discourse systems, and initially expressed in Western language.

The definition of "Western sociologies" here concludes the following basic factors:

First, "Western sociologies" were constructed by the sociologists who worked and lived in Western countries and to some extent, were theoretically abstracted by them through the life experience and historical memory in their own societies.

Second, "Western sociologies" were constructed by the sociologists who worked and lived in Western countries, solely or mainly under the guidance and within the restriction of the traditional Western discourse system (such as the discourse system of ancient Greece–Rome, of Christianity, of modern Enlightenment or anti-Enlightenment).[1]

Third, with the exception that "Western sociologies" were constructed by Western sociologists, solely or mainly under the guidance and within the restriction of the traditional Western discourse system, they were initially expressed in Western language, treating Western audiences as the initial listening object.

A social theory can be categorized into "Western sociologies", only if it has the three factors above at the same time. If:

1. a sociologist, who works and lives in the "West", is unwilling to construct his/her social theory under the guidance and within the restriction of the traditional Western discourse system, but consciously or unconsciously constructs his/her social theory according to some traditional non-Western discourse system, such as the discourse system (concept, statement and clue) of Chinese Confucianism (or Buddhism, Taoism); or
2. a sociologist, who works and lives in the "West", is willing to construct his/her social theory under the guidance and within the restriction of the traditional Western discourse system, but first expresses it in non-Western language (such as Chinese). Therefore, his/her theory (almost) never

---

[1] There are numerous debates about the features of the traditional Western discourse system; however, due to the limited length of the paper, this issue will not be discussed here.

treats Western audiences as the object, or (almost) never has any impact on the field of Western sociology; or
3. a non-Western sociologist is willing to construct his/her social theory under the guidance and within the restriction of the traditional Western discourse system and initially expresses it mostly in Western language, but he/she has never or seldom worked or lived in Western countries, without any concrete experience of Western social life or academic atmosphere.

Then, social theories constructed by these sociologists above are not in the list of "Western sociologies" mentioned here. Therefore, "post-Western sociologies" refer to a new kind of sociology that is formed and developed after these "Western sociologies" defined above, on the basis of cultural interaction between Western and non-Western sociologists. According to the three basic factors about "Western sociologies" above, the basic factors of "post-Western sociologies", in the broadest sense, could be described as follows:

First, "Western sociologies" are constructed not only by sociologists working and living in Western countries but also by both Western and non-Western sociologists together, and they are theoretically abstracted by sociologists from various countries through the social life experience and historical memory of both their own and shared aspects. Compared with the "Western sociologies" defined above, they have more sources of discourse subjects, life experience and historical memory.

Second, "post-Western sociologies" are not constructed under the guidance and within the restriction of the traditional Western discourse system but are constructed by both Western and non-Western sociologists under the guidance and within the restriction of both Western and non-Western discourse systems. Therefore, compared with the "Western sociologies", they have more discourse sources.

Third, "post-Western sociologies" are not initially expressed in Western language, but in various languages including both Western and non-Western languages. Therefore, compared with the "Western sociologies", they have more language carriers and more types of audiences.

The criterion of "post-Western sociologies" is quite different from that of the "Western sociologies". In the broadest sense, to be a member of "post-Western sociologies", a social theory does not have to own all of the three factors above at the same time but has to own only one of the three. Specifically:
1. A social theory can be categorized into "post-Western sociologies", as long as it is not constructed under the guidance and within the restriction of the traditional Western discourse system. This applies regardless of whether it is constructed by sociologists living and working in Western or non-Western countries and whether it is initially expressed in Western or non-Western language.

2. A social theory can be categorized into "post-Western sociologies", as long as it is constructed by sociologists living and working in non-Western countries. This applies regardless of whether it is initially expressed in Western or non-Western language and whether it is constructed under the guidance and within the restriction of the traditional Western discourse system or not.
3. A social theory can be categorized into "post-Western sociologies", as long as it is initially expressed in non-Western language or in Western and non-Western language together. This applies regardless of whether it is constructed by sociologists living and working in Western or non-Western countries and whether it is constructed under the guidance and within the restriction of the traditional Western discourse system or not.

The reason is simple: as previously mentioned, a social theory can be defined as a member of "Western sociologies", only if it has the three basic factors at the same time—proposed by Western sociologist, constructed under the guidance and within the restriction of the traditional Western discourse system, and initially expressed in Western language. If one of the basic factors is missing (it is not proposed by Western sociologist, or not constructed under the guidance and within the restriction of the traditional Western discourse system, or not initially expressed in Western language), it can be defined as "post-Western sociologies".

However, this description might still be ambiguous and vague for understanding. To offer a more concrete and explicit understanding of "post-Western sociologies", more detailed discussion must be made.

2 "Post-Western Sociologies" in Non-Western Countries

The "post-Western sociologies" formed and developed in the wake of the "Western sociologies" include two parts: one is the sociologies formed and developed in non-Western countries; the other is the sociologies consecutively developed in Western countries. A more detailed investigation on the sociologies in these two kinds of countries could be made. First, it is the sociologies formed and developed in non-Western countries.

Generally, non-Western "sociologies", formed and developed in the wake of "Western sociologies", are the result of the transmission of "Western sociologies" to non-Western countries. Therefore, they all seemingly could to be categorized into "post-Western sociologies". However, the truth is that this is not the case. If some theories of Western sociologies transmitted to certain non-Western countries are simply translated in the level of expressive language (translated from some Western language into some non-Western language, such as from English into Chinese) and hence there is no any substantial change in basic concepts and statements, then the theories should still be categorized into "Western sociologies", rather than the so-called "post-Western sociologies" here, although in the process of translation, the connotation and extension of these theories may be different from the connotation and extension in the original mother language. At most, these translated theories could be named "Western sociologies translated into a certain language" (such as "Western sociologies translated into Chinese"). In fact, this is the primary form of almost all sociologies in non-Western countries.[2]

Then, could "post-Western sociologies" be connected with the sociological indigenization in non-Western countries and the sociological theories indigenized in non-Western countries be categorized into "post-Western sociologies"? In my opinion, the answer is still no. For illustration, about the result of "indigenization" of sociologies or social science in non-Western countries, a more detailed analysis could be made.

Through deliberative analysis, it is clear that the "indigenization" of sociologies or social science in non-Western countries can be categorized into the following types:

The first type is the indigenization of research objects, which means the research objects mainly aimed at Western societies have been transformed into those mainly (or even only) aimed at non-Western societies. Meanwhile, in other aspects (such as basic concepts, theoretical propositions, research methods, etc.), the indigenization has not yet happened. Some concepts from Chinese sociologists could be used to describe this type as "object-transformed indigenization". It was the initial expectation for sociologists from non-Western countries in the process of sociological "indigenization" and the primary form of "indigenized sociologies" in non-Western countries. For instance, at the time of formation of Chinese sociologies in the early 20th century, the expectation of sociological "indigenization" initiated by Xu Shilian, Sun Benwen, Wu Wenzao, Li Jinghan, etc., was that, the concepts, propositions and theories from Western societies could be connected with empirical materials from Chinese society.

---

2   It also indicates that similar to "Western sociologies" that cannot be compared to "sociologies in Western countries", "post-Western sociologies" cannot be compared to "sociologies in non-Western sociologies". "Post-Western Sociologies" does not include "Western sociologies", while "sociologies in non-Western sociologies" could include "Western sociologies" or "Western sociologies translated into a certain language".

The second type is the indigenization of both research objects and some other aspects, to some extent, such as basic concepts, theoretical propositions and research methods. For instance, some concepts, propositions and methods originally from the West were modified and transformed based on the indigenous context; for example, distinguishing "*jiating* (家庭)", "*jiazu* (家族)" and "*zongzu* (宗族)" from the concept of "family"; distinguishing "*shequ* (社区)" and "*shequn* (社群)" from the concept of "community"; integrating "nation" and "ethnic" into the concept of "nation (*minzu* 民族)"; some new concepts, such as "*chaxugeju* (差序格局)" and "*danwei* (单位)", propositions and methods were created based on the indigenous discourse resource; and some new theoretical systems, originally from the West but different, were constructed by reinterpretation and reconstruction of the given Western theoretical systems (for example, construction of a Chinese neo-functionalism by integrating English socioanthropological functionalism and the Chicago School of urban ecology). Therefore, the social theories adopted by the native scholars from the West have been more or less supplemented, modified and renewed, and this type could be named as "supplemented-modified-renewed indigenization". Theoretically, due to the differences of cultural tradition, historical experience, natural environment and structure between non-Western and Western countries and the variation in understanding and use of concepts and propositions caused by sociologists, the indigenization of research objects will lead to the indigenization of theoretical concepts and propositions. Most of the results of non-Western sociologies could be categorized into this category. For instance, Fei Xiaotong, based on the research on Chinese rural areas, supplemented and modified Malinowski and Brown's functionalist anthropology and developed a sociological-anthropological theory, which became the model of "supplemented-modified" indigenized sociological-anthropological theory. Since sociology was rebuilt in China, the contemporary Chinese sociologists have consciously constructed numerous indigenized sociological theories with "Chinese characteristics", such as "structural sociology" proposed by Lu Xueyi, "social structure transition" theory by Li Peilin, "structural-institutional analysis" by Li Lulu, Li Qiang, Li Hanlin and Zhangjing, "process-event analysis" by Sun Liping, "school of social operation" or "social mutual-constructionism" by Zheng Hangsheng, sociology of "phenomenology in daily life" by Yang Shanhua, "pluralistic discourse analysis" by me, "emotional choice theory" by Liu Shaojie, "sociological Marxism" by Shen Yuan, "space-time sociology" by Jing Tiankui, "social biology" by Zheng Yefu, and so on, all can be classified into this type of sociologies.

The third type is not only the indigenization of research objects but also the radical and thorough indigenization of theories (concepts and propositions), which means that the Western concepts or propositions are fully or mainly abandoned and a set of indigenized concepts and propositions originating from the native people's social life are adopted instead; however, the thinking patterns and research methods still follow those from Western sociologies (such as positive scientific method, hermeneutics, dialectical method and so on, especially the positive scientific method). Quoting the words from some Chinese scholars, it means using Western modern scientific methods to study the social and cultural contents in indigenous China (Yang Chunhua 2012). This type could be named as "theoretical substitution indigenization". For instance, the indigenization movement in the field of sociology/social psychology, initiated by Yang Guoshu, Huang Guangguo and Yang Zhongfang in Chinese Taiwan and Hong Kong and continued by some scholars in Chinese mainland such as Zhai Xuewei, and the movement of "historical turn of sociology" initiated by some Chinese sociologists such as Qu Jingdong and Ying Xing in recent years, to some extent was the attempt to use Western modern scientific methods (mainly the positive scientific methods, such as the questionnaire survey and experiment) to study Chinese society, culture and behavior and to use some concepts (such as "*renqing* (人情)", "*mianzi* (面子)", "*yuanfen* (缘分)", "*yuanxi* (关系)", "*mingfen* (名分)", etc.) and propositions originating from Chinese society, culture and psychological life to explain Chinese society, culture and behavior.

The fourth type makes a further step on the basis of the third type. It attempts to make radical and thorough indigenization not only of research objects and theories (concepts and propositions) but also of thinking patterns and research methods, which means the thinking patterns and research methods from Western social science have been substituted by non-Western (Chinese) and traditional ones,[3] and meanwhile fully indigenized sociological theories (for instance, Confucianist sociology, Buddhist sociology, Taoist sociology, Islamic sociology, etc.) have been created in three aspects—research objects, theories (concepts and propositions) and research methods, where "the Western" has been completely substituted by "the indigenous". This type could be named as "theoretical-methodical substitution indigenization". Recently, a school of scholars self-proclaimed as "neo-Confucianism in mainland" emerged in China mainland; they claimed a neo-Confucianism and its doctrines with a strong meaning of indigenization, including a set of highly

---

3 "What are the Chinese traditional thinking patterns and research methods?" The debates and controversies on this question never stopped since the Western theories have been introduced. However, there seems to be a common view that a vast or even fundamental difference between the Chinese thinking patterns and the Western patterns exists.

indigenized "neo-Confucianist social theories". If it can be systematically illustrated, its results, to a large extent, can hence be categorized into the type of "theoretical-methodical substitution indigenization". As a matter of fact, the "*qunxue* (群学)" explained by Kang Youwei, Liang Qichao and Yan Fu who were inspired by Western sociologies, in the late of 19th century and the early of 20th century, were quite similar to the theories of "theoretical-methodical substitution indigenization" mentioned here. It is the reason why the scholars of "neo-Confucianism in mainland" appealed to "returning to Kang Youwei" in recent years.

Due to the following reasons, the last type of "indigenized" sociological theories can also be described as "non-Western sociologies". According to the definition of "Western sociologies" above, "non-Western sociologies" can be defined as sociological theories with the following features:

1. merely constructed by sociologists in non-Western countries or regions;
2. merely constructed under the guidance and within the restriction of the traditional non-Western discourse system;
3. merely initially expressed in the non-Western language.

The last type of non-Western indigenized sociologies is exactly the type of sociological theory that is constructed by non-Western sociologists under the guidance and within the restriction of the traditional non-Western discourse system and initially expressed in non-Western language. Therefore, it is fully justifiable to name these types as "non-Western sociologies". In regard to the second and third type of the "indigenized sociologies" in non-Western countries, it is clear that they cannot be categorized into neither "Western sociologies" or "non-Western sociologies". On the one hand, they are different from "Western sociologies" in the aspects of research subjects, theoretical systems (concepts, propositions, etc.) and initiative languages. The most important difference is in theoretical systems. Even "supplemented-modified-renewed indigenization" sociologies (in addition to "theoretical substitution indigenization") are hardly equal to Western sociologies that need to be supplemented and modified by it. For instance, although most of the sociological theories in China mainland belong to the type of "supplemented-modified-renewed indigenization", no one would ever consider them as "Western sociologies". Numerous Western concepts (such as structure, construction, mutual-construction, system, mechanism, function, family, organization, community, class, nation, evolution, progress, etc.) and propositions are adopted, but the connotation of many concepts (such as family, community, class, nation, etc.) has already changed. If these changes are neglected or lack awareness, many works in the sociological literature of contemporary China cannot be fully understood. On the other hand, these sociological theories are crucially or even fundamentally different from "non-Western sociologies", and hence cannot be categorized into them. For instance, although the theories of "supplemented-modified-renewed indigenization" are quite different from their maternal Western theories and they cannot be mixed together, they are still closely linked to each other. Many concepts and propositions, whose connotation (content) and extension (range of application) are still different from those of maternal Western theories, might be developed from the latter. Because of their close relationship, the former cannot be identified as "non-Western sociologies"; although in terms of basic concepts and propositions, the link between the theories of "theoretical substitution indigenization" and Western sociologies has been cut off, the thinking patterns and research methods of the former are still Western (and might be supplemented and modified to some degree according to non-Western societies). Hence, to a large extent, they are still highly westernized, rather than "non-westernized". This is analogous to Chinese medicine that has been transformed based on Western modern science and thus cannot be identified as pure "Chinese medicine", but as a westernized one. They cannot be equal to the fourth type of indigenized theories named as "non-Western sociologies".

Then, what is the relationship between the four types of indigenized sociological theories in non-Western countries above and "post-Western sociologies"? Can they all be categorized into "post-Western sociologies"?

I consider, strictly speaking, that the theories of the first type "object-transformed indigenization" should be categorized into "Western sociologies" rather than "post-Western sociologies". The reason is simple, in that they only supplement Western sociologies with some empirical materials in non-Western societies, while in terms of basic concepts, propositions and theoretical logic, Western sociologies are not supplemented, modified or even replaced. Hence, they are basically still the sociologies constructed by Western sociologists under the guidance and within the restriction of the traditional Western discourse system and initially expressed in Western language, and they are not different fundamentally from the so-called "Western sociologies translated into a certain language".

It is often said that the research object of Western sociologies is Western societies; hence, sociologies whose research object is not Western societies do not belong to "Western sociologies". I consider it incorrect. In truth, both Western sociologies and non-Western sociologies are not simply distinguished by geographical disparities, but by the three factors above (especially the second one—the traditional discourse system that guides and restricts it). As a matter of fact, even though according to the three factors above, the theories of those classic sociologists (such as Marx, Comte, Durkheim, Weber, Tönnies, Parsons and so on) could be categorized into "Western sociologies", their research objects were not limited to Western societies but extended to all the human societies. Although the research objects of the sociological theories constructed by non-Western sociologists are mostly the indigenous social realities, it does not mean that only the indigenous societies rather than other societies (including Western societies) can be their research objects, which is well illustrated by the rise of "overseas ethnography" studies in China mainland during the past few years. Therefore, it is not reasonable to hold that the sociologies of "object-transformed indigenization" whose research objects are no longer Western societies should not continue to be categorized into "Western sociologies".

Therefore, on the basis of the definitions herein, among the four types of indigenized sociological theories in non-Western countries, only the last three could and should be categorized into "post-Western sociologies". In regard to sociologies in non-Western countries, a dual model of "Western sociologies and post-western sociologies" can be offered. According to this model, in non-Western countries, "post-Western sociologies" refer to all the other sociological theories except "Western sociologies translated into a certain language" and sociologies of "object-transformed indigenization". It contain (but are not equal to) "non-Western sociologies" such as "oriental sociologies", "southern sociologies", "eastern Asian sociologies", etc. In other words, "Post-Western sociologies" includes those sociological systems that are "de-Western" or "anti-Western" but are not equal to or limited to these types of sociology.

3 "Post-Western Sociologies" in Western Countries

Now, we turn to "post-Western sociologies" in Western countries.

After "Western sociologies" are spread to non-Western countries, they continue to exist and develop in Western countries. Meanwhile some new changes that gradually occur might stimulate "post-Western sociologies" to form in Western countries. These changes are closely connected with the study and knowledge of Western sociologists on sociologies in non-Western countries.

With the formation and development of sociologies in non-Western countries, some Western sociologists, with a broad sphere of vision and owning the financial and linguistic conditions, chose to walk out of the West and step into non-Western countries to carry out their studies. In regard to these studies carried out by Western sociologists in non-Western countries, their results might contain the following situations:

First, through the field study, empirical materials used to testify Western sociological theories are acquired. As previously mentioned, although many

Western sociologists in their lifetime make their own societies the actual research objects, almost all the worldwide influential Western sociological theorists hope their theory will be applicable to social types at all times and in all places over the world with universal validity. However, due to the limitation of space-time and research resources (for instance, finance, energy, ability, etc.), when they construct their sociological theories, the acquired situations in their own societies are relatively more detailed and accurate than that those in other societies, especially in non-Western societies. Through the field study in non-Western societies, the latter deficiency could be remedied. However, the results only testify or falsify the given theories of Western sociologists and fail to supplement or modify them in terms of basic concepts and propositions; hence, the results are similar to the theories of "object-transformed indigenization" in non-Western countries. This type of study could be named test research by Western scholars in non-Western countries. It only exists in the primary stage of Western scholars' field-studying in non-Western countries. As the study proceeds further, the following results could happen.

Second, through the field study or academic communication and dialogue with non-Western sociologists who are familiar with various types of indigenized theories (including "supplemented-modified-renewed indigenization", "theoretical substitution indigenization", and "theoretical-methodical substitution indigenization"), some new concepts, propositions and methods are acquired, and hence certain theories originating from Western sociologies are supplemented and modified (in particular, when the acquired new concepts, propositions and methods are not only from the field study of realities in non-Western societies but also from the communication and dialogue with non-Western sociologists, they would have more indigenous features of non-Western societies and more supplementation-modification-renew meanings for Western sociologies). The results are similar to the theories of "supplemented-modified-renewed indigenization" in non-Western countries. Therefore, this type of study could be named supplemented-modified-renewed research by Western scholars in non-Western countries.

Third, through the field study in non-Western societies, especially the academic communication and dialogue with non-Western sociologists who are familiar with the theories of "theoretical substitution indigenization", some new concepts, propositions and theoretical systems are acquired that originate completely from indigenous discourse resources in non-Western societies (even constructed by non-Western sociologists); hence, they have highly indigenous features of non-Western societies but can still be understood based on Western thinking patterns and research methods. If Western sociologists working on these types of studies are willing to accept them and adopt them to carry out various types of social studies, including Western and non-Western, then the sociological theories that are considered to be highly indigenous would turn out to be universally valid and become a part of worldwide theoretical systems including Western sociologies. If so, these types of studies could be named theoretical substitution research by Western scholars in non-Western countries.

Fourth, through field studies in non-Western societies, especially the academic communication and dialogue with non-Western sociologists who are familiar with the theories of "theoretical-methodical substitution indigenization", some new concepts, propositions and theoretical systems are acquired that are constructed by non-Western sociologists, and hence different from the given Western sociologies in terms of theories and methods. If Western sociologists working on these types of studies are willing to accept them and adopt them to carry out various types of social studies, including Western and non-Western, then the sociological theories that are considered to be non-westernized, de-westernized or even anti-westernized would turn out to be universally valid and become a part of worldwide theoretical systems including Western sociologies. If so, these types of studies could be named theoretical-methodical substitution research by Western scholars in non-Western countries.

Therefore, as discussed above, the question is "Among all the results of sociological studies carried out by Western sociologists in non-Western countries, which of them could be categorized into the 'post-Western sociologies' mentioned here?"

In my opinion, the answer to this question is almost similar to that above. Obviously, the results of the first research type cannot be categorized into "post-Western sociologies". The reason is as simple as that above: only certain theories of "Western sociologies" are repeated and no new factors (such as new concepts, propositions and methods) or theoretical systems are generated from it. However, the results of the last three research types can be categorized into "post-Western sociologies", because they are formed in the wake of "Western sociologies" and different from their sociological theories.

To summarize, based on the situations in Western and non-Western countries, it is clear that "post-Western sociologies" mainly refer to the sociological theories constructed by Western and non-Western sociologists after the spread of "Western sociologies" to the non-Western world. They have several types as follows:

1. Some new sociological theories are formed after Western and non-Western sociologists supplement, modify or innovate Western sociological theories, based on the context in non-Western countries or through

discourse resources in non-Western countries. These theories are formed on the basis of supplementation, modification and innovation of the given Western sociologies. The connection with each other has not been entirely cut off, but instead, they are still linked in countless ways in terms of concepts, propositions, theoretical logics, thinking patterns and so on. They could be named "non-westernized Western sociologies" (for instance, the situation described by the Chinese phrase "Western systems adopted by China").

2. Some new sociological theories that consist of concepts and propositions of the indigenous social, cultural and psychological life in non-Western societies are extracted by Western and non-Western sociologists, based on the research on social, cultural and psychological life in non-Western societies and by means of Western modern scientific methods. In terms of basic concepts and propositions, the connection between these theories and Western sociological theories might have been fully cut off; hence, the former have highly indigenous features of non-Western societies. However, the fundamental idea of Western sociology has not yet been given up in that modern scientific methods are used to research societies, so these theories are still the results of processing the social and cultural contents in non-Western countries, with Western thinking patterns as its form and instrument. Ultimately, they could be named "westernized non-Western sociologies" (for instance, the situation described by the Chinese phrase "Chinese systems adopted by the West").

3. Some new sociological theories are formed because Western and non-Western sociologists, based on further research and an empathetic understanding of the social, cultural and psychological life in non-Western societies, have fully given up theories and methods from Western sociologies. Meanwhile, they adopted thinking patterns and methods fully originating from non-Western societies to study both Western and non-Western societies. In terms of both research contents and research methods, these theories have features of fully non-Western culture and discourse. Because the connection with Western sociologies has been fully cut off, the characteristics of these theories are completely different from those of Western sociologies, so they could be named "non-Western sociologies".

Therefore, ultimately, regardless of whether the sociologies are those of Western countries or non-Western countries, they might contain both "Western sociologies" and "post-Western sociologies". Some scholars in favor of a certain type of sociology (such as "non-Western sociology") might subjectively expect that this type could replace others, from the point view of sociological development worldwide; however, "Western sociologies" and "non-Western sociologies" are not meant to replace each other but to pluralistically coexist and stimulate each other.

From the above discussion, it is clear that in the formation of "post-Western sociologies", Western and non-Western sociologists will respectively play their different roles. Because "post-western sociologies" aimed at transcending "Western sociologies" are to be constructed through the historical culture and discourse resources in non-Western societies, non-Western sociologists, who are relatively more familiar with the historical culture and discourse resources in non-Western societies, play a more important role. However, if Western sociologists do not participate in the "post-Western sociologies" constructed by non-Western sociologists, then there might only be some indigenous theories, which would preclude worldwide influence and would fail to have universal meanings and values similar to Western sociologies. Therefore, for "post-Western sociologies" to become theories with universal validity, transcending the non-Western world or view, Western sociologists play a crucial role.

Moreover, the formation and development of "post-Western sociologies" rely on constant mutual learning, communication and understanding between Western and non-Western sociologists. On the one hand, for non-Western sociologists, all types of "post-Western sociologies" (including "non-Western sociologies") are not only different from but also transcend "Western sociologies"; hence, learning and understanding of "Western sociologies" become preconditions. On the other hand, for Western sociologists, if they are only familiar with the discourse of Western sociologies and are unaware of the discourse of non-Western sociologies, then they are hardly able to transcend the given view and to construct "post-Western sociologies" transcending "Western sociologies". Therefore, "post-Western sociologies" are to be constructed by neither non-Western sociologists unaware of "Western sociologies" nor Western sociologists unaware of "non-Western sociologies".

4   Why Use the Concept of "Post-Western Sociologies"?

Let us move on to another important question: "Why propose and use the concept of 'post-Western sociologies'?" It seems that the several types of "post-Western sociologies" mentioned here are the direct or indirect outcomes of the "indigenizing sociology" movements in non-Western countries (the "post-Western sociologies" in non-Western countries can be seen as the direct outcomes of the indigenization of the sociologies in these countries. In contrast, the "post-Western sociologies" in the Western world are the imported versions of the former and counted as the indirect results of the indigenization of the non-Western sociologies) and thus can be subsumed under the rubric of "indigenized sociologies" in non-Western countries. Is it then a superfluous endeavor to propose a concept of "post-Western sociologies"?

My answer to this question is no, not at all. In fact, formulating a concept of "post-Western sociologies" would contribute to our more detailed description and profound analysis of the "indigenized sociologies" in non-Western countries. It would further facilitate our appropriate understanding and treatment of the relations between "the West" and "the rest".

What is the "indigenization" of sociology? Scholars have already given diverse answers to this question. However, for a considerable period of time, they basically interpreted it as a process of transforming the sociologies that originated and developed in the Western world to meet the indigenous needs of non-Western countries. It includes translating the original Western sociological notions and propositions into indigenous language, turning their attention from Western societies to non-Western societies for research subjects (more specifically, applying Western sociological concepts, theoretical perspectives and methodology to their study of the historical and practical issues and phenomena in non-Western, indigenous societies, hiring indigenous scholars to study and teach sociology, illustrating the sociological lectures, textbooks, or other scholarly works with indigenous cases and materials), and amending, supplementing, or innovating the original Western concepts and propositions according to their application in indigenous contexts, to strengthen their capacity to explicate the historical and practical phenomena in non-Western societies and to suit their demands of construction and development. Actually, as elaborated above, the various "indigenized sociologies" based upon such an interpretation are exactly "Western sociologies translated into a certain language" and the first two types of "post-Western sociologies" I discussed in this article.

However, in recent years, a brand-new interpretation of "indigenization" emerged, at least in China, which equates "indigenization" to "de-westernization" or "non-westernization" in humanities and social sciences and to the restoration and reconstruction of Chinese traditional scholarship or culture in contemporary China (also called "de-westernization and re-sinicization"; see Hu Xiaoming 2005). The sponsors of this kind of "indigenization" (or "sinicization") trend regard the process of Chinese scholars rearranging and reforming the traditional scholarship according to Western scientific models (such as converting the traditional Chinese studies of the classics into some modern disciplines of Chinese philosophy, history and literature) as a process of "westernization" and harshly criticize it. They suggest an introspection of this "westernization" process in the aspects of disciplinization, systematization, and categorization as well as a restoration or reconstruction of the Chinese traditional culture and scholarship in the current circumstance; for instance, through renaming "Ancient Chinese Critical Theories" or "History of Ancient Chinese Literary Criticism" as "Chinese Critical Theories", they attempt to reach a certain consensus: "Only the tradition of ancient Chinese critical theories can represent the subjectivity of the study of Chinese literature and arts" (see Cao Shunqing and Qiu Mingfeng 2010). These scholars, "concern more about the reconstruction and revival of the ancient Chinese critical theories in modern China [...] about what parts of ancient Chinese critical theories can not only be connected to the modern but also replace the West", or stress that "rooted in Chinese history and culture, Chinese literary theories are utterly different from those in Western cultures. In the vitally important Qi-Ontology system, for example, 'heart (*xin* 心)' and 'things (*wu* 物)', 'principle (*li* 理)' and 'vital energy (*qi* 气)', 'the way (*dao* 道)' and 'instruments (*qi* 器)' are not antithetic but different facets of the same object. Chinese critical theories have their very own cultural and ideological foundations, which are not supposed to be abandoned" (Hu Xiaoming 2005). They believe that "If we want to establish a Chinese modern critical theory, the outmost priority is to de-westernize, to rebuild a unique discourse with our own national characteristics and to seek for the Chineseness during our construction of the Chinese modern critical theory, which only exists in the pre-westernized ancient Chinese critical theories. If only we inherit the uncontaminated tradition from the ancient Chinese critical theories, the hybridity and confusion in modern critical theories would be dissipated and the Chineseness spontaneously displays itself. Since the 1990s, the uniqueness of the so-called 'poetic expression' of ancient Chinese critical theories has drawn unprecedented attention in Chinese academia. It has already become a crucial theoretical orientation in the study of ancient Chinese critical theories to disparage contemporary Chinese critical theories while glorifying their ancient counterparts, to intentionally highlight the heterogeneity between Chinese and Western critical theories, and to strenuously advertise the distinctiveness of Chinese ancient critical theories, without taking into consideration its efficiency in the context of the contemporary literature" (Dai Xun 2007).

It seems that the above ideological tendencies of "de-westernization", "non-westernization" or even "anti-westernization" have not had a considerable impact on the realm of sociology for now. However, logically, the core ideas advocated by these trends can be applied to sociological studies, and then lead to the establishment of the "non-Western sociologies" discussed earlier in this article.

What will actually happen if we do apply the theoretical stand of "de-westernization" or "re-sinicization" to the field of sociology? Most likely, what has already been achieved and developed by Chinese sociologists since the early 20th century would all be labeled as "Western sociology" or "westernized sociology" and be excluded from Chinese sociologies—because unfortunately, the pure "Chinese sociology" has not been built or rebuilt yet.

Can we accept a conclusion such as this?

Based on my elaboration and analysis of the "sociologies in non-Western countries" in this article, I think this conclusion is difficult to accept, and thus virtually cannot be accepted.

According to the description and analysis I made above, the sociologies formed and developed in a non-Western country, such as China, can at least be classified into four possible types: "object-transformed indigenization", "supplemented-modified-renewed indigenization", "theoretical substitution indigenization", and "theoretical-methodical substitution indigenization". Aside from the last one, which falls directly under the rubric of "non-Western sociologies", the other three, more or less, cannot cut off their relations with Western research traditions. However, should we simply repel these three because of their "Westernness"? The answer is in the negative. Let me offer a further explanation.

5 Why Use the Concept of "Post-Western Sociologies": Dialectics of the Relationship between the Universal and Particular

The proponents of "de-westernization" or "re-sinicization" give three reasons to justify their position. First, they indicate that the Western sociologies only reflect and represent the historical experiences of the Westerners and are thus inapplicable to non-Western societies. Second, they hold that the Western sociologies are produced to reveal only the world of meanings (or cultures) of Westerners, so it is irrelevant to the entirely different cultures of non-Western societies. Finally, they believe that "Western sociologies" implicate a sort of discourse power (or hegemony) of Western sociologists over those in the non-Western world. Only an independent "non-Western sociology" would help Chinese sociologists, as well as the sociologists in other non-Western countries, to win an equal opportunity for the academic dialogue. Could these reasons be justified?

Let us first peruse the first reason. The proponents of "de-westernization" usually believe that, as the systems of knowledge formulated by "Western" sociologists, "Western sociologies" are mainly the summation of the social experiences of Westerners and the representation of the historical courses of the development of Western societies. Because of the distinctions between the Western and non-Western societies, the sociologies originally invented to explain the social and historical phenomena of Western societies cannot be applied to the non-Western societies and are thus doomed to be the "particular", instead of "universal" knowledge. Hence, simply adopting such particular knowledge will lead to a misinterpretation or even distortion of the non-Western social phenomena. For a more accurate, objective understanding and representation of the past and present of the non-Western societies, it is necessary to realize the "indigenousness" and "limitations" of Western sociologies, to stop viewing Western sociologies as "universal knowledge", and to formulate and develop some new sociological knowledge that stands on the firm ground of our intensive study of every particular society, that overcomes the limitations of Western sociologies and that is capable of faithfully representing, profoundly understanding, and precisely interpreting the historical and practical phenomena in non-Western societies. This knowledge is the so-called "non-Western sociologies".

In my opinion, this is an ambiguous idea that exaggerates the individual uniqueness of both Western and non-Western societies while disregarding their shared features. We cannot deny the fact that, as the crystallization of the social experiences of the West, the "Western sociologies" are "indigenous" knowledge systems. However, does an "indigenous" knowledge system, derived from the life experiences of the residents of a certain region, only reveal and represent the traits of that particular region? Could it not contain some universally applicable contents that go beyond the geographical limitations? I believe the answer is no! It is mainly because, although the objects of sociologies (i.e., social phenomena) always exist as independent individuals, after being represented and encapsulated by sociologists with highly generalized propositions and abstract concepts, the underlying commonalities of these social phenomena are exhibited, transcending the spatial and temporal restrictions.

I would like to briefly demonstrate it with a schematic example. Let us suppose that:

1. In "Western society", the social phenomena that have been observed are: $A_1, A_2; B_1; C_1, C_2, C_3$.
2. In "non-Western society", the social phenomena that have been observed are: $A_1, A_2, A_3; B_2; C_2;$ and D_1.[4]

As we have noticed, the observed social phenomena in "Western society" are different from those in "non-Western society". Compared to the "Western society", an additional A-type phenomenon (A_3) is observed in "non-Western

---

[4] Neither "Western societies" nor "non-Western societies" are an internally homogeneous world and consist of many different "societies". To simplify our discussion, the internal heterogeneity will be temporarily ignored here.

society"; a completely different B_2 replaces B_1; C_1 and C_3 are missing; finally, D_1, a new type of phenomenon, is discovered.

According to formal logic, we can obtain a set of notions to describe the various social phenomena in "Western society". For instance, A, B, and C (among them, A is the abstract of the observed particular phenomena A_1 and A_2; B is the abstract of the individual phenomenon B_1; and C is the abstract of C_1, C_2 and C_3), as well as a set of theoretical propositions that describe and explain the relations of the phenomena are signified by the notions. When these propositions are linked through a certain format, a sociological system SI, which can be employed to describe and interpret the observed phenomenon in Western societies, is established. Now, here is the question: Does a sociological system based on the empirical materials derived from the observation of the social phenomena of "Western Society" only apply to those phenomena observed in Western societies and is it inapplicable to those observed in non-Western societies? My answer is in the negative.

Let us conduct a thought experiment to examine the possible scenarios when applying the above hypothetical Western sociological system SI to non-Western societies. We are likely to see the following:

1. The concept A does well in describing and explaining the phenomena A_1 and A_2 but likely makes us ignore the existence of the phenomenon A_3.
2. It seems that the concept B can be used to describe and explain the phenomenon B_2, but one might feel that the description and explanation are not felicitous and cannot utterly match the observation.
3. It is more felicitous to apply the concept C to the phenomenon C_2.
4. There is no appropriate concept to describe and explain D_1.

As indicated above, when applying the Western sociological system SI to non-Western societies, it is neither fully suitable nor totally unsuitable: it is basically applicable to some phenomena (such as the type C), generally applicable to some (such as the type A), roughly inapplicable to some others (such as B), and inadequate for a few types (such as the type D). Therefore, simply concluding that the sociological SI is not applicable to non-Western societies because it is from the West is not appropriate. Furthermore, a slight amendment or modification would improve the applicability of SI (such as to formulate a new concept A' by slightly adjusting the connotation and extension of the concept A, to make some essential revision on the concept B to turn it into a new concept B', to convert the concept C to a new concept C', or to add a new concept D, etc.) and turn it into a new sociological system SII, which is a sort of indigenously supplemented-modified-renewed sociology as previously discussed and can be more effectively applied to non-Western societies.

In the above example, we presumed that there are many similarities between the phenomena observed in "Western society" and "non-Western society". To highlight the tension, we now presume that the individual phenomena observed in "Western society" and "non-Western society" are completely different:

1. In "Western society", the social phenomena that have been observed are: A_1, A_2; B_1; and C_1, C_2, C_3.
2. In "non-Western society", the social phenomena that have been observed are: A_3, A_4; B_2, B_3; C_4; and D_1.

Even though the phenomena observed in Western societies seem utterly different from those in the non-Western societies on an empirical level, we cannot arbitrarily conclude that the sociological system sI built from observations in Western societies is entirely inapplicable to non-Western societies. It is because, despite the variations, there are some commonalities between A_1, A_2 and A_3, A_4, similarly with B_1 and B_2, B_3, as well as with C_1, C_2, C_3, and C_4. What we ought to do is, similar to the situation of the former presumption, to complement and amend the system sI (which means, to formulate a new concept A' by slightly adjusting the connotation and extension of the concept A, to make some essential revision on the concept B to turn it into a new concept B', to turn the concept C to a new concept C', or to add a new concept D, etc.) to improve its applicability in the non-Western societies and to convert it into a new sociological system sII that is more universally applicable and would work in both the Western societies and non-Western societies.

Theoretically, there might be nothing in common between the phenomena observed in the Western societies and in the non-Western societies, for instance:

1. In "Western society", the social phenomena that have been observed are: A_1, A_2; B_1; and C_1, C_2, C_3.
2. In "non-Western society", the social phenomena that have been observed are: D_1, D_2; E_1; and F_1, F_2, F_3.

Therefore, the sociological system sI built upon the empirical observation in the Western societies should be utterly inapplicable to the description and interpretation of the phenomena observed in non-Western societies. To efficiently describe and elucidate the latter, we need to start from scratch to construct a brand-new sociological system on the empirical observation in the non-Western societies. However, this kind of extreme case barely happens in practical life.

Although the discussion above mainly focused on the relations between the sociological concepts and social reality, the basic principles can also be extended to the analysis of the relations between sociological propositions and social realities.

WHAT ARE POST-WESTERN SOCIOLOGIES? 81

Thus, obviously, it is untenable to argue that the Western sociologies only apply to the Western societies and are totally impertinent to the non-Western societies because they rest on the empirical materials derived from the observations of "Western society".

6 Why Use the Concept of "Post-Western Sociologies": Dialectics of the Relationship between Insider and Outsider Perspectives

Let us turn our attention back to the second argument proposed by the proponents of "de-westernization" or "re-sinicization": Whether the Western sociologies are endowed with "cultural appropriateness" only in the Western societies?

From the perspective of hermeneutical or phenomenological sociology, every social reality is constructed through the meaningful actions of the members of that society. Therefore, to comprehend a certain social reality, it is necessary to penetrate into their world of meanings, taking an "emic" stand[5] of these actors (instead of an etic stand stressed by positivists), catching the meanings attached by these actors to their own behaviors and the social realities as the consequences through the methods of "understanding", (If the social realities we attempt to explore have been constructed collectively by more than one individual actor, we are supposed to catch the collective meanings attached by all of these actors to their actions and their results. This kind of collective meaning has been assigned different labels, such as "collective consciousness", "group consciousness", "ethnic culture", "regional culture", "institutional spirit", "ethos", "zeitgeist", and so on.), and revealing the relevance between the significances of the actors' meaningful actions and those of the social realities as the consequences of their actions. In the viewpoint of hermeneutical or phenomenological sociology, only the research findings uncovering the connections between the significances of the actors' meaningful actions and those of the social realities have "significant appropriateness" (or as we occasionally put it—"cultural appropriateness") and only these research findings are counted for the social scientific knowledge with the real power of scientific interpretation. From the perspective of classical hermeneutical or phenomenological sociology, researchers might come to diverse versions of interpretations during the research process, but only one version—the one that most accurately reveals the correlations between the meanings of the actors' actions and their

---

5 It is also called the insider's position of the practitioners of a "meaning" or "culture", in contrast to an outsider's position as the observers.

results—is the acceptable research outcome. It can likely be deduced that a sociological doctrine formulated by a scholar who studies Western societies from the stance of hermeneutical or phenomenological sociology only applies to the description and interpretation of Western social realities and is inapplicable to the non-West, even though it precisely uncovers the connections between the significances of Westerners' meaningful actions and those of the social realities. To properly describe and interpret the social realities of the non-Western world, it is necessary to employ the methods of hermeneutical or phenomenological sociology, to start with an "emic" position as members of the non-Western societies, to go deep into the meaningful world of the members of the non-Western societies, and to disclose the relations between the meanings of the members' actions and those of the social realities—only in this way can the non-Western societies be effectively described and interpreted, and only in this way can a sociological doctrine with the "cultural appropriateness" in the non-Western societies be formulated. Simply applying the concepts and theories that reveal the connections between the meanings of the actions of the Westerners and their outcomes to the interpretation of the social realities of the non-Western societies will only lead to a distortion of the latter.

The world of meanings of the actors is constituted with a set of indigenous discourse/semiotic systems (the vocabulary with specific indigenous meanings, narrative approaches with indigenous characteristics, the discourse logic with indigenous essence, and so on). Thus, the so-called "going deep into the world of meanings of the actors", actually means to go deep into the discourse/semiotic system of the actors and to grasp those concepts, narrative modes, and discourse logics that control and restrict the actors' construction of their self-meaning and social world.

This idea makes some sense, in my view, and it is where the significance and value of "non-Western sociologies" are located. Nevertheless, the position of "de-westernization" or "re-sinicization" discussed above is not acceptable. I would like to explain it further here.

First, similar to the situation analyzed above, although the worlds of meanings of the actors in different societies are slightly, or even greatly different, it does not mean that there is not any similarity between them. For instance, there might be vital and indispensable differences between the concept of "God" in the world of meanings of Westerners and the concept of *"tian"* (which can be loosely translated as "heaven") in the world of meanings of the Chinese, between the Westerners' concept of "goodness" and the Chinese concept of *"Shan"* (which can be translated as "goodness"), between "justice" in the west and *"renyi"* (literally "justice" or "rightness"), between the notion of family in the West and Chinese notion of *"jiating"* (literally "family"), between the Western concept of "self" and Chinese concepts of "*ji*" ("self") or "*wo*" ("I"), etc. Ignoring these differences would cause a misunderstanding of the actions and social realities of Westerners or Chinese people. However, it does not mean that there is nothing in common between the above concepts or notions. (There probably, not absolutely, is. We need to conduct an empirical investigation, rather than a transcendental prediction, to decide whether there is or not.) Any commonality testified with empirical evidence makes it plausible to apply a certain layer of meaning with generality from one side (the Western concept of "goodness", for example) to the other (such as China).

Furthermore, although embarking from an emic position of non-Western actors and comprehending the non-Western societies through grasping the meaning attached by the non-Western actors to their own actions and the social realities are surely important approaches, or even the prior approach of understanding and interpreting the non-Western societies, it does not mean that it is the one and only approach. As Geertz elaborates, for those who attempt to understand and interpret (or translate) a world of meanings, an etic stance of an outsider is as valuable as that of an insider. I would like to illustrate it with the following example:

One of my Taoist friends once told me a personal story happened when he was practicing Qigong at home one day. He described that, on that day, he was sitting upright properly at home as usual, according to the Qigong procedure, and soon entered an expected meditation. He found his soul was leaving his body, and heading to a long-admired Taoist palace via a vaguely familiar road. A Taoist priest welcomed him into the palace, in which they had a long conversion. After the conversation, the priest asked him to go back home, but he does not know how. The priest told him "return on the same road by which you came". He tried hard to recall the road, and finally remembered it and went back home. He then opened his eyes, and found himself actually sitting at home.

We can derive two different understandings and interpretations regarding this experience: the first one is based on an emic stance. Suppose that the one with such an experience is a devout Taoist, who believes every doctrine taught by his Taoist master; he would interpret this experience in accordance to the Taoist doctrines and is convinced that he just practiced himself into a higher Taoist level and has already obtained the ability to abandon his secular shell to visit his Taoist predecessor. Hence, in the opinion of the supporters of the emic position, while interpreting this experience, we ought to enter his world of meanings and try to understand the experience, as well as his follow-up actions (such as to practice the Taoist Qigong more frequently, to follow the Taoist doctrines more unswervingly, or to preach the Taoist doctrines more enthusiastically) strictly according to his own explanation. I am not against such a kind of emic interpretation—I completely agree with the idea that we can only understand and even predict the Taoist's experience and actions after acquiring this kind of emic explanation. However, I also think that, aside from this kind of interpretation on the ground of emic points of view, there could be a second kind of interpretation, a sort of interpretation standing on an etic, outsider position. This is exactly the interpretation I attempted to make to my Taoist friend right after I heard his story. My interpretation can be roughly summarized as follows: on that day, you encountered an abnormal mental condition during the Qigong practice. Because you had been cultivating yourself with the Taoist doctrines and standardized Qigong exercises for a long time, those Taoist visons and discourses had penetrated into your subconscious and possessed you to subconsciously experience such a kind of psychological activity. Apparently, this is an interpretation or "translation" based on the modern/Western discourse systems and largely different from the Taoist discourse system. However, who can say this is a pointless interpretation or an understanding that would lead to a misreading of the "authentic" experience of the Taoist? In terms of social, instead of natural sciences, who can make an incontrovertible judgment on which one of the two explanations—the one from the emic stance of the Taoist or the one from my etic standpoint—is a more objective, true, and reliable representation?

Consequently, from the perspective of social sciences, rather than of natural sciences, both the emic and etic interpretations of people's actions and their consequences are meaningful and it is difficult to tell which one of them is more dependable than the other. It also means that, in the case of the interpretation of the non-Western social realities discussed in this article, although the Western sociological perspectives might vary dramatically from the non-Western ones, they are not totally worthless and divorced from the non-Western realities. In fact, for any member of any single society, the understanding of his/her own actions and the social realities should include two perspectives: the insider, "emic" (or "indigenous") perspective, and the outsider "etic" perspective; likewise, for any member of any single society, his/her understanding of an exotic society should also involve these two perspectives: the "emic" perspective of the locals and their own "etic" perspective. As Geertz put it, for one who attempts to understand exotic societies, his/her task is not simply to represent the world of others in their own ways of representing them. Instead, he/she needs to display "the logic of their ways of putting them in the locutions of ours; a conception which again brings it rather close to what a critic does to illumine a poem than what an astronomer does to account for a star" (Geertz [1983] 2000: 11).

Therefore, it is inappropriate and thus unacceptable to claim that the Western sociologies can only be used to describe and explain the social realities in the West and are not applicable to the non-Western social realities because they only reveal the connections between the meanings of the Westerners' actions and of the social realities and that the non-Western societies can only be represented and interpreted by those doctrines disclosing the relations between the meanings of the actions of the members of the non-Western societies and their social realities. "Non-Western Sociologies" are meaningful for us to understand the non-Western societies, but it is not a proper stance to set them up as an antithesis to the Western sociologies and to use it to reject the latter as well as the doctrines derived from them.

7   Why Use the Concept of "Post-Western Sociologies": On the Issue of Academic Hegemony

Let us now take a close look at the third argument of the proponents of "de-westernization" or "re-sinicization". Those scholars who support the "de-westernization" in the domain of social sciences believe that the "Western sociologies" were formulated under the guidance of, and thus restricted by, various discourse systems that originated and developed in the Western societies. If Chinese scholars develop a sociology of their own country only through amending, revising, or renovating the existing discourses of the Western sociologies, rather than to make a breakthrough at the fundamental level of the discourse system and to construct a completely different, independent discourse system based on the traditional discourse system of their own country, they can never win their right to speak on an international academic stage. If the sociologists of the non-Western world, such as China, want to obtain the discourse power on that international stage, they need to formulate a pure, de-westernized "Chinese sociology", which is derived from China's own traditional discourse system.

In my opinion, this argument is also untenable.

First, although making a breakthrough on the level of the discourse system and building a pure, completely "non-westernized" "Chinese sociology" on the traditional discourse system of our own country would help Chinese scholars to win the discourse power from Western sociologists on the international stage, a "de-westernized", pure "Chinese sociology" is not necessarily an essential prerequisite for dominating an academic conversation. The history, regardless of whether the West or the East, can prove this point to some extent: a passive receiver of a foreign discourse can possibly reverse the situation and become the leader of that discourse world after a period of time, as long as it makes an effort to study and innovate that foreign discourse. For example, Christianity was originally a non-Western discourse system and once fiercely prohibited in a Western society—the Roman Empire. However, it was gradually accepted in the Roman world. Some Roman intellectuals became the authorities of the Christian religion and then gained the discourse power in the Christian world. Similarly, Buddhism was not a Chinese traditional discourse system. Instead, it was an imported foreign discourse system, similar to the Western learning we are confronted today. However, after thousands of years of spread and development, Chinese Buddhism has become mainstream and occupies a dominant position in the international Buddhist world today. In the world of Buddhism, the discourse power of Chinese scholars cannot be denied. Therefore, the need to win an academic discourse right per se does not justify the necessity of constructing a completely "non-westernized" "Chinese sociology".

Furthermore, although to make a breakthrough on the level of a discourse system and to build a non-westernized, pure "Chinese sociology" on the traditional discourse system of our own country will help us win the power of academic discourse from Western scholars, obtaining academic discourse power does not necessarily entail the cost of absolute "de-westernization". In contrast, a pure, absolutely non-westernized "Chinese sociology" would peacefully coexist and/or mutually compete with those sociological systems westernized to various degrees.

Here, we need to answer an important question, what is the relationship between the knowledge of sociology and societies as their targeted subjects. This issue opens two sorts of interpretations: a traditional realistic one and a discourse constructionist one. According to the traditional realistic understanding, sociologies are the direct reflections or representations of the societies they study. Hence, the social worlds that sociologists perceive, contemplate, and address is an absolutely "thing-in-itself" and would not be changed and influenced by any discourse system about that world. In contrast, "sociological studies" are the cognitive processes of reflecting and representing those social worlds, through which we would better accustom ourselves to it, and the so-called sociologies are just the products of those cognitive processes. Although there might be several diverse theories or doctrines successively formulated during the cognitive process of one single social phenomenon, there is only one of them—the one that relatively precisely reflects the research object—that can be accepted and labeled as "truth", while other theories or doctrines with relatively more flaws or errors would be excluded from the ultimate system of the sociological knowledge. In the case of the studies of Chinese society, only the sociological theory or doctrine that relatively accurately reflects or represents the Chinese society will be ultimately accepted as the "truth". In particular, for those traditional realists, there is only one theory or doctrine can be accepted, regardless of whether it is about Western societies or non-Western societies, such as China—that is, what we usually call "monist view of truth".

In contrast, according to the interpretation of discourse constructionists, sociologies do not directly reflect or represent the social worlds they depict. We can continue describing the relation between sociologies and the social worlds as a reflection or representation but we have to realize that the reflection or representation is only indirect, not direct. Sociologists do not just "reflect" or "represent" social worlds with their blank brain, as claimed by Émile Durkheim and his logical positivist followers. Rather, they "reflect" or "represent" their research subjects under the guidance and restriction of certain discourse systems. Consequently, the sociological theories or doctrines they finally formulate are shaped by, and thus cannot shake off, the regulations of the relevant discourse systems and thus should be seen as a discourse construction conducted by the sociologists, led and regulated by that discourse system and targeted at the research subjects. Under the guidance and control of different discourse systems, sociologists might produce different research findings on the same research subject and then form different reflections or representations. There is no dependable approach to judge which one(s) is right and which one(s) is wrong. Therefore, in the eyes of discourse constructionists, there could be diverse theories or doctrines proven to be "correct" in the discourse system they belong to, regardless of whether in Western societies or in non-Western societies such as China. This is what is normally called the "pluralist view of truth".

If we take the position of discourse constructionists, we would be able to realize that the "de-westernization" in Chinese sociology is not necessarily the prerequisite or price for a pure, "non-westernized" "Chinese sociology". As we discussed and analyzed above, "non-westernized" sociologies are just a sort of "post-westernized" sociologies, and they can peacefully coexist and/or mutually compete with other "post-Western sociologies" still with Western characteristics to different extents. Thus, developing a pure, "non-westernized" "Chinese sociology" from the discourse system of our own country would help us struggle for the discourse power on the international stage with Western scholars, but it should not necessarily occur at the expense of a complete "de-westernization". Therefore, taking it as a reason to advocate "de-westernization" or "re-sinicization" is scarcely justified.

Different from the concept of "de-westernization", the notion of "post-westernization" is more inclusive and realistic: according to the proposition of "de-westernization", in non-Western countries, except for the "non-Western sociologies", other types of sociologies we categorized as "post-Western sociologies" should be rejected as "westernized". Nevertheless, the "post-westernization" I propose in this article would embrace all of these types of sociologies, including the "non-Western" ones. Compared to the concept of "indigenization", "post-westernization" has two distinctive features: First, it indicates a different attitude toward the "West". The concept of "indigenization" expresses a tendency to seek for and to maintain the differences from the "West" and would easily, if not necessarily, lead people to a kind of extreme "Western/non-Western" dichotomy. Whereas "post-westernization" tries hard to avoid that extreme duality and conveys a tendency to keep the continuity, consistency and commonality while pursuing and maintaining those differences. Second, it expresses an ambition about the "indigenous" sociologies, which differs from that of the concept "indigenization": since "indigenization" implies a tendency to seek the distinction between the "West" and "non-West", it leads people into a "Western/non-Western" dichotomy and confines the validity of "indigenous" sociologies (including "non-Western sociologies" such as "Chinese sociology") within the "indigenous" domain and thus shadows or denies, intentionally or unintentionally, the universal potential of the "indigenous" sociologies. In fact, even the meanings of the abstract concepts and propositions of those extremely "indigenized" "non-Western sociologies" derived from "indigenous" experiences or discourses would exceed the limit of their place of origin and are universally applicable to a certain degree, similar to those of pure "Western sociologies".

Therefore, I propose the concept of "post-Western sociologies" not only because "Western sociologies" might not be applicable to non-Western societies but also because this concept provides us a broader horizon, a more inclusive attitude, and a longer-sighted ambition from the aspect of the theoretical construction of our sociology, multiplies and varies our sociological discourses, and thus paves more paths through which we achieve a better understanding of the social world, and finally contributes to our construction of a brand new social world transcending the Western/non-Western dichotomy.

Acknowledgments

This article was originally published as Xie, L., "Post-Western sociologies: what and why?" *The Journal of Chinese Sociology* 8 (5) (2021): 1–25 DOI: https://doi.org/10.1186/s40711-020-00141-8. Reprinted with permission of this Journal. The author made some modifications and deletions when included in this book.

References

Cao, Shunqing, and Mingfeng Qiu. 2010. "A Journey of Westernization in Chinese Critical Theory". *Journal of Southwest University for Nationalities (Humanities and Social Sciences Edition)*, issue 1: 229–236.

Dai, Xun. 2007. "De-Westernization and Exploration for Chineseness: The Nationalist Discourses of Chinese Critical Theories in the 1990s". *Literature and Art Criticism*, issue 3: 4–10.

Geertz, Clifford. [1983] 2000. *Local Knowledge: Further Essays in Interpretive Anthropology*, translated by Wang Hailong and Zhang Jiaxuan. Beijing: Central Compilation & Translation Press.

Hu, Xiaoming. 2005. "A Rectification of the Name of Chinese Critical Theory: On the Trend of De-Westerncentrism in Chinese Critical Theory Study in Recent Years". *Journal of Northwest University (Philosophy and Social Sciences Edition)* 35 (5): 5–14.

Roulleau-Berger, L. 2011. *Désoccidentaliser la sociologie : l'Europe au miroir de la Chine*. La Tour d'Aigues: l'Aube.

Roulleau-Berger, L. 2015. "Post-Western Space and doing sociology". *Journal of Social Theory* 18 (2): 237–252.

Roulleau-Berger, L. 2016. *Post-Western Revolution in Sociology. From China to Europe*. Leiden and Boston: Brill Publishers.

Roulleau-Berger, L., and Peilin Li, eds. *Post-Western Sociology—From China to Europe*. London: Routledge.

Xie, Lizhong. 2012. "Post-Sociologies: Exploration and Reflection". *Sociology Study* 35 (1): 1–26.

Xie, Lizhong. 2021. "Post-sociologies: What and why?" *The Journal of Chinese Sociology* 8 (1): 1–25.

Xie, Lizhong, and L. Roulleau-Berger, eds. 2017. *The Fabric of Sociological Knowledge: The Exploration of Post-Western Sociology*. Beijing: Peking University Press.

Yang, Chunhua. 2012. "The Fourth Path towards the Localization of Sociology". *Theoretic Observation*, issue 3: 87–88.

Ying, Xing. 2011. *Emotions and Contentious Politics in Contemporary Rural China*. Beijing: Social Sciences Academic Press.

CHAPTER 4

The Oneness Logic: Toward an East Asian General Theory

Kim Seung Kuk

1 Prologue: A New Theory for a New Civilization[1]

1.1 *Background*

We live in a world of historical hybridization between the Western modern civilization and the post-Western post-modern civilization. Some call this transformation the coming of late modernity or second modernity. But I prefer to assess the rise of new civilization in radical terms. Borrowing a prophetic and revolutionary East Asian conception, developed in the Book of Changes (周易) and Korean Right Changes (正易), I introduce a new terminology, "Second Civilization (後天開闢)", after First Civilization (先天開闢).[2] The Second Civilization, foretold in China long ago, but in Korea in the late 19th and early twentieth century, reflects a wishful but realistic utopia where the contradiction between yin and yang decreases and the cooperation between the two increases. The First Civilization full of conflicts and struggles caused by the excessively materialistic greed of human beings is destined to decline. The cyclical principle of things (物極必反) in the Book of Changes (易經) tells us that as modern civilization reaches its peak, it becomes weak.

The ongoing civilizational transformation seems to manifest its mixed image in the two faces of our present world. This duality can be contrasted as follows. On the one hand, artificial intelligence as the culmination of a series of scientific-technological revolutions represents optimistically the coming of "homo deus" (Harari 2015). On the other hand, the pessimistic horizon of the Anthropocene arises with the homo suilaudans (self-worshipper), homo exterminans (terminator), homo carnifex (butcher), and homo delusus (self-deceiver) (Cribb 2017).

---

1 This paper was written as a preliminary and partial version of my book (Kim 2023).
2 I fully respect the logic of Right Changes (正易), written by Ilboo Kim Hang, a Korean scholar. In contrast to the Book of Changes, it uses a framework of 干支度數 (十干十二支). For a more detailed discussion of the first and second civilizations, see Song (2013).

Who knows whether, in the future we may miss our present world of troubles and will be uncomfortable with new world without any human absurdities or mistakes? The new world constructed with the Second Civilization makes no guarantee of promising a total utopia in which everybody feels happy. But we have no other choice than to move forward to a better society.

Given this dilemmatic situation, we social theorists are required to look for a new general theory to plan and prepare for a new world. In this study I propose that a general theory of the Oneness Logic,[3] derived mainly from East Asian wisdoms such as Confucianism (儒家) and the Book of Changes (易經), Buddhism (佛家), Taoism (道家), and Sunism (仙家),[4] can show a way or a Dao in which we discover and invent the Second Civilization as a post-modern and post-Western world. The Oneness Logic can contribute to the rehabilitation of the unity of everything in the universe by going beyond the binary opposition and artificial distinction between human and nature as well as between revolution, socialism, statism, equality and reformism, capitalism, individualism, freedom.

A logic, at least in my usage, is more fundamental or basic than a theory. It does not exclude the mystical way of thinking, often negated as non-rational and unscientific.[5] East Asian (and Western) mysticism is increasingly known to be logical in its own peculiar way, following the world-wide acknowledgment of Heisenberg's uncertainty principle. Our world works simply in terms of probability. Rational civilization of rational Western modernity produced many irrational consequences. Mystical practices and approaches do produce many rational explanations and predictions. The Oneness Logic as a friend of

---

3   Recently, a book, titled *The Oneness Hypothesis: Beyond the Boundary of Self* (Ivanhoe et al. 2018) was published. I believe The Oneness Logic shares some similar theoretical points with it. But my Logic, with its special reference to a general theory, moves in a quite different direction.

4   I add Korean Sunism to the well-known three East Asian wisdoms. The English term, Sunism, used first by me, is based on the common understanding of its focus on the sun as brightness (太陽昂光明), the hermit (神仙), and Sun Dao (仙道). The pronunciation of English "sun (太陽)" is similar to Korean sun (仙). Historically and philologically, the term refers to Choi (908~?)'s "仙史", Kwon's ([1984] 2006) "仙道", and Jung's (2004) "韓國仙道". For a more detailed discussion of Korean Sunism, see *Journal of Korean Sundo Culture* (仙道文化).

5   Any theory can be called "logical" insofar as it demonstrates the capacity to systematically and meaningfully explain things or events in the universe, and predict something useful to them. In this sense, those mystical practices, such as fortune-telling (占), Feng Shui (風水, geomancy), philosophy of destiny (命理), four pillars of destiny (四柱八字), physiognomy (觀相), and (East Asian) exorcism (退魔, 招魂) by a shaman (巫堂) with divine spirituality, that thus far have been stigmatized as magic may be reconsidered as a logic of its own unique (post-)rationality.

East Asian mysticism encompasses both mystic/post-scientific and rational/scientific approaches.[6]

As Beck (2008) sharply observed, with the beginning of the 21st century the return of religions seems to be remarkable. Is it a reaction to the so-called secularization process? Or is it an individualization of belief systems? The Oneness Logic, though historically a form of religious doctrine, has nothing to do with any absolutism or monopoly of the truth. Rather it is directly oriented toward the peace of the world and world religions, providing a common logical ground on which they coexist together as the Oneness.

1.2 The Rise of Post-Western Sociology as Hybridization

The Oneness Logic is to reflect on and respect the spirit of the post-Western sociology project initiated and developed recently by Roulleau-Berger (2016), Xie and Roulleau-Berger (2017), Roulleau-Berger and Li (2018), Yazawa (2019), and Kim (2014). The conception of non-hegemonic dialogue between the East and West as well as the South and North, a core principle shared by post-Western sociologists, is closely connected with my theory of hybridization that constitutes a key empirical theory of the Oneness Logic.

In her formulation of a non-hegemonic post-Western sociology Roulleau-Berger (2021) proposes:

> we can build a new ecology of knowledge in the Western West, the non-Western West, the semi-Western West, the Western East, the Eastern East, and the re-Easternized East to understand our common condition in the world.

What a hybridized world we are living in! To keenly appreciate and correctly respond to this hybridization, we must understand our common condition despite all its diversities. The Common Condition! This is the reason I propose the Oneness Logic to appropriately apprehend the commonality, or, to put it another way, the Oneness of all in our universe with its countless variations. On the basis of this theoretical equivalence, the Oneness Logic will contribute to the advancement of post-Western Sociology.

The Oneness Logic, of course, possesses a uniquely East Asian identity that can be contrasted with certain Western styles of reasoning. The distinction between the two is, however, not always clear cut. If we abandon a fixed idea

---

6 My Logic is influenced by Feyerabend's (2010: 7, 223) principle of "anything goes" which argues that "neither science nor rationality are universal measures of excellence. they are particular traditions, unaware of their historical grounding".

of the established distinction and pay an integrative attention to the two, we may surely find a surprising world of the Oneness across the two. It is not an extraordinary discovery. Since the beginning of human civilization the hybridization between different cultures and values in the world has accumulated many common traits in the world of diversity. Just as nothing in the world is completely the same because of hybridization, so too does everything share something very common in terms of the Oneness. Post-Western sociology too is both a variation from Western sociology and a Oneness as a dialogue between the two sociologies.

1.3 Toward a General Theory for the Oneness Logic

There have been many discussions on the Oneness in the West by Plato (Idea), Plotinus (The One), Christian theologies and Gnosticism, Heidegger, and Deleuze as well as in the East. Most of them are made from a philosophical or religious perspective. The same is true in East Asia. I, as a sociologist, however, am concerned with building a general social theory of the Oneness Logic, while also respecting the heritage of Western theories, such as the system and functionalist approaches developed by Parsons, Alexander, and Luhmann in particular.[7]

My idea of general theory relies on Alexander (1987: 3):

> Theory is a generalization separated from particulars, an abstraction separated from a concrete case…. General theories are theories about everything, about societies as such, about modernity rather than about any particular modern society…. There are special theories about economic classes in society … the middle class, the working class … a general theory, for example, Marxian theory combines all these special theories about classes into a single theory about economic development and class relations as such…. Parsons as a theorist was bent on the reconstruction of European sociology, providing a synthesis which would eliminate the warring schools which had divided it.

Alexander, despite his great respect for Parsons, criticizes him for his more or less one-sided attention to non-Marxist traditions of European sociology. Thus, Alexander turns to a multidimensional approach in which "collective versus individual" and "rational/material versus non-rational/normative" dimensions are juxtaposed with each other, but at the same time he still keeps the

---

[7] Theoretical links between these theories and the Oneness Logic will be fully discussed in my forthcoming book.

legacy of the Parsonian two-value axis of social order and individual freedom. In my view his multidimensional conception of a general theory is not fully developed because of his unwillingness to incorporate resolutely the postmodern concept of hybridization with which he would be able to overcome the dilemma of the micro-macro gap and theoretical conflation and move forward a more integrative functionalist theory. The theoretical issue of the gap or eclecticism may be solved by the Oneness Logic, within which the issue is becoming just a matter of different view points.

Recently, Luhmann made a far more comprehensive and philosophically grounded theory of system/function. Very interestingly, Luhmann's epistemological reliance on mathematician Spencer Brown's Buddhism and Daoism (Lau [2017] 2020) seems to indicate an East Asian dimension of Luhmann's theoretical base. Quite naturally, Spencer-Brown knows and uses the Oneness Logic from which Luhmann's key concepts, such as "einheit (差異同一性)", are derived.

The explicit or implicit Western utilization of East Asian views or conceptions, or, to put it another way, the Easternization of Western theories (Campbell 2007), also seems to be salient in actor-network theory (Latour 2005) and new materialism (Fox 2018; Fox and Aldred 2017). These theories may unconsciously make use of the Oneness Logic that has long argued for the connection, unity, and equivalence between the human and non-human (物我一體), regarding non-human beings also as independent actants, like human beings. Similarly, the rise of post-human perspectives facilitate the tendency of deconstructing human centrism as well as the separation of the human from the non-human.

In this context theoretical dialogue between the West and East requested by post-Western sociology has already begun in the West. Unfortunately, in East Asia such an awakening is not clearly visible, nor has it been remarkably successful. The Oneness Logic will give an impetus to the theoretical dialogue, requesting a hybridization between Western and East Asian theories.

I may be the first sociologist (and social scientist) to coin the term "Oneness Logic". It must be stressed again here that my logic at the moment is just a guideline and hence can be reinvented and reformulated in many other ways. Nevertheless, the basic idea of "all in one and one in all" shared by all students of the Oneness is not to be changeable.

A Western scholar (Ivanhoe et al. 2018) employs the term "oneness hypothesis". He is interested in drawing some psychological hypotheses about positive feelings associated with the Oneness. What's the difference between his "hypothesis" and my "logic"? Simply, his idea is related to special theories of the

Oneness Logic, but mine is related to a general theory. Certainly many Oneness hypotheses can be empirically derived from the Oneness Logic.

1.4   *Discovery of the Oneness*

In 1983, I first met the Oneness in a Western book, *The Tao of Physics: An Exploration of the Parallels between Modern Physics and Eastern Mysticism* written by Capra (1975). He understands the Oneness Logic in terms of the unity of all things, unity of the universe, and unity of opposites in particular. Capra (1975: 130–132, 145) correctly argues:

> The most important characteristic of the Eastern world view—one could almost say the essence of it—is the awareness of the unity and mutual interrelation of all things and events, the experience of all phenomena in the world as manifestations of a basic oneness.... The Eastern traditions constantly refer to this ultimate, indivisible reality which manifests itself in all things, and of which all things are parts. It is called Brahman in Hinduism, Dharmakaya in Buddhism, Tao in Taoism. Because it transcends all concepts and categories, Buddhists also call it Tathata, Suchness.... When the Eastern mystics tell us that they experience all things and events as manifestations of a basic oneness, this does not mean that they pronounce all things to be equal. They recognize the individuality of things, but at the same time they are aware that all differences and contrasts are relative within an all-embracing unity ... the unity of opposites ... constitutes one of the most puzzling features of Eastern philosophy. It is, however, an insight which lies at the very root of the Eastern world view.

Very usefully, Capra (1975: 137–138) continues to indicate:

> Quantum theory thus reveals an essential interconnectedness of the universe.... In the words of Niels Bohr, 'isolated material particles are abstraction, their properties being definable and observable only through their interaction with other systems'.

Capra's precise comprehension of East Asian Oneness in terms of the unity of all things in the universe is very shocking in that East Asian wisdom or mysticism is buttressed by one of the most developed fields of contemporary science, quantum physics. Capra's conception of Oneness as unity may be a bit elaborated. The term unity, like unification or integration sounds more or less strong, orderly, rigid, structured and inflexible. The Oneness in my understanding is rather flexible, unstable or chaotic, changeable, and hence always moving or functioning. The Oneness is logical but not completely definable and explicable. It may rather be referred to as a "tendency" or to risk some oversimplification, a reliable "probability" to appear and disappear. Thus, the Oneness can be defined as both scientifically logical and mystically probable. The unity of the Oneness is likely to become an unstable unity untenable to collapse or disintegration. The ontologically mysterious world of the Oneness is thus to be approached from many imaginative and indeterminist viewpoints. The mathematical framework of quantum theory has passed countless successful tests, while its metaphysics is on far less solid ground. The Oneness Logic can provide a sophisticated and solid model.

2   The Oneness Logic

2.1   *Texts and Theoretical Resources*

There must be many relevant references for my study. Only a small number of them are recognized here. The term, (East Asian) "wisdom" as a school (學派) instead of (institutionalized) religion (宗敎) is intentionally used to express my main interests in theoretical aspects of their original texts. It must be stressed that my knowledge and understanding of these wisdoms are very small and this study is an exploratory attempt to be further elaborated and enriched. If there is some originality in my study, it will be my systematization of ontological constitution and analytical dimensions, and the introduction of three empirical theories.

2.1.1   Civilization

Kim (2019), a pioneer in emphasizing the role of East Asian cultural values in correcting dysfunctions caused by Western modernization, has encouraged me to pay special attention to East Asian classical wisdom. Recently, Shin (2019), with the aid of archeological evidence, meteorological records of the ancient era, and old historical records, established the status of the Old Chosun (古朝鮮) civilization as one of the six origins of World Civilizations, such as Egypt, Mesopotamia, the Indus Valley, China, Mexico and Peru. His discovery provides a solid historical base supporting the existence of the Book from Heaven, known to have appeared sometime during the Old Chosun civilization. Finally, Kim (2021) argues that the inpansive civilization of East Asia will sooner or later succeed the Western expansive civilization, relying on an East Asian conception of the cyclical change of civilizations, i.e., the principle of yin-yang, a derivative of the Oneness Logic.

2.1.2 Religion

The Book of Changes and Confucianism,[8] Buddhism, enlightenment, and mysticism have been sociologically studied by Chung (2000), Kim (2001), Hong (2002), Lee (2008), Woo (2012), Kum (2012), and Ryu (2020). Without these preceding studies, this study would not have been attempted. Graham (2001) also wrote an extensive book on Zhang-tzu. Nan ([1994] 2013; [1991] 2018) gives a good summary and clear interpretation of the Book of Changes. The excellent explanation by Pagels (1980/2012) of Gnosticism as a Christian mysticism testifies to the Western tradition of the Oneness Logic.

There are many interpretations of the Book from Heaven (天符經).[9] I rely on a Christian called a saint, Ryu ([1963] 2021) and Ryu (1997), a philosopher named Ha (1993), a political scientist named Choi (2006), a most respected expert on the Book of Change named Kim (2010) and a famous Sunist and Sun master/his best student, Kwon/Ahn (1999).[10] Choi (2020) gives a historical acceptance of the Book by Daejonggyo (大倧敎),[11] a religion based on the Book. Kim (2005) makes a very useful study of the comparison between the Book and Daejonggyo with special reference to Lee Yong-Tae, a famous believer, proposing that the Book from Heaven is a Pantheism.

2.1.3 The Book from Heaven

My intensive use of the Book from Heaven in this study is never meant to imply its centrality or superiority in comparison to other texts. They are reciprocally interconnected, complementing and enriching each other.[12] To explicate thoroughly the Oneness Logic, we need all texts.

It is, nonetheless, recognized that the Oneness Logic is most intensively and succinctly described in The Book from Heaven, composed of only 81 Chinese letters, in which the word, "one (一)" appears 13 times. The numerical number of 1, 2, 3, 4, 5, 6, 7, 8, 9, 10 (十) is all used in the Book, and is often analyzed in

---

8   For the convenience of discussion, I'll classify the Book of Changes and Confucianism as one category, because the Book of Changes is a philosophical backbone of Confucianism.
9   English translation of the Chinese title, 天符經, was, to the best of my knowledge, first made by me.
10 Lee (2016), in his ontological study of the Book from Heaven identifies three different approaches Daoist, Confucian, and Sunist, expressing, on the Sunist basis, some reservations on the interpretations by Choi (2006) and Kim (2010). While I appreciate his cautious concern, the three approaches can be productively combined (Lee 2016).
11 Three core books of Daejonggyo are the Book from Heaven, Sam-Ilshingo (三一神誥), and Chamjungyegeong (參佺戒經).
12 I agree with Rui (2016) who argues that the Book from Heaven is closer to Daoist and the Book of change than Buddhist. His Daoist interpretation of the Book from Heaven is very useful. But Buddhist perspective is also deeply connected with the Oneness Logic under which all four East Asian wisdom can be independently and properly located.

terms of the mathematical diagram of (河圖洛書) discovered in ancient China as well as East Asian mathematical philosophy (象數學).

My basic theoretical framework of the Oneness Logic is derived directly from the Book from Heaven. More specifically, ontology (本體論) comes from the letter "本" (無盡本, 不動本, 本心本), theory of formation/function/change (變用論) from "變" and "用" (用變), hybridization from "萬往萬來", mind from "心" (本心), the middle way (中道) from "中" (人中), and most importantly the Oneness from "一". Those selected letters can be seen in the below text:

天符經	The Book from Heaven
一始無始一	One begins with one without beginning.
析三極 無盡本	Its differentiation into three does not exhaust its essence.
天一一 地一二 人一三	One heaven is differentiated first, one earth second, and one human third.
一積十鉅 無櫃化三	One accumulates to ten, but has no difficulty with returning to one.
天二三 地二三 人二三	Heaven plus the other two makes three, earth plus two three, and human plus two three.
大三合六 生七八九	Large three makes six and produces seven, eight, and nine.
運三四 成環五七	When three and four are operated, five and seven are made.
一妙衍 萬往萬來	The mysterious function of one makes everything come and go.
用變不動本	Despite its functional changes, its essence does not change.
本心本太陽 昂明	Essential mind is rooted in the sun and respects the brightness.
人中天地一[13]	Human, with its middle way, makes the Oneness with the heaven and earth.
一終無終一	One ends with one without ending.

---

13 This sentence is very important. It emphasizes not only the positive role (主體性, 責任性) of the human subject (人) but also the normative action of the middle way (中道/中庸, 中和, 中正) by humans. My interpretation of 中 in terms of Buddhist 中道 and Confucian 中庸 is first attempted here.

2.2 Four Theoretical Levels of the Oneness Logic

2.2.1 Ontology (本體論)[14]

In East Asia, the conceptual relationship between basis or essence (本體) and its functional change (變用) is the inseparable two sides of one same entity, the Oneness. The latter is just an empirical embodiment of the former. A theory of change comes directly from an ontology. In a similar context, it is not easy to distinguish between the Oneness and one, because the two possess each other within each, though the oneness is used mainly in metaphysical, ontological, and cosmological terms.

2.2.1.1 Mathematical and Numerical Dimension

There are two types of numerical and conceptual differentiation from the Oneness.

2.2.1.1.1 Trichotomy or One-Three Differentiation (三數分化)[15]

The one-three differentiation goes with the differentiation of the Oneness into three. The three is ontologically also a "one" with three different entities (天地人三才) such as one heaven (天一), one earth (地一), and one human (人一). From the hybridization between the above three ones comes all and everything (一妙衍 萬往萬來，三生萬物) in the universe. Figure 4.1 illustrates this differentiation.

I'll employ this one-three model of differentiation as the core principle of constructing the Oneness Logic. I derive correspondingly three formational dimensions by the model and again another three empirical theories corresponding to the above three dimensions. The three-one differentiation model can be most accurately defined in terms of "three in/from one and one in all three" (執一含三, 會三歸一). The whole process of continuing differentiation from the Oneness and its logical constitution is shown in Table 4.1.

FIGURE 4.1 One-three differentiation (三數分化)

---

14 Ontology in East Asian wisdom is directly connected with a cosmological perspective. For a related discussion, see Lee (2011).

15 This trichotomy is based on the Three-One Logic (三一論理) (as a derivation from the Oneness Logic) of Sunism. For a wider discussion of it, see Woo (2012).

TABLE 4.1 Differentiation of the Oneness and constitution of the Oneness logic

Non-Being's Being (有無渾然) (空卽是色) (天地人合一) The Oneness in Chaos (混元一氣)ᵃ (心氣中混合) (一體雜種化) (三一論理)	Ontological Level (本體論) as three in the Oneness (三一)		Formational Level (形成論)	Empirical Level (經驗論) for return to the Oneness (中一, 歸一, 通一)
	Numerical and Compositional Differentiation (量的/構成的 分化)	Qualitative Differentiation (質的分化)		
	one heaven 天(一)	one middle (一)中	天(一)一 axiology (價值論) intermediation	the middle way (中道論)
	one earth 地(一)	one qi (一)氣	地(一)二 functional change(變容論) interconnection	hybridization (雜種化論)
	one human 人(一)	one mind (一)心	人(一)三 epistemology (認識論) inter-communication	solipsist-spiritualist individualism (唯我唯心 個人主義)
	Birth and Death of all things in the universe(萬物萬事 生成消滅)			
Theoretical Significanceᵇ	The Oneness as mysticism for a post-scientific approach, hybridization, communication, peaceful coexistence, ecological balance, self-regulating Epicureanism, and the return of the responsible human subject			

a Choi (2006) uses and explains clearly this term.
b For a more systematic and detailed explanation, see Kim (2023).

2.2.1.1.2   Dichotomy or One-Two Differentiation

(二數分化: 太極 → 兩儀(陰陽) → 四象 → 八卦 →)

The one-two differentiation is used mainly in the Book of Change in which "太極" produces "兩儀(陰陽)", and then "兩儀(陰陽)" produces "四象" (太陽, 少陰, 少陽, 太陰), and "四象" produces "八卦" (乾, 兌, 離, 震, 巽, 坎, 艮, 坤), and "八卦" produces repeatedly and infinitely. The principle of the one-two

THE ONENESS LOGIC   101

```
                    (8) 八卦                              eight bagua
   ↖   ↗      ↖   ↗      ↖   ↗      ↖   ↗
  1    2     3    4      5    6      7    8
                    (4) 四象                              four sanggua
       ↖      ↗                  ↖      ↗
       1      2                  3      4
               (2) 兩儀，陰陽                             yin and yang
                    ↖     ↗
                    1     2
                 (1) 無極/太極                            The Oneness
```

FIGURE 4.2 One-Two differentiation

is governed by yin and yang as two elementary functioning and structuring forces. Figure 4.2 shows this process.

2.2.1.1.3   Integration of the Two Differentiation

The above two models of differentiation each has its own advantages of explaining the way things work. But they can be connected with each other when we employ an approach of hybridization between the Book of Changes and Book from Heaven. The Discussion of Koe (說卦傳) in the Book of Changes clearly states that numbers are constituted by the principle of three from the heaven and two from the earth (參天兩地而奇數). Lao-tzu also acknowledged that the existence of yin-yang (2) penetrated into all beings at the same time when he talked about the one-three evolvement.

Let me explain the process of integration in the following way. One produces first one heaven (the Book from Heaven as BH) as one yang (the Book of Changes as BC) and secondly produces one earth (BH) as one yin (BC), and finally produces one human (BH) as the combination of one yang as male and one yin as female (BC). From this hybridization of the two models the differentiation of one, two, and three from the Oneness proceeds orderly without any conflict. Then from the last three, as the two texts commonly indicate, all are produced in the below order.

The Oneness, 一(太極) = 1 → 天一(陽) + 地一(陰) = 1 + 1 = 2 = 二(陰陽) → 三(天地人) = 3 = 天一 + 地一 + 人一/女陰南陽 = 1 + 1 + 1 = 3 → All things (萬物萬事, 無限).

2.2.1.2   *Qualitative Composition of the Oneness*

I understand the quality of the Oneness in terms of three interrelated components such as, one qi (一氣), one mind (一心), and one middle (一中),

assuming the dynamically chaotic movement of the Oneness rather than the absolutely empty nothingness assumed by Daoists.

2.2.1.2.1 One Qi (一氣)

Qi is usually defined as equivalent to energy or force. In East Asia many debates were made on the relationship between nature (性), qi, ri (理), and mind. I take the theoretical position of unifying the four as an equivalent (性 = 心 = 氣 = 理, 心氣) based on the leading role of qi (主氣論的 一元論). It is assumed that without qi, neither nature nor mind nor ri would be revealing itself.

2.2.1.2.2 One Mind (一心)

Buddhism in particular defines the essential characteristic of the Oneness as one mind. It is well known that Buddhist spiritualism starts from the mind and completes with the mind.

2.2.1.2.3 One Middle (一中 or 中一)

It is really difficult to translate "中" into English. It is not exactly the middle or center. The value-laden connotation of balance, harmony, or distantiation from polarization (過猶不及) must be added to the middle. It may also imply a hybridization between opposite and conflicting objects. Anyhow, whenever we think of and meet "中", we had better associate it with the Buddhist middle way (中道) or Confucian moderation (中庸, 中和, 時中). Confucian praises 中和 as 天下之大本 天下之達道. "中" is a normatively balanced behavior on the basis of hybridization.

2.2.1.3 *One and Zero or Being* (有/存在) *and Non-Being* (無/無存在)

Where does the Oneness come from and return to (何處生一 何處歸一)? Dao Te Ching (道德經) says Dao comes from nothing (無) but produces one (道生一). Does this mean one (一) comes from nothing (無) or zero (o) or emptiness (空)? What is the relation between one (一), nothing (無), zero (o), and emptiness (空)? This is a critical question in discussion of the Oneness Logic. My answer is that all these belong to the "Oneness" that is a hybrid composite of these distinct "ones". The Oneness is not simply a pure one, but a hybrid composition of various ones.

In my view, all conceptually defined things, regardless of their empirical reality or non-reality, are ontologically and numerically "one" thing or "one" nothing or "one" being or "one" non-being or "one" zero or "one" emptiness. All of these distinct states of concepts can be designated respectively as "one". Thus, very logically, they are assumed to return to the Oneness (歸一). This logical connection between the Oneness and one can be clarified by the mysterious fact that numerically one can make zero, but zero cannot make one, as illustrated below:

$1 - 1 = 0 = 1 + 1 - 1 - 1$
$0 - 0 = 0 = 0 + 0 - 0 - 0$

The Oneness is a self-organizing, self-defining, and self-fulfilling concept in that it does not need any other element for its ontological existence. It exists by itself and for itself. It comes from neither Dao nor nothing because the Oneness itself is both one Dao and one nothing. Perhaps Chinese wisdom keenly realized this logical fact and invented neither the number nor the concept of zero that is surely useful in mathematical logic but not so much in the mysterious world of ontology. The holy god or Dao is neither empty nothing nor pure zero. It is the Oneness itself.

2.3   Formational Level: A Theory of Functional Change (變用論)

The following three dimensions are respectively connected to the three ontological differentiations of the Oneness, namely the heaven, earth, and human (一即三).

2.3.1   Functional Dimension

All things/events in the world are done or appearing/disappearing in the field of the earth in that the location and movement of all beings can be specified in terms of the three levels, on the earth (地表), above the earth (地上) and below the earth (地下). Thus, the functional dimension represents the role and status of one earth (地一).

2.3.2   Epistemological Dimension

But who knows and understands this process? The epistemological dimension is logically required. This process of consciousness is made mainly within the inside of human, the realm of one human (人一).

2.3.3   Axiological and Behavioral Dimension

We, humans are destined to do something for our survival. We try to find the best way of doing and the desirable goals in living. The logical outcome of this process of trial and error has led to a quest for normative action. Since the heaven has been respected universally in both the West and East as the mysterious source and guide for proper human action (天道, 天理), it can then be safely assumed that this dimension is closely connected to one heaven (天一).

2.3.4 Formational Functions: Interconnection, Intercommunication, and Intermediation

I identify three formational functions of the Oneness such as interconnection, intercommunication, and intermediation. These three operations are associated, respectively, with the earth, humans, and heaven.

Everything, in the network of interconnectedness (緣起), operates in the realm of the earth. The human with its mind intercommunicates spiritually with other humans and non-humans. Otherwise human cannot find any meaningful values in its existence. Finally heaven, respected as a mysterious and holy entity, is assumed to require humans to behave normatively by intermediating between the earth and itself based on the middle way. Thus, everything's interconnection, the human intercommunication, and heaven's intermediation are conceptually established.

This explanation may be supported by the logic of quantum physics, in which the physical world is divided into two systems, that is, an observed system (object) and an observing system (experimental apparatus and human observers). The object, as quantum physics presupposes, belongs to an interconnected world, while the observing system is operated by a human with some specific goals predetermined by his or her value orientations. Human observation in the world of interconnection can be viewed first as an intercommunication between the object and the observer and second as an intermediation between the observer's own normative value orientations and objective scientific interests/values. Here, too, the three functions are well presented.

2.4 Empirical Level

I introduce, corresponding to the above three logical dimensions, three empirical theories, including hybridization, solipsist-spiritualist individualism (SSI), and the middle way for love. These theories have already been discussed by many. The former two theories in particular and part of the middle way have been reformulated in terms of an East Asian standpoint by me (Kim 2011, 2015, 2018).

2.4.1 Hybridization

Ontologically, the state of the Oneness is chaotic in that its three qualitative components, one qi, one mind, and one middle, are mixed together dynamically into the Oneness. Hybridization as a function of one qi is based on the principle of yin-yang and the Five Ways (五行), which plays a contradictory function of mutual cooperation and opposition, producing functional variations. I define the Five Ways as five functions, including political, economic, social, cultural, and religious functions, reformulating the original concept of the wood (木), fire (火), soil (土), iron (金), and water(水). As already mentioned, cyclically, as the yang reaches its highest strength, then it begins to lose its strength at the same time the yin begins to increase its power.

2.4.2 SSI

One qi makes the spiritually communicative unity between the heaven, earth, and human. The Oneness is perceived, apprehended, and realized only by the specific, unique, and concrete individual I myself. A solipsist view of the human is necessary to individually start and individually finish the way to the Oneness and then collectively share it with others.

An individual may start first from an egocentric and self-limiting individual. But an individual can be reborn, in the quest for the Oneness, as an altruistic self-expanding individual. The mysterious power of the solipsist-spiritual individual can make everything exist within its mindful territory. I am you, we, the world, and the universe.

The practical reason for my inclination toward individualism is to remind people forcefully about the inconvenient truth that you must confront the world of indifference and loneliness and struggle by yourself to survive (各自圖生). An individual is the starting line to live and the finish line to die, though they say you are not alone and there are many friends.

2.4.3 The Middle Way for Love

In East Asia heaven has represented the moral world of all good virtue and values. Since the one middle (中一) is assumed as the qualitative component of heaven, I make a decision to comprehend it in terms of the middle way, the most highly respected behavioral orientation in Buddhism (中道, 中觀) and Confucianism (允其集中, 中庸). Love as a normative behavior has always been regarded as the key to saving the world. No love, no unity between humans and all other beings.

3 Textual Supports and Specification

In this section I clarify and specify the Oneness Logic by quoting some most representative and relevant arguments directly from the four East Asian wisdom.

3.1 *Ontological Oneness*

The Oneness is called different names, such as Dao, Buddha, or God. I delineate the core character of the Oneness in three ways, that is, the chaotic or hybridized (混元/混沌) one qi (一氣), one human mind (一心), and one middle (一中) for or one return (歸一) to the Oneness. The three ones are associated with three functions of interconnection, intercommunication, and intermediation. Many interpretations of the Oneness have focused on the unity or interconnectedness of all things in the universe. But the unity may be better understood as a psychological or mindful communication between I myself and others rather than any materialist or realist unification.

In East Asia, the famous phrase, "from mind to mind (以心傳心, 心心相印)" reflects not only person-to-person mindful communication but also human-to-non-human communication. Human qi is believed to be communicative with non-human qi, because qi as a qualitative component of the Oneness also exist in non-human beings. Without this cosmological communication based on qi as mind, no unity between different things would be plausible.

Table 4.2 shows the ontological level of the Oneness is specified by texts from the four wisdoms.

TABLE 4.2   Ontological level

The Oneness	一 (一者, 道, 佛, 神 …)
	混元/混沌 一氣(主氣論 氣中理一元論), 一心/通一, 中一/歸一/合一
Book from Heaven Sunist	一始無始一, 一終無終一, 無盡本, 不動本, 本心本
	天一一 地一二 人一三, 人中天地一
	(天無形質 無端倪 無上下四方 虛虛空空 無不在 無不容
	一神造群世界 返眞一神)
Book of Changes Confucian	易之爲書也 廣大?備 有天道焉 有人道焉 有地道焉
	兼三才而兩之 故六 六者非他也 三才之道也
	六爻之動 三極之道也
	是故易有太極 是生兩儀 兩儀生四象 四象生八卦
Taoist	有無相生, 得一, 抱一
	道生一 一生二 二生三 三生萬物
	道通爲一 (復通爲一 知通爲一)
Buddhist	萬法歸一, 一卽多 多卽一, 一中多 多中一
	一心爲大乘法 歸一心源(元曉), 佛卽是心
	一中一切多中一 一卽一切多卽一(義湘)

3.1.1   Sunist

Very mysteriously but also very logically, the Book from Heaven (hereafter referred to as BFH) starts with the phrase "one begins with 'no-beginning one' and ends with 'no-ending one'". Here "one" contains the two "seemingly" contradictory meanings of both being (有) and non-being (非有) or nothing (無). This dual conception in the Oneness provides an interesting resolution for the controversy about the connection between being and non-being. According to Sunists, the Oneness includes being as "one" and non-being as "one" in itself.

THE ONENESS LOGIC   107

The disappearance of "one" is either non-being or nothing, while the appearance of "one" makes "one" non-being or one "nothing".

The Oneness is explained by its fundamental and basic nature (本). However much and however long it is used, consumed, and differentiated, the Oneness (本) itself never reduces or changes (無盡本 不動本). Without this everlasting capacity, the Oneness would be unable to exist in the whole universe from its start to the infinite future.

The unity of the heaven, earth, and human within the Oneness (人中天地一 or 天地人合一) highlights the most important role of the Oneness Logic by pointing out the inherent ecological wholeness between the three and requiring the active role of human subject.

3.1.2   The Book of Change(BOC) and Confucian

According to the BOC, there are three dao (三才之道): Dao of the heaven, earth, and human (有天道焉 有人道焉 有地道焉). These three Dao are called three great elements of the Oneness, representing the ultimate being (太極) that is depicted as the symbol of yin-yang dynamics. The Confucian version of the Oneness as "太極" produces first two qi that produce secondly four that produce eight … and finally all things in the universe (是故易有太極 是生兩儀 兩儀生四象 四象生八卦). Here we can discover the connection (兼三才而兩之) between the Sunist three elementary components of the Oneness (the one-three) and the Confucian two elements (兩儀) of the ultimate (太極).

3.1.3   Daoist

Referring to the phrase "everything comes from being, but being arises from non-being … Dao produces one (天下萬物生於有 有生於無 … 道生一)" many have erroneously assumed that Dao stays in the state of non-being and one comes from Dao as non-being because Dao is neither one nor being. Perhaps this interpretation may have only a half-truth.

In my view, as mentioned earlier, Dao is one. When Lao-tzu says "Dao produces one, one produces two, two produces three, and three produces everything (道生一 一生二 二生三 三生萬物)", he is exactly echoing the Oneness Logic in the BFH. Therefore, Dao must be understood first as the Oneness in ontological sense. Second, the one that Dao produces is an existential or empirical one, equal to the first (produced) one heaven (天一一) in the BFC. Following this sequence, Daoist two is the second creation of one earth (地一二) and Daoist three is the third creation of one human (人一三). In short, Dao is the same as the Oneness, an ontological composition of all "ones".

My interpretation is supported also by another of Lao-tzu's arguments for the reciprocality between being and non-being, realization of the Oneness, and encompassing the Oneness (有無相生, 得一, 抱一) as well as Zhang-tzu's mention of Dao's connection to and movement for the Oneness (道通爲一, 複通爲一, 知通爲一). Dao as the Oneness is unquestionably implied by both Lao-tzu and Zhang-tzu.

3.1.4 Buddhist
The idea of the Oneness also is clearly expressed in the Buddhist Book, the Avatamska Sutra (華嚴經), in which one of the most famous Buddhist teachings, "all things are destined to return to the Oneness (萬法歸一)" is declared. Just like the logic of one-in-three and three-in-one in Sunism, Buddhism also proposes that "one is multitude and multitude is one (一卽多 多卽一)". The Korean Buddhist priest Eusang (義湘) used the similar expression of "multitude-in-one and one-in-multitude (一中多 多中一)" in his contribution to Diagram (華嚴一乘法界圖). One Mind (一心), one of three qualitative elements of the Oneness, is most directly and widely used by Buddhists whose ultimate quest is to return to the one mind (歸一心源). Buddha is in your mind and you have Buddha's mind (佛卽是心).

3.2 *Empirical Theories*
3.2.1   Hybridization (雜種化 or 相雜化)[16]

TABLE 4.3   Hybridization

East Asian wisdom	Text
Sunist	一妙衍 萬往萬來 用變不動本, 析三極 一積十鉅 生七八九 一神造群世界, 衆善惡清濁厚薄相雜 從境徒任走 墜生長消病歿苦
Book of Changes Confucian	道有變動 故曰爻 爻有等 故曰物 物相雜 故曰文 文不當 故吉凶生焉 (六爻相雜 唯其時物也, 生生之易) 剛柔相摩 八卦相蕩
Taoist	有物混成 先天之生 故混而爲一
Buddhist	華嚴經 → 雜華經 重重無盡 法界緣起

---

16 Though I respect Western theories of hybridization (Bhabha 1994; Canclini 1995; Nederveen Pieterse 1995, and Leavy and Keri 2008), I have developed it in much wider and deeper terms of ontology, civilizational force, and axis of all functional interactions.

Hybridization as the empirical differentiation from the dynamics of the Oneness is a logical consequence due to the chaotic one qi inherent in the Oneness. Since the Oneness is in the constantly moving state of chaos as hybridization (混沌), its functional differentiation spontaneously follows a way of hybridization in which complexities and changes are incessantly arising according to the principle of yin-yang and Five Ways (陰陽五行) together with their cyclic movements of "win-win and conflict (相生相克)".

3.2.1.1 *Sunist*

Hybridization is symbolically indicated in the phrase, "all things appear and disappear due to the mysterious function of the Oneness (一妙衍 萬往萬來)". Despite this functional hybridization, however, the Oneness as the original source itself never changes (用變不動本). Viewed in this light, hybridization is an inevitable process of making the world. More specifically, people tend to mix the good/clean/thick with the bad/unclean/shallow (衆善惡淸濁厚薄相雜) and fall into the agony of illness and death (墜生長消病歿苦).

3.2.1.2 BOC *and Confucian*

It was astonishing when I read the following wonderful phrase in the BOC: "As Dao changes, Hyo arises (道有變動 故曰爻). As Hyo produces distinction, things arise (爻有等 故曰物). As things hybridize with each other, civilization arises (物相雜 故曰文), As civilization becomes wrong, good and bad arises (文不當 故吉凶生焉)". Hybridization (物相雜) is explicitly used to point to the interaction among things and the formation of civilization. Indeed, our human history as the process of developing various civilizations is possible fundamentally through the mixing role of hybridization. In the advancement of new civilization, the critical function of hybridization must be recognized and respected. Do not be afraid of either being hybridized or hybridizing even with the unfamiliar, reluctant, and strange objects.

The BOC employs similar conceptions, like "the mutual sophistication between the strong and the weak (剛柔相摩) or the mutual cleaning among eight Kyes (八卦相蕩)", that symbolically illustrate the function of hybridization in our everyday life. Hybridization results in producing either the good or the bad(吉凶生焉). Then, the currently bad civilization should again be hybridized with the good civilization guided by the Oneness Logic.

3.2.1.3 *Daoist*

Daoists are aware of the hybridization. Instead of 雜, they use 混. The expression of "雜" or "混" can be used interchangeably. To Daoists, "The hybridization of things means the creation of the world (有物混成 先天之生)". Therefore hybridization is directed toward the Oneness (故混而爲一). No hybridization, no our present world, and no Oneness.

3.2.1.4 Buddhist

"Creation and annihilation due to networking (緣起)", one of the most basic principles in Buddhism, explains the continuing process of the human world from the past to the eternal future. Without this networking, everything loses its existential identity and it becomes an empty nothing (空). The networking in the past, the present and the future (法界緣起) is, empirically, nothing but the process of hybridization between a great many different things (重重無盡).

In this connection between Buddhist networking and hybridization, we are able to correctly understand why the book 華嚴經 has also been called 雜華經 (Buddha decorated with all different kinds of flowers). The meaning of 華嚴 is to magnificently decorate Buddha with beautiful flowers. The notion of 雜華 in this context symbolizes the world of hybridization between good and bad, beautiful and ugly, or clean and dirty. As Buddhism says, Buddha is everywhere and in everything, the conception of "all in one and one in all" is indicative of the world of hybridization. All as a diversity can be constituted only by the hybridization of all different things.

3.2.2 Solipsist and Spiritual Individualism: One Mind (一心)

TABLE 4.4 Solipsist and spiritual individualism: One Mind

East Asian wisdom	Text
	One Mind (一心 = 本心, 天心, 道心, 佛性)
Sunist	本心本太陽 仰明, 自性求子 一神降衷 降在爾腦
	唯衆迷地 三妄着根 日心氣身 心依性有善惡 善福惡禍
Book of Change	天命之謂性
Confucian	格物致知 誠意正心 修身齊家治國平天下, 修己治人 克己復禮
	四端四德: 惻隱之心(仁), 羞惡之心(義), 辭讓之心(禮), 是非之心(智)
	性卽理 心卽理 (心卽性) 心卽氣
Taoist	無心 虛其心 弱其志 心使氣日強
Buddhist	天上天下唯我獨尊 一切唯心造
	一心 有我無我 心爲法本 心尊心使

It is not an exaggeration to say that all East Asian wisdoms are about the mind. The study of the mind is the first and final of all studies. My idea of SSI tries to represent this spiritualist tradition as a distinctive character of East Asian wisdoms or the Oneness Logic.

The SSI is based on the one mind (一心) as a characteristic quality of the Oneness. "一心" was systematically elaborated by Won-hyo (元曉), who also tried to resolve theoretical conflicts among various Buddhist sects by proposing the logic of harmonization (和諍), a methodology of hybridization between different theories for realizing the Oneness.

3.2.2.1   Sunist

According to the BFC, our fundamental mind is rooted in the brightness of the sun (本心本太陽). The notion of brightness (明) related with the sunlight (陽明) is very crucial in all East Asian wisdom as well as Greek philosophies and Christianism. The worship for the sun is to deify its brightness without which the world would be covered with the darkness of absurdity and evil.

The brightness is used by Buddhists in overcoming the ordinary state of non-brightness (無明), by Confucians in achieving bright virtue (明德), by Daoists to reduce the artificiality of human action (有爲), and by Sunists in making the unification of the heaven and earth with a human who respects the brightness (仰明) and takes the middle way (人中天地一).

Sunists say specifically that "the Oneness has already come in your mind and your brain (一神降衷 降在爾腦)". They seem to foretell the rise of modern brain psychology. I believe my mind works within my brain rather than my heart. However, people, deviated from the original nature(自性), begin to acquire three misdirected minds (唯衆迷地 三妄着根).

3.2.2.2   The BOC and Confucians

The BOC is also regarded as a treasure for the study of the mind. Many Koes in the BOC, such as 重天乾 (mind as heaven), 水風井 (mind of love), 重地坤 (acceptance of all), 雷水解 (freedom from mind), etc., tell about the nature of the mind and how to control and cultivate it.

The most popular dictum of Confucianism for establishing one's life career starts with individual efforts, "first, you must study thoroughly and know correctly things surrounding you (格物致知) and then concentrate on building sincerity and right mind (誠意正心), second, after cultivating your mind and body (修身), you may move toward stabilizing your family, governing your state and finally pacifying the world (齊家治國平天下)". This is the most vivid expression of East Asian self-expanding individualism, an individualist quest for his or her own interest as well as all other individuals' interests.

Confucius gives many clear-cut teachings, like "cultivate yourself and then help others (修己治人)",[17] "overcome or regulate yourself and then rebuild social order for others (克己復禮)", "study for yourself for your wisdom (爲己之學)", not for demonstrating your knowledge to others, etc. All these lessons are introduced to stress the priority of cultivating, first, I myself as an individual actor before going out to do something for others. A self-cultivating individual for itself will certainly become a self-expanding individual for others.

Two diversions of Confucian schools, the reason-oriented school (理學派) and the mind-oriented school (心學派) is identifiable in the development of new Confucian school (性理學), established by Chu Hsi (朱熹). In anticipation of some strong criticism and opposition, I support the mind school, mainly because, unlike the reason school's strong criticism of Buddhism and Daoism, it was tolerant of them and it seems to have a closer selective affinity with the Oneness Logic. Wang Yangming (王陽明), a founder of the mind school starts from the declaration of "the mind is the reason (心卽理)" in a bold challenge to the Reason school's dictum, "the (human basic) nature is the reason (性卽理)". Moreover, he goes on to contend that the nature resides within everybody's mind.

3.2.2.3   *Daoist*
The essential value of Daoism is non-action (無爲) or "do-nothing-artificial or involuntary". The non-action is very difficult for us to perform because our mind is full of artificially constructed desires. Thus, Daoists advise us to "empty our mind (無心), or empty it (虛其心), or weaken our intention (弱其志). It is unnatural to try to change forcefully our mind (心使氣曰強)".

3.2.2.4   *Buddhist*
As far as the SSI is concerned, Buddhism provides the most solid theory for it. In fact, it is a Buddhist theory of one mind or the Oneness.

My theory of solipsism and individualism comes directly from the phrase, "there is no other being than only I myself in the universe, who is surely respectful (天上天下唯我獨尊)". The wonderful declaration of "everything in the universe is made by my mind (一切唯心造)" becomes the backbone of my spiritualism.

---

17   I would like to translate "govern (治)" into "help", because the Confucian ideal for political ruling as well as many other actions is benevolence (仁).

The notion of only I/myself (唯我) and only my mind (唯心) is logically equivalent to the notion of individual as a unique subject of thinking and acting. In contrast to Western individualism that is degraded somehow as a selfish egoism, East Asian individualism is self-expanding in that it is ontologically connected with the whole world and normatively and behaviorally demanding the unity with all people and things in the world by discovering a transcendental self in one's present self (無我中有我). The self, whatever it is, is nothing but the omnipotent functional mechanism of one mind in the Oneness (心爲法本 心尊心使).

The SSI does not deny the physical, empirical existence of all other beings, including me. Rather, they are meaningful and realistic to me only when they appear within my conscious mind. Therefore, SSI aims to rehabilitate the role of the human subject I, whom some post-structuralist and structural determinist removed and buried theoretically. Facing an era of post-humanism, the return of I myself and the human subject is becoming an urgent demand for recovering the imbalanced relationship between nature (heaven and earth) and the human being (天地人合一不均衡). The SSI with its inward language (心言) tells us to do something for the ecological Oneness.

3.2.3 The Middle Way (中道) for Love: A Normative Theory of Action (修行論)

TABLE 4.5 The middle way for love: a normative theory of action

East Asian wisdom	Text 無明 昂明 明明德, 明心見性
Sunist	中一, 返妄卽眞, 永得快樂 自性求子 大光明處 性統功完 濟世理化 弘益人間
Book of Change	中正之道, 時中之道, 中節之和, 允執厥中 允執基中
Confucian	仁愛 中庸
Taoist	得一 抱一 通一 上善若水 水善利萬物 不爭 不如守中 無爲自然
Buddhist	大慈大悲, 上求菩提 下化衆生 中道 萬法歸一 萬行歸眞

Unquestionably, the enlightenment or awakening (得道, 成佛, 中一, 得一, 抱一, 通一, 大悟覺醒) is the ultimate and most desirable goal of all East Asian wisdoms. The enlightenment is in the state of brightness (昂明 明明德, 明心見

性). What is then the state of my mind after[18] realizing Dao? Just as Christian teaching says the "truth will make you free", so too does East Asian wisdom say that you will feel free and liberated from all repressing conditions and situations (Bang 2020) when you acquire the Dao. This individual awakening of the Oneness directs us to share our experiences of pleasure and stability arising from the sense of freedom and unity with all other beings in the world.

My freedom becomes a joyful responsibility. How to perform my mission? All wisdom of the West and East gives us a unanimous answer: "LOVE (仁愛, 大慈大悲, 慈愛 弘益)". Love is absolutely requested and demanded all over the world, past and present, certainly in the future too. Now this linkage from enlightenment through freedom as a joyful mission to love completes the normative and behavioral cycle of the Oneness.

In this circulation, I emphasize the middle (中) or the middle way (中道) of enjoying the process itself of acquiring an enlightenment and sharing it. A crucial contribution of the Oneness Logic to contemporary social theory lies in its explicit and strong normative orientations characteristic of East Asian wisdom. They have always been the consistent advocates for cultivating oneself, exploring the truth and doing good, accumulating virtues (積善積德), and helping others. All these normative pursuits can be achieved and internalized through a long and hard self-cultivation in the quest for enlightenment.

Unlike a few Dao-seekers who endure many kinds of long asceticism, however, it is advised that we had better discover and realize the enlightenment in our everyday life. A routinization or secularization of the process of cultivating the enlightenment is necessary for ordinary people to access it. The everyday practices of praying, meditation, and some regular training of body and mind themselves are indispensable part of the realization of Dao. To repeat, Dao is already in ourselves as Buddha is everywhere and everytime in your mind (處處佛 時時佛)! Viewed in this way, our life and living itself is a process of awakening. Furthermore, the process should become a way for hope and expectation, stability and calmness, and perhaps most importantly pleasure and delight in this frustrated, risky, agonizing and heart-breaking world.

3.2.3.1 Sunist

I propose that "中" in the phrase of BFH (人中天地一) can be understood in terms of Buddhist middle way (中道, 中觀) or Confucian moderation (中和, 中庸, 中正, 時中). Thus, a clear normative role by a human subject of mediating between the heaven and the earth can be drawn. Since the equal

---

18 The feeling of ecstasy at the moment of awakening is widely reported.

but independent role is assigned to the three of the heaven, earth, and human by the Oneness Logic, it is neither exceptional nor extraordinary for humans to intervene in the realm of heaven and earth. Humans in bad (凶) civilization may sometimes be antagonistic or destructive to the other two realms. By overcoming Daoist artificial action 有爲 and Buddhist no-light and three harms (無明, 三毒) we can come close to a Daoist "do-nothing-unnatural" (無爲自然) and Sunist unity (天地人合一). Ecological balance is from the start presumed by the Oneness Logic.

The Sunist concept of "caring about all humans or human with great caring for all (弘益人間)" is a final goal for "human action (濟世理化)" after establishing the intercommunication between I myself and my original spirit (自性求子 性通功完)". A self-expanding model of individual for loving/caring for all others is presented at the last stage of the Oneness Logic. We are the world!

3.2.3.2   BOC and Confucians

In the heart of all Confucian teaching is "the value of benevolence (仁) and the performing principle of moderation (中庸, 中正之道, 時中之道, 中節之和, 允執厥中 允執基中)". Benevolence is, mindfully or psychologically, defined as "compassion (惻隱之心)" by Mencius (孟子). Thus, it is equivalent to Christian love and very close to the Buddhist "great mercy and compassion (大慈大悲)", not to mention the Sunist "great man helping others (弘益人間)".

Confucians use the principle of moderation normatively in the empirical world of real human action. It is, however, not easy to specify the meaning and contents of moderation. The way of observing the principle may be different to different men in different situations. One thing unquestionable about moderation is to not fall into any of the two polarized ends of value judgments or actions. We are advised to find a point of moderation in terms of balance, equilibrium, equity, compromise, and reconciliation. Here, too, surprisingly again, a hybridizing point of view is playing a critical role in reaching the moderation in competing or conflicting situations.

3.2.3.3   *Daoist*

The hallmark of Daoism is the non-action or "do-nothing-unnatural" (無爲自然). We may understand Daoism (and Buddhism) as an East Asian anarchism in distinction to but in connection with Western anarchism. The latter, with the exception of pacifist anarchists, such as Tolstoy and Gandhi, relies on revolutionary actions to withdraw the repressive and exploitative state system. Very interestingly, East Asian anarchism embedded in Daoism and Buddhism is not interested in violent revolution. Its preference for gradualism or inactive retreatism seems to be rooted deep in the principle of the middle way. Daoists thus argue that the best way of living a life is "to keep the position of a middle (不如守中)".

We can identify two values, i.e., beneficiality and non-competition, as an expression of Daoist love. Lao-tzu says that water possesses the highest virtue (上善若水), because water benefits all things (水善利萬物) and does not compete and quarrel with others (不爭). The beneficial quality of water is very similar to the Sunist concept of the beneficial man (弘益人間). Daoist non-competition is a very useful method to achieve a Buddhist middle way or Confucian moderation. In this context, we may understand the Daoist dictum of "do-nothing-unnatural" (無爲自然) in a positive way of "do-something-natural". The natural is not to aggressively fight against the unnatural but to coexist peacefully with the latter on the basis of non-competition as moderation or middle way.

Zhang-tzu also informs us of comprehending the Oneness Logic in terms of "realizing (得一), encompassing (抱一) and communicating (通一) with the Oneness". Without mindful communication in particular between human subject and all other beings (通一心), we would be unable to return to the Oneness (歸一).

3.2.3.4 *Buddhist*

There is a famous Buddhist episode: a monk asks, "After everything goes back to the Oneness, where does the Oneness go back" (萬法歸一, 一歸何處)? His teacher gives an incomprehensible answer, "when I was in Chung Joo, I made clothes of seven guns" (我在靑州 作一領布杉 重七斤). My interpretation is that since the Oneness is achieved in our everyday life, it cannot leave us and our everyday. This is the essential teaching of Buddhism, "discover Buddha in your mind and enlighten people outside" (上求菩提 下化衆生). The Oneness Logic asks us to help sad people in miserable situations with a loving mind (大慈大悲). You must go back to your everyday life to do something for people.

"Great sadness" (大悲)! It is worth while paying serious attention to this expression. It must be emphasized that the fundamental or original Buddhist view of the human world and human life was pessimistic (悲觀) and nihilistic (無常) because the human world was just like the sea of agonies (苦海) and had no way out from this damned condition. These days, Buddhist scholars seem to remove or reduce these negative orientations. This attempt is quite understandable but somewhat misdirected.

The pessimistic and nihilistic dimension in Buddhism as well as Daoism is, I stress, an invaluable point of view and a resourceful asset to be fully rediscovered and reinvented to face up to the sad and bad side of our present world and our life in a deteriorating situation. No easy solutions are possible. False hopes for bright near future is useless and harmful. We need first of all a keen sense of pessimism and nihilism about our present condition in order to seek the Oneness. It is advisable first of all to retreat or distance yourself from the reality outside and reflect on yourself and the outside world, then move forward to do something good and productive for yourself and do nothing bad to others.

If you lose the subtle but critical sense of the Buddhist middle way, you are likely to become trapped in either this colorful empirical world (色界) or that empty spiritual world (空界). To avoid the dilemma of choosing either the empirical (色) or the spiritual (空), you must take a middle way (色卽是空, 色空如一). Wonderfully, the middle way can present you all possible worlds, such as 有色無空, 有色有空, 無色有空, 無色無空.

Wonhyo (元曉)'s method of pacifying controversies (和諍) is an exemplary way of achieving the middle way in that he selects good points from all competing arguments and hybridizes them in a harmonious way and proposes a balanced and consistent theory or interpretation. The ancient Chinese school of 雜家 (school of hybridization), as one of the nine famous schools, including Confucian (儒家), Mohist (墨家), Daoist (道家), Buddhist (佛家), Legalist (法家), Naturalist (陰陽家), Nominalist (名家), and Agriculturalist (農家) school in the era of Warring States (春秋戰國時代), brilliantly used the method of an eclectic hybridization between all different schools of thoughts on the basis of Daoist orientations. Buddhist recognition of 雜 (hybridity) leads us to a normative connection between hybridization and the middle way.

4   Epilogue: Dao of Stylish Cultivation (風流道) in the Twenty-First Century

4.1   *Summary*

Thus far, I have tried to construct an East Asian general social theory on the basis of East Asian wisdom, which includes Sunism, Confucianism, Daoism, and Buddhism. I assumed that the four wisdoms share the conception of the Oneness. Relying on this premise, first, I proposed the Oneness Logic to fully explain the logically systematic characteristics of the Oneness. Secondly, some representative texts quoted from the four wisdoms were used to specify and support the Oneness Logic and three theories at empirical levels, such as hybridization, solipsist-spiritualist individualism, and the middle way for love. The major contents of my theoretical construction can be summarized as follows:

1. The Oneness Logic starts from the East Asian ontological recognition of the unity between the heaven, earth, and human (天地人合一).
2. The ontological state of the Oneness is assumed to be chaotic and hybridized with three qualities, such as one qi (一氣), one mind (一心), and one middle (一中). The numerical and compositional dimension of the Oneness is composed of one heaven (天一), one earth (地一), and one human (人一).
3. The Oneness is differentiated into three formational dimensions, such as functional, epistemological, and axiological-behavioral. The functional dimension of one qi and one earth represents movement and change. The epistemological dimension of one mind and one human illustrates the world of the mind. The axiological-behavioral dimension of the middle for love is related to the world of normative behavior.
4. These three dimensions are explained in terms of three empirical theories, such as hybridization for the functional dimension, the solipsist-spiritualist individualism for the epistemological dimension, and the middle way for the axiological and behavioral dimension.
5. The ontological dimensions of the Oneness and three empirical theories are supported and specified by texts quoted from the East Asian four wisdoms.
6. The Oneness Logic advises us to enjoy the process itself of realizing the Oneness in our everyday life.
7. All in all, the Oneness Logic cultivates "a world of the mind within I myself as the Oneness".

4.2   *New Civilization and the Oneness Logic: So What and for What?*

Some 1200 years ago, a Korean scholar named Choi Chi-Won (908~?),[19] who went to China during the Tang (唐) dynasty to study advanced knowledge and pass the state examination and become an official bureaucrat, and to gain a wide reputation as a literary writer of composing "a manifesto for fighting against Hwang-so (討黃巢檄文)", left an epitaph after returning to the Shilla (新羅) dynasty:

> "My country has a mysterious Dao called Wind Flow" (國有玄妙之道曰風流). The history about its foundation is recorded in detail in the history of Sunism (設教之源 詳仙史). The Wind Flow includes within itself three religions of Confucianism, Buddhism and Daoism and cultivates

---

19   For a more detailed discussion of his thoughts, see Jang (2008).

all human beings (實乃包含三敎[20] 接化群生). Its principle of filial piety at home and loyalty outside is the same as Confucianism (且如入則孝於家 出則忠於國 魯司寇之旨也). It's behavior based on non-action and non-speaking is the same as Daoism (處無爲之事 行不言之敎 周柱史之宗也). Its non-doing the bad and doing the good is the same as Buddhism (諸惡莫作 諸善奉行 竺乾太子之化也).

From the above quotation, two concluding points are drawn. First, Choi is known to have discovered first the lost text of the Book from Heaven and to have translated its ancient hieroglyphics into Chinese. As a great scholar he must have had a wide and deep knowledge of the three East Asian wisdoms in China. In this historical context we may safely assume that Korean Sunism and the Oneness Logic shared many common ideas with these wisdoms. He also directly witnessed the historical existence of the Book from Heaven.

Given the universal character of the Oneness as well as the common concern with the Oneness among East Asian wisdom, Hinduism, and Christianity, we may conjecture certain cultural exchanges all over the world. It might be delightful if we would be able to ascertain any kind of dialogue on the Oneness between the East and the West in ancient times. The ongoing project of post-Western sociology may seek such a dialogue.

Second, one distinctive characteristic of Sunism in contrast with other East Asian wisdoms is expressed in its more or less Epicurean tendency to allow or encourage a combination between self-disciplinary study and the enjoyment of artful and stylish pleasures as a way of self-cultivation (設敎之源 相磨以道義, 相悅以歌舞, 遊娛山水). This type of self-regulative Epicureanism based on the middle way is innovative and practical, for most of the great world religions are inclined to prefer an asceticism and deny Epicureanism.

In this regard, Wang Yang Ming (王陽明) and his school, Lee Tak Oh (李晫吾) in particular, must be considered revolutionaries in the orthodox history of Confucianism. They were creative enough to recognize and respect the necessity of human desires (人慾肯定論). Indeed, in East Asia it is recommended to enjoy Dao's pleasure or the delight of following Dao (道樂, 安貧樂道). Dao is not separated from sensual pleasures desired by everybody in everyday life. Korean Sunism explicitly advises us to communicate with the Oneness, enjoying the permanent pleasure (返亡卽眞 性通功完 永得快樂).

Once Freud argued that civilizations were an outcome of human asceticism. It is, however, also true that the history of human civilization is nothing but a process of liberating human desires, iron-caged for a long time by

---

20   The efforts to unite three religions such as Buddhism, Daoism, and Confucianism (三敎統合) was popular and strong in China during the Tang dynasty (Jang 2008).

many hypocritical moralities mainly used for maintaining the establishment. The radical process of hybridization as a powerful catalyst for new civilizational change has been, in this emancipating sense, a struggle for a power shift, deconstructing the old ascetic values of repressing human desires. Of course, as a reaction to this secularizing challenges of hybridization, religious fundamentalism is always ready to play its holy and pure mission of countervailing the rise of Satanic hedonism, often an exaggeration of rational Epicureanism.

Now we are standing at the point of departure toward a postmodern and post-Western civilization. Many different ways or new Daos can guide us to the Second Civilization (後天開闢). The Oneness Logic is one of them. It's unique advantages may be appreciated in terms of its easy access (start at once from your mind), comfortable journey (practice everywhere and every day), and pleasant experiences (enjoy self-regulative Epicureanism). The Oneness Logic can guide us to a way (道) to approach a homo deus (神人) in its ontological sense and realize the communication between god and human I (神人合一 or 通一) within our mind. Or the broken unity between the heaven, earth, and human must be rehabilitated without any additional delay.[21] Would it be a realist quest for a realizable utopia?

Let me finish my unfinished study by quoting Wittgenstein's ([1921] 2006: 15, 116) famous epigram, "we must be silent to the unspeakable … indeed there is something inexpressible. It uncovers itself mysteriously". Undoubtedly this is a contemporary version of Lao-tsu's "An expressible Dao is not a true Dao … Dao is a mysterious and extraordinary way (道可道非常道, 衆妙之門)". The incapacity of human language to express Dao (言語道斷, 不立文字) is clearly appreciated by Wittgenstein, a logician but once (and for all?) a solipsist and mystic. Just like the Buddhist warning, "kill your idols" (殺佛殺祖), Wittgenstein([1921] 2006: 117) too asks us to forget and overcome his logic after comprehending it. Alas! Either Buddha or Wittgenstein or the Oneness Logic may never be an easy target.

References

Classic Texts
天符經, 三一神誥.
周易, 中庸, 大學, 論語, 傳習錄 (王陽明).

---

21 To recover the ecological balance, first of all, a long-term radical policy of reducing the number of the world population is inevitable. The issue of human responsibility becomes an imminent mission.

華嚴經, 法句經, 中論 (龍樹菩薩).
大乘起信論疏 (元曉), 華嚴一乘法界圖 (義湘).
道德經, 莊子內編.

Books and Articles

Alexander, J.C. 1987. *Twenty Lectures: Sociological Theory Since World War II*. New York, NY: Columbia University Press.
Bang, Yung-Joon. 2020. *A Study of Buddha's Political Philosophy*. Inbooks (Korea).
Beck, U. 2008. *Der eigene Gott*. Verlag der Weltreligionen.
Bhabha, H. 1994. *The Location of Culture*. Routledge.
Campbell, C. 2007. *The Easternization of the West*. Paradigm Publishers.
Canclini, N. 1995. *Hybrid Cultures*. Minneapolis: University of Minnesota Press.
Capra, Fritjof. 1975. *The Tao of Physics: An Exploration of the Parallels Between Modern Physics and Eastern Mysticism*. Shambhala.
Choi, Chi-Won. 908~?. *Nanrangbiseo* (鸞郞碑序).
Choi, Min-Ja. 2006. *Chunbukyong·Samilsing·Chamjunkekyong* (天符經 三一神誥 參佺戒經). Mosinunsaramdul (Korea).
Chung, Chang-Soo. 2000. *The I Ching on Man and Society*. University Press of America.
Cribb, J. 2017. *Humanity's Ten Great Challenges and How We Can Overcome Them*. Springer International Publishing.
Feyerabend, Paul. 2010. *Against Method*. Verso.
Fox, N.J. 2018. "Sociology and the New Materialism: Why Matters Matter-Sociologically". In *The Relations Between Human and Things and Future of Social Theory*. Korean Society for Social Theory.
Fox, N.J., and P. Alldred. 2017. *Sociology and the New Materialism: Theory, Research, Action*. SAGE.
Graham, A. 2001. *Chuang-tzu: The Inner Chapters*. Hackeet Publishing Company.
Ha, Ki-Rak. 1993. *A History of Chosun Philosophy*. Hyoungsul (Korea).
Harari, Y.N. 2015. *Homo Deus*. Harvill Secker.
Hong, Seung-Pyo. 2002. *Tao Sociology*. Yemoonsewon (Korea).
Hong, Seung-Pyo. 2005. *Post-modernity in East Asian Thoughts*. Yemoonsewon (Korea).
Ivanhoe, P.J., O.J. Flanagan, V.S. Harrison, and H. Sarkissian, eds. 2018. *The Oneness Hypothesis: Beyond the Boundary of Self*. New York, NY: Columbia University Press.
Jang, Il-Kyu. 2008. *A Study of Choi Chi-Won's Social Thoughts*. Shinseowon (Korea).
Jung, Kyung-Hee. 2004. "The Method of Disciplines of Korean Sundo and the Sacrificial Rituals for Heaven". *Journal of Taoist Culture* 21: 39–80.
Kim, Dong-Hwan. 2005. "Danam (檀菴) Lee Young-Tae (李容兌)'s Religious Thoughts". In *Lee Young-Tae's Life and Thoughts*, edited by the Institute of Regional Cultures, Semyung University. Yyukrak (Korea).

Kim, Jae-Bum. 2001. *I Ching and Sociology*. Yemoonseowon (Korea).

Kim, Kyoung-Dong. 2019. *Social Value: Civilizational Reflections and Visions*. Purunsasang (Korea).

Kim, Sang-Joon. 2021. *Roc' s Wings and the Prospect for Civilization*, Arcanet (Korea).

Kim, Seok-Jin. 2010. *The Book from Heaven* (天符經). Dongbanguibit (Korea).

Kim, Seung Kuk. 2011. "The Coming of Hybrid Society and Theory of Hybridization". *Society and Theory* 21 (2): 423–455.

Kim, Seung Kuk. 2014. "East Asian Community as Hybridization: A Quest for East Asianism". In *A Quest for East Asian Sociologies*, edited by S.K. Kim, P. Li, and S. Yazawa. Seoul: Seoul National University Press.

Kim, Seung Kuk. 2015. *Hybrid Society and Its Friends*. Ehaksa (Korea).

Kim, Seung Kuk. 2018. "Individualism of Unique Self/Mind: Toward a Mind Sociology". *Korean Journal of Sociology* 52 (2): 159–212.

Kim, Seung Kuk. 2023. *The Oneness Logic: An Exploration for East Asian Social Theory*. Ehaksa (Korea).

Kum, In-Suk. 2012. *Mysticism: Yoga, Gnosticism, Alchemy, and Sufi*. Sallim (Korea).

Kwon Tae-Hoon/Ahn Ki-Suk. 1999. *Secrets of Book from Heaven and Culture of Paikdoosan people*. Jeongsinsegesa (Korea).

Kwon, Tae-Woo. (1984) 2006. *Sundo Gongbu*. Sol (Korea).

Lau, Felix. (2017) 2020. *Die Form der Paradoxie*. Translated into Korean by Lee, Chul, and Y. Lee. Theory Publishing (Korea).

Latour, B. 2005. *Reassembling the Social: An Introduction to Actor-network-Theory*. Oxford: Oxford University Press.

Lee, Geun-Cheol. 2011. "Research for 'Cheon(Heaven), Ji(Earth) and In(Humans)' in Cheonbukyung". *Journal of Korean Sundo Culture* 4: 29–58.

Lee, Geun-Cheol. 2016. "A Study on the Definition of 'han' based on "一" in Cheon Bu Kyung". *Journal of Korean Sundo Culture* 9: 169–198.

Leavy, P., L. Smith, and E. Keri, eds. 2008. *Hybrid Identities*. Haymarket Books.

Lee, Seung-Ho. 2016. "The Trial Study on Korean Sundo Ontology". *Journal of Korean Sundo Culture* 9: 328–357.

Lee Young-Chan. 2008. *Paradigms of Confucian Sociology and Social Theories*. Yemoonsewon (Korea).

Nan, Huai Jin (南懷瑾). (1994) 2013. 易經雜說. Translated into Korean by Won-Bong Shin (2013) as *Youkyuongjabsul*. Booky (Korea).

Nan, Huai Jin (南懷瑾). (1991) 2018. 易經繫辭別講. Translated into Korean by Won-Bong Shin (2013) as *Juyoukkesalkangui*. Booky (Korea).

Nederveen Pieterse, J. 1995. "Globalization as Hybridization". In *Global Modernities*, edited by M. Featherstone, S.R. Lash, and R. Robertson. SAGE Publications.

Pagles, E. 1979. *The Gnostic Gospel*. New York, NY: Vintage Books.

Roulleau-Berger, L. 2016. *Post-Western Revolution in Sociology. From China to Europe*. Boston, MA: Brill.

Roulleau-Berger, L. 2021. "The Fabric of Post-Western sociology: Ecologies of Knowledge beyond the 'East' and the 'West'". *The Journal of Chinese Sociology* 8: 10.

Roulleau-Berger, L., and Peilin Li, eds. 2018. *Post-Western Sociology: From China to Europe*. Leiden: Brill.

Ryu, Dong-Sik. 1997. *Pungryudo* (風流道) *and Korean Religious Thoughts*. Yonsei University Press.

Ryu, Joong Wee. 2016. "A Comparative Study of the Book from Heaven (天符經) and Daoist Ontology" 刘 *Journal of Korean Sundo Culture* 4: 135–171.

Ryu, Myong-Jong. 1994. *Neo-Confucianism and the School of Wang Yangming*. Yonsei University Press (Korea).

Rui Seong-Moo. 2020. *Buddhist Sociology of Buddhism*. Parkjongchul Chulpansa (Korea).

Rui, Young-Mo. (1963) 2021. *Korean Interpretation of the Book from Heaven* (天符經)与 *by Daseok Rui Young-Mo*. https://www.youtube.com/watch?v=ctJVeUH6L2I.

Shin, Yong-Ha. 2019. "The Concept of the Ancient Chosun Civilization and Its Location in the History of Human Civilization". In *Why Now Is the Ancient Chosun Civilization?*, edited by Y.H. Shin. Nanam (Korea).

Song, Jae-Kook. 2013. "'Pre' and 'Post Heaven' and 'Gate of Morality' in the Study of Changes". *Journal of Korean Sundo Culture* 14: 437–479.

Wittgenstein, Ludwig. (1921) 2006. *Tractatus Logico-Philosophicus*. Translated into Korean by Lee Young-Chul (2006) as *Nonrichulhaknongo*. Chaesesang (Korea).

Woo, Sil-Ha. 2012. *The World View of Trichotomy*. Sonamu (Korea).

Xie, Lizhong, and L. Roulleau-Berger, eds. 2017. *The Fabric of Sociological Knowledge*. Beijing: Peking University Press.

Yazawa, S. 2019. "Toward a Non-hegemonic Social Science". Seminar at the Toward a Non-hegemonic World Sociology conference. Saint-Emilion, France, June 25–27, 2019.

CHAPTER 5

To Create a Post-Western Sociology: A Brief Sketch of Japanese Sociology

Yazawa Shujiro

1   Translation of Society into Japanese Sociology

Sociology was introduced from Europe and the United States during the formation of a modern nation-state, which was promoted under the slogans of *Fukoku Kyohei* and *Bunmei Kaika*, and by Western talent after the Meiji Restoration. However, even if it was introduced, in order for sociology to take root in Japan and be established, it was necessary to consider at least how the objects and methods of sociology were prepared.

The term *society* was not one found in Japan. It had been introduced into Japan through Dutch studies and English studies since the end of the 18th century.[1] The noun "society" was translated as a verb, like gathering and intersecting (Yanabu 1982). The "society" could be understood as something that was impossible to use as the subject. At the end of the Edo period and the beginning of the Meiji era, "society" came to be translated as *Yoriai* (gathering), *Shukai* (rally), or a *Nakama* (companion). In the French study tradition, it was translated as *Kai* (company). Namely, "society" began to be understood as a noun.

In any case, until the early Meiji era, "society" meant a group of people who knew or knew about in some way. But with this alone, the word "society" would not have been born in Japanese. If this had been all, Japanese has the term *Seken*, which means it. It is said to be a word with a 1000-year history. Amane Nishi wrote *Seken-Ron* in 1873 (Nishi 1873).

The modernization of Japan since the Meiji era has surpassed the above-mentioned relatively narrow world of people. It has created a large number of people who have gathered to achieve a certain purpose. Such a group could not be grasped by the words that had existed in Japan thus far. So much effort was made to figure them out.

---

1   For the translation of the concept of society and individual, I relied on Akira Yanabu. For the cultural background of the translation of foreign words into Japanese, see Masao Maruyama and Shu'ichi Kato (1998).

First of all, the meaning of people-to-people dating, fellowship, and gathering was added to the word "society", which could make certain that the word could be used not only as an adjective and a verb but also a subject. If it is a group of people, it can be the subject. In addition, efforts were made so that people-to-people, people-to-monarch, people-to-state, and state-to-state dating, fellowship, and companion were possible (Fukuzawa 1875).

The creation, independence, and respect of the individual were proposed in order to realize this thought. The thought became widely available by the liberty and people's rights movements.

As a result of these efforts, the term *sha* has come to be attached to a group of people who have come together to achieve a certain purpose. It was often expressed by adding the terms *sha* and *kai* to proper and common nouns. In addition, names such as *Shinbun-sha* (newspaper publisher) and *Zashi-sha* (magazine publisher) have become possible.

The term *sha* was introduced because the term *sha* was applied to traditional Japanese dance groups, music performance groups, etc. Which made it easier. The above developments intersect with the term of *kai* (company, meeting), which is a translation of the term "society" in the tradition of French studies. Thus, society was eventually translated as *ShaKai*, and the term *Shakai* was born and spread in Japanese. It is said that the term *Shakai* was established around 1874–1887.

2   Introduction and Establishing of Sociology in Japan

Let us briefly investigate the introduction of sociology to Japan and the establishment of sociology in Japan. The history of the introduction, establishment, and development of prewar Japanese sociology must be understood as the convergence of several numbers, rather than being single-track, at least with regard to the establishment of sociology.[2]

Amane Nishi studied abroad in the Netherlands at the end of the Edo period. After returning to Japan, in 1871, while working as a bureaucrat, he opened his own private school, where he critically examined the theory of Cheng-Zhu, on which he had relied, and considered the importance of the links between various sciences he preached.

When it came to sociology, he translated it as *Setaigaku* (social science), *Ningengaku* (anthropology), and so on. He introduced the sociology of A. Comte.

---

2   I relied on Takao Kawai (1998, 2003) to write a history of the establishment of Japanese sociology in the earliest days.

He applied the three-step theory of Comte to preach the three-step theory of theology–*Kurigaku* (impractical science)–*Jitsurigaku* (practical science). Therefore, positivism was also translated as partialism (Kawai).

Many of the people who completed their studies of sciences in the Meiji era traveled to the bureaucratic, private, and academic circles. Amane Nishi was no exception. While he had academic achievements in philosophy and psychology, and sociologically wrote the book *Sekenron*, he made a great contribution to the establishment of Japan's military system. Therefore, I would like to call this flow bureaucratic studies.

Shinpachi Shaku belongs to this trend. The influence of relationships does not matter. While working in the translation department of the Ministry of Finance, he founded a private school, the predecessor of a private university. He translated and published H. Spencer's *Theory of Education* in 1880, translating sociology as *Shakaigaku*. This translated book seems to have been read quite a bit, partly due to the rise of the Freedom and People's Rights Movement, but it eventually went out of print (Kawai 1998).

I have already mentioned that Fukuzawa Yukichi played a major role in establishing the concept of society and the individual. In addition, he devoted himself to keen social observations rooted in the daily lives of ordinary people, advocating the importance of a unified scholarship of seeing, listening, speaking, and reading. He emphasized the importance of thinking about the invisible (power) as well as the practical science of unraveling the underlying form of human–human, human–state, and state–state dating.

As mentioned above, it is certain that Fukuzawa Yukichi laid the foundation for the development of social science in Japan, and his achievements are highly evaluated. But he did not consciously develop any particular social science. As a private civilization critic, journalist, and private school owner, he clarified the basic character of modern civilization and preached the construction of economy, politics, society, and culture based on criticism of attitudes toward Asia. Let's define the flow of private science. Baba Tatsui, Masami Oishi, Kotaro Noritake, Sen Katayama, Kakitsu Yamada, etc., belong to this trend.

Tatsui Baba studied at Fukuzawa's private school and studied twice in London. After returning to Japan, he powered the leftmost wing of movement for the development of the Freedom and People's Rights Movement. He extracted and introduced the positive and progressive aspects of Spencer's theory of social evolution and contributed to the realization of a society where freedom was also insidious. This interpretation is valuable because Spencer's theory of evolution was a major piece of idealism on the part of the regime in the early Meiji era. However, the allegations and actions were not accepted, and he traveled to the United States in a form of what was almost asylum and appealed from overseas to prevent the realization of Japan's imperial system and state, but he died in Philadelphia without realizing his dream.

Masami Oishi, along with Tatsui Baba, contributed to the development of the Freedom and People's Rights Movement. He published a translation of Spencer's *Sociology* in 1887. He was also making efforts to establish and manage sociology and socialism studies.

Sen Katayama went to America at a young age and studied urban issues at a university while being interested in the labor movement and the urban socialist movement. He returned to Japan at the end of the century and participated in the labor movement, socialist movement, and general election movement. He also participated in the sociology study group and the socialist study group. After that, he returned to the United States and became interested in the Christian social reform movement, gradually committed to the social subject movement and the communist movement through finding the sociological elements included in theology, and became an international communist activist.

After graduating from Kyoritsu, scholar Kotaro Noritake published a translation of Spencer's *The Principle of Sociology* volume 1, in 1884. He taught at a university for a while, but as freedom was his first principle, from national free economy and free trade, he participated in the Freedom and People's Rights Movement with Ukichi Taguchi, who was said to be the Adam Smith of Japan and published *Tokyo Economic* magazine and *Rokugo* magazine. Sen Katayama's related articles were published in the latter magazine. He also became a bank clerk later.

The final flow is the science of pulpit academic flow. This is a flow that is considered to be the mainstream. After the Meiji Restoration, the Meiji government created Imperial University in 1877. The Faculty of Letters of Tokyo Imperial University was established. All but one of the staff were invited professors from abroad. It was A. Fenollosa who first taught sociology (sociology). His specialty was financial science, political science, philosophy, etc., but sociology was preached as something that must be learned to study these topics. He later turned to aesthetics and Japanese art research.

Masakazu Toyama was the only Japanese staff member of the Faculty of Letters at Tokyo Imperial University. He returned home after earning a PhD from the University of Michigan and joined the faculty. His specialty was chemistry, not sociology. However, he was versatile and probably had excellent organizational management abilities. He actively participated not only in sociology but also in the modernization movement of sentence expression and contributed to the establishment of modern science. Later, he became the first person in charge of sociology, and also the president of the University of Tokyo.

Nagao Ariga was a student of Fenollosa. Immediately after graduating from university he became the first Japanese person to publish three systematically written sociology books in 1883–1884. However, after studying abroad in Germany and studying state theory, he turned to state law.

Around 1886 and 1887 sociology, which had been translated as *Setaigaku* (social science), *Ningengaku* (anthropology), etc., was unified into the translation of sociology, while the above three flows intersected with each other. And the technical terms of sociology were almost fixed. The general sociology of Tongo Takebe can be understood as one of the highest peaks of the development of sociology around the turn of the century (Kawai 2003).

3 Achievement of Prewar Japanese Sociology

Then, how far has Japanese sociology—established as described above—developed?

In Japan, the imperial system was established at the turning point of the century, and after the Sino-Japanese War and the Russo-Japanese War the degree of militarism and imperialism rapidly increased, but sociology was established in the process. After that, through the development of Japanese capitalism and the rise of a political constitutional system following the death of Emperor Meiji, we entered the relatively liberal Taisho era as symbolized by the names "*Taisho* democracy" and "*Taisho* culture".

During that time, sociology developed further. The Japanese Academy of Sociology, the predecessor of the Japan Sociological Society was founded in 1913 and the Japan Sociological Society was also founded in 1924. One of the sociologists who reached the pinnacle of prewar Japanese sociology and created sociology comparable to Western sociology at that time was Shotaro Yoneda.[3]

3.1 *Shotaro Yoneda*

Yoneda obtained his PhD under Giddings from Columbia University and received guidance from G. Tarde in France. After 12 years in two foreign countries, he returned to Japan and served as the first sociology course manager at Kyoto Imperial University.

---

3 Massive manuscripts and the lecture notes of Shotaro Yoneda are kept in the Department of Sociology, Faculty of Letters, Kyoto University. My introduction of Yoneda's theory relies on Hisao Naka (1998, 2003) and Makoto Ogasawara (2003).

What he had to do was to reject social philosophy and social policy tendencies and establish sociology as a realistic empirical science. In other words, it was the establishment of a special sociology that relied on Durkheim, Simmel, Giddings, etc., rather than the synthetic sociology of Comte and Spencer. From there, it was to establish a general, comprehensive sociology that was different from the synthetic sociology.

This task was still a challenge that had to be fulfilled, because although Japanese sociology was established, it was still unclear in society what sociology was, and even in academia it cannot be said that it was well accepted as a science. In this sense, something like "the principle of sociology" had to be written.

Yoneda's basic research attitude was to "absorb normal molecules contained in the ideas of various researchers". This attitude is considered to be quite common, but not many researchers have pushed this attitude as thoroughly as Yoneda. He examined not only sociology but all related things, such as social science, philosophy, and thoughts, and put them together in books. His sociological theory can be summarized in several propositions. The first proposition is that "sociology is pure science". Without this, special sociology as an empirical science that is distinct from philosophy and social policy cannot be formed. But sociology is not completely unrelated to philosophy.

The second proposition is that "sociology belongs to the category of special philosophy". He regarded philosophy as the accounting of intuition and classifies it into general philosophy, which considers fundamental problems such as epistemological problems, and special philosophy, which considers derivative problems. He considered sociology to be a science of concept and believed special philosophy belongs to it. On the one hand, he refers to the establishment of sociology separately from philosophy, and on the other hand, sociology belongs to the category of special philosophy. He did not develop much in-depth discussion of the relationship between philosophy as a science of intuition and sociology as a science of concept, but rather he points out that psychology is a science close to sociology. He pointed out that the combination of the two can be called mental science. In any case, the relationship between sociology and various sciences should be considered in detail.

The third proposition is that sociology consists of three parts: methodological research, abstract research, and concrete research. Based on the above discussion, Yoneda divides sociology into the following three divisions. The first is organizational sociology. It attempts to organize all scientific research on society. The second is genuine sociology. It investigates "the essence of reality 'fundamental facts, and minimum extreme facts' with respect to object recognition". All additional facts must be excluded. It is a highly abstract study. The third is general sociology. It adds additional facts to the essence of reality and recognizes them comprehensively. It must be considered as being different from the former synthetic sociology.

Yoneda examined precisely and extensively related sociology, social science, social thought, philosophy, etc., and he found from those studies the essence of reality, the minimum of extreme facts. For example, consciousness of kind, the interaction of the mind, etc., were taken out. In addition to that, he presented the "law of imitation" (G. Tard) as a result of general sociology. Regarding specific research, Yoneda has published many studies belonging to the sociology of customs (Koseki 1979) and social issues and has been evaluated as a pioneer in those fields. However, for various reasons he did not publish any books on sociology. All that was left were several treatises and a huge number of lecture notes. His great sociological spirit was therefore inherited by the remaining writers and his students.

3.2 *Yasuma Takada*

Yasuma Takada, along with Yoneda, is another sociologist who reached the pinnacle of prewar Japanese sociology. He was Yoneda's first student. Takada inherited Yoneda's sociological spirit, and at the same time, after struggling with Yoneda's theory of sociology, he appeared in the sociological world with *Fundamental Principle of Sociology* (Takada 1919). After that, he published many books, such as *The Study of Social Relations* (Takada 1926), and led the field of sociology.

Ultimately, Takada's aim was to deny synthetic sociology and establish special sociology. To do so, it must be made clear that sociology has its own objectives and theories. According to Takada, the first thing sociology must do is define the object and the essence of society. That is, the development of social essence theory. He thought that in "motivated social relations" (*gewilltes zusammenleben*) "coupling" is the essence of society, the object of sociology rather than social relations in general. In other words, he examined all social relationships but said that "social union" is the one that ranks high.

He called his sociology *union sociology* and thought that only his and Ferdinand Tönnie's forms deserved this name, albeit in widespread sociology. If the essence of reality and the essence of society are taken into consideration, Takada thought that the next thing he had to do was to investigate how society is established and to develop the theory of social establishment.

Society is formed by two types of unions with different properties. The first bond is a room bond. It is brought about by the desire of the herd to bring about a homogenous bond. The second bond is a heterologous bond. It is the desire for power that results in heterogeneity. He further divided the former in two, the desire for physical access and the desire for mental interaction or communication. The latter is also divided into separation, difference relations, and power relations (superiority, struggle, etc.).

In particular, he attached great importance to the last of these and developed the theory of division of labor as an expression of one dimension of power relations. In short, society is established by these various connections, relationships, and combinations. Therefore, Takada was developing social consciousness in relation to these discussions.

Here too, Takada began by abstractly distinguishing between direct and indirect connections. A direct bond is a bond based on the desire for the person itself and is a bond that is unconditional regardless of whether or not the bond can benefit. A society based on this combination is called a direct society. Indirect deficiency, as opposed to direct binding, is a conditional binding for some benefit. Society is based on indirect connection. This is called an indirect society. Of course, this is an abstract division, and the concrete connection or social form is a direct society and a direct indirect society that includes both.

In addition, Takada distinguished between three types of direct and indirect societies. The first is a society in which kinship-based connections are predominant, including families and clans. The second direct and indirect society is a society in which the connection based mainly on the territory is predominant. This includes state and local community. The third is a society in which connections based on indirect connections are predominant and where occupations are positioned, and it was further divided into basic societies and derivative societies. At the end of discussion on social forms. Takada explained social change as a dynamic interaction of various social forms. In short, society is established by these various connections, relationships, and their composites. At the end of the above theory of sociology, Takada considered the relationship between human culture, freedom, and individuality because of the development of society as a social consequential theory.

As mentioned above, Takada's sociology is extremely logical and systematic, and it can be evaluated as having a quality comparable to that of Western sociology at that time. In fact, in Japan today, his theory of power, population, and locality has been restored, as they are developing discussions like Parsons' theory (Kaneko 2003).

But on the other hand, Takada's theory, although not formal sociology, is fairly formal and omits content to be discussed, even considering that he wrote the principle of sociology. In some situations, that had to be the case. The emperor controlled thought, social science, and education by enacting imperial rescript on education, and sociology was to gain its position in academia as a science with its own objects and theories. Scientifically, they were logical and sometimes formal. The end of the Taisho era was the heyday of formal sociology. Yoneda's and Takada's sociology was exceptional; their sociology was beyond formal sociology.

However, it does not seem to have solved the problems of the concept that Japanese sociology had when it was established after the Meiji Restoration. It was the problem of the relationship between society and individuals, and the problem of the system of society and the nation-state. I have to discuss this point a little now. How was the relationship between society and the nation state understood in Takada's sociology (Takada 1922)?

The relationship between the nation-state and society in his theory is, on the one hand, the relationship in existence and, on the other hand, the relationship in transitional development. The relationship in the former is quite clear. Society is included in nations as part of the nation. And the relationship is confrontational. If there is no comprehensive relationship, the two are in conflict or there is no combined communication.

If there is a combined contact, there is the question of whether there is a whole society above the society and the nation. A society in a broad sense is the union of many people. A society in a narrow sense is one with a sense of unity. Societies in the broad sense include occupations, religious groups, classes, family, ethnicities, etc. The relationship between the nation-state and society in transitional development extends to the formation of a world society that has crossed borders through the strengthening and development of unity that accompanies the development of general culture.

Takada was clearly developing discussions from the standpoint of pluralistic power theory and national theory represented by H. Laski and others. The argument is reminiscent of McIver's theory of community. From that standpoint, his argument is understandable. However, when the book was published, Japan was clearly heading toward fascism, a powerful nation-state, and his theory did not capture that direction. However, his argument was valid in the development of democracy in postwar Japanese society.

3.3   *Nyozekan Hasegawa*

It may be better to pay attention to private sectors other than academia in terms of solving the problems of Japanese sociology during the establishment period. In fact, the survey conducted by Yoneda's student who worked in Osaka City is regarded as a pioneering achievement in the history of Japanese social research. It was also private researchers and critics who built the monument of popular culture studies in the Taisho era and later made pioneering achievements called life sciences. Here, I would like to pay attention to the sociological achievements of Nyozekan Hasegawa.

Hasegawa considers the essence of society as a form of life (Hasegawa 1928). And he tried to recapture the form of life as a system of behavior. He was a well-known newspaper reporter who later became an independent critic. Therefore, he did not study the social sciences professionally. Sociology was not particularly important to him. He needed social science to grasp reality and spread it to the masses.

The social form, he said, is "a concrete form of life as an empirical fact" (Hasegawa 1928). To elucidate it, he thought that "although the scientific structure was not strict, it was most important to organize empirical knowledge about the organization of human behavior". In this sense, sociology, especially general sociology, was important to him. Sociology denies foresighted judgments on social phenomena and human behavior, he said.

According to him, "life is a general term for the behavior of organisms". And the life form is a typical example of behavior. He further believed that "behavior is based on scientific law". This statement may seem strange at first glance, but his explanations that "behavior gains science" and "consciousness gains science" make sense. In other words, I would like to say that the reason why human organisms live and act, whether consciously or unconsciously, is because they obtain science at the most fundamental point and are supported by science. So, foresighted ideas are not functional at all with respect to the concrete nature of behavior. Since human life is a life of behavior that uses mental processes as a means, it is important to weed out foresighted knowledge by scientific knowledge. He understood that social science and sociology are also academic consciousnesses that participate in the process.

Hasegawa has so far discussed behavior as individual behavior, but since human life is inevitably social life, he must continue to discuss the nature of collective behavior. Hasegawa thought that even when considering it, it is not separate from individual human behavior, but is typical of that behavior. And the condition that regulates the behavior is "not the internal impulse or environment of the isolated individual, but those of the collective state of the individual".

Finally, Hasegawa discussed how the collective nature of human behavior that emerges in this way leads to group formation. It is human actions that need to be coordinated. However, it should be noted that it is necessary to put the planning and design of cooperation on the mental condition of behavior and the mental communication of human beings. By this, the distant ones are connected by them. Hasegawa concludes as follows: "Thus, the collaboration spatially expanded expands horizontally and further vertically, and human beings are organically connected. The formation of a group of collective actions".

4   Tasks of Postwar Japanese Sociology

From that point, Japanese sociology did not develop much until after the war. In a situation where the Peace Preservation Law was enacted and the gathering of five or more people was prohibited even on university campuses, the development of sociology could not be expected. And even if the results were achieved, it would have been latent.

Postwar sociology is briefly mentioned in my other paper in this book, so I will not go into detail about it here. However, I must mention what happened to the purpose of Japanese sociology, which is the creation of a new civilization, and the evaluation of Japan's modernization after the Meiji Restoration, which is closely related to it.

The creation of Japanese civilization began with the introduction of cultural artifacts from Western Europe to enlighten society and individuals. At that time, in many cases, Western Europe was understood as a civilization and the East was semi-developed and undeveloped. However, the construction of that civilization was soon put into the framework of an imperial system, and education and even scholarship were given by the emperor. As a result, because of the concentration of power on the nation, the rise of nationalism and ethnocentrism, the emphasis on development by power, and the advancement of military personnel into the nation were accelerated, and further, the development by imperialism was carried out following the example of the West.

Of course, the modern social system was put in place following the West's example. Although there were various problems, on the surface it seemed that it had acquired a position comparable to those of the Western powers by around 1930. Attempts were also made to promote modernization with the ideals of the Orient. However, those attempts did not have much influence, and in the Showa era they were absorbed by Japanese romanticism and super-ultranationalism.

Naturally, the problem of modernization in Japan has been pointed out in various ways. Today, the criticisms of Soseki Natsume, John Dewey, Bertrand Russell, etc., are well known. However, it seems that the issues raised were not taken very seriously. Following Japan's defeat in World War II it was Yoshimi Takeuchi, a Chinese literary scholar, who presented the fundamental problems of Japan's modernization in a complete manner, relying on Dewy and Russell (Takeuchi 1981). He was in China before the war for the first time on a trip. He discovered that there were people like him living there. According to him, there was a situation in prewar Japan where even these situations were not visible, the result of Japanese education since the Meiji era. Proceeding from there, he discovered the problems of the modernization of Japan raised by Dewy and

Russell. Japanese modernization was not rooted in the Japanese people and Japanese society. So, even if it was superficially fulfilling, it did not have thick roots in Japanese and Japanese society (Takeuchi 1981). The Japanese people, society, and culture, and the modernization by Western civilization were not well articulated until the Meiji Restoration. Therefore, he proposed to clarify the problems of the modernization in Japan by comparing the three pillars of Japan, the East (at least China and India), and Europe and the United States. He called it "Asia as a method". Of course, this issue cannot be clarified by one person, so he called for the establishment of a sufficient scientific cooperation system.

The above-mentioned issues were raised after the war. It seems that they did not always bring about sufficient results. It was Kazuko Tsurumi, who was doing her research shortly after the war, who accepted and implemented this issue in sociology. Kazuko Tsurumi then introduced Kunio Yanagida and Kumagusu Minakata while studying sociology, and eventually arrived at the theory of endogenous development (Tsurumi 1970, 1988, 1996). Her sociology of history, which tackled the problem of China's modernization based on the inner tree, may be called the step of post-Western sociology probability in Japan. Although it was not located in the mainstream of postwar Japanese sociology, it is thought that the sociology led by Tsurumi had great significance for the future of Japanese sociology.

According to Yoshio Sugimoto, who is actively discussing cosmopolitanism in Europe and the United States today, the same debate as that of cosmopolitanism is being held in Japan under the name of symbiotic society (Sugimoto 2012). This debate, which is rooted in Japan's peace constitution, may have a character that can be called cosmopolitan society in Japan if we study it in detail. Similar attempts may be raised in various fields as cosmopolitan society.

In order for modernization to be rooted in Japanese society and Japanese people, the problem of social movement and the problem of power (Tsurumi 1996) must be solved and many Japanese people must acquire it. Therefore, Japan's post-Western society must be actively involved in the issues of power and social movements.

The subject of postwar Japanese sociology, in other words, is based on the peace constitution that declared the abandonment of war, that is, the values of peace, freedom, equality, human rights, etc., accepted by the national society. It was to contribute to the creation of a society with the power to compete with the nation, and to the creation of individuals who internalized their values. Immediately after the defeat, many Japanese acted by saying things and holding values that were 180 degrees different from those before the war. The values accepted by society must be established in the dimensions of individual, culture, and personality.

This issue is, of course, the relationship between prewar Japanese society, culture, and values, and the relationship between prewar Japanese sociology and postwar sociology. Furthermore, it included issues such as how to overcome the problems of modernization in Japan. However, the influence of Western sociology, especially from the United States, was extremely strong, and Japanese sociologists were inevitably focused on the arrangement of Western sociology, and it was personally done to tackle these issues. Overall, it was inadequate. Therefore, Western sociology and raising issues from the West cannot be of great significance. Raising issues from Western sociology or Western society, such as the importance of dematerialized value or the importance of greening, are already part of the new tradition of Japanese society and Japanese people. From around the turning point of the 20th to the 21st century, many Western issues were raised with the aim of this issue. One of them is raising the issue of provincializing Europe.

Charles Taylor, in his book *Imaginary* (2000), proposed modernity and multiple modernity's based on the following hypothesis.[4] We can shed some light on both the original and contemporary issues of modernity if we can come to a clearer definition of the self-understanding that has been constitutive of it. Western modernity on this view is inseparable from a certain kind of social imaginary and the difference among today's multiple modernity's (Taylor 2003: 1).

Social imaginary, Taylor means, is "… thinking of the way of people imagine their social existence, how they fit together with others, how things go on between them and their fellows, the expectations that are normally met, and the normative notion and images that underlie these expectations" (Taylor 2000: 23). In other words, social imaginary is a self-understanding about what kind of society is shared by ordinary people. And it also has various meanings. It often appears in images, stories, and legends. It is not a theory, but it has a close correlation with theory.

Extensive background understanding lies at the root of social imaginary and social self-understanding. This understanding of background includes the individual's micro selection, the collection of the selection, the perception of the ideal state of the individual's practice, recognition, and the like. And it has a close relationship with the moral order of the society, which is an extension

---

4 I used same sentences that showed my understanding of this book in another paper. See *The Changing Relationship between Society, Affect and Social Movement, Collections of Glocal Studies*. Tokyo: Seijo University (May 2022).

of that. Therefore, for self-understanding and background understanding, it is essential to have a very comprehensive understanding about, for example, what kind of relationships we have, where we have come from, where we are going, and how we have become related to other groups.

Taylor emphasizes components of modernity. In addition to social imaginary and moral order, the following ideas are included: autonomy of the individual, independence of the market economy, public sphere, public/private distinction, people, sovereignty, democracy, civil society (association), direct access society, agency and actors, narrative style (public opinion), secularity, and global acceptance of modernity. Here, he analyzes the development and change of the political society, closely related to the economic and social acts that have been driven by the idea.

Taylor's understanding of multiple modernity through the elucidation of the social imagination of many people makes European localization a reality. Taylor's attempts may be about multiple modernity inside Western modernity, but not about non-Western modern times. Therefore, the discussion of the provinces of Europe is greatly insufficient. However, when it comes to considering Japan's modernization, Taylor's attempts may have great significance. And it is thought that Taylor's method actually was of the best use in the studies of Japanese history, although it is uncertain whether it is factual. For instance, the research of the modernization of Japan by Yasumaru, people's history and popular morality study are very important and useful (Yasumaru 1974, 1996).

5 Conclusion

At the beginning of the 20th century, Kanzou Uchimura placed the spirit and morality of the typical Japanese in his book *Among the Representative Japanese* (Uchimura 2015). And if the spirit and morality of the typical Japanese are justifiably utilized and admonished, then the modernization of Japan is a family state in the process, and Adam Smith's economics, agriculture, the development of the earth's society, and education should have developed independently. The family nation was not achieved because the Japanese spirit and morality had been replaced by them in the West, and it became only an ideology of the Tenno system.

Now I will conclude that the most important task of postwar Japanese sociology has been to analyze and show the Japanese modernization, which is different from Western modernization and one of multiple modernity. Important post-Western sociology will emerge through tackling this task.

References

Fukuzawa, Yukichi. 1875. *An Outline of a Theory of Civilization* [bun-mei ron no gairyaku]. Tokyo: Ogasawara-Bunko.

Hasegawa, Nyozekan. 1928. *The Essence of Society*. In *The Encyclopedia of Grand Thoughts* [daishisou ensaikuropejia]. Tokyo: Shunjyuu-Sha.

Kaneko, Isamu, ed. 2003. *Recovering Takada Yasuma* [takada yasuma recobari]. Kyoto: Mineruva-Shobo.

Kawai, Takao. 1998. *A Short History of Modern Japanese Sociology* [kindai nihon shakai-gaku shouden]. Tokyo: Keisou-Shobo.

Kawai, Takao. 2003. *Development of Modern Japanese Sociology* [kindai nihon shakai-gaku no tenkai]. Tokyo: Kouseisha Kouseikaku.

Koseki, Sampei. 1979. *Human Studies on Adult Entertainment* [fuuzoku no ningen-gaku]. Kyoto: Sekai-Shisosha.

Maruyama, Masao, and Kato Shuuichi. 1998. *Translation and the Modern Period of Japan* [hon'yaku to nihon no kindai]. Tokyo: Iwanami-Shoten.

Naka, Hisao. 1998. *Sociology of Yoneda Shotaro* [Yoneda Shotaro no shakaigaku]. Inaho Shobo. Tokyo: Seiunsha Publishing Co.

Naka, Hisao. 2002. *Yoneda Shotaro: Pioneer of A New Integral Sociology* [Yoneda Shotaro: shin sougou shakaigaku no senkyu-sha]. Tokyo: Toushindou.

Ogasawara, Makoto. 2003. *Introduction to the History of Sociology* [shakaigaku shi heno izanai]. Kyoto: Sekai-Shisousha.

Sugimoto, Yoshio. 2012. "Japan cosmopolitanism". *Routledge Handbook of Cosmopolitanism Studies*, edited by Gerand Delanty. London: Routledge.

Takada, Yasuma. 1919. *Fundamental Principles of Sociology* [shakaigaku genri]. Tokyo: Iwanami-Shoten.

Takada, Yasuma. 1922. *Society and the State* [shakai to kokka]. Tokyo: Iwanami-Shoten.

Takada, Yasuma. 1926. *Study of Social Relations* (shakai kankei no ken'yuu). Tokyo: Iwanami-Shoten.

Takebe, Tongo. 1904–1918. *Futsu-Shakaigaku* (General Sociology, volumes 1–4). Tokyo: Kinkoudou-Shoten.

Takebe, Tongo. 1908. *Principles of Sociology* [shakaigaku kouryou]. Tokyo: Kinkoudou-Shoten.

Takeuchi, Yoshimi. 1981. *Asia as a Method*. Volumes 1–5 [houhou to shiteno ajia zen 5 kan]. Tokyo: Chikuma-Shobo.

Taylor, Charles. 2003. *Modern Social Imaginaries*. Chapel Hill: Duke University Press.

Tsurumi, Kazuko. 1970. *Social Change and Individual: Japan Before and After Defeat in World War II*. Princeton, NJ: Princeton University Press.

Tsurumi, Kazuko. 1988. *Tsurumi Kazuko Mandara IV Tsurumi Kazuko Mandala Volume Earth Yanagita Kunio Ron* [Tsurumi Kazuko Mandara Volume Earth Yanagita Kunio]. Tokyo: Fujiwara-Shoten.

Tsurumi, Kazuko. 1996. *Naihatsuteki Hatten-ron no Tenkai* [A Theory of Endogenous Development as It Evolves]. Tokyo: Chikuma-Shobo.

Uchimura, Kanzou. 1908–2015. *Representative Men of Japan*. Tokyo: IBC Publishing Inc.

Yanabu, Akira. 1982. *On the Establishment of Language Translation* [hon'yakugo seiritu jijyou]. Tokyo: Iwanami-Shoten.

Yasumaru, Yoshio. 1974. *Japanese Modernization and Popular Thought*. Tokyo: Aoki-Shoten.

Yasumaru, Yoshio. 1996. *History of Thought as a Method*. Tokyo: Hasekura-Shobou.

SECTION 2

*Non-hegemonic Traditions and Pluralism
in Asian Social Sciences*

∵

CHAPTER 6

Chinese Sociology: Traditions and Dialogues – Localized Knowledge Production as Post-Western Sociology

Li Youmei

1   **Introduction**

Recently, the discussion of the knowledge or discourse systems of Chinese sociology and the development of "post-Western sociology" has been significantly pronounced in Chinese sociological academia, which is closely related to a country's status in the world system and the development of its own academia. In the "core-periphery" structure of world academia, Western sociology has always occupied the dominant and central position, and its intrusion into the academic periphery increasingly makes that the scholarship on the periphery agrees with the central position of Western sociology, and thus eliminates the authenticity of research on local cultures on the periphery (Gerholm and Hannerz 1982).

During the 1930s and 1940s, when China was exploring the state-building of a modern democratic country and the reconstruction of rural society, sociology was not only involved in specific social movements, but also became an important site for the production of sociological knowledge. After it was tested by China's social practices, it reshaped China's society and social knowledge. Although Chinese sociology has been guided and influenced by Western sociology, it has always stuck to its own authenticity. At the very beginning of the introduction of sociology into China, Yan Fu (严复) tried to interpret sociology on the basis of Confucian philosophy ("studying the nature of phenomenon" and "studying for practical use") in his translation works. The sociological approach with Chinese characteristics gradually emerged thanks to the efforts of several generations of Chinese sociologists. However, Western sociology seems to have ignored these academic efforts and contributions.

The advocacy of the concept of "post-Western sociology" and building the knowledge system of Chinese sociology are actually Chinese academia's desire to transform the global academia, which has been dominated by Western sociology into one characterized by reciprocity. Moreover, this will help Chinese sociology to base its knowledge production on communication and dialogues among different academic subjects. This can be understood as a wave of self-consciousness and enlightenment on the part of Chinese academia, as well as a response to Western sociology; this response is built on the profound tradition of conducting indigenous research.

This article focuses on the study of authentic issues of Chinese society, especially featuring the academic legacy of Fei Xiaotong (also known as Fei Hsiao-tung). The traditions developed by scholars like Fei Xiaotong cannot be neglected when Chinese sociologists conduct conversations with contemporary Western sociology and provide more effective interpretations of Chinese society.

2 Producing New Knowledge beyond the "Civilization/Savagery" Distinction in Anthropology

Social science is typically surrounded by two contradictory expressions. The first approach understands social sciences as sciences pursuing truth and universal knowledge; the second approach understands social sciences from the perspective of liberation and regards them as social activities dedicated to liberation (Seidman 2013). The former is a scientific version, and the latter is a moral one. In the last two centuries, anthropology and sociology have tended to believe that "knowledge can make a difference in our lives" (Seidman 2013: ix), but the idea that legitimate thoughts are only the ones proven to be scientific has pressured Western sociology to increasingly isolate itself from public life; under the prominence of scientific approaches in sociology, textual analysis has replaced social analysis, and the eagerness for comprehensive theories has taken precedence over social criticism (Seidman 2013). This has become a feature of Western sociology. When Western sociology increasingly deviated from social life, an alternative approach of producing sociological knowledge (temporarily called post-Western Sociology) *has* existed, although it has always been ignored.

Fei Xiaotong's sociological work *Peasant Life in China: A Field Study of Country* adopted the moral perspective. In the preface, Fei's PhD supervisor, Bronisław Malinowski, said: "I venture to foretell that *Peasant Life in China* by Dr. Hsiao-tung Fei will be counted as a landmark in the development of anthropological field-work and theory" (Malinowski [1939] 2010: ii). The "landmark" significance of the book for the development of world anthropology is its critical step towards the transcendence of the civil-savage distinction and the fulfillment of Malinowski's wish for "the anthropology of the future" (Malinowski [1939] 2010: vi). In Malinowski's opinion, *Peasant Life in China* freed anthropology from the cage where it was confined to research on "savages" and ushered it into a new and broad space called the "civilized world" (Fei 1996).

Malinowski became conscious of the gap between modern civilization and aboriginal culture when studying the relationship of different ethnic groups in Africa. For this reason, he tried to explore a path and "build a staircase" for the transition from research on "savagery" to the "civilized". *Peasant Life in China* perfectly suited his purpose and negated the previous anthropological approach's focus on the "other". Then, Malinowski realized that anthropology might have a real opportunity to open up a brand-new area, which also implied that the issue of the "other" he discussed might trigger "a methodological revolution". Therefore, he recognized *Peasant Life in China* as follows: "China is the greatest nation in the world ... It contains the observation carried on by a citizen upon his own people. It is the result of work done by a native among natives ... It is an anthropology of one's own people" (Malinowski [1939] 2010: ii).

However, the attitude of the "anthropology of one's own people" was not recognized or accepted by the Western sociology and anthropology of the time. Those scholars found it hard to empathize with Fei Xiaotong in terms of feelings or responsibility, and they believed more in their commitment to scientific truth. Malinowski's moral version did not catch their attention, nor was his proposition "instilled into some of his students" (Fei 1996: 7).

When affirming the "anthropology of one's own people", Malinowski resonated with Fei Xiaotong's *Peasant Life in China* probably because it reminded him of Poland, a country with a long history of civilization and countless hardships. According to Chun Kyung-soo, a scholar from South Korea, "Mr. Fei combined the love and hatred he felt in his fieldwork and wrote *Peasant Life in China*" (Chun 2013: 54). As "a young Chinese patriot", Fei Xiaotong cared unceasingly about "the dilemma of his great Mother-country" (Malinowski [1939] 2010: ii). It was his devotion that made Malinowski recognize what the focus of his research should be, which was "answering how China adapts to the new situation" (Fei 1996: 17). This also shows Malinowski's praise for the patriotic concern and responsibility of Fei Xiaotong's academic works.

Luckier than Malinowski, Fei Xiaotong could closely connect his lifetime academic pursuit with the fate of his nation. Early in 1933, Fei Xiaotong began to seek a remedy for China's economy in decline under the influence of Western industry. He believed that any scholar had his/her motherland, and "if the researcher's country should perish, he/she would suffer from the pains like any other citizen". Therefore, the correct way of saving his nation was to "reconstruct China by understanding the country first". His passionate working style was also encouraged by Pike, who once said: "China's future will take her shape in dreams, practical achievements and in the custom gradually formed among the youths" (Fei 1999b: 103, 366, 124).

After learning about the functionalist school, Fei Xiaotong and others found that, compared with evolutionism and diffusionism, the functionalist school was more scientific and more applicable to the practical demands of Chinese society. Back then, Fei Xiaotong and other scholars had the same confusion Malinowski did, i.e., could ethnography only be applied to studies on simple "savage" communities rather than "our own local 'civilized' communities"? Although they admitted "it is difficult to study the culture where they grow up with an objective attitude", "being difficult" did not mean "being impossible". Guided by the idea of "breaking the stereotypes", Fei Xiaotong visited the village Kaihienkung. This was conducted after his study in Dayaoshan in Guangxi Province, where he adopted the "othering" approach. He hoped to "study a rural place in his own country with the approach used in studying the Hualan Yao ethnic group", so as to "prove our approach can be used to study communities of different natures" (Fei 1999b: 370).

To conclude, it was the methodological thought and exploration combining academic research and social concerns that made Fei Xiaotong "unintentionally" participate in the knowledge production of world social sciences. Although he did not devote academic efforts to pure academic theories, when reflecting on the Chinese nation in peril from a patriotic and responsible perspective, Fei Xiaotong tried to combine the Savage Studies characterized by "othering" with the sociological approach focusing on industrial civilization. In this process, Fei Xiaotong "unintentionally" generated the methodologies that integrate anthropology and sociology.

3   Understanding "Rural China" from the Subject's Point of View Instead of the "Other's"

As mentioned above, in pursuit of scientific legitimacy, Western sociologists were no longer engaged in enlightening the public as educators and advocates. They no longer focused on current social or political issues but were obsessed with meta-theories or philosophical issues. They justified their arguments to form a universal social knowledge and proposed a series of effective standards. Further, these practices have developed orthodox and dominant sociological discourses to guide and dominate sociology. When this orientation was introduced to Chinese academia, it gave rise to the "question-based"[1] approach.

---

1   Here, this term refers to a positivist approach.

Fei Xiaotong did not agree with this, especially the tendency to apply foreign theories to explain Chinese society. He said,

> Due to the import of foreign books and writings, the contemporary Chinese social scientists rely on the knowledge foreign scholars gained in their own countries to speculate what is going on in China. Actually, they assume that cultures follow the same principles everywhere, but these principles per se need to be proven by facts. Moreover, these principles remove the necessity of detailed studies at all.
> FEI 1999a: 405

Therefore, Fei Xiaotong said that he "dare not easily accept the conclusions not drawn from local societies" (Fei 1999b: 405). As for the facts of traditional "rural China", we must first take a detailed look at the nature of the local society and culture. This implied that Fei Xiaotong chose the approach underlining the "practice of peasants as subjects" rather than the "imagination of intellectuals" when studying the modernization of Chinese peasants.

During the first half of the 20th century, the people in rural China were in a situation where "they cannot represent themselves; they must be represented" (Said [1978] 1999: 28). Back then, the Chinese intellectuals mostly viewed the rural people as those who had neither the ability nor the intelligence to express themselves. By this logic, the society needed intellectuals to "stand up" and use more "advanced" thoughts and theories to enlighten and guide the rural people and awaken their consciousness. On the other hand, they spoke loudly as the spokespersons for the proletariat from a people-oriented perspective. In the process, the people who were the subjects of society had always been expressed as "other", and thus they never came on stage.

Fei Xiaotong did not consider himself as a spokesperson for the general public, but he emphasized "going to real places" to explore and discover people's real needs. In his fieldwork in Kaihienkung village during the 1930s, he learned that the real problem of rural China was "starvation" (Fei 1999a: 199). He found that China's economy was not purely based on agriculture traditionally but was "an economy mixed with agricultural production and handicraft industries". Developed handicraft industry had been part of the rural society and economy in China, and it was "a self-sufficient unit in the rural areas characterized by a self-supporting economy". Thanks to traditional handicrafts, peasants had some "spare money" to pay taxes and support sporadic consumption. When the rural industry was destroyed by foreign industries, the balance of the original economic system in rural China was thoroughly broken, and thus the biggest crisis for the peasants was starvation.

In the face of the issue of "starvation", those peasants whom the intellectuals considered as the ones having no stance or being incapable of speaking, showed their subjectivity and made their own choices. They made efforts to restore the unbalanced economic system and to transform the traditional handicraft industry into a modern one. Thanks to technical guidance from intellectuals like Fei Dasheng and the local elites' vigorous advocacy, the peasants became active in joining cooperatives. Under the joint efforts of different parties, the peasants saw hope in constructing the modern industry in rural areas. The transformation of rural industry was also a process of restructuring the unbalanced socioeconomic system.

Rather than generating a set of enlightening knowledge and convincing people by these knowledge, Fei Xiaotong focused on the choices that the peasants made in their actions. Gradually, he immersed himself in the peasants' actions through his academic practices (Fei 1962) and spoke for the public from the peasants' perspective. Epistemologically and methodologically, constructing social sciences theories requires the appropriate knowledge production. It requires knowledge producers to exercise judgment and make choices according to their own culture, to abandon outdated knowledge rules, to learn from others, and further, to produce new knowledge to fill the needs of particular realities. The reason why Fei Xiaotong's thoughts still inspire us today lies in the epistemology and methodology to which he adhered, which was "seeking knowledge from the truth". It requires researchers to develop an understanding of reality and examine their understanding through the real "practices".

Obviously, Fei Xiaotong's approach to knowledge production on "rural China" was rooted in his sufficient fieldwork. Fei Xiaotong's approach has its pronounced feature, viewing the peasants as subjects rather than "others", and further, summarizing their survival wisdom and generating understanding and knowledge about life in Chinese rural societies.

4 Localized Knowledge Is Not Confined to Local Areas

We can learn from Fei's monograph *From the Soil: The Foundations of Chinese Society* that localized knowledge production is neither merely about nor confined to local areas. Fei Xiaotong argues that this book does not provide "the detailed description of a specific society, but some concepts developed from a specific society" (Fei [1947] 1998: 4). These concepts show how the rural Chinese society is working, like "*chaxugeju* (differential mode of association)", "an inactive government", "rule by elders", "social circle", and "rule of ritual". Developing and applying these concepts are also kinds of dialogues with

Western experiences and theories. Further, this is a knowledge production process that integrates the moral and scientific perspective.

"Our pattern is not like distinct bundles of straws. Rather, it is like the circles that appear on the surface of a lake when a rock is thrown into it. Everyone stands at the center of the circles produced by his or her own social influence" (Fei [1947] 1992: 62–63). This is Fei Xiaotong's short description of *chaxugeju* (differential mode of association). It is not a structured definition in strict accordance with academic codes, but a metaphorical description. Fei's introduction of the "rule of ritual" is inspired by the concept of the "rule of law", just like Ferdinand Tönnies' "community" (Gemeinschaft) vs. "society" (Gesellschaft) and Émile Durkheim's "mechanical solidarity" vs. "organic solidarity". Similarly, his concept of *chaxugeju* (differential mode of association) was inspired by *tuantigeju* (organizational mode of association) in Western sociology.

Basically, *chaxugeju* (differential mode of association) refers to the differential mode of interaction among social members based on their differential relationship. With each individual as the center, everyone has a social network that ranges from close to distant relationships. This "concentric circle" mode is not specific to Chinese culture, but a universal type of social networking across the world, one which can be found in almost every culture. Following the Western sociological approach of reasoning to construct unified sociological knowledge, we can surely equate the "differential mode of association" with the "concentric circle" social networking model to highlight its commonality and universality.

However, Fei Xiaotong's comparative study is different from that of Western sociology. According to Stephan Feuchtwang, the comparison conducted by Western sociologists is mostly the comparison "of their own society with the non-Western societies that they have studied" (Feuchtwang 2015: 129); they intend to understand themselves, and further to seek for the general laws of societies through comparison and contrast. Unlike Western sociology, Fei Xiaotong's approach did not emphasize general or universal laws but the consciousness and reflection on the "*si* (私)"[2] nature of Chinese society (developed by the village construction school).

In comparison, Fei Xiaotong found that the difference between Eastern and Western society did not lie in the *tuantigeju* (organizational mode of association) in the West and the *chaxugeju* (differential mode of association) in China, but the difference of "communities" in terms of social structure. *Chaxugeju* actually highlights the dominance of the organizations based on

---

2   This term is translated as "selfishness" by Gary Hamilton and Wang Zheng, and translated as "social egoism" by Stephan Feuchtwang.

the differential orders in Chinese society. In the circles of relationship that spread from the self, "human relations" (*lun*) is the most important principle in Chinese society and culture, which can be understood as differential mode per se (Fei [1947] 1998, [1947] 1992). The *Jiazu* ("small lineage") built on "human relations" is this kind of social organization spreading from the self; it "can condense a kinship network which was originally loose, subordinated to a certain individual's social goals and only coordinated by a certain individual, into a social organization with certain social functions and goals" (Zhang 2010: 12). "Extending ego to family", "extending family to the country", and "extending the country to world" possess the same logic found in constructing "social circles". The "social circle" combines "consensus" and "constraints", making the formation of orders in rural Chinese society both "spontaneous" and "coercive", and thus creates the social norms of rural communities (Zhang 2010). In fact, this direction also reflects the way Chinese cultural tradition views the society, which is not a disciplined perspective and not a view of sociological theories, but a perspective of social life (or human life) in the broad sense (Xiong 2012: 15).

Due to its dominant role in anthropological and sociological discourses, Western academia could accept neither Malinowski's prediction of "methodological revolution" nor his moral perspective, and further failed to understand the theoretical and methodological contribution of scholars like Fei Xiaotong. According to Stephan Feuchtwang, when Western scholars read works by scholars like Fei Xiaotong, they just "read them for the information they provided about Chinese culture and society". Fei's and other scholars' works are just seen as the providers of "Chinese ideas about how to conduct themselves and about the world from their point of view". In other words, Western scholars do not "read them as the products of a Chinese social science, by fellow theorists" (Feuchtwang 2015: 130).

Usually, Western sociology interprets "society" as "a large group or a group of groups" (Feuchtwang 2015: 132). The noun phrase "the social" derived from the adjective "social", is understood as general social relations and various affiliated obligations (Feuchtwang 2015). In contrast, as an "outsider" to Western sociology, Fei Xiaotong explains "the social" in a completely different way. The concept of *chaxugeju* (called "social egoism" by Stephan Feuchtwang) that he proposed went beyond the connotation of "the social" agreed upon by Western sociologists; as a circle of "social relatedness" that extends from every person, it is not confined to (permanent) lineage (Feuchtwang 2015: 132). Furthermore, it is efficient, flexible, and expandable depending on functions and purposes (Feuchtwang 2015).

Fei Xiaotong's comparative research focuses on exploring the origins of social organization that uniquely features the Chinese society, i.e., "*si* (私)" as mentioned above. He did not emphasize the knowledge interest of having theoretical dialogues with Western sociology, examining, correcting, or refuting Western sociological theories through the analysis of non-Western social experience. Instead, he was more concerned with national "liberation" when China faced a national crisis. He viewed Western society as a reference point from which to study his own country and culture, and through the comparison between Eastern and Western societies, to reflect on the cultural inadequacy of the Chinese society impacted by Western civilization. It is "a contrast between ideologies and discourses prevailing in agrarian China and until now, and in the nineteenth-century West until now" (Feuchtwang 2015: 142). Further, it shows the theoretical consciousness beyond the academic binary opposition of the West and the non-West.

5   Knowledge Production as Post-Western Sociology Requires a Cosmopolitan Vision

Over the past four decades, Chinese sociology has leveled criticism at and reflection on the shortcomings of the Western sociological paradigm and tried to rid itself of Western sociology's control in both theoretical systems and research topics. However, Chinese sociologists have unconsciously fallen into the trap of abstract concepts and theories, trying very hard to modify Western sociological theories through unique Chinese experiences, or even have become obsessive about meta-theoretical or philosophical analysis. However, this has made Chinese sociology further entangled in the theoretical and discursive system of Western sociology and has severely limited the vision and imagination of Chinese academia.

In his books like *From the Soil: The Foundations of Chinese Society*, Fei Xiaotong has blazed a trail beyond the binary opposition of the West and the non-West. This approach shows that localization is not a simple emphasis on the "particularity" or "locality" of Chinese sociology, as a response to or refutation of the universality of Western sociology. The knowledge interest of localized sociology is seeking the integration between localization and internationalization, particularity, and universality, and between scientific and moral vision. "Localization may not only create a sociological tradition different from that of the West but may also inspire western sociology and make a distinguished contribution to international sociology" (Xu 2012: 427). In recent years, the concept of "Post-Western sociology" has basically centered on how to change the situation of an international sociological community dominated by Western sociology in terms of discourses and theories, and moreover, how to build a sociological knowledge system breaking the binary opposition of the West and non-West.

In fact, "Chinese sociological knowledge system" and "post-Western sociology" are two complementary concepts. As early as sociology was introduced into China by the end of the 19th century, Chinese intellectuals were making efforts to find a practicable way of "liberation" for China. For this purpose, in his translation Yan Fu connected sociology with the Chinese traditional Confucian philosophy ("studying the nature of phenomenon" and "studying for practical use") in the context of modern China. With the advocacy of the "Sinicization of sociology" by Wu Wenzao, Fei Xiaotong, and others, academic traditions and theoretical knowledge with Chinese characteristics have gradually taken shape after their exploration by generations of Chinese sociologists. It was developed to get rid of Western assumptions and to establish a specific academic paradigm. Fei Xiaotong's works emphasized the understanding of autonomy and further established the specific cognitive framework of Chinese sociology. But regretfully, his academic contribution has not been recognized by Western academia and was even gradually forgotten in the disruption that happened during the development of Chinese sociology. Nevertheless, the academic tradition and theoretical knowledge of Chinese sociology, represented by *Peasant Life in China* and *From the Soil: The Foundations of Chinese Society*, can be seen as the representation of post-Western sociology.

Based on Fei Xiaotong's knowledge production, this article concludes that "post-Western sociology" will show several transitionial trends of sociology:

First, it will change the stubbornness of Western sociology's academic orientation and make science and morality the sociological orientations again. Post-Western sociology emphasizes hermeneutics (or constructivism) that is in opposition to objectivism and will broaden its space to bring subjects back to the stage of sociology. Located in the core of knowledge production, Western sociology has been oriented by objectivism and has excessively emphasized the scientificity of academic analysis. In contrast, post-Western sociology is more based on hermeneutics and emphasized the moral version more in its analysis. In Fei Xiaotong's era, the peasants felt the uneasiness triggered by uncertainties or crises in life. They made active choices and engaged themselves in modern rural industry. This might be a moral economy caused by resistance (Roulleau-Berger 2008), which resonated with Fei Xiaotong, who had moral passion and inspired the moral version in his academic works (Roulleau-Berger 2017). However, in the Western sociology dominated by scientific paradigm, Fei Xiaotong's research could only be at the fringe of knowledge production.

Second, it will change the globalized hierarchy in science, which is caused by the scientific paradigm built on Western academic hegemony. Post-Western sociology aims to establish epistemic equivalence of the connected and separated boundaries of knowledge to resist epistemic injustice in any form (Bhargava 2013). It tries to eliminate the boundary of core/periphery in knowledge production, and it aims to promote the emergence of polycentric academia. The "post"-Western sociology is not simply based on or derived from Western sociology. It is a redefined sociology based on diverse theories, shared methods, certain histories, local politics and local knowledge tradition, and the conversations between Western and non-Western sociology after systematically rethinking and reproducing their local knowledge. It requires the construction of reciprocity where Western and non-Western sociology can learn from each other, inspire each other, and benefit each other in terms of theories, concepts, logic, and forms of reasoning.

Third, it will change the tradition of "truth claims" in Western sociology, increase the pertinence of reflection, and promote academic and theoretical consciousness. On the one hand, Western sociology needs to reflect on its disciplinary paths and traditions, including its singular scientific vision and the scientific norms built by academic hegemony. On the other hand, non-Western sociology needs to strengthen reflection on its previous reflection. Non-Western sociologists have been mainly emphasizing exploiting "local experiences" to resist "Western experiences", which has made non-Western sociology the opposition to Western sociology. Yet, in the future they should spare efforts to develop their own original concepts, theories, and methods to deconstruct the universality of Western sociology. In fact, if sociology as a discipline was developed merely to respond to Western sociology, it would ignore the fact that sociology can provide responses to real social life and solutions to social problems in local contexts. It would also lose its role as a force of social liberation.

The knowledge production of post-Western sociology requires a world or cosmopolitan vision. Cosmopolitanism calls for a reflection on one's own cultural traditions, which implies a shift in cultural identity. Cosmopolitanism is different from other approaches due to its open attitudes towards its own culture and the cultures of others (Han 2017). Post-Western sociology requires such a cosmopolitan vision as well.

With an open attitude, Fei Xiaotong's sociology does not confine his studies to the pure academic dialogues with Western sociology but focuses on real social issues. All the concepts and methods he developed were rooted in practical social needs. Fei's approach of region-based analysis on the three villages in Yunnan Province (seen in *Earthbound China: A Study of Rural Economy in Yunnan*) has not only produced multi-situated knowledge about rural Chinese societies, but also has attempted to correct or balance the mistake of de-contextualization in Western sociology through spatial contextuality (Liu 2017). His approach can be understood as the embryonic form of multi-sited ethnography. The diverse academic products of non-Western empirical studies generated from this approach fully demonstrate how cosmopolitan sociological knowledge production could be.

Likewise, proceeding from his care for the "practices of below" (Deboulet 2017) in rural society instead of responding to Western sociology, Fei Xiaotong questioned the approach used to study the "other", and further developed the approach of "internalization of the other" (Beck and Grand 2010: 419). Then, the "other" was no longer external but part of a researcher's mind. The "methodological revolution" ignored by Western sociology, expands the cosmopolitan vision which is needed by the knowledge production of post-Western sociology.

Regardless of whether the concept of "post-Western sociology" is ultimately established, the emergence and development of this concept per se remind us that it is time to reflect on and transcend the weaknesses and defects of Western sociology. By reviewing *Peasant Life in China* and *From the Soil: The Foundations of Chinese Society*, we find Fei Xiatong's approach to knowledge production is totally different from that of Western sociology. In his practices of knowledge production, he followed the principle of "knowledge from reality" and "aspiration to enrich people", learned from the practices in China, and applied the knowledge back to China's practice. He respected and affirmed the wisdom and choices of ordinary people and viewed people's "liberation" as the criterion with which to judge the effectiveness of his theories and methods. He practiced this principle throughout his academic career, and even in his later years he still traveled around to repeatedly examine the "reality" he aimed to know from the actual situation. By revisiting Fei Xiaotong's works, we once again realize that Chinese sociology has not carried out a systematic reflection on and summarization of localized knowledge production. Therefore, the knowledge reconstruction of Chinese sociology still has a long way to go.

References

Beck, U., and E. Grande. 2010. "Varieties of Second Modernity: The Cosmopolitan Turn in Social and Political Theory and Research". *The British Journal of Sociology* 61 (3): 409–443.

Bhargava, R. 2013. "Pour en finir avec l'injustice épistémique du colonialisme". *Socio* 2: 47–77.

Chun, K.-S. 2013. "On FEI Xiao-tong's Anthropological Research Methods: A Detailed Interpretation of Peasant Life in China—A Field Study of Country Life in the Yangtze Valley". *Journal of Guangxi University for Nationalities (Philosophy and Social Science Edition)* 35 (4): 52–58.

Deboulet, A. 2017. "比较视野下国际都市中的都市公民权" [A Comparative Study of Urban Citizenship in Global Cities]. In 社会学知识的建构:后西方社会学的探索 [The Fabric of Sociological Knowledge: The Exploration of Post-Western Sociology], edited by L. Xie and L. Roulleau-Berger, 443–461. Beijing: Peking University Press.

Fei, X. 1962. "留英记" [My Experience of Studying in the UK]. 文史资料 [Wenshi Ziliao]: 31. Beijing: Wenshi Ziliao Press.

Fei, X. (1947) 1992. *From the Soil: The Foundations of Chinese Society*. Berkeley: University of California Press.

Fei, X. 1996. "重读《江村经济・序言》" [A Review of Malinowski's Preface for *Peasant Life in China*]. *Journal of Peking University (Philosophy and Social Sciences)* (4): 4–18 + 126.

Fei, X. (1947) 1998. 乡土中国 [From the Soil: The Foundations of Chinese Society]. Beijing: Peking University Press.

Fei, X. 1999a. 费孝通文集（第二卷）[Collected Works of Fei Xiaotong, Vol. 2]. Beijing: Qunyan Press.

Fei, X. 1999b. 费孝通文集（第一卷）[Collected Works of Fei Xiaotong, Vol. 1]. Beijing: Qunyan Press.

Feuchtwang, S. 2015. "Social Egoism and Individualism: Surprises and Questions for a Western Anthropologist of China—Reading Professor Fei Xiaotong's Contrast between China and the West". *Journal of China in Comparative Perspective* 1 (1): 128–145.

Gerholm, T., and U. Hannerz. 1982. "Introduction: The Shaping of National Anthropologies". *Ethnos* 47 (1.2): 5–35.

Han, S.-J. 2017. "话语社会学的世界性意涵: 福柯与哈贝马斯在东亚" [Cosmopolitan Implication of Sociology of Discourse: Foucault and Habermas]. In 社会学知识的建构:后西方社会学的探索 [The Fabric of Sociological Knowledge: The Exploration of Post-Western Sociology], edited by L. Xie and L. Roulleau-Berger, 476–490. Beijing: Peking University Press.

Liu, N. 2017. "重返空间社会学: 继承费孝通先生的学术遗产" [Returning to Sociology of Space: Fei Xiaotong's Academic Heritage]. In 社会学知识的建构: 后西方社会学的探索 [The Fabric of Sociological Knowledge: The Exploration of Post-Western Sociology], edited by L. Xie and L. Roulleau-Berger, 383–400. Beijing: Peking University Press.

Malinowski, B. (1939) 2010. Preface. In X. Fei, *Peasant Life in China: A Field Study of Country Life in the Yangtze Valley*. Beijing: Foreign Language Teaching And Research Press.

Roulleau-Berger, L. 2008. "Individuation 'située' et 'globalisée': Grammaires de la reconnaissance et du mépris en Europe de l'Ouest et en Chine continentale". In *La reconnaissance á l'é preuve: Explorations socio-anthropologiques*, edited by J.-P. Payet and A. Battegay. Lille: Septentrion.

Roulleau-Berger, L. 2017. Introduction 2. In 社会学知识的建构: 后西方社会学的探索 [The Fabric of Sociological Knowledge: The Exploration of Post-Western Sociology], edited by L. Xie and L. Roulleau-Berger, 34–58. Beijing: Peking University Press.

Said, E. (1978) 1999. 东方学 [Orientalism]. Beijing: SDX Joint Publishing Company.

Seidman, S. 2013. *Contested Knowledge: Social Theory Today*. Chichester: Wiley-Blackwell.

Xiong, C. 2012. "见证中国社会学重建三十年—苏国勋先生访谈录" [Thirty Years of Rebuilding Sociology in China: A Conversation with Su Guoxun]. In 社会理论:现代性与本土化—苏国勋教授七十华诞暨叶启政教授荣休论文集 [Social Theories: Modernities and Localization], edited by X. Ying and M. Li. Beijing: SDX Joint Publishing Company.

Xu, B. 2012. "心的概念与文化自觉的社会学—从苏、叶两位老师的近期观点谈起" [The Concept of Heart and the Sociology of Cultural Self-consciousness—Discussions Derived from Prof. Su and Prof. Ye's Recent Opinions]. In 社会理论:现代性与本土化—苏国勋教授七十华诞暨叶启政教授荣休论文集 [Social Theories: Modernities and Localization], edited by X. Ying and M. Li. Beijing: SDX Joint Publishing Company.

Zhang, J. 2010. "Charisma, Publicity, and China Society: Rethinking of 'Chaxu Geju'". *Chinese Journal of Sociology* 30 (5): 1–24.

CHAPTER 7

Development of Sociological Thought in the Early Modern Period of Japan

Yama Yoshiyuki

1   Introduction

Starting in the Meiji period (1868–1912), Japan was introduced to many studies from modern Western Europe. In other words, this was the process of translating Western academic languages into Japanese literary languages. This translation was meant to reuse existing Chinese characters with meanings similar to Western academic languages, or to create new Chinese characters. Japan was rapidly introduced to modern Western science during the Meiji period because it already had academic languages comparable to modern Western science; thus, the translation proceeded smoothly. This means that academic ways of thinking comparable to modern Western science were already being developed in the early modern period of Japan (1603–1868).

At that time, modern Japanese society faced sociology as modern science for the first time. Sociology was translated into the Chinese characters "社会学" (Syakaigaku) and introduced to Japan. In the beginning, the Chinese characters "世態学" (Setaigaku) were also used, but the term eventually became accepted as "社会学". However, sociological thought existed in the early modern Japan as well, and although there was no term for sociology, views comparable to those found in sociology in modern Western Europe were developing in Japan during the early modern period.

The situation in East Asia changed significantly following the transition of the Chinese dynasty from Han Chinese to Manchu, which was known as the Ming–Qing transition period (明清交替). The status of the Chinese empire changed, and in the neighboring country of Korea, the Joseon Dynasty implemented "Sojunghwaism" (小中華主義), a movement which situated the country as an orthodox successor to Chinese civilization. Similarly, during the 18th century in Japan, a kind of historical science called "Kogaku" (古学) emerged, with new methods and problem consciousness among Confucianism. The "Kogigaku" (古義学) of Ito Jinsai (伊藤仁斎; 1627–1705) was the first current formed, and then the "Kobunjigaku" (古文辞学) of Ogyu Sorai (荻生徂徠; 1666–1728) appeared in the form of fierce opposition to Jinsai. Ito

Jinsai and Ogyu Sorai developed their thoughts to respond to the "problem of social order" in the early modern period. The Confucian concept of "Michi" (道) is reconstructed by them to recognize and express "social order". The new Confucianism, called "Kogaku" (古学), appeared as a form of criticism to the interpretations of Neo-Confucianism and attempted a direct philological and linguistic approach to Chinese classics. Among them, an original Japanese study of Nativism (Kokugaku, 国学), a philological and linguistic approach to Japanese classics, emerged. In other words, Kogaku and Japanese Nativism were born in the period of post–Neo-Confucianism (Yama 2019).

In the 20th century, Masao Maruyama (1914–1996), a leading political scientist in Japan, recognized the beginning of modern thinking as a process of development from Kogaku to Nativism (Maruyama 1952), and ever since, both Kogaku and Nativism have become the most significant subjects of study in the history of Japanese thought. In particular, Maruyama recognized the political thinking of Ogyu Sorai as being comparable to that of modern Western Europe, and likewise, this paper intends to argue that a type of sociological thinking is recognizable in Kogaku. In the present study, we introduce the development of sociological thought in the early modern period of Japan, especially the sociology of rituals, which adopts the ritualism of Ogyu Sorai to Western sociology theory.

2   The Confucian Concept of "Michi" (道) and "Social Order"

Ito Jinsai was born in Kyoto as the son of a merchant, but he was not suited to the family business and spent his life as a Confucian scholar. In pre-modern China and the Joseon Dynasty, bureaucrats and politicians were selected through an imperial examination called the kakyo (科挙). The content of the examination was based on the Confucian classics; therefore, it can be said that the interpretation of Confucian classics was compatible with the position of the ruling class and the position of the rulers, since the readers also belonged to the ruling class (士大夫層) and the scholar-officials (儒家官僚). Thus, it would have been unthinkable in China or the Joseon Dynasty for a townsman like Jinsai to study Confucianism, which was a discipline for the scholar-officials; however, Jinsai was recognized as famous scholar in Japan during the early modern period, when there was no kakyo.

The reading from the scholar-officials' point of view reconstructs the Confucian classics from the perspective of the ruling class, and in other words, it can be said that the reading is premised on managing and controlling a group of human beings from the standpoint of a politician. The appearance of Jinsai meant that the Confucian classics, which had been read from the perspective of the scholar-officials, were no longer in their context. The reading from the standpoint of the townsmen is completely different from the reading from the perspective of the ruling class.

3   The *Analects* as the "Best Book in the Universe"

Jinsai says in his *Rongokogi* (論語古義) that the *Analects* (論語) is the forever standard for Confucianism and that it is perfectly correct, valid, and consistent, and it is a complete book that does not lack a single character. According to Jinsai, the Michi is all stated here, and the ultimate goal of this study can be found there. Furthermore, Jinsai called Analects as "the first supreme book in the universe" (最上至極宇宙第一書).

Jinsai's remarks emphasize that *Analects* is not so uncomfortable for us today, because *Analects*, along with the Western Bible, is considered as an Eastern classic. However, in Jinsai's time it was not seen as natural for him to consider the *Analects* to be the most important book and to call it "the first supreme book in the universe".

Jinsai also says that, since the Han and Tang dynasties, Confucianists had thought the *Six Classics* (六経) were precious, but they did not consider the *Analects* to be valuable and superior to the *Six Classics*. He also prioritized *Great Learning* (大学) and *Doctrine of the Mean* (中庸) over *Analects* (論語) and *Mencius* (孟子).

Since Confucianism became a national education system in China, the *Six Classics* of *Songs* (詩), *Documents* (書), *Rituals* (礼), *Music* (楽), *Changes* (易), and *Historiography* (春秋), which are pre-Confucius classics, have been regarded as orthodox classics. The Chinese Neo-Confucian philosopher Zhu Xi (朱熹; 1130–1200) reconstructed them into the *Five Classics* (五経). He excluded *music* (楽), which had been lost earlier, and added the four books of the post-Confucius classics *Great Learning*, *Doctrine of the Mean*, *Analects*, and *Mencius*, and made them *"the Four Books and Five Classics"* (四書五経). Among these classics, *Analects* and *Mencius* were ranked the lowest.

Jinsai overturns the position of these classics and places great importance on the *Analects* as the best book in the universe, and the *Mencius* as a clue for understanding the *Analects*. For Jinsai, *Mencius* is a book that correctly continues the thoughts of the *Analects* and thus becomes the second most important book after.

According to Jinsai's book, "*Gomojigi*" (語孟字義), by thoroughly reading the *Analects* and the *Mencius*, the "Context of saints' thoughts and words" (聖人の

意思語脈), that is, the ideological context, is revealed, and based on this, the meaning of the letters, that is, the words, can be accurately understood.

Jinsai also uses the term "Meaning Bloodline of Confucius and Mencius" (孔孟の意味血脈). It means that by contrasting the "ideological context" found in the *Analects* and *Mencius* as a standard, the text of the classics is selected, and only those sentences suitable for the ideological context are read as correct sentences. Jinsai proposes a kind of method of criticizing the literature based on the ideological context.

From this work, Jinsai argues that *Great Learning* (大学), which was ranked high in the four books, is not Confucius's authentic work. The classics should be unquestionable sacred books. Its authenticity can be verified by applying an academic scalpel to it. Thus, it is not subordinate to the Neo-Confucian interpretation, but it is possible to approach the original classics directly and independently, while keeping them close. Given this situation, it is possible to make an attempt to study "Kobunjigaku" (古文辞学) by Ogyu Sorai.

4 The "Michi" Concept for the Daily Life of People (人倫日用の道)

Why does Jinsai assert that *Analects* is the best book in the universe with the best value? He stated in the code of his book *Rongokogi* (論語古義) that *Analects* is the best book because the teachings of Confucius that are documented in the *Analects* refer to the concept of "Michi" that people take for granted in their daily life and preach the "Michi" of humble daily life. It can be said that it is a discovery of "everyday life" by Jinsai. In addition, Confucius, who preached the importance of a humble daily life, is praised the most as "the greatest saint in the universe".

Jinsai calls the "Michi" in *Gomojigi* as "Michi for the daily life of people" and says that human relations are defined by certain relationships, such as sovereign and vassal, father and son, husband and wife, siblings, and friends. In that sense, it says that the "Michi" as "social order" in everyday human relationships has already been realized and does not arise after being taught.

5 Ogyu Sorai's Repulsion

Jinsai regards the *Analects* as "the best book in the universe" and Confucius as "the greatest saint in the universe".

As an opposition against Jinsai's remarks, Ogyu Sorai tries to overcome this. First of all, Sorai emphasizes the importance of the "*Six Classics*" over the

Analects, and also argues that the "Michi of Confucius", which Jinsai found in the *Analects*, is actually the "Michi of the Great ancient kings (先王)". Sorai ranks Confucius as a learner of the "Michi of the Great ancient kings". Confucius is outstanding in that he is the one who learns and conveys the "Michi of the Great ancient kings" as recorded in the *Six Classics*. In that respect, he is a saint, but he is different from the Great ancient kings.

The statement made by Ogyu Sorai indicates that "the Michi of Confucius is the Michi of the Great ancient kings", which means that Confucius did not create the teaching of Confucius's excellent Michi. The Michi of Confucius is the Michi created by the Great ancient kings. The critical view on the "Michi of Confucius" creates a perspective that the Great ancient kings are the creator of the first Michi that cannot be traced back any further.

It means seeing the "Michi" as the production of "saints = the Great ancient kings" from a different angle than Jinsai's position of seeing "social order" already realized in people's daily life. In other words, "social order" has its origins.

Jinsai's remarks, which ultimately evaluate *Analects* and Confucius as "the most extreme in the universe" and value the "Michi for the daily life of people", promoted the formation of Sorai's viewpoint of the production of the Michi by "saints = the Great ancient kings". It is exactly the beginning of the controversy over "order issues" in the early modern period, which took the form of a debate over the "Michi".

6 Discover of "Society"

Before modern times, social phenomena were not regarded as independent phenomena different from natural phenomena and were understood on the same principle. However, social phenomena came to be recognized as phenomena with their own laws. Furthermore, the recognition of the independent law of a social phenomenon leads to the recognition that makes it is possible to manipulate it. This is the discovery of "society" in modern times. Masao Maruyama called this the predominance of "an opportunity for action (作為) against nature (自然)" and tried to find it in the ideas of Jinsai and Sorai (Maruyama 1952). Among the thoughts of the early modern period, regarding Neo-Confucianism, which regards social phenomena as being inseparable from natural laws, Jinsai separated social order from natural laws and identified this as an independent phenomenon. Furthermore, Sorai understood that social order could be artificially reorganized, and Maruyama tried to read the germ of modern thought from Sorai's thought.

In Maruyama's book *A Study on the History of Japanese Political Thought*, he dealt with an episode in Sorai's book, "political talk" (政談), at the beginning of his theory about Sorai (Maruyama 1952: 72). The following is stated:

> Within the territory of Yoshiyasu Yanagisawa, a farmer named Donyu, whose life had become difficult, divorces his wife, disposes of the farmland, and goes on a begging trip with his mother. On the way, his mother became ill, and he went to Edo alone, leaving his mother, so he was arrested for abandonment. When Yoshiyasu asks Confucian scholars for their opinions on the man's disposition, they answer that he cannot be convicted because he did not intend to abandon his mother, but Yoshiyasu is not convinced. On the other hand, Sorai argued that if famine occurs in the world, there will be such people in other territories, and magistrates, chief retainers, and even superiors who have taken the guilty person out of the territory are to be blamed, so the individuals should not be blamed. Yoshiyasu is convinced and makes heavy use of Sorai.

According to Maruyama, the characteristics of the later Sorai studies are expressed "by grasping the social repeatability as an objective type, his innocence was concluded, and the problem was shifted to the political responsibility of the ruler" (Maruyama 1952: 73).

Masahiro Ogino, a Japanese sociologist, describes Maruyama's thoughts:

> As Maruyama pointed out, the fact that farmer's choice of behavior was linked to poverty caused by famine and identified as a "social" problem is certainly a groundbreaking thing that can be called a "discovery of society" by Sorai. The buds of Sorai's sociological thinking have already been plucked; however, Sorai's originality of sociological thinking was sprouting. It is because discussions are taking place over the crimes of parental abandonment.
> OGINO 1998: 55

Maruyama sees the characteristic of Sorai studies as a "divergence between public (公) and private (私)" and understands that there is an objective system on one side and subjective personal morality on the other. According to Ogino, this corresponds to the sociological framework of perception, represented by Émile Durkheim, as the "individual and social dualistic perception framework". In that sense, Maruyama seeks the origin of modernization from Sorai's thought. However, the recognition of parental abandonment as a crime means that parents and children are not independent individuals and have a fateful relationship. According to Ogino, parental abandonment is first recognized as a crime in another sociological perception framework, known as the "interrelational perception framework" based on "relationships", found in Alfred Schütz's theory. No matter how Sorai answers with individual and social dualism, the framework of individual and social dualism cannot be expanded as long as the problem structure itself is interrelational (Ogino 1998: 55–56).

What is interesting to Ogino's point of view is that the recognition of finding order in human relationships, such as parent-child relationships, based on the interrelational cognition framework overlaps with Jinsai's perception of the "Michi".

Sorai's perception of order includes Jinsai's perception of order. In other words, it may be called a "dualistic perception framework for relationships and society". It can be said that it is a position to view "social order" as a relational human relationship and at the same time view "social order" as a unique domain that can be manipulated behind the relational human relationship. These two different orders coexist in Sorai's ideas, and their integration represents an important challenge. As a conclusion, the formation of social order will be explained from the point of view of ritual production.

7 Sociology of Ritual: The Ritualism of Ogyu Sorai

Masao Maruyama especially recognized the political thinking of Ogyu Sorai as being comparable to modern Western Europe. Through the thinking of Sorai, Maruyama tried to find a possibility for Japan's own political science to be comparable to that of modern Western Europe. Similarly, this paper points out the emergence of academic languages in Kogaku as equivalent to the sociology established in modern Western Europe. Because their discussions can be seen, the fundamental question of sociology—namely, "How is social order possible?"—is identified and developed as a question surrounding the concept of "Michi". For example, Sorai said, "The Michi of Confucius is the Michi of the ancient kings". The Great ancient kings (先王) and saints (聖人) were producers of the Michi, or social order, and brought them to the man in distant ancient times. This allowed human beings to acquire "culture" and lead a social life as human beings.

Social thinkers in modern Western Europe have answered this question in the past, stating that humans exist as independent individuals, and they are in a constant unstable state because their interests conflict with each other. Thus, human beings need to form social groups by transferring a part of their rights. After the writings of Thomas Hobbes (1588–1679), social contract theory was based on this way of thinking (Hobbes 1928). This is well known as the "Hobbesian Problem" formulated by Talcott Parsons (1902–1979). This way of thinking explains the transition from the "natural state" before human beings formed social groups to the "social state", in which human beings form social groups. It may be described as a transition from "nature" to "culture". The important point is that the natural state is regarded as a "theoretical model" to explain the origin of society. In this way, it is possible to create theoretical and hypothetical stories about the origin of the society according to the flow from the natural state to the social state (Parsons 1968).

Ogyu Sorai stated the transition of human beings from the natural state to the social state as follows:

> In ancient times, when saints could not take their place, people's lives were all different, so there was no integration, and the people knew the existence of mothers but did not know the existence of fathers. Even if their descendants went around everywhere, they did not ask about that. Although they live in the land and enjoy the produce of the land, they do not know their ancestors. The dead are neither buried nor enshrined. People gathered in wildlife to end their lives and disappeared with vegetation. There was no happy life for people. That is because things that people need to follow are not formed in those days. Thus, Saints (聖人) enacted a feast of souls of the dead (鬼神) to integrate the people, built places where souls of ancestors were enshrined and held festivals of spring and autumn to honor souls of ancestors.
>
> OGYU 1985

This presents a vivid picture of the natural state before human beings formed social groups. Furthermore, Sorai said that when a child is born, it is possible to know the mother who gave birth to the child, but the father's identity could remain unknown. It means that the concept of fatherhood did not exist, which also meant that there was no concept of marriage. Therefore, as a result, groups such as families and relatives were not formed.

Marriage as an institution is an important condition of whether human beings form social groups or not. The early social thinkers of modern Western Europe had a keen interest in the origin of the family. Evolutionary ideas have emerged as scientific; the *Ancient Society* (1877) by Lewis Henry Morgan (1818–1881) is a classic example in anthropology regarding the evolution of the family structure. Thus, the model of the primitive form of the family suggested by Morgan is promiscuity. This means that there is no distinction between those who can marry and those who cannot. For now, it is a thing of the past to explain the differences in family types according to evolutionary stages, but Morgan's theory had a great impact in his time.

Sorai's idea of the "natural state" is very similar to Morgan's idea of the primitive form of family. Surprisingly, Sorai presented a similar idea more than a hundred years before Morgan did. Interest in explaining the transition from the natural state to the social state has continued to the marriage theory of Claude Lévi-Strauss (1949).

Sorai thought about how human beings overcame the natural state and transitioned to the social state. What is noteworthy here is that, as he said, "what people need to follow is not formed", and that an "institution" in a broad sense, which is a criterion for enabling human society, needs to be created. Thus, he clearly described the first institution created by saints to lead the transition of human beings, from the natural state to the social state. In other words, the concept of the dead's souls, especially the institution of ancestral ritual, was created. Human beings are integrated into a social group by overcoming the natural state and performing rituals.

Another discussion may be mentioned here. It is the discussion starting from the premise that "human beings are social beings". According to this way of thinking, it is not necessary to assume the natural state before the origin of society. Instead, the important question is, "How are human social groups maintained?" There is a way of thinking that says that human social groups are maintained by performing various rituals. Rituals are said to have a "function" of integrating human social groups. It is deeply reflected in sociology after Emile Durkheim (1858–1917). It can be seen that the view of Sorai is very close to the sociology of Durkheim. Remarkably, he noticed the role of rituals in social formation more than 200 years before Durkheim.

The social thought of Western Europe considers the transition from the natural state to the social state, but it is thought that human beings formed social groups through the creation of rituals or social contracts, not by saints. In this regard, the view of Sorai is the way of thinking between Hobbes and Durkheim. It may be said to be a "Durkheim-like solution to the Hobbes problem". The difference is that he considers rituals to be produced by saints. His view indicates that Confucian scholars, like politicians, have gained the perspective of managing and controlling human social groups by creating rituals while placing themselves in the position of saints.

8   Symbolic Recovery

In the past, the reconstruction and recovery of disaster-affected communities progressed in the direction of the review and redevelopment of urban planning by mobilizing knowledge and skills from natural science perspectives, especially civil engineering. Thus, as long as the concept of recovery was based on civil engineering knowledge and skills, the contents of recovery also resulted in making something better from a civil engineering perspective. However, it is empirically known that the recovery of disaster-affected communities requires considering not only physical infrastructures but also culture and psychological feelings. If the community members cannot feel that "we have recovered", then recovery has not been achieved, even if it is regarded as being recovered by objective criteria, including a civil engineering perspective. Recovery is realized at the level of people's symbolic semantic systems.

If recovery is ritually directed and realized at the symbolic semantic system level, it is considered effective in recovering cultural heritage and festivals, which are symbols of local communities. Disaster-affected communities have collective traumatic memories. The restoration of local symbols represents a recovery of the community's feelings. What is interesting about this phenomenon is that the recovery of symbols leads to infrastructure recovery.

The author of this paper has suggested the concept of recovery as "symbolic recovery" based on such thinking, distinguished from the conventional concept of civil engineering recovery. Moreover, theoretical reviews have been conducted based on the ritualism, symbolism, and community theory of anthropologists and sociologists, including Émile Durkheim (1912), Arnold van Gennep (1909), Clifford Geertz (1980), Benedict Anderson (1991), Anthony Cohen (1985), Claude Lévi-Strauss (1958), Mary Douglas (1970), and Victor Turner (1969). However, what is important is that our argument introduces a perspective new to their anthropological and sociological ritualism. It is the perspective that people "produce" rituals to build a sense of recovery at the symbolic level, to achieve a feeling of recovery.

Administrators responsible for completing the recovery process, including recovery planners and heads of local governments, recognize that recovery is formed ritualistically, and express the sense of recovery created among people, beyond civil engineering criteria. In other words, it points out the importance of intentionally designing and properly implementing the recovery ritual to create recovery (Yama 2006).

9 Shift to Production Theory

A barrier to argue the "production view of ritual" was the traditional ritualism framework in sociology and anthropology. It is because of this way of thinking that administrators, including recovery planners and heads of local governments, are not suitable for conventional ritualism; this is in spite of the fact that people in such positions are responsible for recovery and are autonomous to decide and implement measures independently of the social group. In conventional ritualism, it is thought that a specific individual also belongs to a social group. An individual's consciousness reflects the social group's unconsciousness; thus, the individual's intention represents the social group's intention. This could be called a "social reductionist way of thinking". Such a process is unavoidable as long as the logic of interpreting the society-related situation to is observed after watching the progress to the end.

However, there will be differences between a specific individual's consciousness and a social group's unconsciousness. Even if it is not one specific individual driving the intentions, there will be substantial differences between the individual's intention and the social group's intention (to which the individual belongs). Even a small community would reflect the same differences. Researchers seem to feel that they can isolate the social group's intention by excluding these differences.

Within a social group, a person who belongs to the group but has a perspective that seems to look at the group from the outside is well aware of the situation inside the group and plays a role in the group's operation. At the same time, the person can acquire external knowledge and skills, obtain external information, and build external networks, thereby changing the situation inside the group while using knowledge, skills, information, and human networks from the outside. The author has named those individuals as the "intermediate intellectuals". It is thought that these intermediate intellectuals trigger actions, and that these actions act on the social group and react to the social group, thereby changing the situation gradually by repeating the interactions, like the two focal points of the ellipse (Yama 2020). It is also thought that these intermediate intellectuals are involved in designing and implementing recovery rituals. These changes of viewpoint on rituals result in a "production theory".

The ritualism theory of Ogyu Sorai was used to reference the production theory viewpoint of ritual.

9.1   *Case Study Review*

This section connects the ritualism of Durkheim with the production view of the ritualism of Sorai. The logic that creates the sense of recovery among people by designing recovery rituals, planning their situation and timing, and implementing them will be introduced, presenting the following case study.

A small fishing village called Kobuchihama, located in Ishinomaki, Miyagi Prefecture, was hit by the Great East Japan Earthquake and subsequent tsunami in 2011, causing important damage to the infrastructure. After this event, only 18 of the 150 houses remained standing. In July 2016, we investigated the revival of the summer festivals in this area. We observed many young people walking in the village, carrying monuments of gods, called "Omikoshi" (portable shrines), and shouting slogans. We found out that the young people who volunteered to carry out the festival were college students from Tokyo, and not area residents. The residents who lost their homes due to the tsunami were living in temporary houses by then. Elder people from temporary houses in the area gathered while hearing the slogans of the festival.

Interestingly, a local shrine festival is generally open only to shrine members, residents called "Ujiko" (shrine parishioners). Others are only allowed to see the festival, not to participate in it. However, after many people lost their homes, died, and went missing in the disaster, external volunteers were allowed to participate. Usually, the festival is used as a barrier for rejecting outsiders, but it becomes a "mediation" tool for accepting outsiders during a crisis.

Disaster-affected communities have collective traumatic memories. The revival of the festival is a symbolic reenactment of the community before the disaster, symbolically expressing the recovery of the community's spirit.

It is important to note that Sorai's ritualism focuses on the ritual that evokes memories of the dead, acts as if the dead are resurrected there, and expresses the exchange between the dead and the living. The recovery ritual also recalls the local community's memories before a disaster destroyed it, acting as if the local community has recovered, and expresses reconciliation and harmony between the past and the present. It is the wisdom of the community that heals collective traumatic memories. In that sense, this ritualism and symbolic recovery are also theories of memory management.

Another example is as follows: Hoichi village, located in the mountainous area of Higashimiyoshi town in Tokushima Prefecture, where we have been investigating for over 10 years, is a typical depopulated area affected by population decline and aging. If depopulation can be seen as "another disaster", then depopulated areas can also be perceived as major damaged areas.

There are two notable activities in this village. Since a single road connected the village with the flatland, the village was isolated every year due to heavy rains and snowfall. For this reason, the president of the residents' association cultivated the land and built a heliport for rescue and for emergency medical helicopters to land. Another activity is the revival of the puppet show through the repairs made on the puppet show stage (cultural heritage), which has not been used for more than 80 years. Moreover, a local arts festival involving music and traditional dance groups, which are the hobbies of nearby residents, is planned and held every year.

Departments within a public office in charge of holding art festivals and disaster prevention activities are different, and each academic field dealing with them is also different. However, for residents, both of them are activities sharing the purpose of protecting the village. The superficial purpose of the art festival is to revitalize the depopulated village. However, a hidden purpose for the president of the residents' association is to establish networks with performers and tourists coming from outside the village, thereby securing supporters outside the village in case of disaster. It creates a system that accepts outsiders by creating a new festival. This case is also an example of how using the cultural heritage and the festival can help recover the local community. The president of the residents' association is a typical "intermediate intellectual".

Researchers involved in the recovery support of the disaster-affected community should engage in a series of recovery ritual processes from production to implementation while coordinating and supporting the intermediate intellectual within the group. This is because the recovery ritual design is an important and indispensable part of community recovery. Furthermore, the knowledge for designing community recovery is thought to be created by aggregating the knowledge through relations, with residents and intermediate intellectuals but also various outsiders, including researchers. The production view of rituals also leads to the potential for "collaboration" among residents, victims, and researchers.

10 Conclusion

In the above chapter, a potential discipline of sociology has been introduced based on the symbolic recovery previously proposed by the author, connecting Western sociology theories with the ritualism of Sorai. Additionally, many pre-modern Confucian scholars of the early modern period who developed thoughts comparable to Western sociology are mentioned.

Japan rapidly introduced modern Western science in the Meiji period because it already had academic languages comparable to modern Western science; thus, the translation proceeded smoothly. This means that academic ways of thinking that were comparable to modern Western science were developed in Japan. The translation is a creative work, but also translating Western academic languages into theoretical academic languages is a process of creating disciplines with new hybrid ways of thinking. Japanese scholars in the Meiji period worked deliberately to create hybrid studies.

Through this study, we hope to contribute to identifying and reevaluating sociology in the non-Western world by understanding sociology in a broad sense that is not limited to Western sociology, to design sociology that integrates Western sociology and non-Western sociology based on these achievements, and to make use of sociology for solving social problems in a globalizing society.

References

Anderson, B. 1991. *Imagined Communities: Reflections on the Origin and Spread of Nationalism*. New York, NY: Verso.

Cohen, P.A. 1985. *The Symbolic Construction of Community*. New York: Tavistock Publications.

Douglas, M. 1970. "Natural Symbols: Explorations in Cosmology". Penguin.

Durkheim, E. 1912. *Les Formes élémentaires de la vie religieuse: le système totémique en Australie* [The Elementary Forms of the Religious Life: Totemism among the Aborigines of Australia]. Paris: Alcan.

Geertz, C. 1980. *Negara: The Theatre State in Nineteenth-Century Bali*. Princeton, NJ: Princeton University Press.

Gennep, A.-V. 1909. *Les rites de passage* [The Rites of Passage]. Paris: É. Nourry.

Hobbes, T. 1928. *Leviathan*. New York, NY: J.M. Dent & Sons Ltd.

Lévi-Strauss, C. 1949. *Les Structures élémentaires de la parenté*. Paris: Mouton.

Lévi-Strauss, C. 1958. *Anthropologie Structurale Deux* [Structural Anthropology]. Paris: Plon.

Maruyama, M. 1952. "日本政治思想史研究" [Studies in the Intellectual History of Tokugawa Japan]. 岩波書店.

Ogino, M. 1998. "資本主義と他者" [Capitalism and Others]. 関西学院大学出版会.

Ogyu, S. 1985. "「徂徠集」『近世儒家文集集成』" [Sorai Collection "Early Modern Confucianism Collection"]. ぺりかん社.

Parsons, T. 1968. *The Structure of Social Action*. New York, NY: Free Press.

Turner, V. 1969. *The Ritual Process: Structure and Anti-Structure*. London: Routledge & K. Paul.

Yama, Y. 2006. "『象徴的復興』とは何か" [What Is Symbolic Recovery]. "先端社会研究", pp. 153–175.

Yama, Y. 2019. "江戸の思想闘争" [Thought Struggle of Edo]. 角川書店.

Yama, Y. 2020. "「媒介的知識人」とは何か" [What Is an "Intermediate Intellectual"?]. "災害復興研究", pp. 83–91.

CHAPTER 8

Sociological Sinicization: A Chinese Effort in Post-Western Sociology

Zhou Xiaohong and Feng Zhuqin

1 Introduction

One of the most notable recent controversies within Chinese sociology has been that Professor Xie Yu, a resident of the United States, published a 2018 article titled "Avoiding the Misleading Trap of Sociology Localization in China" in the journal *Sociological Studies*. The article explicitly asserted that "sociological localization is a pseudo-problem" (Xie 2018). Xie warned against the flawed localization or Sinicization efforts that have been occurring in Chinese sociology since the 1930s and which continue to this day. Xie's article soon saw a strong response. He was supported by the likes of Professor Liang Yucheng, who, despite disagreeing with Xie's view of any effort at localization as a "misconception", "fully agreed with Xie's emphasis on scientism-oriented social science paradigms and his criticism of the ideological trend of localization that ignores universality and only recognizes empiricism based on particularity" (Liang 2018). Xie's article also roused opponents, including Professor Zhai Xuewei who was adamant that Xie's 'judgment of the original meaning of localization is completely misread' (Zhai 2018). These opponents held that there is no localization within Chinese sociology, and that Xie's problem is "fictional". Driven largely by Xie's and Zhai's arguments, comparable discussions have become increasingly frequent. Moreover, they have been an important subject in sociological discourse for some time. It is therefore fitting to further consider the localization of sociology in the context of both Chinese tradition and current practice, with close reference to related historical and theoretical issues, and to provide a Chinese response to the development of post-Western sociology.

2 Localization in Sociology: Origins and Functions

In 1895, Yan Fu, a pioneer of modern Chinese thought, published "Yuan Qiang" (On the Origin of Strength) in the newspaper *Tianjin Zhibao*. In the article, he introduced Herbert Spencer and his *qunxue* (群学/sociology), which is seen as the earliest sign of the arrival of sociology in China (Yan 2010: 3). Subsequently, Yan (1903) translated and published Spencer's *The Study of Sociology*. Thereafter, the American missionary Daniel H. Kulp II convened the first sociology course at the University of Shanghai (沪江大学) and in 1914 founded the university's department of sociology. Then, in 1916, Chinese scholar Kang Baozhong started a sociology course at Peking University. Sociology as a discipline began to take form in China.

2.1 The Inception and Evolution of Sociological Sinicization

From the 1930s, the first generation of Chinese sociologists who had been immersed in modern Western education returned to China and took up faculty positions in the sociology departments of universities. Whether this foreign knowledge system had the capacity to explain Chinese society and to help solve Chinese problems became the main concern of local sociologists. One such scholar, Yang Kaidao, almost joked that "the problem of American sociology is that only domestic materials are used instead of foreign materials; the problem of Chinese sociology is that only foreign materials are used instead of domestic materials" (see Qu 1937: 1). Around the same time, Sun Benwen and Wu Wenzao were working separately on Sinicizing sociology in northern and southern China, respectively (Zhou 2012, 2017). Their work inspired many colleagues, especially those from Yenching University, such as Li Anzhai, Fei Xiaotong, Lin Yaohua, and Qu Tongzu. Their efforts not only succeeded in elevating Chinese sociology to unprecedented historical heights, but, in terms of their influence, also matched the Rural Construction Movement led by Yan Yangchu and Liang Shuming and the Marxist Sinicization Movement presided over by the Communist Party of China and Mao Zedong. These two movements nurtured the Chinese people's collective desire for national independence and the removal of the last vestiges of Western colonialism. For some time, the work of the above sociologists constituted a comparable kind of Sinicization drive, albeit one that was mostly independent of organized politics.

In 1949, when sociology was suppressed across mainland China, the energetic Sinicization efforts within the discipline came to an abrupt halt. It was not until 1966, on the other side of the Taiwan Strait, that Chen Shao-hing's article "Taiwan as a Laboratory for the Study of Chinese Society and Culture"[1]

---

1 Local sociologist Chen Shaoxin pointed out that although Taiwan has experienced fifty years of Japanese colonial rule, it still inherits the traditions of Chinese culture and is a typical Chinese society. Furthermore, due to the small size of Taiwan, its short history of development, and its relatively good collection and preservation of records, 'China can be studied in

reenergized social scientists, many of whom had studied in the United States and Europe and started to return to Taiwan in the mid-1960s. Chen's research urged them to rediscover an enthusiasm for the Sinicization of sociology. Initially influenced by the popular concept of "interdisciplinary integration" and research into "national character" in the United States before and after World War II, Li Yih-yuan (an anthropologist), Wen Ch'ung-i (a sociologist), and Yang Kuo-Shu (a psychologist), all of whom had studied in the United States, jointly initiated research into the "Chinese character". Subsequently, the debate caused by their research, the criticism of the development of sociology in the mid-1970s amid anti-war activism in the United States and Europe (Gouldner 1970), and the localized dependency theory proposed by Central and South American academics who challenged Western ideology during the 1960s, inspired Taiwanese social scientists to establish an academic movement oriented towards sinicization. This led to a comprehensive review of and reflection on the theories and methods of Western social science. Starting in the 1980s, this scholarship started merging with sociological localization movements around the globe. Yet, this process had been and continued to be complicated by the intervention of politics in mainland China. Fortuitously, nevertheless, because of the reform and opening up initiative in 1978, and thus the resurrection of sociology on the mainland, the Sinicization movement was imbued with fresh impetus.

Almost since the reconstruction of sociology began in mainland China, ideas about "localization", "Sinicization", and "Chinese characteristics" have followed it closely. Searching the China National Knowledge Infrastructure academic database reveals that the earliest sociological literature since 1979 with the theme of "localization" or "Sinicization" was the article "Taiwanese Scholars on the Sinicization of Social and Behavioral Science Research", published collaboratively by the members of the Chinese Sociological Research Association in 1982.[2] The piece introduced views on Sinicization among 5 sociologists based in Taiwan and Hong Kong: Hsiao Hsin-huang, Kao Cheng-shu, Ip Kai-ching, Lai Jen-hang, and Ambrose Yeo-Chi King. This was the first time that mainland sociologists had aired the views of their Chinese colleagues in other locales since sociology had been revived in mainland universities. According

Taiwan' (Chen 1966: 13). Refer also to Wang Dong on 'making Taiwan become the best "laboratory" for studying China's social and cultural changes' (Wang 2013).

2 The Chinese Society of Sociology was established at the Sociological Symposium held in Beijing from March 15th to 18th, 1979, which was an important symbol of the reconstruction of Chinese sociology. Three years later, from May 22nd to 26th, 1982, at the 1982 annual general meeting held in Wuhan, the Society was officially renamed the Chinese Sociological Association.

to Ip Kai-ching, "the emergence and growth of Chinese sociology has followed the development of Western sociology, especially American sociology. Thus, it formed its 'empirical', 'practical', 'transplanted' and 'processed' character". In this article, Ip also argued: "the ultimate goal of Sinicized sociology is to reflect on and criticize Western theories and offer a new blueprint for humanity's future through Chinese cultural traditions". Similarly, Ambrose Yeo-Chi King's position here was that "the Sinicization of sociology has at least two different levels of meaning: one is that the establishment of Chinese sociology should give sociology a special Chinese character; the second is to fully develop sociology in China, make it engage actively with Chinese society, be used in China, and take root in China" (Chinese Sociological Research Association 1982).

If we compare Ip's and King's localization views with some of the earliest visions for Chinese sociology conceived by trailblazers such as Sun Benwen and Wu Wenzao, there is a clear continuation between the two. As I argued in 1994, "to some extent, 'localization' is an expansion and continuation of the 'Sinicization' that took place more than half a century ago" (Zhou 1994). Indeed, similar sentiments have been central to the work of another pioneer mentioned previously. In 1993, Fei Xiaotong stated in his address to the New Asia College at the Chinese University of Hong Kong: "the (two) principal features of the Sinicization of sociology are discussing sociology in connection with China's reality and serving the reform and improvement of Chinese society via sociological research" (Fei 1999: 14:7). The parallels between this position and King's understanding of Sinicization are striking. In a sense, both are coherent responses to questions of localization that have been raised by academics and policymakers alike.

2.2 Meanings of Localization in Sociology

Although "the Sinicization of sociology has become a popular topic since the 1980s" (Lin and Tu 1985), "localization" in Chinese sociology has yet to be defined with any measure of agreement. Taking into account the efforts of the first generation of Chinese sociologists, such as Sun and Wu, the upsurge in Chinese nationalism after World War II, and, more recently, globalization, I believe that localization can be seen as "a kind of universal academic movement conceived following World War Two in industrialized nations other than the US and in developing nations including China" (Zhou 1994). In other words, in the field of social science, this can be understood as a "collective effort among 'discourse dependent countries' to overturn to their academic dependence on 'developed countries'" (Wang 2006).

The localization movement first appeared in what was then a somewhat marginalized Western Europe after the war. Not only did Serge Moscovici,

Henri Tajfel, and Joachim Israel establish a second knowledge center of social psychology in Europe through subverting the American tradition of individualism (Fang 2002), but the European school of theoretical sociology represented by the likes of Jürgen Habermas, Pierre Bourdieu, and Anthony Giddens also began to emerge and indeed to flourish independently of US influence. Localization has also appeared in Eastern Europe, Australia, Canada, and Japan (Enriquez 1989; Graham, Brownlee and Esther 2008; Liu 1983; Sandstrom 2008). For instance, Iván Szelényi and Eric Kostello put forward a distinctive theory of social transformation based on social practices in Eastern Europe (Eyal, Szelényi and Townsley 2008; Szelényi and Kostello 1996). Russian sociologists have also highlighted "lessons from Russia's experience in the transition to democracy and from a state to market economy" (Sandstrom 2008: 607).

The social sciences in the developing world also showed a distinct tendency towards localization subsequent to World War II as well. As early as 1957, Gunnar Myrdal, an advocate of dependency theory, urged developing nations not to uncritically absorb Western theories and methods. It was vital, he warned, to tailor economic theories to their specific problems and interests (Myrdal 1957: 309). In the following years, the majority of developing countries sought to foster localization by revising Western practices or creating new practices informed by their own cultures and histories. In the 1980s, owing primarily to increasing globalization, the localization of the social sciences gradually became an academic program with clear goals and a strong sense of identity (Alo 1983; Atal 1981; Clammer 2009; Dirlik, Li and Yen 2012; Kim 2007; Lanuza 2003; Smith 1990). In the words of Syed Farid Alatas,

> such indigenization takes the form of Indianization, Turkicization, Sinicization, Islamization, and so on. Intellectuals in various non-Western societies engage in conscious efforts to develop bodies of social scientific knowledge in which theories and concepts are derived from their respective historical experiences and cultural practices. The culture-specific situation of a society determines, at least in part, the concepts, theories, and methodologies that arise from tackling specifically indigenous problems.
> ALATAS 1993: 310–311

3   Dimensions of Localization: Theoretical and Practical

As a systematic and universal academic movement, localization has two dimensions: theoretical and practical. In the Chinese context, this corresponds to the two aspects of Fei's and King's respective observations. Firstly, whether it is "discussing sociology in connection with Chinese reality" or "giving sociology a special Chinese character", localization centers on how to render sociology, which was imported from the West, especially from the American academic system, consistent with the structure of Chinese society and Chinese people's conduct, and how to ensure that sociology adequately reflects the Chinese nation's values, cultural traditions, ideas, and beliefs, as well as Chinese behavioral patterns. In other words, the first direction or academic dimension of localization relates directly to how Chinese social character and national character can be incorporated into sociology (Lin and Tu 1985), or how these can be understood via sociology.

Sociology is the product of modernity, and its origins lie in early modern Europe (Zhou 2002: 458–459). Gradually, as the United States became a center of Western knowledge at the end of the 19th century, social inquiry was shaped by traditions of pragmatism and individualism, and it gained the legitimacy of an academic discipline due to its employment of quantitative statistical techniques (Chen 2019).

We can recognize that sociology has allowed us to accumulate a wealth of knowledge, but there is no doubt that most of its popular theories are derived from studies of European and American societies, formulated by Western thinkers based on their own social structures and behaviors and informed by the scientific method. Accordingly, as "all theories are themselves cultural products, produced under particular conditions, by particular people in particular places" (King 1990: 408), it follows naturally that social theories can only be regional in their scope, that is, that they can only be somewhat narrow, localized theories. Even those that lay claim to a "universal" scope are scarcely more than the universalization of the particularity of the West. In fact, they can never be truly universal. Looking at sociology from this perspective, it is rather like social psychology, which was also developed chiefly in the United States. Indeed, we can easily imagine that social psychology "would be substantially different if it had been created in a different era or in a different social setting" (Cartwright 1979: 86–87).

In the development of Chinese sociology, given the doubts about the universality or cross-contextual validity of sociological knowledge (Wang 2017), scholars have advocated the notion of Sinicization or localization continuously since the 1930s. From a purely academic perspective, there are two major motivations behind this idea: (1) epistemological motivation, that is, examining imported sociological knowledge with a view to understanding China (Sun 2012: 3:369; Wu 2010: 4) and trying to make it "fit" with the social and cultural contexts of China (Yang 1993) while avoiding its mere "transplantation" (Ip 1982; Zhenglai 2008); and (2) subjective motivations, which are grounded in the knowledge that although Chinese sociology has been developing for more than a hundred years and its revival on the mainland was over 40 years ago, it is still oriented towards the West, and Chinese sociologists often still perceive themselves as "followers" (Ye 1982). Both an "impaired self-esteem" in China due to the underperformance of the planned economy (Zhou 1994) and a "burst of self-confidence" associated with recent economic growth (King 1998) could also be contributors to this subjective pursuit of academic self-sufficiency.

The practical aspects of localization relate to the second element in Fei's and King's respective observations, that is, that sociological research must be made to work for "the reform and improvement of Chinese society", and that it should be "connected to Chinese society and used by China". We might well argue that this kind of expression has become a cliché today, but during the 1930s, when the Sinicization of sociology was being pioneered by the likes of Sun and Wu, the question of how to use Western ideas to transform a troubled, backward China was a pressing one. In this period, the Rural Construction Movement led by Yan and Liang, the Dingxian and Jiangcun surveys of rural life by Li Jinghan and Fei Xiaotong, and the rural research led by the Marxist sociologist and economist Chen Hansheng (based at Academia Sinica in Nanjing) were convergent in practice. Even though they had different understandings of the problems in Chinese society and proposed different remedies, they all hoped to "seek a fundamental solution to China's rural issues" (Yan 2010: 238). It was in this spirit of mutual concern that "understanding national conditions and reforming society" became the main objective of Wu and other sociologists represented by the newly established Chinese School (Li 2008). With the crises precipitated by the Japanese invasion of China in the 1930s, their mission became even more important. A series of field studies conducted in southwest China during this era meant that the social research advocated by the Chinese School prior to the Anti-Japanese War would "become the common ethos of Chinese sociology during the war" (Fei 1999: 5:413).

This "common ethos" applied to all working towards the Sinicization of sociology who adhered to the above-mentioned goal of "understanding national conditions and transforming society". It was not confined merely to the Chinese School, based in the Kuixing Pavilion, Chenggong, Yunan, the members of which conducted research during the war. For example, the department of sociology of Tsinghua University, evacuated from Beiping, not only established the National Census Research Institute in the Confucian Temple in Chenggong, a short distance from the Kuixing Pavilion, but it also provided a scientific and demographic basis for "recruitment for the National Government, local social projects in Yunnan and household registration" (Yang and Shi 2014). Even an accomplished academic like Sun Benwen, under the dual pressure of national and social disintegration, depended on the Central University actively engaging with the social work of the National Government and on it using sociological knowledge to help stabilize Chinese society and ensure national survival (Zhou 2012). Sun participated in the work of the Ministry of Social Affairs of the National Government, "helping in the formulation of social policies, the foundation of social administrative systems, the promotion of social services and the training of social workers" (Yan 2010: 261). By his estimation, through this hands-on sociology, he achieved his lifelong ambition "to be a scholar", that is, by conforming to the Chinese traditional ideal for intellectuals, that they ought to "use their own statecraft and display their ambition to benefit the people" (Sun 2012: 8:1).

The reform and opening up initiative breathed new life into Chinese sociology, which had been suppressed for close to 30 years, and at the same time gave the discipline the historic mission of aiding China's program of socialist modernization. Fortunately, that this reconstruction of sociology was led by earlier generations of sociologists like Fei ensured that it inherited the practicality necessary during the 1930s from the outset. Fei's research had a direct impact on the development of small-town and rural enterprise in southern Jiangsu Province, and Lei Jieqiong's household surveys also facilitated a restoration of the key role of rural households in industrial production. Lu Xueyi, who personally participated in the formulation of rural industrial contract policy in its early stages, later promoted the growth of China's middle class via his insightful research on class. A number of younger sociologists were also involved in closely related research, including work on household units, enterprise restructuring, labor migration, social adaptation among migrant workers, juvenile justice, Confucian social harmony theory, governance, poverty alleviation, ethnicity, border area development, and social consciousness. It now appears that Chinese sociology comprises a meaningful practical component in terms of applying systemic knowledge to solve local problems. This is linked to the confrontation of harsh social realities in the two periods during which sociology was introduced and reconstructed in China. It is also related to what Fei said during his lifetime about Chinese intellectuals, based on traditional Chinese notions: "each one is responsible for the fate of his country" and must focus on "learning in order to practice" (Fei 1999: 1:49). It is precisely under these combined influences that Chinese sociology has come to "emphasize a practical component' or a tradition of 'learning to practice'" (Ip 1982; Zhao 2010; Zhou 2017). Certainly, this practical emphasis could obscure or even undermine the theoretical achievements of Chinese sociology (Su 2005: 162), but this is perhaps the inevitable consequence of a modern industrial nation's discipline having been unnaturally and prematurely "transplanted" into a traditionally agrarian society.

In fact, because the localization of sociology involves the criticism of universalism and Western centralism, its practical dimension includes not only managing new problems encountered by non-Western countries in the process of modernization, but also the drive to curtail Western influence by reducing psychological dependence on the United States in order to bolster national identity (Lanuza 2003; Liu 1983). In the process of Sinicizing sociology, the realization of self-sufficiency and national dignity has been a recurring theme. We have already seen how Sinicizing sociology in the 1930s was closely intertwined with the Chinese national independence movement. Although the sociological Sinicization effort in Taiwan was limited during the 1970s and 1980s, it likewise contributed to maintaining the national consciousness and the cultural identity of the Chinese nation. To date, sociologists in mainland China still strive to realize Sinicism or localize sociology with a view to promoting cultural awareness (Fei 1999: 14:196) and Chinese discourse in the social sciences, including in sociology (Wang and Li 2018; Zhang 2018).

4 Universalism and Particularism: Resolving a Paradox

The relationship between the general and the specific is one of the oldest philosophical questions. As to the applicability of certain value or knowledge systems to different groups, there are at least two roughly corresponding positions, that is, universalism and particularism. The key controversy behind most movements to localize sociology pertains to the cross-border validity of knowledge, or whether sociological knowledge from the West, predominantly the United States, has any universal explanatory power.

4.1 *Universalism and Particularism: Debate and Questioning*
The dispute between universalism and particularism is as old as sociology itself. During the rapid social transformations of the 19th century, Auguste Comte established sociology in the positivist intellectual atmospheres of France and other European countries, introducing the methods of natural science into the study of social order and social change, guided by the notion that "sociology should be shaped by natural science" (Giddens 1987: 11). Soon after, Herbert Spencer and Émile Durkheim further advanced Comte's vision for positivism within sociology, and they gradually developed a hypothesis-testing scientism or a positivism paradigm (Zhou 2002: 248). Although this positivism went on to became the mainstay of sociology in the United States, a completely

different tradition developed in Germany. Influenced by historical criticism and Romantic traditions in German philosophy, Ferdinand Tönnies, Georg Simmel, and Max Weber in particular argued that sociologists did not need to confine themselves to hard data like positivists. Instead, we can learn the things concealed behind such data with a kind of intuitive inquiry (*Verstehen*). Indeed, by seeing sociology as "a science concerning itself with the interpretive understanding of social action and thereby with a causal explanation of its course and consequences" (Weber 1968: 4), the Germans founded the paradigm of humanism or interpretivism, which has been honed further by the Chicago School and continues to this day.

The above two traditions represent the fundamental distinctions in the process of exploring social knowledge. Specifically, scientism encompasses general theories, quantitative analysis, empirical observation, hard data, hypothesis, measurement, verification, formal systems, and models, and it also conceptualizes social processes as natural phenomena. Humanism emphasizes specialized issues, qualitative analysis, synthesis, conceptual reconstruction, topic, meaning, explanation, individuals, and social processes as historical and cognitive phenomena (Alo 1983). For proponents of scientism, the appeal of this approach is related to a popular notion: only the use of scientific methodologies can guarantee objectivity. The key divide within sociology, between the adherents of universalism and particularism, stems from this idea.

One question immediately springs to mind about the concept of scientific objectivity. Is knowledge, including that of natural science, necessarily objective or universal? The answer is a resounding no. All knowledge is generated, or produced, within specific institutional environments containing specific participants. There is nothing that can be applicable and effective at all times in all circumstances. Even Newton's celebrated law of gravitation is no more than a mathematical formula lacking in empirical significance when it is not concerned with gravitational action, let alone the pockets of "local knowledge" discussed by Clifford Geertz in the framework of interpretive anthropology (Geertz 2014). In this regard, the "Iranian Revolution", characterized by the depolarization of secularization, is convincing evidence of the final blow to the modernization theory formed on the basis of Parsons' advocacy of universal structural functionalism (Alatas 1993).

A second question is rather more challenging. Is there any difference between the social science knowledge regarding people, their behavior, and their social structures, and the knowledge associated with natural science? Wilhelm Dilthey, an advocate of German historicism, was among the earliest to point out that the humanities and natural sciences are quite different. Under the influence of Dilthey, Weber further argued that the social world is a world of meaning, so social science should aim to understand social phenomena through human experiences of meaning. Since then, Alfred Schütz has explained from the same standpoint that the social world is experienced by people as a world of meaning from the outset (Schütz 2011: 58). Thus, from this perspective, the quest for objectivity is simply a question of how to return knowledge to the social process or social structure that produced it.

The pursuit of objectivity and universality in the social sciences, especially sociology, originated in 20th-century American sociology. The quantitative traditions pioneered by Franklin Giddings, William Ogburn, and Otis Duncan, as well as Parsons' structural functionalism, which contradicts these others but still pursues scientism in essence, have played an important role in shifting the balance of scholarship in sociology towards positivism (Chen 2019). Yet, even in this era of positivist ascendancy around the world, the voices of criticism are endless, and the questioning of "objectivity" and "universalism" has never stopped. For example, Immanuel Wallerstein pointed out that, in fact, no matter how earnestly scholars pursue universality, so far, across the historical development of the social sciences, expectations of universality have never been realized (Wallerstein et al. 1999: 53).

4.2 Pluralistic Universalism: A Possible Resolution

In fairness, in the discussion of sociological theories and methods, many scholars who emphasize the universal nature of science and usually oppose localization also have varying degrees of vigilance against the abuses of universalism and recognize the Chinese society as being distinct from societies in the West. For example, Professor Xie Yu, noted at the beginning of this chapter, sought to strike a certain balance between universalism and particularism, that is, "on the one hand, we ought not overemphasize particularity, but, on the other hand, we must also recognize that China does have a certain degree of particularity". Thus, he urged, "theories and methods applied to the research of specific social or historical situations must consider the current situation" (Xie 2018).

Yet, while many sociologists may indeed be vigilant and may even concede that "any sociological orientation, theoretical, cultural, historical, or ethnographic, can produce good sociological works" (Xie 2018), they have often assumed the methods of "good" research, that is, the so-called "scientific" methods, are still positivistic in character. They subscribe to the idea that the academic norms by which all scholars should abide are grounded in logic, reason, and evidence. Nevertheless, the "proof" or "evidence" which they prioritize does not typically extend to informal observations, case studies, life histories, oral histories, autobiographies, archives, diaries, letters, and insights gleaned from unstructured interviews conducted by qualitative researchers. Instead, this refers mostly to data that are collected and processed by quantitative researchers. Accordingly, not only do their "suggestions" to young scholars often only involve "sharing your data with academic colleagues" (Xie 2018), but also, in their opinion, qualitative methods are only useful "if good quantitative and operational methods and reliable quantitative data are not available" (Xie 2018).

Some scholars prefer quantitative methods, whereas others prefer qualitative ones. This can be explained by their inclination towards either universalism or particularism. In order to avoid unnecessary attacks on each other, or to achieve an atmosphere of inclusiveness for both quantitative and qualitative research (Goertz and Mahoney 2016), it is imperative to attempt to transcend the traditional confrontation between universalism and particularism. In fact, Weber, Schütz, and Geertz did not need to choose decisively between one or the other; indeed, they established a kind of "pluralistic universalism", as Wallerstein has described it (Wallerstein 1997: 64). The rationale for adopting this position now is that, firstly, it we can recognize that particularity is a manifestation of the differences within the human social community that can be found everywhere, whether across nations and social classes or between urban and rural regions, different ethnic groups, and families. Differences are universal, so simply seeking them out will not lead to an explanatory theory that can account for "all the differences in human society", but such explanation is central to social science (Chen 2015). Secondly, we can acknowledge that since any form of universalism is historically contingent, differences should be admitted and retained: that multiple different interpretations should be allowed to coexist simultaneously, which may enable their incorporation into a "pluralistic universalism" and their expansion into a "larger world of meaning" (Geertz 2014: 3).

In this regard, the attitude of the earlier generations of scholars, described clearly by Wang Mingming, is commendable. They 'respected the universal and cultural characteristics of academics, refusing to lay down the "other's eyes" because of "local" needs. Nor did they neglect the "local" in preference for the "other's eyes"' (Wang 2005: 2). Thus, one feasible attitude is to treat localization as an effective way to achieve "pluralistic universalism", rather than as a supplement to the realization of nationalist aspirations.

5 A Transitional Society and the Practicalities of Localization

Localization has made substantial achievements in in the history of Chinese sociology. In the 1930s and 1940s especially, with the efforts of Sun, Wu, and others, the level of sophistication of sociology and anthropology in China was comparable to that in the West. The activities of the Chinese School and its attempts at Sinicizing sociology were instrumental, as discussed previously (Wang 2005: 41–42). Nevertheless, because of the subsequent suppression of the discipline in mainland China and its advancement globally after World War II, the distance between our scholarship and international scholarship, particularly American sociology, has increased. To this point, we have not yet been able to establish a disciplinary system that can explain the features of Chinese society, and we do not have what Xie calls "first-class research" in China. Further, across international sociology, few scholars have explained societies, including Chinese society, from a "non-Western perspective" (Alatas 1993). Therefore, it can hardly be suggested that the Chinese localization movement has been successful. On the contrary, in light of its course over the past 80 years, we must admit that "the sinicization of sociology is likely to be a very long road" (Chinese Sociological Research Association 1982: 43).

5.1 Social Transformation and Localization: Pseudo-Proposition or Reality?

If the Sinicization or localization of sociology is to be regarded as a "pseudo-problem" that can be cast aside after 80 years of effort, as Professor Xie suggested in his controversial 2018 article, then we ought to keep in mind the 180-year history of sociology: how it began on European soil and how it has been transformed in the United States. Given that China today is undergoing a process of transformation comparable to the changes experienced across the Western world some 200 years ago, we have every reason to believe that the completion of the historical task of Sinicizing the social sciences, including sociology, is closer now than during any previous era. Not only is it not a "pseudo-problem", it is an inescapable reality for contemporary Chinese sociologists.

The Sinicization of sociology is not based on contrived imperatives but on necessity. Since the reform and opening up in 1978, China's extensive social transformation has not only demanded a localizing agenda in sociology, but has also provided the possibility to realize localization. The contributions of Sun, Wu, and other pioneers in Chinese sociology have been recognized both in this discussion and elsewhere (Li 2008; Wang 2005; Zheng 2004; Zhou 2012, 2017). However, even if sociology had not been suppressed in the 1950s, would we have been able to achieve the goal of Sinicization already? We think that the answer is no. The direct motivators of the Sinicization of sociology in the 1930s were the strong anxieties and dissatisfactions that arose from a few or at most a few dozen scholars, such as Fei, "reading many Western books, though remaining ignorant of the situation in China" (Fei 1999: 13:7). While Fei's efforts have led to many first-rate studies—some of which have had considerable international influence—Sinicization still seems beyond our reach, that is, considering how the entire discipline connects with its own civilization and draws raw materials from it. This practice also reveals how an ancient civilization goes about realizing its modern transformation. Indeed, the modern changes in Chinese society had just started in the 1930s, and the era that belongs to our nation has still not yet arrived.

If we remember that sociology is the product of modernity, we can recognize that its achievements as a discipline and its fundamental principles are derived from the transformation from tradition to modernity that occurred in the West, and that its developmental path and the analysis thereof is chiefly the intellectual heritage of Western, or modern, social science (Zhou 2010). That people elsewhere are asking whether or not and to what extent they can similarly examine their own nations' transformative processes is a sign of maturity in the discipline in different countries. Unlike during the 1930s, given the great changes of the past 40 years, it is now possible for those in China with the social sciences as their calling to move beyond anxieties and dissatisfactions, and to recognize that "if such a vast change in China could not be harnessed by academia it would be a loss to both China and the West" (Huang and Liu 2009). It is also in this sense that we can say that the process of sociological transformation in contemporary China might prove to be a model for localizing sociology elsewhere. If modernization around the world is nearly complete, then this is the last chance for Chinese sociologists to start before "the end" is here.

Looking at the transformations of socialist countries like China, the Soviet Union, and Eastern European nations after marketization in the 1980s, we can see that such large-scale social change not only provides new material for international sociology, but it also provides sociologists from various countries the opportunity to propose indigenous theories and do cutting-edge research. In this field, the most influential group is the "New Budapest School" or "Neoclassical Sociological Theory" championed by Iván Szelényi and Gil Eyal (Szelényi 2010). While this research has been warmly received by world sociology—Michael Burawoy even argued that this kind of transformational research is "becoming the mainstream of American sociology"—it still cannot easily be used to explain Chinese practice. Given the continuity in its political system, power structure, and ideology (Liew 2015; Sun 2005), China's unique transformational logic, the "Chinese experience", must still be explained locally by Chinese sociologists. This is a significant challenge, yet it is also an ideal opportunity for Chinese sociology to work on localization.

Even though the Chinese social sciences have not thus far been as influential as the "New Budapest School", the reform and opening up has offered new opportunities for the study of sociology in China. Chinese sociology has made tangible progress over the past four decades; "the amount of academic literature on China's social and economic changes in the West has (also) increased substantially since the mid-1980s" (Tu and Lin 1999: 2).[3] It could be argued, too, that the vast transformation of China after 1978, especially its rapid economic growth, has "become a new source of inspiration and motivation for the development of contemporary sociology and the social sciences more generally" (Sun 2005). Indeed, the changes in Chinese society have a distinctive academic significance for social science. If what China is now undergoing has nothing in particular to call its own, it is just a variation or repetition of what the Western world experienced during its own modernization. In this case, the "Chinese experience" or "Chinese path" is a fallacy. On the other hand, while the transformation of Chinese society might have its own unique historical background and operational logic, it is still a movement towards modernity, much like all of the great changes in modern human society. China is not the "other" of the entire world, so this transformation also has a certain universal value for the development of the social sciences. In acknowledging the particularity of China's social transformation, we can affirm the universal significance thereof to the development of social science and gain new inspiration and legitimacy for its localization and perhaps even for the transformation of human society at large.

5.2 *The Characteristics of a Transitional Society: Agendas and Applied Research*

It could well be said that the great changes in Chinese society and its characteristics initially affected scholarly agendas and applied research in relation to the localization of Chinese sociology. Certainly, many sociologists have recently criticized the state of Chinese sociology. Xie held that prioritizing "research on important and urgent issues" has "to some degree led to homogeneity in domestic sociological research, while also making other relatively small issues and empirical issues seem trivial" (Xie 2018: 3). Zhai Xuewei explained this tendency as a consequence of excessive "state orientation" and an over-eagerness

---

3   We followed Lin Yimin's and Tu Zhaoqing's statistics in 1999 and found that before 1978, the two top sociological journals in the United States, *American Sociological Review* and *American Journal of Sociology* published nothing on China, but the situation has changed since the Reform and Opening Up. In the ten years between 1979 and 1988, the two journals published twenty-two such articles; in the ten years between 1989 and 1998, fifty-three of this type of article were published; during the ten years from 1999 to 2008, the number increased to sixty-six; from 2009 to 2018, there were fifty-one articles. In addition, the number of Chinese authors of these articles has also increased year by year.

to establish a "discourse system" (Zhai 2018). These criticisms are not unwarranted. There was a relevant argument between Sun Liping and Li Yinhe some years ago. At that time, Sun, who was immersed in modernization theory, proposed that academic resources not be invested in research on grand social change. Li retorted by pointing out that studying insect reproduction and studying celestial movement have the same academic value.

From a theoretical standpoint, we naturally support Li, and we concur with Xie and Zhai on the same grounds. However, we also think that this manner of criticism ought to reflect the specific transformational practices of Chinese society. It is these practices that have brought a number of major structural problems to the fore. This makes government departments anxious to draw on social science to address such problems, and it nurtures the practical tendency within social science. Yet, we must also admit that the situation Xie is hopeful for has been gradually taking shape over the years, especially during the last 10 years. There are more micro and empirical studies awarded funding by China's National Social Science Fund each year, and the topics that researchers are concerned with are increasingly diverse.[4] In addition, with the increased availability of research funding, the improvement in foreign language skills among younger scholars, and the simplification of Chinese entry and exit procedures, Chinese sociologists are far more likely to engage with the wider world. For example, the overseas ethnography research promoted by academics including Gao Bingzhong, Bao Zhiming, and He Ming et al. has been having a considerable impact for 10 years, and the phenomenon of "Chinese sociologists almost only studying Chinese society", noted by Xie, is changing as well.

6   Local Traits, International Perspectives, and Post-Western Sociology

At this point in the discussion, there are two crucial issues about the localization or Sinicization of sociology left to be addressed. First, what is the path to realizing the localization of sociology? Second, is localization or Sinicization

---

4   While subject to the needs of Chinese politics and governance, Chinese sociologists' topic choices are concentrated in areas such as social transformation, social governance, community building, population migration and migrant worker adaptation. However, in recent years, the scope of topics has become wider, extending to the lives of truck drivers (Shen Yuan), traditional dance (Zhou Yi), politics and fashion (Sun Peidong), urban migration and social stigma (Guan Jian), bribery and guanxi (Ruan Ji), educated youth (Liu Yaqiu), social memory (Zhou Haiyan), petitions to authorities for help (Ying Xing), suicide (Wu Fei) and gambling on cricket fights (Mou Licheng).

the ultimate goal of Chinese sociology? Regarding the first question, the earliest generation of Chinese sociologists clearly put forward their own ideas. In every subsequent period, sociologists have all been committed to the question, in spite of their different views. As for the latter question, no sociologist has seen localization as the ultimate goal of Chinese sociology. Not only do virtually all sociologists who approve of localization, including Xie, aim to "participate in the dialogue of sociology worldwide" (Xie 2018), but they all identify with Fei Xiaotong's pioneering vision, that is, "first, localization, then globalization" (Fei 2013: 54). In other words, moving from the development of local characteristics to an international perspective is regarded as the final destination on this academic journey.

6.1 The Path of Localization: Some Possible Scenarios

In the 1930s, from the outset of the Sinicization of sociology and the social sciences, two champions of the academic movement, Sun and Wu, proposed specific paths to localization (Zhou 2012, 2017). Half a century later, when the Sinicization drive in Taiwan and Hong Kong had begun, Yang Kuo-Shu, leader of the academic movement, wrote "The Sinicization of Psychological Research: Levels and Directions" (1982). Yang started from the perspective of psychology and laid out the following plan: (1) re-validate foreign research findings; (2) study the vital and unique phenomena of Chinese people; (3) modify or create concepts and theories; and (4) change old methods and design new ones (Yang 1989: 484). This influenced the localization movement in Taiwan and Hong Kong, as well as the development of the social sciences and localization strategies on the mainland to a certain extent, particularly through Yang's social psychology workshops from the 1990s.

Nonetheless, on this topic, Fei once again came to the fore. In the later stages of his life, nearly every 5 years or so, he made a significant breakthrough in promoting the Sinicization of sociology.

First, in 1993, he proposed that sociology should move past its preoccupation with "ecology"[5] and place a stronger emphasis on "psychology" (Fei 1999: 12:315). Later, in 1997, he proposed that through engagement with "different cultures", a sense of "cultural awareness" capable of facilitating self-reflection should be cultivated (Fei 2013: 46). Furthermore, in 2003, Fei, who was 93 by this time, published the article "Extending the Conventional Frontier of Sociology". He focused on people's spiritual world, which he saw as closely related to their psychology, and he proposed that the neglected field of "intuition" is "a very

---

5 Here, Fei Xiaotong uses the word "ecology", which is the living environment corresponding to the mentality of people.

subtle and critical part of the relationships between people". This is similar to the "tacit knowledge" noted by Michael Polanyi and Friedrich Hayek. In this sphere, "Chinese culture has certain preferences and advantages, so developing Chinese sociology may lead to some epoch-making achievements in this regard" (Fei 2003).

Since then, Xie Lizhong has identified four types of localization based on Fei's lifelong academic experience: (1) object-transformational localization, that is, changing the object of study from a Western society to a non-Western society, although Western concepts, theories, and methodologies are not modified; (2) supplementary-modifiable-innovative localization, which involves the variation or adaptation of Western concepts, propositions, and methodologies for local contexts; (3) theoretical-substitution localization, where local concepts are drawn on to replace Western concepts, but the thinking and research methodologies of Western sociology are used; and (4) comprehensive-substitution localization, where theories and methods are comprehensively replaced (Xie 2017b).

Taking Fei's work as an example, the first three types of localization are embodied in *Peasant Life in China* (江村经济), *Birth System*, and *From the Soil: The Foundations of Chinese Society*. The last is the aforementioned research on intuition and the spiritual world. The author regards the last category as a comprehensive-substitution localization because it "touches on the question of the appropriateness of scientific methods like Western thinking models and positivism for the study of Chinese society" (Xie 2017b).

6.2 Post-Western Sociology and Southern Sociology: Expanded Localization?

Within Chinese sociology, it is our position that the task of defining localization should involve the developing world, including China, and the developed world outside of the United States and Western Europe, which dominate international sociology.

A quarter of a century ago, although various forms of localization were underway in different countries and regions, and there were strong commonalities among them, cooperation among countries, especially in the developing and the developed world, was rare. However, this manner of exchange is now commonplace across the world and has become a sign of internationalization in the localization movement.

In the northern hemisphere, cooperation of this order has been occurring between Chinese and French sociologists. According to Laurence Roulleau-Berger, this reflects the relationship of inheritance between Chinese sociology and European sociology, including French sociology (Roulleau-Berger 2009).

In fact, cooperation between sociologists from two or more countries is not uncommon in the era of globalization, but the most important aspect of this exchange, according to many, is the creation of a "post-Western sociology" based on "rebuilt contemporary sociology according to developmental experiences in different countries" (Wei and Li 2018). In other words, this variety of sociology is "constructed by sociologists from different Western and non-Western countries" (Xie 2017a). It could enable us to view the intersection, overlap, and blending of the two forms of sociology constructed in China and the West, and this "postcolonial rupture" may well encourage a "multi-situated sociology" and a gathering of scattered knowledge to create, construct, and recreate heterogeneous and contextual knowledge (Roulleau-Berger 2014: 3, 84). Harold Smith raised the question of how American sociologists should respond to non-Western sociologists' demands for localization in sociology in 1990 (Smith 1990), and the approach shared by Roulleau-Berger and other French sociologists as well as Chinese scholars to rebuild sociological knowledge from the standpoint of "multi-situationlism" is admirable.

Coincidentally, when Chinese and French sociologists in the northern hemisphere came together to create a "post-Western sociology" to resist the dominance of American sociology, Raewyn Connell of the University of Sydney considered the dominant position of the northern hemisphere, especially the United States and Europe, in the production of sociological knowledge over the past 180 years, and implored people to turn their vision to the global south and create a "Southern theory" of social science based on the sociological practices of Australia, Africa, Central and South America, India, and Iran. In the eyes of the American left-wing historian Arif Dirlik, "the south" is only a synonym for "the third world", a fraught term popularized during the 1950s. It is "globalization" that connects "the global" with "the south" and transforms it into this "Global South" (Dirlik 2007). From the perspective of the Global South, Connell challenged the unequal division of labor in producing sociological knowledge between the northern and southern hemispheres, or non-Western (frontier) and Western (urban) countries. But though similar in kind, the problems of producing knowledge in the metropole and the periphery are differently structured *in practice*. "The global inequalities", argued Connell, "have constituted the metropole as the home of theory, or 'science' as such, and the periphery as either the source of data, or the arena in which metropolitan knowledge is applied" (Connell 2007: 106).

Both "post-Western sociology" and sociological "Southern theory" not only aim to be largely independent of American sociology and reflect a clear local research interest or a sense of "alternative discourse" (Alatas 2006), they also have a distinctive feature, that is, cooperation between the developed world and the developing world. This is a new form of localization or expanded localization. It offers possible transitional forms for the establishment of Wallerstein's "diversified universalism" or Roulleau-Berger's "multi-situated sociology" or what Chinese sociologists have come to describe as "global such-and-such sociology".

6.3 Globalized Chinese Sociology: A Chinese Effort in Post-Western Sociology

Across the history of the development of Chinese sociology, the understanding of local and global relationships and the mission of localization have never been static. When the earliest generation of Chinese sociologists advocated Sinicizing sociology, they still only resolved to build a knowledge system that could explain the nuances of Chinese society, and they did not speculate much about the ultimate destination of this academic movement. However, from the 1960s, the next generation of scholars in Taiwan and Hong Kong argued that the ultimate goal of localization should not be to start from scratch. Reflecting on his own branch of the social sciences, psychology, Yang Kuo-Shu clearly stated that "there is only one psychology in the world", and the purpose of "localizing psychological research (including Sinicization) is not to establish a self-reliant national psychology, but to build a better world psychology" (Yang 1989: 485). In 1994, when talking about the localization of social psychology, I also proposed two different kinds of globalization: negative and positive. The former is based on making the world ours, and the latter is based on making ours the world. Of course, in general order, negative globalization came first, followed by localization, and finally positive globalization (Zhou 1994; see also Fei 2013: 54). In this regard, the realization of positive globalization depends on successful localization. We can endow sociology with a distinctive Chinese character through the study of China's long historical tradition and its current transformation, such that we might finally be qualified to participate fully in the discursive exchange of global sociology, dispel the discursive hegemony of American and other Western sociology, and cooperate with other countries to establish a multifaceted global sociology, what Roulleau-Berger and Li Peilin call "post-Western sociology" (Roulleau-Berger and Li 2018). Both prior and subsequent to creation of this type of sociology, it could be argued that a sort of globalized Chinese sociology, or the Chinese version of global sociology, should coexist with it for a period.

Moving from a local to a more global perspective is perhaps the most demanding task to be performed in building a Chinese version of global sociology. To use Fei's words, this relates to "making the good things in our culture clear and making them global" while simultaneously integrating the relatively recent ideas of the West into our ancient traditions (Fei 2013: 54). With this end in mind, Bian Yanjie has begun work on how to encode local knowledge internationally, and on devising a technical path for rendering the "national" "global" (Bian 2017). Wang Ning also hopes to be able to help resolve the problem of the "ineffectiveness" of localization by improving "knowledge-innovation capacity" with a view to disseminating "theoretical knowledge that can be understood and accepted by colleagues around the world" (Wang 2017). Xie has rather more critically argued that Chinese scholars should "make all kinds of contributions to the mainstream of the discipline worldwide, not merely in China" (Xie 2018: 12).

While strong criticism is not unjustified, if we adopt a larger social and historical perspective, I fear that the obstacles that "limit the development of Chinese sociology", especially the barriers that exist in relation to "entering the mainstream", cannot be attributed simply to "the short-sightedness of certain scholars in academic research or other scholars restricting their activities to a designated sphere" (Xie 2018: 11). Indeed, lack of "knowledge innovation" cannot be attributed solely to "the academic system and academic culture" (Wang 2017). Bian's approach might not be able to address this issue either. To resolve the constraints imposed by academic systems and academic cultures on innovation, or, as Xie said, "to have the ability to compete with Western scholars" (Xie 2018: 12), we cannot overlook the long-term and arduous transformation of larger and much more deeply rooted social structures and their institutional backgrounds. To quote Marx and Engels, "the nature of individuals thus depends on the material conditions determining their production" (Marx and Engels 2012: 147).

The establishment of a globalized Chinese sociology and hence a Chinese effort to establish a post-Western sociology is not an unrealistic endeavor. It is based on the historical course of collision, conflict, and uneven exchange between traditional China and the modern West that has spanned over a century. Heavily impacted by the West, China has never stopped resisting Western modernity. This resistance is embedded within the different, even diametrically opposed, contexts of Chinese modern thought. In itself, such resistance constitutes one of the basic elements of Chinese modernity (Wang 2015). From the beginning of the Sinicization or localization movement in sociology in the 1930s, this kind of opposition was concealed. For example, in *Peasant Life of China* (江村经济), Fei first saw Chinese people's desire for a path to modernization beyond "Westernization" from his sister Fei Dasheng's rural industrialization experiment. How to maintain cultural subjectivity without losing cosmopolitanism and how to "emphasize that traditional power is as important as new power" in the process of modernization (Fei 1999: 2:2), however, have frustrated later generations of Chinese intellectuals, including Fei's brother and sister. Yet, so far, what we are facing is still a dual process: on the one hand, the particularity of Chinese society cannot fail to require the localization of social science, which requires researchers to "affirm Chinese identity"; on the other hand, the development of social science "must be connected with the global environment so as not to lose its way in localization" (Dirlik, Li and Yen 2012: 31).

In this sense, the localization of sociology to which we are currently committed comprises necessary preparatory work for the Chinese version of global sociology. This work, as well as the gradual establishment and consolidation of schools of post-Western sociology, including Asian, African, Central and South American, Russian, and Southern schools, and even the Sino-French school, will ideally lead to a multi-contextual global sociology that embraces diverse intellectual traditions and sociological visions and accommodates different national and cultural conditions. This is the only feasible long-term state of sociology in a diversified world.

References

Alatas, Syed Farid. 1993. "On the Indigenization of Academic Discourse". *Alternatives: Global, Local, Political* 18 (3): 307–338.

Alatas, Syed Farid. 2006. *Alternative Discourse in Asian Social Science: Responses to Eurocentrism*. London: Sage.

Alo, Oladimeji. 1983. "Contemporary Convergence in Sociological Theories: The Relevance of the African Thought-System in Theory Formation". *Présence Africaine, Nouvelle série* 126: 34–57.

Atal, Yogesh. 1981. "The Call for the Indigenization". *International Social Science Journal* 32: 189–197.

Bian, Yanjie. 2017. "On the International Codification of China's Local Knowledge" [论社会学本土知识的国际概念化]. *Sociological Studies* [社会学研究] 32 (5): 1–14.

Cartwright, Dorwin. 1979. "Contemporary Social Psychology in History Perspective". *Social Psychology Quarterly* 42 (1): 82–92.

Chen, Shao-hsing. 1966. "Taiwan as a Laboratory for the Study of Chinese Society and Culture" [中国社会文化研究的实验室――台湾]. *Collection of Institute of Ethnology, Academia Sinica* [中央研究院民族学研究所集刊] 14: 1–14.

Chen, Xinxiang. 2019. "The Americanization of Sociology and Lessons for Constructing Sociology with Chinese Characteristics" [社会学美国化的历程及其对建构中国特色社会学的启示]. *Sociological Studies* [社会学研究] 34 (1): 1–28.

Chen, Yingfang. 2015. "How We Practice Academic Localization Today: Taking the Application of the State-Society Relationship Paradigm as an Example" [今天我

们怎样实践学术本土化——以国家-社会关系范式的应用为例]. *Exploration and Contention* [探索与争鸣] 11: 55–60.

Chinese Sociological Association. 1982. "Taiwanese Scholars Talk About the Sinicization of Social and Behavioral Science Research" [台湾学者谈社会及行为科学研究中国化]. *Society* [社会] 1: 45–47.

Clammer, John. 2009. "Sociology and Beyond: Towards A Deep Sociology". *Asian Journal of Social Science* 37 (3): 332–346.

Connell, Raewyn. 2007. *Southern Theory: The Global Dynamics of Knowledge in Social Sciences.* Cambridge: Polity.

Deng, Zhenglai. 2008. "The Contemporary Mission of Social Science in China" [中国社会科学的当下使命]. *Social Sciences* [社会科学] 7: 4–11.

Dirlik, Arif. 2007. "Global South: Predicament and Promise". *The Global South* 1 (1): 12–23.

Dirlik, Arif, Guannan Li, and Hsiao-Pei Yen, eds. 2012. *Sociology and Anthropology in Twentieth-Century China: Between Universalism and Indigenism.* Hong Kong: The Chinese University Press.

Enriquez, Virgilio. 1989. *Indigenous Psychology and National Consciousness.* Tokyo: Institute for the Study of Languages and Culture of Asia and Africa.

Eyal, Gil, Iván Szelényi, and Eleanor Townsley. 2008. *Making Capitalism Without Capitalists: The New Ruling Elites in Eastern Europe,* translated by Peng Lyu and Jialing Lyu. Beijing: Social Sciences Academic Press.

Fang, Wen. 2002. "The Development of European Social Psychology" [欧洲社会心理学的成长历程]. *Journal of Psychology* [心理学报] 34 (6): 651–655.

Fei, Xiaotong. 1999. *Collected Works of Fei Xiaotong* [费孝通文集]. 14 vols. Beijing: Qunyan Press.

Fei, Xiaotong. 2003. "On Extending the Conventional Frontier of Sociology" [试谈扩展社会学的传统界限]. *Journal of Peking University* [北京大学学报] 40 (3): 5–16.

Fei, Xiaotong. 2013. *Globalization and Cultural Self-awareness* [全球化与文化自觉]. Beijing: Foreign Language Teaching and Research Press.

Geertz, Clifford. 2014. *Local Knowledge: Further Essays in Interpretive Anthropology* [地方知识——阐释人类学论文集], translated by Yang Derui. Beijing: The Commercial Press.

Giddens, Anthony. 1987. *Sociology: A Brief but Critical Introduction.* New York: Harcourt Brace Jovanovich.

Goertz, Gary, and James Mahoney. 2016. "A Tale of Two Cultures: Qualitative and Quantitative Research in the Social Sciences" [两种传承——社会科学中的定性与定量研究], translated by Liu Jun. Shanghai: Gezhi Press & Shanghai People's Publishing House.

Gouldner, Alvin. 1970. *The Western Sociology Facing the Crisis.* New York: Basic Books.

Graham, John, Keith Brownlee, Michael Shier, and Esther Doucette. 2008. "Localization of Social Work Knowledge through Practitioner Adaptations in Northern Ontario and the Northwest Territories, Canada". *Arctic* 61 (4): 399–406.

Huang, Wansheng, and Tao Liu. 2009. "The Chinese Value in the Era of Globalization" [全球化时代的中国价值]. *Open Times* [开放时代] 7: 142–158.

Ip, Kai-Ching. 1982. "Research on the Direction and Problems of Sinicization from the Existing Character of Sociology in China" [从中国社会学的既有性格论社会学研究中国化的方向与问题]. In *The Sinicization of Social and Behavioral Science Research in China* [社会及行为科学研究中国化], edited by Kuo-shu Yang and Ch'ung-i Wen. Taipei: Institute of Ethnology, Academia Sinica.

Kim, Kyong-Dong. 2007. "Alternative Discourses in Korean Sociology: The Limits of Indigenization". *Asian Journal of Social Science* 35 (2): 242–257.

King, Ambrose Yeo-Chi. 1982. "The Sinicization of Sociology: A Question of Sociological Epistemology" [社会学中国化:一个社会学知识论的问题]. In *The Sinicization of Social and Behavioral Science Research in China*, edited by Kuo-shu Yang and Ch'ung-i Wen, 91–114. Taipei: Institute of Ethnology, Academia Sinica.

King, Ambrose Yeo-Chi. 1998. "The Argument of Modernity and Positioning of Chinese Sociology" [现代性论辩与中国社会学之定位]. *Journal of Peking University* [北京大学学报] 35 (6): 91–99.

King, Anthony. 1990. "Architecture, Capital and the Globalization of Culture". In *Global Culture*, edited by Mike Featherstone, 397–411. London: Sage.

Lanuza, Gerry. 2003. "Towards a Relevant Filipino Sociology in the Age of Globalization and Postmodernity". *Philippine Quarterly of Culture and Society* 31 (3): 240–254.

Li, Manxing. 2017. "The Rural Reconstruction Movement during the Republican Period" [民国时期的乡村建设运动]. *Yanhuang Chunqiu* [炎黄春秋] 11: 78–84.

Li, Peilin. 2008. "A Chinese School of Sociology in Early 20th Century" [20世纪上半叶社会学的"中国学派"]. *Social Sciences Front* [社会科学战线] 12: 203–210.

Liang, Yucheng. 2018. "Avoiding the Misleading Trap of 'Avoiding the Misleading Trap of the Localization of Sociology in China'" [走出"走出中国社会学本土化讨论的误区"的误区]. *New Horizon* [新视野] 4: 49–54.

Liew, Leong. 2015. "Rethinking Economics in the Asian Century: The Market and the State in China". In *The Social Sciences in the Asian Century*, edited by Carol Johnson, Vera Mackie, and Tessa Morris-Suzuki, 131–151. Acton: ANU Press.

Lin, Nan, and Zhaoqing Tu. 1985. "The Next Step in the Sinicization of Sociology" [社会学中国化的下一步]. *Social Sciences Front* [社会科学战线] 4: 133–138.

Liu, Zhongquan. 1983. "On the 'Indigenization' Tendency in Australian Sociology" [浅谈澳大利亚社会学"本土化"倾向]. *Foreign Affairs Studies* [外国问题研究] 2: 100–102.

Marx, Karl, and Friedrich Engels. 2012. *Selected Works of Marx and Engels* [马克思恩格斯选集]. Vol. 1. Beijing: People's Press.

Myrdal, Gunnar. 1957. *Economic Theory and Underdeveloped Regions*. New York: Harper and Row.

Qu, Tongzu. 1937. *Chinese Feudal Society* [中国封建社会]. Shanghai: Commercial Press [商务印书馆].

Roulleau-Berger, Laurence. 2009. "The Pluralism of Chinese Sociology and Its Construction" [中国社会学的多元性及其建构], *Jianghai Academical Journal* [江海学刊] 3:19–21.

Roulleau-Berger, Laurence. 2014. *Out of Western Sociology: Europe in China's Mirror Image* [走出西方的社会学——中国镜像中的欧洲], translated by Hu Yu. Beijing: Social Sciences Academic Press.

Roulleau-Berger, Laurence, and Peilin Li. 2018. *Post-Western Sociology: From China to Europe*. London: Routledge.

Sandstrom, Gregory. 2008. "Global Sociology—Russian Style". *The Canadian Journal of Sociology* 33 (3): 607–630.

Schütz, Alfred. 2011. *The Problem of Social Reality* [社会实在问题], translated by Huo Guiheng. Hangzhou: Zhejiang University Press.

Smith, Harold. 1990. "Sociology and the Study of Non-Western Societies". *The American Sociologist* 21 (2): 150–163.

Su, Guoxun. 2005. *Social Theory and the Modern World* [社会理论与当代现实]. Beijing: Peking University Press.

Sun, Benwen. 2012. *Collected Works of Sun Pen-wen* [孙本文文集]. 10 vols. Beijing: Social Sciences Academic Press.

Sun, Liping. 2005. "Social Transformation: The New Issue on Sociology of Development" [社会转型:发展社会学的新议题]. *Sociological Studies* [社会学研究] 1: 1–24.

Szelényi, Iván, ed. 2010. *Imagination of Neo-Classical Sociology* [新古典社会学的想象力], translated by Lyu Peng. Beijing: Social Sciences Academic Press.

Szelényi, Iván, and Eric Kostello. 1996. "The Market Transition Debate: Toward a Synthesis?" *American Journal of Sociology* 101 (4): 1082–1096.

Tu, Zhaoqing, and Yi-min Lin, eds. 1999. *The Reform and Opening Up of Chinese Society: A Literature Review of Western Sociology* [改革开放与中国社会:西方社会学文献评述]. Hong Kong: Oxford University Press.

Wallerstein, Immanuel, ed. 1997. *Open the Social Sciences: Report of the Gulbenkian Commission on the Restructuring of the Social Sciences* [开放社会科学:重建社会科学报告书], translated by Liu Feng. Beijing: Sanlian Bookstore.

Wang, Dan, and Youmei Li. 2018. "New Knowledge System: 'Contemporary in Change'—The Contemporary Construction of Chinese Transitional Sociology Discourse System" [新知识体系:"变动中的当代"——中国转型社会学话语体系的当代构建]. *Exploration and Contention* [探索与争鸣] 2: 31–38.

Wang, Dong. 2013. "From 'Sinicization' to 'Indigenization': A Survey of the Academic History of the 'Sinicization Movement' of Social Science in Taiwan" [从"中国化"到"本土化":台湾社会科学"中国化运动"的学术史考察]. *Journal of East China Normal University* [华东师范大学学报] 2: 81–91.

Wang, Hui. 2015. *The Rise of Modern Chinese Thought* [现代中国思想的兴起]. 4 vols. Beijing: Sanlian Bookstore.

Wang, Mingming. 2005. *The Historical Dilemma of "Sinicization" of Western Learning* [西学"中国化"的历史困境]. Guilin: Guangxi Normal University Press.

Wang, Ning. 2006. "Localization in Sociology: Problems and Solutions" [社会学的本土化:问题与出路]. *Society* [社会] 26 (6): 6–11.

Wang, Ning. 2017. "Issues of Sociological Localization: Controversy, Crux and Way Out" [社会学本土化议题:争辩、症结与出路]. *Sociological Studies* [社会学研究] 32 (5): 15–38.

Weber, Max. 1968. *Economy and Society*. New York: Bedminster Press.

Wei, Jianwen, and Peilin Li. 2018. "Post-Western Sociology and Contemporary Chinese Sociology" [后西方社会学与当代中国社会学]. *Journal of Beijing Normal University* [北京师范大学学报] 1: 144–151.

Wu, Wenzao. 2010. "General Preface of Sociology Series" [社会学丛刊总序]. In *On the Sinicization of Sociology* [论社会学中国化], edited by Wu Wenzao. Beijing: Commercial Press.

Xie, Lizhong. 2017a. "Post-Western Sociologies: What and Why?" [后西方社会学:是何以及为何]. *Sociological Review* [社会学评论] 5 (2): 39–55.

Xie, Lizhong. 2017b. "On the Types of Localization of Social Sciences—A Case Study of Fei Xiaotong" [论社会科学本土化的类型——以费孝通先生为例]. *Journal of Jiangsu Administrative Institute* [江苏行政学院学报] 1: 42–47.

Xie, Yu. 2008. "Otis Dudley Duncan's Legacy: The Demographic Approach to Quantitative Reasoning in Social Science" [奥迪斯·邓肯的学术成就:社会科学中用于定量推理的人口学方法]. *Society* [社会] 28 (3): 81–105.

Xie, Yu. 2018. "Avoiding the Misleading Trap of Sociology Localization in China" [走出中国社会学本土化讨论的误区]. *Sociological Studies* [社会学研究] 33 (2): 1–13.

Yan, Fu. 1903. *Qunxue yiyan* [群学肄言]. Shanghai: Shanghai Wenming *Compilation and Translation Bureau*.

Yan, Ming. 2010. *The History of Chinese Sociology—A Subject and an Era* [中国社会学史———门学科与一个时代]. Beijing: Tsinghua University Press.

Yang, Haiting, and Min Shi. 2014. "'Kuige' and 'Wenmiao' in Chenggong County of Yunnan during the War of Resistance against Japanese Invasion as two Schools in the Process of Sinicization of Sociology" [抗日战争时期云南呈贡县的"魁阁"与"文庙":社会学中国化进程中的两大学派]. *Journal of Yunnan Ethnical University* [云南民族大学学报] 31 (6): 53–62.

Yang, Kuo-shu. 1989. "The Sinicization of Psychological Research: Levels and Directions" [心理学研究的中国化:层次与方向]. In *Chinese Transmutation* [中国人的蜕变], edited by Yang Kuo-shu. Taipei: Laurel Books.

Yang, Kuo-shu. 1993. "Why Do We Want to Establish an Indigenous Psychology of the Chinese?" [我们为什么要建立中国人的本土心理学？]. *Indigenous Psychological Research* [本土心理学研究] 1: 6–88.

Ye, Qizheng. 1982. "Research on the Direction and Problems of Sinicization from the Existing Character of Sociology in China" [从中国社会学的既有性格论社会学研究中国化的方向与问题]. In *The Sinicization of Social and Behavioral Science Research in China* [社会及行为科学研究中国化], edited by Kuo-shu Yang and Ch'ung-i Wen. Taipei: Institute of Ethnology, Academia Sinica.

Zhai, Xuewei. 2001. *The Logic of Chinese Action* [中国人行动的逻辑]. Beijing: Beijing: Social Sciences Academic Press.

Zhai, Xuewei. 2018. "Is Sociology Localization a Pseudo Problem—Discussing with Xie Yu" [社会学本土化是个伪问题吗——与谢宇商榷]. *Exploration and Contention* [探索与争鸣] 10: 51–59.

Zhang, Yi. 2018. "Sinicization, Discourse Power and the Discourse System in Sociology" [社会学的中国化、话语权与话语体系]. *Journal of Jiangsu Social Sciences* [江苏社会科学] 2: 17–23.

Zhao, Xudong. 2010. "Transcending Existing Traditions of Sociology—A Review of Fei Xiaotong's Reflections on Sociological Method in His Old Age" [超越社会学既有传统——对费孝通晚年社会学方法论思考的再思考]. *Social Sciences in China* [中国社会科学] 6: 138–150.

Zheng, Hangsheng. 2004. "Localization of Sociology and Its Manifestation in China—A Carding and Retrospect on the Sociological Theories with Chinese Characteristics" [社会学本土化及其在中国的表现]. *Journal of Guangxi Ethnical College* [广西民族学院学报] 26 (1): 144–154.

Zhou, Feizhou. 2017. "From 'Aiming to Enrich People' To 'Being Culturally Self-Conscious': Fei Xiaotong's Turn of Thoughts in His Senior Years" [从"志在富民"到"文化自觉":费孝通先生晚年的思想转向]. *Society* [社会] 37 (4): 143–187.

Zhou, Xiaohong. 1994. "Localization and Globalization: The Modern Double Wings of Social Psychology" [本土化和全球化:社会心理学的现代双翼]. *Sociological Studies* [社会学研究] 6: 13–21.

Zhou, Xiaohong. 2002. *The History and Systems of Western Sociology* [西方社会学历史与体系]. Vol. 1. Shanghai: Shanghai People Press.

Zhou, Xiaohong. 2010. "China Studies: Its International Perspectives and Indigenous Significances" [中国研究的国际视野与本土意义]. *Academic Monthly* [学术月刊] 42 (9): 5–13.

Zhou, Xiaohong. 2012. "Sun Benwen and the Chinese Sociology in the First Half of the Twentieth Century" [孙本文与二十世纪上半叶的中国社会学]. *Sociological Studies* [社会学研究] 3:1–22.

Zhou, Xiaohong. 2017. "Field Research in Jiang Village: Culture Consciousness and Sinicization of Social Sciences" [江村调查:文化自觉与社会科学的中国化]. *Sociological Studies* [社会学研究] 32 (1): 1–23.

CHAPTER 9

Proposing a Global Sociology Based on Japanese Theories

Shoji Kōkichi

1   Introduction

I propose a global sociology based on two of Japan's representative sociological theories after World War II. Tamito Yoshida created a general scheme to reorganize all the natural, social, and cultural sciences with a basic concept of information that patterns materials. Muneske Mita independently revealed the basic program of human individuals and societies by critically applying the cosmic worldviews of peoples who still live pre-modernized lives and some evolutionary theories of genes, such as Ricard Dawkins' theory of "selfish genes". Developing Yoshida's and Mita's theories, I propose a theory of global sociology that can be used by any sociologist of any country to analyze one's own society in the world society backed up by the global ecology. Sociology is a program science to disclose programs that construct societies and their global nexus taking root in the earth's ecological system. Discovering endogenous or human selections in programing processes, sociology can propose to reform programs by rejecting bad selections and inserting new ones to make societies better. Thus, it also can become a policy science.

What kind of social theory can we offer to the world, based on Japan's sociology and the Japanese historical and social realities that have been nurturing it?

2   Science, Altruism, and a New Program of Time

First, I will discuss three theoretical propositions from the legacy of postwar Japanese sociology.

2.1   *Sociology as a Program Science*

I will discuss a proposition that the aim of sociology and social science in a wider sense should be to explore programs of social formation. Science, since it appeared in modern Europe, has been trying to find and systematize laws, such as the law of universal gravitation, supposing that there must be laws to regulate various phenomena of nature. In the 20th century, theories of relativity and uncertainty were proposed; the hypothesis of the Big Bang was presented based on theories about the beginning of the cosmos; and scientists have come to think that the cosmos began from the turning-over explosion of extremely condensed particles and that it has been expanding into the present state, creating various celestial bodies through spontaneous symmetry-breaking processes.

In this trend, societies were first supposed to be regulated by laws since societies were born and developed in nature. Many laws were proposed about their development, such as Auguste Comte's law of three states and Karl Marx's laws of productive forces, relations of production, bases, and superstructures. Meanwhile, in the late 19th century in Germany, a claim was made that nature is different from society, especially in a cultural sense, and that the natural sciences should be nomothetic (establishing laws), while the cultural sciences should be idiographic (describing idiosyncratic features).

However, the cultural sciences or social sciences also have nomothetic aspects, while the natural sciences have come to be considered historical, as the cosmos has been disclosed as expanding to a possible end ever since the Big Bang.

In this process, the solar system appeared, the earth was born, on it life emerged, and through a long evolutionary process humans appeared to become the agents of social history. And in the second half of the 20th century, the biological sciences revealed that lives have in their own bodies genes, which provide programs of their birth, growth, and death. On the contrary, the cosmos has no special place where any program of its Big Bang, expansion, and end is stored, and particles, material bodies, and their fields are regulated by laws that are omnipresent or ubiquitous.

While programs of lives in general are written basically by DNA, signals like traffic lights, programs of humans, and human societies are written not only by biological signals but also by symbols such as language, which has made it possible for complicated cultures to develop. Clearly this has enabled human societies to flower variously.

In this context, a Japanese sociologist named Tamito Yoshida recognized the role of programs in the processes of biological and social evolution. Humankind has been developing its social history with symbol-based programs, which have developed on the basis of biological signal-based programs in individual bodies, by making societies interact with each other against the backgrounds of the biological world and of nature in general. Therefore, Yoshida claimed that the aim of sociology and social science should be to explore programs and their developments and that it has been pseudo-scientific to investigate laws of the market, human relations, power, and such following the model of the natural sciences.

From this standpoint, Yoshida stressed the necessity to make it clear that the aim of the biological sciences also should be to reveal the programs of biological evolution and that the aim of the natural and cosmic sciences should be redefined as the bases of the biological, social, and cultural sciences. He even proposed that we should perform a "Second Scientific Revolution" to reorganize all sciences under the basic idea of program science, not of a nomothetic one (Yoshida 1990a, 1990b, 1991, 2013a, 2013b).

Although we have to discuss more about the points of the second scientific revolution, I will here go further by accepting the proposition that the aim of sociology should be to explore programs of social formation.

2.2 Altruism Overcoming Egoism

The second proposition is, if we use the concept of "program", that there must be a program of altruism for overcoming egoism in social evolution, based on the evolution of lives in general. Since the evolutionist theory emerged in the middle of the 19th century, it has been supposed that the basic laws (programs) should be those of natural selection and mutation. Species, as ensembles of individuals, have made themselves stronger by virtue of the better ones who have survived the struggle of existence. Mutated individuals survive if they are fitter and stronger and make the species stronger. Thus, biological evolution has come to generate the birth of humankind.

Genes are egoistic in the sense that they make themselves stronger in order to make individuals and species stronger, by excluding weaker genes through their death, as Richard Dawkins' theory of selfish genes has claimed (Dawkins 1989).

However, this theory is contradictory, or at least one-sided, with regard to the realities of biological evolution. Beings especially animals, must increase their descendants in order to survive and to protect them in growing. As the higher animals bear fewer offspring at one time, parents must protect children meticulously. Moreover, as higher animals become more social, they protect descendants more and more socially.

As for humankind, we do not need many words to explicate their culture. Since the age of hordes and bands, people have lived in smaller collectivities of smaller families and survived by protecting their children, no matter the groups to which they have belonged. This primitive culture was maintained in processes from segmentary to organic societies in the Durkheimian sense, and this became even more important in connection with private property.

Another Japanese sociologist, Yusuke Maki, revealed that already in the primitive stages of our history the human's ego consciousness or egoism was already programmed as incorporating altruism (Maki 2012a). Humans organized tribes; tribes warred against each other; and kingdoms were built and integrated into huge empires. Even in these processes males and females loved each other and had children and nurtured them meticulously. No society can survive without descendants, however proud it is of victories in sanguinary wars.

Human history is full of terrible wars, even—or much more so—after becoming civilized, but even in passing through wars infinite loves have been made which have enabled humankind to survive. In modern times, wars have been more and more organized, with poison gasses and nuclear arms invented by the leading sciences. This has brought humankind to the brink of extermination and has made people realize that any total war between states would be impossible if we want to survive. We have come to think that there are no ways to progress other than by forming a society that exists beyond nation states.

Japan was barely allowed to build a nation state amidst the world of the 19th century, in which the whole world was being colonized. Japan forced Taiwan, the Korean peninsula, China, and Southeast Asian countries to be hugely damaged by Japan's colonialist and imperialist wars against the big European and American powers. And Japan finally surrendered unconditionally, after losing all its colonies, after having almost all of its cities carpet-bombed and after having Hiroshima and Nagasaki thoroughly destroyed by the atomic bombs that were the first used in the history of humankind. Article 9 of the Japanese Constitution, stating the eternal renunciation of wars as means to resolve international conflicts, has manifested as an altruist program of social formation. This was the first such instance in the history of humankind, and it calls for a condition that we all will have to realize sooner or later.

2.3 Revision of the Program of Modern Time as Infinite Monotonous Ticking

The third proposition is that the most serious program to form the modern world is the monotonous time advancing from the infinite past to the infinite future, "time arrow", that spurs us constantly to better futures and simultaneously nullifies the passing present as evenly pushed away to the past (Maki 2013b). According to Maki, many societies have had more or less "repetitive time" programs to come and go from present to past and to future, as many anthropological surveys have shown. Among them appeared the Hebraist program of "line segment time", which was begun by God's Creation of the World and would be finished by his Last Judgment, while there was the Hellenist program of "circled time", where many stories were developed between gods and humans who would go and come back from the world of the living and that of the dead.

The modern world has created a program of "straight-line time" by destroying the circled line program with negation of the polytheist world on the one hand and by kicking away both the beginning and the end of the world to an infinite past and future with negation of the monotheism on the other. According to this straight-line time, we are able to have hope, since we have a future whenever, but this world is finally naught because everything attained is nullified immediately.

Nietzsche's methodological nihilism was effective in liberating humans from old, large fetters like Christianity, but it plunges us into the world of naught unless we repeat the creation of new values and new worlds as "Superhumans". This is why the modern humans, like ones possessed, have repeatedly changed the world by researching and developing science and technology and by applying these things in innovations in various industries.

Societies that have had rich worlds of life by mixing present, past, and future by their repetitive time programs, have been alienated to outside of this straight-line time program by refusing new commercial goods and other things on the one hand, and have been alienated into this straight time program itself by reluctantly accepting it to survive in the modern world on the other. Alienation from the time and into it!

Infinite virtual space has been created under this straight-line time program by accumulating enormous communication networks, which have been built by the intellectual technology that has made possible immediate communications between any places on the globe. We do not know yet what kind of impact this virtual space has been putting on the straight-line time program and if any new time program has been emerging.

As seen before, we might say that modern science has been reviving a new "line segment" time program by polishing its theory of the beginning and the end of the cosmos. Then, we have to see what kind of time program will fit the altruist tendency that most of contemporary societies have no choice but to ride on for surviving in this drastically changing world.

3 From the World of the Cold War to Citizens' Cooperation in a Global Society

3.1 *Analysis of Japan's National Social Formation to a Sociology of World History*

Under the impact of these propositions, I, as a Japanese sociologist, have been asking since the 1960s what a society is, and in what size it is grasped most appropriately. I started from a study to grasp Japanese society as a whole. I studied analyses and controversies about Japan's capitalist development conducted before and after World War II by economists, historians, and others. I tried to compare and integrate their Marxist methods of social analysis with the sociological theories of Émile Durkheim, Max Weber, Talcott Parsons, and others in order to make an appropriate analytical framework to inquire into a national social formation. And I really tried to analyze Japan's historical development, focusing on causes and effects of its high-speed economic growth performed in the 1950s–1970s (Shoji 1975a, 1977).

While this was to some extent fruitful, I actually realized that a national social formation could not be sufficiently analyzed in itself, since it has been developing in connection with other societies, especially a huge society, the American society, as that of one of the Big Powers.

In the first half of the 1970s, I traveled around Soviet and East-European societies twice, spending 2 months in each. During the second trip, I got the news that China had raised its new worldview that the Socialist Camp had been already substantially taken apart and that China would belong to the Third World if the world consisted of three worlds, the first centered by the United States, the second led by the Soviet Union, and the third of developing countries. Under this impact, I wrote a paper subtitled "Sociology of the World History" where I tried to get a projection of what kind of impact China's view would have on American sociologists' "convergence theory" of American and Soviet societies as industrial societies, on the socialist development theory of the Soviet and most of the Marxist ideologues, and on various attitudes of the theorists and leaders of the third world countries (Shoji 1975b). The conclusion was that the industrial and socialist views would both have to be changed and that we would be obligated to build a worldview with a new sociology which would be able to see a larger society which comprehends not only national societies but also ideological and political camps of liberal (capitalist), socialist, and third world nations.

Just after publishing this paper, I stayed in Cambridge, Massachusetts, USA, for 2 years, 1975–1977, to study and conduct a sort of participatory observation of American democracy. Having lost its self-confidence as a result of the Watergate scandal and the first defeat in its war in Vietnam, American society was even in a bit of a sadistic mood, such as that shown in the movie "Taxi Driver", but I felt American democracy had been rooted in people's everyday life, and I even faced discussions on "not only equality of opportunities but also of results", which might be more socialist than ideological statements by the actual socialist ideologues (Shoji 1980).

3.2 Aggravation of Environmental Disruption and "Bodily" Social Problems

Returning home in the late 1970s and the early 1980s, I proposed a concept of world society and began to funnel all my efforts into how to comprehend it. There were mega-facts, such as the crisis of nuclear war, the mass poverty caused by the North–South disparity, the environmental disruption spreading over frontiers, and the population explosion in developing countries. In the United States, Ronald Reagan, having been elected as president in 1980, hammered out so-called Strategic Defense Initiatives with a hard anti-Soviet line, and this stimulated anti-nuclear movements in Europe, which was supposed to be a major field of possible nuclear wars. The economic disparity between the Northern advanced countries and the Southern developing countries was still huge, and this had been pushing to the fore things like famines caused by mass poverty, and human rights violations at the hands of military dictators forcing policies of nation-building and economic growth.

Environmental disruption was aggravated in American, European, and Japanese advanced societies that had accomplished postwar economic growth to produce "affluent societies". Especially in Japan, which had been called "a pollution-advanced society" in the 1960s and the 1970s, some enterprises began to disseminate environmental disruption by dumping pollutants into the open sea and by exporting polluting factories to developing countries after the internal situation was improved to some extent through various residents' protests and court judgments in favor of those residents. Environmental disruption began to be transferred over national frontiers. The United States was the original source of agricultural pollution symbolized by the "Silent Spring", and the acid raining over frontiers was aggravating pollution in Europe, where many countries bordered each other in an area that was not so vast.

Moreover, population explosion became more and more serious in developing countries where the idea and methods of birth control, let alone feminist movements, were not widely spread. The population explosion, as it increased and mobilized a number of people, brought into relief various problems of discrimination concerning race, ethnicity, sex, handicaps, and sexuality. I called them bodily social problems.

3.3 Communality, Stratification, Social Systems, and Ecological Restrictions

On the other hand, I became interested in and translated into Japanese Charles Smith's *A Critique of Sociological Reasoning*, where he tried to develop a typology of sociological theory into three basic ones of community theories like Durkheim's, of class society theories like Marx's and Weber's, and of social system theory like Parson's (Smith 1979). Based on this idea, I only characterized world society in the following three ways. First, it was actually made a negative community for humankind to survive, however reluctant, by the crisis of nuclear wars. Nevertheless, second, it had to be remained as a huge class or stratified society divided by the North–South disparity that the United States and the Soviet Union had been competing to utilize for their interests. Moreover, third, the United Nations was still too weak as an organization to overview the world as a social system to prevent any nuclear war, reduce the huge disparity, and integrate nation-states with the appropriate power and prestige.

More than that, I thought that we were not able to deal with environmental problems sociologically with these three types of theories and that we needed to develop a theory to analyze these problems on the basis of pollution studies in Japan and a new ecological paradigm (NEP) proposed by some American sociologists. Environmental problems would be generated by societies who, of their own will, would cut some part away from the ecological system and would throw waste out of their space. This would mean that in the world where each nation-state has its own sovereignty and where any coordinating organization has fairly weak power and prestige, waste would be accumulated everywhere in the global ecological system to aggravate more and more environmental problems. In this sense it should be realized that a human society must be originally restricted by the environment or ecology, so that all societies should realize that they were all ecologically restricted.

Since human bodies clearly belonged to the global ecological system, bodily social problems, stated before, should also be those of ecological restrictions. While environmental problems in general were those of external ecological restrictions, bodily social problems should be those of internal ecological restrictions because they were problems of interrelations and communication between human bodies constructing societies. In order to liberate human beings as social existence, societies should accept and internalize different ascriptions, such as race, ethnicity, sex, age, handicaps, and sexuality, which individuals could not change by their own will.

3.4   *From the Concept of World Society to That of Global Society*
In the 1970s and 1980s, the world rapidly changed while I was trying to comprehend the reality of world society and was conducting surveys with my colleagues on how Japanese sovereign people were engendering their consciousness about world society, even if they were not using the same word. Adopting a policy of Reform and Opening-up in 1978, China began to get into a pattern of rapid economic growth under the "socialist market economy" while

keeping the same political system led by the Communist Party. Although being unable to change the economic system centered on the state planning agency, the Soviet Union narrowly opened a road through its remaining democracy for Gorbachev to conduct reforms called perestroika and glasnost, but it was too late for him to stop Eastern European systems from becoming disorganized just after the end of the Cold War, and the system of Soviet Union itself collapsed in 1991.

Adding to the claim for the borderless world had already been spread, the social systems resisting the market economy actually disappeared as soon as the Soviet and Eastern European systems collapsed. Through the whole processes of separation and independence for various parts of the Soviet Union as nation-states, it was made clear that ex-socialist societies, including Russia, had been much poorer than imagined so that the actual environmental disruption was much more serious than had been thought. It was also made clear that ex-socialist societies had not even been able to claim constructing the second world that would compete against the first world centered by the United States, as China's assertion of three worlds had appealed, but rather they were more or less close to developing nations. In the United States, which became the only superpower, and rapidly elsewhere in the world, claims and theories of globalization began to be spread (Shoji 2004).

I have been insisting on the concept of world society for two reasons. First, I would like to keep connections with Wallerstein's theory of the world system (Wallerstein 1974, 1980, 1989, 1995, 2011), and second, I did not want to incorporate my theory into such theories as Meadows' world dynamics (Meadows et al. 1972). Backed up by the Club of Rome, they would rather heatedly discuss the dispersion of environmental disruption and the exhaustion of resources no matter how different social systems and cultures were and no matter how economically rich or poor people lived there in the world. However, global environmental disruption worsened mercilessly through the 1980s and the 1990s, and it interested the whole world such that it became one of the leading political issues, especially after the Global Summit held in Rio de Janeiro in 1992.

Based on these changes, I rearranged basic concepts as following: a world society is defined as a society consisting of all the people living in the world, and as far as the world society locates itself in, and considers itself as outside of, the global ecological system with its collective will, the world society is in the global environment. The global environment would be polluted and disrupted as the world society sees it as its surroundings, exploits what is needed and the desired from there, and dumps garbage and all that is needless and harmful into there through economic and social activities. Now, the human society should redefine itself as a global society by internalizing as much of the ecological system as possible. That is to say, the world society should be leveled up to a global society, which should be defined as a social and ecological system including ecological systems of plants and animals that are needed for the survival of the humankind.

3.5 Toward a Theory of Global Society and Citizens' Cooperation

If we define citizens as the people who run their own society through democracy, a world society is run by world citizens and a global society is run by global citizens. Global citizens should cooperate in order to manage any crisis of nuclear war, to resolve globally extended disparities, not only the North–South gap, to stop the dispersion of environmental disruption, and to liberate all human bodies living on earth. Thinking along these lines, I published my book *Global Society and Citizens' Cooperation* in 1999 (Shoji 1999).

4 Debates on "Empire", Logic of Social Formation, and Civil Society

4.1 The True Meaning of "Empire" Theory and America's "War on Terrorism"

Michael Hardt and Antonio Negri's Empire was published in 2000, just at the end of the 20th century. They presented a truly interesting hypothesis about the structure of the world after the end of Cold War and the collapses of Soviet and Eastern European social systems. To my understanding, the point of this theory is as follows. If we use Michel Foucault's method of bio-political production analysis, the ruling system, which arose from the United States to cover the whole world, is a system like an "Empire" which has the imperative to ask all the people to take and follow an American way of life. Bio-political production means to make our bodies behave in a way through accepting a common lifestyle, like sexuality, to construct a society from the basis and to rule it and the whole world by accumulating minute power exercises while they are noticed by very few people.

If I say this more concretely to my own understanding, we eat food like hamburgers with drinks like Coca-Cola; we wear suits and ties formally and T-shirts and jeans informally; we live in a uniform house, like a Holiday Inn room, which is almost the same all over the world; we have sex like in the movies seen in hotel rooms all over the world; we communicate by personal computers and smart phones; and we fly to any city in the world and drive a rental car to go to any special place. We have been accustomed almost unconsciously to this sort of lifestyle and through it we are forced to conform to "Freedom and Democracy" in the American sense. The concept of sovereignty, which has been formed and polished in a pretty long history, is ineffective under this universal rule.

This hypothesis raised lots of debates around the world because it used as a key term "empire", which we have long used in various senses. If the "Empire" in this hypothesis meant a system as I understood it, it would be extremely important as a ruling mode of the global society. However, as a matter of fact, a way of understanding it simply as an American way of world rule by military forces was spread, since the simultaneous terrorist attacks (September 11) in New York and Washington, DC, in 2001, the year after the book was published, and because President George W. Bush, who had been elected by an extremely narrow margin the year before, hammered out a "war on terrorism" and sent armies to Afghanistan and Iraq.

In 2008 the first black person was elected as president of the United States, huge changes were expected for both the United States and the world. However, Barack Obama only succeeded in some reforms, such as those involving the health insurance system, due to conservative reactions arising from grassroots groups and because Congress was at the time governed by Republican conservatives. In Afghanistan, Iraq, and Syria, situations were rather worsened by half-hearted military operations of the United States so that the worst terrorist groups, such as Islamic State, ran rampant.

4.2 Logic of Social Formation and Empires as Social Systems

In this situation, being pressed to polish and develop my theory of global society and citizens' cooperation, I have been trying to develop it into a new theory of global society and sovereign people's cooperation.

First, it is important to grasp the basic program to construct a society. I pointed out three basic ways to see a society: seeing it as a community, as a class society or a stratified society, and as a system. Since then, I have already considered this not as a typology to observe societies but as a theory of phases of a society because all societies have these three aspects. That is to say, a society is an over-determination (*surdetermination* if we use Althusser's term) of these three moments—communality, stratification, and system. A society seems to be as a community if its aspect of communality is quite strong; a class society if its stratification is strong and solid; and a social system if its system-ness is strong and manifest. If so, the problem is to find how these three moments over-determine each other.

All societies are at first communalities, as members gather and try to live together. Although in them there is some natural division of labor based on sex and age and even some latent rule, they are not recognized under collective consciousness with equality first. Then, if societies of this sort conflict with each other and if the stronger annexes the weaker, the leaders of the stronger come out while those of the weaker are excluded, and the followers of the stronger are put above on the followers of the weaker and such. Thus, stratification becomes manifest and consciousness of inequality spreads. A class society is a society that is stratified more highly and solidly on a wider communality through conflicts of communities or rather tribes.

Moreover, as a class society becomes larger, it is not maintained and developed unless systematized with some integration apparatuses, because heightened consciousness of inequality conflicts with original consciousness of equality. The first integration apparatus is religion. Since people have already developed communication with language and others, they make some stories about reasons why a higher stratification has been built on a widened communality. For example, gods of communities have been in conflict to get a result that the one has beaten others, or another that they have compromised each other. Then, the people persuade themselves by talking and dancing out religious stories in order to maintain and develop their class society. Religion is a series of actions of symbolism of this kind.

However, since these symbolic actions become insufficient as a society grows larger, they organize standing armies to defend themselves from foreign enemies, initiate a tax collection system to maintain themselves and others, and build a bureaucracy to govern the whole society. A state emerges. First, there are instances where a founder or a leader of the religion becomes a head of the state, but as the state grows the head becomes independent as a monarch who runs the bureaucracy with his private properties (patrimonial bureaucracy). The religious leader, keeping his or her status as a nominal speaker of the transcendental, authorizes and follows the monarch, the real ruler of the secular world. On the other hand, as inter-affection and exchanges of goods and services expand markets which jeopardize the basis of society with people's needs, desires, and mobility, the monarch tries to concentrate them under his or her control simultaneously to collect taxes. A city emerges. Since in cities people exchange not only agricultural goods but also all other goods and services, including ideas, the monarch tries to control cities so that the state is morphologically organized as a complex of urban and rural areas. A civilization is born.

Enriched from the bottom by the development of an economy mediated by markets, a civilization starts to try to disseminate culture guided by more and more universalized religion. Being driven by ideas from above and by interests from below (*Idee und Interesse*), a civilization enlarges the state as the center of politics, and expands and pluralizes cities so that the society in a morphological sense is more and more complex and enriched. Monarchies come into conflict with each other, annex or are annexed, and grow into an empire led by an emperor or an empress who is sanctified by the religion. As is widely known, human history was a history of conflicts of empires until the collapse of China's Chin Dynasty and that of Turkey's Ottoman Empire in the 20th century (details in Shoji 2016).

4.3 Formation of Civil Society Systems, Conflicts of Nation-States, and World Wars

Thus, we have explained programs to build empires. Next, we have to explore programs to form an entirely different society, a civil society. Generally speaking, since cities as centers of empires were strictly controlled, citizens were not able to liberate themselves. In the poleis of ancient Greece, where the rule of empires was loosened, citizens were relatively liberated to create and develop literature, philosophy, and democracy, but they did not try to produce and reproduce their way of life, so they were swallowed up by conflicting empires. At last in 11th-century Europe, in cities under a relatively weak empire, citizens began to exchange their own products and agricultural goods from neighbor villages, and they extended their activities to long-distance trade.

Citizens found a joint-stock company as their own way to build and run enterprises and they began to influence churches and monarchs with their stockpiled wealth. Making cities as their bases, citizens extended and controlled the market through their expanding enterprises, and they promoted the Reformation and resisted monarchs with their wealth. Then, taking over the monarchy regimes through their civic revolutions, citizens began to develop democracy and to relativize religions so that they finally opened up a road to atheism. In these processes, they developed science and technology and incorporated them into the industrial revolution so as to globalize the market where they put all kinds of merchandise to change the whole world.

The point here is that citizens, although globalizing the market constantly, succeeded only in building nation-states as imagined communities, because they were bound in traditions of monarchies and by national languages engendered in cities (Anderson 1991; Yoshimoto 1968). While not only the market but science and technology became increasingly globalized, citizens gathered and were condensed in nation-states for geopolitical reasons, and they were drawn into life-and-death battles between each other for the hegemony of the world.

While empires were basically pre-capitalist social formations, imperialism was a way to disguise an empire which nation-states based on capitalist economies took to make false shows to struggle with each other. Becoming imperialist in this sense, British, French, German, American, Russian, and

Japanese nations divided the world into their colonies, desperately struggled for re-division to trigger World War I and II, and finally divided the world into the American-centered capitalist camp and the Soviet-centered socialist camp. The world in the 1960s and the 1970s that I made as the starting point of my global sociology was the world just in the Cold War between these two camps that was bringing humankind to the brink of extermination through their nuclear military buildup races (details in Shoji 2016).

5 Theory of a Global Society with Inclusive Sovereign People

5.1 Pre-sovereign People (Subalterns) and De-sovereignized People (Multitude)

As the Cold War was ended with the collapse of Soviet and Eastern European systems, and because I thought to be able to inquire into worsening global environmental problems and bodily social problems as those of externalization or alienation of the environment and human bodies in processes of social system formations, I conceived of global citizenship studies as developments of my global sociology in the 21st century, and I tried to supply a basic perspective for social movements on various issues (Shoji 2009a). But I came up against a fundamental problem in following three that I have raised in the present essay.

Postcolonialism was already spreading all over the world in the 1980s and the 1990s. Intellectuals of newly emerging nations that had worked to liberate themselves from colonialism learned the most advanced theories in the West and pointed out serious problems that had not been recognized by even ultra-modernist thinkers in 1970s Europe. With Foucault's discourse analysis, Edward Said first brought into relief an Orientalism that has been flowing in the background of even advanced thoughts in the West. And moreover, it was more shocking that a post-colonialist, Gayatori C. Spivak, brought to light the deepest structure of our contemporary world with Jacques Derrida's deconstruction method, which might go over Foucault's one.

Spivak, as an Indian woman, pointed out the massive existence of *satis* who had not been allowed to speak out by themselves, although Western intellectuals and even native leaders mentioned them. Calling them subalterns by using Antonio Gramsci's term, she raised the question of whether we succeeded in comprehending our contemporary world while neglecting this massive layer of people at the bottom of Indian society (Spivak 1988). There are amazing masses, including these satis, of pre-sovereign people, even if they nominally have the right to vote, in India, which introduced democracy by general election after independence.

On the other hand, Hardt and Negri pointed out, in their *Empire*, the existence of the multitudes who are mobilized and made to be wandering around the world to get jobs and to live, by the enormous pressures of the bio-political production. Most subalterns might be included in these multitudes. However, I would rather make a distinction between the subalterns Spivak pointed out and the multitudes in the sense that they were once given sovereignty but are made substantially non-sovereign people by insufficient election systems or by one-sided politics by presidents or prime ministers who are elected through more or less inadequate elections, even in advanced societies. I prefer this use of the term "multitudes" to close up the people who are thus deprived of sovereignty, actually de-sovereignized.

Moreover, there are still some countries, like China, Vietnam, and Cuba, that maintain a people's democracy or one-party politics where people vote to simply recognize a candidate the party has recommended. In this case, people are not actually sovereignized even though they are proclaimed as sovereign people in the constitution, because we are not able to ensure the people's will is reflected in the government. Then, we have to realize that there is still a huge number of people who are considered pre-sovereign or de-sovereignized in our contemporary global society, and we must realize that democracy should be a hereafter task and that it should be repetitively refreshed.

5.2 *Political and Economic Sovereign People: From Citizens to Peoples*

On the other hand, since the end of the 20th century, I have committed myself to leading Japan's university cooperative associations and have contacted similar organizations in Asia, Europe, and the United States, seeing many people of cooperatives (cooperators) in Japan and the world. In Japan there are about 220 university cooperatives, and their members number 1.5 million altogether. Although professors and staff members are joining, the overwhelming majority is composed of students, graduate students, and foreign students. There are many university cooperatives in Asian countries, but most of them are composed of staff members, while students are not necessarily the majority of university cooperatives. While there are some university cooperatives in the United States and Canada, governmental and semi-governmental organizations are providing student support in their restaurants, dormitories, and scholarships in major European countries. And Japan's National Federation of University Cooperative Associations (NFUCA) has been a member of the International Cooperative Alliances (ICA) and has been making many contacts with its member cooperatives, not only in Japan but also around the world (Shoji 2008b, 2015, 2016a).

The first feeling I had through these activities is that the global society is being democratized not only in that more and more of its members have been trying to become its sovereign people in the political sense, but also in that cooperatives are enterprises of these sovereign people in the economic sense. In other words, the sovereign people are economic as well as political, and in many countries workers and peasants, who have gained sovereignty through the general election system, have been trying to build their own societies substantially as economically sovereign people, with cooperative activities as such. And this makes a clear contrast to the fact that in the history of Europe, citizens gained sovereignty in political revolutions with the economic forces they had accumulated in their own enterprises.

Moreover, the decision-making method of cooperatives is, if we are honest to the Cooperative Principles proclaimed in 1995, a one-person-one-vote principle against the one-share-one-vote principle of joint stock companies and corporations as their developed forms where money prevails. Since many NGOs and NPOs as well as cooperatives are engaging in social and economic activities, the global society hereafter will be built by their principally non-profit enterprises so that it is run by political sovereign people on the basis of economic sovereign people's enterprise activities.

Second, I have noticed at the same time that the people of agricultural and fishery cooperatives in Japan and those of cooperatives in general in Asian countries are not easily accepting the word "citizen" and are feeling there is something wrong in its nuances. As a matter of fact, from the standpoint of the people in agricultural, fishery, and mountain villages and of most of those in developing countries, citizens are people living in cities and far from these countryside people, in spite of living with the food and other things these country people produce. Especially with regard to people from the ex-colonial and ex-subordinate countries, it was citizens who selfishly built nation-states, came with their overwhelming military forces, and put the people under the colonial and subordinate rule.

In Europe, America, and urban Japan, the concept of citizens as the sovereign people is conventional, since it is well known that citizens took over sovereignty from the kings through bourgeois revolutions, establishing the principle that the sovereign reigns but does not rule. Intelligent people do not necessarily neglect this historical fact, even in country villages and in ex-colonial and ex-subordinate countries. But, for most of the subalterns and the multitudes seen before, citizens have been the rulers of the world as a matter of fact, and this recognition coincides with the historical processes that citizens, overtaking sovereignty in their revolutions, continued the rule of colonies and subordinate nations even if it was monarchs and their followers who had initiated the European voyage of so-called discovery.

6 Formation of a Global Society with Its Global Sovereign People

Through the 20th century, almost all of the subordinate and colonized people liberated themselves and initiated their own nation-building, although most of them had been disturbed for a while by military and/or development dictatorships.

Then, my fourth proposition is that the sovereign people of contemporary global society is peoples all around the world, including those of ex-colonial and ex-subordinate countries, and that we have to explore, reinforce, and concretize, in going over theories of civil society until now, the programs of democratization of each society and the global society itself from the standpoints of sovereign peoples all over the world, including subalterns and multitudes. The principles are altruism, no war, and public welfare, such as those in the Japanese Constitution, and we have to revise the modern time program of infinite monotonous nicking.

If we look back to history, was the modern world system building inaugurated by European powers' launch into the world and was it conducted by colonizing or forcing subordination upon the rest of the world? Did citizens, taking over sovereignty through bourgeois revolutions, become by themselves the agents of colonialism instead of the old rulers, and did citizens become imperialist on these colonialist bases so as to trigger two World Wars and the US and Soviet Cold War that brought humankind to the brink of extermination? If so, citizens should first establish their own correct view of history, apologize to the people upon whom citizens forced sacrifices in their processes to become affluent, and cooperate and support the nation-building and social development of these people as much as they can.

Japan has responsibility regarding the colonization of Taiwan and the Korean Peninsula, and it tried to colonize first the northeast part and then the entirety of China, as well as Southeast Asian countries. The Japanese people are responsible for having invaded, colonized, and subordinated these people, even though the Japanese people themselves were not the real sovereign people under the Constitution of the Japanese Empire proclaimed in 1889. After the new Constitution became effective in 1948, the Japanese became truly sovereign people and have been repeatedly censured because the Japanese government has not been consistent in reflecting itself and in apologizing to Korean, Chinese, and other Asian peoples. The Japanese sovereign people should have a correct view of history and should be consistent in taking reflective attitudes to apologize to neighbor nations for having seriously damaged them. Only through taking these attitudes can the Japanese sovereign people appeal to European and American nations to seriously reflect upon the modern history of colonialism and imperialism, and to help and support the nation-building and social formation of ex-subordinate and ex-colonial countries.

Summing up, it is not enough to conceive our global society as a global civil society. As far as citizens go, whether they realized it or not, as the agents of the colonial rule of the world by European, American, and Japanese imperialist nations, they were not yet qualified to proclaim Liberty, Equality, and Fraternity such that their civil societies were not sufficiently democratic to be called democratic societies. The true democratic society should be built both in each country and on the earth by making each person and all the people really sovereign people.

As for revision of the modern time program, we can start, for example, from scrupulous considerations regarding those who are weaker in the body. Racial minorities may not be sufficiently educated; women may be inappropriate for performing heavy physical labor; children and the elderly need various elements of care; the handicapped should be cared according to the degree and quality of their handicap: and sexual minorities should be treated depending on their specific character. It takes more time and expense to consider and take care of those who are weaker in body, but it should be an actual revision of the modern time program to have these considerations and cares permeate everywhere into the social system, however time-consuming and costly they are. Along these lines, we should be able to conceive and perform various reforms of our society if we repetitively remind ourselves that Liberty should be always with Equality and Fraternity in a truly democratic society.

References

Japanese Sources

Maki, Y. 真木悠介. 2012a. *Comparative Sociology of Time*『定本真木悠介著作集Ⅱ 時間の比較社会学』岩波書店.

Maki, Y. 真木悠介. 2012b. *The Origin of Ego*『定本真木悠介著作集Ⅲ 自我の起源』岩波書店.

Shoji, K. 庄司興吉. 1975a. *An Introductory Analysis of the History of Social Sciences in Modern Japan*『現代日本社会科学史序説』法政大学出版局.

Shoji, K. 庄司興吉. 1975b. "World Sociology in the Nuclear Age!"「核時代の世界社会学」. *Annals of Social Science Researches* 8『社会科学研究年報』8, 合同出版.

Shoji, K. 庄司興吉. 1977. *Theory of Contemporarization and Contemporary Society*『現代化と現代社会の理論』東京大学出版会.
Shoji, K. 庄司興吉. 1980. *Social Change and Its Agents*『社会変動と変革主体』東京大学出版会.
Shoji, K. ed. 庄司興吉編. 1986. *Structures and Dynamics of World Society*『世界社会の構造と動態』法政大学出版局.
Shoji, K. 庄司興吉. 1989. *Over-managed Societies and World Society*『管理社会と世界社会』東京大学出版会.
Shoji, K. 庄司興吉. 1999. *Global Society and Citizens' Cooperation*『地球社会と市民連携:激性期の国際社会学へ』有斐閣.
Shoji, K., ed. 庄司興吉編. 2004. *America and Asia in Informational Social Changes*『情報社会変動のなかのアメリカとアジア』彩流社.
Shoji, K. 庄司興吉編著. 2009a. *Creating Global Citizenship Studies*『地球市民学を創る:地球社会の危機と変革のなかで』東信堂.
Shoji, K. 庄司興吉. 2009b. *University Reform and University Cooperatives*『大学改革と大学生協:グローバル化の激流のなかで』丸善プラネット.
Shoji, K. 庄司興吉. 2015. *Student Support and University Cooperatives*『学生支援と大学生協:民主協同社会をめざして』丸善プラネット.
Shoji, K. 庄司興吉. 2016a. *Toward a Cooperative Society of Sovereign People*『主権者の協同社会へ:新時代の大学教育と大学生協』東信堂.
Shoji, K. 庄司興吉. 2016b. *Social Analysis by Sovereign People Themselves*『主権者の社会認識:自分自身と向き合う』東信堂.
Yonemoto, S. 米本昌平. 1994. *What Is the Problem of Global Environment?*『地球環境問題とは何か』岩波新書.
Yoshida, T. 吉田民人. 1990a. *Informational Science of Self-Organization*『自己組織性の情報科学:エヴォルーショニストのウィーナー的自然観』新曜社.
Yoshida, T. 吉田民人. 1990b. *Theory of Information and Self-Organization*『情報と自己組織性の理論』東京大学出版会.
Yoshida, T. 吉田民人. 1991. *Theory of Autonomy and Property Structure*『主体性と所有構造の理論』東京大学出版会.
Yoshida, T. 吉田民人. 2013a. *Social Informatics and Its Development*『社会情報学とその展開』勁草書房.
Yoshida, T. 吉田民人. 2013b. *Theory of Program Science*『近代科学の情報論的転回:プログラム科学論』勁草書房.
Yoshimoto, T. 吉本隆明. 1968. *On Communal Fantasy*『共同幻想論』筑摩書房新社.

English Sources

Anderson, B. 1991. *Imagined Communities*. Revised edition. Verso.
Dawkins, R. (1976) 1989. *The Selfish Gene*. Oxford: Oxford University Press.
Hardt, M., and A. Negri. 2000. *Empire*. Cambridge, MA: Harvard University Press.

Meadows, D.H., et al. 1972. *The Limits to Growth: A Report for the Club of Rome's Project on the Predicament of Mankind*. Newgate Press.

Said, E.W. 1978. *Orientalism*. New York, NY: Vintage Books.

Smith, C.W. 1979. *A Critique of Sociological Reasoning*. Basil Blackwell.

Spivak, G.C. 1988. "Can the Subaltern Speak?" In *Marxism and the Interpretation of Culture*, edited by S. Nelson and L. Crossberg. Champaign-Urbana, IL: University of Illinois Press.

Wallerstein, I. 1974. *The Modern World System I: Capitalist Agriculture and the Origins of the European World-Economy in the Sixteenth Century*. The Academic Press.

Wallerstein, I. 1980. *The Modern World System II: Mercantilism and the Consolidation of the European World-Economy, 1600–1750*. The Academic Press.

Wallerstein, I. 1989. *The Modern World System III: The Second Era of Great Expansion of Capitalist World-Economy, 1730–1840s*. The Academic Press.

Wallerstein, I. 1995. *Historical Capitalism with Capitalist Civilization*. Verso.

Wallerstein, I. 2011. *The Modern World-System IV: Centrist Liberalism Triumphant, 1789–1914*. Berkeley: University of California Press.

CHAPTER 10

De-Westernization or Re-Easternization: Towards Post-Western Conceptualization and Theorization in the Sociology of Korea

Lim Hyun-Chin

1   Introduction

When talking about "The End of European History", in 1955, a global historian named Geoffrey Barraclough (1955: 220, 204) declared

> every age needs its own view of history; and to-day we need a new view of the European past, adapted to the new perspectives in which the old Europe stands in a new age of global politics and global civilization ... it does not mean that European history will come to a full stop; it means rather that it will cease to have historical significance.

Barraclough's notion of the fall of Europe includes a view that was not obvious at the time but is now widely shared. He recognized with admirable clarity that history had begun to operate on "a global plane, which only a universal point of view can elucidate" (1962: 91). His comment implies that a Eurocentric social science approach has to be replaced by a historiography with "a global perspective" (92) and that "the political environment of today is world-wide" because "our global age knows neither geographical nor cultural frontiers" (99f.). The final decades of the 20th century have validated Barraclough's insights and re-provincialized Europe (Chakrabarty 2000).

The profound historical change has drawn local histories into global history proper and added value to the globe. Again, this was articulated early on. Lynn White, a leading American historian of medieval technology, wrote in 1956, "The canon of the Occident has been displaced by the canon of the globe" (1968: 12). White, Barraclough, and other perceptive authors, notably Eric Fischer (1943) and Oskar Halecki (1950), decentered Europe accordingly. Contemplating that the Second World War had obliterated the preeminence of Europe and that the globalization of all human action was now on the agenda, they came close to realizing that the supremacy of any other region of the globe had also ended. Searching for an adequate historical perspective to describe that epochal change, they explored a fresh periodization of history.

Looking beyond the Atlantic in the mid-1950s, Barraclough saw a "Pacific age" in the making and "the transition from a 'modern' to a 'post-modern' history" (1955: 207). Of course, "post-modern" came to stand for a great deal more than he and other early users of the term, like Arnold Toynbee and Peter Drucker, had imagined. Departing from the original region of modernity and its overprivileged position, they opened their eyes (and ours) to an inclusive planetary system of regional globalities. From the initial use of "our global age" (Barraclough 1962: 99) to the elevation of global and age into a full-blown theory of The Global Age (Albrow 1996), the globe and its interdependent regions edged into the center of history.

The present chapter takes a multiple modernity perspective that assumes the different sites of modernity in contemporary world. According to Eisenstadt (2003), the ongoing dialogue between globalizing forces of modern reconstruction and specific socio-historical resources embodied by respective civilizational traditions has so far created divergent modernities. I would like to reject the conventional wisdom that Western modernity is a prototype, and Eastern modernity is second modernity (Tiryakian 1990). This revised perspective of multiple modernity tells us that the formation of knowledge and growth of ideas are *seinsgebuden* in the historical context of socio-cultural development on Korean soil. There is a Confucian saying that knowledge and ideas can progress to both openness and closeness: that societies should be open to foreign ideas and knowledge but closed for their own progress.

Sociology under Western tradition has presumed that Europe has pioneered the history of modernization; European modernization has been cemented as the prototype of modernity. With the colonization of Africa, Latin America, and Asia beginning in the 15th century, modernization spread over the world. Marx, Weber, and Durkheim all assumed that the modernity that first emerged in modern Europe would lead to the basic cultural and institutional constellations in modernizing societies throughout the world. I am against this prevalent view of modernization coupled with the convergence of modernizing societies. Among other scholars, Barrington Moore Jr. (1966) has observed the bourgeois, fascist, and socialist paths connected to the modern world: the bourgeois revolution in England and France, the fascist revolution in Germany and Japan, and the socialist revolution in Russia and China.

I am tempted to say that to understand Korean society in a more relevant light, it would be best to utilize its own concepts and theories in social sciences in general and sociology in particular. I aspire to build concepts and theories suited to the Korean socio-historical background. My attempt is geared toward neither de-Westernization nor re-Easternization: it is rather oriented towards building up post-Western concepts and theories.

2 Development of Sociology in Korea

Korean sociology has had to develop a system of knowledge in the intellectual environment where the very concept of society and science, as understood in the West, was non-existent.[1] The poor environment for developing social sciences and the difficulties for the various social science disciplines in establishing their own identities were well illustrated in the cynical remark made by a scholar of the humanities who called Korean social sciences "the discipline borrowed from the West by dishwashers" (Kim 1974). With growth in quantity and in quality, such criticism has become somewhat less valid for Korean social sciences, but many social scientists still see flaws in the field. In fact, it must be admitted that Western scholars such as Weber, Marx, and Durkheim are preferred to the traditional Korean intellectuals, like *Tweh-geh* (退溪李滉), *Da-san* (茶山丁若鏞), and *Yuhn-am* (燕巖朴趾源).

In Korea, there have been some movements towards self-criticism in the area of social sciences. In the case of sociology, there have been several significant movements at different times, in which there was disapproval of the uncritical acceptance of Western concepts and theories, and there was interest garnered with regard to indigenization.[2]

The most striking feature of the recent efforts to reflect the ahistorical nature of Korean sociology has been the attempt to parallel Korean sociology to the discourse of post-colonialism.[3] As Orientalism has inevitably been built upon the Eurocentric framework, so too has the sociology in Korea become

---

1 Historically, in Korea, as well as in the rest of the East Asian region, the concept of "society" has not existed as a countervailing concept of the "state". It was born only after Western ideas began to filter in through the Japanese in the late 1800s. Because of the broad implication of the word and the unfamiliarity of the concept, the Japanese scholars went through great difficulty in finding an appropriate translation. Likewise, the Korean word for science, *Kwa-hak* (科學), implies an academic discipline with a systematic frame of knowledge. The idea of social sciences derived from the natural sciences, with its stress on objectivity and categorical imperative, shows a large disparity from the traditional views of the academic discipline in the Confucian civilization.

2 In 1972, the Korean Sociological Association held a conference titled "Self-Reflection of Social Sciences in Korea", with scholars from economics, government, and history. For the introduction and summary of the conference, see Kim and Lim (1972).

3 For more detailed discussion on the issue, refer to Cho (1994).

dependent on Western academics (Amin 1989; Said 1979). In deliberating upon the dependency of Korean sociology, I cannot totally ignore the effects of the heteronomous background of international political and economic systems over the paths of national development: Sinicism, Japanese occupation, Western imperialism, the Cold War, American influence, and so on. Only in the context of such a tumultuous historical background can I identify the myriad forces that have left Korean sociology in an intellectually crippled state. However, it is ironic that the question of identity of Korean sociology became an issue under the scrutiny of the Western theory of post-modernism raising "fake modernity" in Korea.

Generally speaking, Korean sociology seems to be going beyond the second stage in the process of its own historical development, with the stages as follows: (1) imitation of Western theories, (2) their critical application, and (3) formation of indigenous theories. Thus, sociology in Korea is showing conflicting trends; while some sociologists are attempting a critical analysis of Korean society with readily adapted Western theories, there are others looking for ways to reappropriate traditional thoughts and to produce an independent analysis of Korean society. Though it may outwardly seem that these two contradictory tendencies are clashing with each other, in fact it is a perfectly encouraging sign towards accomplishing the task of the Koreanization of sociology.

Korean sociology faces challenges from the ongoing globalization that is obscuring the boundaries of disciplines and weakening the status of scholars in all social science fields across borders. In the case of Korean sociology, the demand for "nationalization" from one side is offset by the pressure for "internationalization" from another. This has the effect of diluting the identity of Korean sociology and weakening the roots of Korean sociologists.

3   Identity Crisis in Korean Sociology

Sociology in Korea, having modeled itself after and around mainstream European and North American sociology, is an imitation of Western concepts and theories. Diachronically, Korean sociology today is the sum of different patches of ideas since the opening of the nation; German ideas interpreted by the Japanese at first, then American and European ideas as they were imported unilaterally after World War II. In lieu of our beleaguered intellectual history, traditional scholarship—the dominant *Juja-hak* (朱子學) movement of the *Chosun* Dynasty, or the alternative schools of *Shil-hak* (實學) or *Buk-hak* (北學)—was compromised before it had a chance to engage in any sort of dialectic with the imported "sociology in the modern sense". The colonial period

1. Indigenous Roots: *Chosun* Dynasty
A. *Juja-hak* Confucianism: *Tweh-geh Hwang Lee, Yul-kok Yi Lee*
B. *Shil-hak: Byan-kye Hyung-won Yu, Sung-ho Ik Lee, Da-san Yak-young Chung*
C. *Buk-hak: Yuhn-am Chi-won Park*

2. Modern, "Western" Sociology: introduced during the period of the later *Chosun* Era

3. Japanese Colonial Period
Modern Historical Science: *Baik-am Eun-shik Park, Dan-jae Chae-ho Shin, Wi-dang In-bo Chung*
Marxist Historical Science: *Dong-am Nam-eun Baik*

4. Full-scale Acceptance—Transplantation—Settlement of Sociology Since Independence

> Sociology
> Transplantation (1946–1956)
> Simple Application I (1957–1969)
> Critical Application II (1970s–1990s)
> Maturation (2000–)

FIGURE 10.1   The historical development of Korean sociology
Note: Kim (1982), Choi (1974), and Shin (1976).

in Korean history broke the continuity of its cultural and intellectual traditions, and these traditions would be denied the chance to aid in rebuilding the body of Korean knowledge after the occupation (see Figure 10.1 on the development of sociology). Even after the colonial period, the uncritical acceptance of foreign scholarship made it impossible to benefit from the creative transformation in the process of imitation.

In Korea, on the path of national division, the Korean War, student revolution, military coup d'état, and great democratic resistance, authoritarian governments—civilian and military—have, in the name of anti-communism and national security, suppressed freedom of the press, expression, and association. Under the Cold War system, the suppression of academic freedom deprived social sciences of autonomous growth through free and open debates. Therefore, the kind of sociology that upheld the status quo was permitted, whereas the other kind that sought to criticize the status quo was repudiated. Naturally, it was impossible to produce a balanced explanation of and perspective on Korean society. In Korean sociology, liberal theories and Marxist theories have been opposed as modes of explanation. To make matters worse, amid the competition of mainstream paradigms, ideological narrow-mindedness and inflexibility about specific theories have hindered the balanced analysis of Korean society.

Because Korean sociology has expropriated internal relevance from external resources, it has failed to nurture a distinct self-identity. The sometimes excessive theoretical rigidity of sociology is generally due to the tendency to approach reality not via historical evidence but via ideological prophecy. The ability to move from theory to practice—to engender real change in society—is certainly a central function of sociology. Yet, if sociology were to be reduced to a machinery of revolution and solely focus on bringing about changes, the *Wertfreiheit* would have to be compromised. For the mature development of Korean sociology, neither an inclination towards social engineering nor a revolutionary disposition is desirable. It must be understood that the outward orientation of Korean sociology has resulted from a contradictory societal reality as well as from restricted academic freedom.

This does not, however, mean that I am advocating scientism, that is, sociology for the sake of sociology. If sociology becomes too preoccupied with being "scientific" it may separate the object of observation from the observer, thus damaging practical applicability. While it should never become a mere tool for propagating a specific ideology, it, within its capacity to criticize reality, must be grounded in the concept of *Wertfreiheit*.[4] The criticism of ideology is also a central mission of sociology. In that respect, I must be wary not only of technological professionalism as means to preserve the existing system but also of the irresponsibility of practicing ideological pseudo-prophecy (Berger and Kellner 1982).

Korean sociology is highly susceptible to external influences. As a natural outcome of having developed without being rooted in social-historical realities, a change of paradigm in the outside world has been imported in Korean academia without any proper assessment. For example, the disjointed academic styles of structural-functionalism and Marxism, modernization theory and dependency theory, the state theory and globalization theory, modernism and post-modernism well demonstrate such characteristics. Korean sociology has always changed its own paradigm as a response to the shifting changes abroad, thus sentencing itself to its own fate of remaining on the periphery.

It has reached a point where sociology in Korea can no longer delay in creating its own concepts and theories. So far, it has been dominated by imported concepts and theories. Now it is at a place where it can define concepts and theories of its own to explain Korea's social reality. To establish indigenous theories that maintain *Wertfreiheit* with respect to Korean society, the domestication of foreign concepts and theories is important; yet the internationalization of Korean studies is equally, if not more, imperative.

---

4   In Korean academia, there has been a tendency to misinterpret *Wertfreiheit* as removal of values, as translated by Japanese scholars. But *Wertfreiheit* by Weber must be understood as the protection of scholastic viewpoints from external pressures. Refer to Gouldner (1962).

These days, the sociology of Korea share its interests in discourses on East Asia. Underneath such discourses, an idea has been birthed, an idea that sprouted in relation to the "maldevelopment" of Western society, that a cure to the ills of Western development can be found in East Asia. It is interesting to note the development of both the content and the format of these discourses. These East Asian concepts and theories are not only influenced by traces of Occidentalism, but also move towards the universalization of theory in a rather premature manner. Regarding the East Asian region, there have been discourses suggesting diverse directions to their identity development: to follow the path of a traditional discourse on Western modernity, to embrace a resistant discourse about imperialism, or to find an alternative discourse looking for yet a third path.

In the context of the discussion on East Asia, it is important to examine the analysis of "Confucian capitalism" that is underway in international and domestic academic circles. I will investigate the positive and negative implications of East Asia's capitalist development as an apt example to illustrate the peripheral self-identity of Korean sociology. When modernization theory was the dominant paradigm in Western academic circles, the academic community accepted and believed in the theories that emphasize cultural acculturation where Confucianism was conceived as being detrimental to development in East Asia. But the counteraction of a dependency theory contending that politico-economic variables are much stronger forces than cultural factors drove Confucianism off the main stage. In the midst of competition among paradigms, Confucianism once again came to be viewed as the main player behind the remarkable economic growth of East Asia as the significance of culture was rediscovered.

The most notable characteristics of this Neo-Confucian discourse have been attempts to cast off the traditional perspective of equating modernization with Westernization. Confucianism is seen as an explanatory variable with independent, intervening, and circumstantial meanings to explain for East Asia's unique modernization. Confucianism has been understood on a number of levels as having fulfilled a function equivalent to that of the Protestant ethics in Western development, as having brought about changes in both organizations and values with systematized cultural mechanisms, and as having supported social order, hierarchy, and harmony in the formation of a communitarian society.[5]

---

5 It is interesting to note such topics were discussed by American and European scholars of Asian origin. There has been abundant literature on the theme, but for the sake of convenience, refer to the following: Wei-ming (1984) and Morishima (1981, 1988). This article was originally published in the *Observer*, 1978.

What is intriguing is that these discussions have mostly been initiated and led by Western sociology. Asian sociology, including Korean sociology, has continued to act like a consumer, importing and purchasing this product called Confucian capitalism manufactured in the West, whose raw materials are development processes in East Asian countries. Of course, it would be wrong to say that there has been a total lack of such discussions in Asian sociological circles,[6] yet it would be only fair to admit that in the case of Korea, sociology has merely served as a consumer fishing for foreign concepts and theories. So it is only natural that Korean sociology has been wandering aimlessly as the nationless cripple.

It is important to note that rebuilding Korean sociology should begin with an assessment of its past achievements and mistakes. Considering that both exaggeration and undervaluation of history do harm, it is necessary to identify the possibilities and limitations of Korean sociology by investigating the sociological research on Korean society in a comprehensive way, involving such various aspects as research subject, ideological orientation, theoretical perspective, and methodology. The rebirth of Korean sociology for the future is possible only with reflection on the present, which links the past to the future.

A large number of publications have been produced on the establishment and development of Korean sociology. These works point out many ills of Korean sociology, such as the absence of independent theories, the dearth of strategic themes, weak professionalism and disciplinary autonomy, distortions of its critical role, the absence of interdisciplinary studies, weak academic identity, a confusion of history and ideology, dependence on Western theories, an excessive emphasis on textual interpretation, and a disparity between theory and reality. All of these are valid problems with which Korean sociology today should cope.

I believe that what is most important in the self-criticisms of Korean sociology is the lack of a *problematique*, that is, a perspective equipped with an epistemological basis from which to view Korean society. This problematique is more than a paradigm that has methodological characteristics under a particular theoretical perspective. If the paradigms of Korean sociology become rooted in the Korean problematique, they will mature. In order for Korean sociology to form an autonomous academic tradition and creative scholarship, the various paradigms, whether they are transplanted or indigenous, must grow deep roots based on their own problematique.

---

6 For the most internationally renowned research, refer to Kim (1994).

4   Major Tasks for Creating Self-Identity

Generally speaking, theories have always been delayed in explaining social reality. According to Khun, changes in paradigm are the due result of losing its relevancy to the real world. In the case of Korea, the problem of relevancy has been caused in the process of the uncritical acceptance of foreign theories. Because of this, the abnormal phenomenon of the reality being molded after a theory has been justified as a living proof of the practical nature of the sociology. The uncritical reception of foreign theories has also caused the short life span of theories in sociology.

I hold the view that sociology as a social science discipline is distinct from natural sciences in several respects. (1) Sociology, as the product of historical reality, is constrained by time and space. (2) It is almost impossible for any theory to be universal in the sense of its validity. (3) Sociology can be used as a means either to support the existing system or to help overthrow it.

In most Asian countries, like Korea, the need for the indigenization of sociology has been called for due to the lack of autonomous development of the branches of academics such as political science, economics, and sociology, and their consequential failure to meet relevancy in explaining historical reality. Therefore, the task of the Koreanization of sociology must involve not only creating an autonomous social science discipline that bears relevance to Korean reality but also developing the problematiques, meta-theories, and methodologies that are appropriate to Korean social-historical conditions as a whole, which is a mixture of tradition and modernity, the old and the new, and the indigenous and the foreign. The Koreanization of sociology refuses autistic parochialism as well as colonial internationalism. The emphasis must be placed on recognizing the hard reality that sociology is destined to be pluralistic in its time-space nature as major theories pertain their own characteristics of being a multi-paradigm. Therefore, the Koreanization of sociology ultimately aims for the development of middle-range theories that can embrace the Korean peninsula that bears relevance for Asia. To this end, qualitative or/and quantitative methods can be implemented according to the nature of the subjects. Particularly in the case of comparative research, the availability of cases determines the type of research. Variable-oriented research is possible if there are plenty of cases, whereas case-oriented research is usually applied when the cases are scarce.

According to Alatas, in addressing the issue of indigenization and nationalization of social science in the Asian region, the self-identity of sociology in Korea can be catalyzed by creating the discourses that can free themselves from the power and the knowledge of Western societies (Alatas 1993: 332).[7] This means that the disintegration of the colonial ideologies that are internalized in our lives must happen. We will then be able to scrutinize the cultural and institutional foundations of academic dependency, thus exposing the reproductive mechanisms of imitation by creating such liberating discourses as the mental structure that institutionalize the ideas from the major powers of the center, the education system that categorizes academic disciplines in a Western manner, the modernistic scheme in the education system and the school curriculum, the market mechanism that accelerates the homogenization of the standard social sciences, and more.

For the 21st century, Korean sociology must be equipped with essential virtues, such as autonomous creativity, problem relevancy, critical reformism, a humanistic mind, and future orientation.[8] In other words, it is necessary to overcome the modernistic worldview, to develop human potential, to create distinct theories that can appropriately explain Korean realities, to strengthen the ability to criticize, to undo the absurdity of the existing systems, and to prepare for the rapidly changing environment of the future.

Korean sociology must be able to discover its own issues in this century. Upon such development of strategic issues, sociology should take responsibility for a networking academic community by utilizing an interdisciplinary collaboration that integrates academic research with policy research. Also, Korean sociology must make itself more approachable to people by introducing more common vocabularies and working on more down-to-earth applications while taking on roles as educators and researchers.

Korean society provides abundant materials for conducting research in the areas of sociology. In Korea, there are many unique instances where the premodern and postmodern, as well as the anti-modern, coexist on the soil of modernity. It can serve as a rich lab for executing research on the topics such as the dynamics and contradictions of capitalism, clashes among globalism, regionalism, and nationalism, nation-state-building, democratic transition and consolidation, growing social movements and civil society, changing developmental states, and state-guided market economy. For example, there are numerous issues that must be addressed properly in Korea, such as the

---

7   For a comprehensive analysis of this matter, see also "The Philosophy and Sociology of Social Science: Towards an Adequate Conceptualization of Relevance and Irrelevance". Paper presented for the KSA-ISA Joint East Asian Regional Colloquium "The Future of Sociology in East Asia", Seoul, Korea, November 22–23, 1996.
8   For more detailed sociological discussions on the topic, refer to Shin (1994).

history of statehood and nationhood in the course of division and reunification; the meaning of old and new social movements, like protest movements; the absence of religious war and the dominance of foreign religion; harmony and conflict between the market and plans in the economy; and others.

Some methodological considerations must be taken into account when we try to rebuild sociology in Korea.

First, an attempt must be made to create concepts and theories that convey a higher level of concreteness based on our reality, so that they will be able to give an accurate account of Korean society. I would like to introduce some that I have coined to explain Korea more appropriately.

First is the concept of a broken nation-state (缺損國家). A divided state has been used to describe the present separated North and South Korea. It is a static concept that is unable to properly analyze the changing stages from divided to reunified state. Through a broken nation-state, a dynamic process of reunification that goes through federation, confederation, and finally a single nation-state can be imagined.

Second is the state monism theory (國家單元主義). Pluralism and corporatism are useful theories to analyze the underlying nature of Korean politics. In Korea, the state has played a key role in the development process. State monism could be a theory which overcomes the limitation of pluralism and corporatism by grasping the centrality of the state in managing the economy and reorganizing society in Korea.

Third, I would like to introduce *sae* (勢). Class and stratification are used to understand the structured inequality in modern society. I have added a concept of *sae* that as a power bloc influences the formation of people regardless of different social and economic positions. It enlightens the dynamics of Korean society and politics that can be distinguished from class and stratification that are born during the capitalist industrialization process.

Fourth, I have classified the three types of advanced countries based on population size with per capita income of more than $30,000: the small power (强小國) country, which has a population of less than 20 million (the Netherlands, Sweden, Denmark, Switzerland, Norway, and Finland); the middle power country (强中國), which has a population between 50 million and 100 million (Germany, France, England, Italy, and South Korea), and the big power country (强大國), which has a population of over 100 million (United States, Japan). These three types of states can be different from one another in terms of production structure, labor market, banking system, welfare mechanisms, and so on.[9]

---

9 For the sake of discussion, I would like to introduce the following papers written in Korean: Lim (1994), Lim and Kim (1991), Lim (1999), and Lim (2016).

5 Conclusion

This chapter envisions "a sociology of sociology", complete with aspirations for a desirable future of Korean sociology. A relative lack of self-identity in Korean sociology is understood as a natural outcome of marginality accumulated in the process of academic development fostered by imitating sociology from Western countries. Therefore, a Koreanization of sociology must be approached by thoroughly analyzing cultural and institutional foundations of academic dependency that have brought peripheral identity, which is salient on the university and research institutions, rather than by applying the overly simplified dichotomy of inside versus outside or we versus the others.

Sociology in Korea has been sustained by a simple reproduction of imported theories. This explains why it has been so hard to find ways to convert the tremendous amount of accumulated knowledge into the creation of unique theories. The widening disparity between theories and reality exacerbates the chronic dependence of Korean sociology on Western theories.

In fact, it would be quite correct to say that the widespread use of excessive theoretism in Korean sociology had in the past been mainly caused by a lack of attention for empirical research. It is rare to find a case in any country other than Korea of the aptitude and speed for accepting the alteration of the theoretical debates raised in the West over the orthodox and the heterodoxy, the old versus neo, and the pre versus post. Nevertheless, sociology fared worse than humanities in giving an accurate account of the historical turmoil of Korean society. The main reason for this outcome can be found in the fact that the struggle for theoretical hegemony has been blocking concrete narration or an empirical argument.

In this respect, the agenda for relocating Korean sociology lies in developing independent theories. This means presenting problomatiques that reflect the reality of Korea's very own. The task would be impossible without a major epistemological overhaul in the area of sociology in particular and the social sciences in general. With this view in mind, I would like to make three suggestions to conclude.

First, sociology must attempt a holistic approach to the subjects that are unique to Korean society by overcoming the territorialism that prohibits barrier-crossing among academic disciplines. The task is applicable not only for conducting academic research but also in building a more open system of knowledge by lowering the artificially marked barriers, thus promoting interactive dialogue among political science, economics, and sociology. It is also relevant with academic and educational programs for the next generation of sociologists, with its approach particularly designed to widen the breadth of the conceptual frame on the diversity and permeability of social phenomena.

Second, sociology must strengthen exchange and cooperation with historical studies. Historical studies have accumulated a fair amount of research on Korean society both on period-specific agendas or on Korean history as a whole. Sociology will benefit by actively utilizing the rich resources of historical studies in giving more depth to the in-depth analysis of Korean society. If previously focus had mainly been on fact-analysis led by imported theories, now is the time to foster "limited generalization" based on a "thick description" of the Korean reality.

Third, sociology must be strengthened through a concerted effort on the comparative studies with other countries, cultures, and regions. To strengthen comparative studies setting Korean society as a standard, the job of internationalizing domestic research and domesticating area studies must be prioritized. Only through comparative studies can discussions on the universality and the peculiarity of the Korean society be assessed in the theoretical and empirical senses. It is important to take note that comparative studies provide material that helps us overcome provincialism that may come in the process of the Koreanization of sociology and aid in the process of internationalization.

Acknowledgments

This chapter is a revised one based on my previous articles. Hyun-Chin Lim, "Social Sciences in Korea Towards 21st Century: Challenges, Dilemma, and Solutions", *Journal of Korean Studies* 2 (1999): 71–94; and Hyun-Chin Lim, "Sociology in Korea: Achievements and Failures in Explaining Reality", *Korea Journal* 4.1 (2000): 101–137; Wolf Schafer and Hyun-Chin Lim, "New Asiaa and the Rise of Global Regions", in Hyun-Chin Lim, Wolf Schafer and Suk-Man Hwang (eds.), *New Asias: Global Future of World Regions*, Seoul: Seoul National University Press, 2010, x–xxiii.

References

Alatas, Syed Farid. 1993. "On the Indigenization of Academic Discourses". *Alternatives: Global, Local, Political* 18 (3): 307–338.

Albrow, Martin. (1996) 1997. *The Global Age: State and Society Beyond Modernity*. Palo Alto, CA: Stanford University Press.

Amin, Smir. 1989. *Eurocentrism*. London: Zed Books.

Barraclough, Geoffrey. (1955) 1956. "The End of European History". *History in a Changing World*. Norman: University of Oklahoma Press.

Barraclough, Geoffrey. 1962. "Universal History". In *Approaches to History: A Symposium*, edited by H.P.R. Finberg, 83–109. London/Toronto: Routledge & Kegan Paul/University of Toronto Press.

Berger, Peter L., and Hansfried Kellner. 1982. *Sociology Reinterpreted: An Essay on Method and Vocation*. New York, NY: Doubleday.

Chakrabarty, Dipesh. 2000. *Provincializing Europe: Postcolonial Thought and Historical Difference* (reissued in 2007 with a new preface by the author, *Provincializing Europe in Global Times*). Princeton, NJ: Princeton University Press.

Cho, Hae-Jung. 1994. *Reading Books and Lives for the Intellectuals in the Post-Colonial Age 3*. Seoul: Alternative Culture.

Choi, Jae-suk. 1974. "Korean Sociology in the Early Days: Opening to Liberation". *Korean Sociological Review* 9: 10–20.

Eisenstadt, Shmuel N. 2003. *Comparative Civilizations and Multiple Modernities*. Volume 2. Leiden: Brill.

Fischer, Eric. 1943. *The Passing of the European Age: A Study of the Transfer of Western Civilization and Its Renewal in Other Continents*. Cambridge, MA: Harvard University Press.

Gouldner, Alvin W. 1962. "Anti-Minotaur: the Myth of a Value-Free Sociology". *Social Problems* 9: 199–213.

Halecki, Oskar. 1950. *The Limits and Divisions of European History*. London: Sheed & Ward.

Kim, Kyung-dong. 1982. "Sociology". *Korean Scholarships and Academic Traditions*, 202–253. Seoul: Woosuk.

Kim, Kyung-dong. 1994. "Confucianism and Capitalist Development in East Asia". In *Capitalism and Development*, edited by Leslie Sklair, 87–106. London: Routledge.

Kim, Sung Kook, and Hyun Chin Lim. 1972. "Social Sciences in Korea: Discussion and Implication". *Korean Sociological Review* 7: 85–96.

Kim, Yoon-shik. 1974 (June 3). "Culture and Slavery". *Seoul National University Newspaper*, p. 3.

Lim, Hyun-Chin. 1994. "State Building and Nation Formation in Korea: Introduction to A Theory of 'Broken Nation-State'". In *New Horizon for Korean Political Science at a Turning Point: An Essay in Honor of Bum Mo Koo*. Seoul: Nanam Press.

Lim, Hyun-Chin. 1999. "The State and the Structure of Dominance: *Sae* in a Center-Oriented Society". In *Structural Understanding of Korean Society*, edited by Il-Chul Kim. Seoul: Literature and Intellect Press.

Lim, Hyun-Chin. 2016. "South Korea as a Middle Power State". In National Assembly of Korea, *Perspectives on Future*. Seoul: National Assembly, Korea.

Lim, Hyun-Chin, and Byung-Kook Kim. 1991. "Despair of Labor, Betrayed Democratization: Relations of the State, Capital and Labor in Korea". *Quarterly Sasang* (Winter): 109–168.

Moore, Barrington. 1966. *Social Origin of Dictatorship and Democracy: Lord and Peasant in the Making of Modern World*. Boston, MA: Beacon Press.

Morishima, Michio. 1981. *Why Has Japan "Succeeded"?* Cambridge: Cambridge University Press.

Morishima, Michio. 1988. "Confucianism as a Basis for Capitalism". In *Inside the Japanese System*, edited by Daniel I. Okimoto and Thomas P. Rohlen, 36–38. Palo Alto, CA: Stanford University Press.

Said, Edward. 1979. *Orientalism*. New York, NY: Vintage Books.

Shin, Yong-ha. 1976. "The Development and Future Direction for Korean Sociology". *The Seoul National University Social Sciences* 1: 43–59.

Shin, Yong-ha. 1994. "Suggestions for the Autonomous Development of Korean Sociology". In *Korean Sociology in the 21st Century*, 15–31. Seoul: Literature and Intellect Press.

Tiryakian, Edward A. 1990. "On the Shoulders of Weber and Durkheim: East Asia and Emergent Modernity". In *Asia in the 21st Century: Challenges and Prospects*, edited by Kyong-Dong Kim and Su-Hoon Lee. Seoul: Panmun Book Co.

Wei-ming, Tu. 1984. *Confucian Ethics Today*. Singapore: Singapore Development Institute.

White, Lynn. (1956) 1968. "The Changing Canons of Our Culture". In *Machina Ex Deo: Essays in the Dynamism of Western Culture*. Cambridge, MA: MIT Press.

CHAPTER 11

Cosmopolitan Sociology: A Significant Step But Not the Final Task for Post-Western Sociology

Kim Mun Cho

1   Development of Sociology and Changing Concept of Modernity

Sociology, which was born in response to the deplorable state of anarchy of Western Europe in the 19th century, is an outcome of a specific temporal and spatial context of the modern Western society (Zeitlin 1968). That is why sociology is regarded as a derivative of Western modernity.

In its initial stage, sociology pursued a scientific investigation aiming to explore universal truth. Although the discovery of universal truth is known to be the ideal of scientific endeavor, it may not be the case for social sciences because social sciences, including sociology, are highly contextualized disciplines (Gouldner 1970). Therefore, the controversy of universalism and particularism, which has been a hot issue of fierce debate in the whole area of social sciences, needs to be dealt with from a complementary, balanced standpoint rather than a selective, one-sided point of view.

1.1   Predominance of the Functional Paradigm in Sociology

Sociology was institutionalized as an academic discipline when Émile Durkheim founded the department of sociology at the University of Bordeaux in 1895. In the early 20th century, sociology expanded in the United States, including developments in both macro-sociology, concerned with the working of social systems, and micro-sociology, concerned with everyday human social interactions. In the 1930s, Talcott Parsons attempted to integrate them into an overarching paradigm of functionalism. In defense of the criticism pointing out its conservative bias hindering the explanation of social dynamics, Parsons proposed an evolutionary model of continuing progress where a society is moving to a higher stage by the restoring force toward equilibrium. In the mid-20th century, Robert Merton transformed Parsonian "analytic functionalism" into "empirical functionalism" depending on such concepts as latent function, dysfunction, and functional alternatives, and made up the shortcomings of the classical functional paradigm by enhancing the explanatory power for radical social change (Turner, Beeghley and Powers 2012). Owing to their contributions, the functional paradigm would maintain a leading position in sociology between the late 1930s and the early 1960s, especially in North America.

1.2 The Ups and Downs of Modernization Theory

Under the auspices of the functional paradigm, modernization theory resting on the process of industrialization, urbanization, bureaucratization, and secularization became prevalent in the 1950s to 1960s. Originally, the idea of modernization came from Max Weber's discussion on the role of rationality in the transition from a traditional to a modern society (Weber [1919] 1946). But its functionalist version became widely used in sociology and other social sciences afterward. The main thrust of modernization theory is that traditional countries can be brought to development in the same manner more developed Western countries have been (Moore 1963). It implies that the modernization of Western European countries and the United States is so universal that it can be applied to the other areas of the world as well. Underneath the theory of modernization suggesting all traditional societies will develop as they adopt more modern practices of the West lies the following implication, "Modernization is equated with Westernization".

By the late 1960s opposition developed because the modernization theme did not fit all societies in quite the same way. The typical one is the dependency theory. Its central contention is that resources flow from a "periphery" of poor and underdeveloped countries to a "core" of wealthy countries, enriching the latter at the expense of the former. So, poor countries are impoverished and rich ones enriched by the way poor countries are integrated into the system of unequal exchange (Chew and Lauderdale 2010).

Dependency models arising from the southern hemisphere, like Latin America and Africa, are a reaction against the monotheistic stance of the modernization theory that grants universal validity to the following statements: all societies progress through similar stages of development; today's underdeveloped areas are thus in a situation similar to that of today's developed areas at some time in the past; and therefore the task of helping the underdeveloped areas out of poverty is to accelerate them along this supposed common path of development by various means such as investment, technology transfers, and closer integration into the world market (Cohen and Kennedy 2000).

1.3 Critical Reflections on the Western-Centered Conception of Modernity

The sharp confrontation between advocates and critics of the modernization theory not only caused the conflicts of interest between center and periphery or developed and developing countries, but led to a critical appraisal of the concept of modernity derived from the experience of the Western society. Outcomes are themes of alternative modernities, multiple modernities, varieties of modernity, and the like (Eisenstadt 2000; Gaonkar 2001; Schmidt 2006). They all share a view that modernity no longer has a Western "governing center" to accompany it, and forms of modernity are so varied and contingent on culture and historical circumstance that the term itself must be spoken of in the plural. However, more significant advancement can be found in the critical thought of those named "theorists of reflexive modernity" (Beck, Giddens and Lash 1994).

They argue that the modernity characteristic of industrial society (the first modernity) is succeeded by a modernity that involves living with irreducible contingency, living in a more complex and less controllable world (the second modernity). Therefore, reflexivity as a self-monitoring process on the level of both institutions and individual persons becomes not only a necessary process of social life, but also a key focus of social investigation. Beck said, "We are entering the stage of reflexive modernization in which progress can turn into self-destruction and one kind of modernization undercuts and changes another. For him, reflexive modernization means that an initial disembedding is followed by the re-embedding, by another stage of modernity" (Beck 2000). It implies a radicalization of modernity, which breaks up the conditions of industrial society and opens paths to another stage of modernity, and achieves a reform of rationality that creates a new form of modernity. Beck, Bonss and Lau (2003) added, "it is not an excess of rationality, but a shocking lack of rationality, the prevailing irrationality, which explains the ailment of industrial modernity. It can be cured not by a retreat but by a radicalization of rationality, which will absorb the repressed uncertainty".

How to cross the border between the West and the rest of the world? Basically, three scenarios can be postulated in preparation for the declining Western-centric modernization theory: (1) consolidating the hegemony of existing modernization theory by incorporating unexpected events or social anomalies into an extended theoretical framework; (2) developing opposing theories in contrast to the conventional modernization theory, like socialist, Confucian, or Islamic models of modernization; and (3) constructing a new synthetic model that can transgress the boundary dividing "the West and the rest". Among those, the most plausible, preferable, and promising scenario is the third one because in the present era of globalization, national, regional, and continental divisions are rapidly breaking down. Particularly in these days, when globalization is accelerating, cosmopolitan sociology must play a leading role in post-Western sociology to overcome the limitations of Western centrism.

2 Globalization and the Shaping of Cosmopolitan Sociology

2.1 *The Challenge of Globalization*

Globalization has had profound effects and consequences on the world society. The conventional globalization thesis has stressed the positive aspects, such as socio-economic openness, technological innovation, the circulation of various products and services, abundant information and culture, and improved quality of life. But critics have blamed it as the main culprit responsible for the eradication of domestic industrial infrastructures and cultural traditions, the economic and political dependency of poor countries on rich countries, environmental devastation from excess environmental exploitation, and cultural homogenization. Since globalization exhibits such conflicting facets of light and shade, we are bound to ask how to react and cope with the challenge of globalization. Due to this ambivalent nature of globalization, neither absolute acceptance nor rejection is sufficient, as they are both one-sided viewpoints. It is necessary to maintain a balanced stance to recognize its positive and negative effects together. Among the problematic aspects of globalization that should be taken into account seriously, culture sticks out the most because culture is known to be "the formidable machine producing differences (est une formidable machine à produire de la différence culturelle)" (Warnier 1999: 21).

2.2 *Cosmopolitan Turn in Sociology*

Recently, a group of researchers studying culture started to argue that the modern way of life is heading toward differentiated discourses and practices. In order to make a new turn in globalization theory, they focus on something that is local, concrete, particular, and heterogeneous. In other words, emphasis is made on the micro-aspects of everyday life. For example, advocates of post-structuralism, postmodernism, post-colonialism, feminism, and multi-culturalism try to look beyond the macroscopic horizons of globalization and show great interest in differences, otherness, marginality, particularity, and concreteness at the micro level.

In a macroscopic view of globalization based on the dichotomy between global and local, it is hard to do away with the zero-sum dilemma where choosing one over the other necessarily relates to the negation of the importance of the unchosen. Micro-theorists, witnessing such limitations, emphasized the very process where local communities are affected by the driving force of globalization and get structuralized. Their endeavors involve investigating both how the global and the local assimilate and reproduce themselves, and how the interaction of the global and the local constitutes a new hybrid.

With a microscopic perspective, it is only natural that cultural globalization based on lifeworld is the main issue rather than the globalization of the institutional spheres of economy or politics. The reason is that the matter of finding out if people living in limited spaces have ways of lives open to the globe is given more weight than the issues regarding the transnational movement of capital or commodities.

Ulrich Beck describes this kind of new interest in globalization as "cosmopolitanism". Distinguishing between external and internal globalization, Beck argues that external globalization best characterized by the growth in material interconnections across national boundaries is not enough to understand what is happening in our world. Cosmopolitanism corresponds to internal globalization involving not only growing interconnections across national boundaries but transformation of the quality of social life inside the nation-state. Under cosmopolitanism, the exaltation of social consciousness conciliating both spaces of the global (cosmos) and the local (polis) becomes crucial (Beck 2002). Denying the dichotomy between global and local, internal globalization implies the "globalization of mind" where the local within the global and the global within the local can be realized.

2.3 Types and Trends of Cosmopolitanism

Cosmopolitanism comes from a long tradition of scholarly works. In general, it is classified into three types: moral cosmopolitanism, social cosmopolitanism, and cultural cosmopolitanism (Delanty 2006).

Moral cosmopolitanism, more of a classical version, can be traced back to the expansion period under Alexander the Great, when the closed world of polis turned into a vast empire. However, a more direct form of moral cosmopolitanism was first conceptualized by Immanuel Kant. In order to criticize manifest Western imperialism at the end of 18th century, he saw the need for a new perspective where the limitations of narrow nationality-based framework can be overcome. He set out to search for republican political philosophy, and in the midst of these endeavors "A Study on Perpetual Peace" was written (Guyer 1992).

In the third chapter of this study, while stressing that hospitality is not a virtue of sociability towards aliens but the very basic responsibility of all humankind, Kant argues that in truly republican political philosophy, all men should respect human rights by performing moral duty based on humanitarianism (Kant [1795] 1994). Today, such moral cosmopolitanism is very much reproduced in Jürgen Habermas's discursive ethics, forming the foundation of normative universalism (Benhabib 2004).

Social cosmopolitanism is directly related to social civil rights and can be defined as the outcome of the compromise between personal human rights and the civil rights of ethnic minorities. With the foundations for the modern nation established through the Treaty of Westphalia in 1648, the separation of the social and the political followed, and moral cosmopolitanism based on the very concept of human rights gave birth to social cosmopolitanism concentrating on the issue of civil rights. Citizenship based on historicity and locality is the salient subject of discussion in social cosmopolitanism. Social cosmopolitanism, directly related to ethnic prejudices or racial conflicts that heat up hand in hand with transnational migration, concentrates on dealing with the concept of territory as measured by the place of birth in defining citizenship (Arendt [1945] 1978).

Cultural cosmopolitanism, strongly related to the concept of societal pluralization, holds the utmost importance in contemporary societies. Cultural cosmopolitanism assumes pluralist value system to be the foundation of our social world. Put otherwise, instead of treating society as a unitary entity, cultural cosmopolitanism considers society to be the cultural medium free to transform according to the logic of global openness. Manuel Castells, John Urry, and Zygmunt Bauman are considered to have contributed to the theoretical formation of cultural cosmopolitanism (Delanty 2006).

Castells's theory of network society stressed open and flexible structures. It may be proper to say that his theory paved the way for cultural cosmopolitanism. In his theory, society exists in the form of networks rather than territorial spaces (Castells 1996). Urry viewed mobility as the very ontological condition of contemporary society and shared logical traces of cultural cosmopolitanism (Urry 2002). Meanwhile, Bauman described contemporary lives full of ambiguities, uncertainties, embarrassments, and anxieties with the concept "liquid modernity". He argues that the contemporary world contains contending multiple modernities and is heading toward the new stage of cosmopolitanism where post-universalism is sought after (Bauman 2000). Since post-universal cosmopolitanism allows lifestyles or life strategies all individuals, locals, citizens, and simply anyone living on this planet can relish, it goes beyond both moral and social cosmopolitanism that stress human rights and civil rights, respectively.

2.4   *The Making of Cosmopolitan Sociology*

Sociological research on cosmopolitanism resting upon inter-subjective like-mindedness has been led by the scholars of multiculturalism. Cosmopolitan research to date dealing with the human rights, civil rights, and cultural identity of ethnic minorities form not much more than a subfield of sociological investigation in general.

However, a few of the subject-oriented research works did apply or create useful analytical concepts or theories dealing with the problems faced by ethnic minorities. "Theory of otherness", "gender politics", and "study of minority human rights" represent such endeavors to study the subject from a new perspective. The formation of a new perspective corresponding to the changing world tends to usher the cosmopolitan sociology from a subfield of sociological investigation into a new research paradigm. The cosmopolitan sociological paradigm requires people-centered social integration (not system integration aiming at functional efficacy) to be extrapolated from a national to a global level. Following are some ideas that are very crucial to construct a people-based research paradigm of cosmopolitan sociology.

2.4.1   Cultural Creolization
The core of cosmopolitanism can be viewed through the logics of implosion and openness. As the concept of the global village by Marshall McLuhan informs us, internal globalization leading to cosmopolitanism is a convergent process where heterogeneous cultural elements are connected and mixed by "border crossing". This convergent process is the mechanism capable of producing the new mode of solidarity based on cultural sympathy, free of closed and exclusive nationalism and patriotism. In short, diversified cultural creolization is a basic condition for "multicultural politics of otherness", where people with different cultures and various languages live under the shared spirit of egalitarianism respecting difference and diversity, to be constructed (Pieterse 2004).

2.4.2   Dynamism Stemming from Cultural Confrontation or Conflict
Cosmopolitanism assumes the hybridization of various cultural elements. It is important for us to recognize that the emergence of such cosmopolitanism involves a dynamic process instead of a smooth transition or simple alteration. The process of confrontation and conflict between heterogeneous elements is inevitable for various historical experiences and cultural conventions to reach cultural hybridity. In order to overcome such confrontational situations, adhering to an open social system capable of coordinating value differences or moral discords is a necessary step (Benhabib 2004).

2.4.3   Cultural Diversification Out of Different Modernities
Kwame Appiah emphasizes the importance of steering clear of the errors of relativism while putting heterogeneous cultures and societies under the scope of cosmopolitanism. The relativist perspective supported by numerous social scientists, including cultural anthropologists, has a certain level of practical value. However, what we need to be cautious about is a danger of an "exile of

values" obstructing interaction between individuals inherent in said perspective, since relativism is capable of setting a path to silence or skepticism by disconnecting the possibilities of mutual communication (Appiah 2006).

2.4.4 Post-Universal Cosmopolitanism

Universalism contains a risk of inhibiting tolerance or ignoring differences by stressing a single interpretation as an absolute truth. From the pluralist point of view that idealizes a society where various values are realized, universalism is not a goal for us to yearn for but a target of revision. It is supported by such historical examples that include exclusive chauvinism, which gave rise to fascism and closed nationalism. Thus, we need to supplement the conviction of universalism promoting a single and only way of existence with cosmopolitanism where it is not the logic of unidirectional monologue but the logic of reciprocal dialogue that is preferred.

2.4.5 Pluralist Lifestyle and Pluralist Life Strategy

Individuals have the right to enjoy what they like and need different conditions to do so. Just like it is impossible for all plants to coexist under identical physical environment and climates, individuals cannot grow up in the same moral environment. Without guaranteeing diverse lifestyles, individuals cannot pursue their happiness and potential to the fullest (Mill 1863). It is not "solidarity organized through identity" but "solidarity built despite differences" that is necessitated in cosmopolitanism. This is why the diversified combinations of pluralist lifestyles and life strategies at an individual, local, national, or even global level altogether are strongly recommended.

Whereas "cosmopolitan sociology as a subfield of sociological investigation" is a stream of conventional sociological investigation about a specific social phenomenon or subject, and "cosmopolitan sociology as an intellectual resource" reinforces existing sociological study on minorities in general, "cosmopolitan sociology as a research paradigm" can be regarded as an alternative approach that enables us to recast the current sociological enterprises in a quite different way.

3 Beyond the Cosmopolitan Sociology

3.1 *The Coming Age of Convergence*

By seeing human society from an extremely long-term perspective, the entire history of mankind until the 20th century can be described as "the process of differentiation", moving from an undifferentiated to a differentiated or highly specialized state. Such an argument can be illustrated in the works of modern great thinkers, including Immanuel Kant's series of critiques on truth, virtue, and beauty; Herbert Spencer's idea of sociocultural evolution from simple, undifferentiated homogeneity to complex, differentiated heterogeneity; Émile Durkheim's argument on the changing types of social solidarity, from mechanical to organic; and Marx Weber's dictum of the "age of polytheism", which indicates the multiple goals of life to pursue in a modern society (Spencer [1874] 1885; Durkheim [1893] 1984; Weber [1920] 1959).

At the beginning of the second millennium, however, we are witnessing a signal of epochal reversal, in that the centrifugal force of differentiation is substituted by the centripetal force of convergence. Professional knowledge, professional certificate, or professional expertise was an object of respect or trust until a decade ago. Yet, instead of the declining authority of professionalism, a convergence that emphasizes the border-crossing, consilience, fusion, or hybrid has come to be the goal or means of social achievement.

This convergent turn is inspired by digital technology that enables us to deal with a great amount of data on the basis of a binary classification system of 0 and 1. Functions of digital technology, such as receiving, managing, and emitting diverse forms of data, coupled with those of advanced telecommunication technologies that help us exchange messages irrespective of temporal or special boundaries, have contributed much to converging the world of media. In addition, as the effects of convergence diffuse into economic, political, social, cultural, and mental dimensions, radical transformations in industrial arrangement, power structure, interpersonal relations, lifestyles, and social consciousness have followed.

In the past decade, "discourse on difference" has proliferated. It reflects the skepticism about modernity led by the logic of causality, dual mode of thinking, and mechanical worldview. As to the impetus of modernity, Alvin Toffler coined the word "wedging" in order to describe the situation where a social reality is forcibly decomposed in various ways. As a result, separation between cognition and affection, mind and body, rationality and irrationality, civilization and savagery, development and un-development, West and East are carried out, so that one part is ascribed as normal and the other part as abnormal (Toffler 1980). However, the spirit of modernity related with such ideas as progress, rationality, dualism, standardization, universalism, and synchronism have engendered ironical dysfunctions like "civilized violence", "rationalized irrationality", "inclusive exclusion". Such paradoxical conditions tend to stimulate the discourse concerning difference.

In "History and Social Sciences: Long Duration", Fernand Braudel, a leading scholar of the French Annales School, criticizes many historians for using time as one specie and thus spoiling their historical insights. He classified the timespan into three—short-term, mid-term, and long-term durations—and matched these with three types of history: event history, conjuncture history, and structural history (Braudel 1960). As such, Braudel tried to highlight the poly-layered characters of human history.

Stating that "The event is just like dust", Braudel evokes the importance of long-wave history. He stresses deep structural dynamics underlying the series of affairs happening in our ordinary life. Extrapolating Braudel's argument emphasizing long-term societal transition, I am going to introduce an extra–long-term diachronic framework that helps articulate the stages of transitions in our civilization. On the basis of this new conceptual framework, the recent megatrend towards convergence is to be explicated.

3.2 *Nature and Characteristics of the Convergent Society*

Convergence can be defined as the process of merging, mixing, changing, dividing, reproducing, or creating new products or phenomena. Due to this dynamic process of high complexity, convergent society is seen as the prototype of a complexity system of the highest degree (Forrester 1968). However, as a high complexity system, convergence society not only contains interpersonal associations between people, it also includes the interactions between human and non-human that used to be out of consideration in the discussion of complexity system. That is why new definitions, roles, functions, or meanings have to be conferred to non-living things. Accordingly, the asymmetry between human and other organisms or human and non-human, which have been strictly divided as subject and object before, tends to break down and give rise to a radical change in conventional anthropocentric ways of thinking. If reinforced by new epistemology that takes time-space transformation for granted, it is expected that a totally new worldview will emerge, one which is based upon the "the conviction of universal convergence", that is, anything in the universe is able to be a part of a universal movement toward conjunction.

It is true that an increasing degree of freedom reinforced by a series of "con-divergences" (convergence + divergence) tends to amplify social uncertainty. Given the state of excessive chaos, it is expected that a "convergence system" that is substantively different from the conventional complexity system will emerge through the process of reconstructing a new social order. The characteristics of convergence systems can be summarized as follows.

3.3 *Hyper-Openness*

A hyper-open system is a system that postulates free interactions between the subsystems or unobstructed interchange between system and environment.

While the conventional open system theory lays a stress on personal, material, and informational exchanges between system and its environment, the hyper-open system claims unbounded interactions of all kinds disallowing any form of internal or external boundaries.

Consequently, convergence under hyper-open system tends to substitute the concept of a "link-centered network" that resembles the image of thread ball or rhizome for that of a "node-centered network". As long as convergence emphasizes system structures, it highlights the relations of elements or their alliances (Latour 1997). Furthermore, in a hyper-open system, where all conceptual boundaries are imploding, intercourses of any direction, forward or backward, right-hand or left-hand, upward or downward, inside and outside, or whatsoever would be allowed. As a result, it is expected that the image of the world of free association where everything can combine with everything else is going to prevail.

3.3.1   Multiplicity

A convergence system consisting of diverse structured social factors is likely to structure a multi-layered world arranged with variety of overlapped realities. In other words, it implies that the world exists in a multiple state characterized by layers of multiplicity and plurality, not of singularity (Baudrillard 1983). Such an image of multiple worlds that includes both actual and virtual realities was described in the recent movie *Inception*. It shows the coexistence of reality, virtual reality, and another virtual reality inside the virtual reality in a stream of consciousness. It is also supported by a recent astrobiological research reported by NASA (National Aeronautics and Space Administration). An entirely new life form is reported to have been discovered on our planet that "doesn't share the biological building blocks of anything currently living" on Earth: A microbe that lives on arsenic instead of iodine (NASA 2010).

In a multi-society, different parts or part and the whole are related with each other and attempt to reformulate the world. Throughout such complex and dynamic process, a totally new world can emerge. It is shown in Michel Callon and John Law's big science project on space exploration. What they found is local networks that are embedded in a broader network (Callon et al. 1988). Likewise, a convergence system where incessant reconstruction is going on through a series of unbounded interactions tends to gain an amalgamative property due to their intra-systemic and inter-systemic intercourses.

3.3.2   A-linearity

When the factors that structure the system provide the additional effect more than the sum of individual effects, the system is said to possess a non-linear property. Like a strange attractor at a junction point, when it's hard to predict the trajectory of a system, it's a non-linear complexity (Capra 1996). In a mechanical worldview, which is represented by the clock having the cog wheel with the second, minute, and hour hands, a linear logic or solution can be applied. However, the theorists of a complexity system put forth consistent arguments that natural society or individual society gradually becomes non-linear In spite of this, nowadays, more so than the linear simple system and curve-linear complexity, the disconnection, leaping, ramification, confluence, and reversion enter into an a-linear meta-complexity system. It has been seen that individuals' hypersensitive behaviors of multitudes are predominated with inclining, twisting, splitting, and splashing, which cannot even be measured by high-dimensional functional equations (Hardt and Negri 2004).

3.3.3　　Co-production
The theory of autopoiesis is derived by Humberto Maturana and Francisco Varela's: a study of the self-referential organization of living system that maintains itself through dynamic process of reflexive control. In their conceptualization, they emphasize the difference between organization and structure. Whereas living systems' structure implies the actual relation of physical components, the structure denotes the mode of relation that attributes a certain living system to a specific category. Therefore, organization as an abstractive description of relation has no relation with its actual components (Maturana and Varela 1980).

Yet, if the theory of autopoiesis is prolonged with the non-human world, convergent system as a co-production world must be postulated. Here, everything would be combined with everything else and make universal relations, universal collaborations, and universal empathy possible. It helps to reproduce the entire world, including the human sphere, biosphere, ecosphere, and any other types of spheres as well. This view that can be traced back to the emerging stage of radical constructivism is sharply contrasted with that of technological determinism. Regardless of the primacy debate on technology and society, the co-productionist view emphasizing socio-technical ensembles is gaining influence these days (Bijker 1993).

3.4　　*From Complexity System to Convergence System*
The transition of the super complexity system to supra-complexity system is considered as crucial evidence indicating the shift from differentiation civilization to convergence civilization. Through the process of "convergentification", the super complexity system moves beyond its basic properties to a convergence system. In the convergence system, alliance structure is constituted

through the free association of individual elements. The alliance of convergence system can be said to be a series of diagrams or rules indicating the relations of everything, both human and non-human. This equalizes the relationship between subsystem, system, and environment and re-conceptualizes the mutual recognition and collaboration under a new perspective. It also indicates that the order and dynamics of the system are neither planned nor predetermined by any external factor (Latour 1997).

The order of the convergence system is an outcome of internal mechanisms represented by the interactions of its constituents. Therefore, in the concept, idea, and theory of the convergence system, the relationship is more significant than the structure. The network of the convergence system is nothing other than the set of lines that exhibit connective elements of the system. Henceforth, the convergence system is neither exhaustive nor systematic, irrespective of its coverage. The convergence system can be likened to the thread of Ariadne, which presupposes the prospective expansion from local to global or human to non-human realms. It would not remain as a system circumscribed within a human kingdom. As a boundless existence, the convergent system can extend itself to the convergence galaxy encompassing the whole universe.

It should be reiterated that convergence is not just a process of aggregation. It is an articulation process comprising a continuous series of diversifications and confluences. Although the convergent society can be considered as a huge complexity system, it tends to incorporate such properties as hyper-openness, multiplicity, a-linearity, and co-production, and it reaches the state of convergence system substantially differentiated from the conventional complexity system. The convergence system also takes into account the relationships between human and the non-human.

3.5 *Actor-Network Theory, a New Direction of Post-Western Sociology in the Era of Convergence*

Social science before actor-network theory (ANT) was an attempt to analyze a society in terms of the relations of power or interests between people. The human world and the material world were always recognized separately, and the impetus of social change was solely confined to the realm of the human beings. But the actor-network theorists rebelled against such conventional thinking and suggested ANT, emphasizing that attention should be paid to the joint interaction between the human world and material world (Law and Hassard 1999).

Their intellectual planning began with dismantling the objectivity and universality of scientific knowledge, which had been protected by modernity for centuries, arguing that scientific facts were constructed in the process of integrating human interests and inhumane technology through negotiations and combinations. Through elaborate and delicate research on the close interconnection between science and society, they reached the conclusion that nature and society have never been separate but closely intertwined in a hybrid network of human and inhuman elements (Latour 2005).

The ANT demonstrates that everything in the social and natural worlds, regardless of whether it is human or non-human, interacts in shifting networks of relationships without any other elements out of the networks. ANT challenges many traditional approaches by defining non-human as actors equal to human ones. So, it provides a new theoretical and methodological insight transcending Enlightenment humanism, as well as the modern dichotomous boundaries that this humanism influenced, to social sciences and various academic fields. The idea of ANT that perfectly fits the expanded social landscape of the convergence era holds the possibility of expanding the post-Western sociology beyond the human world to the world of all things, including humans, nature, and objects.

4   Conclusion: Prospects for Post-Western Sociology

What made sociology Western? There were at least three crucial occasions that drove sociology to be West-centric: the context in which sociology was launched, the long-term predominance of the functional paradigm in academia, and the diffusion of the modernization theory that equated modernization with Westernization. Neither one of these things fulfilled the purpose of post-Western sociology. In the age of globalization, the cosmopolitan sociology has turned out to be the best alternative that enables to attenuate the intellectual bias that has been embedded in Western sociology. Under the conditions of the current meta-dynamics of convergence, however, the march to post-Western sociology should be continued to the point where all the boundaries besides the continental divide of "the West and the rest" have been implored.

The history of mankind in the past can be regarded as the process of differentiation in which phenomena, perceptions, or activities have kept on dividing by differentiation or specialization. But there are signs of a reversal in which a decentralizing centrifugal force is replaced by a converging centripetal force. Accompanied by such a megatrend, society is transforming into a convergence system going beyond an ordinary complexity system. The convergence phenomena detected everywhere in a contemporary society call for an alternative sociological paradigm coinciding with the new age of convergence civilization.

Given the conditions, ANT appears to provide a very pertinent insight to bring about brand-new alternative theories. At this point, ecosociology studying the patterns of functioning, development, and interaction of the social and natural environments; planetary sociology to explore how closely intertwined and how mutually sensitive the human and geological realms are; and astrosociology focusing on the relationship between outer space, extraterrestrial places, and the wider universe and society seem to be the front-runners to lead the path to post-Western sociology.

References

Appiah, K. 2006. *Cosmopolitanism: Ethics in a World of Strangers*. New York, NY: W.W. Norton.

Arendt, H. (1945) 1978. "Zionism Reconsidered". In *The Jew as Parish: Jewish Identity and Politics in the Modern Age*. New York, NY: Grove Press.

Baudrillard, J. 1983. *Simulations*. New York, NY: Semiotext(e).

Bauman, Z. 2000. *Liquid Modernity*. Polity.

Beck, U. 2000. "The Cosmopolitan Perspective: Sociology for the Second Age of Modernity". *British Journal of Sociology* 51: 79–106.

Beck, U. 2002. "The Cosmopolitan Society and Its Enemies". *Theory, Culture & Society* 19 (1/2): 17–44.

Beck, U., W. Bonss, and C. Lau. 2003. "The Theory of Reflexive Modernization: Problematic, Hypotheses and Research Programme". *Theory, Culture & Society* 20 (2): 1–33.

Beck, U., A. Giddens, and S. Lash. 1994. *Reflexive Modernization: Politics, Tradition and Aesthetics in the Modern Social Order*. Polity.

Benhabib, S. 2004. *The Rights of Others: Aliens, Residents, and Citizens*. Cambridge: Cambridge University Press.

Bijker, W. 1993. "Do Not Despair: There Is Life After Constructivism". *Science, Technology & Human Values* 18: 113–138.

Braudel, F. 1960. "History and the Social Sciences: Long Duration". *American Behavioral Scientist* 3 (6): 3–13.

Callon, M., A. Rip, and J. Law, eds. 1988. *Mapping the Dynamics of Science and Technology*. Macmillan Press.

Capra, F. 1996. *The Web of Life*. Brockman.

Castells, M. 1996. *The Rise of the Network Society*. Blackwell.

Chew, S., and P. Lauderdale, eds. 2010. *Theory and Methodology of World Development: The Writings of Andre Gunder Frank*. Springer.

Cohen, R., and P. Kennedy. 2000. *Global Sociology*. New York, NY: New York University Press.

Delanty, G. 2006. "The Cosmopolitan Imagination: Critical Cosmopolitanism and Social Theory". *British Journal of Sociology* 57 (1): 25–47.

Durkheim, É. (1893) 1984. *The Division of Labor in Society*. Free Press.

Eisenstadt, S. 2000. "Multiple Modernities?" *Daedalus* 129: 11–29.

Forrester, J.W. 1968. *Principles of Systems*. Cambridge, MA: Productivity Press.

Gaonkar, D.P., ed. 2001. *Alternative Modernities*. Durham, NC: Duke University Press.

Gouldner, A. 1970. *The Coming Crisis of Western Sociology*. New York, NY: Basic Books.

Guyer, P., ed. 1992. *The Cambridge Companion to Kant*. Cambridge: Cambridge University Press.

Hardt, M., and A. Negri. 2004. *Multitude: War and Democracy in the Age of Empire*. New York, NY: Penguin.

Kant, I. (1795) 1994. "Perpetual Peace: A Philosophical Sketch". In *Kant: Political Writings, 2nd and Enlarged Edition*. Cambridge: Cambridge University Press.

Latour, B. (1997) 2017. "On Actor-network Theory: A Few Clarifications, Plus More Than a Few Complications". *Philosophical Literary Journal Logos* 27(1): 173–197.

Latour, B. 2005. *Reassembling the Social: An Introduction to Actor-Network Theory*. Oxford: Oxford University Press.

Law, J., and J. Hassard, eds. 1999. *Actor Network Theory and After*. Blackwell.

Maturana, H., and F. Varela. 1980. *Autopoiesis and Cognition: The Realization of the Living*. D. Reidel.

Mill, J.S. 1863. *On Liberty*. Ticknor and Fields.

Moore, W. 1963. *Social Change*. Prentice-Hall.

NASA. 2010 (December 2). "Discovery of 'Arsenic-Bug' Expands Definition of Life". *NASA Science News*.

Pieterse, J. 2004. *Globalization and Culture: Global Melange*. Rowman & Littlefield.

Schmidt, V. 2006. "Multiple Modernities or Varieties of Modernity?" *Current Sociology* 54 (1): 77–97.

Spencer, H. (1874) 1885. *The Principles of Sociology*. New York, NY: D. Appleton and Company.

Toffler, A. 1980. *The Third Wave*. Morrow.

Turner, J., L. Beeghley, and C. Powers. 2012. *The Emergence of Sociological Theory*. 7th ed. Sage.

Urry, J. 2002. *Global Complexity*. Routledge.

Warnier, J.P. 1999. *La Mondialisation De La Culture*. Editions La Decouverte et Syros.

Weber, M. (1920) 1959. *The Protestant Ethic and the Spirit of Capitalism*. Charles Scribner's Sons.

Weber, M. (1919) 1946. *From Max Weber: Essays in Sociology*, translated and edited by H. Girth and C.W. Mills. Oxford: Oxford University Press.

Zeitlin, I. 1968. *Ideology and the Development of Sociological Theory*. Prentice-Hall.

SECTION 3

Heritages and "Re-Asiatization" of Social Sciences

∵

CHAPTER 12

Chinese Economic Sociology: From the Perspective of Post-Western Sociology

Yang Dian

As one of the vital research fields and branches of sociology, economic sociology originated in the academia of Europe and the United States in the late 19th century, and has roughly undergone three stages of development, namely, the peak of classical economic sociology from 1890 to the 1930s; the peak of new economic sociology since the late 1970s; and the trough period, which happened around the 1950s. The research center of economic sociology has moved from Europe to the United States after this fluctuation. Therefore, the influential scholars, academic thinking, schools of theory, and important works in the field of economic sociology have a striking brand of Western sociology. However, the academic research and disciplinary construction of Chinese economic sociology have their own unique background, intellectual tradition, development process, and research findings, although these have been directly affected by the renewal of economic sociology in Western sociology in the 1970s. This is the foundation for us to discuss Chinese economic sociology from the perspective of post-Western sociology.

There is a long tradition of studying economic phenomena in Chinese sociology. The introduction and development of Chinese sociology in the early stages have been closely related to the fate of modern China. The original intention and mission of sociologists engaged in sociological research at that chaotic time were to save the nation from subjugation, advocate new learning, understand the current political situation, and reform society. In the poor and weak China, intellectuals had a strong sense of salvation, and early Chinese sociologists paid special attention to economic development. After the Sino-Japanese War of 1894–1895, Chinese sociologists carried out social surveys focusing on the rural economy, industrialization, and other issues, documenting the transformation of the traditional economic and social structure in China, which brought out a batch of academic masters and academic thinking with far-reaching significance. Among them, Fei Xiaotong's *Peasant Life in China* and Shi Guoheng's *China Enters the Machine Age* can be marked as representative classics of Chinese economic sociology in the early stage. Numerous studies on economic problems completed by early Chinese sociologists demonstrate that the sociological analysis of economic phenomena was an important tradition of Chinese sociology before the abolition of the discipline in the 1950s.

Since the renewal and reconstruction of Chinese sociology in the late 1970s, Chinese economic sociology was rapidly established, developed, and flourished with the endeavor of several generations of scholars. Chinese economic sociologists not only translate and introduce the works of Western economic sociology but also systematically carry out the disciplinary construction of Chinese economic sociology, setting up research institutions, publishing research works, training potential researchers, forming academic communities, and carrying out a large number of fruitful social investigations and theoretical research work based on Chinese experience and guided by theoretical construction. With the miraculous economic development since the reform and opening up, Chinese economic sociologists have made great efforts to explore the core areas, key features, and underlying mechanisms of the Chinese model. Abundant studies have been carried out with focuses on the major practical problems of China's reform and development and essential theoretical issues of Chinese economic sociology, such as the social structure transformation, economic development model, urbanization advancement mechanisms, property rights systems, labor process, and Chinese social relations. These works not only describe and analyze China's unique economic and social development practices, but also form a series of research findings and theoretical viewpoints that are different from Western economic sociology, and initially construct the economic sociology with Chinese characteristics.

The research of economic sociology illustrates that institutions, power, social network, and cognition (idea) deeply shape the economic behavior. The research of Chinese economic sociology reveals that China's unique institutional system (including formal systems, such as political and economic systems with Chinese characteristics, and informal systems, such as family systems and customs), power structure (such as the great influence of state power on various aspects of society), social network (such as *guanxi* 关系 and the culture of *quanzi* 圈子文化), and cultural tradition (such as patriotism and the emphasis on bloodline and the traditional solidarity of common geographic origin) all have great impacts on China's enterprises (property rights and corporate management), market, industry, finance, economic development mode, resource allocation mode, and government-business relationship, which imprint China's enterprise management, market structure, industrial development, financial market, development mode and government-business relationships with strong Chinese characteristics. These characteristics are generally conducive to efficiency and in many ways make some industries even more efficient than those in the Western free market model (such as the high-speed rail industry), although they have some negative impact on economic efficiency. The reason lies in the fact that Chinese enterprises and industries have given full play to the comprehensive advantages of market, social, and governmental mechanisms in the allocation of social resources. It is a mixed mode that has overcome the problems of market, governmental, and social failure.

Both history and current reality strongly demonstrate that efficiency and rationality are the products of social construction. They are not absolute, objective, or exogenous, but relative, interactively constructed, and endogenous in specific social contexts. The East and the West have different institutional arrangements and historical and cultural traditions, while they can both achieve the same level of efficiency and rationality.

We suggest that based on the unique Chinese experience, the following research in the field of Chinese economic sociology has challenged, supplemented, or improved the traditional Western economic sociology theory after more than 40 years of development, which is of great significance for Chinese sociological research to surpass the West-centered sociological model and construct sociology with Chinese characteristics.

1 Another Invisible Hand: The Theory of Transformation of Social Structure

From Adam Smith to John Keynes, from classical and neoclassical economics to contemporary economics, Western economic theories generally believe that market regulation and state intervention are the two key forces and mechanisms that affect resource allocation and economic development and are called the "invisible hand" and "visible hand", respectively. These views have been accepted by other social sciences, including sociology. However, as for China's practice of social transformation, it is not enough to focus only on market regulation and state intervention. The social structural transformation, which China has been and is experiencing, is another critical force affecting resource allocation and economic development. Its mechanism of action is different from that of market regulation and state intervention, which is worth great attention. This is the influential theory put forth by Li Peilin (1992, 1994), a well-known Chinese sociologist.

The theory clearly points out that the social structure transformation is the "other invisible hand" affecting economic development and resource allocation, which is different from market regulation and state intervention. It is not only the consequence of economic growth, but also the driving force of social change. Li Peilin has portrayed the course of China's social transformation and theoretically expounded its characteristics and pattern, which is a remarkable development and supplement to theories of the role of the state and the market in resource allocation and economic development. Various aspects and operating mechanisms of "the invisible hand of social structure transformation" have become important issues in Chinese economic sociology. This new research perspective helps to analyze the various problems, frictions, and contradictions in the economic and social development under the macro background of social structure transformation, which demonstrates the insight, analytical power, and explanatory power of the sociological perspective for macroeconomic and social phenomena. This new research perspective not only possesses distinct Chinese characteristics but also has the universal significance of understanding other societies. It is a supplement to and transcendence of Western theories.

1.1 *Profound Connotation of Social Structure Transformation*

Li Peilin points out that social transformation is a kind of holistic development and special structural change. Social structural transformation is the most essential content of socioeconomic development, substantially determining the modernization of a country; it refers to a comprehensive structural transition at the level of economic structure and other social structures. It is a stage in the process of sustainable development that cannot be portrayed just by general macro description or abstract analysis, since it relates to a category of holistic quantitative relationship and is usually explained by a set of structural parameters. Therefore, it is necessary to employ quantitative analysis to describe and analyze accurately that can show us the timing sequence of change and specific tracks of change at different levels of economic and social structure. In brief, the main body of social transformation is social structure, including structural transformation, mechanism transition, interest adjustment, and conceptual change.

1.2 *The Characteristics of Social Structure Transformation in China*

Li Peilin argues that the transformation of social structure is not an exclusive phenomenon in socialist countries, but rather a common stage in the process of modernization. Yet, the transformation of social structure in China has its own characteristics. First, structural transformation and institutional transformation run in parallel. Unlike in other countries, social structure transformation in China is closely related to the reform of the economic system, and the latter is the direct cause of the former. Second, there is the dual launch of government and market: on the one hand, the Communist Party of China and the Chinese government have promoted a series of reforms that have had a profound impact on the country's transformation in social structure; on the other hand, the market mechanism plays an increasingly important role in the allocation of resources. Third, there is the two-way movement in the process of urbanization: unlike in other countries, the uniqueness of China's urbanization lies in the two-way movement of urban expansion and rural urbanization. Fourth, there is an unbalanced development in the process of transformation: there are a lot of structural imbalances emerging in the process of China's social transformation, including the imbalance of development between regions, between urban and rural areas, between industries, and between economy and society.

1.3 The Influence of Social Structure Transformation

Li Peilin points out that in the process of social transformation, structural changes would become the third force, different from the government and the market. Once the structural transformation starts, it will form an irreversible trend, the driving force of reform and innovation and invisible pressure, such as with township enterprises, the tertiary industry, migrant workers in cities, and the pressure of the reform of state-owned enterprises. In contrast with previous studies that regard structural transformation as the natural result of economic growth, Li Peilin suggests that structural transformation is not only the result of economic growth but also the driving force of social change, which makes structural development an irreversible trend and structural transformation an invisible pressure of change. The structural transformation affects the change of behavioral patterns in the field of micro economics. On this basis, Li Peilin discusses the significance of social structure transformation for developing countries. Firstly, compared with the importance of technology in developed countries, structural transformation may have a greater significance for developing countries. Secondly, the significance of social structural transformation at different stages is different; the lower the level of development, the greater the impact of structural transformation. Thirdly, the more space there is for structural change in the period of social transformation, the greater the role it would play in growth. Fourthly, national development strategies will affect the timing, sequence, and speed of structural transformation.

2 The Development of "*guanxi*" Theory to Western Social Capital Theory

In the 1970s, the American sociologist Mark Granovetter proposed the role of social networks in job mobility. Based on data collected in Western societies, research shows that a weak tie is more effective in job hunting. The reason is that a strong tie is the internal bond within the group, and thus the information obtained from it is highly repetitive. Compared with the strong tie, the weak tie is the link between groups, and thus the information obtained from it is of low repeatability and high heterogeneity. The weak tie plays a bridge role in providing non-repetitive information. Granovetter explained this phenomenon as "strength of the weak tie" and put forward the hypothesis of the weak tie. However, based on the Chinese social experience, Chinese sociologists have demonstrated that the weak tie hypothesis and corresponding propositions have certain limitations, and have made some improvements (Bian 1997; Fu 2011).

2.1   Strong Tie Hypothesis: A Challenge to the Weak Tie Hypothesis

Based on a survey in Tianjin in 1988, Bian Yanjie points out that job opportunity is more often obtained through strong rather than weak ties; both direct and indirect ties are used to obtain help from the people in charge of the distribution of jobs; job seekers and ultimate assistors establish indirect relationships through intermediaries who have strong ties with both sides; job seekers who use indirect relationships rather than direct relationships are more likely to receive better job opportunities (Bian 1997). The mechanism is that strong ties, rather than weak ties, are the network bridge connecting individuals. Social relationship is no longer an information bridge, but a network of favor. The strength of the tie is positively related to getting care and help. A strong tie makes it more likely to get care and help, and vice versa. Bian Yanjie thus put forward the "strong tie hypothesis".

Bian Yanjie (1997) suggests that the existence of the strong tie bridge challenges the hypothesis of weak tie strength, but he does not completely deny the latter. The hypothesis of the weak tie, which refers to the idea that the weak tie has a more practical effect than the strong tie in the market economy, is true even in the unique job distribution system in China, in which resources flow through direct relationships. However, there are limitations to the weak tie hypothesis. The proposal of a strong tie hypothesis implies that the weak tie hypothesis needs to be revised in several aspects: firstly, direct and indirect relationships need to be distinguished; secondly, whether it is information or influence flowing through these relationships needs to be clarified; thirdly, different institutions and the context of the labor market restrict the usage of relationships with different strengths to obtain information or influence in job hunting. Therefore, the practical and valid hypothesis of relationship strength ought to be put forward only after these factors are adequately considered.

2.2 The Effect of the Economic System and Social Networks

After he proposed the hypothesis of the strong tie, Bian led the team to carry out many follow-up research projects, especially in investigating the impact of the transformation of the economic system on social networks in the transition society of China. A representative study of this research discusses the relationship between social network and occupational mobility under the background of transition from planned economy to market economy. It points out that in different economic systems, the relationship mechanisms between social network and occupational mobility may be distinctive; the role of the strong tie not only exists in redistribution systems, but also widely exists in the transition economy. Moreover, the social network of job seekers is mainly composed of relatives and friends. The main form of the functioning of social networks is to provide favors, and the auxiliary form is to pass messages (Bian and Zhang 2001). Another representative study coins the concept of "institution-crossing social capital", suggesting that the stepwise market-oriented reform in China leads to the coexistence of the state sector and the non-state sector and generates two different institutional resources. When people's social relationship network crosses two systems, system-crossing social capital will be generated and enables the system-leapers to obtain various economic returns, including income. This is a supplement to and development of the theory of social capital in the West. In addition, other studies also demonstrate the significant influence of social relationship intensity on enterprises and market operation. Some scholars have shown that relationship (*guanxi*), circle culture (*quanzi*), and the differential pattern of interpersonal relationships have profound impacts on the operation of Chinese enterprises, markets, and industries, such as the familiarization tendency of state-owned enterprises (Zhang 2002) and private enterprises, and the phenomenon of fellow townsman and fellow trader.

2.3 Sociology of Ties: From Theoretical Knowledge to Research Methodology

On the basis of the aforementioned research, the research team represented by Bian Yanjie developed the sociology of ties with Chinese characteristics. Bian Yanjie emphasizes the two levels of connotations of the sociology of ties: first, from the perspective of studying Chinese society, the sociology of ties is a set of theoretical knowledge of relationalism characterized by an ethical basis, relational orientation, and familiarity; second, the sociology of ties has methodological connotations in that it is a thinking methodology and research methodology to explore and analyze patterns of social behavior, that is, to study Chinese society and all other societies from the theoretical perspective of relationalism (Bian 2010). The emphasis on the tie that contains favor, relationship, face, reward, and other elements of interpersonal interaction reflects the unique research object, research perspective, and research method of the sociology of ties, which is the transcendence and development of Western social capital theory.

3 The Transcendence of Property Rights as a Relational Concept and Mixed Ownership Theory over Western Property Rights Theory

Western theories of property rights focus on the field of economics, focusing on the impact of clear property rights on economic performance, and the importance of state, legal, contractual, and other formal systems to define property rights. However, it is difficult to explain the experience of China's market transformation using Western theories of property rights. The field investigation and research of Chinese economic sociologists show that many township enterprises and officially patronized enterprises have achieved rapid development even with unclear property rights. The traditional state-owned enterprises have also achieved preliminary modernization and enhanced market competitiveness. This shows that property rights are embedded in the complex institutional background and social relations, and property rights are not a duality of the public and the private but a "continuum". The primary function of property rights is to provide incentives and constraints. Chinese experience shows that property rights need to be understood in the social institutional environment. Market competition and institutional arrangements (such as well-functioning corporate governance) are more important than property rights in terms of incentives, constraints, and improving enterprise efficiency, or at least they can play the same role (Yang 2013; Zhou 2005).

3.1 *Property Rights as a Relational Concept: Understanding Property Rights from External Social Environment*

The Western theories of property rights emphasize that "property rights are a bundle of rights", including the right to use, the right to earnings, and the right to transfer, and analyze the incentive mechanism of property rights on economic behavior and its impact on the efficiency of resource allocation. Starting from the institutionalism in sociology, Chinese sociologists put forward the concept of property rights as a relational concept, emphasizing that "property rights are a bunch of relationships" and pointing out that the structure and form of organizational property rights are not a kind of independent right emphasized by economists, but the result of organizations establishing long-term stable relations between other external organizations and seeking to adapt to the environment (Zhou 2005). In this sense, the ambiguity of property rights is a strategic choice for an organization to adapt to the external environment, which is conducive to the long-term survival and development of the organization. When an organization transfers part of its property rights to external actors, it can obtain more a abundant and sustained support of resources. The shift from the analysis of rights to the analysis of relations provides a new perspective for the analysis of property rights, that is, to address the role of property rights from a broader external social environment that is a transcendence of Western theories of property rights.

3.2 Possession Institution: A More Basic Concept than the Property Rights System

The Western theories of property rights derive from the clarity or ambiguity of property rights, and emphasize the significance of clear property rights for economic growth. It is with this approach that Western theories of property rights can hardly explain why township enterprises with "unclear" property rights rise in China and promote economic growth. Like property rights as a relational concept, Chinese economic sociologists find that the seemingly unclear property rights are not actually ambiguous in the actual operation, and people involved have a clear definition of property rights. Therefore, we need to find a more basic concept than property rights to describe the actual state of the operation of property rights. From the concept of possession, Chinese economic sociologists put forward the analytical framework of three dimensions of the institution of possession (namely, the exclusive scale of possession, the choice of the mode of possession, and the time limit of possession), which can generate more accurate descriptions and analysis of the state of property rights, and describe the form of possession and social defining mechanism of township enterprises. Chinese sociologists have found that if we observe the various property rights in society from the three dimensions of the institution of possession and the social defining mechanism of possession, the so-called ambiguous property rights have relatively clear status of possession, which has stronger analytical and explanatory power than the Western theories of property rights (Liu 2003).

3.3 Defining Mechanism: Multiple Defining Mechanisms and Dynamic Defining Process of Property Rights

Western economic theories of property rights emphasize the key role of state and law in defining property rights, and they highlight the significance of formal systems for the definition of property rights. Based on the field investigation of the transformation practice, Chinese sociologists point out that there are multiple social defining mechanisms for property rights in practice, including formal identification mechanisms, such as legal identification, administrative enforcement identification, and official forms of identification, as well as informal identification mechanisms, such as civil society norms identification and special interpersonal network identification (Liu 2003). In this sense, the property rights of township enterprises, as the collective property rights of the community, are essentially a kind of social contractual property right. The nature of the social relationship of the community determines the channels for the accumulation and division of assets, and it has an influence on maintaining the order of the property rights of the community. With changes in the external institutional environment, this type of property right is in the dynamic defining process of signing—breaking—re-signing (Zhe and Chen 2005). Therefore, from the sociological perspective, the property rights are not the stable structure set by economics, but a dynamic equilibrium process (Shen and Wang 2005).

3.4   Mixed Ownership: The Relationship between Corporate Governance and Corporate Performance

The Western theories of property rights study the role of the state, as the principal, on the governance and performance of the enterprises in the transitional economy, and suggest that the fatal defect of state-owned enterprises lies in the principal-agent problem. Due to information asymmetry and incentive incompatibility, the managers of state-owned enterprises can hardly maximize the profitability of enterprises. Therefore, the state-owned system is the obstacle to the operation of the market economy, which leads to rent-seeking, corruption, and other corrupt behaviors. However, the research of Chinese scholars shows that the existence of the principal-agent problem does not necessarily equate with the idea that the state-owned shares are inefficient, and the performance of state-owned listed companies is the proof. Unlike traditional state-owned enterprises, state-owned listed companies are no longer completely owned by the state but are of a mixed ownership structure, mostly owned by the state, domestic private shareholders, and foreign shareholders. In the new system of the diversification of property rights, there is a joint influence of different types of shareholders on corporate behavior. Although the state is the largest shareholder in the dominant position in many listed companies, other private and foreign shareholders also have considerable influence, and even the weakest individual shareholders may impose certain supervisions and restrictions on the state shareholders or the corporate executives of state-owned enterprises.

The supervision and balance mechanism among shareholders brought by the diversification of property rights and public listing remarkably reduces the agency cost of state-owned listed companies. Good corporate governance is very important for enterprise performance. Theoretically, property rights should be regarded as a continuum with continuous change rather than the duality of the public and the private, which can not only include the issues of "property rights" with subtle degrees of difference in the scope of investigation, but also help to evaluate and compare the relative strength of various shareholders. This is the transcendence of the Western theories of property rights.

4 The Challenge of the "Chinese Economic Model" to Western Economic Theories of Development

The theory of development economics itself has experienced the debate about the role of market and government, from the classical and neoclassical theories that attach importance to the role of the market, to Keynesian or structural economics that emphasize the role of government, and to the attempt of new structuralist economics to integrate the two mechanisms (the market is the fundamental mechanism of resource allocation, and the positive role of government in guidance is also required for economic development) (Lin 2010). Even if the role of the government was emphasized, it would be the governmental influence on economic growth through macro-control, public goods, infrastructure, and other aspects that drew the most attention, and the deeper governmental intervention into the market, especially the various complex institutional arrangements that the government uses to promote the development of the market economy, would not be the focus.

From the practice of China's development, the rapid development since the country's reform and opening up has created a miraculous economic development that has attracted worldwide attention. The Chinese economic pattern has become a theoretical and empirical topic to which academic circles attach great importance. The research works of relevant scholars have shown that the components of the Chinese economic pattern include at least: the tournament system, the land-revenue-finance trinity of industrial development, the urbanization model, the government-led financial system (commercial banks, stock markets, policy banks), Chinese political-business relationships (growth alliance), industrial policy, and the system of development zones/industrial parks/high-tech parks/cultural industry gardens (Zhou 2009). These components reflect the great role played by the government in economic development, put forth a challenge to the Western development economics that adheres to the free market orientation, and form an important supplement to the discussion on the role of government in development economics.

4.1 Tournament System

The duality of political centralization and economic decentralization is an important feature of China's system, and it is a critical factor in the relationship between the central and local governments. In this context, the central government has set economic development indicators for local governments. Local governments compete around the indicators, and the winners have a higher chance of promotion, which fully mobilizes the enthusiasm of local governments in economic development. This system is called "tournament system" by sociologists (Zhou 2009). Either in the period of the Great Leap Forward or after the reform and opening up, the tournament system has been a distinctive feature of the relationship between the central and local governments. The seemingly decentralized tournament is actually based on highly centralized power and the state's control over important social resources. This kind of control is manifested in three aspects: political control, media control, and resource control, which firmly grasp and influence the personnel promotion of local officials, social information systems, and public opinion, as well as important economic resources in all aspects (Zhou 2009). With these three aspects of control, the decentralization of the central government in the economy can have an immediate effect that results in the rapid climax of economic construction in a short period of time, in the form of behaviors by local government, such as "corporatization", "soft budget", and "adding at every lower level".

4.2 The Land–Revenue–Finance Trinity of Urbanization and Industrialization

The fiscal relationship between central and local governments is an important dimension to understand the behavior of local governments and the developmental pattern of China. If the tournament system had a significant influence on the political motivation of local government officials to seek economic development, the fiscal system would have a direct impact on the economic motivation of local government officials. Chinese economic sociologists have conducted systematic and in-depth studies of the tax distribution reform in 1994 and the transformation of development patterns brought by the reform. The reform of the tax distribution system has had a profound impact on the relationship between the central and local governments and between government and enterprise, which causes the local governments to urgently seek ways to make money out of their budgets. From the fiscal contract system to the tax distribution system, in the wave of marketization and urbanization, the local government behavior has changed from managing enterprises to managing cities. Through the acquisition, development, and transfer of land, the local government can obtain a huge amount of revenue, such as land transfer fees and land-related taxes and fees, as fiscal expenditure. On the one hand, it is used for land acquisition compensation and development costs, on the other hand, it is used to develop more land, and to mortgage land to leverage bank loans. Three aspects cooperate to promote the construction of urban infrastructure and the rapid expansion of urban scale. Scholars summarize this development pattern as the land–revenue–finance trinity of the urbanization and industrialization model (Zhou 2012).

4.3 *The Government-Led Industrial Policy and Chinese Political-Business Relationships*

In the transformation and upgrading of industrial systems, especially in the development of high-tech industry, a series of industry policies led by the government are the key factors. The research of economic sociology has found that the innovation system of the coexistence of competition and cooperation under government regulation is the foundation of the success of China's high-speed train industry innovation. This system consists of three interrelated organizational mechanisms, namely, government coordination and control, oligopoly competition among equipment manufacturers, and collaboration among the industry, academia, and research institutions. Among these aspects, government regulation is vital. This government-led innovation system has successfully solved the incentive problem of specific technology investment and the supply problem of complementary technology capacity in high-speed rail innovation (Li 2019). Meanwhile, under the tournament system, Chinese governments at all levels have launched fierce competitions for regional economic growth. By vigorously building development zones, industrial parks, and high-tech parks, the government has invested in infrastructure projects and attracting investment, especially attracting foreign-invested enterprises to settle in, so as to actively promote regional economic growth in a variety of ways (Li and Hou 2011). In addition, local governments have greatly shaped China's grassroots market activities, industrial structure, and economic performance. There is close interaction among and common pursuit between local governments and enterprises, forming a Chinese political-business relationship of a growth alliance, which plays an important role in building market systems, developing characteristic industries, attracting foreign investment, and promoting economic growth (Fu 2018; Geng and Chen 2015).

4.4 *The Government-Dominated Financial System*

The sociologists have analyzed the improvement of the state control and resource mobilization ability in China from the perspective of finance, suggesting that China's financial system is a government-dominated financial system and the state is in the central position in the power structure of the financial system. The state has realized the improvement of national capacity through the mechanisms of revenue financialization, foreign exchange growth, land financialization, and the dual-track system of interest rates, to guarantee the strong resource input for high-speed economic growth (especially the development of state-owned enterprises, industries, and regions), to lay a solid resource foundation for coping with financial risks, and to provide resource support for the governance of social differentiation and the maintenance of social stability (Liu, Young and Yu 2020). From the perspective of economic growth mechanisms, the Chinese economy is characterized by government-driven growth. Since the reform and opening up, the capitalization of state-owned enterprises, the separation of banking and government, and the reform of the tax distribution system have been conducive to the improvement of the investment capacity of the central government. Although the tax distribution system and the separation of banking and governmenthave weakened the investment capacity of local governments, local governments have made use of land fiscalization and financialization to overcome the conditional restrictions and realize the great improvement of investment capacity (Liu, Chen and Yong 2014).

5 The Contribution of Chinese Labor Sociology to Western Labor Process Theory

The study of the labor process is a critical part of labor sociology. In *Das Kapital*, Marx laid the foundation for the study of the labor process. *Labor and Monopoly Capital*, published by Braverman in 1974, marked the formal establishment of labor process theory. Inspired by Burawoy's works, there is more and more research on workers' subjectivity. In addition to paying attention to the factors of class and gender that are emphasized in Western studies of subjectivity, Chinese labor studies include the particularity of China's reform process to develop a labor sociology with Chinese characteristics (Wen and Zhou 2007).

5.1 *The Reformation of the Working Class in China's Transitional Society*
Understanding the labor issues in China's transitional society is the first problem that needs to be solved by labor sociology with Chinese characteristics. Chinese sociologists point out that China's labor issues need to be examined in the macro social background of the two "great transformations". The

institutional arrangement of the starting stage of China's social transformation, especially the dual structure of urban–rural division, causes the reformation of the working class to be divided into two different segments, the old and the new, which develop along different paths and show a complex and diverse labor process (Shen 2006). Unlike the labor groups in other countries, the history of China's reform has created two groups: old workers and new workers. Before the reform, the industrial working class was concentrated in the city and was entitled to various state social welfare systems, according to the state industrialization strategy of the central city, while the farmers engaged in agricultural production lived in rural areas, bound to the land, benefited little from the welfare provided by the state, and were not allowed to move at will. After the reform and opening up, the original industrial working class and the peasant class started to evolve towards the working class of market society, but through a different approach and logic. On the one hand, the previous workers of the state-owned enterprises are gradually incorporated into the labor market and become "old workers"; on the other hand, the farmers who flow out of the countryside enter the factories and are tempered and forged into "new workers". To be specific, "old workers" and "new workers" have great differences in the subjectivity of workers in the following three ways:

First, there is the formation of class consciousness. New workers enter the city from the countryside and work in foreign-invested enterprises, joint ventures, and private enterprises. Facing the labor–capital relations in a typical market society, they often form a working-class consciousness in the production field. The class consciousness of old workers in the former state-owned enterprises is closely related to the marketization process promoted by the state, which is formed in the living community after they quit the original production field (laid off and dismissed).

Second, there is the pattern of labor reproduction. The residences and workplaces of "old workers" are in cities, and their cost of labor reproduction includes not only the reproduction of their own physical and mental power, but also their families. Yet the families of "new workers" are in rural areas. New workers often come to work alone in the city. This leads to their "split" pattern of labor reproduction. This "split" pattern of labor reproduction determines that "new workers" may accept much lower wages than the "old workers". The arrangement of state power strengthens the effect of the reproduction pattern of labor force. The state can reduce the production cost, reduce the pressure of urbanization, and promote the industrialization process based on cheap labor with this pattern.

Third, there is the capacity of collective action. The power of the working class is divided into two aspects: the power of association and the power of structure. "Old workers" tend to display "association power" or semi-"association power". But "new workers" display more "structure power", especially "bargaining power in the market". Even with the almost unlimited labor supply, "new workers" can still show this power by "voting with their feet". In short, these three aspects are not within the scope of Western labor theory. Different segments of the working class in the transitional period have different structural characteristics and ability to act, which are deeply affected by the initial institutional arrangements in the transitional period.

5.2 The Core Characteristics of the Labor Process with Chinese Characteristics

Chinese labor sociologists have carried out abundant in-depth field research and have enriched, promoted, and revised the Western labor process theories based on this research. Shen Yuan, an influential Chinese scholar in the field of labor sociology, systematically summarized the characteristics of labor process with Chinese characteristics revealed by these studies (Shen 2020).

First, there are the social attributes of workers. Western theories of labor sociology define labor from the economic dimension and comprehend labor from the perspective of the subordinate of production relations. However, Chinese sociologists have found that labor groups have rich social attributes, which implies that the definition of economic dimension would not be sufficient to describe Chinese labor. It is necessary to include the social regulations carried by labor groups, especially the broader urban–rural relations and local social characteristics, to comprehend the labor group and labor process in China.

Second, there are the production regimes of migrant workers. "Factory regime" is a core concept of Western labor sociology, aiming at the grasp of the relationship between micro characteristics of the labor process and the macro background, such as market relations and state policies. Chinese sociologists have found that the concept, type, and operation mechanisms of the Western factory regime are not enough to explain the complex labor process of Chinese society, especially the phenomenon of migrant workers' labor process. There are various forms of factory regimes in China's transitional society, and its influence mechanism is not only the relationship between the state and the market, but also involves various factors, such as social relations, gender, and cultural cognition.

Third comes labor consciousness and culture. Most Western theories of labor sociology suggest that the group consciousness of labor is formed in the production workshop. However, Chinese labor sociologists have revealed that the production of labor consciousness in the transitional society is extremely complex, which may be in the workshop or outside the workshop, and the latter is more important. Compared with the old generation of workers, the formation of consciousness and culture of the new generation of workers is more complex.

Fourth we have the labor organization and the labor struggle. The research of Chinese sociologists finds that labor organizations confront the dual pressure of institutionalization and marketization. To obtain the resources for survival, labor organizations are either absorbed by the official system or integrated into the market, with a fundamental defect of the lack of "social as the standard". In the labor struggles, researchers have discovered that, rather than pursuing grand class unity or challenging the abstract dominant pattern, migrant workers would flexibly employ the official discourse, cultural symbols, and daily life resources to achieve pragmatic unity (Wang 2013) within the group and the mobilization effect of social forces. It shows a more diverse struggle mechanism than that revealed by Western labor sociology research.

Fifth, there is the politics of life. Western labor sociology always emphasizes the "politics of production" and ignores the life of labor groups outside the production process. Rather, Chinese labor sociologists pay close attention to private lives and action spaces outside the production workshop. Research shows that the daily life of migrant workers has an important impact on their group consciousness, organization mode, and action strategy. Based on this, Chinese labor sociologists put forward the concept of "politics of life", paralleling with the concept of "politics of production", which expands the theoretical vision and research space of labor sociology.

6   The Challenge of Chinese Urbanization Model to Western Urbanization Theory

In 1954, Lewis established the binary structure model of economic development (Lewis 1954). This model separates the economy in developing countries into two sectors—agriculture and industry—and summarizes the process of economic development as the process of economic structural transformation, that is, the gradual decline of the agricultural proportion and the rise of the industrial proportion. In this model, there is a large amount of surplus labor in the rural areas of developing countries, and the industrial sector that represents advanced productivity is still in expansion. Since the marginal productivity of the industrial labor force is obviously higher than that of agriculture, its wage is higher than that of agriculture, which continuously draws the agricultural labor force out of the countryside to the city. This process will not cease until the rural surplus labor force is completely absorbed by the city, the rural wages and urban wages reach an equilibrium, the urban–rural differences gradually disappear, and the national economy achieves modernization.

A striking feature of China's urbanization process is its breakthrough in the binary development mode (Zhang 2013). Many elements of this non-binary also exist in other developing countries, but the breakthrough in China is the most outstanding, which specifically is reflected in two ways.

6.1   The Development of Township Enterprises and the Breakthrough of Urban–Rural Dual Structure

The springing up of township enterprises is a great initiative on the part of Chinese peasants. With their emergence and development, the boundaries between urban and rural areas in many areas in China, especially in the economically developed coastal areas, have become increasingly blurred. Peasants "leave the land but not the hometown", work in township enterprises, and remain in rural communities. The small towns developed in rural areas have increasingly obtained the functions and characteristics of traditional urban areas, functioning as the political, economic, and cultural centers of rural areas. The construction of small towns is the way to develop rural areas and solve the problem of population (Fei 1984), thus breaking through the traditional urban–rural dual structure.

6.2   The Conflict between the Bottom-Up Urbanization Model and the Theory of Dual Regional Structure

Since 1978, one of the important characteristics of China's urbanization has been the emergence and development of bottom-up urbanization. A significant consequence of this urbanization is the reduction of the regional urban primary index. This kind of non-polarization phenomenon in the early stages of development is not only a challenge to the traditional dual regional development theory but also a development in the non-polarization regional development theory. The development is embodied in the following three aspects.

First, studies of rural urbanization in China can make up for the neglect of the role of marginal areas in the process of regional development in the framework of dual analysis. Many studies show that the main driving force behind China's rural industrialization comes from the rural areas themselves. The rural areas at the edge play a major role in early development, either in the aspect of the source and spread of innovation, which is very important in the center–periphery theory, or in the aspect of funding sources, which are not just driven by the diffusion effect of the core cities after the industrialization has reached a certain stage, as the traditional dual regional structure theory suggested. With both the Wenzhou model and Jinjiang model, which are far away from big cities, and the southern Jiangsu model, which is greatly influenced by big cities, the initiative of local communities and the funding by peasants or local communities all play a major role (Li 1996; Lu 1995). These models summarized by Chinese scholars are a breakthrough in Western urbanization theory.

Second, studies of rural urbanization in China will help to gain some new understanding of the spatial effect of foreign investment in the process of urbanization in developing countries. The urbanization research based on the traditional regional development theory does not pay much attention to the role of foreign investment, or it generally emphasizes the negative impact of foreign investment on the urbanization of developing countries. At the same time, it argues that foreign investment is a major factor leading to the phenomenon of urban primacy. Many empirical studies conducted outside China also reflect that foreign investors are generally more likely to invest in the core economic areas, with the obvious "big city tendency". The practice of Chinese development demonstrates that a large amount of foreign investment would target rural and small towns and other marginal areas. Some scholars even think that there is a new type of urbanization called "external-oriented urbanization" (Li 2004). This phenomenon strengthens the position of small towns rather than big cities in the urban system in the Pearl River Delta and southeast Fujian Province.

Third, rural urbanization in China can provide new connotations for the theory and strategy of "bottom-up" urbanization and regional development. China's rural urbanization and regional development strategy attaches great importance to the role of industrial development in absorbing rural surplus labor. At the same time, since the reform and opening up, in the process of urbanization the connection between Chinese rural areas and international and domestic economic systems has also been deepening. From the perspective of the dual analysis framework of urbanization, a significant feature of China's bottom-up urbanization is that it breaks through the traditional view of the duality of urban industry–rural agriculture, the opposition between urban and rural areas, and that rural development must be dominated by central areas, especially big cities.

6.3 *The Leading Role of Government in the Mode of Urbanization*

Sociologists point out that the main characteristics of China's urbanization include: government-led, large-scale planning, holistic promotion, state or collective ownership of land, the obvious separation of old downtown areas and new city districts, etc. Based on this, they point out that there are seven types of urbanization promotion modes in China, namely, the establishment of development zones, the construction of new districts and towns, urban expansion, old city reconstruction, construction of central business districts, township industrialization, and village industrialization (Li, Chen and Liu 2012). Some other studies have shown that China's urbanization is particularly different from Western urbanization due to the trinity model of land–revenue–finance that promotes the rapid development of urbanization and highlights the important role of local governments in promoting the process of urbanization, which is different from the Western urbanization mainly promoted by marketization and industrialization. In the urbanization promotion mode that balances urban and rural development, the combination of government leadership and capital intervention has brought a series of changes, such as peasants "going upstairs" (peasants leaving the original homestead to live in a new place) and capital "going to the countryside" (the large-scale agriculture operated by the city capital), which plays an important role in promoting the process of urban and rural integration and reflects the urbanization mode centered on land management (Zhou and Wang 2015). This phenomenon has strong Chinese characteristics.

In the development of Chinese economic sociology in the previous 40 years, Chinese sociologists have always adhered to the research approach of the combination of investigation, research, and theoretical construction based on the great journey and vigorous practice of reform and opening up. Chinese economic sociologists learn from and absorb Western theories with no intention of simply copying them. Based on Chinese experiences, they put forward the theoretical viewpoints of economic sociology with Chinese characteristics represented by the above six topics, and thus supplement, develop, and transcend Western economic sociology. From the above six topics, it is reasonable to argue that China's economic sociology has made significant theoretical innovation on the macro, meso, and micro levels. On the macro level, theories of the other invisible hand, the tournament system, the government-led financial system, the trinity of the land–revenue–finance development model, and the two-way movement of urbanization process have explanatory power for the phenomenon of social transformation in various fields in China and have reference and inspiration for understanding the economic and social development of other countries, especially developing countries. It reflects the competence of Chinese economic sociology to respond to and comprehend economic and social phenomena at the macro level and illustrates the transcendence and development of Western macroeconomic and social theory. On the meso level, theories of the government-led industrial policy, Chinese political-business relations, and the reformation of the working class demonstrate the unique organizational processes and mechanisms in the economic and social development in China, which has irreplaceable value for understanding the role of the Chinese government, especially for different levels of government in social transformation and economic development, and challenges the overemphasis of the role of the free market in the Western theories. On the micro level, the theories of property rights as a relational concept, the institution of possession, mixed ownership, labor process, and relational sociology reveal the complex reality and underlying logic of China's economic and social micro-operation, which makes an important contribution to the construction of the basic theory of economic sociology with Chinese characteristics and complements and perfects the general knowledge system of sociology. Chinese economic sociology from the perspective of post Western sociology will continue to explore and innovate on the basis of these research accumulations, especially in the face of various new trends, new problems and new challenges under the background of remarkable global changes and the great rejuvenation of China.

References

Bian, Y. 1997. "Bringing Strong Ties Back in: Indirect Ties, Network Bridges, and Job Searches in China". *American Sociological Review* 62 (3): 366–385.

Bian, Y. 2010. "Relational Sociology and its Disciplinary Status". *Journal of Xi'an Jiaotong University (Social Sciences)* 3: 1–6.

Bian, Yanjie, and Wenhong Zhang. 2001. "Economic Systems, Social Networks and Occupational Mobility". *Social Sciences in China* 2: 77–89.

Fei, Hsiao-Tung. 1984. "Big Problems in Small Towns". *Outlook Weekly* 2: 18–20.

Fu, Ping. 2011. "Transaction Pattern Based on Secondary Clientelism, Business Ideology and Market Development: The Case of Lime Market in Hui Town". *Sociological Studies* 5: 1–30.

Fu, Ping. 2018. "Market Regime and Industrial Advantages: A Sociological Study of Regional Disparity in Agricultural Industrialization". *Sociological Studies* 1: 169–193.

Geng, Shu, and Wei Chen. 2015. "Government-Corporate Relations, Two-Way Rent Seeking and the FDI Miracle in China". *Sociological Studies* 5: 169–193.

Lewis, W.A. 1954. "Economic Development With Unlimited Supplies of Labour". *The Manchester School* 22 (2): 139–191.

Li, Guowu. 2019. "Competition and Cooperation Under Government's Coordination and Control: The Innovation System of China Railway High-speed and Its Evolution". *Nankai Journal (Philosophy, Literature and Social Science Edition)* 3: 121–137.

Li, Guowu, and Jiawei Hou. 2011. "The Tournament System and the Growth of Provincial Development Zones in China: Evidence from Provinces". *Chinese Journal of Sociology* 2: 42–72.

Li, Peilin. 1992. "Another Invisible Hand: Transformation of Social Structure". *Social Sciences in China* 5: 3–17.

Li, Peilin. 1994. "On 'The Other Invisible Hand'". *Sociological Studies* 1: 11–18.

Li, Peilin. 1996. "Social Network and Social Status of Migrant Workers". *Sociological Studies* 4: 42–52.

Li, Qiang, Yulin Chen, and Jingming Liu. 2012. "On the 'Development Mode' of Chinese Urbanization". *Social Sciences in China* 7: 82–100.

Li, Shenglan. 2004. "A Study of the Development Mode of External-Oriented Urbanization". *Journal of Sun Yat-sen University (Social Science Edition)* 5: 11–15.

Lin, Yifu. 2010. "New Structural Economics: Reconstructing the Framework of Development Economics". *China Economic Quarterly* 10: 1–32.

Liu, Changxi, Yong Gui, and Qin Yu. 2020. "Financialization and State Capacity—A Sociological Framework". *Sociological Studies* 5: 123–146.

Liu, Changxi, Chen Meng and Yong Gui. 2014. "Sociological Analysis on Governmental Investment Driven Economic Growth Model: A Perspective From Capacity Theory". *Sociological Studies* 3: 77–99.

Liu, Shiding. 2003. *Possession, Cognition and Interpersonal Relationship—An Economic Sociological Analysis of China's Rural Institutional Change*. Beijing: Huaxia Publishing House.

Lu, Xueyi. 1995. *Jinjiang Model and Rural Modernization*. Beijing: China Knowledge Publishing House.

Shen, Jing, and Hansheng Wang. 2005. "The Practical Logic of Collective Property Rights in Rural China Life: The Process of Contracting Property Rights From the Sociological Perspective". *Sociological Studies* 1: 113–148.

Shen, Yuan. 2006. "The Social Transformation and Reformation of Chinese Working Class". *Sociological Studies* 2: 13–36.

Shen, Yuan. 2020. "The Development of China's Labor Sociology in the Past 30 Years". *Sociological Review of China* 5: 3–17.

Wang, Jianhua. 2013. "Pragmatic Solidarity: An Analysis on the Case of New Workers' Collective Action in Pearl River Delta". *Sociological Studies* 1: 206–227.

Wen, Xiang, and Xiao Zhou. 2007. "Western Labor Process Theory and Chinese Experience: A Critical Review". *Social Sciences in China* 3: 29–39.

Yang, Dian. 2013. "Corporate Governance and Firm Performance: A Sociological Analysis Based on Chinese Experience". *Social Sciences in China* 1: 72–94.

Zhang, Hongyan. 2013. "China's New Urbanization Theory and Strategic Innovation". *Sociological Studies* 3: 1–14.

Zhang, Yi. 2002. *The Familialization of State Owned Enterprises*. Beijing: Social Sciences Academic Press.

Zhe, Xiaoye, and Yingying Chen. 2005. "Defining the Property Rights in the Context of Township and Village Collective Enterprises". *Sociological Studies* 4: 1–43.

Zhou, Feizhou. 2009. "Tournament System". *Sociological Studies* 3: 54–77.

Zhou, Feizhou. 2012. *Profit for Profit: Financial Relationship and Local Government Behavior*. Shanghai: Shang DXJ Publishing Company.

Zhou, Xueguang. 2005. "Property Rights as a Relational Concept: A Sociological Approach". *Sociological Studies* 2: 1–31.

CHAPTER 13

Thirty Years of Labor Sociology in China

Shen Yuan

1   Introduction

The origin and development of contemporary labor sociology in China can be divided into three periods: the first period comprises the decade of 1990s, when Chinese sociology faced the labor group in the reformation process after reconstruction; the second period is the first decade of the 21st century, when labor research based on labor sociology began to develop; finally, the third period is the second decade of the 21st century, when the new fields and new horizons of labor sociology were further expanded. The sorting of the three periods constitutes the theme of this paper. It is necessary to explain that the principle on which this paper divides the three periods is "the unity of history and logic". Therefore, the division of each period on the timeline is not so detailed and precise, but rather an outline. In this paper, the comments on the research results of different periods are not completely sorted by time but classified according to their logic. The purpose of this formulation is to reveal the agreement between the outline of the periods and the academic logic of labor sociology, and to illustrate the structural extension and internal tension of the latter.

2   The First Decade: Newly Formed Labor Group

Chinese sociology was restored and reconstructed in the 1980s, with two important factors in its macro background. First, reform and opening up has made China a "world factory"; second, this has led to the reformation of Chinese labor groups. After the reform and opening up, a large number of farmers left rural areas and agriculture, and they moved to the emerging industrial areas in the east and to large and medium-sized cities to work as migrant workers. Together with the original "old workers" in state-owned enterprises, they formed a labor group in the transition period. The number of migrant workers was large at the beginning of formation. Today, according to official statistics, there are nearly 300 million migrant workers, which shows that when China becomes a "world factory", the largest labor group in the world has been formed (Shen 2006a).

At the beginning of its restoration and reconstruction, Chinese sociological studies involved different aspects of the labor group, such as "Analysis of Chinese Contemporary Class Stratum", presided over by He Jianzhang, former director of the Institute of Sociology, Chinese Academy of Social Sciences; "Investigation of Township Enterprises", engaged by Professor Ma Rong, Wang Hansheng, and Liu Shiding, which focused on migrant workers in township enterprises who are "Agricultural Household Entrepreneurs" (Ma et al. 1994); influential research results on the large-scale mobility of migrant workers at that time (Sun 1997); and the primary systematic study on workers in state-owned enterprises by researcher Li Peilin (Li et al. 1992). It is particularly worth mentioning that it is sociology that first put forward the concept of "migrant workers", which was quickly accepted by academic circles and society. According to Zhang Yulin, a researcher at the Institute of Sociology, Chinese Academy of Social Sciences, as this emerging group is constituted by farmers who engage in industrial production, they should be called "migrant workers" so as to express the contradiction between their identity and occupation.

If there are still some shortcomings in the labor research in this period, it is hard to ignore that the biggest limitation lies in the misuse of the theoretical framework, that is, the labor group and labor issues are investigated under the mainstream sociological theoretical framework, such as with "social mobility", "social stratification", and "social issues", instead of being analyzed with the labor theoretical lens, namely, "labor sociology". What the author emphasizes here is that this approach includes the most important perspectives of observing the labor group, such as "Control and Resistance in Labor Process", and the most important methods, such as "Factory Ethnography", that had been omitted by researchers. Even though Chinese sociology faced huge theoretical demands from labor group research, the initial theoretical introduction focused on mainstream theories without taking this into account. At this point, an important task faced by Chinese sociology in the next period has emerged: Systematically introducing a labor sociology theory and conducting labor research in the transition period on the theoretical basis of labor sociology.

3 The Second Decade: Labor Research Based on Labor Sociology Theory

In the first decade of the 21st century, a remarkable trend of sociology was to begin the construction of the discipline of labor sociology and to carry out research work based on labor sociology theory. Limited to the scope of personal cognition, the author takes Tsinghua Team as an example here. The department of sociology at Tsinghua University, where the author taught in the past, has established labor sociology as one of the disciplinary directions of the department since its reestablishment in 2000. At that time, the construction of labor sociology was carried out in two directions. One direction was the systematic introduction of labor sociology theory. The department of sociology at Tsinghua University has established an academic cooperation with Professor Lee Ching Kwan of UCLA, and has systematically introduced the most fundamental theories of labor sociology, such as the "Theory of Labor Process and Factory Regime", the "Theory of Working Class Formation", the "Theory of Labor Protest and Movement", and the "Theory of Globalization and Labor Issues" to China (Lee 2003, 2006). Meanwhile, the most commonly used qualitative research methods of labor sociology were introduced and promoted, including "Factory Ethnography" and the "Extended Case Method".

In parallel, another direction is to carry out field research facing Chinese labor under the guidance of labor sociology theory. The characteristic of labor research carried out by the Tsinghua Team during this period was that the idea of "labor process" lay at the core of research, whereas observation, description, and understanding of the labor process in the workplace were taken as the basic directions of the entire research. In summary, six points in our research are worthy of praise.

3.1 The Social Character of Labor

We paid special attention to the social character of labor. While emphasizing the leading role of the labor process, we also strove to explore the influence and shaping of various social factors on labor. Labor research in classical Marxism considers labor to be based on economic categories. It mainly regards labor as being dominated by production relations, as having the group characteristic of the exploited, and as the conscious or unconscious subject in the labor process. Labor sociologists after Burawoy have tried to return to labor the social characters, such as gender, race, and civil rights, which had been abandoned by classic writers in their studies (see Lee 2008). The work is often referred to as the process of "rising from abstract labor to specific labor". The research of the Tsinghua Team was carried out along with this process. The study of "household workers" in North China's rural areas by Tong Genxing reveals that when migrant workers are taken into "household factories" located in local villages, such a rural factory regime forges a kind of "atypical labor" through double action (Tong 2005). Focusing on the influence of China's unique regional relations on labor politics, Wen Xiang's research discussed the "differential politics" caused by the cultural category of the "native place" (Wen 2008). It can be seen that when defining the category of labor and exploring the labor process, only by incorporating various social regulations and rural characteristics of labor into the analytical framework can China's labor and its action logic be truly understood.

3.2 The "Production System of Migrant Workers"

The concept of the "Production Regime of Migrant Workers" is born out of "factory regime", which is one of the most important concepts in labor sociology. After its reform and opening up, China has actually evolved into a "museum of factory regime". China has various factory regimes, from the most primitive factory regime in history, to the extensive factories in early industrialization, to the hierarchical manufacturers under the modern market system, and then to the "flat" work organization of high-tech industries. For example, the "factory regime" of North China's rural luggage industry is the so-called "patriarchal regime". Such a factory regime also commonly exists in the rural areas of the Pearl River Delta and other regions, which is a very old form of "factory regime" (Chen 2011; Liao Bingguang 2012).

The field investigation also suggests that the power creating a "factory regime" is diverse and not limited to institutional power. The "hegemonic" domination in China's construction enterprises is based on the social relations brought into enterprises by migrant workers. When looking for employment, migrant workers frequently depend on relatives and friends, so they are widely associated and jointly active. Therefore, when entering the labor process, these relationships are also brought into enterprises. These relationships can be changed into the resource on which labors are organized to resist control. But they can also be the approach used by employers to manage labor. When these relationships are applied to governance by managers, a special hegemonic system is formed in the workplace. We define it as "relationship hegemony" to distinguish it from the "institutional hegemony" put forward by Burawoy (Shen 2006a; Zhou 2007). Through a long-term field investigation of a service enterprise in a city in southwestern China, He Mingjie found a unique factory regime based on the gender management of female workers. That is, the same system contained the dual orientation of "despotism" and "hegemony" for different female workers—for middle-aged female workers who are engaged in rough work, a "despotism" management method is adopted; and for beautiful young female workers who directly deal with customers, such as waitresses, a "hegemony" management method is adopted. This complex "factory regime" is based on the distinction and utilization of the "Gendered Age" of middle-aged female workers and young female workers (He 2009).

The different characteristics of labor affect the structure of "factory regime", and different factory regimes impact the character-shaping process of labor, playing a very important role in molding the cognition and behavior of labor. The Tsinghua Team strives to show the diversity of the "factory regime" and the complexity of the dynamic mechanisms in the transition period. Later, we collectively call these "factory regime" forms, which are numerous and distributed at each end of the spectrum, the "Production System of Migrant Workers" and define this as the unique form of factory regime in the transition period, one based on the domination and utilization of migrant workers. The frequent protests of migrant workers are inevitably caused by the conflict with the "Production System of Migrant Workers" (see Guo et al. 2011; Shen 2013).

3.3   *Labor Consciousness and Culture*

The subjectivity of labor is one of the most important research fields in labor sociology, which is mainly defined by their own subjective world, namely, group consciousness and self-mentality. During the transformation of Chinese society, the production of labor consciousness was very complex. In terms of "old workers" in state-owned enterprises, Wu Qingjun's field investigation of the restructuring process of a state-owned tractor factory in northeast China found that when these state-owned enterprises' labors still had the status of formal workers and were still in the labor process, they only had a "unit consciousness". Only after the enterprise restructuring forced them to leave the production process and struggle in the labor market could the laborer's group consciousness be generated (Wu 2010). Xia Xue made a comparative study on the different consciousness and mentality of two generations of workers in a large state-owned textile factory in a city in central China, trying to reveal the processes and mechanisms of change and dissipation of the sense of unit identity and dependence of workers in state-owned enterprises (Xia 2007). Guo and Chang investigated the life courses of workers at some large state-owned enterprises in northeast China, as well as the reform of social security system, revealing the mentality changes in laid-off workers (Guo and Chang 2005). The field investigation of construction workers by Qi Xin found that the unique phenomenon of "wage arrears and wage seeking" in China is closely related to certain institutional heritages left over from the period of the redistribution system and the general recognition of migrant workers thereof: At the end of the "Cultural Revolution" a small number of construction teams, mainly farmers, moved to cities to build houses. And their income settlement was carried out according to the year-end dividend method in rural areas. After the reform and opening up, the highly market-oriented construction industry followed the year-end dividend settlement method in terms of distribution (Qi 2011). The inspiration of the study is that certain institutional elements of the redistribution system can be retained and continue to function in the marketization period.

3.4 Labor Organizations and Labor Protest

In terms of labor organizations, the research of the Tsinghua Team mainly focused on the Pearl River Delta Region, where about 40 of the most influential labor non-governmental organizations (NGOs) in China were active. The research of Lv Jialing was based on four aspects: source of funds, management mode, service object, and right-safeguard way. It was found that "institutionalization" and "marketization" have constituted a double pressure on labor NGOs, which leads them to be absorbed by the system for acquiring resources or integrating into the market (Lv 2008). Of course, these judgments were made according to the situation at that time. Today, most labor NGOs have fallen silent and disappeared in the long history of transition.

Concerning the research of migrant workers' protests, Zheng Guanghuai analyzed how local power and capital colluded and set up an "institutional trap" by means of "de-legality", thus depriving disabled migrant workers of their ability to defend their rights (Zheng 2005). In the later period, the Tsinghua Team focused on the protest of the new generation of migrant workers. The "new generation" refers to the fact that the relationships these migrant workers have with rural areas, cities, and country changed fundamentally. The actions of the new generation of migrant workers have produced a series of new characteristics, among which "short-term employment" and "leap-type job change" are two of the most important manifestations (Shen 2013). Wang Jianhua emphasized the orientation of "pragmatic solidarity" in labor action. Most ordinary workers are not interested in pursuing grand group goals or challenging the abstract dominance pattern, but they can expand the influence of their actions as much as possible by flexibly using mainstream ideological discourse and resources in daily life (Wang 2013). Similar action logic can be also reflected in the collective protest tide of sanitation workers in the Pearl River Delta Region. In addition to various structural conditions, sanitation workers were mainly winning on the skillful application of cultural symbols. The "weak symbol" they generated spread very quickly across society, mobilizing most of the citizens, who got involved in layers and helped each other (Dou 2016; Tang 2016). The mechanism of such protests is clearly more complex than the classic labor protest.

3.5 The "Politics of Life"

The concept of the "politics of production" put forward by Burawoy means that categories such as politics and culture do not exist outside the production process, which differs from classical Marxism. On the contrary, they are all rooted in the production process, and they synchronically exist and function (Burawoy 1985). When we define the main research object as migrant workers, their characteristics as "migrant workers" immediately come to us. Migrant workers left their hometown to work in factories. They not only engage in labor production in factories, but also live in factory dormitories or urban corners (mostly urban villages) to complete the reproduction process. The daily life field of migrant workers is of great significance for forming group consciousness, formulating action strategies, and forging independent organizations. For example, in 2010, the protest action of "Guangzhou Honda" workers was first conceived, organized, and launched through QQ and MSN chat in the daily life field rather than in the workshop. Wang and Quan systematically discussed the influence of the daily life field on migrant workers and put forward the concept of the "politics of life" (Wang and Quan 2013).

3.6 "Public Labor Sociology"

Labor sociology itself is public and should not be confined to the ivory tower of universities (Burawoy 2007). The highest level we pursue in labor sociology is that the knowledge produced is not only for the sake of academic achievement but should be used in direct dialogue with labor groups as a tool for their liberation. The Tsinghua Team has tried for many years to establish "public labor sociology".

The methods of "strong intervention" and "weak intervention" have been adopted for the "BG Night School for Migrant Workers" and the "NGO Film and Television Training Course", respectively. The former is a possible way for migrant workers who are deeply trapped in the household factories to break the ideological cage and develop group consciousness. For 2 years, the intervention team, composed of teachers and students from the department of sociology and the Law School of Tsinghua University, have been working in the BG Luggage Industrial Zone in North China every weekend to set up the "Night School for Migrant Workers" and carry out legal education for migrant workers (Hu 2007). The "Film and Television Training Course" aims to help workers in labor NGOs improve their cognition and organizational ability. We held two such courses where we distributed hand-held video recorders to 40 participants and had professional film and television directors explain collecting and editing skills to them, and then we asked the participants to return to their work sites. The participants recorded and compiled their daily work scenarios and processes, and then returned to the course to show their works to other participants, along with explanations (Wang 2009). In addition, teachers and students from the department of sociology at Tsinghua University have also participated extensively in major labor development issues, such as the reform of local trade unions and the construction reform of industrial worker teams, thus realizing "public labor sociology" in practice.

Of course, the Tsinghua Team is confined to a small department that was recently reestablished, with limited resources and capabilities. In fact, the labor sociology in this period was a great development starting from a small point. The long-term, systematic, and large-scale questionnaire survey and in-depth field research by Professor Cai He and other professors from the department of sociology at Sun Yat-sen University on migrant workers in the Pearl River Delta Region, especially the discussion on the transformation of migrant workers' protests from "bottom-line" to "incremental"; the research of migrant workers in the construction industry and the "Foxconn Migrant Workers Survey" by Professor Lu Huilin and other professors from the department of sociology at Peking University, and the research of employees in service industry and the discussion of labor and gender issues by Professor Tong Xin; the discovery and description of "the 'Making Out' Game outside the Factory" by Professor Huang Yan from the South China University of Technology, and the research of mentoring relationships, skills training, and labor politics by Professor Wang Xing of Nankai University (see Cai 2010; Pan, Lu, Guo and Shen 2012; and Pan, Lu and Zhang 2010; prepared by Pan et al. 2012; Huang 2012; Tong 2009, 2012; and Wang 2009). These are some prominent cases.

The growth of the Tsinghua Team reflects the development of Chinese labor sociology from one aspect, as noted above. We admit that our labor sociology is based on the theories and methods of Burawoy, and we will not hide the fact that the research results of this period are characterized by distinctive features, such as "production center" and "factory regime". One thing we must emphasize is that we will not stop conducting research.

4 The Third Decade: New Fields and New Horizons of Labor Sociology

Labor sociology has obviously entered a new stage in its third decade. The new stage means that there is a new trend in labor research, which is mainly manifested in two aspects: first, the research of new groups; and second, the formation of new horizons.

Studying different labor groups has always been the main research field of labor sociology. In the past 10 years, truck drivers born out of the rapid development of the road freight transport industry, as well as food deliverymen, couriers, and ride-hailing drivers born out of the growth of platform economics, have become the new focus of labor sociology.

According to the data provided by the China Road Transport Associations, there are about 15 million freight trucks and 30 million truck drivers in the road freight transport industry (China Road Transport Associations 2016). By chance, some labor sociology researchers from Tsinghua University, the Capital University of Economics and Business, the China University of Labor

Relations and the Beijing Academy of Social Sciences were able to team up and start a systematic research project focusing on this labor group. On the basis of collecting a large amount of empirical data, the five characteristics of the truck driver's labor process have been summarized. (1) Truck drivers are mostly "self-employed", with the dual attribute of being small private owners and workers. (2) The labor process of high mobility and atomization contains many labor forms such as physical strength, mental power, and emotion. (3) Drivers consider trucks as their home, so the production and reproduction are integrated. (4) Male-dominated occupations are full of strong masculinity and regulate the labor process. (5) A high dependence on smart phones and mobile Internet brings the organization the feature of "virtual solidarity". The research of "professional gender minority", that is, female drivers and the wives of truck drivers, revealed the significance of gender in the labor politics of the road freight transport industry. We also studied the basic institutional arrangements of the road freight transport industry, and two professional groups closely related to the labor process of truck drivers, namely, logistics operators and loaders. The research has been continued for 3 years, and the research results were published in the form of a "social survey report" published in three volumes (Research Group of Chinese Truck Drivers of Transfar Foundation Philanthropy Research Institute 2018a, 2018b, 2019). In spring 2020, the sudden outbreak of the COVID-19 epidemic interrupted the normal production and living order of the whole society. Our two investigation reports on "truck drivers under the epidemic" and "truck drivers' work resumption" reflect in a timely manner on the track of the anti-epidemic, production, and daily activities of truck drivers during this period (Research Group of Chinese Truck Drivers of Transfar Foundation Philanthropy Research Institute 2020a, 2020b).

The intervention of the Internet in the logistics and service industry has created the operational form of a new economy, and "platform economics" is one of them. "Platform economics" has generated unique labor groups, such as the food deliverymen called "take-out riders" and the couriers called "delivery guys". Chen Long, from the department of sociology at Peking University, meticulously described the daily labor process of "take-out riders" in Beijing through 6 months of observation and in-depth interviews (Chen 2018). Lian Si's team from the University of International Business and Economics adopted various methods to describe the work of "delivery guys" (Lian 2019). Zheng Guanghuai's team from the School of Social Sciences at Central China Normal University systematically investigated the labor process and daily life of food deliverymen and couriers in Wuhan, and they tried to summarize the labor characteristics of "platform economics" with the concept of "download labor" that they forged on the basis of their investigation (Zheng et al. 2020).

"Platform economics" reflects the typical characteristics of Zuboff's so-called "Surveillance Capitalism" (Zuboff 2015). Similarly to the above research, Wu Qingjun's research on ride-hailing drivers by means of the participation observation method also revealed that platform economics blurs real labor relations and strengthens systematic surveillance (Wu and Li 2018).

Studies on urban gas station workers are another case of such research. Gong Baohan and Song Qi, two master's degree program students with the Tsinghua Team, took 385 of the 1,441 gas stations in Beijing for investigation, depicting the unique factory regime of gas stations and the basic characteristics of the "nested labor" of gas station workers: They "nested" two different jobs, namely, filling vehicles with oil and selling commodities to drivers, in the same labor process (Gong and Song 2020).

With the further expansion of the category of "labor" into the broad category of "work", people beyond blue-collar workers and their work have been gradually included in the scope of labor sociology. In recent years, two aspects are worth noting. One aspect is the research of "digital labor". Since Professor Qiu Linchuan of the Chinese University of Hong Kong took the lead in discussing the "network society of the new working class" (Qiu 2013), "white-collar workers" in the computer and Internet industries, i.e., programmers, have been gradually included in the scope of labor sociology. Since then, the research scope of labor sociology has increasingly extended to "knowledge labor" and labor organizations in Internet enterprises (See Liang 2019; Hou and He 2020). Another aspect is the research on live webcast platforms and the work of network "anchors" (see Xu and Zhang 2019), and the amount of such research is increasing.

The expansion of the research field is only one aspect of the recent development of labor sociology. Another aspect that must be explained is the emergence of a number of new horizons. The author roughly groups these into the following seven points.

1) *Looking forward to the macro: towards regional comparative institutional analysis.* The advancement of the theoretical framework is reflected in multiple aspects, among which the framework of "regional comparative institutional analysis" has profound implications. Wang Jianhua initiated this framework and took the farthest course in this direction. He put forward that there are two urgent problems to be solved in current labor sociology. First, due to an excessive concentration on the experience of the Pearl River Delta and the insufficient consideration of other regions, the different impacts of differentiated economic and social development among regions on labor cannot be fully presented. Second, due to the insufficient amount of importance attached to the role of local

government for the centralized analysis of the micro factory regime and labor process, the research on the relationship between the state and labor needs further exploration. He believes that it is necessary to discuss labor issues within the framework of comparative analysis of economic and social development models among large regions, especially so as to grasp the different strategies and roles of local governments in labor management, which brings a new horizon for analyzing "state intervention" and further adapts the theory of factory regime to China's situation (Wang 2017; Wang, Fan and Zhang 2018).

2) *Deeper into the micro: attempting a more delicate emotional labor analysis.* Since Hochschild, "emotional labor" has become a basic conceptual tool for analyzing the particularity of service industry labor (Hochschild 1992). It is also widely used in the labor sociology of China. Early classical analysis includes that on domestic workers' labor carried out by Ma Dan from the department of sociology of Peking University (Ma 2012), while recent novel analysis includes that on the "pleasure" of cultural and entertainment producers carried out by Jia and Zhong from Shanghai University (Jia and Zhong 2018). When studying truck drivers, we also found that their labor also includes emotional labor and can be divided into two categories with two directions. One direction involves the "emotional labor" facing others. When truck drivers interact with traffic police, freight forwarders, and loaders, such emotional labor is widely needed. The other direction entails the "emotional labor" facing one's inner world, which is an inner self-psychological experience of truck drivers throughout their driving labor (Research Group of Chinese Truck Drivers 2018). Wang Fan's research continues along the direction of "emotional labor". He put forward that the labor process is never an absolutely continuous process, but is often interrupted. It is the unity of continuity and discontinuity. "Waiting" is a continuous interruption, but it is different from "resting". During waiting, labor force is not needed, but labor's mind is worn, and psychological experiences, such as anxiety, impatience, uneasiness, and tension, are produced in the laborers' minds, resulting in a special mentality and social consequences (Wang Fan 2019).

3) *Relationship-oriented: Towards the "two-point theory" position of labor research.* When it comes to the classic research of labor sociology, its self-evident basic position is "labor-oriented"—limited to the research of labor itself and presenting the characteristics of "one-point theory". Such a research position is conducive to an in-depth exploration of and thinking about the characteristics of labor itself, but at the same time it often leads to an insufficient amount of attention being given to the

other party of the labor process, namely, capital and managers. That is what is meant by the statement "class struggle is a two-sided body" (see Fantasia 1985). In recent years, more and more scholars have realized this limitation of labor sociology and have tried to enrich their research by connecting with labor relations and introducing its horizons about the interaction between labor and capital. In this respect, the research on the collective transformation of labor relations, trade union reform, and collective negotiations carried out by Professor Chang Kai of Renmin University of China and Professor Wen Xiaoyi of the China University of Labor Relations, is of instructive significance (See 2013; Wen 2014, 2017).

4) *Towards technology: exploring the impact of new scientific and technological factors involved in the production field on labor.* As mentioned earlier, the new labor groups generated by platform economics and digital governance and the domination on them are an example. Operating platform economics under the current social framework not only fails to fully realize its great potential in effectively providing public goods, but exposes its orientation of concealing labor relations and intensifying labor control. The impact of AI technology involved in the production field on labor is another example. Professor Xu Yi of Sun Yat-sen University and others have creatively explored the application of robots in the labor process and its impact on labor, with quite thought-provoking results (see Xu and Xu 2019). And the impact of driverless technology on the career prospect of truck drivers has also become an increasingly concerning issue.

5) *Internationalization: focusing on overseas laborers and their work and organizations against the background of globalization.* Foreign capital entering the country and the situation of domestic labor have been a concern of labor sociology for many years, but only little attention has been paid by labor sociology to Chinese capital going abroad and the work and life of overseas Chinese laborers. Recently, this situation has begun to improve. Domestic scholars have started conducting research in this field (see Liu and Wang 2019), thus enriching the global horizon of labor research.

6) *Exploring history: understanding and learning from the sociological tradition of the Republic of China.* Older sociologists, such as Chen Da and Shih Kuo-Heng, began research on labor issues from different theoretical angles. Their research seems to emphasize the role and influence of indigenous factors in the machine age. Shih Kuo-Heng's discussion on the "Consensus Relationship" in modern enterprises is an example (Shih 1946). Such a perspective is quite beneficial to today's discussion on migrant workers. The labor sociology of today has begun to explore the

sociological tradition of the Republic of China and to integrate it into the current theoretical framework as much as possible. Wen Xiang's recent research reflects such a direction (Wen 2018).

7) *Open mind: engaging in a constructive dialogue with new foreign theories.* The most influential Western labor theory at present is the theory of so-called precarious work and precariat (see Yao and Su 2019). Such a theory put forward by attempts to summarize the current situation of labor groups in the neoliberalism era in the Western world. If the theory is used as a reference for the research of Chinese migrant workers, we can find that, on the one hand, Chinese migrant workers do have many "precarious" characteristics, which are quite similar to the current predicament of Western labor. On the other hand, the roads experienced by Chinese and Western labor are just the opposite. In the West, in the era of neoliberalist globalization, labor groups have been deprived of all of the welfare systems and rights frameworks they had previously acquired through their 200-year-old struggle. The labor groups are suffering indescribable pain, and such pain may be reflected in the theory of the "precariat". Compared with this, Chinese migrant workers have had few welfare benefits from the beginning. The urban–rural segmentation system and household registration system have defined migrant workers as "second-class citizens" in cities from the very beginning. On the contrary, in the past two decades, the state has promulgated the *Labor Law* and the *Labor Contract Law* to promote the citizenization of migrant populations; to try to establish the minimum wage standard; to implement a series of laws, regulations, and institutional arrangements, such as social insurance; and to gradually empower and provide guarantees for migrants, thus laying an institutional foundation for them to become a real modern labor group.

5 Conclusion

This paper aims to describe the "history and development" of Chinese labor sociology in general. It should be noted that a large part of this narrative is based on the labor research of the Tsinghua Team. This is the result limited by the author's horizon, but it is also based on objective history: it is from the reestablishment of the department of sociology of Tsinghua University that the labor sociology theory was introduced and carried forward. In this sense, the labor sociology of Tsinghua University can be compared to a small milestone, indicating that contemporary Chinese labor sociology has begun to develop. Today, although labor sociology has become an obsolete in Tsinghua University, the ideology has been spread outside the campus and developed so prosperously in China. The increasingly fruitful research results of labor sociology are the best commemoration of the milestone.

References

Burawoy, M. 2007. *Public Sociology*. Translated by Yuan Shen, et al. Beijing: Social Sciences Academic Press.

Burawoy, M. 1985. *The Politics of Production*. London: Verso.

Burawoy, M. 2008. *Manufacturing Consent*. Translated by Rongrong Li. Beijing: The Commercial Press.

Cai, He. 2010. "From 'Bottom-line Interests' to 'Incremental Interests': Change of Migrant Workers' Interest Demands and the Labor-capital Relations". *Open Times* 9: 37–45.

Chang, Kai. 2013. "The Collective Transformation of Labor Relations and the Improvement of the Government's Labor Policy". *Social Sciences in China* 6: 91–108.

Chen, Long. 2019. "Labor Order Under Digital Control: A Study on Labor Processes and Capital Control in the Platform Economy". Doctoral dissertation. Department of Sociology, Peking University, Beijing, China.

Chen, Qiuhong. 2011. "Family Is Factory: Rural Industrialization Survey in Beizhen Town, Hebei". Master's thesis. Department of Sociology, Tsinghua University, Beijing, China.

China Road Transport Associations. 2016. *Green Driving Report on the Survival of Truck Drivers*. Available at www.jsjtxx.com.

Dou, Xuewei. 2016. "Appeal and Intermediary: Sanitation Workers' Power of Protest". Doctoral dissertation. Department of Sociology, Tsinghua University, Beijing, China.

Fantasia, R. 1985. *Cultures of Solidarity: Consciousness, Action, and Contemporary American*. Oakland, CA: University of California Press.

Gong, Baohan, and Song Qi. 2020. "'Nested Labor' and 'Service': A Survey on Gas Station Workers in City B" (Preprint), Collected Papers Database of Social Sciences Academic Press, https://www.jikan.com.cn/infoDetail/article/30000005 (accessed April 17, 2020).

Guo, Yuhua, and Aishu Chang. 2005. "Life Circle and Social Security: A Sociological Probe into the Life Course of Workers Out of Work". *Social Sciences in China* 5: 93–107.

Guo, Yuhua, Yan Shen, Yi Pan, and Huilin Lu. 2011. "Contemporary Migrant Workers' Protest and the Transformation of Labor-Capital Relations". *The Twenty-First Century Review* (April): 4–15.

He, Mingjie. 2009. "Labor Process and the Differentiation of Sisterhood". *Sociological Studies* 2: 149–176.

Hochschild, Arlie Russell. 1992. *The Managed Heart: Commercialization of Human Feeling*. Taipei: Laureate Book Co. Ltd.

Hou, Hui, and Xuesong He. 2020. "No Survival Without Overtime Work: Why Employees of Internet Companies Become Assembly Line 'Overtime Dogs'". *Exploration and Free Views* 5: 115–123.

Hu, Lina. 2007. "Baigou Migrant Worker Night School: An Attempt of Sociological Intervention". Master's thesis. Department of Sociology, Tsinghua University, Beijing, China.

Huang, Yan. 2012. "The 'Making Out' Game Outside the Factory: A Case Study of "Making Out" Production in Pearl River Delta Area". *Sociological Studies* 4: 187–203.

Jia, Wenjuan, and Kaiou Zhong. 2018. "Another Way of 'Amusing Ourselves to Death'? Experience, Ideological Fantasy, and Labor Control in Variety Entertainment Production". *Sociological Studies* 6: 159–185.

Lee, Ching Kwan. 2003. Lecture Notes on Labor Sociology. Not published.

Lee, Ching Kwan. 2006. *The Politics of Working-class Transitions in China, Social Stratification in Contemporary China: Theory and Demonstration*, edited by Liping Sun, et al. Beijing: Social Sciences Academic Press.

Lee, Ching Kwan. 2008. *Engendering the Worlds of Labor: Women Workers, Labor Markets and Production Politics in the South China Economic Miracle, Teaching Materials for the Labor NGO Seminar*, edited by the Department of Sociology of Tsinghua University (internal printing), Beijing, China.

Li, Peilin, et al. 1992. *Chinese State-Owned Enterprises in Transition*. Jinan: Shandong People's Publishing House.

Lian, Si, ed. 2019. *The Development Report on Chinese Youth No. 4*. Beijing: Social Sciences Academic Press.

Liang, Meng. 2019. *Overtime: Research on Work Stress of Internet Companies in China*. Beijing: Social Sciences Academic Press.

Liao, Bingguang. 2012. "A Case Study on Bag and Suitcase Manufacturing Industry Clusters in Baigou Town". Master's thesis. Department of Sociology, Tsinghua University, Beijing, China.

Liu, Xinghua, and Yong Wang. 2019. "Labor Export, Transnational Production Politics and the Formation of Exploitation Relationship—A Case Study of Chinese Workers in Japan". *Chinese Journal of Sociology* 3: 123–153.

Lv, Jialing. 2008. "Manufacturing Unity? A Paradox of Labor NGOs in China". Doctoral dissertation. Department of Sociology, Tsinghua University, Beijing, China.

Ma, Dan. 2012. "Commercialization of Private Life: A Study on the Labor Process of Live-in Domestic Workers in Beijing". Doctoral dissertation. Department of Sociology, Peking University, Beijing, China.

Ma, Rong, et al. 1994. *Development History and Operating Mechanism of China's Township Enterprises*. Beijing: Peking University Press.

Marx, Karl. 1979. *Capital*. Beijing: People's Publishing House.

Pan, Yi, Huilin Lu, and Huipeng Zhang. 2010. "The Formation of Class: Labor Control on Construction Sites and the Collective Resistance of Construction Workers". *Open Times* 5: 5–26.

Pan, Yi, Huilin Lu, and Huipeng Zhang. 2012. *Large Construction: The Survival View of Rural Migrant Workers in Construction Industry*. Beijing: Peking University Press.

Pan, Yi, Huilin Lu, Yuhua Gou, and Yuan Shen, eds. 2012. *I Am in Foxconn*. Beijing: Intellectual Property Publishing House.

Qi, Xin. 2011. "The Formation and Reproduction of Wage Back-Payment Mechanism in Chinese Construction Industry". *Sociological Studies* 5: 55–79.

Qiu, Linchuan. 2019. *World Factories in the Information Age: The New Working-Class Network Society*. Guilin: Guangxi Normal University Press.

Research Group of Chinese Truck Drivers of Transfar Foundation Philanthropy Research Institute. 2018a. *Chinese Truck Drivers I*. Beijing: Social Sciences Academic Press.

Research Group of Chinese Truck Drivers of Transfar Foundation Philanthropy Research Institute. 2018b. *Chinese Truck Drivers II*. Beijing: Social Sciences Academic Press.

Research Group of Chinese Truck Drivers of Transfar Foundation Philanthropy Research Institute. 2019. *Chinese Truck Drivers III*. Beijing: Social Sciences Academic Press.

Research Group of Chinese Truck Drivers of Transfar Foundation Philanthropy Research Institute. 2020a. "Truck Drivers During the COVID-19 Epidemic" (Preprint). Collected Papers Database of Social Sciences Academic Press, https://www.jikan.com.cn/infoDetail/article/30000001 (accessed March 10, 2020).

Research Group of Chinese Truck Drivers of Transfar Foundation Philanthropy Research Institute. 2020b. "Survey Report on Work Resumption of Truck Drivers" (Preprint). Collected Papers Database of Social Sciences Academic Press, https://www.jikan.com.cn/ (accessed April 15, 2020).

Shen, Yuan. 2006a. "The Social Transformation and Reformation of Chinese Working Class". *Sociological Studies* 2: 13–36.

Shen, Yuan. 2006b. "'Strong Intervention' and 'Weak Intervention': Two Approaches Of Sociological Intervention Method". *Sociological Studies* 5: 1–25.

Shen, Yuan. 2007. *Market, Class and Society*. Beijing: Social Sciences Academic Press.

Shen, Yuan, ed. 2013. "Social Transformation and New Generation Migrant Workers". *Tsinghua Sociological Review* 6.

Shen, Yuan, and Xiang Wen. 2012. "Labor Studies in the Perspective of Transitional Sociology: Problems, Theories and Methods". *Tsinghua Sociological Review* 5.

Shih, Kuo-Heng. 1946. *China Enters the Machine Age*. Beijing: The Commercial Press.

Silver, Beverly J. 2016. *Forces of Labor*. Translated by Zhang Lu. Beijing: Social Sciences Academic Press.

Sun, Li, ed. 1997. *Chinese Society in Transition: Chinese Social Survey*. Beijing: Reform Press.

Tang, Lingyue. 2016. "Protest of the Weak and Symbolic Production: Taking the Sanitation Workers' Strike for Rights Protection in Guangzhou as an Example". Master's thesis. Department of Sociology, Tsinghua University, Beijing, China.

Tong, Genxing. 2005. "Household Workers in Beizhen Town: The Logic of Macro Political Economics and the Logic of Daily Practice". In *Sociological Master Degree Papers From Three Universities*, edited by Yefu Zheng, et al. Jinan: Shandong People's Publishing House.

Tong, Xin. 2009. "Gender, Division of Labor, and Social Mobility in Small-Scale Restaurants in China". *Jiangsu Social Sciences* 3: 1–8.

Tong, Xin. 2012. "Labor Relations and Labor Rights Protection in the Security Service Industry in China". *Comparative Economic & Social Systems* 5: 36–46.

Wang, Chi. 2009. "Power of Images: From the Perspective of Migrant Workers". Master's thesis. Department of Sociology, Tsinghua University, Beijing, China.

Wang, Fan. 2019. "Waiting at Work: Time Experience, Consequences and Metaphors". Master's thesis. Department of Sociology, Tsinghua University, Beijing, China.

Wang, Jianhua. 2013. "Pragmatic Solidarity: An Analysis on the Case of New Workers' Collective Action in Pearl River Delta". *Sociological Studies* 1: 206–227.

Wang, Jianhua. 2017. "Packaged Government-Business Relations, Localized Employment and Labor Protest in Small and Medium-sized Mainland Cities". *Sociological Studies* 2: 51–75.

Wang, Jianhua, Lulu Fan, and Shuwan Zhang. 2018. "Regional Differences in Industrialization Patterns and Migrant Workers' Problems—A Comparative Study Based on the Pearl River Delta and Yangtze River Delta Regions". *Sociological Studies* 4: 109–136.

Wang, Jianhua, and Quan Meng. 2013. "Patterns of Collective Resistance Among the New Generation of Chinese Migrant Workers: From the Politics of Production to the Politics of Life". *Open Times* 1: 165–177.

Wang, Xing. 2009. "Contracting the Mentor-Apprentice Relationship and Labor Politics". *Chinese Journal of Sociology* 4: 26–58.

Wen, Xiang. 2008. "'Ethnicity' in Bag Factories: Revisiting Household Workers in North Town". Master's thesis. Department of Sociology, Tsinghua University, Beijing, China.

Wen, Xiang. 2018. *The Sanctity of Labor*. Beijing: The Commercial Press.

Wen, Xiang, and Xiao Zhou. 2007. "Western Labor Process Theory and Chinese Experience: a Critical Review". *Social Sciences in China* 3: 29–39.

Wen, Xiaoyi. 2014. "Direct Labor Union Elections: Lessons from Guangdong". *Open Times* 5: 54–65.

Wen, Xiaoyi. 2017. "From 'State Steering' to Multielement Promotion: The New Trend of Collective Negotiation and Its Typology". *Sociological Studies* 2: 28–50.

Wu, Qingjun. 2010. *Reform of State-owned Enterprises and Transition of Old Industrial Workers*. Beijing: Social Sciences Academic Press.

Wu, Qingjun, and Zhen Li. 2018. "Labor Control and Task Autonomy Under the Sharing Economy: A Mixed-method Study of Drivers' Work". *Sociological Studies* 4: 137–162.

Xia, Xue. 2007. "Attachment and Alienation: A Comparative Study on the Sense of Belonging of Two Generations of State-owned Enterprise Workers". Doctoral dissertation. Department of Sociology, Tsinghua University, Beijing, China.

Xu, Linfeng, and Hengyu Zhang. 2019. "The Game of Popularity: Earning System and Labor Control in Live Streaming Industry". *Chinese Journal of Sociology* 4: 61–83.

Xu, Yi, and Hui Xu. 2019. "Two Models of Machine Replacing Human and Their Social Impacts". *Culture Crossings* 3: 88–96.

Yao, Jianhua, and Yihui Su, eds. 2019. *Bringing Labour Back in: Precarious Workers in the Global Economy*. Beijing: Social Sciences Academic Press.

Zheng, Guanghuai. 2005. "Injured Migrant Workers: A De-powered Social Group". *Sociological Studies* 5: 99–118.

Zheng, Guanghuai, et al. 2020. "Platform Workers and Download Labor: Group Characteristics and Labor Process of Couriers and Food Deliverymen in Wuhan" (preprint), Collected Papers Database of Social Sciences Academic Press, https://www.jikan.com.cn/infoDetail/article/30000002 (accessed March 30, 2020).

Zhou, Xiao. 2007. "Relation-Based Hegemony: A Field Study on the Labor Process on Construction Sites". Master's thesis. Department of Sociology, Tsinghua University, Beijing, China.

Zuboff, S. 2015. "Big Other: Surveillance Capitalism and the Prospects of an Information Civilization". *Journal of Information Technology* 30: 75–89.

CHAPTER 14

Voice of the Dead: Hibakusha Collective Memory against the Western Ethos

Nomiya Daishiro

1   Introduction

Japan's modernization project started in the late 19th century, when it transformed a longstanding feudal system into a western-style political and economic system. Change in the economic infrastructure came first, when silk and cotton spinning industries, employing a western factory system, saw substantial development in 1880s (Okawa and Rosovski 1973). Soon mining and ship construction industries picked up, followed by the rapid development of railroad, trafficway, and shipyard industries.

Behind this modern economic development was a strong push by the Meiji Japanese government to move fast toward an industrialized country. In 1850s, after 200 years of national isolation policy, Japan opened its seaports to foreign countries. After the opening of the country, mounting pressure from western powers, including the US, Great Britain, and France, forced Japan to transform itself to a modern state. This foreign pressure also instigated intense domestic conflicts among local feudal powers. Increasing voices form strong local powers in turn weakened the central government, culminating in the revolution of 1868 called the Meiji Restoration. In less than 20 years after the Restoration, new modern state Japan saw the development of western-style economic activities.

In addition to a strong push to agricultural and manufacturing development, the Meiji government took a gigantic step toward militarization. This was partly an effort to confront possible invasions by the strong western countries, but more to it, Japan faithfully followed the path the strong militaristic western countries had paved in the previous centuries. It was in the late 19th century that Japan began its own invasive action toward neighboring East Asian countries. Starting with the Sino-Japanese War in 1894, the Russo-Japanese War in 1904 and Japan's annexation of Korea in 1911 followed. In less than a decade from the domination of Korea, Japan entered itself in another humongous war, World War I, which ended with the victory by the military alliance Japan sided with.

Invasion and expansion were the core of Japanese foreign policy in the early 20th century. During this period, Japan's invasions to neighboring countries resulted in massive land seizure by the Japanese military forces and their domination of peoples residing in newly acquired territories. Extensive use of science and technology, together with the development of heavy industries, provided the foundation for the construction of military arsenals and high-technology weapons. To the world in the early 20th century, Japan was a rapidly emerging state that would soon rank with advanced western powers. Japan appeared invincible—at least to the eyes of those who led military operations in Japan. It was in this context that Japan's aspiration to a stronger military state led itself further to the participation in another war, this time, the World War II, the biggest war mankind has ever experienced to this date.

The route Japan chose to develop itself by can be interpreted as that of reflexive modernization. Giddens and Beck argue that the pursuit of modernity should give rise to a new set of risks, such as destruction of natural environment, development of military arms with high lethal potential, and resultant military confrontations and totalitarian regimes (Giddens 1985; Giddens 1990; Beck et al. 1994). This set of risks is a combinatory result of the development of capitalism and industrialism, increase in state's monitoring and centralizing capacity, and state's monopolization of the means of violence (Bauman 1989; Giddens 1990). Japan has exactly followed the developmental trajectory Giddens and many others lay out in the theory of modernity. This trajectory is that of westernization as well, as Japan in the late 19th century drew its developmental plan modelling after western powers (Tominaga 1990).

In the World War II, Japan lost. Not only Japan lost the war, but it did so devastatingly, as exemplified by the complete destruction of the cities of Hiroshima and Nagasaki by the dropping of the US atomic bombs, which mankind had used as war weapons to kill others for the first time in human history. The bombs turned two beautiful local-capital cities into barren lands, claiming to this date the death of more than 500,000 only in these two cities.[1] For Japan, the defeat in the World War II meant a failure in its effort to modernize itself by becoming a military giant.

Entering in the post-war era, a new developmental project immediately took off. The next few decades were marked by a series of gigantic rebuilding work in Japanese sociopolitical, economic, and military fields. Interestingly,

---

1 As of August 2019, the atomic-bomb related death toll counts close to 320,000 in Hiroshima, and over 180,000 in Nagasaki, according to the List of the Atomic Bomb Dead Victims compiled by the cities of Hiroshima and Nagasaki respectively (City of Hiroshima 2019, City of Nagasaki 2019).

the guiding principle of the post-war rebuilding project was, again, westernization. In the political field, Japan transformed itself from an imperialistic militant state to a democratic state. Following western democracies, it put popular sovereignty, pacifism, and respect for basic human rights as the core values to be pursued both in the new Constitution and in the actual formation of sociopolitical institutions and organizations. In the economic field, too, Japan continued its insistence on the western pattern of growth, with the adoption of capitalistic mode of production and added-profit trade model as the central mechanisms with which to lead the future of Japanese economy.

Especially in the economic field, this westernization project was a big success. It led Japan to a miraculous economic recovery, punctuated by the enactment of the "Income Doubling Plan" in 1960, trade liberalization in the early 1960s, and the participation to the OECD in 1964, and finally becoming the second-largest country in GNP in the world in 1968 (Nakamura 1995).

Amid an unprecedented economic boom and a renewed sense of development in the post-war era, there was one area that Japan did not follow western countries: development of nuclear weapons. After the World War II, advanced countries, including the US, Russia, France, and England, brought a lot of time and energy into their respective nuclear weapon development projects. Starting with the invention of the atomic bombs during the war, they successively went on to the creation of hydrogen bombs, missiles with nuclear warhead, nuclear submarines and nuclear-powered aircraft carriers. Indeed, it seemed that the post-war western powers continued their way to becoming even stronger military giants. Japan, however, did not take the same route.

What lies behind this move of Japan to stay away from the nuclear weapon development race by western countries? Why did Japan stop following the footsteps of western countries? This chapter claims that the "*hibakusha*" collective memory, non-western ethos emerged out of the defeat of the war, provides a sentimental basis with which to oppose to the development and forceful use of nuclear weapons as well as other military arms.

Entering in the post-war era, people in Japan started to ponder on the past experiences of the war, trying to understand the impact the war had left on their lives, together with the burdens they would have to carry into the future (Maruyama 1956; Ishida 1956; Kamishima 1961; Ohtsuka 1969; Wada 2015). This was especially true to the residents of Hiroshima and Nagasaki, as they were most severely torn apart by the atomic bombs (Takayama 2016; Nemoto 2018). In their agonizing effort to quest for the meanings of life and death, killing and surviving, and war and nations, they found hibakusha as a reference point where they would start their search for the meaning of life, how to make sense of the world they have in their surroundings, and what they would choose in the next crossroads in their lives (Ishida 1986; Yoneyama 2005).

Hibakusha is a collective name; it literally means those exposed to the atomic bomb explosions. Many victims died at the precise moment of the explosion; most of those who survived the moment of the explosion also died in the following days and months due to heavy exposure to radiation, which resulted in the body malfunctioning leading to fatal diseases. Then left are alive hibakusha, whom we call atomic-bomb survivors today.

As the only group of people in the world history who became the direct target of the atomic bombs, atomic-bomb survivors paved a way for new Japanese ethos to take root in post-war Japan. As the individual that nearly escaped from death, the survivor started to talk about him/herself, about how they saw the flash of the atomic bomb explosion, what they saw on the ground in the aftermath, and how they managed to stay on to continue their lives into the post-war era. The sheer fact that the survivors collectively own the traumatic experience of the exposure to the explosions had them share a sense of helplessness, grief, sorrow, and hope for a world without war. One individual narrative heavily loaded with the memory of the destruction and innocent death, together with a sense of inescapable sorrow and agony, was tied to another to form collective memory.

Away from the western ethos, this new collective memory began to influence the understanding and interpretations of the past and to limit future routes Japan should take. The hibakusha collective memory has embodied itself in some of the major controversies and events that represented significant turning points in the post-war history of two atomic bomb-laden cities, Hiroshima and Nagasaki, and of Japan. This hibakusha collective memory often puts strong influence on the political decisions both at a local and national level. In a way, hibakusha collective memory has given rise to a route to escape from the curse of the West, and to walk into a new road in the future.[2]

---

2   The author does not claim that the hibakusha collective memory is the decisive factor in the decision-making process in the local and national political scenes, nor argue that the hibakusha collective memory always weighs heavily in the deliberative processes in local and national arenas. Typically, in the political decision-making process, a host of multiple factors, such as stakeholders and relevant institutions, are to be taken into considerations. This was particularly true in the early phase of post-war period in Japan, as the GHQ (General Headquarters, the Supreme Commander for the Allied Powers) heavily intervened in Japan's major political processes and exerted significant influence over Japan's choice for a future road to reconstruct itself (National Diet Library on website; Shibata 2015). The argument here is that, despite such historical fact, the hibakusha collective memory has always been in

There have been incidents and cases where we can observe the working of the hibakusha collective memory in the decision-making processes and activities of the individuals, groups, and organizational bodies. Among the most well-known examples in the area of civil activity is perhaps the representation of hibakusha by Setsuko Thurlow, who delivered the lecture in December 2017 in Oslo, Norway, in commemoration of ICAN's (International Campaign to Abolish Nuclear Weapons) reception of the Novel Peace Prize in 2017. She has been among the leading figures of the campaign and was instrumental in the birth of the Treaty on the Prohibition of Nuclear Weapons in July 2017 (ICAN 2017; Henley 2017). Setsuko Thurlow herself is a hibakusha. The fact that a hibakusha was elected to the lecturer to represent a long-standing international peace activity reveals the extent of importance the ICAN puts onto the individual who has embodied the hibakusha collective memory throughout her life.

In other civil activities, the hibakusha collective memory often works as a point of reference that guides the interpretations and mental make-up of those involved in the activity. This is clearly seen in the case of the signature-collecting campaign in 1954, which raised a voice against the development of nuclear and hydrogen bombs. The 1954 signature campaign started in response to Japanese fishermen's deadly exposure to the nuclear fallouts caused by the hydrogen bomb experiments by the US near the Bikini atoll. One characteristic slogan employed in the campaign was the "third exposure to radiation", as participants counted the number of instances for Japanese people to be exposed to radiation. The first was Hiroshima, and the second, Nagasaki. Without a doubt, this slogan shows the working of hibakusha collective memory in the minds of campaign participants. Using the hibakusha collective memory, they established a strong connection between the incident of 1954 and those of Hiroshima and Nagasaki in 1945. This slogan instantly evoked the memory of disastrous past and instigated a humongous civil action. This civil action eventually collected more than 30 million signatures, well over one-third of the entire population of Japan back then, the largest signature-collecting campaign that gathered a vast number of participants and supporters in the history of Japan (Maruhama 2011; Ubuki 1982).

Instances of the working of the hibakusha collective memory is not restricted to occasions in a distant past; even today, this collective memory emerges as a strong internal voice that molds the minds of involved individuals when necessary. Employing the network analysis technique, Nomiya et al.

---

existence and remained to be one of those factors; it emerges on the surface when it matters most, and it often influences the political outcome.

(2019) draw a mental map of the movement participants to demonstrate how the hibakusha collective memory contributed to the mental make-up of the movement participants and supporters in the anti-nuclear power plant demonstrations in 2011–2012. The anti-nuclear power plant campaign was the largest civil movement in Japan since 1970s (Chiavacci and Obinger 2018).

The hibakusha collective memory entails anti-war sentiment; for hibakusha, it was war that gave them continuous torture throughout their lives. This sentiment occasionally appears in Japanese media. In the national poll in 2021, more than 60% of the Japanese citizens are in support of the preservation of Article 9 in the Constitution of Japan, which provides the renunciation of war, non-preservation of war potential forces, and the denial of the right of belligerency (Asahi Newspaper 2021).

As shown above, instances of the working of the hibakusha collective memory are scattered through the post-war history of Japan. The next section presents in detail how the hibakusha collective memory shows itself to make a counterargument against the movement formulated around the modern western ethos of progress and physical force. For this purpose, we take up a heated debate that took place in Hiroshima during the 1960s. A sudden announcement by the SDF (Self Defense Forces) plan to enter the Hiroshima Peace Memorial Park on its way to marching into the Peace Boulevard aroused a much-heated debate among residents of Hiroshima, civil groups, political parties, and the city government of Hiroshima. This debate ended with the SDF's revocation of its original plan to march into the Peace Memorial Park. In this debate, we can observe strong influence of the hibakusha collective memory on the emotions of concerned individuals and parties, which were gradually formed into one grand voice against SDF's entrance to the Peace Memorial Park.

2 Battle between the West and the Non-West: Debate on the Military March in Hiroshima[3]

In late October 1965, news broke out that the Japan's Self-Defense Forces (SDF) was planning to enter the Peace Memorial Park in Hiroshima on its way to the troop inspection march in an avenue in Hiroshima city. Also, it became apparent that the Hiroshima city government was in favor of this plan, having already given the SDF and its solders a permission to enter the park. The march would consist of 1600 soldiers, together with tanks, cannons, and other vehicles for the battle. The city march by the SDF had been performed since

---

3 Much of the content in this section is quoted from Nomiya (2022).

1962. The planned march in 1965 was the first, however, for the SDF's soldiers to enter the Peace Memorial Park.

A heated debate ensued, involving Hiroshima citizens and civil groups, atomic-bomb survivors, politicians and political parties, religious groups, and the SDF. What was on the line was whether the SDF was allowed to enter the Peace Memorial Park. Behind this debate was the characteristics of the SDF and the nature of the Peace Memorial Park.

The root of the SDF goes back to 1950, when the National Police Reserve was established. Due to the change in international circumstances, the National Police Reserve was transformed into the Self Defense Forces (SDF) in 1954. Despite its name, the SDF was a de facto military force, carrying weapons and equipment with which to attack and start the battle when necessary.

The Peace Memorial Park, on the other, was designed to honor the war victims and to pray for eternal peace, as its name suggests. In the monument placed at the center of the park, an oath is carved out that reads, "we shall not repeat the mistake". It is not only the holistic nature of the park that arose a sense of uneasiness by SDF's plan to enter the park; but also a vast number of atomic bomb victims, it is said, have been left buried under the ground of the park. In the eyes of Hiroshima citizens, those victims would have been downtrodden by the military forces again if the SDF had entered in the park.

In the debate, some threw in doubts, questioning the legitimacy of SDF's plan to bring in soldiers and military weapons to the Peace Memorial Park. Others claimed the SDF was an institution to protect people, not attack others, thus was no problem in having the SDF to enter the park. The debate intensified, turning itself into a possible physical collision, when some opposition groups and organizations threatened to resort to the use of forces to stop the SDF if they dared to enter the park. As early as October 25, 1965, several university students started camping in front of the monument (cenotaph) in the park to express their resistance. One labor union group, too, announced that it would start sit-ins in the park from October 29 by mobilizing ten thousand supporters; on October 31, when the SDF planned to enter the park, the group would continue to stay in the park before they would go on to the street march (Chugoku Newspaper, October 26, 1965).

This debate ended by SDF's concession. On October 27, the SDF announced that it would send, not 1600 soldiers, but only some representatives with no weapons to carry to the monument in the park. Opposition groups' contention not to allow weapons nor soldiers to enter the Peace Memorial Park was, at least in formality, preserved.

Probably it is not difficult to treat this debate as an unimportant passing event that does not impact much the political configuration of the city of

Hiroshima. Nonetheless, if seen as a discursive field, it vividly shows a clash of ideas and meanings attributed to the Peace Memorial Park and to the SDF's attempt to enter the park.

In one side of the discourse lies a claim by the SDF. Faced with a rapidly growing opposition, the headquarters of the Hiroshima SDF Division made an announcement on October 23, 1965, arguing that the SDF sought to attain peace by force, given the international situations at that time (Chugoku Newspaper, October 24, 1965).[4] This logic of peace by force continued to be employed in later years, as in April 3, 1974, when the headquarters of the SDF Hiroshima Division made a claim, asking the opposition parties and Hiroshima citizens in general to reconsider what they should do, including a possible use of weapons, as a nation to protect the peace and safety, and national independence in the real world (Chugoku Newspaper, April 4, 1974). It is clear that the spirit of the SDF to attain peace through the use of force is the reverberation of the Japanese military forces prior to the end of the World War II.

Another strand of the argument in the debate came from the city government of Hiroshima. Against opposition groups calling for the cancellation of the permission given to the SDF to enter the Peace Memorial Park, the city mayor Hamai announced that the city would not cancel the permission. The mayor went on to explain the reason, saying that the SDF was not a military force that would challenge other nations (Chugoku Newspaper, October 21, 1965). This statement by the mayor implied that SDF's effort to protect the nation was permissible, while SDF's act to attack others was not. This logic was further strengthened in later years when the city mayor Yamada downplayed the power of the SDF, characterizing it as a "toy" unable to go to a real battleground (Chugoku Newspaper, October 23, 1972). Hiroshima city's effort to conceal the offensive nature of the SDF by trivializing its physical forces, coupled its effort to read the SDF as only protective mechanism, was intended to persuade opposition parties, and possibly transform a civil perception toward the SDF into a positive one.

Against the arguments made by the SDF and the city of Hiroshima, various groups and organization raised oppositional voices. Among all these oppositions, beliefs, ideas, and sentiments behind respective arguments varied substantially. One straightforward argument came from groups of the atomic-bomb survivors, who strongly disagreed with the troop inspection march by the SDF. They claimed that Hiroshima citizens would not allow the SDF to perform the

---

4   In their effort to defend their legitimacy to enter the park, the SDF had made its first statement that the SDF shared the spirit of seeking peace on October 20th (Chugoku Newspaper, October 21, 1965).

troop inspection march with canons and tanks, adding also that the Peace Memorial Park was designed to swear our allegiance not to engage in wars in the future (Chugoku Newspaper, October 21, 1965). Behind this argument was a strong sense of opposition to the war and arming the military.

This sense of refusal was also shared by the peace movement groups and student movement bodies, who maintained that the troop inspection march via the Peace Memorial Park would constitute a sacrilegious act against Hiroshima citizens wishing for eternal peace (Chugoku Newspaper, October 21 and October 26, 1965).

Some religious groups, notably Hiroshima church branches and Christian organizations, issued a similar statement. They made it clear that they were against the use of the Peace Memorial Park by the SDF, adding that the personnel from the SDF must disarm should they enter the park (Chugoku Newspaper, October 27, 1965). The essence of their argument was that lethal weapons were incompatible with peace.

The Socialist Party and prefectural labor unions reasoned that the SDF was a national organization and thus the march by the SDF would mean a demonstrational act to show its national military power. They also argued that the military forces would never help attain nor protect peace (Chugoku Newspaper, October 24, 1965). A radical version of this argument was found in the claim by the youth division of the Socialist Party, who vehemently opposed the existence of the SDF. For them, the SDF would even point their guns at the citizens (Socialist Party Hiroshima Branch and Japan Socialist Youth Alliance 1973). Their voice was also directed against the city mayor of Hiroshima, criticizing mayor's decision to give the SDF a permission to use the Peace Memorial Park as a thoughtless action. In essence, the Socialist Party, its youth division, and the labor unions opposed to any military forces, national militarization and their legitimization.

With all these counterarguments made by various civil organizations and political groups, the SDF was pushed against the wall. On October 27, 1965, three days prior to the planned march, the SDF announced a change of the original plan. In the new plan, a small number of unarmed SDF personnel would enter the Peace Memorial Park to do worship service, and the troop inspection march would be performed away from the park (Chugoku Newspaper, October 27, 1965).

Behind this heated debate existed a special meaning that had been attributed to the Peace Memorial Park. For many, the Peace Memorial Park means a sanctuary, in which countless citizens of Hiroshima lie underground as the atomic bomb victims. These victims were the sacred as they died an innocent death; they were sacrificed, as it were, to end the war. The sacred victims were not to be violated nor outraged by a military force again. Thus, the opposition groups argued against any weapons to be brought into the park, denying any military show displaying tanks and canons of lethal capacity. For them, an act by a military force to enter the park would mean an act of ravage on the sacred soil.

This meaning attribution stood behind most of the discourses. Arguments and ideas issued by the opposition groups were based on the identification of the Peace Memorial Park with a sanctuary where the sacred were buried. This identification took over the discursive sphere of the debate in 1965, which eventually ended with a concession made by the side of the SDF.

In this debate, one can see the clash between western and non-western ethos. The SDF intent to attain peace by using physical forces, as exemplified by its plan to bring in soldiers to the Peace Memorial Park, represents modern western ethos, which is easily found in the formation of the state in pre-1945 Japan. Against the working of western modernity detected in the move made by the SDF, citizens, social groups and political parties raised counterarguments from a different perspective, most of which were rooted in the hibakusha collective memory and the emotions and cognitions associated with the Peace Memorial Park. In 1965 Hiroshima, the hibakusha collective memory, non-western ethos, appeared to dominate the discursive battlefield.

3   Implications and Discussions

This chapter examines the developmental trajectory of post-war Japan, and finds that one category of social memory, the hibakusha collective memory, helped mold post-World War II Japan by providing new opportunities and limitations to the Japanese society; it has provided opportunities for new peace movement bodies to arise in the post-war Japanese political scene, and gave a chance to the citizens of Hiroshima to voice against the plan put forth by the national institutional body, the SDF, and found a way to stop a military march into the sacred soil, the Peace Memorial Park. All in all, strong emotions and recognitions inscribed in the hibakusha collective memory worked against the proposals that would otherwise lead post-war Japanese society to take the same route as that of advanced western societies.

In a large context, we may read in this examination instances of clash between western ethos and that of non-western. The hibakusha collective memory stopped the national military organization's move to put Japanese society back into the pre-war developmental route guided by the western modernity, and thus contributed to pushing Japan to take a non-western route to reconstruct post-war Japanese society. Also, the hibakusha collective memory provided a huge emotional and cognitive base for the creation of a national drive aiming to materialize a world without nuclear weapons and nuclear wars, a route many advanced western societies do not take. Thus, it may well be that the emergence of the hibakusha collective memory became a turning point that separated Japan from advanced western countries in the post-World War II era.

How does this examination of Japan's case relate to the construction of non-western or post-western sociology? A few implications may be drawn from this research result. A first is a need to define the western in the outset of the research. Very simply, one cannot detect the non-western nor post-western unless one has a rather clear idea as to what constitutes the western. This chapter employs the concept of modernity as the guiding principle for the construction of modern western world. Emergence of a modern state has been considered as the phenomenon peculiar to the western world in the past few centuries (Giddens 1990; Wagner 1994, 2001; Heller 1998; Beck 2012). Only with this understanding can we pick up a societal element considered to be non-western and discuss what characteristics it displays and how it exerts an influence on the society from which it originally took route and emerged on the surface of. We may also discuss how different this societal element is from those found in western societies, and characteristics of the route such an element helps the society to move in.

A second is the importance of social memory in determining a future direction with which a society may develop itself into. There are instances where forces residing outside of a society forcefully alter the future developmental route of the society. The examination in this chapter shows that an experience of failure to follow the western developmental route and subsequent contemplations of the past by the citizens somehow led to the creation of new collective memory within the society, and this internal creation contributed to the alteration of the future developmental route of the society itself. Collective memory is not a material force; it does not forcibly compel one to move or act; it is an internal set of mentalities that provides an emotional and cognitive base for an interpretive effort of those who share the collective memory. The examination in this chapter shows that such mentalities may contribute to turn the society from western to non-western.

This chapter does not claim that post-war Japanese society has transformed itself into a new non-western society; as shown in the previous section, political institutions and economic organizations in post-war Japan have continuously followed a western route to orchestrate various efforts to construct post-war Japan. Rather, this chapter maintains that new ethos emerged in the civil sphere in post-war Japan, and it has guided Japan to derail itself from the developmental route directed by the western ethos.

Acknowledgments

Portion of the materials and illustrations referenced in this chapter have been used in author's previous work (Nomiya 2022). However, discussion focus and arguments expounded in this chapter are different from those in the previous work.

References

Asahi Newspaper Company. 2021. "Need for Change in Constitution 45 percent, No Need at All 41 percent, Maintaining Article Nine 62 percent". *Asahi Shimbun Digital*, May 3, 2021. Website accessed on March 22, 2022. https://www.asahi.com/articles/ASP52632JP47UZPS009.html.

Bauman, Zygmunt. 1989. *Modernity and the Holocaust*. United Kingdom: Polity Press.

Beck, Ulrich, Anthony Giddens, and Scott Lash. 1994. *Reflexive Modernization: Politics, Tradition and Aesthetics in the Modern Social Order*. United Kingdom: Polity Press.

Beck, Ulrich. 2012. *An Introduction to the Theory of Second Modernity and the Risk Society*. London and New York: Routledge.

Chiavacci, David, and Julia Obinger, eds. 2018. *Social Movements and Political Activism in Contemporary Japan: Re-emerging from Invisibility*. London and New York: Routledge.

Chugoku Newspaper Company. 1965. *Chugoku Newspaper*, October 21st, 23rd, 24th, 26th, and 27th. Hiroshima, Japan.

Chugoku Newspaper Company. 1974. *Chugoku Newspaper*, April 4. Hiroshima, Japan.

City of Hiroshima. 2019. *List of the Atomic Bomb Dead Victims*. Website accessed on September 2, 2020. https://www.city.hiroshima.lg.jp/site/atomicbomb-peace/15513.html.

City of Nagasaki. 2019. *List of the Atomic Bomb Dead Victims*. Website accessed on September 2, 2020. https://www.city.nagasaki.lg.jp/heiwa/3020000/3020100/p002235.html.

Giddens, Anthony. 1985. *The Nation-State and Violence: Volume Two of a Contemporary Critique of Historical Materialism*. United Kingdom: Polity Press.

Giddens, Anthony. 1990. *The Consequences of Modernity*. United Kingdom: Polity Press.

Heller, Agnes. 1999. *A Theory of Modernity*. Malden, MA: Blackwell Publishers.

Henley, Jon. 2017. *Nobel peace prize 2017: International Campaign to Abolish Nuclear Weapons wins award—as it happened.* Website accessed on April 7, 2022. https://www.theguardian.com/world/live/2017/oct/06/nobel-peace-prize-2017-winner-live.

ICAN. 2017. Website accessed on April 9, 2022. https://www.icanw.org/nobel_prize.

Ishida, Hiroshi. 1956. *Study of the Political Structure in Modern Japan* [*kindai nihon no seiji kouzou no kenkyū*]. Tokyo: Miraisha.

Ishida, Tadashi. 1986. *Theorizing Experiences of the Exposure to the Atomic Bomb* [*genbaku taiken no shisouka*]. Tokyo: Mirai-sha.

Kamishima, Jiro. 1961. *Spiritual Structure of Modern Japan* [*kindai nihon no seishin kouzou*]. Tokyo: Iwanami Shoten.

Maruhama, Eriko. 2011. *Creation of the Anti-Nuclear and Hydrogen Bomb Signature Campaign* [*gensuikin shomei undo no tanjyou*]. Tokyo: Gaifuu-sha.

Maruyama, Masao. 1956. *Thoughts and Actions in Modern Politics, first and second volumes* [*gendai seiji no shiso to koudou, jyou ge*]. Tokyo: Mirai-sha.

National Diet Library. *Birth of the Constitution of Japan* [*nihon koku ken-pou no tanjyou*]. Website accessed on March 20, 2022. https://www.ndl.go.jp/constitution/.

Nakamura, Masanori. 1995. "Japan in the 1950s and 60s: Rapid Economic Growth" [1950–60 nen-dai no nihon: koudo keizai seichou]. In *Iwanami Lecture Series Overview of Japanese History, Vol. 20, Modern Period 1* [*iwanami kouza nihon tsuushi dai 20 kan, gendai 1*], 1–68. Tokyo: Iwanami.

Nemoto, Masaya. 2018. *Hiroshima Paradox* [*Hiroshima paradokkusu*]. Tokyo: Bensei shuppan.

Nomiya, Daishiro, Isamu Sugino, and Risa Murase. 2019. "Social Movements as Network of Meanings: Constructing a Mental Map of the 2012 Antinuclear Movement Campaign in Japan". In *Economic and Social Changes: Facts, Trends, Forecast. Vol. 12. Issue 5*, 158–174. Vologda Research Center of the Russian Academy of Sciences.

Nomiya, Daishiro. 2022. "Stranded Modernity: Post-war Hiroshima as Discursive Battlefield". In *Global Modernity from Coloniality to Pandemic: A Cross-disciplinary Perspective*, edited by Hatem Akil and Simone Maddanau, 81–104. Netherlands: Amsterdam University Press.

Ohkawa, Kazushi, and Henry Rosovski. 1973. *Japanese Economic Growth: Trend Acceleration in the Twentieth Century.* Stanford, CA: Stanford University Press.

Ohtsuka, Hisao. 1969. *Human Foundation of Modernization—Ohtsuka Hisao Collection, vol.8* [*kindaika no ningen-teki kiso—Ohtsuka Hisao chosaku-shu dai 8 kan*]. Tokyo: Iwanami shoten.

Shibata, Yuko. 2015. *Hiroshima and Nagasaki, Deconstructing Experiences of the Exposure to the Atomic Bombs* [*Hiroshima Nagasaki hibaku taiken wo kaitai suru*]. Tokyo: Sakuhin-sha.

Socialist Party Hiroshima Branch and Japan Socialist Youth Alliance. 1973. *The Nose of the Gun Is Pointing at You: Blocking the SDFs March* [*jyu-ko wa anata wo neratteiru: jiei-tai pareido soshi*]. Hiroshima, Japan.

Takayama, Makoto. 2016. *Becoming a Hibakusha* [*hibakusha ni naru*]. Tokyo: Seria-shobo.

Tominaga, Ken-ichi. 1990. *Japanese Modernization and Social Change* [*nihon no kindai-ka to shakai hendou*]. Tokyo: Iwanami shoten.

Ubuki, Jun. 1982. "The beginning of the anti-nuclear and hydrogen bomb campaign in Japan: 1954 Signature-collecting campaign" [nihon ni okeru gensuibaku kinshi undo no shuppatsu: 1954 nen no shomei undo wo chuushin ni]. In *Hiroshima Peace Science*, vol. 5, 199–223. Peace Center, Hiroshima University. Hiroshima, Japan.

Wada, Haruki. 2015. *Birth of a "Peaceful Country": Origin and Transformation of Postwar Japan* [*"heiwa kokka" no tanjyou: sengo nihon no genten to henyou*]. Tokyo: Iwanami shoten.

Wagner, Peter. 1994. *A Sociology of Modernity: Liberty and Discipline.* London and New York: Routledge.

Wagner, Peter. 2001. *Theorizing Modernity: Inescapability and Attainability in Social Theory.* Sage Publications.

Yoneyama, Risa. 2005. *Hiroshima: Politics of Memory* (originally published as *Hiroshima Traces; Time, Space, and the Dialectics of Memory* in 1999 by the University of California Press). Tokyo: Iwanami shoten.

Zwigenberg, Ran. 2014. *Hiroshima: The Origins of Global Memory Culture.* Cambridge, UK: Cambridge University Press.

CHAPTER 15

COVID-19 and Hegemonic Modernity: Post-Western Sociological Imaginations

Han Sang-Jin

The key issue we need to clarify in our joint project of this book is to explore and establish the meaning and criteria of post-Western sociology as the key concept we use. The concept of post-Western sociology is highly imaginative yet also involves many ambiguities. It is imaginative in that we often confront with critical approaches to the hegemonic consequences of Western sociology (knowledge production in general) as deeply related to such trends as colonialism, imperialism, instrumental domination, turbo-capitalism, Eurocentrism, and American superpower. Disillusioned by these hegemonic consequences of the Western domination of the world, there have emerged various intellectual movements from the South, for example, towards a non-hegemonic, post-Western sociology. Yet the term "post-Western" sociology is multi-dimensional and ambiguous, since "post" can connote many things. Thus, it needs to be defined more precisely.

My position in this regard is to focus on hegemonic modernity as an essential characteristic of Western sociology. We can trace back this problem to Weber's famous thesis of global universalization of instrumental rationality which serves as a rational foundation of capitalist enterprise, state bureaucracy, global markets, professional organization, rule of law, and religious and art institutions. In this chapter, I contend that such hegemonic modernity has come to an end deeply challenged and threatened by the COVID-19 pandemic and the world crisis it has created. And I want to examine how a global metamorphosis has been taking place and speaks of post-Western sociological imagination based on the analysis of the survey data collected from the citizens of 33 metropolitan cities.

Before that, I want to pay attention to the efforts drawn by colleagues such as Xie Lizhong (Beijing), Kim Seung Kuk (Seoul), and Laurence Roulleau-Berger (Paris) to define the concept of post-Western sociology in their own characteristic manner.

1   An Inclusive Classification by Xie

The concept of post-Western sociology is fluid, slippery, and ambiguous. Thus, defining it clearly is not an easy task. In this situation, Xie (2021) draws attention to Chinese sociology and attempts to define this notion in a logically consistent and procedurally step-by-step manner. More specifically, he takes two approaches: a formal approach in the first half of the paper and a critical approach in the second half of the paper. The formal approach is to draw boundaries of a post-Western sociology, and the critical approach is to identify and problematize certain trends related to the indigenization of sociology in China. The latter offers a set of polemics and thus is more attractive than the former. Yet this polemic is based on the outcome of the formal approach. Though he shows quite a systematic and comprehensive analysis, there are some issues that call for further reflection and clarification.

The initial question we face is how to delineate the boundaries and/or relations among three types of sociology: Western, non-Western, and post-Western. Xie offers three criteria by asking (1) the identity of researcher (whether he or she is Western or non-Western), (2) the location of research problems (whether they are Western problems or non-Western problems), and (3) the cultural background of the discourse (whether it is a Western discourse or a non-Western discourse). The three criteria may work well. It may be not difficult to examine whether a researcher is Western or not, whether the problem investigated is Western or not, and whether the main discourses are Western or not. Thus, one can say that the definition of Western sociology is clear-cut. The definition of non-Western sociology is less clear-cut than the former, but Xie presupposes that it is possible to distinguish between Western and non-Western sociology. Then, the key question is how to construct the concept of a post-Western sociology by examining the varieties of Western and non-Western sociologies.

In this regard, Xie pays attention to the interaction between Western Chinese sociologies and identifies 4 different categories of non-Western sociologies. The first strategy is to apply a Western theory to the non-Western problem. Xie regards it as an extension of Western sociology and thus eliminates it from the category of non-Western sociology as well as a post-Western sociology. He argues that this type of research should be treated as part of Western sociology. The other three types of non-Western sociology refer to (1) a Western theory conceptually innovated to meet non-Western societies, (2) a Western theory methodologically innovated for culture-sensitive research in non-Western societies (like Fei Xiaotong), and (3) a complete indigenization of social theory.

Xie includes these three types of non-Western sociology in the concept of a post-Western sociology.

Following the same logic, he goes further to examine the formation of a post-Western sociology not only from non-Western countries but also from Western countries. Thus, a post-Western sociology refers to the shared trend of research that both Western and non-Western sociologists have constructed, being aware of each other's traditions and discursive systems. This analysis is illuminating and sensitizes our attention to the reciprocal interaction and hence dialogic relations between Western and non-Western sociologists and sociologies rather than a simple and rigid dichotomy.

Thus, from his perspective of a formal approach, the outcome is rather simple. We can distinguish a post-Western sociology from both Western sociology and certain types of non-Western sociology. The boundaries of post-Western sociologies are quite broad and inclusive. This is an outcome of the formal analysis taken in the first half of the paper.

In the second part, Xie develops polemics in four sections addressing the issues of the indigenization of sociology. The purpose of this debate is to identify the trends within the theoretical camps of indigenization in China that are incompatible with a post-Western sociology, insofar as they claim either anti- or de-Westernization or the advocacy of Chinese traditions as superior to and distinguished from the Western ones.

One of the key points of this paper is to acknowledge the significance of indigenized Chinese sociology in general for a post-Western sociology. But Xie argues that indigenization is not equal to de- or anti-Westernization. With the concept of post-Western sociology, Xie keeps a distance from certain Chinese intellectual circles that have gained influence advocating the superiority of Chinese intellectual traditions. This critical debate is very constructive and suggestive of the future of Chinese sociology.

Yet, ultimately, we come up with the following question: In thinking of a post-Western sociology, what do we gain by taking a formal approach as found in the first half of the paper? This goes back to the initial question from which he started, that is, what is the meaning of "post"? Post means "after" or "different". Post in the sense of after or different can be diverse, complex, inclusive. But post also means going beyond. If we want to go beyond Western sociology in the name of post-Western sociology, it is necessary to discuss the main problems or difficulties or inherent limitations of Western sociology. Eurocentrism may be a case in point. However, Xie shows no such attempt. Consequently, the theoretical significance of the concept of post-Western sociology remains rather limited.

There seem to be two options. The first option is the concept of post-Western sociology which is broad, inclusive, but weak in terms of its critical significance. The second is to confront Western sociology and develop a strong version of post-Western sociology that goes beyond the limitation of Western sociology but without advocating an anti-Western attitude.

2 Two Diverging Discourses by Kim and Roulleau-Berger

Though Xie shows a cautious classification model of post-Western sociology within the context of Chinese sociology, Kim (2021) and Roulleau-Berger (2021) extend Xie's imagination further to envision the notion of post-Western sociology, but they are more diverging than converging. When they deal with the future of sociology as an antidote to the limits of the Western hegemonic sociology, Kim pursues a post-Western civilization from the cultural perspective of East Asian tradition. He thinks it possible to defend a grand theory of a new civilization of general relevance as a goal of post-Western sociology. He speaks of the logic of oneness as well as an East Asian general social theory. The goal he sets before himself is much more ambitious than Xie's. In contrast, Roulleau-Berger is more eclectic than essential. She extends Xie's focus on China to global diversities involved in knowledge production and pays attention to such knowledge niches as located in "the Western West, non-Western West, semi-Western West, Western East, and re-Easternized East" (Roulleau-Berger 2021: 17).

Consequently, the foci of Kim and Roulleau-Berger are different. Crucial for the former is to grasp East Asian philosophical roots of a general theory of a new civilization for humanity. He did not clearly state so, but obviously he feels the hegemonic modernity deeply embedded in Western sociology to be frustrating and paradoxical. This is the reason why he advocates a normative alternative to this disillusioning modernity when he deals with post-Western sociology. He emphasizes one overlapping logic in the cultural transformation in the world. Contrastingly, Roulleau-Berger pays attention to concrete diversities involved in knowledge production in different regions of the world and grasps commonalities among them converging into post-Western sociology.

> In Post-Western sociology, we will be considering both the local and transnational dimensions of academic research as part of our attempt to analyze the effects of social context on the production of theoretical methodologies based on local research situations. However, we will

also be analyzing the transnational flows between the various contexts of knowledge linked to research methodologies and considering both the processes involved in the production of sociological knowledge and cultural variations in research practices. Theories, knowledge, and methods cannot circulate until these equivalences have been established and appear to be relatively stable, and the framework is based on common conventions and norms governing academic research that have been put in place. Practices give rise, in these very different contexts, to sociological knowledge obtained in response to questions that are similar but situated in sociologists own societal experiences; we will be posing questions about the universal value of sociological knowledge.

ROULLEAU-BERGER 2021: 18

Roulleau-Berger rejects the hegemonic aspects and implications of Western Eurocentric sociology and yet wants to defend the universal value of sociological knowledge while greatly sensitizing our attention to the diversities, multiplicities, and complexities involved in sociological knowledge production in different regions and diverse cultural contexts.

Both seem to share a certain normative view of post-Western sociology, whereas Xie is reluctant to raise this issue. The baseline of this normative view may be that the post-Western sociology we pursue in this book jointly should be at once non-hegemonic and not simply relativistic. This is the reason why Kim advocates a general social theory of upcoming civilization which can show the hybridization of concrete manifestations from the common logic of oneness. Yet Kim's discourse is more philosophical than empirically informative social scientific. Thus, we call for further dialogue between Xie, Kim, and Roulleau-Berger to define more precisely how a new paradigm of post-Western sociology differs from the conventional paradigm of Western sociology theoretically and normatively.

3   Paradoxical Characteristics of Modernity

In this context, I want to make clear the critical intent of the concept of post-Western sociology by bringing out a hegemonic modernity deeply built into the conventional paradigm of Western sociology. As I wrote in the preface to my book *Confucianism and Reflexive Modernity* (2020), "much vigilance is needed when we talk about modernity", simply because "discourses of modernity are abundant". Despite many critiques of the deficiencies of Western modernity, what has come out of these efforts is "far from being uniform". The proposed solutions are so divergent that one is liable to "end up highly confusing". In this regard, I argued:

> It is of fundamental significance to see how deeply the Western capitalist modernity has been entangled with the historical processes of colonialism, imperialism, and hegemonic use of power over the non-Western third world, particularly what we now call the Global South. This process entailed a systematic exploitation, a brutal suppression as evidenced by slavery institutions, and the dehumanization of the colonized people. There is no doubt that the Western modernity has become hegemonic only by externalizing costs and sacrifices to the peripheries in the world system of stratification. Granted that, however, it is also indisputable that it still carries within itself an unfinished normative endeavor concerning an enlightenment-oriented, moral-ethical, and aesthetic deliberation.
> HAN 2020: XI

More in detail, I suggested 10 salient characteristics of paradoxical modernity.
1) The rise of the nation-state in Europe, as a key function of modernity, paved the way for a colonial and imperial power which ruled the third world by imposing a stereotyped divide between the West as civilized and the rest as barbarian. This aspect of modernity is paradoxical in that the role of the state is under siege by globalization, which heightens disparities among the countries beyond the ability of nation-states to keep them under control.
2) Since labor issues have tended to stand at the forefront of the social conflicts awakened by modernity, the ideological and political landscape has been powerfully shaped by the competition between the left and the right. However, modernity marked by this confrontation is largely gone even in cradles of social democracy, such as Scandinavia. The labor movement and left-wing organizations appear to be rigid, power-oriented, and preoccupied with securing their own interests without paying enough attention to other pertinent issues, such as the environment, the rights of minorities, and various risks imposed on ordinary citizens.
3) Characteristic of modernity is the expansion of the bureaucratic regulation of human interaction and the role of professional experts. However, unbridled faith in the superiority of bureaucratic rationality as a key element of modernity has largely gone away today, as evidenced by many post-bureaucratic reforms, such as teamwork, autonomous decision-making, flexible modes of production, and bottom-up as well as horizontal communication.

4) Modernity refers to a specific civilizational form in which science and technology reign supreme. Yet the paradoxical consequences are obvious. It is high time that science together with industry also takes responsibility for the wholesale destruction of the environment as global warming, and the carnage of war spread by the weapons of mass destruction. Furthermore, the scientific mentality subjugates normative concerns to those of technical management and delegates the increasingly desperate call for the moral-ethical, emotive, and aesthetic dimensions of human life to second place.

5) Modernity means representative democracy in terms of political parties and parliaments. Today, however, politics is widely seen as corrupt, under the sway of powerful lobbies for sundry, self-motivated interests. Consequently, voters are seeking ways to participate in a more direct manner, like through town hall meetings, citizen protests, referendums, and participatory governance. Political modernity faces the challenge of answering the call of anti-politics from all quarters, reflecting the general apathy and cynicism of people.

6) The modern family system is the nuclear family. Even here tremendous changes are taking place because the age-old relationship between two sexes—love, marriage, and the institution of the family based on it—has been undergoing a fundamental transformation.

7) Modernity means the stability of life in terms of occupation. People were expected to follow a fixed and stable course of life once they took on a regular occupation. But this is no longer true. For many reasons, our life is becoming more fluid with the disappearance of the *idée fixe*. The future life will be more nomadic than ever since people will have to enter or leave various jobs as they see fit.

8) As modernity entailed a sharp distinction between the private and the public, women who were considered more emotional and relational than men have been forcibly related to remaining in the private realm in society. However, a modernity characterized by male domination in terms of formal and instrumental rationality faces serious challenges today because women are actively resisting such division and the structural inequalities deeply embedded in it.

9) Modernity means functional specialization and differentiation. As society becomes highly complex, however, new countertrends emerge calling for reintegration, recombination, fusions, and hybrids, as can best be seen in the information industries.

10) Originating from the idea of individual freedom and sovereignty, modernity has promoted the constant expansion of individual choice and

self-determination. Consequently, the value of community tends to collapse, producing various side effects such as the surge of materialistic values, self-centered egoism, social isolation, suicides, mental illnesses, etc. Thus, there has emerged a deep need to reconcile individual freedom and a flourishing community.

These paradoxical characteristics of modernity as well as the alternative trends do not mean that they are intrinsic only to the West. We can see these everywhere in the world. Thus, we need to be more specific when we talk about hegemonic modernity in relation to post-Western sociology. As we have seen in the cases of analysis by Kim and Roulleau-Berger, we consider it possible to imagine the possibility of *non*-hegemonic world sociology as an antithesis of hegemonic Western sociology. A non-hegemonic world sociology may be viewed as a normative picture of post-Western sociology. Then, we should ask: What do we mean by hegemonic modernity? How can we go beyond it while doing sociology? Even further, how can we grasp hegemonic modernity and alternative trajectories by empirical data?

These questions are indeed complex, sensitizing attention to new frontiers of sociology related to the paradigm of modernity and what comes after that, like second modernity. I attempted to answer these questions in part by drawing attention to the hegemonic consequences of instrumental rationality via a critical confrontation with Max Weber on the one hand, and the possibility of "affective reasonable rationality" coming from the Chinese cultural traditions on the other. I argued the necessity and desirability of reconciling cognitive (instrumental, scientific) and moral and affective rationality through a non-hegemonic dialogue between the West and East (Han 2020a). This argument touches deeply on the first four paradoxical characteristics of modernity suggested above.

4 What Do We Mean by Hegemonic Modernity?

Hegemonic modernity as I use it in this paper should be more specifically defined, since I do not want to overstretch this notion. In particular, I want to discuss hegemonic modernity not as a general theoretical problem of modernity but within the context of the COVID-19 global pandemic and the crisis it has produced.

To be blunt, the core of hegemonic modernity lies in my view in the belief and trust in science and technology as the most reliable way of understanding, diagnosing, and prescribing the puzzles we face in the changing world as well the progressive view of history it promotes. Quite unexpectedly, the COVID-19 global crisis has given rise to an interesting competition between modern scientific and risk-sensitive outlooks of the future. For the sake of convenience, I call the latter a *second-modern reflexive outlook*. The modern outlook is characterized by the belief that the key solution to the COVID-19 pandemic crisis lies in the production and inoculation of COVID-19 vaccines. In this sense we can observe "the return to science at the turn of modernity" (Joshi 2021). On the other hand, however, serious doubts have arisen as to whether we can effectively deal with the complexities of global risks we face along the modern paradigm of the scientific regulation of such risks. The dispute already apparent will continue. Given the basic paradoxical characteristics of modernity outlined above, we can define the vaccine-centered, scientific approach to COVID-19 as an outlook of hegemonic modernity. Intensive studies are required to deal with the complex and uncertain boundaries between modern and second-modern outlooks in this regard (Han 2021). Yet, I consider this to be beyond the limits of this paper.

Instead, in this paper I will focus on the aspects of hegemonic modernity deeply entangled with the COVID-19 global crisis. I want to go beyond the conceptual parameter of Eurocentrism by paying attention to the hegemonic struggle between the United States and China as a real global problem. To be sure, Eurocentrism has been deeply entangled with the colonialism dictated by the European powers from the turn to modernity. However, I consider it more realistic to discuss the hegemonic aspects of modernity today in relation to such thrusts as "making America great again". The United States is the most powerful superpower in the world, dominating science and technology, high-tech industries, commerce, military capability, and advanced education, as well as cultural industries. Yet the United States faces serious challenges from many bottlenecks, and thus its hegemonic status is not as stable as before.

Let us look at Habermas's criticism of hegemonic modernity in the form of the American neo-liberal project of global management. By globalization, Habermas (2006:175) refers to "the cumulative processes of a worldwide expansion of trade and production, commodity and financial markets, fashions, the media and computer programs, new and communications networks, transportation systems and flows of migration, the risks generated by large-scale technology, environmental damage and epidemics, as well as organized crime and terrorism". We face a new task of how to distribute life chance in the global community. In this context, Habermas (2006: 181–182) distinguishes a genuinely cosmopolitan approach and "the particular American ethos armed with a claim to universality". He worries about the tendency to impose certain "national territorial and security interests in the name of the ethos of a new liberal global order" and declares that "once the globalization of a particular ethos has replaced the law of the international community, whatever is then dressed up as international law is in fact imperial law". Habermas rejects such hegemonic liberalism as an expression of world-dominating instrumental, bureaucratic, and market-based rationality.

> With regard to the concrete form of the new global order, hegemonic liberalism does not aim at a law-governed, politically constituted world society, but at an international order of formally independent liberal states. The latter would operate under the protection of a peace-securing superpower and obey the imperatives of a completely liberalized global market. On this model, the peace would not be secured by law but by imperial power, and the world society would be integrated, not through the political relations among world citizens, but through systemic, and ultimately market, relations.
> HABERMAS 2006: 183–184

As we know well, Donald Trump, former president of the United States, loudly proclaimed a new ground foreign policy and attitude of "making America great again". He also launched a war of hegemony against China as G-2 power. We can take this as a good example of hegemonic modernity or what Habermas calls the American neo-liberal project of global management. What I want to do in this respect is to examine the extent to which such hegemonic modernity is sustainable in terms of the global citizens' evaluation of the American performance of COVID-19 governance.

Not only does hegemony entail surveillance and subjugation, it also involves a moral and ethical dimension. A good case in point is the concept and norm of "noblesse oblige", which refers to a moral economy wherein privilege must be balanced by duty towards those who lack such privilege or who cannot perform such duty. On this condition, hegemony entails a voluntary acceptance of the ruling power by the ruled in terms of certain normative conceptions of politics.

Above all, protecting the life of the people from epidemics and pandemics is the raison d'être of state power as a public institution. In the case of the liberal democratic state, it is also important to protect and promote civil liberties. Independently of it, all state power in the form of the nation-state is morally required to do its best to protect the life of its populace. Failure in this regard may produce a moral crisis of hegemony. In this sense, bio-politics is of fundamental significance for the sustainability of the hegemonic exercise of power.

5 Global Citizens' Evaluation

In what follows, I will show global citizens' evaluation of COVID-19 pandemic governance. The Joongmin Foundation stationed in Seoul has conducted three rounds of global citizens' surveys on the topic of COVID-19 governance and citizen life, with various questions, in more than 30 global cities in June 2020, September 2020, and September 2021. I will:
- compare how global citizens evaluate the performance of the United States' COVID-19 pandemic governance from June 2020 to September 2021;
- show data regarding how global citizens compare the United States and China in this regard; and
- examine whether global citizens regard the West (America) as being capable of managing global hegemony or whether they endorse the view that the axis of civilization is now moving to East Asia.

A comparative study of the collected data requires considerable effort to check the different collective standard of evaluation in the regions and cities. For instance, in our first global survey, we suggested 30 metropolitan cities and asked about 500 citizens chosen in each city according to the standard method of sampling how they evaluated the COVID-19 performance of each country. The suggested scale was: "very competent", "largely competent", "so-so", "largely incompetent", and "very incompetent". We also included "don't know" but excluded it from analysis. As can be seen easily, the citizens of certain cities (regions and cultures) were consistently more generous in their evaluation than the citizens of other cities. This means that the global average of the citizens of each city varied significantly. For instance, the global average of Seoul citizens is 2.15 (maximum, 5.0), whereas that of Tokyo is 2.62. New York is 3.24, Paris is 3.1, Moscow is 3.24, São Paulo is 3.38, and New Delhi is 3.41. Thus, care must be taken to consider this collective diverging in cultural inclinations. It is methodologically dubious to compare global citizens' evaluation flatly. Figure 15.1 shows how the global average fluctuates from one city to another.

Figure 15.2 demonstrates clearly that the state image of the United States is consistently below the global standard of the citizens of 30 metropolitan cities. As shown in Figure 15.1 and Figure 15.2, the global standard of evaluation is up and down from one city to another. Assessed by this standard, global citizens evaluate the United States' COVID-19 pandemic governance has having completely failed as of June 2020.

Figure 15.3 shows the same pattern. The gap between the global standard by each city and the United States' pandemic governance seems to be enlarged except for among New York's citizens.

COVID-19 AND HEGEMONIC MODERNITY   317

FIGURE 15.1   Global average of evaluation of COVID-19 performance by each city's citizens (June 2020)

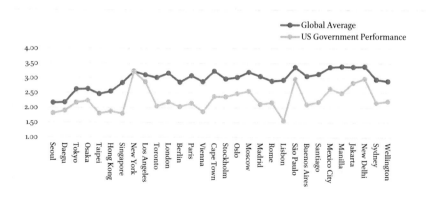

FIGURE 15.2   The United States' image as assessed by the global average of each city's citizens (June 2020)

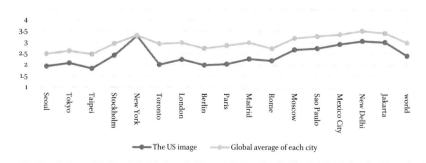

FIGURE 15.3   The United States' image as assessed by the global average of each city's citizens (September 2020)

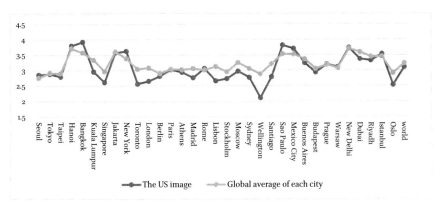

FIGURE 15.4   The United States' image as assessed by the global average of each city's citizens (September 2021)

However, Figure 15.4 shows considerable improvement in the state image of the United States, perhaps because the United States was moving ahead of other countries in producing vaccine treatments and implementing the necessary medical policies. As of September 2021, for instance, the global standard of evaluation by Seoul citizens was 2.75. Yet their evaluation of the United States' performance was 2.85. Likewise, the assessment of the United States' performance by Bangkok citizens was 3.92, significantly higher than their global standard. We can see a similar pattern in Hanoi, Rome, São Paulo, Mexico City, Prague, Warsaw, New Delhi, and Istanbul. Yet it should be noted that the general trend of evaluation of the United States' COVID-19 pandemic governance is still negative.

Given the aggressive campaign of "making America great again" by the United States and the hegemony competition launched against China, the citizens' survey provides a good opportunity to examine how global citizens compare the United States and China in terms of their COVID-19 performance. Figure 15.5 shows that as of June 2020 global citizens largely saw China performing better than the United States except in New York and Los Angeles. An interesting exception is East Asia. In Seoul, Daegu, Tokyo, Osaka, and Taipei, citizens saw the United States as performing better than China. Here their evaluation of both the United State and China was significantly lower than their global standards. Yet they are sensitive to the issue of global hegemony, taking the side of the United States.

Figure 15.6 shows that the gap between the United States and China grew larger as of September 2020. We may say that a global consensus emerged among global citizens that insofar as the role of the state as the protector of

COVID-19 AND HEGEMONIC MODERNITY 319

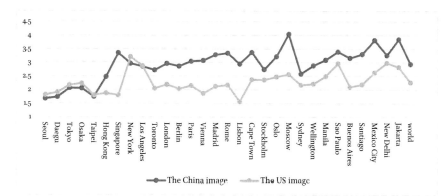

FIGURE 15.5   The state image of the United States and China by global citizens (June 2020)

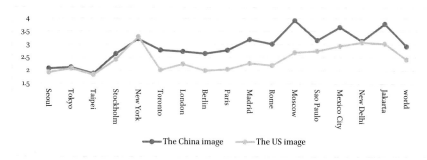

FIGURE 15.6   The state image of the United States and China by global citizens (September 2020)

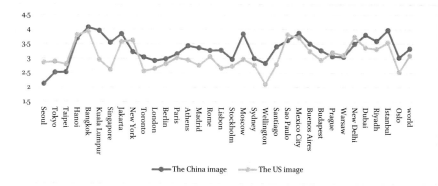

FIGURE 15.7   The state image of the United States and China by global citizens (September 2021)

human life against pandemic disease is concerned, China performs better than the United States.

However, as of September 2021, the general picture becomes a bit mixed. East Asian cities, like Seoul, Tokyo, and Taipei, evaluated the United States as doing better than China, together with Hanoi, São Paulo, Mexico City, Prague, Warsaw, and New Delhi.

To assess hegemonic modernity as the A merican neo-liberal project of global management, as Habermas put it, we used another set of questions in our global citizens survey on COVID-19 and citizen life. We included the following questions in the second round of the global survey, conducted in September 2020.

In the third round of the global survey, conducted in September 2021, we attempted a comparative assessment of the United States and China with regard to COVID-19 health governance. We will use only one item directly related to issue of hegemonic modernity.

I will present a data analysis of the questions referred to in Table 15.1 and Table 15.2. In the scale of 1 to 5, the average score of the 4 issues in Table 15.1 is 3.40 in the case of the United States losing hegemony, 3.33 in the case of the priority of human survival, 3.17 in the case of the civilization axis moving to East Asia, and 2.79 in the case of the Chinese superiority in bio-politics. Overall, except for the last issue, the average score was higher than 3, which means that there is a general tendency to accept the view, although variations are significant from one city to another.

The tendency to accept the United States as losing global hegemony was greater in Western cities (New York 3.49, Toronto 3.72, London 3.58) than in other regions. It was significantly lower in East Asia (Seoul 3.31, Tokyo 3.35, Taipei 3.17).

The tendency to accept the priority of human survival was particularly strong in New Delhi (3.79) and Jakarta (3.71). It was relatively strong in East Asia but was rather weak in other regions, like Southern Europe and Latin America.

The tendency to accept the civilizational axis moving to East Asia calls for careful attention. I will show the second round of data analysis first and then move to the third round of the global citizens survey to examine this issue in more detail. As of September 2020, citizens of Seoul and Tokyo differed significantly. Seoul citizens (3.20) tended to accept the view, whereas Tokyo citizens (2.82) tended to deny it. Taipei citizens also tended to support the view. As usual, the citizens of New Delhi and Jakarta supported the view most willingly. Overall, there was found to be no rejection of this view except among Tokyo citizens.

TABLE 15.1 The following statements describe how COVID-19 is changing the world. How strongly do you agree or disagree with each statement?

		Strongly disagree	Disagree	Neutral	Agree	Strongly agree
(a)	The US is losing its global hegemony.	①	②	③	④	⑤
(b)	Human survival is more important than human dignity.	①	②	③	④	⑤
(c)	The axis of civilization is moving to East Asia.	①	②	③	④	⑤
(d)	The Chinese system is more capable than liberal democracy at protecting human life.	①	②	③	④	⑤

TABLE 15.2 The following survey items are concerned with a comparative assessment of the United States and China with regard to COVID-19 health governance. On a scale from 1 to 10, please identify the point you feel most closely matches your opinion

d. Their global influence

Western liberal democracies maintain global hegemony				Middle			The axis of civilization is moving to East Asia		
1	2	3	4	5	6	7	8	9	10

One distinctive finding of this analysis is that New York citizens tended to be more critical of the American system than any other citizens. For instance, New York citizens supported the view that the United States is losing hegemony with 3.49, higher than the global average of 3.40. They supported the priority of human survival with 3.51, much higher than the global average of 3.33. They accepted the view that the civilization axis is moving to East Asia with 3.26, higher than the global average of 3.17. Even regarding the view that

TABLE 15.3 Aspects of global change from the COVID-19 pandemic (September 2020)

City	The United States is losing hegemony	Priority of human survival	Civilization axis moving to East Asia	China is superior in bio-politics
Seoul	3.31	3.36	3.20	2.22
Tokyo	3.35	3.21	2.82	2.28
Taipei	3.17	3.49	3.19	2.32
Stockholm	3.40	3.27	3.05	2.57
New York	3.49	3.51	3.26	3.16
Toronto	3.72	3.41	3.16	2.67
London	3.58	3.39	3.19	2.85
Berlin	3.40	3.18	3.09	2.72
Paris	3.38	3.17	3.14	2.91
Madrid	3.24	3.17	3.14	2.91
Rome	3.38	3.22	3.11	2.79
Moscow	3.42	3.05	3.21	3.18
São Paulo	3.25	3.16	3.12	2.74
Mexico City	3.29	3.17	3.21	3.11
New Delhi	3.47	3.79	3.39	2.88
Jakarta	3.61	3.71	3.45	3.29
All	3.40	3.33	3.17	2.79

China is superior in protecting human life, they endorsed this view with 3.16, much higher than the global average of 2.79.

Overall, however, the tendency to regard China as superior in bio-politics compared with the United States remains not well supported, except a few cities like Moscow, Mexico City, and Jakarta.

Global citizens' response to the view of the civilizational axis moving to East Asia is a good indicator of how the global perception of world hegemony is changing or transforming. Deeply related to other indexes in global change, such as second modernity, the advocacy of in-between commonality, and the preference of community value to individual freedom, this civilizational variable shows mixed attitudes and evaluations of Western hegemony among countries and regions. In East Asia, only Seoul is positive of this view, whereas Tokyo and Taipei are negative. In Southeast Asia, many countries accept this view, as can be seen in Figure 15.8, as evidenced by New Delhi, Bangkok, Jakarta, and Kuala Lumpur. Contrastingly, almost all Latin American cities are

COVID-19 AND HEGEMONIC MODERNITY 323

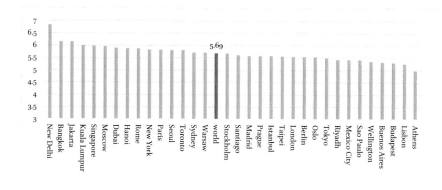

FIGURE 15.8   Index of the civilizational axis moving to East Asia (September 2021)

reluctant to endorse this view, as can be seen in Buenos Aires, Sao Paulo, and Mexico City. Rome in Southern Europe, Dubai in the Middle East, and Warsaw in Eastern Europe stand out as supporting this view. In Western Europe, New York, Paris, Toronto, and Sydney are positive, while Stockholm, London, Berlin, and Oslo are negative.

6   Concluding Remarks

We started this enquiry by asking what we mean by post-Western sociology as a collective topic of this handbook. Previous studies have been critically reviewed to point out that post-Western sociology calls for a normative vision against the hegemonic modernity deeply built into the history of Western sociology. Ten paradoxical characteristics of modernity have been outlined to show the complexities involved in the discourses of modernity. Theoretically and practically, the key question we face is to identify the types of human actor that are capable of carrying out the project of non-hegemonic global sociology against the conventional paradigm of Western sociology associated with hegemonic modernity. The present paper falls short of providing a solid answer to this task.

Instead, this paper has shown the profound challenge to hegemonic modernity posed by the COVID-19 pandemic and has paid particular attention to the project of 'making America great again', which Habermas has sharply criticized as the American neo-liberal project of global management. Global citizens survey data collected in June 2020, September 2020, and September 2021 have been shown to demonstrate how the United States' normative assumption of hegemonic power is threatened, if not collapsed, and how global citizens compare the COVID-19 pandemic performance of the United States and China in terms of their global standards, which differ from one city to another.

Finally, the paper has shown data analysis to demonstrate the tendency of global citizens to accept the contending views directly related to hegemonic modernity. Regarding the view that the United States is losing global hegemony, the general trend accepts this view, although variations are considerably large. In contrast, regarding the view that the Chinese system is superior in protecting human life, no visible support for this view is found in the world except in a few cities.

Concerning the thesis that the civilizational axis is moving to East Asia, there can be found cleavages among cities as well as among regions. All Latin American cities and Southeast Asian cities are negative on this view. In East Asia, only citizens of Seoul accept this view, while Taipei and Tokyo reject it. In Eastern Europe, only Warsaw tends to accept it, while Prague and Budapest reject it. In Southern Europe, only Rome tends to be positive, while Madrid, Athens, and Lisbon are negative. In Western Europe, New York, Paris, Toronto, and Sydney are positive, while London, Stockholm, Berlin, and Oslo are negative.

The key question that we need to discuss further is not whether the United States (or Western countries) will continue to manage global hegemony nor whether it will be replaced by China. Rather, the key question is how we can carry out a non-hegemonic global sociology based on coercion-free civilizational dialogues. To the extent to which COVID-19 reveals the fundamental limit and crisis of hegemonic modernity, we should extend post-Western sociological imaginations to conceptualize the possibility of non-hegemonic global sociology that we can create and share by combining theory and empirical data.

References

Habermas, Jürgen. 2006. *The Divided West*. Cambridge: Polity Press.
Han, Sang-Jin. 2020. *Confucianism ad Reflexive Modernity*. Leiden: Brill.
Han, Sang-Jin. 2021. "Can Science Lead the Post-COVID-19 Era: A Second Modern Outlook". Paper presented at the 2nd EASA Meeting, "Social Transformation in Asia: Before and After COVID-19". Busan, Korea; October 29–30, 2021.
Han, Sang-Jin. 2020a. "Specialization and Fusion of Rationalities: A Reinterpretation of Weber's 1913 Essay on Understanding Sociology". *Phenomena and Knowledge* (in Korean) 44(4): 51–74, 273–274.

Joshi, Javat. 2021. "The Return to Science at the Turn of Modernity". doi:10.5281/zenodo.4027624.

Kim, Seung-Kuk. 2021. "Toward an East Asian Theory Construction: A Cycle of Oneness, Hybridization, Solipsist Spiritual Individualism, and Enlightenment". Paper presented at the 2nd EASA Meeting, "Social Transformation in Asia: Before and After COVID-19". Busan, Korea; October 29–30, 2021.

Roulleau-Berger, Laurence. 2021. "The Fabric of Post-Western Sociology: Ecologies of Knowledge Beyond the 'East' and the 'West'". *The Journal of Chinese Sociology* 8 (10). http://doi.org/10.1186/s40711-021-00144-z.

Xie, Lizhong. 2021. "Post Western Sociologics: What and Why?" *The Journal of Chinese Sociology* 8 (1): 1–25.

CHAPTER 16

Wanderers and the Settled: Perspectives of Kunio Yanagita and Kazuko Tsurumi on Social Change

Okumura Takashi

1   Introduction: "Square Words" and "Round Words"

When American sociologist Marion Levy Jr. came to Japan in 1960 to study "social structure in the Tokugawa era", Kazuko Tsurumi, who became his research assistant, took him to Kunio Yanagita's residence in Seijo, Tokyo. Tsurumi had a close relationship with Yanagita's daughter Chizuko, as a classmate at the Tsuda English School, and since 1947 Tsurumi and her family had lived in a house just in front of Yanagita's. At this meeting Yanagita told Levy, "There are two kinds of people in Japan, one who speak round words, and one who speak square words. If you want to know Japan, you have to get acquainted with people who speak round words" (Tsurumi 1977: 8).

According to Tsurumi, "square words" refer to *kanji* (Chinese characters) and written language, and those who speak to them are the "intelligent class". On the other hand, "round words" are *kana* (letters unique to Japan born from *kanji*) or spoken words, and "*jomin* (common people)" are their users (ibid.: 8). Tsurumi, who called Levy and Yanagita "my two academic mentors" (ibid.: 229), said that Yanagita's studies were focused on the latter. "Yanagita regarded common people as the bearers of social change, and he tried to understand their ways to live without relying on the government in economics, politics, and faith" (ibid.: 233).

Kunio Yanagita, the founder of folklore studies in Japan, was a person who lived between square and round words. Born in 1875 in a rural area of Hyogo Prefecture, in western Japan, as the sixth son of doctor and Confucian scholar Misao Matsuoka, Yanagita can be said to have mastered "square words" among the people using "round words". After moving to Tokyo in 1887, he was active as a new style poetry writer. He entered the Imperial University of Tokyo in 1897, majoring in agricultural politics at the School of Law, and was assigned to the Ministry of Agriculture and Commerce in 1900.

While traveling throughout Japan as a bureaucrat, he found the way to the world of "round words" in each region, and he published *Post-Hunting-Words*, describing the lives of hunting people in the Kyushu area, in 1909, and *Tales of Tono*, a collection of folk tales from Tono, Iwate Prefecture, in 1910. He was promoted to secretary general of the House of Lords in 1914 but resigned in 1919, and he became a guest writer at the Tokyo Asahi Shimbun in the following year. After 19 years of bureaucratic life and 11 years of transition (2 years of which he was in Geneva as a member of the League of Nations mandate), he resigned from the Asahi Shimbun in 1930, to concentrate on his work as a freelance folklorist.

On the other hand, Kazuko Tsurumi was born and raised in an exceptionally elite family. She was born on June 10, 1918, at the official residence of the Ministry of Foreign Affairs in Tokyo, as the eldest daughter of Yusuke and Aiko Tsurumi. Kazuko's father, Yusuke, was a bureaucrat of the Ministry of Railways at the time, and he was later elected as a Member of Parliament five times. Due to the position he took during the war, he was expelled from public office in 1946. This expulsion was lifted in 1950, and he served as Minister of Health and Welfare in 1954. Kazuko's mother, Aiko, was the eldest daughter of Shimpei Goto, who had served as president of the South Manchuria Railway, Minister of the Interior, Minister of Foreign Affairs, and mayor of Tokyo.

Despite her elite family, Tsurumi was also a person who moved back and forth between several kinds of words, including the "square words" of the intellectual class, foreign words acquired by studying in the United States, and "round words" encountered in the life-composition movement of the postwar period. Particularly by reviewing Yanagita's works, she reconsidered the relationship between "round words" and "square words", and confronted new words in the research project on Minamata disease in 1970s. This paper mainly follows Tsurumi's personal trajectory of explorations, with a special reference to Yanagita's ideas on social change, through Tsurumi's book *Wandering and Settling: Kunio Yanagita's Theory on Social Change*, published in 1977. The key concepts Tsurumi took from Yanagita were those of "wanderers" and "the settled", which will be the focus of this discussion.

2 Between "Common People" and America: Tsurumi before and after the War

2.1 *"Conversion" from Marxism to Pragmatism*

After graduating from the Tsuda English School in March 1939, Tsurumi enrolled at Vassar College in Poughkeepsie, New York, in September. Tsurumi recollected in a 1992 interview that she chose Vassar because it was the "mecca of the student union movement", and the "forbidden books", including Marx, Engels, and Lenin, were listed as must-reads there. Her master's thesis, "A Comparative Study of Historical Materialism and Instrumentalism as Methods of Social Sciences", criticized pragmatism from the standpoint of dialectical materialism (Tsurumi [1992] 1997: 65).

Tsurumi confessed two reasons for her fascination with Marxism. One was "a sense of guilt that I have grown up with since I was a child". When she heard the maids working at home telling stories such as "a communist has just been arrested", she was worried about "the relationship between the maids' kitchen and my family's living room", and it was her first awareness of the existence of "classes". The second reason was her experience of reading *The Capital* in the United States, which excited her in its ability to analyze society beautifully. At the time, Tsurumi thought that because the Japanese imperial system was an extremely strong opponent, it was necessary to have a powerful weapon with a sharp edge, rather than a dull weapon like pragmatism (ibid.: 69).

Tsurumi moved to Columbia University's Graduate School of Philosophy in September 1941, but after the Pacific War began in December, she boarded a Japan-US exchange ship in June 1942 with her younger brother, Shunsuke Tsurumi, who had been majoring in philosophy at Harvard, to return home. In 1943, she became a researcher with the Pacific Association (*Taiheiyo-kyokai*) and studied the national character of the United States. After experiencing Japan's defeat in August 1945 at the age of 27, she began preparing for the publication of a new magazine, and in May 1946, *Science of Thought* (*Shiso no kagaku*) was launched.

The publication goals of the magazine, written by Shunsuke, were as follows:

> First and foremost, we will consider the implications of the defeat of the war and continue to learn lessons from it.... We feel ashamed that the thoughts and words of Japanese intellectuals have been separated from the Japanese public until now. Therefore, we would like to think as one of the masses, by reducing the intellectual-likeness of our way of thinking.... We want to learn from the public and change our senses, thoughts, and actions.
>
> TSURUMI [1981–1982] 1997: 20–21

Intelligentsia who use "square words" should learn from the masses who speak "round words". According to Tsurumi, there was pragmatism at the base of this idea. The "common man's philosophy" in *Science of Thought* was derived from John Dewey, and "if the thoughts of ordinary people contain important truth, the role of the philosopher is to pick up the truth and systematize it" (Tsurumi [1992] 1997: 67).

In the 1992 interview, Tsurumi noted, "In my case, the experience of struggling between Marxism and pragmatism was very valuable". She pointed out that both Marxism and pragmatism are modernism, but the former is historical determinism, while the latter's view of history is centered on uncertainty. While Tsurumi had been in a position to criticize uncertainty from the viewpoint of certainty, she "gradually changed to take the uncertainty more seriously", and that was "my conversion". The decisive moment was her involvement in the life-composition movement. "When I entered reality through the movement, I realized that from the standpoint of determinism one could not help imposing an ideology to others, instead of drawing out the thoughts of their own lives", she said (ibid.: 68).

2.2 *Learning from the Life-Composition Movement*

In August 1952, Tsurumi was invited to the 1st National Council for Writing Education held in Gifu Prefecture, where she gave a lecture on "How to think about urban life for writing education". Here, Tsurumi raised the notion that Japanese intellectuals' ideas and surveys were about "a group that does not include oneself", gaining a significant response from the audience. In her article "Learning From Life Writing Education", published two months later, Tsurumi stated that the characteristics of Japanese intellectuals who played a part in modernization could be called "heterological". In her words, "When Japanese scholars discussed 'Japan' and 'Japanese', it was as if they did not include themselves" (Tsurumi [1952] 1998a: 323), Tsurumi stressed that if a "scientific survey" conducted by scholars "objectively" does not cause any changes to the scholars themselves, or the villagers who are surveyed, it is a "dark" one. However, if both the investigators and the investigated are given the opportunity to change, we can find "the brightness in the darkness", and that is the life writing movement (ibid.: 324). Tsurumi concluded that life-composition projects were not just a matter of children's education, but that "in order for us adults to be reborn, especially intellectuals and scholars, we need life writing self-education" (ibid.: 327).

Tsurumi recollected in the 1992 interview, "So I joined the life-composition movement with downtown housewives in Tokyo, and female textile workers in Yokkaichi, Mie Prefecture. I realized that individuals are more important than anything else. Big theories, inevitable laws, and so on are not that important" (Tsurumi [1992] 1997: 69–71).

However, it was not easy for Tsurumi, who had learned "square words" thoroughly, to enter the world of "round words". In her 1954 essay, "Companions to Talk and Write With", Tsurumi said that the last two years of writing practice "have made us much more self-confident", but any "group of people of different ages, occupations, and educational backgrounds like us has a problem". She added, "Another problem is myself". She mentioned a criticism made by a young female textile worker: "We, the workers at a textile factory, are sentimental and dark. But Tsurumi-san is neither sentimental nor dark.... Your voice, your way of speaking, the impression of your entire body are too bright for us" (Tsurumi [1954] 1998a: 376–378). The same worker sent Tsurumi a letter, which she also quoted deliberately in this essay.

> We have been working very hard since we were small, and grew up with jealousy and twisting. We have been exposed to the contradictions and darkness of society.... On the contrary, Tsurumi-san is far from us, a baby who has never felt the jealousy and contradiction.... You do not know the darkness of Japan today. Then, even if you try to improve society, you will end up steadily targeting only the honor students in the world. I am afraid the distance between us is widening.
>
> IBID.: 379–381

Tsurumi's response to this letter was only "banal phrases" (ibid.: 383). The life-composition movements came to fruition in publications such as *Housewife Who Holds a Pencil* (1954), *History of Mothers: Lives of Japanese Women* (1954), and *Love Among Colleagues* (1956). But the distance was "widening".

In December 1954, Tsurumi's father became the Minister of Health and Welfare. In the same month, the female workers who joined the movement were pressured by the factory over their "dangerous" ideas. In February 1955, Tsurumi headed to Geneva to attend the World Mother Convention. In October 1957, an article was posted in the Textile Labor Union bulletin, demanding that the life-composition group disband immediately, and the female workers who had been named were fired. Tsurumi and other intellectuals supported the legal struggle against this, and in April 1958, the dismissal was invalidated.

However, starting in late 1957, due to pleurisy and pulmonary infiltrates after the flu, Tsurumi was treated at her home in Seijo and villa in Karuizawa for 1 year, unable to go out or receive visitors for much of this time.

2.3   *Doctoral Dissertation at Princeton*

From July to September 1959, Tsurumi was engaged in a survey of Japanese immigrants from Wakayama Prefecture in Steveston near Vancouver, Canada. This survey was organized by Ronald Dore, a professor at the University of British Columbia, who invited Tsurumi to participate, assigning her three themes: everyday life, education, and a sense of belonging or self-identity.

Tsurumi interviewed the immigrants to understand how their loyalty fluctuated between their country of origin and Canadian society (Tsurumi [1995] 1998a: 15–17). The results were published in 1961 as *A Tale of Steveston: Japanese in the World*.

When Tsurumi's father collapsed due to cerebral softening in November 1959, she returned to Japan. However, in 1960, Professor Marion Levy came to Japan, and he hoped Tsurumi to become his research assistant. In September 1962, she entered Princeton University Graduate School "to learn research methods" as one of the first 8 female graduate students, and she passed her doctoral qualification in April 1964. Her dissertation, "Social Change and the Individual: Japan Before and After Defeat in World War II", earned her a PhD in sociology in December 1966, and it was published in 1970.

In her dissertation Tsurumi wanted to analyze Japanese society before and after World War II with the concept of "socialization". At the time, however, the concept was only used as "childhood socialization". In her search for a theory that could discuss "adulthood socialization", she met with Princeton psychology professor Silvan Tomkins. Tsurumi attempted to analyze Japanese society using Levy's theory of social structure and Wilbert Moore's theory of the tension management system, both of which were derived from Talcott Parsons, and Tomkins' theory of affect and socialization (Tsurumi 1998b: 10–13).

The dissertation consisted of two parts, one dealing with prewar Japan, and one with postwar. Chapter 1 dealt with personality changes in six cases of "ideological conversion" in the 1930s, including Takiji Kobayashi, a proletarian novelist "ever committed" to communism; and Manabu Sano and Sadachika Nabeyama, leaders of the Japanese Communist Party "reversely converted" from Marxism. Chapters 2 and 3 discussed the socialization in Japan from the Manchurian Incident in 1937, to the 1945 defeat in the war, characterized as "socialization for death" dominated by the imperial system, while the education at schools and in the army was explored with "pattern variables" and "affect socialization model".

Chapter 4 explored the International Military Tribunal for the Far East as "the agent of socialization for peace". Tsurumi noted that the war tribunal established in January 1946 was intended to shock the defeated nation by punishing war criminals, and it had the educational effect of shifting from affirmative values to negative ones of war as an "explicit function". Of 4,000 arrested war criminals, 1,068 were executed or died in prison from 1946 to 1951. Meanwhile, 701 of them left personal documents in the forms of letters, diaries, essays, and poems, which were collected and published in 1951 as *The Last Testament of the Century* (Tsurumi 1977: 138–139). Tsurumi analyzed this to find that 87.4% of the prisoners were "unconverted" from the prewar values, and only 8.9% were "converted" (ibid.: 146). She considered the reason for this to be the failure of adult re-socialization (ibid.: 153), stating that while the socialization of the Japanese army into the war ideology was through "negative affect", such as pain, fear, contempt, and humiliation, the war criminal trials, which advocated re-socialization to the denial of war, relied on the negative affect of the death penalty (ibid.: 177–179).

Part 2 commenced with chapter 5, "Postwar Social Change: The Eclipse of the Emperor System". In the following chapter Tsurumi regarded the circle of the life-composition movement by textile workers to have "characteristics that are the exact opposite of the military as a socialization institution" (ibid.: 213), with the possibility "to become intermediate groups that can be a leader in creating a multidimensional society" (ibid.: 246–247).

Chapters 7 and 8 analyzed the roles of women in their families during and after the war. Prewar adult socialization of women was conducted with the role regulation of "mother or wife of a soldier", which forced an "enduring negative affect of self-sacrifice" (ibid.: 257). Concerning women after the war, Tsurumi first extracted strong normative consciousness from the case of the life-writing group of upper-class housewives in Tokyo. Committed to the peace movement, they began with the awareness that "mothers or wives of soldiers" were ignorant, and such incorrect roles should be altered (ibid.: 271–274). On the other hand, rural women innovated ways of communication within families to rationalize households by bookkeeping and to create cooperative forms of small-scale farming realistically (ibid.: 285–290). Tsurumi estimated that in the case of city women, "ideal type precedes real type", while in the case of agrarian women "real type precedes ideal type" (Tsurumi 1998b: 219).

When recalling her dissertation in 1998, Tsurumi noted that while writing it, she tried to "construct a comprehensive typology and analytical framework in my own way", but it could be regarded as "a very wasteful task". However, "Only after this work could I reach my own thoughts and theories", so "my English dissertation was a necessary step, but now it can be discarded" (ibid.: 584). Certainly, this work, which analyzed the "round words" of the war criminals and the women in the life-composition circle, with "square words" learned at Princeton, and was written in "English", can be said to investigate Japanese society as a "group that does not include oneself". If this dissertation could not make a change to either the investigator or the investigated, it should be called "a dark one".

Tsurumi returned to Japan in March 1966 and became an associate professor at Seikei University. In April 1969, at the age of 51, she was appointed as a professor at Sophia University, remaining there until March 1989. In the next section, we will see how Tsurumi got away from the round trip between "common people" and America.

3 From "Common People" to "Wanderers": Tsurumi's Interpretation of Yanagita

3.1 "Common People" or "Primitive Men within Us"

Wandering and Settling: Kunio Yanagita's Theory of Social Change, published in 1977, contains 9 articles from 1969 to 1976 in the order in which they were written. The book's postscript mentions how Levy recommended "Kunio Yanagita" as the subject of Tsurumi's PhD dissertation, but she was not confident about it. According to Tsurumi, it was through her "foreign studies" of modernization and social change that she discovered clues to Yanagita's works. "If I had just passed through Yanagita's gate straight from my father's house in Seijo, I would not have had any ambition to solve the mystery of Kunio Yanagita" (Tsurumi 1997: 231).

Tsurumi's interpretation of Yanagita in this book seems to be divided into three phases. First, let us take a look at "Primitive Men Within Us: Rethinking Modernization Theory Centered on Kunio Yanagita", published in 1969. This article opens with the sentence, "There is a recurrence of Kunio Yanagita now". Tsurumi says that the question of whether "modernization of Japan" brought happiness or not was related to this "recurrence". Yanagita was enthusiastically talked about after the 1960 struggle against the Japan-US Security Treaty. The Marxists in the 1930s experienced "a conversion and a setback of the movement because their universalism was separated from the masses", whereas young people in the 1960s reconsidered how they could reach "universalism rooted in the masses" and sought to change Japanese society without relying on ideas transplanted from the outside, such as Marxism and modernism. In this context, they were attracted to Yanagita. Similarly, Tsurumi considers Yanagita's ideas "a theory of social change that has grown indigenously in Japan" (ibid.: 3–4).

According to Tsurumi, Yanagita aimed to create a homological social science, whereas Japanese social science after the Meiji era was heterological. As already mentioned, "heterological" refers to using a methodology created outside the society that is the subject of research, and it is premised that the researchers belong to a different group from that of the research subject. "Homological" means that the research method is born from the society of the research target, and the researchers belong to the same group as the research target. Yanagita broadly surveyed overseas ethnology, folklore studies, and anthropology, such as Tyler and Fraser, but he tried to build a "homological" folklore that could capture Japanese folklore from the inside. Its methodology should be called "particularism", and Yanagita sought "a way to reach universalism starting from particularism" (ibid.: 5–7).

The main character of Yanagita's world is "*jomin* (common people)", which is close to Dewey's "common man". Dewey saw the prototype of common man as "a lumberjack without a single letter in his eyes", a person who thinks without relying on written language, and Yanagita's *jomin* overlaps with this. Here, Tsurumi contrasts Yanagita with Talcott Parsons. Parsons divided macro-social development into primitive, middle (ancient/medieval), and modern. Primitive society is a society that has spoken language but no written language, middle society is one that has written language, and in modern society, social norms are legally institutionalized. According to Tsurumi, Yanagita's "common people" are close to the "primitive people" defined by Parsons. Yanagita was convinced that they were the "bearers of social change, rather than intellectuals" (ibid.: 7–9).

Tsurumi stresses that Yanagita's theory of social change is most comprehensively shown in *History of Meiji and Taisho Era: Volume on Everyday Life*. This book, published in 1930, was prefaced,

> As a result of my dissatisfaction with the traditional biographical history, I deliberately refused to list even one proper noun in this book…. I described only what people omnipresent in the country can watch and listen if they open their eyes and ears and can think if they reflect themselves without difficulty.
> YANAGITA [1930] 1993: 7

Tsurumi argues in her 1973 article "Common People and History of Everyday Life" that there is a "contradiction" in this remark. Yanagita was an outstanding intellectual who specialized in writing as a professional and was objectively "not a common man". However, he has a feeling of one of the common people. Yanagita was aware of "the part of common man and the part of uncommon man in himself, that's why there was a conflict". It is this self-awareness that made this book stimulating (Tsurumi 1977: 68).

One important point Tsurumi notes from the book is the "transformation in senses". While values and ideology are regarded as important factors of social change, Yanagita described affect changes by observing facial expressions and gestures, senses for colors, sounds, scents, and tastes of common people (ibid.: 71–74). To take an example from chapter 2, "Individual Freedom of Food", Yanagita states, "the scent of the village was still one for a long time" (Yanagita

[1930] 1993: 62). In other words, every house consumed the same seasonal food, and the dishes prepared on festival days were the same. However, the scents of the houses became different from each other recently, changing from "unification" to "separation". Formerly, the food was cooked by the "official fire" in the kitchen derived from *kojin* (the god of fire), and was distributed to the family members in order, so it was cold to eat. In the last 50–60 years, the warmth of foods became more valued than the togetherness of eating, and *konabedate* (individual hot pot dishes) developed rapidly. Yanagita called this "the division of fire (*kamado*)" or "the concession of the worship (*Shinto*) of fire", and emphasized how different foods and scents had spread in the family and in the village (ibid.: 63–69).

These changes occurred over a long period rather than on a predetermined date. Tsurumi says that "history from the standpoint of the rulers" will develop at certain stages, but from the ordinary people's viewpoint, the past, present, and the future coexist intricately, and human personalities are also layered with old and new affects or sensations. One of Yanagita's key achievements, according to Tsurumi, was "to get rid of the habit of evaluating the new as better than the old" (Tsurumi 1977: 78–79).

3.2 Confrontation with "Modernization Theory"

What kind of "modernization theory" is possible from such attention to *jomin*? The second phase of Tsurumi's interpretation of Yanagita demanded a direct confrontation with her own academic position cultivated in the United States.

In the final section of "Primitive Men Within Us", Tsurumi says that modern American sociologists, such as Parsons, Levy, and Moore, defined "modernization" as the changes that occur with "industrialization", synonymous with "westernization". The process of modernization is roughly divided into two types based on the time of its starting point. "Indigenous development" is a modernizing process that has created its own model of modernization, occurring over a long period of time. "Exogenous development" is a process in which modernization must be achieved in a relatively short period by seeking a model of modernization outside its own society. Many latter societies are "latecomers" and seek models from the most modernized societies (ibid.: 19–20). But for Yanagita, "modernization" involved the process of molting many times, occurring not "after traffic with the West" but "naturally in the private sector" (ibid.: 21–22). Rather than the Western "model of stages", Yanagita proposed the "model of icicles". In Japan, "it has moved slowly and unobtrusively", and now "primitive, ancient, medieval and modern are existing like an intricate work" (ibid.: 26).

Tsurumi boldly compared the methodologies of "my two academic mentors" in her 1971 article, "Particularism and Universalism in International

Comparison: Kunio Yanagita and Marion Levy". In Tsurumi's view, the conventional international comparative theory of modernization assumed a "universal measure" based on the modernization of Western society. Tsurumi termed this as "strange", given that the theory was constructed on a hypothesis that deals with the experiences of a particular society as if they were universal to human society. "My suggestion is to restart by clearly admitting that the universality of the Western world is fiction", she noted. This does not advocate abandoning the universal type of modern Western Europe, but "if it is a hypothetical construction, other images of modernization can also be set to be universal. It is a proposal to analyze international comparisons using various types of universality" (ibid.: 36–38).

According to Tsurumi, although Levy made efforts to break away from the prejudice that regards modern Western Europe as universal, his model of a "modernized society" was generalized from the experience of Western society, especially the United States. On the other hand, Yanagita's theory of social change was modeled on "a society without a break between modern and pre-modern times". If one applies the Yanagita model to "developing countries" and "West European societies", one will see facts overlooked by the idea of seeing a clear break between "modernized society" and "non-modernized society" (ibid.: 51–52). While Levy's theory of modernization is a "single-line development theory", Yanagita's theory of social change is a "multi-line development theory", and the process by which "originally the same" becomes "multiple different things" can be clarified (ibid.: 53–56).

This "indigenous development theory" made progress in "The Paradigm of Social Change: Focusing on the Works of Kunio Yanagita", contributed to *Adventure of Thought: A New Paradigm of Society and Change* in 1974. In this article, Tsurumi dared to regard Western modernization theory as Thomas Kuhn's "normal science" and discussed how the premise and hypothesis of Yanagita's theory of social change can innovate it, making the following six contrasts: (1) Is the academic goal value-neutral or value-statement? (2) Is the view of evolution "single-line" or "multi-line"? (3) Does it emphasize breaks or continuity in history? (4) Are exogenous or indigenous factors emphasized when discussing the modernization of non-Western societies? (5) Are the elite or ordinary people assumed to be bearers of social change? (6) Is ideology or affect emphasized as the basis of mental structure? (ibid.: 83–92).

3.3   *Resistance, Discrimination, and Wandering*
Tsurumi's interpretation of Yanagita changed greatly in two articles in 1975 and 1976, which could be called the "third phase". In "The Prototypes of

Discrimination and Nonviolent Resistance: *Tales of Tono, Considering Kebozu, The Story of Ancestors* and So On" of 1975, Tsurumi newly discovered the subjects of "discrimination" and "resistance" in Yanagita's work.

Regarding resistance, Tsurumi states that, "Viewed from the theory of indigenous development, *Tales of Tono* is an indirect and realistic critique of the emperor system as an ideology of the centralized state" (ibid.: 164). It testified that "the morals of the emperor's belief and patriotism are completely different from the beliefs and norms alive in the hearts of the villagers" (ibid.: 176). The Imperial Rescript on Education (*Kyoiku Chokugo*) taught "filial piety to parents" and "marital harmony", but this book described the bullying of a wife by a mother in law (Yanagita [1910] 1975: 7–8), and a heterogeneous marriage (ibid.: 20–21). Mountain gods, mountain people (ibid.: 5–7, 28–29), *tengu, kappa* (kinds of apparition) (ibid.: 17–18, 28), and so on appeared in Tono, but the emperor god worshiped in the Imperial Rescript did not appear at all. Tsurumi found here the "non-violent resistance" of *jomin* (Tsurumi 1977: 179–180).

In "Materials on Side Stories of Mountain People" (1913–1917), and "Considering Mountain People" (1917), Yanagita developed the hypothesis that "mountain people", who wandered in the mountains, were descendants of the indigenous people (ibid.: 181; Yanagita [1913–1917] 1975: 144, 160). Yanagita regarded the ancestors of the imperial family called "*amatsukami* (gods of heaven)" were foreigners who conquered the indigenous people, and the people called "*kunitsukami* (gods of countries)", who had lived in the Japanese archipelago before, were subjugated by them and were otherwise driven deep into the mountains (Yanagita [1917] 1975: 132–134). Some of them were ostensibly repatriated because they could not compete with force, but they took the path of instilling their religion in the conquerors from below (ibid.: 140). In his *Lives in Mountains* published in 1926, Yanagita wrote that the religions of modern villages included the religion of the conqueror (leading to State *Shinto* and the religion of the imperial god) and the religion of the conquered (leading to private *Shinto*, or worship to the nature of the hometown) (Yanagita [1926] 1975: 130–131). Tsurumi notes that the method of protecting one's religion by "not making a head-on conflict with the conqueror's religion" could be said to be "less dangerous resistance". Besides, those who could not assimilate or did not want to give in would "leave the community and wander in the mountains", which Tsurumi termed "courageous resistance" (Tsurumi 1977: 182).

With regard to Yanagita's approach to discrimination, Tsurumi examined "Considering *Kebozu*" (1914–1915). *Kebozu*, priests with hair, were private priests who chanted the funeral sutra when asked, but were farmers on a daily basis. Yanagita opposed the 1906 "Enshrinement Ordinance" by the Takashi

Hara Cabinet mandating only one shrine in each village, and felt the need to investigate the religious life of the locals. While tracing the origin of *kebozu*, "he encountered the problem of the *Buraku* people" (ibid.: 185).

Yanagita argued that medieval pilgrim priests were the origin of *kebozu*. In this context, he treated all professions other than "court nobles, samurai, shrines, temples, farmers" in the same category, including religious people, craftsmen, entertainers, beggars, and so on, in line with the *Buraku* people. Tsurumi insists that this was "to show how discrimination is associated with wandering and how discrimination is unreasonable". Yanagita's idea was that discrimination occurred because those who were originally *jomin* became wanderers for some reason, and some of them were settled in the communities under bad conditions. In order to eliminate discrimination, they should return to the ordinary people and be treated as *jomin* (ibid.: 186; Yanagita [1914–1915] 1975: 356–375). Tsurumi criticizes this solution of "returning to *jomin*" as too optimistic (Tsurumi 1977: 189) and notes that Yanagita's analysis only shows "the process leading up to discrimination" without explaining how "discriminated former wanderers" would contribute to reorganization of order (ibid.: 192).

3.4 *"Wandering" and Social Change*

"Wandering and Settling: The Connection of Nature and Society as Seen by Kunio Yanagita", published in 1976, can be seen as the peak of the third phase of Tsurumi's interpretation of Yanagita. Here, she examines how Yanagita considered "common people" and "wanderers".

Yanagita criticized the centralized modernization policy promoted by Japanese government bureaucrats, emphasizing that decentralized development by the governed was possible, and set "common people" as the subject. The concept of *jomin* has been widely used since 1932–1933, and Yanagita's interest in wanderers preceded this. Tsurumi believes that Yanagita's clarification of the relationship between wanderers and the settled raised the concept of "the common people as the bearers of social change" (ibid.: 199). Here, she tries to overcome Yanagita's argument by noting

> On the one hand, common people as permanent residents are awakened and energized by encounters with wanderers. On the other hand, the common people, who have usually settled down, open up new perspectives and regain vitality through temporary wandering. For common people to become bearers of social change, they need to go through a settling-wandering-settling cycle, or a shocking encounter with wanderers.
>
> IBID.: 202

Yanagita saw that the settled people had a conflicting relationship of "discrimination or contempt and longing or respect" for the wandering people. Regarding "discrimination or contempt", Yanagita stated that among the people who were deprived of land by the ruler and entered the "lifelong traveler's life", some were forced to settle on the outskirts of the village and work as removers of animal skins, and they were discriminated against by villagers due to both their "state of being wanderers" and "forced occupation". Yanagita clearly argued that this was "discrimination without reason" (ibid.: 203–204). Regarding "longing or respect", hospitality to "*marebito* (rare people)" could be said to cause "respect for those who bring excellent happiness" (ibid.: 205).

According to Tsurumi, Yanagita covered seven types of "wanderers". The first type is the "propagator of faith", such as the hair priest or shrine maiden, whom Yanagita termed "prototypes of wandering". The second is the craftsman group, including brush makers, basket makers, blacksmiths, lacquer scrapers, and so on. The third type are "performing artists", including blind singers (*goze* and *zato*), female dancers (*shirabyoshi*), monkey trainers (*sarumawashi*), and comedians (*manzai*). Yanagita pointed out that these professionals were "related to worshipping gods in some way" (ibid.: 206–207).

The fourth type were the "mountain people", who, as hypothesized in "Considering Mountain People", were descendants of the indigenous people. The fifth category is "travelers". Some of them traveled for a lifetime, while others had settling places and used them as bases for occasional wandering trips. Yanagita highly valued common people going on temporary trips for "self-education". The sixth type is "temporary drifting as profession" or "in search of jobs" (ibid.: 207–209).

Finally, Tsurumi cites "the settling and wandering of the gods" as the seventh category. At the festival (or *hare*, contrasted with *ke* as everyday life), "the gods settled in the local community" and "the gods drifting from foreign regions" meet, and when faith in the indigenous gods declines, it regains vitality with this meeting. Additionally, the indigenous gods themselves "temporarily drift" on the festive day (Yanagita thought the ancestral spirits were at the top of high mountains behind the villages, and they "played out" to the shrine at the festival). "The encounter between the gods and the settled people is *matsuri* (the festival)", and gathering at the festival are not only the settled but also travelers from other villages and towns, priests, craftsmen, and merchants who are wandering. "The festival is the place for the gods and humans of all forms of wandering and settling to meet" (ibid.: 209–210).

Tsurumi concluded her interpretation of Yanagita's idea of social change as follows:

> People who have been settled in a particular community tend to have restricted vision and flow to inertia, and their mental vitality is easily exhausted by settling there for many years. At that time, there were two ways to rejuvenate. One is to go on a journey. The other is to welcome wanderers from outside and learn new knowledge, beliefs, and skills.... For the settled, temporary wandering and encounters with wanderers bring about self-awakening effects. In particular, encounters at the festival provide strong inspirations to the settled. It can be the driving force that rocks the settled, and drives them into new social movements.
>
> IBID.: 217–218

This gave Tsurumi an "analytical framework of social movement" to see her contemporary reality.

4   Minamata Seen from a Wanderer's Perspective: Reflections to the Present

4.1   "A Wanderer" in Minamata

In January 1976, the "Shiranui Sea Comprehensive Investigation Team" was established. This was in response to Michiko Ishimure's request to Daikichi Irokawa, a historian focusing on peoples' movements in modern Japan, who visited Minamata in December of the previous year.

Minamata disease is a pollution-caused disease officially confirmed in 1952. Since 1946, the Minamata Plant of Chisso Co., Ltd. had been discharging untreated waste liquid from the acetaldehyde production process, which contaminated the Shiranui Sea with organic mercury. People who consumed such contaminated fish and shellfish found their central nervous systems severely affected. Furthermore, fetal Minamata disease was first confirmed in 1961. In June 1969, a total of 112 patients and their families filed a proceeding in the Kumamoto District Court with Chisso named as a defendant.

Michiko Ishimure was the author of *Paradise in the Sea of Sorrow: Our Minamata Disease*, published in 1969, a novel depicting the suffering of patients in Minamata. She recalled that when this research team was launched, Tsurumi's participation was "so powerful" (Ishimure 1999: 137). Tsurumi wrote about the research team at the time as follows: "What does it mean to 'investigate' such human suffering 'academically'? Is the scholarship we have been doing useless for real human suffering? We wondered about these questions desperately" (Tsurumi [1995b] 1998c: 30). Ishimure noted, "the whole thing came alive when Tsurumi-sensei was there" (Ishimure 1999: 138).

Noriaki Tsuchimoto, a documentary filmmaker, recollected that Tsurumi

> always wore indigo-colored kimono, and never hesitated to stand out. She was accepted as "the expulsion of the noble species" by the patients, and finally, they opened their mouths. If she enjoyed with sake, she would dance in the traditional Japanese style. But everything was natural, which relaxed the patients so much.

According to Tsuchimoto, Tsurumi's nobleness and closeness to the people made it possible for all the families in the Minamata disease prone villages to be investigated, and "the people of Minamata still have not forgotten her" (Tsuchimoto 1999: 141–144).

At that time, Tsurumi must have realized that she was "a wanderer". In the final section of "Wandering and Settling", she wrote that Yanagita's hypothesis that "the encounter between wanderers and the settled awakens the settled and becomes a source of vitality for their movement" was "suggestive for Minamata" (Tsurumi 1997: 223). Presumably, she was referring to her own encounter with the people who had settled in Minamata.

Furthermore, Tsurumi discovered that in the seaside villages of Minamata City, those who had settled there generations ago were called "*jigoro* (the grounded)", while those who (or whose ancestors) had migrated were called "*nagare* (drifters)". The ratio of *jigoro* and *nagare* varied depending on the district, and in Minamata disease-prone areas, the number of *nagare* was overwhelmingly higher than that of *jigoro*, with residents' movements more active (ibid.: 223). Starting from this awareness, she continued investigating the relationship between "wanderers" and "the settled" in Minamata.

4.2 *"Wandering and Settling" in Minamata*

Tsurumi visited Minamata once or twice a year for five years from 1976, and she investigated the personal histories of 32 patients and healthy people from 4 disease-prone villages. The result was published in 1983, when she was 65 years old, as "Structural Changes and People in the Disease-Prone Villages: From Destruction of Nature to Endogenous Development".

As Tsurumi mentions at the beginning of part 1, "Structure and Change of Settling and Wandering in Disease-Prone Villages", *jigoro* are the people who have owned the land for a long time, and *nagare* are new people who have no land. "*Amakusa nagare*" refers to people from the Amakusa area who have the occupation of fisherman. From the standpoint of "farmers who have settled down and own the land", it was a word that discriminates against "fishermen who have drifted from outside and have no land". Not being used ostensibly, it appeared on the surface of people's consciousness in serious situations, and the patients were severely alienated and isolated by comments such as, "Minamata disease is *nagare*'s bizarre disease" (Tsurumi [1983] 1998c: 154–158). Tsurumi tries to redefine these "indigenous words" (≒ round words) to the concepts of "settling and wandering" and use them as "analytical tools" (≒ square words) (ibid.: 153).

Tsurumi calculates in detail the ratio of "the settled" and "wanderers" in each village, and finds that the four villages were not "closed microcosms", but there were cycles of constantly accepting migrants from the outside, while also releasing residents to the outside. "These villages were places of discrimination and repulsion between the settled and wanderers, as well as encounters and exchanges between them" (ibid.: 170). Tsurumi further describes how the outbreak of Minamata disease changed people's livelihoods and relationships. Due to the pollution of the Shiranui Sea, people could not live without compensation for fishing and certified Minamata disease. At the same time, compensation money caused conflict between villagers (ibid.: 182).

However, this does not mean there was a "collapse" of the village community. From her experience of visiting Minamata for five years, Tsurumi says, "The bonds that once existed have been broken, but new bonds have been created". Then, in part 2, "The Leaders of Endogenous Development", she tries to draw the building of cooperative relationships between "residents, wanderers, and newcomers" (ibid.: 186).

According to Tsurumi, there were two aspects of rehabilitation from the destruction of the natural environment and livelihood in Minamata. The "first aspect" focused on "trial struggle and voluntary negotiation" in which the Minamata disease patients claimed damages from Chisso. In this phase, "the settled and wanderers of villages" and "supporters who are travelers from outside" joined forces (ibid.: 187). Tsurumi depicts the cooperation between Teruo Kawamoto, a *nagare* who led the "voluntary negotiation movement", and Takeharu Sato, a *jigoro* from the oldest family among the four villages, who encouraged this movement (ibid.: 190–196). In addition, for the sit-in protests conducted by Kawamoto and other patients at the Chisso Tokyo Headquarters from December 1971, support from lawyers with specialized knowledge and members of the "Group for Accusation of Minamata Disease" in Tokyo, Osaka, and other cities was indispensable (ibid.: 197).

The "second aspect" was an attempt to regenerate the region by patients, who realized that modern medicine had no therapeutic ability and "relied on their own creativity to restore their inner nature" (ibid.: 198). Yoshiharu Tanoue, a *jigoro* from an old family, was severely afflicted with Minamata disease at the age of 26 in 1956; he refused admission to the rehabilitation center after being hospitalized and began beekeeping at home. When Tsurumi first visited Tanoue's house in 1977, she found a "microcosm in which various creatures coexist" (ibid.: 199–202). Tanoue eventually decided that he could not sustain his livelihood on his own, so in 1978 he bought an old mandarin orange field, and ran it together with Akira Sunada. Born in Kyoto, Sunada presided over a theater company in Tokyo but moved to Minamata in 1972 after traveling on a "pilgrimage" from Tokyo to appeal the suffering of patients. He became friends with Tanoue, who taught and discussed with him indigenous farming methods, and the two couples formed a "community of four" to work the field equally (ibid.: 206).

Lastly, Tsurumi describes her encounter with Teruo Kawamoto. They first met on the streets of Toronto, Canada, in fall 1975, when Kawamoto and his colleagues returned from a visit to the indigenous people's reservations named White Dog and Grassy Narrows, which were located near a mercury-contaminated lake. The people of both settlements were able to unite for the first time by meeting Kawamoto and others, and to file a proceeding for damages against the multinational corporation responsible. Tsurumi says that for Kawamoto, the encounter with them was an "awakening", and for the people of the reservations, the encounter with Kawamoto was a "soul-shaking shock" (ibid.: 212–213).

Here, the people in the reservations were "the settled", and the Minamata disease patients were "travelers or temporary wanderers". When indigenous Canadians visited Minamata, they were "temporary wanderers", and the Minamata people were "the settled". "From such exchanges, Minamata disease patients in Japan and patients in Canada could be aware of the particularity and commonality of their experiences by collating with each other". Tsurumi says that the relationship between settling, wandering, and temporary wandering can be regarded as "an analogy of the circulation structure of soil, water, and living things in the thinking way of ecology". Her closing remark of this article is, "It is my remaining task to reconsider the universalization of the experience of Minamata disease from this point of view" (ibid.: 215).

4.3 *Implications for Post-Western Sociology*
In terms of Tsurumi's own wandering and settling, she kept "global wandering" in her fifties and sixties. She served as a visiting professor at the University of Toronto in 1973–1974, and at Princeton in 1976–1977. She also visited China in 1978 to meet Fei Xiaotong, and she formed a delegation with leading Japanese sociologists in 1981. While continuing these vigorous activities, in January 1989, 70-year-old Tsurumi delivered her final lecture, "Three Cases of Endogenous Development", and retired from Sophia University in March. In the final

lecture, she examined the rural self-help movement in Thailand, the industrialization of Xiaocheng Town in China, and the regional revitalization movement in Minamata.

On December 24, 1995, Tsurumi collapsed at home with a cerebral hemorrhage. Her motor nerves were destroyed, resulting in left hemiplegia, but her language and cognitive abilities were unaffected. After moving into a facility with long-term care in Kyoto, where Tsurumi last "settled", she compiled 9 volumes of complete works named *Collection Tsurumi Kazuko Mandala*, and published more than 30 books. She was busy working until May 2006, but was hospitalized in June owing to a broken spine, and on July 31, Kazuko Tsurumi passed away at the age of 88.

It would be better to leave it to the readers to decide the implications of post-Western sociology from the works of Yanagita and Tsurumi. However, in their attempts to approach the world of ordinary people in Japan, they reorganized the frameworks of Western social sciences, which both of them had learned deeply, into the indigenous frameworks born from their own society. They questioned the universality of Western models and tried to build the theory of endogenous social change.

For Yanagita, *jomin* as the common people were its bearers, and Tsurumi initially agreed with this. However, upon reviewing Yanagita's early works, Tsurumi discovered that he repeatedly portrayed the lives of "wanderers" and the dynamic relationship between "wanderers" and *jomin* as "the settled". From the perspective of wandering and settling, Tsurumi extracted the issues of resistance and discrimination from Yanagita's text and analyzed the encounter between the settled and wanderers as a crucial opportunity to encourage social movements. Moreover, her monograph on Minamata depicted discrimination and repulsion between the settled (*jigoro*) and wanderers (*nagare*), and the collaborative relationship between the two toward social movement and resistance.

These analytical frameworks, derived from the world of "round words", would have great potential as indigenous conceptual devices that can capture social changes in non-Western societies, and in Western societies. As Tsurumi in Minamata showed distinctly, attempts by sociologists or intellectuals who have acquired "square words" to consciously define themselves as "wanderers" and establish connections with ordinary people, could be a reference point for considering the position of social science and knowledge in non-Western societies. To realize post-Western sociology, where in society should its bearers be located, and what can and should they do to the common people? I believe that Yanagita's and Tsurumi's quests will provide significant clues to the answers to these questions.

References

Ishimure, Michiko. 1999. "Primordial Power Revived, Kazuko-sensei". In Kawai, et al., *The World of Kazuko Tsurumi*, 137–140. Tokyo: Fujiwara Shoten.

Kawai, Hayao, et al. 1999. *The World of Kazuko Tsurumi*. Tokyo: Fujiwara Shoten.

Tsuchimoto, Noriaki. 1999. "Tsurumi Kazuko-san in Minamata". In Kawai, et al., *The World of Kazuko Tsurumi*, 141–144. Tokyo: Fujiwara Shoten.

Tsurumi, Kazuko. 1952. "Learning From Life Writing Education". In Tsurumi, 1998a, *Collection Kazuko Tsurumi Mandala II: Life History of the Japanese: in Japan and Abroad*, 322–327. Tokyo: Fujiwara Shoten.

Tsurumi, Kazuko. 1954. "Companions to Talk and Write With". In Tsurumi, 1998a, *Collection Kazuko Tsurumi Mandala II: Life History of the Japanese: in Japan and Abroad*, 370–384. Tokyo: Fujiwara Shoten.

Tsurumi, Kazuko. 1970. *Social Change and the Individual: Japan Before and After Defeat in World War II*. Princeton, NJ: Princeton University Press.

Tsurumi, Kazuko. 1977. *Wandering and Settling: Kunio Yanagita's Theory on Social Change*. Tokyo: Chikuma Shobo.

Tsurumi, Kazuko. 1981–1982. "*Science of Thought* in Postwar". In Tsurumi, 1997, *Collection Kazuko Tsurumi Mandala I: The Works of Tsurumi Kazuko: A Guidance*, 19–63. Tokyo: Fujiwara Shoten.

Tsurumi, Kazuko. 1983. "Structural Changes and People in the Disease-Prone Villages: From Destruction of Nature to Endogenous Development", In Tsurumi, 1998c, *Collection Kazuko Tsurumi Mandala VI: Minamata: An Approach to Animism and Ecology*, 152–219. Tokyo: Fujiwara Shoten.

Tsurumi, Kazuko. 1992. "The Departures Were Overlapped". In Tsurumi, 1997, *Collection Kazuko Tsurumi Mandala I: The Works of Tsurumi Kazuko: A Guidance*, 64–76. Tokyo: Fujiwara Shoten.

Tsurumi, Kazuko. 1995a. "Significance of Immigration Research". In Tsurumi, 1998a, *Collection Kazuko Tsurumi Mandala II: Life History of the Japanese: in Japan and Abroad*, 9–39. Tokyo: Fujiwara Shoten.

Tsurumi, Kazuko. 1995b. "The World of Minamata People and the Endogenous Development". In Tsurumi, 1998c, *Collection Kazuko Tsurumi Mandala VI: Minamata: An Approach to Animism and Ecology*, 28–79. Tokyo: Fujiwara Shoten.

Tsurumi, Kazuko. 1997. *Collection Kazuko Tsurumi Mandala I: The Works of Tsurumi Kazuko: A Guidance*. Tokyo: Fujiwara Shoten.

Tsurumi, Kazuko. 1998a. *Collection Kazuko Tsurumi Mandala II: Life History of the Japanese: in Japan and Abroad*. Tokyo: Fujiwara Shoten.

Tsurumi, Kazuko. 1998b. *Collection Kazuko Tsurumi Mandala III: Social Change and the Individual*. Tokyo: Fujiwara Shoten.

Tsurumi, Kazuko. 1998c. *Collection Kazuko Tsurumi Mandala VI: Minamata: An Approach to Animism and Ecology*. Tokyo: Fujiwara Shoten.

Yanagita, Kunio. 1910. *Tales of Tono*, In Yanagita, 1975, *Series Modern Japanese Thought 14: Kunio Yanagita Collection*, 3–39. Tokyo: Chikuma Shobo.

Yanagita, Kunio. 1913–1917. "Materials on Side Stories of Mountain People". In Yanagita, 1975, *Series Modern Japanese Thought 14: Kunio Yanagita Collection*, 144–163. Tokyo: Chikuma Shobo.

Yanagita, Kunio. 1914–1915. "Considering *Kebozu*". In Yanagita, 1975, *Series Modern Japanese Thought 14: Kunio Yanagita Collection*, 307–383. Tokyo: Chikuma Shobo.

Yanagita, Kunio. 1917. "Considering Mountain People". In Yanagita, 1975, *Series Modern Japanese Thought 14: Kunio Yanagita Collection*, 132–143. Tokyo: Chikuma Shobo.

Yanagita, Kunio. 1926. "Lives in Mountains". In Yanagita, 1975, *Series Modern Japanese Thought 14: Kunio Yanagita Collection*, 40–131. Tokyo: Chikuma Shobo.

Yanagita, Kunio. (1930) 1993. *History of Meiji and Taisho Era: Volume on Everyday Life*. Tokyo: Kodansha.

Yanagita, Kunio. 1975. *Series Modern Japanese Thought 14: Kunio Yanagita Collection*, edited by Kazuko Tsurumi. Tokyo: Chikuma Shobo.

SECTION 4

Epistemic Autonomies and Located Knowledge

∴

CHAPTER 17

Case Studies towards the Analysis of Total Social Construction

Qu Jingdong

1 Introduction: Sociological Studies Starting from Total Social Construction

Any social science research is bound to be motivated by two basic pursuits: the pursuit of 'truth', which is exploring the real social existence in life; and the pursuit of 'comprehensiveness'; if the truth of life is unable to explain the venation and logic of the whole society, then the research can hardly be called 'social' science. Without doubt, all the confusions come from being focused on these two pursuits, since there is neither absolute truth nor absolute comprehensiveness. People often cannot even recognize the 'self', let alone the so-called comprehensive 'social reality'. Therefore, sociologists can only do so much to approach truth and comprehensiveness. There is truth in society nevertheless, which is truth to the whole society; otherwise, everyone would talk alone and there would be no learning.

Weber's discussion on social sciences methodology was entangled with this question. He criticized Wilhelm Georg Friedrich Roscher, the historical jurist, who on the one hand attempted to find an empirically based 'natural law' for the society, and on the other hand wished to rely on the intuition of individual experiences to reproduce historical experience. This is a purely contradictory method (Weber 2009). What Weber meant was clear: just because people's social world is defined by 'subjective meaning', it does not mean that there are universally applicable laws or that there is any kind of connatural truth that applies to comprehensiveness. In other words, anything concerned with society based on the general assumptions of the whole is invalid. Conversely, if an individual truth does not include the whole, it will lose 'objective validity', and the truth that does not include the whole is not true. Thus, Weber (2009: 125) might say that among the social sciences related to human beings, or to sociocultural phenomena, 'we have a special kind of satisfaction in the standard of causal explanation'.

A special way of seeking causal association is a special research method in the social sciences (represented by sociology) that has saved cultural phenomena. The difference between sociology and other disciplines is that it does not embark on certain universal presuppositions to infer the true face of the total society, nor does it start from the sensory synthesis and empathy mechanism of individuals or groups to reflect the true total society; rather, it tends to build an interpretable bridge between objective experiences and subjective meanings. Here, we would not elaborate on Weber's view. No matter how splendid his explanations are, they would be confined in the meaning of culture and cannot fully confirm and reveal the mechanism of our own social life. However, the enlightenment we receive from Weber is that if we cannot feel the value form and meaning of our own culture, or make a breakthrough not based on the objective validity of the historical (also real) empirical world, we cannot have sociological reflections in the true scientific sense.

2   Techniques of Case Study: The Methods of -graphy

A good case is certainly not limited to a specific time and space; it may be deeply imprinted by history or reflect the traits of the era. More typical cases may become an epitome of social functioning and transition, like the 'monad' proposed by Leibniz, which is a dynamic and indivisible spiritual entity that reflects the whole world. Theoretically, any case has extensibility to some extent, since it is in infinite space and time, as the intersection point of history and reality. The historical heritage and transition, the spirit of the times and policy tendency, system rules, customs, and mores may be infused into the society of a specific time and space.

For any case, although it is just a point at first sight, either the intrinsic connection between the elements within itself or the multidimensional relationship with the external world would form a linear relationship by connecting points. However, in forming a kind of chain-like social logic mechanism, such different relationships may extend to other, broader social aspects and establish linkages with other mechanisms, forming a plane. Thus, the intersection of different domains in society may further be presented as a three-dimensional social structure that reflects the panorama of the whole society. Starting from a kind of idealized case study, we should form the order from point to line to plane, describe the social aspects that are carried by the case, sort out the main points that constitute the society, and prepare for a specific case study.

Both the edification of phenomenology and the homely style of ethnography remind us that a case study cannot enter the analysis level too early. Any case is located in a specific time and space, which may produce multiple social linkages, and therefore, it is start-up work to record and describe such linkages. Such work is similar to operations such as classification, cataloging, tabulation, and drawing, which are the basic work of social science studies. The description from a case study to the whole society only starts from the case study but is not limited to the domain of the case. The reason is simple: no partial society is molded completely by itself. Its micro-operation is affected by macro-conditions, such as rules and regulations from central and local governments, the economic systems of China, and the world or other linkages, and the realistic structure and historical legacy also embrace such grand dimensions. Cases are only microscopic sections from which to examine the overall structure and changes of society, to 'see a world in a grain of sand, and heaven in a wildflower', while how far and how deep the case can reach is determined by its own property and capacity. The typicality of cases is the scale of measurement. Therefore, starting from each dimension, we should at first seek the technology of describing cases in different disciplines. Various kinds of -graphy are easy-to-use methods.

From the perspective of space, geography (historical geography or human geography) can provide effective methods for case study and its natural distribution and anthropogeographic study. Whether it is the layout and configuration of the internal social space to which the case belongs, or the relationship between external factors and the environment, these are important topics for case studies. In essence, any social unit is embedded in multilayered social systems, as a site in such systems. In other words, in many situations, cases do not form an independent unit for observation or analysis. Only by starting from space to understand the relationship between the case and the multilayered social system can its property be obtained. For example, in south China, some villages are inhabited by descendants of concubines' sons, and unless we track the kinship sacrifice system made by an ancestral shrine, we can hardly determine its specific position in the kinship system; thus, case study may be carried out without a specific purpose. In northern China, many water resource distribution systems and their customary laws that come down from history form a unique social arrangement in the sense of geography, which is intertwined with kinship relations or kinship relation systems. If we only study a single unit among them, we may miss the forest for the trees.

In this respect, the studies of historical anthropology offer excellent examples. In the research design of the 'Settlement Form and Ritual Alliances in Putian Plain', Zheng (2010) explicitly mentioned the advantages of human geography. He stated that "our plan is to introduce the concept of space into the study of historical process. The geographic spaces that we are concerned about include ecological, administrative, social, and cultural ones; these are multilayered and mobile spaces. We are also concerned about the mutual constraints and effects of different geographic spaces". This means that in discussing the characteristics of Chinese society and culture, we should include villages into an interrelated regional system, rather than isolate them. In the historical case of the development of Putian Plain, due to the development of water conservancy and the irrigation system, some strips or belts of settlements were formed along the channels and dams; therefore, finding the factors that influenced the settlement relation, especially the space distribution of water conservancy, administrative regions, clans, weapon fights, and ritual alliances, was the supporting point of this study. That is to say, by using the information system of historical human geography and considering raw materials such as village history, inscriptions, ritual notices, and religious literature, we should try to explore the regularization function of ritual alliances in social competition and integration, family order and religious faiths.

It can be stated that finding the mechanism of social formation from spatial relations can highlight the logical relation between cases and the larger social structure or system. In addition, such studies are not confined to the level of space distribution and mobility; they can also serve as a set of governance technologies that transform complicated actual space into abstract space that can be analyzed and controlled (Lefebvre 1991), namely, so-called 'cartography' (Du 2017). As Foucault stated, in modern 'governmentality', demography takes population governance as its aim, and cartography takes land governance as its aim, that is, governance related to the supervision and distribution of land categories, land area, and land quality, as well as governance over state territory security (Foucault 2007, 2010).

Starting from the grand issue of land economy and governance in contemporary China, Du (2017) did a case study on the implementation process of land projects, such as overall urban-rural development, linking increase in urban construction land with reduction of rural construction land, cultivated land requisition-compensation balance, and found an essential phenomenon: on the one hand, the central government established a nationwide land information system on the basis of survey and remote sensing and supervised and governed local governments on this basis; on the other hand, cartography offered local governments possibilities for new methods of governance by abstracting the actual geographic space through mapping. By means of space reorganization, selecting layers, and over-lapping and remodeling them, the social contradictions created by expanding and merging projects are concealed. Therefore, a game on space focusing on cartography by the central and local governments reflects the new characteristics and tendencies of project governance. In conclusion, whether acting as a means of social configuration or as a governance technology, space needs to be described first by a method of -graphy. As a matter of fact, tabulation and mapping in any case may take different forms according to different social systems or governance hierarchies, and the correspondence, interrelation, or dislocation in between are sources of inspiration for new discoveries in research.

Along with spacial techniques in case studies, time is also an important dimension. Generally speaking, historiography is frequently referred to as 'the theory and history of historical writing' by historians and is considered to be the study of the relationship between the written content and form of historical classics, that is, 'the relevance between historical issues and historical trends' (Zhu 2006). However, the main part of the study was more explicitly explained by Pocock (2014: 4): historians should pay special attention to the complexity of context and discourse in historical explanations and should include the meaning in texts and speeches in the social context and structure of the times. Therefore, discourse analysis is the core of historiography. The focus of Pocock's study was classical texts of political thought, but it is still inspiring to the carriers of history, the texts or speeches formed in people's daily lives. Fundamentally, historic significance exists when the entire past has effects on the present. Croce, Bloch, and Foucault all used similar words stating that all history is contemporary history. Therefore, both text or speech memories of macro-history or the micro-history of anonymous individuals or a small village have the characteristics of historical compilation. In addition, another feature of history is that there must be various forms of material carriers, since even things that have not been said in memory, or the everyday lives that people are accustomed to, have potential historical significance. Interviewing in a case study is a means to reveal and realize such historical significance.

Strictly speaking, the pure present is only a form of time. It is the connection between the past and the future that constitutes the present, which cannot do without all the contents provided by history. Apart from the cases with historical accumulation, even every person and the existing relationships between individuals are largely given by history. In case study, the time dimension with historical significance endows the case with very broad meaning; however, to determine how real life is shaped and transformed through history, it is necessary to find the traces of history as much as possible through the method of -graphy, to describe the process by which history continually receives multilayered memories and unlimited interpretations. Wang Guowei once proposed the 'method that applies to origin and development of history', or 'the method for time, geography and ways of the world' (Wang 1998); Chen (1980: 219) also drew a conclusion that he called a method that integrates 'explanatory proof', 'supplementary proof', and 'referential proof'. In the same way, in summarizing 'the method of collating historical facts by textual research', Chen Yinke also described three levels: '(1) Collecting related materials; (2) Comparing similarities and differences and collating historical facts after making choices; (3) Doing textual research, explaining contradictions and questions, referring to each other, and writing a book' (Wang 1998). Although what these two masters did were grand research studies, and the theory of 'three proofs' mainly relates to the areas of philology, archaeology, or transportation, such methods also offer references to specific case studies.

The historiography of case studies is also extensible. First, material collecting should never be restricted to a local area. The totality or specificity of policy documents issued by the central and local governments during a particular period, including all kinds of archives kept by the grassroots society, physical transcripts, and interview materials related to people from all walks of life, records of daily activities, and abnormal events in local communities, all belong to this category. This is the so-called 'collecting related materials'. As Chen Yinke (1980) stated, the method of collecting related materials is to establish a list of historical facts, which is attached to a great quantity of historical materials in the sequence of time, and then organize the list into a series, the materials being 'never too much'. Nevertheless, the materials that record the past are not inherently historical. Historical research first needs to compare the differences among various materials, the misplacement of different speeches, the omission of a storyline, the repairing of past memories, and so on. The so-called 'selecting materials after weighing' is part of the work of 'the method of collating historical facts by textual research', aiming at working out solid evidence according to clear topics. In essence, all the past materials are 'seemingly true' or 'half-genuine and half-sham'. Different interpretations come out due to different motivations, intentions, planning, or evaluation orientations of subjects in writing and speaking. Taking researchers' input of understanding into account, there is no absolute truth. However, through comparative analysis of multiple facts, verification of multiple materials, and tension adjustments between subjectivity and objectivity, it is possible to find historical links with contexts, clues, and logic.

The purpose of using the -graphy method of the temporal dimension in case study is not to completely restore historical facts. The key is that all historical facts are to undergo 'transformation through narration' and 'explanation resetting'. Without doubt, started from their own meaning contexts, researchers continue to offer 'reasonable reinterpretations'. Nevertheless, since they have done all kinds of textual research studies such as abundant comparisons and verifications, they possess objectivity to some extent. Furthermore, such objectivity is not limited in the cases themselves since the above-mentioned work has included cases on all related levels in the whole society and their periodic changes. The cases have extended into a social network for the whole society: from partial space and time points of cases, like running ripples, they extend to a broader social range horizontally and longitudinally, even building substantial logical relations with the highest-level social systems, such as transformation of political powers, adjustments of central government policies and reform of industrial structures, or building relations in the analytical sense with long-inherited and deep-rooted cultural phenomena ethics, and codes of conduct (like the 'social background' described by scholars).

For example, Zhe and Chen (2005)'s study on 'social contracting' is a reinterpretation process on collective property rights in the transformation of enterprises in the 1990s, which is a typical case for analysis. In addition, the two authors also paid special attention to cases of 'registration of land contracting management rights. Then, to determine the 'common owner' of a farmer's land property rights, namely the membership rights, it is necessary to clarify the basic standards through legal principles in the sense of systems and policies, while in the meantime, suitable coordinative screening is required according to specific reasonability principles. However, in such research a more important point is that right affirmation is, in essence, a process of constantly tracing history. First, taking the population unit in membership rights as an example, it is necessary to determine four kinds of stock rights according to four categories of 'marginal man' caused by changes in urban–rural structures. Although some people neither experienced land compensation recourse nor participated in joint entrepreneurship with villagers, nor made a fortune outside of the village for a long time, they still claimed stock rights sharing. All such 'marginal men' would constantly do historiography according to past and realistic policies, history associated with the village community and the individual's life history and offer different justifications for 'rationality'. As a matter of fact, the crucial point in social operations does not lie precisely in institutional rules themselves, but in the problem-solving process brought about by the continuous interpretation of various related systems and history by such marginal men in expanding time and space. Thus, this shaped the theoretical 'boundary effect' in institutional practice. That is to say, the formulation, adjustment, and implementation of social systems come from the 'hard points' generated from all groups of people or all situation in cases. The discovering, adjusting, and solving processes of such hard points form the source points for the generation of social logic. This case shows that the village community's acceptance or rejection of the marginal man in the empowerment process constitutes a kind of judgment and decision about the whole society after integrating all historiographic work and explanations of related parties from problematized paths of systematic practice. The determination of degree is realized based on tracing or reshaping many historical facts and the process of logicization through a problematized process (contradictions or paradoxes). This is the unique vision of case study by sociologists.

We can also see that although sociology draws upon the methods of historiography to explore the processes of social operation, all the 'transformation through narration' and 'explanation resetting' are realized by every individual in the society. Therefore, for the people and groups who are key to social operations and the history molding process, it is a method for further exploring the historical dimensions of cases. In this respect, the methods of biography or even autobiography bear the nature of life-course study; however, in essence, they are still used to reveal social mechanisms. The research method of autobiography here is not from autobiographical texts by the researchers themselves, but rather, takes auto-biographical texts as the object of study. For example, the diary written by a member of the local gentry named Liu Dapeng in Shanxi province during the late Qing Dynasty was not an autobiography of himself but contained the local gentry's thoughts on the changes in national affairs (history of mind) (Yang 2012). According to historical texts such as Official Admonitions and the behaviors of some authors in the administration, local conditions during a specific historical period and the ideological traces of scholars in the administration can be observed (Zhou 2012a).

There is a classic case in academic history in which case studies were carried out through the skilled use of the biographical method. The famous book written by Lin Yueh-Hwa, The Golden Wing, was first published in 1944. When it was published in New York, its subtitle was once 'A Family Chronicle'. The author wrote frankly that the method used in this book was the 'biographic method'. Lin (1990: v) stated, in the English version of the foreword, that 'in talking about the fate of the emperor, families or individuals, what we try to explore is interpersonal relationships. Indeed, the description of someone's life course, which is biography, is an upgraded version of historiography. Since what historiography is concerned with is a specific individual's historical history and reinterpretation process, the biographical method has the following advanatages in case studies. First, it enables social studies to return to the people themselves; the feelings, behaviors, thoughts, and aspirations of specific individuals in the society form the engine that launches social linkage, while the overall structure of a people itself is the result of molding by history; only the structure of a people itself has potential continuity in a civilization. Furthermore, culture has substantive meaning only for specific individuals. People are the fruit of civilization, and culture exists in the vivid relationships among people. Cultivation is the fundamental mechanism of society. 'The existence of human beings is a process of responding to stimulations continuously'

(Lin 1990: 28). Therefore, Lin Yueh-Hwa said, 'we can comprehend "the Heaven" as a human being itself, and regard "destiny" as human society' (Lin 1990: 28; also, Firth 1990: ix–xii). Second, people live in changing interpersonal relationships and may be faced with contingencies such as opportunities or accidents; therefore, only by releasing such contingencies in analysis can we resume the true social living status; contingency is not an error in variable thinking, but a kind of social mechanism that plays an even more important role.

The Golden Wing narrates the ups and downs of the life histories of two families, Huang and Zhang. As for the life course, social construction may occur along with the developmental trajectories of the main family members, from rural areas to towns to cities; from farming to small trades and business operations; from getting married to family break-ups to the collision between family and politics and even foreign invasions. Along with such trajectories, the concept of family is also continually extended. In Lin's opinion, such an extended life history was still linked to two kinds of destinies for the Chinese: the first destiny was the long-cherished wish to go home, indicating the overlapping of destinations and starting points in a life cycle; the second destiny was that people are always involved in activities of production operations or sacrifice ceremonies. No matter how the scope of life expands, a sustainable equilibrium of interpersonal relationships is maintained between normality and changes, the balance and imbalance of life. This dynamic balance mechanism is the source of social order. It can be stated that the case study based on biography has deepened descriptive analytic principles and changed the abstract ideas in hypothesis thinking starting from measurement, also improving perspectives in qualitative observation starting from analytical interpretation. Because, regardless of whether research is quantitative or qualitative, all studies try to set aside the changing and accidental flow of life for presuppositional or slice analysis of society, rather than finding the real connotations of society from the continuous life flow to realize understanding of human life molded by its own civilization.

From this perspective, starting from biography, a kind of research method can be developed based on historiography but different from other methods. The presentation of life history is somewhat different from the strategy of historiography. As Lin Yueh-Hwa stated, 'External materials for measurement should rely on introspective explanation, so as to realize the truths of society and understand the value of life' (Lin 2000; Zhang and Wang 2000). Therefore, the understanding based on 'intuition, empathy, and introspection' is the most expressive, substantial, and intuitive sociological explanation.

The kinds of -graphy technologies in case study are not limited to those listed above. For example, lexicography is also of high value for the application of sociology. This method takes social concepts as the object of study, meaning that the frequently used concepts or categories in social life should be studied within a specific historical context. Durkheim once proposed in his religious study that, as a basic form of social structure, the concept in religious thinking is collective representation, which is a kind of social mental activity; the epistemological foundation laid by religion always takes the distribution and form of social groups as its basis; social configuration, and classification is the highest form of knowledge schema (Durkheim and Mauss 2000: 88–89; Qu 2017). What Durkheim referred to is the concepts in daily use in which society is implied; therefore, tracing the sources of concepts is just studying the formation of the social mechanism.

For example, in studying the early revolutionary history of the Communist Party of China, Meng (2016) proposed that the discrimination and disputes about the concept of 'rich peasant' are key points in the hierarchical division and ideological mobilization mechanism in the early 1930s. The concept of rich peasant came from the Soviet Union, and therefore, 'the differences between landlords and rich peasants, rich peasants and well-to-do middle peasants are generally vague and hard to judge' (Meng 2016). However, in the narrative discourse of hierarchical revolution, such a definition is directly related to the judgment on the holistic crisis of Chinese society in modern times as well as to the political and ideological relation between the Communist Party of China and the Communist International, which is related to the specific practice of transferring the revolutionary strategies regarding hierarchy as the core of revolution and to the operation that realizes hierarchical division in agrarian revolution (Meng 2018). Especially around the Sixth National Congress of the CCP, rich peasants were regarded as experiencing a change from the middle class to an 'enemy of revolution' and this evolved into the issue of taking 'the route of rich peasants' in the complicated struggle situation, which finally turned out to be the internal logic of the dynamic mechanism of revolution. In the specific evolution of the introduction and operation of such a term, it is clear that the social focus and its connotation of the concept have gone far beyond a mere part of society and become the criteria for judging the logic of political revolution. In the same way, in studying the agricultural cooperation movement in the mid-20th century, Luo (2013) found, after analyzing the texts of Planting the Millet by Liu Qing, that the social transformation in rural areas brought about by cooperation took defining the concept of 'middle peasant' as the focus of the social movement. Through the theoretical identification of the private properties of 'middle peasants' and taking them as the entry point for social transformation, the logic transfer was finished by replacing 'for the private' with 'for the public' and replacing 'the multitude' with 'the state'. These two studies show that, whether used to label people as 'rich peasants' in the early revolution or 'middle peasants' in the socialist transformation, such words and concepts reveal the core logic of the social construction of a specific historical period, and therefore, as the engine that generated the society, they present the appearance of the total society.

By describing the above specific case studies, I have described the analysis and operation processes of all kinds of -graphy technologies. On the whole, however, in the time–space dimension formed by the cases, the processes can be regarded as the elaborated and deepened methods of ethnography. Above, I have described how recent ethnographic studies have been challenged by many theories, such as phenomenology, linguistics, and hermeneutics, and without a doubt, such challenges can be comprehended as opportunities for the further development of the ethnographic method. Seen from the overall orientation related to such studies, ethnography still occupies the leading role.

Starting from the comprehension clues on ethnos, Yang (2010) discussed the evolvement process from cultural setting to research paradigm related to the history of civilization in the life of Fei Xiaotong. She pointed out that Fei's initial interpretation of ethnos refers to the separation and reunion between clans; around the year 1928, when Fei considered transitioning from field investigation to integration of historical study and field study, he began to comprehend the historical process of ethnos as a process of cultural transition and to discuss 'how an ethnic unit as cultural unit develops in the interaction between ideas and society'; in his late years, he rethought the influence that Shi Luguo had had on him, and by further expanding his research boundaries, he fully integrated social study and scholar study, proposed a cultural study paradigm in the sense of 'cultural self-consciousness', and took the spiritual associations between society and culture and its carrier as the keys to understanding ethnos. Here, the reason for discussing the ethnographic method from Fei Xiaotong's thought progression is to illustrate that ethnography is not a descriptive technology based on the forms of ethnic groups. Bridging the time and space of a society, correlating the whole structure of the civilization body to fulfill its role as the carrier of culture, which is the mental status of scholars or intellectuals and the spiritual life course, is the fundamental essence of doing so. Therefore, it could be said that ethnography serves as the aggregation of all -graphy methods and the actual spiritual core of case studies.

3   Eventalization: Activation of 'Society'

The -graphy methods in case studies are techniques that deepen and expand cases from the inside out, and the path that can constantly present the whole society as embodied and involved in cases. However, pure description is not the final goal of case studies; even if the restoration by phenomenology provides some primary basis, the so-called 'constant' societal mechanisms still need reinterpretation. The 'thick description' Geertz proposed seems to aim in this direction. Geertz once said, describing a colleague:

> Alfred Schütz covered a multitude of topics—almost none of them in terms of extended or systematic consideration of specific social processes—seeking always to uncover the meaningful structure of what he regarded as 'the paramount reality' in human experience: the daily life as men confront it, act in it and live through it.
> GEERTZ 1999: 18

In social studies, phenomenology can remind us of where we should return to, rather than tell us where we are, while ethnography after introspection tells us what is here, instead of telling us why.

Heidegger's criticism of phenomenology also comes out of this reasoning. He wrote: 'The questioning in phenomenology indeed approached the question of phenomenon related to being, but it failed in answering the question of "geschehen (coming into being)", namely the original initiation of being' (Heidegger 2014: 50–52). To this, sociologists may add: As a social being itself, it is not a revelation of the state of being, but a question from the perspective of Dasein; it is not a restoration process of a social form, but rather the way "the people in society" exist in the form of questioning. For the question of 'what is history', Heidegger held a similar view in Introduction to Metaphysics:

> The history of 'what is asked about' is not the reorganization and recording by history, nor the linear link of the flow of time. Its essence lies in 'being', which comes into being from 'what is asked about and what is replied'. Therefore, the activity of questioning has the essence of history (Geschehnis),
> HEIDEGGER 2018: 6

rather than the facts generally stated by people, or a kind of continuous description process. Exploring what is 'social being' also requires a kind of 'openness in thinking'. Social being is not a presentation of a series of social elements and their correlations, but the onset effect activated by them. Here, we call it 'eventalization', which is not equal to the event that emerges in everyday life. An 'event' is the emergence of a matter that can be sensed by almost everyone. It is a matter only related to emergence, a one-time dynamic representation process. Although eventalization emerges focusing on an event, it is an emerging or generating process and a phenomenon with a tint of phenomenology presented by the effect of a specific social mechanism. Therefore, eventalization is a questioning process throughout the society by way of emergence of an event, which cannot be perceived daily by all people. It can only be conducted by people who ask, 'what is asked about'. The social mechanism eventalization presents is permeated in society with the possibility of ubiquity and repetitive effects. It is not an instantaneous reality, but a continuous mechanism existing in various phenomena through a one-time event.

The most prominent characteristic in case study is eventalization, which is a 'coming into being' process of the socially related beings in cases. In other words, any case study would have a kind of special opportunity or beginning that causes parties to get involved and allows involved parties to get out of the previously covered status and pose questions, which is why they encounter such a special social situation under the specific status of Dasein. Whether through the occurrence of an extraordinary event; an occasional encounter in daily life; a certain chance, change, or abnormality; or even the researcher interviewing involved parties, eventalization may provoke questioning activity by the involved parties concerning 'what is being asked about' and enable the parties to launch a series of concepts that reorganize social beings.

All such social becomings are not a result of presetting, nor the reproduction of the existing social order, but a process that really occurs in society. In the tradition of qualitative research in sociological studies in China, the 'process-event' paradigm proposed by Sun (2005) is very representative. He found that social life in rural areas is at a very low stylized or patterned level compared with that in urban areas, since there are some secret points the 'delicacy' of which needs exploration, as in the concept of 'constancy' proposed by Yang Shanhua (Yang and Sun 2015). The delicacy here is reflected in two points. "Firstly, the uncertainty, that is to say, there is no unchanging link between elements or between matters and the environment; and secondly, the invisibility in static structure". In this case, 'process-event analysis' is an appropriate way to demonstrate such secret or delicacy: "Process can be taken as a relatively independent source of explanation or explanatory variable". Sun adopted two concepts, 'minor practice' from De Certeau and 'deep play' from Geertz, to illustrate the transformation of the explanation logic above, which is the change of perspectives from unit to context, from nature to relation, and from cause and effect to event. He pointed out that, for such a research strategy, "in dealing with social phenomena, just like Impressionist painters see flowing air and sunlight, they regard social phenomena as fluid, fresh, and dynamic, full of 'secrets'" (Sun 2005). In the process of eventalization, various social factors may be inactivated from a potentially dormant status, and social construction is going on continually in frequent social interactions to release all kinds of possibilities into society.

The studies above fully illustrate the characteristics of eventalization: (a) only through the occurrence of events, can a society 'pose a question' and the social elements that are perceived through our description generate correlation; (b) only through the occurrence of events can all social aspects be revealed and visible and can the possibilities associated with society be released; (c) eventalization has phe-nomenological significance, since it can present the important elements that have not been discovered previously; (d) one event can evolve into a series of eventive processes to mobilize the investment of more social elements and form a chain of infinite interconnections of social mechanisms; (e) through eventalization, we can explore current system boundaries and the extremity possibilities after continuous adjustments in the derived realistic effects; (f) only through eventalization can all social processes return to the Dasein status of specific individuals and can the people concerned be treated as an integrated body of social relevance; only through eventalization can the society return to human beings themselves and to the question of civilization's origin constituted by human nature.

Sun Liping's discussion on 'process-event analysis' is mainly focused on the level of state mobilization. He once pointed out that 'the grand visit', 'changing climate', and 'ten-thousand people meeting' are cases of key eventalized processes. Meanwhile, the case of the 'government's purchase of grains' also illustrates that the informal use of formal administrative rights in local society blurs the boundary between state and society, and in the same way, it is also utilized by the state (Sun and Guo 2000). In response, Fang (2003) proposed the concept of the 'no-event situation', referring to 'all kinds of repetitive event sequences in life' or a 'repetitive event flow in daily life'; for example, the routine activities and social linkages in social life and the 're-routinization' process after eventalization. These two kinds of interpretation of eventalization are basically from the perspective of the relation between the state and society. Although events in case studies become extraordinarily complicated under bidirectional effects, the interpretations of eventalization from both positive and negative sides illustrate that the state's power in permeating and transforming local society lies in defining 'eventalization', or on the contrary, the focus of the 'no-event situation' may emerge.

As a matter of fact, the process of activating society by way of eventalization is not limited to the category of interaction between the state and society: there are many cases of question forming in common people's daily life and ethics. Therefore, the no-event situation or repetitive event sequence in daily life are still methods of eventalization, and thereby, daily life not only exhibits the process of continually being activated, but also absorbs and integrates all kinds of external elements, constantly building a kind of extended 'self', and 're-mold[ing] the perception of the world' (Fang 2003). Here, what I want to emphasize is that only through eventalization, especially repetitive eventalization, can a society continue to 'pose questions' and become open on the basis of returning to its origins. In other words, we should not merely regard eventalization as a process of social production, but as a kind of process of backtracking to the origins of a society; the eventalization process is not the essential point, the questioning of what the civilization's foundation of daily life is forms the foundation of social studies. This is what Fei Xiaotong implied in proposing 'cultural self-consciousness' in case studies. The differentiation and analysis above intend to illustrate that so-called 'eventalization' in case studies is by no means caused by the intervention of external powers from top to bottom; it also comes from the dilemmas in people's daily lives; the sociological meaning embodied in the power relation is not inherently higher than the seemingly trivial things in ethical life.

Nevertheless, how can we find the process of eventalization itself? This is indeed the lifeline of case study. Generally speaking, when people say an event takes place, it means there is something abnormal. Eventalization in sociological studies inevitably has abnormal elements in it; the phenomena that go against normality, convention, and common-sense pose challenges to people's routine lives or theoretical ideas. The phenomena of question forming or 'paradox' (Ying and Jin 2000; Zhe 2018) are the beginnings of questioning. This is quite similar to Garfinkel's 'breaching experiment' (Garfinkel 1967). Unreasonable things may not eventually deny common sense but reactivate the logic in people's daily lives through contradictory or conflicting methods and construct a new social reality or mechanism with various external factors that trigger events.

The 'carrot and stick' method of grassroots government mentioned in the grain purchasing case by Sun and Guo (2000) is a feasible working method that was found after absorbing nutrients from local knowledge. Grain purchasing is a hard nut to crack. This work is the most difficult and most troublesome, and it may easily cause contradictions. Generally speaking, grassroots government is merely the performer of national policies, carrying out its duty according to rules; however, in reality, the conflict is made more serious by working according to rules, and therefore, there is the process of eventalization or question forming. There is no such 'carrot and stick' method in the rules and regulations of the government, and the most commonly used methods in people's daily lives are the most effective. In short, to manage a large family, to control a group of people, some low-end methods, such as teasing, cheating, bullying, frightening, lying, and fabricating might be used. Grassroots governments have to use such methods to solve problems. Apparently, the abnormalities of such administrative operations are not uncommon, although they are not in line with people's usual impressions. Through the questioning of eventalization, we understand a plain but profound principle: there is no prescribed path by formal system for administrative operation, and the commonly used methods by the people are equally effective in governance. Indeed, are there any organizations, units or higher departments that do not use such methods? With such an acknowledgment, we will have an open understanding of the social structure, and it is eventalization that gives us such an opportunity.

The abnormality in eventalization has another meaning in it, which is the unexpected result derived from events. Normally, people tend to take social life for granted, and analytical realism regards society as the existence of established systems; therefore, social studies become a reality that can be proved by various facts through empirical evidence (Yeh 2018: 253). However, eventalization does not pursue the following logic: there are chances everywhere in life, and the interactions between various elements often produce unexpected results. Case study is the best way to release social possibilities. Zhou Xueguang wrote a paper on collective debt caused by building roads in rural areas and revealed a series of unexpected events in cases. The road network construction was aimed at promoting public transportation facilities in rural areas; however, due to fiscal gaps for this project, the village had to rely on self-raised funds and to use various means or even 'deceive acquaintances' to collect funds. After the project was finished, the villagers even used collective assets to repay collective debts, impawning collective assets to foreign contractors for ten-year or twenty-year periods. In particular, the village with the greatest enthusiasm for the project not only consumed the collective assets accumulated over the years, but also added a huge amount of debt to the village collective, which could only be paid off over several years (Qu 2012b; Zhou and Cheng 2012) As a matter of fact, only through eventalization can the various social elements obtained by description generate unexpected interactive relations, and the possibilities of potential social relations become infinitely open, to establish a kind of in-depth explanation of the whole society. In many cases, in which a long chain of social effects was produced by eventalization, there was more room for explanation, and the scope extended to the society was wider.

Seen as a mechanism of social evolution, eventalization might occur when motivated by sudden events, or be caused by variations in the social mechanism itself. Therefore, it tends to present some abnormal forms which are different from those used in the past. However, purely emphasizing the abnormal significance of events may bring about the risk of overinterpretation of the cases. Case researchers should frequently remind themselves that, especially in the abnormal evolutionary process of events, it is easy to provoke researchers' association on the macro-structure of society, intensify existing social opinions, and produce the temptation to produce a 'strong explanation'. Therefore, abnormality is not the prerequisite that defines 'eventalization'. There are some other events in social life presented in the form of sublimation—for example, festival, ritual, or sacrificial activities—which combine and organize people periodically through existing procedures and realize the presence of social essence from secularity to sacredness. The ritual is a kind of eventalization process. Either the symbolic rituals in the 'citizen religion' described by Robert N. Bellah, or the 'Balinese cock fight' Geertz described, are a process of rejuvenating and reshaping the norms by means of a collective event. The 'rite order' Chinese describe is a more prominent reflection of Confucius's 'What is necessary is to rectify names' (Fei 1985; Wang 2007).

An episode from The Golden Wing illustrates the unexpected social function produced by rituals. When the brothers of the Huang family broke up the family and began living apart due to disputes, the elders and arbitrators in the locality came over to help make judgments and conclude an agreement. But they failed at last, and two brothers even came to blows. Before long, their grandmother Pan died of an illness. The Huang family held a grand funeral ceremony, and although the ceremony had nothing to do with family conflicts, it produced unexpected effects, and then the brothers stopped fighting. Lin (1990: 113) wrote: "During the funeral ceremony of the grandmother Pan, the life of the Golden Wing was completely different from the past. The ceremony lasted for several days. The Huang family and the mourners who came over reconsolidated their relations through this ceremony. After the crisis brought about by death broke the routine of life, the funeral ceremony once again became a force for unity to re-establish the common feelings among people". Compared with the eventalization provoked by external elements, the eventalization promoted by ritual life can go deeper into the endogenous mechanisms in society and can better embody the intrinsic mechanisms accumulated in history. It is the path to discovering so-called 'local knowledge' and even the more common civilization tradition. It could be said that the process-event analysis paradigm emphasizes the way to seek the explanatory logic for the expansion of power from grassroots society to the state by exploring local resources; however, the ritualized eventalization process can help us to explore how such so-called 'local resources' can be formed on a more profound basis of civilization.

Overall, we found that only by motivating the society through eventalization can the social elements captured by the -graphy methods mentioned above really be gathered, integrated, and expanded in specific social life and form a dynamic process in the sense of restoration and generation, and present multiple kinds of constitutive characters. According to such analytical clues, case study can unfold the multiple aspects linking to the whole society. The many points in eventalization constitute the story, with plots that are connected and transformable. It is the only story that regards all those involved in social life as people who live and experience life. In the same way, only by tracking these stories infinitely and searching for the ins and outs of the events and people in them can all the elements that constitute social life be unfolded like a map or biological drawing; only in this way can sociologists construct a picture of the whole society and find clues for solving the case.

4   Discussion: From Mechanism Analysis to Structural Analysis

Discovering society from the perspective of eventalization and comprehending it as a kind of constantly moving and developing body is different from the kind of thinking that verifies a hypothesis from a predetermined structure. Society, from the perspective of case study, not only has long-standing social and historical conditions and milieux on different levels, but also has conventional paths based on all kinds of institutions, such as the standardized public time coordinate (Elias 2007); it has not only the stocks of knowledge and thinking schemes required for people's social action, but also the emotional patterns provided by the mores people are accustomed to; it has not only the integration of all kinds of social factors or even the events formed by the occasionally appearing stimulation, but also the community after the long-term cultivation in history or personalities of individuals. All of these are substantial and important parts of society.

Therefore, case study itself has the characteristics of 'extensibility' in nature (Burawoy 2007). Taking the event as the starting point, the topological relationship of 'folding-cutting-expanding' is constantly formed between tiny events and world history (Li 1996; see also Ying 2018), from point to line, and from line to plane, a panorama with interlaced and mutually convertible images. I have mentioned above that a case is an occurrence point, which is like every individual in the life flow, with all sensations, images, and thoughts taking place at the moment. However, this point may gradually develop into a new life process and establish an association with surrounding life elements in a specific time and space, activate each locus in all associations by means of eventalization, and extend it to the past or the future as the 'present moment' to produce projection, reflection, and diffraction effects to the infinite depth of history and the broader societal world; as with physicists exploring the quantum world, it is a probe into the vast universe.

From its birth, what sociology has tried to discover in scientific exploration is not purely linear relations between cause and effect, but the relations between all social elements in an extremely complicated social field, or, in the words of Durkheim, a co-variant relation. Whether it is correlativity or a covariant relation, at first, it is an arrogant questioning against a kind of 'one-dimensional science'. According to Weber, no social phenomenon can do without its historicity. Each person's conceptual structure is closely associated with their historical destiny, so how can a purely objective reality be constructed in a complete manner? Therefore, the objectivity that sociology intends to procure, or the research methods that sociology goes by, are something different.

In the eventalization process, discovering how to establish the abovementioned correlativity or covariant relation and find the linkage in the event series is the very first step in case study. The linkage can be established through expounding and convergence. Petitions and Power: The Story of the Migrants of a Dam in China by Ying Xing (Ying 2001) is an example for study which expounds upon the multi-fold social linkages through the structure of continuous deduction. Precisely because petitioning is a kind of behavior with a 'logical paradox' that resorts to the superior government directly, it inevitably has a strong and extensible story-telling ability; moreover, with the associations established between petitioners and governments and administrative officials level by level, both sides would inevitably reshape the resistance and dominance logic and significance every time. It could be said that, just like in Liu Zhenyun's novel, *I Am Not Madame Bovary*, the unfolding process of the event is also a constantly turning and extending process of logic of both sides, thus forming the reciprocally acting covariant relation. Like the 'petitioning genealogy' proposed by Ying Xing, the natural process of eventalization presented all logical aspects of society running: how to judge the breakpoint of individual and collective petitioning, the degree of skip-level petitioning, the break-point of rational petitioning and trouble-making petitioning, attitude differences between authorities and the grassroots level toward petitioning, the breakpoint between a normal period and a special period, along with the evolution of the event, have become the key links in governance gaming between people and the state (Ying 2001: 315–317). Among such phenomena, people's techniques in question forming, states' governmentality, the mode of production of facts, and discourse in specific society running were all presented in a subtle and complicated manner.

Compared with related or covariant analysis, there is also a social association form in the sense of generative theory, which can be called 'mechanism analyses. Some scholars believe that 'social mechanism' refers to a series of events that constitute a sequential logic chain, among which the crystalization of the properties and activities of different social entities can generate specific social outcomes sustainably (Hedstrom and Ylikoski 2010). Or, in a common sense, it means that the social association formed during an event may continue to play a role in a series of subsequent events, embodying the possibility of producing similar results to those of previous events. This does not mean that the events will show a completely consistent evolution process, because the social conditions in different times and spaces will undergo significant variations, so the final result may not be similar; so long as there are no significant changes in social structure, this kind of correlation may always exist and very likely play similar roles under similar conditions. Therefore, even if the social mechanism has potential social associations, which are also sustainable, it can be said that such a combination of multiple correlations or covariant relationships has constituted a network of dynamic links of the entire society, demonstrating a prominent leading role and agency mechanism.

Finally, let us talk about the analysis form that enables the whole society to form a structural linkage by establishing the point in the above-mentioned eventalization, the line in the covariant relationship, and the plane created by the social mechanism, which is structuration. The compositional conditions for social structuration are certainly all kinds of social elements and their distribution and linkage forms revealed by the above-mentioned -graphy methods; however, the real onset of a society should rely on the eventalization process. Structural analysis is the advancement of mechanism analysis, which is the social linkage of all kinds of mechanisms further established by what was arrived at, based on mechanism analysis. On the contrary, if we have mastered the structural elements and their linkages in the whole society, this would offer inspiration and clues for micro-social research.

Here, I need to explain that the structuration explanation of cases is not realized by a single case study, and even comparative studies between cases may not be able to achieve this level of interpretation. Going from mechanism analysis to structure analysis constitutes a leap in the research process, and the real linkage is established between micro-analysis and macro-analysis. Although structure analysis also starts from the eventalization process of cases, however, the formed social mechanisms therein constitute all the important links in the whole body of social structure. Therefore, the transition in the analysis inevitably demands a panoramic vision of the whole society on the part of researchers, which not only helps us to discover the linkages among all leading mechanisms, but also to intuit the basic system and its spiritual background throughout an era.

The leap from mechanism analysis to structural analysis is a cause that propels case study toward a vision of the total society and extends the traditional boundary of sociology. The academic history that sociological predecessors have experienced serves as a portrayal of this extraordinary cause. From the case study of his 'Peasant life in China' and the comparative case study of 'Three villages in Yunnan', Fei Xiaotong combined historical research with field research in the late 1940s to move the research vision toward the issue of the dual-track politics of Chinese traditional society and the issue of basic social structure stated in 'From the soil' and 'The institution for reproduction', which are typical academic approaches that progress from mechanism analysis to structural analysis. Fei's introspection in his late years further upgraded sociological studies in the spirit of the humanities and incorporated issues such as religious integration, ethnic fusion, and civilization history into the great structural issues related to the theory of 'the Chinese nation as a unity of cultural diversification' and the existence of world civilizations. He has significantly promoted the research state of sociology (Yang 2010).

In short, the extension of case studies does not simply mean the extension of the eventalization process itself, but rather it starts from the event, extends it toward correlative or covariant relationships with the event's evolvement chain, then progresses toward the society-generation logic of mechanism analysis, and finally undertakes a structural analysis of the total society. The complete process of such an explanatory construction is the path along which to lead case study to analysis of the total society and is also the scientific mission of case study. The purpose of case study lies not in the case itself, but rather, it provides a possible explanation for the total society. This possibility is not brought about by direct hypothesis or judgments on the total society, but by the reflection of occurrences or questioning from the society. Therefore, individual cases should go toward the total society. It is a requisite academic responsibility for the research strategy of 'providing a kind of unique satisfactory method to the causal explanation standard' (Weber 2009: 125). However, to take this step, extraordinary efforts should be made in case study. This comes not only from researchers extricate descriptions, perceptions, and comprehensive abilities regarding the eventalization of cases, but also from their prudence in adjusting their judgments on cases based on all components of the society, which comes from thorough mastery of the structure, temperament, and spirits of the times they are living in. All of these are supported by researchers' rich life experiences and academic accomplishments.

5 Discussion

Fei (1999: 26) once stated, in his later years, that the whole human world is not a mathematical collection of individuals. Indeed, what are the differences between the social world and the human world? People are different from one another. If the truths of the whole society could be found on the faces of everybody, the world would become a grand union. The difficulty of social science research lies in the aspect of 'people'. Individuals have basic life demands, but they also have thoughts. People cannot do without great political and economic systems, but they are also the products of culture and history. This is the case for people in the social world, and also for people who study the social world. They can never become mere observers who look at the ups and downs of the world without any devotion or emotion. To be honest, case study itself has a sense of 'immersion'. Even if science requires us to stay calm at all times, with the progress of each story, researchers naturally tend to see themselves as the main character in the story, to understand the circumstances, to make judgments, and to embrace the story's ending. Hegel (1977: 11) wrote: "The truth is the whole. The whole, however, is merely the essential nature reaching its completeness through the process of its own development".

Acknowledgments

This article has been translated into English and first appeared in the Chinese (simplified character) language in the *Chinese Journal of Sociology* (Chinese version). For permission to reprint all or part of the article in Chinese (simplified characters), please contact CJS@oa.shu.edu.cn. For all other reuse requests, please email permissions@sagepub.co.uk for permission.

Corresponding author:
Jingdong Qu, Department of Sociology, Peking University, 5 Yiheyuan Road, Haidian District, Beijing 100871, China.
Email: qujingdong70@163.co

References

Burawoy, M. 2007. "Extended case method". In *Public Sociology*, translated by Y. Shen, 77–138. Beijing: Social Sciences Academic Press.
Chen, Y.K. 1980. Foreword of Records on Plunder on Dunhuang by Chen Yuan. In *The Second Edition of the Manuscript Series of Jinming House*. Shanghai: Shanghai Ancient Books Publishing House.
Du, Y. 2017. "Cartography: A new framework of national governance". *Sociological Studies* 32 (5): 192–217 (in Chinese).
Durkheim, É. 1995. *The Rules of Sociological Method*. Translated by Y.M. Di. Beijing: The Commercial Press.

Durkheim, É. 1999. *Les formes elementaires de la vie religieuse* [The Elementary Forms of the Religious Life]. Translated by D. Qu and Z. Ji. Shanghai: Shanghai People's Publishing House.

Durkheim, É., and M. Mauss. 2000. *Primitive Classification*. Translated by Z. Ji. Shanghai: Shanghai People's Publishing House.

Elias, N. 2007. *An Essay on Time*. Dublin: University College Dublin Press.

Fang, H.R. 2003. "'No-event situation' and the 'reality' in the life world—memories of social life in the farmer land reform of Xi village". In *Chinese Sociology* (Vol. 11), edited by Institute of Sociology, Chinese Academy of Social Sciences, 282–371. Shanghai: Shanghai People's Publishing House.

Faure, D. 2015. *What do historical anthropologists do in the field?* Translated by M. Cheng. The Paper 11 October.

Fei, X.T. 1985. *From the Soil: The Foundation of Chinese Society*. Beijing: SDX Joint Publishing Company.

Fei, X.T. 1999. Foreword to Peasant Life in China after rereading. In *Selected Works of Fei Xiaotong* (Vol. 14), 13–49. Beijing: Qunyan Press.

Firth, R. 1990. *Introduction in the English Edition*. In Y.-H. Lin, *The Golden Wing: The Sociological Study of Chinese Familism*, translated by K.S. Zhuang and Z.C. Lin, 9–13. Hong Kong: SDX (Hong Kong) Co., Ltd.

Foucault, M. 2007. *Security, Territory, Population: Lectures at the College de France, 1977–78*. London: Palgrave Macmillan.

Foucault, M. 2010. *Security, Territory, Population*. Translated by S.J. Qin. Shanghai: Shanghai People's Publishing House.

Garfinkel, H. 1967. *Studies in Ethnomethodology*. New Jersey: Prentice Hall.

Geertz, C. 1999. "Person, time, and conduct in Bali". In *The Interpretation of Cultures*, translated by Naribilige, 360–411. Shanghai: Shanghai People's Publishing House.

Guo, Y.H. 2013. *The Narratives of the Suffering People: The History of Village Ji and the Logic of One Type of Civilization*. Hong Kong: The Chinese University of Hong Kong Press.

Hegel, G.W.F. 1977. *Phenomenology of Spirit*. Translated by A.V. Miller. Oxford: Clarendon Press.

Heidegger, M. 2014. *Being and Time* (revised translation). Translated by J.Y. Chen and Q.J. Wang. Proofread by W. Xiong. Beijing: SDX Joint Publishing Company.

Heidegger, M. 2018. *Introduction to Metaphysics*. Translated by Q.J. Wang. Beijing: The Commercial Press.

Lefebvre, H. 1991. *The Production of Space*. Blackwell: Oxford University Press.

Li, M. 1996. *Power technology in daily Life: A sociological analysis toward a kind of relationship/event*. Master's thesis, Department of Sociology, Peking University, Beijing, China (in Chinese).

Lin, Y.-H. 1990. *The Golden Wing: The Sociological Study of Chinese Familism*. Translated by K.S. Zhuang and Z.C. Lin. Hong Kong: SDX (Hong Kong) Co., Ltd.

Lin, Y.-H. 2000. *From Study to the Field: Selection of Lin Yueh-Hwa's Early Academic Works*. Beijing: China Minzu University Press.

Luo, L. 2013. "Practice of mutual assistance and cooperation as an ideological construction: A sociological analysis of Liu Qing's novel Cultivating Millet Log (Zhonggu Ji)". *Chinese Journal of Sociology* (Chinese version) 33 (6): 180–216 (in Chinese).

Meng, Q.Y. 2016. "Quantification of social class in the Chinese Communist land reform: 'The School of Counting' in the Communist Party's Land Revolution". *Chinese Journal of Sociology* (Chinese version) 36 (4): 40–75 (in Chinese).

Meng, Q.Y. 2018. "Party, politics and policy: The multi-logic of the 'Rich Peasants Problem' in the early CCP revolution". *Chinese Journal of Sociology* (Chinese version) 38 (5): 70–105 (in Chinese).

Pocock, J.G.A. 2014. "Virtue, Commerce and History", translated by K.L. Feng. In *State Building and Government Behavior*, edited by X.G. Zhou, S.D. Liu, and X.Y. Zhe, 238–276. Beijing: China Social Sciences Press.

Qu, J.D. 2012. "Project system: A new system of state governance". *Social Sciences in China* 5: 113–130 (in Chinese).

Qu, J.D. 2013. "Possession, operation and governance as three conceptual dimensions of town and township enterprises: An attempt back to classical social sciences (II)". *Chinese Journal of Sociology* (Chinese version) 33 (2): 1–32 (in Chinese).

Qu, J.D. 2017. "After sacred society: Commemorate the 100th anniversary of the death of Émile Durkheim". *Chinese Journal of Sociology* (Chinese version) 37 (6): 1–32 (in Chinese).

Qu, J.D., F.Z. Zhou, and X. Ying. 2009. "From macro-management to micro-management—reflections on thirty years of reform from the sociological perspective". *Social Sciences in China* 6: 106–129 (in Chinese).

Sun, L.P. 2005. "'Process-event analysis' and the practice form of the farmer relationship in contemporary China". In *Tsinghua Sociological Review* (Volume 1), edited by Department of Sociology, Tsinghua University, 1–20. Beijing: Social Sciences Academic Press.

Sun, L.P., and Y.H. Guo. 2000. "'Carrot and stick': A process analysis of the informal operation of formal power—a case study of the purchase of grains in b town of north China". In *Tsinghua Sociological Review* (Special volume), edited by Department of Sociology, Tsinghua University, 21–46. Xiamen: Lujiang Press.

Wang, M.M. 2007. "Viewing Chinese social theory from etiquette". In *Experience and Mentality: History, World Imagination and Society*, 235–270. Guilin: Guangxi Normal University Press.

Wang, M.M. 2016. "Part as the whole: The broadening of the scope of community study from the perspective of a village". *Sociological Studies* 31 (4): 98–120 (in Chinese).

Wang, Y.X. 1998. *Historiographic Drafts of Chen Yinke*. Beijing: Peking University Press.

Weber, M. 2009. *Roscher and Knies: The Logical Problems of Historical Economics*. Translated by R.S. Li. Shanghai: Shanghai People's Publishing House.

Wu, W.Z. 1990. "On the cultural table". In *Collected Works of Anthropology and Sociology Researches by Wu Wenzao*, 190–253. Beijing: The Ethnic Publishing House.

Yang, Q.M. 2010. "The history of Fei Hsiao-t'ung's mind: Ethnos as a clue to his community study and ethnic study". *Sociological Studies* 25 (4): 20–49 (in Chinese).

Yang, Q.M. 2012. "Writings and intellectual history: An interpretation of the gentry Liu Dapeng and his Tuixiangzhai Diary". In *Qizhen* (1), edited by Z.Y. Wang, 81–103. Hangzhou: Zhejiang University Press.

Yang, Q.M. 2015. "The ideas and practices of 'Yanching School' about the sociology of knowledge: A comparative study on Wu Wenzao, Fei Xiaotong, and Li An-che". *Chinese Journal of Sociology* (Chinese version) 35 (4): 103–133 (in Chinese).

Yang, S.H. 2009. "Perception and sight: Phenomenological sociology in the practice of research". *Chinese Journal of Sociology* (Chinese version) 29 (1): 162–172 (in Chinese).

Yang, S.H., and F.Y. Sun. 2005. "Depth-interviewing as meaning exploring". *Sociological Studies* 20 (5): 53–68 (in Chinese).

Ying, X. 2001. *Petitions and Power: The Story of the Migrants of A Dam in China*. Beijing: SDX Joint Publishing Company.

Ying, X. 2018. "'The imagination of fieldwork': Between science and art—a study of Petitions and Power: The Story of the Migrants of a Dam in China". *Chinese Journal of Sociology* (Chinese version) 38 (1): 30–53 (in Chinese).

Ying, X., and J. Jin. 2000. "The 'problemization' process in collective petitions: The story of migrants from a hydropower station in the southwest". In *Tsinghua Sociological Review* (Special volume), edited by Department of Sociology, Tsinghua University, 80–109. Xiamen: Lujiang Press.

Zhang, H.Y., and Y. Wang. 2000. "Lin Yueh-Hwa's early academic thoughts". In *From Study to the Field: Selection of Lin Yueh-Hwa's Early Academic Works*, 507–522. Beijing: China Minzu University Press.

Zhe, X.Y., and Y.Y. Chen. 2005. "Defining the property rights in the context of township and village collective enterprises". *Sociological Studies* 20 (4): 1–43 (in Chinese).

Zheng, Z.M. 2010. Settlement pattern and ritual unions of Putian Plain. In: *Geographical Review* (2nd Volume). Beijing: The Commercial Press, 25–37.

Zhou, F.Z. 2012a. "'Confucian Classics' and 'political affairs': The practice of governance in ancient China—a study outline of Official Admonitions". In *Social Theory: Modernity and Localization*, edited by X. Ying and M. Li, 502–513. Beijing: SDX Joint Publishing Company.

Zhou, X.G., and Y. Cheng. 2012. "Toward collective debt: Government organization, social system, and public product supply in rural China". *Journal of Public Administration* 1: 46–77 (in Chinese).

Zhu, W.Z. 2006. "The process and modality of historiography". *Fudan Journal* (Social Sciences Edition) 6: 1–13 (in Chinese).

CHAPTER 18

Risk Governance, Publicness, and the Quality of the Social

Yee Jaeyeol

COVID-19 has revealed clearly that what is needed for immunity is publicness. The essence of immunity is the recognition of mutual dependence among individuals and communities. Pandemics can only be overcome through cooperative collective action. Individuals must consider each other to save each person's own safety; meanwhile, the community should consider individuals to secure the safety of the whole. COVID-19 made us understand that there is a wide variation in quarantine regimes in dealing with this type of risk across the world. Traditional belief on the Western ideal of the social based on individualism and the social contract has proved to be lacking in dealing with the pandemic. The relatively successful response of East Asian countries, which have been regarded as having less developed publicness, reveals that there must be an alternative type of publicness that is better fitted to solve the problem of collective action in cases of risk governance against pandemics. To answer this problem, I want to reconstruct the concept of "publicness" by incorporating the main ideas of social quality approaches, and then interpret recent developments of new forms of publicness by introducing three dimensions of social systems, i.e., power distribution, actor traits, and the transparency of social rules. Traditionally, West and East have been regarded as opposite in all three dimensions, and Western ideals, such as democracy and the market, have been regarded as the superior solutions to social issues in modern times. But I want to propose an alternative framework: publicness as a measure of *the social*, combining the degree of public interest, fairness, civic participation, and transparency. East Asian societies have developed their own concept of publicness, based on the ideas of the socially embedded self, a hierarchically situated social order, and deeply contextualized social rules. By linking the idea of publicness and these countries' relative success with quarantine in the process of spreading COVID-19, I want to propose a theory of risk governance that is based on the different empirical realities of Western and East Asian countries.

1 Introduction

We need multifocal lenses to understand the publicness and the quality of the social in Korea as well as in East Asia in the age of the pandemic and expanding digital economy. It took only a century to transform a self-sufficient rural society dominated by Confucian ethics into a hybrid society mixed with tradition and Western influence (Kim 2015). Counting from the civil revolution and industrial revolution, European countries took hundreds of years to nurture the bourgeoisie and industrial occupations, rendering the issue of *the social* as a core topic in classical sociology. Hundreds of years of transition from a traditional to an industrial society, so-called modernization, was the history of invention: the invention of modern institutions and ideas based on the concept of the social. In Korea, by contrast, modernity did not naturally evolve from within the tradition, but was transplanted from the outside and acculturated in a local context. The process was not smooth and peaceful. Ports were opened by military power. Before the country had enough momentum for modernization from within, Korea was colonized, and as a result, modernity was colonial from the beginning. The Korean War gave a shock to the lingering traditional elements. As such, Korean modern history is filled with inconsistencies, conflicts, and contradictions between tradition and modernity.

After the colonial period in early 20th century, turbulent events, such as war, political upheaval, and military coup, swept through before Korea rose as a newly industrializing country. Considering the breadth, speed, and depth of tremendous change in a short period of time, we cannot imagine the extent to which the modernity was compressed (Chang 2010). One of the distinguishing features can be described as the "simultaneous coexistence of the asynchronous". With these circumstances as a background, the view on the transition from tradition to modernity is divided into two: the discontinuity and the continuity perspective.

The discontinuity perspective asserts that a new modern and rational society should replace the inherited traditional and natural social system, eliminating familism and an outdated Confucian way of life. Behind this perspective lies modernization theory (Inkeles 1981) and Marxist theory. The discontinuity perspective gains strength from the fact that *yangban* (aristocratic literati) and *nobi* (slavery) have been completely abolished, and a new industrial society has been built on top of the dismantling of the traditional rural society. The neoliberal transformation of Korea, strongly carried out after the economic crisis in 1998, puts the acceptance of the global standard as the highest value and contributed to this awareness of the problem. Also, many research results from Korean sociologists confirm Western theories and concepts are well fitted to Korean reality.

On the contrary, the continuity perspective argues that the root on which the Korean society is based has not changed, even under the heavy influence of the West and rapid industrialization. These researchers argue that the ethics and morals of the traditional era have not changed much, and Confucian habits of the heart is still the basis of the lifestyle and behavior of current Koreans, even under the transition to a post-modern society. The recently spotlighted theory of Confucian capitalism and Neo-Confucian philosophy represent these views (Chang 1980; Lew and Jang 1998; Lew, Jang and Kim 2000).

However, to decide how continuous or discontinuous the change is, it is necessary to reveal at what level and how much it has changed (Kim 1993). The foundation of the discontinuity perspective focuses more on changes in the industrial structure, the abolition of traditional status, and changes in official norms and ideology. On the other hand, the continuity perspective emphasizes the continuum in practical rules of conduct and order in everyday life (Ogura 2017). Therefore, in Korean society, there is a considerable discrepancy between the structure of the explicit norms (laws, institutions, rules, etc.) and the customs and belief of ordinary people. The root of this type of decoupling is the result of such a rapid modernization: outwardly visible normative aspects are modernized, while the traditional Confucian influence remains inside.

Based on the observation records of foreign visitors, social psychologists, such as Cha (1994), analyzed three major periods of change in the values, beliefs, attitudes, and behaviors of Koreans over the past 100 years: before 1910, between 1910 and 1945, and after 1945. As a result, he concluded that, beliefs and attitudes, i.e., de jure norms and legislation, changed a lot, but behaviors, i.e., de facto practices and behaviors, did not change much. Specifically, he found that 50% of values and 89% of beliefs and attitudes changed, whereas only 29% of behaviors changed. He interprets this discrepancy as a result of decoupling between drastic change in the formal aspects and the continuing effects of deep structural forces, such as social grammar (Cha 1994: 55; Na 1998).

With this context in mind, I propose a concept of "transformative continuity" that is a compromise between the two. In other words, there is a drastic break from the traditional dynasty, as is expressed by the expansion of the market, fundamental industrial transformation, and political democratization. But less dramatic change is observed in the social relationships in everyday social life.

2 Review of Previous Literature

2.1 *Relationalism and Substantivism: Theoretical Reinterpretation of Publicness* (公共性)

We can find diverse ideas about publicness, from Plato, Rawls, Habermas, Arendt, Jorgensen, and Bozeman in the West, and ancient Confucian literatures and neo-Confucian debates in East Asia. Recent research emphasizes the multidimensional aspects of publicness. For example, publicness is defined as a combination of political democracy and social justice as an ethics (Im 2010), or it is combination of the formal institutional process of democracy, and the substantial realization of equality and justice as a goal (So 2003).

There are two different views on explaining social reality: relationalism and substantivism. Relational perspective, the main basis for this paper's ideas, is best explained by Emirbayer's "sociology of relationships" (Emirbayer 1997). Relationalism contrasts ontologically with substantivism, and it contrasts with methodological individualism or strategic choice theory. Substantive thinking presupposes an independent actor, or a group with clear boundaries and an internally well-structured role system. Focusing on communities, villages, specific groups, organizations, or people with specific boundaries, strict internal structures, and strong leaders, substantivists treat identity as immutable.

On the other hand, according to relational thinking, identity is not a constant, but rather is dependent on the context of various events or actions, and consequently is consolidated over recurring differences. Community formation, in this perspective, is also contingent upon shared norms, identity, and sense of cohesion (Park Hyo-Jong 2008: 128–129).

Substantivism and relationalism have different implications for explaining publicness. According to the substantivist view, publicness is closely linked to the question of who is responsible for the important issues. It is the state or ruling political regime that is responsible for public issues, and remaining areas are defined as private. For example, Japanese modern history tells us that the public meant the emperor or the state. The Chinese communist state also defines the public as the ownership of the state. Private space is composed of independent individuals interacting with each other. According to the substantivist theory, the strategic choice of the government and political leaders is the most important requirement for working of the public sphere. The state-centered view assumes that the state pursues absolute publicness and a top-down implementation of publicness (Cho 2012). On the other hand, from a relational point of view, it is not only the government but also the role of citizens that is important in the working of publicness. We may call it civic publicness, implying that the state is a tool for the improvement of the safety and welfare of the people, and it is secured by voluntary participation from below, compassionate solidarity, and active communication. There is a micro-foundation of the macro-social effects like publicness. Civic publicness emerges from the below, once everyone recognizes that they are sharing the same destiny, and thus trust the social rule and strengthen social cohesion.

The relational basis of publicness has close links with communitarianism, which supposes that personal fulfillment and self-realization are only possible in a healthy and open community. Communitarianism originally started as a reaction to the problems generated by both "individualist libertarianism" and "totalitarian statism". Communitarian thinkers argue that a community with publicness requires free individuals and their gathering as a neighborhood and civil society. The problem is that community-based publicness does not evolve naturally but is frequently challenged by extreme individualism and libertarianism on the one hand, and by extreme collectivism or statism on the other (Se-il Park 2008). Extreme individualism makes it difficult to form a communal publicness, and extreme statism stifles the vibrant communal public sphere.

Although communitarianism can be traced back to Greek philosophy, early Christianity, or ancient Buddhism, it was in Europe after the 1980s that it became decisively important. There are several reasons for the renewed attention on community in Europe: Firstly, excessive individualism has unleashed various social problems, such as disorder, crime, school failure, drugs, moral hazards, and mental illness; and second, as competition became excessive due to market-oriented policies during the era of Reaganomics or Thatcherism, only economic policies survived, and most social policies disappeared. As a result, there was widespread dissatisfaction and resistance from those who were left out of competition.

The emphasis on social quality, proposed by scholars in the European Union since the mid-1990s to comprehensively capture people's quality of life, goes beyond the traditional dichotomy between the conservatives and progressives or the public and the private. As an elaborated framework it overcomes the shortcomings of the dichotomy. Basically, a social quality approach assumes dynamic tension between de jure rule and de facto reality, or between the state and the lifeworld. The active participation of individuals and demand create tension with the state until it is recognized and absorbed as an institution. Such conflicting but balancing tension between the state and the lifeworld, and between the individual and the society implies that the emergent community or publicness is not a fixed entity but an ongoing process. It is in the process of being continuously formed through creation and reproduction. The emergence of publicness can be explained as occurring in the horizontal dimension of the "field of interaction" and the vertical dimension of the "field of construction/appearance" (Beck, van der Maesen and Walker 1997; Beck et al. 2001).

2.2 Publicness as an Emergent Property of the Social

A group of scholars define an ideal publicness as a "good quality" of society. Social quality is a highly value-laden concept: It refers to the degree to which individuals can form a mutually beneficial relationship to maximize their potential and well-being by participating in the social, economic, and cultural life provided by the community. In other words, the character of society is a function of the dynamic and balanced tension between "individual self actualization" and "various collective identities constructed in a social context". One tension occurs on the axis separating individual life course from societal development (actor-structure), and another tension occurs on the axis separating formally organized systems from the intimate lifeworld (Beck et al. 1997, 2001).

The vertical axis that separates actors and structures is the field where the publicness is constructed and manifested. Social values and norms are expressed through interactions between individuals, but at the same time, individual behaviors and value orientations are restricted by macroscopic structures. Individual self-actualization cannot be considered in isolation from the group identity, such as family, community, company, institution, etc. The principle of duality operates between individual self-actualization and collective identity formation. In other words, a social norm is a collective manifestation that is formed as a result of individual choices, but at the same time it has coercive influences over individual choices. Social structural change and personal life course development can sometimes conflict with each other. For example, a society that focuses only on the individual may cause excessive inequality or exclusion, and it is difficult to expect neither publicness nor social cohesion. On the other hand, in strong collectivism, individual freedom is stifled. Therefore, there is a need for balanced tension between individuals and groups, or between individuals and society.

What separates the system from the lifeworld is the arena of interaction. Tensions or conflicts arise here between formal systems, such as formal administration, and the informal world of life. As Habermas points out, hypergrowth of the system tends to lead to colonization of the lifeworld. A sense of alienation and deprivation increases when emotions, communication, and values in life are overwhelmed by the formality and efficiency logic of the system. Conversely, various voices and demands in the life world or the participation of individuals can affect the operation of the system. Such a system change from below is energized by "political participation" until it is "socially recognized".

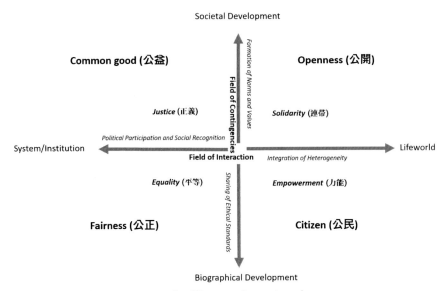

FIGURE 18.1   Four components of publicness and pursuing values

In addition, the process by which system and institution permeate into the lifeworld is called integration or compromising the heterogeneity. An integrated system has a legitimacy that penetrates everyday life. The most important thing here is communication. This is because through communication, heterogeneous interests and conflicts can be resolved and compromises can be made (Yee 2015a,b).

The publicness of society is determined by the values pursued in the four areas and the practical conditions that can materialize those values. European social scientists, who first theorized the character of society, identified (distributive) justice, solidarity, equality, and human dignity as the most fundamental social values. The conditional factors responding to the publicness include public interest, fairness, participative citizen, and openness (Beck et al. 2001; Yee 2007; Yee et al. 2015b).

Look at each component. Common good refers to how much the goods and services are pertinent to the benefit of the total society. Openness is a measure of how the information is openly accessible to the whole population. Fairness refers to how much citizens can access various services without discrimination based on factors ascribed by bestowed traits such as gender, age, ethnicity, etc. Participation refers to the role of active citizens who are willing to participate in the political process by which their destiny is determined, either by institutional or non-institutional methods.

If we can measure the specific conditions of these four areas with observable and comparable indicators, we can construct and index of the publicness of a society. In other words, publicness is measured by the social quality.

The first component is public interest (公益), implying the promotion of common goods closely related with society-wide safety provision, and realizing distributive justice. Common goods include military defense, which provides protection against external threats; a public welfare system against poverty; public education against incompetence; and public health service against pandemics.

The second is fairness (公正), measuring how much the various institutions and services are universally accessible without discrimination based on ascribed status such as gender, race, age, etc. All citizens should have equal access to the various institutions as a member of the society. We call the society inclusive when the fairness works well, and we call it discriminatory when the fairness is not working. Without fairness, publicness cannot be maintained.

The third component is the participative citizen (公民), who actively participates in decision-making on public issues. The capabilities of ordinary people can be measured by literacy, newspaper subscriptions, Internet penetration rate, voter turnout rate, and participation in voluntary associations. The existence of various political decision-making mechanisms is also an indicator of participative citizenship. A society where citizens are politically empowered tends to be vibrant, while a society without participative citizenship tends to be lethargic.

The final component of publicness is openness (公開). Open information and transparency contribute to social cohesion, if the relationship between people operates on common rule. The base of solidarity is general trust: trust in institutions, altruism, tolerance and solidarity. Without general trust, publicness cannot be achieved. We call it "trust society" when there is transparent rule and general trust is built among people, and we call it "distrust society" when there is neither trust nor transparency regarding the operation of the system. In the Korean context, trust deficit in institutions has a critical negative impact on the public space. The trust deficit, coupled with a lack of open information, undermines publicness by raising doubts as to the equitable burden on resource allocation and taxation.

2.3 *Publicness as a Measure of Risk Governance*

Sequences of man-made disasters during its rapid economic growth, as well as the Sewol Ferry disaster (2014), reflect the lack of publicness in Korean society. After successful industrialization and democratization, the state-centered concept of publicness that was the driving force in authoritarian top-down mobilization has been disassembled, yet Korea has not attained citizen-based publicness. As a result, Korea has suffered from the void of publicness. Since the developmental era, the main value has still been materialism and competitive efficiency. To make things worse, increasing socioeconomic inequality across generations and classes provoked anxiety and distrust, and traditional ties and personalist ethics have rapidly dissolved. In such a growth-oriented and materialist environment, public interests, such as universal welfare and distributive justice, were ignored, and social cohesion was undermined by competition.

Recent research conducted by the Institute for Social Development and Policy Research found that Korea's publicness is ranked 33rd among 33 OECD countries. Nordic countries, such as Norway, Sweden, and Finland, ranked top in the overall score, followed by the Netherlands and Germany. In case of the United States, participatory citizen and openness was very high, but the country ranked at the bottom in public interest and fairness. Japan and Korea share similar profiles, showing the lowest rankings in all four components of publicness (Chang et al. 2015).

How can we explain the repeated man-made disasters in Korea? There are two types of organizational learning: learning from past failures will contribute to the prevention of similar disasters. In most cases, single-loop learning is chosen. Set a certain goal, and if the result is failure, try to improve within the existing system. Increasing input and strengthening efforts are believed to bring better results. However, if failure is repeated despite increased efforts, the goal and strategy must be radically revised by reviewing the premises and assumptions of the system that have been taken for granted. This is called double-loop learning. Only through this double-loop learning can we achieve fundamental innovation.

Let us take a recurring disaster as an example. After experiencing a major disaster 20 years ago, the Korean government created a new Fire and Disaster Prevention Agency. After another big disaster the Ministry of Public Administration and Security became the Ministry of Security and Public Administration. When a disaster occurs, it is customary for the minister to resign and for the person in charge to be punished. However, it did not prevent future disasters, such as Sewol Ferry accident. Why? Because implicit assumptions about the workings of the system are wrong. Changing the name of government departments and creating new agencies did not automatically change the way they worked. Resignation of ministers does not automatically mean that responsible administration has been strengthened after that. Unless we find the systemic elements of the disaster, we try to find a scapegoat for the mishap. Double-loop learning starts by questioning the assumptions structured in the existing system. In order not to tolerate risk, a system that recognizes the value of safe investment is necessary. In order to solve the regulatory problem, a fundamental solution to corruption is required, and efforts should be made to increase the on-site response capacity of each institution and improve the coordination capacity between ministries.

From this point of view, the Sewol Ferry disaster was an "incubated accident" that emerged as a result of repeated single-loop learning and misuse of technology despite its safety-proven technology. Disasters are incubated if the risk factors are scattered, signals of risks are overlooked, the worst case is not seriously assumed, and the organizational-level system is not working, even if individuals recognize the risk factors. As Heinrich's Law explains, incubated disasters are not an exception, but rather the tip of the iceberg with numerous omens.

What is the cause of incubation? We often believe we do not have a good system design, but we find that the best systems and practices around the world are imported and implemented. But the problem is that it does not work. Transaction cost economists point out a trade-off relationship between the market and hierarchy: the government solves the problem of market failure, and the market solves the government failure. Various types of ideal governance are discussed; however, what is crucially missing is fairness or transparency. If publicness is not resolved, all ideal coordination systems will be distorted and deformed.

For example, the traditional ideal model that we think works well is the Rule of Right model. A virtuous and wise leader, followed by the people educated with righteous principles, is the essence. The charismatic leadership of Park Chung-hee in politics and Chung Ju-young in industry are good examples of the Rule of Right model. However, the strength of this model deteriorates into private patrimonial regimes like the mafia unless publicness is secured by righteous principles. In that sense, the relaxation or decay of the publicness can be seen as a hotbed for such repeated accidents.

It is a complicated issue to trace the trajectory of a social system, but by crossing the general trust and transparency, we can figure out a simple but powerful model of the context of publicness in Korea. In the era of authoritarianism, Korea maintained relatively high general trust despite having low transparency. The hierarchical authoritarian model, as seen in China and Vietnam today, worked actively during 1970s and 1980s. However, after democratization, institutional trust has fallen rapidly, while transparency did not improve accordingly. Korea has not yet reached a position where both a high level of institutional trust and high transparency are combined. The democratic procedures are clearly secured, but political process is not yet consolidated. Without enhanced transparency, it looks very difficult to solve the deficit of publicness. The core issue is the changing nature of corruption. The monopolistic corruption chain surrounding the top political leaders in the era of authoritarianism is replaced by an "elite cartel" in all sectors of society.

3 Discussion

3.1 *Personal Ethics and Righteous Principle* (義理)

The key phrase to analyze the dual aspect of discontinuity at the macro-material level and continuity at the micro-psychological level is *personal ethics* or *personalism*. The concept, originally proposed by Y.S. Chang, means "a normative system that is repeated in social life in which the principle of mutual aid, which was the principle of rural community in the traditional era, is transformed and remains in the modern urban community" (Chang 1991). Personal ethics are well represented by *righteous principle* (義理). Righteous principle contrasts with justice in individualist contract society. By maintaining affectionate relationships among individuals as an end, righteous principle asserts the superiority of the relationship over the abstract principle of justice in the formal contract.

In the Western tradition, where the notion of an individual with an independent self and ego is very strong, a very radical concept of individualism and freedom is derived. A key problem in liberal democracy is the conflict between individual selfishness and the concept of community. That is why Adam Smith emphasized the role of sympathy and the importance of morality in the working of market economy. Dewey argued a good community is a necessary condition for ensuring individual freedom. The reconciliation of individualism and common prosperity has been the key issue in Western social theory.

In East Asian culture, the concept of human is relational, implying that individuals are not independent but are always in the context of family, community, nation, and universe. The core concept is well expressed in the family. Family is a building block of the Confucian culture, linking the totality to the parts or elements. For example, family is the expansion of self. Diverse social entities are expressed as family: blood-related family, business company as a family, nation as a family, etc. During the traditional dynasty, the realization of self was identified as the realization of family, business company, or country. Conceptual expansion of family means that 'I' as an individual and 'we' as a social group is identified (Choi 1998).

Another difference between East Asia and the West lies in the concept of transcendence, which is a universal concept in Western civilization. In Greco-Roman civilization, the pursuit of truth and certainty was pursued as the logic of ultimate form that governs human experience. They thought logic governs meaning. Religiously, Europeans believed that the perfect monotheistic God provided the ultimate formal structure that governs the universe and human behavior. Politically, the Constitution of the United States was believed to be "an immutable structure that regulates political actions and thoughts".

In Confucian culture, on the contrary, there is a tendency to emphasize the concrete reality surrounding a person than abstract and logical order. Religiously, they believed that God is not a transcendental logical being, but their dead ancestor. Even though the cultural traditions were different, Europeans tended to look down on the East because of the absence of the concept of transcendence. They had culturally imperialistic attitudes, such as Orientalism. The attitude of the Jesuit missionaries in East Asia and the US foreign policy that imposes a universal concept of human rights have something in common in this respect.

The core concept for understanding relational society is *personal ethics* and *righteous principle*. However, the definition of righteous principle has changed historically. The first dictionary definition of righteousness is "the principle that human beings ought to do". The concept of "righteousness" originally used by Confucius is in contrast to "justice" in Western philosophy. For Confucius, "being human" means being formed into an "authoritative person" through the embodiment of courtesy (禮) and "righteousness". "Righteousness" is the source of courtesy and at the same time a standard for situational behavior. It is situational ethics and has a very flexible conceptual extension, rather than a transcendental and abstract standard. Ames interprets "righteousness (義)" as "appropriateness (宜)" through etymological analysis. Therefore, "righteousness" is not a fixed and immutable measure, but a situational ethical standard in the changing reality. He also sees that "righteousness" is characterized by "flexibility". In other words, "righteousness" is not a transcendent and universal standard of action, but a "context-dependent" moral judgment in a specific situation. "Righteousness" does not follow external standards as in Western rule-centered ethics, but rather "creative ability" to judge and act morally in a unique situation given to one. In this sense, "righteousness" has creative and aesthetic characteristics rather than logical and rational ones (Hall and Ames 1987). In Neo-Confucianism, it was distinguished from exegetical studies after the Han and Tang dynasties by putting forth righteousness as a study field that elucidates the morality. We find many people with righteous principle in Korean history; all of them showed loyalty to the declining monarch, in contrast to the realists who followed newly emerging power.

The second definition of righteous principle that has emerged from modern period saw the meaning changed into a "reciprocal principle to be followed in relationships with people". It is like the etiquette in personal exchange, or appropriate rule of give-and-take. In modern times, a person with righteous principle is regarded as a person properly fulfilling a moral obligation by performing a balanced exchange of gifts. This version of righteous principle is very close to the idea of the gift exchange rule portrayed by Marcel Moss. He found that Maori tribes thought that there is a spirit in the belongings of a people, so that gift exchange is more than receiving a physical item; rather, it is an exchange of spiritual essence. Keeping the righteous principle for a friend is also more than a utilitarian calculation of give-and-take. In a culture that emphasizes relationships, as shown in expressions such as "person with no righteousness", "good righteousness between friends", or "keep a righteous attitude to comrades", friends and acquaintances are regarded as a different form or extension of the self, and I must approach them as a whole person.

The third and most recent deteriorated definition of the righteous principle is "the principle of integration of a patron–client relationship formed by non-rational factors" (Choi 1976: 157). Choi points out the following elements as the nature of the patron–client group: (1) It is organized under non-rational factors; (2) a master–slave relationship, not an equal relationship, dominates, but actors are not conscious of this tilted relationship; (3) the patron protects the clients, without explicit demand for protection or loyalty; (4) they are extremely exclusive to outsiders; and (5) righteous principle is the principle of group solidarity. Like a mafia, an obligation to the interests of the group dominates (Choi 1976: 157–158). Choi argues the patron–client group solidarity originated from the father–son relationship, and he found much similarity in Korean political parties.

We find that "righteousness" as a source of personalism has historically evolved and appeared as different social facts depending on the contexts. In the original neo-Confucian tradition, righteousness meant human moral principles and basic human ethics consistent with the metaphysical principles that govern the universe. However, the concept was narrowed down to the axiomatic reciprocity, and finally deteriorated to the mafia-style bonding principle.

In a personalist culture, an individual's identity is defined in relation to others. Therefore, the distinction between "I" and "we" is not clear, and "I" is not separated from "us". Individual identity overlaps within a group, while the boundaries between groups are very clearly distinguished. On the other hand, in individualistic culture, individual identity is very clear, but psychological boundaries between groups are not clear (Na 1998). As the density and overlap of the relationships between individuals increases, the cohesion of the informal group appears as a clique, and the formation of a clique soon leads to the rift of the formal group. In such a situation, loyalty, acting as a facilitator of "in-group" solidarity, produces the unintended result of intensifying rifts between groups.

3.2   Types of Social System

Keeping in mind the idea of publicness as interpreted by social quality framework, the tension and balance between the system and the lifeworld, and between the community and individuals, can be reinterpreted as a culturally refined concept of individualism versus a personalist ethic.

Different regimes of social quality produce different types of publicness, depending on the cultural and historical heritage of dealing with the issue of risks, such as pandemics, earthquakes, and natural disasters. Comparative historical research reveals different coping mechanisms of publicness in cases of disasters, such as moral implosion or explosion against witches.

I would like to point out that most social facts, such as righteousness, social capital, publicness, solidarity, etc., are formed into different shapes, depending on the context of the social relationship. Therefore, in order to conceptualize and properly grasp the core mechanisms of social systems, we need to overcome the dichotomy between the personalist and the individualist society. We need a multidimensional framework to understand the shaping of publicness in a pandemic.

TABLE 18.1   Comparison of K-type and W-type

	K-type	W-type
1. Actor traits	Personalist Relational being based on familial bond	Atomistic self Independent being based on egocentric identity
2. Power distance	Unequal, hierarchical order justified by legitimate elements such as age, ability, and tradition	Equal, democratic order justified by equality among individuals
3. Social rule	Extension of internal sincerity to the external relation and wider society Intergenerational responsibility based on moral obligation	Explicit contract among individuals Intergenerational responsibility based on contract of utility

First, as is shown in Table 18.1, the first axis relates to the traits of the actor, the unit of social relations. The rational and self-interested agent, which is the assumption of modern economics, is at one extreme, the other extreme is a more sociological view of the human being, that is, internalizing the norms and rules of society, resulting in a sense of duty and responsibility, and it is a human view that strives to meet the expectations of others. In other words, the individual with the personalist ethic does not act opportunistically as he internalizes social norms. Some philosophers argue that even the concept of human being is different between the two cultures (Hall and Ames 1987). A very clear concept of self and conscience are very common ideas in individualist culture, and the concept of the self has been examined by numerous philosophers, such as Plato, Locke, Mill, and Rawls. A radical concept of individual freedom, nurtured in the individualist tradition, became the basis of democracy and the market economy on the one hand, and a source of violence, alienation, and isolation on the other.

In contrast, the notion of a human as a relational being is a central notion in personalist cultures, where an individual is not an independent but an interdependent being embedded in the family, community, nation, and the universe. The Confucian way of thinking resembles collectivism and emphasizes the context of concrete relationships (Hall and Ames 1987). Chen, a Chinese philosopher, enlists dichotomies corresponding to the contrast between two cultures: energy versus atom, organic versus formal thinking, dialectic versus logic, family versus individual, collectivism versus individualism, epistemological versus axiological freedom (Chen 1999). Such contrasts are echoed in Nisbett's distinction between causal attribution versus causal modeling, relationships and similarities versus categories and rules, and so on (Nisbett 2003). Asian countries have developed a personalist ethics that is quite different from the individualism valued in Western societies. This resembles the contrast between the economist's vision of the egocentric agent and the sociologist's vision of social being, for which obligation and compliance are important.

The second axis, power distance, considers the effect of inequality among actors. Power distance refers to the way in which power is distributed and the extent to which the less powerful accept this distribution as legitimate. It can be measured as the degree of authoritarian hierarchy, unequal distribution of power, or unequal distribution of economic resources. In a society with a hierarchical order in which authority is unequally distributed, the power distance between people increases, and the social relationship will become tilted by domination-subordination, or a patrimonial relationship. A gerontocracy is an example of power distant domination where age, as an informal standard, exerts a powerful influence. A well-developed honorific system in everyday language and the development of courtesy are other signs of a K-type society (Choi 1976). In a hierarchical society, people occupying the lower ranks usually have difficulty registering their opinions. The hierarchy is often seen as reflecting individuals' innate ability. At the other extreme, where the power distance is short, equally endowed agents interact on an equal basis. Horizontal coordination is most important. Those who are nurtured in a culture that allows a short power distance expect and accept power relations that are more consultative or democratic (Hofstede 1991).

The third axis is closely related to the transparency of the rules that define social relations. It is the institutional opacity caused by the lack of clarity in communication and unequivocal interpretation of social rules. The existence of de jure stipulation, such as laws and regulations, mean the public institutionalization, but more fundamentally transparency in rules is closely coupled with trust in the impartiality of public authorities and government. Rules are transparent when a set of universal rules that are both publicly documented and respected by social actors exists. Violators can then be punished, in principle, without exception. Opacity in rules means that no universal set of rules govern social relationships; rather, the rules are constantly under negotiation by participants. A series of social surveys conducted in Korea shows that public trust in public authorities and institutions declined very quickly during the democratization process.

By combining the three different dimensions (actor traits, power distance, and social rule), we can figure out a typology based on relational elements (Yee 1998). Publicness of any social system, including the political system and a market economy, exists within a cultural and social context, which I refer to as the institutional template.

Let me start with survival of the fittest. It combines self-interested agents competing without consistent and universal rules. In this social Darwinism neither interpersonal trust nor institutionalized rule exists. As power and authority are distributed unequally, it is referred to as the law of the jungle. The Machiavellian view of politics and a realist approach to international politics represent this kind of social system. A Hobbesian society is a situation where individuals with equal rights compete under conditions where there is neither legitimate rules nor interpersonal trust.

A community is a setting where individuals with equal rights live with interpersonal trust. Cooperatives, credit unions, and traditional villages can be examples of this. A community does not have universal rules applicable to the larger society, but individuals have high levels of trust and respect reciprocal ethics vis-à-vis other members of their group. The community is an island of trust in the sense that the scope of trust is limited to face-to-face

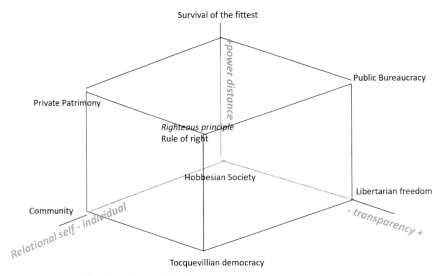

FIGURE 18.2 Typology of a social system

relationships. Thus, ties of blood, regional background, and religion tend to be vital to the operation of communal systems. Patrimonial office involves the exchange of loyalty and patronage within hierarchically organized groupings. Although communal order is often idealized, in practice communities often tend to be coupled with a hierarchy in which patron–client relationships play an important role. It is this relationship that distinguishes patrimonial office from community.

Market is a system where equal agents make exchanges to maximize their individual utility. It requires a clear set of institutional rules. Economists emphasize that the voluntary participation of independent actors is crucial for the existence of equilibrium consistent with the interests of the different participants in the market. According to neo-institutional economists such as North (1990), the rise of the market in Western Europe was crucially conditioned by the development of such rules. In this view, clearly defined and enforced property rights are essential for the development of the market economy because they enable transparent exchange among individuals. In a capitalist market economy, actors are assumed to behave opportunistically when possible; in the absence of clearly defined property rights, that opportunistic behavior may be corrosive to the operation of the market.

Although democracy is an ideal, there is also the view that it is impossible to have a humane society based on procedural justice and arm's-length contracts alone. The additional element that is required for the smooth functioning of such a system is publicness and consensus for the common good. Under substantive democracy, citizens actively participate in voluntary associations in both the private and public spheres, giving rise to civic norms that regulate their behavior. We call this Tocquevillian democracy.

In the bureaucratic ideal type as formulated by Weber, system efficiency depends on excluding the use of personal influence and attributes in roles. Predefined rules and procedures enable the organization to operate efficiently regardless of the attributes of the individual who occupies the bureaucratic positions at any point in time.

3.3 *Risk Governance and Social System*

A strong personalist culture without transparency decreases the publicness of the system and exacerbates the misgovernance of risk. According to a survey of workers working in chemical plants, most believe that safety-related standards are uncompromising principles. However, they reported that sticking to the principle undermines human relationships. There is a dilemma for workers. Formally, safety-related norms must be followed, but people feel the pressure to treat friends and acquaintances as an exception to the strict rule. A strong personalist ethic may promote nepotism.

For ordinary people, personalism is a lubricant for social life. But the distribution of social networks is far more unequal than income or asset. Most of the available, effective networks are concentrated at the top of the hierarchy, and top elites in the hierarchy can control the vast amount of information and resources. That is why the Rule of Right model can easily deteriorate into private patrimonial nepotism.

There is a strong relationship between low publicness and the fragile risk governance. Previous research showed that Korea ranked at the bottom in the comparison of social quality among 30 OECD countries. Quality of the social is critically influenced by not only the system capacity, but also the civic capacity (Yee and Chang 2011).

Korea is in a double-risk society. Koreans are exposed to the risk of future-type new disasters without proper preparation, and we have not yet resolved the risks of old disasters derived from the compressed industrialization. Boundaries are gradually disappearing due to increasing uncertainty, worldwide networking, and destruction of the global ecosystem. Polluted dust crosses spatial boundaries, and radioactive waste crosses the time boundary that separates present and future generations, and environmental disasters have left many problems that cannot be solved through established institutions and regulations, resulting in organized irresponsibility.

A normal accident, proposed by Perrow (1999), is another new type of risk. Normal accidents are difficult-to-avoid accidents that occur unexpectedly and are triggered by small human errors or minor mechanical faults in highly complex and tightly coupled systems. Subways, high-speed rails, communication networks, and pipelines, which are composed of complex networks, always have the possibility of falling prey to normal accidents.

Although similar earthquake damage occurred, the reason why there were far more victims of the Sichuan earthquake in China than the Kobe earthquake in Japan, and the reason why North Korea suffers more than 200 times more casualties than South Korea even when the same typhoon or heavy rain passes over the peninsula, is because the ability to respond was weak not only in terms of economic resources, but also with regard to social and organizational dimensions.

The foundation of disaster response and resilience is publicness and social quality. In a society with high system capacity, catastrophic anxieties, such as natural disasters and financial crises, can be reduced, and social risks, such as unemployment and poverty, can be prepared. High trust and social capital help prevent major disasters and heal trauma. And highly empowered participative citizens reduce anxiety. By improving the publicness, we will be able to achieve a transition from a growth-oriented society that values speed, appearance, and results to a sustainable society that emphasizes safety, stability, and process.

4   Conclusion

Disaster provides an opportunity to observe the hidden weaknesses of a society, and the pandemic allows us to check the vulnerability of diverse social systems. The Chinese response to COVID-19 at an early stage vividly showed the dark side of the statist response: shutdown of a megacity overnight by blocking all traffic in and out of Wuhan, and surveillance-based quarantine over the people utilizing big data and artificial intelligence. The Japanese response revealed the rigidity of a manual society where the formalized bureaucratic procedures blocked a prompt and flexible response in the case of mass infection in a cruise ship. The response of the United States was rather shocking, as there were violent protests against mask requirements and vaccination. The libertarian culture coupled with weak publicness, especially in terms of public interest, caused the collapse of the medical system and mass layoffs, and ultimately produced huge economic inequalities.

Throughout the long history of the pandemic, we have known that the essence of quarantine is collective action based on mutual dependence. The community and individual must consider each other. Prompt government

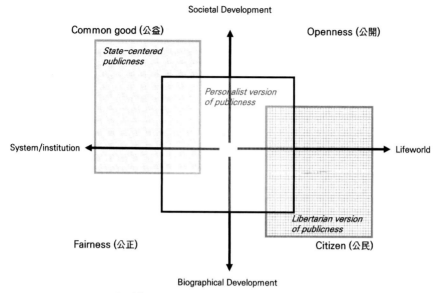

FIGURE 18.3 Types of publicness and risk governance

measures must be supported by private hospitals and citizens. To save the usage of limited capacity of intensive care unit, buffering the technical core is essential. One must code potential patients so mild cases, rather than being hospitalized, are classified through screening and stay in a treatment facility transformed from existing training facilities run by public and private institutions.

By combining the theoretical and historical arguments, the paper tries to answer the puzzle of why East Asian societies that are believed to have lower social quality and weak publicness are doing better in the quarantine against COVID-19. As Figure 18.3 shows, different publicness regimes emerged to confront the pandemic. The typical US response shows the Libertarian publicness that is skewed to the individual freedom and openness, thus ignoring the public interest and fairness. Such biased publicness contributed to the explosion of patients dying on the street without being properly hospitalized in the market-driven medical system. The Chinese response fits the state-centered publicness. A strong state initiative coupled with surveillance over the people thanks to digital technology contributed to the quarantine, but it seriously ignored individual autonomy and the openness of the system. The Korean, Taiwanese, and Japanese model shows the personalist publicness. Although there are some differences in terms of degree, all four components of publicness, such as public interest, fairness, participatory citizens, and openness, are satisfied.

The transformative continuity of the personalist ethic has contributed to the working of disaster solidarity, by providing bonding power to the people and treating the community as an extension of their family and following the policy initiative of government agencies based on moral commitment.

In the Korean case, we cannot go without mentioning the effect of the government's double-loop learning. The Korea Disease Control and Prevention Agency (KDCPA) experienced a total failure in controlling the MERS outbreak in 2015. After the failure, the KDCPA organized a group to review the whole process of the quarantine, and it published a white paper containing a thorough review of the basic assumptions and the cause of the failure, and it redesigned the process for possible future pandemic outbreaks. Fortunately, when COVID-19 started, the head of KDCPA was the former executive officer of the MERS white paper.

The Korean case of successful quarantine, especially in the early stages of the pandemic, vividly shows the importance of publicness. By showing a highly prepared, prompt leadership on the part of the government, paired with open information provided by the well-developed digital platform; fair treatment of all members of the society, including foreigners; and the active voluntary participation of citizens, personalist publicness emerged and showed its impact.

In this paper, I constructed a typology of a social system based on actor traits, social distance, and clarity of social norms, and argued that by maximizing the balanced tension between the system and the lifeworld, and between the individual and society, we can enhance the social quality, and ultimately effectively conduct quarantine. The Asian way of publicness, traditionally idealized as the rule of right, is qualitatively different from the Western ideal of Tocquevillian democracy. But both ideals can result in low publicness unless four components, such as public interest, fairness, participatory citizenship, and open transparency, are met.

References

Beck, Wolfgang, Laurent J.G. van der Maesen, and Alan Walker. 1997. "Theorizing Social Quality: The Concept's Validity". In *The Social Quality of Europe*, edited by Wolfgang Beck, Laurent J.G. van der Maesen, and Alan Walker. The Hague: Kluwer Law International.

Beck, Wolfgang, Laurent J.G. van der Maesen, Fleur Thomese, and Alan Walker, eds. 2001. *Social Quality: A Vision for Europe*. The Hague: Kluwer Law International.

Cha, Jae-ho. 1994. "Changes in Koreans' Values, Beliefs, Attitudes and Behaviors Over the Past 100 Years" [jinan 100nyeongan-ui hangug-in-ui gachi, sinnyeom, taedo mich haengdong-ui byeonhwa]. *Journal of the Korean Psychological Association: Social Psychology* [hangugsimlihaghoeji: sahoe] 8 (1): 40–58.

Chang, Duk-jin, Byung-hee Cho, Jaeyeol Yee, Hye-ran Koo, and Ji-young Kim. 2015. *The Sewol Ferry Asks Us: The Sociology of Disaster and Publicness* [sewolhoga uliege mudda: jaenangwa gong-gongseong-ui sahoehag]. Seoul: Hanul.

Chang, Yunshik. 1980. "Changing Aspects of Hamlet Solidarity". In *Economic Development and Social Change in Korea*, edited by Sung-Jo Park, Taiwhan Shin, and Ki Zun Zo. Frankfurt: Campus Verlag.

Chang, Yunshik. 1989. "Peasants Go To Town: The Rise of Commercial Farming in Korea". *Human Organization* 48 (3): 236–252.

Chang, Yunshik. 1991. "The Personal Ethic and the Market in Korea". *Comparative Studies in Society and History* 33 (1): 106–129.

Chang, Kyung-Sup. 2010. *South Korea Under Compressed Modernity: Familial Political Economy in Transition.* New York: Routledge.

Chin, Wei Pung. 1999. *Comparative Philosophy with Seven Themes* (中西哲學比較面面觀), translated by Ko Jaeuk. Seoul: Yemunseowon.

Cho, Die Yop. 2012. "Transition of Modernity and Restructuring of Publicness: Logic of Social Constructive Publicness and Structure of Micro Publicness" [hyeondaeseong-ui jeonhwangwa sahoe guseongjeog gong-gongseong-ui jaeguseong—sahoe guseongjeog gong-gongseong-ui nonliwa misigong-gongseong-ui gujo]. *Korean Society* [hangugsahoe] 13 (1): 3–61.

Choi Bong-young. 1998. "Confucian Culture and Modernization of Korean Society" [yugyo munhwawa hangug sahoeui geundaehwa]. *Society and History* [sahoewa yeogsa] 92 (53): 61.

Choi, Jaesuk. 1976. *Social Characteristics of Koreans* [hangug-in-ui sahoejeog seonggyeog]. Seoul: Gaemunsa.

Emirbayer, Mustafa. 1997. "Manifesto for a Relational Sociology". *The American Journal of Sociology* 103: 281–317.

Hall, David L., and Roger T. Ames. 1987. *Thinking Through Confucius.* New York: State University of New York Press.

Hofstede, Geert. 1991. *Culture and Organizations: Software of the Mind.* New York: McGraw Hill.

Im, Young-young. 2010. "Types of Publicity" [gong-gongseong-ui yuhyeonghwa]. *The Korean Journal of Public Administration* [hangughaengjeonghagbo] 44 (2): 1.

Inkeles, Alex. 1981. *Convergence and Divergence in Industrial Societies.* Abingdon: Routledge.

Kim, Kyoung-dong. 1993. *Theory of Social Change in Korea* [hangugsahoebyeondonglon]. Seoul: Nanam.

Kim, Seong-guk. 2015. *Hybrid Society and Its Friends: Anarchist Liberal Civilization Theory* [jabjongsahoewa geu chingudeul: anakiseuteu jayujuui munmyeongjeonhwanlon]. Seoul: Yihaksa.

Lew, Seok-Choon, and Mi-Hye Jang. 1998. "The Non-profit/Non-Government Sector and Social Development in Korea: Focusing on Related Groups" [hangug-ui biyeongli bijeongbu bumungwa sahoebaljeon: yeongojibdan-eul jungsim-eulo]. *East-West Studies* [dongseoyeongu] 10 (2): 121–144.

Lew, Seok-Choon, Mi-Hye Jang, and Tae-eun Kim. 2000. "East Asian Ties and Globalization" [dong-asiaui yeongojuuiwa segyehwa]. *Tradition and Modernity* [jeontong-gwa hyeondae] 13: 87–115.

Na, Eun-Young, and Kyung Hwan Min. 1998. "Theoretical Study on the Duality of Korean Culture and the Source of Generation Gap, and Reinterpretation of Existing Research Data" [hangugmunhwaui ijungseong-gwa sedaechaui geun-won-e gwanhan ilonjeog gochal mich gijon josajalyo jaehaeseog]. *Journal of the Korean Psychological Association: Social Issues* [hangugsimlihaghoeji: sahoemunje] 4 (1): 75–93.

Nisbett, Richard. 2003. *The Geography of Thought: How Asians and Westerners Think Differently, and Why*. New York: FreePress.

North, Douglas. 1990. *Institutions, Institutional Change and Economic Performance*. Cambridge: Cambridge University Press.

Ogura, Kizo. 2017. *Korea is a Philosophy: Korean Society Interpreted with Li and Ki* [hangug-eun hanaui cheolhag-ida: li wa gi ro haeseoghan hangug sahoe]. Seoul: Mosinunsaramdul.

Park, Hyo-Jong. 2008. "Reflection on communitarianism" [gongdongchejuuie daehan seongchal]. In *Communitarian Liberalism: Ideology and Policy* [gongdongche jayujuui: inyeomgwa jeongchaeg], edited by Se-il Park, Seong-rin Na, and Do-cheol Shin. Paju: Nanam.

Park, Se-il. 2008. "Why Community Liberalism—An Answer to Skepticism" [wae gongdongche jayujuuiinga—hoeuilon-e daehan dabbyeon]. In *Communitarian Liberalism: Ideas and Policies* [gongdongche jayujuui: inyeomgwa jeongchaeg], edited by Se-il Park, Seong-rin Na, and Do-cheol Shin. Paju: Nanam.

Perrow, Charles. 1999. *Normal Accidents: Living With High-Risk Technologies: With a New Afterword and a Postscript on the Y2K Problem*. Princeton, NJ: Princeton University Press.

So, Young-Jin. 2003. "Crisis of Public Administration and Public Issues" [haengjeonghagui wigiwa gong-gongseong munje]. *Government Studies* [jeongbuhag-yeongu] 9 (1): 5.

Yee, Jaeyeol. 1998. "Democracy, Social Capital, and Social Trust" [minjujuui, sahoejeog jabon, sahoejeog sinloe]. *Quarterly Thought* [gyegansasang] 37 (2, Summer): 65–93.

Yee, Jaeyeol. 2007. "Social Quality Korea: Change and Its Prospect". In *Financial Crisis +10, How Has It Changed Korea?*, edited by U.C. Chung and H.S. Cho. Seoul: SNU Press.

Yee, Jaeyeol. 2015a. "Social Capital in Korea: Relational Capital, Trust, and Transparency". *International Journal of Japanese Sociology* 24 (1): 30–47.

Yee, Jaeyeol, ed. 2015b. *Social Quality in Korea: From Theory to Application* [hangug sahoeui jil: ilon-eseo jeog-yongkkaji]. Seoul: Hanul Academy.

Yee, Jaeyeol, and Dukjin Chang. 2011. "Social Quality as a Measure for Social Progress". *Development and Society* 40 (2): 153–172.

CHAPTER 19

The Korean Wave as a Glocal Cultural Phenomenon: Addressing the New Trends in Korean Studies

Jang Wonho

1   Introduction

The Korean Wave can be defined as the spread of Korean cultural products, predominately dramas and K-Pop, all over the world. When the Korean Wave first emerged as a cultural phenomenon in Asia at the beginning of the 21st century, many scholars thought that it was a transient occurrence and would soon end. Much to the chagrin of those who held that view, it has lasted more than 20 years and has even spread beyond Asia. As we witness the popularity of BTS all over the world, it is safe to say that Korean cultural content has in fact increased in popularity. Accordingly, many scholars specializing in cultural studies are now involved in explaining the dynamics of the Korean Wave.

The studies of the Korean Wave are different from conventional scholarship practices in Korean Studies in many ways. While the traditional approaches of Korean Studies have mainly emphasized Koreanness or taken a regional focus, many studies on the Korean Wave emphasize non-Koreanness as a part of the success of the Korean Wave. Some scholars even argue that the "K" in K-Pop denotes anything but "Korea" (Lie 2012).

While globalization can be defined as the worldwide hegemony of Western culture, and localization involves adapting global cultural content to suit local domestic markets, glocalization refers to the mixture of global and local culture that can have its own competitiveness and be re-exported to other countries, even those of the hegemonic culture.

This study argues that the Korean Wave is a representative case of glocal culture and demonstrates how it can contribute to cultural exchange between Korea and the countries consuming its cultural products. The process of the manifestation of glocal culture is as follows: First, there is the phenomenon of globalization in which hegemonic Western culture has an impact on nearly all parts of the world. Then, there is the intermingling of this hegemonic culture (in the form of foreign culture) with local cultures in local contexts. This interaction produces glocal culture, which can be consumed transnationally as well as locally. Furthermore, accompanying the transnational consumption of glocal culture has been the emergence of new glocal culture and the formation of transnational cultural communities that embody it.

Another theoretical implication of Korean Wave studies is their contribution to the new trends of female universalism. Female universalism is a universal value system shared by all women in the world who want to sever the chains that tie them to traditional and male-dominated cultures. While globalization has witnessed the spread of Western male universalism, as clearly depicted in such globally popular cultural products as *Sherlock Holmes* and *Superman*, the Korean Wave has provided the cultural content for the flourishing of female universalism in which female characters free themselves from their gendered, racial, and postcolonial melancholia without fears of social or state violence against them. In so doing, the Korean Wave has helped female consumers explore the possibilities of constructing and eventually realizing female-dominated communities.

2   Glocal Culture and the Korean Wave

The term "glocalization" was first used in the business field to refer to local adaptations of global products. For example, McDonald's has developed various hamburgers according to local tastes, such as the Maharaja Mac in India, the Teriyaki McBurger in Japan, and the Bulgogi Burger in Korea. In this sense, glocalization involves the penetration of global products into local markets. However, glocalization also can also be defined as the globalization of local materials and cultural content. Scholars who interpret glocalization as such stress the intersection of regional tendencies and global characteristics, and the simultaneity of both universalizing and particularizing tendencies (Robertson 1995).

Glocal culture has the same characteristics as glocalization, meaning it has a hybridity of global factors and local characteristics. That is, glocal culture has developed under the circumstances of mixing global content with local specialties. The specific sociocultural traits of local society reshape and change global cultural content, producing a new hybrid culture which has both universal and particular cultural characteristics. Jang and Lee (2015) elaborate on the concept of the glocal culture, focusing on cultural material and content related to pop culture. More importantly, since glocal culture has universal characteristics, it can be consumed in other societies. As glocal culture spreads, its particular features also play an important role in transnational consumption practices. The final stage of the process is the development of new glocal cultures in the countries that consume the foreign glocal culture.

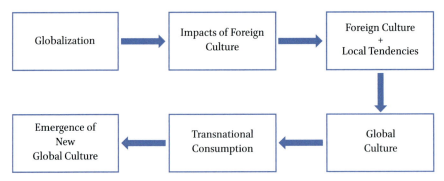

FIGURE 19.1   The process of glocal culture development

To explain the characteristics of K-Pop glocal culture, which exhibits a combination of foreign culture and local tendencies, I posit two major features of it: its contemporaneity of the uncontemporary and its synchronized dancing to melodic music (Jang and Kim 2013).

The idea of the contemporaneity of the uncontemporary has developed from Korea's status as a semi-peripheral country, a midpoint in the modern world system between the core (i.e., the world's most developed countries) and the periphery (i.e., newly developing and less developed countries). Such a position gives the Korea the advantage of being able to offer both highly advanced and developing cultural elements to foreign visitors. For example, visitors from G7 countries feel nostalgic when they come to Korea, perceiving it as reminiscent of their immediate past, whereas tourists from developing countries find it very modern, clean, and cutting-edge. This particular state of being in the middle of the world system reflects the "contemporaneity of the uncontemporary" (i.e., the coexistence of modernity and premodernity at the same time). The ability to exhibit both modern and premodern characteristics can mean separate things to audiences in core and peripheral countries. To core country audiences, Korean singers appear innocent and pure, unlike singers in Europe and America. However, to peripheral audiences, who are mostly Asian, Korean singers do not look pure or innocent but instead appear sophisticated, modern, and polished, much like the "Western" idols they have stereotyped or imagined them to be. Being subject to influence from the United States, Europe, and Japan has led Korea to develop its own hybrid culture. Such hybridity has resulted from an experience of compressed modernization that has allowed for the complementary existence of the past and present, or rather tradition and modernity (Chang 2010).

The second special feature of K-Pop is its unique success in combining synchronized group dancing with melodic music. It is typical for boy and girl groups all over the world to dance to rhythmic music in a synchronized fashion. The preference of melodies over beats in synchronized group dancing, however, is not common because it is hard to dance to certain types of trendy beats while singing a song that has a complex choral combination of melodies. A stereotypical argument as to why K-Pop group members have been able to master synchronized group dancing while singing complex melodies is that these singers are either disciplined harshly or are carefully controlled by slave-like contracts. It is true that K-Pop trainees undergo an arduous training period of singing, dancing, acting, and even foreign language learning for more than six hours every day (and more than ten hours during weekends and holidays). However, the trainers at the entertainment companies stress that the trainees endure this difficult training because they are aware of the "red queen race" of the Korean education system.[1] The red queen race is a situation in which everyone works hard but remains in the same place. It is the state in which most Korean students find themselves because of the educational craze in Korea. Thus, just like students preparing for university entrance exams, the would-be K-Pop singers also practice as hard as possible to get selected as members of idol groups.

With these special features, K-Pop has attracted a wide audience from all around the world. Table 19.1 below shows how much K-Pop is being consumed currently.

The total number of views for the top 10 K-Pop idol groups reached 40 billion on YouTube in a single year. As shown in Table 19.1, the music videos of BTS were viewed more than 15.5 billion times by people from around the world. The girl group Blackpink has almost 10 billion views. Seven idols were viewed more than 1 billion times during year shown in the table.

Lastly, I would like to illustrate the final stage of the glocal cultural process, that is, the emergence new glocal cultures in the local areas that consume K-Pop. As conveyed in the glocal culture concept diagram, glocalization spawns new glocal cultures in local societies that consume the foreign glocal culture. K-Pop has influenced local music scenes, leading people in these areas to create new-style music that follows the styles of K-Pop. We can consider the creation of new glocal culture as an example of cultural communities that are based on the cultural content of the Korean Wave.

---

1 The concept of "red queen race" comes from the novel *Alice Through the Looking-Glass*. In a scene from the novel Alice is constantly running but remains in the same spot. Looking at Alice, the Red Queen says, "If you want to go somewhere else, you must run at least twice as fast as that".

TABLE 19.1 The number of YouTube views of the Top K-Pop groups from October 2020 to October 2021

Rank	Name	Total views	Gender	
1	BTS	15.4B	Male	
2	BLACKPINK	9.92B	Female	
3	TWICE	3.54B	Female	
4	Stray Kids	1.59B	Male	
5	ITZY	1.42B	Female	
6	SEVENTEEN	1.02B	Male	
7	MAMAMOO	1.01B	Female	
8	EXO	960M	Male	
9	Red Velvet	959M	Female	
10	aespa	875M	Female	Debuted 11/17/2020
11	TXT	823M	Male	
12	(G)I-DLE	713M	Female	
13	NCT 127	656M	Male	
14	TREASURE	654M	Male	
15	IZ*ONE	531M	Female	
16	GOT7	483M	Male	
17	iKON	437M	Male	
18	EVERGLOW	386M	Famale	
19	OH MY GIRL	363M	Female	
20	ENHYPEN	352M	Male	

1B = 1 billion, 1M = 1 million
SOURCE: HTTPS://WWW.YOUTUBE.COM/YT/ARTISTS (OCTOBER 6, 2020–OCTOBER 2, 2021)

TABLE 19.2 Idol groups outside of Korea inspired by K-Pop

Nation	Name	Number of members	Gender
Japan (18)	NiziU	9	F
	JO1	11	M
	G-EGG Team A,B,C,D	24	M
	INI	11	M
	ORβIT	7	M
	and 13 more groups		

TABLE 19.2 Idol groups outside of Korea inspired by K-Pop (*cont.*)

Nation	Name	Number of members	Gender
Taiwan (11)	Per6ix	6	F
	G.O.F. (Girls on Fire)	7	F
	H.U.R. (Hurricane)	6	F
	C.T.O.	6	M
	MIRROR	12	M
	6 more groups		
Myanmar (2)	Alfa	7	M
	Project K	7	M
Laos (1)	PAPAYA	4	F
Vietnam (8)	Lime	3	F
	Lip B	4	F
	O2O Girl Band	8	F
	MONSTAR	5	M
	Super 9	8	M
	Uni5	5	M
	3 more groups		
Thailand (46)	Hi-U	3	F
	DAISY DAISY	7	F
	White Out	9	F
	4TEEN	4	M
	AXIS	5	M
	NKO	7	M
	41 more groups		
Indonesia (16)	BE5T	5	F
	S.O.S.	6	F
	StarBe	4	F
	BFORCE	5	M
	UN1TY	8	M
	Smash	6	M
	10 more groups		
China (72)	Bonbon Girls 303	7	F
	Chic Chili	5	F
	FANXYRED	4	F
	Teens in Times (TNT)	7	M
	WayV	7	M
	INTO1	11	M
	and 67 more groups		

TABLE 19.2 Idol groups outside of Korea inspired by K-Pop (*cont.*)

Nation	Name	Number of members	Gender
Philippines (13)	BINI	8	F
	CLOVER	4	F
	BOSS	4	F
	1ST.ONE	6	M
	SB19	5	M
	Press Hit Play	6	M
	7 more groups		
Hong Kong (1)	Super Girls	5	F
Kazakhstan (9)	IMZ1	6	F
	Ice Blue	4	F
	Newton	4	M
	Ninety One	4	M
	NIKI	5	M
	4 more groups		
Kyrgyzstan (2)	BirAi	5	F
	Love IZ	4	F
UK (1)	KAACHI	3	F
France (1)	ALIIFE	4	M
USA (4)	PRETTYMUCH	5	M
	Brockhampton	13	M
	In Real Life	5	M
	Unwritten Rule	6	M
International (3)	Z-Girls	7	F
	Z-Boys	7	M
	NOW UNITED	18	Mixed

SOURCES: KPROFILES.COM, HTTPS://NAMU.WIKI/W/%EC%95%84%EC%9D%B4%EB%8F%8C, HTTPS://TPOP.FANDOM.COM/WIKI/MAIN_PAGE, HTTPS://CPOP.FANDOM.COM/WIKI/CPOP_WIKI

As shown in Table 19.2, more than 200 idols inspired by K-Pop are now actively performing their music and dance routines in their own countries and internationally. The international idol groups Z-Girls, Z-Boys, and NOW UNITED deserve special attention here because they clearly demonstrate the emergence of transnational cultural communities sharing in the enjoyment of K-Pop.

3 Female Universalism and the Korean Wave

Having provided a rundown of the glocal cultural process of K-Pop, it is now time to turn to the second theme of this paper, namely the topic of female universalism. This will help address the question of why the majority of Hallyu fans are women who range from teenagers to women in their seventies.

3.1 Female Universalism and the Gender Divide

The "K" in K-dramas and K-Pop is now obvious to us: the Koreanness represents a female universalism that is vividly conveyed in major works of Hallyu that are exported all over the world. The "K" deliberately targets a female fandom that appreciates female universalism, which can be considered a ubiquitous value system shared by most women in the world (that is, among those with gendered melancholia). This is the area where Korean tacit knowledge is most present and where it performs most effectively. The subtle emotional actions that Korean TV drama actresses engage in are the best example of this. Often, these actresses do not receive any prompting and sometimes ad-lib while exhibiting a wide range of emotions, including impromptu—and real—tears. Female K-Pop singers blend difficult aerobic movements with the facial expressions of K-drama actresses, as they are full of subtle facial expressions and body gestures. A dominant theme for Korean actresses and girl group singers alike is the universalism of their physical beauty—in other words, women across the world now feel Korean beauty is the ultimate look to replicate (Epstein and Joo 2012). Here, physique is not used as a tool of sexual suggestiveness but rather as a way for women to overcome everyday gender limitations.

The gender divide that facilitated the rise of Hallyu worldwide came about from three factors: gendered melancholia, racial melancholia, and post-colonial melancholia (Oh 2011; Oh and Kim 2019). Hallyu fans may inevitably have at least one of these three types of melancholia. Melancholia is defined as an emotional state that results from the suppression of sorrow caused by the lack or loss of something or someone that is cherished (Butler 2011). Gendered melancholia is an archetypal form of melancholia that arises out of a mournful realization that a woman cannot weep openly about the natural sex with which she is born. Her duty as a woman is to denounce her mother, sisters, and other girl friends as lifetime companions in order to accept male partners instead. Thus, her adult or sometimes even adolescent sexual partners force her to live with gendered melancholia (Butler 2011). We can also ascertain that males who go through similar gender troubles can also experience gendered melancholia, as many gay men cannot openly bemoan the fact that they are born male.

Racial melancholia occurs in men and women who are not born as members of the hegemonic racial group in their society. The fact that one cannot openly lament about the racial category in which she was born constitutes the beginning of her melancholic experiences (Eng and Han 2000). Finally, postcolonial melancholia refers to the suppressed sorrow imperialists feel when they lose their colonies to the people indigenous to the regions that they colonized (Gilroy 2005). Postcolonial melancholia is felt among people in former imperialist nations and then re-manifests itself as racism against their former colonial subjects who are living in the former imperial motherland, such as the United Kingdom, Japan, France, Germany, Italy, Spain, the United States, and so on. Victims of racism who are minorities living in the global cities of former imperialist countries therefore feel enhanced racial melancholia that leads to a collective urge to seek cultural and emotional comfort from their strong ties to their homeland (Appadurai 1990). When myriad minority women find that the cultural content from their homeland is also filled with sexist, racial, and postcolonial biases, they may turn to Hallyu's female universalism.

Hallyu's glocal ascendance as an important entertainment genre for women around the world is due to its female universalism. Particularly important is K-drama's femininity, which espouses heroines who represent wisdom, rationality, tenderness, care, and scientific reasoning, along with active social participation, all of which were once considered characteristics of Western male universalism. In Hallyu dramas, it is these heroines who assume the roles of attorneys, prosecutors, politicians, doctors, artists, and ordinary, struggling, unemployed college graduates who want to realize their dreams. Female universalism is therefore a universal message of gendered melancholia and struggle shared by all women in the world who want to break free from the chains of traditional and male-dominated communities, such as Confucianism, Catholicism, and Islam. It is the will among women to explore the possibilities of building and eventually realizing equal communities, where they can freely relieve their gendered, racial, and postcolonial melancholia without fear of social or state violence. Like K-Pop, K-drama's success lies in its portrayal of Korean women breaking free from the yoke of Confucianism and other oppressive local values in order to embrace Western values and create a free and inclusive global humanity.

For the first time in Korean popular music history, K-Pop girl groups have elevated their corporeal beauty to the level of acceptable defiance of the Confucian repression of Korean women. Their dancing and singing have also appealed to many female fans from traditional Catholic, Islamic, and Confucian backgrounds in Asia, the Middle East, and Latin America. Unlike the typical phenomenon of female fans being infatuated by boy groups, female fans in the K-Pop scene provide enormous support to girl groups. Girls' Generation, for example, has the most YouTube views among K-Pop singers, and in 2017 another all-girl group, Red Velvet, garnered the number one spot on the K-Pop charts for the greatest number of weeks.

Put together, Hallyu cultural content, in its K-Pop and K-drama forms, has captured the attention of female fans across the globe as the only truly postcolonial cultural industry, vis-à-vis the so-called conviviality cultural industries of the United Kingdom, the United States, and Japan. Hallyu, as a whole, deals with gendered and racial/ethnic melancholia on a global scale. Its success is now corroborated by the ongoing observation and empirical evidence that Korean entertainers have excellent tacit knowledge in mixing Western cultural content with Korean-style female universalism. Furthermore, it has demonstrated that it can attract a majority of female fans from all over the world who are tired of pop culture from Japan and/or Hollywood (Oh 2011).

3.2 *Gender Fluidity and Androgynous Men: A Glocal Phenomenon within the K-Community*

Within the world of female universalism, how does Hallyu package and market Korean males? Are the males scientific and rational universal men, like white males or their Japanese variations? What value do Korean men have in the world of K-drama and K-Pop? These are our final questions in the second part of this paper.

In both K-Pop and K-dramas, male actors and singers tend to be presented as fluid in their gender identities, much to the initial dismay of the South Korean cultural community, where traditional male and female gender roles had—until the emergence of Hallyu—been strictly upheld. To compete with local and global celebrities and cater to female fans all over the world, male K-Pop singers and K-drama actors alike had to undergo a rapid evolution from being macho characters to promoting images of androgynous males with feminine looks and trim, hairless bodies (Oh 2015).

"Beautiful boys" (*misonyeon* or *bishōnen*) has been a universally popular term in the West and in East Asia for literary and opera characters. In Renaissance Italy, beautiful boys were often perceived by artists as modern manifestations of beauty, whereas in Japanese *kabuki* plays, beautiful boys, as *yakusha*, elicited enormous fan support, mostly from older women (Rocke 1998). Beautiful boys, along with beautiful girls [*bishōjo*], also occupy significant positions in much of modern Japanese *manga* or comic book stories. However, in Korea, such a concept did not exist, especially because of the strict Confucian values that distinguished men from women in terms of gender from the age of seven. It is only through Korean TV dramas and K-Pop that the concept of beautiful boys emerged in Korea and later proliferated through a careful use of tacit knowledge. Since Koreans had not really been familiar with the Renaissance or the Japanese concept of *bishōnen*, it may seem unlikely that they would possess any tacit knowledge of how to manufacture pretty boys. Yet the reality has proven otherwise. In the Hallyu industry, pretty boys were manufactured according to the demands of the female beholders who knew how to create them.

Korean drama and K-Pop producers have a vast array of beauty techniques at their disposal, including cosmetic products and makeup skills, or outright cosmetic surgery (Epstein and Joo 2012). Most beauty technicians are women who define what constitutes the K-drama or K-Pop "pretty" boy look. Korean boy groups and actors maintain Renaissance-style facial features and body composition (for example, golden ratios) rarely found in Japan or other Asian countries. Korean beautiful boys, therefore, have garnered enormous fan loyalty from both Chinese and Japanese women, which has resulted in a wider rush of female fan support from Southeast Asia, the Middle East, Latin America, North America, and Europe.

In this sense, the K-community, where global fans of K-dramas and K-Pop interact either offline or online, is filled with glocalized beautiful boys. These males serve the demands of female universalism shared among female Hallyu fans who want to defy traditional gender roles. Physical beauty is not a given trait, but something manufactured in the K-community through proactive applications of beauty and athletic techniques. The modification of their bodies is not for the purpose of enhancing their physical appeal to the opposite sex, but to relieve Hallyu fans of their gendered, racial, and postcolonial melancholia. If 20th-century Europe and North America embodied white male universalism, East Asia in the 21st century epitomizes female universalism in the form of gendered melancholia. In short, female entertainers in Hallyu culture constitute "the other" whom female fans want to become or emulate, whereas Korean male actors and singers represent their ideal gender-neutral sexual partners. Often, it is observable that many of these female fans want to be bewitched by the androgynous male idols who can act as both males and females (Oh and Kim 2019). All these gender-bending techniques are part of the Hallyu glocalization thought process, which attests to how the Korean Hallyu industry has perfected its tacit knowledge in creating and manufacturing beautiful boys and girls for the new world of female universalism. It is therefore only natural that female universalism in K-Pop and Hallyu has promoted a proactive fandom, including Hallyu pilgrimage tourism to Korea, Korean culture and language learning, K-Pop cover dance video production, participation in K-Pop auditions, and ultimately joining the K-Pop industry as production staff and singers (see Kim, Mayasari and Oh 2013; Oh 2009, 2011).

4 Conclusion

This paper has introduced the new concept of glocal culture and subsequently demonstrated that the Korean Wave is an exemplary glocal culture. To do so, the paper has described the process of glocal culture, in which the impacts of global culture, mixed with Korea-specific sociocultural characteristics, have led to the emergence of a hybrid culture that can be consumed transnationally. The final stage of the glocal cultural process is the newly emerging glocal cultures in societies where people are actively consuming the Korean Wave.

The glocalizing dynamics of the Korean Wave can be seen in the processes of consumption as well as the creation of new pop cultures in the counties that consume the Korean Wave. An important factor for the creation of transnational cultural communities is the practice of people of different countries sharing cultural identities and tastes based on the Korean Wave and developing a sense of mutual understanding and cooperation.

In addition to the glocal cultural process, this paper introduces two theoretical concepts about Hallyu: female universalism and gender fluidity. Based on these concepts, the following findings about Hallyu from the (Korean) producers' perspective can be considered. First, Hallyu is not really about Koreanness or Asianness, but instead entails the global cultural values of female universalism. Female universalism does not intend to replace white male or scientific male universalism, but rather aims to liberate women from the yoke of gendered melancholia, a suppressed desire to distinguish oneself from her prescribed gender identity. In so doing, some of these women also suffer from racial and postcolonial melancholia, both of which can be liberated by the same worldview of female universalism. In short, female universalism is the realization of female identity by people who experience gendered melancholia, but not necessarily the other two forms of melancholia.

Secondly, the gender divide in the appeal of Hallyu is not an accidental occurrence but is instead the product of a prolonged period of planning and experimentation by Korean drama writers (mostly women), K-Pop producers, K-Pop choreographers, voice coaches (again, mostly women), and Hallyu performance artists. In hindsight, appealing to female universalism has turned out to be much more successful than appealing to male scientific universalism. The gender divide has created an uneasy outcome for Hallyu, as its fandom is predominantly female with only a small fraction of male followers. One estimate by the World Association of Hallyu Studies is that that more than 90% of the 100 million registered fan club members in the world are female.

Thirdly, Hallyu's success is based entirely on its glocal strategy of business expansion in a way that has bypassed the lure of globalization or localization strategies. However, the glocal strategy will find it difficult to sustain its "L" process (that is, localization), which necessitates the employment of Korean talent. As the global popularity of Hallyu expands to Europe and North America, more fans, most of whom are proactive learners themselves, will likely demand the opening of the "L" to international contenders. When Hallyu opens up its "L" to global contenders, it will have to abandon its glocal strategy in favor of a global strategy, where "L" itself will have to be globalized or transnationalized, just like its input and distribution. If BTS one day were to feature global and transnational boys other than Koreans, would its female universalism be sustainable? Or would it perhaps attract more male fans than female ones? These are some of the immediate questions we can raise about Hallyu's future based on the glocalization framework it has maintained so far.

Regarding the international success of the Korean Wave, various suggestions have been raised for utilizing it. Focusing on economic benefits, some scholars and bureaucrats argue that Korea should collaborate with the cultural content of other industries, such as electronics and cosmetics. Others contend that Korea should use the Korean Wave to enhance Korea's soft power. However, if Korea tries to use the Korean Wave only for enhancing the interests of Korea, either economically or culturally, it will face opposition and anti-Korean Wave movements in other countries where people seek to protect their own interests. The authors therefore believe that building a transnational cultural community and thus enhancing intercultural understanding and cooperation are the keys to the sustainable development of the Korean Wave. In the long term, this will lead to an increase of economic benefits and cultural influence.

Let us close with a story from Jerusalem that attests to the role glocal culture can have. This episode was reported in *Dong A Ilbo* (*Dong A Ilbo*, May 13, 2013), one of the leading newspapers in Korea. In Jerusalem, the areas of Jewish and Palestinian people are strictly divided, and so there is seldom communication between them. A Palestinian student at the Hebrew University of Jerusalem had never talked with Jewish people until she met some friends in a K-Pop fan club. There, she became acquainted with Jewish students and shared her ideas about K-Pop with them, which led her to understand Jewish people more. She has now become friends with many Jewish students and shares her enjoyment and interest in the Korean Wave with them. This, we believe, is the future that the Korean Wave should pursue; that is, it should produce content that delivers hope and bridges the divide between conflicting groups in transnational cultural communities.

Acknowledgment

Some parts of this paper have been published in Jang and Kim (2013), Jang and Lee (2015), and Oh and Jang (2020).

References

Appadurai, A. 1990. "Disjuncture and Difference in the Global Cultural Economy". *Theory, Culture and Society* 7 (2–3): 295–310.
Butler, Judith. 2011. *Gender Trouble: Feminism and the Subversion of Identity*. New York, NY: Routledge.
Chang, Kyung-Sup. 2010. *South Korean Under Compressed Modernity: Familial Political Economy in Transition*. New York, NY: Routledge.
Eng, D., and S. Han. 2000. "A Dialogue on Racial Melancholia". *Psychoanalytic Dialogues* 10 (4): 667–700.
Epstein, S., and R. Joo. 2012. "Multiple Exposures: Korean Bodies and the Transnational Imagination". *Asia-Pacific Journal* 10 (33.1): 1–24.
Gilroy, P. 2005. *Postcolonial Melancholia*. New York, NY: Columbia University Press.
Jang, Wonho, and Youngsun Kim. 2013. "Envisaging the Sociocultural Dynamics of K-pop: Time/Space Hybridity, Red Queen's Race and Cosmopolitan Striving". *Korea Journal* 53 (4): 83–106.
Jang, Wonho, and Byungmin Lee. 2015. "The Glocalizing Dynamics of the Korean Wave". *Korean Regional Sociology* 17 (2): 5–19.
Kim, A.E., F. Mayasari, and I. Oh. 2013. "When Tourist Audiences Encounter Each Other: Diverging Learning Behaviours of K-Pop Fans From Japan and Indonesia". *Korea Journal* 53 (4): 59–82.
Lie, John. 2012. "What Is the K in K-pop? South Korean Popular Music, the Culture Industry and National Identity". *Korea Observer* 43 (3): 339–363.
Oh, C. 2015. "Queering Spectatorship in K-pop: The Androgynous Male Dancing Body and Western Female Fandom". *The Journal of Fandom Studies* 3 (1): 59–78.
Oh, Ingyu. 2009. "Hallyu: The Rise of Transnational Cultural Consumers in China and Japan". *Korea Observer* 40 (3): 425–459.
Oh, Ingyu. 2011. "Torn Between Two Lovers: Retrospective Learning and Melancholia Among Japanese Women". *Korea Observer* 42 (2): 223–254.

Oh, Ingyu, and Wonho Jang. 2020. "From Globalization to Glocalization: Configuring Korean Pop Culture to Meet Glocal Demand". *Culture and Empathy* 3 (1–2): 23–42.

Oh, Ingyu, and Seol-Ah Kim. 2019. "Comprendre la communication de la gender mélancolie autour du fan féminin de Hallyu". *Societes* 145: 11–24.

Robertson, Roland. 1995. "Globalization: Time-Space and Homogeneity-Heterogeneity". *Global Modernities* 2: 25–45.

Rocke, M. 1998. *Forbidden Friendships: Homosexuality and Male Culture in Renaissance Florence*. New York, NY: Oxford University Press.

CHAPTER 20

Development of Critical Theory Based on the Analysis of Literary Works on Tenderness: Habermas's Thesis and Akira Kurihara's Work

Deguchi Takeshi

1   Introduction

This study focuses on Akira Kurihara's work to highlight the uniqueness of Japanese critical sociology that developed under the influence of German critical theory.[1]

Akira Kurihara (1936–) is a professor emeritus at Rikkyo University in Tokyo, Japan. He is one of the most influential personalities in political sociology and disaster studies. His body of sociological work can be classified into three categories: (1) the critical theory of the totally administered society, which examines the general populace's spontaneous submission to control; (2) psychohistory, which elucidates the formation of the identity and mentality of youth from the 1970s to the 1980s; and (3) studies of social movements, which include volunteer activities, religious movements, commune movements and environmental movements. In the present study, I will examine Kurihara's concept of *yasashisa* (tenderness), which he presents as a state of youth identity; this is a crucial intersection point for his various research themes.

In this study, I aim to conduct historical or philological research on Japanese critical sociology both for a Japanese readership and to introduce it to non-Japanese critical theorists around the world. Therefore, I wish to shed light on the domestic context in which Japanese critical sociology has developed, as well as the content of the theory itself.

First, it may be helpful to explain the term "galapagosization".[2] The term is used to refer to a Japanese product that is too local and unusual to be available outside Japan. It is derived from the Galapagos Islands, which are inhabited

---

1 The present study is based on earlier studies presented at the ISA World Conference of Sociology RC16 in Japan on July 14, 2014; at the 9th international critical theory conference in Rome on May 7, 2016, and at the inaugural congress of the East Asian Sociological Association in Tokyo on March 9, 2019.
2 For galapagosization, see Deguchi (2014).

by rare, endemic flora and fauna species because the islands are isolated from other lands and have unique evolution processes. In daily conversation, this term is used to refer to Japanese mobile phones (*Gala-kei* or *Galapagos-keitai*) that have various precision-made but unnecessary functions. Therefore, the term carries a negative and disparaging implication. However, I would like to transform "galapagosization" into a methodological and heuristic concept that enables the rediscovery and reappraisal of Japan-localized sociology with due regard to its relevant context.

So far, Japanese social theory has been protected by a strong language barrier and a large Japanese readership and market. Therefore, it was not essential for social theorists to discuss issues that dominated discussions elsewhere or write in other languages. However, on the one hand, sociologists could focus on daily Japanese terms or adopt them into theoretical concepts to gain a deeper understanding of their own society, whereas, on the other, they could reflect on the same society using Western social theories made available through Japan's advanced translation culture.

Having completed this initial overview of the Japanese sociology situation, I will begin by outlining Kurihara's social theory against the backdrop of Japanese critical sociology. Next, I will explore his critique of the totally administered society, influenced by the critical theory of Herbert Marcuse, Theodor Adorno, and Jürgen Habermas, the psychohistory of Erik H. Erikson, the phenomenological sociology of Peter Berger and Thomas Luckmann and the Marxist phenomenology of Trân Duc Thao from Vietnam. Following this, I will discuss the idea of *yasashisa* (tenderness) that is generated by and opposed to the totally administered society by examining Japanese literary works from the 1960s and 1980s. Finally, I will compare Kurihara's theory of the totally administered society with Habermas's thesis of the colonization of the lifeworld.

2 Background

2.1 *Japanese Theory of Social Consciousness and Erik H. Erikson*

Before closely examining Kurihara's social theory, I will touch briefly upon the theory of *shakai ishiki* (social consciousness), which was uniquely developed in postwar Japanese sociology under the influence of Marxist historical materialism (Deguchi 2016).[3] According to Marx, objective material conditions—the forces and relationships of production—form the foundation or substructure

---

3 The theory of *shakai ishiki* has been a unique research field that eliminates interaction between substructure and superstructure in the sense of Marxism. For the theory of *shakai ishiki*, see Deguchi (2013).

of human society. Correspondingly, its superstructure, including legal or political forms, ideologies, culture, and forms of social consciousness, is then constructed. The Japanese theory of *shakai ishiki* (social consciousness) originally focused on the intermediating processes through which ideology and social psychology are generated based on the substructure; in particular, it focuses on the birth of revolutionary subjects in the historical process and their consequent effect on social changes.

Kurihara gives importance to the subjects' identity formation and, in contrast with Habermas's introduction of Kohlberg's stages of moral development, adopts Erik H. Erikson's developmental psychology (Kurihara [1967] 1982). According to Erikson, psychological development aims to attain a "sense of ego identity", that is, the accrued confidence that one's ability to maintain inner sameness and continuity matches the sameness and continuity of one's meaning for others. Furthermore, Kurihara uses Erikson's opinion to argue that the sense of ego identity is closely related to change in historical society; namely, society's historical crisis causes a crisis of identity in individuals; consequently, individuals' actions to attain their sense of ego identity lead to social changes. In short, Kurihara reconstructs Marx's historical materialism by adopting developmental psychology and describing the dynamic relationship between individual psychology and society in general.

In reality, political movements declined through the 1950s and 1960s, and therefore, the *shakai ishiki* (social consciousness) theory transitioned from a search for revolutionary subjects to an exposition of the mechanism of the general populace's spontaneous submission to control. Throughout this process, Kurihara maintains that the fact that in the everyday lifeworld people accept political domination as a natural fact or as something taken for granted without resistance should be emphasized; he tackles this problem in terms of the social construction of reality using phenomenological sociology context (Kurihara 1976).[4]

2.2 *Human Praxes and Social Realms*

The phenomenological sociology of Peter Berger and Thomas Luckmann is the most appropriate approach for illuminating people who consider social reality as the taken-for-granted. Kurihara introduces this approach to describe the possibility of control by power in the everyday lifeworld. Berger and Luckmann argue that the social construction of reality comprises three elements: externalization, objectivation, and internalization. The relationship between these

---

4 The following discussion is based on a lengthy paper written by Kurihara in Japanese (Kurihara 1976).

elements is as follows: "Externalization" is the process by which the products of human activity come into existence outside of individuals; these products are attributed the character of objectivity and the taken-for-granted by "objectivation"; finally, through "internalization", the objectivated social world is retrojected into the individual consciousness during socialization. Furthermore, Berger and Luckmann attach importance to the role of language in the objectivation process. Although language has its origins in face-to-face situations, it can be readily detached from them. Language, as well as signs and sign systems, can transcend subjective intentions here and now and form an independent system; therefore, it can provide objectivity and integrated meanings for human products of individual activities.

Kurihara, however, criticizes the narrowness of human activity in Berger and Luckmann, and, following Habermas's article "Work and Interaction", distinguishes such activities into three types of human praxes: "work", which is bound to the human organism and desire; "interaction", which is determined by others; and "symbolic behavior", which uses and responds to symbols. In contrast to Habermas, who highly prioritizes linguistic communication, Kurihara believes that work, interaction, and symbolic behavior are equivalent and are never separated from each other. Kurihara employs the origin of language theory proposed by the Vietnamese Marxist phenomenologist Trân Duc Thao and argues that human work is essentially collective and interactive and that this behavior process leads to language; in reality, these three elements permeate each other.

Having developed the concept of human praxes, Kurihara explores a relationship between human praxes and social realms. According to him, the three human praxes correspondingly construct three "social realms" as subfields of society in general: realms of "functionality", "communality", and "symbolicity". The social realm of functionality is where individual work bound to the human organism and desire is accumulated into collective forces of production that aim at a quick and efficient satisfaction of desire. It is compared in reality to an economic area. The communal realm is where interactions with others develop into social institutions that lead to common decision-making behaviors and thus maintain solidarity among citizens. This realm also contains the so-called public sphere. The realm of symbolicity comprises various kinds of signs and sign systems. They integrate fragmented social phenomena into a single social world and give them a frame of reference or interpretation; consequently, they provide the character of objectivity to social phenomena. This realm is, in fact, mass media and culture.

3   Social Pathologies and Predominance of Functionality

3.1   *Predominance of Functionality*

Let us move on from Kurihara's basic concept of human praxes and social realms and turn to his diagnoses of social pathologies in a totally administered society.

Kurihara supposes that in a traditional and egalitarian society, work or functionality is also rooted in the communality of human interaction and solidarity. Furthermore, symbolic systems combine work with interaction at a micro level and maintain harmonic social integration at a macro level. But once such a society modifies into an industrial and stratified society, the functionality interferes in and dominates other social realms and an additional subfield aiming at administration and coordination is created, namely, an "intentionality" realm, which appears as a state in the social world. Discussing Kurihara's concept of the state and his history as a whole is beyond the scope of the present study. Therefore, I would like to focus exclusively on the "administering state" and its social realms.

In a totally administered society, functionality transforms into "universal operability". This creates a system in which members of the society are polarized into technocrats and mass workers, and both groups are integrated into the system simultaneously only as parts. Functionality permeates into the communal and political realm and forms "a double-binding system". To more efficiently realize functionality and operability, this system provides people with a fictitious image of democratic agreement or participation. In administering the state apparatus in the intentionality realm, "integrative devolution" can be observed. As functionality interferes with intentionality, state power appears to be decentralized and democratized; however, it is, in fact, only devolved into an "ideological state apparatus", in the sense of Althusser (the family and the educational system) and intermediate groups (the community and the union), under the influence of the state apparatus. In the media and symbolic systems subfield, mass media is employed to gain control through the taken-for-granted. People interpret and accept social reality per the frame of reference provided by mass media, and they consequently regard control by power as natural and as the taken-for-granted.

Kurihara identifies that the predominance of functionality and its permeation with other social realms are the causes of social pathologies in the totally administered society of the 1970s. Next, I will focus on the dysfunctionality in the reproduction of the social world.

3.2 Birth of yasashisa (*Tenderness*) and Dysfunctional Reproduction

In Kurihara's social theory, no outside world is free from the predominance of functionality; he explores a way of being emancipated in functionality itself. The expansion and intensification of functionality lead to a contradictory situation that is opposed to it. Owing to the social development of science and technology, social organizations have become increasingly complicated and people need to learn to use extremely high-level technology and obtain knowledge to control every societal realm. At the institutional and individual identity levels, the educational period and the psychological moratorium, respectively, are extended. During the psychological moratorium, adolescents are given sufficient freedom and are exempted from social duties. This enables them to find their proper positions in society and gain a sense of ego identity, which is attained by inner sameness and continuity that matches the sameness and continuity of one's meaning for others.

However, in a totally administered society, so-called productivism prevails. With regard to this productivism, Kurihara prioritizes the efficiency and functionality of organization and augments forces of production through high levels of scientific technology, bureaucratization, and non-democratic administration. With productivism permeating educational systems, students face a more oppressive and competitive situation. Therefore, the school exerts strict contorol, with students being deprived of their freedom and psychological moratorium. Kurihara supposes that this leads to a so-called "internalisation of moratorium". Kurihara says that the intensification of productivism causes the psychological moratorium to be interrupted, and consequently to be given up in reality but internalized as an inner ideal utopia. He defines this kind of consciousness as "double consciousness" or "double thinking". It includes a dispassionate realism and a utopian idealism; the latter arises from an internalized moratorium during socialization. This double consciousness is a matrix of *yasashisa* (tenderness) towards others (Kurihara [1971] 1994, [1977] 1994).

While *yasashisa* contradicts the principle of productivism and the predominance of functionality in a totally administered society and is a generally accepted orientation to success and achievement, it neither attacks power with violence nor criticizes a state openly. It represents a flexible and soft mental attitude towards external factors. In the following, I will explore the *yasashisa* mentality in four literary works considered by Kurihara.

4 Analyzing Literary Works

4.1 *Four Categories of* yasashisa

Before analyzing literary works, Kurihara presents the theoretical framework for categorizing four types of *yasashisa* (Kurihara [1995] 1996). First, Kurihara classifies *yasashisa* (tenderness) into two categories: one is emotional and the other is structural. Emotional *yasashisa* does not have any contact with the social system, while the structural form links to social structure and sometimes tries to actively change people's place or social systems. Second, Kurihara introduces the difference between openness and closedness. The attitude of open tenderness is literally ready to open to the outside world and communicate with others. In contrast, the attitude with closed tenderness is that it does not reach out to others. It cares only for itself in a narcissistic way. By adopting two kinds of criteria, such as emotional/structural and open/closed, we can get four types of *yasashisa*: namely (1) emotional and open *yasashisa*, (2) emotional and closed *yasashisa*, (3) structural and closed *yasashisa*, and (4) structural and open *yasashisa*.

(1) Emotional and open *yasashisa* can be seen in the late 1960s and early 1970s. According to Kurihara, this kind of tenderness is realizable only among intimate people, such as family or friends.

(2) Emotional and closed *yasashisa* was spread in the late 1970s and early 1980s. As mentioned earlier, *yasashisa* results from the internalization of moratorium as an inner utopia. With domination and administration being reinforced through the 1970s, *yasashisa* was put under more repressive pressure from outside reality. *Yasashisa*, however, was never lost, but was preserved. Kurihara considers *yasashisa* to be protected under such situations like "people would slip in front of the enemy with something dear to them in their arm".

(3) Structural and closed *yasashisa* can be seen during the 1980s. People with this *yasashisa* lost their interest in other people or society in general and disliked any change in society. *Yasashisa* in this case just means a negative state of mind in which people simply do not want to hurt other people or themselves. This mentality sometimes assumes a conservative and narcissistic tendency. What is more, it structurally links to social reality. As a result, *Yasashisa* helps maintain or reinforce the present social structure.

(4) The last category of *yasashisa* is, as Kurihara says, an ideal attitude but has not yet been realized. People who have this *yasashisa* would act proactively towards social change to eliminate the cause of people's suffering. I will discuss this type in the conclusion section.

Kurihara uses literary works to clarify the characteristic features of the four types of *yasashisa*. Japanese sociologists sometimes analyze literary works to elucidate the inner state and the mechanism of the mind (Deguchi 2016). They think that it is difficult for sociological theory to touch upon the subtleties of human nature, and, to the contrary, that novelists can depict human conduct and nature vividly, especially the inner experience, which is caused by new social changes.[5]

4.2 Be Careful, Little Red Riding Hood *and* yasashisa *to Others*

Let us move away from the theoretical discussion and turn to the analysis of the first two literary works, written from the end of the 1960s to the 1970s: Kaoru Shoji's *Akazukin-chan kiwotsukete* (*Be Careful, Little Red Riding Hood*) and Masahiro Mita's *Bokutte nani* (*What Am I?*). Both works were very popular among the youth and were considered serious literature, and both won the Akutagawa Prize, a prestigious award given to new novelists. What is of importance here, however, is not the novels' plot or conclusion but the characters and behaviors of their heroines and heroes: *yasashisa* (tenderness). Kaoru, who is a protagonist of *Be Careful, Little Red Riding Hood*, and Boku (a personal pronoun referring to the first person), who is a protagonist of *What Am I?*, embody a man who is emotionally *yasashii* (adjective form of *yasashisa*) and communicatively open to others.

The novel *Be Careful, Little Red Riding Hood* was published in 1969.[6] The Japanese student movement ended the year before, and since that time, the Japanese universities have entirely transformed into predatory schools set up only to train people to obtain a job and to progress in life as an elite salaried worker for Japanese companies. The hero Kaoru, sharing the author's name, is a student at one of the distinguished senior high schools known for its high ratio of graduates who are successful applicants to *Todai* (University of Tokyo). During his last year at school, however, he loses an opportunity to attempt an entrance examination for admission to *Todai* because the exam was canceled by the authorities due to the chaos caused by student movements and campus disputes.

Kaoru is openly and superficially very submissive and obedient towards adults and their values (double consciousness). However, he is also a typical *yasashii*, or a tender young man. His *yasashisa* is demonstrated through his

---

5 In Japanese sociology, the sociology of literature forms one field. A famous sociologist of literature, Keiichi Sakuta deals with works by F. Dostoyevsky, J.-J. Rousseau, and the famous Japanese novelists Soseki Natsume and Osamu Dazai. For Sakuta's sociology of literature, see Deguchi (2016).
6 For Kurihara's analysis of *Be Careful, Little Red Riding Hood*, see Kurihara ([1983] 1996, [1985] 1996, [1995] 1996).

attitude towards three women. The first is Yumi, a female friend whom he has known since childhood. Kaoru is always taking care of Yumi fondly and indirectly, although he is not dating her. The second is a strange woman he meets in the subway. One day he sees a young woman weeping inconsolably on the subway. Initially, the crying woman weighs on his mind and he is unable to get off at his destination; however, after a while, he finds the crying unbearable and suddenly gets off the train. He is distressed by the fact that although he tried to speak with her, he could not do anything. Once on the platform, he strongly decides that he will never make a woman unhappy in the future. The third person is a little girl who is referred to as Little Red Riding Hood in the novel. One day Kaoru's nail is taken off and he is forced to walk with a pair of crutches. While walking outside, a little girl suddenly steps on his wounded toe and he feels unbearable pain. The girl apologizes and, caring about him from the bottom of her heart, makes every effort to smile at him tenderly. Her care and tenderness for him touch his heart and he feels very happy. He goes to the bookstore with her to find a book she wants, *Little Red Riding Hood*.

In the novel's last scene, on his way home, Kaoru is walking with Yumi. He tells her that he has decided against going to the university, the passport to a successful life, and wants to carve out a future for himself. He holds her hand and chooses to become a big, tender man like the sea and a simple, sturdy man like the woods and to protect her all her life.

Kaoru's tenderness reflects the paternalism that still remained in Japanese society at the end of the 1960s. However, what is of consequence here is that Kaoru gives up a university education, which promises progress in life. The university symbolizes two contradictory futures: success and achievement in life and a violent battle with the establishment. Kaoru refutes both these futures and chooses the tender but independent lifestyle.

4.3   *What Am I?* and *Sensitivity to Life*

What Am I? was published in 1977.[7] The political climate at the time was completely distinct from that of 1969, and Japanese society's administration system was stronger. The novel's unnamed hero is a first-year student at a famous private university in Tokyo. He has been persuaded to join a sect of radicals and now cohabits with one of its executive female members. The leftist sects repeatedly engage in violent internal struggles due to serious antagonism concerning their principles and policies. However, the hero is apolitical and follows his cohabitant girlfriend's orders in everyday sect activities. In the course of the novel, he changes sects twice, being persuaded by members of other sects to do so, and decides to break up with his girlfriend. After escaping

---

7   For Kurihara's analysis of *What Am I?*, see also Kurihara ([1983] 1996, [1985] 1996, [1995] 1996).

sanctions by the sects that he has just left, he comes back to his flat and sees his separated girlfriend and his mother, who has come to Tokyo from his hometown to meet him. They have waited for him overnight and cooked his favorite dishes together. The hero feels happy and thanks his girlfriend for returning to him and for getting along with his mother.

The hero's indecisiveness is not interpreted as a weakness; rather, it is a typical symptom of the diffusion of identity, which can be seen during a period of psychological moratorium. What is significant here is that he definitely refuses violence. In fact, he secedes from one sect because the sect uses fierce violence; members of this sect are responsible for injuring an opposite sect's member and leaving him unattended. Furthermore, he leaves the second sect because of the antagonistic sectionalism among sects and the betrayal of a member who had initially invited him to join the second sect. To sum up, his seriousness forces him to leave two groups because of betrayal and sectionalism. He appears to be indecisive and opportunistic, but in fact he dreams of a non-violent and tender utopia like the one of his childhood days with his mother and the happy cohabitating life with his girlfriend. Later, Kurihara referred to such non-violent tenderness as "sensitivity to life".[8] According to him, this passive but non-violent attitude changed into the emotional and structural motivation that led people to participate in various kinds of peaceful social movements in the 1970s.

4.4 Almost Transparent Blue *and* yasashisa *in Confinement*
Almost Transparent Blue was written by Ryu Murakami in 1976, the year before *What Am I?* was published, and it, too, won the Akutagawa Prize.[9] However, Kurihara thinks the protagonist of this novel belongs to the second category of emotional and closed *yasashisa*.

The main character of this novel, Ryu, who shares the author's name, lives in a "House" in a small town in Tokyo. The House refers to a kind of residence that was used by the US military before and is now rented out to the Japanese. Even after Japan became independent of the United States, the American military has been stationed in various parts of Japan. The House is indeed supposed to represent a Japanese semi-colonial status, but in this novel it symbolizes a sense of being hopeless in a repressive administered society. In fact, Ryu and his friends are always indulging in drugs and orgies in the House, and at the

---

8 Kurihara often defines *yasashisa* as "extreme sensitivity to life". This idea results from Kurihara's engagement in the pollution problem of Minamata disease. Minamata disease was caused by mercury poisoning around 1952.

9 For Kurihara's analysis of *Almost Transparent Bule*, see Kurihara ([1983] 1996, [1985] 1996, [1995] 1996).

same time they want to break free from their corrupt lives. As violent sensations appear repeatedly, it is next to impossible to read *yasashisa* from superficial texts. Only Okinawa, Ryu's friend, and his girlfriend, Reiko, play a very important part in dragging out Ryu's inner *yasashisa*. "Okinawa", which is a nickname the author gives one of Ryu's friends, is also the name of a prefecture where more than 70% of US military facilities in Japan are concentrated. The Okinawa prefecture is a symbol of subordination to the United States. Okinawa likes Ryu's flute. It is a symbol of Ryu's inner *yasashisa*. Okinawa talks to Ryu.

> Hey, you should play the flute, playing the flute's what you're supposed to do, try to do it right without running around with shit like Yoshiyama, hey, remember how you played on my birthday? It was over at Reiko's place, I really felt great then. That was when somehow my chest felt all crawly, like, I can't really say how to say it but I felt, you know, like trying to make up with this guy I'd been fighting with ... you could make people feel that way.
> MURAKAMI 1977: 98

Yasashisa results from lost moratorium and inner utopia. In the last part of the novel, Ryu sees an illusion of a palace, city, and bird. He says that there is a blank in his mind that is filled with various scenes of his experiences. Ryu creates his own utopia in his fantasy, and the palace and the city symbolize his inner utopia. Ryu says to Lilly, one of his female friends.

> We've got to kill the bird, if it's not killed I won't understand about myself anymore, the bird's in the way, it's hiding what I want to see. I'll kill the bird, Lilly, if I don't kill it I'll be killed, Lilly, where are you, come and kill the bird with me, Lilly, I can't see anything, Lilly, I can't see a thing.
> MURAKAMI 1977: 122

When the bird came to Ryu to destroy the city in his fantasy, he hurt his own arm with a small broken piece of glass, and at the same time he passed out with the bird. In the very last scene, the fragment of glass, as it soaked up the dawn air, turns almost transparent blue. Ryu thinks he wants to become like glass and reflect a smooth white curving and show it to other people. This smooth white curving is a metaphor for a utopia he sees.

Kurihara interprets the bird as a state that has enormous power. He argues that the fragment of glass is a sharp weapon with which the tender man, Ryu, fights against the state.

4.5   Somehow, Crystal *and* yasashisa *Harmless to Both Others and Self*

Somehow, Crystal was published in 1981. Kurihara argues that this novel is ahead of its time and the heroine Yuri's personality shows structural and closed *yasashisa*, which can be seen throughout the 1980s.[10] Ryu's *yasashisa* is closed but stands against the repressive social structure of a totally administered society. In contrast, that of Yuri is structurally and intrinsically linked to the social system in a passive manner.

Yuri is a student at a university located in a fashionable area of Tokyo and works as a part-time fashion model. She cohabits with a boyfriend, Jun'ichi, who is also a university student and a semi-professional musician. Although in Japan, university students typically depend on their parents' monthly allowance, Yuri and Jun'ichi live independently and enjoy living together in a rented luxury condo. However, they have sexual relations with people other than each other and tolerate these love affairs.

What is noted in this novel is its unique style; the right-hand pages are the main body of the text, and the left-hand pages are all footnotes. These footnotes explain famous restaurants and shops where Yuri and her friends visit and the expensive brand-name goods they wear. Furthermore, the manners and customs of young people, as well as their slang, are explained in detail in the footnotes. This means that the way of life and the latest fashions Yuri and her friends follow diverge from that of the general public in Japan. The background of the novel, however, depicts precisely some aspects of Japanese society, which is enjoying an unprecedented economic boom after the Second World War. It was in 1979, two years before this novel was published, that Ezora Vogel highly praised Japanese-style management in her book *Japan as Number One: One Lesson for America*. Yuri looks very happy and enjoys her "somehow moods" life.

> I guess I'm living these 'somehow moods'.
> Some might say that such a degenerate lifestyle so lacking in agency is disgraceful. But for me, born in 1959, 'moods' drive my behaviour more than anything.
> TANAKA 2019: 30

According to Kurihara, Yuri's mental attitude is to avoid hurting both her partner and herself. She does not want to keep her boyfriend on a tight leash, nor

---

10 For Kurihara's analysis of *Somehow, Crystal*, see also Kurihara ([1983] 1996, [1985] 1996, [1995] 1996). This work did not win the Akutagawa Prize but did win the Bungei Prize. It also won an award for the best new talent.

does she want to be by him. The free and boundless relationship with lovers is characterized as "crystal" in the novel. The following is a conversation in which Yuri and Masataka, her affair partner, talk about *yasashii* (adjective form of *yasahisa*), or tender relationship, with their partner and about their lifestyle.

> 'We're not just indulging each other. I love Jun'ichi, and he loves me too. I think I always want to live with him. And for that, I think we both need our freedom.'
> 'I really get that, how you feel.'
> 'I don't think there's such a thing as love without constraints, true. But at the same time, I think love with more constraints than necessary just makes both people stop feeling for each other.'
> Masataka was silent for a moment.
> Then,
> 'Maybe my lifestyle sense is similar to yours', he said.
> 'It's crystal, that lifestyle. Not worrying about anything. Nothing to worry about in the first place, ...' I said.
> TANAKA 2019: 128–129

Their *yasashisa* is not at all greedy but somewhat distant. Yuri recognizes that she lives such a free and fashionable life because she is a university student who is exempted from social duties, and at the same time is a fashion model who is a highly paid part-time worker. She knows well that her present life is passing happiness. She has a feeling that she may marry someone (other than Jun'ichi) and become a housewife when the time comes. It was undoubtedly a standard and not necessarily the free way of life for Japanese women in the early 1980s.

> So even ten years from now, I still wanted to be together with Jun'ichi.
> What kind of musician would Jun'ichi be by then?
> I wanted him to be someone who did first-rate work, not just as a keyboardist, but as an arranger and a producer as well.
> Would I still be modelling?
> I wanted to be a model who could still work in her thirties.
> When I'm in my thirties, I want to be a woman who can wear a Chanel suit well.
> TANAKA 2019: 132

She has a *yasashii*, or tender dream, inside as an inner utopia; it never changes but reproduces present consumption or a totally administered society.

5 Discussions and Conclusions

In conclusion, I would like to discuss four points in relation to Habermas's thesis of the colonization of the lifeworld and current Japanese society.

First, the "colonisation of the lifeworld by system" thesis assumes that the ideal lifeworld where people aim at developing mutual understanding can be separated and made independent from the domination of the capitalist market or bureaucracy. In contrast, Kurihara indicates the presence of three equal social realms and sheds light on the fact that every social realm (the economic system, solidarity and public decision-making, mass media and culture, or state power and bureaucracy) cannot but change into pathological forms because of the intensification and permeation of functionality.

Second, by reconstructing historical materialism using Erikson's theory of ego identity, Kurihara is able to illuminate individual motivations that lead to individuals criticizing or protesting the totally administered society. While Habermas finds the causes of the protests against late capitalist society in the "seams of the lifeworld and system", Kurihara identifies them as a psychological drive to attain a sense of identity, that is, individuals' attempts to find recognizable relationships with others and their own position within society. This consideration can contribute to deepening the understanding of the psychological mechanism of colonization and the protest against it in relation to Axel Honneth's struggle for recognition.

Third, I will return to *yasashisa* in terms of an agency that gives a revolutionary impact on the social system. By the dominant and conservative position of society, *yasashisa* might be regarded as an immaturity characteristic of the youth. This idea of immaturity is, however, acceptable on the premise that present social structure functions adequately and reproduces itself automatically or to make an in-depth remark, only on the assumption that existing society should be preserved without reformation. Once the existing social system causes social pathologies, such as crime, deviations, poverty, inequality, exclusion and so on, the legitimacy of the current social norms and values which protect social structure is in question. Following that, the prevailing way of life as a subjective agency that takes a part of productive labor and the reproduction of social systems is transformed into shackles for people who would reform the society. Instead, a new type of way of life will be needed. Kurihara introduces here "neoteny" in the theory of evolution. Neoteny refers to a state in which animals become mature in a larval form without reaching adulthood and have unlimited possibilities of evolution. Kurihara argues that *yasashii* people are in a state of neoteny and have the ability to react to social problems in a flexible and reformative manner. We could say that we must be free from maturity to be free from existing society.

Finally, we are in a position to consider the fourth type of structural and open *yasashisa*. The Japanese government enacted very conservative laws in 2015. These include legislation on state security and a set of security-related laws. Young university and senior high school students attracted people's attention because they demonstrated in front of the Diet building. After the Great East Japan earthquake, coupled with the Fukushima Daiichi nuclear plant disaster in 2011, a lot of volunteers took part in the relief operations for the earthquake and tsunami victims. It should be noted that not only young people but also adults stopped their own everyday lives and, even if briefly, stayed in the disaster area of east Japan, close to the victims. These volunteers have structural and open *yasashisa*. An American writer named Rebecca Solnit remarks that in the event of a serious disaster, a utopia appears temporarily in which people help each other. The action of those volunteers can be explained with Kurihara's concept of a structural and open *yasashisa* which is free from maturity in the sense of a modern subject.

References

Berger, P., and T. Luckmann. 1966. *The Social Construction of Reality*. New York, NY: Anchor Books.

Deguchi, T. 2013. "Critical Theory and Its Development in Post-war Japanese Sociology: Pursuing True Democracy in Rapid Capitalist Modernization". In *Japanese Social Theory: From Individualization to Globalization in Japan Today*, edited by A. Elliott, M. Katagiri, and A. Sawai. Abingdon: Routledge.

Deguchi, T. 2014. "Beyond Shame and Guilt Culture to Globalised Solidarity: Reappraising Keiichi Sakuta's Sociology of Values as a Galapagosized Sociology". *Theory*, 19–24. Accessed December 8, 2021. www.isa-sociology.org/uploads/files/rc16newsletter_winter_2014.pdf.

Deguchi, T. 2016. "Sociology of Literature After the Great East Japan Earthquake: Analysing the Disaster's Underrepresented Impacts". In *The Consequences of Global Disaster*, edited by A. Elliott and E.L. Hsu. Abington: Routledge.

Habermas, J. 1968. *Technik und Wissenschaft als "Ideologie"*. Frankfurt: Suhrkamp.

Habermas, J. 1987. *Theory of Communicative Action*. Vol. 2: *Lifeworld and System: A Critique of Functionalist Reason*. Boston, MA: Beacon Press.

Honneth, A. 1995. *Struggle for Recognition: Moral Grammar of Social Conflicts*. Cambridge: Polity Press.

Kurihara, A. (1967) 1982. Rekishi niokeru sonzaishomei wo motomete [In Search for Identity in History]. *Rekishi to identity* [History and Identity]. Tokyo: Shin'yo sha.

Kurihara, A. (1971) 1994. Mikan no sonzaishomei [Uncompleted Identity]. *Yasashisa no yukue* [Whereabouts of Tenderness]. Tokyo: Chikuma Shobo.

Kurihara, A. 1976. Nihongata kanrishakai no shakai ishiki [Social Consciousness in Japanese-type Administrated Society]. In *Shakaigaku koza 12 Shakai ishiki* [Sociological Library 12 Social Consciousness], edited by M. Munesuke. Tokyo: Tokyo daigaku shuppan kai.

Kurihara, A. (1977) 1994. Yasashisa no yukue [Whereabouts of Tenderness]. *Yasashisa no yukue* [Whereabouts of Tenderness]. Tokyo: Chikuma Shobo.

Kurihara, A. (1983) 1996. Yasashisa no wa no monogatari [Tale of Ring of Yasashisa]. *Yasashisa no sonzai shomei* [Identity of Tenderness]. Tokyo: Shin'yo sha.

Kurihara, A. (1985) 1996. Yasashisa [Tenderness]. *Yasashisa no sonzai shomei* [Identity of Tenderness]. Tokyo: Shin'yo sha.

Kurihara, A. (1995) 1996. Yasashisa no hen'yo [Tenderness in Change]. *Yasashisa no sonzai shomei* [Identity of Tenderness]. Tokyo: Shin'yo sha.

Marcuse, H. 1964. *One-Dimensional Man: Studies of Technology in Advanced Industrial Society*. Boston, MA: Beacon Press.

Solnit, R. 2009. *A Paradise Built in Hell: The Extraordinary Communities That Arise in Disaster*. New York, NY: Penguin Books.

Trân, D.T. 1973. *Recherches sur L'Origine du Langage et de la Conscience*. Paris: Éditions Sociales.

Literary Works

Mita, M. 1977. *Bokutte nani* [What Am I?]. Tokyo: Kawade Shobo.

Murakami, R. 1977. *Almost Transparent Blue*. Translated by Nancy Andrew. Tokyo: Kodansha International. First published in Japanese in 1978 as *Kagirinaku tomei ni chikaiburu*. Tokyo: Kodansha.

Shoji, K. 1969. *Akasukinchan kiwotsukete* [Be Careful, Little Red Riding Hood]. Tokyo: Shincho Sha.

Tanaka, Y. 2019. *Somehow, Crystal*. Translated by Christopher Smith and Sugizaki Megumi. Tokyo: Kurodahan Press. First published in Japanese in 1981 as *Nantonaku, kurisutaru*. Tokyo: Kawade Shobo.

CHAPTER 21

From Social Equilibrium to Self-Production of Society: The Transition of China's Sociological Recognition on China's Society

Sun Feiyu

In 1897, Yan Fu, a famous important Chinese scholar at that time, started to translate a sociology book written by H. Spencer, *The Study of Sociology*. After seven years, the book published with the name of *Qun Xue Yi Yan* (群学肄言), which means the textbook of collective studies. This is the first sociology book that was translated into Chinese from the Western world. Why did Yan translate this book? In 1895, in his book *Yuan Qiang*, which means an investigation into why a country could become rich and powerful, Yan Fu explained this. In this book, Yan says:

> Mr. Spencer is also from England. He named his doctrine as Sociology … I conclude his theories and find out that his essentials are pretty much close to the essentials of our *Great Learning* (大学) on the self-cultivation, the family regulation, the state governance, and on bringing peace to all under the heavens. However, our Great Learning does not have a detailed discussion on those topics, and Spencer's excellent books are profound and delicate, rich and speculative … his works especially focus on the principle of a country's rise and decline, the reason why people's morality becomes honest and why it becomes ruined.
>
> YAN 1895

This article explains why Yan Fu translated this book and introduced sociology into China. He did those things because he wanted China to become powerful and rich. For him, sociology could change China's society. And this is the earliest understanding and expectation of Chinese scholars regarding sociology. This type of understanding and expectation is very typical among Chinese scholars in the early 20th century.

1   Survive or Perish: Early Sociologists' Concern in China

The most famous work of Professor Fei Xiaotong in the entire academic world is his book *Peasant Life in China*. It has been taken as a classical work of both sociology and anthropology by both Eastern and Western sociology. Jing Zhang believes that this book should be taken as a new type of study on China, written by a new type of scholar that did not exist in the history of China (Zhang 2017). In other words, it represents a new era in China's knowledge production and a new type of understanding of China's society. In the preface of this book, Malinowski calls Fei a "citizen": "The book ... contains observations carried out by a citizen upon his own people" (Malinowski 1939: xix). This is a word that traditional Chinese scholars never used in the history of China to describe themselves.

Fei also considers himself a modern scholar who was influenced by the May Fourth Movement and belonging to the generation of May Fourth (Zhang 2000: 645–646), which confirms the image of "citizen".

However, recent studies from Chinese scholars found that Fei also had an aspect of Chinese traditional "gentry". And he also admits to having such an aspect (Yang 2010). In other words, Fei is a Chinese sociology scholar with dual characteristics: that of a traditional Confucianism scholar and that of a modern social science scholar.

Such a duality of Fei comes from a wide-ranging influence. What we would like to point out in this paper is that his early works, the works before *Peasant Life in China*, could give us a clue in understanding this book and his duality.

Various early works that Fei had written before his *Peasant Life in China* focused on one topic: the transition of China's cultural and society. We can take it as a direct reflection of a bigger trend of social thought in early 20th-century China: saving the nation from subjugation and ensuring its survival.

The current materials provide evidence that Fei started his academic writing around 1933. In 1932 he wrote a preface for a translated article named "Eyewitness to War between China and Japan". In this preface, Fei shows his concern with *saving China* clearly and says that he wants to find a way out for China. Thus, like Yan Fu, sociological and anthropological study had become a method for Fei at that time to explore the way of modernization for society in traditional China. The basic question he raised in his early works is how could a traditional culture find its own way of adapting modern society? From 1933 to 1937, many studies by Fei did show such a concern. He clearly understood that China was on the verge of huge change and wanted to find out that where China would go and how to understand such a huge transition.

For example, in 1933 he wrote a book review of *The Pilgrims of Russian Town*, written by Pauline v. Young and published by the University of Chicago Press in 1932. In this book review, Fei's concern focuses on how a religious community, Molokan clan, which is totally different from American society in every aspect, survives in American cities and adapts to them. Such a perspective clearly shows Fei's concern about how China's traditional society, with its long history and with influence from the outside, could transform into a modern society.

This concern even shows up in his reading of Max Weber's classic work *The Protestant Ethic and the Spirit of Capitalism*. Fei is probably one of the earliest scholars who read the English version of this book. Around 1940, Fei wrote a long book review of this book. The perspective in which he chose to read this book is also the transition of a traditional culture in modern society.

Such clues as to his thoughts were directly shown in his work *Peasant Life in China*. In the preface for this book, Malinowski says: "the book, moreover, though it takes in the traditional background of Chinese life, does not remain satisfied with the mere reconstruction of the static past. It grapples fully and deliberately with the most elusive and difficult phase of modern life: the transformation of the traditional culture under the Western impact" (Malinowski 1939: xix). Moreover, Malinowski notices that Fei's village represents a bigger question of his country: "his great Mother-country to westernize or to perish?" (Malinowski 1939: xx). In order to answer this question, just like Fei himself argues, sociological studies should respect the "live social reality" (Fei 2009: 104).

Such a work and concerns do not only exist in Fei's works. With many other sociologists and many practitioners of the rural construction movement, we can also find these kinds of concern and understanding of China's society.

There are two standpoints regarding this question. Some scholars believed that China's society is undergoing a huge change and needs change in order to adapt to modern society. Scholars and doers, such as James Yen, had a very typical standpoint on this when he raised his own understanding about China. He carried out social investigation in China's rural society in the early 1920s and concluded that poverty, weakness, selfishness, and foolishness are the four main characteristics of traditional Chinese society. His trial of reforming China's society, which is called the civilian educational movement, started in 1921 in Ding County of Hebei Province. Basically, the idea of this civilian educational movement is to reform China's society through four kinds of education: arts education, livelihood education, citizen education, and hygiene education.

However, many other scholars, including Shuming Liang and Guangdan Pan, had different standpoints on such a question. They believed that China's society and culture have their own value and vitality, and they are different from Western society and Western culture. In his famous book *Eastern and Western Cultures and Their Philosophies*, regarding Western civilization as being doomed to eventual failure, Liang did not advocate for a complete reform of China's society and the adoption of Western institutions. He nonetheless believed that reform was needed to make China equal to the rest of the world. Instead, he pushed for changes to socialism starting at the grassroots level and learned from the traditional Chinese Confucianism method. To this end, he founded the Shandong Rural Reconstruction Institute and helped found the China Democratic League. Like many other sociologists, Liang believed that the rural village was the most important aspect of Chinese society. However, in the last few hundred years, China's history had been characterized by its destruction. Thus, the most important part of saving China was to save China's rural society. Since such a society has been and is different from Western society, China should not simply learn from the West.

Liang argues that while China's culture stresses the importance of family, Western society focuses on the relationship of the individual to the community. He insists that this leads China down a path dedicated to an ethics-based society, while Western society produces an individual-based one instead. China was led down its path because of feelings of kinship and emotional bonds, which dominated its society. The West, due to its emphasis on mutual rights, proceeded down a path revolving around class distinction, economic independence, and laws. The Chinese, however, had a society of professional divisions due to greater social mobility, mutual responsibility, and personal bonds to maintain orders.

Finally, Liang brings up his three-culture theory and China's position in it: the West–China–India culture model. He states that although China was in the second stage, she had skipped the first and consequently lacked the development of profit and power. Rather than suggesting she go back to the first cultural stage, Liang suggests the introduction of Western science and democracy into Chinese society to promote development in those areas. He tries to promote a kind of modern township treaty, which means education and politics together, education is politics and vice versa. Through such a treaty, he was trying to build up a basis for modern China's politics.

2   Comparative Studies between China and Western Society

Besides Liang, many other scholars started to reflect on the characteristics of China's society and its difference from Western society. Among those scholars,

Professor Guangdan Pan's works are representative. Pan was one of the very early scholars who used European theory to explain Chinese society. In 1922, he wrote a paper about Xiaoqing Feng, a narcissistic girl in the Late Ming dynasty whose story was recorded in many books and poetries in the Ming and Qing dynasties. Pan borrowed theories from Sigmund Freud and used them for his explanation of Ms Feng. This approach was very successful, such that Mr Qichao Liang, his professor, praise it a lot. After he wrote this paper, Pan went to Dartmouth College and then Columbia University. He stayed about five years in the United States and then went back to China. At this time, as a scholar who was influenced heavily by Western civilization, he started to think about the difference between China's civilization and Western civilization, especially the difference between Confucianism and Christian civilization. And his writings also reflected his thoughts.

In 1927, Pan expended his paper into a book and published it. In this book he put two epilogues where he explains the reason he performed the research of Xiaoqing Feng. Both are related to his concern with China's society. First, he placed Feng's case as one diagnosing China's society, especially its attitude toward women. Secondly, he took Feng as a case of narcissism and used it as a starting point for his understanding of the trend of individualization in early 20th-century China. He believes that the trend of individuation in China comes from Western civilization and it is a symbol of modernization that China cannot avoid. However, excessive individualization has already endangered China's society, especially marriage and the family.

The second epilogue had already shown Guangdan Pan's complicated attitude toward modernization. As a sociologist, he performed a series of studies on comparing the difference between Eastern civilization and Western civilization. And he believed that the two civilizations and societies are totally different.

In 1928, Pan published another book, *China's Family Issues*. In this book, he argues that family issues are especially important in China's sociology because traditionally, "In the country of China, family is at the center of its society"; however, in the modern transformation of China's society, the idea of family in China's younger generation has changed a lot (Pan [1928] 2000: 71).

In this study, Pan analyzes the data that he collected through his questionnaire investigation for China's younger generation on family issues. And he found the trend of individualization in 1920s China. The data show that younger generations prefer romantic love more than family and marriage. However, Pan believes that in modern society, family still has value and can "fit modern ethics". The reason is that family represents a bigger function for human society: ethnic continuity (Pan [1928] 2000: 132).

Pan finds from his research the trend of individualization of young generations. He believes that this is a big change in modern China. More importantly, such a trend is especially obvious in those people who have higher education. He uses the theory of Freudian narcissism on the analysis of such a trend of individualization in modern society, and explains the crisis of China's society from the perspective of the Eastern–Western comparative model. such a train of thought was very typical in Pan's works in the 1920s to 1930s. In these comparative works between China's Confucianism and Western culture, he posited that a big difference is the sentimentalism of the West and the moderation of emotions in China. He mentioned a very similar point with Xiaotong Fei's Cha-Xu-Ge-Ju and argued that traditional Chinese people would prefer the moderation of his feelings and emotions in daily life. Thus, he believes that if modern Chinese people stress individualism and the emotional part of marriage, they will fall onto the path of narcissism. In this essay, he criticizes some behaviors of the young generation at that time in the name of "romantic love" and argues that this is nothing but a reflection of individualism. Thus, we could say, Pan's works on Feng reflected his concerned thoughts on China's social transformation and the change of identity.

In his study on China's family, Pan also compares the cultural difference between China and Western society and criticizes individualism and how it harms traditional China's familyism. He emphasizes that in China, "family is the biggest pivot for an individual's emotions" (Pan [1928] 2000: 236). He believes that China's scholars must look for the solutions for the social problems that are caused by individualism from China's traditional culture.

What is the difference between Eastern and Western culture and society? Pan believes that the idea of God in Christian culture cannot be understood by China's culture, especially by Confucian culture in daily ethics. In China, the factor of human relations is the most important thing for the understanding of society. However, in Christian culture, human relations is not the most important thing because God is far beyond human beings. Simply speaking, China's culture is a culture of family, and Western culture is a culture of individualism. If China follows Western culture in a simple way, it will cause severe social problems.

As an influential professor, Pan's other research efforts focus on higher education, especially on liberal arts education. His thoughts on higher education and liberal arts education are closely related and come from his own sociological theory: Zhong He Wei Yu, meaning equilibrium, harmony, and sociologists should investigate any social issue from its own cultural, historical, and social background. When he uses this theory for the study of China's new higher education in the early 20th century, he criticizes such an education for being "totally failed" (Pan [1933] 2000). This failure can be proven by the bad performance of those government officials in the desperate situation of China, which means the invasion of the Japanese into China. And the reason for this failure, Pan believes, is this "new education" that focused only on professional education and did not emphasize the cultivation of human beings. His understanding of the cultivation of human beings mostly means the cultivation of traditional Confucian scholars. In other words, Pan believes that traditional Confucianism is still valuable and even necessary for modern China. Modern university education in China did not provide such an education, and thus failed. For that reason, he advocates liberal arts education, which can play such a role. This kind of liberal arts education, he believes, is even more important than professional studies.

3 Social Ground and the Self-Production of the Society

After the Cultural Revolution, Chinese scholars translated Weber's book *The Protestant Ethic and the Spirit of Capitalism* into Chinese. In the 1980s, this book suddenly became a phenomenon. Sociologists and even wide academic circles read and discussed it enthusiastically. In this book, Weber explains the cultural elements of European modernization and emphasizes the unique rationalization of Western culture as its very essence of Western modernization. Chinese scholars studied it passionately because they wanted to discover the possibility of modernization for Chinese culture. Scholars wanted to find their own answers as to such a Weberian question: Why didn't modern capitalism (modernization) happen in China?

This question is related to another question directly: How should we understand China's society? Since the 1980s, many works by foreign scholars on China have been translated into Chinese and introduced into Chinese academia. This new wave of translation reflects Chinese scholars' concerns about this question. Among these newly translated books, many of their topics focus on the relationship between state and peasants or local society.

In this period, some scholars argued again that China's society should reform into a society similar to Western society. For example, when comparing China's society and Western society, some scholars found that China does not have its own civil society. Thus, China's society should produce its own civil society. And many scholars started to study social organization. That is why in China's sociological studies, how social organizations that envision social reforms interact with existing social and political structures in their practices is the key for some scholars to study. A "social production" perspective and related study on the structural features and poverty alleviation practices of a philanthropic organization, which has successfully solved the entry problem and meanwhile clearly recognized and maintained its independence, was used by Feiyu Sun in one of his papers (Sun 2018). Sun studied how an organization with a clear vision, actionable goals, compatible, and strictly managed, as well as having monitoring systems, encountered many obstacles that are inconsistent with its goals. The organization thus may not be able to realize its goal in practice, and thus might fall into a detached state, and even become a structural space for the reproduction of local society. From a "state-society" perspective, Sun tries to understand the obstacles that this organization encountered and studies it by re-embedding the organization into the local social-political context. Sun argues that the reason this organization became an academically interesting issue is because it shows the complexity of the transitional process of Chinese society and allows us to observe the self-reproduction process of the society.

In their study on China's transition, especially the transition of the rural society, some scholars take an inclusive view of the peasant village in their discussions on intersections between state and society (Oi 1989; Strauch 1981). Oi concludes that there are two contrasting models for understanding the relation of state and society in communist states. The first one is a totalitarian model which stresses mostly state power and its influence on society, such as the works of Friedrich and Brzezinski. Another model is called the "interest group model", which places the influence of local identifiable groups on state power. Oi uses the peasant village as the meaning of society in his functionalism society-state model. Different from the two models, Oi describes the village politics in China as "clientelist" and choose a "clientelism model to describe the village politics, especially on the elite-mass linkage" (Oi 1989: 7).

However, from the studies of land reform, some scholars find that the relationships between individual, community, and state are more complicated. CPC's trial of entering local society was immediately involved in the local social and political structure. Local power structure started to influence the power from outside (Guo and Sun 2002; Sun 2013).

Similarly, Philip Huang also points out that there are three traditions of Chinese peasant studies from different dimensions. The first tradition, which is represented by Western economists, such as Theodore Schultz (1964) and Samuel Popkin (1979), describes the peasant as a kind of capitalist entrepreneur. The second tradition, which is represented by Karl Polanyi (1957), suggests a "substantive" economics "that would stress the social relationships in which economic behavior in premarket societies was 'embedded'" (Huang 1985: 5). The third tradition, which is contrasted against both the formal and substantive points, is the Marxism tradition from Karl Marx to Mao Tse-tung.

In his famous book *The Peasant Economy and Social Change in North China*, Huang presents his critic to all three traditions: a common tendency in the studies above about Chinese villages is to take villages as units that are "socially and economically integrated" into larger social and economic systems. Meanwhile, peasants have "generally been depicted as a single 'peasant class' that transcended villages and acted as one" (Huang 1985: 27). Huang tries to put peasants within their own village communities and to explore the political function of Chinese villages in 20th-century from this "community"-state perspective. He argues that China's "village-state" relations "were shaped not only by the nature of governmental power, but also by the internal structures of villages" (Huang 1985: 32).

By showing how the state power met the "indigenous village political organizations" in early and middle 20th-century China, Huang notes: "how the larger processes of agricultural involution and social differentiation ... affected village communities and their relations with the state" (Huang 1985: 32).

In this paper, I would like to choose a case from the fieldwork in Western China in order to describe the transition of China's rural society from the perspective of relationships directly between peasants and state. In this perspective, I will refuse to describe the peasants as chessman that are controlled, or mobilized, or constructed passively in a large transition of the history: I would like to describe them as an initiative social group from the perspective of social self-production. I want to emphasize that, they have their own thoughts, interests, and plans about their own choice.

3.1 *Case History of a Peasant*

On the basis of our fieldwork in Xichuan city, the provincial capital of M municipality in western China, I would like to analyze a case history of unequal contests between local government and the peasantry in contemporary China within a background of urbanization.

Unequal contests between local government and the peasantry refers to their confrontation and struggle because of related but opposite purposes given the background of a great disparity in their status and strength.

In order to upgrade the level of urbanization and develop local economies, in the last 30 years, many local governments in China have extended their city areas, which directly changes the populations, locations and administrative organizations of local society. The lives of millions of traditional rural peasants changed from being in a rural area to an urban one by local governments' actions of expanding the scale of cities. However, such a transition doesn't necessarily follow up with supportive industrial networks or good business that could provide enough work opportunities. Thus, it is not a rare phenomenon for suburban peasants to have a negative attitude and even to resist this kind of urbanization, and their urbanization could be described as passive (Yu 2005).

In this case history, the village peasants had already encountered this kind of passive urbanization since early 1990s. During their process of passive urbanization, confrontations would happen between the local government and peasants due to the different appeals of interests. Obviously, local government usually controls far more resources than peasants and could achieve its purposes. However, from this case history we will find out that there is another aspect for us to understand the relationship between local government and peasants.

In 2002, Xichuan city government carried out the "Large Xichuan Strategy" and brought about a typical phenomenon of passive urbanization in its suburb area.

Ba village is located in a connecting zone between urban and rural areas, and it confronted the problem of land expropriation very early. In 1990, 1995, 1998, and 2001, local government performed land expropriation four times. The price that the government paid to local peasants was different in each time. In 1995, the price of each Mu land that the local government gave peasants was 8,000 RMB. After 2000, following the rise of land prices in the market, and at the request of the peasants, the price of land expropriation started to rise. Along with this urbanization and land expropriation, after 2000, more and more peasants in this village went to Xichuan City and tried to find a job there. Agriculture was no longer the most important livelihood in this village.

We met this story in our fieldwork under such a circumstance.

4 The Rural Democracy Event

4.1 *The Village Politics*

Ba village has 104 households and more than 300 people. The largest kinship in Ba village is the S family, which has more than 30 households. This family kinship is a very tight social group. And this is one of the most important reasons that this family kinship was the most powerful family in Ba village before 2001. Among this kinship, the Old-S-father worked as village head from 1966 to 1978. After 1978, his three sons—SYL, SYK, and SUL—followed him and continued to take key positions in this village, such as the village head (SYK and SUL), CPC committee member and accountant (SYL). Since this family kinship had been at the center of village power before 2001, they were called the S-dynasty in Ba village by peasants. Another large family kinship in this village is Z family. The Z family also has more than 30 households. However, Z family members were not as tight as those of the S family, nor were they enthusiastic about village politics. Besides S and Z families, there were some other small families in the village, including a household with family name of W. Family W is a migration family. They moved into the Ba village in 1990s. In Ba village, the W family was in a marginal status in village politics. Most of the villagers did not like them because none of the three brothers from this family did farm work, which usually means non-stable life in local culture. In the villagers' opinion, they did not have decent jobs and were like idlers. Among the three brothers, the big brother, WS, is their head. He used to work in large cities and had several different jobs, including some odd jobs in construction business. Later on, he became a labor contractor. Besides the S family and Z family, most of the families in this village were ordinary peasants before 2001. And these kinds of families consist of the largest groups in this village.

The story of this rural democracy started from WS's request.

4.2   Checking Account

Along with the process of urbanization, the land expropriation fees for local government were getting higher and higher. And as a rule, a certain percentage of the expropriation fees were kept by the village committee as collective property. According to the rule, the property of the village was kept and managed by the local government as collective property. So, a large amount of the money that belongs to the villagers was held by local government. In our fieldwork, villagers told me that they were not satisfied with this kind of distribution. And they were worrying that the money was being illegally allocated or spent by the local government officials. However, they did not have any clear evidence, so the general attitude among villagers was to bet the village head to "watch" the money for them and would return to them someday in the near future.

Meanwhile, all of the villagers knew that an important reason that the S family could stay at the center of the village politics was because they were very "obedient to the local government" and "the local government liked them". So, they had every reason to believe that S family was not very honest with them.

In early 2001, WS, the big brother from the W family, reported to the local government that the village head of the Ba village, the SYK, had an "economic problem": he had embezzled part of the land expropriation fees. It seemed that WS prepared very carefully before doing this: he wrote a report and listed 21 issues about SYK's bad behaviors in order to prove that he was not qualified to work as village head anymore. Given the strong evidence he reported, the local government had to send out a work team to Ba village to investigate SYK's economic issues. As the result of this investigation, 2 issues of the 21 items were confirmed. Although the related money was less than 9,000 RMB, and SYK himself had found excuses to explain it, he could no longer maintain his position. WS's purpose was to hit the S family, to shake their powerful position in the village but he only achieved the target partly. The S family was still strongly supported by the local government and the village committee. The decision they made was to ask the S family's big brother, SYL, to replace his second brother, continuing the S family's powerful status in the village.

There was an unpredicted effect for WS: the trust from villagers. WS started to build up his own authority and get support from many villagers because he did successfully prove that the "checking account"—the investigation—was a reasonable request and SYK did have economic issues. However, WS was not satisfied with this ending.

4.3   *The Petition Event*

The aim of WS was very simple: to become the village head. To achieve this target, he had to successfully persuade the local government to carry out a new village election. However, his influence was not strong enough in the local government, this work seemed just about impossible.

In June 2003, WS and his close supporters wrote a letter to the local government. In this letter, WS stated very clearly that most of the land expropriation fees were kept by the local government. And he expressed a strong will that the villagers wanted the money back. With this letter, WS visited almost all of the households in the village and asked peasants to sign it. He promised that he would negotiate with the local government as the villagers' representative to retrieve the money for them. Most of the villagers signed the letter, even including those people from the S kinship. So WS got a letter, with almost all of the signatures from the village.

However, before he went to the local government, WS changed the content of the letter. He kept those signature page but changed the content page. The letter became a petition with most of the villagers' names subscribed: they wanted to change the village head, and they wanted to hold a new village election.

The local government had concern about this letter because of those signatures. However, this was not enough to change their minds. WS also prepared another gift. As a former labor contractor, he was familiar with the contracting market. He performed a personal investigation and had found that the properties were allocated by the local government in order to build up a new local market zone. And in this process, there must be some officers who were not clean. With this guess, he warned the local government that the only thing he wanted to have was a new round of election in his village. If he could not get what he wanted, he would reveal the evidence, which he actually did not have, and report them to the upper level's authorities.

With message from the S family, local officers had already known that WS was not an easygoing ordinary peasant. On the other hand, after all, all he wanted was a new round of election. Given the powerful position of the S kinship in village, the local government believed that this request was only WS's own farce. Thence they agreed with WS's request and decided to hold another election in Ba village. It was not until this decision was made that most of the villagers, including S family members, realized that the content of the letter was not about retrieving money for them. But it was too late: the local government had already started the procedures.

On the other hand, in order to appease the villagers' anger about his cheating behavior, WS made a bolder promise to the villagers: if he was elected, not only would he get their money back, he would also find a construction company and build two-story houses for each household at a very low price so that they did not have to pay too much for it besides the money that the local government kept away from them.

His plans and budget seemed very clear. He knew how much money they would get back from government: 4.5 million RMB in total. Surely there was still a shortfall in the budget for his plan of houses for villagers. However, he promised that he could find a construction company that would like to do the job first and take the money after. And WS believed that the villagers could get more money in the near future from further land expropriation from the local government. And they could pay the rest of the money with that new income. The purpose of WS was clear: he wanted to show the villagers that he did not want to become village head only for his own interests, but for the interests of all the villagers. In our fieldwork of 2003, we knew that the only thing that most of the villagers worried about was the possible corruption from the new village head. However, WS clearly indicated that since the budget of building houses for them was clear and clean, he could not embezzle any money for himself. On the country, he might even put his own money into this construction budget. Throughout this clear budget, WS successfully rebuilt his new positive image in front of the villagers. And he thus made a fully preparation for the election with two candidates: WS and the present village head SYL.

4.4 *Two Rounds of Elections*

The first round of election was resisted by whole kinship of the S family. The reason was simple: WS persuaded the local officers to put the ballot box in his own house. WS thought that this could make himself influential in the election. However, as a tight group, all of the people from the S kinship refused to go. According to the election rule, the peasants who actually voted must exceed the half of the village who should vote. Thus, with the boycott from S family kinship, the first round of election did not get enough tickets to be valid.

WS still believed that he could get elected if there were enough votings. The only problem for him was to get enough people to vote. His plan for the second election included three parts: (1) he suggested the local government use the local middle school for the election, and he asked the chief executive of the local township government to come to supervise the election; (2) he asked the local government to announce that everybody who came to vote, no matter for whom he/she voted, would get an award of 50 RMB (after he was elected, he paid those voters through the village's public funds); and (3) he secretly mobilized enough people who would vote for him. He did the mobilization work under the table mostly because he clearly realized that no family in this village would like to offend S family on his behalf. So this kind of secret mobilization made him even more popular.

Meanwhile, the S family was too optimistic about the election. And the successful boycott of the first round made them believe that WS was nothing but a clown. Thus in the second round of election, all of the 33 households of the S kinship went to vote. Their thoughts were just like what SYK's wife told us in our fieldwork: "at that time, our chief executive of government called us to vote. Everybody who went there will get 50 RMB, no matter if you vote or not, and no matter who you vote for. So, who would not like to go? Everybody went there and voted happily".

The S family thought that they would get the money and that WS would still lose this election.

However, the result was that WS got more than 60 votes and SYL only got 33, exactly the number of the S household. This brought a huge change in Ba village and the S dynasty finally ended. However, many people from the S family could not accept this result and in our fieldwork, SYL's wife even told us that she believed WS cheated in the counting of the ballots. However, her claim got no evidence to prove. Even the leader of the S family at that time, Mr SYL, did not have doubts about this result. This rural democracy that was supervised by local government was totally valid.

4.5   *The Weapon of the Peasants*

Thus, WS became the new village head. But what kind of village head would he be? In our fieldwork of 2003, we heard about some of his performances after he became the village head.

Firstly, he did ask for the money back. There were more than 4 million RMB that he asked back from the local government. And he did use the money to start fulfilling his promise about the houses. There was another story about how he used the strategy that the S family would not use in the time of S dynasty. He threatened the local government with two things: (1) the evidence that he had about their corruptions; and (2) in 2002, Xichuan City hosted an international Auto And Motorcycle Tourism Festival. That was the largest international event for Xichuan in 2002. Right before the opening ceremony of the festival, WS went to the local government and threatened the chief executer that he would mobilize his villagers to protest in front of the ceremony if the government did not return the money back to them. Given that thousands of foreigners and journalists were coming to the city, the local government decided to give him what he wanted and made him satisfied.

Secondly, however, in our interview with WS's daughter, we realized that the construction company that WS hired to build up houses for villagers had a very close relationship with him. And not surprisingly, we heard that he got a lot of interests from that company.

Thirdly, in 2003, the city government did carry out a new round of land expropriation in this village. As part of the plan of building up "big Xichuan", the Xichuan city government decided to expropriate a large amount of land from suburban areas, including 200 Mu of land from the Ba village. However, local villagers were not satisfied with the price that the Xichuan government gave them, and the negotiation between the villagers and government broke up, the government decided to expropriate their land by force. And thus, conflict broke out between the peasants and government. Many local peasants were arrested in the conflict. According to the words of a peasant, "all those men who wear peaked caps (policemen) in Xichuan city came to our village". However, in this conflict, WS disappeared. Some of our interviewee told us that he might be there on the scene but did not do anything. On the night of the conflict, he signed the contract and started to persuade his villagers to sign it. He still had a strategy to do this. He let people know that the first 20 households who signed the contract would get 300–500 RMB higher than other people in terms of the price per Mu. His strategy was proved to be successful again. Most of the peasants went to his house and signed the contract. Not long after he worked as the village head, he proved that he had no difference from anyone in the S-dynasty.

In 2005, when our team went back to revisit our interviewee, my teammate found that the townhouses that he promised the villagers were almost finished. However, he asked every household that wanted to buy the house to pay a certain percentage of the fee before they were allowed to move in. And of course, some families could not afford the price. Thus it was becoming another public issue in the village and WS did not provide a solution before our fieldwork team left.

In our later fieldworks we learned that after 2010, along with the progress of urbanization, this village became part of Xichuan city. WS lost his position due to many reasons, including his age, his education background and different political structure in urban area. "he was just not qualified anymore to work in urban area", a local officer told us. It seems that urbanization in China has already abandoned the traditional peasants, but we found more similar stories in our fieldwork with the story of WS. Young generations in China, no matter in countryside or in urban area, repeat the stories of their parents again in urban China.

The various aspects of social realities we observed from this case can be seen as an analogy to China's current political and social issues. It thus helps us to develop a holistic understanding of the phenomena, mechanisms, and issues in China's political and social transition process.

In the interactions between government and peasants, surely there is space for peasants to make a bargaining. The peasants also had their own thoughts on the local politics, community, and their own choices. From this perspective, we refuse to describe the peasants as chess men that are controlled, mobilized, or constructed passively in a large transition of the history: we would like to describe them as a social group with initiative. Meanwhile, those officers who work in the government are also part of this social group. The community that they live in makes it easy for them to choose a similar attitude. They have their own thoughts, interests, and plans about their own choices. And it is hard to change them, not even through revolution and urbanization.

5   Self-Production of Society and Sociological Studies in China

In their works, Yang and Sun ask this question: How can we understand the internal operational mechanism of Chinese society? As the core question of Chinese sociological scholars' efforts in building up the subjectivity of China's sociology, the answer to this question demands a thorough understanding of China's society and even the sociology itself. Yang and Sun raise the concept of *social ground*, which refers to those "unchanged/stable subjects" in the history of Chinese society. They find that after the Cultural Revolution, some factors of traditional China's culture emerged quickly, especially family-oriented culture. Although China's society is undergoing a huge change, just like what we can observe from the story of WS, there are some traditional cultural factors that are always unchanged. On the contrary, traditional cultural factors can come back, combine with the new historical condition and produce new possibilities of history while keeping its deepest historical meanings. We call this self-production of society in China.

Such finding is very close to the famous term *cultural self-consciousness* (文化自觉) that was raised by Fei Xiaotong in his late period (Fei 2013). It might even be proper to say that the studies of social self-production in China and the *social ground* are part of efforts of sociological studies on cultural consciousness in China.

Thus from the social equilibrium to the self-production of society or social ground, there is a transition of China's Sociological recognition on China's society. This transition, however, cannot answer the question of where China should/would go and only bring more questions. Certainly China should have its own way of modernization and China's sociology should respect its own society. However, this brings more questions for China's sociologists: Can we say that China's society cannot be transformed eventually into modern society and will remain its core characteristics forever? Or can we say that China's sociological studies actually confirm the famous comments made by some Western scholars such as Hegel and Max Weber? There are no answer to these questions. China is still going on huge changes. Where China would go? It might take more than one hundred of years to answer these questions since these questions have been raised around 1900s.

References

Fei, Xiaotong. 2009. *Complete Works of Fei Xiaotong*. Huhhot: Inner Mongolia People's Publisher.

Fei, Xiaotong. 2013. *Globalization and Cultural Self-Awareness*. Beijing: Foreign Language Teaching and Research Press.

Guo, Yuhua, and Liping Sun. 2002. "Shuku: yizhong nongming guojia guannian xingcheng de zhongjie jizhi" [Speaking Bitterness: The Formation of Peasant Concepts of Nationalism]. *China Scholarship* 12 (4): 130–157.

Huang, Philip. 1985. *The Peasant Economy and Social Change in North China*. Palo Alto, CA: Stanford University Press.

Malinowski, B. 1939. "Preface of Peasant Life in China: A Field Study of Country Life in the Yantze Valley". In *Peasant Life in China: A Field Study of Country Life in the Yantze Valley*, edited by Xiaotong Fei, xix–xxvi. London: George Routledge and Sons Ltd.

Oi, Jean C. 1989. *State and Peasant in Contemporary China: The Political Economy of Village Government*. Berkeley: University of California Press.

Pan, Guangdan. (1928) 2000. "China's Family Issues". In *Collective Works of Pan Guangdan*. Vol. 1. Beijing: Beijing University Press.

Pan, Guangdan. (1933) 2000. "The Education That Forgets Roots". In *Collective Works of Pan Guangdan*, Vol. 8, 554–557. Beijing: Beijing University Press.

Strauch, Judith. 1981. *Chinese Village Politics in the Malaysian State*. Cambridge, MA: Harvard University Press.

Sun, Feiyu. 2013. *Social Suffering and Political Confession: Suku in Modern China*. Singapore: World Scientific Press.

Sun, Feiyu, Huijuan Chu, and Yanlong Zhang. 2018. "Producing Society or the Self-Producing of Society? A Study of an NGO's Difficult Situation on Poverty Reduction". *Chinese Journal of Sociology* 4: 151–185.

Yan, Fu. 1895. *Yuan Qiang*. Zhi Bao (直报).

Yang, Qingmei. 2010. *The Last Gentry: Taking Fei Xiaotong as a Case Study of Anthropological History*. Beijing: World Publishing Corporation.

Yang, Shanhua, and Feiyu Sun. 2015. "On Social Ground: Fieldwork Experience and Thoughts". *Chinese Journal of Sociology* 35: 74–91.

Yu, Hongqiang. 2005. *Unequal Contests Between Local Government and Peasant as Viewed from Passive Urbanization: A Reinterpretation of State and Society in China*. PhD dissertation. Sociology Department, Peking University, Beijing, China.

Zhang, Guansheng. 2000. *Fei Xiaotong Biography*. Beijing: Qunyan Press.

Zhang, Jing. 2017. "What Makes a Unique Peking Sociology? Fei Xiaotong's *Peasant Life in China* as an Example". *Sociological Studies* 32: 24–30.

CHAPTER 22

Sociology without Society: The Dreyfus Affair, the Taigyaku Affair, and the Sociology of Life

Kikutani Kazuhiro

1   Introduction

While writing this article, which took almost a year, I suddenly received some disturbing news. I was informed that I had cancer. Soon after this, I had to undergo a series of heavy medical treatments, which hurt me physically and mentally a great deal. Having no choice in the matter, this special year of time had me fundamentally reconsider the meaning of social life and Life itself.

I would like to take this opportunity to present my reconsideration in line with the theme of this book through reviewing two affairs, one of which took place in France and the other in Japan. The persistent question that lies throughout this article is whether or not "society" that is originated from the Occident could also exist in the Orient, and whether or not the Orient could have some form of "sociology".

2   Dreyfus Affair

We will look first at the Dreyfus Affair as an introduction to the subject of this article, which is to "pose a question about society itself". The reason for this is because the Dreyfus Affair radically shows the conflicts that exist between society, the state, and individuals. At the same time, it also displays differences in "society" between the Occident and the Orient, which are clarified in the latter part of this chapter in an attempt to compare France's Dreyfus Affair to Japan's Taigyaku Affair.

The Dreyfus Affair is widely known today, along with the name of Émile Zola, a great French novelist, not only in France, where the incident occurred, but also in other parts of Europe and the world. It has been repeatedly made into movies. Therefore, instead of going into detail about the incident, I will just cover the outline within the range of the main subject of this article.

The Dreyfus Affair is an incident of false accusation that took place in France in the late 19th century. It is no doubt remembered as an epoch-making event in modern social history that shook the foundation of the French Third

Republic itself. The Dreyfus Affair first broke out as spying allegations made against a soldier. Combined with anti-Semitic sentiment, the case triggered a conflict over the principle of social integration, which later divided the society between those advocating for the reign by the military and the state, whose authority comes from the sacred and inviolable nature on which Catholicism forms its backbone, and those advocating the reign of a republic that claims universal human rights.

Back in 1894 a memo was found in France, where a mood of bitterness that stemmed from being defeated in a war with Germany was still lingering. The memo bore information providing evidence that confidential communication exchanged among military members had been leaked to the German side. Based on the fragile evidence that "an artillery officer whose name begins with D" was behind the leakage of military secrets, Lieutenant Alfred Dreyfus was marked as the suspect of this incident.

However, a survey conducted on Dreyfus revealed different images about his background and personality, all of which hinted he was far from a spy. Dreyfus was born into a wealthy family who came from Alsace to seek shelter. He was a promising soldier who graduated from a military college with honors. He was in no debt and was leading a pleasant life. But there was one thing counting against him. He was a Jew.

France was the nation in Europe that first gave citizenship to the Jews. Because of this policy, Jews in France had more chances to participate in various fields of society. This also brought the consequence of anti-Semitism sweeping across the nation at all levels of society.

Dreyfus was arrested on the spot on suspicion of treason when the Department of the Army, which had ordered him to appear, reasoned that his handwriting patterns on a letter he was asked to write were identical to those on the memo.

The arrest of Dreyfus was treated as a military secret at first. But it was not long before the secret was leaked to the media and became widely known as a political scandal across France, especially after some anti-Semitic papers made headlines out of the incident. It was obvious that the arrest of Dreyfus was no longer a personal spy case. The fact that a spy was found inside the French military, which was considered sacred, and he was a Jew added a sense of shock among people from various backgrounds who were already appalled just by the arrest of a German spy. The Dreyfus case posed a question regarding the fundamental principles of how to integrate the people of France. The issue here is whether the sovereign power to integrate the people of France lies in the state (embodied by the military), even if there is no choice but to make an innocent Jewish man a scapegoat for national reasons (*raison d'État*), or in universal human rights that are equally given to all individuals.

A court-martial was held. Whether right or wrong, the French military needed to make Dreyfus guilty to defend authority as a national force. In the end, the military succeeded in convicting him by fabricating the evidence against him. Dreyfus was stripped of the status of a soldier. Only a year and a half after the incident, he was transferred to a sweltering prison on Devil's Island, off the coast of French Guiana, South America, where he eventually spent 4 long years in confinement.

3   Émile Zola: Proponent of Naturalism

The situation surrounding those backing Dreyfus was overwhelmingly disadvantageous. To make matters worse, the "Affair" gradually faded from people's memory after Dreyfus' imprisonment, with a growing sense that the "Affair" itself had become a past event. However, on the January 13, 1898, Émile Zola, the proponent of naturalistic literature who had been known for a number of sharp social criticisms, expressed his view in an open letter titled "J'Accuse…!" (I Accuse…!), addressed to the president of the republic. The letter was published in the paper *L'Aurore*.

Zola's letter reversed the situation. In the open letter, Zola aggressively argued for Dreyfus' innocence based on bare facts by disclosing the conspiracy inside the military with the real names of those who were involved in it. Zola's acts of revealing the truth of Dreyfus' case were presented in such a way that an accusation was widely directed to all the people living together in society rather than restricting the boundary to the parties who were closely related to the "Affair", such as the military staff and Jewish people.

> People take fright at the appalling light that has just been shed on it [French War Office] all by the Dreyfus Affair, that tale of human sacrifice! Yes, an unfortunate, a "dirty Jew" has been sacrificed. Yes, what an accumulation of madness, stupidity, unbridled imagination, low police tactics, inquisitorial and tyrannical methods this handful of officers have got away with! …
>
> … and now the rogues are triumphant and insolent while law and integrity go down in defeat…. France, the great and liberal cradle of the rights of man, will die of anti-Semitism if it is not cured of it. It is a crime to play on patriotism to further the aims of hatred. And it is a crime to worship the sabre as a modern god when all of human science is labouring to hasten the triumph of truth and justice.
>   ZOLA 1898: 928–929 = 50–51

Zola's letter sparked a wave of shock and much controversy among the common people. It provoked such huge responses that public opinion was sharply split, and clashes between anti- and pro-Dreyfus protesters erupted on the streets of France, some of which escalated into large-scale riots. Zola's attempt to appeal to the public by putting his article in a paper certainly aroused people's awareness that the Dreyfus case should be understood not as a personal spying issue or, in other words, a mere Semitic issue, but as a human rights issue involving all human beings. Conversely, it can be said that Zola's letter of accusation attracted public attention based on the existence of the "people" who are ready to take in Zola's calling in the process of forming public opinion.

Whether it was tragic or inevitable, Zola was arrested for slander for causing the social confusion that his accusation brought about. Although there was a short period of legal battle, he was soon convicted. Upon receiving judgment, he was forced to go into exile in the United Kingdom. Zola, a novelist, who had no personal connection with Alfred Dreyfus or the other parties concerned, confronted the injustice with a belief that the truth and universal humanity rather than the State are the basis of human association, knowing his involvement brings no benefit to him. In spirit, Zola martyred himself for his faith in "people", so to speak.

Owing to Zola's selfless act of accusation, the "Affair" had gathered a great deal of international attention. Facing the situation this way, the national military could no longer ignore public opinion, and the retrial was started in 1899, a year after "J'Accuse…!" was published. Surprisingly, or in fact rather naturally, the national military stuck to the initial allegation at the retrial. As a result, Dreyfus was convicted again, yet 10 days later he received a pardon granted by the president. Therefore, the Dreyfus case was politically settled.

Even after the settlement, Dreyfus and his supporters continued their efforts to seek approval of the truth and redemption of his honor, which became a reality seven years later when the Court of Appeal revoked his conviction in 1906. Dreyfus was finally readmitted to the military service with his honor restored. That incident symbolizes a victory of trust in humanity that Émile Zola, a naturalistic novelist, had persistently held in his pursuit of human truth.

4   Taigyaku Affair

Here we turn our eyes to the Orient, namely Japan. I will note a false accusation case similar to the Dreyfus Affair that took place a little while after it. However, the incident, which is called the Taigyaku Affair (literally, the affair of high treason), took a different course, ending with a contrasting result, when compared to the Dreyfus Affair. What this incident symbolizes is the absence of a litterateur like Zola, a failure to arouse public opinion, and the execution of innocent persons who were accused of a crime.

I will start by going into the details of this incident, which is probably not well known in the Occident, before examining the aspects that differ from the Dreyfus affair, as well as their meaning. Consequently, comparing these two affairs will provide us with an insight into "society" in both Occidental and Oriental terms. Unlike the Dreyfus Affair, in which Alfred Dreyfus was the only defendant, the Taigyaku Affair is more complex in that there were a large number of defendants, and it is not right to say all of them were falsely accused.

Therefore, in the following part, to make a clear comparison with the Dreyfus Affair we will focus on Shusui Kotoku, a socialist and an anarchist who was regarded as the mastermind behind the Taigyaku Affair, even though it was undeniable that he was falsely accused. Back in early 20th-century Japan nationalism was gradually rising. At the same time, socialism and anarchism were also gaining momentum as an opposing force, one against which the imperial Japanese government stayed vigilant, marking this movement as a threat. Especially following the assassination of ex-Prime Minister Hirobumi Ito in 1902, extreme tension had taken hold of the government, where a sense of "might be murdered" had become realistic, and this sense of insecurity shaped an attitude of "take action first or be killed".

Meanwhile, on May 25, 1910, some materials for the production of explosives were found in the hidden part of a sawmill building located in Akashina, Nagano Prefecture. This was the moment that the Taigyaku Affair broke out, later known as a big event in which Shusui Kotoku and his followers were accused of planning to assassinate the emperor, and were finally executed for high treason.

Immediately the police investigated Takichi Miyashita, the owner of these materials. Based on his confession on May 29 that the purpose of the explosives was for the assassination of the emperor, a preliminary trial of Shusui Kotoku and 7 others was requested of the Great Court of Cassation (today's Supreme Court) only two days later, on May 31. The trial began immediately. Kotoku was prosecuted on the same day, without being given a chance to be examined, on suspicion of violating the Penal Code Article 73, which regulates the acts of harming or intending to harm the imperial family. In other words, it was concluded as high treason.

Penal Code Article 73 states: "A person who harms or intends to harm the Emperor, Grand Empress Dowager, Empress Dowager, Empress, Crown Prince, or Grandson of the Emperor shall be punished by the death penalty". In other words, it permits authorities to accuse those having motives to harm the imperial family even they do not take action to do so. Furthermore, the death penalty is the only option prescribed in the law. On the June 1, the day after the prosecution, Shusui Kotoku was arrested in Yugawara, where he was editing and writing his works.

In the following 4 months, the government identified a number of possible suspects nationwide who could have been involved in the assassination plan, and detained them for reasons such as "he is the author of an article that has influenced Miyashita", "he was once close to Miyashita", or "he could do, he should be doing", etc., all of which had no substantial grounds. Eventually, a total of 26 suspects had been prosecuted as defendants for high treason.

The trial began on the December 10 at the Great Court of Cassation. However, the trial was never made open to the public due to the reason that an open trial was detrimental to public peace and order. Moreover, all requests for calling a witness were rejected. In short, the whole process was carried out in a secretive manner in which nobody other than legal professionals and the defendants themselves was given a chance to witness the trial process, and there was no sufficient investigation into the evidence. On the December 25, the prosecutor demanded the death penalty for all the defendants, and the trial was concluded on the December 29, less than 3 weeks from the beginning of the trial. The judgment was delivered on the January 18, only 39 days from the beginning of the trial. Of course, the trial at the Great Court of Cassation was "the first and the final trial". That is what it was: there were no other options, and there was no chance of appeal.

In this judgment, Kotoku and 23 of his close associates were sentenced to death as was requested, and two others were sentenced to imprisonment with a definite term. However, on the January 19, the Meiji emperor granted a special pardon, and 12 of the defendants had their sentences commuted to life imprisonment. Then on the January 24, which was 45 days from the beginning of the trial and 6 days from the delivery of the judgment, and the following day, the execution of all the 12 defendants, including Kotoku, was carried out at the gallows in Tokyo Prison. Thus, the "Affair" was politically settled. Later research found that the direct evidence used to implicate Kotoku's involvement in this incident was only his chats in November 1908.

On the November 19, 1908, Kotoku seemed to have enjoyed chats with his old friends. The chats may have gone as far as talking about the topic of how to grab the power of the nation overnight with reference to Paris Commune, which could be interpreted as having motives for a revolution. This meeting, later named the "November Conspiracy", was only a drinking party, an informal gathering of its kind, containing some casual chats or free discussion. However, this gathering was interpreted as a "conspiracy" to plan an assassination of the emperor, with Kotoku believed to have been taking part in it, and later became definitive evidence of Kotoku's guilt in the Taigyaku Affair. Kotoku was identified as the mastermind of this incident, based on an unsubstantiated scenario made up by the national authority in which it concluded, according to the authority, that what they called "members of a suicidal mission" were recruited to carry out an assassination plan decided in what is regarded as a "Conspiracy for Treason", where some informal chats were exchanged.

In fact, Matsukichi Komiyama, the prosecutor in charge, later confessed as follows;

> All the government officials then agreed the possibility that *Denjiro Kotoku* [= *Shusui Kotoku*] *was not part of the incident could hardly be ruled out*.... Miyashita, inspired with anarcho-communism by Kotoku, had become his follower and so it was impossible to conclude that Kotoku was not part of the incident.... *Although evidence was fragile*, government officials had come to a conclusion that it was right to accuse Kotoku as well.
>
> KOYAMA 1929: 351–352; italics mine

The fact is that Kotoku seemed to have opposed Miyashita's plan to assassinate the emperor. For example, the following statement remains as Miyashita's response to the investigation: "When I talked about this [the plan to assassinate the Emperor] with Kotoku around January 1909, he did not agree with me, saying he can't do it and should not be doing such a violent thing" (ibid.: 350). After all, just like Alfred Dreyfus, Kotoku was arrested, accused, and sentenced by the national authority for being "suspicious", just for that reason alone, and unlike Alfred Dreyfus, Kotoku was sentenced to death.

Here, the following questions can be raised. What causes these differences? Why is it that Zola didn't appear in Japan?

5 Kafu Nagai: A Literary Giant Who Could Not Become "Japan's Zola"

> In 1911 when I was on my way to Keio University where I was teaching, I chanced to see five or six prisoner wagons go past Yotsuya in succession, heading toward the Court House in Hibiya. Of all the public incidents I have ever witnessed or heard of, I have never felt as unspeakably ghastly as I did at this moment. As a litterateur, I must not keep silent about this question of principles. I know Zola, a French novelist, had to go into exile because he cried for justice in the Dreyfus Affair. But I, along with other litterateurs, said nothing. I somehow feel an unbearable agony

of conscience. I was extremely ashamed of myself as a litterateur. Since then, I considered that I could do no better than dragging the quality of my own art down to the level produced by the writers of frivolous and vulgar fiction in Edo Era.... The frivolous writers and Ukiyo-e masters at the end of Edo Era saw such things as the coming of the Black Ships to Uraga, and the assassination of the Senior Minister at Sakurada Gate as a matter of no interest to them, the common people. They thought it is better to know their place and remain silent. Instead of denying this, I thought I'd better respect rather than despise their intentions in the moment of creating their erotic novels and prints.

NAGAI 1919b: 256

This is a part of an article written by Kafu Nagai (1879–1959), a Japanese novelist who by accident witnessed the prisoner wagons on which members of the accused—Shusui Kotoku and others—were riding. It was written 8 years after the Taigyaku Affair (also known as the Kotoku Affair) by recalling his impressions and thoughts at that time. As he was aware, Kafu Nagai, a literary giant, was certainly standing in the same position as Émile Zola. However, Nagai, a naturalistic novelist who had respected Zola and been greatly influenced by him, did nothing to protest Kotoku's case, in spite of his personal knowledge about the human condition of French society from his valuable experience of staying in France in those days. No, to be accurate, he could not. The news about Kotoku's court trial was secretly conveyed to him from some sources. It was clear that Kotoku was falsely accused. He tried to stand up as "Japan's Zola" in spirit but failed in that. Because of his quietness, he was so ashamed and recognized himself as a hypocrite or a fake, just like the frivolous writers and Ukiyo-e masters would do. Why?

It is not difficult to assume that Nagai's resisting spirit might have been hindered before the strong power of the imperial Japanese government. However, the situation was the same as with the French Third Republic in the Dreyfus Affair. In fact, Zola was put on trial and was forced into exile. Therefore, the reason Nagai could not become Japan's Zola lies in a problem deeper than just a political one. There is some "social" reason. Here is Nagai's account on the issue of the government's ban on the publication of his work *Furansu Monogatari* (*Tales of France*), which was written based on his valuable experience of staying in France in those days. He describes as follows, suggestive of Zola in the Dreyfus Affair:

What I am up against is the government, a strong power, and I am only a weak man of letters. The art of France is now enjoying its liberty and independence. But how many men of letters in France fought desperately for their rights of art…. I have looked back on some court cases in France. Given that no man of letters in Japan has ever fought for liberty before, we cannot help the situation where liberty of art is not recognized in Japanese society. So, I feel I must fight for liberty, yet when it comes to the issue of whether my effort is worth a victory, my heart goes hesitant once my thought is on *the general public spirit of French society. Gaining sympathy from people in society is indispensable if we want to win rights in a battle with the authority.* Judging from many cases, *how much power is given to that movement of a man of letters by sympathy that flows from the people of France in general who love liberty and respect art.*

Now turning our eyes to Japan, *Japan does not seem to need liberty and art as much as France does. Only a small number of social outsiders who have read Western books want them.* Having a thought of establishing independent art in such a society is just like growing fruits in a desert.

NAGAI 1909: 332–333; italics mine

In addition, Nagai recorded as follows in his diary in the same year that he wrote the beginning part of the above citation: "*The absence of awakenedness to being an individual* is no different from the feudal Era" (Nagai 1919a: 76; italics mine). The meaning of these words becomes increasingly clear in the course of Japan's history in which the nation had intensified militarism and rushed toward the war. Nagai's diary continues as follows:

It's unbelievable that the social condition of the present day resembles that of Edo town in the Tenpo Era in a sense that the government and its officials exercise their power in everything and *ordinary people accept the authorities obediently.*

NAGAI 1929: 297; italics mine

[Even when the government prohibits them from eating polished rice and order them to eat half-polished rice instead,] they just keep quiet and follow the instruction. I'm amazed that *the nationals are obedient and passive.*

NAGAI 1939: 328; italics mine

I have learned … *the difference between Christian culture and Confucian culture.*… Corruption of the government, extremism of the military, and poor awareness among nationals are the sources of modern Japan's calamity. Corruption of the government and extremism of the military all *stem from poor awareness among ordinary nationals.* These are attributable to the *absence of awakenedness to being an individual.* Therefore, it is meaningless to put hope in the prospects for individuals' awakenedness.

NAGAI 1936: 387; italics mine

In other words, unlike the French people in the Dreyfus Affair, the Japanese had been obedient to the state for a long period of time. They were just obedient to such an extent that no complaints were expressed even about the food that affects directly their lives. The Japanese did not feel the need for liberty, let alone art, in the first place. Inevitably, the Japanese have never experienced the history of confronting the state in the process of winning the status of the people, in other words, "social human beings". *The universal human rights that Zola cried out and the human society that assisted with Zola's accusation did not exist in Japan when Nagai lived.*

It is exactly this situation, the reality of Japan in those days that Nagai's cries in which he expressed "poor awareness among ordinary nationals" and "the absence of awakenedness to being an individual" reflected. The Japanese nationals are not aware that they are individuals. In that sense, the Japanese nationals are not awakened to the fact that they are all human beings. At the root of this issue lies the fundamental difference between Christian culture and Confucian culture. Nagai assumed that the prospects of the Japanese awakening to it were bleak. This is the very despairing "social" reason Nagai could not stand as Japan's Zola.

People did not exist in Japan, so neither did individuals. What existed were only nationals of the imperial Japanese government, or, precisely speaking, the emperor and his subjects. They were nationals with no originality and creativity, which was the same as being replaceable segments and parts constituting the state of Japan, the empire that continues its policy of modernization and nationalization.

That means that a society in the Western sense did not exist in Japan. It seems that such a society, which consists of individuals, or, in other words, consists of human beings with universal humanity, does not exist at least in a sufficient form in this constitutional monarchy, which even today still has an emperor over our heads. The definition of nationals is mistaken for that of human beings, and also there is no clear distinction between the state, which consists of the former, and the society, which consists of the latter. There is no clear line that distinguishes the state from society. For this reason, the family that has neither Japanese nationality nor citizenship, and, in that sense, whose human rights are not granted, is still institutionalized as the indispensable "crown" of the nation.

6 Reality of Society and the Individual, Reality of Sociology

The above is an overview of two similar affairs of false accusation that took place almost at the same time, one in the Occident, France, and the other in the Orient, Japan. What causes were involved in these contrasting results? It was the "presence or absence of people in general" and the "presence or absence of awakened individuals"—in simple terms, the "presence or absence of society". Unlike in Zola's France, in Nagai's Japan there was no awakening of an individual's creativity, no ordinary people in pursuit of liberty and art, and no people who confronted the state to win these. This means that Japan had been unable to produce the soil, namely, society. Then, a question arises as to whether or not it is possible for such "a nation without society" to have "sociology", a discipline that has its origins in the Occident and takes the Occidental society as a given.

We are reminded of Nagai's words as saying that the Japanese are obedient and passive, the Japanese have no will to seek liberty and art. There is no awakening to being an individual among the Japanese. Considering that Nagai was a writer and a creator, these words can be interpreted as pointing out that the Japanese are short of creativity or, more precisely, lack "the will to create".

However, what exactly is "society", the "individual", or a "human being" anyway? And what is sociology?

6.1 *Creation of Sociology: Émile Durkheim, the Founder of Sociology*

We try to ask this radical question of Émile Durkheim, a founder of sociology, who insisted on "treating social facts as things" and declared their objective reality. Durkheim's positivist sociology, which became a foundation of modern sociology, was established through critically reviewing and overcoming the metaphysical approach proposed by the "sociologists" of the previous generations, such as Auguste Comte and Herbert Spencer. It has unexpectedly inherited quite a bit of the social organism theory in terms of the notion of society itself. The following part of Durkheim's work, *The Rules of Sociological Method*, typically explains this.

> The living cell contains nothing save chemical particles, just as society is made up of nothing except individuals. Yet it is very clearly impossible for the characteristic phenomena of life to reside in atoms of hydrogen, oxygen, carbon and nitrogen…. Life cannot be split up in this fashion. It is one, and consequently cannot be located save in the living substance in its entirety. It is in the whole and not in the parts….

> Let us apply this principle to sociology. If ... this synthesis *sui generis* [italics by the author], which constitutes every society, gives rise to new phenomena, different from those which occur in consciousnesses in isolation, one is forced to admit that these specific facts [social facts] reside in the society itself that produces them and not in its parts—namely its members. In this sense therefore they lie outside the consciousness of individuals as such, in the same way as the distinctive features of life lie outside the chemical substances that make up a living organism.
>
> DURKHEIM 1895: XIV–XV = 10–11

> Now, once the individual is ruled out, only society remains. It is therefore in the nature of society itself that we must seek the explanation of social life.... it transcends infinitely the individual both in time and space....
>
> IBID.: 101–102 = 85

Durkheim insists that the individual is, first of all, the objective reality, comparable to molecules and atoms. In his theory, society is conceived to be just like an entirety of a biological organism, which is clearly distinguished from individuals, existing externally to individual's consciousness. Thus, Durkheim shows society is such an objective reality, but this has to be taken as more than a mere metaphor. The reason can be seen in the logic in which it explains society is no longer created by the individual. It can even be interpreted as if it tells whether an individual's consciousness is not the origin of society but rather its component, such that society is an objectively existing body of consciousness.

A counterargument will be raised immediately. It goes, "it is rather true that society is created from the synthesis *sui generis* [some kind of unique synthesis] of the individual, and, in that sense, it is created by the individual who is the only subject of consciousness". However, this synthesis is by no means an explanation of the course of facts, the formation process of society. It is the same argument as the fact that living cells are made up of a synthesis of inorganic molecules does not necessarily mean that the latter literally give rise to the former. It only explains the principles of synthesis, the composition of association.

In short, what Durkheim conceives as society is, contrary to the realistic feeling of consciousness that each individual experiences today, not such as to require the existence of the individual prior to that of society, in other words, not such as to be created by an individual's cooperation and association based upon the existence of the individual as a subject of consciousness, regardless of the existence or non-existence of society. Durkheim conceived of society as a condition in which the individual and society are in a relationship that is neither too close nor too distant, living conditions of humanity where both (the individual and society) are inseparable in its entirety.

Accordingly, the distinction between the individual and society emerges only when we spotlight the same life, inseparable human life from two different angles. In other words, for Durkheim, who tried to grasp the entire reality of the people living together as an objective fact, both are two different aspects of the reality of life, and are the same entity. Therefore, the individual is not the beginning of subjective action. It is the entirety viewed from the perspective of division. It is just "individuals" in which the essential sociality of the individual emerges.

6.2   *Objectivity of the Social*

As society is not material, society is not an organism in itself to begin with. However, as long as every one of us is an individual, a society inevitably has to exist. This, on the other hand, means that if each one of us wishes to lead an independent life or to be an individual as an independent being—not a solitary ego, the only and unique consciousness existing in the world—then we have to make certain efforts to form and maintain the society. It is because society is not a natural object.

This effort is nothing but to treat others—friends or enemies—as a human being, and actively act to make others exist as other human beings. It is an action of objectifying others as a human being in exactly the same sense as you regard yourself as a human being. In this sense alone, society as a place where individuals live together appears to us as a "sensible" object, and it can stand as an objective reality. The basis for Durkheim's objectivity of social facts ultimately lies here. It is a daily practice, synonymous with living as a social being, in other words, living a social life. Society exists "objectively" as constantly elaborating "individuals".

Earlier, I mentioned that the synthesis *sui generis* that gives rise to society is not the actual process of its formation but only the principle of its composition. We can understand this principle precisely here. In other words, the formation of society is literally a process of constant human effort, and in this process, an individual as a social being is created at the same time. The proposition that society is created by the association of individuals only represents one aspect of this process. Individuals can exist only on the premise that society is the place where they live together. Individuals are subject to living a social life. The principle that covers the entire process of this constant effort is the "synthesis *sui generis*". It is a dynamic principle, a principle that is a process.

6.3   *Creation of Another Person: Endless Negation and Free Will*

We try to make sure of the above facts by looking back on our own experience. We all lead a "social life" with others. In our day-to-day life, we associate with, cooperate with, bother, or stay indifferent to each other. However, when we consider if this "social life" is a reality or not, the following question comes across our mind instantly. "Are others around me really individuals or human beings in the same way that I identify myself to be an individual or a human being?" In other words, "Are we all people?" What we instantly know is that our experience does not support an affirmative answer to this question. It is not a surprise to think of others as "other human beings" in our daily life. We think of every such being—including ourselves—as "individual", and their aggregation as "people" or "society".

However, this is not an empirically self-evident fact. Evidence can be seen in the fact that others' thoughts, feelings, and wills are not directly given to our consciousness. All that is given are "my thoughts", "my feelings", and "my wills". Others' spirits are not given to my senses. What is given is "another (person's) body". The content of another person's consciousness or another person's will can only be speculated. That is why our expectations of others are often betrayed.

This does not necessarily mean that "another person (alter ego) does not exist". Rather, the opposite is true. Among the "human bodies" that are given senses, only "my body" can experience the consciousness, and consciousness that "dwells" in "my body" can become "self-consciousness" only in the form of the residue that resulted in the process of endless failure in which it says, "I am unable to feel the consciousness in others' bodies". Therefore, my consciousness is something that emerges in the process of endless negation, the ceaseless discomfiture of understanding others, and in that sense it is the attribute of an exceptive body of one's own but not of all others which can never experience consciousness. Otherwise, the self is the only and a single—capitalized, so to speak—"Consciousness" or "Spirit" and cannot become "the consciousness of human individuals".

Upon this recognition, the ego, or self-consciousness, makes "another person (alter ego)"—in other words, "another individual"—exist by regarding "the ego which cannot be sensed to other bodies" as existing *even though it is, in reality, not sensed*. It is to treat another person as existence of having the consciousness in the same sense as ourselves, in other words, to treat another person as a human being. As long as it is groundless, it is a purely creative act, a kind of bet that makes another person exist.

It is in this "even though" that the liberty of human will exists. This "even though" is the manifestation of free will and sharply characterizes human life in the material world. The recognition that another person is a human being in the same sense that we are is not given to experience. The ego emerges in the negative process of constantly failing to experience others' consciousness. "Nevertheless", by the free-willed act of regarding another person's body as an agent in which humanity dwells, another person, a self, an individual, a human being in general is created.

6.4 Network of Mutual Creation: Society and the Social

Now, you may have understood that if these creations are mutually exercised, Kafu Nagai's "awakened individual" is created by Durkheim's "synthesis *sui generis*", and that synthesis shapes an elaborately woven network. This is what "human society" is all about. In this sense, Nagai's cry of "the Japanese lack the will to create" profoundly and perceptively indicates the absence of society. And therefore, the world with another person does not necessarily mean an aggregate consisting of multiple egos. The ego exists on the condition that the alter ego is not given to experience. (Occidental) society consisting of independent individuals, on which Zola and Nagai stood, is only a manifestation of "the world of life with another person".

In other words, the social precedes society. Society is not about social institutions. It is neither about political institutions nor about judicial institutions, much less about military organizations. It is not "a structure that must be maintained". The social is a daily act of will to make another person be a universal being. It is a creation and a bet. The existence of society means a state in which this bet of creating another person, a human being, is constantly carried out. Hence, even if society appears to be a solid structure, it does not have sociality in itself. The sociality of society exists in the social as a creative act of will. It is about unceasing creation and re-creation. Society which seems as if it were "established" is only the emergence showing one frame of constant and continuous creation. It is never a corporeal entity.

6.5 Sociological Creation

But if that is the case, a question is raised concerning the reality of sociology and its viability. Can the discipline of sociology, a science that covers research on society, be established in the first place? If your intuition is good, you might have noticed the following. This social creation is the creation of sociology. That is embedded in the very establishment of sociology by Durkheim. Acting on the recognition of society and the individual as described above will lead to the constant creation of society and sociology both in the Occident and the Orient, since it is directly derived from the reality of human life.

Therefore, it is possible for a nation without society to have sociology. It is because sociology is a practice of creating society. It creates awakened individuals, people, and human beings in such a nation without society. In this sense, it is certain that sociology in the future will inevitably become non-hegemonic, post-Western in that it goes beyond the distinction between Western and Eastern, and universal in that it is based on "human life".

7 Conclusion

After all, the fact I am writing this article with undeterred spirit at this moment even after I was hit by an upsetting event of cancer means that you make me live, and the fact that you read this article means I make you live. In this way, we all make each other live. This is the reality of life, and human society is the manifestation of life in such a way. The following criticism Henri Bergson once indirectly made of Durkheimian sociology is right, and it also indicates the direction of what the next generation of sociology—as it were, the "Sociology of Life"—shall create.

> The mistake would be to think that moral pressure and moral aspiration find their final explanation in social life considered merely as a fact. We are fond of saying that society exists, and that hence it inevitably exerts a constraint on its members, and that this constraint is obligation. But in the first place, for society to exist at all the individual must bring into it a whole group of inborn tendencies; society therefore is not self-explanatory; so *we must search below the social accretions, get down to Life, of which human societies, as indeed the human species altogether, are but manifestations*.... If society is self-sufficient, it is the supreme authority. But if it is only one of the aspects of life, ... *we shall have had to push on as far as the very principle of life.*
> BERGSON 1932: 102–103 = 100; italics mine

References

Bergson, Henri. (1932) 2000. *Les Deux Sources de la Morale et de la Religion*. Paris: Presses Universitaires de France. In English: (1935) 1977. *The Two Sources of Morality and Religion*. Translated by R. Ashley Audra and Cloudesley Brereton, with the assistance of W. Horsfall Carter. Notre Dame, IN: University of Notre Dame Press.

Durkheim, Émile. (1895) 2013. *Les Règles de la Méthode Sociologique*. Paris: Presses Universitaires de France. In English: 2014. *The Rules of Sociological Method and*

Selected Texts on Sociology and Its Method, edited by Steven Lukes. Translated by W.D. Halls. New York: Free Press.

Kikutani, Kazuhiro. 2015. "*Shakai (Convivialité)*" *no nai Kuni Nihon—Dreyfus Jiken, Taigyaku Jiken to Kafu no Hitan* [A Nation without "Society (Conviviality)"—The Dreyfus Affair and the Taigyaku Affair, and Kafu's Grief]. Tokyo: Kodansha.

Koyama, Matsukichi. (1929) 1957. "Nihon Shakaishugi Undo-shi" [History of Socialist Movement in Japan]. *Tokubetsu You Shisatsunin Jousei Ippan* [A Report on the Activities of Persons Under Close Surveillance], 264–423. Tokyo: Meiji Bunken Shiryo Kanko-kai [Publishing Association of the Documents of the Meiji Era].

Nagai, Kafu. 1909. "Furansu Monogatari no Hatsubai Kinshi" [Ban of *Tales of France*]. In *Kafu Zenshu* [Complete Works of Kafu Nagai]. Vol. 6, 331–333. Tokyo: Iwanami shoten.

Nagai, Kafu. 1919a. "The 20th of July 1919, Danchotei Nichijo" [Dyspepsia House Days]. In *Kafu Zenshu* [Complete Works of Kafu Nagai]. Vol. 21, 76. Tokyo: Iwanami shoten.

Nagai, Kafu. 1919b. "Hanabi" [Fireworks]. In *Kafu Zenshu* [Complete Works of Kafu Nagai]. Vol. 14, 252–260. Tokyo: Iwanami shoten.

Nagai, Kafu. 1929. "The 18th of October 1929, Danchotei Nichijo" [Dyspepsia House Days]. In *Kafu Zenshu* [Complete Works of Kafu Nagai]. Vol. 22, 297. Tokyo: Iwanami shoten.

Nagai, Kafu. 1936. "The 14th of February 1936, Danchotei Nichijo" [Dyspepsia House Days]. In *Kafu Zenshu* [Complete Works of Kafu Nagai]. Vol. 23, 387. Tokyo: Iwanami shoten.

Nagai, Kafu. 1939. "The 2nd of December 1939, Danchotei Nichijo" [Dyspepsia House Days]. In *Kafu Zenshu* [Complete Works of Kafu Nagai]. Vol. 24, 328. Tokyo: Iwanami shoten.

Zola, Émile. 1898. "Lettre à M. Félix Faure, président de la République (J'Accuse …!)". In *La Vérité en Marche, Œuvres complètes d'Émile Zola*, edited by Henri Mitterand. Vol. 14, 921–931. Paris: Cercle du Livre Précieux. In English: 1998. *The Dreyfus Affair—"J'Accuse" and Other Writings*, edited by Alain Pagès, translated by Eleanor Levieux, 43–53. New Haven, CT: Yale University Press.

CHAPTER 23

Weber "Fever" in China (1980–2020): Scholarly Communication and Discipline Construction

He Rong

Weberian study has become a hot field since the reconstruction of Chinese sociology. The translation of Weber's works, the translation and introduction of research literature on Weber, and the emergence of this special research field are all manifestations of the development of the Chinese Weberian academics. Chinese scholars, on the one hand, actively introduced and studied Weber's theory; on the other hand, they showed their initiative and independence based on academic quality and question consciousness, indicating the real rise and wave of Weberian study in Chinese academic circles, and echoing the practical needs of Chinese society since the country's reform and opening up. It is not only a typical example of academic reconstruction and independent academic discourse construction in contemporary China, but also a part of global academia with Weber's works as the platform.

1 Introduction: Weber Fever in Chinese World, an Accident, or a Necessity?

Since the 1980s, a noticeable phenomenon in Chinese academic circles has been the so-called Weber fever—that is, Max Weber (1864–1920) has continued to be a focus in all fields of humanities and social sciences, and even in the broad public reading field. In the two decades since 1980, scholars in mainland China, Hong Kong, Taiwan, and overseas coincidentally have devoted themselves to discussions on such propositions as Protestant ethics, Chinese civilization, and the development of capitalism, which aroused interest in Weber in a variety of fields, including sociology, economics, philosophy, religious study, history, law, and politics, and promoted the translation and introduction of Weber's works. During the first two decades of the new century, Weber's important works continued to be published in different translations. Echoing the compilation of the complete works of Weber in German, the Chinese translation of such works especially has also been comprehensively promoted. Many works of internationally renowned experts in Weberian study have been introduced to the academic circle, and Weber's works have attracted wide attention from many fields of sociology and adjacent disciplines and have occasionally aroused public topics.

In fact, the translation and dissemination of Weber's works is a worldwide phenomenon. E. Hanke put forward a proposition with the meaning of "profound or radical change", that is, a Weberian study wave often arises at times of change in scientific paradigms, changes of social economy, and the emergence of legitimacy crises of a political order (Hanke 2016). With respect to the reception of Weber in China, Po-Fang Tsai listed the diversity of Weber's works as an important influential factor. He comprehensively organized the Chinese literature that researches Weber, and he expressed his viewpoint that the centralized translation and introduction of secondary literature have promoted the recognition of Weber in Chinese academic circles since the 1980s (Tsai 2020).

Based on the standpoint of the above two studies, a preliminary hypothesis can be put forward, i.e., Weber's works and related literature echoed the ideological needs in the changing society, thus triggering the Weberian study wave. Indeed, the Weberian study wave in the Chinese world existed precisely in the period when the Four Asian Tigers and mainland China were experiencing economic takeoff and social changes one after another, especially China, which was in its important period of reform and opening up (1980–). The development of Weberian study is characterized by multiple translated works, diverse research themes, and multidisciplinary participation. There is almost no other counterpart that can compare to it in academic attention, no matter in classical theory research or contemporary theory. Weber fever emerged in mainland China synchronously with the reconstruction of Chinese sociology and China's reform and opening up. Its emergence and development not only depend on the favorable institutional environment, but also respond to people's needs for spiritual nourishment in the changing era.

However, it is worth noting that when researching Weber reception, the international academic circle often describes the Weberian study in China as Weber fever. This is different from the understanding of Chinese scholars. On the one hand, the term "fever" implies such derogatory senses as "worship" and "irrationality". On the other hand, it is suspected that it particularly makes the Chinese academic circle independent from the global academic circle. Besides, Chinese scholars have seen that Weberian study wave successively emerge in many countries in the world. For example, Su Guoxun researched the Chinese "Weber fever" in the context of the overall development of global academics, and then pointed out that Weber fever originated in the United States in the 1950s; then, the "Weber Renaissance" appeared in the Federal Republic of Germany in the 1960s. From that point the Weberian study wave in Western academic circles began to spread eastward, triggering the translation and research of Weber's works in Japan, Korea, Taiwan, Hong Kong, Singapore, and other countries and regions. Weberian study with special features also even developed in the Soviet Union and Eastern European countries that experienced political turmoil multiple times (Su 2016: 13–20). Therefore, Weber fever in mainland China since the 1980s has just been part of the worldwide Weberian study wave.

Then, a question arises: All the classics of social sciences have returned to the academic field since China's reform and opening up, and their starting points are basically the same. Why does Weberian study have such a prominent and extensive influence? Moreover, in terms of time and environment, Weber's works have no advantages in dissemination in China compared with those of other theorists. The emergence of Weber fever is somewhat "unexpected".

First, Weber's works entered China relatively late, and they did not have favorable opportunities for dissemination. Weber's works initially entered Chinese academic circles at a relatively late time, 1936, with *The Social Economic History*, translated by Zheng Taipu, a famous translator of the Commercial Press. Before that, *The Methodology of Social Sciences* and *The Division of Labour in Society* by Durkheim were successively translated into Chinese in 1929 and 1935. Second,[1] Chinese sociology has been deeply influenced by the Anglo-American or Western sociological tradition since its establishment,[2] and less influenced by German sociology. Third, Weber had a broad academic vision and carried out his research in diverse fields. In the late 1890s, his illness led to his alienation from the academic circle for a long period of time. His influence was relatively scattered from the beginning and was limited. To sum up, Weber's works did not enter China in an advantageous period. Chinese scholars initially influenced by his works were more likely to be economic historians rather than sociologists.

---

1 In 1948, Sun Benwen pointed out at the beginning of *Modern Chinese Sociology* that during the fifty years of sociology's introduction to China, there were 14 "popular and important works", including the works of Comte and Spencer, three works of Durkheim, and the works of Tönnies, Gumplowicz, and Schaffle in German sociology, except for Max Weber and his works (Sun Benwen [1948] 2017).
2 The so-called "Western Sociology" refers to the sociology of England, the United States, and France, as opposed to "German Sociology", in Wu Wen-tsao's *The German School of Systematic Sociology* (1934). In fact, German thought had a long-standing self-perception in society as opposed to the "Western (Britain and France)" thought, so that the "West" of Weber's time was still relative to Germany, which changed only after the 1940s. The gradual evolution of the concept of "West" can be seen in the acceptance and translation of Weber's works. Please refer to He Rong's *Where is the West? – The Conceptual Basis and Change of Weber's Cultural History* (2015).

In this paper, we believe that apart from the above-mentioned factors, e.g., social transformation and economic takeoff, the situation of Weberian study is closely related to the efforts of Chinese Weberians, so we should return to the core text and key scholars to understand Weber's reception in China. It should be noted that the reception of Weber by Chinese scholars is not only a kind of passive "learning" but also an active "choice" based on their cultural identity and academic mission. Weber's works, due to their open characteristics and diverse themes, echo with Chinese academic reading to some extent. His theoretical framework to some extent fits the internal concerns of Chinese academics have had since the reform and opening up. His broad vision in comparative historical research makes an open, diversified, and mutually communicative global academia possible. Therefore, Weberian study in China naturally has the vision and position of post-Western sociology.

2 The Beginning of Chinese Weberian Study: Translation and Introduction

Generally speaking, the specialization of Chinese academics tends to set Chinese scholars in a "follower" position in aspects of things such as theoretical paradigms, i.e., forming a kind of leader/follower difference based on the dichotomy method of "the West/the rest". However, Weberian study in China is positive and initiative, not just passive "learning". The rise of the Weberian study wave in China is not the imitation of followers. Moreover, as mentioned by Su Guoxun, Weberian study in postwar Germany, the United States, Japan, the Soviet Union, Eastern Europe, East Asia, and other countries and regions basically emerged after the 1950s.

Let's take the English academic circle as an example. Only *The Protestant Ethic and the Spirit of Capitalism* and *The General Economic History* were translated into English by the 1940s. Thereafter, the English translation and research of Weber's works were greatly promoted with the efforts of Parsons, Shils (Edward Shils), Gerth (Hans Gerth), Mills (Charles Wright Mills), and other Weber scholars. The English version of *Economy and Society* compiled by Guenth Roth and Claus Wittich through the efforts of Weberian studies scholars, made an important series of Weber's works present. By the late 1970s, Parsons' great influence on social theory had gradually declined, but most of Weber's works on methodology, comparative religion, economy, and society were translated into English one after another, and new generations of Weber scholars constantly emerged, grew up, and enjoyed an international reputation through the influence of English academics.

Weberian study in German academic circles also experienced ups and downs. The academic community of German sociology was seriously destroyed by both World Wars. Even after World War II, West Germany still needed to invite Raymond Aron, a French scholar, to explain Weber's theory. From the perspective of the influence of international academics, German scholars began to enter the field of Weberian studies and made great efforts to make progress in the late 1970s and 1980s. The results of Weberian study of German scholars, such as Wolfgang J. Mommsen, Wolfgang Schluchter, Friedrich Tenbruck (Friedrich H. Tenbruck), and Dirk Kaesler, attracted wide attention. Their works, based on Weber's writing history and German academic tradition, greatly deepened the international academic community's understanding and explanation of Weber from the perspectives of text context, ideological background, perspective, and paradigm.

Therefore, Weberian study in China started in the 1980s, meeting the new (a colorful and flourishing) atmosphere of the international Weberian study community, and a valuable "bonus" was obtained, i.e., the change in direction of international Weberian study at this time. To be specific, with respect to the research method, scholars began to focus on the path of Weber's "writing history", that is, to research Weber from his textual context and background of the times. In terms of text choice, the research was no longer limited to *Economy and Society*, derived from Weber's posthumous works *Economy, Social Fields, and Power*. From the perspective of research groups, the "German Weber" described by German scholars gradually replaced the so-called "Americanized Weber" (Gan 1997). When scholars in Chinese academic circles paid attention to Confucian ethics, the international scholars kept their eyes on such works as *Collected Essays in the Sociology of Religion* and *The General Economic History*. Thus, the former can be incorporated into and become part of the latter.

On the one hand, the Weberian study wave in China emerged basically synchronously with the Weber renaissance in the international academic circle. On the other hand, when Weberian study in Chinese sociology started, the reconstruction of sociology was being carried out in mainland China. The reform and opening up policy launched in 1978 marked the beginning of the change of the isolated, ill-informed, and lacking in materials Chinese academic circle. In 1979, Deng Xiaoping pointed out in a speech that missed lessons should be made up for sociology and other disciplines. Since then, sociology has finally ushered in new opportunities. The academic circle in mainland China started to revive sociology by accumulating academics in the Republic of China and through the efforts of overseas Chinese scholars.

Therefore, Weberian study since the 1980s has enjoyed an academic "bonus" in the Chinese cultural circle. One bonus is that Weber's works and important

Weberian study works were translated and written by scholars in mainland China, Taiwan Province, and other places, showing the characteristics of multiple translations and a remarkable improvement in quality. Weber's important works, e.g., *The Protestant Ethic and the Spirit of Capitalism*, *The Religion of China: Confucianism and Taoism*, methodology, academics, and political speeches, were translated into Chinese in each historical period. Since 2010, some of Weber's works that were generally neglected in the past, such as studies of medieval commercial partnerships, Roman land law, and music sociology, have also been translated into Chinese. Weber's works on methodology were also translated into Chinese by Zhang Wangshan, who is known for the comprehensive selection and compilation of works and proper translation. Compared with English-language selected works published in the same period, each edition has its own advantages. Thus, some important translators and/or researchers appeared. All of these things have further promoted Chinese Weberian study.[3]

On the other hand, scholars from East Asia generally paid attention to Confucian ethics and economic development, making Chinese Weberian academics rooted in reality and Chinese culture. In the 1980s, Weberian study in East Asia was accompanied by a very strong realistic care. Facing the economic takeoff in Japan, Taiwan and Hong Kong, China, and Singapore after World War II, scholars hoped to explain the modernization of East Asia from the perspective of Confucian tradition. Therefore, their Weberian study focused on Protestant ethics and China, especially "the relationship between Confucianism as an ideology and economic development and seeking the transformation and enrichment of Confucianism in order to play a positive and active role in social, economic, and political modernization in today's situation" (Su 2016: 17). Based on this theory and the reality, Chinese scholars at the three "Chinese Culture and Modernization" Seminars held in Hong Kong, China, in 1983, 1985, and 1988, respectively, discussed the relationship between Chinese traditional ethics and economic development in East Asia,

---

3   In addition to the translation of Weber's text, the introduction of secondary literature, and the publication of professional academic journals, there are also some special publications on social theory, such as *Foreign Sociology* by Mr Su Guoxun as editor-in-chief, formerly a compilation of reference materials in the early days of the Institute of Sociology, Chinese Academy of Social Sciences and became an internal publication after 1986. Theoretical trends in foreign sociology are translated and introduced, including many classic texts of Weberian study. Moreover, specialized works and collected papers on Weberian study, etc. (a collection of classic literature on related topics and new and emerging research from domestic academia) have been published, which have a wide and profound impact on the entire social science community.

and questioned Weber's assertions about China, deepening the thinking on the social structure and culture of China. In the warm atmosphere, *Dushu* magazine in Beijing held a symposium with the theme "Max Weber: Portrait of a Thinker" in 1985, marking the beginning of the Weberian study wave in mainland China. After the financial crisis in 1997, the research on Confucian ethics and the development of capitalism declined, but the complex relationship between Weber and China's modernization, the ideological framework behind the academic construction of China and the West, etc., were still within the concern of the Chinese academic circle, and new reflections on these things are still on the way (Luo 2007; Wang 2007).

Therefore, the Weberian study wave in China presents a superposition state, one where learning, selection, and echoing reception mechanisms occur simultaneously. For example, 1987 is such a typical year. In that year, Ding Xueliang published his article "An Introduction to Weber's Comparative Study of World Civilization" in *Social Sciences in China* to introduce Weber's comparative historical studies; Joint Publishing published *The Protestant Ethic and the Spirit of Capitalism*, translated by Yu Xiao and Chen Weigang; and Su Guoxun completed the first doctoral dissertation with the theme of Weber's thought in mainland China, marking the simultaneous appearance of a Chinese translation, secondary literature introduction, and local Weberian study.

On the whole, Chinese Weberian study in the 40 years stretching between 1980 and 2020 can be divided into three stages: introduction and dissemination, in-depth text, and synchronous development with the international academic circle. Let's take the Chinese version of *The Protestant Ethic and the Spirit of Capitalism* as an example. The Chinese version of that book included in "Toward the Future Series" in 1986 should be its earliest Chinese version, but there are some major defects, for example, some important notes of the book are not included. Thereafter, in 1987, Joint Publishing published its translation of Yu Xiao, Chen Weigang, etc., with all the annotations of the original book and annotations added by Parsons included and translated. Thus, a usable translation has formed. In the next 20 years, this translation was the basic choice for the academic circle in mainland China to read Weber. This undoubtedly had a far-reaching influence. Another translation is Taipei Yuan Liou's version, introduced by Guangxi Normal University Press in 2004. This version was translated by Kang Le and Jian Huimei, and it contained the content of *The Protestant Sects and the Spirit of Capitalism* on the basis of the German version as it is, together with annotations on background knowledge. It was widely distributed and benefited a lot of people. In 2010, Social Sciences Academic Press (China) published new translations of Su Guoxun, Qin Fangming, Zhao Liwei, Qin Mingrui, etc. These translations are based on the new English translation of Stephen Karlberg, and they can reflect the new knowledge accumulation and research trends of international Weberian study. It can be said that the three Chinese versions of Weber's works on Protestant ethics have their own characteristics, providing a reliable basis for scholars of different generations to read Weber. From the perspective of Weber's reception history, these translations echo the three stages respectively: the enthusiasm of the academic circle in mainland China to study Western social theories in the 1980s, the emphasis on deepening Weberian study and closing the gap between the scholars and the original German text after the 1990s, and the synchronous development with the international academic circle since the start of the 21st century.[4]

3 "Fever" and "Calm": Weberian Study as the Academic Construction of Chinese Sociology

By organizing (combing) the academic history of China in modern times, we can see that this article introducing Weber's works have been available in the Chinese world since the 1920s. Moreover, Fei Xiaotong, the most famous sociologist in China, devoted himself to reading *The Protestant Ethic and the Spirit of Capitalism* in the 1930s (Fei 2016). However, it was not until more than half a century later, when Su Guoxun published his doctoral dissertation in 1988, that the real sense of Weberian study in the sociological circle in mainland China actually took root and developed synchronously with China's reform and opening up and the reconstruction of Chinese sociology. Since then, Weber fever in Chinese academic circles has never abated. It includes not only the specialized Weberian study but also Weber's theory-based discussions in various fields and on different themes of social science, including basic translation

---

4 This classification is basically consistent with Xiao Ying and Guo Qi's studies. They argue that the social theory research team since the reform and opening up includes three generations: The first generation shifted from philosophy and other disciplines to the field of social theory at the beginning of the recovery of sociology and was credited with initiating social theory research; the second generation emerged at the turn of the century and established a framework, research norms, and cultivated a research echelon for theoretical research in Chinese sociology; the third generation became active around 2010 in social theory in the fields of social theory, and formed an academic community with substantial exchanges and common progress (Xiao Ying and Guo Qi 2019). The academic inheritance in the field of Weberian study is also typically characterized by this intergenerational feature. According to the institutions researching Weberian studies, the Institute of Sociology under Chinese Academy of Social Sciences, Peking University, Shanghai University, etc. have made outstanding achievements in the academic accumulation and talent cultivation of Weberian study.

and text analysis, and the application, reflection, and further development of Weber's theory, like a symphony with complex structure and rich rhythms.

From the perspective of the world, Chinese sociology started late in the 1980s and was isolated from the international academic circle for a long time; however, the international Weber academic circles also ushered in a new interpretation pattern during this period. Therefore, Weberian study in China in the past 40 years is basically synchronized with the processes of organizing and publishing the new complete set of Weber's works, and the Chinese Weber academic circle is deepening and developing its understanding of the translation of Weber's works.

On this basis, what needs further reflection is the wording "Weber fever". The term "Weber fever" used by Su Guoxun in his works means the wave of reading and studying Weber's works in different countries and periods around the world. The term itself is neutral and is used to refer to the Weberian study wave that has emerged or is emerging in different countries around the world. However, after being translated into China's "Weber fever" (Hanke 2016), it added a sense of "fanaticism" to China's Weberian study to some extent, whether intentionally or unintentionally. Coincidentally, there is similar wording in international academic circles. After the mid-20th century, some kind of "Weber cult" (Radkau 2011: 178) spread all over the world through the efforts of German scholars in exile in the United States. In recent years, the Chinese academic circle also has been reflecting on or debating whether there are "fairy tales" or "myths" around Weber (Su et al. 2016).

In fact, the importance of classic works will not change with changes in the attitude or number of readers. Weber is an open-minded thinker. He regards science as a process of continuously approaching reality. It is especially meaningless to be "fanatical" towards him or "worship" him. The Weberian study wave has been discussed in detail in the previous text, including the translation of Weber's works, translation and introduction of Weberian study literature, and reflection on Weber's theory, but what the essence of the Weberian study wave is and whether it constitutes some kind of fanaticism or worship need further discussion. In the following text, we make a preliminary comparison between "Weber fever" in the United States and in China in order to get some answers to these questions.

To a considerable extent, Weber's status in contemporary sociology is also due to his "Americanization" (Hinkle 1986). With the support of German scholars who went to the United States in the 1930s and 1940s, American sociology in the 1950s and 1960s, represented by Parsons, regarded Weber as the founder of sociology and modern social science. *The Protestant Ethic and the Spirit of Capitalism* translated by Parsons became a sociological "sacred scripture"

(Scaff 2005), which is arguably the most significant academic-historical construction in the history of sociology. From the viewpoint of American ideology building, the mission of American academic circles after World War II was to continue the "Western" tradition, and the modern man shaped in the Protestant ethic met precisely the self-fulfilling expectations of American society. So, the popularity of Weber's works was also due in part to social psychological factors.

Accordingly, from American sociological publications of the time, the specialized fields of Weberian study as well as Weber's extensive influence on sociological research in general, reflected Weber's Americanization. In terms of the quantity of publications from the 1950s onwards, approximately 75% of the papers related to Weber in the *American Journal of Sociology* were published between the 1970s and 1980s (Rijks 2012); an analysis on 156 articles published in 4 mainstream journals, including the *American Journal of Sociology* (AJS), from 1964 to 1975 showed that Weber was highly cited, while only 36% of the articles actually centered on Weber's ideas (Adatto and Cole 1981). In other words, Weber's influence in the United States extended beyond specialized study fields, and he was held in high esteem by studies addressing a wide range of topics in politics, economics, law, management, and social life, despite the possibility of "ritual" or "decorative" citations.

To make a contrast, we can examine as examples some basic features of contemporary Weberian study by the articles of specialized Weberian studies and studies relying significantly on Weberian texts published in *Sociological Research* since its establishment in 1986. From 1986 to 2020, *Sociological Studies* published 30 articles on the subject of Weber or relying mainly on Weberian texts, with 3 years (1988, 2001, and 2017) each having 3 articles, reaching the highest level. And from 2012 to 2015, no Weberian studies or related articles were published. Among these 30 articles, thematically, the largest number of articles on methodology (5) indicated to some extent the concern of sociologists for disciplinary infrastructure; the second largest number of articles on Marx or Marxism (4) were related to academic resources and orientation. In terms of writing style, the articles published around 2000 were obviously based on a more solid literature foundation, and they delved into classical propositions, such as Protestant ethics on the one hand and theoretical reflections based on Chinese society and Chinese experiences on the other. Also, they delved into specialized fields, such as economic sociology, sociology of religion, urban sociology, agricultural sociology, and sociology of the state, which not only reflected the in-depth advancement of Weberian study but also became an important achievement in the construction of Chinese sociological disciplines.

From a cursory comparison between Chinese and American sociological journals and the fact that *Sociological Studies* was the only professional sociological journal in China for a long time, the publication quantity of less than one article per year raises some doubts about the wording of "Weber fever". Moreover, Weber's theory has never reached a dominant position in China, but Parsons' theory has, and general empirical research does not require "ritual" references to Weber, so the content about Weber in professional sociology journals is not as great as one might expect.[5]

To corroborate the above observations, we further combed through the articles of two later professional sociology journals, *Chinese Journal of Sociology* and *Sociological Review of China*,[6] and found that *Chinese Journal of Sociology* published 19 articles in 16 years (2005–2020) and *Sociological Review of China* published 11 articles in 8 years (2013–2020). Compared to the 30 articles published by *Sociological Studies* in 35 years, the publication quantity of those two is significantly greater. One reason, of course, is that 2020 marks the centenary of Weber's death, and both *Chinese Journal of Sociology* and *Sociological Review of China* set dedicated commemorative columns. The good thing is that most of the authors of Weberian study in both journals are young, up-and-coming sociologists.

This phenomenon shows indirectly that the development of Chinese Weberian study is also the development of a sociological disciplinary system, the accumulation of academic discourse, and the cultivation of academic talent, and reflects the expansion of various specialized research fields in sociology, such as politics, religion, comparative history, and national issues, as well as the in-depth thinking based on Chinese history and Chinese culture.

Therefore, this paper argues that there has been a "coldness" among the "Weber fever" in Chinese academic circles over the past decades. The first "coldness" refers to the fact that Weber's influence in Chinese sociology is mainly in the field of theoretical research, with limited impact on empirical

---

5 In this regard, a comprehensive search of Weber-related papers, Weber works cited, and other basic information can be done technically through the database information of the publication in order to show the proportion of Weber-related texts in the overall scholarly publication. However, both translations and studies have to some extent shown mixed results since the emergence of Weberian study was largely synchronized with the revival of the discipline of sociology and lacked a disciplinary foundation. Therefore, this paper focuses on the leading publications and research groups.

6 Liu Yang and Li Junyin, PhD students (admitted in 2019) of the Graduate School of Chinese Academy of Social Sciences, are gratefully acknowledged for their help in sorting through the Weberian study literature published in Sociological Studies, Chinese Journal of Sociology and Sociological Review of China.

research in sociology, as opposed to the dominance and widespread influence in American sociology in the 1970s and 1980s. The second "coldness" refers to the "calm" selection and reflection of Chinese researchers in their Weberian studies. Contemporary Chinese Weberian studies reflect the independence, reflection, and critical self-consciousness of authors in terms of themes and positions. For example, Su Guoxun, the earliest professional researcher in the field of Weberian studies, has a clear understanding of Weber's shortcomings or limitations and keeps deepening his own understanding of Weber. In his final work, Su pointed out that we should benefit from and be enlightened by the bridging of the conflict between action and structure, plural causal analysis and the opposition beyond materialism and idealism, etc., in Weber's theory, and based on cultural self-awareness, have a dialogue with Weber from the perspective of the comparison between Chinese and Western cultures (Su 2021).

In addition, we should understand the state of Weberian study across disciplinary boundaries, because the group of people who read Weber and are inspired by Weber's works is not limited to the sociological community but includes the vast majority of contemporary Chinese people in all fields of humanities and social sciences. Thus, Weber fever in contemporary China consists of translations of Weber's works, specialized Weberian study, specialized fields of sociological research based on Weber's texts, and the results of adjacent disciplines in the humanities and social sciences. On the one hand, it represents sociology's intellectual contribution to the entire academic community; on the other hand, it means that sociology has been able to establish disciplinary academic status and theoretical value, and to establish channels of communication with the academic community. Weber's works, together with other classical works, constitute the academic backbone of sociology as a discipline. In addition, the all-encompassing and open-ended nature of Weber's works, as well as the research fever in the last 40 years, makes Weber's contribution to Chinese sociology particularly distinctive.

4 Establishment of Post-Western Academic Research: Possibility of Global Academia Based on Weberian Study

The history of the reconstruction and revival of contemporary Chinese sociology is also a process of opening up and learning from the international academic community and a process of constantly liberating one's creativity from the Western imagination and building one's own academic identity. To emphasize learning while ignoring the independent choices, reflections, and critiques of Chinese scholars would be to ignore the intrinsic connections between various countries and different academic communities which is the foundation upon which post-Western sociology is built.

For example, although a Weberian study wave appeared later in the 1980s, we can find from Weber's texts that there are some implicit connections between Weber and early Chinese sociology, namely, some coincidences in intellectual resources and problematic awareness. For example, when writing *The Religion of China: Confucianism and Taoism*, Weber used the writings of the missionary Arthur Henderson Smith to understand Chinese character and civil society, and Pan Guangdan also used the missionary's writings to develop his Eugenics (Pan [1937] 2010). The coincidences and differences between them should be a topic worthy of in-depth discussion. For another example, the source of social history cited in *The Religion of China: Confucianism and Taoism* is an English work called *Village and Town Life in China*, published by sociologist Tao Menghe and his classmates Liang Yugao during their study in England (Weber 2004: 145, 147). This shows that the temporal, thematic, and informational differences between Weber's work and early Chinese sociology are not very serious, and that there may even be some parallel development, a potential cross-reference, or a nearly contemporaneous relation. It is such a potential affinity that allows for a certain inherent concert between Weber and Chinese sociology.

Professional Weberian studies in China have emerged since the 1980s, but historical changes in modern China unexpectedly allowed Weber's work to influence a scattered group of scholars, namely Chinese scholars in American academia after the 1950s. From them, one can see the stirring of Western scholarship and Eastern identity, and the tortuous development of Republican scholarship (1911–1949) in China. At the right time, they were influenced by Weberian theory. To name just the most influential, in addition to the sociologists Shu-qing Lee, Ch'ing K'un Yang, and T'ung-tsu Ch'u, the representatives also included many literary and historical scholars, such as Lien-sheng Yang, Ray Huang, Ying-shih Yu, and Chuo-yun Tsu.

By the time Weber's theory became popular in American academia in the 1950s, Lien-sheng Yang was teaching at Harvard University and had been invited by the French sinologist Demiéville to lecture at the Collège de France and was well known in international sinology circles. The influence of Weber's theory can be reflected in several of his writings. For example, in *The Concept of Pao as a Basis for Social Relations in China*, Lien-sheng Yang states that interactivity is a foundational principle for social relations in China. In response to Weber's discourse on Chinese culture as described by Parsons, Lien-sheng Yang attempted to engage in dialogue, demonstrating cultural self-awareness and independence (Yang [1973] 2011). Later, Lien-sheng Yang's student Ying-shih Yu responded directly to Weber's Protestant ethics and Chinese religious studies with *China's Modern Religious Ethics and Merchant Spirit*, which was an important question based on Chinese culture within the framework of Western scholarship and has gained a reputation in international East Asian studies, especially Chinese cultural studies, since the 1980s. The importance of this work can be understood without further explanation. In 2021, the book was compiled and published in English by H. Tillman, bringing the culmination of Weberian study in Chinese literature into a more internationally influential channel of dissemination.

Unlike general scholars who attempted to explore and understand the spirit of capitalism in Chinese society, Ping-ti Ho questioned the efforts to explore the occurrence and development of capitalism in Chinese history through specific studies. In the study on salt merchants from the cities of Huainan and Huaibei published in 1954, he sorted out data on the scale, organization, wealth, and costs of salt production and sales in the cities of Huainan and Huaibei, pointing out the phenomena of conspicuous consumption and the high proportion of family members joining the government in the salt merchant community. Despite the wealth of the salt merchants, they were unable to generate capitalism. So, he advocated that there was no "Merchant Spirit" in modern China and was not convinced by studies on the sprouting of capitalism. He held an ambition to use Western learning as the intellectual framework for and Chinese learning as the foundation of his scholarship. His academic ideal was to use the highest level of Western historiography as a standard, and to break through the limits of sinology and access the field of social science by his insights into national history. In 1964, he participated in a multidisciplinary seminar on "The Crisis of the Family System" at the University of California, where he presented a paper titled "The Chinese Family System in the Eyes of Historians" and exchanged ideas with Parsons, a leading scholar in the field of researching Weber's theories (Ho 2005).

In general, with the exception of a few works, these scholars have had a limited impact in the mainstream academic circles in the United States. However, even with all the difficulties and setbacks, their work has had some impact in the field of American sinological studies.[7] In particular, with mainland China's opening up to the outside world and its intellectual prosperity after the 1980s, these scholars' humble academic work spread Weber's influence to

---

7 Please refer to *Guest Historians of the Republic in the United States and American Sinology* written by Wu Yuanyuan, Academy Press, 2018 Edition.

the wider Chinese academic circles, which formed a scattered and tortuous scope chain. From the perspective of the reception history of Weber's thought, both Ying-shih Yu's attempt to sort out the counterpart of the capitalist spirit in Chinese society and Ping-ti Ho's creativity in penetrating into Chinese institutions and culture with the theoretical and methodological tools of the social sciences reflect the independent choices of Chinese scholars. With the achievements of this group of scholars, Weber has impacted the humanities and social sciences as a whole in China since the country's reform and opening up.

The real occurrence and development of Weberian study in China reflect the academic literacy and cultural consciousness of Weberians. Weberians choose consciously and actively to situate Weber's works in the thought river of philosophical and social sciences, the fundamental questions of modernity, and the fundamental concerns of Chinese society, and to delve into the more fundamental theoretical system of Weber's works.

In 1988, Su Guoxun's doctoral dissertation *Rationalization and its Limitations – An Introduction to Weber's Thought* was published, which was the groundbreaking work of Chinese sociology specializing in Weberian study, and also the first specialized treatise on the Western social theory since the reconstruction of Chinese sociology. At a time when much of Chinese academic circles was still limited by such propositions as Confucian ethics and capitalist economic development, Su Guoxun began to delve into the more fundamental issue of rationalization, placed it in the context of Western modern philosophical reflection, and pointed out that rationalization itself had its limits and inherent tensions. Based on China's cultural and historical situation, Su believed that the path of modernization was neither unique nor dominant. His exploration brought social theory research in China to the forefront, and his work led a new generation of social theory scholars. With his profound theoretical insight, Su Guoxun continued to advance his Weberian study in the 21st century based on the Chinese context, and he effectively discussed the value of Weber's theories for the practice of modernization in China.

Li Meng is a model of the new generation of social theorists and follows the system of Weberian academics flourishing in the 1980s. As a Weberian who grew up in the era of reform and opening up, Li Meng has been more nourished by Chinese and Western academic thoughts, and his personal experience has made him more obviously self-conscious. In 2001, Li published his paper *The Disenchanted World and Guardian of Ascetics: The "England Law" Problem in Weber's Social Theories* which synthesized the German and American scholarly traditions of Weberian study. He proposed "ethical rationalization" based on the ideas of Schluchter and Karlberg, further extending the issue of modernity to a broader field of social science and penetrating into the inner tensions of Western modernity. Therefore, a dialogue with international social theory research on fundamental issues was established and the second landmark of Weberian studies in China was formed.

In addition, the academic leadership and significant influence of scholars such as Su Guoxun and Li Meng are reflected in the emergence of a new generation of social theory scholars and their numerous contributions to the building of a public academic community. It is foreseeable that the work in Weberian studies in China will continue to be passed on from generation to generation and flourish in the near future.

As Kaesler says, "Weber never became mainstream while he was alive, but he became a great master afterwards". In addition to his works, his reputation was driven by the trustees represented by Weber's wife Marianne Weber, the promoters represented by Winckelmann, and the interpreters and the international propagandists represented by Parsons. However, many of those who tried to disseminate Weber's works and ideas were marginalized in academia or were not sociologists. Thus, during the dissemination of Weber's theories, so-called invisible colleges of international Weber scholars emerged, where someone concerned with the historical contextualization of Weber's works, and someone concerned with the theoretical continuation of Weber's works more. Due to these Weber researchers from different countries and cultures, Max Weber became a "living classic" (Kaesler 2016).

Whether called "Weber scholars" or "Weberians", Weber researchers themselves are the point of penetration for understanding the "fever" and "calm" of Weberian study. In China, Weber's works have received extra attention because the pattern and themes inherently echo the dramatic changes in China over the past 40 years. Chinese scholars with cultural self-consciousness have found in his works new perspectives for understanding Chinese civilization and Chinese history, and they are important foundations for building post-Western sociology.

Therefore, a Weber scholar who recognizes Weber's open academic spirit will follow Weber's scientific spirit and expand into areas beyond Weber's reach; a Weber scholar with Chinese cultural self-awareness will take on the task of reflecting on, innovating, and inheriting Chinese culture with the spirit of academia. This may be the convergence of fever and calm, inheritance, and development, and has the potential to constitute a "world academia" with Weber as its object, Weber's works as its platform, and reality and truth as its goals. In this sense, Weber transcended his time and became what Raymond

Aron called "our contemporaries"; moreover, Weber transcended his place or country and belonged to a part of the world of science, the meaning of which is constantly reflected in the highest values of each generation.

Likewise, Weberian academics in China embodies the effort of paradigm innovation in post-Western sociology. The issue of post-Western sociology emerged from the concern of Chinese and French scholars about the relationship between universal theory and local experience. Post-Western sociological theorists observed continuities and discontinuities in the conceptualization of sociological theory (Roulleau-Berger 2016), which suggested that the essence of claimed universalism was the conscious or unconscious academic hegemony of Western theory. Conversely, since reconstructed, Chinese sociology, on the one hand, has had the self-awareness of discipline construction to enhance theoretical perspectives and refine methodological tools with an open and global perspective; on the other hand, based on the development and transformation of Chinese society and economy over decades of research, it enriches theories and thinks through the lens of Chinese experiences to refine several important theoretical paradigms and advance theoretical innovations, thus revealing further research for the paths of post-Western sociology (Wei and Li 2018).

In terms of material, Chinese Weberian academics is a classic sociological work, or a "Western" one. But it is open-minded, open-hearted, and global in its ambition, with the mission of reaching a consensus among scholars and sharing scholarship. Thus, the "reception" of Weber's theories is not uncritical acceptance, but an active choice based on his own academic vision and heartfelt realistic sentiment, which excavates and develops specialized fields such as religious ethics and economic development, social science methodology, sociology of religion, political sociology, sociology of the state, etc. The fundamental concern is consistent with the analysis of property rights, the unitary system, class, and mobility, etc., which are the concerns of the empirical research of Chinese sociology, i.e., that is to say, it is the construction of the academic system of Chinese sociology itself and the concern for the study on local problems in China.

Therefore, the Weberian study wave in China is not a late following after predecessors, nor is it an uncritical acceptance of the universality over the particular, rather it is the excavation and discernment of common experience. It is based on the local, but its vision is global. In this way, the classical paradigm is directed toward new interpretative boundaries with a new vision, promoting the enrichment and innovation of a constructive, post-Western sociological paradigm.

References

Adatto, Kiku, and S. Cole. 1981. "The Foundation of Classical Theory in Contemporary Sociological Research: The Case of Max Weber". In *Knowledge and Society: Studies in the Sociology of Culture Past and Present*, edited by R.A. Jones and H. Kuklick, 137–162. Greenwich, CT: JAI.

Fei, Xiaotong. (Lost draft) 2016. *On the Rational Relationship of Protestant Doctrine and the Spirit of Capitalism*, Wang Mingming, Zhang Rui (Organizer), *North West Ethno-national Studies* 2016 (1): 5–24.

Gan, Yang. 1997. "Weberian Study Restart—Preface by the Editors of the First Volume of Selected Weber Works". In Max Weber, *The Nation-State and Economic Policy*, 1–11. Translated by Yang Gan, Qiang Li, Yijun Wen, and Yongjian Bu. Beijing: Joint Publishing.

Hanke, Edith. 2016. "Max Weber Worldwide: The Reception of a Classic in Times of Change". *Max Weber Studies* 16 (1): 70–88.

He, Rong. 2015. *Where is the West—The Conceptual Basis and Change of Weber's Cultural History, Qiaoyi*. Vol. 2. Beijing: Social Sciences Academic Press.

Hinkle, Gisela. 1986. "The Americanization of Max Weber". *Current Perspectives in Social Theory* 7: 87–104.

Ho, Ping-ti. 2005. *60 Years of Reading History*. Guilin: Guangxi Normal University Press.

Kaesler, Dirk. 2016. "Max Weber Never Was Mainstream, but Who Made Him a Classic of Sociology?" *Serendipities* 1 (2): 121–137.

Luo, Gang. 2007. "'Modernization' Expectation or 'Modernity' Concern—Western Imagination in Terms of 'Weber's Translation' since the 1990s". In *The Self-Disintegration of Enlightenment: A Study on the Major Debates in Chinese Ideological and Cultural Circles since the 1990s*, edited by Jilin Xu. Changchun: Jilin Publishing Group.

Pan, Guangdan. (1937) 2010. *Ethnic Characteristics and Ethnic Health*. Beijing: Peking University Press.

Radkau, Joachim. 2011. *Max Weber: A Biography*. Translated by Patrick Camiller. Cambridge, UK: Polity Press.

Rijks, Marlise. 2012. "Max Weber in the *American Journal of Sociology*: A Case of Circulating Knowledge". *Journal of the History of the Behavioral Sciences* 48 (1): 55–63.

Roulleau-Berger, L. 2016. *Post-Western Revolution in Sociology: From China to Europe*. Leiden and Boston: Brill Publishers.

Scaff, Lawrence A. 2005. "The Creation of the Sacred Text: Talcott Parsons Translates *The Protestant Ethic and the Spirit of Capitalism*". *Max Weber Studies* 5 (2): 205–228.

Su, Guoxun. 2016. *Rationalization and Its Limitations: An Introduction to Weber's Thoughts*. Beijing: The Commercial Press.

Su, Guoxun. 2021. "Weber's Thoughts in China". *Academia Bimestrie* 2021 (1): 68–80.

Su, Guoxun, Wansheng Huang, et al. 2016. "Going Out of Weber Myth: Reflection on the 100 Years After the Release of *Confucianism and Taoism*". *Open Times* 3: 11–62.

Sun, Benwen. (1948) 2017. *Modern Chinese Sociology*. Beijing: The Commercial Press.

Tsai, Po-Fang. 2020. "Between Translation and Monographs: An Exploratory Analysis of the Secondary Literature on Max Weber-Reception in the Chinese Context". *Max Weber Studies* 20 (1): 57–81.

Wang, Hui (汪晖). 2007. "Weber and the Question of Chinese Modernity". In *The Politics of Imagining Asia*, edited by Hui Wang and Theodore Huters, 264–308. Cambridge, MA: Harvard University Press.

Weber, Max. 2004. *The Religion of China: Confucianism and Taoism*. Translated by Le Kang and Huimei Jian. Guilin: Guangxi Normal University Press.

Wei, Jianwen, and Peilin Li. 2018. "Post-Western Sociology and Contemporary Chinese Sociology". *Journal of Beijing Normal University (Social Sciences)* 1: 143–150.

Wu, Wen-tsao. (1934) 1990. *The German School of Systematic Sociology, Anthropological and Sociological Studies*, 85–121. Beijing: The Ethnic Publishing House.

Xiao, Ying, and Qi Guo. 2019. "Social Theory Research in China: From Introduction to Reconstruction". *Hebei Academic Journal* 3: 13–25.

Yang, Lien-sheng. (1973) 2011. "The Concept of Pao as a Basis for Social Relations in China". In *The Powerful Families of the Eastern Han Dynasty*, 179–202.

PART 2

*Translation and Ecologies of Knowledge:
Dialogues East–West*

∴

SECTION 5

Globalization and Social Classes

∴

CHAPTER 24

Wealthization and Housing Wealth Inequality in China

Li Chunling

1   Introduction: Wealthization in the Western World and China

In recent years, there has been a new trend of social stratification and inequality, one in which wealth differentiation has become the most prominent inequality in today's society. Many economists and some sociologists have studied the issue in depth and concluded that the dynamics of wealth in the Western world is a central element of the inequality (Piketty 2014, 2020; Saez and Zucman 2016; Wolff 2016). Chauvel and colleagues (2020) also revealed the phenomenon of the comeback of wealth and rewealthization in American and European countries. The rising importance of wealth inequality has challenged traditional class analysis and the concept of occupation-based class. Wealth differentiation is dissolving the hierarchical system of modern society based on occupation status. In the past, social stratification theorists usually emphasized that occupational prestige or employment status determines class position, social status, and class consciousness (Shin 2020). However, due to increasingly prominent wealth inequality, this traditional theory of social stratification has been questioned. Some sociologists argue that wealth has become a crucial resource for defining one's social position in the conceptualization of social class (Chauvel 2006; Jodhka, Rehbein and Sousa 2017; Savage 2014; Savage and Schmidt 2020; Savage et al. 2015).

Over the past three decades China has shared a similar wealthization process with Western countries. However, Chinese wealthization is a slightly different story from that of Western countries. In Western countries the process has been characterized by rewealthization and inherited wealth primacy (Chauvel et al. 2020), but Chinese wealthization is characterized by the newly rich. This is a process of new wealth accumulation and aggregation driven by marketization and privatization, which are dynamics of wealthization different from those of Western countries. Such a process is most prominent in housing wealth because housing property is the most important wealth of Chinese families, which on average accounts for 71% of total family wealth (Li and Fan 2020). The inequality of housing wealth is creating a new form of social stratification in China, which is different from the traditional stratification of occupation-based classes. This new trend of social stratification has caused researchers to rethink traditional stratification theory.

2   Housing Wealth Growth: From a No-Property Society to a Booming-Property Society

China's housing wealth distribution has undergone dramatic changes over the past several decades. During the public ownership movement in the 1950s, most of the houses in cities and towns were nationalized, while the rough houses in rural areas were privately owned but had no market value. Very few Chinese families had private housing property until the late 1970s, when the reform and opening up began. Forty years later, however, more than 90% of Chinese families have private houses, and family housing wealth has increased dozens of times. China has changed from a society with scarce private property to a society with growing private property during the past four decades.

Figure 24.1 illustrates this process. In the late 1980s, the Chinese government implemented the pilot housing reform to promote the privatization of public houses in urban areas and allow self-built houses. The number of families owning private houses began to increase. In 1988, the home ownership rate of urban families in China was 13.7%. In 1995, the ownership rate rose to 42% with the promotion of nationwide housing reform. In the late 1990s, housing reform was accelerated. Almost all public housing was sold to individuals, and the

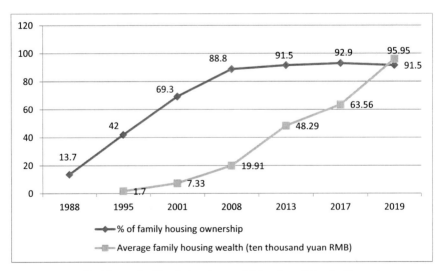

FIGURE 24.1   Rapid growth of family housing wealth in urban China (1988–2019)
Note: The data of Figure 24.1 are from the Chinese Household Income Project (CHIP) and Chinese Social Survey (CSS).

housing ownership rate reached 69% by 2001. In the 21st century, the Chinese government has vigorously developed the real estate market, which has further increased the housing ownership rate. The housing ownership rate has exceeded 90% in urban areas since 2013. The vast majority of Chinese families have owned private property. At the same time, family housing wealth has also increased. In 1995, the average housing property value for urban families was only 17,000 yuan, and it rose to 960,000 yuan in 2019. The average household property has increased by 56 times in 24 years.

3   Change in the Major Source of Economic Inequality: From Income Inequality into Housing Wealth Inequality

The wealthization has brought about a shift in the major source of economic inequality from income inequality into housing wealth inequality. In 1980s and 1990s, income inequality was a major source of economic inequality, and income Gini coefficient increased quickly. However, since 2000, with the growth of housing wealth, housing wealth inequality has become the major source of economic inequality, and its Gini coefficient is much higher than the income Gini coefficient (Figure 24.2).

FIGURE 24.2   Trends of income and housing wealth Gini coefficient in China (1981–2017)
Note: The data of income Gini coefficients are from the National Bureau of Statistics of China. The data of housing wealth Gini coefficients are from the Chinese Household Income Project (CHIP) and Chinese Social Survey (CSS).

Figure 24.2 compares the trend of income and housing wealth Gini coefficient in China. The income Gini coefficient of China had increased significantly during the late 1980s and the 1990s, which has led to a strong public concern about income inequality. Since 2000, income inequality has not been increasing rapidly and has entered a period of fluctuation. Income Gini coefficient even declined for the period of 2007–2015 but the public has not perceived the reduction in economic inequality. On the contrary, the public media has continued to discuss the widening gap between the rich and the poor. This is mainly because wealth inequality, particularly housing wealth inequality, increased. In the 1980s and 1990s, the housing wealth Gini coefficient was quite low because most urban families lived in public housing. The privatization of public houses and the development of the real estate market since 2000 have quickly lifted the housing wealth Gini coefficient. Surging house prices since 2004 have further strengthened this trend.

4 Shift in the Mechanism of Housing Wealth Distribution: From the State to the Market

The rapid growth of housing wealth as well as the rapid rise of housing wealth inequality has pushed forward the process of Chinese wealthization. In this process, there has been a shift in the mechanism of housing wealth distribution from domination by the state to domination by the market.

Figure 24.3 shows the sources of private house property in different years. In 1995, most families (68.6%) acquired their housing property by purchasing public houses for a much cheaper price than market value, and very few families (5.5%) bought their houses from the real estate market. Since the allocation of public houses depended on the type of work unit, administrative rank, and length of service in the public sector, the position of individuals in the state system determined the amount of housing wealth in that period. The state was the major force driving housing wealth inequality during the late 1990s and the early 21st century. But in 2019, about half of families (47%) bought their houses from the real estate market, 38.8% were self-built houses, and only 8.9% purchased public houses for favorable prices by the government. That displays a shift in the mechanism of housing wealth distribution with marketization. The market has replaced the state as the main force causing housing wealth inequality. The amount of family housing wealth mainly depends on the individual's market capacities including residential location, income, occupation, education, and so on. The distribution of housing wealth has been increasingly dominated by the market. However, the role of the state has not been completely eliminated in the distribution of housing wealth. Therefore,

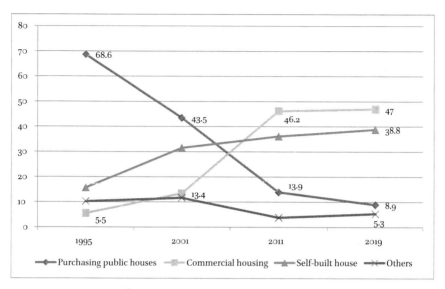

FIGURE 24.3 Source of housing property in different years (%)
Note: The data for Figure 24.3 are from the Chinese Household Income Project (CHIP) and Chinese Social Survey (CSS).

the interaction of the state and the market is the main driving force of housing wealth differentiation as well as wealthization in the past two decades.

5 Creating a New Social Stratification: The Occupation-Based Classes Split by Wealth Class

The wealthization has created a wealthy class, which holds an enormous amount of housing property. The wealthy class refers to people who hold more than 5 million (RMB) of housing wealth (no mortgage debt). CSS survey data of 2019 show that the members of the wealthy class are not only from the upper class and the middle class, but also the working class and peasants. Among the wealthy class, about 5% are "wealthy elites" who are business owners, senior managers, and professionals; 65.2% are "the wealthy middle class" who are the middle- or low-level managers, professionals, technicians, and small business owners; and 29.8% are "wealthy laborers" who are blue-collar workers and peasants. In other words, nearly one third of the members of the wealthy class are from the class of manual laborers, which are defined by the traditional theory of social stratification as the lower class.

Unlike European and North American societies with a relatively stable social structure, China, as a transitional society, has experienced a reconfiguration of social stratification and also wealth distribution. Some persons from

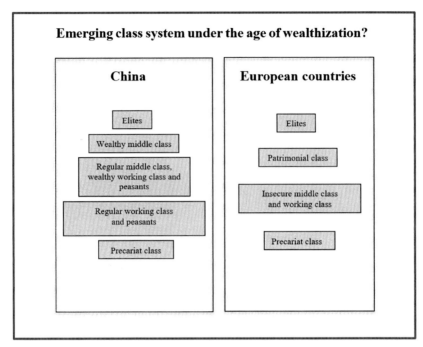

FIGURE 24.4   A new social stratification created by wealthization

the lower classes had taken advantage of some special opportunities to obtain wealth—for example, poor peasants living around the city and laid-off workers living in the city center got huge compensation in the form of housing wealth by land acquisition and the demolition of old houses during the rapid urbanization of recent decades so that they became members of the wealthy class. At the same time, some members of the middle class, while holding a decent job and earning a good salary, are unable to afford an apartment or are overwhelmed by the mortgage. The wealthization has created division within each class—for example, the middle class has been divided into the wealthy middle class and the regular middle class, and there are differences between the two groups in terms of their living conditions and social-political attitudes. This also happens among the working class and peasants. Wealth differentiation has been splitting the original social classes and reconstructing a new social stratification system.

The aggravation of wealth differentiation and the inconsistency with the traditional social stratification have been implying a new trend of social stratification. This new trend is manifested not only in Chinese society, but also in European and American society. Some European scholars (Savage 2014; Savage et al. 2015) believe that the wealth inequality has led to a new class system and reconstructed the social structure in today's European countries, one in which an upper middle class has been separated from the middle class. The upper middle class, the members of which usually inherited property from their parents, enjoys property security and stable economic status while the regular members of middle class without economic security have fallen living conditions similar to those of the working class. Similarly, in Chinese society, the wealthization driven by housing wealth inequality is also leading to fissions in the original social classes and is creating a new class system. A difference from European and American society is that the wealthization separates not only the wealthy middle class from the middle class but also the wealthy labor class from the working class and peasants. Figure 24.4 outlines the rudiments of the new social stratification in China and compares them with the new class structure of European society developed by Savage and other European scholars. In both China and Europe, there has been an emerging precariat class at the bottom who have neither employment security nor property security.

6   Conclusion

China has experienced a process of wealthization different from that of Western countries but experienced social consequences similar to those of Western countries. That is an emerging class system under the age of wealthization. Class position has not depended entirely on occupational status. Wealth, especially housing wealth, has been playing an increasingly important role in the formation of class identity. This will challenge the traditional theory of social stratification and class analysis, and urge sociologists to think deeply about the influence of wealth inequality on the social stratification of contemporary society.

References

Chauvel, L., E.B. Haim, A. Hartung, and E. Murphy. 2020. "Rewealthization in Twenty-First Century Western Countries: The Defining Trend of the Socioeconomic Squeeze of the Middle Class". *The Journal of Chinese Sociology* 8 (4).

Chauvel, L. 2006. "Are Social Classes Really Dead? A French Paradox in Class Dynamics". In *Inequalities of the World*, edited by G. Therborn. London: Ed. Verso.

Jodhka, S.S., B. Rehbein, and J. Souza. 2017. *Inequality in Capitalist Societies*. London: Taylor & Francis.

Li, C., and Y. Fan. 2020. "Housing Wealth Inequality in Urban China: The Transition From Welfare Allocation to Market Differentiation". *The Journal of Chinese Sociology* 7 (16).

Piketty, T. 2014. *Capital in the 21st Century*. Cambridge, MA: Harvard University Press.
Piketty, T. 2020. *Capital and Ideology*. Cambridge, MA: Harvard University Press.
Saez, E., and G. Zucman. 2016. "Wealth Inequality in the United States Since 1913: Evidence From Capitalized Income Tax Data". *The Quarterly Journal of Economics* 131 (2): 519–578.
Savage, M. 2014. "Piketty's Challenge for Sociology". *The British Journal of Sociology* 65 (4): 591–606.
Savage, M., N. Cunningham, F. Devine, S. Friedman, D. Laurison, L. Mckenzie, A. Miles, H. Snee, and P. Wakeling. 2015. *Social Class in the 21st century*. London: Penguin.
Savage, M., F. Devine, N. Cunningham, M. Taylor, Y. Li, J. Hjellbrekke, B. Le Roux, S. Friedman, and A. Miles. 2013. "Social Class in the 21st Century". *Sociology* 47 (2): 219–250.
Savage, M., and C. Li. 2021. "Introduction to Thematic Series 'New Sociological Perspectives on Inequality'". *The Journal of Chinese Sociology* 8 (7).
Savage, M., and C.M. Schmidt. 2020. "The Politics of the Excluded: Abjection and Reconciliation Amongst the British Precariat". *The Journal of Chinese Sociology* 8 (7).
Shin, K.Y. 2021. "A New Approach to Social Inequality: Inequality of Income and Wealth in South Korea". *The Journal of Chinese Sociology* 7 (17).
Wolff, E.N. 2016. "Household Wealth Trends in the United States, 1962 to 2013: What Happened Over the Great Recession?" National Bureau of Economic Research: Working Paper 20733 December 2014, https://www.nber.org/papers/w20733.

CHAPTER 25

Squeezing the Western Middle Class: Precarization, Uncertainty and Tensions of Median Socioeconomic Groups in the Global North

Louis Chauvel

1 Introduction

Three decades of earning stagnation and increasing economic inequality (Savage and Li 2021) have exacerbated social tensions in Western Europe, Northern America and several other "post-industrial societies" that constitute the "Global North" (Therborn 2021). These trends are very significant (Reeves 2017; OECD 2019) since they express a major issue of our age, a comeback of extreme classes after the development of a Western olive-shaped society (Li and Zhu 2016). In his prophecy of the 21st century, Hobsbawm's (1994) conclusion focused on the major risk of future darkness that could be generated by the comeback of extreme inequalities. The consequences of these trends are particularly visible in the difficulties of different segments of the middle classes.

In this paper, I re-evaluate my previous contribution (Chauvel 2009) on the Western "middle class adrift" diagnosis of the last 30 years. After definitions of "middle classes" in terms of social stratification and of "middle class society" in terms of process of civilizational change, this paper identifies different facets of de-middlization that follow the former trend of middlization (Lu 2010). Ruptures in the social trends in the former "middle class society" (such as stagnation, new inequalities and social precarization, among others) happen to constitute new trends of the current backlash after decades of middlization. The demographic and social consequences of the new trends are analyzed to finally highlight the importance of this problem for social stability. When large segments of the middle class have less interest in the maintenance of the social order, the risks of political anomie grow. I finally underline the necessity to balance social individualism promoted in Western middle-class societies with a stronger collective conception of social "middlization" thought as a holistic process of social unification and harmony through the construction of an "integrating whole" (Fei 2015).

2 Defining the "Middle Class" (Singular) and "Middle Classes" (Plural) within the Class System

The complexity of the middle-class debate comes from the diversity of the Middle Classes (MCs). The middle class, no plural, is generally defined in terms of the relative level of living in relation with the median of the income distribution: the middle class can be defined as the population with incomes between 50% and 150% of the median. A broad, systematic example comes from the project of Gornick and Jäntti (2013): many Western societies, in particular in English-speaking countries, show obvious trends of increasing inequalities associated with a loss of density of this middle class, squeezed between deepening poverty and the income expansion of the rich. My own update (January 2022) of middle-class dynamics confirms that poverty and richer categories progressively absorb the middle class (Figure 25.1).

Yet this middle class (singular) conception is not sufficient to understand the different facets of the problem: in the sociological literature, the realities of middle classes (MCs) are plural (Chauvel 2009) with two main cleavages:

– A clear vertical division between the central middle class, having short tertiary education and living close to the median of incomes, and the upper middle class that might reach the elites (Méndez and Gayo 2019).
– A second divide between the "old" middle class based on wealth and control of assets (middle size shop owners, petty entrepreneurs, etc.) and the "new" middle class of skilled workers with more education than economic resources, typical of the intermediate credentialed workers with recognized skills (Wright 1997). This second divide draws the difference between wealth and education.

The two axes of social inequality and differentiation structure the whole class system, not only the middle class. A clear design of this structural system, resulting as a hybridization of Bourdieu (1979) and or Wysong and Perrucci (2017) conceptualizations, is presented on the "Bourdieusian diamond" (Figure 25.2). In post-industrial Western countries where agriculture represents a small minority of the workforce, the vertical axis opposes the elites at the top to the underclass (synonyms: the poor, marginalization, *Lumpenproletariat*, exclusion, etc.) at the bottom. This first axis defines mainstream inequalities, but is completed by the opposition between economic resources, on the right, and educational/cultural resources, on the left. The multidimensional structural system, typically Bourdieusian, comes with internal social divides and segmentations that generalize the "double-diamond diagram" of classes (Wysong and Perrucci 2017).

The transformations of the "Bourdieusian diamond" help us to understand class structure changes through time and between countries. Northern

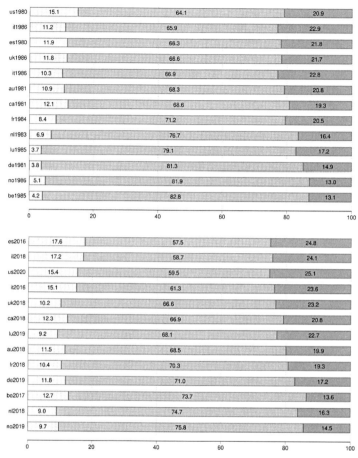

FIGURE 25.1 Population shares in poverty (lightest grey, incomes below 50% of the median), in affluence (darkest fray, incomes above 150% of the median), and in the middle class (medium grey, neither in poverty nor affluence) based on equivalized disposable income circa 1985 and 2020.
Note: Countries ISO standard codes: Australia (au), Belgium (be), Canada (ca), France (fr), Germany (ge), Israel (il), Italy (it), Luxembourg (lu), Netherlands (nl), Norway (no), Spain (es), United Kingdom (uk), United States (us)
SOURCE: LIS DATACENTRE

European countries of the early 1980s, defined by a strong conception of socioeconomic equality, present clear "olive shaped" distributions (Li and Zhu 2016). On the contrary, the American double diamond is typically stretched between the economic elite and extreme poverty, with a squeezed middle-class in-between. Some countries like France show a larger second axis opposition, with a clear divide between the economic (wealth) based middle

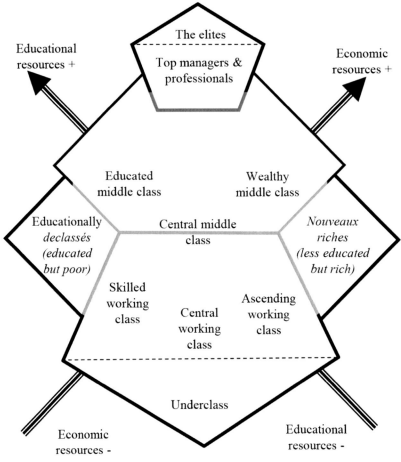

FIGURE 25.2   The "Bourdieusian diamond" in twenty-first century Western societies

class and elite on the right, opposed to elite educated higher civil servants of the state selected within an upper middle class of selectively educated intelligentsia. France, compared with the United States, presents a stronger division between the private business elite and the public management system: "money alone cannot buy culture and education" is a common statement in Paris. In the recent American trends, by contrast, we notice an increasing relation between the wealthiest and the most selectively educated ones (Pfeffer 2018): the American Bourdieusian diamond becomes unidimensional, reduced to a stretched vertical line where the middle is squeezed.

3 Defining "Middle Class Society" and Its Historical Dynamics

Above are the definitions of the "middle class" (close to the median individuals on the income scale) and the "middle classes" (subgroups of individuals in the two-dimensional Bourdieusian space), but we still need another definition: what is the middle-class society?

Western sociologies prefer individual definitions of sociological concepts, and it is particularly evident in the traditions of English-speaking sociologies, with major exceptions (Malinowski 1945; Wright 1997; Savage 2021). The French sociological tradition, with prominent examples in Durkheim and Bourdieu, is more opened to holistic trends where collective conceptions and the point of view of the whole social reality (整全觀) are predominant aspects of sociological analysis. For this reason, French sociology is particularly open to Fei Xiaotong's approach of the "integrating whole" associating individuals, collectivity, and space (Roulleau-Berger 2021). Fei (2015: 11), developing on the "emphasis on a holistic and systematic approach to human biology and social structures", is able to underline that the whole integrating collectivity is more than the sum of individuals in a society: Western sociology must work more on Fei's concept of the "integrating whole", that is a stronger concept than the one of "system integration", relatively common in the Western sociology (Lockwood 1964).

In this precise sense, middle classes are not simply close sets of similar individuals, they also integrate them in a whole collective dynamic to construct a "middle class society". From the literature on the Western middle classes until the 1970s, we can draw the main lines of this process of "middlization" that promotes a middle-class society. Based on various classical sociological studies (notably Galbraith 1958), the typical middle-class societies of the late industrial age, which peaked in the Western world on the eve of the 1980s, can be described by seven important parameters—or seven "pillars" of middlization:

1. Well above the level of the proletariat, a new group of wage earners emerges with stable and secure incomes around the median wage. Career stability and security is promoted and accessible to larger social groups of wage earners. Work stability becomes the typical model of the public sector and large companies, including banks and insurance companies, etc. This model of the average employee generates a whole dynamic of integration including lower and upper wage earner classes.
2. In Galbraith's (1958) affluent society model, the standard of living rises over the life course, leading not only to a consumption society, but also to

modest home ownership opened even to the lower middle class. Housing property is accessible to the median wage earner, because of lower land prices and accessibility of long-term mortgages that household can reimburse from age 25 to 55 years old. This model promotes relative equality through wage moderation at the top of the distribution in a context of rapid and sustained economic growth that reduces risks of frustration in the different social classes.

3. The development of the welfare state increases lifelong security that helps extend "social citizenship" where individuals are integrated in a system of collective responsibility in relation with social risks (widowhood, retirement, health, unemployment, poverty among the elderly, etc.). This collective social protection is an alternative to private wealth accumulation and promotes a trend of "dewealthization": wealth is no longer a condition of security.

4. Middle class society promotes educational expansion. Education is not only acquisition of selective skills that defines the "new middle class" compared to the old one but is also a major process of successful socialization of the young generation. Education is not only based on individual merit, thought of as personal talent and effort: it integrates a third dimension of moral values and actions for the collectivity. The middle-class society is characterized by a growing, state-funded higher education sector ("education boom") promoting human capital, social upward mobility, and also political integration of the young in a holistic conception of merit.

5. Middle class society is also a vision of progress and an optimistic conception of an endless quest for personal and collective improvement through human development and economic, technological, and scientific progress. In the history of the American middle class, the late 1960s was the climax of the belief in progress ("Man on the Moon").

6. In the context of the post-World War II golden age in Western countries, the middle class became the barycenter of local political power, trade unions, but also central governmental action—in European countries more precisely. Traditional politics was based on the struggle between the dominant conservative bourgeois class and the social revolutionary trends of proletarian currents. The early 20th century trade unions were working class-based movements, generally excluding middle class who often joined bourgeois parties in elections. In the middle-class society, the new middle class gained a central place in democratic politics, especially in continental Europe.

7. Middle-class values in a middle-class society correspond to the Aristotelian ideal of moderation, stability, and rationality in a harmonious society. Middle class becomes a central and moderate actor, as prophesied by Georg Simmel or Eduard Bernstein.

These seven parameters or trends are typical of the golden age of the equalitarian growth in the golden age Western societies. These trends created not only a convergence of centripetal forces, but also a social entelechy (Mannheim 1928), a social force that connects individuals to form a collectivity and have a socializing effect. They generate class-consciousness, collective streams, social calling that includes not only middle class members, but motivates the working class for upward social mobility and at the same time could integrate some children of the bourgeois classes, who find in progressive politics convincing moral and philosophical arguments they prefer to the traditional selfishness of the elites.

In the Global North (GN), typified by the countries of the initial OECD founding members, this middle-class society dynamics culminated fifty years ago, in the 1970s, when a large group of wage earners close to the median income exemplified this typical "olive-shaped" society (Li and Zhu 2016). This process had begun in the late 19th century and was observed by key thinkers of the coming "new middle class", including Simmel, Schmoller or Bernstein (see Charle 2002). The two world wars had interrupted this process for an entire generation in a violent "age of extremes" (Hobsbawm 2003). In particular the brutal economic recession of the 1930s in the European context transformed this new middle class (Lederer and Marschak 1926) in a potentially anomic group that eventually contributed to the rise of fascist empires in the "panic in the middle class" (Geiger 1930). In the post-WWII era, in a context of rapid and egalitarian reconstruction of Western economies, a new model of society emerged: the middle-class society that resulted from a process of middlization. Economic growth was the motor of this trend, but with stagnant wages and economic slowdown of the GN, a new trend developed: "de-middlization".

4 Diagnosing Demiddlization and Symptoms of a Destabilized Social Class?

The inversion of Galbraith's seven parameters is typical of centrifugal dynamics from the middle class. The destabilization of the former middlization trends gains in importance in times of economic decline and could produce a generation of young adults shaped by a pessimistic *Zeitgeist* ("spirit of the time", Mannheim 1928). The sketch here is more programmatic than a definitive demonstration because it would require a more systematic, comparative, and long-term validation. The main claim here, however, is that the elements of social destabilization that have affected the working class since the 1980s are moving upward on the socio-economic ladder and reach at least the level of the lower middle classes. In this section, the seven arguments presented above are systematically reassessed in order to test the hypothesis of a "destabilizing middle class": are we witnessing a general reversal of the seven trends of the post-*Golden Age* period? Does it mean the coming decay of the middle-class society in the GN?

1. The loss of career stability and fluctuations in the labor market create wage insecurity and therefore increasing difficulties in the middle class to plan life-course perspectives. A massive new precariat (Standing 2011) is emerging in middle class societies, especially in the younger generation. This status uncertainty brings new risks of debt distress and vulnerability (Russell et al. 2012; Ahlquist and Ansell 2017). One of the biggest changes in the middle class is its relationship to safety in terms of controlling adverse events across the lifespan. Securing stable employment or adequate and scheduled work contracts is a central goal for the majority of the population, which was generally achieved early in adult life by the 1970s' wage earners. In the American case, the growing vulnerability of large segments of the lower middle class (Newman and Chen 2007) is becoming an obvious threat for the children of the *Golden Age* middle class. Health consequences have been widely documented with "deaths of despair" resulting from growing collective uncertainty (Case and Deaton 2020).

2. The slowdown in economic growth negatively affects wage earners, even in Western "affluent societies". Income stagnation is even clearer for net wages after payroll and income tax. Globalization (Milanovic 2016), market competition between continents, robotization and digitalization are accelerating this trend. These adverse trends might be mitigated by social protection systems. Depending on welfare regimes, protection against job uncertainty could fade faster or slower, over-indebtedness could become a major issue or not, housing crisis could have been mitigated or accelerated, but the tide of destabilization is exacerbated everywhere by other demographic trends like ageing or increasing family complexity and general precarization (Oesch 2015; Chauvel and Bar-Haim 2016) that intensified social risks.

3. The model of strong middle class wage earner's protection faces welfare state retrenchments and the replacement of public insurance systems

by private alternatives has a devastating impact on household incomes and stability. Targeted, means-tested social protection schemes gradually exclude the middle class from public social redistributions: the poor receive protection and the richer benefit from market-based solutions to retirement, health care, and quality education; but the median is too rich to be protected and too poor to benefit from market competition. As a result, savings and capital gains generate an increasing gap between wage earners unable to build wealth accumulation on their own and the upper classes able to grasp new market opportunities. This signifies a major turning point after a full twentieth century of welfare state construction and promotion of de-commodification as described by Esping-Andersen (1990). The new trend of re-modification and provision of social protection through private market solution means a rewealthization. This destabilization opens up new vulnerabilities over the entire life cycle (Spini et al. 2017).

4. In several countries (e.g., Italy, Spain), even highly educated people have difficulty entering the labor market, resulting in a mismatch between education and socio-economic positions. also known as "overeducation". Beliefs in the intrinsic value of mass education are eroding and the middle class become conscious of the risks of sudden social decline. This is not specific to Southern Europe or the lower middle class: in countries like Britain, a college degree in young adulthood becomes a weaker protection against risks of being NEET (Not in employment, education, or training) (Holmes et al. 2019). After 40 years of rising unemployment rates (with fluctuations), France offers an interesting example of this drop in job predictability. On the one hand, we can say that education offers relatively increasing protection against unemployment as the gap between the educated and the less educated has widened over time. On the other hand, in this process of acceleration of inequalities, diplomas lose their absolute protective power. In this regard, education becomes a more necessary and less sufficient resource (Bar-Haim et al. 2019). This contributes to the long-term development of insecurity and malaise in the wage earner society, especially in the younger generation (Yeung and Yang 2020).

5. In Europe, the decreasing trust in the European Union political construction and populistic trends are obvious symptoms of political anomie (Mau 2015). In America, after long-term trends of increasing difficulties in civil society participation, worrisome examples of political destabilization are obvious, along with declining trust in the future, progress and science, and public authorities. In Geiger's (1930) model of "panic

in middle class", economic degradation, downward mobility, and lack of stable regulatory framework create fear, frustration, and social disorganization. A strong core of shared values and a sense of solidarity can limit centrifugal tendencies, but if they are absent, societies are threatened by anomie and social unrest. These tendencies are typical of the French "yellow vests" riots of 2018 that expressed the negative or adverse sentiments of frustrated and downwardly mobile individuals from the lower middle class (Chauvel 2019). In the current context of the COVID-19 pandemic, that is exacerbating anxiety in Western populations, systemic distrust in authorities and even Western science as well as the erosion of collective discipline generates new problems and hamper any solution.

6. The decline in participation in the institutions of social democracy, in particular the trade unions, marks the loss of the political centrality of the middle class (Chauvel and Schroeder 2017). This comes with a trend towards the elitization of politics in a winner-take-all process (Hacker and Pierson 2010; Jensen and van Kersbergen 2017) that excludes the poor and the middle class as well.

7. Problems that were previously limited to socially excluded groups or the working class are now spreading to the lower middle class, or even higher. Gradually, populist parties succeed in winning votes in the middle class, such as the Front National in France or the FPÖ in Austria (e.g., Pastor and Veronesi 2018). Western countries such as France, Italy, Hungary, and the Netherlands face worrying deviations from their democratic ideals. In France, the "yellow vests movement" illustrates the anomic tendencies and the populist temptations in the lower-middle-class fractions experiencing downward mobility (Chauvel 2019). The situation in Northern America or Australia underlines the global threats coming from anomic consequences of destabilized middle-class politics. Increasing tensions in the Western populations might cause the comeback of aggressive politics.

5 Individualism and Holism in Middle Class Dynamics

The diagnosis of the Western "new middle-class squeeze" is as follows: in the United States, the general landscape is a clear middle-class process of shrinking trend and squeeze, in economic and cultural terms. In Europe, it is more complex in terms of incomes, but the analysis of wealth dynamics shows similar traits. Political and cultural dimensions complete the perspective of the endangered middle class and of the problematic reversal of the middle-class society in Western countries.

Such a dynamic, which is particularly clear in France, has a strong impact on the legitimacy of the educational and university system, on top of trust in science, progress, and even in the whole system. In terms of downward mobility, compared to Americans, the French are less subject to intra-cohort disruption than to inter-generational declines. In other words, France is less a country of "falling from grace" (Newman 1988) than a country of a specific incapacity of the young generation to inherit the wage earner middle class status of their parents due to a lack of positions in the "new" middle class.

The younger generations, often the children of upwardly mobile baby boomers, are experiencing a strong rise in education, and many are experiencing downward dynamics of lower middle-class positions; this contradiction is likely to produce a kind of generational dismemberment of the "new" middle class. If the French social structure seems to be quite stable in recent decades, the young face a collective concern of a shrinking new middle class. Their own parents, who are growing increasingly conscious of the challenges of the next generation, are likely to share the pessimism of their children.

If wealth makes a difference and develops a larger number of potential heirs of substantial fortune, this new trend is still seen as an additional element of injustice because inherited wealth is, by construction, the opposite of merit. The consequences of these trends, in political terms, are quite pervasive: in France, the 2018 yellow vests movement, inspired by a radical critique of extreme injustice, demonstrates the destabilization of the lower middle classes and of the younger generations. Revealing a deepening generational rift, these increasingly frequent "earthquakes" among the younger generations foreshadow the "big one". The American situation of democracy is problematic as well. By comparison with Western pessimistic trends, the Chinese transformations over the last 20 years are much more optimistic because educational investments have received better rewards. The fantastic situation of massive economic growth in China provides collective certainties of better situations for all that have no equivalent in the West. In Western countries, a deep slowdown in this trend explains increasing inner tensions in the middle classes.

Another aspect of middle-class societies in the West and in China must be underlined in reference to the inspiration of Fei Xiaotong: Western middle-class society of the 1960s—and the Chinese middle-class society today—is not simply a question of positions of atomistic individuals in job markets, social pyramids, or consumption lifestyles. Middle class society is also an "integrating whole" where the seven characteristics generate a collective trend of socialization. In this holistic vision where the whole is more than its individual parts, a collective culture and project of progress happens. In Western societies, the individual is generally seen as more important than collective entities, a typical trait of the American movie industry that promotes a conception of individual heroes. In this individualist vision, collective entities are seen as the simple sum of individual contributions, like in the Western conception of "human rights" that generally gives preference to single individuals at the expense of rights of large groups to benefit from collective progress. The intrinsic risk in the development of the middle-class society is to forget this collective vision of progress. In this Western conception, the success of middle class is undermined by the development of centrifugal trends: individual appetites and competition, loss of integrative vision in collective progress, transformation of solidarity and welfare provision as a due and not a collective responsibility. The radicalization of individualism that is intrinsic to Western cultures, and is exacerbated in the process of middlization, might (and will, in the West) accelerate the inverse process of demiddlization. The promotion of middle-class as an "integrating whole" "building harmony in diversity" (Fei 2015) is a more sustainable way that China might promote and experience in the future.

References

Archer, M. 1996. "Social Integration and System Integration: Developing the Distinction". *Sociology* 30 (4): 679–699. doi:10.1177/0038038596030004004.

Bourdieu, P. 1979. *La Distinction, Critique Sociale Du Jugement.* Paris: Editions De Minuit.

Case, A., and A. Deaton. 2020. *Deaths of Despair and the Future of Capitalism.* Princeton University Press.

Charle, C. 2002. "The Middle Classes in France: Social and Political Functions of Semantic Pluralism from 1870–2000". In *Social Contracts under Stress. The Middle Classes of America, Europe and Japan at the Turn of the Century,* edited by Olivier Zunz, L. Schoppa, and N. Hiwatari, 66–88. New York: Russell Sage Foundation.

Chauvel, L., and A. Hartung. 2016. "Malaise in the Western Middle Classes". World Social Science Report 2016. *Challenging Inequalities: Pathways to a Just World,* edited by UNESCO, 164–169. https://unesdoc.unesco.org/ark:/48223/pf0000245860.

Chauvel, L. (路易・肖韦尔). 2009. "The transformation of the European class system and the middle classes adrift" [欧洲阶级体系的转型以及中产阶级的飘零]. In Li Chinling (李春玲), *Formation of Middle Class in Comparative Perspective: Process, Influence and Socioeconomic Consequences* [比较视野下的中产阶级形成], 371–396. Beijing (北京): Social sciences academic press [社会科学文献出版社].

Chauvel, L., and M. Schroeder. 2017. "A Prey-Predator Model of Trade Union Density and Inequality in 12 Advanced Capitalisms over Long Periods". *Kyklos* 70 (1): 3–26.

Chauvel, Louis, Eyal Bar-Haim, Anne Hartung, and Emily Murphy. 2021. "Rewealthization in twenty-first century Western countries: the defining trend of the socioeconomic squeeze of the middle class". *Journal of Chinese Sociology* 8 (4): 1–17.

Esping-Andersen, G. 1990. *The Three Worlds of Welfare Capitalism*. Princeton, NJ: Princeton University Press.

Fei, X. 2015. "Building Harmony in Diversity". In *Globalization and Cultural Self-Awareness*. China Academic Library. Berlin and Heidelberg: Springer. https://doi-org.proxy.bnl.lu/10.1007/978-3-662-46648-3_2.

Galbraith, J.K. 1958. *The Affluent Society*. Boston: Houghton Mifflin.

Geiger, T. 1930. "Panik Im Mittelstand". *Die Arbeit* 7 (10): 637–654. http://library.fes.de/cgi-in/digiarb.pl?id=01021&dok=1930&f=637&l=654&c=637.

Gornick, J., and M. Jäntti, eds. 2013. *Income Inequality: Economic Disparities And The Middle Class In Affluent Countries*. Stanford, CA: Stanford University Press.

Hacker, J.S., and P. Pierson. 2010. "Winner-Take-All Politics: Public Policy, Political Organization, and the Precipitous Rise of Top Incomes in the United States". *Politics & Society* 38 (2): 152–204. https://doi.org/10.1177/0032329210365042.

Holmes, C., E. Murphy, and K. Mayhew. 2019. "What accounts for changes in the chances of being NEET in the UK?" SKOPE working paper, No. 128 (July). Oxford.

Hobsbawm, E.J. 2003. *Age of Extremes: The Short Twentieth Century, 1914–1991*. London: Abacus.

Jensen, C., and K. van Kersbergen. 2017. *The Politics of Inequality*. London: Palgrave.

Lederer, E., and J. Marschak. 1926. "Der neue Mittelstand, in Grundriss der Sozialökonomik", *Das soziale System des Kapitalismus, Grundriß der Sozialökonomik*, IX. Abteilung, I. Teil, 120–141. Tübingen: Mohr.

Li, C. 2010. "Characterizing China's Middle Class: Heterogeneous Composition and Multiple Identities". In *China's emerging middle class: beyond economic transformation*, edited by Cheng Li. Washington, DC: Brookings Institution Press.

Li, C. 2014. "A Profile of the Middle Classes in Today's China". In *Chinese Middle Classes: Taiwan, Hong Kong, Macau and China*, edited by Hsin Huang and Michael Hsiao, 78–94. London and New York: Routledge.

Li, P. 2016. "Transition of Occupational and Social Stratum and Innovation of the Social Management System". In *Great Changes and Social Governance in Contemporary China*, edited by P. Li. China Insights. Berlin and Heidelberg: Springer.

Li, P. 2013. *People's Livelihood in Contemporary China: Changes, Challenges and Prospects*. Singapore, SGP: World Scientific Publishing Company.

Li, P., and D. Zhu. 2016. "Make Efforts to Develop an Olive-shaped Distribution Pattern: An Analysis Based on Data from the Chinese Social Survey for 2006–2013". *Social Sciences in China* 37 (1): 5–24. DOI:10.1080/02529203.2015.1133432.

Liu, X. 2020. "Class structure and income inequality in transitional China". *Journal Chinese Sociology* 7 (4). https://doi.org/10.1186/s40711-020-00116-9.

Lockwood, D. 1964. "Social Integration and System Integration". In *Explorations in Social Change*, edited by G.K. Zollschan and H.W. Hirsch. Boston: Houghton Mifflin.

Lu, H. 2010. "The Chinese Middle Class and Xiaokang Society". In *China's emerging middle class: beyond economic transformation*, edited by Cheng Li. Washington, DC: Brookings Institution Press.

Malinowski, B. 1945. *The Dynamics of Culture Change*. Connecticut: Yale University Press.

Mannheim, K. 1928. "Das Problem der Generationen". In *Kölner Vierteljahrshefte für Soziologie* 7, S. 157–185, 309–330.

Mau, S. 2015. *Inequality, Marketization and the Majority Class: Why Did the European Middle Classes Accept Neo-liberalism?* Springer.

Méndez, M.L., and M. Gayo. 2019. *Upper Middle Class Social Reproduction: Wealth, Schooling, and Residential Choice in Chile*. New York: Palgrave Pivot Series.

Milanovic, B. 2016. *Global Inequality: A New Approach For The Age Of Globalization*. Cambridge, MA: Belknap Press.

Newman, K., and V.T. Chen. 2007. *The Missing Class: Portraits of the Near Poor in America*. Boston: Beacon Press.

OECD (Organisation for Economic Co-operation and Development). 2019. *Under Pressure: The Squeezed Middle Class*. Paris: OECD Publishing.

Oesch, D. 2015. "Welfare regimes and change in the employment structure: Britain, Denmark and Germany since 1990". *Journal of European Social Policy* 25 (1): 94–110.

Pfeffer, F.T. 2018. "Growing Wealth Gaps in Education". *Demography* 55: 1033–1068. https://doi.org/10.1007/s13524-018-0666-7.

Piketty, T. 2014. *Capital in the Twenty First Century*. Translated by A. Goldhammer. Cambridge, MA: Belknap Press, An Imprint of Harvard University Press.

Reeves, R. 2017. *Dream Hoarders: How the American Upper Middle Class is Leaving Everyone Else in the Dust, Why That Is a Problem, and What to Do About It*. Washington, DC: Brookings Institution.

Roulleau-Berger, L. 2021. "The fabric of Post-Western sociology: ecologies of knowledge beyond the "East" and the "West"". *Journal of Chinese Sociology* 8 (4). https://doi.org/10.1186/s40711-021-00144-z.

Russell, H., C.T. Whelan, and B. Maître. 2012. "Economic vulnerability and the severity of debt problems: An analysis of the Irish EU-SILC 2008". *European Sociological Review* 29 (4): 695–706.

Savage, M. 2021. *The Return of Inequality: Social Change and the Weight of the Past*. Cambridge, MA: Harvard University Press.

Savage, M., and C. Li. 2021. Introduction to thematic series "new sociological perspectives on inequality". *Journal of Chinese Sociology* 8 (4). https://doi.org/10.1186/s40711-021-00145-y.

Spini, D., L. Bernardi, and M. Oris. 2017. "Toward a Life Course Framework for Studying Vulnerability". *Research in Human Development* 14 (1): 5–25.

Standing, G. 2011. *The Precariat: The New Dangerous Class*. Bloomsbury Academic.

Therborn, G. 2021. "Two epochal turns of inequality, their significance, and their dynamics". *Journal of Chinese Sociology* 8 (4). https://doi.org/10.1186/s40711-021-00143-0.

Whelan, C.T., B. Nolan, and B. Maitre. 2017. "Polarization or "Squeezed Middle" in the Great Recession?: A Comparative European Analysis of the Distribution of Economic Stress". *Social Indicators Research: An International and Interdisciplinary, Journal for Quality-of-Life Measurement* 133 (1): 163–184.

Wright, E.O. 1997. *Class counts: Comparative studies in class analysis*. Cambridge University Press.

Wysong, E., and R. Perrucci. 2018. *Deep Inequality: Understanding the New Normal and How to Challenge It*. Boulder, CO: Rowman & Littlefield.

Yeung, W.-J., and Y. Yang. 2020. "Labor Market Uncertainties for Youth and Young Adults: An International Perspective". *The ANNALS of the American Academy of Political and Social Science* 688 (1): 7–19. https://doi.org/10.1177/0002716220913487.

CHAPTER 26

A New Approach to Social Inequality: Inequality of Income and Wealth

Shin Kwang-Yeong

1   Introduction

This paper attempts to explore income inequality and wealth inequality and their relationship, revealing that the two main indicators of inequality have different dynamics of making economic inequality in contemporary South Korea. Analyzing *the linked data* of the Survey of Household Finance and Living Conditions (HFLC) collected by the Statistical Office with the administrative data on household income by the National Tax Office in South Korea, this paper identifies contributing factors to household income inequality and wealth inequality. It also shows that the traditional approaches to social stratification have limitations to fully understand the issue of rising economic inequality in the post-industrial society characterized by the growing elderly population and changing the family system as well as the transformation of industrial production.

While economic inequality has become an important political issue as well as an academic issue all over the world in the 21st century (Piketty 2013; Atkinson 2016; Stiglitz 2012), sociologists have not been successful in explaining the rise of income inequality. Piketty has shown how income and wealth have been concentrated into top income groups in the advanced industrial democracies since the late 20th century. As many sociologists have already argued, however, sociologists have not been successful in providing sociological explanations of the rising inequality (Western 1999; Myles 2003; Kenworthy 2007; Savage and Burrows 2007). While sociologists have been concerned with inequality of mobility chance or social fluidity between social groups such as social class, gender, and race, sociologists have not significantly contribute to an understanding of the rising income inequality and wealth inequality.

The traditional approach to social stratification has focused on *individual* work and occupation. The work-based approach to social inequality has been a core of social stratification and class analysis in sociology. It has formed a research paradigm in social stratification which focuses on the role of *education* mediating the relationship between family background and individual occupation (see Blau and Duncan 1965; Breen and Muller 2020; Erikson and Goldthorpe 2000; Featherman and Hauser 1975; Hout and DiPrite 2006; OECD 2018). Occupation has played a key role as an origin (father's occupation) and destination (children's occupation) in the social mobility research, while education has worked as a social elevator for upward spcoa; mobility over generations. Thus, the *O-E-D model* has been the core research framework in social stratification for the past decades, called 'a disciplinary default' (Savage 2016).

There have been good reasons why sociologists have focused on occupation rather than income and wealth. There have been *practical* reasons for occupation rather than income as a key area on research on social stratification. In practice, measurement error is serious in getting information about income and wealth. For example, many respondents don't know their income exactly, or they don't want to tell their income to others. Therefore, almost all survey questionnaire asked income in an interval scale with the open-ended top income, making a precise measurement of income inequality impossible.

Sociologists have been preoccupied with the working population, excluding the elderly mostly out of the labor forces. The majority of the elderly population who are not working has been excluded from the research on social stratification. In the past, women were excluded in the social stratification research until the 1970s, whereas the elderly were excluded in the social stratification research in the late 20th century (see Acker 1973). Much of the research on social mobility and sex segregation of jobs has focused on the working population.

Sociologists have assumed *individuals* as a unit of analysis of social stratification, while they have conceived family background as an essential factor to shape children's education and occupation. Household as a social institution of pooling family member's income has not been emphasized. Educational investment in children's education has been made by family or household level, not an individual level. Family or household is a unit of family consumption, children's education, and daily social life.

Finally, most of the research on social stratification has not paid attention to *wealth inequality*, while wealth inequality is much more severe than any other dimension of inequality in almost all countries (Alvareto, Chancel, Piketty, Saez and Zucman 2018; Therborn 2012; Piketty 2013). Some magazines such as *Forbes* report the global rich with narratives of the success story of the people in business (Kroll and Dolan 2019). But there has been little research in sociology on how wealth is associated with social stratification and inequality. Research on the labor market and gender has focused on wage disparity among the employees. Owners of capital, such as stockholders or building owners, get a much higher income than the earnings of employees, though some of them don't have jobs and occupations.

This paper investigates two dimensions of inequality, income inequality and wealth inequality, and examines the relationship between the two by using linked administrative and survey data. In the next section, we will discuss the relationship between income and wealth and explore the relationship between wealth and income inequality. In the third section, we will explain the Survey of Household Finance and Living Conditions (HFLC) and the linking the survey data to administrative data from different governmental agencies to get accurate information about income. Then we will briefly explain *the regression-based-inequality decomposition* method used in the statistical analysis. The fourth section reports the results of an empirical analysis, identifying major contributing factors to income inequality and wealth inequality. In the last section, some implications of the finding of this research will be addressed concerning research on social stratification.

2   Household Income and Wealth

Recently income has been a focal point of discourse on inequality. While income has been considered as a primary dimension of economic inequality in social sciences, income has seldom been the main topic of theoretical discourse or a subject of empirical research in sociology. Research on inequality and stratification has paid more attention to structural or institutional factors that are assumed to generate socio-economic inequality that we observe every day. For example, status attainment approaches have focused on the relationship among social origins (parents' occupation), education (respondents' education), and destination (respondents' occupations), called the OED model. However, the relationship between occupation and income has not been fully elaborated. The only average of earnings of occupation has been assumed to represent the income level of each occupation without recognizing the variation of an individual's earnings has been affected by other factors than occupation, such as industry, firm size, employment status, and gender.

Individual occupation has been considered as a proxy of socioeconomic status or social stratification in sociology. Does an individual's occupation represent one's economic wellbeing? Does it affect the distribution of household income that influences family expenditure and educational investment for children? The answer is yes, but only partially true. With an increasing diversification and flexibility in the labor market, there have been increasing numbers of non-standard workers who get less paid by employers, less secured by unions, and less protected by the state (Kalleberg 2000; OECD 2019; Shin 2013). The rise of precarious work challenges the validity of occupation as a cornerstone of earnings inequality.

Earnings refer to economic rewards from work and there are many other economic gain from other than work. Income refers to a flow of money that include not only economic rewards from work but also economic gains from factors such as capital, land, and pension and entitlement. Thus, it has a variety of forms, such as wage, public transfer, profits, rent, interest, and dividends. As the capitalist economy develops and employment relation becomes a dominant form of the economic system, the majority of the people receive wage or salary in exchange for their work as employees. Those who hire others in their business get profits. Thus wage or salary comes from a part of the profits gained by employers.

However, new forms of income derived from non-producing capital. Nowadays, as the financial sector dominates the economy and everyday life, more people tend to own stocks and bonds to get more economic benefits. Those who own stocks and bonds get capital gains through a transaction of them in the stock market or a dividend given to stockholders by a corporation. Financialization of the economy leads to the increasing importance of the financial sector in the economy relative to the economy, and the growing number of people engages in the financial market and get income from financial capital (Davis and Kim 2015). The ascendancy of the financial sector has led to the new rules of accumulation without producing material goods, enabling middle-class members to engage in the stock market transaction and real estate markets for short-term profits. Now with the help of digitalization of the daily trading of stocks at home, 'profits without producing' has been possible for middle-class households as well as the global financial investors (Sawyer 2014). Financialization has completely transformed the distribution of income and wealth through the mediation of financial institutions such as investment banks and financial firms specialized in real estate speculation. At the household level, households utilizing credit systems begin to use leverage to purchase an asset, mostly housings and stocks, with the expectation of the increasing return of investment. In particular, the rising housing price in many countries has instigated middle-class households and wealthy investors to use debt financing or bank loans to invest in the housing market and real estate markets. Increasing household debt has been observed in several countries where housing bubbles were made, generating high household indebtedness ratio. South Korea displays a very high level of household indebtedness and debt-to-total asset ratio among OECD countries (OECD 2020).[1]

Income is determined by the monthly economic gains derived from economic activities or profits from investment or rent, including houses or offices. In this case, for the majority of the people, one's occupation or social class is an essential factor in explaining an individual's income. However, substantial social changes that occurred in the late 20th century challenged the long tradition of approach to income inequality. The first challenge is that an individual's income may be quite different from household income because the growing number of married couples jointly participates in the labor force (Esping-Andersen 1999: ch. 4). Thus, household income is a pooled income of individual household members when more than one family member engaged in economic activity. The growth of dual earners family contributes to the divergence of household income from individual income in the labor market in post-industrial societies.

Household income is also affected by the development of welfare programs to cope with social problems such as poverty and unemployment. An effect of the development of the welfare state has been an increase of public transfer to the people with low income or unemployment. Also, the rise of the aged population retired from the labor market also increases the proportion of the people who receive pension or benefits not associated with work. The growth of the population getting pension benefits contributes to the growing impact of public transfer in income distribution. The impacts of welfare programs on income distribution have been associated with the level of public social expenditure and tax rate. On average, OECD countries reduce more than one-quarter of market income inequality via tax and cash transfers. Korea was one of the least redistributive countries with less than 10 percent in 2014 (OECD 2020).

Wealth is a stock of valuable assets, including a share of stocks of companies, savings in banks, the ownership of property, insurance schemes, pension, and luxury goods. Some form of wealth, such as a house or a car, is visible, whereas other forms of wealth, such as ownership of stocks and insurance, are entirely invisible to outsiders. As some wealth such as savings, lands or estates themself generate income, "a disproportionate share of the highest income comes from wealth" (Davis 2019: 128). Besides, parts of wealth itself are convertible to market income by selling stocks and houses.

---

1 In South Korea, the level of household debt was 184.20 percent of the net household disposable income in 2018, which was more than twice that of Germany and Japan. It was 147.53 percent in 2010. See OECD (2020) for the details.

Wealth can function as a private safety net in case of unemployment, severe illness, divorce, industrial injury industry, and retirement. In particular, housing ownership plays a role as a social safety net against the various social risks in one's life in countries where social welfare is not sufficiently institutionalized. Housing ownership can be a functional equivalence to social welfare in South Korea. Thus the ratio of housing ownership has increased even after the income has decreased in their 60s. When earners decease, of course, the earned income disappears. But, the wealth of the deceased is inheritable to children. Thus, wealth inequality is much more stable than income inequality over time.

Then, how is wealth formed? There are many pathways through which wealth is formed, and wealth inequality is generating. The typical pathway is the accumulation of some part of disposable income as savings for a period at an individual level or the household level. Thus, the surplus income, that is, income minus expenditure, are kept in banks or invested in the stock market or real estate markets. The formation of a financial asset can be a stock of saved income. Higher-income earners tend to save a more substantial part of income. Those who have their own housings can save more than renters of housings. For example, in South Korea, the top 10 percent of income group has 22.39 times higher savings than the lowest 10 percent of income groups in 2017.

The second pathway is the rise of values of possessed wealth, such as ownership of capital, houses, or other property. Thomas Piketty (2013) argues that the dynamics of increasing wealth inequality is simply based on the fact that the rate of return on capital r is greater than the rate of return to labor g ($r > g$). Also, financial assets and real estate multiply itself through capital value change. The rise in the price of real estate, stocks, and bonds also contributed to the growth of wealth for renters. In addition, the rise in rent also played a vital role in the growth of wealth. Wealth has been more severely affected by market fluctuation than income. Sometimes, the asset bubble bursts out when the price of an asset-inflated exceeds the intrinsic value of the asset.

The third pathway is the role of wealth as leverage of loans. Wealth can function as a collateral for borrowing loans from banks. Financial organizations utilize a credit system to reduce the risk of bad credit. Even speculative mortgage loans has been possible for new investment in the financial market. Thus, profits without producing real values dominate the global economy in recent years. The wealthy people can utilize the loans to invest in the stock market and the financial market. Therefore, credit inequality becomes a new type of inequality emerging in the period of financialization. While debt-to-equity ratios increased on average, the wealthy people utilizes more financial resources than the poor in new investment.

The fourth pathway is the transmission of parent's wealth to children through private transfer or inheritance after the death of parents. Thus, the family's wealth has contributed to the wealth formation of descendants over generations. Children of the rich family acquire the properties of their parents after or before their parents pass away. The impact of inheritance of wealth on wealth inequality depends on the inheritance tax rate and the number of heirs in each country. Persistent wealth inequality and the stability of wealthy people have been common across countries. In short, economic inequality is largely ameliorated by the unequal ownership of income-producing assets and rent saving property.

3 Data and Method

3.1 Data and Variables

In this paper, we used the survey data of the Household Finance and Living Conditions (HFLC), which is the linked data of the survey data and administrative data. The HFLC has been collected by the Statistical Office in South Korea since 2010. The Statistical Office of South Korea began to collect information about household income, debt, wealth, and welfare to know the dynamics of finance after the global financial crisis in 2008–2009. The sample size was 10,000 cases until 2011, and after that, it increased to 20,000 households since 2012. The HFLC has been replaced by 20 percent of the total sample every year. Thus the HFLC will be utterly new after five years.

In this paper, we used HFLC 2017 with the sample size 18,497 in 2017. The Statistical Office in South Korea began to link the HFLC with the administrative data to overcome shortcomings of the survey data on income. Linking survey data with registered administrative data provides a new research possibility on inequality research with more accurate information on personal and household income (Medalia, Meyer, O'Hara and Wu 2019). Administrative registered data in the HFLC included the various data source to measure household income: The annual income and tax from the National Tax Office, the transfer income and pension from the Social Insurance Office, the health insurance and health service information from the National Health Insurance, educational allowance from the Ministry of Education, and child allowance from the Ministry of Health and Welfare.

Table 26.1 reports different measures of inequality of income and wealth in the survey data and the linked data in 2017. As we expected, the linked data displays a higher maximum income than the survey data, revealing that the survey data underreport the income of the top income. It also shows that the

TABLE 26.1 Measurement of income inequality and wealth inequality, 2017

	Survey data	Linked data
Income		
Median	3,698	3,966
Maximum	102,400	161,310
Gini coefficient	.4236	.4416
Share by top 10 percent	.2883	.3165
Share by top 20 percent	.4598	.4901
p90/p10	12.5800	12.3469
Palma ratio	2.4542	2.6421
Wealth		
Median	21,482	21,482
Maximum	2,670,220	2,670,220
Gini coefficient	.5738	.5738
Share by top 10 percent	.4389	.4389
Share by top 20 percent	.6147	.6147
p90/p10	55.6727	55.6727
Palma ratio	7.2046	7.2046

Note: The unit of income and wealth is 10 thousand Wons, which is equivalent to roughly 9 US Dollars. The linked data use information about income from the tax agency, but it uses information about wealth from the survey data.

survey data do not accurately identify the income of the low-income groups since the median shifts from 3,698 to 3,966. As a result, Gini coefficients measured by the linked data, 0.4416, is higher by 4.25 percent than that of the survey data, 0.4236.[2] The linked data that uses income from the administrative recode shows the fact that the survey data collected by the Statistical Office in South Korea tend to underestimate the level of the top income and the degree of inequality of the household income. The concentration of income on the top 10 percent and 20 percent of income groups also increases from .2883 in

---

2   The Gini coefficient in the HFLC 2017 is much larger than the Gini coefficient reported to the OECD by the Statistical Office Korea. The Gini coefficient reported to the OECD is based on the Household Income and Expenditure Survey (HIES) with a smaller sample size than the HFLC. Instead of the HIES, the Statistical Office Korea began to report the statistical indicators of income distribution from the HFLC since 2015. For example, the Gini coefficient in 2017 was 0.355, whereas it was .307 in 2012. The difference mainly came from the data with sample size.

the survey data to .3165 in the linked data. The share by the top 10 percent and the top 20 percent also show a similar pattern of the rising concentration of income. However, p90/p10, indicating the income gap between the income of the lowest 10 percent and the highest 10 percent income group, shows a little bit different pattern, by reducing the ratio by 1.85 percent. On the contrary, the gap between the poor 40 percent and the richest 10 percent becomes widen when the linked data is used. The Palma ratio, the ratio of the richest 10 percent of the households' share of income divided by the poorest 40 percent, shows an increase from 2.4542 to 2.6421.

Wealth inequality is much higher than income inequality across the whole countries (Zierminska, Smeeding and Allerezza 2013; Jäntti, Sierminska and Kerm 2013). On average, the popular perception of the rising inequality has been derived by not only income inequality but also wealth inequality. Wealthy persons consume luxury goods and cars and live expensive housings in gated communities. Also the rising housing price contributes to the perception of wealth inequality as well as wealth inequality itself. In South Korea, the rising housing price in recent years has contributed to the fear of the youth of the middle class and the working class, as housing ownership was very low among young adults (see Figure 26.1). The Korean youth has shown the lowering marriage rate and birth rate of the married couple mainly due to the housing shortage and housing bubbles over the decades as well as the high rate of unemployment (Kim 2017).

In this paper, income is measured by annual household income containing the market income and public transfer income. The market income includes earnings from work, profits from business, property income such as interests or rents, and the private transfer. Pre-tax income will be used in the following to focus on the impacts of contributors to before-tax income inequality. Wealth is measured by the price of a variety of possession, including properties such as houses, lands, buildings, and cars. Linking the survey data with the administrative data provides more accurate data on income than any other data set in South Korea.

The joint distribution of income and wealth shows highly polarized distribution, characterized by the two poles around income poor-wealth poor and income rich-wealth rich. Figure 26.2 displays a topographic picture of the joint distribution of income and wealth in 2017. We can see that the lowest 5 percent income and wealth group displays one pole with 3.56 times higher proportion than the average. The highest 5 percent of income and wealth shows 7.19 times higher proportion than the average. The lowest 10 percent and the highest 10 percent in both income and wealth distribution show the second-highest density. However, in the middle of income and wealth distribution in Figure 26.1,

A NEW APPROACH TO SOCIAL INEQUALITY 519

FIGURE 26.1 Distribution of earnings and housing ownership, 2017
Notes: Earnings ratio refers to the ratio of earnings relative to average earnings, and the ratio of housing ownership indicates the proportion of housing owners among each age group.

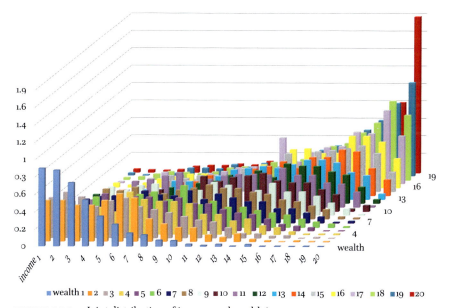

FIGURE 26.2 Joint distribution of income and wealth in 2017

there is more frequent mobility than any other parts of the joint distribution of income and wealth. It shows that there is a low level of association between income and wealth in the middle of income group and in the middle wealth group. High income and high wealth clusters are formed in the both poles.

Table 26.2 reports the summary of the description of major independent variables. Those are mostly the characteristics of the head of households

TABLE 26.2 Descriptive summary of major variables (*N*=18,497)

Variables	Explanation	Percent	Standard deviation
logY	Log of annual income	8.4173	0.9841
logW	Log of wealth	9.5869	1.7747
Sex	0 = Male	75.51%	
	1 = Female	24.49%	
Age	Average	55.2066	14.8992
Education	Years of education	11.0702	4.7102
Occupation	Managers	2.42%	
	Professionals	13.13%	
	Clerics	12.32%	
	Service	6.38%	
	Sales	7.85%	
	Peasant	5.11%	
	Skilled workers	9.42%	
	Semi-skilled workers	12.14%	
	Unskilled workers	10.29%	
	Soldier	0.28%	
	Non-working	20.64%	
Employment Status	Regular	43.54%	
	Non-regular	11.78%	
	Employer with employees	5.50%	
	Employer without employees	17.48%	
	Atypical workers	1.02%	
	Non-working	20.67%	
Family Size	Average family members	2.8413	1.2846
Elderly Household	Age of household head > 65	19.75%	
Housing Ownership	Owners of housing	61.13%	

Note: The proportions of non-working are slightly different between occupation and employment status due to the collapse of family workers without pay to non-working in the distribution of employment status.

except family size. Thus, sex in the HFLC refers to the sex of the household head. The majority of the household head is male (75.51 percent), relative to females (24.49 percent) in South Korea. The measurement of education is done by the calculation of years of education rather than categories based on the level of education. Family size refers to the number of family members. In the subsequent analysis, family size is categorized from one to six since there is a non-linear relationship between family size and income. Occupation includes non-working people as well as the working population since it deals with the entire household. Employment status also includes the category of non-working people. Soldiers in the occupational category are excluded in the following analysis because the market does not determine their incomes.

3.2 Analytical Methods

To identify the extent to which some factors contribute to inequality of income and wealth, we use the regression-based inequality decomposition developed by Gary Fields (2003).

Assuming that the income is

$$\ln y = X\beta + \varepsilon \qquad (1)$$

where: y is an n×1 vector of incomes; X is an n × (K + 1) matrix of individual and household characteristics (age, education, employment status, occupation, household size, etc.) including the constant; β is a (K + 1) × 1 vector of coefficients, and ε is an n × 1 vector of residuals. A sample of observations {$y_i, x_i, i = 1,2,... n$} can be used to estimate the model.

The linear model (1) can be rewritten as:

$$\ln y = \beta_0 + \beta_1 X_1 + \beta_2 X_2 ... + \beta_K X_K + \varepsilon \qquad (2)$$
$$= \beta_0 + Z_1 + Z_2 ... + Z_K + \varepsilon \qquad (3)$$

Where each Z_k is a "composite" variable, equal to the product of a regression coefficient and its variable ($Z_k = {}_K X_K$), with k = 0,1,... K and $X_0 = 1$.

For inequality decomposition calculations, the value of β_0 is irrelevant as it is constant for every observation.

The OLS estimate of (3) can be used for inequality decomposition:

$$\ln y = b_0 + \hat{b}_1 X_1 + \hat{b}_2 X_2 ... + ... + \hat{b}_K X_K + \hat{\varepsilon} \qquad (4)$$

Marginal contribution of the kth factor ($\hat{Z}_k = \hat{b}_k X_k$) to the variance of logarithm of income is as follows:

$$S_k = \widehat{b_k} cov(Xk, \ln y) / \sigma^2(\ln y) \tag{5}$$

$$\sum_{i=1}^{k} S_k = \sum_{i=1}^{k} \widehat{b_k} cov(Xk, \ln y) / \sigma^2(\ln y) = \sigma^2(\ln \hat{y}) / \sigma^2(\ln y) = R^2 \tag{6}$$

The less $\hat{\epsilon}$ in equation (4), the larger the explanatory power (R^2).

3.3 Results

How can we explain the high level of household income inequality and wealth inequality in South Korea? Which factors contribute to inequality of income and wealth? Does individual's occupation explain inequality of household income? Do demographic factors and family change affect the distribution of household income? How is income inequality associated with wealth inequality? The regression-based inequality decomposition method might be helpful for getting answers to some of those questions.[3]

We take two steps to decompose inequality of household income and wealth by each contributing factor. The first step is to specify income functions and wealth functions respectively, and estimate coefficients of variables in those functions by linear regression analyses. The second step is to estimate the variance of household income explained by the covariance of each independent variable and household income. It is a decomposition of the total explained variance (R^2) into contributions by each independent variable based on Shapley value.

Table 26.3 reports the results of the regression-based inequality decomposition based on the model that specify some income functions. The best-fitting models, that is, the model with the highest R^2 and significant coefficients, are used to estimate the contribution of each variable to the variance of household income and wealth. The residuals refer to the unexplained variance of inequality of household income by the model, $1 - R^2$. The number indicates the proportion of the variance of household income explained by each variable. For example, the sex of household head explains 2.0593 percent of the total variance of household income, whereas education explains 4.8322 percent of it. Those are relatively low because household dynamics are different from individual earnings in the labor market.

In Table 26.3, the occupation of the household head is the largest contributor to the variance of household income.[4] It explains 31.0587 percent of the

---

[3] We used *ineqrbd*, the STATA module to calculate the regression-based inequality decomposition, proposed by Carlo Fiorio and Stephen Jenkins (2007).

[4] The contribution of categorical variables to inequality is based on dummy coding. For example, the occupation in this data has 11 categories; 9 occupational categories, one non-working, and soldiers. Managerial occupation is a reference (base) category. The contribution of each

TABLE 26.3 Household income inequality decomposed through multivariate variables (%)

	Model 1		Model 2	
Sex	2.0593	3.3936	1.5893	2.6488
Age + Age-squared	3.4320	5.6558	0.2023	0.3372
Education	4.8322	7.9632	5.8808	9.8001
Employment status	2.7471	4.5271	13.1029	21.8382
Occupation	18.8469	31.0587	–	–
Industry	4.9104	8.0921	–	–
Wealth	16.9161	27.8768	17.5451	29.2418
Family size	13.3810	22.0512	16.5935	27.6558
Residuals	39.3184	–	39.9171	–
R^2	100.00	60.6816	100.00	60.0000
Total	100.00	100.00	100.00	100.00

explained variance of household income. Individual characteristics such as sex and age do not contribute to the variance of household income, while education exerts modest influence on it by 7.9632 percent. Household wealth is the second largest contributor to the variance of household income by 27.8768 percent. Family size plays a significant role in household income inequality. It explains 22.0512 percent of the explained variance of household income.

Model 2 in Table 26.3 provides a more parsimonious model in which occupation and industry of household head are excluded, and only the employment status of the household head is included. Employment status consists of regular employment, non-regular employment, employing other employees, self-employment employees and typical workers, and non-working person. Model 2 fits the data as good as the Model 1 with the almost same explained variance, R^2, 0.606816 vs. 60.0000. The impact of employment status on household income inequality comes from inequality between working persons and non-working persons. Both occupation and employment status include non-working persons, who increased inequality substantially.

Table 26.4 displays the contribution of each variable to the total variance of wealth, following the same equation for household income and a modified equation dropping occupation and industry and adding loans. Model 1 in Table 26.4 includes household income in the independent variables to explain

categorical variable to inequality is the sum of the contribution by each category. It will generate the same result though we change the reference category for any reason.

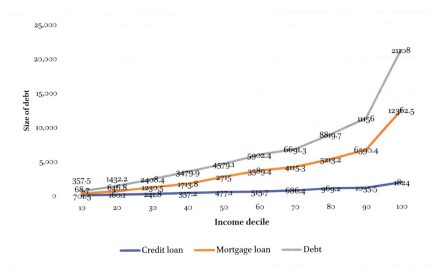

FIGURE 26.3 Debt by income decile

wealth. Unlike the decomposition of income inequality, individual characteristics and work-related variables do not display large impact on wealth inequality. Household income and education explain more than 60 percent of wealth inequality. Model 2 introduces loans and drops occupation and industry in the wealth equation to explain wealth inequality. While debt might be a survival resource for the poor, it can be a resource for the middle class and the rich for new investment. Thus loans can be a leverage for enhancing wealth for the rich. As Figure 26.3 illustrates, the high-income groups are more likely to utilize loans than low-income groups. The high-income groups have more chance to alleviate their wealth and promote their life chances through the financial markets. We observe the polarization of the financial markets in favor of the wealthy class.

Significant contributors to wealth inequality are quite different from those of income inequality. When we apply the same variables in the equations, we find out very different impacts on income and wealth. First of all, human capital variables are very weak in their impact on wealth inequality. Therefore, we include only selected variables that were significantly affecting wealth inequality. The model selected through regression analysis is presented in Model 2 in Table 26.4 in which income and loans explain almost 75 percent of inequality of wealth. Loans contribute to wealth inequality by 43.9148 percent, and household income contributes to 32.6228 percent. Although the accumulation of income for a period could contribute to the growth of wealth, loans seem to be more directly associated with wealth. As housing price has continued to increase in the 21st century, the deregulation of financial markets and severe

TABLE 26.4 Wealth inequality decomposed through multivariate variables (%)

	Model 1		Model 2	
Sex	0.7435	1.3959	0.8202	0.6488
Age + Age-squared	−1.2328	−0.0216	0.8311	0.3372
Education	6.9042	12.1185	3.5798	6.9621
Employment status	1.1242	1.9732	4.0311	7.8399
Occupation	0.3763	0.6605	–	–
Industry	4.8705	8.5489	–	–
Income	24.5113	48.9305	16.7739	32.6228
Loans	–	–	22.5800	43.9148
Family size	5.9041	10.3631	3.9844	7.7490
Residuals	56.9722	–	48.5823	–
R^2	100.00	43.0278	100.00	51.4177
Total	100.00	100.00	100.00	100.00

competition among financial institution has promoted the mortgage loans to the middle class. As the real estate bubble grows for a while, wealth inequality will continue to increase as well.

The above results display two things. First, the dynamics of income and wealth are different from each other. While income inequality and wealth inequality are significant dimensions of economic inequality, the mechanisms of the formation of income and wealth are very different. Income is an outcome of economic activities as well as profits from the capital, whereas loans are a financial resource based on income and wealth. The credit system as a core institution in the financialized economy functions for the social group, which already enjoys the advantage. That exacerbates income distribution and economic inequality.

4   Conclusion

Analyzing the HFLC data that linked the survey data with administrative data in South Korea, this paper attempts to explore income inequality and wealth inequality and their reciprocal relationship mediated by financial behavior. While income inequality and wealth inequality are the two major dimensions of social inequality, sociologists did not pay much attention to income inequality and wealth inequality. Rather, individual social mobility has been a core research topic among sociologists in social stratification. Wage inequality has been a focal arena among sociologists in the research on the labor market and gender gap. Therefore, sociologists have stopped at the individual's occupation, fall short of a comprehensive understanding of the rising inequality of income and wealth since the late 20th century.

The analysis of inequality of income and wealth in this paper reveals at least four findings. First, the linked data combining the survey data with administrative data shows higher income inequality than the survey data. The HFLC data provide more accurate information about household income, which was registered information around different governmental agencies. It provides a new possibility for social scientists to investigate income inequality.

Second, wealth inequality is much severe than income inequality in South Korea. Almost all indicators of inequality, such as the Gini coefficient, the top 10 percent share, and p90/p10, displays that wealth is much more concentrated into the top 10 percent than income. While ordinary people perceive wealth inequality as a core of economic inequality, sociologists did not pay much attention to it for various reasons.

Third, the joint distribution of income and wealth shows the highly bi-polarized distribution in which the pole with the highest 5 percent of income and the highest 5 percent of wealth shows the highest density, indicating the concentration of both income and wealth at the top 5 percent of the rich household. The opposite pole with the lowest 5 percent income and the lowest 5 percent wealth shows the second-highest density, revealing the concentration of poverty in the lowest 5 percent of the household.

Fourth, the dynamics of income and income inequality are different from the dynamics of wealth and wealth inequality. Household income has been affected by occupation and family size as well as work-related variables, such as employment status and occupation. Unlike the expectation of researchers on occupation, the effect of occupation on income inequality is not based on the technical division of labor but the division between working and non-working population. Thus, employment status rather than occupation provides a better fitting model with fewer variables. Wealth has been most affected by household income and loans in South Korea. It indicates that income directly affects wealth, and loans mediate the formation of wealth. As the housing market bubble has grown for the last decade, loans and credit systems play a significant role in aggravating wealth inequality.

Fifth, the positive feedback loops are working between income and wealth through capital income and credit systems. The multiplicative effect of the feedback loops has contributed to the concentration of income and wealth on the top 5 or 10 percent in recent years, widening the gap further between the rich and the poor. As wealth is the most significant factor of income inequality and income is the second most important factor of wealth inequality, income inequality tends to increase further with the rise of the real estate price in recent years in South Korea.

There are some limitations to this paper. One is the problem of the representativeness of the survey data. Although the size of the Survey of the Household Finance and Living Conditions is much larger than the previous survey data, the wealthy families reported in the media are not sufficiently included in the data. Furthermore, the extremely poor are also excluded due to the limitation of accessibility to them. Thus the underestimation of income and wealth inequality may be possible. While the linked data was used, at least the problem of under-representation and inaccessibility remains unabated. In particular, underrepresentation of the super-rich may result in a much lower estimation of income inequality and wealth inequality.

Another limitation is the lack of information about an inheritance from parents to children. The survey data used in this research cannot capture the exact amount of inheritance because the information entirely depends on respondents' answers to survey questionnaires. Information about inheritance may be a piece of sensitive information that cannot be revealed by survey interviewers. In addition, most of the heirs of property do not pay inheritance tax because the tax bracket is too high and most of the heirs are exempted from taxation. Nevertheless, inheritance has been an essential part of wealth formation of the people and wealth transmission over a generation has been an institutionalized pathway of the rich maintain to their socioeconomic positions across all societies. We need different data, such as the fully merged administrative data, as so to thoroughly investigate the dynamics of income and wealth inequality.

References

Acker, Joan. 1973. "Women and Social Stratification: A Case of Intellectual Sexism". *American Journal of Sociology* 78 (4): 936–945.
Alvaredo, Facundo, Lucas Chancel, Thomas Piketty, Immanuel Saez, and Gabriel Zucman. 2018. *World Inequality Report 2018*. Berlin: World Inequality Lab.
Atkinson, Tony. 2015. *Inequality*, Cambridge, MA: Harvard University Press.
Breen, Richard, and David Muller. 2020. *Education and Intergenerational Social Mobility in Europe and the United States*. Stanford: Stanford University Press.
Cagetti, Marco, and Mariacristina De Nardi. 2008. "Wealth Inequality: Data and Models". *Macroeconomic Dynamics* 12: 285–313.

Causa, Orsetta, and Mikkel Hermansen. 2019. *Income Redistribution through Taxes and Transfers across OECD Countries*. OECD Economics Department Working Papers No. 1453.

Chetty, Rey, David Grusky, Maximilian Hell, Nathaniel Hendren, Robert Manduca, and Jimmy Narang. 2016. *The fading American dream: Trends in absolute income mobility since 1940*. NBER Working Paper 22910. National Bureau of Economic Research.

Connelly, Roxanne, Christopher I. Playford, Vernon Gayle, and Chris Dibben. 2016. "The role of administrative data in the big data revolution in social science research". *Social Science Research* 59: 1–12.

Cowell, F.A., and C.V. Fiorio. 2011. "Inequality decompositions: a reconciliation". *Journal of Economic Inequality* 9: 509–528.

Davis, Gerald F., and Suntae Kim. 2015. "Financialization of the Economy". *Annual Review of Sociology* 41: 203–211.

England, Paula. 1994. "The gendered valuation of occupations and skills: earnings in 1980 census occupations". *Social Forces* 73: 65–100.

Esping-Andersen, Gøsta. 1999. *Social Foundation of the Postindustrial Economies*. Oxford: Oxford University Press.

Fields, G.S. 2003. "Accounting for income inequality and its change: A new method, with application to the distribution of earnings in the United States". *Research in labor economics* 22: 1–38.

Fiorio, Carlo V., and Stephen P. Jenkins. 2008. "INEQRBD: Stata module to calculate regression-based inequality decomposition". Statistical Software Components S456960. Boston College Department of Economics, revised April 2, 2010.

Goldin, Claudia. 2008. "The rising (and then declining) significance of gender". In *The Declining Significance of Gender?*, edited by F. Blau, M. Brinton, and D. Grusky, 67–95. New York: Russell Sage Foundation.

Jäntti, Markus, Eva Zierminska, and Philippe Van Kerm. 2013. "The Joint Distribution of Income and Wealth". In *Income Inequality: Economic Disparity and the Middle Class in Affluent Countries*, edited by Janet Gornick and Markus Jäntti, 285–311. Stanford: Stanford University Press.

Kalleberg, Arne L. 2000. "Nonstandard employment: Part-time, temporary and contract work". *Annual Review of Sociology* 26 (1): 341–365.

Kenworthy, Lane. 2007. "Inequality and Sociology". *American Behavioral Scientist* 50 (5): 584–602.

Kim, Keuntae. 2017. "The changing role of employment status in marriage of formation among young Korean adults". *Demographic Research* 36 (5): 145–172.

Kroll, Luisa, and Kerry A. Dolan. 2019. "Billionaire: The richest people in the world". *Forbes*, March 5, 2019.

Medalia, Carla, Bruce Meyer, Amy O'Hara, and Derek Wu. 2019. "Linking Survey and Administrative Data to Measure Income, Inequality, and Mobility". *International Journal of Population Data Science* 4 (1): 1–8.

Meyer, Bruce D., and Nikolas Mittag. 2019. "Using Linked Survey and Administrative Data to Better Measure Income: Implications for Poverty, Program Effectiveness, and Holes in the Safety Net". *American Economic Journal: Applied Economics* 11 (2): 176–204.

Milanovic, Blanko. 2016. *Global Inequality: A New Approach for an Age of Globalization*. Cambridge, MA: Harvard University Press.

Myles, John. 2003. "Where Have All the Sociologists Gone? Explaining Economic Inequality". *The Canadian Journal of Sociology* 28 (4): 551–559.

OECD. 2018. *A Broken Social Elevator? How to Promote Social Mobility*. Paris: OECD.

OECD. 2019. *Employment Outlook 2019: The Future of Work*. Paris: OECD.

OECD. 2020. *Household Debt*. http://lps3.www.oecd-ilibrary.org.proxy.cau.ac.kr/econo mics/household-debt/indicator/english_f03b6469-en (accessed on January 13, 2020).

Piketty, Thomas. 2013. *Capital in the 21st Century*. Cambridge, MA: Harvard University Press.

Piketty, Thomas. 2015. "Putting Distribution Back at the Center of Economics: Reflections on *Capital in the Twenty-Century*". *Journal of Economic Perspectives* 29 (1): 67–88.

Piketty, Thomas, and Emmanuel Saez. 2003 "Income Inequality in the United States, 1913–1998". *Quarterly Journal of Economics* 118 (1): 1–39.

Savage, Mike. 2014. "Piketty's Challenge for Sociology". *The British Journal of Sociology* 65 (4): 591–606.

Savage, Mike. 2016. "Are we seeing a new "inequality paradigm" in social sciences?" https://blogs.lse.ac.uk/politicsandpolicy/are-we-seeing-a-new-inequality-paradigm-in-social-science/ (accessed on January 10, 2020).

Savage, Mike, and Rogers Burrows. 2007. "The coming crisis of empirical sociology". *Sociology* 41 (5): 885–899.

Sawyer, Malcolm. 2013. "What Is Financialization?" *International Journal of Political Economy* 42 (4): 5–18.

Shin, Kwang-Yeong. 2013. "Economic crisis, neoliberal reforms, and the rise of precarious work in South Korea". *American Behavioral Scientist* 57 (3): 353–355.

Stiglitz, Joseph. 2012. *The Price of Inequality: How Today's Divided Society Endangers Our New Future*. New York: W.W. Norton.

Therborn, Goran. 2014. *The Killing Fields of Inequality*. Cambridge: Polity.

Zierminska, Eva, Timothy M. Smeeding, and Serge Allergrezza. 2013. "The Distribution of Asset and Debt". In *Income Inequality: Economic Disparity and the Middle Class in Affluent Countries*, edited by Janet Gornick and Markus Jäntti, 285–311. Stanford: Stanford University Press.

CHAPTER 27

Globalization and Social Inequality in the Context of Japan

Sato Yoshimichi

1   Introduction

Globalization seems to increase social inequality in a country. Some people who can enjoy the fruits of globalization become richer, while other people who lagged behind in globalization become poorer. As a result of this polarization, social inequality—and income inequality in particular—becomes larger.

This theoretical argument is not necessarily valid, however. My point in this chapter is that the effects of globalization on local inequality (inequality in a country) are not direct but indirect. That is, the effects are enhanced or mitigated by local institutions (institutions in a country). Take temporal change in income inequality by country, for example (Figure 27.1). Although they are advanced countries and similarly exposed to globalization, the United States, United Kingdom, Sweden, France, and Japan show different patterns. Income inequality in the United States, United Kingdom, and Sweden steadily increases, while that in France steadily decreases. By contrast, the level of inequality in Japan is lower than these countries. However, it has been steadily increasing since the 1980s. (I will get back to this point later in this chapter.)

Why do we witness these differences even though the countries are similarly affected by globalization? One might argue that several factors other than globalization affect the patterns, and I argue that local institutions are the main factor creating the different patterns. If we compare the patterns of income inequality in the United States and Japan, we come up with an idea that regulatory institutions in the United States are weaker than those in Japan, which contributes to the steady increase in income inequality in the United States and the suppressed pattern in Japan.

Sato and Arita (2004) show another example of how local institutions affect the impact of globalization on the inequality of social mobility in Japan and South Korea. Analyzing the 1975, 1985, and 1995 Social Stratification and Social Mobility data sets in Japan and the data of the Survey on Inequality and Equity conducted in South Korea in 1990, they compared intergenerational and

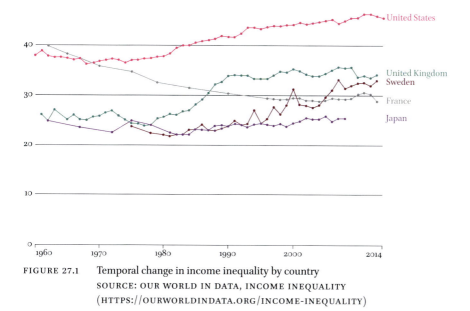

FIGURE 27.1   Temporal change in income inequality by country
SOURCE: OUR WORLD IN DATA, INCOME INEQUALITY
(HTTPS://OURWORLDINDATA.ORG/INCOME-INEQUALITY)

intragenerational mobility in Japan and Korea in detail. Their findings related to this chapter are as follows:

– Globalization has not substantively affected the social mobility of the new middle class in Japan, while the new middle class in South Korea is more mobile than its Japanese counterpart.
– The old middle class in Japan became more mobile from 1985 to 1995 in terms of intergenerational mobility. In their study, the old middle class consists of the self employed and employers who are managers, clerks, sales workers, service workers, or technicians/laborers (Arita 2002).

Sato and Arita (2004) attribute the findings to different levels of "inertia" of protective institutions in Japan. Protective institutions, such as Japanese employment practices—the long-term employment practice, the seniority-based wage scheme, and corporate unions—were not substantively affected by globalization. That is, they have a high level of inertia. Because of this inertia, the new middle class in Japan has not been substantively affected by globalization. The protective institutions mitigated the effects of globalization on the new middle class in Japan.

In contrast to Japanese employment practices, they argue, the inertia of protective institutions for the old middle class became weaker. Thus, globalization made the Japanese old middle class more mobile. One possible reason for that is that protective institutions for the old middle class were mainly laws, such as the large-scale retail store law that protected small retail stores, and it is

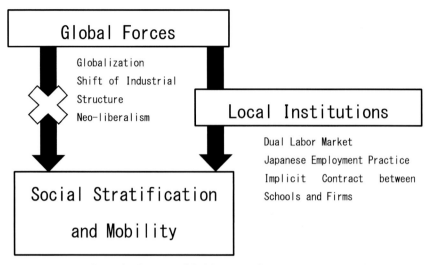

FIGURE 27.2   Relationship between global forces, local institutions, and social stratification and mobility
SOURCE: MODIFIED SATO AND HAYASHI (2009)

easier to change laws than it is to change practices or conventions in general. Therefore, we can guess that the Japanese government revised protective laws for the old middle class in response to globalization.

To generalize the abovementioned argument, global forces, such as globalization, the shift of industrial structure from the heavy to the service industry, and neo-liberalism do not directly affect local inequality, such as social stratification and social mobility. Rather, they indirectly affect it via local institutions. Figure 27.2 summarizes this point and adds concrete examples of local institutions in Japan, which will be examined in the next section.

2   Local Institutions in Japan

I focus on the three local institutions in Japan that I think are major factors affecting inequality in Japan: The dual labor market, Japanese employment practices, and the implicit contracts between schools and firms.

The dual labor market has been a prominent characteristic of the labor market in Japan (Odaka 1984). Before examining Odaka's argument on the dual market, let us check the theory of the internal labor market proposed by Doeringer and Piore (1971). Focusing on the labor market in the United States, they argue that there are two segments in the labor market: the primary market, or the internal market, and the secondary market, or the external market. They show the differences in the characteristics between the two segments. For example, workers enjoy high wages, job security, and opportunities for promotion in the internal labor market, while the external labor market lacks such benefits. In response to this difference, workers in the internal labor market have higher human capital than their counterparts in the external labor market.

Odaka (1984), by contrast, studies the historical development of the dual labor market in Japan. Being different from Doeringer and Piore's categorization of the internal and external labor markets, he pays attention the wage differential between workers at large firms and workers at small/mid-sized firms. He attributes this difference to the difference in productivity between the two sectors, and the difference in productivity comes from the difference in technology the two sectors adopt. Large firms are more likely to adopt modern technology than small/mid-sized firms. Then he analyzes the history of the labor market to show how the difference evolved over time.

As Okada's theory of the dual labor market points out, the dividing line between the large-firm sector and the small/mid-sized-firm sector was a main factor creating social inequality in tandem with social class in Japan. Therefore, the abovementioned Social Stratification and Social Mobility project, which has been the main research project on social stratification and social mobility in Japan, created a class scheme using occupations and firm sizes. The scheme consists of eight classes: professionals, managers, white-collar workers at large firms, white-collar workers at small/mid-sized firms, white-collar self-employed individuals, blue-collar workers at large firms, blue-collar workers at small/mid-sized firms, blue-collar self-employed individuals, and farmers.

Okada's theory of the dual labor market and the class scheme created by the Social Stratification and Social Mobility project once reflected the actual situation of social inequality in Japan. However, they cannot properly capture social inequality in the labor market in contemporary Japan. This is because the share of non-regular workers has been increasing even in large firms. As will be shown in the next section, social inequality between regular and non-regular workers is large and persistent. If we compare a part-time lecturer and a full professor at the same university, inequality in income, job security, and social security between them is very high even though they belong to the same class, that is, the professional class.

Therefore, I would argue that the labor market in contemporary Japan is "quadruple", not dual (Imai and Sato 2011). What is more important is that workers at the core of the labor market, that is, regular workers at large firms, are still protected by the Japanese employment practices consisting of the long-term employment practice, the seniority-based wage scheme, and corporate unions (Abegglen 1958).

The Japanese employment practices, I would argue, have contributed to suppressing inequality among workers. It is true that income inequality among

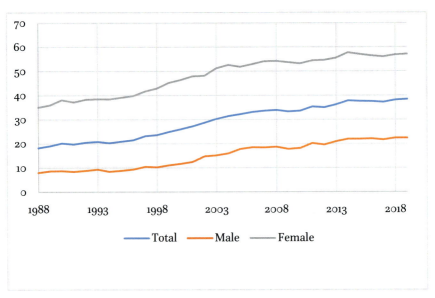

FIGURE 27.3 Temporal change in non-regular employment rate by gender
SOURCE: LABOR FORCE SURVEY

workers at the same firm exists, but the seniority-based wage scheme keeps income inequality among workers in the same cohort low.

The Japanese employment practices, however, have become weakened because of Japan's increasing exposure to global forces, such as globalization, the shift of industrial structure from the heavy to the service industry, and neoliberal policies. The increase in the percentages of non-regular workers is strong evidence for this. Figure 27.3 shows that the percentages have been increasing since the 1990s both for male and female workers. The percentage of female non-regular workers is higher than that of male non-regular workers in general because most of the female non-regular workers are married women. The male single-breadwinner model, in which a husband works as a regular worker earning decent income and a wife is a housewife or a non-regular worker, was established during the high economic growth period in Japan and was influential. Feminists have criticized the combination of Japanese employment practices and the male single-breadwinner model because they say that it pushes women to the periphery of the labor market and creates inequality within the family. Economically, however, households with the combination were able to have a stable, decent life, so it became dominant in Japan.

However, the recent increase in the percentage of male non-regular workers reflects the weakening of not only Japanese employment practices but also the male single-breadwinner model. Young male non-regular workers find it difficult to get married (Tarohmaru 2011), mainly because they think they cannot afford to support their family. If they marry female regular workers with decent income, their family can have an economically stable life. However, in reality, they hesitate to do that because they are trapped by the ideology of the male single-breadwinner model.

The implicit contract between schools and firms (Kariya 1991; Rosenbaum and Kariya 1989) effectively matched students and jobs in Japan. Recruiters and teachers exchange information on job openings and students to learn the detailed characteristics of jobs and students. Then teachers know who is suitable to a job offered by a firm, which contributes to the efficient allocation of students to jobs.

Thus, the implicit contract placed graduates in the regular employment sector. This prevented graduates from becoming non-regular workers or unemployed upon graduation. Low unemployment rates for young Japanese were partly attributed to the implicit contract.

However, the implicit contract is said to have weakened (Honda 2005).[1] Theoretically, Honda's argument is understandable. The implicit contract is a long-term relationship between schools and firms based on mutual trust. Therefore, it functions well when the labor market is stable. However, firms have to abandon it because of the increasing flexibility in the labor market, such as the increase in the percentage of non-regular workers.

Brinton (2008) examined this argument empirically by analyzing the 2005 Social Stratification and Social Mobility data set. She reports that the percentage of graduates who got a job by the implicit contract was 40.4% for people graduating from school before 1978, 41.9% for those graduating from school between 1978 and 1991, and 37.6% for those graduating from school between 1992 and 2005. It seems that the youngest cohort used the implicit contract less than the two older cohorts, but the difference is not statistically significant. This implies that the implicit contract has not necessarily weakened.

What is more interesting in Brinton's analysis is that people getting a job through the implicit contract are more likely to get a regular job than those applying for a job through job advertisements. Combining this finding with the abovementioned one, we could say that even though the implicit contract might have become weaker than before, those who could use it are more likely to get regular jobs than those who could not.

The implicit contract once covered many students, which had a social function mitigating inequality in getting jobs among them. However, if it has become weaker, the proportion of students who can use it when finding jobs

---

1 The description of the implicit contract in the text depends on Sato (2010).

will become smaller, and inequality between those who can use it and those who cannot use it will become wider.

3 Globalization and Local Institutions in the Creation of Social Inequality

I focused on the three institutions and their changes in Japan: the dual labor market, Japanese employment practices, and the implicit contract. My arguments about them based on the discussion in the previous section are summarized as follows:
- The local institutions have kept social inequality in a narrow range.
- Their changes increase social inequality.

Let me explain these arguments in detail below.

The dual labor market has maintained inequality in terms of income, job security, and social security between workers in the large-firm sector and their counterparts in the small/mid-sized firm sector. However, even regular workers in the small/mid-sized firms enjoyed more income, job security, and social security than non-regular workers in contemporary Japan. In this sense, the dual market has suppressed inequality between regular workers in the two sectors.

However, as pointed out in the previous section, another dividing line—employment status—emerged in the dual labor market, which forged the quadruple labor market. The quadruple labor market consists of four segments: (1) regular workers at large firms, (2) regular workers at small/mid-sized firms, (3) non-regular workers at large firms, and (4) non-regular workers at small/mid-sized firms.

As Figure 27.3 in the first section shows, the percentage of non-regular workers has been increasing. This means the first and second segments of the quadruple labor market are becoming smaller, while the third and fourth segments are becoming larger. In addition to this, the percentage of non-regular workers at large firms has also been increasing (Figure 27.4). Figure 27.4 shows that the percentage of non-regular workers has been increasing at firms of any size and that the gap between small/mid-sized firms and large firms has become smaller. This means that the core—the first segment—in the quadruple labor market has been shrinking, while the periphery—the second, third, and fourth segments—has become larger.

The change in the Japanese employment practice reflects this change in the labor market. The practice has protected regular workers, and non-regular workers have been excluded from it. There are historical reasons for this

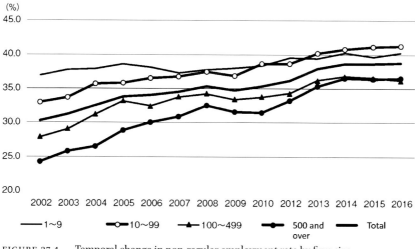

FIGURE 27.4 Temporal change in non-regular employment rate by firm size
SOURCE: FIGURE/TABLE 10 IN EGUCHI (2018)

inequality (Sato 2013). There was a huge inequality between white-collar and blue-collar workers at the same company before World War II. The two groups differed not only in income but also in their payment scheme. In general, white-collar workers had higher incomes than blue-collar workers, and the former earned a monthly salary while the latter earned daily or weekly wages. The job security of the former was much better than that of the latter. The former enjoyed a generous social benefit package while the latter did not. In sum, only white-collar workers were protected by Japanese employment practices. To put it differently, "white-collar workers" and "blue-collar workers" meant not only different occupations (or occupational classes) but also different social statuses, like the samurai status and the artisan status in the Edo period.

This status hierarchical system was harshly criticized by labor unions, which were influenced by the democratization promoted by the occupying army after World War II. Labor unions claimed that the system was a holdover of Japanese feudalism and that white-collar and blue-collar workers should be treated equally as members of the same company. Eventually, the status hierarchical system was abolished, and inequality between white-collar and blue-collar workers became mitigated because the latter became protected by Japanese employment practices like white-collar workers were. In this sense, the practice reduced inequality between the two types of workers in postwar Japan.

However, it should be noted that "workers", no matter whether they were white-collar workers or blue-collar workers, were presumed to be regular workers. Non-regular workers were excluded from Japanese employment practices.

The long-term employment practice and the seniority-based wage scheme were not applied to them, and they were unable to become union members. Therefore, inequality between regular and non-regular workers stayed intact while inequality between white-collar and blue-collar workers diminished. This did not become a serious social issue, however. This is because, as mentioned above, most non-regular workers were women married to regular workers. Even though their income was lower than that of female regular workers, their economic situation as a family was decent because of the husband's stable income.

However, recent increases in the percentage of male non-regular workers are weakening the combination of Japanese employment practices and the male single-breadwinner model. Male non-regular workers are less likely to get married than their counterparts in the regular employment sector because they do not think they can afford to feed their family. In this sense, male non-regular workers are pushed to the periphery in the labor market as well as the marriage market. Therefore, the deterioration of Japanese employment practices increases inequality between regular and non-regular workers. The weakening of the implicit contract also contributes to inequality between graduates who can still use it and those who cannot. When the implicit contract functioned effectively, many graduates used it. Therefore, it reduced inequality among graduates in terms of getting regular jobs. However, if it becomes weaker, those who could use it are more likely to get regular jobs than those who could not. This increases inequality between the two types of graduates.

The abovementioned analysis of the change in the structure of the labor market, Japanese employment practices, and the implicit contract shows that the weakening of the three local institutions increases inequality between people at the core of the labor market and those at its periphery. The core means the regular employment sector at large firms, which is still protected by Japanese employment practices. I would argue that the increase in the level of income inequality in Japan in Figure 27.1 is caused by this weakening of the local institutions.

4   Coexistence of the Stable Core and the Flexible Periphery

Reviewing findings on various segments in the labor market and social stratification in Japan in the 2005 Social Stratification and Social Mobility Survey Project, I proposed the thesis that the core was stable, but flexibility was increasing on the periphery of the labor market as well as on the periphery of social stratification (Sato 2010).

This coexistence of the stable core and the periphery becoming more flexible was forged by the interaction between local institutions and global forces. The protective local institutions, such as the dual labor market, Japanese employment practices, and the implicit contract, have become weaker because of their increasing exposure to global forces. However, their inertia in the core is still high, so workers in the core are still protected by the institutions. By contrast, as indicated by the increase in the percentage of male non-regular workers, the institutions no longer protect workers at the periphery, making it more flexible. In other words, their inertia in the periphery is low.

My study of the mobility barrier between the regular and the non-regular employment sectors using the 2015 Social Stratification and Social Mobility data set adds new findings to the abovementioned thesis (Sato 2018). Still, the stable core and the flexible periphery coexist, but the core has become smaller, and the mobility barrier from the non-regular to the regular employment sector has become higher. Sato (2018) compares the hazard rates of mobility from the non-regular to the regular employment sector by period: The high economic growth period (1955–1973), the slow economic growth period after the oil crises (1974–1984), the bubble economy period (1985–1991), and the post-bubble economy period (1992–2015). As mentioned above, the Japanese employment practice was established after World War II and became dominant during the high economic growth period (Brinton 1993).

Compared to the high economic growth period, Japanese employment practices are thought to have become weaker during the post-bubble economy period because the influence of global forces became stronger during that time. Therefore, the mobility from the non-regular employment to the regular employment sector should have become more frequent during that period. This would lead to the increase in the hazard rate of mobility from the non-regular to the regular employment sector. However, the result of my analysis shows that the hazard rate in the post-bubble economy period is lower than that in the high economic growth period. This means that mobility became less frequent in the former period than in the latter period. In addition to this finding, as shown in Figure 27.3, the percentage of non-regular workers has been increasing, which reflects the shrinkage of the core.

5   Conclusions: Globalization, Differential Inertia of Local Institutions, and Social Inequality

If the inertia of local institutions in the labor market in Japan did not exist, social inequality among workers would be smaller. For example, as mentioned above, Japanese employment practices suppressed inequality between white-collar and blue-collar workers, although they kept inequality between workers in large firms and their counterparts in small/mid-sized firms intact. However, global forces insert another dividing line into the labor market: inequality between regular and non-regular workers. In response to the "invasion" of global forces, Japanese employment practices try to protect workers at the core of the labor market. As a result, workers at the core are still protected by the practices, but the core has become smaller and the mobility barrier from the non-regular to the regular employment sector has become higher. These contribute to the widening of inequality among workers.

As pointed out above, local institutions used to mitigate social inequality, which would have become wider without them. However, their differential inertia creates new inequalities, protecting workers at the core and simultaneously increasing the flexibility at the periphery. Although the core is shrinking, the mobility barrier to the core becomes higher. It is unpredictable as to whether local institutions will survive in the era of globalization and whether social inequality will become larger or not.

References

Abegglen, James C. 1958. *The Japanese Factory: Aspects of Its Social Organization*. Glencoe, IL: Free Press.

Arita, Shin. 2002. "The Process of Emergence and the Social Consciousness of Middle Classes in Korea". In *The Emergence and Features of the Asian Middle Classes*, edited by Tamio Hattori, Tsuruyo Funatsu, and Takashi Torii. Institute of Developing Economies, Japan External Trade Organization. (In Japanese).

Arita, Shin. 2016. *The Sociology of Reward Inequality among Employment Positions: A Comparison of Non-standard Employment and Social Stratification in Japan and Korea*. Tokyo: University of Tokyo Press. (In Japanese).

Brinton, Mary C. 1993. *Women and the Economic Miracle: Gender and Work in Postwar Japan*. Berkeley: University of California Press.

Brinton, Mary C. 2008. "After the Bubble: Young Men's Labor Market Entry Experiences in the 1990s and Beyond". In *Social Stratification and Social Mobility of Young Japanese*, edited by Hiroshi Tarohmaru. The 2005 SSM Research Committee.

Doeringer, Peter B., and Michael J. Piore. 1971. *Internal Labor Market and Manpower Analysis*. Heath.

Eguchi, Masahiro. 2018. "Shortage of Manpower and Non-regular Employment at Small/Mid-Sized Firms: An Analysis of Customized Aggregated Data of Labor Force Survey". *Shoko-Kinyu* 68 (1): 30–62. (In Japanese).

Honda, Yuki. 2005. *Young People and Employment in Japan: Beyond the "School-Mediated Job Search"*. Tokyo: University of Tokyo Press. (In Japanese).

Imai, Jun, and Yoshimichi Sato. 2011. "Regular and Non-regular Employment as an Additional Duality in Japanese Labor Market: Institutional Perspectives on Career Mobility". In *Japan's New Inequality: Intersection of Employment Reforms and Welfare Arrangements*, edited by Yoshimichi Sato and Jun Imai. Trans Pacific Press.

Kariya, Takehiko. 1991. *Sociology of School, Occupation, and Selection: The Japanese Mechanism of Labor Market Entry of High-school Graduates*. Tokyo: University of Tokyo Press. (In Japanese).

Odaka, Konosuke. 1984. *An Analysis of the Labor Market: Japanese Development of the Dual Structure*. Iwanami Shoten. (In Japanese).

Rosenbaum, James E., and Takehiko Kariya. 1989. "From School to Work: Market and Institutional Mechanisms in Japan". *American Journal of Sociology* 94 (6): 1334–1365.

Sato, Yoshimichi. 2010. "Stability and Increasing Fluidity in the Contemporary Japanese Social Stratification System". *Contemporary Japan* 22: 7–21.

Sato, Yoshimichi. 2013. "Regular Employment and Non-regular Employment: Disparity Issue in Japan". In *Exploring Inequality-generating Mechanisms*, edited by Yoshimichi Sato and Toshiaki Kimura. Minerva Shobo. (In Japanese).

Sato, Yoshimichi. 2018. "Intragenerational Mobility Between the Regular and Non-Regular Employment Sectors in Japan: From the Viewpoint of the Theory of Mobility Regime". Working paper for the 2015 Social Stratification and Social Mobility Project. https://www.l.u-tokyo.ac.jp/2015SSM-PJ/07_04.pdf (accessed on October 15, 2021).

Sato, Yoshimichi, and Shin Arita. 2004. "Impact of Globalization on Social Mobility in Japan and Korea: Focusing on Middle Classes in Fluid Societies". *International Journal of Japanese Sociology* 13: 36–52.

Sato, Yoshimichi, and Yusuke Hayashi. 2009. "Change and Stability in the Social Stratification System in Contemporary Japan: Coexistence of Stability and Fluidization". Paper presented at the 2009 Spring Meeting RC28, Beijing, China.

Tarohmaru, Hiroshi. 2011. "Youth Non-regular Employment and Marriage". In *Disparity and Diversity*, edited by Yoshimichi Sato and Fumiaki Ojima. Tokyo: University of Tokyo Press. (In Japanese).

SECTION 6

Youth and Education

∴

CHAPTER 28

Educational Expansion and Its Impacts on Youth in Transitional China

Wu Yuxiao

In China, the past four decades since the marketing reform have witnessed tremendous achievements in the development of education. China is in the transition from a country with a huge population to a country rich in human resources. Meanwhile, the return to education also has been increasing steadily, and education is becoming more and more important in the status attainment ladder for Chinese youth. These trends have had a profound impact on Chinese society and Chinese youth. First of all, we see a consistent trend of a declining gender gap in educational attainment, especially for young cohorts that show a reversal gender gap in academic performance in schools and overall educational attainment. Secondly, empirical studies have detected that rapid educational expansion is accompanied by an increasing level of school socioeconomic segregation in elementary and middle schools, and by a rising class gap in higher education. The increasing class-based inequality in educational opportunities may lead to furious competition in educational opportunities and labor market outcomes among Chinese youth. Thirdly, educational expansion is associated with later marriage (more so for women than for men) and a declining fertility rate that may affect the Chinese population's structure in the long run. To reveal these trends and to unpack the underlying mechanisms may shed light on the theoretical discussions of post-Western sociology.

1 Educational Expansion in Post-Reform China

In recent decades, particularly since the reform and opening up launched in 1978, the educational attainment of the Chinese population has been increasing steadily, mainly due to the educational opportunities provided by the Chinese government.

In 1985, China started to push forward the nine-year compulsory education system. In 1986, the Compulsory Education Law had been promulgated to provide the legal basis for universalizing the nine-year compulsory education nationwide. Starting in 2008, all students in the compulsory education stage have been able to attend school free of charge. By 2010, China finally reached its

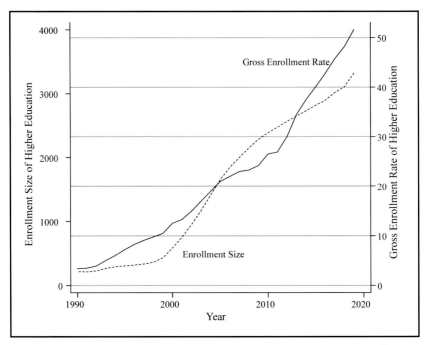

FIGURE 28.1 Gross enrollment rate and enrollment size of higher education in China, 1990–2019
DATA SOURCE: EDUCATIONAL STATISTICS YEAR BOOK OF CHINA (1990–2019)

ultimate goal—that is, the nine-year compulsory education has reached all children and adolescents of school age throughout the country. At the same time, high school education in China, including the academic senior high school track and vocational track, has been rising and moving to be universal. As indicated by the official statistics, high school gross enrollment rate has increased from 35.1% in 1978 to 89.5% in 2019; the number of students in high school education increased from 18.85 million in 1978 to 39.95 million in 2019, of whom about 24.1 million were senior high school students in the academic track, and about 15.8 million students were in the secondary vocational education track.

The most significant change in Chinese education since 1978 might be the substantial expansion of higher education. During the last four decades, higher education in China has been moving rapidly from elite education to mass education. At the beginning of the reform (in 1978), the gross enrollment rate of higher education in China was only 1.56%. By 1990, the gross enrollment rate of higher education was merely 3.4%. In those 12 years, the gross enrollment rate of higher education had only increased by 1.84 percentage points. After entering the 1990s, the development of higher education in China shifted into

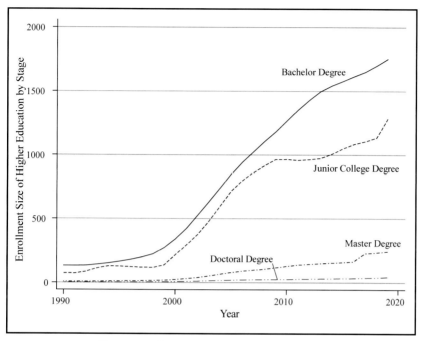

FIGURE 28.2 Enrollment size of higher education in different types of degree in China, 1990–2019
DATA SOURCE: EDUCATIONAL STATISTICS YEAR BOOK OF CHINA (1990–2019)

an express lane. Especially after the great expansion of enrollment in 1999, the gross enrollment rate of higher education rose rapidly to 10.5% in 1999. By 2003, the gross enrollment rate had risen to 15%, reaching the internationally recognized level of popularization. In 2019, the gross enrollment rate of higher education in China reached 51.6%, which has exceeded the standard of the popularization stage (that is, 50%). Figure 28.1 shows the trends of gross enrollment rates and enrollment sizes of higher education in China since the 1990s.

With the rapid rise of the gross enrollment rate of higher education, the scale of higher education in China has also expanded substantially. According to the latest statistics published by the Ministry of Education, in 2019 the total number of students in all kinds of institutions of higher education in China reached 40.22 million, including 2.86 million graduate students and 30.32 million general college students. Compared with the 12.29 million in 2000 (the first year after the expansion of higher education), the total number of students in school increased by 272%, and it rose by 1664% compared with 1978. In all kinds of higher education, the largest increase in the number of students is in the general undergraduate and junior colleges. As can be seen in Figure 28.2, from 1990 to 2019, the number of undergraduate and junior college students increased from 1.32 million and 0.74 million in 1990 to 17.51 million and 12.81 million in 2019, with increase rates of 1226% and 1624%, respectively. In addition, the scale of graduate education is also on the rise. In 2019, there were about 2.44 million postgraduates in China; the number of doctoral students on campus reached 0.42 million, increases of 2.36 million and 0.41 million, respectively, over 1990, with increase rates of 2824% and 3539%, respectively.

2 The Decreasing Gender Gap in Educational Attainment

The rapid expansion of education in China is accompanied by a decline in gender inequality in educational attainment. Figure 28.3 depicts the differences in educational attainment between men and women for different birth cohorts, using pooled cross-sectional data from the Chinese General Social Survey (CGSS 2010, 2011, 2012, 2013, 2015).[1] It can be seen that the younger the birth cohort, the smaller the gender gap of educational attainment, either in terms of average years of school (left panel) or the proportion of people of

FIGURE 28.3 Gender disparities in educational attainment in China by cohort
DATA SOURCE: CGSS 2010, 2011, 2012, 2013, 2015

---

1 The Chinese General Social Survey (CGSS) has been launched jointly since 2003 by the Hong Kong University of Science and Technology and Renmin University of China. Starting in 2010, it has been organized independently by the National Survey Research Center (NSRC) at Renmin University of China.

each sex holding a college degree or above (right panel). Moreover, for those born around 1990, the gender disparity almost disappears, and even shows a trend that women exceed men.

The rapid decline in educational gender inequality can be attributed to many factors. For example, the nine-year compulsory education system (established by the Compulsory Education Law in 1986) has legally guaranteed women's right to receive an education. In addition, the continuous expansion of education in China, the practice of gender equality ideology in the period of the redistributive economy between 1949 and 1977, the decline of the birth rate caused by the country's population policy, and the change in population structure are also the main factors for the decline of the educational attainment gender gap in China (Wu 2012; Ye and Wu 2011). The rapid narrowing gender gap in education plays an important role in the improvement of women's social and economic status, and, as a result, contributes to the progress of gender equality in China.

3   The Growing Urban–Rural and Class Gap in Educational Attainment

It might be reasonable to believe that the expansion of education will reduce the effects of family background on educational opportunities. However, empirical studies have found that although the overall level of education of Chinese residents has increased over the years, the gaps between urban and rural areas and between classes in educational attainment have shown an increasing trend, in particular in higher education (Li 2010; X. Wu 2009; Y. Wu 2013). Again, using pooled data from CGSS 2010, 2011, 2012, 2013, and 2015, this chapter maps the trends of urban–rural disparity and class-based inequality in educational attainment over time. As can be seen from Figure 28.4, there is a persisting, or even growing, urban–rural gap in education for the Chinese population. Specifically, the left panel of Figure 28.4 shows that the urban–rural inequality persists over different cohorts in terms of average years of schooling, while the right panel depicts a clear growing gap between urban and rural residents over time in terms of proportion of people who have a college degree or more. Compared to older cohorts, the urban–rural disparity in educational attainment among younger cohorts is more pronounced. That is, young people in rural China have benefited less from the continuous expansion of the supply of education, compared to their counterparts in urban areas.

By analyzing the same data sets as in Figure 28.4, Figure 28.5 shows the trends of class-based disparities in educational attainment in different cohorts. The left panel shows the relationship between parents' educational attainment

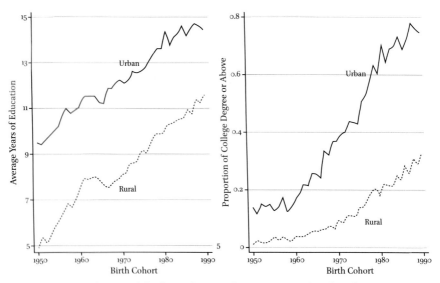

FIGURE 28.4   Urban–rural divide in educational attainment in China by cohort
DATA SOURCE: CGSS 2010, 2011, 2012, 2013, 2015

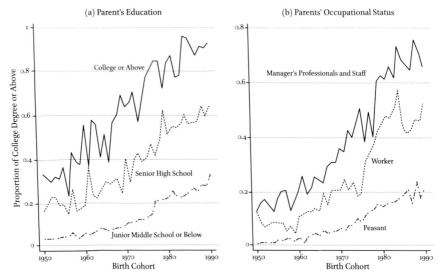

FIGURE 28.5   Disparities in educational attainment in China by parents' education and occupation
DATA SOURCE: CGSS 2010, 2011, 2012, 2013, 2015

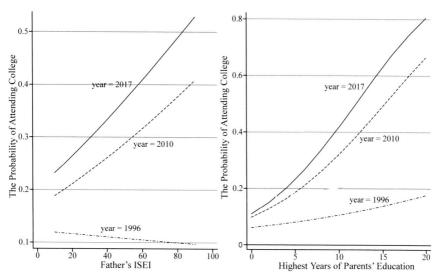

FIGURE 28.6 Predicted effects of fathers' ISEI and parents' education on children's probabilities of entering college in 1996, 2006, and 2015
DATA SOURCE: LHSCC 1996; CGSS 2006, 2015

and children's higher education opportunities in various cohorts. As can be seen, the higher the parents' educational level, the higher the odds for children to enter college. Moreover, the gaps have become larger for younger cohorts, meaning that the effect of parental education on children's educational attainment has been increasing over time. The right panel of Figure 28.5 shows the relationship between family socioeconomic status (measured by the father's occupations) and children's odds of entering higher education. Overall, children from higher socioeconomic background obviously have more opportunities to go to college. Similarly, the gaps between children from different classes have been widening for younger cohorts.

Figure 28.5 shows the pattern of increasing class-based inequality in educational attainment over time. To further confirm this trend, I use logistic models to estimate the marginal effects (after controlling for gender, age, and *hukou* status) of fathers' International Socioeconomic Index (ISEI) and parental educational attainment on children's probabilities of entering college in 1996, 2006, and 2015, respectively, using data from the Life Histories and Social Change in Contemporary China (LHSCC 1996)[2] and CGSS 2006 and 2015. Figure 28.6 shows the findings. As can be seen, the impact of fathers' occupational status (measured by ISEI) and educational achievement on children's

---

2 See Treiman (1998) for detailed information about these data.

access to higher education has been increased over time, providing more convincing evidence that class-based inequalities in educational opportunities have been growing.

4   Education and Youth in Transitional China

4.1   *Increasing Educational Competition and Rapid Growth of Private Tutoring*

Since the reform and opening up in 1978, although the supply of education has been increasing, the competition with regard to education has become increasingly intense. The key-point school system in the early stage of reform and opening up took the entrance examination scores as the exclusive admission standard, which placed a heavy burden of learning and mental pressure on students. Although the Ministry of Education later canceled the key-point school system to ease educational competition, replacing it with the policy of "going to schools nearby", educational competition has not been relieved for students in elementary and high schools. On the one hand, getting the qualification of education at high-quality public or private schools has become a competitive process for most families. The housing prices of districts with quality schools and the tuition fees of private schools have been rising rapidly and steadily. On the other hand, the policy of "reducing the burden" implemented by the Ministry of Education has not achieved the expected outcome, but to some extent it has contributed to the rapid growth of the after-school supplementary education market. According to a recent study, in 2017 the rate of primary and secondary school students' participation in after-school tutoring was 47.2%, the average cost was 5615 RMB yuan per student, and the overall scale of the after-school education industry in China had reached more than 458 billion RMB yuan nationwide (Huang and Wei 2018). It is worth mentioning that the main purpose of the extracurricular supplementary education for most Chinese students is "enrichment" (improving test scores for high-performing students) rather than "remedial" (helping the poorly performing students) that is the more common type of tutoring offered in most Western countries. When most students in the classroom have learned the materials in advance in after-school tutoring, the teachers in formal schools have to make adjustments to the teaching content, so that those students who did not participate in after-school supplementary education have been forced to join in this form of game.

Extracurricular private tutoring, in the context of intense educational competition, has obvious implications for social inequality. High-income families can afford greater quantities or higher quality of private tutoring than middle-income and low-income families. Therefore, participating in private tutoring has been considered one of the mechanisms of reproduction of educational inequality in China (Xue 2015).

4.2   School Socioeconomic Segregation and Its Consequences

As mentioned above, although educational supply has been expanding in China in recent decades, the class-based inequality in educational attainment persists or even shows an increasing trend. Moreover, in the compulsory education stage, the problem of unequal distribution of quality educational resources (schools) among groups from different social classes is becoming increasingly noticeable. The intense competition over entering quality schools leads to school socioeconomic segregation. By analyzing data from the China Education Panel Study (CEPS),[3] a recent study revealed that marked segregation currently exists in Chinese high schools; students from higher socioeconomic status families are more likely to enter high quality schools (Wu and Huang 2016). The Dissimilarity Index (one of the popular indices to measure segregation) is about 0.45, indicating that to achieve integration (i.e., completely eliminate segregation), about 45% of high school students in China would need to change their schools (Wu and Huang 2016).

The phenomenon of school class segregation is not only a hot topic in academic research, but it is also one of the core issues in education policy-making. The problem of class segregation in China's elementary and high schools is not only detrimental to educational equity, but it also leads to growing social inequality. If the children of the upper class gather in the high-quality schools, they will take advantage of this to achieve better educational and occupational outcomes. Meanwhile, when most children of the disadvantaged families gather in the low-quality schools, their educational achievements may be undermined. Due to the fact that education determines status attainment for individuals to a great extent (and its role is becoming more and more important), school class segregation will lead to the expansion of class disparities in the long run.

4.3   Impacts of Education on Marriage among Chinese Youth

One of the important effects of educational advancement on young people's life chances is the postponement of the age of first marriage. According to previous studies, in recent decades, the age of first marriage has shown an obvious

---

3 CEPS data are collected by the National Survey Center at the Renmin University of China (see http://ceps.ruc.edu.cn for detailed information about the survey).

upward trend in Western countries, and in China as well (Wang and Wu 2013). The influence of education on the age of first marriage is reflected in two aspects. First, higher educational attainment means the extension of school time that may delay the marriage age naturally (Sweeney 2002; Thornton, Axinn and Teachman 1995). The main reason is that most of the students rely on their parents economically, so the role of students is incompatible with the role of marriage. For most people, students are expected to complete their education first, and then take on the responsibility of marriage and family. Secondarily, from the perspective of human capital, getting ahead in education means the accumulation of knowledge, skills, and a quality diploma valued by the labor market. That is, the higher the education level, the higher the expected income in the labor market. With the improvement of educational status, the individual's competitiveness in the labor market is enhanced, while the comparative worth of marriage becomes smaller, which may depress the willingness to enter marriage and, as a result, delay the age of first marriage.

Previous studies disclosed that, in China, educational expansion plays an important role in the delay of the age of first marriage (Wang and Wu 2013). In this chapter, I depict the trend by analyzing a youth sample (aged 18–35 years) in multiple waves of CGSS data (namely, CGSS 2003, 2005, 2006, 2008, 2010, 2011, 2012, 2013, and 2015). We can find from Figure 28.7 that for the young people aged 18–35 years, the proportion of "never married" has been increasing

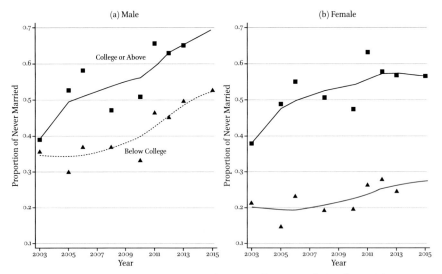

FIGURE 28.7   Proportions of "never married" among Chinese youth (aged 18–35) for years between 2003 and 2015, by gender
DATA SOURCE: CGSS 2003, 2005, 2006, 2008, 2010, 2011, 2012, 2013, 2015

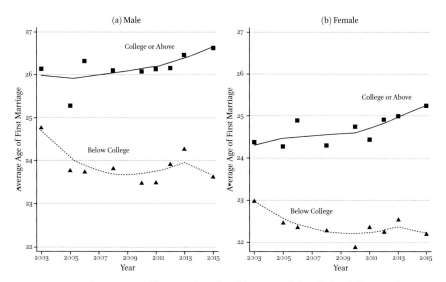

FIGURE 28.8 Average age of first marriage for Chinese youth (aged 18–35) for years between 2003 and 2015, by gender
DATA SOURCE: CGSS 2003, 2005, 2006, 2008, 2010, 2011, 2012, 2013, 2015

over the years for both men and women. Moreover, the proportion of "never married" for those with a higher education diploma is much higher than that of those without a college diploma. This is particularly true for women. The right panel of Figure 28.7 shows that highly educated women are much more likely to be "never married" than their less educated counterparts. When looking at the trends from 2003 to 2015, we can find that with the passage of time, the gap between the two groups of different educational levels shows an expanding trend.

When looking at the average age of first marriage for the young people aged 18–35 years, as shown in Figure 28.8, we find more interesting patterns. First of all, highly educated youth married much later than their low-education counterparts for both men and women. Secondarily, we see clear increasing trends (for both men and women) of the average age of first marriage over time for young people with a college degree, while there are obvious decreasing trends for those without a college diploma. That is, highly educated young people get married later and later over time, but groups with low education levels are getting married earlier and earlier.

4.4 *Education and Chinese Youth's Employment*

According to the human capital theory in neoclassical economics, in a fully competitive labor market the employment opportunities and monetary returns

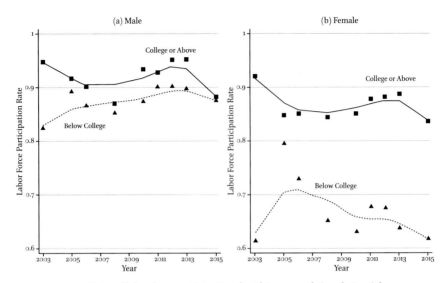

FIGURE 28.9 Rates of labor force participation for Chinese youth (aged 18–35) for years between 2003 and 2015, by gender
DATA SOURCE: CGSS 2003, 2005, 2006, 2008, 2010, 2011, 2012, 2013, 2015

of jobs depend on their investment in different forms of human capital (mainly in education) (Becker 1975; Mincer 1962). Following this logic, the higher the education level of an individual, the higher the expected income in the labor market and the higher the opportunity cost of not getting employed, which may result in a higher rate of labor force participation for highly educated people. The existing literature shows that in China, level of education is truly one of the important factors that affect individuals' participation in the labor market (Cai and Wang 2004; Wu 2010).

For Chinese young people, what is the relationship between education and their labor participation and occupational status? What is the trend of this relationship over time? These are questions that are worth exploring in the context of the continuous educational expansion. I answer these questions by analyzing various waves of CGSS data.

It can be seen from Figure 28.9 that, in general, educational attainment has a positive impact on labor participation. For both men and women, the labor participation rate of young groups (aged 18–35 years) with a higher education degree is higher than that of those without college diploma. In particular, education has a significant impact on women's labor participation. The impact of a college degree for young men is not very obvious (as shown by the left panel of Figure 28.9), which indicates that men, as the breadwinners of families, have to participate in labor regardless of their educational achievements. However, the labor participation rates of highly educated young women and young women with a low amount of education are hugely different.

If we examine the trend of labor participation, we can find that from 2003 to 2015, the labor participation of young men 18–35 years old with a higher education degree fluctuated over time and has presented a slightly downward trend recently, but the labor participation rate of less educated groups shows an upward trend. For young women, whether they are highly educated or less educated groups, their labor participation rate presents an overall downward trend. This shows that in the context of education expansion in China, the labor participation rate of highly educated groups is declining.

5 Summary and Discussion

In this chapter, I illustrated the trends of educational development in China since the market reform launched in 1978, and I analyze how education, on the individual level and on the group level, has an impact on the life chances of Chinese youth. The findings can be summarized as follows:

- In the past decades, China has made substantial achievements in educational development, as indicated by the rapidly increasing gross enrollment rates and sizes of student bodies at all school levels.
- Gender disparity in education has been declining over time. Like with most Western countries, we have even seen a reverse gender gap in education for newly born cohorts in China.
- The urban–rural gap and class-based educational inequality persist and have even grown over time, which may have important implications for the reproduction of social inequality in the long run.
- Education expansion in China has an impact on young people's life chances, including intense competition in educational advancement, school class segregation at various school levels, the rising average age of first marriage for young people, and the patterns of labor force participation for young men and women (especially the declining rate of employment for highly educated youth).

The relationship between education and youth has important implications for the changes of gender and class structure and population structure in China. Therefore, from the perspective of education and youth, China provides an important empirical context for the theoretical debates of international post-Western sociology.

References

Becker, Gary. 1975. *Human Capital.* New York, NY: Columbia University Press.

Cai, Fang, and Meiyan Wang. 2004. "Changing Labor Force Participation in Urban China and Its Implications". *Chinese Social Science* 4: 68–79. (In Chinese).

Huang, Xiaoting, and Yi Wei. 2018. "Development Status of After-School Training Industry: Based on the China Institute for Educational Finance Research-Household Survey (CIEFR-HS) in 2017". In *Report on the Development of Education New Forms in China (2017)*, edited by Rong Wang. Beijing: Social Sciences Academic Press. (In Chinese).

Li, Chunling. 2010. "Expansion of Higher Education and Inequality in Opportunity of Education: A Study on Effect of 'Kuozhao' Policy on Equalization of Educational Attainment". *Sociological Studies* 3: 82–113. (In Chinese).

Mincer, Jacob. 1962. "Labor Force Participation of Married Women: A Study of Labor Supply". In *Aspects of Labor Economics*, 63–97. Princeton, NJ: Princeton University Press.

Sweeney, Megan M. 2002. "Two Decades of Family Change: The Shifting Economic Foundations of Marriage". *American Sociological Review* 67: 132–147.

Thornton, Arland, William G. Axinn, and Jay D. Teachman. 1995. "The Influence of School Enrollment and Accumulation on Cohabitation and Marriage in Early Adulthood". *American Sociological Review* 60: 762–774.

Treiman, Donald J., ed. 1998. *Life Histories and Social Change in Contemporary China: Codebook.* Los Angeles, CA: UCLA Institute for Social Science Research.

Wang, Peng, and Yuxiao Wu. 2013. "Determinants of the Age of First Marriage: A Study Based on CGSS2006". *Chinese Journal of Sociology* 3: 89–110. (In Chinese).

Wu, Xiaogang. 2009. "Economic Transition, School Expansion, and Educational Inequality in China, 1990–2000". *Chinese Journal of Sociology* 5: 88–113. (In Chinese).

Wu, Yuxiao. 2010. "Impacts of Individual Factors on Women's Employment in Urban China: Comparison of 1995 and 2002". *Chinese Journal of Sociology* 6: 136–155. (In Chinese).

Wu, Yuxiao. 2012. "Gender Gap in Educational Attainment in Urban and Rural China". *Chinese Journal of Sociology* 4: 112–137. (In Chinese.)

Wu, Yuxiao. 2013. "Educational Opportunities of Chinese Rural and Urban Residents in 1978–2008: Inequality and Evolution". *Social Sciences in China* 3: 4–21. (In Chinese).

Wu, Yuxiao, and Chao Huang. 2016. "Stratification of the School Hierarchy and Educational Expectations of Students in Basic Education". *Social Sciences in China* 4: 111–134. (In Chinese).

Xue, Haiping. 2015. "From School Education to Shadow Education: Education Competition and Social Reproduction". *Peking University Education Review* 3: 47–69. (In Chinese).

Ye, Hua, and Xiaogang Wu. 2011. "Fertility Decline and the Trend in Educational Gender Inequality in China". *Sociological Studies* 5: 153–177. (In Chinese).

CHAPTER 29

Exploring Educational Institutions' Major Roles and Norms to Understand Their Effects: The Example of France

Agnès van Zanten

In order to understand what educational institutions do, as well as their effects both on individual students and on society as a whole, it is important to resort to general models for their analysis or, more widely, for the analysis of organizations fulfilling functions similar to those of schools. While it is always possible to create new models, testing the robustness of existing ones by integrating new elements and changes over time, as well as concepts and theories developed to explain them, is more conducive to reinforcing the cumulative character of scientific knowledge. These general models present two main advantages; the first is that they provide interpretations about crucial phenomena that take into account, and in turn try to account for, many different factors and processes. The second, directly relevant to the purpose of this book, is that they allow for cross-national dialogue while avoiding the risk of focusing on a term-to-term comparison of specific national goals or structural arrangements.

1 Two Seminal Models for Analyzing Educational Institutions' Roles and Norms

1.1 People-Changing and People-Processing Dynamics in Educational Institutions

We will use two ideal typical models to analyze the roles that schools, and higher education institutions (HEIs) assume in French society and the norms that inform their goals and activities. Y. Hasenfeld, an American organizational sociologist specializing in the study of human service organizations, devised the first of these models. In a seminal article focusing on organizations whose raw materials are people (rather than objects), Hasenfeld (1972) introduced a useful distinction between two types of organizations: those aimed at changing the people they take charge of and those that focus on "processing" them. As shown in Table 29.1 below, these two organizational types differ in several key dimensions.

TABLE 29.1 Main features of people-changing and people-processing organizations according to Hasenfeld (1972)

	People-changing organizations	People-processing organizations
Main goal	Alter the physical, psychological, or cultural attributes of clients	Alter the status of clients and relocate them to other contexts
Dominant technologies	Socialization and resocialization techniques widely based on human interactions	Classification and disposal techniques based on human interaction but also on ranking and allocation devices
Duration of staff-client relationships	Long-term interactions	Short-term interactions
Degree of customization of staff-client relationships	High degree of customization	Low degree of customization
Organizational boundaries	Most activities are intraorganizational	Most activities take place at organizational boundaries

Hasenfeld underlines that these two types can correspond to different subunits within a single organization. In this chapter, we take this perspective but complicate it by considering that in spite of a formal separation concerning the processes and persons involved in each type of activity, in reality they are closely intertwined in educational institutions. Although teachers are expected to engage mostly in people-changing activities, their actual teaching "charter" (Meyer 1970) includes two dimensions related to people processing. The first is that teaching contents, methods, and evaluations both adapt to students' previous trajectories and are influenced by teachers' beliefs about their probable future educational and professional paths, leading them to engage in a process of "anticipatory socialization" (Merton 1968). The second is that teachers play a major role in the classification of students in different categories according to educational performance (i.e., "good", "average", "failing"), which plays a major role in the future distribution of students into different paths. Guidance counselors, on the other hand, who are expected to focus mostly on students' relocation (Ciccourel and Kitsuse 1963), frequently engage in people-changing actions in order to encourage them to accept educational options that they initially refuse to consider. The hybridization of these two roles, changing students and participating in their circulation, has moreover been reinforced in the last decades by neoliberal educational policies encouraging all actors to get involved in the management of students' transitions and in their assessment and counseling, not only to rank and relocate them but also to encourage them to adopt attitudes and behaviors that fit more closely with the expectations of employers and policy-makers.

1.2 Contest Mobility and Sponsorship in Contemporary Educational Systems

The second model that we will use in this article was also devised by an American sociologist, Ralph Turner (1960). In a frequently cited article, Turner draws an ideal-typical distinction between two modes of upward mobility through education: contest mobility and sponsored mobility. For Turner, "contest" and "sponsorship" are normative patterns or organizing norms able to guide representations and practice, not through legal constraints but rather by spreading through groups and institutions in the form of folk concepts. However, because they have been embedded in institutional practices for so long, these types also refer to the mobility channels (Kerckhoff 1995) that make upwardly mobile trajectories possible. As shown in Table 29.2 below, these two norms differ in several key dimensions.

TABLE 29.2 Distinctive features of contest and sponsorship according to Turner (1960)

	Contest mobility	Sponsored mobility
Access to elite status, main mechanism, and underlying metaphor	Status is taken by aspirants' own efforts Competition Sporting event	Status is granted on the basis of the qualities established elites wish to see in fellow members Co-opting Private club
Organization of school careers	Keeping everyone in the running until the final stages, by delaying absolute judgments as long as possible Focus on principles and rules allowing a fair race.	Early selection of "elected" individuals into tracks allowing access to elite positions Focus on preparing recruits for their elite position

TABLE 29.2 Distinctive features of contest and sponsorship according to Turner (1960) (*cont.*)

	Contest mobility	Sponsored mobility
Teaching priorities	Education is valued less for its content than as a means of getting ahead. Help is provided to the less successful	Schooling is valued for its cultivation of elite culture. Educational resources are concentrated on "those who can benefit most from them".
Mechanisms through which elites join the normative system in place	Insecurity of elite position because each contest, rather than ensuring a definitive position, serves to qualify the participant for competition at the next higher level.	Early and thorough indoctrination in elite culture, combined with a sense of responsibility toward inferiors
How loyalty is controlled among the disadvantaged classes	Combination of futuristic orientation, the norm of ambition, and a general sense of fellowship with the elite, as each individual is encouraged to think of himself as competing for an elite position	Control is maintained by training the masses to regard themselves as incompetent, by restricting access to the skills and manners of the elite, and by cultivating belief in the superior competence of the elite

Any serious attempt to use this distinction today has to incorporate the changes that have marked school systems over the past 60 years, as well as the sociological interpretations that have tried to account for them. To update his typology, it is especially important to add three complementary clauses. The first, introduced in the sociological literature by James Rosenbaum (1979), is the need to distinguish between open competition, which is inclusive, and close competition or "tournament mobility", where the candidates' chances of rising up through the ranks grow weaker with each competitive test. We have elaborated ourselves on the last two clauses based on our previous research (Van Zanten 2018). The second is that the two norms coexist, that they are closely intertwined and complementary in the way they contribute to the social closure of access to elite positions and to the reproduction of inequalities in current education systems. The third is that it is necessary to distinguish between two sets of actors that play a key role in updating both norms—parents and teachers—and to examine their joint participation in two distinct types of sponsorship: family sponsorship and institutional sponsorship. The first of these notions relates to all the actions through which social groups belonging to the elite—or those with the necessary resources to be "pretenders" to elite status—influence school processes or adapt to them efficiently; the second, to the institutional arrangements offered by the teaching system and its professionals to allow certain children access to elite positions.

2 Dominant Mechanisms and Norms in the French Educational System and Their Effects

2.1 *Excellence, Merit, and Tolerated Sponsorship*

French schools and HEIs' official goals are to educate children and youngsters to become reflexive citizens and competent workers, to favor individuals' sociopolitical and economic integration and their social cohesiveness and progress. They enact these goals through institutional arrangements and key principles combing the norms of merit and sponsorship. One of these key principles is academic excellence, which articulates the Enlightenment ideal of individuals' intellectual and moral development and social development and integration through the diffusion of knowledge with the French Revolution meritocratic ideal of selection of the most competent to occupy positions of power irrespective of their social origins. The sponsorship norm is, however, also at the heart of how academic excellence is defined and evaluated in at least three ways. First, although official institutional discourses tend to equate excellence with merit-as-effort, in practice teachers tend to reward talent rather than effort, which is a dimension of merit more easily associated with membership into the upper classes. Second, the cultural knowledge and skills that schools transmit and the criteria used to evaluate students' acquisition of them are much closer to those of this social group (Bourdieu and Passeron 1977; Bourdieu and Saint-Martin 1988). Finally, even if schools enjoy a relative autonomy concerning who deserves to be promoted, thus individualizing the social reproduction process, upper-class parents still can use their cultural, social, and economic capital to circumvent, adapt to, or partially modify school expectations and rules (Lareau and McCrory Calarco 2012; Van Zanten 2013).

This emphasis on academic excellence goes together with the importance of institutional arrangements devoted to the regular testing and classification of students more to detect and reinforce the intellectual progress of the best than to provide help to the less successful. However, due to pressures in favor of inclusiveness and widening participation as well as to the penetration of psychological concepts and of a liberal ideology emphasizing personalization, choice, and responsibility, the importance of exams has been reduced except for the competitive *concours* for access to the most prestigious and selective HEIs, the *grandes écoles*: the secondary entrance exam was abolished in the 1960s, and the *baccalauréat*, still required to continue into postsecondary education, has become much less selective, and it is less important than grades in admission to higher education. Selection now takes place through a series of both informal and formal "gateway encounters" (Ridgeway 2013). In preschools and primary schools, for instance, qualitative assessments of children's results and behavior determine whether they can remain on the "normal" route or benefit from specific programs which, rather than helping them overcome their difficulties, frequently lead to their marginalization or exclusion.

At the end of middle secondary school, these encounters become official and take the form of evaluations of students' capacity to attend one of the three tracks—academic, technological, or professional—that will channel them into very different higher education and professional paths. Although grades play an important role in these evaluations, students' relocation into these tracks is not as meritocratic at it is officially claimed. Since the 1960s, different studies have shown that social dimensions play an important role in this process, with teachers more likely to endorse upper-class parents' systematic wish for their children to continue into the academic track, even when their grades are low, and to discourage lower-class parents and students from doing so even when the latter have average academic results (INED 1970). This combined process of institutional and family sponsorship is still very much at work, but now rather than the state and schools taking official responsibility for making final decisions about students' educational and social destinies, these decisions are presented as the result of a compromise between students' and parents' projects, and teachers' judgments. This new context has both given more leeway for advantaged families to obtain the desired academic tracks and forced teachers to develop more sophisticated strategies to influence the choices of disadvantaged students and parents (Cayouette-Remblière 2014).

These tracks also constitute a powerful mechanism of institutional sponsorship because, together with grades and the kind of feeder school students come from, they strongly determine student careers in higher education. While selective HE tracks are allowed to accept only a tiny proportion (around 5%) of students from the technological track and none from the professional one, non-selective universities have in the past developed various ways to discourage them (Beaud and Pialoux 2001). State policy-makers claim that with the introduction of a new online platform for managing applications to HE the power balance has changed in favor of users who are allowed many choices and receive additional information on HE fields of study and institutions.

In fact, however, HEIs, now including universities, still strongly consider the tracks attended in secondary school when ranking students' applications, while the complexity of the platform gives additional advantages to students who receive help from their school and family to interact with it effectively (Frouillou, Pin and Van Zanten 2020).

2.2   Winners, Losers, and a Divided Society

The ways in which the French school system enacts its people-changing and people-processing role as well as the dominant norms of merit and sponsorship generate different perceptions among students, depending on their experiences, of their place in society and of the justice of the social system. The winners of the series of closed competitions organized by schools and HEIs strongly feel they deserve their position at the top of the educational system, either because of their talents or efforts or both, and that their educational status should automatically give them the right to monopolize highly desired positions in other spheres. They are less likely to acknowledge that in addition to their own merit, what has made this status possible is the fact that they have benefited from various forms of institutional sponsorship and, for the great majority of those who come from advantaged social groups, of family sponsorship as well. This is due to the fact that some of these processes have been at least partly invisibilized by school agents and parents who, for different reasons, want to emphasize the fact that schools reward those who win in open competitions (Van Zanten 2015) and also to the fact that, when students are conscious of them, they tend to see them as rewards for their merit. Moreover, the fact that these students tend to be socialized and to circulate in environments where they are surrounded by students with similar trajectories and profiles makes them neither open to the difficulties experienced by those students whose learning and trajectories take place in less favorable contexts nor, contrary to what Turner (1960) hypothesized, prone to feel in any way responsible for their condition.

On the other hand, losers of the competition, who in the vast majority of cases did not benefit or only benefited to a small degree from institutional or family sponsorship, tend to internalize opposite perspectives. Some of them, as predicted by Turner's sponsorship model, develop strong feelings of personal incompetence, and accuse themselves rather than the system for their position at the bottom, and even more so as the educational system now encourages all students to feel responsible for their results and trajectories. These students tend to accept their situation but to become disengaged from the political and social system. Others instead, and among them many students of immigrant origin who are likely to view the lack of institutional support as a form of discrimination (Brinbaum, Moguérou and Primon 2010), become highly critical of educational and state institutions more generally and might engage in different forms of protest or violence against them. Contrary to Turner's (1960) prediction, neither the first nor the second type of student tends to identify with the elite, this being mostly the case for those students from disadvantaged backgrounds who manage to become winners in the competition either solely because of their own efforts or by additionally benefiting from some kind of compensatory sponsorship (Grodsky 2007).

There are multiple societal effects of the internal dynamics of the French educational system. On the one hand, the system manages to produce a competent elite able to exercise important roles in the economy, the state, and the professions, and confident about its intellectual capacities but one that tends to reproduce itself rather than innovate. On the other hand, although it also manages to raise the general level of education of each generation and prepare most students for different occupations, it does so imperfectly because of its main focus on sponsoring the best students rather than stimulating the progress of the rest and providing help for the unsuccessful ones, whose educational progress and experiences made them less likely to become effective and satisfied workers. Due to the high level of inequality that such a system generates, its goals of training reflexive citizens and building a just and cohesive society are also only partly realized. The most "enlightened" individuals are not encouraged to develop a comprehensive understanding of social contexts and groups, while feelings of divorce from, mistrust and even hate of, elites develop among those who have not received the full benefits of education, creating a divided society riddled with deep political tensions.

3   Conclusion

This general overview of the French educational system in light of Hasenfeld's and Turner's model shows some specific ways in which schools and HEIs fulfill their roles of changing students' identities and of making them circulate within the educational system and out of it and interpret the norms of competition and sponsorship. Nevertheless, comparisons of educational systems with these theoretical tools help us see that other choices are possible. Rather than focus on encouraging and rewarding the excellence of the few through close competition, specific institutional pathways, and tolerance towards different forms of support from advantaged families, policy-makers and educational professionals can give priority to the acquisition by a maximum of students of the knowledge and skills required to be future responsible citizens and competent workers. They might also orient their efforts towards the creation of inclusive educational systems with few or no tracks until postsecondary education and many possibilities to move from one type of training to another. These comparisons are also useful to perceive both the structural and ideological obstacles that prevent educational systems to change in positive directions and imagine possible solutions to reduce or eliminate them.

References

Beaud, S., and M. Pialoux. 2001. "Les 'Bacs pro' à l'université. Récit d'une Impasse". *Revue française de pédagogie* 136: 87–95.

Brinbaum, Y., L. Moguérou, and J.L. Primon. 2010. "Parcours et expériences scolaires des jeunes descendants d'immigrés en France". In *Trajectoires et origines. Enquête sur la diversité des populations en France*, edited by C. Beauchemin, C. Hamel, and P. Simon, 47–57. Paris: Ined.

Bourdieu, P., and J.C. Passeron. (1970) 1977. *Reproduction in Education, Society and Culture*. London: Sage Publications.

Bourdieu, P., and M. de Saint-Martin. (1975) 1988. "Categories of Professorial Judgment". In P. Bourdieu, *Homo Academicus*, 194–225. Cambridge: Polity Press.

Cayouette-Remblière, J. 2014. "Les classes populaires face à l'impératif scolaire. Orienter les choix dans un contexte de scolarisation totale". *Actes de la recherche en sciences sociales* 205 (5): 58–71.

Ciccourel, A., and J. Kitsuse. 1963. *The Educational Decision-Makers*. Indianapolis: The Bobbs-Merrill Company.

Frouillou, L., C. Pin, and A. van Zanten. 2020. "Les plateformes APB et Parcoursup au service de l'égalité des chances ?" *L'Année sociologique* 70 (2): 337–363.

Grodsky, D. 2007. "Compensatory Sponsorship in Higher Education". *American Journal of Sociology* 112 (6): 1662–1712.

Hasenfeld, Y. 1972. "People-Processing Organizations: An Exchange Approach". *American Sociological Review* 37 (3): 256–263.

INED. 1970. *"Population" et l'enseignement*. Paris: Presses Universitaires de France.

Kerckhoff, A. 1995. "Institutional Arrangements and Stratification Processes in Industrial Societies". *Annual Review of Sociology* 21: 323–347.

Lareau, A., and J. McCrory Calarco. 2012. "Class, Cultural Capital and Institutions: The Case of Families and Schools". In *Facing Social Class*, edited by S. Fiske and H. Markus, 61–86. New York, NY: Russell Sage Foundation.

Merton, R. (1957) 1968. *Social Theory and Social Structure*. New York, NY: The Free Press.

Meyer, J. 1970. "The Charter: Conditions of Diffuse Socialization in Schools". In *Social Processes and Social Structures: An Introduction to Sociology*, edited by R. Scott. New York, NY: Henry Holt Co.

Ridgeway, C. 2013. "Why Status Matters for Inequality?" *American Sociological Review* 79 (1): 1–16.

Rosenbaum, J. 1979. "Tournament Mobility: Career Patterns in a Corporation". *Administrative Science Quarterly* 24: 220–242.

Turner, R. 1960. "Sponsored and Contest Mobility and the School System". *American Sociological Review* 25 (6): 855–867.

Van Zanten, A. 2013. "A Good Match: Appraising Worth and Estimating Quality in School Choice". In *Constructing Quality: The Classification of Goods in the Economy*, edited by J. Beckert and C. Musselin, 79–99. Oxford: Oxford University Press.

Van Zanten, A. 2015. "A Family Affair: Reproducing Elite Positions and Preserving the Ideals of Meritocratic Competition and Youth Autonomy". In *Elites, Privilege and Excellence: The National and Global Redefinition of Educational Advantage*, edited by A. van Zanten, S. Ball, and B. Darchy-Koechlin, 29–42. London: Routledge.

Van Zanten, A. 2018. "How Families and Schools Produce an Elite: Paths of Upward Mobility in France". In *Elites in Education*. Vol. 4, edited by A. van Zanten. London: Routledge.

CHAPTER 30

Youth and Transition from School to Work in Japan

Asano Tomohiko

1   Introduction: Youth, Who Are They?

The question of who "youth" are may serve as a good starting point for "East–West Dialogue" under the title "Youth and Education". "Youth" is related to the fact that someone is young in a biological sense. The root of the English word "youth" is "young", while the Japanese word for youth, *wakamono*, consists of the Chinese characters *waka* [young] and *mono* [person]. Similarly, the Chinese word for youth, *nianqingren*, consists of the words *nianqing* [young] and *ren* [person]. However, an examination of the age range covered by these various words reveals that there are some differences. For example, the online resource Education and Childhood Studies, published online by Bloomsbury, contains 60 articles on youth, where youth is defined as individuals between the ages of 13 and 21 years. In Japan, *wakamono*, as defined in national government policies, includes individuals between the ages of 15 and 39.

These age differences imply that the concept of youth is not simply defined biologically but is a construct related to the institutions in each society. Age coverage is one aspect of how an institution deals with people, the simplest example of this being the ages to which wide varieties of laws apply. In Japan, crimes committed by individuals younger than 20 years are dealt with under the Juvenile Law of Japan. Individuals under 20 are not allowed to buy cigarettes or alcohol. On the other hand, all individuals over the age of 18 years now have the right to vote in elections (the minimum age was 20 until 2015). The Child Welfare Act also defines children as "a person under 18 years of age".

In order to study "youth" from a post-Western sociological standpoint, the concept should be understood in the relationship to relevant institutions in each country. Education is one such institution, but not the only one.

2   The Divided Worlds for Youth and Its Unification

Japan, China, and South Korea each have their own education system. These three systems are similar in some respects but different in others. One of the common trends in the postwar era has been the expansion of secondary and higher education, with some disparities between genders, classes, and regions. Some differences have been observed in relation to the school-to-work transition.

Interestingly, from the post-Western sociological point of view, Japanese has two different words for "youth". One of those terms, mentioned above, is *wakamono* [young person]; the other is *seinen*, which is written using the same characters as *qingnian* in Chinese. The first part of the word, *sei*, means "blue" and refers to something new and immature. "Adolescence" is sometimes translated into Japanese as *seishun*, which is the characters *sei* [blue] and *shun* [spring].

The important difference between *wakamono* and *seinen* is that *seinen* has some developmental implications, while *wakamono* does not. *Seinen* are youth who are on the way to adulthood and are subject to education and guidance from adults. *Wakamono* is used to refer to lifestyles rather than development. Youth culture, for example, is translated as *wakamono bunka* [culture]. In the context of education, therefore, young people are usually referred to as *seinen*.

The Japanese education system was totally reformed after the country's defeat in World War II. In the reformed system, primary and secondary education is called the 6-3-3 system—which means 6 years for elementary school, 3 years for junior high school, and 3 years for high school. Beyond this 6-3-3 system is 4-year university education.

Elementary school and junior high school are compulsory, while high school is not. That said, high school education rapidly expanded during the period of the high-growth economy from the late 1950s to the early 1970s. According to the Basic Survey of Schools conducted annually by the Ministry of Education, Culture, Sports, Science and Technology (MEXT), around 50% of youth went to high school in the 1950s. This rose sharply to 70% in the 1960s and to 90% in the 1970s. The figure today is 98.8% (2020).

College enrollment rate also rose during the same period, albeit at a more moderate pace. The rate was around 10% in the 1960s but increased to 20% and 30% in the 1970s and 1980s, respectively. Since then, the enrollment rate has increased at a slightly accelerated rate to 50% in the 1990s.

Until the late 1960s, young people were divided at the age of 15 into two groups: students and workers (including farmers). After graduating from junior high school, young people in these two groups started to live in such different environments that it was almost impossible to capture their circumstances in the single category of "youth". During this period, young people who started to work after leaving junior high school were called *kinro seinen* [working youth] or *nouson seinen* [youth working in farm villages]. *Kinro seinen* worked in factories in urban areas, while *nouson seinen* worked as farmers in rural areas. *Kinro seinen* and *nouson seinen* are distinguished from individuals who went to high school, who were simply referred to as *gakusei* [students]. There were many junior high school graduates who were able to go to high school in terms of their grades but did not do so due to their economic circumstances. These youth had to work to support their families. As pointed out by Fukuma (2020), there was likely tension between those who could afford to go to high school and those who could not.

One interesting example is the national speech contest for 20-year-olds that is broadcast by the public station NHK. Despite its title, "Opinions of Young People", until the 1970s almost all of the speakers were workers in urban areas and farmers (Sato 2017). There were no university students.

As can be seen from the above, during this period, youth were hardly monolithic. With regard to the education system, there were two distinct worlds—one for those working in urban areas or rural villages and another for high school and university students.

However, these two distinct worlds were integrated in the 1970s. The high school enrollment rate rose rapidly in the early 1970s, to more than 90%, which transformed the worlds of young people that had been separated up to that point. That is, since this period, most youth spend 3 years, from the ages of 15 to 18, as high school students. Most young people in this age bracket experience similar life circumstances, and therefore it has become possible to capture them as one group, youth.

What these youth have in common is that they spent a lot of hours in school every day. This is why "student culture" was adopted by scholars as a framework for the analysis of "youth" during this time period.

3   Japanese System of School-to-Work Transition

Along with the unification of the youth worlds, a system for school-to-work transition was established during the high-growth period. The system is called "simultaneous recruiting of new graduates" or "periodic recruiting of new graduates". This is a core part of the Japanese employment system, which is often characterized as providing lifetime employment, seniority-based wages, and corporate unions.

Most students engage in job hunting in their last year of school and start their career as full-time regular workers in April, just after graduating from university and high school. It is as if individuals in the same age group move from schools to corporations together as one group. Workers of the same age who enter the same corporation move up the ladder in the organization together through to the end of their career (the seniority-based wage system and lifetime employment).

Keiichirou Hamaguchi, a scholar of labor law, explained that this employment system is membership oriented as opposed to job oriented (Hamaguchi 2013). Workers in Western societies as well as in South Korea and China are employed to do perform a specific job. That is, what happens in a job-oriented system of employment is that jobs come first, and then people having the required skills or qualifications are hired. In Japan, employing workers is more like accepting new members into a community, town, or village. Firms bring on a certain number of new graduates of the same age as new members in April every year, irrespective of the jobs that need to be performed. This is what Hamaguchi calls a membership-oriented system of employment wherein new members are first taken on and then are periodically assigned to different position within the company.

Thus, what is required of young job applicants in Japan is quite different from job applicants in other societies. In job-oriented employment systems, young applicants are required to have certain skills or qualifications to do a specific job. When university graduates are employed, the student's area of study matters a lot. In contrast, in a membership-oriented employment system, it is not the skills or qualifications that matter. Young applicants are required to be new graduates, honest, hard-working, loyal to the company, and possessing a general facility to learn. They do not have to prove that they can do specific jobs, but instead must prove that they can learn everything and that they can adapt to any job to which they are assigned. As a criterion for evaluating this general ability to learn, employers often rely on the name of school or university. The more prestigious the school or university, the more highly the job applicant is evaluated. Therefore, the student's major does not matter in the job-hunting process.

From a job-oriented point of view, many aspects of the membership-oriented job-hunting process are strange. One example is the postponement of graduation by university students for the sake of job hunting. As mentioned above, young job applicants are required to be new graduates. Applicants who spend a year or two after graduation without full-time regular employment face difficulties in job hunting. To avoid the disadvantage, many students choose to postpone graduation and to pay tuition for another year even though they already have the credits required for graduation.

Sociologist Mary Brinton described this transition system as a move between shared places, using the concept of *ba* [shared place] proposed by Japanese anthropologist Chie Nakane. Students occupy the shared place (*ba*) of school, then move as a group to the next shared place of work. Another metaphor used by sociologist Masahiro Yamada is that of a pipeline. Students in the same grade move together through the pipeline into the labor market at the same time of year.

It is this move between *ba* and "pipeline" that was lost in the mid-1990s.

4 Postwar Regime of Youth

The high enrollment in high school, which led to the unification of the formerly divided worlds of youth, and the above-described transition system provide the groundwork for a certain life stage, which we could call "youth". This life stage is a function of institutions such as schools, the labor market, and companies. The sociologist Akio Inui referred to this as the "post-war regime of youth" (Inui 2010). What is important from a post-Western sociological view are the various functions of different institutions that constitute this "youth" regime, not just young people themselves.

This regime was established during the high-growth period, mainly during the 1960s, and stabilized later in the 1970s. Young people living in this regime had a clear image of their transition and even of their subsequent life course, such as when they would get married, have children, buy a house, and so on. An individual's life trajectory was highly predictable as long as the regime was well maintained.

It is in this context that young people have become less interested in school education and transition-to-work and more interested in a wide variety of cultural activities. Around the mid-1970s, Japanese society entered a new stage of capitalism in which products were bought not based on their function, but rather for their symbolic meaning. The ability of the product to distinguish the owner from others was more important than what could be done with the product. Japan became a consumer society in Baudrillard's sense (Baudrillard 1970).

Young people are leading actors in this consumer society. They signify themselves as someone different from the others through the purchase and enjoyment of some products and services. When the focus is on this aspect of young people, young people are referred to as *wakamono* (literally, young people). As mentioned earlier, *seinen* is used to refer to youth in the context of the education system, while *wakamono* is used to refer to youth in the context of the consumer society.

Shinji Miyadai, a prominent sociologist in the field of youth studies, wrote that youth as consumers or bearers of consumer culture do not adhere to a "class code" or do not identify themselves with positions in the class structure of the society (Miyadai 2006). Miyadai argues that instead, *wakamono* have started to use a "consumption code" to indicate the cultural tribes to which they belong or to distinguish themselves from certain other tribes. From the *wakamono*'s perspective, these cultural distinctions are horizontal rather than vertical, as is the case for class structure.

Education and transition-to-work serve as core mechanisms for the reproduction of class structure. From the late 1970s to the early 1990s, these lost importance for young people and were replaced with consumption, culture, and lifestyle. Studies on youth in this period have also paid attention mainly to these aspects of youth (Kotani 1993, 1998). For example, Miyadai chose comics, music, and the dating culture of youth as topics for youth studies (Miyadai 2007). The journalist Soichiro Matsutani wrote a 30-year history of the "culture war" among girls' tribes (Matsutani 2012), which seems to have something in common with the conflicts between *feizhuliu wenhua* [non-mainstream culture] and *shamate wenhua* [smart culture] among Chinese youth in the 2000s.

Another change that has been observed in the horizontal perspective of youth (i.e., lifestyle) is a declining political interest among young people. Politics is a process that involves the distribution of a wide variety of resources, which results, to a certain extent, in the vertical structuring of society. However, the horizontal and cultural perspectives have obscured this structuring and rendered it invisible. Until the end of 1960s, young people, including high school students in Japan, were quite active in politics and social movements, much like students in other advanced societies at that time (Kobayashi 2012). However, since the early 1970s Japanese youth have rapidly lost their interest in politics. Fewer youth are voting in elections and participating in politics.

5   Transformation in the 1990s

Since the collapse of the bubble economy in 1991, the postwar regime of youth seems to have entered a process of decline. The long-lasting recession, which is often referred to as the "lost 20 years" or "lost 30 years", has spoiled the basic conditions under which the postwar regime of youth was maintained.

In response to the recession, companies have curbed the employment of new graduates to avoid having to dismiss current regular workers. In addition, various jobs that had been assigned to full-time regular workers have been transferred to part-time non-regular workers. This new orientation of employment has been justified by the Japan Federation of Employers' Association, the biggest interest group of prestigious corporations, as the "Japanese Style of Management in a New Age".

The group hit first and hardest by this change of orientation was the high school students who were going about applying for jobs in the same way as before, as those jobs for new workers with high school diplomas were the first to be transferred to part-time workers. Then, a few years later, university students began to face similar difficulties in job hunting. A lot of young people in this cohort could not get jobs when they left school or university and started to work as part-time workers.

As explained above, when young people apply for jobs for the first time they are required to be new graduates, otherwise they find themselves in a difficult situation. This is what happened to the individuals who had to start their careers as part-time workers. Those impacted by the change in the school-to-work transition system in the mid and late 1990s were subsequently relegated to unstable life conditions. In the early 2000s, the media began to widely cover the plight of such workers as a new social problem, and those affected by it were named the "lost generation".

To use Brinton's word *ba* [shared place], a lot of youth lost their place in the *ba* while moving from school to work. Or, to use Yamada's metaphor, the "pipeline" was cracked, and a lot of youth fell out through the cracks. Once they have fallen out of the *ba* or "pipeline", it is difficult for young people to return to where they are supposed to be. Because the transition system does not assume the routine dropout of many individuals as a matter of course, there is no safety net or public support for those dropouts.

The reason the system had worked well without a safety net is because it was based on cooperation between companies, families, and schools, which the sociologist Yuki Honda called the "cycle model of post-war Japan". In this system, families are in charge of taking care of children and sending them to schools, schools are in charge of educating them and sending them to companies, and companies are in charge of paying them enough to provide for their families. The school-to-work transition system is a part of this "cycle model" and is sustained by families, schools, and employers, with the government and public organizations playing almost no role. Therefore, when companies began to gradually withdraw their cooperation in the cycle model in response to the recession of the early 1990s, no actor in society was prepared to provide a safety net for those young people who dropped out of what was formerly a stable transition course.

It is clear that the increase of young part-timers and casual workers was caused by the structural transformation of the school-to-work transition system. The public reaction at the end of 1990s, however, was more akin to "moral panic". Public sentiment was quite critical of young people who were not able to find full-time regular jobs. At the time, it was said that these young people's inability to find employment was due to their low motivation and poor work ethic. The situation was attributed to a lack of "individual responsibility".

This view was also shared by policymakers. The new labor policies for young workers passed in the early 2000s were mainly focused on changing young people's attitudes, not on changing the labor market or the school-to-work transition system itself. Efforts were made to train young people who were unable to obtain regular jobs to become more adaptable to the labor market and in the workplace (Komikawa 2010; Miyamoto 2015). Such policies, however, could not function as a safety net because even if the young people were well trained and highly motivated to get jobs, the fact remained that there was a shortage of decent and stable jobs.

Without the existence of a public safety net and with the cycle model remaining unchanged, the brunt of the burden falls on families. Young people who are part-timers and cannot earn enough to support themselves have no choice but to rely on their parents. Many continue to live with their parents after graduation and to rely on their parents' earnings or even their pensions. It is clear that this parasitic relationship cannot be sustained over the long haul. Thus, the postwar regime of youth began to collapse without any alternative in view.

6   Youth as Social Problem

As the postwar regime for youth began to collapse, youth could not simply be characterized as "working youth", "students", "consumers", and "bearers of the new cultures". Today, they find themselves at the intersection of a wide variety of social problems.

First, youth are the central element of labor market problems. A lot of commentators and journalists in the early 2000s, and even some today, criticized young people for their lack of motivation and work ethic. Unemployment or unstable conditions were seen to be the fault of the individuals, when in reality these young people had simply been forced out of the market due to structural transformation.

During the period from the end of the 1990s to the early 2010s, a wide variety of harsh criticisms of youth that were not at all based on empirical data resulted from this image of "lazy youth", which was encouraged by mass media. One such criticism had to do with juvenile delinquency. The media reported repeatedly that juvenile delinquency, and particularly homicides committed by minors, had increased both in number and seriousness, although public statistics showed the opposite. Yet, a lot of people, including politicians, believed these false claims, ultimately resulting in the revision of the Juvenile Law in 2000 to make it stricter for the first time since the end of World War II.

Second, youth are placed at the center of the problem of Japan's declining birth rate and decreasing population, particularly the declining labor population, which may cause the welfare system to go bankrupt. Like other East Asian societies, or for longer than them, Japan has been facing a rapidly declining birth rate. The birth rate, which was a little higher than 2.0 in the early 1970s, has since plummeted to 1.57 in 1989, 1.26 in 1995, and 1.34 in 2020.

One reason for this decline is most certainly the deterioration of the youth labor market. Many youth are avoiding getting married or are postponing having children until they can obtain a job that is stable enough to support a family or until they find a partner with full-time regular employment.

Another reason has to do with the fact that the abovementioned "post-war cycle model" in large part depends on the "male breadwinner model". This system does not work as well as it did in the 1980s, yet gender inequality in the labor market remains as strong as before. Women have been facing difficulty not only in finding partners but also in obtaining employment. Japan's male breadwinner model is a "zombie category" in Beck's sense.

Third, youth are seen to embody the problem of inequality through education. In the mid-2010s, the media started to report on research and studies indicating that educational achievement is significantly affected by the family environment. That is, the higher the socioeconomic status of a family, the higher the academic achievement of that family's children. In advanced societies, education is an important way, and in some case the only way, to climb the social ladder. If this is true, education reproduces inequality starting in the early stages of life. Sociologists of education are afraid that this might divide Japan's society (Kikkawa 2018; Matsuoka 2020).

One of the best solutions would be to increase public spending on education to support students in disadvantageous environments; however, this approach is not supported by the general public, according to several opinion polls (Ohoka 2014). This is because people believe that education is an investment by each family and that the beneficiaries of education are the families themselves and not society. People do not think it is fair to spend public money on supporting some families and not others. This is another zombie category that may have enjoyed life in the "post-war cycle model".

Fourth and lastly, the boundary of the concept of "youth", which finds itself at the intersection of several social problems, is gradually becoming blurred. For example, when the Juvenile Law was made stricter, the distinction became "juvenile" and "adult" became less clear. This is because the amendment made the Juvenile Law more like the Penal Code by which adults are judged.

Another example of the boundary of youth becoming blurred has to do with the Ministry of Labor, Health and Welfare's definition of young labor. In the 1960s and 1970s, the term covered individuals from 15 to 19 years old. However, the age range has gradually been expanded to include individuals between the ages of 15 and 24 in the 1980s, 15 and 29 in the 1990s, and 15 and 34 in the 2000s (Toivonen 2011). This reflects the increasing instability of younger workers during this period. Thus, the definition of young labor has changed along with changes in relevant policies, laws, and institutions, including the labor market.

In post-Western sociology, "youth" may not be suitable as a common frame of reference between East and West, or even between Japan, South Korea, and China; however, what should be examined is the social processes by which the concept of "youth" has been constructed in each society, which is historically inherent to each society. Young people in each society are framed and designated with different nicknames, such as the *Satori Sedai* [resignation generation] in Japan, Generation Z in Western societies, or *Tang Ping Zu* [lying flat tribe] in China. In order to compare these generations across cultures, we need to understand the social processes that underlie these categories in each society.

References

Baudrillard, Jean. 1970. *La société de consommation: ses mythes, ses structures*. Paris: Éditions Denoël.

Brinton, Mary. 2010. *Lost in Transition: Youth, Education, and Work in Postindustrial Japan*. Cambridge: Cambridge University Press.

Fukuma, Yoshiaki. 2020. *"Kinrou Seinen" no Kyouyou Bunkashi* [Cultural History of Working Youth]. Tokyo: Iwanami Shoten.

Hamaguchi, Keiichirou. 2013. *Wakamono to Roudou* [Youth and Labor]. Tokyo: Chuoou Kouron Shinsha.

Honda, Yuki. 2014. *Shakai wo Musubinaosu* [Reconnecting the Society]. Tokyo: Iwanami Shoten.

Inui, Akio. 2010. *"Gakkou kara Shigoto he" no Henyou to Wakamonotachi* [Transformation of "School-to-Work Transition" and Youth]. Tokyo: Aoki Shoten.

Kobayashi, Tetsuo. 2012. *Koukou Funsou 1969–1970* [Student Power in High School 1969–1970]. Tokyo: Chuoou Kouron Shinsha.

Komikawa, Ichiro. 2010. "Wakamono jiritsu chousen plan ikou no wakamono shientaisaku no douko to kadai" [Trends and Challenges of Youth Support Policies Since the "Youth Independence Support Plan"]. *The Japanese Journal of Labour Studies* 602: 17–26.

Kotani, Satoshi. 1998. *Wakamonotachi no Henbou* [Transformation of Youth]. Kyoto: Sekaishisousha.

Kotani, Satoshi, ed. 1993. *Wakamonoron wo yomu* [Reading Youth Studies]. Kyoto: Sekaishisousha.

Matsutani, Soichiro. 2012. *Gal to Fushigichan* [Cultural War Between "Gals" and "Floaters"]. Tokyo: Hara Shobo.

Miyadai, Shinji. 1994–2006. *Choice of School Girls*. Tokyo: Asahi Shimbunsha.

Miyadai, Shinji, Hideki Ichihara, and Meiko Otsuka. 1993–2007. *Subculture Shiwa Kaitai* [Anatomy of Subculture Myths]. Tokyo: Chikumashobo Shinsha.

Miyamoto, Michiko. 2015. "Jakunen mugyousha to chiiki wakamono support station jigyou" [Workless Youth and the Local Youth Support Station]. *The Quarterly of Social Security Research* 51 (1): 18–28.

Ohoka, Yorimitsu. 2014. *Kyoiuku wo Kazoku dakeni Makasenai* [Let's Not Make Education Dependent on Family]. Tokyo: Keisoshobo.

Sato, Takumi. 2017. *Seinen no Shucho* [Speech Contest of Youth]. Tokyo: Kawade Shobo Shinsha.

Toivonen, Tuukka. 2011. "NEETs: The Strategy Within the Category". In *A Sociology of Japanese Youth*, edited by R. Goodman, Y. Imoto, and T. Toivonen, n.p. (20 pp.). London: Routledge.

Yamada, Masahiro. 2004. *Kibou Kakusa Shakai* [Hope Gap Society]. Tokyo: Chikumashobo Shinsha.

CHAPTER 31

Education as an Institution and a Practice: Issues and Perspectives in Korean Sociology

Kim Byoung-Kwan

1   Sociological Quests and "Western" Sociology

If we regard the birth and the development of "modern" social sciences, including sociology, as an indispensable element of the grand historical project of modernization, it becomes only natural that we would regard the whole endeavor of sociological projects as a pivotal part of modernization. And if we associate the historical era of the past two centuries with the grand theme of modernization, and adopt the term "the West" to delineate the initiator and the main actor of this historical project of modernization, we may think of the conceptual term of "Western sociology" as the dominant designing device of the sociological reality of our world and of our times.

But such a conception, with natural appeal in itself regarding the bare reality of uneven sociological playing fields, is bound to face challenges from several angles. What exactly is "Western" sociology? It seems to be the conjoint concept of two dichotomizing criteria: an ongoing tradition of social scientifically and epistemologically dominant contributions, and a certain region.

How much dominance and even hegemony are flexed by this academic tradition in sociology? Has there been a shift in the playing fields in recent years? What exactly are the ingredients of this intellectual tradition that characteristically distinguish it from others and sustain its status and roles? How monopolistic, self-righteous, self-sufficient, closed, parochial, autistic, and hegemonic is this tradition to be called by names? Is it to be perceived as a Kuhnian paradigm? Is it something that hinders the indigenization of the knowledge field in other regions?

How would one delineate the "Western" in Western sociology? Is there a sufficient amount of within-group homogeneity and between-group heterogeneity to merit the dichotomy based on region? If this dichotomy can be understood with the analogy of academic "core, semi-peripheries, and peripheries" or with the finer classification of six different divergent categories on an epistemological continuum (Roulleau-Berger 2021), an ecology of knowledge of many different shades of gray situated along an epistemological continuum, can we pose the picture in the context of the west versus the others? Is it possible to think of the sociology of the East, and if so, what would be the delineating characteristics of such? (see Park 2019).

The dominance of a certain perspective, especially when it was conceptualized and justified in an alien context, can be both inspiring and detrimental in nurturing any pertinent intellectual environment and activities at the importing ends. The reason why this tradition is being called by names, however, is that the academic dominance and hegemony, whether intended by the proponents of it or not, are perceived to be a hindrance to fulfilling the true nature of the sociological endeavor of empiricism. Perspectives developed in different contexts can sometimes exert not-so-constructive influences in developing pertinent concepts, theories, and explanatory logics that reflect the diverse differences in reality. Perspectives dictate every step of the whole process of the recognition of the problem, analytical understanding, prediction, and response.

When the sociological perspectives developed in the West dominate the epistemological field of the sociological enterprise in other parts of the world, problems arise with the irrelevant choice being made to the situation where different perspectives are called for. Despite the constellation of different agendas and issues in different societies and in different times, it often is the case that less relevant or even erroneously conceived sociological perspectives influenced by the experiences of Western institutions and the reality of the modern era play out. This in turn renders situations where only the problems and issues that are suited for such perspectives are picked up, and so many of the other pieces of pivotal social reality become unnoticed or are unfairly treated with less attention.

Sociology from its very inception 200 years ago has been driven by its desire to explain the social reality, not by a divine revelation but by a scrutinization and representation of the rich concreteness of social phenomena. If the alien perspectives stand in a way of a real sociological understanding of the concrete reality in any place at any time, that is the time when the right thing to do is to thoroughly scrutinize the validity and relevance of the imported perspectives in the local soil and pick and choose the analytical value of each detail of those perspectives. If we are to call the 200 years of sociological accumulation a vain enterprise, it is not just a groundless claim, but rather an injustice to much of human civilization. If any of us call for a Kuhnian paradigm shift at this juncture, such efforts with irony will be suspected as a hegemonic move. Still, it is quite advisable that sociological communities around the world must keep a keen eye on staying firm on the ground with the focus more on the concrete reality of social beings.

1.1 Components of Analytical Tools for Sociological Scrutinization of Social Reality

The task of sociology as an intellectual endeavor is to pursue the interests in the dynamic interrelationship unfolding between the social actors, including individuals, and structural forces in the realm of diverse social institutions. "Western" sociology can be characterized by methodological orientations and by a certain number of so-called perspectives and theories. In between, sociology has mid-level explanatory tools called approaches.

In studying the social reality and phenomena in diverse social institutions, including education, sociological research has utilized diverse resources in the name of approaches and explanatory models. They include institutional approaches, political approaches, historical approaches, cultural approaches, and others. The typical sociological research, regardless of which approach they resort to, shares the characteristics of emphasizing an empirical orientation and dealing with concrete social reality.

In studying a concrete social reality in different social settings, sociologists often have adopted comparative approaches to better and effectively reach the categorical substance of the matter. A comparative approach is both a conceptual model and a set of methodological tools at the same time. A minimum set of rules of a comparative approach include spatial and temporal comparative analyses. A spatial comparison can involve a geographical dimension and a categorical dimension as well. In sociological research on education in Korea, many studies took the form of either spatial or temporal comparative approaches to increase the validity and comprehensiveness of the research findings.

To understand the very characteristics of the social institution in any society, sociologists have dug into the cumulated body of knowledge to come up with the most useful pertinent concepts. Sociological concepts that served as the base of sociological comparative studies include the concepts of developmental paths between origin and destination positions. And the concepts of developmental paths are based on the concepts of convergence and divergence. The convergence and divergence of developmental paths involve the dynamic unfolding of inertia and isomorphic forces.

To find the consistency and differentiation of sociological paradigms, the concept of inertia has been adopted in many kinds of research. The concept of inertia has been summoned to describe the mechanisms of consistency or divergence of social beings that started at different initial positions. Structural inertia, institutional inertia, and cultural inertia are some of the specific examples of the usage of the concept. The concept of inertia is about the accumulation of resources and different developmental paths in that while minor discords and changes are possible, there needs to be some exceptional mechanism in effect to overcome the differences accumulated from the initial points. Concepts such as path dependency and cumulative advantages or disadvantages are popular examples of inertia.

In a contrasting model of comparison, the mechanism of convergence between different societies that come from different initial positions are studied. A concept that has been frequently utilized in this context is an isomorphism or isomorphic force. Institutional isomorphism or structural isomorphism has been called up to describe the shifts in overall forms without any specification of a detailed mechanism.

The idea that all societies begin their developmental paths at the same position and they tend to stay in the same direction toward a shared common end because the similarities and commonalities of the essential traits among them far outweigh the differences is not greatly appreciated in contemporary sociology. In the same vein, the idea that the initial differences between societies are so overwhelming that any kind of isomorphic pressure cannot suppress the emergence of fundamental differences is not a popular one in sociological research as well.

Hence, in between these two major social forces of inertia and isomorphic mechanisms lies the third perspective of the comparative approach. In this comparative conception, we focus on the tendency of two different societies that share a large number of similarities but keep developing and displaying the emergent differences as a result of small incidents or choices.

Such a conception renders researchers interested in what kinds of incidents and choices make the differences emerge more visibly and what kinds of triggers set off the detachment from the inertia or path dependency. Concepts for sociological comparison serve as the analytical tools that support researchers in staying focused on the institutional arrangements, historical incidents, and changes in social mechanisms that are bringing in certain policies, and vice versa. These are some of the tools that we can utilize in our search for a sociological understanding of education in Korea.

1.2 *Sociological Research on Education*

Sociological understanding of education as a social institution and practice involves a conception of both commonality and peculiarity. For both commonality and peculiarity, we can resort to sociological perspectives, theories, and methodologies from the cumulated body of knowledge of sociology, but apply them to particular problems and issues at the local level. The unit of analysis is no bigger than a country. The comparative study of education as institutions or practices is conducted with single country as the unit of analysis; seldom is the research done with multiple countries as the unit of analysis, for education is a social institution and a practice so deeply rooted in the context of the institutional, legal, political, economic, and cultural underpinnings of each nation-state.

For sociologists, education has been regarded as one of the most salient social institutions that form the foundations of a society, and it is responsible for several vital functions. Sociologists maintain that education is responsible for the social reproduction of various kinds of valuable functions for the maintenance of society; to ensure the functional prerequisites of society through the training and socialization of the members of society; to fulfill the function of the effective and efficient sorting of its members for the reproduction of status and roles; and to transmit the social arrangements of apparatus for shape-forming, including power relations and the structure of resource allocation.

Education is a contested field of different ideological, political, economic, and cultural interests. Education carries very strictly identified stakeholder relations. Direct stakeholders of education as social institutions include the state, the schools, teachers, parents, and students. In addition, we must reckon with indirect stakeholders of education as well, although their interests in education can vary widely, depending on what they want from education as social institutions. They include businesses, labor unions, media, and the community. Issues of control over the whole process, curriculum, finances, pedagogy, assessment, selecting and sorting the students, and equality of educational opportunity all become the objects of intense dispute and negotiation among the stakeholders.

In the case of Korea, the ideological underpinnings of educational policy and curriculum have been an object of intense conflict between the government, parents, the teachers' union, and the shadow education, or private tutoring, industry. The conflict over the curriculum and the university entrance exam, particularly in Korea, has been a battle nobody can afford to lose.

1.3 Recent Major Issues in the Sociology of Education

The field of the sociology of education reflects the social formation of salient issues, policies, and theories in constant flux. More recently, a group of members of the Board of the Sociology of the Education Research Committee (RC04) of the International Sociological Association examined a selection of the significant and emerging issues (Dworkin et al. 2013). According to them, emerging issues in the sociology of education include the following topics: education and globalization; education and stratification; educational inequalities in developing countries; the politics of multicultural education in developed nations; educational assessment and accountability from a global perspective; the effects of peer groups on schooling; school-to-work transition;

adult education and lifelong learning; teacher supply and demand, status, and morale; and social control. As will be discussed below, many of the emerging issues listed above are shared in the sociological research of education in Korea.

2   Characteristic Features of Education in Korean Contexts

2.1   *Research Problems for Sociologists*

To make a partial contribution to a collaborative search for the enrichment of sociological understanding, I will discuss some of the most salient characteristics and traits of education as both institutions and practices by overviewing and describing the current states and the developments in the past several decades in education in the Korean context.

No one would claim that the characteristic features of Korean education discussed below are peculiar to Korea. Some of them are the features widely found in most countries simply because they are the characteristics of a modern educational institution. Others are to be found in countries with similar developmental experiences. Yet others are commonly found in societies with similar cultural backgrounds. For each different type of sociological understanding, we would summon diverse analytical tools, theories, and methodologies from the accumulated body of knowledge in sociology.

In many cases, sociologists in Korea in their search for the understanding of social phenomena are no different from their peers in other countries in that they would take the strategy of looking for conceptual and analytical tools and theories developed in other social contexts, including Western countries, and make an assessment of to what degree and in what way they are applicable with validity. If they find the fit is not good enough, they invent their own wheels to explain the concrete reality of Korean society. While doing that, they would be interested in figuring out whether the concepts, explanatory models, and theories developed reflecting the Korean context would be valid in other countries' contexts. Although Korean sociologists are all keenly aware of the difficulties and problems ensuing from the different degrees of hegemonic influences that the sociology of the Western countries, most notably the United States, exerted on sociologists in the rest of the world, including Korea, sociologists in Korea tend not to disapprove of the body of knowledge that the sociological tradition in the Western countries has accumulated during the past two centuries of the sociological enterprise.

To understand the social phenomena and mechanisms associated with education in Korea, one needs to take institutional, developmental, historical, and cultural contexts into consideration. The modern history of rapid "compressed" economic, political, and social developments of the past decades; the overall reshaping and modernization of social institutions, value systems, and behavioral patterns; and parts of the persistently remaining historical and cultural heritage are worth noticing.

2.2 Topics of Research Interests in Sociology of Education in Korea

The issues that researchers in the field of the sociology of education in Korea have worked on include ones similar to what one would find in other countries. In the bibliographical review papers of recent decades of research in the sociology of education in Korea, Kim and An (2003) and Kim (2012) came up with a summary of the trends of research topics in the sociology of education in Korea. As is the case in many other countries, research topics tend to reflect particular national profiles and the shift in them at different times (see Dworkin et al. 2013; Power and Rees 2020). Research topics in the sociology of education are heavily influenced by the shifting winds of social, political, and economic situations, conceptual and theoretical developments in the fields, and methodological advances, often with their origin in Western countries, especially when they are available in the English-language medium.

From 1990 to 2002, the topics that were heavily researched in Korea include educational attainments and academic achievements, juvenile delinquency (including school dropouts), educational fervor and competition, curriculum reform, gender, digital society, equality, control over the classroom, returns on education, school effects, the social capital of the family, curriculum, alternative schooling, socioeconomic attainment, career choice, and the school-to-work transition (Kim and An 2003). Kim (2012) analyzed the papers published in an influential academic journal in Korea, the *Korean Journal of Sociology of Education*, during the two decades of 1990 to 2010. He shows that the most frequently researched topics include gender, theories, educational policy and institutions, higher education, child and youth problems, school effects, educational disparity, and school choice. Even within this short period, it was quite clear that there was a shift in research topics, reflecting the impacts of the socioeconomic trends. The Asian financial crisis of 1997 and the global financial crisis of 2008 left the issue of educational disparity and justice more at the forefront of research interests. One finding that is worth noting is that the availability of large data sets of new and advanced types provided a surge in certain research topics (Kim 2012).

2.3 Educational Expansion and Educational Fervor

Of the characteristics that should be discussed in any efforts for a sociological understanding of education in Korea, educational fervor is the most salient phenomenon. Researchers mobilized the economic explanation with the concept of returns on education, the economic gains in the form of wage differentials for the high school diploma in the earlier phase of economic development in the middle of the 20th century, and the university diploma in the later period. In an institutional approach, researchers discuss the supply side factor of educational expansion as a partial explanation for the rise of educational enrollment. In a historical approach, researchers summon the historical practices of education and learning to be regarded as the ultimate goal of one's self-fulfillment. In a cultural approach, educational credentials as symbolic capital and means to differentiate the credential holders themselves are often referred to as the roots of educational credentialism in Korea.

The credentialism in Korea extends not just to the quantitative aspects of educational attainments in the form of degrees and amounts of schooling, but the qualitative aspects of educational achievements in the form of prestige and rankings of individual institutions as well. There is a rather clearly identified, recognized, and even taxidermied hierarchy of educational institutions, especially of universities, in the public perception, and they are the criterion used by all of the parties involved in this process to gauge the academic success and even prospects of students.

Educational expansion and educational fervor in Korea are in a mutually causal relationship. The expansion of educational opportunity by establishing more schools and increasing the capacity of the nationwide school system was not just unsatisfactory but stimulated and escalated educational fervor to the next level. At the same time, educational fervor never ceased to demand more educational opportunities. Spiral effects of the positive reinforcement were in action. This system of education, despite the expansion of size, stimulates the perpetuation of educational practices as a fiercely competitive arena in Korea.

2.4   *Competitive Race in Education*
The competitive nature of education in such situations becomes even worse when the educational opportunity is associated with family resources. In Korea, partly because of the lack of the state's financial capacity to fully meet the expanding demand for tertiary educational opportunities, especially in the initial phase of industrialization, a significant portion of the tertiary educational institutions were privately founded and are being run as not-for-profit private institutions, which are heavily dependent on tuition fees for their financial viability.

With such a historical backdrop for tertiary education, the privatization of university finances has remained the same despite the growth of the state's financial capacity. It has been only in recent years that the state began to significantly expand financial assistance to university students. As a result, without much institutionalized financial assistance for students without sufficient means, university education became an object of strategic decision-making and resource mobilization, and a channel for active and passive status attainment at the family level.

For most families in Korea, sending someone in the family to a university reflected a family strategy for economic and social upward mobility, with a pertinent resource allocation. Even in recent decades, with the tertiary education enrollment ratio hovering close to 70%, the highest level in the world, it still is true that attending a "prestigious" university is a family business in Korea.

And as such, education became a means and channel for social mobility with the family as a unit. The competition for family socioeconomic achievement through education became a nationwide race with the advancement of economic development. Although perfectly rational for individuals as a strategic choice, this race resulted in over-education at an aggregate level. A university diploma in the past was the means to gain an edge in the race for socioeconomic achievement and provided social justification for achievement of any sort. As time passed, it became no more than an indispensable minimum credential to be accepted into the labor market for most Koreans. And the race continues to be shifted for the next level of credentials, in terms of both the quantity and quality of schooling.

As individuals and families seek to gain advantages in this competition, the industry of private tutoring services, or "shadow education", is growing in Korea (Bray 1999; Lee and Shouse 2011; Park, Byun and Kim 2011), which has been a persistent problem in the country. A shadow education system is an undeniable and firmly institutionalized element in the Korean education system, both in a positive and in a negative sense. Shadow education includes a range of after-school academic activities, including individual or group tutoring, most often from for-profit cram schools, and increasingly in recent years from online learning services. Shadow education, or private tutoring, when sought after by individuals as a surefire way of providing the needed competitive edges in the race to gain entrance to more prestigious educational institutions, causes social complaints and conflicts mostly over two issues. It is named as the main culprit contributing to unequal access to educational opportunities. It also has been blamed as the main disruptive force that disturbs the normal operations of the public education system.

One peculiar thing that has been a problematic concern in Korea is the disparity of the quality of formal schooling and the availability of quality private tutoring services between the so-called metropolitan Seoul area and the rest of the country. The private tutoring industry in Korea, much earlier than its formal school counterparts, made an innovative move to adopt various online learning technologies to provide the private tutoring of the "metropolitan Seoul" area to the underserved student customers in other regions and in other economic segments.

2.5   *Educational Inequality and the Strategic Choice of the Family*
The concept of credentialism itself carries some aspects of class prejudice in that the educated class does not want such a rapid expansion of education, especially at the university level, attenuating the value of their monopolistic holds on the economic and symbolic capital of higher education. The expansion of higher education in Korea did result in the expansion of opportunities for all classes and provided a significant but diminishing economic and social return for education over time.

Sociological research has focused on the inequality of educational opportunities by the economic status of family, gender, and region, at both the higher education level and the secondary education level. Such inequalities have shifted in different directions over time. The impact of family on school choice, academic achievements, and eventually status attainment and marriage were found to increase as Korean society went through the economic development stages, and the consolidation of socioeconomic classes took shape as the overall amount of resources increased. The difference between the genders in education has diminished to zero in the same period. The increase of family resources and the reduction in the number of children in each family, together with the rapid retreat of patriarchal orders in society in general, resulted in the evaporation of male centrism in education. Some research noted that women tend to work harder than men for academic achievement within both curricular and extracurricular activities, for they will eventually face discriminatory practices in the school-to-work transition. Although it is diminishing, for most women gender discrimination has been a harsh reality in the Korean labor market.

Given the rapid expansion of educational opportunities over time in Korea, has the equality of educational opportunities increased over time? Based on multiple empirical data analyses, Lee and Byun (2021) argue that educational inequality has decreased over time. The relationship between the educational levels of fathers and children showed a decreasing tendency, showing the diminishing educational inequality. Looking at the qualitative aspects of educational inequality, however, they conclude the educational inequality in the qualitative aspects, measured as the direct relationship between the parents' socioeconomic status and the children's academic achievements, have gained in strength, showing an increased inequality. The increase in educational inequality in qualitative aspects can be ascribed to the worsened income distribution after the Asian financial crisis of 1997. Another factor that contributed to the increase in educational inequality is the shift in government policy from a more egalitarian approach to education to the neo-liberal approach, in which educational and academic excellence is emphasized more as the goal in public education (Lee and Byun 2021).

Kim and Byun (2021), through their extensive empirical study, argue that the labor market value of university education in Korea has held at a steady level over time in terms of the attainment of occupational prestige. With regard to economic returns, however, a slight and steady decrease in the income-generating value of university education has been found. They argue that the shift toward a more equalizing trend in the economic return for education is due to the societal shift toward more equality than to the dynamic re-valuation of the university degree itself.

Regarding gender inequality in the value of education for women, Shin and Kim (2021) show that the educational attainments and academic achievements of women are no longer lagging behind men in Korea. In fact, in many aspects of educational attainments, women already have surpassed their counterparts. In labor market outcomes, however, women are struggling to secure a foothold in both entry to and advancement in labor markets, due to the tendency of gender differentials in university majors, and the corporate culture of hiring, which is lagging.

2.6   *Education as a Contested Terrain and the Role of the Government*

Different governments in different times have adopted varied policies toward the shadow education industry, with not much of a decisive outcome. The debate over how to assist the formal educational institutions to better function as "the great equalizer" and as the effective setting to better serve most students' learning needs for careers has become a contested agenda for the stakeholders of not just the state, students, and family, but also teachers' unions and the media. In the meantime, the problematic situation of the physical and psychological well-being of the youth has been a major social issue in Korea, with the dire competition for better academic performance in national tests and university entrance exams being cited as an offender.

To take more control of the curriculum and management of the schools and classrooms, the roles that teachers' unions played are noticeable. In Korea, two contrasting trade unions, or associations, of teachers are in operation, vying against each other for control of the schools. The Korean Federation of Teachers' Association was the first one on the scene with a tendency to take a conservative stance on issues. In contrast, the Korean Teachers and Education Workers' Union (KTEWU), which came into being later in the 1980s, takes a progressive stance on issues. KTEWU, while having not gained much popular support for its radical positions over some issues of the curriculum, has brought about the democratization of education and schools, and has overly politicized education as well.

In the competitive race for educational achievements, the most meaningful trophy for individuals has been the prestige of the university that one attends. Given the fact that the enrollment ratio of tertiary education has hovered close to 70% in Korea in recent decades, the highest level when compared to other countries, a university diploma alone is not enough of a differentiator for individuals and families. In this context, the institutional arrangements of university entrance exams inevitably become objects in a clash of the stakeholders' different interests. With such high stakes for individuals and families, the curriculum and the practices of learning and education in secondary educational institutions became dependent on the criteria and the practices of the university admission process. It should be the role of the government to ascertain the systemic incorporation and accordance of the curriculum of secondary education, the need for students' learning to fit the demand of the labor markets, and the university admission process. There have been numerous attempts through policy shifts and adjustments, but the whole process and the arrangements for such an accordance are still in precarious flux, with only partial support from the public. As different administrations come into power, the emphasis on the educational curriculum tends to swing. The values driven by the market demands collide with the values supported by social causes. And the struggle in the educational arena affects mechanisms behind the operation of the educational apparatus.

In the same vein, questions have been raised over the mismatch of university education and the demand of society regarding the contents and relevancy of university education and training. The concept of tertiary educational institutions as the great training robbery (Berg 1970) and credentialism has been an object of public concern in Korea. While it is quite true that the massive pace of the expansion of higher education in the past several decades in Korea has served its intended role in supporting economic growth at the national level and socioeconomic advancement at the individual level, it is also true that it raised concerns about overeducation and resource inefficiency at both the individual and the collective level.

Educational assessment and accountability of the school system are also contested realms. The call for educational reform to bring about "new workers" anticipating the reality of the "new" labor market of the 21st century has placed a huge amount of pressure on education in recent years. The education of talent with the skills and readiness for creativity, innovation, collaboration, and global minds is perceived as the new mission of schools. All of the educational institutions at different levels are running for more innovative and paradigm-changing educational models out of fear of falling behind or even being weeded out. Times are difficult for the whole system of educational institutions in Korea, facing the dual pressure of educational reform and the diminishing population of school-enrollment age individuals. Universities and colleges are in the biggest crunch, with a dire financial situation on top of the dual pressure situation. The role of the government in coordinating the conflicting interests in education, maintaining a viable ecosystem of educational institutions, and securing financial resources for universities in their efforts of reform and innovation for the 21st century has become more vital than ever before.

3 Closing Remarks

As part of the concluding remarks of this piece, where I tried to review some of the accomplishments of the Korean sociology of education in recent decades, it seems pertinent to ask a question that has recurred for many sociologists in Korea in recent decades. Are the efforts of redefining and reconfiguring the traditional sociological knowledge on education taking place in Korea? Are there any noticeable outcomes of such efforts being cumulated to form their mass?

Overall, I would not say this question itself is fair or even what we need at this point. And a fair assessment of the current states of sociological research on education in Korea would be a partially favorable one at this moment. It is quite true that Korean sociology as a whole has long passed the earlier phase where the de facto role of most sociologists was to "import" the concepts, theories, and methodologies from the main, in this case "Western", sociology to apply them in Korean contexts. Such efforts of the earlier phase have proven to successfully provide the basis of sociological research in Korean contexts, with self-reflection that provided the fertile ground for the next generation of sociology in Korea.

After several decades of efforts on the part of Korean sociology to come up with its own explanatory models, sociologists in Korea are struggling, with some success, to emphatically display the possibility of the balance of the body of knowledge developed and accumulated globally, with Korean society as a part of it. It is still quite true that a hugely disproportionate contribution comes from Western contexts, but at least in Korean sociology, such an imbalance is being remedied. What matters the most is the awareness of the sociologists themselves to stay open and flexible to embrace the intellectual dialogue and communication in both domestic and global directions.

"Post-Western sociology" may not be a proper conceptualization of the efforts in which sociologists in Korea and other countries are engaging. "Western sociology" as an overarching concept may well be a scarecrow of someone's invention. The devil is in the details. Each concept and theory should be tested in different social contexts, and some will survive and some won't. And it may not be a good frame to incorporate what is taking place among Korean sociologists. As long as sociology as an academic discipline and a frame of perspective keeps distancing itself from exclusive and hegemonic practices and remains firmly rooted in empiricism and flexible enough to stand against determinism, sociology around the world has a chance to make a more meaningful contribution to the betterment of social and human beings. It is high time to talk about global sociological enterprise with the balance of diverse local knowledge conjoining together to form the basis of sociology, with universal elements in it as well.

References

Berg, Ivar. 1970. *Education and Jobs: The Great Training Robbery*. New York, NY: Praeger.

Bray, Mark. 1999. *The Shadow Education System: Private Tutoring and Its Implications for Planners*. Paris: International Institute for Educational Planning. UNESCO.

Byun, Soo-yong, and Seong-Kyun Lee. 2021. *Educational Attainments and the Socioeconomic Status of Parents* [in Korean]. Seoul: Bakyoung Books.

Dworkin, A. Gary, Jeanne Ballantine, Ari Antikainen, Maria Ligia Barbosa, David Konstantinovskiy, Lawrence J Saha, Shaheeda Essack, Jason Chang, Marios Vryonides, and Antonio Teodoro. 2013. "The Sociology of Education". *Sociopedia.isa*. doi: 10.1177/2056846013122.

Kim, Chang-Hwan, and Soo-yong Byun. 2021. *Educational Premium in Korea* [in Korean]. Seoul: Bakyoung Books.

Kim, Kyung-Keun. 2012. "Twenty Years of Korean Journal of Sociology of Education: Its Traces, Accomplishments, and the Tasks Ahead" [in Korean]. *Korean Journal of Sociology of Education* 22 (1): 25–49.

Kim, Kyung-Sik, and Woo-Hoan An. 2003. "The Exploration of Research Areas in Korean Sociology of Education" [in Korean]. *Korean Journal of Sociology of Education* 13 (2): 47–64.

Lee, Soojeong, and Roger Shouse. 2011. "The Impact of Prestige Orientation on Shadow Education in South Korea". *Sociology of Education* 84 (3): 212–224.

Park, Hyunjoon, Soo-yong Byun, and Kyung-Keun Kim. 2011. "Parental Involvement and Students' Cognitive Outcomes in Korea: Focusing on Private Tutoring". *Sociology of Education* 84 (1): 3–22.

Park, Myoungkyu. 2019. "What Can Sociology Do for East Asia, and Vice Versa?" *Journal of Asian Sociology* 48 (2): 169–178.

Power, Sally, and Gareth Rees. 2020. "Conceptualizing the Sociology of Education: An Analysis of contested Intellectual Trajectories". *British Journal of Sociology of Education* 41 (6): 778–793.

Roulleau-Berger, Laurence. 2021. "The Fabric of Post-Western Sociology: Ecologies of Knowledge beyond the 'East' and the 'West'". *The Journal of Chinese Sociology* 8 (10): 1–28.

Shin, Kwang-Young, and Chang-Hwan Kim. 2021. *Education, Gender, and Social Mobility* [in Korean]. Seoul: Bakyoung Books.

SECTION 7

State and Governance

∴

CHAPTER 32

Urban Renewal, Urban Restructuring: The City as Inescapable Western Representation

Agnès Deboulet

This chapter builds on a parallel between two very different case studies to underline the persistent presence of a Western paradigm within urban planning practice. But rather than speaking about a single paradigm, we should rather elaborate on a variety of sub-paradigms that can be seen in various contexts of urban renewal. Across metropolitan fabrics, urban renewal programs take different shapes and names but convey at least 4 common elements: the combination of state and private interventions with an increased financialization; a persistent top-down and somehow opaque set of mechanisms; the insistence on social mix and in any case of strategies to reinvigorate the spatial fabric with attributes of middle to upper-class landscape, housing and services; the hidden and hard to trace mechanisms of displacement and dispossession. Needless to say, these policies are conducted in a quite different manners in major urban French large cities and in Cairo, the first one being caught between a large range of local urban actors (decentralized) and a national agency and the second one between mostly state national agencies, the army and no local stakeholder. In both cases, a post-Western analysis invites us to draw some parallels in situations often deemed as very different because of the nature of the state, the construction of citizenship and furthermore the complete alterity that is attributed to "South" planning by contrast with planning in the North. If some researchers have clearly marked their distance with a Western theory of planning, practitioners of the North remain mostly convinced of the superiority of their model, as respectful of human or housing rights. On another side, Western representations of the city may be seen as a hidden mantra of urban renewal projects taking place in a broad frenzy of restructuring. This symbolic construction is nevertheless rarely questioned within a post-Western perspective, and we often remain caught within a dialectic between Western representations of dominant actors and post-Western analysis by public research and its effects.

1 Urban Renewal in France Large Social Estates: Revival of an Old Republican Song

The starting point for discussions about the socio and political justification for urban renewal in France is both the notion of ghetto and "communautarism". Here these terms mostly used in the medias and by state apparatus point to a collective imaginary of "social separatism" reactivated by political Islam and lack of integration measured spontaneously by "incivilités" (or "misbehaviours") and other deviant behaviours. The on-going presidential campaign perfectly illustrates the perpetuation of this imaginary and moreover, its efficiency to flatter extreme-right electors. Valérie Pécresse, candidate of Les Républicains is using the once very polemical image of the necessity to clean up the "suburbs" with a karcher, a metaphor used by N. Sarkozy in 2005 in La Courneuve and Argenteuil.[1]

In a famous article Loïc Wacquant (1992) showed how, despite adverse conditions, residents of Paris' popular estates could not be described as living in the ghetto as compared with Chicago's, a statement that could be discussed, at least in some places, three decades later. Nevertheless, recent research have pointed some similarities in French and North American urban renewal programs, almost all tackling the large visible symbols of stigma and segregation with a forecast of 400,000 demolished dwelling (160,000 after the first phase). Starting from 2010, the program is reactivated but this time acknowledging the lack of residents and the necessity to give more impetus to the human environment (such as employment or services) and the term "urban renewal" with its dreadly connotation has dropped. The new program is called "Nouveau Programme de renouvellement urbain". As underlined in the case of Jerusalem urbanism vs. Palestinian places of residence, these "imagined societal binaries and hierarchies (...) are entrenched in wider political discourses" (Lemanski 2021).

As most of urban policies in Europe since the 90s, urban renewal is justified by a quest for urban mix (Lelévrier and Noyé 2012).[2] Findings of many research reveal that demolitions tackle firstly social housing and in some cases popular deteriorated housing. In the first case, the buildings deemed for demolition concentrate the highest proportion of large apartments typically those attributed in a first place to the "large families", which means mostly African first generation of migrants and their family. In some extreme cases, one of the women living in polygamous households have been forced to move-out

---

1 See the documentary by Samir Adballah, "Les enfants de la dalle", ISKRA, 2007.
2 These two paragraphs are an adapted translation from chapter 3 of A. Deboulet, *Sociétés urbaines au risque de la métropole*, Paris: Dunod, published in 2022.

(D'Orazio and de Villanova 2010). The systematic introduction of private housing is not as such a problem, but it does mostly go along a decrease in the share of social housing. Unfair competition between these kinds of housing stock is also played detrimental to the first generation of migrants, but also poor European families and all the "social cases (cas sociaux)" as described in local parlance. A good example of this substitution is Housing for students, a profitable investment that could sometimes also replace this middle age housing stock and at the same time reassign original residents or part of two new locations. Considering the targeted housing stock is also telling about the hidden post-colonial management, modulated according to the political alliances with the municipalities.

After the dismantling of all the slums (at these times mostly workers slums) in Paris peripheries in the 60s (Collet 2019) and the massive rehousing in large social estates or transit camps, a similar mythology allows a massive demolition program of the social housing stock. If the initial demolition and disruption of collective life was initiated on the sake of dignity and integration into the republic, the urban renewal program is clearly introducing the idea that urban mix is the solution to poverty and segregation. Several research have challenged the view on urban mix arguing that (a) its benefits have never been proven (b) its ambition and definition is terribly vague and allows for programmes that rarely succeed (Lelévrier 2018). Following a post-Western perspective, we argue that public norms (of social mix) is conducive of social violence and disruption in immigrants neighborhoods or places considered as mostly populated by migrants. Analyzing the impacts and perceptions of social mix among these populations brings out the necessity to deconstruct the official political and technical narratives carried out by the national agency for urban renewal (ANRU) and its local representatives, the social landlords and local political actors. We must bear in mind that the current urban renewal programs have been designed as the only financial tool to regenerate and refresh a housing stock that has been left out for decades and to bring in potential new private builders, therefore offering an opportunity to "open up the lock" to urban regeneration. This intrinsic logic also needs to be assessed within the framework of the legal consultation needed to validate the official multi-partner agreement between all the parties (ANRU, prefecture, sovereign fund, municipalities …).

2 A Post-Western Analysis for a Post-colonial Urban Regeneration

Post-Western lenses are even more appropriate to unravel the planning endeavours of urban renewal in deteriorated central or peri-central locations of major cities. Marseille's case until the recently elected municipality based on an alliance with the green party and activists engaged in supporting non-rehoused households from the rue d'Aubagne mortal accident. In 2018 there were still 70 inhabited "hôtels meublés (furnished hostels)" (Dahdah et al. 2017), cheap accommodation for mostly for old single migrants from North Africa leaving in dreadful condition. We followed at this time a program of refurbishing of these hostels and a large number of private buildings was going on with a clear ambition of ethnic and social substitution, that did accelerate once the High-speed train started to arrive in the city. "In the neighbourhood, it seems that the municipality wants to settle Europeans, they don't want any more people from the maghreb countries, they want to get rid of the hostels [...] you renovate the hostels for the Europeans, or you sell" (former grocer located adjacent to the Saint-Charles railway station, Tunisian, 2010).[3]

There is no place in this short peace to unpack these very complex planning interventions, also playing, in the private sector, with a series of financial incentives targeted to wealthy investors interested by the heritage component of the building and the added value it represents. What remains is that even more in urban renewal within the private/old neighbourhoods than in social estates, planners neglect any form of consultation and play the division among inhabitants. It is striking though to consider to what extent the intentions of displacement are rarely explicated. As for risk-induced displacements, "decision ad implementation is based on stakeholder visions, concepts, mindsets" (Johnson, Jain and Lavell 2021) and are not explained or even mentioned to the affected residents or when they are, it is always felt and resented as "brutal". The violence of displacement induced, in the first case by demolition and in the second case by rehabilitation with eviction both carry a lot of violence. If not restricted to migrants, programs are conducive of the idea that upgrading urban environments and attracting new middle/upper class populations worth intentional displacements and relocations of the populations belonging to the "quartiers à problèmes" (or problematic areas). Planning is undertaken without them but also against them but always, as in colonial planning strategies "for their own good". In several occasions, planners would confess that "these people don't know what is good for them" and attachment to the place is seen as an impediment to social upward mobility, comparable to the encroachment of the ordinary evoked by A. Bayat (2017) in Middle-Eastern cities and to what he calls "social nonmovements".

In the course of neoliberalization and authoritarianism that remerged after the Arab revolutions, Cairo is one of the cases where the gaps between a tiny

---

3 A survey conducted with Isabelle Berry-Chikhaoui.

elite and a large poor segment of the population added to a growing middle class still fighting to get out of budget restrictions have widened to an extreme extent In a few years. Yet the current metropolis reproduces former colonial divides and somehow accentuates them since the physical distance between social strata is bigger than ever and all infrastructures are deemed to serve them (especially hundreds km of new highways in Cairo only). This rupture is even more pronounced with the construction of a new administrative capital in the desert. I follow here Bayat by suggesting that enclosure and the city "inside out" are the double face of the same failure to make an inclusive city, despite all international donors injunctions. This appears clearly as a call to renew the expression of dissent (Bayat, Scott) through the lenses of ordinary resistances, critics, encroachments.

This suggests that a post-Western approach would maybe prevent us from a systematically use of the notions frequently defining the transformation of most of Western cities. My assumption here is that we should mark Cities in transition with a specific scope of analysis: urban renewal and gentrification are not predicated in the same way in Cities in transition (with a population growth of 3% or more per year, especially located in Africa and Asia) than in Europe or in the Ameriques. If gentrification is based on the predicament of former alliances or common interest between dwellers and investors, this is clearly not true in a city like Cairo where most of the population (above 60%) live in precarious neighbourhoods (Deboulet 2016). The recent wave of demolitions (official 240,000 households in the 5 last years) reflects heteronomous decisions from public authorities, the army, and private investors. On the ground, nobody knows when the housing stock will be destroyed, neither really why and where they will be rehoused or compensated. Urban renewal erected as a systematic policy to evict informal neighbourhoods has clearly very little room for negotiation. In addition, its massive character prevents from describing this as gentrification as explained by Van Criekingen (2020) and many others but rather calls for an urban reconquest and masking growing inequalities.

3   The Denial of the Ordinary City Fabric and Its Networks

Coming back to urban renewal in France, planning regulations and interventions in "priority neighborhoods" have broadly failed to understand the diversity of ordinary responses to segregation and growing deprivation. It is only thanks to the spotlight of the recent pandemic of COVID-19 that state agencies and other donor agencies (respectively l'Agence Nationale pour la

Cohésion des Territoires and the Abbé-Pierre foundation) have respectively financed a specific report of the "resources of the priority neighborhoods" and an action-research on health and urban initiatives in these territories. Romain Leclercq report (2021) draws on a few decades of research displaying the subtle refusal of discriminations and of top-town policies and even institutionalized participation. It is interesting to see that his report precisely opens to a South–North nonlinear trajectory since he started his young researcher journey in Dakar's peripheries. In fact, this work as other researchers' warns against: frequent denial of ordinary politics; informality as a material and social resource; the blindness to the reliance on social networks and especially those supporting immigrants communities despite the official republican neutrality on race and religion. First example, the action-research undertaken in some of the large housing estates in a wealthy "departement" of the Ile-de-France region (APPUII 2021) also reveals the scope of solidarities among immigrants communities and their descent and even the role of local mosques in fostering food distribution and alternatives to health care or transportation imbalances. It calls for a real consideration given by public policies to these subterranean initiatives. Second, several recent researches point on hidden but still very pervasive economies in a post-industrial liberal context. For instance, street mechanics has proven to be a crucial "public good" in many popular neighborhoods as the price of official repair in legal garages is one of the most rapidly increasing constituent of the budgets, but still the overwhelming majority of local authorities refuse to accept their existence and chase the workers (coming overwhelmingly from recent immigration) with no attention to the know-how invested in these activities of this truly circular economy (Ndiaye et al. 2019).

This speaks about a recent rediscovery of what really makes popular politics and local ties and resists to the tyranny of urban renewal. But yet many other research in urban sociology and anthropology have echoed these politics of the ordinary, starting with the seminal work on slums relocations of the 70s in the newly built suburban dystopias that creates social confusion and heteronomy (Petonnet 2002) or Victor Collet's books on Nanterre slum (2019) before its destruction in the mid 60s, calling for an unseen solidarity despite the stigma and the filth. To start with, rehousing in large social estates is a typically reminiscence of the colonial vision of the city and the "indigenous". Rehousing in these estates has been open to non-migrants but the housing segregation has immediately echoed the initial division between Arabs, Gypsies, European migrants and French (Giband 2010). And this renewed perspective on cities of the West (North) through the lens of subalternity (Spivak, Chakrabarty) can really work if it goes along with a reading of Gramsci. Exactly as the attention to "ordinary cities" according to J. Robinson despecify the non-global cities. I suggest here that looking at global processes of urban renewal/regeneration allows us to hybridize our thinking and go beyond the unicity of views of politics, resistance, citizenship but also dispossession. We advocate understandings and knowledges to circulate South–North and North–South and not only to be inspired by Southern epistemologies. This brings us to pay more attention to "non Western West" (Roulleau-Berger 2021), what we used to call "urban development situations" and to open up to the unprecedented transformation carried out by the massive urbanization race soon bypassed by climate change agency mostly in Countries in huge demographic, urban and social transition.

References

Bayat, A. 2017. *Revolution without revolutionaries. Making sense of the Arab Spring*. Stanford, CA: Stanford University Press.

Collet, V. 2019. *Nanterre, du bidonville à la cité*. Marseille: Agone.

Dahdah, A., G. Audren, and F. Bouillon. 2017. "La ville (in)hospitalière : parcours scolaire et résidentiel d'une famille syrienne à Marseille". *Espaces et Sociétés* 2018, 1–2 (172–173): 73–91.

Giband, D. 2014. "La mixité sociale à l'épreuve de l'ethnicité territoriale dans trois quartiers en rénovation urbaine de Perpignan". In *Rénovation urbaine en Europe*, edited by C. Lelévrier and A. Deboulet, 201–210. Rennes: Presses Universitaires de Rennes.

Johnson, C., G. Jain, and A. Lavell. 2021. *Rethinking Urban Risk and Resettlement in the Global South*. London: UCL Press.

Leclercq, R. 2021. In Observatoire Nationale de la politique de la ville, rapport (2021). *Vulnérabilités et ressources des quartiers prioritaires* (Agence Nationale de la Cohésion des Territoires).

Lelévrier, C., and C. Noyé. 2012. "La fin des grands ensembles?" In *A quoi sert la rénovation urbaine*, edited by Jacques Donzelot, 185–221. Presses Universitaires de France.

Lemanski, C. 2021. "Afterword: Citizenship and the politics of (im)material stigma and infrastructure". *Urban studies*, 11 Nov., https://doi.org/10.1177/00420980211055301.

Ndiaye, A., K. Mamou, and A. Deboulet. 2019. *La mécanique de rue: vertus cachées d'une économie populaire dénigrée*. *Métropolitiques*, https://hal.archives-ouvertes.fr/hal-02615305.

Pétonnet, C. 2002. *On est tous dans le brouillard*, edited by CTHS.

Robinson, J. 2006. *Ordinary cities. Between modernity and development*. London: Routledge.

Roulleau-Berger, L. 2021. "The fabric of Post-Western sociology: ecologies of knowledge beyond the "East" and the "West"". *The Journal of Chinese Sociology* 8 (10): Online.

Van Criekingen, M. 2021. *Contre la gentrification. Convoitises et résistances dans les quartiers populaires*. Paris: La Dispute.

Wacquant, Loïc. 1992. "Pour en finir avec le mythe des "cités-ghettos": Les différences entre la France et les Etats-Unis". *Les Annales de la Recherche Urbaine* 54 (1): 21–30.

CHAPTER 33

State and Society in Urban Renewal and Social Governance

Shi Yunqing

1 Introduction

In the context of the great transformation of China, how society is produced is not only a social practice task, but also a social cognitive one (Shen 2007). This key question not only reveals distinct located knowledge in Chinese sociology but also inspires discussion with Western sociological theories with a solid foundation. Based on social participation during different phases of urban renewal in China, this research elaborates the changing pattern of the relationship between the state and the society/individual in China's social transition, and discusses two different ways of "Chinese-styled society making", tying to start a dialogue with a post-Western sociology perspective.

2 Chinese-Style State–Society Relationship in Urbanization

China is in a state of grand transition in which the state in grand unification is creating a market and freeing its society up. This process is entirely different from those in the Western history, where the market was established and states were built in civil societies. Over the past 40 years since the reform and opening up, China's economy and society have achieved remarkable development, and China's state–society/individual relationship has been changing. The following characteristics could be pointed out with the perspective of international comparison: Firstly, space for the society has been gradually generated with the unfolding of a "gradual" reform, in which the political system remains unchanged while the reforms of the economic system have gradually deepened. Secondly, with the emergence of social space, the intermediary between state and individuals has become pluralistic, ranging from the early completely spontaneous citizen groups to the current social organizations promoted by the government. Women play an increasingly important role in those organizations, which makes the cushion between the state and society softer and more flexible at the grassroots level. Thirdly, from the deep cultural and social psychological structure of the Chinese people, the permeated boundary between state and individuals still exists, which makes the relationship between the state and society remain unified as a whole. However, different ways of response are adopted in different periods.

Urbanization is an extremely important driving force of social transition in China. During the past three decades, urban renewal of the big cities in China has gone through three phrases: the commercialization of space (1990–2004), the commercialization of culture (2005–2014), and community revitalization and the construction of public culture (2015–present). Along with this process, the scale and pace of spatial renewal are slowing down, and the focus of renewal is sinking to everyday life. The perspective of the "people", which was neglected in the early stages, is now gradually being taken into political account.

Regarding the state–society relationship, the power of the society released from the transition that was at first contradictory to the state has been gradually integrated into the state again, along with the public policy discourse, which was upgraded from "social management" to "social governance". During this process, the production of citizens and society in a "Chinese style" developed into two types, both of which balanced the inner tension and achieved a correspondence between state and society. The first type is "the active production of society", which started from the society and tried to appeal for legitimacy from the state, while the second one is "the state-dominated production of society", which originated from the state and tried to call for an echo from the society. The converging on the duality of the state and society with the mutual interacting dynamics between them inspires post-Western sociology.

3 Rapid Urbanization Driven by Land-Based Finance in the Early Stage

In the several decades after reform and opening up, China has been going through the fastest and largest-scale urbanization in the world. According to data from the National Bureau of Statistics, the urbanization rate was 10.64%, with an urban population of 58 million, in 1949; then, 17.9%, with an urban population of 170 million, in 1978; it rose tremendously to 51.2%, with an urban population of 690 million, in 2011; and recently, in 2019, the urban population reached 60.60%, with 850 million. From 1980 to 2017, China's urbanization increased at an average annual rate of 3%, which is much higher than the world's average annual rate of 0.82%.

It is the great driving force released by the commercialization of state-owned land that has stimulated the rapid growth of urbanization in China. As a starting phase, 1990–1998 was the testing period, key for introducing market mechanisms into the policy system of the public ownership of land. The "Interim Regulations of the People's Republic of China Concerning the Assignment and Transfer of the Right to the Use of the State-owned Land in the Urban Areas" was issued in 1990, which marked the new era of the compensated use of state-owned land. After that, the "Regulations on the Administration of Urban Housing Demolition and Relocation", issued by the State Council in 1991, initiated the great urban transformation influencing the following decades regarding the great potential for turning the residential use of the land located at the centers of the old cities into the commercial use, called inner city renewal. During this period, "massive demolishing and massive building" was the major form of action with the idea of "operating cities". Through population replacement and industrial upgrading, local governments attracted foreign investment with land, while they resettled the evicted residents in housing on the outskirts of the cities. In the middle of this period, the State Council issued "The Decision on Deepening the Reform of the Urban Housing System" in 1994, laying a foundation for a commercialized housing market. Followed by "The Notice of Further Deepening the Reform of Urban Housing System and Accelerating Housing Construction", issued by the State Council in 1998, the transformation from housing allotments and tangibles to payments was officially set up. Therefore, beginning with the commercialization of land and ending with the commercialization of housing, the testing period of 1990–1998 gave birth to the subsequent decades of land finance-driven economic growth. Since then, the urbanization rate for every 10 years has increased from 4.68% (from 26.2% in 1989 to 30.9% in 1999) to 15.7% (from 30.9% in 1999 to 46.6% in 2009), and China has entered a period of rapid growth.

The essence of this process could be called "the commercialization of space", which lasted until 2005 in Beijing. Driven by power and capital, the texture of the old city has been quickly removed while shopping malls and business districts have sprung up. According to the statistics of the Surveying and Mapping Institute of Beijing in 2004, a total of 639 Hutongs were demolished from 1990 to 2003, which is 3.1 times that of the previous 40 years (199 Hutongs were demolished from 1949 to 1989). This was followed by the destruction of social structure: according to the *Real Estate Yearbook of Beijing*, between 1991 and 2000, a total of 878,600 residents from 281,200 households were removed from their previous dwellings and 647,800 rooms were demolished, with a total floor area of 9,155,300 m^2. The disappearance of the ancient capital caused public opinion to exert pressure with regard to cultural protection, while the incomplete infrastructure in the remote resettlement community also rose lots of complaints from citizens; both of these factors led to the end of this model of "massive demolishing and massive building". In 2005, the "urban organic renewal" model was put on the agenda, elaborated as "small-scale, microcirculation, diversification and gradual". Although more attention had been paid to cultural elements, such as architectural style and spatial form, the renewal process was still driven by the economic benefits generated by land development. Shopping streets upgraded from traditional buildings in the city center had prevailed all over the country while local people were resettled to the suburbs. The renewal logic had further developed from the commercialization of space to the commercialization of culture, while the daily life was still missing.

4   The Active Production of Society: Claiming Citizenship and Clearing the Boundary

Behind the high-speed urbanization in the early and middle stages was the excessive invasion of the state and market into social and personal life, which produced great tension between the state and society, and stimulated an active response from society. China had experienced a period of high incidence of collective actions, most of which were caused by demolition and resettlement. Compared with Western social movements, Chinese actors were facing a difficult situation: there was no room for collective action to take place legally with the fine institutional control shaped by the total state; furthermore, individuals who had just undergone the social transition remained subordinate to the state, but in the meantime they were turned into an atomized situation after the dismissal of the unit system. Thus, for sociological research, the key question is: How could these collective actions occur in such environments and conditions that do not support their occurrence? How could actors handle this dilemma? They have to create opportunities and space for the action and establish the legitimacy that can be recognized by the system in the meantime.

As a result, making full use of institutional space and normalizing movements that defended people's rights became the most important and unique form of protest, for citizens to claim their own property and civil rights in the process of urbanization in China, which is prominently reflected in various legal and legislative rights protection strategies (Chen 2010). Therefore, "law" has a very important and unique practical significance in the Chinese context, and it has become a carrier of multiple meanings of text, symbol, and practice. It was typically shown in an administrative collective litigation caused by demolition in 2000, in which citizens employed the multiple strategy of using the law to claim their citizenship. Through the textual meaning of law, the actor claimed property rights for their demolished house and lands; through the symbolic meaning of law, the actor maintained consistency with the highest level of national interests and obtained the legitimacy of action. Finally, through the practical significance of law, actors traced back to the tradition of political movement in the early days of the founding of the People's Republic of China, making the self-organized law-popularizing group a unique social mobilization mechanism (Shi 2018).

Behind the multiple functions of law is the complex relationship between the state and society in the early stages of China's transformation, as the two entities were in the process of differentiating from each other while remaining adherent and involved with one another (Yang 2008). At the beginning of the transition, the state nurtured the market, while society had little space. Because of the excessive extrusion of the alliance of the state and the market, the society was forced to sprout, with urban movement as the main form, and this caused a great tension between state and society. Citizens tried to claim their property rights and citizenship from the bottom up in order to resist the invasion of individual life by the commercialization of land and culture, indicating a tendency to separate society from the state. But even so, citizens were fully aware of the importance of aligning the framework with the state ideology at the highest level, so as to seek the legitimacy from the top down. To deal with the tension, the government's initial response was to "maintain social stability" and try to absorb people's protests with various strategies (Zhang and Lee 2012), but it could not solve the deep contradiction hat society was unable to obtain space for itself. Beginning in 2013, the "innovating social governance system" has gradually become the dominant discourse of social policy, which means that state has begun to realize that it should actively absorb social forces.

5 Slowing Down Urban Renewal Characterized with Social Participation in the Current Stage

After nearly 20 years of renewal, the appearance of the central urban areas of China's big cities has completely changed. Around 2015, the original development-oriented renewal mode gradually came to an end, which is reflected in the following aspects: first, from the perspective of land reserves, the attractive space to be renewed has disappeared, the current renewal detention area is scattered in scale, limited in expected ways of land use, and has a high density of residents, all of which weakened the motivation for commercial development. Second, from the perspective of social forces, movements to defend citizens' rights in the past decades have generally enhanced the awareness of law and rights of residents in old urban areas, and the popularization of technology, such as the Wechat Group, has also enhanced the collective action ability of citizens. Third, from the government itself, the arbitrary space of its power of operations has been reduced by the improvement of internal normative operation requirements and increasing external public opinion supervision from the developing social media. Under the constraints of many conditions, in order to further promote the renewal of big cities in China, it is urgent to transform the mode.

At the same time, with the rise of global cultural capitalism, more and more attention has been paid to the "singularity" (Reckwitz 2019) of the cultural and historical value of the old urban areas. In addition, the new generation of young people gradually entering the mainstream of society grew up in an environment of individualism and consumerism, are well educated, and have a strong awareness of civic participation, with a high demand for aesthetic life, as their daily life and the city are inextricably linked. Promoted by those factors, the idea in recent years has changed from "old city renewal" to "ancient city revival", from the "material renewal" that is dominated by developers and pays attention to architectural forms to the "cultural renewal" that encourages social participation and pays attention to daily life. The "multi-governance" principle, as "government-led, market operation and public participation", has become a suitable governance mechanism, and residents are expected to complete the renewal process together, as one of the multi-subjects.

Compared with the previous period, the concept of social governance can be regarded as the initiative of the state to release a certain amount of space for the society, in order to seek a bottom-up response, and to eliminate the tension between the state and society caused by the rapid urbanization in the early and middle stages. With this change, urban renewal projects have been defined as being for the "public interest", and the control has become normative, soft, and flexible. The production of society is no longer full of confrontation with the state and the market, as it was in the early stage, but increasingly closely intertwined with the two at the grassroots level. Society has gained a certain space for growth, but it has been more restricted in form, scope, and ways of operation.

6 The Government-Dominated Production of Society: Blurring the Boundary Once Again

With a focus on daily life, urban renewal in China has entered the third stage based on community revitalization and public culture construction. It is characterized by "the government-dominated social participation", the essence of which is to bring back the social structure evacuated by the rapid urbanization in the early stage, and to make it increasingly integrated with the changing grassroots governance, reflecting the efforts of the state to actively absorb society so as to present a new state of integration between the two. According to the degree of state intervention, the type of intermediary, and the way society is absorbed, it can be roughly divided into the following three types, which are promoted in different regions.

Firstly, for the renewal detention areas that need to be continuously promoted, the government directly intervenes and leaves room for the society in its rules. In 2013, "Opinions on Accelerating the Reconstruction of Shantytowns", issued by the State Council, which proposed to improve 10 million shantytowns in five years, and supported several preferential policies, known as the "New Shantytown Reconstruction Movement". Subsequently, the renewal detention areas were integrated into projects initiated under this movement. Compared with the previous demolition, this shantytown reconstruction was mainly characterized as "for public welfare" and "people's livelihood project", which adopted the expropriation procedure and operated on the principles of being government-led and of resident participation. Government leadership is embodied in the direct financing of the project by the government, state-owned enterprises, and the State Development Bank, and the responsibility for work was taken by the grassroots officials of the government. Resident participation is reflected in taking the contract signing rate into account and setting a starting point in the rate, as a condition to decide whether each building is renovated or not; what is more, this emphasized that the whole process of expropriation was transparent and open, the policy was consistent, and residents were encouraged to supervise each other as well as the government officials (Shi 2021).

Secondly, for the historic areas that need to be preserved, the government introduced third parties to promote the cultural revitalization indirectly. Various pilot projects of community revitalization have been carried out by diversified social organizations and small market institutions. As a concept originating in Japan and Taiwan, community revitalization has a strong folk color. However, it has been promoted as an important strategy of social governance with an official color in China's urban renewal. Therefore, how to connect top-down government-led and bottom-up social participation has become a unique problem of community revitalization in China. The effort to build those connections leads to various explorations of the cooperation between grassroots governments and third-party organizations. In recent years, community revitalization has also changed from urban planning and design to more inclusive activities and public cultural construction, even taking a close focus on social participation and mobilization. Therefore, the daily life of local residents has been dis-embedded from the original environment and context and has become an important element in the cultural regeneration to create "authenticity". Citizens have been endowed with a certain subjectivity as the producers of traditional culture expressed in a new fashion style, during their interactions and dialogue with young people who are introduced into those areas by the third parties. In this way, the society presents its vitality while still absorbed in the state.

Thirdly, for the old communities without distinct characteristics, the government holds an expectant attitude and absorbs the emerging grassroots social organizations at the right time. In recent years, urban agricultural gardens and community gardens have become an important type of community revitalization, one in which "family" is used as a new intermediary between the state and society/individuals. In those cases, individuals are brought into the public sphere through three dimensions carried out under the specific meaning and function of "family" in the Chinese background, including the social network mobilized by the kids and diffusing to the whole community via a quasi-family relationship among neighbors, the public space produced by the social participation of "seeding" (exchanging seeds among neighbors, growing them on an individual's own balcony, and planting the adult plants into the community garden), as well as the collective memory mobilized by the storytelling around how different generations grew up. Based on the social participation of those community gardens, a new kind of grassroots social organization is emerging, called the "mothers' group", which regards urban space as an educational space for children and tries to combine social participation and children's education. In these cases, the subjectivity of society is obvious, but in the way of trying to let itself be accepted by the government so as to obtain resources to sustain the organizations. As for the grassroots government, these groups have real significance for its ability to mobilize young and middle-aged people, who were hard to reach under previous administrative systems, so the government selects the right time to make those grassroots groups as officially registered organizations in order to bring them into the system.

These practices are closely linked to daily life, reflecting the characteristics that did not exist in the previous stage. Firstly, intermediary organizations have emerged between the state and society. This shows that the state has retreated at the grassroots level, but the society is still produced under the dominance of the state. Secondly, the tension between the state and society is weakened, and the control from the state appears to be human-based, flexible, and soft. It is reflected in the increasing participation of women, as well as the domination of women in public culture-based and parent–child-focused types of community revitalization. Thirdly, the boundary between the state and society has been blurred once again. At this stage, the nature of "public welfare" in renewal projects has been defined and emphasized. The logic of the state absorption of society has been continued as financing relying on big state-owned enterprises or small but diversified market institutions, while foreign capital has been withdrawn. In addition, flexible governance also makes the interaction between the state and society at the grassroots level more integrated and permeable.

7   "Located Knowledge" from China with a Post-Western Sociology Perspective

This study reviews China's urban renewal in the past 30 years, and it compares two different types of society-making during different stages of urbanization. During the early age of high-speed urbanization, as people's daily lives had been heavily invaded by real estate development-driven urban renewal, urban movements had been evoked. However, for the actors, the claim for citizenship fighting against the local government had to be constructed under the premise of expressing their loyalty to the central state, which sustained the correspondence. During the current stage, the speed of urbanization starts to slow down, as it faces the growing social force, the development of citizen's legal awareness as well as the institutionalization of administrative procedure. With regard to these changes, a new model of urban renewal called "government-dominated social participation" has been created, which pays more attention to local people and their daily life, trying to adapt to the developed society. With this transition, the great tension between the state and society at the beginning has been partly dissolved. The governance of the state indicates its soft but resilient pattern.

Looking into those two types of "Chinese-style" productions of society, a "located knowledge" with a post-Western sociology perspective could be produced. The first is the correspondence between state and society. With a Chinese background, the duality of state and society does not oppose but converges, as Xiang (2010) and Huang (2019) have discussed. What this research further pointed out is the dynamic way in which both ends try to adapt to each other and push the great transition to go forward. The progress achieved during the solving of inner tension between the state and society in China indicates a more complicated way considering how states and societies transform and constitute one another (Migdal 2001). The second is the diversity of intermediary agents between the state and individual/society. In a Chinese background, both social organizations and "family" are closely related to the state and play the role of bridging between the individual/society and the state. Unique contributions to post-Western sociology could be made by digging into the negotiating mechanism between various boundaries during different historical periods, and how the corresponding system between the state and the society/individuals changes during the social transition with Chinese experiences.

Both aspects above show the complexity and dynamics in "Chinese-style" society production. Under the influence of Western sociological theory, a balanced relationship among society, state, and market during China's transformation has always been a subject of great concern. In the early stage of urbanization, the society actively responded to the extreme pressure of state and market, showing a strong "subjectivity" (Touraine 2008) in the citizens, as well as great effort from the bottom to create an "egalitarian state-individual relationship" out of the prevailing "subordinate state-individual relationship". However, along with the public policy discourse being upgraded from "social management" to "social governance", social forces have been intentionally absorbed into the state and "social participation" has become mainstream. But it is very different from the Western experience, as the upper state still maintains an absolutely dominant position while the grassroots government has retreated, which makes "the government-dominated producing of society" more like a "means" than an "end". As a result, the boundary between the state and the society/individuals made clear in the early stage has become blurred once again. The clues of state, market and society are connected and bonded in the grassroots interaction, but the complete independence of society and the internal equality among the three seem to be even more difficult to achieve. All of these things are not available in Western experience, which enriches the discussion of the subjectivity and practical ways of making a society.

References

Chen, Peng. 2010. "Legal Rights Activism Among Proprietors in Cities in Modern China: An Analytical Framework For Proprietors' Rights Defense Activities". *Sociological Studies* 1: 38–67.

Huang, Zongzhi. 2019. "Rethinking 'the Third Sphere': The Dualistic Unity of State and Society in China, Past and Present". *Open Times* 3: 12–36.

Migdal, J.S. 2001. *State in Society: Studying How States and Societies Transform and Constitute One Another*. Cambridge: Cambridge University Press.

Reckwitz, A. 2019. *The Society of the Singularities: The Structural Change of the Modern*. Translated by Jie Gong. Beijing: Social Sciences Academic Press.

Shen, Yuan. 2007. *Market, Class and Society: Critical Issues on Sociology of Transformation*. Beijing: Social Sciences Academic Press.

Shi, Yunqing. 2018. "Individualization in China under compressed and contradictory modernity". *Temporalités*. http://journals.openedition.org/temporalites/3853; DOI: 10.4000/temporalites.3853.

Shi, Yunqing. 2021. "'One Ruler Measures to the End': Rule Hardening in Grassroots Governance—Taking a Pilot Project in Urban Renewal as an Example". *Chinese Journal of Sociology* 7 (1) :74–106.

Touraine, A. 2008. *Return of the Actor*. Translated by Shiwei Shu. Beijing: The Commercial Press.

Xiang, Biao. 2010. "The 'State' Theory of Ordinary People". *Open Times* 10: 117–132.

Yang, Yiyin. 2008. "A Pre-Test of Citizenship in Contemporary China". *Sociological Studies* 2: 58–72.

Zhang, Y.H., and C.K. Lee. 2012. "The Making of Consent: How Do Grassroots Government Absorb People's Protest". *Open Times* 7: 5–25.

CHAPTER 34

The State, Civil Society, and Citizens through Local Governance in Japan

Yamamoto Hidehiro

1   Introduction

Since the 1990s, civil society as a public sphere independent of the state and the market has been attracting significant attention, especially in Western countries, and has eventually spread throughout the world. Civil society associations are private, but they differ from economic entities such as corporations in that they are nonprofits. They monitor the activities of the state and engage in advocacy to express the values and interests of society in politics, while providing public services that cannot be adequately covered by the state. The number of associations fulfilling these civil society functions has been increasing around the world, to the extent that it has been called the "association revolution" (Salamon 1994). In Japan, the rise of nonprofit organizations and volunteers since the late 1990s has brought attention to civil society working for the public interest. Furthermore, as decentralization reforms progressed, there were more opportunities for citizens to participate in the management of local governments. These trends seem to be in line with the global trends in civil society.

However, civil society in Japan has traditionally had a dual structure of strong local communities based on people's participation and weak social groups under the control of the state (Pekkanen 2003, 2006). At the community level, mutual aid based on closeness, which is considered as bonding social capital (Putnam 2000), has been used to provide public services and support the government (Pekkanen, Tsujinaka and Yamamoto 2014). Social groups with close ties to the government have also gained policy benefits while supporting the provision of public services (Tsujinaka 2002; Tsujinaka and Mori 2010). On the other hand, activities to oppose and challenge the state, such as social movements, have been weak (Yamamoto 2017). Pekkanen symbolically refers to this as "membership without advocacy" (Pekkanen 2003, 2006). This may be somewhat different from the picture of civil society or state-society relations according to the perspective of the West, which is independent of the government, cooperating with it, but monitoring its role. In this chapter, I review the relationship between the state and civil society in Japan, focusing on the local, and discuss its post-Western development.

2 Japan's Administrative Resources and Social Groups

In considering the relationship between the state and society in Japan, it is necessary to review Japan's administrative resources as a precondition. According to OECD (2021), the share of civil servants in Japan's total workforce in 2019 was 5.9%, which is very low compared with other Western countries, such as Germany (10.6%), the United States (14.9%), the United Kingdom (16.0%), and France (21.2%). As for public finances, public sector spending as a share of GDP in 2019 was 39%, about the same as the OECD average of 41%. This proportion was the smallest among Western countries until the 1970s, and although the proportion has been increasing since then, the fiscal size is relatively small (Soga 2013).

In this sense, Japan's administrative resources are small, and thereby Japan has consistently been a "small government". What has compensated for this lack of resources has been the various groups existing in society. In what the public administration scholar Michio Muramatsu calls the "maximum mobilization system (*Saidai Doin System*)", social groups have assisted in the enforcement of government policies and provided public services (Muramatsu 1994). Thus, the state and the society are not separated in Japan, and it can be described as a state that is open to society.

Nevertheless, the relationship between the state and society has never been one of equality. The state has always had strong legal control over social groups. Article 34 of the former Civil Code, enacted in 1890, stipulated that public interest groups require approval from the government agency in charge to obtain legal personality. In other words, the legal status of an organization was determined by the government. In addition, there were other systems in place for the government to supervise the activities of social groups in the form of licensing and administrative guidance. As a result, groups that support the government were more likely to obtain legal status, while groups that challenge the government and grassroots citizen groups were forced to operate as arbitrary groups. This is the reason why advocacy activities are still weak in Japan (Pekkanen 2003, 2006). Here, we find a characteristic of a state that is small in terms of resources but has a strong authority over society.

Based on this state–society relationship, how have individual social groups interacted with the state, and how have they changed over time? In the following sections, I examine the relationship between the government and society at the local level, focusing on neighborhood associations, local governance, and nonprofit organizations.

3 State–Society Relations at the Local Level: Neighborhood Associations

The largest number of social groups in Japan are neighborhood associations located in almost every area, called "jichi-kai" or "chonaikai"; there are about 300,000 of these associations. In principle, all residents are required to join these associations, which provide public services such as welfare, crime prevention, and disaster prevention, as well as maintenance of the living environment through road management and garbage collection. In addition, they are also involved in social activities such as helping with local festivals and funerals (Kurasawa and Akimoto 1990; Nakata, Kuroda and Itakura 1998; Pekkanen et al. 2014).

To carry out these activities, they also coordinate various functional groups in the community, such as crime prevention associations and social welfare councils. At the same time, they have a close relationship with the local government. They cooperate in the implementation of the public services mentioned above, as well as in communicating administrative information and undertaking administrative tasks, and representing the local community. Although several neighborhood associations have their origins in the pre-modern era, varying from region to region, it was not until the Meiji era (1968–1912) that organizations in their present form were established. Since then, these organizations have cooperated with local governments and assisted with the lack of administrative resources.

Later, due to the recession and social disturbances after World War I, there was a widespread movement to position neighborhood associations as subordinates of the government in order to maintain local social order. Furthermore, during World War II, they were incorporated into the national mobilization system. Thus, neighborhood associations have sometimes been institutionally regarded as terminal administrative structures. Therefore, after the war, under the occupation regime of the General Headquarters (GHQ), the neighborhood associations were ordered to be dissolved, as they were part of the mobilization system for the war. However, due to the need for mutual support among residents in the turbulent society immediately after the war, the group was maintained informally and was revived again after the restoration of Japan's sovereignty.

Since then, new neighborhood associations have been formed in urban areas as a result of rapid industrialization and population growth, while people's dependence on their local communities has decreased. In rural areas, the outflow of population has made it difficult to maintain the organizations. Despite these problems, expectations for community-based organizations have rather increased with the progress of decentralization and local governance, as described below. While neighborhood associations are based on the lives of local residents, as mentioned above, their relationship with the government has always been questioned. For this reason, a controversy has raged over the nature of neighborhood associations, between the view that they are a relic of the feudal system because they were positioned at the terminal of the government, and the view that they are a part of Japanese culture because they continue to be maintained even through social changes (Yoshihara 2002).

However, there is also a view that neighborhood associations are for the common interest of living together in a region (Iwasaki, Ajisaka, Ueda, Takagi, Hirohara et al. 1989). In comparative politics, the concept of "straddling civil society" has been proposed as an association that mediates between both the state and its residents in East and Southeast Asia (Read with Pekkanen 2009). In other words, one of the characteristics of the civil society that is distinctive to Asia when compared to the West is that it is a bridging association based on both the state and society. Japan's neighborhood associations are a typical example of this. In any case, it was essential for Japan's under-resourced local governments to make good use of neighboring associations.

4 Decentralization and Local Governance

I will review the trends of various social groups formed by citizens, focusing on the period after the decentralization reform in the 1990s. Before that, it is necessary to mention the 1960s and the 1970s, when innovative local governments were established in urban areas and the citizen participation system was introduced. Japan's economy was growing rapidly, and the population concentrating in urban areas. However, the improvement of the living environment could not keep pace, and various regional problems arose.

These problems inspired many local movements aimed at improving the living environment and opposing industrial pollution. The central government of the Liberal Democratic Party (LDP) was unable to adequately deal with these problems, and as an antithesis to the LDP, innovative governors and mayors with the support of the Socialist Party and the Communist Party emerged in many places. These innovative local governments aimed for a pluralistic democracy that would incorporate the voices of citizens in the formulation of civil minimums, the minimum standard of living for residents (Matsushita 1971; Muramatsu 1974). Thus, even in Japanese civil society, considered to be weak in advocacy, it is important to confirm that protests were held against problems caused by the strains of industrialization and urbanization, and that opportunities were created for citizens' political participation in local areas.

Since the 1970s, Japan, like the West, have entered a period of low growth, and financial constraints have made it difficult for the state to provide centralized public services as envisioned by the welfare state system. With the rise of small government and neo-liberal policy orientation, there has been a shift in the direction of emphasizing market competition and reducing the role of the state, including the supply of public services. Furthermore, with the expansion of globalization, several problems that cannot be controlled by a single state have emerged. In the face of this situation, the traditional methods of control through laws and regulations are becoming less effective, and the state is already unable to function adequately in the realization of social problems and public interests (Pierre and Peters 2000). This is the emergence of what is called the "hollowing out of the state" (Rhodes 1997, 2000).

To respond to this situation, various actors other than the state are required to play an active role. In other words, there is a trend for the private sector, whether commercial or non-commercial, to collaborate with the state under the provision of public services and public decision-making (Bevir 2012; Pierre 2000; Pierre and Peters 2000). In essence, there has been a shift from the unilateral governance of the government to the governance of a network of stakeholders, including the state and social actors.

Governance is particularly important in the context of local and urban politics. This is because it is at the local level that public services are provided, and there is a great deal of room for collaboration between local governments and private organizations. Moreover, the socioeconomic environment has been changing rapidly in recent years, especially at the local level. As mentioned earlier, the global economy and the shrinking functions of the state have led to the need for autonomous management of local cities themselves. In addition, the government sector has also begun to emphasize the principle of competition and has adopted methods such as New Public Management and quasi-markets.

In Japan, in response to these changes in the international environment, decentralization reforms began earnestly in the 1990s. In the past, local governments had been characterized by strong control by the central government, but the delegation of administrative tasks from the central government to local governments was eliminated, and tax sources and authorities were devolved. These reforms aim to encourage independent local management.

For the local governments of Japan, which originally lacked resources, the cooperation of citizens became increasingly necessary. As part of this movement, various groups have been established to promote local activities and the collaboration between the government and local residents. Systems to encourage these activities have also been developed (Hagai 2007; Tamano 2006). In addition, basic self-governing ordinances (*Jichi Kihon Jorei*) that include citizen participation in their regulations have been enacted, creating a system that reflects the voices of citizens in policy formation.

Furthermore, municipal mergers were promoted after peaking in 2005–2006 to improve the management efficiency of local governments. As the scope of the merged municipalities has become wider, there is a growing expectation for residents' groups, such as neighborhood associations, which are managed by the residents of each district (Okada and Ishizaki 2006). As described above, Japanese social groups have supported the Japanese government with small resources, but with the autonomy of local communities, they are playing an increasingly important role under the guise of "citizen participation" (Tokuhisa 2019).

5 The Rise of Nonprofit Organizations

Volunteer activities and nonprofit citizen organizations emerged at the same time. In Japan, the Great Hanshin-Awaji Earthquake of 1995 triggered a huge increase in the interest for volunteer activities, and the number of citizen groups engaged in public interest activities also increased. This can be seen as a phenomenon of the global association revolution in Japan, as mentioned earlier. This trend resulted in the Law for the Promotion of Specified Nonprofit Activities (NPO Law) enacted in 1998, and since then, the number of incorporated nonprofit organizations has been increasing drastically. In addition, a new system of public interest corporations came into effect in 2008, allowing social groups to obtain corporate status without administrative permission, and abolishing the competent authority system in which the government controlled social groups.

According to a survey conducted across a wide range of nonprofit organizations in 2017, the most common field of activities were health and welfare organizations at 19.4% (32.9% of incorporated NPOs), and education and youth development at 12.0% (15.1% of incorporated NPOs) (Ushiro and Sakamoto 2019). In addition, the number of organizations that have abolished the competent authority system due to institutional reform has increased, while the fields of activities have diversified and the employment environment for full-time staff has improved (Ushiro, Yamamoto and Kotagiri 2019). Thus, while institutional reform can be seen as part of neoliberal deregulation, it is also creating an environment in which many civil society organizations can freely engage in public interest activities.

Based on their own missions, these nonprofit organizations perform public interest activities independent of the state, which enables them to overcome the so-called government failures and supply flexible and novel services. In this sense, they are civic activities distinguished from the state as envisioned by the civil society theory. However, these nonprofits lack human and financial resources, and being contracted by the government in order to continue their activities would help them considerably. Particularly for Japanese civic groups with insufficient donation funds, it is important to earn money through business income (Ushiro 2009). As discussed in the previous section, with the adoption of methods such as new public management and quasi-markets, they will become increasingly committed to a contractual relationship with the government, competing with other actors such as corporations. Some argue that this is a subcontracting of the state (Ogawa 2009; Tanaka 2006).

In addition, a phenomenon called mission drift has been pointed out (Kotagiri 2019; Minkoff and Powell 2006), in which the more a citizen group is involved in the competition for commissioning, the more its activities become disconnected from its original mission. It has also been argued that there is a possibility of business-like characterization, where the nature of the organization resembles that of a commercial enterprise (Maier, Meyer and Steinbereithner 2016; Nihei 2019).

6   Concluding Remarks

In this chapter, I discussed the relationship between the state and society in the Japanese locality. In Japan, the government originally relied on a variety of social groups to provide public services. However, due to institutional regulations, the government approved the public interest of the social groups and controlled their activities. Thus, while the state and society were in an integrated relationship, the state had the upper hand. In response to the global trend of the decline of the welfare state and the rise of neoliberalism, and the accompanying withdrawal of the state from the social sphere, the presence of civil society has increased in Japan as well. As seen in this chapter, opportunities for involvement in local government policy formation are expanding with the decentralization of power. Nonprofit organizations have also emerged, and the institutional environment for them is being developed.

However, the reality is that local governments, which have always lacked resources, are forced to rely on the efforts of citizens. Civic groups are also lacking in resources and are involved in policy implementation in the form of contracted services from the government, which may undermine their freedom to work on their own missions. In this way, the rise of civil society and the focus on local governance in Japan can be seen as a deepening of the traditional relationship that symbolically utilizes "citizen participation" in a different form, rather than an interconnection between a mutually independent state and society as envisioned in Western discussions.

It should be noted, however, that such state-society relations do not mean that the social groups themselves are stable. In principle, all households in Japan are members of neighborhood associations, but based on a survey of the general public, the membership rate has been declining over the years (Zenkyo 2019). In fact, the aging of leaders and the lack of successors have been recognized as problems, and the development of local governance has increased the burden on neighborhood associations (Pekkanen et al. 2014). For the rest of the groups, there has been a basic downward trend in membership rates; and conversely, there is an increase in the percentage of people who are not members of any group (Zenkyo 2019).

The shrinking participation of individuals not only leads to a decrease in the resources of the social groups, but also means a narrowing of the values and benefits realized through the groups. Therefore, it can be said that the achievement of public interest through the integrated relationship between the state and social groups in Japan is at a crossroads.

References

Bevir, Mark. 2012. *Governance: A Very Short Introduction*. Oxford: Oxford University Press.

Hagai, Masami, ed. 2007. *Jichi to Sanka, Kyodo: Rokaru Gabanansu no Saikochiku* [Self-Governance and Participation/Collaboration: Reconstruction of Local Governance]. Kyoto: Gakugei Shuppansha.

Iwasaki, Nobuhiko, Manabu Ajisaka, Tadaichi Ueda, Masao Takagi, Moriaki Hirohara, and Naoki Yoshihara. 1989. *Chonaikai no Kenkyu* [The Study of Neighborhood Associations]. Tokyo: Ochanomizu Shobo.

Kotagiri, Yasuhiko. 2019. "Hieiri Soshiki no Zaigen to Missyon Dorifuto" [Nonprofit Financial Resources and Mission Drift]. In *Gendai Nihon no Shimin Shakai: Sado*

Skuta Chosa niyoru Jissho Bunseki [Changing Japan's Civil Society], edited by Fusao Ushiro and Haruya Sakamoto, 200–211. Kyoto: Horitsu Bunkasha.

Kurasawa, Susumu, and Ritsuo Akimoto, eds. 1990. *Chonaikai to Chiiki Shudan* [Neighborhood Associations and Regional Groups]. Kyoto: Minerva Shobo.

Maier, Florentine, Michael Meyer, and Martin Steinbereithner. 2016. "Nonprofit Organizations Becoming Business-Like: A Systematic Review". *Nonprofit and Voluntary Sector Quarterly* 45 (1): 64–86.

Matsushita, Keiichi. 1971. *Sibiru Minimamu no Shiso* [The Idea of Civil Minimum]. Tokyo: University of Tokyo Press.

Minkoff, Debra C., and Walter W. Powell. 2006. "Nonprofit Mission: Constancy, Responsiveness, or Deflection?" In *The Nonprofit Sector: A Research Handbook*, 2nd ed., edited by Walter W. Powell and Richard Steinberg, 591–611. New Haven, CT: Yale University Press.

Muramatsu, Michio. 1974. "Gyosei Katei to Seiji Sanka: Rokaru Reberu ni Shoten wo Okinagara" [Administrative Process and Political Participation: Focusing on Local Level]. *Annual Review of Japanese Political Science* 25: 41–68.

Muramatsu, Michio. 1994. *Nippon no Gyosei: Katsudo gata Kanryosei no Henbo* [Japanese Public Administration: The Transformation of an Activity-Based Bureaucracy]. Tokyo: Chuo Koron sha.

Nakata, Minoru, Yoshihiko Kuroda, and Tatsufumi Itakura. 1998. *Chiiki Kyodo Kanri no Genzai* [Community Co-management Today]. Tokyo: Toshindo.

Nihei, Norihiro. 2019. "Sado Skuta Soshiki no Bijinesu Raikuka to Koyo" [Becoming Businesslike of Third Sector and Employment]. In *Gendai Nihon no Shimin Shakai: Sado Skuta Chosa niyoru Jissho Bunseki* [Changing Japan's Civil Society], edited by Fusao Ushiro and Haruya Sakamoto, 184–199. Kyoto: Horitsu Bunkasha.

OECD. 2021. "Government at Glance 2021". Accessed September 1, 2021. https://www.oecd.org/gov/government-at-a-glance-22214399.htm.

Ogawa, Akihiro. 2009. *The Failure of Civil Society? The Third Sector and the State in Contemporary Japan*. Albany, NY: State University of New York Press.

Okada, Tomohiro, and Seiya Ishizaki, eds. 2006. *Chiiki Jumin Soshiki to Jumin Jichi* [Local Community Organizations and Resident Self-Governance]. Tokyo: Jichitai Kenkyusha.

Pekkanen, Robert J. 2003. "Molding Japanese Civil Society: State Structured Incentives and the Patterning of Civil Society". In *The State of Civil Society in Japan*, edited by Frank J. Schwartz and Susan J. Pharr, 116–134. Cambridge: Cambridge University Press.

Pekkanen, Robert J. 2006. *Japan's Dual Civil Society: Members Without Advocates*. Stanford, CA: Stanford University Press.

Pekkanen, Robert J., Yutaka Tsujinaka, and Hidehiro Yamamoto. 2014. *Neighborhood Associations and Local Governance in Japan*. New York: Routledge.

Pierre, Jon, ed. 2000. *Debating Governance: Authority, Steering, and Democracy*. Oxford: Oxford University Press.

Pierre, Jon, and B. Guy Peters. 2000. *Governance, Politics and the State*. London: Macmillan.

Putnam, Robert. 2000. *Bowling Alone: The Collapse and Revival of American Community*. New York: Simon & Schuster.

Read, Benjamin L., with Robert J. Pekkanen, eds. 2009. *Local Organizations and Urban Governance in East and Southeast Asia: Straddling State and Society*. Abingdon: Routledge.

Rhodes, R.A.W. 1997. *Understanding Governance: Policy Networks, Governance, Reflexivity and Accountability*. Philadelphia: Open University Press.

Rhodes, R.A.W. 2000. "Governance and Public Administration". In *Debating Governance: Authority, Steering, and Democracy*. edited by Jon Pierre, 54–90. Oxford: Oxford University Press.

Salamon, Lester M. 1994. "The Rise of the Nonprofit Sector". *Foreign Affairs* 73 (4): 109–122.

Soga, Kengo. 2013. *Gyoseigaku* [Public Administration]. Tokyo: Yuhikaku.

Tamano, Kazushi. 2006. "90 Nendai Ikou no Bunken Kaikaku to Gabananasu" [Decentralization Reform and Governance Since the 1990s]. In *Chiiki Shakaigaku Koza 3 Chiiki Shakai no Seisaku to Gabananasu* [Regional Sociology Series 3: Policy and Governance of Regional Societies], edited by Nobuhiko Iwasaki and Sumiko Yazawa. Tokyo: Toshindo.

Tanaka, Yayoi. 2006. *NPO ga Jiritsu Suru Hi: Gyosei no Shitauke ni Mirai ha Nai* [The Day NPOs Become Self-Sustaining: No Future in Government Subcontracting]. Tokyo: Nihon Hyoron sha.

Tokuhisa, Kyoko. 2019. "Chiiki Kyodo no Kanousei" [The Possibility of Local Co-Production]. *Ritsumeikan Hogaku* 387/388: 162–197.

Tsujinaka, Yutaka, ed. 2002. *Gendai Nihon no Shimin Shakai, Rieki Dantai* [Civil Society and Interest Groups in Contemporary Japan]. Tokyo: Bokutaku sha.

Tsujinaka, Yutaka, and Hiroki Mori, eds. 2010. *Gendai Shakai Shudan no Seijiteki Kino: Rieki Dantai to Shimin Shakai* [The Political Function of Contemporary Social Groups: Interest Groups and Civil Society Organizations]. Tokyo: Bokutaku sha.

Ushiro, Fusao. 2009. *NPO ha Kokyo Sabisu wo Ninaeruka: Tsugi no 10 nen no Kadai to Senryaku* [Can NPOs Carry Out Public Services?: Challenges and Strategies for the Next Decade]. Kyoto: Horitsu Bunka sha.

Ushiro, Fusao, and Haruya Sakamoto. 2019. "Sado Sekuta Soshiki no Kihon Zokusei" [Basic Attributes of Third Sector Organizations]. In *Gendai Nihon no Shimin Shakai: Sado Skuta Chosa niyoru Jissho Bunseki* [Changing Japan's Civil Society], edited by Fusao Ushiro and Haruya Sakamoto, 30–57. Kyoto: Horitsu Bunkasha.

Ushiro, Fusao, Hidehiro Yamamoto, and Yasuhiko Kotagiri. 2019. "Sado Sekuta Soshiki no Jizoku to Henyo" [Persistence and Transformation of Third Sector Organizations]. In *Gendai Nihon no Shimin Shakai: Sado Skuta Chosa niyoru Jissho Bunseki* [Changing Japan's Civil Society], edited by Fusao Ushiro and Haruya Sakamoto, 117–134. Kyoto: Horitsu Bunkasha.

Yamamoto, Hidehiro. 2017. "Shakai Undo Ron: Kokka ni Taiko suru Shimin Shakai" [Social Movement Theory: Civil Society Against the State]. In *Shimin Shakai Ron: Riron to Jissho no Saizensen* [Civil Society Theory: Frontiers of Theory and Evidence] edited by Haruya Sakamoto, 39–54. Kyoto: Horitsu Bunka sha.

Yohihara, Naoki. 2002. "Chonaikai Ron: Komyuniti Keiseiron niokeru Kindai Ninshiki" [Neighborhood Association Theory: Modern Recognition in Community Formation Theory]. *The Annals of Japan Association for Urban Sociology* 20: 45–62.

Zenkyo, Masahiro. 2019. "Shimin Shakai heno Sanka no Suitai?" [Decline in Participation in Civil Society?]. In *Gendai Nihon no Shimin Shakai: Sado Skuta Chosa niyoru Jissho Bunseki* [Changing Japan's Civil Society], edited by Fusao Ushiro and Haruya Sakamoto, 239–251. Kyoto: Horitsu Bunkasha.

SECTION 8

Ethnicity and Space

∴

CHAPTER 35

The Border of Ethnicity Worlds

Ahmed Boubeker

The idea of society as a referent of behaviours based on a mono-cultural model of nation states no longer holds. This new situation requires the construction of new paradigms, and the question of interethnic relations appears as an analyser of the current stakes of social, cultural, and political mutations and of the stakes of diversity management. Beyond the old primordialist perspective of ethnic groups, most sociologists agree to consider ethnicity as an activity of group-making and maintenance of boundaries between "us and others" in line with the work of the anthropologist Fredrik Barth (boundary work).

As far as Western sociology is concerned, while this interactionist conception of ethnicity has made it possible to revitalise research in the Anglo-Saxon academic world, in France the concept of ethnicity still comes up against the reservations of a research tradition which identifies it, if not as an ideological weapon for updating racial theories, at least as a concept localised in the context of relations between groups in the United States. Nevertheless, since the 1980s, in a French version of postcolonial studies, a growing body of sociological research (Joseph 1984; Poutignat and Streiff-Fénart 1995; Boubeker 1999) has made it possible to discover the new faces of French society and the heuristic stakes of a socio-anthropology of ethnicity: far from being passive in the face of discriminatory and segregative social relations, populations of immigrant origin give new meanings to their solidarity, thus opening new fields of economics, politics or territorial identification. Thus, starting from different figures of ethnicity the narration of which translates movements of identity renewal, I proposed a reflection on the notion of "worlds of ethnicity" (Boubeker 2003) articulating a perspective of "social worlds" specific to symbolic interactionism to different regimes of historicity. In the context of the decline of the nation-state (at least in its European version), these figures shed new light on the meanings which subtend the cultural rather than state cohesion of our social realities.

In this article, I propose to highlight some characteristics of this interactionist perspective of ethnicity, while suggesting some timid cross-views with the Chinese situation based on Barth's approach to interethnic boundaries.[1]

---

1 Fredrik Barth, *Ethnic Groups and Boundaries: The social organization of culture difference.* Bergen/Oslo: Universitetsforlaget; London: George Allen & Uwin, 1969.

1 Ethnicity as a Fact Far from Anglo-Saxon Multiculturalism

Sociological theory on ethnicity comes from English-speaking societies, but the question of ethnicity is not posed in the same terms in France, where it is difficult to answer the question: What kind of minorities live in a country that claims to be the republic of the universal? We will discuss this question, but first let us emphasise that in the perspective of a post-Western sociology, in France as well as in other non-Anglo-Saxon countries such as China, scholars should exchange experiences with other international scholars. As the sociologist Rong Ma writes "When we study issues of ethnicity, it is very important to establish a scientific discourse that corresponds to the history and situation of the country concerned at the same time, it is essential to share the knowledge accumulated by scholars in other multi-ethnic countries such as the United States even if it is still situated knowledge".[2] The Chinese sociologist adds that beyond any national ideology, scholars should be allowed to think, study and discuss openly the social phenomena and theoretical issues related to ethnicity: "what do concepts like race, ethnicity, mean to all social groups in a multi-ethnic society? What are the cultural, social, and political meanings of ethnicity in the daily lives and social activities of people? How these meanings and resulting ethnic identities have been produced in the past".[3]

In China as in France or in other European countries, there is an obvious gap between existing "nation theories" and the social realities. Nevertheless, it seems impossible to realise a comparative study of a small nation state of 67.5 million inhabitants and a country-continent of 1.45 billion people. What could be more different than the French political model of integration and the official Chinese "nation/*minzu*" theory and discourse? There is no French equivalent of the 56 Chinese "nationalities/*minzu*" and even fewer collective rights granted to separate minority identities.[4] France is indeed the "nation of nations": a thousand-year-old state and a political community born of the Revolution of 1789 and founded on the universal figure of the citizen. No other European country has been the home of so many regional cultures, some of them prestigious, such as those of the Breton or Occitan people. The borders of

---

2   Rong Ma, "Reconstructing 'nation' (*minzu*) discourses in China", *International Journal of Anthropology and Ethnology* 1 (8) (2017), https://doi.org/10.1186/s41257-017-0003-x.
3   Ibid.
4   Official policy recognises the multiethnic nature of the Chinese state, within which all "nationalities" are formally equal. Minority nationality is a legal status in China. The Chinese government decides whether or not a group is a minority nationality.

the French political nation were founded by laminating these "ethnic nations"[5] and the contribution of generations of immigrants was forgotten, melted into the "French melting pot"[6] of a national identity. A symbol of a national culture and universal political values, the French nation-state does not recognize differences and leaves no other choice than silent assimilation through individual and cultural integration.[7] Some observers thus denounce "the republican myths": their analyses tend to show that before the advent of the welfare state and the generalisation of the wage-earning system, modernity was largely based on community-based modes of socialisation.[8]

Long a country of immigrants which does not recognise itself as such, France is now a shameful multi-ethnic society. Many migrants have taken up citizenship or had children in France. But far removed from multiculturalism, the French melting pot is colourblind to differences. There are no public policies in France which confer recognition on ethnic groups, and for many French people, race or ethnicity are taboo terms.[9] These words tend to recall the atrocities of Nazi Germany with the complicity of the French government of Vichy. The Republic thus maintains the myth of a French exception which is addressed to everyone without regard to origin or race. There indeed exists a shameful memory of the Republic and, Michel Foucault recalled the role of French historians in the invention of the concept of "race war"[10] which, for the little story which became big, would have directly inspired the Marxist concept

---

5   Robert Lafont, *Sur la France*, Gallimard, 1968. Like other Occitan authors (Yves Rouquette, Joan Larzac …), the academic, Robert Lafont, inscribes his work in the current of regionalist movements of the sixties and he is one of the theorists of the "internal colonialism" (*Décoloniser en France*, Gallimard, 1971) which notably inspired the Corsican nationalists. In his critique of the French conception of the nation inseparable from the dogma of unity and republican indivisibility, Lafont opposes regional "ethnic primary nations"—in a conception close to the Germanic cultural conception of Herder or Fichte—to "a secondary nation, founded by the political contract of citizenship" which would have betrayed its own foundations through the national myths of a nationalist drift and an appropriation of the ethnic traits proper to a primary nation.
6   Gérard Noiriel, *Le creuset français*, Seuil, 1988.
7   The first failure of this model founded on the invisibility of differences is that minorities are increasingly visible. A particularity of France is that minorities are always referred to as "immigrés". So, the first problem of visibility is a major confusion between real immigrants and the youth of the suburbs. They are born in France and their invisibility as citizen in contrast with their visibility as a minority suffering severe discrimination is part of the question of ethnicity.
8   Paul Genestier, Jean Louis Laville, "Au-delà du mythe républicain", *Le Débat*, December 1994.
9   The word race was even removed from Article 1 of the constitution on July 12, 2018.
10 Michel Foucault, *Il faut défendre la société, Cours au Collège de France. 1976*, Gallimard/Seuil, 1997.

of class struggle. The racial argument was defended by politicians and famous writers like Gobineau, Barrès, Lapouges, as well as by the ethnologists of colonial thought. It was also a biological theory of the foreigner which inspired the demographer-inventors of immigration policy at the beginning of the 20th century. And probably because of this shameful memory but also for reasons related to the centrality of the social question, even today, there is still no such thing as "ethnic relation studies" in France. Yet, in contemporary Western societies, ethnicity, through interrogations on immigration and national identity, has become a focus of political problems.

2   The Inter-ethnic Border Model as a New Paradigm

Fredrik Barth is a Norwegian anthropologist trained in Chicago and Cambridge whose research on ethnic boundaries was introduced late in France as well as in China and yet transformed the conceptions and approaches of many scholars in the field of ethnicity. Barth's pragmatic approach, inspired by Goffman's interactionism, allows him to understand the border as the place where the mutations of identities can best be read, always reconstructed or deconstructed in the test of interactions beyond any biological or culturalist dimension. In China, as professor Fan Ke says: "Many scholars have suggested to go beyond categories the state classified, exploring how people see each other and if they have their own categories".[11] He adds: "For Barth, ethnicity is an intersubjective phenomenon and ethnic boundaries do not assume the absence of mobility, contact, and encounters with others. In contrast to the *minzu* concept, an ethnic group is not formed because of the isolation of the group and defined by its cultural distinctions; instead, it always involved encounters with the other. Ethnicity thus is a practice of categorization by interacting people rather a set of shared cultural traits".[12] This position could also reflect the French experience of ethnicity, so the constructivist approach appears to be a common heritage for French and Chinese sociologists. But if we can speak of "ethnic groups" in China, France and the United States which share common characteristics as a result of many years of interaction, we must not forget the different historical conceptions of the border from one country to another.

China has a millennial history of a political entity composed of a multitude of groups, with very different languages, cultures and territories. According to Fan Ke, in China Frontier and *minzu* have mutually constructed one another,

---

11   Fan Ke, ENS Lyon Conference, 2018, June 28th.
12   Ibid.

they are inseparable in public representations "even in professional Chinese ethnology": "It is not hard to understand why so many scholars were involved in these projects of ethnic identification and the related debates over the meaning of *minzu*. The state urgently needed to narrate histories [...] Scholars were now given the task of legitimizing these newly established ethnicities by showing how they connected to forbears in ethnic groups of the historical past".[13] The anthropologist explains: "In order to generate historical facts to fit to the logic of this narrative, of course, scholars had to be very selective. They were required to provide material to prove the hypothesis that China had been a unified country of multiple nations since ancient times".[14] Andrew Jacobs wrote something similar in the New York Times, "When it comes to China's ethnic minorities, the party-run history machine is especially single-minded in its effort to promote story lines that portray Uyghurs, Mongolians, Tibetans and other groups as contented members of an extended family whose traditional homelands have long been part of the Chinese nation" (New York Times, August 18, 2014).

In France, the school of the Republic was able to teach "our ancestors the Gauls" to children who did not have the same origins because of the multiple invasions (Germans, Normans, Saracens ...) then waves of immigrants, Italian, Portuguese, Polish, or Spanish people first, before migrants from Africa, North Africa, and South-East Asia. Many came from countries colonised or formerly colonised because we must not forget that the French Republic has long been an empire which at its peak covered an area larger than that of China. It should be remembered that the construction of ethnic representations is first and foremost the work of ethnology and colonial thought. For the policy of colonial administrators in Africa and Asia, to which French ethnology contributed its theoretical support, the question was that of identifying races and reducing them to a subordinate position. A specific quality was thus denied to exotic societies which remained in the "infancy stages of humanity": historicity. To believe in its civilising mission, the Republic has long protected a colonial border seen as a line of colour between "us and the others". And despite its claims to Enlightenment values against cultural archaism, who could say that the French colonial frontier was more open than that of the Han domination in China? And in the French historical context as well as in the Chinese, Fan Ke's words are appropriate: "All descriptions and narratives about ethnic minorities in media, textbooks, and other sources, portray them as economically and

---

13   Ibid.
14   Ibid.

culturally backward".[15] Today, in France, the increasing attention to the effects of discrimination in society, to racism and ethnical assignations among the French citizens of colonial descent draws new internal boundaries for French society. Like a socio-ethnic partitioning of the Hexagon, a new colour line or a radical rupture between recognized citizens and second-class citizens.

3   Urbanity and Ethnicity

In terms of analogy—for I repeat, there is no question of claiming a comparative dimension between the French and Chinese situations—it should be added that in both countries, minorities are generally poor; and their income levels are generally much lower than those of the majority population. But it seems to me that the analogy ends there. In France, the question of ethnicity arises essentially in an urban context, which is not the case in China, even though recent studies (Roulleau-Berger 2010; Roulleau-Berger and Jun 2017) have shown that ethnicity linked to immigration in large metropolises is a current issue. Even if the lure of well-paid work in the cities draws young people away from traditional village life, most of the members of the Chinese minorities live in southern China, Tibet, or the western Province of Xinjiang or near the borders of Asian countries. They constitute only about 7 percent of the total population but are distributed over 60 percent of the land. Many are located in frontier areas, live on steppes, or in high mountains, and are dependent on pastoral nomadism or shifting cultivation.

In France, the question of ethnicity arises essentially in an urban context: the French suburb is not the American ghetto, but a quarter of a century of social disdain has already put the flame to the powder keg in certain French suburbs, which have become concentrations of misery and resentment. In terms of social achievements, the significant investment in urban public policy had been essentially wasted. Equal access to employment and housing and social participation remained no more than a mirage for immigrant children, those on welfare, perpetual trainees, the long-term unemployed, or those in prison. The first way in which French society came to recognize the French ethnicity was through the involvement of second-generation citizens of foreign origin in suburban riots. The authorities, incapable of addressing the social roots of the malaise, gradually began to adopt a moralising, even sanctimonious tone. The public suspicion with respect to immigrant families is that they are deemed

---

15   Ibid.

responsible for their own condition. There are suspicions of duplicitous double play or community manipulation. This is the theme of the mafioso, ethnic, islamist, communitarian tendencies in these areas. It represents a new version of Louis Chevalier's "dangerous classes" (1978) aligned against the Republic. Images of riots and urban crisis fed the public's greatest fears and fantasies, buttressed by repeated expressions of concern over security made by the extreme Right but also by certain intellectuals who denounced communitarian groups. By the mid-1990s, the focus shifted away from the concern with forms of the social divide toward the ways in which Islam in the suburbs provided examples of the now increasingly invoked "postcolonial divide" (Bancel et al. 2010)—as a "clash of civilizations" (Huntington 1997). When they are not portrayed as budding Islamists, the immigrant children are seen as foreigners and treated as such. According to this view, ethnicity and religion are the causes of social and economic marginality. The children of postcolonial immigration would hang on to their cultural and religious traditions and it is because of this cultural difference that they would not want to assimilate into French society.

But ethnicity is not shaped by macro-structural processes alone. Like other types of social identity, ethnicity results from processes of identification which people mobilise in specific contexts to assert, contest, resist, negotiate, give meaning to their place in society. The city is a heterogeneous space in which the control of diversity cannot be reduced to an ideology of integration. Taking into consideration the narratives of the journeys of the inheritors of immigration, one always ends up by getting out of the confinement of suburbs. Not only do "those people" play at getting beyond the fortress, but their means of escape outside of the walls of the suburbs participate in a new urban dynamic, in the construction of relay spaces (Roulleau-Berger 1991) anchor points, thresholds of passage, a meeting place between the local and the global. Certain neighbourhoods of "ethnic business" thus constitute crossroads of mobility, of a "globalisation from below" (Tarrius 2004). That which escapes from the feeble knowledge of the urban crisis, is precisely this capacity of the inheritors of immigration to cross over boundaries, to bet on the miracle of a path to perpetuate a nomadic construction of doors and bridges between fragmented universes. Between the world, the Hexagon, the city, and neighbourhoods, new territories of mobility tie together the courses of exile in networks across which circulate men, merchandise, and information. We thus find a logic of the city which makes wealth and social productivity from its capacity to arrange activities and groups, to polarise flows of people, goods, and information, to play on hybridisations and encounters which are at the foundation of the urban phenomenon as a way of life and of the constitution of the public space.

This is because immigration is still the occasion of encounters at the crossroads of values which are reinterpreted and of meanings which are re-negotiated through generational conflicts and interactions with the whole of society. Where official statistics see only problems of integration or stigmata of exclusion, we must re-situate the living subject of ethnicity. We must also ask "how do the individual and collective existences of the children of migrants construct themselves in encounters, alliances and conflicts, through relations of memory and forgetting, through individual choices and collective movements?"

4   Figures of the Worlds of Ethnicity

The ambiguity of the concept of ethnicity, already underlined by Weber,[16] nevertheless takes on an empirical dimension in the complex fabrics and uncertain horizons of our contemporaneity. Beyond the debates of political philosophy, my work on ethnicity is part of a pragmatic perspective: I have tried to outline some figures, from the point of view of the heirs of postcolonial immigration in France, based on a hypothesis, suggested by the sociologist Abdelmalek Sayad,[17] of a relative autonomy of the world of migration with respect to the societies of immigration and emigration. Against a perspective of immigration condemned to domination, a plural figure of "heirs" testifies to the metamorphosis of life paths, through different places of anchorage, different configurations of "worlds of ethnicity", between reinterpretation of the legacy and confrontation with the actuality of French society. In line with the work of F. Barth, I thus find an interactionist perspective of ethnicity. Far from a substantialist conception of identities, the figures of ethnicity are always constructed in a tension, between individual strategies and collective perspectives, between logics of the self and a dynamic of conflict or sharing with other social worlds and public and institutional actors.

Any logic of identity in the working-class neighbourhoods where these populations reside seems in fact to pass through a superimposition of family or neighbourhood ties and through a re-appropriation of the stereotypes of social designation. Beyond a cultural heritage, part of the ethnicity attributed to or claimed by the heirs of immigration thus appears to be the result of a negotiation with their environment: the neighbourhood, the family, the school, but

16   Max Weber, *Economie et société*, Plon, 1971.
17   Abdelmalek Sayad, *La double absence : des illusions de l'émigré aux souffrances de l'immigré*, Seuil, 1999.

also the media, which appear to be the vehicles of internalised public images. From this perspective, the urban context appears as a superposition of territories and intermediate spaces in which new identities are negotiated. The experience of working-class neighbourhoods is thus valid for the generations inherited from immigration both as an initial place of socialisation and as a place of elaboration of shared convictions which build worlds of meanings between cities of urban legends and cities adrift from actuality. Nevertheless, it is important to be wary of an overly globalising use of the concept of "ethnic borders" which tends to obscure the diversity of migratory paths, forgetting the depth of field, the historical reliefs or the backgrounds on which the snapshot of interaction scenes is based. The figures of ethnicity, on the other hand, make it possible to schematise the very course of these relations and to configure experiences which are inscribed in different temporalities, different rhythms, different blocks of space-time.

At the end of the 1990s, in France, new ethnic agents understood that the essential issue was to update references to identity and to align a pluralist memory of immigration within the context of the present. More precisely, it became important to reflect on the very historicity of forms of experience. The focus shifted to finding new ways of posing age-old questions: What exactly does it mean to be an Arab, a Berber, black, West Indian, Sino-Vietnamese or a French Muslim? Hence, the legacy of immigration is the creation of a referential, identitary "us" which can be evoked by different systems of signs incarnated by specific figures in those sights of emergence which are the "worlds of ethnicity". Figures, then—figures of the Imaginary of worlds of ethnicity, with its pioneers, heroes or victims; figures of individual and collective destinies; figures which symbolise a communitarian ethos and generational rupture, modes of expression and of communication with the other worlds of French society. Beyond the dispersion of itineraries, it is indeed a narrative of several voices which is expressing itself by means of an interplay of individual histories and collective references—a narrative by immigration, and by the suburbs about themselves—an alternative to the golden legend of the French melting pot. What these ethnic groups did affirm was the variety of ways one could live in French society while simultaneously valorising forms of collective empowerment and weaving together the disparate threads of a society built around inclusion. The eclecticism of these groups best translates the diversity of ethnic/postcolonial legacies and the myriad ways in which the historical struggles[18] relate to immigration.

---

18   In fact, only a handful of researchers in France have explored the political history of postcolonial immigration (Boubeker and Hajjat 2008). The various immigrant struggles

5 Conclusion

In France, for the majority of researchers and political actors, ethnic categorisation implies a connection between biological inheritance and culture. Nevertheless, discrimination is a fact of life for minorities in France. This fact has forced the issues of ethnic diversity onto the French policy agenda. Despite this, France has begun to move away from its strict colour-blind model, and we can discover ethnical objects at the borders of sociology. Researchers have identified various factors of social and economic marginality reinforced by discriminations in areas such as employment, educational opportunities, and the stigmatisation of teenagers from working-class suburbs, which makes them appear as outsiders to French society. Far from abolishing differences in the public sphere, the French model of equalisation of conditions has only succeeded in imprisoning the inheritors of immigration in stigmatised identities. But French society is paralysed by the questioning of national categories of political understanding and refuses to look at the ethnic dimension of social inequality, which crosses over from problems of urban segregation, from racial discrimination, and from the denial of recognition.

If today the question of identity spills into the public sphere in the context of globalisation, this is partially as a result of the actions taken by minorities against the stifling of their singularity. For it is precisely the refusal to accept the kind of dehumanising representations which result in feelings of disenfranchisement, by daring to express themselves in their own words and by exposing their wounds and their imperfections, that those who are excluded from the French model of integration can escape public disdain and even attain recognition. What else are these new activist minorities seeking to compensate for if not the shortcomings of the state, the contradictions between the values and principles of the social Republic, and the discriminatory reasoning at play on the ground?

In the end, if the most essential personal identity should be citizenship, it is necessary to specify that some problems of ethnicity in France are also posed—in different socio-historical terms, of course—in other countries such as China (the Han are the dominant group, and many maintain prejudice and discrimination against minority groups). As Rong Ma writes: "In a

---

which span the twentieth century—from the workers' movement to anticolonialist solidarity, from May '68 to the struggle for housing rights, from the Palestinian councils to the "Mouvement des Travailleurs Arabes" (MTA: Mouvement des travailleurs arabes (Arab workers' movement)—reveal the tremendous diversity of political and social engagement and the emergence of an "immigrant consciousness" distinct from a "class consciousness".

modern society, all citizens should be treated equally in political, social and cultural affairs. [...] So, the government should take all possible measures to improve the educational and employment achievements of minority members and increase their participation in the national development and modernization process [...] so that minority members can live and work as the majority group on the basis of self-respect and self-confidence".[19] And the warning of the Chinese sociologist could be adapted to the French society: "If we don't engage in introspection and eliminate the 'Han chauvinism', prejudice, and discrimination that is deeply held by people across the country, then the goal of improving ethnic relations in China will be impossible".[20]

Acknowledgment

I would like to thank warmly Senior Translator Nigel Briggs for his rigourous translation in English.

References

Bancel, N., et al., eds. 2010. *Ruptures postcoloniales*. Paris: La découverte.
Barth, F. 1969. *Ethnic Groups and Boundaries: The social organization of culture difference*. Bergen/Oslo: Universitetsforlaget; London: George Allen & Uwin.
Boubeker, A. 1999. *Familles de l'intégration, les ritournelles de l'ethnicité en pays jacobin*. Stock.
Boubeker, A. 2003. *Les mondes de l'ethnicité*. Paris: Balland.
Boubeker, A., and A. Hajjat. 2008. *Histoire politique des immigrations postcoloniales*. Paris, Amsterdam.
Chevalier, L. 1997. *Classes laborieuses, classes dangereuses*. Paris: Librairie générale française.
Foucault, M. 1978. *Il faut défendre la société*. Paris: Gallimard.
Genestier, P., and J.-L. Laville. 1994. "Au-delà du mythe républicain". *Le Débat*, 22–34.
Gobineau, A. 1967. *Essai sur l'inégalité des races humaines*. Paris: Belfond.
Huntington, S. 1997. *Le choc des civilisations*. Paris: Odile Jacob.
Joseph, I. 1984. "Urbanité et ethnicité". *Terrain* 3: 20–31.
Lafont, R. 1968. *Sur la France*. Paris: Gallimard.
Lafont, R. 1971. *Décoloniser en France*. Paris: Gallimard.

---

19 Rong Ma, *op. cit.*
20 Ibid.

Lapouge, George V. 1909. *Race et milieu social: essais d'anthroposociologie*. Paris: M. Rivière.

Ma, R. 2017. "Reconstructing "nation" (*minzu*) discourses in China". *International Journal of Anthropology and Ethnology* 1 (8).

Noiriel, G. 1988. *Le creuset français*. Paris: Seuil.

Poutignat, P., and J. Streiff-Fenart. 1995. *Théories de l'ethnicité,* suivi de *Les groupes ethniques et leurs frontières* de F. Barth. PUF.

Roulleau-Berger, L. 1991. *La ville intervalle*. Paris: Editions Klincksieck.

Roulleau-Berger, L. 2010. "Migrant(e)s dans les villes chinoises, de l'épreuve à la résistance". *Multitude* 2010/4 (no. 43): 94–103.

Roulleau-Berger, L., and Jun Yan. 2017. *Travail et migration: Jeunesses chinoises à Shanghai et Paris*. Editions de l'Aube.

Sayad, A. 1999. *La double absence: des illusions de l'émigré aux souffrances de l'immigré*. Seuil.

Schnapper, D. 1994. *La communauté des citoyens*. Paris: Gallimard.

Tarrius, A. 2004. *La mondialisation par le bas*. Paris: Balland.

Weber, M. 1965. *Économie et société*. Paris: Plon.

CHAPTER 36

Ethnicity, Space, and Boundary-Making among the Hui in Nanjing

Fan Ke

1   Introduction

This chapter deals with ethnicity, space, and boundary-making in association with an ethnographical case in Nanjing. After an examination of the main concepts (terminologies) that concern this study in the first place, this chapter briefly discusses how ethnicity has been generally understood in Chinese academia; drawn on field data collected in Nanjing, the capital city of Jiangsu Province, the third and fourth parts of this chapter examine the main argument of this study: ethnicity could become an issue among the people whose ethnic identifications are identical, according to the state's categorization of the population along ethnic lines. To support this argument, the meanings generated through ethnic encountering taken place among the Hui Muslims will be explored.

Ethnicity is a social phenomenon, or, subjectively a social action, concerned with "boundaries". This means that the phenomenon in question should be something happening "between" rather than "in"; ethnicity is thus considered to be a social fact centering around social relation (Barth 1969; Eriksen 1992: 7). It is true if one agrees that the emergence of ethnicity, regarding if, as a consequence could be from interactions taken place among subjects, such as the state and its policy toward cultural or ethnic diversities, local elites, neighboring groups of ethnicities, mobility of people, and even the impacts of globalization, among many others. In recent years, however, there also have been scholars arguing ethnicity could be understood as recognition, and suggest doing studies of "everyday ethnicity" (Brubaker 2005, 2009; Brubaker et al. 2004). This approach is impressive in terms of its ambition of going beyond the debates among primordial and instrumentalist and Barthian approaches. In line with this approach, we could even go beyond to consider ethnicity to be something as hybrid collective, or the phenomenon of the social reassembling, phrasing from Bruno Latour (2005). Virtually, ethnicity results from human action in terms of boundary-making and, in the meantime, of building up interconnectedness among different actors (subjects). Exploring how this has come about is impossible without thinking of the space within which the phenomenon in question has taken place.

The concept of space in this chapter functions in the theorization of the process of the ethnicity phenomenon having taken place. Through an investigation of the phenomenon in question, this chapter examines the fact that ethnic boundaries could emerge among the same ethnic group, which, as a case this chapter will examine, was identified by the state to be a *minzu* (民族), or nationality. It is argued that ethnicity could be examined through the everyday experiences of the people who have migrated spatially from one place to another and been able to be back and forth between places they have lived and are living.

Following the German philosopher Immanuel Kant, space and time, in this chapter, are not discovered by humans to be objective features of the world, but imposed by humans as part of a framework for organizing experience. More precisely, the concept of social space Pierre Bourdieu analyzes in the field of power is more appliable to understand the phenomenon of ethnicity. Bourdieu considers conflict to be the fundamental dynamic of all social life. At the heart of all social arrangements is the struggle for power. One of Bourdieu's key claims is that this struggle is carried out over symbolic as well as material resources (see Swartz 1997: 136). Space could thus be socially constructed in which people act. In an ethnography he wrote in accordance with his observation of Berber House, Bourdieu suggests the space also could be structured, and fraught with the meaning of gender opposition in the Berber Houses. Though Levi-Strauss has obviously had an impact on this argument, it indeed unfolds how a physical space generates its social meanings to present itself as social space (Bourdieu [1971] 2003).

In general, anthropological study of space and place recognizes that landscape, space, and the body represent important sites for cultural meaning, social and political memory, and public discourse. Space can be used to carry social meanings that are culturally and historically constructed as well as contested (Aucoin 2017). In line with these considerations, space, whether social or symbolic, is a representation featured in interactions either among people or between humans and nonhumans, and thus is fraught with meanings of human action. Accordingly, we can also understand space in relation to either a place or a locale. Having focused on how people and things move around, change positions, and so on and so forth, space could be just like a collective in Latour's sense, where things happen and human and nonhuman meet together.

Boundary-making, or maintenance, and context are two central concepts in the study of ethnicity (Banks 1996: 27). The idea was originally a suggestion from Max Gluckman. What he found in Angola is, when Africans (in this case,

Zulu people) and European colonial officials ran into one another, Africans would behave differently; he regarded that as a boundary maintained to distinguish Africans from Europeans (Gluckman 1958). Fredrik Barth's cutting-edge chapter has further argued that ethnic boundaries could emerge from the situation when people of different cultural backgrounds encountered one another (1969). The phenomenon in question, therefore, is not cultural but social, as an aspect of social relations (also see Eriksen 1992: 7). In line with this stance, one would agree that it is impossible for the ethnicity phenomenon to have happened without existence of the other group of people. Sociologically, therefore, the precondition of an ethnic group to have existed is the existence of the other ethnic group.

As a consequence, through boundary-making space is imposed for people to change, displace, and move their positions, when encountering others. In this conjunction the ethnicity phenomenon takes place. What this chapter provides ethnographically is a description of how boundary-making has shifted from ethnic to religious. As a social process, however, ethnicity might have unnecessarily had to take place among peoples who are holding onto their respective ethnic identities under the conditions of the nation-state. Indeed, as Benedict Anderson (1998: 29) suggested, governmentality, through modern political action, such as state censuses and elections, has produced the bound seriality, which, according to Partha Chatterjee (2004: 5), is a small, limited, countable number of categories (classes, as he said). This means that one could be only 1, and cannot be 1.25 or anyone else. Accordingly, the degree of ethnic diversity that the state has produced should be *de facto* lower than that before categorization. Nonetheless, still, it is diversity, such as the 56 *minzu* or nationalities in China, for example. Most of the ethnic identities in contemporary China resulted from the campaign of ethnic identifications, and were eventually assigned by the state. This is a reason why the phenomenon in question could even have emerged among people whose ethnic identity is identical.

William Skinner used to argue (1987; Honing 1996) that place identity, once it was in association with labor division, could also generate the meaning of ethnicity. Skinner's insight is relevant to this chapter, since it casts light on the question asked in this chapter. Accordingly, ethnicity, as a sentimental representation of belongingness or social phenomenon, could possibly emerges from a group of people who share a common identity. Nonetheless, unlike the situation we usually see and understand, in this study it is the religion, rather than anything else, that replaces other ethnic or cultural characteristics to underline ethnicity. Ironically, however, the religion in question is shared and practiced by the people who are subject to this scrutiny. How could a group of people make a boundary shift from ethnic to religious to differentiate themselves from the other group who share a common identity (ethnic identification) with them? This is what will be discussed in this chapter.

2   Understanding of Ethnicity in the Chinese Academia

Though ethnicity has been an important issue and concept in anthropology from the 1950s and 1960s on, until the middle of the 1990s the concept in question was almost unknown to the vast majority of Chinese scholars. It was, however, immediately attracting Chinese scholars' attention soon after it was introduced to Chinese academia. Nonetheless, before the concept was introduced, Chinese scholars had their own way of approaching the situation of ethnicity. For quite a long period of time, there was not even Chinese terminology for ethnicity, despite the fact that traditionally, a great deal of scholars had been studying ethnic minorities in terms of ethnic history (*minzushi* 民族史), interethnic relation (*minzu quanxi* 民族关系), and ethnic linguistics (*minzu yuyanxue* 民族语言学), among several other topics. Accordingly, it is better for this chapter to comprehend ethnicity as a synthetic one, covering almost everything related to things related to ethnic minorities in a particular Chinese context.

Elsewhere I have suggested that the study of ethnicity in China has experienced research paradigm changes.[1] For a half-century-long period after the establishment of the People's Republic, Chinese scholars focused especially on three paradigmatic problems concerning ethnicity: (1) what was the *essential aspect* in the history of interethnic relations in China; (2) which *stage of social evolution* did each minority nationality or *minzu* (hereafter *minzu*[2]) occupy; and (3) how to describe the role of the *frontier* in each group's formation. The

---

1   I am using "paradigm" in Thomas Kuhn's sense but with a little different. According to Kuhn (1996), a paradigm forms when some new academic achievement breaks through earlier problems and shapes other scholars' academic enterprises. In the long run, however, such a paradigm can limit the development of a discipline, because paradigms discourage thinking along lines outside themselves. In this sense, paradigms also mean making boundaries. As Kuhn suggested, every breakthrough academic achievement succeeds by overcoming the limitations or boundaries of the old paradigms. In China, however, rather than seeing a breakthrough that gets rid of the old and establishes a new paradigm, however, paradigms established in social sciences and humanities have been strongly shaped by what the state wants academia to do. In other words, the state determines the formation of a paradigm more than any academic innovation.

2   *Minzu* (民族), the Chinese translation for almost all terms regarding peoplehood. Stevan Harrell (2000 [1990]) questions the quality the translation that could not fully match criteria terms of nation or nationality or ethnic group so it is better to leave *minzu* as it is. This

paradigms built around these three questions attracted almost all the academic enterprise in the study in question during that period, and the question of the frontier is still ongoing, albeit with some minor changes. The need to determine social policy underlay this long period of paradigm sovereignty (for details, see Fan 2019).

How the paradigms in question came about should be attributed to two projects the state carried out in 1953 and 1958, respectively. They are ethnic identification (民族识别工作) and the sociohistorical investigation of ethnic minorities (少数民族社会历史调查). Carrying out the first project was an action congruent with an ongoing larger project of state-making. For its purposes the national population should be categorized along ethnic lines in order for the state to have applicable ethnic representation in its power system. The project fixed 55 minority nationalities in China, and with inclusion of the majority Han, there are 56 nationalities in total. After most of the ethnic identifications were fixed, it was necessary for the state to narrate historiographies for these newly categorized ethnicities.[3] This is the reason why the second project was initiated 5 years later. With these projects being carried out, most scholars were led to engage in studies relevant to the projects. This is the reason why the paradigms came about.

As a consequence, around these paradigms a lot of works and articles were produced. More often than not, however, these works or articles seemed to take on the same general shape. In general, one had to examine how every separate *minzu* could be tied together throughout history in the first place, for instance. All narratives of ethnicities had to have such a thematical statement: "China has been a unified country of multiple nations since ancient times". Every *minzu*, however, has to be differentiated from one another, because not all of them are on the same level of social development. And the level or stage of social evolution each separate *minzu* occupied must be documented in a framework differentiating each *minzu* in accordance with the theory of the five stages of social evolution. An alternatively ethnic hierarchy presented as the brotherhood was therefore constructed in association with kind of "family ethic": One should help others if one occupied a position higher than other people in social or economic development. The majority Han was considered to be the most advanced; therefore, the oldest brother had the burden of

---

suggestion is reasonable if one had to deal with problems particularly caused by translation of these terms from Western languages to Chinese, or the other way around.

3 Jinuo (基诺族) was the last one to be ethnically identified in 1979. Afterward, no any of new groups of peoples was defined to be a separate nationality. It was officially announced that the government would no longer carry on the ethnic identification, and the mission of ethnic identification project was completed.

helping all of the others. Peoples other than the Han were evaluated in order to locate each of them on a suitable stage represented by their degree of social development. Eventually, these were critical tasks assigned by the state in order to construct a Chinese nation that should be congruent with the reality of variations of ethnicities in a configuration of brotherhood.

Here, I would like to elaborate in more detail the third of these, the "frontier paradigm" (*bianjiang fanshi* 边疆范式). It appeared much earlier but maintained its vitality even today. It first appeared in the Republic era. That was a time the state engaged in the work of nation-building within a framework of nation-state, and this work cannot be done without a consideration of sovereignty (*zhuquan* 主权) for a newly established modern state. As a concept sovereignty did not even exist in China until the second half of the 19th century (Schrecher 1971). In imperial China, state penetration was increasingly downplayed from the core toward the frontier in the territory. Sometimes, the state was even absent from the marginal regions of its territory. Such a situation might have actually helped preserve demographic and cultural diversities. For imperial rulers, territory had no hard borders; the spectrum of power faded from the darkest to the lightest throughout the imperial territory. Accordingly, as Anthony Giddens (1985: 4) pointed out, the traditional country, such as an empire, had frontiers rather than borders, and in the transition to the modern state, borders would replace these frontiers. The imperial frontiers were more often than not overlapping lands that were shared with other political units; it was a space in which peoples of different countries could move back and forth.

Shortly after China began to construct itself to be a modern state, however, its frontier was no longer a free-contact zone, but a crucial site for the state to practice its sovereignty. Since the sovereignty concerns the state so much, it is impossible not to have had an impact on either policymakers or ordinary people. For example, as long as this concern has continued to exist, national security rather than people's livelihoods would be given first priority. Since the vast majority of ethnicities have been living in the frontier areas, such as the northwest, southwest, and northeast, *bianjiang* thus became a term juxtaposed with *minzu*, and to a great degree one can replace the other cognitively; they are inseparable in current representations of either *minzu* or *bianjiang*. For a long time after the sociohistorical investigation of ethnic minorities, all descriptions and narratives about ethnic minorities in the media, textbooks, and other sources portrayed them as economically and culturally backward. The representation of ethnic minorities as such has always occurred in association with the conditions of *bianjiang*. This inseparability has persisted in Chinese ethnology even today. It is not an overreaction to address the fact that *biajnjaing* and *minzu* have mutually constructed each other; at the same time, they serve as metaphors or rhetoric for each other (Fan 2017).

Though many of these old paradigmatic concerns and questions remain today, a new paradigm has emerged to actively take part in the old debates, if not to replace them. From the last decade of the 20th century, Fredrik Barth's theory of ethnicity gained popularity in the community of Chinese anthropology. Having Barth's theory of ethnic boundary introduced, the theoretical body of ethnicity has gained abstraction from Chinese scholars. Accordingly, many of them have tried to understand China's ethnic issues from the perspective of ethnicity theory. Barth has thus become one of the most cited scholars. Since a conceptual sign for this new approach is *zuqun* (族群, ethnic group) I have named this new approach *zuqun* (hereafter *zuqun*) paradigm (Fan 2019). Nonetheless, even though Barth has been cited or mentioned everywhere in the research on ethnicity, many scholars just take concepts, such as ethnic groups or ethnic boundaries, for granted. Some even understand "ethnic boundaries" the other way around, treating ethnicity as something "in" rather than "between", defining ethnic boundary as cultural one. This is exactly what Barth wanted to correct.

3 Who Are the Nanjing Hui?

To answer this question, it is better to know who the Hui are in the first place. To make a long story short, the Hui, as a group of people, was formed in the historical past of China; they are Chinese speakers and part of their ancestry might have descended from foreign Muslims. Under the early Yuan, a large number of foreign Muslims came to China with the return of the Mongolian expeditionary army through the Eurasian landmass. They had integrated into Chinese society but have through one way or another maintained the practice of Islam. A point of view generally accepted is that the Hui identity emerged mainly under the Ming. Nowadays the Hui population is nationwide spread out, and it reached 10,586,087 in 2010.

Nonetheless, most of the Hui before 1949 did not regard themselves as a *minzu*, although the practice of Islam had differentiated them from other people, including the Han; and, as Chinese speakers, the Hui have been different from other groups of Muslim peoples in China. In the past many Hui people could not accept being regarded as a "*zu*" (族, an ethnicity) just because they had practiced Islam (Fan 2012). The Hui is not a homogeneous entity because there is cultural diversity among them (see Gladney 1989). For this reason, no one in the Hui study would treat the subject under study as a representative of the Hui as a whole. Accordingly, place identities are always in association with the Hui as groups of peoples. In other words, scholars usually may use a place identity to describe the Hui in their studies.

Following this rule, this chapter defines the Nanjing Hui as a group of people who have lived in the Nanjing area for generations. Historically, the Nanjing Hui made conspicuous contributions to the study of Islamic teachings, thinking, and doctrines. For a few great figures who emerged from the Nanjing Hui community, Islamic principles and doctrines in the Quran were interpreted through ways of *yiruquanjing* (以儒诠经)—interpretation of Islamic principles through Confucian concepts). Only after diffusion of their pioneer works were teachings from the Quran ultimately accessible to ordinary Hui Muslims. Without them, it is doubtful whether Islam could really be revitalized among the Hui. It would therefore not be overemphasized to argue that Nanjing was one of Islamic centers in historical past of China.

As described elsewhere (Bai 2005), one of legacies of Nanjing Muslim history is that there were 36 mosques in the city areas before 1949. Although we do not know exactly the size of the Hui population before 1949, the number of mosques suggests that it should have been relatively larger than it is today. Like many Hui communities south to the Yangtze River, Nanjing Hui had experienced ups and downs throughout history. Although I am unable to detail the history of the Nanjing Hui in this chapter, one fact that cannot be ignored is that the legacies from the peak of Nanjing Hui in history are endogenous resources underpinning the integration of Nanjing Hui today, especially after the vast majority of its physical sites were demolished during a radical urbanization starting in the middle 1990s.

Nowadays, there are only three mosques in Nanjing, and two of them have even been restored in recent years. Islam declination in the city after 1949 was, of course, due to sociopolitical conditions. The "cultural revolution" (1966–1976) was disastrous. Only after 1976, the year of end of cultural revolution, was Islamic practice be able to revitalized in the Hui community. In addition to changes before the reform-open era, urbanization taking place since the middle 1990s is a factor physically tearing down the Hui community.

Traditionally, the Hui were concentratedly living in association with mosques. The place Nanjing Hui have traditionally resided around is *qijiawan* (七家湾, literally means seven-home bay). Probably, no one knows exactly where or for what this place was named; the Nanjing Hui were living here for generations. Only at the turn of the 21st century, however, was *qijiawan* facing pressure to be torn down. In the end, *qijiawan* was demolished. Its residents were therefore moved to somewhere else. Fairly speaking, the Nanjing Hui community as a physical site is gone.

Another event that cannot be ignored in the Nanjing Hui history is, in the period of socialist reform (社会主义改造) starting in 1952, several businesses the Hui traditionally owned were either being confiscated or forced to become public-private joint ventures. This event harmed the Hui community seriously. Ironically, as is described in the pages that follow, the ownership in question even became an issue later on. The Hui migrants raised the question of whether these Nanjing Hui restaurants are halal enough.

From the late 1970s on, as the capital city of Jiangsu Province, Nanjing has been increasingly increased, and the population of regular residents has grown from 612,6165 in 2000 to 931,468 in 2020.[4] The expansion of the city has brought a large number of migrants coming to search for opportunities. Among migrants, there are ethnic minorities. According to results from the seventh state census carried out in 2020, the growth of migrant population was up to some 739,200, and 38.64% of them were grown in the second decade of the 21st century; the average annual growth rate is 3.32%, far beyond than the growth of the regular residents, which took only 1.53%. Today, there are some 265,1800 migrants living in Nanjing, comprising 28.47% of the regular resident population.[5] Though we cannot find specific numbers of migrants of each *minzu*, they should be certainly considerable as a whole.

4 Ethnic Encountering among the Hui in Nanjing

The students of ethnicity may ask why ethnicity phenomena emerged among the people who are supposed to hold on to a common identity. As one may know, 56 nationalities assigned by the state are significantly political more than anything else. The categorization of the population along ethnic lines, in Benedict Anderson's sense, forms a "bound seriality" (1998: 29). This means that in this seriality a person can only be 1, impossible to be 1.25, 1.5, and so on. This means ethnic diversities in China were actually less after the ethnic identification. As we know, the major work in the campaign of ethnic identification was fundamentally a process of incorporation, regrouping, and categorizing. Apparently, some of these categories may not be certificatory to the

---

4 Source: Nanjing Bureau of Statistics: Report from the 7th state census, 2020 (https://tjgb.hongheiku.com/11126.html).
5 Source: Ibid.

people who are included. The Hui identification is a case, among others. In other words, there are diversities among the Hui. This is all about the question asked in the beginning of this section.

Northwestern China has been celebrated for its Islamic heritage and existence. The dynamics or reasons for the northwestern Hui to move to cities in the east, such as Nanjing, Shanghai, and Hangzhou, to mention just a few, are not different from the vast majority of migrants worldwide who are looking for "work" and "love". No matter where they are, migrants are dreaming of making more contributions to the well-being of their families through hard work elsewhere rather than staying in their home villages. They will not go out if they are sure that staying home can make more money. This chapter is exclusively dealing with the Hui migrants from Linxia (临夏), Gansu Province. These migrants have almost exclusively made a living by running small businesses, and what they are mostly doing is the provision of service by nature. In the study of migration in sociology and anthropology, they are typically the middle-man minority. The nature of what they do may bring different feelings or attitudes from the local people toward them. We can find numerous examples for this argument. If they are concentratedly doing jobs not favored by the locals they might have been looked down on. Accordingly, according to C. William Skinner (1977), in association with place identity, labor division may generate meaning of ethnicity.

Interestingly enough, however, these Hui migrants have never complained about whether or not they were put in such a situation. And they cannot believe that what they are doing could cause them to be lower in a hierarchy. They think they just do whatever they can. Nonetheless, in the very beginning what determined what they should take must be a rational choice from some individuals. It is a common situation where migrants from the same place tend to do the same kinds of jobs or hold the same kinds of businesses. It is not hard to understand this situation. Migrants usually follow their successful kinsmen or villagers, who have left their hometowns and moved to cities or other countries. Place identity in this case makes sense for the migrants. Most of the Linxia Hui in the areas of the Yangtze River Delta are running restaurants with the brand of Lanzhou Lamian (兰州拉面—Lanzhou *ramen*, hereafter Lanzhou *ramen*). Interestingly, however, this brand cannot be found in Lanzhou. In turn, we need to know where Linxia is and who the Linxia Hui are.

5   Linxia and Its Hui Migrants in Nanjing

Linxia was called Hezhou in ancient times. Today, it is one of the two Hui Autonomous Ethnic Prefectures under the administration of Gansu Province.

The prefecture was established in November 1956. Until April 2021, according to the state census, the population of Linxia reached some 2,437,000; of these, regular residents were some 2,071,000. With the name of Little Mecca (*xiao maijia* 小麦加), Linxia was very important in China's Islamic history. Several Islamic sects or *menhuan* (门宦, hereafter *menhuan*)[6] were formed here, then diffused to other areas in northwestern China. Today, Islam is still the central force in Linxia Hui's daily life. However, from numbers that have been provided previously, we know that there are some 366,000 Linxia people living elsewhere rather than in their hometown. They are migrants living elsewhere. Many of them have settled down in cities in the east. Nanjing is one of their destinations.

Geographically, Nanjing is not difficult to reach. What we need to explain briefly is the people of Nanjing. The people of Nanjing have long been regarded as culturally being neither north nor south (*bunan bubei* 不南不北). This could mean that the people in question are more easygoing or tolerant in general. It could be true because the city used was the capital for six dynasties in the historical past. As the political center of these dynasties, Nanjing residents should have consisted of peoples from different places. One can find cultural ingredients considered to be both northern and southern in the city. "Neither north nor south" also means cultures of different regions could be found in Nanjing. Possibly because of its historical condition, traditionally Nanjing people have not been so sensitive to others. In addition, compared with other cities in the Yangtze River delta areas, Nanjing has been much more impressive in terms of its local Muslim history and Islamic legacy. After all, Nanjing seems to be an ideal place for the Hui migrants to start their new lives.

The Linxia Hui started to migrate to Nanjing in the 1990s. In this chapter we focus on a group of people tied by kinship or close friendship from the same place in Linxia. With them, Tong Teng, a formal MA student of mine, conducted excellent fieldwork. Ma Yuanxing (马远行), one of our main informants, left Linxia when he was 17. Before coming to Nanjing, he worked in Wuhan, Hangzhou, and elsewhere. He learned his ramen skills in Hangzhou. Also, in Hangzhou he contracted for a "window" in a canteen at a university to start his own ramen business in 1993. Next year, because something bad happened to him, he lost money, and so he had to find a cheaper place to restart the business. This is the reason that he moved to Nanjing. In a ramen restaurant owned by his uncle he worked as a cook in the first place.

---

6 *Menhuan* is the Chinese term refers to socioeconomic and religious organization of Sufi brotherhood liked to "leading descent line" of the original Sufi founder, extending through his appointed descendants to the leader himself and from him to Muhammad (Gladney 1996: 42, 350 and 110).

For Hui Muslims from the northwest to live elsewhere, the first thing they have to deal with is where to find foods that follow Islamic law. "Obey Islamic law" produces meanings of being a good Muslim, while "where to buy them" carries meanings shared among a group of people. It is in such a process of practice of meaning produced and shared that a bonding system of food exchange was built to differentiate the northwestern Hui from the outside world (Tong 2014: 20). Accordingly, whether or not it is *"qingzhen"* (清真, Chinese translation of Halal), or absolute in all aspects of Muslim life, was the first concern for them. This concern also means that it is impossible to live in their own world if have no contact with the outside world.

Therefore, as usual, they were of course having to make new friends among the local Hui Muslims. In Nanjing, to begin with, these Linxia Hui Muslims were going to the Jingjue Mosque, the only mosque in the city in the 1990s. As suggested, the Jingjue Mosque is a spatial representation of Nanjing Hui. As elsewhere in the past, the Nanjing Hui lived in association with mosques. Not until recent years were the vast majority of them living next to one another in Qijiawan; a Hui neighborhood was thus formed in the history. From the 1990s on, it was finally demolished completely to develop a space for businesses and other economies. Many new buildings have been erected while the old neighborhoods have gone. To what degree does this demolishment leave social trauma? To many people, especially those aged Hui Muslims, it is serious. They did not worry about where to live; the government built housing for them before starting demolition—what they really worry about is if their social network can remain the same. As arranged by the government, they are going to live in different communities (*xiaoqu* 小区) in different locations. One fact that cannot be denied is that most residents in Qijiawan were happy with this change; they had expected to improve their living conditions. This fact tells us that for Qijiawan, as Nanjing Hui's spatial representation, most of its people were quite secularized in everyday life. No doubt this is the result of several political movements after the communists attained power in 1949, and especially a result of the "cultural revolution".

Presumably, the Jingjue Mosque is the main space where the Linxia Hui meet the Nanjing Hui. In addition to religious congregation, such as practice of the Friday worship, they hope to find the right individuals to be partners for their business. What they need most are the suppliers of the halal food materials. Beef is a crucial ingredient for the business, for most of the Linxia Hui migrants are running ramen restaurants. Very soon, however, they found that they were wrong because some suppliers they met around the mosque seemingly were not halal enough—they even wondered whether these suppliers just pretended to be the Hui; most likely some of these suppliers were the Han from the surrounding areas. This brought anxiety to Linxia Hui individuals. These individuals therefore refuse to even go to the local *qingzhen* restaurants. (Tong 2014, 16). Yuanxing Ma pointed out that quite a few of these suppliers are the Han. He thus felt that many of Nanjing Hui are not dedicated to Islam; they are not strictly obeying the principle of halal.

To me, this is understandable. Islam in Nanjing has suffered from political movements much after 1949 than it is in the northwestern China. The Nanjing Hui must have gotten used to the situation that the power of Islam had progressively downplayed over times. On the one hand, they might have kept practicing Islam in some ways; however, they might have also put up with the fact of fewer *qingzhen* in their daily routine on the other; reading words from the Quran before the slaughter of animals was no longer serious to them, for example. For the Linxia Hui, however, this is absolutely unacceptable. For them, Muslims are forbidden to buy beef from non-Muslims. For Muslims, "trust" should not be a problem among them according to Islamic teachings. What they experienced in their early days in Nanjing turned out to be a question they asked themselves: Have these suppliers been trustworthy? Why have the Nanjing Hui not even asked for the credibility of these suppliers' Hui status?

In the ramen business, whether or not beef and other materials come from a trustworthy halal source determines the quality of the business. This is why the suppliers concerned them; this is also a reason that they tended to regard the Nanjing Hui, compared with themselves, to be less religious—they are not so dedicated to Islam; these suppliers should not be allowed to exist if the Nanjing Hui were faithful Muslims. Accordingly, Yuanxing Ma decided to shift business to the supply. Only by doing this does he feel safe, he said. This change also significantly means a lot more opportunities in the market. Except for Ma, at that time in Nanjing there was not a single beef supplier originally from Linxia. Intimacy, based in religion, culture, and where they came from, has brought him a bright future in the business. Indeed, he achieved this accomplishment later on.

6 The Halal Discourse and Trust

As long as halal concerns the Linxia Hui migrants, the boundary-making went on. Through looking at things that concerned the legitimacy of being Hui, the discourse regarding "what a Hui should be" emerged among these migrants. According to them, things that characterize a person to be Hui could be questionable if these criteria were applied to Nanjing Hui. They agree that Nanjing Hui had suffered unfair treatment over the decades since 1949; they do not deny the fact that Nanjing used to be one of the Islamic centers in imperial China, "but it was several hundred years ago". "And, today, only the northwest (*xibei* 西北) can be considered as the center of Islam in China". What's the matter, why are these Hui migrants are so suspicious of the Nanjing? They think that a few facts in association with the Nanjing Hui identity have blurred the boundary between Muslims and others, Yuanxing Ma thus suggested.

According to Ma, it would be a little hard for him to recognize a Hui without having a *jiaomen* (教门, the other term for *menhuan*, the Chinese version of the Sufi brotherhood). In addition, according to Huaizhai Ma, whom Teng Tong has interviewed, in their everyday language, *jiaomen* is the other term for faith (*xinyang* 信仰). One has a *jiaomen*, which means one is Islamic (Tong 2014: 20). It goes without saying that for a Hui in the northwest, having a *jiaomen* background means legitimately being Hui. How important a *jiaomen* was for a Hui from northwest China can be exemplified by a story of Quanzhou, a port city in south Fujian. Because of its maritime history, the city used to have a great number of foreign Muslims living there. Nonetheless, for some reason Islam had increasingly declined since the late Yuan. When Chen Yougong, a Hui from Yunnan in the southeast, came to Quanzhou for his military official duty sometime under the Qing, he found that Islam was almost gone. He tried hard to help restore the Islamic faith among the local Muslims and said that what he wanted to do was restore *jiaomen* (*chongzhen jiaomen* 重振教门), although no *jiaomen* had ever existed among the Quanzhou Hui (see Fan 2003). This is also a case of using *jiaomen* to replace the term of Islam in everyday usage.

Since the Nanjing Hui do not belong to any *jiaomen*, the Linxia Hui thus consider themselves to be the much more legitimate Hui. They call the Nanjing Hui *shenfengzheng huimin* (身份证回民, the ID Hui) because they have only the Hui status and many of them probably never really practice Islam. Yuanxing Ma suggested that without a *jiaomen*, one would be much more laid back in terms of religious life. Thus, how can these Hui possibly maintain *qingzhen*? *Qingzhen* means halal. For it, the Linxia Hui have the other term, *halali* (哈拉里), that sounds directly from halal. A difference in the use of the terms is that *halali* is generally used in communication among themselves, while *qingzhen* is used in communication when they meet the others. By the choice of the respective terms, they are actually making boundaries, which are based on the degrees of closeness to the others in a social network rather than in religion.

Another aspect for which the Linxia Hui think that the Nanjing Hui are not so *qingzhen* is their attitude toward slaughtering animals. The ideal animal slaughter should best be undertaken by the *ahung* (阿訇). The process of slaughter goes through steps. In the first place, animal would be placed facing west; then, an *ahung* will read a few words quoted from the Quran; in slaughtering, the animal must be quickly cut into deeply, so the blood from the animal's body can be emptied. It is best to have animal's trachea, throat, and two main arteries chopped off at once. If these "four tubes" (四管) are chopped off by one cut, the beef is considered to have a "cutting point" (*daokou* 刀口, hereafter *daokou*). In so doing the beef would be perfectly halal. For this process if there's no *ahung* around, it is best to invite a Muslim from the *jiaomen*. For the Nanjing Hui, however, they practice *qingzhen* by avoiding eating pork. They are apparently not so serious about beef, as long as they can have it. In general, they trust these beef suppliers. For the Linxia Hui, these suppliers are far from being trustworthy, however.

"*Daokou*" thus becomes an interesting and meaningful metaphor centered in the halal discourse. One will be disappointed if wants to find a *daokou* in the beef. In reality, there is no difference between beef with or without *daokou*. Hence, *daokou* is not in beef but in people's hearts (Tong 2014, 20). Logically, when the Linxia Hui left their homes behind, especially in a place where non-Muslims are the vast majority of population, "eating" became an issue. On the one hand, their habitus requires them to pick food congruent with Islamic law; on the other hand, lack of social capital in a non-Muslim place would force them rely greatly on *jiaomen*. This is what the *daokou* is all about. And, this is also what *qingzhen* means to them.

The other thing is that traditional brands of *qingzhen* foods in Nanjing also led to the discourse of halal or *qingzhen* among the Linxia Hui migrants. According to Sydney Mints (1985: 3), people's "food preferences are close to the center of their self-identification: people who eat strikingly different foods or similar foods in different ways are thought to be strikingly different, sometimes even less human". In the historical past the population of Nanjing Hui was relatively much larger than it is today. For a long time there were 24 mosques in the Nanjing Hui communities (Bai 2005).[7] The growth of businesses was quite prosperous. At the turn of the 20th century there were brands, such as Ma Xiangxing (马祥兴), Jiangyouji (蒋友记), Wufangzhai (五芳斋), and Anleyuan (安乐园), that emerged from the Hui communities. The birth of these brands articulated what the Nanjing Hui eat; it is certainly different from what the Han usually eat, although the local Han also like to go for foods under these brands. As elsewhere, many of the Han accept the *qingzhen* foods; not all of them, however, understand why the Hui refuse to eat pork. Thus, whether or not one eats pork, to many Han people, becomes a sign of differentiating them

---

7 As have pointed out, historically Nanjing used to have 36 mosques. However, during the Taiping Rebellion (1851–1864), they were all demolished. There 24 were rebuilt after the rebellion.

from the Hui. In other words, from a Han perspective, eating or not eating pork seems to be the only boundary between the Han and the Hui.

As I have mentioned, the Linxia Hui refuse to go to *qingzhen* restaurants in Nanjing. This contingently happened at the very beginning, but it seems to have become synthetic later on in the halal discourse of the Linxia Hui migrants. They first found that the Nanjing Hu were not religiously meticulous in their daily life; second, Nanjing Hui do not have *jiaomen*. These are the downsides of Nanjing Hui if they are considered to be Muslims. What I want to say here is that *qingzhen* is also a category of food, and in addition to Islamic principles in the food, in everyday life, foods must have different flavors in accordance with different regions or locales. Therefore, for the flavor of *qingzhen* foods, for example, with a few sweet dishes of some sort, the Nanjing *qingzhen* foods should be no problem in general. So, we should look into factors beyond the foods themselves. Accordingly, what we found is that it is about the ownership of these brands of the *qingzhen* food businesses. Anyway, to these Hui from Linxia, who actually own these businesses, that is a serious question.

For understanding such an attitude, we need to trace back the issue of ownership a little bit. After the establishment of the PRC, as happened nationwide, the businesses of these brands were confiscated, becoming public–private joint ownership (公私合营) in the first place; then, they changed to completely public ownership (国营), owned by the government from the early 1950s on. The slaughter industry is another business traditionally run by the Hui Muslims that was also changing its ownership from the private to the public. From private ownership to state ownership, these businesses finally fell into the hands of communist officials of the bureaucratic system. Ultimately, no doubt, in this process the exchange system of Islamic foods was completely broken, leading *qingzhen* to have much less religious meaning.

Although from the Linxia Hui's stance the businesses of Nanjing Hui may not be *qingzhen* enough, the local people, no matter if they are the Han or the Hui, have no doubts regarding the businesses in question as *qingzhen*. The cultural revolution (1966–1976) had a huge impact on and rendered the businesses almost lifeless. In the reform–opening up era, especially since the 1990s the government has found that the old business brands (*laozihao* 老字号) could be used for increasing the GDP; therefore, they decided to restore them. The *qingzhen* restaurants are thus encouraged to address their traditions. Because of the experience these businesses suffered during that period of time, the Hui migrants do not fully recognize these businesses as fully *qingzhen*. "Their ownerships are unclear"—these words were heard all the time when talking about these old brands with our Linxia Hui informants. According to their point of view, it does not matter what the property is, if it belongs to a religious body the government should not be in charge of it. "How can foods under these brands maintain *qingzhen*, if the owners are not Muslims?" And "the state" (国家) is atheist, so how religion can really be respected? They are suspicious that under the conditions as such, food materials cannot maintain halal status. Some of them even doubt if there is prayer and reading of the Quran taking place before animals are slaughtered.

In an urban space everything is industrialized. There were things these Hui migrants felt it was difficult to accept in the very beginning. For the beef supply, they have visited the slaughterhouses. What they found in the slaughterhouses alerted their sensibility in terms of halal. According to what they said, they heard the sound of praying but found that the sound came out of a tape or recording. Again, they asked a question: How could God's messages be delivered by these lifeless machines? All modern things, when they appeared, were being challenged by the forces of traditionalism. These Hui migrants are not afraid to emphasize their traditionalism, and Islamic doctrines and principles measure everything. Lifeless machines play a role pretending to be *ahung* that touches upon the issue of trust, according to these Hui migrants. Though many of them finally adapted to this situation, this was the juncture for Yuanxing Ma to find a chance to shift his job to become a beef supplier. This decision was of course made by not only the religious passion but also a "rational man" choice; he believed that he might become the only one among the Linxia Hui in the slaughter industry, through which he may create a market among the owners of ramen business of the Hui migrants.

In the first decade of the 21st century, globalization accomplished its new stage, globalization 3.0 (Friedman 2007: 9–11). The world became tiny and flat; it was actually becoming a platform, on which individuals were empowered to participate in the global competition. Besides, companies or individuals from the third world are also increasingly being seen in the global market. In the hallah food market there were several foreign companies taking part in competition. This also faced a challenge from those Hui migrants in the beginning.

In 2005, there was a person who said that he was Hui, working at a trade company in Nanjing. The company is for importing meat products. He introduced Yuanxing Ma to the frozen beef brand Allana, which is a hallah food industrial company based in India. The price of beef was quite cheap. At that time the retail price of beef Ma Yuanxing offered was 30 RMB for 0.5 kg, which was much expensive than the price of frozen beef offered by the Allana, which was less than 20 RMB for 0.5 kg, much cheaper than the fresh beef. If the market profit was the only concern, the frozen beef is of course more acceptable. Nonetheless, for many Hui migrants this is problematic because whether or not ingredients are halal is most important.

In the first place, Ma did not want to buy the frozen beef. He did not trust that supplier at all. He felt that that supplier was not a serious Muslim and regarded him as the ID Hui. He was hence suspicious as to whether the beef was from animals that were slaughtered under the Islamic law. But through that person he met the other person who shared the same experience with him. People called this guy Laoda Ma (马老大). Laoda was almost in charge of the hallah beef supply in Shanghai at that time. According to Yuanxing Ma, compared with the ramen industry in Nanjing, in which there were more than 500 of this type of restaurant at that time, in Shanghai the number was much larger, at least more than 2000. Laoda Ma was not unknown to Yuanxing Ma. Through social networks of the Linxia Hui migrants, Yuanxing Ma had known about him for quite a while. The representative of the Allana, who is an Egyptian, looks exactly like what an Arabic Muslim looks like in the Chinese imagination. Laoda Ma was finally persuaded by that ID Hui, coming to trust in him. Accordingly, Yuanxing Ma followed Laoda Ma to accept Allana. Soon, frozen beef started to ship from Mumbai to Nanjing.

Nonetheless, it seems much easier to import beef from India than to retail it to the owners of ramen businesses. Not all of the owners accepted frozen beef without other considerations. They just had never sold frozen meat before. It was natural to think of the issue of halal when they first encountered this frozen beef. Trust was built among those "big bosses" (*da laoban* 大老板), such as Laoda Ma and Yuanxing Ma, but it had not yet been built among the vast majority of the Hui migrants, including Yuanxing Ma's younger employees. Previously, the businesses owners had always had fresh beef; if they had to use frozen beef that must be shipped from Linxia. This time, what they received were packs of beef with English and Arabic signs. According to what they said, for the fresh meat they always knew the whole process of animal slaughtering, so fresh meats were accordingly directly embodied by ways of slaughtering the animal, and because the suppliers and even butchers were familiar to them. For the frozen beef, however, because of a long journey from foreign countries to China, many things before and during these journeys were actually unknown to the buyers. Many Linxia Hui business owners felt uncertainty toward the beef from foreign countries in spite of mark of halal. Obviously, the concern of trust is all about.

Trust as a social fact came about because human life was full of uncertainty and risk. For this reason, networks of trust relations facilitate social exchanges (Cook 2005). This is common to see in situations where people meet strangers or happen to be in a place totally alien to them. Anthropologist R.N. Adams (1951) in his paper on ethnocentrism argues that humans used to have a consciousness he termed "wegroup consciousness", which came into being because the collective is highly valued and collectivism is emphasized; under such conditions, people always said "we" instead of "I". This situation may have hatched a sense of ethnocentrism, which not only highly values one's own culture and looks down on that of others, but it also sees outsiders as the enemy. Within the group, however, trust was never an issue and there was not even any sense of trust in the group. In Ferdinand Tonnies's sense, it is a community that is face-to-face society. From this point of view, trust as a feeling only takes place when "us" meet "them". Accordingly, it is not overemphasized to say that trust is an important factor in dividing "you" and "I", or even "enemy" and "us" (see Fan 2015: 116).

It goes without saying that trust concerning human society in general had to wait until the arrival of industrial society. This was also a time in which the context of social relations of human beings were dis-embedded from the local ones and extended to a much large space (Giddens 1990). People had to encounter strangers everyday under urban conditions, and, according to sociologist Peter Blau (2002), social relationships based on trust were thus popularized. Through management of social capital people built their trust relationships centering on reciprocity in the beginning. This relationship, however, with some nature of contracts in modern society, namely transaction. The difference between transaction and reciprocity is that a clear goal is in the former, while for the later, it is naturally an expectation among interactive parties. This is an inevitable factor in the process of establishment of social relationship among strangers (ibid.). Karen Cook (2005) even goes so far as to suggest that making social relations optional became popularized among strangers, and this changes the nature of social order, and thus to divide societies into modern ones or traditional ones.

Above discussion suggests that the Linxia Hui migrants in Nanjing are exactly in such a situation. After they have seemingly adapted to an unfamiliar urban space, they need to further adapt to the situation of ongoing changes in this space. Some of them are following up quickly, but there are still quite a few individuals who are insistently maintaining their traditions, and what the Allana has encountered is a case exemplifying this argument. Those who do not trust the Allana argued that this beef should be produced through the processing line; can producers then critically follow the Islamic way in such a highly productive process? "Who reads the Quran when animals were slaughtered?" "By machine?" "Then, how can the machine read the Quran?" "Machine doesn't have a *jiaomen* and is lifeless!" "If the *jingwen* (scriptural phrases, hereafter *jingwen*) is read by the person who controls the machine, then, I want to ask, how can one do it?" "If one has to slaughter a large number of animals one by one through the machine, can he read the *jingwen* to animals in every kill?"

"I would be going crazy if I had to do this!" said Chouchang Ga (尕惆怅), one of those who challenge the credibility of imported foreign beef.

They moved on to argue whether or not the beef of the Allana is *daokou*. To me, however, the situation is a bit worse, because we all know that *daokou* eventually is a metaphor and cannot be found in the meat. According to what Chouchang Ga said, there seemed to have an intensive quarrel between individuals such as Ga and Yuanxing Ma. Though the quarrel has come down, we believe, in some Linxia Hui hearts, it is still there. To many Linxia Hui migrants, only "tradition" can be congruent with Islamic way.

7 Conclusion

The suggestion of the post-Western society attempts to go beyond the theoretical domination of the Western sociology in the discipline. The suggestion opens up a horizon for sociologists in Western and non-Western countries to work together and to have many more interactions in the exchange of ideas and innovations with one another. As long as questions such as how to write our own theory concern scholars of non-Western countries, what we may have kept in mind is that the idea of post-Western sociology does not mean leaving behind the sociological theories Western scholars have produced; rather, it is an advocation that the students of sociology should not take these theories for granted without thinking of its feasibility if practiced in one's own social and cultural conditions. If one could test the given theories in one's own social context in particular, the research result then is relevant. Post-Western sociology is, on the other hand, not to mean the nativization or localization (本土化) of sociology in any sense, but argues that the study must touch more on the lands of particular contexts, from which the research questions come and in which the social facts are problematized. Only through this way could one's research be more specific on the one hand, and more universal on the other. But I do think what we face is how to deal with the social problems and answer the questions. For purposes as such where the theories come from should not be a matter, as long as they are valuable to inspire us in answering questions and solving the problems as well.

Drawing on the above considerations, this chapter first discussed concepts such as ethnicity, space, and boundary-making (boundary maintenance) in order to set up a theoretical context for an ethnographic examination that follows. Standing in line with Fredrik Barth, this chapter considers ethnicity as a social phenomenon that takes place only in "between" rather than "in", which means that it is only emerged when different agencies encounter one another. For space, this chapter follows relevant ideals from Immanuel Kant's tradition.

Rather than seeing space as objective features of the world, this chapter considers that it is imposed by humans as part of a framework for organizing experiences. For "boundary-making", the concept is eventually situated in Barth's view of ethnicity in an interactive context, in which mobility seems to be a main factor to lead to the phenomenon in question taking place.

Drawing on the ethnographical data collected in Nanjing, this chapter further examine the fact of boundary making taken place among the people who are sharing the same ethnic status but with different local identities that are the Linxia Hui migrants and the Nanjing Hui. In this case, space is a zone, in which actors meet and contacted, in which feelings, emotions, speculations, actions, and things, among many others, are all to have interacted, forming a brand-new phenomenon of ethnicity. In this juncture, the practice of categorization by the Hui migrants in question has turned out to be more religious, differentiating them from the Nanjing Hui, despite the fact that they share the same ethnic identification that was assigned by the state. At the turn of the 21st century and facing the flow of globalization, these Hui migrants were once again feeling uncertain. They kept asking if the beef they purchased for their small business from foreign companies of *halah* foods is *halah* enough? Can a machine listen to or understand Allah's words being read before the slaughtering in the process of beef production? These questions that they have frequently asked are the reflections are typically produced in the juncture of "old" and "new" coming across. Trust thus is the only way to solve the questions emerging actually from human nature.

References

Adams, R.N. 1951. "Ethnocentrism and Ingroup Consciousness". *American Anthropologist* 53 (4): 598–600.

Anderson, Benedict. 1998. *The Spectre of Comparison: Nationalism, Southeast Asia and the World*. London: Verso.

Aucoin, Paulline McKenzie. 2017. "Toward an Anthropological Understanding of Space and Place". In *Place, Space and Hermeneutics*, edited by Bruce B. Janz, 395–412. New York: Springer.

Bai, Youtao. 2005. *Pangencao: Chenshihua Beijing xiade Huimin Shequ* [Vetiver Glass: The Hui Community in the Context of Urbanization]. Yinchuan: Ningxia Renmin Chubanshe.

Banks, Marcus. 1996. *Ethnicity: Anthropological Constructions*. London: Routledge.

Barth, Fredrik. 1969. "Introduction". In *Ethnic Group and Boundaries: The Social Organization and Cultural Differences*, edited by Fredrik Barth, 9–38. Boston, MA: Little Brown.

Blau, Peter. 2002. "Reflection on a Career as a Theorist". In *New Directions in Contemporary Sociological Theory*, edited by Joseph Berger and Morris Zeldith Jr., 3345–3357. Lanham, MD: Rowman and Littlefield.

Bourdieu, Pierre. (1971) 2003. "The Berber House". In *Rules and Meanings*, edited by Mary Douglas, 98–110. London: Routledge.

Brubaker, Rogers. 2004. *Ethnicity Without Groups*. Cambridge, MA: Harvard University Press.

Brubaker, Rogers. 2009. "Ethnicity, Race, and Nationalism". *Annual Review of Sociology* 35: 21–42.

Brubaker, Rogers, Mara Lovemen, and Peter Stamatove. 2005. "Ethnicity as Cognition". *Theory and Society* 33 (1): 31–66.

Chatterji, Parthan. 2004. *The Politics of the Governed: Reflection on Popular Politics in Most of the World*. New York: Columbia University Press.

Cook, Karen. 2005. "Networks, Norms and Trust: The Social Psychology of Social Capital". *Social Psychology Quarterly* 68 (1): 4–14.

Eriksen, Thomas Hylland. 1992. *Ethnicity and Nationalism: Anthropological Perspectives*. Boulder, CO: Pluto Press.

Fan, Ke. 2019. "Paradigm Chang in Chinese Ethnology and Fredrik Barth's Influence". In *It Happens Among People: Resonances and Extension of the World of Fredrik Barth*, edited by Keping Wu and Roberta P. Weller, 268–299. London: Routledge.

Fan, Ke. 2017. "bianjiang yu minzu hugou de lishi guocheng jiqi yingxiang" [Mutual Construction of Frontier and Ethnic Minorities: Historical Process and Realistic Impacts]. *Minzu Yanjiu* [Ethno-National Studies] 6: 58–73.

Fan, Ke. 2016. "Representation of Ethnic Minorities in Socialist China". *Ethnic and Racial Studies* 39 (12): 2091–2108.

Fan, Ke. 2012. "Ethnic Configuration and State Making: A Fujian Case". *Modern Asian Studies* 42 (4): 919–945.

Fan, Ke. 2003. "Ups and Downs: Local Muslim History in South China". *Journal of Muslim Minority Affairs* 23 (1): 63–87.

Friedman, Thomas I. 2007. *The World Is Flat: A Brief History of the Twenty-first Century*. New York, NY: Picador/Farrar, Struss and Giroux.

Giddens, Anthony. 1990. *The Consequences of Modernity*. Palo Alto, CA: Stanford University Press.

Giddens, Anthony. 1985. *The Nation-State and Violence: Volume Two of a Contemporary of Critique of Historical Materialism*. Berkeley: University of California Press.

Gladney, Dru. 1989. *Muslim Chinse: Ethnic Nationalism in the People's Republic*. Cambridge, MA: Harvard University Press.

Gluckman, Max. 1958. *Analysis of a Social Situation in Modern Zululand*. Manchester: Manchester University Press for the Rhodes-Livingstone Institute.

Honing, Emily. 1996. "Reginal Identity, Labor, and Ethnicity in Contemporary China". In *Putting Class in Its Place: Worker Identity in East Asia*, edited by Elizabeth Parry, 225–243. Berkeley: University of California.

Latour, Bruno. 2005. *Reassembling the Social: An Introduction to Actor Network Theory*. Oxford: Oxford University Press.

Mints, Sidney. 1985. *Sweetness and Power: The Place of Sugar in Modern History*. New York: Penguin Books.

Schrecher, John E. 1971. *Imperialism and Chinese Nationalism: Germany in Shangdong*. Cambridge, MA: Harvard University Press.

Skinner, C. William. 1977. "Introduction: Urban Social Structure in Ch'ing China". In *The City in Late Imperial China*, edited by C. William Skinner. Palo Alto: Stanford University Press.

Stalin, Joseph. 1935. *Marxism and the National and Colonial Question*. Moscow: Co-operative Publishing Society of Foreign Workers in the USSR.

Swartz, David. 1997. *Culture and Power: The Sociology of Pierre Bourdieu*. Chicago, IL: University of Chicago Press.

Tong, Teng. 2014. *Sanzhong Qingzhen—Bianjie Shang de Shiwu Xinren* [Three-Qingzhen: Halal Food Trust on Border]. Master's thesis, Nanjing University, Nanjing.

CHAPTER 37

Considering Super-diversity in Immigration: Post-Western Sociology and the Japanese Case

Tarumoto Hideki

1   Introduction

Following the World System schema of Emanuel Wallerstein (2011), East Asia might not have a position at the core or the periphery but rather in the semi-periphery of the world system of academic knowledge production. Regardless of their own academic interests and activities, East Asian sociologies tend to be subject to the Western academic paradigm composed of theories, methods, languages, and customs. They might suffer from epistemic injustice such that their capacities to develop their own frameworks are discouraged (Bhargava 2013). How can East Asian academics create post-Western sociology where they can acquire more epistemic autonomy while being independent from Western academic hegemony? (see Roulleau-Berger 2016, 2021). One possible way, albeit not an exclusive one, is for academics to examine and overturn Western theoretical assumptions with reference to East Asian theories and/or empirical cases.

This chapter aims to examine a Western theoretical concept in migration studies, that is, super-diversity. Around the latter years of the 1980s, the globe entered a new era, the so-called globalized migration era where cross-border migration has become more accelerated, more diverse, and more complicated than ever before (Castles and Miller 2009). As such, it is often argued that some highly industrialized countries experience "super-diversity" in their immigration and multicultural reality. The concept has now become familiar among scholars who research multicultural situations that appear globally in the 21st century. Peláez et al. (2021) found that 78 academic papers on the subject of super-diversity were published in English and Spanish from 2007 to 2019. However, the concept of super-diversity is clearly a Western academic product. Is super-diversity a universal trend across the globe beyond the West? Does super-diversity prevail among non-Western countries too? Does super-diversity hide non-Western social realities and/or distract from non-Western academic perspectives?

To address these super-diversity puzzles, this chapter focuses on an East Asian highly industrialized country, Japan, as an empirical case, then poses three questions. Firstly, what is super-diversity in the Western academic world? Secondly, has Japan experienced super-diversity in immigration? Finally, can Japanese experiences provide any implications for post-Western sociology?

2 What Is Super-diversity?

2.1 *The British Experiences*

Firstly, we should make sure to specify what the concept of super-diversity means.[1] The pioneer research by Steven Vertovec (2007) observes British experiences in immigration between the early 1990s and the early 2000s, naming them super-diversity. Then it defines the concept of super-diversity as follows: A "level and kind of complexity surpassing anything the country has previously experienced" in immigration and multicultural diversity (Vertovec 2007: 1024). Surely, Britain had already accepted European immigrants, mainly before World War II, and subsequently received immigrants from former colonial Commonwealth countries, such as the Caribbean islands, India, Pakistan, Bangladesh, and additionally Hong Kong after 1950s. But new types of immigrants started to rush into Britain in 1990s. It is argued that these immigration flows resulted in the emergence of super-diversity in Britain.

Firstly, in terms of net immigration flow, 2,857,000 foreign-born immigrants without UK citizenship lived in the United Kingdom in 2004. This number denotes an increase of 857,000, by 40%, since 1993.

The second point is that new immigrants increasingly came from countries of origin with thin historical links to Britain in immigration. Migrants from the Old Commonwealth countries dropped from 30% (1971) to 17% (2002), and migrants from the New Commonwealth countries decreased from 32% (1971) to 20% (2002). In contrast, migrants from the European Union (EU) countries increased from 10% (1971) to 17% (2002), and migrants from Middle Eastern and other countries rose from 16% (1971) to 40% (2002).

Thirdly, languages have become diverse too. Although it is not easy to count the number of languages used, it is reported that around the year 2000,

---

[1] This chapter uses "super-diversity" rather than "super diversity" only to fit in with other concepts for a notational purpose. In addition, it does not use "hyperdiversity" because of the research tradition and its negative and uncontrollable connotation (see Meissner and Vertovec 2015).

schoolchildren in London spoke about 300 languages at home (Baker and Eversley 2000). According to other research, Turkish, Arabic, Yoruba, Akan, and Somali were mainly brought by new immigrants (Storkey 2000: 65).

Finally, the present residents in Britain mainly follow Christianity, Hinduism, Sikhism, and Islam as religions. Above all, the presence of Islam is rapidly growing, with increasing heterogeneity within the group.

2.2 Cross-cutting Sociocultural Dimensions in Great Britain

Along with the influx of immigrants, immigration channels and statuses have expanded in size and type into workers, students, family migrants, refugees, irregular migrants, and new citizens. Such myriad channels and statuses cross-cut sociocultural and economic dimensions. In gender, it is said that more female immigrants enter and stay in the receiving country, although it varies across ethnic groups. In age, new immigrants highly concentrate in the younger cohort of ages 25 to 44 years. In space and place, new immigrants tend to concentrate on specific areas like London, noting that the asylum dispersal policy and employment opportunities disperse migrants to different parts of Great Britain. In transnationalism, remittances, phone calls, transnational marriage, and engagement in the homeland development have grown significantly.

As a result, it is argued that diversity in immigration flow, countries of origin, language, and religion has produced highly diversifying transnational connections, socioeconomic positions, and legal statuses of the immigrants between and within groups.

The concept of super-diversity is "a multi-dimensional perspective on diversity" (Vertovec 2007) originating from Western origin, which leads to having a significant impact on social sciences; public policy practices, such as social work for immigrant clients; maternal welfare provisions; and other research fields, such as history (Boccagni 2015; De Bock 2015; Meissner and Vertovec 2015; Phillimore 2015). Then, it is insisted that not only Britain but also some other countries, such as the British settler country of New Zealand, have experienced super-diversity (see Spoonley 2015).

3 Has Japan Experienced Super-diversity?

3.1 Immigration Flow and Countries of Origin

As the second question of this chapter, among various countries across the globe, has the East Asian country of Japan experienced super-diversity?

Before World War II, Japan received its immigrants mainly from the colonies of the time, largely Korea and Taiwan. This type of immigrants is called Oldcomers. Although there was no influx of immigrants during the period of

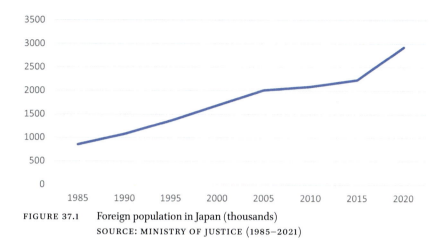

FIGURE 37.1   Foreign population in Japan (thousands)
SOURCE: MINISTRY OF JUSTICE (1985–2021)

high economic growth from the middle of the 1950s to the early 1970s, around 1980 new immigrants started to enter from various places around the globe. They are called Newcomers (Tarumoto 2015). Then, compared to 1990, the number of foreign stayers has increased rapidly: 57% (2000), 94% (2010), and 172% (2020) (Figure 37.1). As of 2020, foreign stayers account for 2.3% of the whole population in Japan.[2]

With the increase of immigrants, countries of origin are becoming diverse, especially among countries in Asia (Table 37.1). In particular, Vietnam, Nepal, and Indonesia have newly emerged as sending countries, even if they had only thinner historical links with Japan in migration flow.

TABLE 37.1   Foreign population in Japan by countries of origin (thousands)

	1985	1990	1995	2000	2005	2010	2015	2020	2020
China (Taiwan)	74.9	150.3	223.0	335.6	519.6	688.4	655.8	778.1	27.0%
Vietnam	4.1	6.2	9.1	16.9	28.9	41.4	147.0	448.1	15.5%
South/North Korea	683.3	687.9	666.4	635.3	598.7	560.8	–	–	
South Korea[a]	–	–	–	–	–	–	457.8	426.9	14.8%
Philippines	12.3	49.1	74.3	144.9	187.3	200.2	229.6	279.7	9.7%
Brazil	2.0	56.4	176.4	254.4	302.1	228.7	173.4	208.5	7.2%

a   South Korea had been in the same category as North Korea until 2011.

2   Calculated by the author based on SBIAC (2021) and the MOJ (1985–2021).

TABLE 37.1 Foreign population in Japan by countries of origin (thousands) (cont.)

	1985	1990	1995	2000	2005	2010	2015	2020	2020
Nepal	..	..	1.3	3.6	7.0	17.1	54.8	96.0	3.3%
Indonesia	1.7	3.6	7.0	19.3	25.1	24.4	36.0	66.6	2.0%
Taiwan[b]	–	–	–	–	–	–	48.7	55.9	2.3%
United States	29.0	38.4	43.2	44.9	49.4	49.8	52.3	55.8	1.9%
Thailand	2.6	6.7	16.0	29.3	37.7	38.2	45.4	53.4	1.8%
Others	18.5	70.0	117.7	179.1	255.9	248.2	321.5	418.0	14.5%
Total	850.6	1075.3	1362.4	1686.4	2011.6	2087.3	2232.2	2887.1	100.0%

b Taiwan had been in the same category as China until 2011.
SOURCE: MINISTRY OF JUSTICE (1985–2021)

3.2 *Language and Religion*

Diversity in language is developing gradually year by year. According to countries of origin in Table 37.1, a large portion of foreign residents in Japan are expected to speak Chinese, Korean, Vietnamese, Tagalog, Portuguese, Nepali, English, Thai, or Indonesian.

The central and local governments and other agencies are under pressure to deal with speakers of these multiple languages. In particular, schoolchildren who need Japanese language instruction are rapidly growing in the field of education (Fig. 37.2). In addition to children with foreign nationality, children

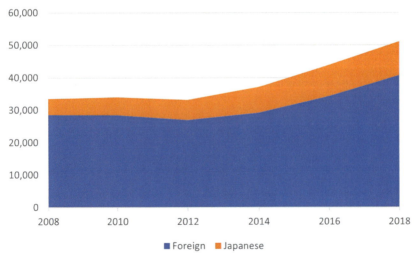

FIGURE 37.2 Foreign schoolchildren needing Japanese instruction
SOURCE: MEXT (2019, 2020)

with Japanese nationality and immigrant background could possess limited Japanese language skills. Considering both groups together, the number of these individuals increased from 33,470 (2008) to 51,126 (2018), by 53% (MEXT 2019, 2020).

Along with the influx of immigrants, the number of religions in which they believe also has increased. Among them, Islam is the one that has been rapidly increasing its presence in recent years. When the so-called bubble economy attracted illegal unskilled workers from Pakistan, Bangladesh, and Iran in the late 1980s, Japan encountered Muslim people collectively for the first time. It is estimated that the number of foreign Muslims in Japan increased from 91,744 (2011) to 152,744 (2018), a 66% rise, with Japanese Muslims reaching 43,000 (2018) (Tanada 2019: 260). The number of mosques also increased rapidly, from 4 in the early 1980s to 102 as of 2018 (Tanada 2018, 2019).

As such, there is a great deal of linguistic and religious diversity in Japan, but still fewer languages and fewer Muslims than in the United Kingdom, which is a super-diverse country.

3.3   *Immigration Channels into the Labor Market*

Along with the increasing flow and diversity in countries of origin, language, and religion, immigration channels and statuses have also become diversified in Japan.

In recent years, the number of foreign workers has risen dramatically, 3.5-fold from 486,398 (2008) to 1,724,328 (2020). A look into the labor market composition shows that foreign workers are employed through a variety of channels (Figure 37.3). As of October 2020, the foreign workers mainly consist of those who have the following types of residential status: professional and technical (359,520), designated activities (45,565), technical internship (402,356), activities beyond granted status (370,346), and status based on "position" (546,469) (see Tarumoto 2020).

Under the immigration policy principle "No introduction of unskilled foreign workers", the Ministry of Justice (MOJ) has targeted professional and technical workers primarily for introduction into the country. However, a severe labor shortage due to depopulation has opened channels for other types of workers. The Minister of Justice has some discretion to grant designated activities status to certain immigrants who are eligible to work under this status, such as working holidaymakers, construction workers, and shipbuilders.

While the official purpose of the technical internship is for foreign interns to stay in Japan to acquire skills and bring them back to their home country, activities beyond granted status are granted to a large part of foreign students who have officially come to Japan for the purpose of study. Despite their official purposes, both of them de facto make up for the shortage of unskilled

FIGURE 37.3   Foreign workers by residential status
SOURCE: MHLW (2021)

labor: While a large portion of technical interns are engaged in unskilled work without any opportunity to acquire skills, foreign students work at part-time jobs for up to 28 hours a week as permitted by law, or sometimes longer against the law.

Finally, although status based on "position" is not a residential status for workers, a large part of its holders enter into the labor market. This residential status is composed of five parts: (1) special permanent resident (for Oldcomers), (2) permanent resident, (3) spouse and child of a Japanese national, (4) spouse and child of a permanent resident, and (5) setter (granted to a large part of *Nikkeijin*, Japanese returnees from Latin America).

3.4   *Cross-cutting Sociocultural Dimensions*

The next issue is whether there has been any development in diversity outside the labor market or not. Asylum seekers/refugees and new citizens seem to be exceptions to the development for Japan. Conventionally, Japan has granted refugee status to a very small number of applicants, 20 cases (2017), 42 cases (2018), 44 cases (2019), and 47 cases (2020) in recent years. This has provoked severe criticism that the numbers are too small for an advanced country (Tarumoto 2019). In new citizens, the number of naturalizations has remained stable at a low value, like 9,074 cases (2018) and 8,453 cases (2019).

Concerning gender, Japan has received a significant number of female migrants, such as Filipino entertainers, since the 1980s. The number of female migrants has been relatively stable: it comprised 53% of total foreign residents in 2008 and 50% in June 2020. In terms of age, foreign residents in Japan concentrate in the age cohort of 25 to 44 years, comprising more than 90% of the total foreign population in July 2020. These gender- and age-related characteristics are similar to those of super-diversity.[3]

Just like in the London area in Britain, some specific spaces and places in Japan attract far more immigrants than others. Out of all 47 prefectures in Japan, only 7 of them—Saitama, Chiba, Tokyo, Kanagawa, Aichi, Osaka, and Hyogo—accounted for 63% of foreign stayers in 2019.[4] Moreover, some cities and towns hold a large number of foreign residents, thus having led to the establishment of the Committee for Cities with Concentrated Foreign Population in order to discuss various issues concerning foreign residents (Tarumoto 2018).

Due to a lack of data, it is not clear to what degree transnationalism has developed along with the immigration flows to Japan. One piece of evidence can be drawn from cases of so-called international marriage, where a Japanese person marries a foreign partner across borders of nationality. While international marriage was only 1 in 100 (0.9%) in 1980, it has since risen to 1 in 27 (3.7%) couples married in 2019.[5]

As another example, Burmese refugees had engaged in democratic campaigns for their own country beyond the national border from the late 1980s to 2010. The democratic campaigns resumed against the newly emerged military government after the coup d'état in February 2021, making a demonstration in Tokyo on the "Day of Origin of the Democratization Movement", August 8, 2021, for example (NHK 2021). This shows one piece of evidence that political transnationalism emerges in Japan. As a result, it has been found that the Japanese experiences above ride along similar lines to the super-diversity discourses stating that increasing channels and statuses of immigrants cross-cut sociocultural dimensions.

4 Some Implications on Super-diversity

4.1 *Deepening Diversity*

Regarding super-diversity, what implication can we draw from the Japanese case? As mentioned earlier, Japan has accepted not only Oldcomers but also the increasing number of Newcomers from countries with little historical connection to Japan. Along with the immigration flow, speakers of foreign languages and religious believers have also increased and diversified, with a rapid

---

3 The ratios in gender and age are calculated by the author based on the MOJ (1985–2021).
4 The ratio in prefecture is calculated by the author based on the MOJ (1985–2021).
5 The ratios of international marriage are calculated by the author based on the MHLW (1980–2019).

increase in the presence of Muslims especially. Foreigners staying in the country are concentrated in the younger age groups of between 25 and 44 years, and in certain regions and spaces, such as 7 prefectures and member cities/towns of the Committee for Cities with Concentrated Foreign Population. Transnationalism has developed, as illustrated by examples such as international marriage and transnational political movements.

These phenomena clearly show that Japan has experienced a deepening diversity in immigration, following other industrialized countries, such as Britain.

4.2 Is It Super-diversity?

If Japan's increasing diversity has followed that of other industrialized countries, can we conclude that super-diversity emerges in Japan as well? There are some points left to be explored. Even if immigration flows are larger and countries of origins became more diverse than before, the scale of immigration and the range of countries of origin are not as great as in some other industrialized countries: foreign residents in Japan consist of 2.3% of the total population, and they are mainly from Asian countries. In particular, there are fewer Middle Eastern immigrants in Japan today, a group that has contributed greatly to creating super-diversity in Britain.

In a similar manner, even after Newcomers started to enter and stay in Japan, they brought fewer kinds of language with them. In terms of religion, not as many immigrants have brought Islam to Japan. Certainly, immigration channels and statuses became diverse in Japan as well, but the proportions of unskilled workers, recognized refugees, and new citizens remain smaller. Finally in transnationalism, even if there are some cases of international marriage and political transnationalism, Japan can be estimated to have fewer transnational activities of immigrants than advanced immigrant-receiving countries.

As such, these facts suggest that although diversity is deepening in Japan, the level and scope of diversity are limited. In other words, even though Japan experienced a certain degree of diversity, it was not super-diverse when it came to immigration. This finding brought with it a new challenge: the need to elaborate conceptually and theoretically on the relationship between super-diversity and other forms of diversity.

5 Constructing a Diversity Framework

5.1 *Medium-diversity*

The concept of super-diversity primarily refers to the increasing spread, speed, and scale of migration-related diversification processes and can be a malleable Western lens to guide the research process (Meissner 2015), but it is not the only type of migration-related diversity and still requires specifying its meaning with relation to diversity in general. East Asian perspectives and experiences could contribute to the development of this Western concept. The Japanese case strongly suggests that it is required to clarify the types of diversity in society. Above all, it is necessary to distinguish super-diversity and other forms of diversity that have not yet reached super-diversity regarding their size and degree of difference.

As can be seen in the Table 37.2, super-diversity refers to societies that have experienced large-scale migration and where the migrants have made greater differences than before. Then, we need to set up a type of society in which differences due to migration are large but the scale of migration is smaller. Here we propose to name the type "medium-diversity", after the Chinese idea *Zhōngyōng*.[6] According to the Analects, Confucius (1999) first identified *Zhōngyōng* as the highest virtue in the 5th or 6th century BC, saying that *Zhōngyōng* means not extremes and excesses but moderation and fairness, which has always been rare among people. Medium-diversity is not only consistent with the Japanese experiences, but is also likely to apply to other cases—for example, the Belgian city of Ghent accepting Mediterranean immigrants from 1960 to 1980 (De Bock 2015), housing experiences of immigrants in a neighborhood of Istanbul (Biehl 2015), and diversification processes in Mexico (Acosta-García and Martínez-Ortiz 2015), among others.

In addition, Table 37.2 represents two other types, in addition to super-diversity and medium-diversity. Of the two types, the first indicates societies in which numbers of immigrants are large but differences bought about by immigration are small. This type can be called plurality. The second type refers to societies where the scale of immigration is small and differences created by immigration are small. This type can be named homogeneity.

TABLE 37.2 Types of diversity and beyond

Scale of immigration	Difference of immigrants	
	Large	Small
Large	Super-diversity	Plurality
Small	Medium-diversity	Homogeneity

---

6 Acosta-García and Martínez-Ortiz (2015) use the term "already-existed diversity" prior to super-diversity. Although the term seems to share a part of the idea in medium-diversity, it refers to diversity that only people of indigenous or African descent create in Mexico without undertaking a theoretical exploration.

This diversity framework pursues addressing the actual pattern of societies, with clarifying some assumptions behind the super-diversity discourses.[7]

6 Conclusion: Towards a Post-Western Sociology on Migration

With reference to the Japanese experiences, this chapter examines the Western theoretical concept of super-diversity, then proposes a framework on diversity in immigration, including the type of medium-diversity. This theoretical proposal pursues avoiding some epistemic injustice based on the academic World system, realizing the plural epistemic autonomy of East Asian sociology, and creating intercultural spaces for active dialogue between East Asian and Western sociologies. However, it is followed by some challenges to establishing post-Western sociology.

Firstly, we should elucidate criteria to distinguish super-diversity, medium-diversity, and two other types of diversity in the framework. To ensure this, the number of and difference in immigrants could be clues. Secondly, the period and timing of the observations must be clearly defined. Finally, it should be examined whether super-diversity leads to positive effects on the society, like conviviality (see Padilla et al. 2015) in East Asia or not.

Overall, the examination of super-diversity contributes to an understanding of unprecedented social change and social transformation under globalized migration. Moreover, it must lead to the advancement of the intervals between East Asian and Western sociologies to create post-Western sociology.

References

Acosta-García, Raúl, and Esperanza Martínez-Ortiz. 2015. "Mexico Through a Super Diversity Lens: Already-Existing Diversity Meets New Immigration". *Ethnic and Racial Studies* 38 (4): 636–649.

Baker, Philip, and John Eversley. 2000. "The Languages of London's Schoolchildren". In *Multilingual Capital: The Languages of London's Schoolchildren and Their Relevance to Economic, Social and Educational Policies*, edited by Philip Baker and John Eversley, 5–60. London: Battlebridge.

Bhargava, Rajeev. 2013. "Pour en finir avec l'injustice épistémique du colonialisme". *Socio* 1: 41–75.

---

[7] The framework presented in this chapter does not deal with theories of diversity as described by Hartmann and Gerteis (2005).

Biehl, Kristen Sarah. 2015. "Spatializing Diversities, Diversifying Spaces: Housing Experiences and Home Space Perceptions in a Migrant Hub of Istanbul". *Ethnic and Racial Studies* 38 (4): 596–607.
Boccagni, Paolo. 2015. "(Super)diversity and the Migration-Social Work Nexus: A New Lens on the Field of Access and Inclusion?" *Ethnic and Racial Studies* 38 (4): 608–620.
Castles, Stephen, and Mark J. Miller. 2009. *The Age of Migration: International Population Movements in the Modern World*. 4th ed. Basingstoke: Palgrave Macmillan.
Confucius. [1963] 1999. *Analects* [Japanese translation]. Tokyo: Iwanami Shoten.
De Bock, Jozefien. 2015. "Not All the Same After All? Super Diversity as a Lens for the Study of Past Migrations". *Ethnic and Racial Studies* 38 (4): 583–595.
Hartmann, Douglas, and Joseph Gerteis. 2005. "Dealing with Diversity: Mapping Multiculturalism in Sociological Terms". *Sociological Theory* 23 (2): 218–240.
Meissner, Fran. 2015. "Migration in Migration-Related Diversity? The Nexus between Super diversity and Migration Studies". *Ethnic and Racial Studies* 38 (4): 556–567.
Meissner, Fran, and Steven Vertovec. 2015. "Comparing Super-Diversity". *Ethnic and Racial Studies* 38 (4): 541–555.
Ministry of Education, Culture, Sports, Science and Technology (MEXT). 2019. "Results of the 'Survey on the Acceptance of Pupils in Need of Japanese Language Instruction (FY2008)'". Accessed July 30, 2021. https://www.mext.go.jp/content/1421569002.pdf.
MEXT. 2020. "Corrections to the results of the 'Survey on the Acceptance of Students who Need Japanese Language Instruction (Fiscal Year 2008)'". Press release. Accessed July 30, 2021. https://www.mext.go.jp/b_menu/houdou/31/09/1421569_00001.htm.
Ministry of Health, Labor and Welfare (MHLW). 1980–2019. "The Statistics of Population Survey" [in Japanese]. Accessed August 3, 2021. https://www.Mhlw.go.jp/toukei/list/81-1.html.
MEXT. 2021. "A Summary of Reports on 'Employment Situation of Foreigners' (As of the End of October 2020)" [in Japanese]. Accessed July 31, 2021. https://www.mhlw.go.jp/stf/newpage16279.html.
Ministry of Justice (MOJ). 1985–2021. "The Statistics on Foreign Residents" [in Japanese]. Accessed July 30, 2021. http://www.moj.go.jp/isa/policies/statistics/toukei_ichiran_touroku.html.
NHK (Japan Broadcasting Corporation). 2021. "Protest Demonstrations in Tokyo on Myanmar's 'Day of Origin of the Democratisation Movement' (August 8 2021)". Accessed August 10 2021. https://www3.nhk.or.jp/news/html/20210808/k10013189631000.html.
Padilla, Beatriz, Joana Azevedo, and Antonia Olmos-Alcaraz. 2015. "Super diversity and Conviviality: Exploring Frameworks for Doing Ethnography in Southern European Intercultural Cities". *Ethnic and Racial Studies* 38 (4): 621–635.
Peláez, Antonio López, María Victoria Aguilar-Tablada, Amaya Erro-Garcés, and Raquel María Pérez-García. 2021. "Super Diversity and Social Policies in a Complex Society:

Social Challenges in the 21st Century". *Current Sociology.* https://doi.org/10.1177/00113921209833344.

Phillimore, Jenny. 2015. "Delivering Maternity Services in an Era of Super diversity: The Challenges of Novelty and Newness". *Ethnic and Racial Studies* 38 (4): 568–582.

Roulleau-Berger, Laurence. 2016. *Post-Western Revolution in Sociology: From China to Europe.* Translated by Nigel Briggs. Leiden and Boston, MA: Brill.

Roulleau-Berger, Laurence. 2021. "The Fabric of Post-Western Sociology: Ecologies of Knowledge beyond the 'East' and the 'West'". *The Journal of Chinese Sociology* 8 (1): 1–28.

Spoonley, Paul. 2015. "New Diversity, Old Anxieties in New Zealand: The Complex Identity Politics and Engagement of a Settler Society". *Ethnic and Racial Studies* 38 (4): 650–661.

Statistics Bureau, Ministry of Internal Affairs and Communications (SBIAC). 2021. "The Estimate of the Population: The Report in June 2021" [in Japanese]. June 21 2021. Accessed July 30, 2021. https://www.stat.go.jp/data/jinsui/pdf/202106.pdf.

Storkey, Marian. 2000. "Using the Schools Language Data to Estimate the Total Numbers of Speakers of London's Top 40 Languages". In *Multilingual Capital: The Languages of London's Schoolchildren and Their Relevance to Economic, Social and Educational Policies,* edited by Philip Baker and John Eversley, 63–66. London: Battlebridge.

Tanada, Hirofumi. 2018. "Islamic Religious Groups and Community in Japan" [in Japanese]. *Social Analysis* 45: 75–94.

Tanada, Hirofumi. 2019. "Estimate of Muslim Population in the World and Japan, 2018" [in Japanese]. *Waseda Journal of Human Sciences* 32 (2): 253–262.

Tarumoto, Hideki. 2015. "Emergence et gestion des nouvelles tendances migratoires: le cas Japon". *Migration Société* 27 (157): 97–109. Translated from the English by Catherine Wihtol de Wenden and Myrna Giovanella.

Tarumoto, Hideki. "The Limits of Local Citizenship in Japan". In *International Migrations and Local Governance: A Global Perspective,* edited by Thomas Lacroix and Amandine Desille, 191–213. London: Palgrave Macmillan.

Tarumoto, Hideki. 2019. "Why Restrictive Refugee Policy Can Be Retained? A Japanese Case". *Migration and Development* 8 (1): 7–24.

Tarumoto, Hideki. 2020. "Immigrant Acceptance in an Ethnic Country: The Foreign Labor Policies of Japan". In *The Wiley Blackwell Companion to Race, Ethnicity, and Nationalism,* edited by John Stone, Rutledge Dennis, Polly Rizova, and Xiaoshuo Hou, 379–401. Hoboken, NJ: John Wiley & Sons.

Vertovec, Steven. 2007. "Super-diversity and Its Implications". *Ethnic and Racial Studies* 30 (6): 1024–1054.

Wallerstein, Immanuel. (1974) 2011. *The Modern World-System: Capitalist Agriculture and the Origins of the European World-Economy in the Sixteenth Century.* Berkeley: University of California Press.

CHAPTER 38

Spatial Confinement of Migrant Workers in Korea

Choi Jongryul

1 The Myth of Temporariness and Isolation: Policies on Migrant Workers

Migrant workers have increasingly become a conspicuous presence in Korea since the late 1980s. As of December 2019, the number of foreign residents is about 2.5 million, representing 4.9% of the nation's total population. Among foreign residents, migrant workers account for most foreign residents. Right before the 1988 Summer Olympics in Seoul, Korea had maintained a strong border control policy, especially prohibiting any low-skilled laborers from entering the Korean labor market. But the Korean government opened the gate temporarily during the 1988 Summer Olympics in order to draw foreign tourists, and hundreds of thousands of Asians entered Korea on a visitor's visa and did not return home even when their visa expired. At the time, Korea was suffering from a severe labor shortage in the so-called 3-D (dirty, difficult, and dangerous) jobs, and small- and mid-sized firms tried to solve this problem by employing Asian migrant workers. But hiring low-skilled migrant workers was legally banned then, and thus Asian migrant workers naturally became "illegal migrant workers". The Korean government tolerated this illegal hiring of migrant workers for economic reasons. Without any systematic policy on migrant workers, illegal migrant workers suffered from delayed payment of wages, extremely poor working conditions, industrial accidents, physical and verbal abuse, sexual harassment, etc. (Yoo 2005).

In November 1991, the Korean government finally introduced the Industrial Skill Trainee Program (ISTP), which allows overseas-invested firms to introduce their workers into Korea under the legal status of trainee. Authorized duration of stay under this program is six months, but it can be extended up to six additional months. While the main beneficiaries of ISTP were large overseas-invested enterprises, small- and medium-sized firms could not find a legitimate means of hiring foreign labor. Therefore, the Korean government introduced the Industrial Trainee System (ITS) in November 1993 to help resolve the labor shortage problem in small- and medium-sized firms. Under ITS, migrant workers could work as trainees for a period of one year, and the training period could be extended for another year when necessary.

But migrant "trainees" were not protected by any Korean labor law because of their status as trainee. Under very limited legal protection, trainees suffered from severe labor exploitation, which forced most of them to flee from their designated workplaces to ones that exploited them less. In this way, most trainees became undocumented migrant workers, a situation that seems to be taken advantage of by small- and medium-sized firms as well as the Korean government. But this short-sighted policy was soon faced with strong protests from non-governmental organizations and the media because of the inhumane treatment of migrant workers (Kim 2011), and even migrant workers' own union movements (Grey 2007). Reluctantly, the Korean government partially amended ITS to allow trainees to acquire the status of worker after working as a trainee for a certain period. In 2000, a 2 + 1 system (2 years as trainee and 1 year as worker) was carried out; it was changed to a 1 + 2 system (1 year as trainee and 2 years as worker) in 2002 until its absorption into EPS in 2007. This revision was not a systematic migration policy but a short-term supply-and-demand policy for migrant workers (Kong, Yoon and Yu 2010). But the real problem lies in the fact that labor shortage is not a temporary and transitory incident; rather, it a chronic structural problem intimately related to the loss of Korea's comparative advantage in low labor costs within the world economy system (Kim 2004) and to the limited domestic supply of unskilled workers mainly due to the aging of the Korean population and the country's low birth rate (Kim 2009; Kim and Torres-Gil 2009).

On October 17, 2004, the Korean government finally implemented the Employment Permit System, which allows Korean employers who cannot hire domestic workers to legally hire migrant workers. Under EPS, migrant workers can work legally for less than 3 years, after which they should return to their home country. Those who leave Korea after working for three years, however, can re-enter after six months from their departure and work for an additional three years. If employers want to continue to hire their migrant workers after the initial three-year visa period expires, those workers can re-enter Korea and work for three years more after only one month from their departure. Seemingly, migrant workers under EPS are stipulated to be protected by labor laws and hence treated the same as domestic workers, and migrant workers could file a suit in court if their employers violated the law (Kim 2011). But in reality, EPS restricts migrant workers to working in only four areas: the manufacturing industry, the construction industry, agriculture and stockbreeding, and the fishing industry. Furthermore, migrant workers cannot change their workplace more than three times during their three-year stay, and only twice after their sojourn beyond the initial three-year period. If a migrant worker is not employed by a new employer within three months of termination from previous employment, he or she must leave the country. Considering the supply-and-demand aspect of the labor market, the Foreign Workforce Policy Committee established under the Office of the Prime Minister annually determines important issues, such as the number of migrant workers needed, industries in need of migrant workers, the countries chosen to send migrant workers to Korea, etc. As of 2010, there are 15 countries with which the Korean government signed a bilateral employment permit agreement: Bangladesh, Cambodia, China, East Timor, Indonesia, Kyrgyzstan, Mongolia, Myanmar, Nepal, Pakistan, Sri Lanka, Thailand, the Philippines, Uzbekistan, and Vietnam (Shin 2011).

EPS was originally established in order to change the status of undocumented migrant workers into that of legitimate migrant workers, but its actual implementation proceeded according to the three principles of the nation-state's economic growth as follows rather than for the benefit of migrant workers. First is the principle of displacement, according to which employers can employ migrant workers only in the areas in which domestic workers cannot be found, resulting in migrant workers' over-concentration in 3-D jobs. In this sense, EPS severely restricts migrant workers' freedom to choose their jobs and workplaces. Second is the principle of supplementation that stipulates employers should hire domestic workers first and migrant workers can be hired only when domestic workers cannot be hired, which threatens the job security and stability of migrant workers. Last is the principle of anti-settlement, the most important clause of EPS, the goal of which is the prevention of migrant workers from settling down permanently in Korea by restricting their sojourn period to a maximum of 3 years. Migrant workers who leave Korea after having worked under EPS cannot be employed again under EPS unless they stay outside of Korea for 6 months or more (June 2009).

On April 10, 2010, the Ministry of Employment and Labor revised the Act on Foreign Workers' Employment in order to solve the potential problem of a re-increase in illegal residents as the first EPS was about to expire. One of the most significant changes is in the requirement for reemployment: The previous condition of reemployment was that a migrant worker may be reemployed after leaving Korea for at least one month (originally six months when EPS was first established). However, this clause has since been changed so that migrant workers could be reemployed for two more years without having to leave Korea for one month. Originally, an employer had to submit an application for a migrant worker's reemployment 30 days prior to the expiration of employment, but this has been changed to 45 days before the expiration of employment. This aims to provide migrant workers with some avenue of predicting what the near future holds for them. As well, in cases where migrant workers have to change their workplace due to unavoidable situations, they are required to receive permission to do so from the Korean government, and the period for receiving permission for this has changed from two months to three months, which gives migrant workers one more month to sojourn in Korea even if their application is rejected. In addition, it is no longer counted as a change of workplace if migrant workers cannot continue their work due to circumstances beyond their control, including the workplace going out of business.

In July 2012, the Korean government passed a special revision in re-entry employment restrictions. Before this revision, foreign migrant workers had to voluntarily leave Korea when their employment period of a maximum of 4 years and 10 months end, and to become employed again, they had to re-enter Korea 6 months later and go through the procedure of searching for a job again. Under the revised law, if an employer applies for re-employing a foreign migrant worker and that worker also wishes to continue working there, the foreign migrant worker can re-enter Korea three months after leaving it and work again for a maximum of 4 years and 10 months. This is because Korean businesses that relied on cheap foreign labor suffered tremendously when foreign migrant workers returned to their hometowns when their legal sojourn period ended. Thus, the Korean government has adopted a policy of extending the length of legal residence of foreign migrant workers in Korea by making exceptions that change the legal status of residence of foreign migrant workers.

Since then, Korean government has continued to revise regulations on the legitimate sojourn of foreign migrant workers in Korea under the name of multicultural society. Nevertheless, Korean government did not fundamentally change its policy of requiring foreign migrant workers to go back to their countries of origin after the legally permitted period of sojourn because the main purpose of its policy revision is to meet the needs of small- and medium-sized businesses that permanently need (un-)skilled foreign laborers to fill the shortage of domestic workers in 3-D jobs, not to encourage multicultural society in Korea. EPS is, in fact, very similar to Europe's guest worker system or temporary foreign worker policies (TFWPs) in terms of its narrow economic view, such as the anti-settlement and short-term rotation policies (Castles 1986, 2006; Lin 2009; Martin and Miller 1980). Like many Western European states that wrongly assume "the economic man could be divorced for the purposes of public policy from the social, political, and cultural being" (Martin and Miller 1980: 327), the Korean government is trying to import labor, not people. Migrant workers in Korea under EPS cannot legally reside in Korea permanently, let alone sojourn long-term. They are treated as cheap disposable commodities that can make Korea's small- and mid-sized firms survive longer in global competition. In this respect, EPS is based on the so-called "myth of temporariness", i.e., "the belief that migration is motivated by short-term economic considerations and will not lead to long-term settlement" (Castles 1998: 221). This myth is intimately associated with another "myth of isolation", according to which migrant workers are supposed to migrate by themselves without families, work in designated workplaces isolated from society, and voluntarily go back to their countries of origin before their visas expire. Migrant workers are expected to be "asocial atomic economic individuals" who are totally severed from the network of home and not able to make any networks in Korea.

2   Absolute Juridical Strangers

In spite of this short-sighted economic view of migrant workers, undocumented migrant workers have emerged as a social force in Korea. Korea has been increasingly dependent on "temporary" migrant labor in meeting the "permanent demand for workers who are willing to labor under unpleasant conditions, at low wages, with great instability, and facing little chance for advancement" (Massey et al. 1993: 443). On the one hand, the Korean government has tried to exercise a high level of control over temporary documented workers in order to prevent them from being illegal residents. On the other hand, the Korean government has tolerated the employment of undocumented migrant workers for economic gain. It is not easy to ask small- or mid-sized firms to relinquish the profits obtained through poor wages and poor working conditions under which undocumented migrant workers work.

EPS seems to have succeeded in the short term, but undocumented migrant workers begin to settle in specific neighborhoods and form ethnic minority groups. The official ideology of the state has denied that ethnic minority groups exist in Korea. This denial is based on the historical belief in the natural correspondence between the nation and the state. The nation is imagined as a cultural community (of same language and history) with its own territorial political authority, i.e., the state. Korean nationals' belief that we are all siblings descended from one great ancestor used to serve the function of denying and repressing class fissures and status discrimination among Koreans.

But the financial crisis in 1997 and the following neoliberal transformation of Korean society began to shatter this belief in an unrecoverable manner. Under the pressure from the IMF, the Korean government implemented labor market flexibilization as a means for economic recovery and regrowth. As one route towards more flexibility, the Korean government increased atypical or non-standard forms of employment, which led to a strong segmentation of the labor market. As a consequence, labor contracts became less stable, less guaranteed, and contained lower wages, robbing Korean nationals of job security. As this neoliberal regulation spread throughout society, all kinds of inequalities in terms of class, age, region, gender, education, etc., that had been repressed began to abruptly manifest themselves and tear Koreans apart. Rather than caring for nationals, the Korean government accelerated universal deregulation, such as "the unbound freedom granted to capital and finance at the expense of all other freedoms" (Bauman 1997: 22), which in turn aggravated the process of polarization (Kim 2004; Park 2012).

The myth of nationalism—that the nation-state will take care of all nationals—is beginning to be shaken from its roots. Under this gloomy circumstance, Korean nationals are uncomfortably witnessing the advent of an increasing number of undocumented migrant workers in their "precious territory". The advent of undocumented migrant workers is challenging the modern notion of the social, introducing ambiguity and contingency into the binary modern order of nationals and non-nationals. The nation-state hires undocumented migrant workers to perform "dirty jobs" that no nationals want to do, but the meaning of their existence has yet to be established, or it is reduced to their juridical status, i.e., potential criminals: "The Semantic under- and/or over-determination of the strangers corrupted neat divisions and marred the signposts" (Bauman 1997: 18). It is this feature of undocumented migrant workers that challenges the modern notion of the social, the natural correspondence between nation and state.

In order to preserve the modern notion of the social, the Korean government invented a new form of sociation, ethnic labor. To ethnic laborers, ethnic and national solidarity are forever forbidden by the nation-state. Ethnic laborers are juridically confined to designated places where they produce something useful, like productive hens within a tiny overcrowded henhouse. The nation-state coerces them to preserve their tribal, primitive, and backward ethnie from which their usefulness for the nation-state comes. The strangehood they want to preserve and the one the nation-state wants are contradictory, and if this contradiction worsens, organized racism might arise.

Classical sociology assumes that strangers are (potential) citizens or denizens despite their foreign origin. It supposes that their structural status of "inbetweenness" would give them special benefits that are not available to normal members of the host society. Simmel's "strangers" are Jewish people living in Germany; their "special union of closeness and remoteness" makes them enjoy their special benefits, such as mobility, objectivity, and freedom: as a potential wanderer, the stranger "is the freer man, practically and theoretically. He views his relation to others with less prejudice; he submits them to more general, more objective standards, and he is not confined in his action by customs, piety or precedents" (Simmel 1971: 146).

Park's "marginal man" is the Jewish person living in urban cities, liberated from the walls of medieval ghettos,

> a cultural hybrid, a man living and sharing intimately in the cultural life and traditions of a two distinct peoples.... He was a man on the margin of two cultures and two societies, which never completely interpenetrated and fused. The emancipated Jew was, and is, historically and typically the marginal man, the first cosmopolite and citizen of the world.
> PARK 1928: 892

Schütz's "stranger" is the newcomer who is eager to adjust himself to new circumstances, "an adult individual ... who tries to be permanently accepted or at least tolerated by the group which he approaches" (Schütz 1944: 499). The first time he approaches the host society, he has a difficult time in defining the situation, mainly due to the lack of a natural attitude toward the cultural pattern of group life. "[T]he cultural pattern of the approached group is to the stranger not a shelter but a field of adventure, not a matter of course but a questionable topic of investigation, not an instrument for disentangling problematic situations but a problematic situation itself and one hard to master" (Schütz 1944: 506). This initial process, of course, includes "his own bitter experience of the limits of the 'thinking as usual', which has taught him that a man may lose his status, his rules of guidance, and even his history and that the normal way of life is always far less guaranteed than it seems" (Schütz 1944: 507), but paradoxically, it will give him objectivity. Certainly, Schütz's emphasis is on the possibility that the process of adjustment is one of the accumulation of an enlarged and adjusted stock of experiences. In this sense, the stranger can enjoy his special traits of objectivity and cultural hybridity.

This classical sociology of strangers is limited in accounting for undocumented migrant workers in Korea where, unfortunately, they cannot enjoy their structural status of "inbetweenness" at all. Undocumented migrant workers are not the Simmelian cosmopolitan strangers with mobility, objectivity, and freedom; they are confined to designated workplaces, with their possibilities juridically blocked. They are also not Park's marginal man, a cultural hybridity, because they left their home but are denied participation in the Korean way of cultural life. They are forbidden to mix their culture with Korean culture. Lastly, they are not Schütz's stranger, who can enjoy the adventure of adjustment into the approached group; they are forced to stick to poor workplaces as working machines. In short, undocumented migrant workers are not the strangers characterized by the classical sociology of strangers, "the insiders-outsiders who have access to a different type of knowledge not available to insiders" (Marotta 2002: 45).

Undocumented migrant workers should preserve their strangehood because the reason they can stay in Korea is their usefulness as strangers: "They are useful precisely in their capacity as strangers; their strangehood is to be protected and caringly preserved" (Bauman 1997: 30). They are "absolute strangers" who

> are not estranged from their world, because the world where they live has never been theirs.... Their relation to the world is accidental, for the territory of their actions has nothing to do with their roots, upbringing, and tradition. Moreover, the whole world around them, with all their ranks and classes, is alien to their own tradition.
> HELLER 2000: 150

If they want to stay in Korea as long as they wish, they should maintain their status of absolute stranger to the utmost because their usefulness comes from it. The best way to make undocumented migrant workers preserve their strangehood is spatial confinement, "the prime method of dealing with the unassimilable, difficult-to-control, and otherwise trouble-prone sectors of the population" (Bauman 1998: 106). As "slaves were confined to the slave quarters" (Bauman 1998: 106), so too should undocumented migrant workers be confined to designated workplaces. Thus, they cannot accumulate human capital to help them move upward or social capital to help them settle in Korea. If they lose their strangehood by way of accumulating human and social capital, then their existence in Korea will be jeopardized.

3   Concluding Remarks

When migrant workers enter Korea, they are not considered as future citizens or long-term residents; they are expected to leave soon. In this sense, they are supposed to be conditional strangers whose ultimate orientation is back toward their home countries. Following this supposition, through the rigid enforcement of laws the Korean government has attempted to prevent migrant workers from forming ethnic minority groups. Undocumented migrant workers are determined and maintained by their juridical status with regard to the nation-state. They are without legal entitlement to settle in Korea, which gives them a unique existence as illegalized outsiders. The Korean government imported migrant workers to meet Korea's needs but has forced them to remain as absolute strangers forever via having an accidental relationship with Korean society. The Korean government in particular and Koreans in general want migrant workers to perform dirty jobs forever. Migrant workers are "servants" who are invited to work in menial dead-end jobs, not fellow humans who can construct a cosmopolitan society together.

For Koreans, migrant workers from Asia appear "to be far too 'traditional', too 'backward', too community-oriented, too little educated, and unskilled" (Karakayali 2006: 326). Koreans seem to think that Asian migrant workers deserve the most primitive, dirtiest tasks which too modernized, too forward, too individuality-oriented, too educated, and highly skilled Koreans do not want to perform. A grotesque mixture of racialism and modernism is underpinning Korea's imaginary of the social, in which a polarized, dichotomous symbolic structure of modern versus traditional, productive versus unproductive, superior versus inferior is widely used among Korean nationals (cf. Alexander 2004; Choi and Choi 2012).

Undocumented migrant workers are "absolute juridical strangers" who are forced to live as atomic economic individuals without a past or a future. They exist in the eternal present, only laboring in designated workplaces without mobility. They do not have a home to go back to because they lost it permanently, mainly due to political or economic reasons. They are forbidden to become members of the political community by the nation-state. Like ethnic groups, they want to maintain their own ethnie. But unlike ethnic groups, they cannot preserve their own ethnie because the nation-state does not allow them to form their own ethnic groups. In this sense, undocumented migrant workers disturb the natural identity of exclusive territorial authority and national rights (Fraser 2005).

References

Alexander, J.C. 2004. "Rethinking Strangeness: From Structures in Space to Discourse in Civil Society". *Thesis Eleven* 79: 87–104.

Bauman, Z. 1997. "The Making and Unmaking of Strangers". In *Postmodernity and Its Discontents*, edited by Z. Bauman, 17–34. Oxford: Blackwell.

Bauman, Z. 1998. *Globalization: The Human Condition*. Cambridge: Polity.

Castles, S. 1986. "The Guest-Worker in Western Europe: An Obituary". *International Migration Review* 20 (4): 761–778.

Castles, S. 1998. "New Migration in the Asia-Pacific Region: A Force for Social And Political Change". *International Social Science Journal* 156: 215–227.

Castles, S. 2006. "Guestworkers in Europe: A Resurrections?" *International Migration Review* 40 (4): 741–766.
Choi, J., and I. Choi. 2012. "T'alyŏngt'ohwa toen konggong changso esŏ 'esŭnisit'i chŏnsi hagi': Ansan e daehan kwan'gwanggaek ŭi munhwa kisuljijŏk tansangdŭl" ["Displaying ethnicity" in Deterritorialized Public Places: A Tourist's Ethnographic Fragments in Ansan]. *Han'guk sahoehak* [Korean Journal of Sociology] 46 (4): 1–44.
Fraser, N. 2005. "Reframing Justice in a Globalizing World". *New Left Review* 36: 1–19.
Grey, K. 2007. "From Human to Workers' Rights: The Emergence of a Migrant Workers' Union Movement in Korea". *Global Society* 21 (2): 297–315.
Heller, A. 2000. "The Absolute Stranger: Shakespeare and the Drama of Failed Assimilation". *Critical Horizons* 1 (1): 147–167.
Jun, H.B. 2009. "Oegugin kŭlloja koyong chŏngch'aek" [Employment Policy on Migrant Workers in Korea]. *Chŏsŭt'isŭ* [Justice] 109: 290–315.
Karakayali, N. 2006. "The Uses of the Stranger: Circulation, Arbitration, Secrecy, and Dirt". *Sociological Theory* 24 (4): 312–330.
Kim, A.E. 2009. "Global Migration and South Korea: Foreign Workers, Foreign Brides and the Making of a Multicultural Society". *Ethnic and Racial Studies* 32 (1): 70–92.
Kim, B.J., and F. Torres-Gil. 2009. "Aging and Immigration: The Case of South Korea (With a Look at Italy and Japan)". *Generations* 32 (4): 80–86.
Kim, D. 2011. "Promoting Migrants' Rights in South Korea: NGOs and the Enactment of the Employment Permit System". *Asian and Pacific Migration Journal* 20 (1): 55–78.
Kim, W.B. 2004. "Migration of Foreign Workers Into South Korea: From Periphery to Semi-Periphery in the Global Labor Market". *Asian Survey* 44 (2): 316–335.
Kong, D., K. Yoon, and S. Yu. 2010. "The Social Dimensions of Immigration in Korea". *Journal of Contemporary Asia* 40 (2): 252–274.
Lin, T.C. 2009. "Will South Korea Follow the German Experience? Democracy, the Migratory Process, and the Prospects for Permanent Immigration in Korea". *Korean Studies* 32: 28–55.
Marotta, V. 2002. "Zygmunt Bauman: Order, Strangehood and Freedom". *Thesis Eleven* 70: 36–54.
Martin, P.L., and M.J. Miller. 1980. "Guestworkers: Lessons From Western Europe". *Industrial and Labor Relations Review* 33 (3): 315–330.
Massey, D.S., J. Arango, G. Hugo, A. Kouaouci, A. Pellegrino, and J.E. Taylor. 1993. "Theories of International Migration: A Review and Appraisal". *Population and Development Review* 19 (3): 431–466.
Park, K. 2012. "Neoliberalization of the National Institutional Framework of Immigration Policies in the Era of Transnationalism: The Case of South Korea". *Journal of the Korean Urban Geographical Society* 15: 141–161.
Park, R.E. 1928. "Human Migration and the Marginal Man". *American Journal of Sociology* 33 (6): 881–893.

Schütz, A. 1944. "The Stranger: An Essay in Social Psychology". *American Journal of Sociology* 49 (6): 499–507.
Shin, J.J., ed. 2011. *Key Migration Issues for the Republic of Korea, 2010*. Seoul: International Organization for Migration.
Simmel, G. 1971. "The Stranger". In *On Individuality and Social Forms*, edited by D.N. Levine, 143–149. Chicago, IL: The University of Chicago Press.
Yoo, K.S. 2005. *Foreign Workers in the Republic of Korea*. Seoul: Korea Labor Institute.

SECTION 9

Social Movements and Collective Action

∴

CHAPTER 39

Contributions of Japanese Environmental Sociology in Non-Western Contexts

Hasegawa Koichi

1   Introduction

The influences of Western sociology on Japanese and Asian sociologies are varied and dependent on research fields. In the case of environmental sociology, the Japanese version has developed many original perspectives, including the social structure of victims (Iijima [1984] 1993), life environmentalism (Torigoe and Kada 1984), and benefit versus victimized zone theory (Funabashi et al. 1985). The history of serious industrial pollution incidents, like Minamata disease from the 1950s to the 1980s and high-speed traffic pollution, defines the characteristics and concerns of Japanese environmental sociology. The damage of the 2011 Tohoku earthquake and tsunami and the Fukushima nuclear disaster brought new research topics on academic responses to disasters and those who suffer them. The unique characteristic of Japanese environmental sociology has been reflecting on the historical backgrounds of this study and the Japanese unique contexts of environmental issues, redesigning traditional local commons which are shared resources by locals and the 2011 disasters. Finally, the author's original scheme of a "sociology of downstream perspective" as a unified perspective on environmental problems is examined.

2   Unique Perspectives and Contributions of Japanese Environmental Sociology

To date, the Japanese social sciences have generally demonstrated strong tendencies to debate earlier theories and to introduce the latest theoretical developments from the West. Efforts to face and tackle the concrete social problems and policy issues confronting Japanese society and to develop theories based on primary research have remained relatively weak. However, the influences of Western sociology on Japanese and Asian sociologies are various and dependent on research fields. In the case of Japanese urban sociology, the influences of the Chicago School, Castells, and other leading Western sociologists have been substantial. See Matsumoto (2021) which focused on the Chicago School. The urbanization process of a population shift to urban areas and the diffusion of urban lifestyles has been almost similar in Western societies and Japan. However, in the case of Japanese rural sociology, the influence of Western sociologists has been very limited. The Japanese rural communities are very traditional and unique, based on small-scale and self-sufficient rice and crops farming, and several joint kinship groups called "ye".

In my view, the sociology of social structure, sociology of social movements, sociology of immigrants, sociology of medicine, and feminist sociology are typical examples strongly affected by Western perspectives. Simply speaking, these issues and phenomena are common and less unique. How about in the case of Japanese environmental sociology?

In conclusion, Japanese environmental sociology has developed many original perspectives and unique characteristics. Especially major vibrant research interests include (1) pollution and local development, the processes by which environmental issues emerge, and perpetrator–victim relationships; (2) intersections of daily life and culture with the environment, ecology, environmental perspectives, and consciousness; (3) disaster effects and recovery processes; (4) redesigning local commons; and so on.

To the best of my knowledge, perspectives on the social structure of victims (Iijima [1984] 1993), life environmentalism (Torigoe and Kada 1984), and benefit versus victimized zone theory (Funabashi et al. 1985), which emerged from analyzing high-speed traffic pollution incidents, are topics to which Japanese environmental sociology has made particular and excellent contributions. This is supported by *The Blackwell Encyclopedia of Sociology* (Ritzer 2006), which includes several entries by Japanese environmental sociologists. Hasegawa's contributions were on "daily life pollution", "high-speed transportation pollution", "residents' movements", "pollution zones, linear and planar", "social structure of victims", and "structural strains, successive transition", and Yamamoto's involved "life environmentalism".

There have been many other pioneering studies in Japanese environmental sociology. However, most of these were written in Japanese, and very few English editions have been published (Furukawa 2007; Hasegawa 2004, 2015; Horikawa 2021). Thus, except for those few environmental sociologists who have personal contacts abroad, the significance of this research has not been sufficiently recognized by the international academic community.

2.1 Comparison of Western and Japanese Textbooks

Let us compare Western texts and Japanese texts in the field. Humphery and Buttel (1982) recently revised as Humphrey, Lewis, and Buttel (2002), was the first environmental sociology textbook published in the United States and has been very popular across the world except in Japan. Five of its eight chapters explore global and macro resource topics, including population, energy, and food (see Table 39.2). Bell et al. ([1998] 2021) focus on dominant environmental ideologies and values. Hannigan (1995) uses case studies to explore issues such as acid rain, threats to biodiversity, and biotechnology.

TABLE 39.1 Contents of the Japanese environmental textbook

Similarity to the US version	Chapter titles
x	1 Social History of Environmental Problems
x	2 Social Mechanism of Environmental Degradation
x	3 Environmental Policy as Social Regulations
x	4 Mechanism of Environmental Degradation
o	5 Environmental Problems and Social Movements
x	6 Life Environment and Local Community
x	7 Environmental Problems and the Way of Life
x	8 Environmental Problems in Developing Countries
o	9 Challenges and Methodologies of Environmental Sociology
o	10 Sociological Study of Environmental Problems

SOURCE: IIJIMA ED. (1993)

TABLE 39.2 Contents of the US environmental textbook

Similarity to the Japanese version	Chapter titles
o	1 Exploring Environmental Sociology
x	2 Social Theory and the Environment
x	3 Population and the Environment
x	4 The Struggle over Hunger: Social and Ecological Dimensions
x	5 Energy and the Environment: the Reemerging Energy Crisis
o	6 The Environmental Movement: Historic Roots and Current Trends
x	7 The Sociology of Sustainable Development
x	8 Environmental Sociology and Alternative Environmental Futures

SOURCE: HUMPHERY, LEWIS AND BUTTEL ([1982] 2002)

Iijima (1993), the first environmental sociology textbook as the Japanese original version, highlights the unique characteristics of Japanese research. The discipline has used local area field studies to attain solid achievements in the areas of pollution-related social research, environmental destruction, citizen participation, and local communities (see Table 39.1). It has not, however, made much of a contribution to global-scale problems or resources, or to developing macro perspectives. Then, four edited volumes (Funabashi and Furukawa 1999; Funabashi and Miyauchi 2003; Iijima 1993; Torigoe and Obitani [2009] 2017) were published and four single-author textbooks emerged (Hasegawa 2021b; Kada 2002; Mitsuda 2005; Torigoe 2004). We have the five-volume *Environmental Sociology in Japan*, a comprehensive and systematic series, and another introductory six-volume set, *Environmental Sociology: A Series (Shiriizu kankyo shakaigaku)*. Both were published between 2001 and 2003. Together, these publications make Japan exceptional as one of the first non-English-language countries where students can study environmental sociology systematically in their mother language.

In these Japanese versions of textbooks and teaching materials, how have authors dealt with Western environmental sociology?

For a typical example, the latest and the most popular version of a Japanese textbook for an introduction to environmental sociology (Torigoe and Obitani [2009] 2017) includes only a short piece of one page on Western environmental sociology and another one-page piece on eco-feminism. The latest 207-page textbook (Torigoe and Obitani 2017) devoted only 2 pages to describing Western perspectives. The index has a few names of Western environmental sociologists and their statements: Catton and Dunlap (1980) for the ecological paradigm, Schnaiberg (1980) for a "treadmill of production" framework, Mol and Spaargaren (2000) for ecological modernization, and Beck (1986) for the theory of risk society.

Searching the total 27 volumes of back issues of the *Journal of Environmental Sociology* (JES) for these 27 years, the author found more evidence of a scarcity of articles on Western theories. There were only 7 articles discussing Western theories and perspectives among more than 500 articles. Among them were two articles by the guest contributors Dunlap and Broadbent, and another four articles by Japanese environmental sociologists in which the main focus point is the paradigm dispute by Dunlap and Buttel (Buttel 1987; Catton and Dunlap 1980). There were no articles on recent trends of theories and perspectives of Western environmental sociology.

2.2 Involved in East Asian Contexts

Another notable thing is that in paying attention to East Asian environmental sociology, Torigoe and Obitani (2017) include one page on East Asian environmental sociology, the same amount as for Western environmental sociology, focusing on South Korean, Taiwanese and Chinese versions as well as the Japanese one.

It was very stimulating to find the special issue titled "Coming East Asian environmental sociology" in volume 15 of JES, 2009. Korean and Chinese scholars contributed. Japanese environmental sociologists were interested and involved in East Asian contexts rather than Western contexts.

In 2008, the biennial International Symposium on Environmental Sociology in East Asia (ISESEA) was established in Tokyo. Eight symposia have now taken place, hosted twice each by Japan, Taiwan, South Korea, and China, allowing for academic exchange between East Asian environmental sociologists on topics that include environmental degradation, the role of environmental sociologists in disasters, energy shifts, climate change protection, promoting organic farming, collaborating with environmental non-governmental organizations, and depopulating rural areas. These topics indicate the major research contents of East Asian contexts. Two edited volumes on East Asian and Asian environmental issues, focusing on energy shift and climate change, led by Taiwanese environmental sociologists (Chou 2017; Chou et al. 2000) have been published.

3 Major Contributions in the Early Stage

The social and historical origins of Japanese environmental sociology have led to the discipline's unique characteristics (Hasegawa 2021a). The years prior to 2001 marked the organizing of a distinct group of scholars who could call themselves environmental sociologists. In 1992, the Japanese Association for Environmental Sociology (JAES) was established, with the publication of its official journal, JES, starting in 1995, making it the world's oldest specialist journal in the field of environmental sociology. Case studies of local environmental destruction were a major focal point. I will examine the typical major contributions.

3.1 *Nobuko Iijima: A Global Pioneer*

The late professor Nobuko Iijima (1938–2001), called the "mother of environmental sociology", was a global pioneer and the first president of the JAES. Professor Iijima began her sociological research into environmental issues in the late 1960s, exploring the lives of the victims of mercury poisoning at Minamata and Niigata (Iijima 1970). Her master's thesis at the University of Tokyo, finished in November 1967, as the first academic contribution in the world on industrial pollutions from sociological perspective. It was ten years before the emergence of environmental sociology by Catton and Dunlap

(1978). She continued to almost single-handedly tackle Japanese environmental issues until the 1980s.

Her notion of the social structure of victims is the distinguished example of Japanese original contributions (Iijima [1984] 1993; Tomozawa 2014). She captured the multidimensional and multilayered nature of the damage caused by pollution. The physical damage done to victims is relatively easy to discern, but this is only one aspect of pollution damage. Equally costly is the mental and social damage that occurs in the wake of the physical impact. Iijima attempted to describe comprehensively the complex structure of the suffering of victims, from physical suffering to worsening relationships between family members and neighbors who may be indifferent to the pollution problem or wish to keep it hidden. This approach reveals the flow-on effect of the physical damage. In fact, Iijima demonstrated how such suffering affects every aspect of the family's daily life, including loss of income and an increase in medical expenses, and often leads to family breakdown or the destruction of the family's living conditions. Through her research on Minamata disease, mercury poisoning of Canadian Indians, and drug-induced Subacute-Myelo-Optico-Neuropathy (SMON) disease, Iijima discovered that the social mechanism of suffering victims was very similar regardless of whether the damage was caused by a work-related accident, a drug-induced disease, or an environmental hazard. The source of the pollution that caused Minamata disease was a malfunctioning factory already known as the troublesome site where numerous labor accidents often happened. A systematic and institutional lack of care or consideration by industry and the government for both the safety of working conditions and people's environment nurtured the endemic problems that led to the outbreak of Minamata disease.

Iijima's argument regarding the social mechanism of suffering victims represented a practical contribution to the sufferers as well as a theoretical contribution to the field. In the case of drug-induced SMON disease, Iijima testified as to her research findings in court, and her argument became the basis for the plaintiffs' demands for financial compensation for their suffering, including the mental damage inflicted on them and the destruction of their daily lives. The compensation was legally admitted and performed.

More broadly, Iijima discussed the way that the suffering caused by environmental damage was not evenly distributed in society but reflected the disparities between majority and minority groups. Hence, in Japan, where small farmers or fishermen occupy the lowest strata of society, they are most likely to suffer from environmental hazards. In this way, she found some similarities with US scholars of environmental justice and racism with regard to African Americans and Native Americans, such as Bullard (1994).

3.2 Life Environmentalism: Traditional Management Practices

In 1984 Hiroyuki Torigoe and others published "Environmental history of water and people" (Mizu to hito no kankyō-shi), a distinguished study unique to Japan, utilizing folklore to reveal how the local culture of the people around Lake Biwa was intertwined with their relationship to the water and water management system. They called their theoretical and methodological paradigm "life environmentalism". They stress the points of view of local residents: how they define the issues based on their own local knowledge, experiences, way of life, and traditions. Torigoe and others criticize the "modern-technofix approach" through which engineers, professionals and bureaucrats try to handle any environmental problems with a technofix approach based on engineering experiences and scientific knowledge. Torigoe et al. also criticize "natural environmentalism", which is the mainstream approach in Western nature conservation movements and in which "reserves" are retained as protected areas for wildlife where extracting natural resources, drilling, fishing, and mining are banned. They question how the locals near the reserves can maintain their way of life using these resources from the area, *satoyama* is a good example of this. The word means literally a hill in a village, a mosaic of mixed community forests, rice fields, grasslands, streams, ponds, and reservoirs for irrigation. It consists of secondary and coppiced woodlands, and grasslands managed for thatch, fodder, and compost. Fallen leaves are gathered to use as fertilizer in rice fields. Farmers also use wood for construction and heating, and they use the grasslands to feed cattle. Streams, ponds, and reservoirs play an important role in adjusting the water levels of rice fields. Villagers and many plant and animal species have been able to live together in these forests because traditional management practices and regulations have been followed. Torigoe and others found many examples of using forests and water resources by fieldwork run for several years.

3.3 Learning from Traditional Lifestyles to Redesign Local Common Resources

Similar practices of *Satoyama* management are found in some Pacific islands and in tropical Asia. As we face a serious environmental crisis resulting from globalization's drive toward privatization and the market economy, the non-Western social and historical context of Japanese environmental sociology offers a unique approach to our understanding of local commons which are shared resources by locals, the environment, and sustainability. Local commons present excellent opportunities for stimulating sociological theory and for contributing to local practices, such as understanding traditional and indigenous concepts regarding commons, the wise use of shared resources, ingroup and outgroup relationships, varieties and types of ownership of resources, roles and legitimacy of local actors, environmental governance, environmental justice, and the interaction between local communities and the globalizing world. Lessons learned from the management and utilization of local commons can specifically contribute to the redesign and reactivation of the Tohoku area devastated in 2011.

In Japan, environments such as *satoyama* have long been maintained as sustainable common resources. More recently, however, they have fallen into disuse because of the energy revolution, urbanization, dependence on foreign resources, and Japan's declining birth rate and aging population. Japan's environmental sociologists have now begun to explore issues such as the increasing number of vacant houses, abandoned farms, and devastated *satoyama* forests in rural areas. Earlier common resources research by Inoue (2004), Miyauchi (2001), Suga (2001), and others, focused on the role of local residents and the prevention of overuse. Today, the maintenance of *satoyama* by local residents is increasingly difficult due to declining and aging rural populations. Therefore, reactivating *satoyama* and other local common spaces are current topics of interest for Japanese environmental sociologists (Yamamoto 2003).

3.4 *High-Speed Transportation Pollution*

Another example is the joint research of Harutoshi Funabashi, myself, and others, published as "Bullet train pollution" (Shinkansen Kogai) (Funabashi et al. 1985). This is the world's first dedicated sociological study of high-speed transportation pollution. It revealed social factors that contributed to the noise and vibration pollution arising in the shadow of Japan's world-class bullet train, the social mechanisms that made the issues difficult to resolve, and the social forces that carried forward the measures to rectify the bullet train noise and vibrations.

High-speed transportation pollution refers to a type of environmental pollution consisting of high levels of noise, vibration, and air pollution brought about by high-speed transportation systems, such as the airplane and airport, the "bullet train" (super-express trains), or the expressways for car traffic. These disturbances cause damage to daily life through things such as sleep deprivation or the disturbance of conversation at home, as well as stress-related health issues, like heart disease or gastrointestinal disease. Bullet trains, jet airplanes, and high-speed expressways are essential to highly industrialized modern urban life. They are basic conditions for developing efficient modern economies, greatly reducing the time and cost of moving goods and people over large distances. In most countries, high-speed transportation pollution is serious along the train line, the expressway, or the area surrounding the airport. It is especially serious in metropolitan areas and in high popular density countries like Japan.

In many ways, high-speed transportation pollution is quite distinct from industrial pollution. At first glance, the impact on the environment for each flight, bullet train service, or individual automobile on the expressway looks inconsequential. It comes and goes away very quickly, at most within a few minutes. But an airplane takes off every several minutes at a major airport, and, in the case of Japan's Tokaido line, a bullet train also passes through every several minutes. They keep coming every day, including holidays, from early morning to the middle of the night (for the airport and bullet train) or all day and night (for the expressway). The cumulative effect is great. In fact, as the number of flights and trains rapidly increased in response to growing demand, the pollution from bullet trains and jet planes became a serious social problem.

For many years planners, engineers, suppliers and administrators of the transportation system focused only on the "benefit sphere": speed, safety, convenience for passengers or drivers, economy of the system, and economic effect for the surrounding area. They overlooked the "negative" environmental effects for local residents near the transportation system. Effective regulation of the environmental effects only came about with the beginning of protest movements and the advent of serious social issues. This contrast highlights the social conflict between the benefit and victimized zone (Funabashi et al. 1985). In large-scale projects like high-speed transportation systems, the benefit and victimized zones, those who benefit and those who are victimized, the area where benefit and the area where are victimized are fully separate. Actors of the benefit zone, including passengers, tend to overlook and be indifferent to those who sufferer noise pollution.

In some cases of industrial pollution, determining cause and effect is not always simple. But in most cases of high-speed transportation pollution, the cause is usually obvious: we feel the noise and vibration. Despite this obviousness, planners, suppliers, and passengers tend to miss the negative effects. The principles of remedy or countermeasure are very clear—making the polluter pay (the PPP or polluter-pays principle) and fixing the problem at the point where it occurs. These are basic and relatively cheap principles. But in Japan, the government administration and the railway companies tended to reject these principles.

In Japan, during the years of rapid economic growth in the early 1970s, high-speed transportation pollution, especially in the high-density areas of large metropolises, became a major issue for local residents' movements. This was because the national government tried to continue high economic growth by constructing many airports for jet planes, bullet train lines, and expressways.

This special social background at that time made high-speed transportation pollution a major nationwide social problem.

Representative examples of these protest movements include movements to rectify the Osaka Airport pollution problem, oppose the construction of Narita Airport, rectify the Nagoya bullet train pollution problem, and oppose the construction of the Tohoku and Joetsu bullet train lines in the metropolitan Tokyo area. In all of these cases, large groups of residents rapidly and successfully organized a powerful local residents' movement that reminded active for a long time.

In smaller-scale projects it is relatively easier to reach a consensus because both sides can more readily understand others' situation and position. Disputes over the construction of light-rail transit systems are typical of the conflict of overlapped types of the benefit and victimized zones, where some people are asked to move but oppose doing so. This classification and their hypothesis that the "benefit zone" is expanding while the "victimized zone" is becoming locally grievous (Kajita 1988) has been significant for understanding, for example, the specifics of expressway traffic pollution as a social problem, the interrelationship between the social costs and benefits when evaluating both large- and small-scale projects, and the major social characteristics of consensus-building processes.

High-speed transportation pollution is just one example of the unintended but harmful pollution caused by transportation technology. As mass consumer society becomes increasingly technological, the environmental problems caused by new technologies extend well beyond noise and vibration into new areas like destruction of the ozone layer by chlorofluorocarbons.

The Chuo Shinkansen, a new Japanese maglev line project running 286 km in distance providing service that takes only 40 minutes (currently it takes 100 minutes) between Tokyo and Nagoya has been under construction from 2014, with plans for extension to Osaka. It will be scheduled to start operation in 2027. The planned maximum speed is 500 km/h, whereas the current maximum speed is 285 km/h. Some citizens filed a lawsuit in 2016 concerning the various environmental effects of this new line project, including noise and vibration, damages to the landscape, surplus construction soil disposal, and running out of groundwater. This issue of the maglev line project is the new type of high-speed transportation pollution.

4   Unprecedented Triple Disaster

Earthquake, tsunami, and nuclear power plant accident led to 21,000 people dying, including disaster-related dead, and estimated losses of USD $200 billion to $300 billion. Many Japanese environmental sociologists immediately turned their attention to these disasters, their related effects, and recovery processes. With prior pollution and environmental degradation research, environmental sociologists have mainly focused on the victims of this triple disaster and their communities.

In 2011, 2012, 2013, and 2021, JES published special issues on these disasters. Research published elsewhere also referred to the disasters, including studies by Tanaka, Funabashi, and Masamura (2013) and contributions to the three-volume *Sociological Perspective on Tohoku Disaster-Stricken Areas* (Hasegawa and Yamamoto 2017; Tanaka et al. 2019; Yoshino and Kato 2020).

The 2011 Fukushima nuclear accident revealed another aspect of Iijima's social structure of victims. She stressed the multidimensional and multilayered damage caused by pollution (Iijima [1984] 1993). Fujikawa, Watanabe, and Horihata (2017) provide a good example of this approach to the Fukushima accident, where family life and fertile farmlands were devastated, forcing people to live apart from their families for more than a decade, worrying about the effects of radiation. No one knows when relief will come, and many are skeptical of official announcements. Farmers in highly contaminated areas hesitate to grow crops, and many fishermen refrain from fishing. Residents can only despair and resent the fumbling attitude of the electric company and the national and prefectural government. The location of nuclear facilities in peripheral areas means that the poorest, such as small farmers and fishermen, have been forced to face potential and very real nuclear risks in order to make a living.

Iijima stressed the difference between natural and human disasters. In cases of environmental pollution and human disaster, the attribution of responsibility, and determining who are the perpetrators and who are the victims, is essential. In natural disasters, these relationships are not so clear. However, human factors are critical in cases such as the Fukushima nuclear accident or in the delayed release of flood evacuation information. In 2011, a natural earthquake and tsunami triggered a total loss of power supply to cool the fuel rods at the nuclear power plant. The three former heads of TEPCO (Tokyo Electric Power Company Holdings, Incorporated) were charged with criminal negligence, having ignored the scientific warnings issued by a government committee[1] (see Soeda 2017). Contrary to Iijima's thesis, most serious disasters comprise a complex mix of human and natural factors. This is also true for the current climate crisis. At a glance, typhoons, flooding, and extreme heat appear to be natural disasters. However, they are all underpinned by the phenomenon

---

1 On September 19, 2019, a Tokyo local district court found the former top executives of TEPCO not guilty.

of climate change, where human factors are critical in accelerating CO_2 emissions (Hasegawa and Shinada 2016).

5 Sociology of the Downstream Perspective

The author has proposed that environmental problems should be viewed as downstream problems, and that the sociology of environmental issues should be a "sociology of the downstream perspective" (Hasegawa [2000] 2004). The terms "upstream" and "downstream" have come to be deployed in various fields in the sense that they are used to describe water flows. We can also distinguish between the upstream side of water supply/intake and the downstream side of waste water disposal. Using terms of water supply as a guide, I have proposed to define the term "upstream" to refer to the processes preceding the consumption of valuable resources—"environmental goods"—and "downstream" to indicate the processes that follow the use of those resources, including the release and disposal of waste and other environmental burdens—"environmental bads". Similarly, Yoshimura (1984) argued that pollution should be viewed as a "downstream" problem. From this perspective he refers to waste incinerators and sewage treatment plants as "downstream facilities".

The term of "goods" in economics means valuable resources, substances, and services to be used for production or consumption. They are demanded, and therefore treated as commodities with some positive price. On the other hand, "bads" is a new concept recently developed in environmental economics in contrast with goods. Typical bads are waste. Nobody demands them; therefore, they must be dealt with at some negative price. If you want to pass "bads" on to somebody else, you must pay some price, not receive some payment in exchange. So, for a long time bads were neglected in both the business/government world and the academic world. Bads are one of the key terms for thinking about a transformation towards a sustainable society. Conceptually, goods includes services. So, I propose that we consider environmental bads to include energy flows and conversions that result in environmental burdens, such as noise pollution. General waste, industrial waste, radioactive waste, dioxins, environmental hormones and CO_2 emissions that cause the climate crisis constitute environmental bads. Likewise, development projects and activities that harm historical landscapes, historical places, and natural coastlines should be classified as environmental bads. Thus, the definition of environmental bads used here is: "all substances, energy flows, and activities that harm the environment".

I also consider the production process in its widest sense, including traffic and distribution. Doing so provides a unified perspective through which to discuss the whole of environmental problems, including industrial, high-speed transportation, and global environmental issues. I therefore have proposed a new definition of environmental problems: they arise as a result of the upstream side, through both production processes and everyday activities, and result in the generation of environmental bads on the downstream side that must somehow be released and disposed of in the environment.

5.1   *The Downstream Perspective and Its Significance*

What is the significance of revising the perspective on environmental problems and treating these as downstream problems? First, this perspective allows us to develop a unified scheme of increasingly diverse and dispersed environmental problems and hazards.

Second, by examining the interrelationships between the upstream and downstream sides, we can analyze environmental problems produced by upstream activities. Each of us, albeit in varying degrees, contributes to the total accumulation of most types of everyday activities, pollution, and the climate crisis, and we all suffer from the accompanying problems. The perpetrator–victim relationship raises questions of responsibility as well as legal, social, and moral liability.

Third, the upstream–downstream approach is significant because it makes it possible to identify downstream problems at the focal point of all contemporary social issues. Before the 1960s, the main focus of social research and discourse was on the upstream side of production processes and daily activities. Later, however, with the growth and growing awareness of environmental pollution and environmental problems, it has become necessary and unavoidable to shift attention to the downstream side of society. The climate crisis is an example of how downstream problems may decrease the scale of the upstream processes and where a radical shift in approach is most pressing. Our societies and each member within them need to fundamentally change the dominant view of the relationship between the environment and society that tends to be biased towards upstream problems and develop an alternative perspective that focuses on downstream issues.

Fourth, we can interpret Beck's conception of a "risk society" from a downstream perspective (Beck 1986). Contemporary life is filled with a multitude of multidimensional risks, but environmental risks are the most acute and essential ones. Radioactive contamination from the Chernobyl reactor crossed national borders, affecting the entire world. Risk society theory assumes a critical perspective on modern society, defining contemporary society as one of the increasing risks whose effects are complex, difficult to control, and often invisible to the naked eye. The argument is that we are witnessing a transformation from an industrial society characterized by interclass struggles for the allocation of resources to a risk society in which the central struggle is about the distribution of risk. We can restate this argument by saying that the transformation from an industrial society to a risk society demands a change in focus—from upstream oriented to downstream oriented.

Fifth, the downstream perspective allows us to address issues of environmental justice and social surroundings, as well as social discrimination and social disparity. If we consider the downstream side from spatial and sociological perspectives, as Bullard (1994) has done in his work on the conception of environmental justice and equality, areas populated by ethnic minorities and the very poor as well as remote areas suffering from depopulation tend to be located at the peripheries and in the downstream areas of a society. On a global scale, such communities tend to be concentrated in the special peripheral area known as the "South". The dichotomies of center–periphery and upstream–downstream often correspond to one another. Residents of the center have relatively high incomes and are better endowed with access to information and human networks. In other words, they have more resources to mobilize against environmental problems and are more independent, which makes it easier to attract alternative, environmentally friendly industries and contribute to regional development. Moreover, it is easier for core regions to minimize their involvement in downstream activities and processes, and thus avoid related problems. The periphery, on the other hand, tends towards much higher rates of involvement in downstream activities, and already polluted regions attract new polluting sources. In some cases, the presence of one type of environmental burden contributes to the development of another, thus resulting in a double, triple, or multilayered structure of pollution.

5.2   *Reflecting on Modern Societies*

Sixth, the distinction between upstream and downstream processes can help with the development of a new perspective on the modern societies that have brought about this polarization. In pre-modern, pre-urbanized societies, the upstream and the downstream were not polarized. The two sides were unified in the realm of everyday life, constituting a whole. Based on field research on traditional lifestyles in hamlets along the shores of Lake Biwa, Furukawa, a research colleague of Torigoe, notes that before modern water systems were introduced, water supply and disposal were not separate processes. It was therefore possible to maintain clean water. It can be said that the two could be viewed only as interrelated and complementary. That is because in traditional water management systems, if water supplies and waste were not scrupulously separated, to a much greater extent than nowadays, there was a risk that waste water would be mixed with supply water. Furthermore, one person's waste water would often become somebody else's supply water (i.e., those who lived downstream). Thus, there was a continuous cycle of water use that, importantly, could be easily observed with the naked eye. That is, the people could see that their waste water affected others. (Furukawa 2007).

5.3 Environmental Sociology as Sociology of the Downstream Perspective

Environmental sociology is a discipline that uses sociological methods to focus on the interrelationships between individuals, society, and primarily the natural environment. If we apply the upstream–downstream approach, we can say that whereas mainstream sociology has primarily focused on upstream issues, such as production processes and social activities, environmental sociology is the sociology of downstream perspective and issues.

I argue that the significance of environmental sociology lies in its focus on downstream issues and its conceptualization of society in terms of sustainability and resource circulation. The sociology of environmental problems focuses on pollution, environmental contamination, and other environmental burdens that affect various social fields, as mentioned. As I have repeatedly stressed, environmental problems are those caused by environmental burdens downstream.

5.4 Toward Policy Studies Inspired by Environmental Activism

Environmental activism—social movements motivated by environmental problems and the promotion of environmental safety—at its best serves to mediate between perpetrators, victims, and policymakers. It can also be seen as a protest voiced from downstream. "Without the environmental movement of the late 1960s, environmental sociology would probably not have emerged" (Humphrey and Buttel [1982] 2002: 7). In both the United States and Japan, the fact that the academics who specialize in the study of environmental activism have been the ones to secure leading positions in the field is indicative of the strategic importance of environmental activism.

It may seem that in terms of affecting policy, environmental sociology lags behind environmental economics and legal study, but the achievements of environmental activism indicate another strategy. Environmental sociology should therefore move from research on activism in reaction to environmental damage to research on a policy-making orientation inspired by activism. Then,

Japanese environmental sociology would have the potential to have a unique impact on environmental policy.

Sustainable development is one of the prerequisites for achieving a sustainable lifestyle and society. How can we integrate the upstream and downstream sides so that they are once again understood to be a unified system collaborating with Western environmental sociologists and sociologists in any other research field? How to reunify the upstream and downstream processes in order to create a new system of reuse and recycling, and reduce waste?

Developing concrete policies based on analysis of the downstream perspective will require sociological imagination. This is the challenging task we are now facing.

References

Beck, U. 1986. *Risikogesellschaft: Auf dem Weg in eine andere Moderne*. Frankfurt/Main: Suhrkamp Verlag.

Bell, M.M., I.S. Leslie, L.H. Schlachter, and L.L. Ashwood. (1998) 2021. *An Invitation to Environmental Sociology*. 6th ed. New York, NY: Sage.

Bullard, R.D. 1994. *Dumping in Dixie: Race, Class, and Environmental Quality*. 2nd ed. Boulder, CO: Westview Press.

Buttel, F.H. 1987. "New Directions in Environmental Sociology". *Annual Review of Sociology* 13: 465–488.

Catton, W.R. Jr., and R.E. Dunlap. 1978. "Environmental Sociology: A New Paradigm". *The American Sociologist* 13: 41–49.

Catton, W.R. Jr., and R.E. Dunlap. 1980. "A New Ecological Paradigm for Post-Exuberant Sociology". *American Behavioral Scientist* 24: 15–47.

Chou, K.-T., ed. 2017. *Energy Transition in East Asia: A Social Science Perspective*. London: Routledge.

Chou, K.-T., K. Hasegawa, D. Ku, and S.-F. Kao, eds. 2020. *Climate Change in Asia*. London: Routledge.

Fujikawa, K., S. Watanabe, and M. Horihata. 2017. *Kogai · Kankyomondai Hochikozo to Kaiketsukatei* [Finding a Solution to the Hidden Pollution and Environmental Incidents]. Tokyo: Toshindo.

Funabashi, H., and A. Furukawa, eds. 1999. *Kankyo Shakaigaku Nyumon: Kankyo Mondai Kenkyu no Riron to Giho* [Introduction to Environmental Sociology: Theories and Techniques of Research into Environmental Problems]. Tokyo: Hakubunsha.

Funabashi, H., K. Hasegawa, S. Hatanaka, and H. Katsuta. 1985. *Shinkansen Kogai: Kosoku Bunmei no Shakai mondai* [Bullet Train Pollution: Social Problems of a High-Speed Civilization]. Tokyo: Yuhikaku.

Funabashi, H., and T. Miyauchi, eds. 2003. *Kankyo Shakaigaku* [Environmental Sociology]. Tokyo: Hosodaigaku Kyoiku Shinkokai.

Furukawa, A. 2007. *Village Life in Modern Japan: An Environmental Perspective*. Melbourne: Trans Pacific Press.

Hannigan, J.A. 1995. *Environmental Sociology: A Social Constructionist Perspective*. New York, NY: Routledge.

Hasegawa, K. (2000) 2004. "Sociology of Environmental Issues: A Look at the Downstream Side". In *Constructing Civil Society in Japan, Voices of Environmental Sociology*. Melbourne: Trans Pacific Press. (Original work published in 2000).

Hasegawa, K. 2004. *Constructing Civil Society in Japan, Voices of Environmental Sociology*. Melbourne: Trans Pacific Press.

Hasegawa, K. 2015. *Beyond Fukushima: Toward a Post-Nuclear Society*. Melbourne: Trans Pacific Press.

Hasegawa, K. 2021a. "Japanese Environmental Sociology: Focus and Issues in Three Stages of Development". *International Sociology Reviews* 36 (2): 289–301.

Hasegawa, K. 2021b. *Kankyo Shakaigaku Niyumon: Jizokukanouna Mirai wo Tsukuru* [Introduction to Environmental Sociology: Building a Sustainable Future]. Tokyo: Chikuma Shobo.

Hasegawa, K., and T. Shinada, eds. 2016. *Kikohendo Seisaku no Shakaigaku: Nihon wa Kawarerunoka* [Sociology of Climate Change Policies: Can Japan Happen to Change?]. Kyoto: Showado.

Hasegawa, K., and K. Yamamoto, eds. 2017. *Siriizu Hisaichi kara Mirai wo Kangaeru. Vol. 1, Genpatsu Shinsai to Hinan: Genshiryoku Seisaku no Tenkan wa Kanouka* [Sociological Perspective on Tohoku Disaster-Stricken Areas. Vol. 1, The Fukushima Nuclear Disaster, Evacuation from the Disaster-Stricken Areas and Possibility of the Energy Shift]. Tokyo: Yuhikaku.

Horikawa, S. 2021. *Why Place Matters: A Sociological Study on a Historic Preservation Movement in Otaru, Japan, 1965–2017*. Cham: Springer.

Humphrey, C.R., T.L. Lewis, and F.H. Buttel. (1982) 2002. *Environment, Energy and Society*. Belmont: Wadsworth.

Iijima, N. 1970. "Sangyo Kogai to Jyumin Undo" [Industrial Pollution and the Community Residents' Movement: The Case of the Minamata Disease]. *Shakaigaku Hyoron* [Japanese Sociological Review] 21 (1): 25–45.

Iijima, N. (1984) 1993. *Kankyo Mondai to Higaisha Undo: Kaiteiban* [Environmental Problems and Victims' Movements: Revised edition]. Tokyo: Gakubunsha.

Iijima, N., ed. 1993. *Kankyo Shakaigaku* [Environmental Sociology]. Tokyo: Yuhikaku.

Iijima, N., H. Torigoe, K. Hasegawa, and H. Funabashi, eds. 2001. *Koza Kankyo Shakaigaku, 1: Kankyo Shakaigaku no Shiten* [Environmental Sociology in Japan. Vol. 1, Perspectives of Environmental Sociology]. Tokyo: Yuhikaku.

Inoue, M. 2004. *Komonzu no Shiso wo Motomete: Karimantan no Mori de Kangaeru* [In Searching for Commons: Thinking in Forests, Kalimantan]. Tokyo: Iwanami Shoten.

Kada, Y. 2002. *Kankyo Shakaigaku* [Environmental Sociology]. Iwanami Shoten.

Kajita, T. 1988. *Tekunokurashi to Shakai Undo: Taikoteki sohosei no Shakaigaku* [Technocracy and Social Movements: The Sociology of Conflicting Complementarity]. University of Tokyo Press.

Matsumoto, Y. 2021. *"Shikago gakuha" no Shakaigaku: Toshi Kenkyu to Shakai Riron* [Sociology of the Chicago School: Urban Studies and Social Theory]. Tokyo: Yuhikaku.

Mitsuda, H. 2005. *Kankyo Shakaigaku he no Shotai: Gurobaru na Tenkai* [An Invitation to Environmental Sociology: A Global Development]. Tokyo: Asahi Shimbunsha.

Miyauchi, T. 2001. "Komonzu no Shakaigaku: Shizen Kankyo no Shoyu, Riyo, Kanri wo megutte" [Sociology of the Commons: Ownership, Utilization and Management of the Natural Environment]. In *Koza Kankyo Shakaigaku 3: Shizen Kankyo to Kankyo Bunka* [Environmental Sociology in Japan. Vol. 3, The Natural Environment and Environmental Culture], edited by Hiroyuki Torigoe, 25–46. Tokyo: Yuhikaku.

Mol, A.P.J., and G. Spaargaren. 2000. "Ecological Modernization Theory in Debate: A Review". *Environmental Politics* 9 (1): 17–49.

Ritzer, G., ed. 2006. *Blackwell Encyclopedia of Sociology*. Malden, MA: Blackwell.

Schnaiberg, A. 1980. *The Environment: From Surplus to Scarcity*. New York, NY: Oxford University Press.

Soeda, T. 2017. *Toden Genpatsu Saiban: Fukushima Genpatsujiko no Sekinin wo Tou* [The Criminal Action Against Former TEPCO Executives: Criminal Responsibility of the Fukushima Nuclear Accident]. Tokyo: Iwanami Shoten.

Suga, Y. 2001. "Komonzu toshite no Mizube: Teganuma no Kankyoshi" [The Waterside as Commons: Ethnography of Teganuma]. In *Komonzu no Shakaigaku* [Sociology of Commons], edited by M. Inoue and T. Miyauchi, 96–119. Tokyo: Shinyosha.

Tanaka, S., H. Funabashi, and T. Masamura, eds. 2013. *Higashi Nihon Daishinsai to Shakaigaku: Daishinsai wo Umidashita Shakai* [Sociological Analysis of the Aftermath of the 2011 Tohoku Earthquake and Tsunami: A Society Produced Heavy Disaster]. Kyoto: Minerva Shobo.

Tanaka, S., Y. Kuroda, N. Yokota, and J. Oyane, eds. 2019. *Siriizu Hisaichi kara Mirai wo Kangaeru. Vol. 2, Bosai to Shien: Seijukushita Shimin Shakai ni Mukete* [Sociological Perspective on Tohoku Disaster-stricken Areas. Vol. 2, Disaster Prevention and Relief, Rethinking the Civil Society of Japan]. Tokyo: Yuhikaku.

Tomozawa, Y. 2014. *Toi toshiteno Kogai: Kankyo Shakaigakusha Iijima Nobuko no Shisaku* [Philosophy of Japanese Environmental Sociology: From the Thoughts of Nobuko Iijima (1938–2001)]. Tokyo: Keiso Shobo.

Torigoe, H. 2004. *Kankyo Shakaigaku* [Environmental Sociology]. Tokyo: University of Tokyo Press.

Torigoe, H., and Y. Kada, eds. 1984. *Mizu to Hito no Kankyoshi: Biwako Hokokusho* [Environmental History of Water and People: The Lake Biwa Report]. Tokyo: Ochanomizu Shobo.

Torigoe, H., and H. Obitani, eds. (2009) 2017. *Yokuwakaru Kankyo Shakaigaku 2nd ed.* [Environmental Sociology for Beginners]. Kyoto: Mineruba Shobo.

Yamamoto, S., ed. 2003. *Sinrin Borantia Ron* [On Volunteers in Forestry]. Tokyo: Nihon Ringyo Chousakai.

Yoshimura, I. 1984. *Gomi to Toshi Seikatsu: Kankyo Asesumento wo Megutte* [Garbage and Urban Life: The Role of Environmental Impact Assessment]. Iwanami Shoten.

Yoshino, H., and M. Kato, eds. 2020. *Siriizu Hisaichi kara Mirai wo Kangaeru. Vol. 3, Shinsai Fukko to Tenbo: Jizoku Kanona Chiikishakai wo Mezashite* [Sociological Perspective on Tohoku Disaster-Stricken Areas. Vol. 3, Reconstruction from Disaster: Reflective and Critical Analysis for Sustainable Society]. Tokyo: Yuhikaku.

CHAPTER 40

Social Movements and Collective Action

Lilian Mathieu

1   Introduction

The notion of "social movement" emerged during the 19th century with the development of the workers movement; as such, it is historically linked to the formation of an industrial proletariat and to socialist activists and thinkers. This explains why the study of social movements has mainly developed among Western sociologists analyzing Western social conflicts. It also explains why this field of research has been infiltrated by normative issues, with some left-wing analysts expressing their support for the movements they studied, while conservative scholars showed contempt or fear of working-class unrest. The situation changed during the 1960s with the emergence of social movements standing apart from the workers movement, its organisations, and its mass base. This provoked a substantial renewal of theoretical approaches and gave birth to the so-called "US" and "European" research traditions. Each one met a distinct fate: if the US tradition is nowadays dominant in the Western world, its European counterpart is still influential in the South, and especially in Latin America.

2   The Progressive Predominance of US Approaches

After the trauma of World War II and the beginning of the Cold War, some American analysts focused on what they called "mass movements" (such as German Nazism and Soviet Communism) and tried to explain their development invoking the psychological strains or frustrations of socially disintegrated individuals. The idea that in modern societies, it is not deprivation as such, but relative frustration caused by unfulfilled expectancies which feeds discontent became dominant as the 1960s drew to a close (Gurr 1971). But the same era was also marked by the development of a broad and strong movement, that of the Black Americans demanding the abolition of segregation and the recognition and protection of their civil rights. Their mobilisation saw the emergence of prominent leaders (such as Malcolm X and Martin Luther King) and gave rise to new forms of collective action such as bus boycotts, sit-ins, or freedom rides. It also encouraged White sympathisers—especially among the educated youth—to join the fight against discrimination, such as the high risk 1964 Freedom summer operation, aimed at helping Black citizens register to vote in Mississippi (McAdam 1988).

Their spirited contribution to the civil rights movement encouraged many students to pursue their activism in the defence of other causes during the 1960s. For example, some female activists were strongly affected by the sexism that prevailed within the radical left and started to express their own feminist grievances. Their struggle for equality and for sexual rights was soon joined by an emerging lesbian and gay movement. Most of all, the beginning of the war in Vietnam led many leftist students to mobilize for peace, but they were quickly confronted with academic repression and had to fight for free speech on their campuses. Some of them were sociology or political science students and felt discomfort when they were taught in class that those who protest, like them, are frustrated or socially maladjusted people. They had to look for alternative intellectual resources in order to study the mobilisations in which they were participating, and found them in economist Mancur Olson's book, *The Logic of Collective Action* (1965).

Olson's approach leaves no room for psychological maladjustment; on the contrary, it presupposes a complete rationality among those who can consider mobilisation as a way to improve their situation. But this rationality can itself be an obstacle to collective action, even among those who know perfectly well that uniting their efforts is the best way to reach a collective good: as mobilisation is costly, each individual prefers to stay on the sidelines while expecting the others to pay this cost. This egotistical *free riding* strategy, which precludes any collective action, can be overcome only if some *selective incitation* (an individual benefit that exceeds the cost of collective action) is available.

Olson's framework has been criticised for being overtly disembodied and utilitarian, but it has contributed to "normalise" the study of social movements: activists are no longer deemed to be psychologically or socially fragile people but are considered to be normal actors who try to achieve some goals by collective means. Olson's legacy also lies in the idea that knowing that mobilisation is the best way to achieve these goals is not enough: many obstacles have to be surmounted, and many unsatisfied people would prefer to remain silent or to retreat from a negative situation rather than publicly voice their discontent (Hirschman 1970). McCarthy and Zald (1977) have stressed that what prevents most people from collectively and publicly expressing their grievances is the non-availability of resources, such as time, money, and skills to dedicate to the cause. This impediment can be surmounted by specific organisations, designed to gather, and mobilize the required resources. What McCarthy and

Zald call *social movement organisations* (SMOs) compete for resources within *social movement industries* (SMIs)—meaning causes such as feminism, ecology, migration, peace, etc.—which are components of a wider *social movement sector* (SMS). SMOs themselves attract different kinds of activists. *Cadres* are permanent paid staff who lead the action while others are *volunteers* who devote their free time to the movement. Some participants can expect to be *beneficiaries* of the mobilisation (such as migrants in hunger strikes in support of regularisation) whereas others, mainly motivated by altruistic reasons, assume the posture of *conscience constituents*.

Historian and sociologist Charles Tilly (1978) has coined the concept of the *repertoire of collective action* to study one decisive resource: the set of means of protesting which a specific group has at its disposal at some moment in its history. Tilly shows that the unification of the repertoire of collective action is parallel to the constitution of the nation state, with street demonstrations and public meetings becoming the core of the modern Western repertoire. His concept also enables us to study the strategic dilemmas of groups which have to choose, within their own repertoire, the best way to express their grievances, be it strike, demonstration, occupation, sit-in, or petition. Identity (what public representation of the group will be displayed during its contentious performance) and strategy (what is the best way to overcome an antagonist, be it the government or a firm) are closely intertwined in such choices.

More recently this basic framework has been doubly completed, first with a focus on the political context in which social movements develop. The concept of *political opportunity structure* (POS) has been developed by sociologists such as Tilly (1978) and Tarrow (1994) to stress that political institutions can be unevenly receptive to a movement's grievances, whether they offer an open attitude (e.g., when sympathetic members of the political system are ready to channel claims) or demonstrate a closed one (e.g., when the state responds with harsh repression). The POS concept has been used both diachronically—in studies of the fluctuations of the state's responsiveness to a movement's claims—and synchronically—in comparative studies demonstrating that some nation states prove more open or closed to the same movement (e.g., ecologist, feminist ...) and its claims. Closed POS are deemed to provoke more radicalisation among challengers, whereas open ones tend to facilitate a peaceful channelling of grievances within institutions.

Secondly, the way social movements strategically express their grievances in order to enlist new public support and challenge authorities has been addressed using Goffman's *frame analysis* (Benford and Snow 2000). The idea is not only to study how the adoption of an injustice frame—the perception of a given situation as unfair and deserving to be challenged—is a precondition for individual mobilisation, but also to show that frame alignment—a homogeneous definition of a situation as requiring a collective protest for it to be changed—is what permits an SMO to gain new sympathisers and activists.

This theoretical triad—organisational resources, POS, and framing—has become internationally dominant since the 1990s and, differently combined, adapted or revised (McAdam, Tarrow and Tilly 2001), it nowadays inspires many studies, whether they focus on Western or non-Western mobilisations. It has been recently completed or amended with considerations for emerging issues such as the transnationalisation of social movements (e.g., Della Porta and Tarrow 2005), pathways from protest to revolution (e.g., Della Porta 2016), gender and sexuality (e.g., Staggenborg and Taylor 2005), and culture and emotions (e.g., Goodwin, Jasper and Polletta 2001).

3 A French Acclimatisation

Before becoming dominant, the US tradition had to overcome a competing European paradigm, the so-called "New social movement" approach, notably elaborated by French sociologist Alain Touraine. Touraine (1981) reads the May 68 revolt as a turning point in modern history, more precisely as the inaugural act of a *post-industrial society*. While, since the 19th century, the workers movement, and the materialist claims it expressed, had been the main historical actor within the industrial society, a new social movement would be, according to Touraine, called upon to play the same role within the post-industrial society. This new historical actor would emerge from a set of "new social movements"—among them the ecologist, feminist, regionalist, student ones—expressing *post-materialist* (meaning moral or identity) claims and recruiting mostly within the educated middle class.

The research program Touraine and his colleagues conducted during the early 1980s in order to identify the new social movement that would replace the "old" workers movement proved unsuccessful. Many of his assumptions were not met empirically (not only materialist issues are still predominant in contemporary Western social movements but also the distinction between materialism and post-materialism appears irrelevant), and his definition of the social movement is overly demanding to be used as a heuristic tool. This is the reason why many French analysts who, like myself, started studying social movements in the early 1990s turned away from the Tourainian (mostly interpretative) approach and borrowed their concepts and methods from the US tradition.

Preceded as it was by the theoretical perspectives opened by Dobry (1986) and Chazel (1993), the development of a new trend in social movement research in France at that time coincided with a renewal of social conflict, and more specifically with the emergence of new poor people's movements. Studies have been devoted to the mobilisations of undocumented migrants, homeless families, unemployed workers, AIDS victims, etc. My own PhD research (see Mathieu 2003 for an English synthesis) contributed to this trend as it was dedicated to the mobilisation of prostitutes. Its main aim was to study how such a stigmatized group, deprived of any contentious tradition or organization, has however been able to overcome the many obstacles to its collective action and to launch mobilisations, such as the occupation of a church in Lyon in 1975 to protest against police harassment. Appealing to the US tradition was very helpful for me (and colleagues working on similar movements), as it incited us to focus on the resources which deprived people need in order to mobilize but cannot find within their own group. The main result of my research was that people without resources have to forge alliances with more privileged groups in order to launch a collective protest—like the Lyon prostitutes who were advised to occupy a church by leftist catholic sympathisers, who helped them to negotiate their action with the local priests and were supported by feminists who helped them to frame their grievances as gender domination issues. Such alliances usually prove to be very ambiguous: they are necessary for those McCarthy and Zald call the beneficiaries, but they involve some dependency on the skilled conscience constituents.

This appropriation of the US tradition has however not been without selection (the static POS concept has been globally rejected, while framing has been severely criticised for being overly strategist) and acclimatisation to the French intellectual context. The economical metaphor on which McCarthy and Zald's framework is built has been revised in order to stress that relationships between SMOs and SMIs are not only composed of competition but also of alliance (e.g., when AIDS activists join forces with the unemployed movement) and antagonism (e.g., when feminists confront anti-abortion groups). Bourdieu's field theory has inspired an approach focusing on the interdependence between groups, organisations or causes within what I have called a *space of social movements*, which I define as the relatively autonomous microcosm of practice and meaning in which contentious mobilisations are linked by various relationships of interdependence (Mathieu 2021). By socially situating protest activities, the concept helps us to understand not only the internal dynamics of the relationships between multiple movements, but also the relationships the space of social movements maintains with other social microcosms, such as the political field. The recent history of protest in France can thus be analysed as a succession of phases of *autonomisation* (for example during tremendous contentious cycles) of quasi-disappearance (when there is a complete deflation of contentious activity) with a strong dependence on the political field and its own (electoral) temporality.

Bourdieu's sociology has also proven helpful to study individual activists' socialization: in other words, what, in their own trajectory, has predisposed them to develop some interest and inclination for contention. Biographical elements like family inheritance (e.g., when one's parents were themselves politically engaged), personal experience of injustice (e.g., based on colour, religion, gender, or sexual orientation), exposition to transformative events (like May 68), a politicised cultural capital, etc. shape a habitus that fits with protest practice. Whether it relies on the concepts of trajectory or career, or on qualitative or quantitative methods, French research has proven able to identify recruitment clusters and typical profiles specific to various social movements.

4   Some Insights from the South

Himself a historian, Tilly (2004) stressed that the "social movement form" is a historically situated phenomenon, not a universal one. As previously stated, that form, and the expression "social movement" itself, appeared during the 19th century in Western countries at the time they were experiencing an industrialisation process. This leads to two opposite analytical risks when embarking on the study of collective protest in non-Western contexts: first the risk of ethnocentrically applying maladjusted (Western) concepts and theories to a reality upon which they cannot correctly shed light; second, the risk of ignoring what, in the various non-Western ways of contention, is nevertheless close to the social movement form. Siméant (2013) has warned against both risks, stressing that in Africa, for example, contention might be labelled by other concepts—resistance, politics from below, consent refusal, street politics, etc.—which prevent us from recognising its forms as social movements, but also from being aware of the risk of denying any specificity to the non-Western context and forcing empirical data to fit a maladjusted (Western) analytical framework. Theoretical approaches or concepts (such as POS) which focus on the state-movement relationship, for example, might appear ill-adapted to analyse contention in countries where the state hardly exists.

This is also what happened to the Tourainian paradigm, which has been internationally extended, and most notably in Latin America (e.g., Calderón 1995; Bizberg and Zapata 2010; Alonso 2013). This extension might be related to Touraine—who in the 1970s welcomed many researchers from the Southern cone fleeing from authoritarian regimes—and his personal links with that continent, but also to the Latin American traditional stance against US (academic) imperialism. Without doubt, there is a strong tradition of social (even revolutionary) contention in Latin America, but Touraine's approach to social movements can somehow seem ill-suited to many countries. As previously stated, he asserts that, headed by the middle class, the new social movements of the post-industrial society are intended to succeed and replace the workers movement of the industrial age. Since many Latin American countries are characterised by their restricted industrial sector and the weakness of their workers movements, it seems that they are not "ready" to welcome any "new social movement" with "post-materialist claims". Nor does the narrowness of the middle class allow it to become a central political actor in countries in which the majority of people live in poverty (de Sousa Santos 2001)—a reason why many analysts prefer to talk about "popular movements". The fact that, until the 1990s, many Latin-American movements had to confront authoritarian regimes using harsh repression is also a major trait that differentiates them from the Western "new social movements" (Goirand 2010). As a matter of fact, the global political context in which movements develop—or are impeded by state violence if not terror—is not a secondary variable.

This epistemic inadequacy and the intellectual imperialism of Western theories it expresses (de Sousa Santos 2011) have been all the more resented as recent contention in South America has placed colonialism at the forefront. In many countries, mobilisations have emerged out of indigenous claims for identity recognition and political autonomy and have confronted oppressive states inherited from colonial times. The Zapatista movement in Chiapas, Mexico, is the most well-known of those indigenous protests, but it is surely not isolated in the continent. Many such mobilisations have developed around environmental and economic issues, for example when mega-projects (such as canals, dams, or petrol extraction sites) threaten a traditional way of life based on agriculture. Mobilisations criticise both capitalism and the state for submitting indigenous communities to poverty, political subjugation and cultural alienation. The idea of de-colonialsation stands at their core, as they promote traditional auto-government procedures they postulate more egalitarian than institutional democracy. However, their goal is not to return to pre-colonial social life, but to consider tradition as a means to regain political autonomy and to define better and more egalitarian ways of life; some new issues—such as gender equality and leadership mistrust—have thus appeared on their agenda.

Some sympathetic academics have asserted that the concept of social movement itself is unable to shed light upon such contention of post-colonial dominations, and Zibechi, for example, has coined the notion of *people in movement* (2020) to stress both that indigenous communities collectively mobilize, but also move from a historically inherited situation of material and symbolic oppression to a political and cultural emancipation. Nevertheless, the de-colonial approach has been severely criticised among Latin American scholars themselves, who have denounced its poor empirical grounding, geographical determinism, cultural essentialism, homogenisation of the Western world, and political Manichaeism (Makaran and Gaussens 2020). It is also worth stressing that the fact that many analysts are sympathisers of the causes they study, if not their organic intellectuals, may lead them to give enchanted accounts of their mobilisations. Be they from the North or from the South, the balance between involvement and detachment (Elias 1987) is an epistemic challenge for all sociologists.

References

Abizberg, I., and F. Zapata, eds. 2010. *Los grandes problemas de México, t. 6: Movimientos sociales*. México: El Colegio de México.

Alonso, J. 2013. *Repensar los movimientos sociales*. México: CIESAS/Publicaciones de la Casa Chata.

Benford, R.D., and D.A. Snow. 2000. "Framing Processes and Social Movements: An Overview and Assessment". *Annual Review of Sociology* 26: 611–639.

Calderon, F. 1995. *Movimientos sociales y política : la década de los ochenta en Latinoamérica*. México: Siglo XXI.

Chazel, F., ed. 1993. *Action collective et mouvements sociaux*. Paris: Presses universitaires de France.

De Sousa Santos, B. 2001. "Los nuevos movimientos sociales". *Revista del Observatorio Social de América Latina* 5: 177–188.

De Sousa Santos, B. 2011. "Épistémologies du Sud". *Études rurales* 187: 21–49.

Della Porta, D. 2016. *Where Did the Revolution Go? Contentious Politics and the Quality of Democracy*. Cambridge: Cambridge University Press.

Della Porta, D., and Tarrow Sidney, eds. 2005. *Transnational Protest and Global Activism*. Lanham: Rowman & Littlefield.

Dobry, M. 2009. *Sociologie des crises politiques*. Paris: Presses de Sciences-po.

Elias, N. 1987. *Involvement and Detachment*. Cambridge: Blackwell.

Goirand, C. 2010. "Penser les mouvements sociaux d'Amérique latine. Les approches des mobilisations depuis les années 1970". *Revue française de science politique* 60 (3): 445–466.

Goodwin, J., J.M. Jasper, and F. Polletta, eds. 2001. *Passionate Politics: Emotions and Social Movements*. Chicago: University of Chicago Press.

Gurr, T. 1971. *Why Men Rebel*. Princeton: Princeton University Press.

Hirchman, A.O. 1970. *Exit, Voice, and Loyalty*. Cambridge: Harvard University Press.

Makaran, G., and P. Gaussens, eds. 2020. *Piel blanca, máscaras negras. Crítica de la razón decolonial*. México: Baja Tierra.

Mathieu, L. 2003. "The Emergence and Uncertain Outcomes of Prostitutes' Social Movements". *European Journal of Women's Studies* 10 (1): 29–50.

Mathieu, L. 2019. "The Space of Social Movements". *Social Movement Studies* 20 (2) (2021): 193–207.

McAdam, D. 1988. *Freedom Summer*. Oxford: Oxford University Press.

McAdam, D., S. Tarrow, and C. Tilly. 2001. *Dynamics of Contention*. Cambridge: Cambridge University Press.

McCarthy, J.D., and N. Zald Mayer. 1977. "Resource Mobilization and Social Movements: A Partial Theory". *American Journal of Sociology* 82 (6): 1212–1241.

Olson, M. 1965. *The Logic of Collective Action*. Cambridge: Harvard University Press.

Simeant, J. 2013. "Protester/mobiliser/ne pas consentir. Sur quelques avatars de la sociologie des mobilisations appliquée au continent africain". *Revue internationale de politique comparée* 20: 125–143.

Staggenborg, S., and V. Taylor. 2005. "Whatever Happened to The Women's Movement?" *Mobilization* 10 (1): 37–52.

Tarrow, S. 1994. *Power in Movements*. Cambridge: Cambridge University Press.

Tilly, C. 1978. *From Mobilization to Revolution*. Addison-Wesley.

Tilly, C. 2004. *Social Movements. 1768–2004*. Boulder: Paradigm Publishers.

Touraine, A. 1981. *The Voice and the Eye*. Cambridge: Cambridge University Press.

Zibechi, R. 2020. "Los pueblos en movimiento como sujetos anticoloniales". In *Piel blanca, máscaras negras. Crítica de la razón decolonial*, edited by Makaran Gaya and Gaussens Pierre, 227–250. México: Baja Tierra.

CHAPTER 41

State's Temperament and the Control of Collective Action in Contemporary China

Feng Shizheng

1   Introduction

Control of collective actions ("stability maintenance") is an important political agenda of the Chinese state. Central to the work of "stability maintenance" is the concept of "mass incident" (*quntixingshijian*), which is a Chinese equivalent of social movement and collective action. Probing the "mass incident" and the state interaction with it provides a window to understand China's social movement and the general political temperament of the Chinese state. This chapter traces the formative process of the concept of the "mass incident" as well as its later politicization. It reveals a significant transition the concept of the "mass incident" underwent: initially it was a technical term referring to a disturbance to public security, and later it was a political term connoting a threat to regime survival. The author suggests that this transition embodies a profound change in the Chinese state temperament, from a revolution-celebrating ideocracy to a calculation-based technocracy.

2   Predecessor of "Mass Incident": Between Revolutionary Heroism and "Naoshi"

Massive social contentions started as early as the foundational years of the PRC. From the second half of 1956 on, workers' and students' strikes as well as petitions and demonstrations increased significantly. "Within half a year, over 10000 worker and 10000 student strike of various scales have been reported nationwide" (CCP Central Research Office on Literature 1994: 154). Nowadays these events would be framed as "mass incidents", but in that period, when the concept had not yet come into being, they were all referred to as "naoshi" (trouble-making).

In the aftermath of these incidents, Mao Zedong made his historic speech "On Correctly Handling Contradiction Among the People" (CCP Central Research Office on Literature 1999: 204–244). "Naoshi" was a very frequently used word in this talk—Mao cited this term nine times in the 1,000-word-long part IV, "On Some People's Naoshi". Leaders after Mao continued to use this concept in the ensuing decades until the 1980s. In 1978 Deng Xiaoping referred to the student-petitioners in Yunnan as "Naoshi" (1994a: 370), and the student movement in the 1980s was referred to by Deng as "Naoshi" as well (1994b: 194–197).

In Chinese language, "naoshi" (trouble-making) is an everyday life word that originated in the 19th century. Conveying a negative connotation, "naoshi" means "making conflict in a people-gathering manner to challenge authorities". In the early 1950s, "naoshi" occurred frequently—in some places they reached a large scale. Yet, hardly distinguishable from the still ongoing revolutionary movement, these incidents were often sympathetically interpreted by the state as a distorted heroism. Accordingly, there was no coherent effort to conceptualize such incidents or counter them. To signify such incidents, the state randomly assigned a simple everyday life word, "naoshi".

An example can be drawn from Mao Zedong's attitude. In the speech "On Correctly Handling Contradiction Among the People", Mao referred to "naoshi" in a casual manner: "Naoshi is not good and we don't support it, but once it takes place, it forces us to learn lessons. Naoshi is helpful in overcoming bureaucratism, educating cadres and masses. We can thus transform bad into good. Naoshi is chaos, but we should learn to view chaos in such a dual perspective". Later on, in the CCP Central Committee's Directive on Workers' and Students' Strikes, Mao furthered that "naoshi" should not be forbidden but could be used as an opportunity for the masses' self-education, as a supplementary form to regular thought work (CCP's Central Research Office on Literature 1994: 154–163).

The decade between 1978 and 1989 was a period of transition and exploration. On the one hand, the Chinese state officially declared a farewell to Mao's Cultural Revolution, denouncing as "turmoil" (*dongluan*). On the other hand, the state was reluctant to add "stability" to its political goals, but rather continued to prefer the traditional language of "solidarity" (*anding tuanjie*). At this stage, the Chinese state retained a high level of self-confidence in legitimacy, which led it to think that "stability" was so easy to achieve that there was no need to make it a goal. It was as late as February 1989 that Deng Xiaoping changed the language. In a meeting with US President George H.W. Bush, Deng acknowledged that stability was under severe threat and maintaining stability should be China's first priority (Deng 1994b: 284).

Throughout the 50 years from 1949 to 1989, the Chinese state, with high confidence in its political legitimacy and capacity, celebrated social contention, viewing it as the continuation of the pre-1949 revolutionary momentum. To the Chinese state, social contentions like strikes, demonstrations, and petitions were all positive, which could function to punish corruption, educate the people, and increase popular support. The labeling of such incidents as "trouble-making" did contain a condescending and condemning tone, but it also implied a strong belief of the Chinese state that the Communist Party's legitimacy was so secure that any state reactions to mass contention would not undermine it.

3 The Shift of State Notion and the Birth of the Concept of the "Mass Incident"

From the early 1980s onward, the state changed its initial conception of social conflicts. This shift was shaped by three waves of collective actions since 1978. The first wave occurred at the turn of the 1980s nationwide. The participants were mainly college students and intellectuals. Pursuing Western-style democracy, this movement was denounced by the state as "bourgeois liberalization" and ended up with the Tiananmen Event of 1989.

The first wave of social contention, though it was finally put down, sent a warning to the state that its legitimacy was not as secure as it had imagined. A lengthy process of cognitive adjustment was thus inaugurated. The state attitude toward "trouble-making" gradually switched from tolerance to containment. In dealing with everyday riots, the preexisting ad hoc responsive regime came to be replaced by a routinized preventive one. This turn was marked by the restoration of the "Political and Legal Affairs Committee" in 1990 and its later continuous expansion. Stability maintenance as an institutional component formally entered the state political body, assigned with a clear and accountable agency.

The first wave of social contentions put the concept of "trouble-making" into question but did not remove it. Nevertheless, several significant shifts occurred. First, the state recognized the need to create a more technical and moderate concept to substitute the old frame of "trouble-making". Second, a consensus was emerging that stability maintenance was necessary. Though vague, this notion paved the way for the collective acceptance of the concept of "mass incident" by state sectors. Third, the initial frame of "mass incident" as a technical public security affair formed a special historical starting point, which gave the department of public security a significant voice in the ensuing agenda setting.

The second wave of social contentions took place in the period of 1992–1998, when China's reform advanced into a new stage. Unlike the elite-led first wave, this round of contentions was grassroots-level, non-political, small-scale, and scattered. Most participants came from the classes of peasants and workers. In rural areas, protests targeted "three arbitrary" things perpetuated by local cadres (arbitrary fine, arbitrary toll, arbitrary withholding). In urban areas, contention stemmed from the massive bankruptcies of state-owned enterprises and the ensuing layoffs. Most protesters only had economic claims, such as burden-reduction, welfare protection, and re-employment. Most incidents broke out due to common emotional reaction, but they were ad hoc, unorganized, and spatially and temporally isolated.

With the lesson of the early 1980s in mind, the state took the second wave of contention vigilantly and seriously. In 1994, *People's Public Security*, a ministerial official magazine, warned in an editorial article that "mass incidents are mounting, potential to threaten social stability … apparatus of public security must be well prepared, so that they are capable of preventing and appropriately dealing with such incidents". This is the first time the term "mass incident" appeared in an official public writing, which marks the birth of this concept.

The official confirmation of the concept of "mass incident" embodies many significant changes. Unlike the old frame of "trouble-making", "mass" subtly acknowledges the reasonableness of popular discontent, and "incident" appears to be less judgmental. "Trouble-making" trapped the state in a repressive stance, likely to irritate the masses; "incident" evades a clear characterization and thus leaves the state sufficient leeway in dealing with social contention. Such a language shift also implies a changed state–society relationship, where the state is abandoning a condescending stance, presenting a will to draw equal conversation with social movements.

TABLE 41.1   The use of "mass incident" in 1994

	Article title	Author	Author's affiliation	Journal title
1	Jiejin quanli wending zhi'an (Make Every Effort to Guarantee Public Security)	Editorial commentator	Renmin Gong'an Press, Ministry of Public Security	*Renmin Gong'an*
2	Guanyu tuoshan chuzhi quntixing Shijian weihu shehui wending de sikao (Some Thoughts on Correctly Handling Mass Incidents and Maintaining Social Stability)	Li, Jinwu	Deputy Director of the Administrative Office, Bureau of Public Security, Yantai, Shandong	*Shandong Gong'an Congkan*

TABLE 41.1 The use of "mass incident" in 1994 (*cont.*)

	Article title	Author	Author's affiliation	Journal title
3	Guanyu dangqian shehui zhian wenti de diaocha yu sikao (Survey and Thought on the Current Public Security)	Huang, Songlu	Director and Party Secretary, Department of Public Security, Fujian Province	*Gong'an Yanjiu*
4	Guanyu dangqian yingxiang shehui wending de bu'anding yinsu de diaocha (Negative Factors on the Social Stability)	—	The Third Bureau, Department of Public Security, Shanxi Province	*Jingxue Yanjiu*
5	Zhengque chuli quntixing Shijian, renzhen zuohao weihu shehui wending gongzuo (Correctly Deal With Mass Incident and Maintain Social Stability)	Guo, Yongyun	Department of Public Security, Guangxi Autonomous Region	*Zhengfa Xuebao*
6	Guanyu Taizhou diqu nongcun shehui zhi'an de diaocha baogao (A Survey Report on the Social Security of Taizhou Rural Area)	Ye, Deyu	Research Office of the Social Security Committee, Zhejiang Province	*Qingshaonian Fanzui Wenti*
7	Shilun chengshi gong'anju juece zhihui xitong jianshe de yuanze (Principles on Decision-Making and Command System of Public Security in Urban Areas)	Wang, Xiuquan	Bureau of Public Security, Nanyang City, Henan Province	*Henan Gong'an Xuekan*
8	Guanyu henan nongcun shehui zhi'an de diaocha yu sikao (Survey and Thought on the Public Security in Henan Rural Areas)	Wang, Jisheng	Department of Public Security, Henan Province	*Henan Gong'an Xuekan*

TABLE 41.1 The use of "mass incident" in 1994 (*cont.*)

	Article title	Author	Author's affiliation	Journal title
9	Dangqian qiye bu'anding yinsu ji duice (Negative Factors on Enterprise Security and Some Suggested Solutions)	Ren, Jinxian	Director, Shunqing Branch, Bureau of Public Security, Nanchong City, Sichuan Province	*Gong'an Daxue Xuebao*
10	Shichang jingji tiaojian xia renmin neibu maodun he quntixing Shijian jiqi chuzhi (Some Thoughts on Handling Contradictions Among People and Dealing With Mass Incidents)	Huang, Guangzu	Bureau of Public Security, Taizhou City, Jiangsu Province	*Gong'an Yanjiu*
11	Qianxi jizhong jingji liyi maodun yinfa de quntixing shijian (Economic Factors That Arouse Mass Incidents)	Zheng, Xunbin	Bureau of Public Security, Fuqing City, Fujian Province	*Gong'an Yanjiu*

Note: This table is collected and coded from CNKI. If an article has more than one author, only the first author is listed. All subtitles have been omitted.

In its incipient years, the term "mass incident" was a technical concept only connoting disturbances to public security. Most early users of the concept "mass incident" came from the public security system. Their writings mostly appeared in organs of the public security apparatus and the academic journals of policing schools. A search of the CNKI database shows that within the first two years after the term "mass incident" was coined, a total of 27 articles cited this concept. Except for 1 article whose author information is unclear, all the remaining 26 articles were authored by public security staff, and most of them were first-string policemen (see in Table 41.1 the 11 articles that were published in 1994).

4 The Politicization of the Concept "Mass Incident"

In the late 1990s, the state reconceptualized "mass incident". In the new frame it was interpreted as a threat to national political stability rather than a disturbance to local public security, as it had been defined before. As China's old social welfare system was undergoing massive reforms, this period saw a new wave of social contentions, in urban as well as rural areas. This wave of social contentions involved features that had rarely been seen before, which aroused the vigilance of the PRC state. In comparison with previous waves, contentions of this wave were more organized, large-scale, and politicized. In many reported cases, protests entailed Internet mobilization, which allowed a broader population to provide support from long distance. This change indicated that the boundary between technical and political had been blurred. An isolated and local incident of public security could escalate to a massive and nationwide political contention. It was in this situation that the concept "mass incident" was officially made. In a speech on December 7, 1998, Jiang Zemin, then CCP General Secretary, issued a clear warning: "We are at a crucial period in advancing reform and development ... certain social problems were dealt with appropriately, but some others were not. The latter had aroused mass incidents.... These incidents, if taken incorrectly, may grow into a threat to general social stability, or even worse, escalate to an overall political risk". It is in Jiang's 1998 speech that "mass incident" was for the first time conceptualized as a potential connector between public incident and political risk.

Closely after Jiang Zemin's speech, the CCP's and the Central Government's central offices jointly issued a document on preventing and correctly dealing with mass incidents (Zhongyang zhengfawei yanjiushi 2001: 7–8). This document marked the entering of the concept of "mass incident" into the national agenda. In 2003, following General Secretary Hu Jintao's suggestion, a new institution, "the Central Joint Meeting of Dealing with Letters and Mass Incidents", was created, with a staff covering 28 departments, 6 working teams, and 3 "joint meeting summoners" (Wang 2008: 286). In 2004, in a follow-up document issued by the two central offices, local governments were required to establish local branches of this joint institution (Zhao 2005). Thereafter, handling mass incidents was officially reframed as a trans-ministerial affair rather than the internal affair of the department of public security.

The upgrading of "mass incident" from a ministerial affair of public security to a national political issue at the turn of the 2000s indicates a changing state perception of social conflicts. When mass incident was framed as a disturbance to public security, it connoted no more than a local disorder that could be technically fixed by the regular police department. In a politicized frame, however, mass incident was interpreted as the early symptom of an overall and systematical dysfunction. Accordingly, mass incident as the potential to be the starting point of political turmoil should gain sufficient state attention, even at its incipient stage. Since a mass incident involves complicated social factors, it can only be addressed by comprehensive measures, which could entail top-down adjustments of social structure, state-society relations, and patterns of stratification. Such overall adjustments must involve coordination among multiple state sectors.

5   Conclusion: The State Concept, Notion, and Temperament

This chapter traces the historical formation of the concept of the "mass incident" since 1978. "Mass incident" was created as a technical term, referring to skirmishes and conflicts that disturbed public security. Eventually, however, "mass incident" came to be reframed as a political threat, connotating a challenge to the regime's stability and legitimacy. Such a transition must be understood within a broader social context. Although "mass incident" as a concept was initially created and prompted by the state, its historical change stemmed from the interactions between state and society. While the repertoire of social protests is changing, the state keeps adjusting its norms and strategies as well. Such an interactional cycle drives the concept of "mass incident" to transition from a technical term to a political concept. The three waves of social protests China underwent since 1978 are vital to understand this cycle.

The reconceptualization of "mass incident" embodies a profound change: the Chinese state has completed a transition from an ideocracy to a technocracy. In the foundational years, the PRC state, bearing a high level of self-confidence in its legitimacy, welcomed collective action as a continuation of revolutionary authenticity but tended to neglect its cost. At this stage, technical calculation was overwhelmed by ideological celebration. The birth of the concept of the "mass incident" marks a turning point. Massive official promotion of this term suggests that the Chinese state came to view collective action as a political threat. Transiting into a technocracy, the state, far more cost-sensitive, insists that social contention must be controlled at its incipient stage—it is by no means permissible for an "incident" to grow into political turmoil.

While the scholarship on China's mass incidents has been extensive, few researchers have realized that the concept of "mass incident" has a history of formation of its own. This chapter bridges this gap. The present historical analysis of the concept of "mass incident" helps in understanding not only how the Chinese state perceives social conflicts in the past and at present, but also offers insights into general theoretical thinking on state-building.

References

CCP Central Research Office on Literature (Zhonggong Zhongyang wenxian yanjiushi), ed. 1994. *Selection of Important Literature since the Foundation of the PRC* [*Jianguo yilai zhongyao wenxian xuanbian*]. Vol. 10. Beijing: Central Literature Press [Zhongyang wenxian chubanshe].

CCP Central Research Office on Literature (Zhonggong Zhongyang wenxian yanjiushi), ed. 1999. *Anthology of Mao Zedong* [*Mao Zedong Wenji*]. Vol. 7. Beijing: Renmin Press [Renmin chubanshe].

CCP Central Research Office on Literature (Zhonggong Zhongyang wenxian yanjiushi), ed. 2000. *Selection of Important Literature Since the CCP's Fifteenth Congress* [*Shiwuda yilai zhongyao wenxian xuanbian, shang*]. Beijing: Renmin Press [Renmin chubanshe].

Deng, Xiaoping. 1994a. *Selected Works* [*Deng Xiaoping wenxuan*]. Vol. 2. Beijing: Renmin Press [Renmin chubanshe].

Deng, Xiaoping. 1994b. *Selected Works* [*Deng Xiaoping wenxuan*]. Vol. 3. Beijing: Renmin Press [Renmin chubanshe].

Editorial Commentator. 1994. "Make Every Effort to Guarantee Public Security" [Jiejin quanli wending zhi'an]. *People's Public Security* [*Renmin gongan*] 5: 4.

Research Office of the Central Political and Legal Affairs, ed. 2001. *A Collection of Survey Reports on Maintaining Social Stability* [*Weihu shehui wending diaoyan wenji*]. Beijing: Law Press [Falv chubanshe].

Wang, Xuejun, ed. 2008. *One Hundred Questions and Answers on the CCP's Central Committee and Central Government's Directives on Dealing with Mass Petition of New Period* [*Xuexi Guanche zhonggong Zhongyang guowuyuan guanyu jinyibu jiaqiang xinshiqi xinfang gongzuo de yijian baiti jiedu*]. Beijing: Renmin Press [Renmin chubanshe].

Zhao, Baichuan. 2005. "Joint Meeting on Petition Is an Efficient Solution to the Problem of Mass Petition" [Xinfang lianxi huiyi shi jiejue xinfang tuchu wenti de yizhong youxiao xingshi]. *Bulletin of Xi'an Municipal People's Government* [*Xi'an shi renmin zhengfu gongbao*] 5: 44–46.

SECTION 10

Gender and Inequalities

∴

CHAPTER 42

Gender and Inequalities in France

Christine Détrez

1 Introduction

How to think about the concept of gender in the framework of a post-Western sociology? In order to answer this challenge, from the point of view of French sociology, which is mine, it is important to first recall the foundations of gender studies since the 1970s. We will then consider the evolutions, which allow us to start a work apparently favorable to the de-Westernization of the notion of gender, before concluding on the avenues to pursue.

2 The Heritage: Social Sciences of Gender within the Constructivist Framework

The French approach to the concept of gender is to be placed in the continuity of Western studies, especially Anglo-Saxon ones, but also in two opposing traditions, constructivism, more defended by the social sciences, and essentialism, more developed by the humanities, especially literary studies. These two schools of thought also strongly structured the French feminist field of the 1970s.

The essentialism, mainly represented in the 1970s by Hélène Cixous or Luce Irigaray, intends to rehabilitate the "feminine" as principle of creation. It is a question of returning to the body, and to the supposed specificities of the female body, to nourish creation: fluids, maternity, intuition, long devalued, become matrices which must be rehabilitated against the supremacy of the intellect, of the reason, traditionally attached to the male. The claim is to create, to write "like a woman", as the concept of "feminine writing" testifies. On the contrary, the social sciences are going to build themselves against this risk of essentialization and naturalization of a supposed feminine nature, whose specificities would have to be rehabilitated. For the social sciences, the problem does not reside only in the hierarchy which inferiorizes the feminine against the masculine, but in the very existence of this duality.

Conversely, in social sciences, the path followed is that of constructivism. The Western heritage comes first from anthropology, and in particular from

Margaret Mead's work. Through a study of three New Guinea societies, she questions the essentialization, the universalism and the naturalization of the concepts of "masculine" and "feminine" in the United States. If, among the Chambulis, the Arapeshs or the Mundugumors, the characters traditionally attributed to men and women are not distributed in the same way, then one can conclude that they are not natural, but products of culture (Mead 1935). In the 60s, the work of psychiatrists continues this deconstruction, and will lead to the invention of the term "gender identity". Finally, historians such as Joan Scott (Scott 1986), or sociologists such as Ann Oakley (Oakley 1972), will enrich the notion of "gender": it does not only designate the constructed character of gender identities, as well as the roles to which society socializes us, as men and women, but it also designates the whole of a system—the gender system—where these notions of masculine and feminine, as well as the places occupied by the individuals who belong to them, are strongly hierarchical.

Gender is, then, understood as a classifying system, which allows us to understand both the material positions of individuals and the values and symbolic representations attached to each of the binary poles of this gender system: as Pierre Bourdieu (Bourdieu 1980, 1998) shows, just like Françoise Héritier with the concept of differential valence of the sexes (Héritier 1996), space and its directions (up/down; left/right …), the tasks devolved to men and women in the domestic space as in the field of work, but also characters (gentle/violent, passive/active, weak/courageous …) or even physical characteristics (hot/cold, dry/wet …) are organized according to this internal hierarchy of the gender system. The concept of differential valence is then extremely enlightening: the attribution of such or such characteristic can vary according to the studied society (for example, the hot, in a society can be attributed to the man, and the cold, to the woman, whereas it will be the opposite in another society). What does not vary, however, will be the fact that everything that is related to the male will be valued, to the detriment of the female, whatever the society in question: if the hot is attributed to the man in society A, then in this society, the hot is valued over the cold. If, in society B, the cold characterizes the man, then the cold in this society, will be valued (Héritier 1996). This is the material and symbolic basis of male domination, whether we call it that or patriarchy.

In France, the social sciences develop this constructivist and materialist model: following Simone de Beauvoir's famous quotation—one is not born a woman, one becomes one—, the sociologists and historians demonstrate the multiple forms of domination: the sociology of work is going to emphasize "the blind spot in the rearview mirror" (Kergoat 2012), showing, for example, the specificity of the condition of female workers, forgotten by the studies on male workers: being a female worker is not exactly the same as being a male worker, because to this condition is added the fact of being a woman. In the same way, domestic work becomes susceptible to economic analysis, in order to measure its quantitative value and the extent of this free work granted by women (Delphy 1998; Guillaumin 1978). The investigations carried out in this vein since the 1970s are innumerable, cross all the fields of sociology and are extremely fertile. Without being exhaustive, it is thus a question of demonstrating, for the sociology of the family, the always unequal distribution of tasks in the family, and the places of each one in the couple; in sociology of work, the gendered distribution of the professions as well as the inequalities of wages, or still the differences of the working time (with the imposition to the women of the part-time, and the question to know if it is a question of chosen or undergone part-time) or still the phenomena of glass ceiling, or glass escalator (Williams 1992); In sociology of culture, the works question cultural consumption and their gendered attributions; in sociology of education, the phenomena of pierced pipe describes the disappearance of girls as one advances in the courses of study and the glass corridors explain the different school orientations according to the gender. Still in the sociology of education, the study of hidden curricula analyzes everything that is taught, through teachers' remarks, through the multiple interactions in class, in addition to and outside the official programs contained in books and manuals. In political sociology, the work focuses on demonstrating the difficult representation of women in politics, while in health sociology, the most recent work shows how medical research and the practice of medicine itself are still based on biased criteria and representations, the consequences of which can be fatal: for example, these studies show that cardiovascular accidents or heart attacks are less diagnosed for women, because public health policies do not communicate on the gendered difference in symptoms, thus leading to a misunderstanding of them in common sense: who knows, for example, that the symptoms of a heart attack, for a woman, are fatigue rather than pain in the left arm? In the same way, management varies, as well as the care brought to the recovery.

These studies in the sociology of health question once again the notion of the neutral masculine, which has already been elaborated by women's history (Thébaut 1998, 2007; Perrot 1998): what passes for neutral and universal is in fact only the generalization of the masculine model, and the forgetting or erasure of women. In history, this led for example to reread the history of literature, sciences, art. If museums and encyclopedias abound in male figures, this comes from a triple system of exclusion (Le Doeuff 1989, 1998). The first stage is the denial of existence, which by the laws, exclude the women from the education, and thus from the knowledge. The second stage is the denial of reality: even though women artists, musicians, scientists, etc. have existed, history does not remember them, because it privileges men. Finally comes the denial of value: when the existence of these women is recognized, their contribution is minimized, devalued. It is thus to a true rereading of History that it is necessary to proceed, and the initiatives multiplied these last years, in order to work out a "matrimoine" which gives back their place to the forgotten and erased women of the history (Détrez 2016).

Once the classical framework of Western gender studies has been established, what are the main evolutions and questions in the context of a post-Western sociology?

3 The Questioning of the Western-Centric Framework of Gender Studies

The first questioning of the Western model of gender studies, which already questioned the supremacy of the model of the neutral masculine and of male domination, can be linked to postcolonial studies. "Can the subaltern speak?", asked Spivak (Spivak 1988), while Audre Lorde, or bell hook pointed to the same impasse: who are the studies talking about, even though they claim to be feminist or inspired by constructivist gender theories? Can all women recognize themselves in these models promoted by white, Western women, most often from the bourgeoisie or at least the middle class, endowed with cultural and/or economic capital? By creating two blocks—men and women—and by basing their theory on the domination of the women's block by the men's block, do these white women not force black women, for example, to betray the men of their community, who are also subject to social domination and extremely strong violence? Should they consider themselves first as women, or first as black, Latina, Indian, Arab, or any other minority on Western soil? Feminists of color and non-Western feminists (with the movements of black feminism or Chicana feminism) are thus challenging the foundations of Western, white, middle-class feminism (Dorlin 2008; Moraga and Anzaldua 1983; Kian 2010).

Thus, we have again the risk of essentialization and standardization of these reified categories, the category of "women", versus that of "men". The other risk is the disregard, by white and Western intellectuals, of the specificities experienced by other women. The concept of intersectionality, elaborated by Kimberlé Crenshaw in 1989, thus aims at restoring the combination of multiple dominations at the crossroads of which individuals are situated, as soon as they escape the unquestioned, hegemonic, Western model. Intersectionality refers to the situation of people who are simultaneously subjected to several forms of stratification, domination, or discrimination in a society. Intersectionality studies the links between the different forms of domination, oppression, and discrimination. This is based on the premise that social differentiations such as gender, race, class, color, nation, religion, generation, sexuality, or sexual orientation ... are not compartmentalized: the relations of domination between social categories cannot be fully explained if they are studied separately from each other. Moreover, it analyzes social relations at the macro-sociological level (in particular the way in which systems of power explain the maintenance of inequalities) and at the micro-sociological level (in particular via the analysis of systems of inequalities in individual trajectories). This macro/micro duality characterizes intersectional research.

The notion of intersectionality is still often misunderstood in France and is often at the root of a very vehement opposition between the new generation of researchers and the older generation. Indeed, French sociology remains more marked by the Marxist tradition, and the importance given to social class rather than race, which is more effective in the United States. Moreover, intersectionality is not only the product of a classical crossing of variables, as it has been criticized: the ambition is indeed to show how discriminations combine, in a dynamic movement of consubstantiality. Oppressions are not added to each other in a mechanical way, successively in time and space. If the notion of intersectionality is also questioned by the shift towards militancy that it sometimes entails, it is on the other hand essential to question the white, Western framework that is still often dominant in Western social sciences.

Another challenge to this Western framework, particularly welcome in gender studies, comes from the work of situated viewpoint epistemology. Here again, it is a question of breaking with the illusion of universalism, as well as with an often-abusive reading of the concept of axiological neutrality, taken from the work of Max Weber. Indeed, recent translations have gone back on the translation of *Wertfreiheit* by "axiological neutrality" and have contradicted its use in French sociology (Freund 1990; Pfefferkorn 2014). Without going into the details of the controversy over this abuse of translation, and in particular its use by Raymond Aron in the preface he wrote in 1959 to *Le savant et le politique*, it suffices to note that the concept of Wertfreiheit does not signify the demand for an absolute and ideal objectivity that is impossible to achieve. It is only the putting forward of the importance of the conscience of the values which animate us, and the necessity, in the scientific work as in the teaching, to get rid of them, or at least, not to put them at the basis of our judgments. The epistemology of the situated point of view insists on this dimension: rather than advocating an overhanging vision or arguing for an illusory objectivity, the sociologist must imperatively reflect on his place in the field of knowledge and exercise a necessary reflexivity. Here again, this shaking of the foundation of Western certainties comes from the knowledge situated on its margins.

If the notion of race is less classical in French social sciences, gender studies have shown their difficulties to keep the Western hegemonic framework as soon as they have been confronted, also, to the questioning of the omnipotence of the white feminist model. The shaking came from the questioning of racist and colonialist images presenting Muslim women as eternal victims: historically, the literary, historical or pictorial representation of these women depicted them as prisoners of the harem, uncultured, ignorant, passive and powerless (Mernissi 2001; Tarraud and Sebbar 2010; Détrez 2012). Studies have shown the stereotypical and wrong character of this description, deeply marked by orientalist fantasies. In the same way, colonial feminism has been widely questioned, especially in its actions in India, Egypt or Algeria, with, for example, the actions of public "unveiling". In France, in a very contemporary way, the various questions raised by the wearing of the veil, for example, are characteristic of this perpetuation of an orientalist and Western-centered frame of thought and of the difficulty, but also of the necessity, to get rid of the belief in the omnipotence, or the superiority of its intellectual frame: thus, should we not question the binary idea of the internalization of the principles of domination by dominated women, as Bourdieu defended? If women wear the veil, are they only their men's consenting victims? Are they unconscious of the principles which maintain them in this domination? Are white and Western feminists the best placed to tell these women the very principles of their actions (Mernissi 1975)? On the contrary, can we not claim that there is a true Islamic feminism (Ali 2012)? Gender studies and postcolonial feminist theories then criticize the homogenization of women and the obscuring of their diversity by Western feminist theories (Kian 2010). According to Aihwa Ong, "the process of otherness, which characterizes colonial discourse, resurfaces within Western feminism producing the epistemological and political divides between us 'feminists' and them 'the oppressed women'" (Ong, as cited in Kian 2010). For Ong, feminist scholars tend to situate non-Western women in a subordinate position within theoretical and textual productions: "These self-validating exercises affirm our feminist subjectivity while denying it to non-Western women".

We can clearly see with the previous developments how these interrogations can be inspired, initially, by the critique carried by postcolonial studies, and continue the awareness of the orientalism of Western worlds (Said 1978; Agamben 2007): thus, "it is above all orientalisms that have set boundaries to knowledge perceived, experienced, represented as more legitimate than others" (Roulleau Berger 2016, 2017).

4 Questions for a Post-Western Theory of Gender?

The questions raised are fundamental for gender studies in the post-Western situation, but also for sociology in general: they question the place left to the statements of the respondents by the model of critical sociology in its most rigid and deterministic version. It also questions the possibility of "translating", in the strong sense of the term, ways of thinking, intellectual frameworks from one language to another, or even from one cognitive system to another: the post-Western sociology program, notably on gender issues, should thus be inspired by the achievements and the questions of the sociology of emotions. The danger is indeed to be unable to understand the existence of other ways of thinking, notably because our language fails to translate them. Abu Lughod's or Lutz' work insist on this primordial warning (Abu-Lughod and Lutz 1990): it is not because our language fails to translate, or that our cognitive system fails to understand a profoundly foreign concept that it does not have its raison d'être and its value just as heuristic as the concepts that have forged our reasoning and our culture. It can thus be extremely difficult to transpose from one language to another, from one system of thought to another, questions relating to different temporalities, to the different meanings given to the term "migrant" in China and in France, for example, to multiple modernities (Eisenstadt 2000) or social transitions, or to definitions of gender as a mosaic (Ji Yingchun 2017) or the meaning of the intimacy or self-government, very different from the Western meanings (Roulleau-Berger 2012). This shows the permanent necessity of collective work, and of the confrontation of ways not only to interpret a field, but even to name it, and to restore it in different languages.

Applied to the concept of gender, the post-Western sociology program reflects the same "desire to do away with the 'epistemic violence' of reifying categorizations, the Eurocentric myths of humanism and progress, the linear and historicist narrative of modernization, and finally the elitist historiographies blind to the specific consciousness and modes of action of the dominated" (Kian 2010). Just as post/decolonial feminist theories have rejected the myth of passivity of colonized and racialized women through highlighting the creative process of interpreting, appropriating, or hijacking Western colonial and racial discourse, post-Western sociology of gender could interrogate the place of dominations and resistances, and Laurence Roulleau-Berger herself reminds us of Scott's place in Chinese sociology (2016). The post-Western sociology of gender should thus draw more inspiration from works sensitive to the deployment of the agency of individuals. If it is not a question of denying the strength of structural social dominations, which are very real, a closer attention to resistances, as to ordinary lives, is essential, in order to show the diversity of situations: This is demonstrated, as one example among many, by a study of domestic workers in China, with the segmentation of the domestic labor market between urban women experiencing a process of downward social mobility and "migrant" women seeking to free themselves from the constraints of peasant life (Roulleau-Berger 2021).

Gender studies undoubtedly offer a privileged terrain for developing a post-Western sociology: indeed, in their very premises, they have had to question the claim to universalism, by forging for this purpose the critical concept of the neutral masculine. Through the emergence of situated thinking, and the questioning, by researchers engaged in postcolonial studies, of the orientalist character of feminisms, both in academic and political fields, gender studies, here too, have begun the path towards a more advanced interrogation of their Western centrism. Just as it had been clearly said by the first theorists, it is not a question of adding a chapter to the already written histories of gender sociology, nor of adding columns to the already existing statistical tables: on the contrary, the stake is to question and to make evolve the bases of the knowledge considered as legitimate, but also our way of thinking the problematics, of making our fields, and of writing our works, in the back and forth, the reading and the mutual listening.

Acknowledgment

I would like to thank warmly Senior Translator Nigel Briggs for his rigourous translation in English.

References

Agamben, G. 2014. *Qu'est-ce qu'un dispositif*. Dijon: Rivages.
Ali, Z. 2012. *Féminismes islamiques*. Paris: La Fabrique.
Bourdieu, P. 1980. *Le sens pratique*. Paris: Editions de Minuit.
Bourdieu, P. 1998. *La domination masculine*, Paris, Editions du Seuil.
Crenshaw, K. 1989. "Demarginalizing the Intersection of Race and Sex: A Black Feminist Critique of Antidiscrimination Doctrine, Feminist Theory and Antiracist Politics". *University of Chicago Legal Forum*, vol. 1989, issue 1, article 8.
Delphy, C. 1998. *L'ennemi principal* (Tome 1): *économie politique du patriarcat*. Paris: Syllepse (réédité en 2009 par Syllepse).
Détrez, C. 2012. *Femmes du Maghreb, une écriture à soi*. Paris: La Dispute.
Détrez, C. 2016. *Les femmes peuvent-elles être de Grands Hommes?* Paris: Belin.

Dorlin, E., ed. 2008. *Black Feminism. Anthologie du féminisme africain-américain, 1975–2000*. Paris: L'Harmattan.
Eisenstadt, S. 2000. *Multiple modernities*. New Brunswick: Transaction Publishers.
Freund, J. 1990. *Etudes sur Max Weber*. Paris: Librairie Droz.
Guillaumin, C. 1978. "Pratique du pouvoir et idée de Nature. L'appropriation ds femmes". *Questions féministes*, n°2, Les corps appropriés, (février 1978): 5–30.
Héritier, F. 1996. *Masculin-Féminin, tome 1 : la pensée de la différence*. Paris: Odile Jacob.
Ji, Yingchun. 2017. "A Mosaic Temporality: New Dynamics of the Gender and Marriage System in Contemporary Urban China". *Temporalités. Revue De Sciences Sociales Et Humaines* 26: 1–16.
Kergoat, D. 2012. *Se battre, disent-elles*. Paris: La Dispute.
Kian, A. 2010. "Introduction : genre et perspectives post/dé-coloniales". *Les cahiers du CEDREF* 17: 7–17.
Le Doeuff, M. 1998. *Le Sexe du savoir*. Paris: Aubier (rééd. en mars 2000 chez Champs Flammarion).
Le Doeuff, M. 1989. *L'Étude et le Rouet. Des femmes, de la philosophie, etc*. Paris: du Seuil.
Li, S. 2012. "Employées domestiques: les implications de la hiérarchie urbain-rural". In *Chinoises au XXIe siècle, ruptures et continuités*, edited by Marylène Lieber and Tania Angeloff. Paris: Editions La Découverte.
Lutz, C.A., L. Abu-Lughod, eds. 1990. *Language and the politics of emotion*. Cambridge: Cambridge University Press.
Mead, M. 1935. *Sex and temperament in three primitive societies*. William Morrow and co.
Mernissi, F. 1975. *Beyond the veil: male-female dynamics in modern Muslim society*. Cambridge: Schenkman Publishing Company; also Indiana University Press, 1987; Saqi Books, 2011.
Mernissi, F. 2001. *Le Harem et l'Occident*. Paris: Albin Michel.
Moraga, C., and G. Anzaldua. 1981, 1st edition. *This Bridge Called My Back: Writings by Radical Women of Color*. Persephone Press. 4th edition State University of New York Press, 2015.
Oakley, A. 1972. *Sex, Gender and Society*. London: Temple Smith. Reprinted with new Introduction, London: Gower, 1985.
Perrot, M. 1998. *Les femmes ou les silences de l'histoire*. Paris: Flammarion.
Pefferkorn, R. 2014. "L'impossible neutralité axiologique. Wertfreiheit et engagement dans les sciences sociales". *Raison présente* 3 (no. 191): 85–96.
Roulleau-Berger, L. 2012. "En guise de conclusion. Femmes chinoises, modernités multiples et individuation". In *Chinoises au XXIe siècle, ruptures et continuités*, edited by Marylène Lieber and Tania Angeloff. Paris: Editions La Découverte.
Roulleau-Berger, L. 2016. *Post-Western Revolution in Sociology. From China to Europe*. Leiden/Boston: Brill Publishers.

Roulleau-Berger, L. 2017. "L'invention de la sociologie post-occidentale: de l'Asie à l'Europe". *Le Portique*: 39–40.

Roulleau-Berger, L. 2021. *Young Chinese Migrants. Compressed Individual and Global Condition*. Leiden/Boston: Brill Publishers.

Saïd, E. 1978. *Orientalism*. London: Routledge & Kegan Paul.

Scott, Joan W. 1986. "Gender: A Useful Category of Historical Analysis". *The American Historical Review* 91 (5): 1053–1075.

Spivak Gayatri, C. 1988. "Can the subaltern speak?" In Nelson Cary, Grossberg Lawrence (ed.), *Marxism and the interpretation of Culture*. Chicago: University of Illinois Press, 271–313.

Tarraud, C., and L. Sebbar. 2010. *Femmes d'Afrique du Nord, Cartes postales (1885–1930)*. Paris: Bleu Autour.

Thebaud, F. 1998. *Écrire l'histoire des femmes*. Lyon: ENS Éd. (2e édition: *Ecrire l'histoire des femmes et du genre*, ENS Éd. 2007).

Williams, C. 1992. "The Glass Escalator: Hidden Advantages for Men in the "Female" Professions". *Social Problems* 39 (3): 253–267.

CHAPTER 43

Changing Gender Dynamics and Family Reinstitutionalization in Contemporary China

Ji Yingchun

1 Introduction

In this chapter, I would like to discuss three concepts/theories—i.e., mosaic gender ideology, mosaic familism, and mosaic modernity—that I have developed in the last decade regarding gender dynamics and family changes. In the last 40 years, Chinese society has transitioned from a centrally planned economy to a profit- and efficiency-driven market economy; different social forces at the macro level constitute a traditional-modern mosaic of temporality in the transitional society, the sturdy return of once contained Confucian patriarchal tradition (Cook and Dong 2011; Ho et al. 2018; Ji et al. 2017), likely in the 1990s and more remarkable after the 2008 Beijing Olympics, the pre-reform socialist version of modernity and its heritage, the market version of modernity, and the sweeping influence of globalization and neoliberalism after China entered the World Trade Organization (WTO) in 2001 (Ji 2017; Ji et al. 2017). These complex historical and institutional dynamics resulted in a mosaic modernity in contemporary China, one which simultaneously shapes gender and family changes as conceptualized by mosaic gender ideology and mosaic familism, and is defined by these changes in post-reform China. In the following sections, I will elaborate the three concepts, respectively.

2 Mosaic Modernity: An Interplay between Tradition and Modernity

The conceptualization of mosaic modernity is related to concepts of first modernity, second modernity, and cosmopolitan modernity (Beck and Grande 2010); further, Yan (2010 and 2020) demonstrated a coexisting of premodernity, first modernity, and second modernity in the Chinese society, whereas Chang (1999 and 2010) described a landscape of compressed modernity due to rapid socioeconomic development and the modernization process of East Asia within several decades compared to 300 years in Western societies.

Yet, to a large degree mosaic modernity is distinct from these above concepts. Tradition and modern not only coexist (Yan 2010) but are compressed (Chang 2010), reshuffled, or out of order (Beck and Grande 2010). Mosaic modernity is not merely a variant of the Western modernity, particularly in Beck's term of first modernity and second modernity, but relates more to the terminology of cosmopolitan modernity and the logics of post-Western theory (Roulleau-Berger 2015; Wei and Li 2018) in that it is complex, multidimensional, dynamic, plural, and contextual. Tradition is not necessarily replaced by modernity, but is a part of, shapes, and refines the Chinese modernity, thus creating an alternative or parallel to the Western modernity. And at the same time, it interacts with, is influenced by and likely influencing, and potentially clashing with modernity. Some tradition is not to be disregarded, or merely obeyed subconsciously without reflection. Ordinary people sometimes deliberately and reflexively choose, modify, and remold tradition to make it relevant in their lives; here, tradition is not necessarily constraining and oppressive, but meaningful to individual Chinese people in modern China and salient in their daily motivations and behaviors. Thus, it merits note here that tradition is not necessary static and it is renewing, renovating through the temporality of daily life.

This plural, complex modernity of Chinese characteristics, i.e., mosaic modernity, is the key context in which to understand the concepts of mosaic gender ideology and mosaic familism, which are defined by this mosaic of tradition and modernity coexisting and entangling with each other. To elaborate on these three concepts, I will discuss the structural and cultural changes that largely contribute to gender dynamics and family changes and the Chinese modernity as well in the post-reform period; hence, I will focus on the decline of the dual state apparatus during the planned economy to marketization transition, the collapse of the danwei system, and the waning of dominant Marxist ideology, whose vacuum is refilled by the reinstitutionalizing private families and resurging patriarchal tradition (Ji 2020; Ji et al. 2017).

The collapse of the danwei system and the decline of the dominant ideology have shaped the Chinese pathway to the separation of public and private spheres, which is different from how it historically occurred in the West and features the Chinese way towards modernization. Driven by early industrial revolutions, men left home to work while women stayed at home, where economic activities and livelihood used to be highly integrated in feudal agricultural societies. This gave rise to the separation of so-called man's domain in the workplace and women's domain in the private home. With women's large-scale participation in the labor market, women have had to shoulder a large bulk of housework and care work at home in addition to paid labor in the workplace, while men did very little to share women's second shift in the private sphere.

During the socialist time the Chinese government promoted women's emancipation through employment via the danwei system, which provided lifetime employment and comprehensive services for social reproduction and care (Cook and Dong 2011; Liu 2007). This brought about one of the highest female employment rates and lowest gender wage gaps in the world during that time. As analyzed in the Chinese feminists' terms of "private embedded in the public" (Song 2011) and "simultaneous construction of both family and state" (Zuo and Jiang 2009), the danwei system in urban China factually created an integration of the public and private spheres. Yet, during the transition to marketization, through the "unburdening" and downsizing to increase efficiency and productivity for the sake of profit, the danwei (particularly the state-owned enterprises) successfully transferred the responsibilities for social reproduction and care to individual families, which disproportionally fell upon women's shoulders (Cook and Dong 2011), producing a historical pathway transiting to the separation of the two spheres in China (Ji et al. 2017). The implication is that the historical Western path to the two-sphere separation is not a universal monologue; gender inequality is highly complex and contextually induced, and so is the road towards modernization, including family modernization.

3 Mosaic Gender Ideology: Complexity and Multidimensionality of Gender Ideology

The collapse of the danwei system and the decline of the mainstream Marxist gender egalitarian ideology as the dual state apparatus to organize gender equality in the socialist era have led to the separation of the public and private spheres in post-reform China. These changes have resulted in Chinese women's intensified work–family conflicts and have fundamentally shaped their disadvantaged status both in the family (private sphere) and labor market (public sphere). Corresponding to the two-sphere separation, the resurgence of Confucian patriarchal tradition (Cook and Dong 2011; Ho et al. 2018; Ji et al. 2017), the rise of gender essentialism (Wu 2009), and the newly introduced neoliberal rhetoric (Sun and Chen 2015) plus the once dominant Marxist gender ideology have forged a mosaic gender ideology to echo and justify the structural changes (Ji et al. 2017), where traditional, modern, conservative, progressive, and collectivist and individualist discourses/norms form a unique hybrid landscape of gender culture/ideology (Ji 2017; Ji et al. 2017). This mosaic gender ideology subtly promotes women's traditional role as wife and mother in a relative individualistic and modern tune. The tiles of different components in the mosaic gender ideology may assemble differently across different dimensions in individuals' life choices in their daily lives who belong to different social groups concerning gender, cohort, rural/urban divide, education, etc. For example, a high-achieving single woman in Shanghai on the one side enjoys being independent and successful in her career in the public domain, while on the other side she approves the normative imperative of marriage being the highest success of a woman but at the same time laments "men are brainwashed by 5,000 years of feudalism" in China (Ji 2015: 1068). Some people may largely live under traditional constraints without much reflection, while others may choose to obey, negotiate with, modify, or disregard some traditional components concerning their daily choices and behavior, and this may vary through different stages of life.

Recent research supports the complex and multidimensional feature of the changing gender ideology in present-day China. Husbands' migration facilitated couples to develop a strategic gender egalitarianism to deal with different dimensions of work and life, i.e., being progressive regarding labor structure and their daughters' education, but remaining traditional regarding male primacy and sons' duty for old age support (Zhang and Fussell 2017). Related, the trend of housewifization among some women in China, in opposition to the ongoing dehousewifization in Japan (Ochiai 2010), is not always due to constraints from traditional gender norms, but also is likely to be born of personal choice (Wu 2014). Although Chinese educated women are becoming more egalitarian, their male counterparts seem to stagger farther behind, likely due to the backlash from men's increased share of household work (Pimentel 2006). In general, Chinese are becoming more modern and egalitarian in gender ideology. Yet, there is a visible turning-tradition trend when it comes to gender role divisions in work and family, such as "men charge the outside, and women charge the inside" and "men are superior to women". Further, the Chinese are increasingly supportive of children taking the mother's surname and of equal inheritance between daughters and sons (Yang, Li and Zhu 2014).

Following the logic of modernization theory, in any society the process of modernization associated with economic development will eventually lead to an egalitarian attitude concerning gender roles (Inglehart and Norris 2003). As Knight and Brinton (2017) pointed out, this assumption of a linear tradition-egalitarianism continuum is built upon the Western-centric modernization mentality. Based on analyses of 26 European countries, they developed the conceptualization of multidimensionality of gender ideology and identified its three variants in different countries: liberal egalitarianism, egalitarian familism, and flexible egalitarianism. Similar in terms of multidimensionality yet different in ideology configuration, in Japan and South Korea the prevailing pro-work conservative ideology deviates from the traditional-egalitarian dichotomy, which stresses women's paid work in the market and at the same time promotes their primacy at home (Brinton and Lee 2016). Following the theoretical critique over the turning towards the two-sphere separation in post-reform China (Ji et al. 2017), empirical research identifies the tension in gender ideology. Across cohorts and gender, individual Chinese are positive about women's labor participation in the public sphere but remain supportive of gendered division in both paid work in the labor market and unpaid labor inside the family, and there is a marked gender gap in egalitarian gender ideology (Qian and Li 2020).

The conceptualization of mosaic gender ideology echoes the newly emerging conceptualization of multidimensionality of gender ideology and corresponding empirical findings in that it both stands against the Western-centric modernization theory, recognize the tension between the public and private spheres related to women's life constraints, and attempt to provide a plural, non-linear, and more complex version of the modern world.

4   Mosaic Familism: The Rise of a Bilateral Family System

I have developed the theory of mosaic familism focusing on intergenerational relations in the last decade (Ji 2017, 2020, 2021; Ji et al. 2020; Ji, Liu and Yang 2021). It describes an emerging bilateral family mode in today's Chinese society featuring both traditional norms and modern practices, where parents and adult children are interdependent on each other through financial, emotional, and caregiving support to withstand the rising cost of living and uncertainties in the era of marketization and globalization. Here, due to the collapse of the danwei system, individuals are disembedded from the almighty danwei system which provided lifetime employment and comprehensive welfare (Ji 2017; Yan 2010, 2020), and reembedded in the family, which factually becomes a micro welfare system providing care services to individuals (Ji 2020). More specifically, a loop of caregiving exchange among generations of women along bilateral family lines is the micro mechanism driving the emergence of this mosaic familism (Ji 2020; Ji et al. 2020), and this gendered pattern echoes the mosaic gender ideology in that women's traditional role as wife and mother in the private family is strengthened while egalitarian gender roles in the public sphere are supported.

There are five pillars of the mosaic familism theory. First, the mosaic configuration of tradition and modernity in the transitional society of China contextualizes the ongoing family reinstitutionalization and is the macro force driving the family changes. Second, with the decline of the traditional patriarchal extended family, an intimate bilateral-multinuclear, symbiotic family system is emerging, where parents and young adults are interdependent and young couples are embedded in close relations with both paternal and maternal parents following a gendered pattern. Third, in this bilateral intergenerational relationship, exchanges of money, emotional caregiving and housework, and norms, obligations, and rights are interwoven. Fourth, the exchanges of unpaid care work among women of different generations along the bilateral lines are the micro force driving this ongoing family reinstitutionalization. Traditional gender and family norms and modern practices coexist and interplay in daily life and on a cultural level, which influences and consists of mosaic modernity in a reciprocal manner (Ji 2020).

In the following, I will elaborate on heterosexual family supporting the elderly and providing child care, and homosexual women coping with intergenerational relations when faced with severe heterosexual marriage pressure from their parents. I will stress the gender dimension of this complex, mosaic relationship.

With the collapse of the danwei system, the public and private spheres are increasingly separating, resulting in women's intensifying work–family conflicts. Related to the long-term one-child family planning policy, the rising normative of intensive mothering, and the weak social welfare services, working mothers have to depend on bilateral parents, the paternal and maternal parents of the couple, to help with child care. Ji et al.'s (2020) investigation on women's second birth intention at a county-level city in the Yangtze Delta shortly after the initiation of the comprehensive two-child family planning policy shows a family relay of child caregiving mainly undertaken by generations of women in a bilateral way, "Grandparents on both sides and parents work together to provide day care, night care, preschool care, and educational involvement at different times of the day and at different stages of a child's development" (Ji et al. 2020: 126). Paternal and maternal grandmothers take turns in fulfilling the second shift in their life after retirement to help with child care, whereas the mother takes over the second shift to care for the child(ren) after her daytime work.

The practice of bi-locality and bi-surnaming is rather common at the research site in that young couples and their child(ren) live with grandparents of both sides during different times of the year and children sometimes follow either their father's or their mother's family name when there are two (Ji et al. 2020). And son preference has become much weaker, with some residents preferring to have a daughter. Yet, the emergence of a modern bilateral family pattern seems to both cripple the patriarchal and patrilineal tradition, but sometimes consolidates the patriarchal tradition, which indicates a complicated interaction between tradition and modernity. For example, the logic of the bi-surnaming system actually follows the patrilineal name of grandfathers on both sides but never gives credit to either paternal or maternal grandmothers who actually have given unpaid child care to two generations. Further, related to the son preference tradition, local parents usually buy a wedding house for sons, but they only buy a wedding car for daughters. This leads to the paradox that if a couple's first child is a son, it would prevent them from having a second child due to the giant future financial expenditure for sons. In contrast, a first birth being a daughter tends to encourage a second birth. Here, the patriarchal tradition sabotages itself in a modern context of rising property prices by potentially preventing more boys from being born (Ji et al. 2020).

When the downward intergenerational support seems to follow a bilateral pattern, this is also true for the upward old age support. In another county-level city in the same Yangtze Delta, married women continue their intimacy and financial and caregiving exchange with their own parents (Ji 2020). They try to treat their parents-in-law the same as their own parents. This rising practice of daughters providing for parents is in stark contrast with the patriarchal and patrilineal norm of raising sons for old age support, which was factually practiced by daughters-in-law, who were then expected to practice filial piety to their parents-in-law rather than their own parents. Amid this modern, bilateral practice of old age support by married women, there is a clear, simultaneous trend towards a decline in patrilineal power and a rise in matrilineal power. For example, Siyu, a married woman born in the late 1980s, was willing to provide for her mother-in-law in her old age the same as for her parents, but she also expressed that the old age support would have been degraded if her mother-in-law had not had helped with child care. In her logic, her mother-in-law's partial intention to help with child care was for her own old age support. Yet, Siyu was rather disdainful toward her father-in-law and refused to provide for him when he grew old, because he had been living with his mistress for years, and thus was not worth her respect and support. Another interesting story is that of Yanping, a working grandmother. She was not able to help take care of her newly born grandson because she had to work. Her son's mother-in-law thus came to live with Yanping's family to help with child care. Yanping was struggling about her "duty" and "right" as well being taken by her in-laws, but she also seemed to be understanding that sometimes married women even did not "allow" the mother-in-law to help considering they were usually close to their own mothers. Runan, a nurse born in the 1990s, further pointed to the fragility of the patrilineal connection and the unreliability of patriarchal power when a woman faces a divorce. In her narrative, her own parents would never fail her, but the in-laws would always be on the husband's side even if he was wrong.

In different locales, from a small city to a big city in inland China and to metropolitan Shanghai on the east coast, young lesbians are under various degree of pressure from their parents to form a heterosexual marriage (Ji et al. 2021). The small city girl Shitou provided her parents' definition of filial piety, which she apparently cannot fulfill as a lesbian: "Being filial is getting married at the right age, having a family, and then providing eldercare and burying their dead bodies in the end" (543). Mumu, from an inland big city, always felt guilty and unfilial being a lesbian, and she gradually changed her mind regarding the patriarchal norm of filial piety, i.e., "raising sons for old age support". She found that her uncle, the only son of her maternal grandparents, failed to provide for his mother. She started to help her mother learn new skills and technology to adopt to the fast-changing world and defined growing up together with her mother as the modern practice of the traditional norm of filial piety, being the only daughter who happened to be lesbian.

Put together, the above studies regarding bilateral grandparents caring for grandchildren and married women providing bilateral old age support, we can find that a loop of generations of women following bilateral lines to exchange care, including child care and old age care, factually drives the rise of a bilateral family system with a clear gendered pattern, where the declining patriarchal tradition is negotiating with modern gender and family practices. Whereas the lesbian study shows how the traditional patriarchal norm of filial piety is transformed into a relatively egalitarian, intimate modern intergenerational relationship, yet one that is still in the name of "filial piety", which fits well with the essence of mosaic modernity and mosaic gender ideology.

5 Discussion and Conclusion

The separation of the public and private spheres and the mosaic gender ideology, and the consequent gender dynamics thus contextualize complex family changes and ongoing demographic transition in the private sphere in contemporary China. Partially thanks to the long-term one-child family planning policy, the traditional patriarchal and patrilineal Chinese family mode is transitioning to mosaic familism, a new family mode with relatively egalitarian and intimate intergenerational relationships. This mosaic model is different from both the traditional, distant, and hierarchal patriarchal family dynamics, and the so-called modern Western nuclear family of a clear individualistic orientation. It bears witness to a simultaneous decline in traditional, patriarchal, and patrilineal authority, and a rising influence along the matrilineal family line. The exchange of and cooperation in care services (mostly raising children and elder care provision) by women of different generations following the bilateral family lines propel the rise of mosaic familism. Further, mosaic familism and mosaic gender ideology are both shaped by and constitutive of the mosaic modernity in the transitional society of China, where tradition and modernity coexist and interplay with each other. It merits note here:

> The complex interplay of traditional, modern, local and global influences that contribute to mosaic modernity and mosaic familism are not uniform across China. Not only should we expect variation in such a large country, but also need to take account of the differences in the pace of modernization and degrees of exposure to diverse new ideas and values across China, as well as differences and inequalities in the life choices open to Chinese citizens.
>
> JI et al. 2021

The above localized theorizing and conceptualization regarding two-sphere separation, mosaic gender ideology, mosaic familism, and mosaic modernity are directly based on Chinese people's daily practices deeply rooted in the historical and institutional context in China, which actually has never been isolated from, but well embedded in, globalization, particularly since China entered the WTO in 2001. Of course, this mosaic nature of the Chinese modernity can even date back to the very beginning of the Chinese modernization course, the Self-Strengthening Movement in the late 19th century, featured by the tenet of Chinese Essence and Western Technology. Yet, in terms of knowledge production and reproduction, we draw insights from Western scholars, such as Western feminists' critique of two-sphere separation and Ulrich Beck's reflections on the Western modernity. We are also inspired by ideas from Chinese and East Asian scholars, such as Shaopeng Song, Yunxiang Yan, and Kyung-Sup Chang. Further, the above theorization of gender dynamics, family changes and demographic transition has direct implications for East Asian and other transitional societies. It is also relevant to the Western societies that do not necessary embody a monotonic modernity or follow the only path to modernization, but simultaneously have both modern and traditional forces within.

Therefore, the process of theorizing the above dynamics concerning gender, family, and modernity in contemporary China is simultaneously local and global, reflecting the continuities and discontinuities of knowledge, tradition, and modernity. Moreover, it shows the significance of knowledge production in multiple sites across the globe that is parallel to and interactive with knowledge production in Western societies. This pluralistic and dynamic process of knowledge production and reproduction vividly embodies the essence of post-Western sociology.

References

Beck, U., and E. Grande. 2010. "Varieties of Second Modernity: The Cosmopolitan Turn in Social and Political Theory and Research". *The British Journal of Sociology* 61 (3): 409–443.

Brinton, M.C., and D.J. Lee. 2016. "Gender-Role Ideology, Labor Market Institutions, and Post-Industrial Fertility". *Population and Development Review* 42 (3): 405–433.

Chang, K. 1999. "Compressed Modernity and Its Discontents: South Korean Society in Transition". *Economy and Society* 28 (1): 30–55.

Chang, K. 2010. "The Second Modern Condition? Compressed Modernity as Internalized Reflexive Cosmopolitization". *The British Journal of Sociology* 61 (3): 444–464.

Cook, S., and X. Dong. 2011. "Harsh Choices: Chinese Women's Paid Work and Unpaid Care Responsibilities Under Economic Reform". *Development and Change* 42: 947–965.

Ho, P.S.Y., S. Jackson, S. Cao, and C. Kwok. 2018. "Sex With Chinese Characteristics: Sexuality Research in/on 21st-Century China". *The Journal of Sex Research* 55 (4–5): 486–521.

Inglehart, R., and P. Norris. 2003. *Rising Tide: Gender Equality and Cultural Change Around the World*. Cambridge: Cambridge University Press.

Ji, Y. 2015. "Between Tradition And Modernity: 'Leftover' Women in Shanghai". *Journal of Marriage and Family* 77 (5): 1057–1073.

Ji, Y. 2017. "A Mosaic Temporality: New Dynamics of the Gender and Marriage System in Contemporary Urban China". *Temporalités. Revue De Sciences Sociales Et Humaines* 26: 1–16.

Ji, Y. 2020. "Mosaic Familism: Daughters Providing for Parents and the Reinstitutionalization of Chinese Families". *Twenty-First Century Bi-Monthly* 180 (4): 77–79. (In Chinese.)

Ji, Y. 2021. "A Migrant Girl Coming of Age: A Zigzag Journey of Life". In *Sociology of Migration and Post-Western Theory*, edited by L. Roulleau-Berger and Y. Liu, 134–140. ENS Éditions.

Ji, Y., X. Wu, S. Sun, and G. He. 2017. "Unequal Care, Unequal Work: Toward a More Comprehensive Understanding of Gender Inequality in Post-Reform Urban China". *Sex Roles* 77 (11): 765–778.

Ji, Y., Y. Liu, and S. Yang. 2021. "A Tale of Three Cities: Distinct Marriage Strategies among Chinese Lesbians". *Journal of Gender Studies* 30 (5): 536–548.

Ji, Y., H. Wang, Y. Liu, R. Xu, and Z. Zheng. 2020. "Young Women's Fertility Intentions and the Emerging Bilateral Family System under China's Two-Child Family Planning Policy". *China Review* 20 (2): 113–142.

Knight, C.R., and M.C. Brinton. 2017. "One Egalitarianism or Several? Two Decades of Gender-Role Attitude Change in Europe". *American Journal of Sociology* 122 (5): 1485–1532.

Liu, J. 2007. *Gender and Work in Urban China: Women Workers of the Unlucky Generation*. Routledge.

Ochiai, E. 2010. *Twenty-First Century Japanese Families: Where to Go*. Translated by Y. Zheng. 3rd ed. Shandong People's Publishing House. (In Chinese, translated from Japanese.)

Pimentel, E.E. 2006. "Gender Ideology, Household Behavior, and Backlash in Urban China". *Journal of Family Issues* 27 (3): 341–365.

Qian, Y., and J. Li. 2020. "Separating Spheres: Cohort Differences in Gender Attitudes About Work and Family in China". *China Review* 20 (2): 19–51.

Rouleau-Berger, L. 2015. "Post-Western Space and Doing Sociology", translated by J. Ren. *Journal of Social Theory* 18 (2): 237–252. (In Chinese, translated from English.)

Song, S. 2011. "The Private Embedded in the Public: The State's Discourse on Domestic Work, 1949–1966". *Research on Women in Modern Chinese History* 19: 131–172. (In Chinese.)

Sun, S., and F. Chen. 2015. "Reprivatized Womanhood: Changes in Mainstream Media's Framing of Urban Women's Issues in China, 1995–2012". *Journal of Marriage and Family* 77 (5): 1091–1107.

Wei, J., and P. Li. 2018. "Post-Western Sociology and Contemporary Chinese Sociology". *Journal of Beijing Normal University (Social Sciences)* 265 (1): 143–150. (In Chinese.)

Wu, X. 2009. "The Transformation of Gender Discourse in the Context of Marketization". *Social Sciences in China* 2: 163–176, 207–208. (In Chinese.)

Wu, X. 2014. "The Rise and Decline of the Housewifization: From the Perspective of Individualization". *Nanjing Journal of Social Sciences* 2: 62–68, 77. (In Chinese.)

Yan, Y. 2010. "The Chinese Path to Individualization". *The British Journal of Sociology* 61 (3): 489–512.

Yan, Y. 2020. *The Individualization of Chinese Society*. Taylor & Francis.

Yang, J., H. Li, and G. Zhu. 2014. "Changing Trends in Gender Outlook in China from 1990 to 2010". *Collection of Women's Studies* 126 (6): 28–36. (In Chinese.)

Zhang, H., and E. Fussell. 2017. "Strategic Gender Egalitarianism in Rural China: The Impacts of Husbands' Migration on Gender Relations". *American Behavioral Scientist* 61 (10): 1192–1213.

Zuo, J., and Y. Jiang. 2009. *Urban Women's Work and Family in Social Transition*. Contemporary China Publishing House. (In Chinese.)

CHAPTER 44

Revisiting Comparative Frameworks and Gender Inequality in Japan

Nemoto Kumiko

1   Sex Segregation and Gender Inequality in Japan

Japan's gender inequality is characterized by a high level of vertical sex segregation at work, a large percentage of irregular women's employment, and a distinct gendered division of labor in the family. Women are highly concentrated in clerical and low management positions, with few female executives in top management. The percentage of female managers in Japan is only about 13%, while it is 43% in the United States and 39% in Sweden (Aizawa 2018). In postwar corporate Japan, a gendered division of labor has long been maintained through firms' customs. For example, a large number of companies have hired only a small number of elite female college graduates for positions in which men have typically been hired while relegating a large number of women to non-career-track, part-time, and temp positions. This custom of track hiring has been a major means of labor cost savings for Japanese firms (Nemoto 2016).

Japan ratified the UN Convention on the Elimination of All Forms of Discrimination Against Women (CEDAW) in 1985, which led to Japan's enactment of the Equal Employment Opportunity Law (EEOL) in 1986. However, the EEOL has no effective enforcement mechanism and offers little incentive to firms to follow the law. Women's quitting work upon marriage and childbirth was common until the late 1990s. In the 1990s, Japanese firms employed liberal reforms by partially introducing a style of US employment management, which included such practices as downsizing, restructuring, and instituting performance-based wage systems, for the purpose of saving on labor costs and increasing the hiring of irregular and temporary female workers, which only furthered the gender gap in the labor market. The Japanese business community opposed a revision of the EEOL or legal sexual harassment prevention in the 1990s. In 2013 Prime Minister Shinzo Abe announced "Abenomics", a plan to revitalize Japan's long-depressed economy; it included "womenomics", meant to increase the number of women leaders in all decision-making positions in society to 30% (Dalton 2017). Womenomics reflected Japan's aspiration to incorporate the global business standard, including corporate social responsibility and pressure from foreign shareholders. For the same reasons as above, the Japanese government promoted corporate efforts to increase female managers. Although the Abe government's emphasis on "women's empowerment" was a popular slogan, few reforms were mandatory, and a large number of women continued to be economically insecure.

A high level of corporate gender segregation in the workplace is one of the major characteristics of gender inequality in Japan. Japanese companies have long used women mostly in non-managerial positions, and thus as cheap labor. During the postwar period, the Japanese state has promoted the explicit gendered division of labor in work and family, emphasizing women's devotion to the family and men's focus on work. The government-led initiatives such as EEOL were mostly guideline-based, with few penalties to employers and with little protection of women's employment. Until recently, governmental and corporate responses to gender inequality in Japan did not derive from civil demands but instead related to international pressures, including the rise in corporate social responsibility with regard to global business imperatives and the increase in foreign shareholders in Japan (Nemoto 2016). Thus, Japan differs from social democratic countries such as Sweden, where explicit gender egalitarianism and employment security are emphasized in government policies. It also differs from the liberal market economies such as the United States, where liberal reforms incorporating women into the labor market have been emphasized.

2　Japan's Coordinated Capitalism and Gender Inequality

According to scholars of varieties of capitalism (Hall and Soskice 2001; Vogel 2006), Japan belongs to the category of coordinated market economies, differing from the liberal market economies in its close relations between the state and firms, its lack of labor mobility and employment protection, and its industries' close ties. In the postwar period, Japan's close relationships among the state, the banks, and industry are known to have propelled national economic growth. They also stabilized employees' lifelong employment security by rarely resorting to layoffs, offering financial security to men as breadwinners, and thus reifying the gendered division of labor in the family. Lifelong employment and an age-based hierarchy made companies operate like "community firms", valuing loyalty and long service while women were mostly treated as "quasi-members ... or non members" (Inagami and Whittaker 2005).

Indeed, this framework left out aspects of gender inequality or the role of the family in relation to businesses and the state. Some argue that firms in the coordinated capitalist countries emphasize long-term employment protection and require employees to continue to stay at one firm and that they therefore have a negative impact on women, who may interrupt their careers for childbearing and leave a firm (Estevez-Abe 2006). In Japan, such a gender bias or a cultural expectation of a gender division has been normalized, not limited to employment customs, although it has a close relationship to the dimension of family dynamics.

The family is critical to understanding coordinated capitalism in the postwar economic development of Japan. As the stable state-firm ties secured lifetime employment and employment security, women shouldered the caretaking obligation in the family and thus the state welfare burden; women's cheap labor as temps or part-time workers saved companies large labor costs. Tax policy provided strong incentives for a housewife to work only part-time and to be financially dependent on her husband. Marriage became a major means for women to attain economic security in the 1980s because unmarried women had a hard time being economically independent and not falling into poverty (Osawa 2009). The status of "housewife" became widely viewed as a socially desirable one. This was because housewives were provided security by both the Japanese state and their husbands, in tax and pension benefits as well as in the traditional role of managing their husbands' entire income. The ideological normalization of the housewife peaked in the 1960s and 1970s. In 1999, about 80% of women who were regular full-time employees before marriage quit their jobs upon marriage (Abe, Hamamoto and Tanaka 2003: 31). Marriage in postwar Japan has been strongly based on gender-divided obligations and responsibilities rather than couples' emotional ties and satisfaction. Not only have women been expected to serve as the major caretakers of the family, but because of the strong emphasis on men's economic duties and financial responsibilities, men have been expected to devote themselves single-mindedly to work (Mathews 2003). Given that the family has been the locus of this "reproductive bargain" (Gottfried 2016), or mutual exchange of obligations and benefits not just within the family but within the state and the business community, gender and family can be understood as a critical dimension of Japan's coordinated capitalism.

3   Gender Relations during the Conservative Modernization of Japan

The gendered division of labor in work and family life and the marginalization of women in the labor market have been the default setting of Japan's coordinated capitalism (Nemoto 2016). However, the belief in the gendered division of labor is not based in the traditional culture of Japan but instead derived from the gender orders in the development of Japan's authoritarian modernization. Prior to World War II, the patriarchal belief in the family system was imposed as an institutional apparatus, enforced by legal codes, by the authoritarian Japanese state for the sake of the country's economic growth and as a means of modernization during the Meiji period.

Shire and Nemoto (2020), extending Walby's theory of the gender regime to non-Western contexts, argued that gendered families and gendered public orders in the modernization process of Japan and Germany was different from what occurred in the liberal market states and social democratic states. Examining gender relations in Japan and Germany within Barrington Moore's theoretical framework of "conservative modernization", we explained that both Japan and Germany developed authoritarian imperial projects of warfare, colonization, and the state-led development of heavy industry, and also legitimized distinctively gender-divided social orders. The conservative modernization of Japan "codified the patriarchal family to both subordinate wives to husbands and to constitute the family in the interest of the authoritarian state" (Shire and Nemoto 2020: 435). According to Moore (1966: 414), Japan and Germany differ from other countries in that both lacked the elite class of the bourgeoisie, whose revolutions in England, France, and the United States led to the evolution of democracy. In Japan and Germany, the socially and politically weak business class did not adopt democratic political reforms but just reacted to circumstances, culminating in fascism. Economic development before modernization in Japan was mostly led by the state, and thus the bourgeoisie had a weak role and never carried democratic ideas in Japan as it did in other European countries (Moore 1966: 298). Importantly, Japan's conservative modernization under the authoritarian state also mobilized wives and mothers for nationalistic and militaristic pursuits (Shire and Nemoto 2020: 435).

The ideology of gender and family was employed for the sustenance of imperial Japan, as a nation with the belief that it was to be governed by an emperor. Similarly, the family was to be controlled by a man, or the father, and thus women's submission to men was legitimized (Tsujimura 2008: 155) in public and private. The Meiji Civil Code refers to wives' dependence on husbands and wives' subordination to their husbands due to their quasi-incompetence (Shire and Nemoto 2020: 435). Women during the Meiji period were doubly exploited by the nation and family (Tsujimura 2008: 151). As Japan relied on the textile industry, a large number of young women at the age of 12 or 13 years entered the workforce, often sold by their fathers, in poor families, or abducted by an outsider.

Patriarchal lineage in marriage and family was emphasized during this time. A woman registered to enter into a man's family. Children born out of wedlock did not have rights of inheritance equal to those of legitimate children until 2013. In short, gender relations in conservative modernization are distinguished by weak individual rights, a legally codified gendered division of labor, and an emphasis on the importance of the family in the public sphere (Shire and Nemoto 2020: 443). The patriarchal family in conservative modernization in Japan was not constrained within the private sphere, but rather was "cut loose from the household to produce a social order that subordinates women to men in the nation" (Shire and Nemoto 2020: 438). In the postwar period, the patriarchal family transformed into the male breadwinner-led family, in which women are paid for their traditional roles through their husband's employment; they are classified as "dependent" on the husband and given tax and pension benefits (Osawa 2004: 90). Due to strong nationalistic mobilization and the embracing of women's role as good wives and wise mothers in modern Japan, even progressive feminists ended up supporting this (Kano 2006: 197). With the decline of grassroots feminism in Japan, gender equality has become a project developed mostly by the government (Yamaguchi 2018). It has continued to shape gender dynamics and the gendered characteristics of family and employment in Japan.

4 Gender and Liberalism

As my discussions of both conservative modernization and the coordinated market economies have pointed out, Japan's economic and industrial growth was state-led; the Japanese state also led Japan's social and economic modernization with a strong emphasis on "catching up" with the Western mindset. Japan's weak liberal and democratic reforms in its attempts at modernization related to the state-led economic and social reforms that placed too little value on individual rights. Schwartz and Pharr argue that Japan's civil society has been state-led to such a great degree that workers are willing to subordinate themselves to the state (2003: 4). Worker relations with firms have been based on intense conformity and exploitation, characterized by a lack of autonomy or fairness, as seen in the frequency of workers' deaths and suicide by overwork (Barshay 2003: 76–77). The economic survival of the state has also made the maintenance of the gender hierarchy and the division of labor in work and family imperative to national growth.

Gender egalitarianism is a critical component of democracy and human advancement in modern nations (Inglehart and Welzel 2005: 282–284). A country's economic development leads to an increase in democratic values and thus to gender equality (Inglehart, Norris and Welzel 2002). Societies that are all about survival place the highest value on materialism and hard work while having little tolerance for difference and diversity. According to Welzel and Inglehart's discussion of democracy and gender equality, economic development and the subsequent increase in individual material and social autonomy leads to an aversion to authority and a preference for freedom and equality (2008). As they point out (and I agree), the development of a liberal democracy may be a key to gender equality because of the development of a public consciousness opposed to traditional authority, collectivism, and conformity (Nemoto 2016). But, as seen with conservative modernization, economic development and individual freedom of choice do not necessarily lead to fast progress in gender equality due to the persistence of conservative gender ideology. Liberalism may enhance opportunities for individuals to choose, but it does not lead to gender inequality because the types of choices themselves may be limited.

Liberalism emphasizes one's autonomy, freedom, and personal choice, and thus it would appear to promise equality (Levey 2005: 127). But the types of choices one can make are socially and culturally shaped or limited. Interestingly, much of the current gendered division of labor is perpetuated through women's voluntary choices. Levey discusses Rawls' views of the gendered division of labor, which address the idea that the family has produced an unjust system in which women, as the main caretakers, bear an unequal share of the tasks, but Rawls state that such a gendered division of labor may not result from, or lead to, injustice, as it is voluntary and a part of one's basic liberties (138). Levey concludes that liberalism is not useful for responding to acts and attitudes that are driven by voluntary choice, such as the gendered division of labor within the family or gendered preferences for jobs and occupations; by contrast, involuntary discrimination, or coercing one to engage in involuntary gender roles, can be addressed by laws and states (139). While liberalism appears to be generous to individuals as it offers us the opportunity to choose, it cannot address the logic of gender, and thus it may perpetuate inequality. Similarly, gender inequality in Japan is not so much a matter of liberalism as it is a matter of normalized gendered options themselves in Japan needing to be questioned.

In the United States, liberal individualism encouraged "free choice" gender egalitarianism, especially since it resonated with the feminist message that promoted equal access to jobs and education for women, paving the way for the "gender revolution" (England 2010: 162). The logic that individuals should have equal rights to education and jobs with the social values of achievement and upward mobility led women to find their "true selves" and undergo "self-realization" by undertaking high-paying, traditionally male jobs (159). But England argues that, due to a strong degree of gender essentialism remaining in the United States, women from working-class backgrounds have remained in traditionally female-dominated jobs, such as teaching and nursing, while women with middle-class backgrounds have been integrated into male-dominated professional and managerial jobs. Therefore, increased liberal choices do not necessarily lead to the eradication of gender inequality in jobs and occupations. Further theoretical and empirical comparisons of Japan with other Western and non-Western countries, with regard to how democratic values and liberalism permeate the gendered division of labor, will be critical.

5   Discussion

Following insights gained from post-Western sociology's exploration of intersecting points among various countries in order to open up the Western/non-Western dialogue rather than merely making a structural comparison among countries (Roulleau-Berger 2021: 17), this paper revisited the theoretical frameworks of the coordinated market economies and the conservative gender regime and extended their perspectives on Japan to include the gendered division of labor in work and family life. These comparative frameworks, which are often criticized for overgeneralizing diverse national differences, need to be developed by examining national variations in gender ideologies and their relationships with national modernization processes and histories. While the state-governed ideology of gender in work and families in modern and contemporary Japan differs from gender evolution in Anglo-Saxon liberal nations or social democratic nations, there needs to be a further large-scale dialogue for future progress in gender equality in families and work in many more countries. The comparative frameworks I discussed offer useful starting points for identifying some commonalities among nations and societies. Future research should add more complexity to these frameworks so that there is more clarification on the similarities and distinct characteristics of gender.

References

Abe, M., Chizuka Hamamoto, and Shigeto Tanaka. 2003. *Reconciling Work and Family: Issues and Policies in Japan*. Geneva: International Labor Office.

Aizawa, Y. 2018. "Gender Equality in Japan Remains Bottom". NHK *World Japan*. December 16, 2018. Accessed August 16, 2021. https://www3.nhk.or.jp/nhkworld/en/news/backstories/335/.

Barshay, Andrew E. 2003. "Capitalism and Civil Society in Postwar Japan: Perspectives from Intellectual History". In *The State of Civil Society in Japan*, edited by Frank J. Schwartz and Susan J. Pharr, 63–82. New York: Cambridge University Press.

Dalton, E. 2017. "Womenomics, 'equality' and Abe's Neo-liberal Strategy to Make Japanese Women Shine". *Social Science Japan Journal* 20 (1): 95–105.

England, P. 2010. "The Gender Revolution: Uneven and Stalled". *Gender & Society* 24 (2): 149–166.

Estevez-Abe, M. 2006. "Gendering the Varieties of Capitalism: A Study of Occupational Segregation by Sex in Advanced Industrial Societies". *World Politics* 59: 142–175.

Gottfried, H. 2016. *The Reproductive Bargain: Deciphering the Enigma of Japanese Capitalism*. Leiden: Brill.

Hall, P.A., and David Soskice. 2001. "An Introduction to Varieties of Capitalism". In *Varieties of Capitalism: The Institutional Foundations of Comparative Advantage*, edited by Peter A. Hall and David Soskice, 1–68. Oxford: Oxford University Press.

Inagami, T., and D.H. Whittaker. 2005. *The New Community Firm: Employment, Governance and Management Reform in Japan*. Cambridge, MA: Cambridge University Press.

Inglehart, R., and C. Welzel. 2005. *Modernization, Cultural Change, and Democracy: The Human Development Sequence*. New York, NY: Cambridge University Press.

Kano, A. 2006. "Motherhood and Sexuality". In *Feminism*, edited by Yumiko Ehara and Yoshiko Kanai. Tokyo: Shinyosha.

Levey, A. 2005. "Liberalism, Adaptive Preferences, and Gender Equality". *Hypatia* 20 (4): 127–143.

Mathews, G. 2003. "Can 'a Real Man' Live for His Family? Ikigai and Masculinity in Today's Japan". In *Men and Masculinities in Contemporary Japan*, edited by J.E. Roberson and N. Suzuki, 109–125. London: Routledge Curzon.

Moore, B. 1966. *Social Origins of Dictatorship and Democracy: Lord and Peasant in the Making of the Modern World*. Boston, MA: Beacon Press.

Nemoto, K. 2016. *Too Few Women at the Top: The Persistence of Inequality in Japan*. Ithaca, NY: ILR Press/Cornell University Press.

Osawa, M. 2009. "Women's Resistance". In *Feminism in Japan*, edited by Syoko Amano, Kimiko Ito, Ruri Ito, Teruko Inoue, Chizuko Ueno, Yumiko Ehara, Mari Osawa, and Mikiyo Kano, 1–39. Tokyo: Iwanami Syoten.

Osawa, M. 2004. *Making Gender Equal Society*. Tokyo: NHK Books.

Roulleau-Berger, L. 2021. "The Fabric of Post-Western Sociology: Ecologies of Knowledge Beyond the 'East' and the 'West'". *The Journal of Chinese Sociology* 8 (10): 1–28.

Shire, K., and Kumiko Nemoto. 2020. "The Origins and Transformations of Conservative Gender Regimes in Germany and Japan". *Social Politics* 27 (3): 432–448.

Schwartz, Frank J., and Susan J. Pharr, eds. 2003. *The State of Civil Society in Japan*. Cambridge: Cambridge University Press.

Tsujimura, M. 2008. *Jenda to jinken* [Gender and Human Rights]. Tokyo: Nihonhyoronsya.

Vogel, Steven K. 2006. *Japan Remodeled: How Government and Industry Are Reforming Japanese Capitalism*. Ithaca, NY: Cornell University Press.

Welzel, C., and Ronald Inglehart. 2008. "The Role of Ordinary People in Democratization". *Journal of Democracy* 19 (1): 126–140.

Yamaguchi, T. 2018. "The Mainstreaming of Feminism and the Politics of Backlash in Twenty-First-Century Japan". In *Rethinking Japanese Feminisms*, edited by Julia C. Block, Ayako Kano, and James Welker. Honolulu: University of Hawai'i Press.

CHAPTER 45

Two Contradictory Trends in Korea in the COVID-19 Era: "Condensed Radicalization of Individualization" and "Community Orientation"

Shim Young-Hee

1   Introduction

Gender inequality in Korea, particularly gender discrimination in the job market and the family against married women with children, is well known (Shim 2011; Shim, Kim and Kim 2002). The Gender Gap Index ranked Korea 108th in 2018, 115th in 2017, and 118th in 2016 (Joo et al. 2019). Since the COVID-19 pandemic, socioeconomic polarization has worsened. According to *World Inequality Report 2021* (World Inequality Lab 2021, quoted in Lee 2021), the inequality in assets as well as income in the world has worsened since the COVID-19 pandemic, and some civil society organizations like Oxfam called the coronavirus an "inequality virus".[1] Korea is no exception. As to gender inequality, the share of women's income in world labor income ended up in increasing from 31% in 1990 to 35% in 2021. In Korea the share of women's income increased slowly, from 27.3% in 1990 to 30.9% in 2010 and 32.4% in 2020, but it did not reach the world average. According to the report, "In the case of Korea, even though the share of women's income is higher than that of Japan (38%), India (18%), it does not reach that of Western Europe (38%) and Eastern Europe (41%)" (World Inequality Lab 2021, quoted in Lee 2021).

---

1   According to the report, inequality in terms of assets is bigger than income inequality in the world. Korea is no exception to this. In terms of asset inequality, the top 1% hold 25.4%, and the top 10% hold 58.5% of assets in Korea. Compared with 2019, both rose 0.1%. However, the lower 50% remained the same, with 5.6%. In terms of income inequality Korea is in a better state than the world average. However, the phenomenon of leaning toward higher strata is remarkable. The top 1% holds 14.7% of income, and the top 10% holds 46.5% of income. The income of the top 10% is 14 times greater than that of the lower 50% in Korea, showing a bigger gap than France (7 times more), Italy (8 times more), and Germany (10 times more). The report said "Korea achieved rapid industrialization and economic development in the 1960s–1990s, during which time deregulation and liberalization were made while the social safety net was weak. As a result, the share of the top 10% increased from 35% to 45% since 1990, while the share of the lower 50% decreased from 21% to 16%".

Most of the recent studies on women and COVID-19 have focused on the impact of COVID-19 on women. For example, some say that COVID-19 is "a disaster for women" (Berkhout and Richardson 2020), some others have opposed the phrase "war with COVID-19" (Enloe 2020). A special issue of *Feminism and Philosophy* in September 2020 that deals with the theme of "Feminist Responses to Covid-19 and Pandemics" published articles on the increase in domestic violence due to COVID-19 (Pilipchuk 2020), child care issues (Harbin and MacLachlan 2020), mental health issues (Gotlib 2020), and sympathizing political leaders (Betzler 2020). Domestic research also focuses on the impact of COVID-19 on women, particularly on women's care work. Caring democracy is also a big issue in domestic research (e.g., Kim 2020; Tronto 2013). The double burden on women has been a hot issue for a long time (Hochschild 2012). However, in the time of the COVID-19 pandemic, it burst out again because the time of people staying at home grew longer and women's care responsibilities became heavier. Most of the gender and COVID-19 discussions focus on this issue.

Women could respond to this situation in one of two ways: to get away from the family or to stick to the family. I discuss individualization issues because they are supposed to be related to a decrease in marriage, an increase in divorce, and a decrease in fertility, and women and the family in general. Here, individualization refers to "a categorical shift in the relationship between individual and society", as Beck has defined it (Beck 1992; Beck and Beck-Gernsheim 2002).

In this regard I will focus on two contradictory aspects of "condensed radicalization of individualization" on the one hand and the still lingering "community orientation" on the other.

This coexistence of the two contradictory trends shows a trend that follows the individualization trend of the Western society on one hand, but also another trend which goes over and tries to restore the cherished community orientation on the other. This community orientation seen together with "condensed radicalization of individualization" among the Koreans indicates a post-Western tendency going beyond the "West" and the "East" (Roulleau-Berger 2021; Roulleau-Berger and Li 2018). By "post-Western" I mean not only "after" but also "critical of" or "overcoming" Western sociology (Han, in this book). And in this sense the coexistence of the two contradictory trends also suggests a direction which may unfolded in the future.

2 "Condensed Radicalization of Individualization" in Korea

2.1 Change of Individualization in Nine Years

With regard to "condensed radicalization of individualization", which is a term I coined to describe the individualization changes in Korea, I will start with a recent survey conducted in 33 global cities around the world in September 2021 (Han 2021).

To measure the concept of individualization, I tried to use the two aspects of individualization aptly pointed out by Howard (2007: 8–9): one is emancipation from tradition and the other is emancipation from the group. My colleague and I have worked on the measurement of individualization according to these two aspects since 2012 and developed the following three questions: one is related to marriage, the second to children, and the third to divorce. And we have conducted several surveys since then (Han and Shim 2016; Shim, Kim and Kim 2014). The first of them was in 2012. In the first survey the individualization questions were asked in a dichotomy style.[2]

In later surveys, we changed the questions a little bit, making them into a Likert scale. After asking "How strongly do you agree or disagree with the following statements?" we gave the following three items: a) "Marriage is not a necessity. Living alone is acceptable to me"; b) "I don't need to have children after marriage. Living without children is acceptable"; and c) "I would get a divorce if my marriage didn't work out as expected". And the answers were measured on a Likert scale: "Strongly Disagree" (score 1), "Disagree" (score 2), "Neutral" (score 3), "Agree" (score 4), and "Strongly Agree" (score 5).

In a recent survey conducted in 33 global cities in September 2021 (Han 2021), the findings were as follows (Table 45.1). As to the item "Marriage is not a necessity. Living alone is acceptable to me", Seoul turned out to be second highest, with a score of 3.41; as to the item "I don't need to have children after marriage.

---

[2] The questions were changed somewhat since the first survey. In the first survey conducted in Seoul, Korea; Beijing, China; and Tokyo, Japan, in 2012, the questions were as follows: "How would you respond 1) if your child says he/she will live alone without getting married, 2) if he/she says that he/she will not have a child after getting married, 3) if he/she says that it is too difficult to live together and he/she will get divorced". And the respondents were asked to choose among the following two choices. Each of the three had either the traditional and/or collective way of thinking/acting or the emancipation from it, that is, individualization.

1) a. I would advise him/her to get married by using various method such as matchmaking. b. Living alone is a way of life, if he/she wants it.
2) a. I would advise him/her to have children anyhow. b. Living without children is a way of life, if the couple wants it.
3) a. I would advise him/her not to get divorced. b. Getting divorced is a way of life, if the couple wants it (Han and Shim 2016; Shim, Kim and Kim 2014).

TABLE 45.1 Degree of individualization by three questions on marriage, children, and divorce: based on answers to the question "How strongly do you agree or disagree with the following statements?" 2021

	Mean score of Seoul	Mean score of 33 cities	Ranking of Seoul among 33 cities	The highest score and city	The lowest score and city
a. Marriage is not a necessity. Living alone is acceptable to me.	3.41	3.08	2nd	3.44 Bangkok	2.38 Riyadh
b. I don't need to have children after marriage. Living without children is acceptable.	3.29	2.92	2nd	3.33 Toronto	2.23 Riyadh
c. I would get a divorce if my marriage didn't work out as expected.	3.36	3.34	19th	3.7 Budapest	2.56 Jakarta

SOURCE: HAN ET AL. (2021), GLOBAL SURVEY TO 33 GLOBAL CITIES

Living without children is acceptable", Seoul turned out to be the second highest, with a score of 3.29; as to the item "I would get a divorce if my marriage didn't work out as expected", Seoul turned out to be 19th, with a score of 3.36 (Table 45.1). This shows that the citizens of Seoul are very radical in living alone without getting married, and living without children, but they are not so radical in getting divorced. For space reasons I will return to this issue later and to discuss the individualization issue.

When we compare these results of the 2021 global survey with the 2012 survey, we can see a radical increase in Seoul. More specifically, in the 2012 survey, respondents agreeing with "Living alone without getting married is a way of life" was 70.3%, those agreeing with "Living without children is a way of life" was 53.9%, and those agreeing with "Getting divorced is a way of life" was 56.4%. And when we break down the results by gender, female respondents show higher degree of individualization, with 81.9%, 62.9%, and 61.4%, than male respondents, who show 58.6%, 44.7%, and 51.4%, respectively, for the three items in order (Table 45.2).

Among the three items, we could see a rapid increase particularly in the second item, "Living without children is a way of life", even though the scale is somewhat different. When we compare Seoul with Tokyo, which showed the highest individualization among the three cities in 2012, Tokyo turned out to be 30th for the first item, 26th for the second item, and 28th for the third item

TABLE 45.2 Individualization score in terms of marriage, children, and divorce in Seoul, 2012

	Seoul (total)	Male	Female
Living alone is a way of life, if he/she wants it.	70.3	58.6	81.9
Living without children is a way of life, if the couple wants it.	53.9	44.7	62.9
Getting divorced is a way of life, if the couple wants it.	56.4	51.4	61.4

Note: The score is out of 100.
SOURCE: HAN AND SHIM (2016). BREAKDOWN BY GENDER WAS ADDED (2012 SEOUL, BEIJING, TOKYO SURVEY RESULTS).

in 2021. This shows how quickly the attitude of citizens of Seoul has changed in comparison with Tokyo. This radical change of attitude may be related to a rapid decrease in the fertility rate in Korea. As to the other two items, the proportion agreeing with the individualization part of the first item was already high nine years ago, and as to the third item, there seems to have not been such a big change. To the divorce issue I will return later.

The three questions turned out to be a good indicator for individualization in 2021 as well as in 2012. A factor analysis of the three items in 2021 shows that the three questions make a one factor (cumulated distributed discretion is 68.64, Cronbach's alpha = .771). The individualization index was made by adding the average score of each of the three questions. The interpretation is that the higher the score, the higher the individualization.

When we compare the individualization index by city in 2021 (Figure 45.1), Seoul turned out to be fourth highest, with 3.35 among the 33 global cities. Toronto (3.38), Budapest, and Wellington were the three highest cities. The average of the total 33 cities was 3.11. And the lowest score was 2.49 of Riyadh, Saudi Arabia. Among the East Asian cities, Taipei was 15th, Singapore 23rd, Hanoi 26th, and Tokyo 29th. Through this comparison we can see how high Seoul's individualization index is.

When we compare the individualization index in 2021 with that of the three cities in 2012, the individualization index of Seoul was the lowest among the three cities in 2012: at that time Tokyo was the highest with 86.7, Beijing second highest with 68.6, and Seoul the lowest with 62.7. In 2021 Seoul turned out to be the fourth highest, higher than Tokyo (29th), which was the highest among the three cities surveyed in 2012. We can see how rapidly the individualization index of Seoul has risen.

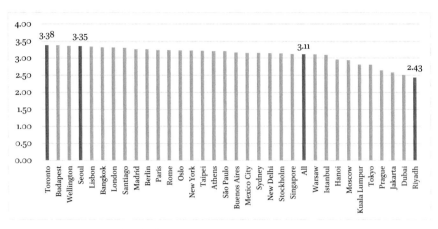

FIGURE 45.1   Degree of individualization by city
SOURCE: HAN ET AL. (2021), GLOBAL SURVEY TO 33 GLOBAL CITIES

2.2   *Attitude Toward the Value of Children*
In order to better see the attitude toward low fertility and its reasons, we developed questions on the value/burden of children on the one hand, and value of the family and work on the other. The questions were as follows: "The following questions are related to the value of family, children, and work. To what extent do you agree or disagree about the following statements?" And six items were presented: a) "Watching children grow up is life's greatest joy"; b) "Having children interferes too much with the freedom of parents"; c) "Children are a financial burden on their parents"; d) "A job is alright but what most women really want is a home and children"; e) "Being a housewife is just as fulfilling as working for pay"; f) "Having a job is the best way for a woman to be an independent person". Among these six items, a, b, and c are concerned with the value/burden of children, and d, e, and f are concerned with value of the family and a job. And the choice of answers was "Strongly Agree" (5), "Agree" (4), "Neither Agree nor Disagree" (3), "Disagree" (2), and "Strongly Disagree" (1) in the Likert scale.

The findings were shocking (Table 45.3). Seoul turned out to be either highest or lowest among 33 global cities as to the questions concerned with the value/burden of children. More specifically, as to the item "Watching children grow up is life's greatest joy", the mean score of Seoul turned out to be 3.63, the lowest among the 33 global cities. The mean score of the world average of 33 cities was 4.03, and the highest mean score was 4.5, in Jakarta. As to the item "Having children interferes too much with the freedom of parents", Seoul turned out to be 3.55, the second highest among 33 global cities. The mean score of the world average was 3.02, and the lowest mean score was 2.13, in Jakarta.

TABLE 45.3 The following questions are related to the value of family, children, and work. To what extent do you agree or disagree about the following statements? (Mean score by city) 2021

	Mean score of Seoul	Mean score of 33 cities	Ranking of Seoul among 33 cities	The highest score and city	The lowest score and city
a. Watching children grow up is life's greatest joy.	3.63	4.03	33rd	4.5 Jakarta	3.63 Seoul
b. Having children interferes too much with the freedom of parents.	3.55	3.02	2nd	3.61 New Delhi	2.13 Jakarta
c. Children are a financial burden on their parents.	3.61	2.95	1st	3.61 Seoul	2.21 Jakarta
d. A job is alright but what most women really want is a home and children	2.96	3.14	23rd	3.81 Hanoi	2.5 Mexico City
e. Being a housewife is just as fulfilling as working for pay	3.14	3.23	21st	3.72 Jakarta	2.75 Lisbon
f. Having a job is the best way for a woman to be an independent person	3.58	3.69	25th	4.16 Hanoi	3.28 Budapest

As to the question "Children are a financial burden on their parents", Seoul turned out to be 3.61, the highest among the 33 global cities. The mean score of the world average was 2.95, and the lowest was 2.21, in Jakarta (Table 45.3). The other three items on the value of the family and a job turned out to be the 23rd, the 21st, and the 25th, respectively, and do not seem to be noticeable.

These results clearly fit well with the individualization analysis discussed above, and confirm that Seoul is extremely individualized as far as children (and fertility) issues are concerned. Seoul's citizens certainly individualized faster and more radically as far as children issues are concerned than Western people, for whom it took more time and more institutionalization to be individualized. I would call this phenomenon of Seoul citizens "condensed radicalization of individualization", which is similar to but different from the Western path of individualization.

3   Family-Oriented Individualization in Korea

On the other hand, we can also see a trend contradictory to the "condensed radicalization of individualization" in Korea. My colleague and I worked and discovered a trend which we called "family-oriented individualization" and conducted related research (Han and Shim 2016; Han, Shim and Kim 2018; Shim 2013, 2018; Shim and Han 2010).[3] Very recently we also found this phenomenon in the recent COVID-19 pandemic situation. According to a global survey on the COVID-19 situation people in Korea as well as those in some other East Asian countries are more worried about their families than their Western counterparts. We could find these contradictory trends above all in the higher community orientation in Seoul than in other cities in the 2021 survey. And we could also see this trend in other parts of family life, such as there being almost no change in the ideal number of children, hesitation to get divorced, and relatively high acceptance of patriarchal attitudes.

3.1   *Higher Community Orientation in Seoul*

To measure the degree of community orientation since the COVID-19 pandemic, we asked the following question: "The following statements are observations of the results of COVID-19. How much do you agree or disagree with the following observations?" Among the six items presented, the first item was "The coronavirus pandemic has brought communities closer together". And the choice of answers was: "Strongly Agree" (5), "Agree" (4), "Neither Agree nor Disagree" (3), "Disagree" (2), and "Strongly Disagree" (1) in a Likert scale. I will call the result "degree of community-orientation".

The results are shown in Table 45.4 and Figure 45.2. Seoul turned out to be the fourth highest in the degree of community orientation, with a score of 3.16. New Delhi (3.34), Hanoi (3.31), and Bangkok (3.17) were the three cities with the highest scores. The mean score of the 33 cities was 2.26. And the lowest score was 2.12, in Lisbon. Among the East Asian cities, Hanoi was the 2nd with 3.31, Taipei was the 5th with 3.05, Singapore was the 8th with 2.80, and Tokyo was the 32nd with 2.13. Through this comparison we can see that Seoul's ranking in community orientation and mean score is very high.

The findings are very surprising. Seoul, which was the fourth highest in individualization index (Figure 45.1), turned out to be also the fourth highest

---

3 This tendency is also seen in various aspects of family life in Korea and East Asia, such as the case of female marriage migrants (Shim 2015; Shim and Han 2010), and among elderly women (Shim 2013).

TABLE 45.4 Mean score of community orientation, 2021

	Mean score of Seoul	Mean score of 33 cities	Ranking of Seoul among 33 cities	The highest score and city	The lowest score and city
a. The coronavirus pandemic has brought communities closer together.	3.16	2.63	4th	3.34 New Delhi	2.12 Lisbon

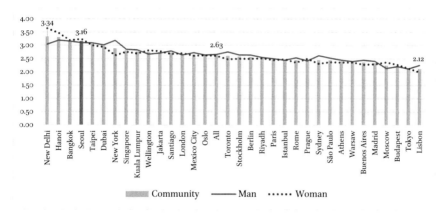

FIGURE 45.2   Degree of community orientation (total, male, female), 2021

in the degree of community orientation (Figure 45.2). And in contradiction to our expectation, women showed even higher levels of community orientation. Individualization and community orientation are opposite to each other, and if one turns out to be high, the other should turn out to be low. Most of the Western cities follow this pattern. In order to better see the relationship between the individualization index and community orientation, I compared the individualization index with community orientation.

As can be seen in Figure 45.3, the individualization index was higher than community orientation in most of the Western cities, as expected. However, in some East Asian and Southeast Asian cities, we can see different patterns. For example, Seoul, Bangkok, and Taipei show a pattern in which the individualization index and community orientation are both high (Table 45.5). And in New Delhi, Hanoi, Dubai, and Riyadh, community orientation is even higher than the individualization index. What does this mean?

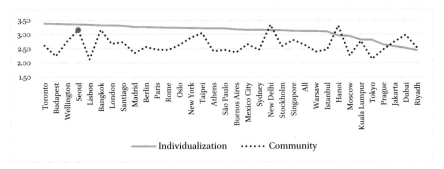

FIGURE 45.3   Comparison of individualization index and community orientation, 2021

TABLE 45.5   Comparison of individualization index and the degree of community orientation of some East Asian and Southeast Asian cities, 2021

	Individualization index	Degree of community orientation
Seoul	4th (3.35)	4th (3.16)
Bangkok	6th (3.32)	3rd (3.17)
Taipei	15th (3.22)	5th (3.05)
Singapore	23rd (3.12)	8th (2.80)
Hanoi	26th (2.96)	2nd (3.36)
Tokyo	29th (2.81)	32nd (2.13)

The answer to this question can be found in the two contradictory trends I mentioned above, "condensed radicalization of individualization" on the one hand and "community orientation" on the other, found in Seoul, Korea. This is something that is different from Western societies and shows a future prospect for going beyond the discourse of Western sociology. And in this sense it can be called a "post-Western" phenomenon. Tokyo is also an exception in that both individualization index and the community orientation degree are low. This phenomenon is a something to be explained later, in a post-Western way in post-Western sociology.

3.2   *Almost No Change in the Ideal Number of Children*

For more detailed scrutiny, I looked at the number of ideal and expected children. And it turned out that even though the number of expected children decreased, there was almost no change in the ideal number of children

TABLE 45.6 Expected and ideal number of children of women by marital status

	Married women		Never-married women	
	Expected number of children	Ideal number of children	Expected number of children	Ideal number of children
1976	3.4	2.8	–	–
1985	2.5	2.0	–	–
1991	2.2	2.1	–	–
2000	2.0	2.2	–	–
2015	1.9	2.3	2.0	2.0
2018	1.9	2.2	1.9	1.8

SOURCE: GENDER STATISTICS IN KOREA 2019

according to the flow of time. According to *Gender Statistics in Korea* 2019 (Joo et al. 2019), the number of ideal children turned out to be 2.2 and 1.8, and the number of expected children was 1.9 and 1.9 for married women and never-married women, respectively, in 2018 (Table 45.6).

For a more recent trend, we included questions on the ideal and expected number of children in the aforementioned survey in 33 global cities. The questions were as follows: a. "Given the social and economic constraints on individuals as you find them today, how many children do you think are suitable?" And the respondents could choose from "1. I don't want to give birth, 2. One child, 3. Two children, 4. Three or more children". And b. "How many children of your own would you like to have if there were no limitations in your resources?" And the choices were from "1. Zero, 2. One, 3. Two, 4. Three or more, 5. Not sure". The findings are shown in Figure 45.4.

As seen in Figure 45.4, in Seoul the ideal number of children is 1.8, and the expected number of children is 1.4. When we compare the results with those from other cities, we can find that the ideal number of children is greater than the number of expected children in most of the global cities except New Delhi and Riyadh, where there is almost no difference between the two numbers. The mean score of difference between the two in the 33 global cities was 0.28. The biggest difference was seen in Athens, with 0.46, the second was Seoul and Tokyo with 0.42, the third was Santiago with 0.41, and then there was Istanbul with 0.38.

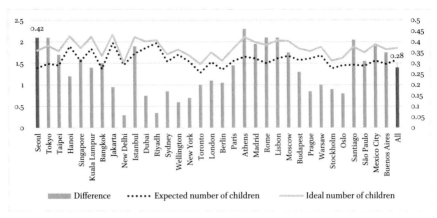

FIGURE 45.4   Ideal and expected number of children and the difference by city

When we compare this finding with 2018 statistics in *Gender Statistics in Korea 2019*, the ideal number of children dropped from 2.2 (for married women) and 1.8 (for single women) to 1.8, and the expected number of children dropped from 1.9 (for married women) and 1.9 (for single women) to 1.4. The difference between 2018 and 2021 is smaller in the ideal number of children (0.3 for married women and –0.1 for single women) than the number of expected children (0.5 and 0.5, respectively).

What is the meaning of these indices? The fact that there was only a small change in the number of ideal children in the flow of time and a big difference between the ideal and expected number of children in a given time means that women want to give birth if the circumstances allow. This result seems to support the above discussion of community orientation.

In addition, there are other statistics that show a hesitation to get divorced. When we get back to the divorce question, the third of individualization questions in the 2021 survey conducted in 33 global cities, we can see that the answer to the divorce question in Seoul is relatively low in the world ranking (19th) compared with living alone without marriage (2nd) and living without children (2nd). I think this means Korean women hesitate to get divorced. Many Korean women might not want to get married and/or might not want children, but once they get married, they hesitate to get divorced.[4] Together with this hesitation to get divorced, we can also find a relatively higher level of

---

4   The *Gender Statistics in Korea 2019* shows that those who agree with "should not get divorced" and "don't get divorced if possible" decreased from 18.1% in 1998 to 6.7% in 2018 and from 38.9% in 1998 to 22.2% in 2018, while those who agree with "better to divorce if there are reasons" increased from 8.3% in 1998 to 18.8% in 2018, respectively. However, it also shows that those women agreeing with "cases by case" increased from 31.4% in 1998 and occupies almost half (49.2%) in 2018. This, I think, also implies women's hesitation to get divorced.

acceptance of patriarchal attitudes,[5] which seems contradictory to the individualization index and also supports the community orientation in one way or other. However, there is no space to discuss those issues here. I think a discussion of the fact that there was only a small change in the number of ideal children in the flow of time and a big difference between the ideal and expected number of children is enough to support the community orientation.

What does this mean? On the one hand we see a phenomenon in which people in Korea are disembedded from the family and have fewer children: they want to live alone, and they do not want any children. And the degree of individualization far exceeds that of Western cities. However, when we look at these in more detail, we also see a phenomenon that in times of emergency people in Korea try to rely on the family[6] and the community, showing higher community orientation. That is, the individualization process in the Western sense is occurring, but it is faster and more radical than at the Western level, and the family orientation in the Eastern sense is still there at the same time. Thus, this can be interpreted as a post-Western trend, something which goes beyond the "West" and the "East" (Roulleau-Berger 2021).

---

5 In a 2021 survey on 33 global cities Seoul shows a relatively high acceptance of patriarchal attitude: *The following statements are related to gender issues. How strongly do you agree or disagree with each statement?* a. "On the whole, men make better political leaders than women do": mean score of Seoul = 2.71; mean score of 33 cities = 2.58; ranking of Seoul among 33 cities = 22nd; highest score and city = 2.75, Bangkok; lowest score and city = 1.93, Lisbon. b. "A university education is more important for a man than for a woman": mean score of Seoul = 2.39; mean score of 33 cities = 2.36; ranking of Seoul among 33 cities = 15th; highest score and city = 3.17, New Delhi; lowest score and city = 1.77, Lisbon. c. "When jobs are scarce, men should receive priority for job openings": mean score of Seoul = 2.49; mean score of 33 cities = 2.43; ranking of Seoul among 33 cities = 21st; highest score and city = 3.32, New Delhi; lowest score and city = 1.72, Lisbon.

6 Especially in the time of disaster like COVID-19 pandemic, there seems not much choice for women due to many reasons, socio-economic, caring of the children, etc. This might be particularly so in a society where there is only a weak safety net. In such a society people in difficult situations have no choice but to rely on the family, and the family might be the only resort to rely on. The 2012 Seoul, Beijing, and Tokyo survey, clearly shows this. In 2012 survey, we asked the following question, "If a disaster occurred, how much help do you think the following people or groups could give you?" And six institutions were presented, the family, friends, neighbors, government, insurance company, and civic group (NGO). The answers to the question of are as follows: Among the six institutions mentioned, the family turned out to be highest in the degree of expected help when in disaster, showing strong solidarity among the family (showing 64.3 points in Seoul, 92.9 points in Tokyo and 90 points in Beijing among 100 scores). Next was friends, neighbors, government, insurance company, and civic group (NGO), with Beijing being exceptionally high in expected help from the government (67.0). When we break it down by gender, those expecting help from the family was 69.0 for male respondents and 59.6 for female respondents. Even though female respondents showed lower expectation of help from the family than male counterpart, it can be considered still high with 59.6.

4 Concluding Remarks

In this paper I tried to show two contradictory trends in relation with women and the family in Korea. I asked the following question: Which new trends are found with regard to women and the family in the situation of deepened inequality since the COVID-19 pandemic. For an answer to the question, I focused on two contradictory trends in Korea: one is what I call "condensed radicalization of individualization" and the other is "community orientation". And I found a coexistence of these two contradictory trends, one of which follows the individualization trend of Western society on the one hand, and another which goes over and tries to restore the cherished community orientation in the East on the other.

If we understand "post-Western" as meaning not only "after" but also "critical of" or "overcoming" Western sociology (Han, in this book), this coexistence of two contradictory trends can be seen as a post-Western trend. The community orientation seen together with "condensed radicalization of individualization" among Koreans indicates a post-Western tendency in the sense that it goes beyond the "East" and the "West" (Roulleau-Berger 2021). And in this sense I think it also suggests a direction that may unfold in the future.

References

Beck, U. 1992. *Risk Society: Towards a New Modernity*. Translated by M. Ritter. London: Sage.

Beck, U., and E. Beck-Gernsheim. 2002. *Individualization: Institutionalized Individualism and Its Social and Political Consequences*. London: Sage.

Berkhout, Suze G., and Lisa Richardson. 2020. "Identity, Politics, and the Pandemic: Why Is COVID-19 a Disaster for Feminism(s)?" HPLS 42 (49). http://doi.org/10.1007/s40656-020-00346-7.

Betzler, Riana. 2020. "What Does It Mean to Have an Empathetic Leader? Lessons From COVID-19". *Feminism and Philosophy* 20 (1): 32–35. Special Issue: Feminist Responses to COVID-19 and Pandemics.

Enloe, Cynthia. 2020. "'Waging War' Against Virus Is NOT What We Need to Be Doing". *WILPF International* (March 23, 2020). Leverage Feminist Perspective on Peace.

Gotlib, Anna. 2020. "'Surviving and Getting Your Life Back Are Two Different Things': COVID-19, ICU Psychosis, and the Coming Mental Health Crisis". *Feminism and Philosophy* 20 (1): 28–32. Special Issue: Feminist Responses to COVID-19 and Pandemics.

Han, Sang-Jin. 2022. "COVID-19 and Hegemonic Modernity: Post-Western Sociological Imaginations". In *Handbook of Post-Western Sociology*, edited by L. Roulleau-Berger, et al. Leiden: Brill.

Han, Sang-Jin. 2021. *An International Comparative Study on Citizen Participatory Governance Model and Health and Welfare Policies in the COVID-19 Era*. Report to the Ministry of Health and Welfare, Republic of Korea.

Han, Sang-Jin, and Young-Hee Shim. 2010. "Redefining Second Modernity for East Asia: A Critical Assessment". *British Journal of Sociology* 61 (3): 465–488.

Han, Sang-Jin, and Young-Hee Shim. 2016. "Dual Individualization in East Asia: Individualization in the Society and in the Family". In *Liberalism and Chinese Economic Development: Perspectives From Europe and Asia*, edited by Gilles Campagnolo, 281–290. New York, NY: Routledge.

Han, Sang-Jin, Young-Hee Shim, and Jung-su Kim. 2018. "Comparative Study of Neighborhood Community Reconstruction in Seoul and Beijing: An Action-Theoretical Approach". *Korea Journal* 58 (2): 113–140.

Harbin, Ami, and Alice McLachlan. 2020. "Pandemic Parenting". *Feminism and Philosophy* 20 (1): 22–26. Special Issue: Feminist Responses to COVID-19 and Pandemics.

Hochschild, Arlie. 2012. *The Second Shift: Working Families and the Revolution at Home*. New York: Viking Penguin.

Howard, Cosmo, ed. 2007. *Contested Individualization: Debates About Contemporary Personhood*. New York: Palgrave Macmillan.

Joo, Jae Seon, et al. 2019. *Gender Statistics in Korea*. Korea Women's Development Institute.

Kim, Hyun-Mi. 2020. "'Gender Crisis' and the Future of Ecological Social Reproduction". COVID 19 and the Future of Gender Equality: The 123rd Gender Equality Policy Forum of KWDI (Korea Women's Development Institute). December 16.

Kim, Ji Young. 2016. *People Living Alone in Three Cities* [*Sedosiui Honja Saneun Saramdeul*]. Research report. ISDPR, SNU. Seoul: Seoul National University [Sahoebaljeonyeonguso].

Lee, Jung-Hoon. 2021. "Inequality Accelerated with COVID 19: Assets of Top 10% 190 Times More Than Lower 50%". *Hankyoreh Daily*. December 9.

Pilipchuk, Miranda. 2020. "A Crisis Ignored: Domestic Violence and the COVID-19 Pandemic". *Feminism and Philosophy* 20 (1): 15–22. Special Issue: Feminist Responses to COVID-19 and Pandemics.

Roulleau-Berger, Laurence. 2021. "The Fabric of Post-Western Sociology: Ecologies of Knowledge Beyond the 'East' and the 'West'". *The Journal of Chinese Sociology* 8 (10): 1–28. http://doi.org/10.1186/s40711-021-00144-z.

Roulleau-Berger, Laurence, and Peilin Li, eds. 2018. *Post-Western Sociology: From China to Europe*. Leiden: Brill.

Shim, Young-Hee. 2011. "Toward a Community-Oriented Family Model of the Twenty-First Century: From a Perspective of Second Modernity and Individualization Theory". *Journal of Asian Women* 50 (2): 7–44. (In Korean.)

Shim, Young-Hee. 2013. "Two Types of Individualization: Family-Centered Survival-Oriented Type and Twilight Divorce Type". *Society and Theory* 23: 277–312. (In Korean.)

Shim, Young-Hee. 2015. "Research Methodological Debate on Emancipatory Catastrophism: The Case of Transnational Marriage". *Current Sociology* 63 (1): 105–109.

Shim, Young-Hee. 2018. "East Asian Patterns of Individualization and Its Consequences for Neighborhood Community Reconstruction". *Korea Journal* 58 (1): 41–69.

Shim, Young-Hee, and Sang-Jin Han. 2010. "'Family-Oriented Individualization' and Second Modernity: An Analysis of Transnational Marriages in Korea". *Soziale Welt* 61 (3/4): 235–253.

Shim, Young-Hee, and Sang-Jin Han. 2013. "Individualization and Community Networks in East Asia: How to Deal With Global Difference in Social Science Theories?" In *Theories About and Strategies Against Hegemonic Social Sciences*, edited by M. Khun and S. Yazawa, 197–214. Tokyo: Seijo University.

Shim, Young-Hee, M. Kim, and B. Kim. 2014. "Two Dimensions of Family Risk in East Asia: Variations and Contextualization". *Development and Society* 43 (2): 239–267.

Shim, Young-Hee, Y. Kim, and E. Kim. 2002. *Achieving Gender Equality Together*. Seoul: Nanam. (In Korean.)

Tronto, Joan C. 2013. *Caring Democracy*. New York: New York University Press.

World Inequality Lab. 2021. *World Inequality Report 2021* (quoted in J.H. Lee, 2021). https://wir2022.wid.world/www-site/uploads/2021/12/wir2022-full-report-english.pdf.

SECTION 11

Environment and Mistrust Crisis

∴

CHAPTER 46

How Ecological Civilization Contributes to Post-Western Sociology

*Wang Xiaoyi and Anier**

1 Introduction

After coining the concept of the Anthropocene in 2000, Professor Paul J. Crutzen published his paper "Geology of Mankind" in *Nature*. In this short paper, the author mentioned, "For the past three centuries, the effects of humans on the global environment have escalated" (Crutzen 2002). Although environmental problems have been caused by the rapid expansion of mankind in numbers and per capita exploitation of Earth's resources, these effects have largely been caused by only 25% of the world population.

Although the paper is very short, it reveals three issues that are central in the discussion on environment: (1) human activities since industrialization have affected the environment where humans have been living; (2) injustice exists in the environmental problem, that is, some people benefit from it while others have been affected by environmental destruction; and (3) we should guide society towards sustainable environmental management in the era of the Anthropocene, but we still have not found the way out.

In the past two decades, China has been in the same situation, even worse than that in the developed societies. In the second decade of 21st century, China formed the ecological civilization discourse for shifting the mode of development and achieving sustainable development. Ecological civilization has been considered the way to save society from the environmental crisis.

2 From Environmental Protection to Ecological Civilization

After 20 years of rapid growth, China's environmental problems became prominent around 2000. In the ecologically fragile areas in the central and western regions, they have mainly been manifested in ecological degradation, such as

---

* Anier is her full name; she is Mongolian.

how the grassland was severely degraded, which brought about the large-scale sandstorm weather; soil erosion has affected the environment of the mountainous areas and threatened the downstream areas; and the forest coverage has dropped sharply, which brought about frequent occurrences of flood disasters. At the same time, the damage in developed eastern regions is mainly manifested in increasingly serious pollution problems, such as water, land, and air pollution caused by industries; and the excessive use of chemical fertilizers and pesticides has entered soils, rivers, and food systems, which exacerbates the deterioration of water quality and food safety.

The problems emerging in China are very similar to those discussed by Paul J. Crutzen, but these problems broke out in a short period in China. First of all, China has rapidly improved its level of industrialization and urbanization. Compared with the global industrialization of three centuries, China completed it within 30 years; secondly, China has become the world's factory, with many high energy-consuming and high-polluting enterprises concentrated within it, and therefore China bears more industrial waste and pollution and consumes more energy; third, China has a huge population base. With the improvement of the Chinese people's living standards, although their consumption level is still far lower than that of Western developed countries, it has already formed a huge pressure on the environment. The environmental problem embodies the characteristics of China's "compressed modernization".

China has adopted a series of policies trying to reverse the trend of environmental degradation. For example, it has introduced the grassland protection policy for grassland degradation, by limiting the number of grassland livestock to reduce the pressure on the grasslands; for the development of mountain agriculture, it has introduced a policy of returning farmland to forest to restore the environment in mountainous areas; in response to the degradation of the environment, a natural forest protection policy has been introduced, which prohibits the logging of natural forests to expand forest coverage; for the industrialized areas, a strict environmental protection policy has been introduced, requiring companies to safely dispose of waste generated in the production process to prevent pollution; an action plan has been issued to reduce the use of chemical fertilizers and pesticides in order to protect the agricultural environment and improve food safety.

However, the intensive introduction of these policies has not fundamentally changed the trend of environmental degradation. First, the core of the environmental problem is the system problem. If the system is not improved, the environmental problem cannot be solved. John Foster points out that the ecological crisis facing today's society is actually a crisis of the mode of production, and the destruction of the environment is caused by the capitalist mode of production. Capitalism takes the accumulation of wealth in the form of capital as its supreme goal, and pursues rapid economic growth at any cost. This single-value production mode allows people to destroy the environment and benefit from it, thus making it impossible to adopt wide-ranging actions to solve environmental problems; second, environmental problems are highly complex issues, and a single problem-oriented environmental policy cannot completely solve environmental problems. For example, some grassland areas replaced grassland grazing by planting trees to reduce the pressure of grazing on the grasslands. However, the industry has brought about a drop in the groundwater level in arid and semi-arid areas, and has created new effects on the environment of the grassland. In the face of complex and comprehensive environmental problems, a single environmental protection policy often cannot solve practical problems. Third, new environmental problems continue to arise. On the one hand, industrialization and urbanization continue to bring about new environmental problems. For example, domestic waste has caused a series of social problems in recent years. A series of social actions have emerged around the construction of garbage treatment facilities, which is typical of "not-in-my-backyard". But so far, no matter whether it is landfill or incineration, the existing garbage disposal mechanism has not been able to solve more and more garbage disposal problems. On the other hand, with China's globalization process, more and more global environmental issues have entered China, which requires China to take corresponding actions. For example, the issue of climate change, especially carbon neutrality, will have extensive effects on China. For China to achieve sustainable development, new systemic thought is needed.

It is against this background that China has proposed the development strategy of ecological civilization.[1] As a development strategy, ecological civilization has four meanings below:

1. Development aimed at the happiness and sense of gain of the people. Modernization is a long-term development goal that China has been pursuing. In particular, the growth of economic aggregate represented by GDP is the main goal of the Chinese government's attention. However, in the pursuit of rapid development, the destruction of the environment and resources has harmed people's lives. Life experience, pollution, smog, and other environmental issues have reduced the happiness of the people living in it. In the strategy of ecological civilization, the goal of people's happiness in life is put first, and environmental governance is emphasized to enhance people's happiness in life.

---

[1] In April 2015, the Central Committee of the Communist Party of China and the Chinese government adopted the "Opinions on Accelerating the Construction of Ecological Civilization", which systematically explained the Chinese government's opinions on ecological civilization.

2. Development model that is different from the development model of industrial civilization. From the last two decades of the 20th century, China's development has been called extensive development, which is mainly manifested in high energy consumption and high investment in industrial development. This development mode is also an important cause of environmental problems. In the strategy of ecological civilization, China has established a new development mode that conserves resources, improves efficiency and benefits, and controls the intensity of resource exploitation through the transformation of development mode.
3. Rebuild the relationship between man and nature. It is necessary to fully realize the enhancement of man's effect on nature and its consequences after entering the Anthropocene period, learn to respect and conform to nature, recognize the principle that man and nature are an organic whole, and establish a harmonious and symbiotic relationship between man and nature.
4. In environmental protection, a more comprehensive and systematic strategy would be adopted to avoid a single policy in environmental governance. Human factors must be taken into consideration in ecological governance, as well as the integrated comprehensive management of mountains, water, forests, fields and lakes, fully cognizing the high degree of interrelationship between various elements in the ecosystem.

The strategy of ecological civilization is an exploration of how to achieve sustainable development in the era of Anthropocene under the background of China's development.

3   The Response of Environmental Sociology

As in developed societies, environmental sociology developed very late compared to other subfields of sociology in China. The number of papers in environmental sociology has increased sharply since the first decade of 21st century.

In the beginning, the studies concentrated on environmental conflicts. As China's environmental damage has worsened, people have paid more and more attention to the impact of environmental issues, and China has begun to have more and more environmental conflicts. In the economically developed eastern regions, the construction of chemical companies, the location of waste incineration plants, and food pollution often lead to mass incidents. Fear of environmental pollution often makes residents take action to avoid the impact of environmental pollution. Social conflict is one of the most important themes of sociological research. Social conflicts caused by environmental problems can easily enter the vision of environmental sociology scholars and become an important topic of environmental sociological research.[2]

The problem behind the environmental conflict is the issue of environmental justice or injustice. Especially in the period of rapid economic growth, environmental destruction and environmental protection will bring about different reactions from various stakeholders. For example, the development of the mining industry has had a serious impact on the environment. In turn, it conflicts with the traditional resource utilization methods of local residents and affects the development of local agriculture and animal husbandry; river pollution would affect the development of domestic water and aquaculture of downstream residents. Not only will environmental damage affect the interests of local residents, but environmental protection will also have an impact on the lives of local residents. Especially with the expansion of China's nature preserves, the development and utilization of resources in the preserves and surrounding areas are restricted to varying degrees, which in turn has had an impact on the employment and income of local residents.

With the implementation of the strategy of ecological civilization, the issue of environmental governance has gradually become the core issue of environmental sociology. From the perspective of the Anthropocene, the impact of human activities on the environment is mainly negative, but from the perspective of ecological governance, whether it is the development of science and technology or the increased investment in environmental protection, it will reverse the trend of environmental pollution and environmental degradation. However, any technology and investment in environmental governance are embedded in society, and Chinese environmental sociology has gradually shifted its focus from environmental protests to environmental governance (Hong and Gong 2015).

The research of environmental sociology first restores the complexity of environmental issues, pays attention to the participation of residents and the formation of environmental governance mechanisms with Chinese characteristics, and makes preliminary explorations of China's participation in global environmental governance.

Industrialized society has brought about many environmental problems, and pure technological input cannot solve these problems. Environmental sociology hopes to find answers to the problems in traditional wisdom, such

---

2 A large number of studies on the "not-in-my-backyard" movement have appeared in China, reflecting the high level of attention paid to environmental events during this period. See Xiaoyun Chen, 2017, "Fight for Technological Citizenship: Why NMIBY Transform into Social Movement—A Case Study of Anti-incinerate Event in China (2009–2013)", *Journal of Gansu Administration Institute* 124 (6).

as relying on the ecologically recycling economy of agricultural society to solve environmental problems caused by pesticides and fertilizers (A. Chen 2019), or relying on traditional nomadic knowledge to protect the grasslands (Zhang and Ai 2018). Traditional wisdom emphasizes the recycling of resources and regards people as a part of nature, which provides an important reference for rethinking the relationship between man and nature, as well as necessary technical means for the establishment of ecological civilization.

Citizen participation in environmental protection is an important topic of environmental sociology. In particular, citizens' participation in environmental protective actions through public welfare organizations has become an important part of China's ecological civilization. There are a large number of organizations engaged in environmental protection at all levels, which extensively carry out environmental information collection, perform environmental protection research, and encourage citizens to take protective actions for the environment. Environmental non-governmental organizations have become an important force in China's environmental governance and an important channel for citizens to participate in environmental protection. In China, non-profit organizations engaging in environmental protection have played an innovative and leading role in various fields, such as biodiversity, community participation, water protection, and pollution control.

The characteristics of China's environmental governance are to emphasize the overall plan, formulate a responsible implementation mechanism, and ensure the completion of various tasks of environmental protection through an accountability system. For example, in the face of increasingly serious water pollution problems, China has established a "river chief" system, that is, making the main local administrative leaders assume responsibility for preventing and controlling river pollution. This system has worked, but with the generalization of this system, the "river chief" has gradually evolved into a form that cannot function (T. Chen 2019). In addition, the research on rural environmental issues is also becoming more and more in depth. From the perspective of Anthropocene, industrialization, urbanization and population growth are the main causes of environmental problems. However, in the context of rapid population decline, China's rural environmental problems have become more and more serious, because with the decline in rural population, the logic of industrialized production and life begins to dominate the countryside, and how to improve the rural ecological environment in the context of ecological civilization has also become an issue of environmental sociology.

Through the study of environmental governance, China's environmental sociology has gradually shifted its focus from the criticism of the industrialization development model to formulating a way to construct its new civilization form and achieve sustainable development.

4 The Contribution of Ecological Civilization to Post-Western Sociology

Western sociology began with the explanation of modern society, especially the explanation of industrialized society, but from the perspective of resources and the environment, industrialized society is facing a crisis of development. Since the publication of *Silent Spring* in 1962, human society has been exploring the path of sustainable development. In this sense, ecological civilization can contribute to post-western sociology than sustainable development can.

As we all know, people live in the environment to the end; however, classical sociology pays more attention to the relationship between people and seldom discusses the environment (Woodgate and Redclift 2005), while environmental sociology introduces the issue of environment into sociological discussions. It should be said when we introduce environmental issues into sociological discussions that the research orientation of sociology is already different from that of classical Western sociology.

References

Chen, Ajiang. 2019. "Governance With Inaction: Exploration and Effect of Compound Symbiosis Agriculture" (in Chinese). *Academia Bimestrie* 179 (5): 80–87.

Chen, Tao. 2019. "Generalization of Governance Mechanism: An Analytical Dimension of the Reproduction of River Chief System" (in Chinese). *Journal of Hohai University (Philosophy and Social Sciences)* 21 (1): 97–103 + 108.

Chen, Xiaoyun. 2017. "Fight for Technological Citizenship: Why NMIBY Transform Into Social Movement—A Case Study of Anti-incinerate Event in China (2009–2013)" (in Chinese). *Journal of Gansu Administration Institute* 124 (6): 77–92 + 127.

Crutzen, Paul J. 2002. "Geology of Mankind". *Nature* 415 (6867): 23.

Hong, Dayong, and Wenjuan Gong. 2015. "China Environmental Sociology Stepping onto Express Lane" (in Chinese). *Journal of Nanjing Tech University (Social Science Edition)* 14 (4): 5–16.

Woodgate, Graham, and Michael R. Redclift. 2005. "Introduction". In *New Development in Environmental Sociology*, edited by Graham Woodgate and Michael R. Redclift. Cheltenham: Edward Elgar Publishing Limited.

Zhang, Qian, and Li-kun Ai. 2018. "Adaptive Governance and Climate Change: Case Analysis of Inner Mongolia Grassland and Counterplan Study" (in Chinese). *Climate Change Research* 80 (4): 411–422.

CHAPTER 47

The Post-Western Anthropocene

Paul Jobin

At the turn of the 21st century, Nobel Prize-winning chemist and atmospheric specialist Paul Crutzen and marine biologist Eugene Stoermer posited in a short article that, around the time of the Industrial Revolution in the 18th century, the earth left the Holocene—the post-glacial geological epoch of the past 12,000 years—to enter a new geological period marked by the serious effects of anthropic activity, which they proposed to name the Anthropocene (Crutzen and Stoermer 2000). Two years later Crutzen published another one-page article in *Nature*, and the neologism "Anthropocene" became instrumental in raising awareness of a large range of man-made disasters, from an alarming acceleration of global warming to the massive depletion of biodiversity also known as "the sixth mass extinction". These apocalyptic issues are often discussed under the catchword of "the Anthropocene".[1]

The international community of geologists has received the neologism with reserve, preferring thus far to stick to the previous era, the Holocene; however, this was no great surprise, since it had taken 50 years of discussions to finally validate that designation at a conference in 1885. The term has also stirred fierce resistance among social scientists, although a great number of researchers have endorsed its use, particularly in the subfields dealing with environmental issues, such as environmental history. As Jason Moore puts it, "like globalization in the 1990s, the Anthropocene has become a buzzword that can mean all things to all people" (Moore 2016: 3).

Much of the discussion on the Anthropocene has consisted in the debate around where and when it started. Did it happen in Western Europe during the first industrial revolution, prompted by the invention of the steam engine and the sudden use of large quantities of coal? Or did it start after the Second World

---

1 In addition to a burgeoning number of articles using the Anthropocene in their title or as keyword (for literature reviews in humanities and social sciences, see Marquardt 2019; Simangan 2020), there are already three academic journals entirely devoted to it. The quarterly *Anthropocene*, which started in 2013 with Crutzen on the editorial board, is hosted by the scientific publisher Elsevier; *Elementa: Science of the Anthropocene*, an online open access journal, was launched the same year by the University of California; and the *Anthropocene Review*, another quarterly that welcomes scholars in the humanities and social sciences, debuted in 2014 and is hosted by Sage.

War with the "great acceleration" in the consumption of natural resources, driven in particular by the "American way of life" (Bonneuil and Fressoz 2017)? Although the idea that human activity was effecting cataclysmic changes to the Earth's systems was not new, this theoretical framework reminds us that environmental destruction has entered a scale that was unknown some 20 years ago; this is not just another crisis that will soon end.

This chapter presents some salient points of the debate on the Anthropocene, and why it matters for post-Western social sciences. I also advocate for an understanding of the Anthropocene that goes beyond its current Western focus.

1 Postcolonial Criticism of the Anthropocene

A major criticism of the Anthropocene concept is that it ascribes responsibility for the environmental crisis to humans in general, whereas many feel that the blame rightly belongs to just a portion of mankind. To some, the problem is its inherent Western-centrism, which deflects the responsibility of Western Europe and North America for the ecological crisis. In other words, the *anthropos* of the Anthropocene discourse is another version of the capitalist white male who finds in this narrative a renewed way to impose his neo-colonial domination (e.g., Baldwin and Erickson 2020; Davis and Todd 2017; Hecht 2018; Simangan 2020; Simpson 2020). This postcolonial criticism is of importance for a post-Western approach of social sciences, as advocated in this volume.

An unexpected challenge to this postcolonial criticism, however, has come from Dipesh Chakrabarty (2009), a prominent author of postcolonial and subaltern studies. Chakrabarty admits that all the anthropogenic factors contributing to global warming are part of the imperial domination imposed by the West on the rest of the world. Western countries bear a moral burden, and other countries like China—which has now surpassed the United States as the largest emitter of carbon dioxide—now share responsibility for the years ahead. Chakrabarty concludes that while postcolonial scholarship's "hermeneutics of suspicion" "is an effective critical tool in dealing with national and global formations of domination", it is of little help in addressing global warming. Chakrabarty's article has provoked heated debates. Andreas Malm and Alf Hornborg (2014), for instance, endorse the notion of the Anthropocene, but they tag Chakrabarty's approach as a "flawed argument" that overlooks the differentiated vulnerability inherent in the power game between the rich and the poor (see also Resznityk 2020).

Other scholars believe that while the West was undeniably the primary source of anthropogenic activities, the true culprit is capitalism. Its conception and early development were Atlantic-centered, but its subjugation of nature to capital accumulation has been adopted by much of the world, exponentially accelerating its devastating effects on the environment. Historian Jason Moore argues that capitalism seized on a completely new attitude toward nature: one that ceaselessly expanded the use of free—or almost free—labor, food, energy, and raw materials, through their appropriation and exploitation in lands both near and far. This reliance on "cheap nature" (2015) became the fundamental capitalist law of value. For this reason, it has been suggested that the term "Anthropocene" should be replaced or at least completed by the concept of the "Capitalocene" (Moore 2016). The bulk of the many suggested alternatives for the Anthropocene have had little or no theoretical impact; the Capitalocene is a notable exception.

Another left-wing criticism of the Anthropocene discourse argues that it tends to depoliticize the debate. For instance, Erik Swyngedouw (2015) posits that the Anthropocene discourse neglects the impact of global corporations and tax-free polluters, thereby reducing the political discussion to a consensual and managerial approach within the neoliberal framework of "good governance". Harvey Neo (2021) thus draws on Swyngedouw's criticism to debunk the discourse on Singapore as a perfect model of resilience in the Anthropocene.

Nonetheless, the Anthropocene is not necessarily a depoliticizing concept. Bruno Latour, who has generally endorsed the term (e.g., 2014, 2015), has also addressed a sharp criticism of the consensual "good governance" and the mirage of a world government that would be able to impose the right decisions on everyone. The problem, as Latour argues, is rather to fully acknowledge the *geo* in geopolitics. For instance, the COVID-19 pandemic, which has disrupted the traditional world order, is a dramatic reminder of the geopolitical force of the Anthropocene, provided that we take seriously the geological forces that are reshuffling traditional views on national sovereignties (Latour 2020). Latour accordingly invites us to look "down to earth" as closely as possible to the ground level of politics, so as to gradually map the frontlines of conflicts at different levels—local, national, regional, and international—step by step (Latour 2015, 2017).

But how different regions of the world fit in the Anthropocene? How do these regional views affect Western-centered understanding of the Anthropocene? The next section examines the case of Asia.

2 The Asian Anthropocene, or an Asian Perspective

An overwhelming proportion of authors who discuss the Anthropocene, both advocates and opponents of the notion, are from Western Europe, North

America, and Australia. Moreover, scholars from other regions have so far shown little enthusiasm for this debate. This discrepancy engenders empirical shortages and theoretical flaws, sometimes openly assumed (e.g., Corlett 2013). Departing from the domination of Western paradigms in the Anthropocene literature (Marquardt 2019), a few scholars have therefore deemed it necessary to redefine the concept from the perspective of Africa (Hecht 2018) and Asia (Chatterjee 2020; Hudson 2014; Simangan 2019, 2020; see also Horn and Bergthaller 2020, chapter 12). This regionalist approach includes elements of the postcolonial criticism already presented, but it also offers further perspectives.

As a concept aiming to define a very long period of time on a universal scale, the Anthropocene is not supposed to be confined within a particular place. From that angle, there should be nothing like a "Post-Western Anthropocene" or an "Asian Anthropocene". But I use these formulas to reverse perspectives on the Anthropocene. Let us further look at the case of Asia, largely defined (South Asia, Southeast Asia to East Asia).

Hudson (2014) paved the way by identifying three research axes: the role of Asia in Anthropocene histories, the social and ecological vulnerabilities this epoch poses for Asia today, and how Asia addresses these global challenges. But as Dahlia Simangan, a researcher from the Philippines based in Japan, aptly notes: "In a discourse saturated by universalising agenda, a regional level of analysis is an attempt to bridge global action and local capacity" (Simangan 2019: 565). Moreover, in an echo of *Provincializing Europe*—Chakrabarty's seminal book for subaltern studies—the historian of India Elisabeth Chatterjee (2020) invites researchers to "provincialize" the notion and depart from the Western focus on the history of coal and oil (e.g., Malm 2016) to study other drivers of the Anthropocene, such as hydroelectricity, which has been instrumental in the modernization of Asian countries.

However, the geography of contemporary Asia is intertwined with the logic of asymmetrical world exchanges. Consider, for instance, that the Organization for Economic Co-operation and Development (OECD), which includes Japan and South Korea, accounts for more than two thirds of the world's gross domestic product, but less than 20% of its population. What Alf Hornborg (2013) terms "time-space appropriation" and an "unequal ecological exchange" have meant a huge transfer of wealth and resources from the "rest of the world" to Europe and North America. As he further observes (Hornborg 2018), this transfer still operates to the advantage of economic alliances, such as the OECD, because while these countries import and consume merchandise from China, carbon emissions resulting from the production of these imports are attributed to China (see also Sims Gallagher and Xuan 2018; Zhang et al. 2017).

The philosopher and member of the Australian Greens Clive Hamilton (2017) tackles the argument of unequal relations: not only China is now the world's biggest carbon-emitter, but as China reorients its economy toward domestic consumption, its share of emissions arising from export manufacture is declining; it is thus becoming harder to place all of the responsibility on its exports. At the 2015 climate conference in Paris, Chinese diplomats were compelled to give up this line of argument, which had sabotaged the negotiations at the 2009 Copenhagen conference. Following on Chakrabarty, Hamilton therefore fully endorses the notion of the Anthropocene: "If the 'Anthropocene' was a Eurocentric idea when it was coined, it is now Sino-Americo-Eurocentric, and in a decade or two it will be Indo-Sino-Americo-Eurocentric" (Hamilton 2017: 31). Or as Horn and Bergthaller (2020: 173) put it: "The old industrial nations of Europe and North America may have started the recent transformation of the Earth system, but they are no longer in the driver's seat. Today the Asian nations are as much a part of the problem—and they must be a part of the solution, if there is to be one".

Indeed, from 1998 to 2017, five of the top ten countries most affected by climate change were in Asia: Myanmar, the Philippines, Bangladesh, Pakistan, and Vietnam (Burck et al. 2020). Inversely, Taiwan, Japan, and South Korea rank in the bottom of those most on duty to reduce their carbon emissions (Eckstein, Hutfils and Winges 2019). The Asia Pacific region as a whole is the highest contributor of greenhouse gas emissions to the atmosphere, with 40% of global emissions in 2015; this percentage is projected to increase until 2030, with 89% of Asia-Pacific's contribution coming from China, India, and Indonesia (Simangan 2020).

Regarding the concrete consequences of what the Anthropocene means for Asia, a great deal of discussion has so far focused on climate change and its most immediate consequences, like rising sea levels or stronger typhoons. For instance, Jakarta has been proclaimed "the city of the Anthropocene" for its vulnerability to rising sea levels and the resilience of the *kampong*—its floating slums (Chandler 2017). The Indonesian government is thus planning to transfer the capital to East Kalimantan (on the island of Borneo), with possibly detrimental effects for local indigenous populations and lush rainforests that are home to orangutans and countless other animal species. Singapore is another city threatened by rising sea levels, with 35% of its territory lying less than 5 meters above sea level; but from Lee Kuan Yew's vision of a "Garden City" to its iconic Supertrees, Singapore's techno-nature and green-washing policy reflect the firm intention of the city-state to become a champion of resilience in the Anthropocene (Schneider-Mayerson 2017; cf. Neo 2021).

Along with rising seas, biodiversity loss in Southeast Asia is a major issue— if not the main issue—of the Asian Anthropocene. In addition to the oceans' depletion of fish and corals, the rivers' flora and fauna have been drastically decreasing due to the astounding number of hydroelectric dams under construction (Middleton and Allouche 2016). Terrestrial species are similarly under attack, due to continued deforestation. After the Amazon and the Congo, Southeast Asia is the world's third-largest zone of tropical forests and a concomitant repository of terrestrial biodiversity, now at the forefront of "mass destruction" and at such a rapid rate that current data quickly become obsolete (Zeng et al. 2018).

The deforestation of tropical rain forests has long been a core research topic of Western political ecology (e.g., Dauvergne 2001; Peluso 1994; Ross 2001). Since the 1990s, mobilizations of local people and transnational networks against deforestation by agribusiness (such as palm oil) have continued unabated. Nevertheless, the last two decades have seen an acceleration of forest loss in the region, as if no human force or any law could possibly stop the chainsaws and bulldozers from encroaching further on "protected" forest areas, not until the very last tree is cut down. Furthermore, the construction of large hydroelectric dams and the expansion of mining and monocultures are almost inevitably accompanied by the displacement of entire communities, massive pollution of land and rivers, and a homogenization (and oversimplification) of human and natural ecology.

3   Western Legacy and Beyond

This violence is nothing new; it started during colonial times, was further aggravated by postcolonial regimes of European to Japanese domination and has been described by an abundant literature (e.g., Hirsch and Warren 1998). What is more specific to the Anthropocene paradigm is a departure from the naïve belief that brutal infrastructure projects and the expansion of agribusiness are "sustainable development", and there is now a large consensus among international organizations that further destruction of "cultural and natural heritage" must be avoided.

These considerations on the Anthropocene of Asia intertwine also with geopolitical concerns. As a mark of its ascendancy, China has undertaken a comprehensive global investment program, the Belt and Road Initiative (BRI), with the aim of fashioning a China-centered economic sphere, by developing and economically integrating the countries along the historic Silk Road. With an estimated value by 2049 of USD $8 trillion spread over a total of 72 countries, the BRI could be the largest infrastructure project in human history, with possibly devastating consequences for biodiversity (Middleton and Allouche 2016; Morris-Jung 2018; Wang 2021) and a further increase in global warming emissions due to the export of coal-burning power plants (Maréchal 2018).

To my limited knowledge, thus far publications on the Anthropocene in Asian vernacular languages have been very limited. The "indigenization" of the notion has started only recently. For instance, in Taiwan, the notion of the Anthropocene has prompted some academic discussions, although these are limited to a small circle of social science scholars and artists engaged in ecological issues (e.g., Chuang and Gong 2020; Lin 2018). The perspectives include various angles, such as eco-feminism (Chuang 2020b) or the land and custom rights of indigenous peoples (Lee 2020; Wu 2020). The theoretical frameworks include local literature as much as a long list of Western scholars—with some recurrent figures, such as Bruno Latour, Dona Haraway, and Anna Tsing.

In Bahasa Indonesian, a special issue of *Balairung*, which was edited by a group of students from Gadjah Mada University (Raja et al. 2018), argued that the Anthropocene concept opens a brand-new theoretical gateway for understanding the specific role of Indonesia in the global ecological crisis (Sugandi and Najjah 2018). Here, too, bringing the focus away from the West does not necessarily mean a rejection of its academic literature; instead, what prevails is a reinterpretation of that legacy. For example, Haekal and Suci (2018) draw on Mann and Wainwright's theoretical framework of a "Climate Leviathan" and a "Climate Mao".

In spite of the limited indigenization of the Anthropocene in Asian languages thus far, we must keep in mind that all over Asia, environmental movements have played a significant role in curbing the massive forces of destruction presented above (Jobin, Ho and Hsiao 2021), with emblematic examples such as the litigations for climate justice initiated from the Philippines and Indonesia (Magno 2021; Suharko 2021). It remains to be seen, however, to what extent these social movements can cope with the pace and scope of the ongoing destruction. Will these mobilizations be able to act quickly and efficiently enough to prevent the last forests from being completely erased, or the Mekong and other rivers from becoming so dammed up that only a few dozen species out of thousands will survive? As I conclude in the next section, the answer lies in a reset of geopolitics and a post-Western re-politicization of the Anthropocene.

4   For a Geopolitics of the Anthropocene

Since Beeson (2010) posited China's and Singapore's environmental governance as alternative models, a thread of literature has advocated that environmental authoritarianism could do a better job of fixing the climate emergency and other urgent environmental issues. To this argument, Shahar (2015) replies that eco-authoritarianism is only capable of matching the performance of market liberalism, and at the clear cost of renouncing individual and political rights.

Dryzek and Pickering (2019: 149) further argue that democracy must be redeemed in the Anthropocene because only it allows the ecological reflexivity needed to cope with its challenges, whereas environmental authoritarianism prescribes the solutions through top-down directives with uncertain results. Today's environmental problems are exceedingly daunting, and response to them too long delayed, but the protection of democracies and human rights is no less legitimate than the global concern for the climate.

The problem is therefore: can the two models—liberal and authoritarian—of environmental and climate governance coexist at different levels of national sovereignties, and cooperate on global issues (through the United Nations organizations, among other platforms of discussion and coordination)? In Geoff Mann and Joel Wainwright's *Climate Leviathan* (2018), the authors draw on Hobbes' famous political model and Schmitt's reading of Hobbes to introduce their concepts of "Climate Leviathan" as a global capitalist regime, and "Climate Mao" as its anti-capitalist equivalent.

A good example of this confrontation between two climate regimes can be found in the recent evolution of climate change diplomacy between the two great powers. After years of climate change denial under the presidency of Donald Trump, the US administration of Joe Biden has assigned to John Kerry the difficult mission of boosting cooperation with China on the climate emergency, while Kerry's colleague, Secretary of State Antony Blinken, would keep a strong stance on human rights and traditional geopolitics (such as on the Xinjiang, Hong Kong, Taiwan, and the South China Sea). But in the rare meetings launched thus far, Chinese delegates, including Chinese Special Envoy on Climate Change Xie Zhenhua and Minister of Foreign Affairs Wang Yi, have replied sharply that climate cooperation would not be possible without better overall US–China relations, thus rejecting the American call for compartmentalization of the issue.

In their essay on the Anthropocene, Horn and Bergthaller (2020: 84) bring back Michel Serres' interpretation of 19th-century Francisco Goya's painting "Duel with Cudgels" (*Duelo a garrotazos*) as two men fighting in the midst of quicksand: obsessed with their struggle against one another, they are blind to the fact that every move they make is gradually burying them both. This allegory of the limitations of traditional approaches to political conflicts applies perfectly to the Anthropocene: while nations show their military muscles, the very ground which makes these conflicts possible is swallowing the conflicting parties.

When all territories are threatened by *mega-disasters* (mega-fires, giant typhoons and floods, etc.), long drought, and rapid sea rise, except perhaps a few ecological niches, no place on Earth can be safe. It means that, except perhaps for a few niches, the ongoing climate emergency is a national security threat for every country. The Anthropocene is a geopolitical threat in the traditional meaning of geopolitics, i.e., the international order inherited from the Treaty of Westphalia, Napoleon, and Clausewitz. In other words, the Anthropocene makes climate and environmental issues a threat on traditional boundaries. Unless the *geo* of geopolitics is put at the center of security issues and international relations, humanity is likely to end like Goya's fighters.

Consequently, we need new perspectives to reconsider geopolitics, both from state and non-state actors, as well as from peoples living in interstitial territories of the new cold war, such as indigenous peoples, peoples of the Arctic, nomads, gypsies, and sailors. Moreover, given the ongoing Sixth Mass Extinction, the politicization of the Anthropocene should necessarily include a much larger diversity of "stakeholders" far beyond human species: from a larger range of animals and plants—not just garden flowers, house dogs, and cats—down to microbes and viruses (Chuang 2020a; Neo 2021; Wu 2020).

Moreover, during our journey in the Anthropocene, to avoid Goya's nightmare, we may keep in mind another powerful image: the Song Dynasty famous painting "Travelers among Mountains and Streams" by Fan Kuan (范寬，谿山行旅圖), as an allegory of what should remain the exact proportion between humans and the geological forces of the Earth. But this is not to say that Chinese culture has a better understanding of "Nature"; one should beware of culturalist traps, be them Western-centric, Sino-centric, or anywhere-centric, for in the Anthropocene there is no more center but humanity as the worst threat to life.

References

Baldwin, A., and B. Erickson. 2020. "Introduction: Whiteness, Coloniality, and the Anthropocene". *Environment and Planning D: Society and Space* 38 (1): 3–11.

Beeson, M. 2010. "The Coming of Environmental Authoritarianism". *Environmental politics* 19 (2): 276–294.

Bonneuil, C., and J.-B. Fressoz. 2017. *The Shock of the Anthropocene: The Earth, History and Us*. London: Verso.

Burck, J., U. Hagen, N. Höhne, L. Nascimento, and C. Bals. 2020. *Climate Change Performance Index*. Bonn: Germanwatch Institute.

Chakrabarty, D. 2009. "The Climate of History: Four Theses". *Critical Enquiry* 35: 197–222.

Chandler, D. 2017. "Securing the Anthropocene? International Policy Experiments in Digital Hacktivism: A Case Study of Jakarta". *Security Dialogue* 48 (2): 113–130.

Chatterjee, E. 2020. "The Asian Anthropocene: Electricity and Fossil Developmentalism". *The Journal of Asian Studies* 79 (1): 3–24.

Chuang, C.M. 張君玫. 2020a. "Renleishi de duoyangxing zhengzhi" 人類世的多樣性政治 [The Politics of Diversity in the Anthropocene]. *Chung-Wai Literary* 中外文學 49 (1): 7–11.

Chuang, C.M. 張君玫. 2020b. "Renleishi zhong de nuxing zhuyi: lizudian, difang yu shijian" 人類世中的女性主義:立足點、地方與實踐 [Feminism in the Anthropocene: Standpoints, Places and Practices]. *Chung-Wai Literary* 中外文學 49 (1): 13–60.

Chuang, C.M., and J.J. Gong, eds. 2020. "Yishu celiang, renleishi meixue pipan" 藝術測量・人類世美學批判 [Artistic Measuring, Aesthetic Critique in Anthropocene Epoch]. *ACT: Art Critique of Taiwan* 藝術觀點 80: 4–128.

Corlett, R. 2013. "Becoming Europe: Southeast Asia in the Anthropocene". *Elementa: Science of the Anthropocene* 1:000016. doi:10.12952/journal.elementa.000016.

Crutzen, P.J. 2002. "Geology of Mankind". *Nature* 415 (6867): 23.

Crutzen, P.J., and E.F. Stoermer. 2000. "The Anthropocene". *Global Change Newsletter IGBP* 41: 17–18.

Dauvergne, P. 2001. *Loggers and Degradation in the Asia-Pacific: Corporations and Environmental Management*. Cambridge: Cambridge University Press.

Davis, H., and Z. Todd. 2017. "On the Importance of a Data, Or, Decolonizing the Anthropocene". *ACME: An International Journal for Critical Geographies* 16 (4): 761–780.

Dryzek, J., and J. Pickering. 2019. *The Politics of the Anthropocene*. Oxford: Oxford UP.

Eckstein, D., M.-L. Hutfils, and M. Winges. 2019. *Global Climate Risk Index*. Bonn: Germanwatch Institute.

Haekal, L. and P. Erfika Suci. 2018. "Kuasa dan Eksklusi: REDD+ sebagai 'Climate Leviathan' dan Alih Fungsi Lahan di Indonesia". *Balairung: Jurnal Multidisipliner Mahasiswa Indonesia* [Multidisciplinary Journal of Indonesian Students] 1 (1): 108–125.

Hamilton, C. 2017. *Defiant Earth: The Fate of Humans in the Anthropocene*. Sydney: Allen & Unwin.

Hecht, G. 2018. "The African Anthropocene". *Aeon* (online), February 6.

Hirsch, P., and C. Warren, eds. 1998. *The Politics of Environment in Southeast Asia; Resources and Resistance*. London: Routledge.

Horn, E., and H. Bergthaller. 2020. *The Anthropocene: Key Issues for the Humanities*. London: Routledge.

Hornborg, A. 2013. *Global Ecology and Unequal Exchange: Fetishism in a Zero-Sum World*. London: Routledge.

Hornborg, A. 2018. "La magie mondialisée du Technocène. Capital, échanges inégaux et moralité". In *Penser l'Anthropocène*, edited by Rémi Beau and Catherine Larrère, 97–112. Paris: Sciences Po.

Hudson, M. 2014. "Placing Asia in the Anthropocene: Histories, Vulnerabilities, Responses". *The Journal of Asian Studies* 73 (4): 941–962.

Jobin, P., M.S. Ho, and M.H. Hsin-Huang. 2021. *Environmental Movements and Politics of the Asian Anthropocene*. Singapore: ISEAS.

Latour, B. 2014. "Agency at the Time of the Anthropocene". *New Literary History* 45: 1–18.

Latour, B. 2015. *Facing Gaia: Eight Lectures on the New Climatic Regime*. Cambridge: Polity.

Latour, B. 2017. *Politics in the New Climatic Regime*. Cambridge: Polity.

Latour, B. 2020. "Is This a Dress Rehearsal?" *Critical Inquiry* 47 (2): 26–27 (March 26).

Lee Yi-tze 李宜澤. 2020. "Renlei shixia de yuanzhumin: dijing xushi yu jichu jianshe renshilun" 人類世下的原住民:地景敘事與基礎建設認識論 [Indigenous People in the Anthropocene: Landscape Narratives and Epistemology of Infrastructure]. *Chung-Wai Literary* 中外文學 49 (1): 133–143.

Lin Chun-Yin 林春銀. 2018. "Liugei ziran bange diqiu: shenmei de tiyan" 留給「自然」半個地球—審美的體驗 [Preserve Half the Surface of the Earth to Nature: The Aesthetic Experience]. *Applied Ethics Review* 應用倫理評論 64: 217–237.

Magno, F. 2021. "Environmental Movements in the Philippines: Contestation for Justice in the Anthropocene". In *Environmental Movements and Politics of the Asian Anthropocene*, edited by Paul Jobin, Ming-sho Ho, and Hsin-Huang Michael Hsiao, 139–170. Singapore: ISEAS.

Malm, A. 2016. *Fossil Capital: The Rise of Steam Power and the Roots of Global Warming*. London: Verso.

Malm, A., and A. Hornborg. 2014. "The Geology of Mankind? A Critique of the Anthropocene Narrative". *The Anthropocene Review* 1 (1): 62–69.

Mann, G., and J. Wainwright. 2018. *Climate Leviathan*. London: Verso.

Marquardt, J. 2019. "Worlds Apart? The Global South and the Anthropocene". In *The Anthropocene Debate and Political Science*, edited by Thomas Hickmann, Lena Partzsch, Philipp Pattberg, and Sabine Weiland, 200–218. London and New York: Routledge.

Maréchal, J.-P. 2018. "La Chine nouvel *hegemon* du régime climatique mondial". *Monde Chinois Nouvelle Asie* 56 (4): 9–27.

Middleton, C., and J. Allouche. 2016. "Watershed or Powershed? Critical Hydropolitics, China and the 'Lancang-Mekong Cooperation Framework'". *The International Spectator* 51 (3): 100–117.

Moore, J., ed. 2016. *Anthropocene or Capitalocene? Nature, History, and the Crisis of Capitalism*. Oakland, CA: PM Press and Kairos Books.

Morris-Jung, J., ed. 2018. *In China's Backyard: Policies and Politics of Chinese Resource Investments in Southeast Asia*. Singapore: ISEAS.

Neo, H. 2021. "The Post-politics of Environmental Engagement in Singapore". In *Environmental Movements and Politics of the Asian Anthropocene*, edited by Paul Jobin, Ming-sho Ho, and Hsin-Huang Michael Hsiao, 109–137. Singapore: ISEAS.

Peluso, N. 1994. *Rich Forests, Poor People: Resource Control and Resistance in Central Java*. Berkeley: University of California Press.

Raja, Muhammad Unies A., ed. 2018. "Antroposen". *Balairung: Jurnal Multidisipliner Mahasiswa Indonesia* [Multidisciplinary Journal of Indonesian Students] 1 (1): 6–143.

Reszitnyk, A. 2020. "The Descent into Disanthropy: Critical Theory and the Anthropocene". *Telos* 190: 9–27.

Ross, M.L. 2001. *Timber Booms and Institutional Breakdown in Southeast Asia*. Cambridge: Cambridge University Press.

Schneider-Mayerson, M. 2017. "Some Islands Will Rise: Singapore in the Anthropocene". *Resilience* 4 (2–3): 166–184.

Shahar, D.C. 2015. "Rejecting Eco-Authoritarianism, Again". *Environmental Values* 24 (3): 345–366.

Simangan, D. 2019. "Situating the Asia Pacific in the Age of the Anthropocene". *Australian Journal of International Affairs* 73 (6): 564–584.

Simangan, D. 2020. "Where Is the Asia Pacific in Mainstream International Relations Scholarship on the Anthropocene?" *The Pacific Review* 34 (5): 724–746.

Simpson, M. 2020. "The Anthropocene as Colonial Discourse". *Environment and Planning D: Society and Space* 38 (1): 53–71.

Sims Gallagher, K., and X. Xiaowei. 2018. *Titans of the Climate: Explaining Policy Process in the United States and China*. Cambridge, MA: MIT Press.

Sugandi, Ahmad T., and A. Hakam Najjah. 2018. "Panggung Megah Itu akan Roboh: Di Ambang Batas Paradigma dan Harapan akan Revolusi" [The Magnificent Stage Will Crumble: On the Brink of Paradigm and Hope of the Revolution]. *Balairung: Jurnal Multidisipliner Mahasiswa Indonesia* 1: 20–39.

Suharko, S. 2021. "Environmental NGOs in 'Post-New Order' Indonesia: Saving the Forests Through Democracy". In *Environmental Movements and Politics of the Asian Anthropocene*, edited by Paul Jobin, Ming-sho Ho, and Hsin-Huang Michael Hsiao, 171–201. Singapore: ISEAS.

Swyngedouw, E. 2015. "Depoliticized Environments and the Promises of the Anthropocene". In *The International Handbook of Political Ecology*, edited by Raymond Bryant, 131–145. Cheltenham: Elgar.

Wang, James W.Y. 2021. "The Cambodian Neopatrimonial State, Chinese Investments, and Anti-dam Movements". In *Environmental Movements and Politics of the Asian Anthropocene*, edited by Paul Jobin, Ming-sho Ho, and Hsin-Huang Michael Hsiao, 295–328. Singapore: ISEAS.

Wu Chuang-hsien 吳宗憲. 2020. "JiàngòuJiangou renleishi de dongwu baohu zhili jizhi" 建構「人類世」的動物保護治理機制 [To Construct an Animal Governing Mechanism in the "Anthropocene"]. *Chung-Wai Literary* 中外文學 49 (1): 95–132.

Zhenzhong, Z., L. Estes, A.D. Ziegler, and C. Anping, et al. 2018. "Highland Cropland Expansion and Forest Loss in Southeast Asia in the Twenty-First Century". *Nature Geoscience* 11: 556–562.

Zhang, Q., J. Xujia, D. Tong, S.J. Davis, Z. Hongyan, G. Guannan, F. Tong, Z. Bo, L. Zifeng, D.G. Streets, N. Ruijing, M. Brauer, A. van Donkelaar, R.V. Martin, H. Hong, L. Zhu, P. Da, K. Haidong, Y. Yingying, L. Jintai, H. Kebin, and G. Dabo. 2017. "Transboundary Health Impacts of Transported Global Air Pollution and International Trade". *Nature* 453: 705–717.

CHAPTER 48

East Asian Compressed Ecological Modernization: Modus of Developmental State and Technological Response to the Environmental Crisis

Satoh Keiichi

1   Introduction

Ecological modernization theory (EMT) is one of the major environmental theories/discourses among scholars and policymakers (Mol 2002). By extending the discussion of reflexive modernity (Beck, Giddens and Lash 1994), EMT argues that environmentally adaptive socioeconomic reforms can be a source of future innovation and development in late modern societies. At the actual policy level, the EMT tries to use the inherent pressure for innovation in competitive market economies to transform the resource- and environment-intensive industrialism mode. Such policies include the emission trading of greenhouse gas, feed-in-tariff to renewable energies, and carbon tax (Jänicke 2020).

The EMT draws its perspective mainly from the Western countries that have experienced a set of late modernity characteristics, such as post-industrialization, severe environmental degradation caused by industrial technology, and the cultural shift into the post-materialism. By contrast, although the degree varies, the East Asian societies (here we refer to Japan, South Korea, and China) generally experienced modernization and a second modernization at once (Han and Shim 2010). These multiple modernizations, or "compressed modernization", resulted in East Asia's unique response to the environmental crisis, particularly the climate change problem.

In the remainder of this chapter, the literature of multiple modernizations in East Asia is briefly reviewed, followed by the discussion about the how such multiple modernizations shape the East Asian response to the climate change problem.

2   Asian Multiple Modernization

In the sociological literature, first modernization and second modernization (or often referred to as reflexive modernity) are conceptually distinguished.

The first modernization is typically characterized by industrialization, urbanization, nationalization of boundaries, and modern rational identities (Han and Shim 2010: 470). Notably, each characteristic of first modernizations is interwoven, and the process of first modernization involves the institutionalization of social systems, such as a capital market economy and national state-building, that drive and cause such modernization.

However, such a first modernization induces risks that can eventually break down the first modernity. Manufacturing plants, for example, polluted the air, imposed health risks to residents, and destroyed the ecosystem. Hence, on the one hand, second modernization is the consequence of and self-critique for the first modernization. On the other hand, second modernization is also a radicalization of first modernization, because such unintended consequences of risks also push globalization and cosmopolitanization further (Beck 2014).

EMT shares this notion of second modernity that global society currently faces. But it is connected more directly to the specific set of assumptions, mechanisms, and actual policy. The basic premise of EMT is the centripetal movement of ecological interests, ideas, and considerations within the social practices and institutional developments of modern societies (Mol 2006: 33). In other words, as a response to the adversarial consequences of the first modernization, ecological perspective and ecological rationality become autonomous, independent, differentiated perspectives vis-à-vis other perspectives and rationalities in the second modernity (Mol 1996; Spaargaren and Mol 1992). The concrete example includes the growth of green ideology, environmental organizations, and environmental policies. Ecological modernization is also seen as the radicalization of advanced accountability in democracy and individualization. The EMT based policies try to reform the market system in such a way that the ecological considerations become an inevitable aspect of the rationality.

As the term already implies, such a distinction is deeply embedded in the historical context that mostly Western advanced industrial societies experienced. In contrast, East Asia experienced the development of first modernity and the transition to second modernity almost at once within a very short period (Han and Shim 2010). Notably, such compressed modernization in East Asia were led by a bureaucratic-authoritarian developmental state whereby the states play a central role in investment and coordination for the socio-economic modernization process without the democratization. The Japanese developmental state can be traced back to the Meiji restoration (1862), when it launched a modernization that moved quickly to catch up. The Korean developmental state was established by President Park Chung-Hee, who led the military coup in 1961 and conducted Yushin reform subsequently. China's development after the opening and reform (1979) can be seen also an example of developmental state-led reform (Han and Shim 2010: 473). Consequently, reflexivity means quite different things in Western and East Asian contexts (Beck and Grande 2010).

Viewed from the theoretical considerations about East Asian modernization, it is important to ask how such a compressed modernity characterizes environmental reform in East Asia. The fact that East Asian societies already experienced first modernization implies that they are also ready for further transformation. However, some key institutions, especially those related to democratization, are still in the process of transforming from the premodern to the first modern. Culture in East Asian countries also preserves several elements that the Western scholars may call premodern. How is this complex mixture of premodern, first modern, and second modern elements interwoven? In the next section, we will focus on the climate change problem and discuss how compressed modernity stipulates the East Asian response to this problem.

3 East Asian Response to Climate Change

3.1 *Technological Response by the East Asian Society*

The climate change problem is discussed as the typical environmental problem of reflexive modernity (Giddens 2011). Since industrialization in the modern era, the burning of fossil fuels has emitted massive amounts of CO_2 gas into the air, which mantles the atmosphere, causing the greenhouse effect. If no effort is taken to reduce CO_2 gas emissions, it is predicted that the global average temperature will rise more than 4 degrees Celsius (IPCC 2015). In order to avoid the catastrophic consequences caused by climate change, the latest IPCC report argues that the global net greenhouse gas emission needs to be zero by the 2050s at the latest (IPCC 2021). Such net zero emissions of greenhouse gas can be achieved by reducing the total amount of energy consumption, switching energy sources from fossil fuels to non-fossil fuels, and/or capturing greenhouse gas in the air and storing it somewhere. Note that scholars disagree about how to combine each method.

The sociological question is thus how to achieve such a transition into the net zero greenhouse gas society. Roughly speaking, there are three approaches to achieve such goals. The first camp advocates for the business as usual (BAU) path that preserves the current socioeconomic system. This camp stresses the cost of the transition of the socioeconomic system and commonly sees technological innovation (or extension of the current technology) as originating from the current system. In the actual policy, most of the advocates prefer the voluntary approach by the business sector to mitigate greenhouse gas. By contrast, the second camp, EMT, sees the necessity of the adjustment of the socio-economic system toward the net zero greenhouse gas society. Such an adjustment can be induced by changing the incentive and profit structure in the market. The actual policy involves, for example, the introduction of carbon tax, emission trading systems, and a feed-in-tariff system for promoting renewable energies. The third camp, a treadmill of production theories (TPT; Schnaiberg and Gould 2000), criticizes EMT in that such an amendment of a capitalist economy cannot reduce the environmental impact. Any efforts to enhance resource productivity will be overwhelmed by expanded production, on which governments rely, and therefore those governments will be reluctant to regulate them (Perrow and Pulver 2015). Hence, TPT argues for the fundamental change in the socioeconomic system. In the actual policy process, however, the conflict between BAU and EMT is the major fault line.

TABLE 48.1 Greenhouse gas emissions and economic indicators in East Asia (2018)

	Japan	South Korea	China	US	Germany	Sweden
CO_2 emission[a]						
CO_2 emission (Mt)	1080.72	605.78	9528.21	4921.13	696.13	34.51
world rank	5	7	1	2	6	67
% of change since 2000	-5.9	40.3	207.4	-14.1	-14.3	-33.6
per GDP CO_2 emission (kg CO_2/USD)	0.20	0.30	0.40	0.25	0.16	0.07
% of change since 2000	-20.0	-25.0	-33.3	-37.5	-36.0	-53.3
Economic indicators[b]						
GDP (billion USD)	4549.9	1506.0	13446.5	19468.7	3585.5	3585.5
% of change since 2000	16.06	94.61	383.93	41.49	26.22	26.22
MVA (billion USD)	961.1	413.6	3892.4	2211.9	760.4	760.4
% of change since 2000	27.8	148.0	436.0	25.7	39.7	39.7
MVA per capita (Billion USD)	7485	8084	2726	6762	9148	7526
% of change since 2000	27.0	129.7	384.2	8.3	36.8	17.8
MVA share in GDP (%)	21.1	27.5	28.9	11.4	21.2	14.0
% of change since 2000	9.9	27.3	10.7	-10.9	10.4	-10.3

Abbreviations: GDP = gross domestic product; USD = US dollar; MVA = manufacturing value added.
SOURCES: [a] IEA (2021); [b] UNIDO (2021)

East Asian countries have a unique combination of opportunity and challenges to pursue BAU and EM paths. To comprehend the macro-economic context, Table 48.1 summarizes key indicators related to socioeconomic activity and climate change in 2018. China, Japan, and South Korea are, respectively, the first, fifth, and seventh largest emitters of the greenhouse gas in the world. Together with the other major Western industrial countries, such as the United States and Germany, they compose the largest emitters in the world. Note that non-large emitter Sweden is also added into Table 48.1 because it is often considered as the frontrunner of the ecological modernization.

The trend of East and West large emitters makes a vivid contrast. While Western large emitters reduced CO_2 emissions by approximately 15% from 2000, Eastern large emitters, except Japan, greatly increased emissions and have not yet reached peak emissions. This trend is largely accounted for by the countries' rapid industrialization, as shown by their change in manufacturing value added (MVA) since 2000, which is the indicator that measures the manufacturing output as a share of a country's gross domestic product (GDP). Assessed by MVA per capita, these Eastern and Western societies, except for China, are now at almost the same level as industrialized societies that produce highly valued manufactured products. However, in terms of decoupling of economic growth and decarbonization, East Asian societies are not at the stage of transition observed in Western industrial countries. Even Japan, which has been the front-runner of industrialization in East Asian societies, has not shown as clear a trend of transition as its Western counterpart Germany (Mez, Okamura and Weidner 2020).

The different trend in the paths is also observable in its energy supply (Table 48.2). Because most of the greenhouse gas originates from energy that human beings use, both reducing the total amount of energy use and switching energy sources from fossil fuels (i.e., oil, coal, and natural gas) to non-fossil fuels (e.g., nuclear energy, wind, and solar) are necessary to reduce the amount of greenhouse gas.

The East Asian emergent industrial countries, Korea and China, greatly increased their amount of energy consumption, while the Western industrial countries of Germany and United States slightly reduced energy usage. Notably, Japan is an exceptional case here, as it dramatically decreased its total energy usage. This decrease is partly due to the aging of the country's society. However, the clear decrease first happened since the Fukushima Daiichi Nuclear Power plant accident in 2011, where citizens and businesses installed lots of technologies to increase the efficiency of their energy usage.

TABLE 48.2 Total energy supply in West and East countries

	Japan		Korea		China		Germany		US		Sweden	
	2018	change[c]	2018	change	2018	change	2018	change	2018	change	2018	change
Total (ktoe)	425,999	−17.9%	282,206	50.0%	3,197,631	182.8%	306,270	−8.9%	2,237,045	−2.1%	51,025	9.0%
Fossil fuels[a]	377,647	−9.8%	238,624	51.0%	2,819,842	211.1%	240,364	−14.6%	1,840,992	−6.4%	13,569	−19.2%
Nuclear	16,918	−79.8%	34,786	22.5%	76,865	1662.6%	19,804	−55.2%	219,216	5.5%	17,861	19.6%
Renewables[b]	31,434	89.4%	8,796	397.2%	300,924	36.8%	46,102	332.3%	176,837	60.5%	19,595	30.1%
% of composite by source												
Fossil fuels[a]	88.6%	8.0%	84.6%	0.6%	88.2%	8.0%	78.5%	−5.2%	82.3%	−3.8%	26.6%	−9.3%
Nuclear	4.0%	−12.2%	12.3%	−2.8%	2.4%	2.0%	6.5%	−6.7%	9.8%	0.7%	35.0%	3.1%
Renewables[b]	7.4%	4.2%	3.1%	2.2%	9.4%	−10.0%	15.1%	11.9%	7.9%	3.1%	38.4%	6.2%

Notes: [a] Fossil fuels include oil, coal, and natural gas. [b] Renewables include solar, wind, hydro, and biofuels. [c] Change in % since 2000.
SOURCE: IEA (2021)

By breaking down to the energy sources, the different trends become clear. While Western emitters decreased their fossil fuels usage, Eastern countries, including Japan, increased it. Notably, in terms of the composition of the energy, Eastern countries increased the ratio of fossil fuels in the total energy supply, meaning that they became more dependent on fossil fuels. Renewable energies (e.g., solar and wind) also increased in these countries both in terms of total amount and the composite ratio. However, the trend is weaker than in Western counterparts.

The other non-fossil fuel energy is nuclear energy. For this energy source, there is no clear difference between the East and the West. Yet, in terms of future plans, a clear difference exists. As of 2021, 22 entirely new nuclear power plants are under construction in East Asia (i.e., 18 in China and 4 in Korea), while only 2 are being built in the aforementioned Western countries (i.e., 2 new power plants in the United States). Put in other words, around 40% (22 of 519) of new reactors around the world are located in East Asia (WNA 2021), which will make East Asia the world's most densely populated area with nuclear reactors.

Most of these reactors are located across coastal areas. It is worth mentioning that due to climate change, rise in sea levels, flood risk, and the intensification of typhoons are expected (IPCC 2015). Such a sea rise can cause an additional risk to keep nuclear power plants in coastal areas, if we recall that the direct cause of the Fukushima accident was the hit of the tsunami to the nuclear power plants.

To summarize, East Asian countries' socioeconomic response to the climate change problem is characterized by (1) ongoing economic growth coupled with an increase in greenhouse gas, (2) increased dependence on fossil fuels, and (3) a possible transition toward nuclear energy from fossil fuels. In other words, East Asian countries appear to be pursuing the BAU path rather than the EMT path.

3.2   Driver of the East Asian Society's Response

How can the East Asian response to climate change be understood? Three different drivers that consist of the different levels are discussed below.

The first aspect is the role of East Asian countries in the global market. Many of the Western industrial countries started to shift toward a postindustrial society as early as the 1970s, and the proportion of the laborers that work in the service sector has increased. The shift toward a postindustrial society by the Western industrial countries created a new opportunity for Eastern industrial countries, particularly Japan at that time, where the labor wages were lower than in Western countries. The proportion of laborers in the industrial sector peaked in 1992 in Japan, which implies that Japan started to shift toward a postindustrial society as late as the early 1990s (Oguma 2012). The position of Japan as the manufacturing plant for the world economy was then replaced by Korea and China. Hence, the different characteristics of the Western and Eastern industrial countries can be better understood in that the former features of Western industrial societies were taken over by their Eastern counterparts. The current position by the Eastern countries in the world economy makes them keep their modus of production that is characterized with the coupling of growth and greenhouse gas emission.

Notably, despite their "old" modus of production, East Asian countries are known to be efficient users of natural resources compared with former Western industrial societies (Sugihara 2020). Between 1925 and 1990, when Japan experienced rapid economic growth together with industrialization, energy intensity in Japan (i.e., energy uses per unit of GDP) remained around 0.2 TPES/GDP, which was roughly around one third to one half of those in the United States (Sugihara 2020: 156). The similar trend applies to Korea during its industrialization between 1971 and 2000. While the energy intensity in China dramatically worsened during its first heavy industrialization in 1950–1960, from 1960 onwards Chinese energy intensity also improved rapidly (Sugihara 2020: 174–175).

Sugihara (2020) argues about the different resource availability between Western countries and East Asia. In Western countries industrialization was driven by the intense use of the coal that was widely available in this region. By contrast, East Asia is known to have scarce natural resources except for the internal area in China. Hence, East Asia's industrialization was accomplished through the efficient use of natural resources and the creation of industrial cities in coastal areas, to which natural resources are imported. Notably, such industrialization was led by the developmental state that planned for and invested in the creation of industrial cities and the hard-working workers supplied from farm areas to industrial areas through the state-led education system.

It is important to point out that modernization in East Asia, especially for Korea and China, coincided with the development of environmental policy (Mol 2006). Pollution control in China began in the early 1970s and the National Environmental Protection Office was established in 1974, in the same period as the economic reforms. Moreover, in Korea the environmental movement since the 1980s has been very tightly knit with the country's democratization process (Ku 2011). The economic and political reforms knotted with the environmental reform generally contributed to the economic success in the East Asian path of development, because such processes generally increased efficiency in the use of resources and the mobility of skilled labors, which are key for their development.

This unique combination of economic and political modernization processes and the institutionalization of environmental policy in East Asia created a complex impact on further development in climate policy.

First, the developmental state tradition is connected to noninstitutional environmental regulation by bureaucracy, which is reportedly quite common in China (Mol 2006) and Japan (Schreurs 2002). Specifically, the voluntary action by business sectors to reduce greenhouse gas emissions in Japan is arguably the largest in the world (Sugiyama and Wakabayashi 2013). Importantly, despite being termed "voluntary", the voluntary action among the businesses should be seen as a quasi-regulation with oversight by the state bureaucracy (Satoh 2017). The other side of coin of this noninstitutional regulation is that it prevents the introduction of institutionalized environmental policy. Moreover, while successful modernization led by the developmental state resulted in the strong *output legitimacy* (Scharpf 1997) of the state bureaucracy, which is the different causality from the EMT. What EMT assumed has assumed is that such environmental reform is driven by the increased *input legitimacy*, such as through participation and accountability.

Second, the East Asian modernization process created several conditions that support the building of nuclear power plants. Given the initial setting that the East Asian modernization is the process of overcoming resource scarcity, it is a natural direction for these societies to aim to obtain their own energy. Nuclear energy was an attractive choice for them to be independent from resource scarcity (Yoshioka 2011). East Asian large industrial cities that are the result of its modernization path also require a large amount of energy which nuclear power plants can produce from a relatively small site. Furthermore, the success in East Asian industrialization made citizens trust in their own technologies. Notably, while Western countries, except France, decreased the number of their operating nuclear power plants after the Chernobyl accident in 1986, Japan kept building the plants until the Fukushima accident. Honda (2005) reported that the common perception across the business and civil societies during this period was that the technology for power plants in Japan was better than it is in Russia. Similarly, according to Kim et al. (2013), citizens in Korea and China showed the highest acceptance of nuclear energy among the 47 countries they examined before the Fukushima accident. Even though the acceptance dropped, especially in China, after the accident, the acceptance rates of the two countries are still second and third highest, respectively.

4 Conclusion

In the sociological literature, two ideal types of modernity, first and second/reflexive modernity, have been distinguished. Following this general notion, EMT hypothesized that environmentally adaptive socioeconomic reforms are the significant forces of development in reflexive modernity. Such development is arguably backed by the autonomous ecological rationality, which is the self-critique against the growth-oriented first modernity. While Western industrial societies have been experiencing such gradual shifts toward second modernity, East Asian societies have experienced compressed modernization, that is, they experienced first and second modernization at once. Hence, in this chapter we asked how such a unique East Asian path toward modernization affected the region's reactions toward the environmental problems, especially climate change.

The most important characteristics of East Asian countries' responses toward the environmental problem are that the environmental reform itself is deeply embedded in their project in the compressed modernity. East Asian countries are known to be a geographically resource-scarce region. Overcoming this handicap has been a key factor from the beginning of their modernization. Modernization was done by the creation of relatively energy-efficient industrial large cities in the coastal areas, where hard-working workers have been supplied from farm areas and where there have been resources from abroad. Such modernization was effectively led by the developmental states that are a common feature of these regions.

Ecological rationality hereby played two different but interwoven roles. On the one hand, the efficient usage of energy was a key requirement for modernization as well as economic strength in the global market. On the other hand, environmental movements in this region were strongly associated with the democratization that is the other important tier of modernization but had lacked in the developmental state.

This way in which ecological rationality played out in environmental reform makes a strong contrast to Western industrial countries. In the latter cases, ecological rationality originates from the critique against economic growth, modern technology, and eventually the whole societal systems that advanced the first modernity. By contrast, in East Asian societies in which environmental reform is the integral part of first modernity, these societies try to counter the environmental risks by advancing the first modernity.

An iconic example is nuclear energy. East Asia is known to be the region where citizens' acceptance of nuclear power plants had been very high. According to the recent projection based on the planned new power plants,

East Asian coastal areas will be one of the densest regions with nuclear power plants. Such an advancement of nuclear technology will impose other risks to coastal large cities which are already known to be quite vulnerable against the sea level rise and typhoons caused by climate change.

Having said that, it is also important to point out that the Fukushima accident in Japan had a significant impact on society. The number of nuclear power plants operating in Japan dropped dramatically after the accident. The trend of energy usage went downwards in Japan, and the decoupling of economic growth and energy consumption is ongoing. It is also worth mentioning that South Korea introduced the national greenhouse gas emission trading system in 2015, which is the second largest trading market in the world. These changes in the growth modus in Japan and environmental institutional reforms exemplified in South Korea had been lacking in the technological response to the climate problem in East Asia. Hence, it may be not accurate to assume that the East Asian response to the environmental problem, which is the extension of compressed modernity, will continue in the future. Nevertheless, its transformation toward the other modus of response will be not the same as what the Western industrial societies experienced.

References

Beck, Ulrich, Anthony Giddens, and Scott Lash. 1994. *Reflexive Modernization: Politics, Tradition and Aesthetics in the Modern Social Order*. Palo Alto, CA: Stanford University Press.

Beck, Ulrich, and Edgar Grande. 2010. "Varieties of Second Modernity: The Cosmopolitan Turn in Social and Political Theory and Research". *The British Journal of Sociology* 61 (3): 409–443. doi:10.1111/j.1468-4446.2010.01320.x.

Beck, Ulrich. 2015. "Emancipatory catastrophism: What does it mean to climate change and risk society?" *Current Sociology* 63 (1): 75–88. doi:10.1177/0011392114559951.

Giddens, Anthony. 2011. *Politics of Climate Change*. 2nd edition, revised and updated. Cambridge: Polity.

Han, Sang-Jin, and Young-Hee Shim. 2010. "Redefining Second Modernity for East Asia: A Critical Assessment". *The British Journal of Sociology* 61 (3): 465–488. doi:10.1111/j.1468-4446.2010.01322.x.

Honda, Hiroshi. 2005. *Datsu Genshiryoku No Undō to Seiji: Nihon No Energy Seisaku No Tenkan Wa Kanō Ka*. Hokkaidō: Hokkaidō Daigaku Shuppan Kai.

IEA (International Energy Agency). 2021. "Data and Statistics". Accessed September 3, 2021. https://www.iea.org/statistics/.

IPCC (Intergovernmental Panel on Climate Change). 2015. *Climate Change 2014: Synthesis Report*. Geneva, Switzerland: IPCC. Contribution of Working Groups I, II and III to the Fifth Assessment Report of the Intergovernmental Panel on Climate Change.

IPCC (Intergovernmental Panel on Climate Change). 2021. "Summary for Policymakers". In *Climate Change 2021: The Physical Science Basis. Contribution of Working Group I to the Sixth Assessment Report of the Intergovernmental Panel on Climate Change*, edited by IPCC, 1–41. Cambridge: Cambridge University Press.

Jänicke, Martin. 2020. "Ecological Modernization: A Paradise of Feasibility but No General Solution". In *The Ecological Modernization Capacity of Japan and Germany: Comparing Nuclear Energy, Renewables, Automobility and Rare Earth Policy*, edited by Lutz Mez, Lila Okamura, and Helmut Weidner, 13–23. Wiesbaden: Springer VS.

Kim, Younghwan, Minki Kim, and Wonjoon Kim. 2013. "Effect of the Fukushima Nuclear Disaster on Global Public Acceptance of Nuclear Energy". *Energy Policy* 61: 822–828. doi:10.1016/j.enpol.2013.06.107.

Ku, Dowan. 2011. "The Korean Environmental Movement: Green Politics Through Social Movement". In *East Asian Social Movements: Power, Protest and Change in a Dynamic Region*, edited by Jeffrey Broadbent and Vicky Brockman, 205–229. New York: Springer.

Mez, Lutz, Lila Okamura, and Helmut Weidner, eds. 2020. *The Ecological Modernization Capacity of Japan and Germany: Comparing Nuclear Energy, Renewables, Automobility and Rare Earth Policy*. Wiesbaden: Springer VS.

Mol, Arthur P.J. 1996. "Ecological Modernisation and Institutional Reflexivity: Environmental Reform in the Late Modern Age". *Environmental Politics* 5 (2): 302–323.

Mol, Arthur P.J. 2002. "Ecological Modernization and the Global Economy". *Global Environmental Politics* 2 (2): 92–115. doi:10.1162/15263800260047844.

Mol, Arthur P.J. 2006. "Environment and Modernity in Transitional China: Frontiers of Ecological Modernization". *Development and Change* 37 (1): 29–56. doi:10.1111/j.0012-155X.2006.00468.x.

Oguma, Eiji. 2012. "Sōsetsu: Sakinobashi to More Ochita Hitobito". In *Heisei Shi*, edited by Eiji Oguma, 13–89. Tokyo: Kawade Shobō Shinsha.

Perrow, Charles, and Simone Pulver. 2015. "Organizations and Markets". In *Climate Change and Society: Sociological Perspectives*, edited by Riley E. Dunlap and Robert J. Brulle, 61–92. New York, NY: Oxford University Press.

Satoh, Keiichi. 2017. "Nihon No Kikohendo Taisaku Ni Okeru Private Governance: Keidanren Jisyukodokeikaku No Sado Mechanism". *Kankyo Syakaigaku Kenkyu* 23: 83–89.

Scharpf, Fritz W. 1997. *Games Real Actors Play: Actor-Centered Institutionalism in Policy Research*. Boulder, CO: Westview Press.

Schnaiberg, Allan, and Kenneth A. Gould. 2000. *Environment and Society: The Enduring Conflict*. Caldwell, NJ: Blackburn Press.

Schreurs, Miranda A. 2002. *Environmental Politics in Japan, Germany, and the United States*. Cambridge: Cambridge University Press.

Spaargaren, Gert, and Arthur P. Mol. 1992. "Sociology, Environment, and Modernity: Ecological Modernization as a Theory of Social Change". *Society & Natural Resources* 5 (4): 323–344. doi:10.1080/08941929209380797.

Sugihara, Kaoru. 2020. *Sekaishi No Naka No Higashi Ajia No Kiseki: The East Asian Miracle in Global History*. Nagoya: Nagoya Daigaku Shuppankai.

Sugiyama, Taishi, and Masayo Wakabayashi, eds. 2013. *Ondanka Taisaku No Jisyuteki Torikumi: Nihonkigyo Wa Do Kodo Shitaka*. Energy Forum.

UNIDO (United Nations Industrial Development Organization). 2021. "UNIDO Statistics Data Portal". Accessed September 3, 2021. https://stat.unido.org/.

WNA (World Nuclear Association). 2021. "Plans for New Reactors Worldwide". Accessed September 8, 2021. https://world-nuclear.org/information-library/current-and-future-generation/plans-for-new-reactors-worldwide.aspx.

Yoshioka, Hitoshi. 2011. *Genshiryoku No Shakaishi: Sono Nihonteki Tenkai*. Asahi Shimbun Shuppan.

CHAPTER 49

The Legacy of the Developmental State and the Rise of Fragmented Green Growth

Hong Deokhwa and Ku Dowan

Can the greening of capitalism be a solution to the ecological crisis? This long-held question has become one of the most controversial issues in environmental sociology. Simply put, the carbon-neutral plans announced by the leading countries in the world maintain that the climate crisis may be solved through green capitalism. However, as suggested by the slogan of the climate justice movement, "system change, not climate change" or "uproot the system", there is a growing voice that a post-capitalist society must be sought to overcome the climate crisis. As the ecological crisis has accelerated, no one denies the need to transition to a sustainable society. However, as shown in the difference between the Anthropocene and the Capitalocene, or between green capitalism and de-growth, the analyses of the causes of the ecological crisis and the transition strategy to a sustainable society differ considerably.

Ecological modernization theory (EMT) has attracted worldwide attention as an influential theory that explains the environmental improvement in modern society. It has also provided a theoretical background for various policy discourses seeking ways to solve the ecological crisis within capitalism, such as green growth and green capitalism. However, in contrast to what is expected by EMT, the planetary rift has continuously expanded (Foster 2012; Hickel and Kallis 2020). In addition, as the contention over the transition pathways intensifies, criticism of EMT or green capitalism is spreading further. The contrasting responses to EMT—acclamation and sarcasm—stem from the fact that EMT is based on the experiences of Western Europe. Therefore, the dynamics of environmental improvement must be examined from historical and comparative perspectives. This article reviews major studies in Korean environmental sociology, which has struggled with the legacy of a developmental state, and reexamines EMT in the context of Korea's export-led economy and democratization. The differences between the historical contexts in which environmental sociology has developed imply the issues that environmental sociology should solve as a global knowledge system.

1   The Legacy of the Developmental State

The developmental state is regarded as the starting point for explaining Korea's rapid economic growth in the second half of the 20th century. According to developmental state theory, the embedded autonomy of the developmental state in the context of the Cold War system and authoritarian rule was the driving force of the compressed economic growth (Evans 1995; Kim 2017). What draws attention from the environmental perspective is that public enterprises took the initiative in large-scale development projects, such as the construction of infrastructure, including dams, roads, power plants, and land reclamation projects. Since the export-led economic growth model is dependent on overseas demand, which is uncontrollable, it is critical to increase price competitiveness in the global market by lowering domestic production costs. Therefore, decreasing the cost of using infrastructure was a crucial means of managing supply costs. The developmental state rapidly constructed infrastructure through public enterprises and increased the price control power, supporting large export companies to achieve price competitiveness in foreign markets. Such infrastructure construction served as a basis for Korea's incorporation into the global production network and helped foster export industries. In the 1970s, as the heavy and chemical industrialization policy was promoted and the relocation of polluting industries from Japan increased, environmental pollution increased around industrial complexes and spread into major cities.

After the 1980s, the relative autonomy of the developmental state diminished. The persistent democratization movement ended military dictatorship in 1987, and new social movements emerged in civil society. Furthermore, technological catch-up in major export manufacturing industries not only became the driving force behind the continuous economic growth but also served as the foundation for strengthening corporate power. However, there were divergent views about whether neoliberalism deconstructed the developmental state (Kim 2017). Those who emphasized the path dependency of the developmental state argued that it had adopted neo-liberalization rather than be dismantled by neoliberalism. A neoliberal developmental state was typically associated with environmental issues. Large-scale development projects led by public enterprises were carried out continuously, and powerful price controls on infrastructure, such as energy, water, and transportation, were employed as an essential means of managing supply costs. In addition, with an increase in preferences for eco-friendly products in the global market, the Korean government has strengthened industrial policy interventions and expanded support for green technology and the green industry. However, fostering the green industry without internalizing environmental costs is likely to reach a breaking point. The solution of the government and large manufacturing companies was to separate the domestic market from foreign markets. Rather than investing resources to create the domestic environmental market, exporting companies, including *chaebols*, conglomerates in Korea, chose to strengthen their competitiveness in the global market by continuing to use "cheap" infrastructure and receiving governmental support through industrial policies. Their choice was also affected by the profits that the *chaebols*, including large manufacturing companies, gained by participating in large-scale development projects through their subsidiary construction companies.

The legacy of the developmental state should also be considered to understand the environmental movement in Korea, which was born in a close relationship with the democratization movement. Even after the democratic transition in 1987, large-scale development projects were often promoted without consensus among the residents. Fierce campaigns against development projects occurred repeatedly; however, the government and public enterprises continued to promote development projects as they used to do in the past. While environmental non-governmental organizations (NGOs) in Korea expanded their influence by organizing campaigns against development projects, participation in policymaking procedures has emerged as a fundamental requirement of the environmental movement. As a social movement framework, democratization was highly effective when the environmental movement organized campaigns against the government and public enterprises. In addition, organizational networks formed during the democratization movement provided the basis for environmental NGOs to nationalize campaigns in solidarity with other social movement organizations. Around 2000, environmental groups managed to delay or stop large-scale development projects through successful environmental campaigns (Ku and Hong 2013). On the other hand, the *Saengmyung* (Life) movement led by *Hansalim*, which criticized the mechanistic view of nature by reinterpreting Korean traditional ideas, found its space in consumer cooperatives and alternative communities and grew continuously as interest in ethical consumption increased in the 2000s.

Although environmental NGOs grew rapidly in the 1990s, they had a narrow ideological spectrum. The division system of the Korean peninsula, the product of the Cold War, prevented radical ideologies, such as eco-socialism and eco-anarchism, from being rooted in the environmental movement. The anti-pollution movement, which grew in solidarity with the radical social movement in the 1980s, argued that monopoly capitalism should be abolished to solve the pollution problem. However, after the democratic transition and the collapse of the Soviet Union, the radical environmental movement rapidly weakened and turned into an institutionalized reformist environmental movement in the early 1990s (Hong and Ku 2014). Overall, the environmental movement seeking radical repertoires of contentions was very weak, and the entry of the Green Party into the National Assembly was far off. However, when the democratization movement camp seized the government, environmental NGOs were given more opportunities to participate in policymaking procedures. The demand for procedural democracy by environmental NGOs was accepted to some extent, especially when environmental conflicts intensified. In most cases, individual activists, not organizational representatives, participated in temporary organizations limited to specific issues, but this was a change that could not be ignored.

2 Environmental Movements against the Construction State and Development Projects

Developmental states and large-scale development projects have long been researched in environmental sociology in Korea. The concept of the construction state has been extensively used to analyze and criticize development projects led by the government and public enterprises. In the early 2000s, interest in neo-liberalization increased in Korean environmental sociology, and environmental studies were extended to various fields. However, analyzing the legacy of the developmental state was a difficult task to avoid. For example, in 2008, the Lee Myeong-bak administration declared green growth as a national vision, but the green growth policy was explained more by the concept of the construction state than by EMT (Bluemling and Yun 2016). As the Four Major River Projects, accompanied by the construction of large-scale barrages, and the nuclear power expansion policy, including the export of nuclear power plants, were projects that symbolized the green growth of the Lee administration, the criticism of the construction state was considered more appropriate than EMT. There has been a steady interest in the theories of critical environmental studies, such as metabolic rift and the neo-liberalization of nature, but only a few studies have actively used these concepts to investigate Korean cases empirically (Korean Association for Environmental Sociology 2013). Studies that aimed to reconstruct the form and function of the state, such as the green state and the ecological welfare state, regarded the dismantling of the developmental state as a starting point.

With an interest in the socio-ecological problems of the construction state, many environmental sociologists in Korea have actively conducted studies on the movement against development projects (Korean Association for Environmental Sociology 2013). While directly or indirectly involved in the environmental movement, environmental sociologists have explored the movement against large-scale development projects for nuclear power plants, dams, and land reclamation. As the environmental movement has often claimed the participation of citizens and residents as an essential requirement, environmental sociologists have responded by analyzing the environmental movement from the perspective of democratic politics, including local referendums, deliberation models, and ecological democracy. Also, environmental justice has often been employed as a tool to reveal what was behind the environmental conflicts around development projects.

In the 2010s, studies were conducted in new areas, such as energy transition, climate change, agri-food systems, and disasters. New theories and concepts, including a multi-level perspective, sustainability transition, commons, and resilience, were widely applied. However, the task of explaining the legacy of the developmental state and the trajectory of the environmental movement remained unfinished. With the spread of commons studies, for example, there was a growing need to systematically investigate the role that the Korean government played in the process of deconstructing traditional commons and constructing new commons.

3   Greening of Capitalism and Exportism after Democratization

EMT aims to harmonize economic growth and environmental protection through decoupling based on technological innovation (Mol, Sonnenfeld and Spaargaren 2009). More precisely, ecological modernization implies the optimistic narrative that, as ecological principles are applied more to technological innovation and economic activities, the ecological crisis may be resolved through the greening of capitalism. There are certainly various criticisms of EMT. For example, Jevons paradox questions whether decoupling in capitalism can occur on a full scale (Foster 2012). Some specific companies or industries show signs of greening, but evidence for decoupling on the global scale is still weak. Considering the tendency of capitalism, in which competition continues to pursue profits by creating more products, it is overly optimistic to argue that the ecological crisis may be resolved through green technologies and green industries. However, it should be noted that EMT drew attention to a critical issue as it showed temporal and spatial variations of capitalism in environmental management. Even when the inherent tendency of capitalism to deteriorate the environment is admitted, the problem of explaining the differences between states, industries, and companies remains to be solved. Both the merits and demerits of EMT capture the possibility of improving the environment within capitalism through empirical case studies.

The legacy of the developmental state, which Korean environmental sociology has struggled with, allows the reexamination of ecological modernization in the context of comparative history. First, as the case of Korea reveals, green growth tends to be fragmented in late-coming industrial countries seeking an export-led economy. The Korean government and companies have promoted green growth policies by separating the domestic and overseas markets, and consequently, green growth strategies have been utilized mainly by a small number of specific industries and companies. EMT has been continuously criticized because it is based on European conditions, including coordinated market economies and corporatism (Buttel 2000). Although studies based on EMT have been conducted globally, the differences in the conditions and contexts have continuously questioned its validity. The signs of the greening of capitalism in Korea have been distorted by the path dependency of the developmental state. The post-developmental state has repackaged its development projects as green growth. As revealed in the green growth policy implemented by the Lee Myeong-bak administration, fostering green industries through industrial policy intervention has connected with construction projects as an accumulation strategy, rather than replacing them. From the perspective of comparative history, the developmental state has concentrated productive resources on the fostering of manufacturing and export industries, in contrast to the predatory states based on extractivism. Furthermore, unlike the Fordist welfare state, the export-led growth model tends to limit investment to the reproduction cost (Sum 1998). In the context of the preserved legacy of the developmental state, the greening of capitalism in Western countries urged manufacturing export companies to change, and the outcome was fragmented green growth. The fragmented green growth born in the exportism of late-coming industrial countries has served as a mediator between the extractivism of the global South and ecological modernization in Western countries. This implies that in the analysis of global environmental problems, East Asian exportism should be employed as a key parameter. It also highlights the need to address the problem of the heterogeneity of environmental management in the capitalistic world economy rather than ecological modernization on a global scale.

Second, the environmental movement in Korea, which has developed in connection with the democratization movement, may contribute to the understanding of the political process of environmental improvement. EMT focuses on the phenomenon of expanding citizen participation in the field of environmental policy in place of bureaucratic control (Mol, Sonnenfeld and Spaargaren 2009). Critics, however, highlight that ecological modernization has emerged as a counter strategy for capitalists, technocrats, and some environmental activists against radical and subversive environmental movements (Hajer 1995). The signs of ecological modernization in Korea appear in a considerably different context. Taking advantage of the political opportunities formed in the process of democratic consolidation, the Korean environmental movement has actively responded to environmental pollution and organized campaigns against development projects. Since the 1990s, the growth of environmental movements has greatly contributed to the development of environmental policies and environmental improvements in several areas. However, in the process of developing the Korean environmental movement, the main targets have been the developmental state and undemocratic public enterprises, not private companies. As a result, many environmental NGOs often take an ambiguous position in responding to market-friendly environmental policies introduced along with neo-liberalization. As described above, the change in the export market serves as a driving force for promoting fragmented green growth. Citizen participation, to which EMT pays attention, has been dependent upon the seizure of governmental power by the democratization movement camp, rather than being conducted in connection with the de-radicalization of the environmental movement. The rule implemented by the democratization movement camp has increased the opportunities for activists to enter the government and/or governance and introduce democratic procedures in the process of promoting development projects. However, the procedural democracy that has been introduced without changing the growth model is often employed as a means of justifying development projects and green growth policies. The attempt to overcome the growth ideology through procedural democracy has frequently generated frustration. Furthermore, the absence of a radical environmental movement narrows the transition strategy of the environmental movement. When the environmental movement was sluggish in the 2000s, the introduction of democratic procedures accelerated the institutionalization of the environmental movement and therefore weakened the strength of the environmental movement. The boundary between participation and inclusion was highly ambiguous. This situation raises the need to systematically analyze the contention among the state, capital, and environmental movements around capitalistic environmental management, as well as the condition of political compromise under which ecological modernization can progress.

4 Towards a Post-Western Environmental Sociology

As already suggested by the debates on green capitalism, the theory of environmental sociology should be elaborated to analyze the ecological crisis and the transition pathway. Although the phenomena on which EMT focuses occur globally, the assumptions of EMT are still questionable. Considering this, the history of environmental deterioration and improvement in Korea raises the need to reexamine EMT from a relational perspective that encompasses Western and non-Western societies. The signs of ecological modernization in advanced industrial countries, such as the EU member states, have not only emerged as a condition of the export-led economy of East Asian countries but also served as a driving force to promote fragmented green growth in East Asia, especially in Korea. Ecological modernization and fragmented green growth are part of the capitalistic environmental management that occurs worldwide. The export-led growth model of Korea has been accompanied by a counter mechanism of democratization. Even in a situation where developmentalism has persisted for a long time through the success of the catch-up, the environmental movement has contributed to consolidating democracy and leading to environmental improvement, at least in several sectors. However, the absence of a radical environmental movement has postponed the debate on green capitalism and caused the underdevelopment of the transformative movement seeking system change. What is called ecological modernization, if it has occurred, reflects an uneven development in which heterogeneous elements are intertwined. Tracking the historical development of capitalistic environmental management may be one of the starting points of post-Western environmental sociology.

References

Bluemling, Bettina, and Sun-jin Yun. 2016. "Giving Green Teeth to the Tiger? A Critique of Green Growth in South Korea". In *Green Growth: Ideology, Political Economy and the Alternatives*, edited by G. Dale, M. Mathai, and J. de Oliveira. London: Zed Books.

Buttel, Frederic. 2000. "Ecological Modernization as Social Theory". *Geoforum* 31: 57–65.

Evans, Peter. 1995. *Embedded Autonomy: States and Industrial Transformation*. Princeton, NJ: Princeton University Press.

Foster, John. 2012. "The Planetary Rift and the New Human Exemptionalism: A Political-Economic Critique of Ecological Modernization Theory". *Organization & Environment* 25 (3): 211–237.

Hajer, Maarten. 1995. *The Politics of Environmental Discourse: Ecological Modernization and the Policy Process*. Oxford: Oxford University Press.

Hickel, Jason, and Giorgos Kallis. 2020. "Is Green Growth Possible?" *New Political Economy* 25 (4): 469–486.

Hong, Deokhwa, and Dowan Ku. 2014. "Environmental Movement after Democratization in Korea: A Protest Event Analysis". *ECO* 18 (1): 151–186. (In Korean.)

Kim, Yun-Tae, ed. 2017. *The Developmental State: Past, Present and Future*. Paju: Hanul. (In Korean.)

Korean Association for Environmental Sociology, ed. 2013. *Environmental Sociology and Environmental Problems in Korea*. Paju: Hanul. (In Korean.)

Ku, Dowan and Deokhwa Hong. 2013. "The Growth and Diversification of the Korean Environmental Movement: Focusing on Institutionalization". *ECO* 17 (1): 79–120. (In Korean.)

Mol, Arthur, David Sonnenfeld, and Gert Spaargaren. 2009. *The Ecological Modernisation Reader: Environmental Reform in Theory and Practice*. Abingdon: Routledge.

Sum, Ngai-Ling. 1998. "Theorizing Export-Oriented Economic Development in East Asian Newly-Industrializing Countries: A Regulationist Perspective". In *Dynamic Asia: Business, Trade and Economic Development in Pacific Asia*, edited by I. Cook. Burlington, VT: Ashgate.

SECTION 12

Individuation, Self, and Emotions

∴

CHAPTER 50

Management, Experience, and Performance: Emotional Regimes in Contemporary Society

Cheng Boqing and Wang Jiahui

1   Introduction

In contemporary society, the concept of emotion has been problematized in an unprecedented way and commands particular attention. for example, social resentment, public anxiety, and social involution have become representative social topics recently in China. Not only the middle-aged but also the young, and even children, suffer from anxiety and emotional stress in contemporary Chinese society. The prominence of emotional phenomena is undoubtedly related to the transformation in social structure and social interaction patterns. The issue should be investigated through a sociological lens because "the sociological imagination enables us to grasp history and biography and the relations between the two within society" (Mills 2000: 6).

Although many current sociologists have focused on emotional factors, they failed to offer an in-depth analysis of the internal mechanism of emotions due to ineffective conceptual tools and observation methodologies. Since the mid-1970s, the "affect revolution" (Tangney and Fischer 1995: 3–24) has swept across numerous disciplines, giving a new face to emotional research in sociology. With the establishment of the Emotions Section of the American Sociological Association in 1986, the status of Emotional Sociology as a subfield of sociology has been consolidated. Related research has been continuously conducted. However, most current sociological theories of emotion, the American school in particular, focus on explanations in particular contexts but neglect the macro-context of social structures.

From a sociological perspective, the above deficiency is first due to the fact that existing theoretical constructs are too restrictive to accommodate macro social structures. The current structural analysis of social phenomena is based merely on the power and status of individuals in different social positions (Turner and Stets 2006). Secondly, the aforesaid deficiency is due to a lack of historical perspectives. Certain emotional phenomena that belong to "a particular social form" (Marx 2000: 501) are deemed as universals, making it impossible to accurately analyze emotional phenomena that arise only out of specific social contexts. Furthermore, the positivism tendency in sociology has resulted in the neglect of the social meaning dimension of emotions, often overly simplifying socially meaningful emotions to emotions solely based on physiological responses. Also, the existing conceptual framework presupposes that the generation and transmission of emotions originate from social interaction, and thus cannot organically link individual emotional stories with the grand narrative of the times. Therefore, as Calhoun (2001: 45) stated, "Nonetheless, wide-reaching though efforts in the sociology of emotions have been, they have not yet deeply transformed sociological theory in a general way, nor have they reshaped many subfields of the discipline".

In view of this, there is a need for an analytical approach that connects the ostensible emotional experience of individuals with general social trends. In other words, this analytical approach allows us to understand the social mechanism of emotional issues through investigating those emotions which are formed and expressed under general social conditions. Our zeitgeist can, consequently, be diagnosed through the understanding of emotional phenomena.

2   The Perspective of Emotional Regime

The concept of "feeling rules" proposed by Hochschild (1979: 551–575) is highly relevant to the discussion of the relationship between individual emotions and general social structure. Feeling rules are norms acquired through socialization. They are used to instruct individuals how to experience, interpret, and manage their own emotions, including the emotions that should be felt in a particular scene and expressed in a particular manner. For example, the guests at a wedding should feel happy, whereas the guests at a funeral should feel sad. Feeling rules guide individuals to confirm, name, adjust, and manage their emotions by retrieving specific feelings from the complex of social life. However, feeling rules, as a mediator between emotional experience and social structure, suffer from shortcomings that echo the previous problem: feeling rules help explain micro or middle-scale scenarios, but they cannot grasp the emotional mechanism in a macro social context. This is because rules may vary with situations. The concept of feeling rules can barely explain some universal emotions related only to the fundamental social structures.

In fact, it is striking that many scholars, in order to find an appropriate approach, have carried out fruitful explorations in the history of emotions. They also proposed many enlightening concepts, such as: emotional community (Rosenwein 2007); emotional styles (Guo 2010); and emotionology

(Stearns and Stearns 1985). The concept of "emotional regime", more suitable as an analytical perspective for us to investigate the issue, is proposed by Reddy (2004: 129). According to Reddy's definition, the emotional regime involves a set of emotions, and the development and expression of this set of emotions must conform to certain rules, reinforced through rituals and practices. In Reddy's opinion, emotion, central to individual life, is deeply influenced by society, is politically significant, and provides indispensable support for a stable political regime. Therefore, understanding emotional regimes is essential to the stable operation of political regimes.

Reddy's emotional regime is obviously contained in a specific political regime, and it is potentially assumed that a unified and single emotional regime exists under a political regime. However, this essay attempts to utilize the emotional regime as a general sociological concept and believes that there may be emotional regimes that can transcend a specific political regime. There may also be multiple emotional regimes under a specific political regime. Compared with the concept of feeling rules, the emotional regime allows us to transcend the interactive and situational analysis of emotions and to understand the practice and discourse of emotion in a specific time frame from a relatively higher and more fundamental level. The adoption of the regime is to emphasize social arrangements outside the context of interpersonal communication and interaction. Such arrangements may not be expressly stipulated, but they permeate the core areas of social life. Only by revealing the mechanism of emotional regimes can we discover the logic of the evolution of the emotional field and see the common causes and trends of current emotional issues.

3   Contemporary Social Structure and Consciousness Background

The "contemporary society" in this essay refers to the general social forms that have existed since the 1970s. As for developed countries, it means the advent of the post-industrial era, the rise of the service-oriented economy, and the maturity of the consumer society. As for developing countries, such as China, these countries are involved, voluntarily or forcibly, in the process of globalization, stepping onto the modernization and post-modernization path and experiencing a comprehensive impact from developed countries, in particular to daily lifestyles. In terms of the emotion field, the freedom of emotional expression might have reached an unprecedentedly high level; in fact, the discipline and manipulation of emotions have also become more severe and comprehensive, and Bentham (2009) described this kind of phenomenon as "measuring pleasure and pain". Without any doubt, the transformation in social structures and social consciousness plays a significant role in causing this condition.

As far as social structure is concerned, how to grasp the mainstream and the primary characteristics of contemporary social structure? Work and everyday life, the two most basic social activities, might be a starting point. In the field of work, driven by the new technological revolution and development of the economic system, more and more laborers enter the service industries (Bell 1973), such as flight attendants, which not only requires physical strength and skills but also emotional engagement. In the field of everyday life, the improvement in material living standards and the rise of leisure time have changed the form of consumption and social interaction. For consumption, it is not limited to satisfying basic survival needs, but to pursue unique styles and tastes and acquire stimulations and personal experiences (Baudrillard 2001). For social interaction, the rapid social changes and flows, especially the use and popularization of the Internet, have made the originally strong interpersonal bonds looser. The relationships between individuals have become short-lived, even virtualized. More individuals feel lonesome, at the same time deriving more communication needs from their loneliness (Giddens 2001). We can grasp the social structure and its transition from other aspects. Work, consumption, and social interaction, for example, are the relatively major ones. Thus, it is vital to understand our emotional regimes through these approaches.

Moreover, the spread and infiltration of emotional discipline and manipulation has resulted from the contemporary social consciousness. Firstly, with the evolution of social value orientation, the idea of "amusing ourselves to death" is prevalent, and has even become a threat to cultural spirit (Postman 2011). Under these circumstances, individuals seem to increasingly submit themselves to the manipulation of fashion. The modification of inner character also gives way to the pursuit of emotional experience. With the rapid changes in society, the constant external reference systems, such as religious or moral systems, gradually decline (Taylor 1989). Thus, individuals could only experience fragmented and disembedding feelings rather than emotions that have a strong connection to an integrated and steady society. Consequently, emotions can be manipulated easily.

4   Three Emotional Regimes

According to the previous explanation about social structure and consciousness transitions, the investigation of the emotional regimes could be focused on the three main spheres of contemporary everyday life: work, consumption, and social interaction. Based on integrating and refining the existing research achievement in the field of sociology of emotion, it can be constructed that there are three ideal types of emotional regimes correspondingly in the three main spheres: the managerial regime in the field of work, whose dominant normative emotion is cordial; the experiential regime in consumption, whose dominant normative is joyful; and the performative regime in social interaction, whose dominant normative emotion is caring. It is worth pointing out that political and cultural difference is not considered, because the main purpose is to establish an analytical framework to explain the emotional issues caused by some common trends of contemporary society, such as industrialization, marketization, individualization, and informatization (Cheng 2013).

4.1 The Managerial Regime

The managerial regime requires individuals to manage and regulate their emotions to suit external organizational and occupational requirements in the field of work. The requirements of modern occupations for workers at first were only physical effort and time. Later, professional skills on top of physical strength were required as well. To date, physical strength, professional skills, and emotional devotion are all involved in, although there may be a slight flexibility in terms of time. Correspondingly, the role of emotion in the occupational field goes through an evolution process from rejection to conquest. For instance, the Taylor system and bureaucracy are designed to eliminate people's emotions from work. However, emotional intelligence nowadays is greatly emphasized in the field of work. This situation can be seen as the colonization of emotion, the last fortress of nature—human nature, by rationalization and mechanization. This, of course, has to do with the increasing sophistication of the disciplinary web of civilizing process (Elias 1982).

More specifically, the role of emotion in occupation depends on the stage of economic development. With the rise of the service-oriented economy, interactive services have become the main production activity. Thus, emotional labor is highlighted. Emotional labor means that employees express the emotions required by the organization to customers or others through publicly visible facial expressions and body postures (Hochschild 1983). That is, individuals are required to adjust their emotions to be consistent with organizational expectations or professional norms, regardless of whether they are in line with their intrinsic feelings. Emotional labor requires individuals to show pleasing emotions in service, such as kindness, friendliness, and consideration, which is intended to induce in customers a certain emotional state or reaction so that they boost their intention to purchase or in order to increase their satisfaction.

Some occupations may have different emotional requirements. For example, doctors are asked to show sympathy to patients; debt collectors must show anger and fierceness. In general, the atmosphere in which consumers are superior, pleasing clients is the mainstream orientation of emotional labor.

When dealing with emotional labor requirements, employees usually have two strategies: "surface acting" and "deep acting" (Hochschild 1983). The former means employees only adjust their emotional expression to suit the organizational and occupational requirements without changing their true feelings, which is like an act of drama; the latter means adjusting their true inner emotions to not only meet the requirements of emotional expression but also express themselves naturally and sincerely. Generally, emotional labor places more demands, adds extra burdens, and may cause psychological harm to employees (Hochschild 1983). It's indicated that surface acting could cause more emotional issues to employees than deep acting because they must act out emotions they do not have while suppressing what they really feel. Gradually, employees might alienate their selves and true feelings. However, some studies have pointed out that emotional labor does not necessarily lead to emotional exhaustion or reduced job satisfaction, which mainly depends on the nature of the work, especially the degree of autonomy at work. If the degree of autonomy is relatively high, emotional labor may also be a fulfilling and enjoyable process (Bryman 2004).

Regarding emotional labor, two tit-for-tat views exist. One argues that emotional labor is a further labor alienation, which constitutes a heavy burden on laborers and causes self-estrangement and the exploitation of emotional surplus value. This is a further step of Marx's classic thesis. Another view is that emotional labor is a kind of personal ability and quality, one which can be used to achieve a win-win situation, and even some marketing and management experts believe that the emotional value created by emotional labor is a huge commercial treasure to be developed (Barlow and Maul 2000). Indeed, the treatment of emotional labor cannot be generalized, but so far, the value of emotional labor is often overlooked. The salaries for emotional labor are low, and most of the jobs are borne by women, which is a reality that cannot be ignored. For example, with the intensification of aging, the elder care industry is becoming more and more important in China, but the emotional labor expended in the process of caring for the elderly has not yet been fully quantified or even recognized.

With reference to the McDonaldization Thesis (Ritzer 1998) of society, the essence of the managerial regime is the McDonaldization of emotion, which means that emotion is involved in the scope of rationality to promote production.

4.2 The Experiential Regime

The experiential regime requires individuals to pursue the pleasure brought by novel experiences so that they can highlight the value of their own existence and demonstrate their own personality. The experiential regime is mainly reflected in the field of consumption. The basis of modern consumption is hedonism. Hedonism has an evolution from tradition to modernity, and one of the major turning points is that the trigger of hedonic pleasure has moved from sensations to emotions. Sensory organs may be satisfied quickly due to their own adaptation and stimulus saturation, while emotions can be continuously strengthened. Pleasure could be developed from any emotions, including pain and fear from watching thrilling movies or riding roller coasters. In fact, the modern division of labor also causes the involution of emotion into the consumption field. Simmel (1997: 94) reveals the connection: "it seems as if the modern person wishes to compensate for the one-sidedness and uniformity of what they produce within the division of labor by the increasing crowding together of heterogeneous impressions, by the increasingly hasty and colourful change in emotions".

Contemporary emotional experience no longer relies solely on personal exploration but has a trend of industrialization. In terms of emotional consumption, industries that are worth paying attention to are the psychological consultation industry (providing psychological comfort and emotional relief), popular art industry (emotional expression, support, and resonance), entertainment industry (sales and creating happiness), sports industry (catharsis, tension, excitement, pride, recognition), tourism industry (pleasure, novelty, alternative experience), and mass media industry (emotional communication, satisfaction, and support) (Wang 2000). In addition, the Internet industry has popularized video games. Many individuals are addicted to video games because game players can immerse themselves in the specific situations presented by video games, namely, "narrowing the distance", thereby triggering emotional devices to experience happiness. Although the satisfaction of game players is achieved by virtual means, it is real in terms of emotional effects.

There are two main operation modes of the emotional industry. Firstly, it intends to release people's tension and pressure. The rationalization of everyday life has caused self-restraint for modern individuals. Meanwhile, the accelerated pace of life and intensified work competition have increased the tension and pressure for modern individuals. Therefore, the pursuit of excitement and escape from reality is often "utilized to release control and overcome the boredom and monotony of everyday life" (Williams 2001: 116). Secondly, it intends to provide artificial emotions. From nostalgia to laughter, movies to theme parks, everything is incorporated in the consideration and plan of

McDonaldization. Thus, the emotions generated in this process are difficult to distinguish between true and false. Some individuals even claim that they have entered a post-emotional society. In other words, their nature, intensity, and correctness have been cognitively evaluated before all emotional experiences occurred. We can thus no longer experience spontaneous and genuine emotions (Meštrović 1997).

4.3   The Performative Regime

The performative regime requires the emotional expression in social interaction to be dramatic, either by exaggerating the performance or by reinforcing the atmosphere of a particular situation, or by deliberately creating a (micro-) spectacle to attract the attention of the public. Although in a broad sense, social life is performance (Goffman 2008), performance appears more in various ceremonies and formalities. However, performance has now increasingly become a feature of social interaction in everyday life. One of the most common performances is the overflow of all kinds of love, such as romance, affection, or fraternity. In current politics and other public life, public expression of emotions has also become a style. It is now widely accepted and even praised for public figures to shed tears publicly. Ironically, this would have been considered a gaffe in the past. On the contrary, the sense of sublime and solemnity is shrinking in the public social sphere. Weber (2010: 151) stated that this is precisely because "the world has been disenchanted". Those noble and ultimate values have disappeared from the realm of public life. They have either escaped into the transcendental realm or entered the friendship of private interactions. The emotionalization of the public sphere is presumably a correction of the depersonalization of the bureaucracy.

Performance not only has constructive meaning in public life but also constructs meaning for everyday life. Facing the trivial and boring everyday life, the performance highlights or creates exciting stories through an exaggerated narrative, with specific regard to the so-called surprises that make the monotonous world colorful, and transform everyday life into many self-contained fragments. In the contemporary context, the lack of the ultimate meaning of life causes individuals to pursue it through dramatic emotional expressions in everyday life so that their passion of life can be ignited constantly.

From the background of an increasingly individualized contemporary society, performance is also a strategy of "struggling for recognition". Individuals who are submerged in the torrent of a changeable society can easily be washed away. Therefore, planning spectacular events, becoming a figure in the spotlight, creating fifteen-minutes-of-fame moments, is a common way to highlight individual existence. As this type of fabrication has become more and more complex, specialized institutions have emerged. In marketing activities, merchants often package the goods and services they provide dramatically and use exciting stories to enhance attractiveness. These merchants even appropriate emotional symbols to increase their value. The prevalence of this marketing strategy has also made performance a common sight that permeates every part of our everyday life and causes further imitation.

In addition, performance has another function, and that is to gather or create an emotional community. Performances often use dramatic and visual expressions, and vivid images to make an emotional impact on individuals. Psychological identification is generated through this emotional connection to attract like-minded individuals and form new modern tribes (Maffesoli 1996). With more and more new tribes based on common emotions, such as various fan groups, to meet the needs of common emotions, these tribes will also participate in the image shaping of their emotional symbols, which is called "fan culture". This has been increasingly prevailing in recent years. Most of these tribes have a high sense of self-identity, and their members embrace and strengthen each other's ideas, and even work together to reject dissidents. For example, common controversies between fan groups of different idols can be seen online. This is thus particularly worthy of attention in the Internet age because some extremist organizations tend to take advantage of this new form of community.

5   The Relationship among Three Emotional Regimes

Although unlike previous emotional control with strict hierarchy and clear rules, the contemporary emotional regime presents a certain degree of differentiation and ambiguity. However, a dominant trend that remains difficult to be identified. Namely, a happy regime with the pursuit of happiness as its goal. It is believed that since Bentham established the legitimacy of modern society on the pursuit of maximum happiness for most people, and at the same time simply defined happiness as hedonism, the entire modern society has moved towards the pursuit of tragalism and entertainment.

Since the emotional regime has split in different fields, what is the relationship among the different regimes? An obvious certain degree of tension and even opposition among the principles of different regimes can be found. Thus, different regimes should be discussed separately. This kind of confrontation is particularly reflected in the field of work and consumption between the managerial and the experiential regime. As Bell (1976) proposed, on the one hand, commercial companies want people to work hard, establish professional loyalty, and become organizational people. On the other hand, the company's products and advertisements foster a climate of ecstasy, relaxation, and indulgence. There is certainly tension between the managerial regime and the performative regime: do individuals perform to display themselves, or do they perform to please the audience? Between an experiential regime and a performative regime a certain tension exists as well: whether to immerse yourself in your own experience, or to show your own experience to others to appreciate. The desire or responsibility of performance may sometimes spoil the interest of experience, or performance may even hinder the true experience. Individuals usually adapt to this situation through the compartmentalization of specific areas of life and time.

On the other hand, intersecting and blending relationships among the three regimes exist as well, which is shown in Figure 50.1 below:

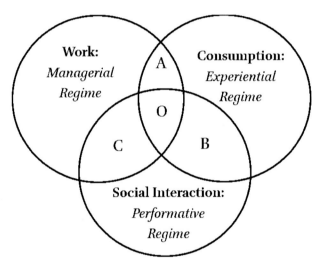

FIGURE 50.1   The figure of the relationship among three emotional regimes

The first is the intersection of the managerial regime in the work field and the experiential regime in the consumption field, which is the area A in the above figure. There are two tendencies with different emphases: either the producer enjoys the process at the same time, or the consumer participates in the production of the consumer object. The former is actually a successful deep acting, which is an idealized state; the latter is a related phenomenon typical of Do It Yourself (DIY). Not only can the participation of consumers satisfy the pleasure of doing it yourself, but it can also strengthen the sense of autonomy, belonging, and identity under the premise of participation. As far as pure emotion is concerned, there have been various activities with the nature of treatment, development, and training, such as salons, summer camps, etc. The participants are consumers (one can only participate with a fee), and at the same time they follow the guidance of the instructor or expert, under certain emotional managerial strategies to create their own novel experiences. Such activities are often in a relatively closed environment through ritualized and dramatic means to stimulate the desired emotions. As for whether they can get out of this "emotional utopia" and enter the real world, whether the effect will last, is uncertain. In fact, emotional consumption has made the most thorough interpretation of the so-called prosumer—the consumer involved in production activities. Thus, they are both consumers and producers.

The second is the intersection between the experiential regime in the consumption field and the performative regime in the social interaction field, that is, the B area in the figure above. This is also divided into two situations with their own emphasis: either the consumption activity itself is revealing and socially connected, or the social interaction activity itself is realized through consumption. Considering that many consumption activities are becoming more and more social, and what is being consumed has more and more symbolic value, the boundary between the two situations is becoming more and more blurred (Cheng 2012). Here, we might as well take the commercial method to interpret the story of romantic love as an example. Romantic love is originally an emotional utopia to resist the tool world based on exchange relations, trying to accept and overcome the loneliness and powerlessness of individual existence with purity, profoundness, and tolerance for the complete individual. But gradually, contemporary people use consumer goods and even luxury goods as the symbolic expression of their emotional relationship, and love is thus materialized and commercialized (Zelizer 2007). However, people can still use dramatic performances to relive, reinforce, or confirm the existence of pure relationships based on emotions from time to time. However, the infinite work pressure brought about by the new capitalist network structure puts a huge amount of pressure on long-term love and intimacy: the increasing shortage of time and resources, the increasing mobility, and the increasing demand for emotional investment in work make the creative arts, which are necessary to maintain pure relationships, rare (Hartmann and Honneth 2006). As a result, romantic expression began to be outsourced, and agencies specializing in planning and directing shows of emotional appeared. This kind of romantic love represented by others is greatly reduced in the authenticity and purity of the experience, and even reduced to a pure and serious dramatic performance.

The third is the intersection between the performative regime in the field of social interaction and the managerial regime in the field of work, that is, area C in the figure above. Among them, it can also be divided into roughly two types of sub-regimes with different emphases: those that need to be presented in a performance during production, and those with productive purposes or effects in social interaction. Taking into account the competition and mobility of the workplace, at the same time teamwork is required at work. Therefore, handling the relationship between colleagues is the core requirement of today's so-called emotional intelligence. Therefore, in most places where emotional labor is needed, it is not only the emotions towards the client that need to be managed, but also the emotions towards other members of the "performance crew". Bryman (2004), who put forth the Disneyization of society proposition to supplement Ritzer's "McDonaldization" proposition, changed "emotional labor" to "performative labor". As for the sub-regime with a production purpose, in social interaction it is nothing more than all kinds of commercial social activities. In essence, it is still a kind of performative labor. This is particularly reflected in some strategies in marketing or the emotional industry. In fact, more and more occupations have become similar to a performance on stage. As the two management experts who put forward the "experience economy" claimed, at any level of any company, employees must know that any business is a stage, so work is acting. According to Bryman, the staff at Disneyland can be regarded as a model of contemporary performative labor culture in this respect. They not only directly use metaphors, such as casting members, audit, front desk, backstage and so on, but they all smile sincerely and naturally, as if they are not working but participating in the game. It is true that jobs are called roles by them, as if they are experiencing a pleasant journey, just like tourists.

Finally, it is the overlapping part of the three regimes in the three fields, that is, the O area in the figure above. Just imagine if the above-mentioned Disneyland staff successfully acted as producers, consumers, and performers at the same time, immersed in the joyful fairytale world: Wouldn't it be cool? So cool! And nowadays there is nothing more that can better embody the essence of the O area than the highly respected "cool". Cool is actually a unique emotional style, with a bit of perseverance (managerial), a bit of intoxication (experiential), and a bit of pretentiousness (performative). Cool is a kind of process and state that individuals seem to enjoy with a status that includes self-examination, calm performance, and keeping a distance from their own feelings. One of the signs of coolness is sunglasses. Sunglasses, in fact, do not allow people to perceive the emotions in the eyes. Therefore, the sunglasses also reveal the limit of coolness. As far as the Chinese context is concerned, although cool is imported from foreign culture, the reason why this foreign buzzword can become popular in China as well is obviously related to the similar and cross-bordered structural situations and experiences. American emotional history expert Stearns traced the formation of American emotional styles in the 20th century in *American Cool: Constructing a Twentieth-Century Emotional Style*, including the shrinking family size, the growth of management agencies, the increase in dating, the prevalence of consumerism, and the decline of religion. All have led to historical changes in emotions. New modes of emotional expression encourage self-control and restraint, and increasingly rely on the means of scientific psychology (Stearns and Stearns 1994). From "cool" we can get a glimpse of the comprehensive effect of contemporary emotional regimes.

6 Conclusion

Emotional regime is bound to be mandatory and restrictive because it is still categorized as a regime. Individuals would be punished if they violated it. In the meantime, emotional regime strengthens the emotions that conform to its norms and excludes the emotions that do not match them. In fact, emotions that are contrary to the three regimes above have become suppressed or even eliminated in the discourse of contemporary emotional studies. For example, painful emotions shall not exist because avoiding trouble is encouraged. Hatred shall not appear; at least, it shall be forgotten. Anger is harmful because complaints can only lead us to be self-defeating and so on. What the contemporary emotional regime encourages is to find happiness and create happiness in a planned and systematic way.

We hope that through exploring the emotional regime we can reflect upon the spirit of the time in contemporary society. Due to the complexity and ambiguity of the contemporary emotional regime's evolution and the contradictory nature of emotion itself, it is difficult for us to discern a clear trend. However, emotion has increasingly become an indispensable dimension for us to accurately depict the social picture and its dynamic process.

The concept of "affective turn" (Clough and Halley 2007) in many disciplines is not only a theoretical orientation but also a reflection of reality. Sociology should maximize the imagination of sociology in the interpretation of emotional phenomena to make its unique contribution. What forces are trying to turn contemporary individuals into "cheerful robots" as Mills (1951: 233) described? We must return to the social, public, and moral perspectives to find the social roots of contemporary emotional problems.

The sociological exploration of the emotional regime in this essay is just a preliminary attempt. How does emotional regime form and change in a specific structural background? How do individuals who are in the emotional regime escape and even resist the system? Are there variations in different social classes, and what are the political consequences of this difference? How can contemporary emotional regimes and different cultural traditions coexist or compromise? These are questions that need to be studied in the future.

Acknowledgment

A slightly different version of this article was published in the 5th issue of *Social Sciences in China* in 2017.

References

Alexander, J.C. 2006. "Cultural Pragmatics: Social Performance Between Ritual and Strategy". In *Social Performance*, edited by Jeffrey C. Alexander, Bernhard Giesen, and Jason L. Mast, 54–55. Cambridge: Cambridge University Press.

Alexander, J.C. 2015. "A Theory of Social Performance: Modeling Cultural Pragmatics between Ritual and Strategy". *Chinese Journal of Sociology* 35 (3): 1–36.

Barbalet, J.M. 1998. *Emotion, Social Theory, and Social Structure: A Marcosociological Approach*. Cambridge: Cambridge University Press.

Barlow, J., and D. Maul. 2000. *Emotional Value: Creating Strong Bonds With Your Customers*. San Francisco, CA: Berrett-Koehler Publishers.

Baudrillard, J. 1988. *Selected Writings*, edited with an introduction by Mark Poster, 48. Palo Alto, CA: Stanford University Press.

Baudrillard, J. 2001. *The Consumer Society*, translated by Liu Chengfu and Quan Zhigang. Nanjing: Nanjing University Press.

Bauman, Z. 2004. *Work Consumerism and the New Poor*. 2nd ed. Philadelphia, PA: Open University Press.

Bauman, Z. 2012. *Liquid Times: Living in an Age of Uncertainty*. Translated by Gu Lei and Wu Yuanyuan. Nanjing: Jiangsu People's Publishing House.

Bell, D. 1973. *The Coming of Post-Industrial Society: A Venture in Social Forecasting*. New York: Basic Books.

Bell, D. 1976. *The Cultural Contradiction of Capitalism*. New York: Basic Books.

Bentham, J. 2009. *The Principles of Morals and Legislation*. Translated by Shi Yinhong. Beijing: The Commercial Press.

Bourdieu, P. 1984. *Distinction: A Social Critique of the Judgement of Taste*. Cambridge, MA: Harvard University Press.

Bryman, A. 2004. *The Disneyization of Society*, 122. London: Sage Publishers.

Calhoun, C. 2001. "Putting Emotions in Their Place". In *Passionate Politics: Emotions and Social Movements*, edited by Jeff Goodwin, James M. Jasper, and Francesca Polletta, 45. Chicago, IL: The University of Chicago Press.

Campbell, C. 1987. *The Romantic Ethic and the Spirit of Modern Consumerism*, 69. Oxford: Basil Blackwell.

Cheng, Boqing. 2012. *Emotion, Narrative and Rhetoric—Exploration of Social Theory*. Beijing: China Social Sciences Press.

Cheng, Boqing. 2013. "The Sociological Meaning of Emotion". *Shandong Social Sciences* 211 (3): 42–48.

Clough, P.T., and J. Halley. 2007. *The Affective Turn: Theorizing the Social*. Durham, NC: Duke University Press.

Elias, N. 1982. *The Civilizing Process*. Oxford: Blackwell.

Frisby, D. 1988. *Fragments of Modernity: Theories of Modernity in the Work of Simmel, Kracauer and Benjamin*, 94. Cambridge, MA: MIT Press.

Giddens, A. 2001. *The Transformation of Intimacy*. Translated by Chen Yongguo, et al. Beijing: Social Sciences Academic Press.

Goffman, E. 2008. *The Presentation of Self in Everyday Life*. Translated by Feng Gang. Beijing: Peking University Press.

Guo, Jing Ping. 2010. *60 Years of Changes in China's Emotional Civilization—The Perspective of Social Transformation*. Beijing: People's Publishing House.

Hartmann, M., and A. Honneth. 2006. "Paradoxes of Capitalism". *Constellations* 13 (1): 52.

Hirschman, A.O. 2002. *Shifting Involvements: Private Interest and Public Action*. Princeton, NJ: Princeton University Press.

Hochschild, A.R. 1979. "Emotion Work, Feeling Rules, and Social Structure". *American Journal of Sociology* 85 (3): 551–575.

Hochschild, A.R. 1983. *The Managed Heart: Commercialization of Human Feeling*, 7. Berkeley: University of California Press.

Illouz, E. 2007. *Cold Intimacies: The Making of Emotional Capitalism*. London: Polity Press.

Kapferer, B. 1979. "Emotion and Feeling in Sinhalese Healing Rites". *Social Analysis* 1: 154.

Krieken, R.V. 1998. *Norbert Elias*, 130. London: Routledge.

Maffesoli, M. 1996. *The Time of The Tribes: The Decline of Individualism in Mass Society*. London: Sage Publications.

Marx, K. 2000. *Manuscript of Economics and Philosophy in 1844*. Beijing: People's Publishing House.

Massey, D. 2002. "A Brief History of Human Society: The Origin and Role of Emotion in Social Life". *American Sociological Review* 67 (1): 1–29.

Meštrović, S.G. 1997. *Postemotional Society*. London: Sage Publishers.

Mills, C.W. 1951. *White Collar: The American Middle Classes*. New York: Oxford University Press.
Oatley, K., and J.M. Jenkins. 1996. *Understanding Emotions*, 62. Malden, MA: Publishers Inc.
Plamper, J. 2020. "The History of Emotions: An Interview with William Reddy, Barbara Rosenwein, and Peter Stearns". *History and Theory* 49 (2): 237–265.
Postman, N. 2011. *Amusing Ourselves to Death*. Translated by Zhang Yan. Guilin: Guangxi Normal University Press.
Reddy, W.M. 2004. *The Navigation of Feeling: A Framework for the History of Emotions*, 124–129. Cambridge: Cambridge University Press.
Ritzer, G. 1998. *The McDonaldization Thesis: Exploration and Extensions*. London: Sage Publications Ltd.
Rosenwein, B.H. 2007. *Emotional Communities in the Early Middle Ages*. Ithaca, NY: Cornell University Press.
Simmel, G. 1994. "Tendencies in German Life and Thought Since 1870". In *Georg Simmel: Critical Assessments*. Vol. 1, edited by David Frisby, 9. London: Routledge.
Simmel, G. 1997. *Simmel on Culture: Selected Writings*, edited by David Frisby and Mike Featherstone. London: Sage Publishers.
Solomon, R.L. 1980. "The Opponent-Process Theory of Acquired Motivation: The Costs of Pleasure and the Benefits of Pain". *American Psychologist* 35 (8): 691–712.
Stearns, P.N., and C.Z. Stearns. 1985. "Emotionology: Clarifying the History of Emotions and Emotional Standards". *The American Historical Review* 90 (4): 813–836.
Stearns, P.N., and C.Z. Stearns. 1994. *American Cool: Constructing a Twentieth-Century Emotional Style*. New York, NY: New York University Press.
Stets, J.E. and J.H. Turner, eds. 2006. *Handbook of The Sociology of Emotions*. New York, NY: Springer.
Tangney, J.P. and K. Fischer, eds. 1995. *Self-Conscious Emotions*. New York, NY: The Guilford Press.
Taylor, C. 1989. *Sources of the Self: The Making of the Modern Identity*, 21. Cambridge, MA: Harvard University Press.
Turkle, S. 2011. *Alone Together: Why We Expect More From Technology and Less From Each Other*. New York, NY: Basic Books.
Turner, J.H. 2007. *Human Emotions: A Sociological Theory*, 126. London: Routledge.
Wang, Ning. 2000. "The Consumption of Emotions and the Industry of Emotions: A Note on the Sociology of Consumption". *Journal of Sun Yatsen University (Social Science Edition)* 40 (6): 109–113.
Weber, M. 1978. *Economy and Society: An Outline of Interpretative Sociology*, 1150. Berkeley: University of California Press.
Weber, M. 2010. *From Max Weber: Essays in Sociology*, 151. Translated by Yan Kewen. Beijing: People's Publishing House.

Wharton, A.S. 1999. "The Psychosocial Consequences of Emotional Labor". *The Annals of the American Academy of Political and Social Science* 561: 158–176.

Williams, S.J. 2001. *Emotion and Social Theory: Corporeal Reflections on the (Ir)Rational*, 116. London: Sage Publishers.

Xu, Yibing, and Hubert Petit. 2014. "Research on the Theory of Tribes According to Michel Maffesoli". *Journal of Northwest University (Philosophy and Social Sciences Edition)* 2014 (1): 21–27.

Zelizer, V.A. 2007. *The Purchase of Intimacy*. Princeton, NJ: Princeton University Press.

Zhao, Dingxin. 2006. *Social and Political Movements*, 290. Beijing: Social Sciences Academic Press.

CHAPTER 51

The Individual and Society: The End of an Alliance and the Burden of Emotions

François Dubet

1   The Embeddedness Model

Sociology is a scion of modernity insofar as it was at the outset a narrative of modernisation born in some European countries. This narrative is structured by a number of constant themes, notably, the division of labor, rationalisation and democratic individualism (Nisbet 1984). The project of a science of society arose in a democratic culture and in the wake of the Enlightenment, which valued the individual and his or her subjectivity as the very triumph of modernity over tradition. The sociology of the "founding fathers" thus sought to combine the assertion of individual freedom and autonomy with the functional necessities of social integration. The solution proposed by classical sociology, born in some modern, industrial, and democratic Western countries, was one of embedding the individual in society.

The first stage of the reasoning is perfectly holistic: social action is defined by the internalisation of models, norms and values which allow one to act in accordance with systemic necessities. However, the universality of modern values introduces a reflexive distance and autonomy between the individual and the social actor, thus opening the space for a real personal subjectivity. I am free when I act in the name of Reason, Liberty, Equality … but this is, nevertheless, a freedom which is strongly framed by social forces, self-control and social control, the mechanisms of which constitute, strictly speaking, society: institutions, social classes, roles, codes, norms …

This intellectual strategy for constructing the individual has been largely synthesised by Parsons (1959) who proposed a whole system of successive embeddings from culture to personality via society (roles, status, etc.). In modern societies, the individual is defined by the internalisation of values, norms, and roles. But the universality of values and the complexity of roles also mean that the individual is not a fiction because he or she is obliged to constantly reconstruct his or her action by adapting to contexts which are not always perfectly pre-established and formalised, contrary to what was imagined to be the way of tradition. No role is total, and no personality is perfectly adequate for it; this can be attributed to functional reasons in modern societies in which change is as important as order, in which individuals incessantly jump from one role to another. The modern individual does not emerge "against" the system, but is the result of transformations in social control, which is gradually individualised and "subjectivised" (Elias 1991). Insofar as each individual perceives social obligations and codes as intimate, personal and freely accepted constraints, social actors see themselves as individuals, as the authors of their own action and, at the same time, are tempted to perceive the social world as a "landscape" which is external to themselves and onto which they project their own feelings (Martuccelli 2002; Riesman 1964). Social constraint has become a subjective habitus, a freedom.

This conception of the individual presided over the vocation of classical sociology, which consisted in establishing a system of close correspondences between social situations and individual attitudes experienced as free and autonomous, between objective variables and subjective variables which had to be shown to be, in reality, deeply articulated. In France, Bourdieu's theory (1972) is today the most familiar construction of this theory of action in which the individual is the crystallisation of a set of precociously acquired dispositions, of several habitus experienced as self-evident and as manifestations of a real individual autonomy even though they are closely correlated to the material and social conditions of their creation.

In this intellectual framework, emotions are perceived as a double symptom of the breakdown of the individual's embeddedness in society. On the one hand, emotions are seen as an *excess* of socialisation, as a return of the traditional community in which the individual consciousness is invaded by the collective consciousness: religious or patriotic emotion, the passion of the crowds are like the trances of traditional societies described by Durkheim. Collective emotion cancels out the individual and threatens the democratic subject, it aspires to authority and calls for totalitarianism. On the other hand, at the other extreme, emotions result from the *detaching* of the individual from society, from his or her distance from socialisation. Personal emotions, especially feelings of love, prove that the individual is not totally social. Modern art, like all fictional literature, constantly reveals individual authenticity "against" social constraints and routines. With modern art, one sees the world in a singular way, one has a view of one's own; with the novel, one loves and acts outside social roles, one is "misunderstood", alone, singular … From this point of view, psychoanalysis has been a sociology of modernity insofar as it highlights this double nature of emotions: the dissolution of the individual in the crowd and an irreducible status as outsider to the world.

2 Exiting Embeddedness

The social thinking of the last fifty years has been dominated by the exit from this conception of the embedding of the individual based on the correspondence and reversibility of the actor and the system. The departure from the embeddedness model results from the transformation of the long-dominant representation of society, dominant both on the critical, Marxist side and on the conservative, functionalist side of sociology. Indeed, the image of embedding necessarily relies on an integrated conception of social life in which culture is diffracted into a relatively homogeneous social structure, into a set of more or less integrated roles and, ultimately, into the most intimate personalities. Placing either values or the division of labor at the center of the integration mechanism changes nothing: society is a highly integrated system in which systemic integration and social integration are two complementary facets of the same whole. This "tranquil" representation of modern, industrial, democratic and Western societies has come undone with what we, with others, will call late modernity rather than post-modernity insofar as the breakdown which can be observed today was largely inscribed in the various narratives of modernity: increasing complexity, continuous rationalisation, disenchantment with the world, anomy, broadening democratic individualism, market extension... To put it differently, we are experiencing the exhaustion of the idea of society conceived as the integration of an economy, a culture and a national political sovereignty, an integration which is necessary for the establishment of a continuity between the subjectivity of the actors and the objectivity of their positions and, therefore, for the embedding out of which the individual emerges. The fact that many a society has modernised and developed outside the Western road to modernity has obviously contributed to destroying the Western (and imperialist) illusion of being at the forefront of evolution: one can be economically and technologically "modern" within cultures and political systems which differ from Western models.

This observation can be described in a less abstract way. The old class structures "explode" in the face of the multitude of divisions and discriminations which individualise inequalities (Dubet 2019). Modern societies which used to perceive themselves as culturally homogeneous, or destined to be so, are now culturally plural societies. The institutions of socialisation, starting with the family and school, are described as being in crisis: the conjugal family is less stable, and school is more a machine for sorting pupils than an institution of socialisation comparable to the churches ... (Dubet 2002). And when society is not perceived as being an integrated system, the individual ceases to be "embedded".

Whatever the paths chosen, it seems clear that contemporary sociological theory is no longer structured by a central conception of the individual, by a program of embeddedness based on a representation of society in terms of a homogeneous system of action. We can always wonder whether it is the economic, cultural, and social transformations which have induced these changes in sociological thinking, or whether it is the dynamics of the academic and theoretical domain itself which explain these changes, but, in any case, we have to take note of the decline of a long-hegemonic response, asserting simultaneously the unity of the individual and the unity of society. At the cost of an extreme, even caricatural, simplification, three major sociological conceptions of the individual can be distinguished.

The first is that of the *social individual*, inspired by the classical conception: the individual is the product of socialisation. But this individual is "hyper-embedded" because the "enchanted" representation of a fully social and autonomous subject is replaced by that of an individual reduced to the internalisation of social domination. When norms, values and identities are nothing more than the vectors of social domination, the individual becomes an illusion. Thus, "deconstruction" highlights the power which constitutes the individual as the product of domination: sex is the product of the patriarchy, cultural identity is the product of Western domination, the "free" worker is internalised capitalism ... This logic is even more powerful because the less society is perceived as a system of social relations, the more everything becomes social and constructed: the body, nature, subjectivity, identities ... are entities constructed by domination. In the end, only the sociologist would escape the dominations he or she denounces!

Opposite this hyper-socialised conception of individuals, one finds the model of the *rational individual*, which is resolutely individualistic and reverses the reasoning of classical sociology (Boudon 1984; Coleman 1990). This model postulates that the core of sociological analysis is a rational individual acting as a strategist in a social context defined in terms of competition and resources. In fact, the more or less rational and utilitarian individual is seen as the atom of a society conceived as a compositional effect resulting from the multitude of individual strategies. The individual of methodological individualism is not a mere *homo oeconomicus*, but always resembles one because he or she is, above all, an epistemological tool, more a convenient theoretical fiction than a real singular person. Moreover, from a methodological point of view, it is quite rare that research claiming to belong to this orientation concerns itself with concrete and singular individuals; the individual is a cognitive and strategic machine the action of which is inferred from aggregated macro sociological data: opinion polls, school course choices, various beliefs, political attitudes, market equilibria ... While the social individual is supported by a psychology of identity, the rational individual seems strangely devoid of subjective substance: an individual with neither passions nor personality.

Advocates of the third figure, the *ethical individual*, consider that the individual builds himself or herself by wresting autonomy from social constraints. This is an individual insofar as he or she wants to be an individual, as imposed on him or her by a cultural model which values moral autonomy and a system which is sufficiently open to allow him or her to detach himself of herself from the constraints of his or her roles and interests. Given this, the individual is conceived as a subject capable of producing meaning, of constructing his or her world in a continuous distance and tension with society (Dubet 1994). This is the thesis of the growing separation between the experienced world and the system, of the continuous rupture between social integration and systemic integration. In this case, the individual is defined by his or her reflexivity, by the fact that he or she is never totally adequate for his or her social roles, on the one hand, and interests, on the other. Here, the individual is a subject insofar as he or she is not fully socialised and insofar as he or she tries to tear himself or herself away from the other two ways of being an individual. He or she is an individual because he or she claims to be one, either personally or collectively because he or she needs the recognition of others to perceive himself or herself as an individual.

3   The Burden of Emotions: Contempt

When what we used to call society is no longer the integration of a culture, a structure of classes, and social roles, the individual experience is a work on the self, an attempt to articulate one's various relationships of belonging and habitus with the rational pursuit of one's interests in the multiple ever-expanding markets (economic, academic, symbolic ...). This experience is driven by ethical ideals which invade the social vocabulary: authenticity, autonomy, the project, singularity, "agentivity" ... (Archer 2003). Everyone is expected to be the actor of his or her own life and to be recognised as such. Consequently, social criticism adopts a "psychological" vocabulary centered on emotions rather than on the denunciation of socio-economic inequalities and exploitation. When each individual has to be the subject of his or her own social experience, the dominant emotion is the feeling of *contempt*. An emotion which breaks down into several dimensions.

The first dimension is the feeling of being invisible and forgotten, not recognised for what one uniquely is. I am despised because I am not seen, because

I am reduced to the anonymity of the market, of mass cultures and of blind bureaucratic procedures. I am despised because I am discriminated against by those who forget who I am: a woman, a member of a minority, a sick person, an old person ... But I am also despised because I am too visible, because my singularity is incarcerated in a thousand stereotypes—racist and sexist in particular—which impose on me a collective identity which is not my own. Invisible or too visible, I am always despised because I am never adequate for the identities assigned to me. Contempt is the dark side of the demand for recognition.

The second dimension of contempt stems from the stranglehold of the ideal of the equality of opportunity. In societies which promote equal opportunities to achieve unequal positions, everyone is expected to be responsible for his or her social destiny. Therefore, the winners of meritocratic, economic, and educational competitions, but not only them, think they deserve the inequalities which they enjoy. But, in this case, the losers of these competitions "deserve" their failures and must only blame themselves. They not only feel despised, but to some extent despise themselves. Therefore, to escape this feeling of contempt, they have no choice but to despise others, especially those poorer, more foreign, weaker than them, while denouncing the contempt of the elites and the "intelligent" towards them. From this point of view, contempt is not a social relationship, it is a continuous chain of interactions, it is a basic social emotion when self-realisation becomes the norm (Honneth 2000).

Contempt is the basic emotion of societies which "oblige" individuals to construct themselves, to do what society and institutions used to but no longer do for them. European and North American societies are no more "contemptuous" than the old class-based societies: on the contrary even, they assert equality of all and the right to be different much more than the old class societies did. But contempt becomes the basic emotion of inequalities and injustices when they are experienced as singular experiences, when individuals are required to construct their own experience.[1] The transfer of the construction of society to individuals reinforces the burden of emotions, and this is all the heavier to bear as the development of information technologies, screens, and networks, allows everyone to access the public space and to be a one-person social movement in their own right.

The emergence of emotions is not only a matter of social climate and singular subjectivities insofar as it profoundly transforms the political life of old

---

1 This analysis is close to Axel Honneth's (*La société du mépris*, Paris: La Découverte, 2006). It diverges, however, on one point: contempt is less a form of domination than the emotion of the individuals expected to be the authors of their respective lives.

modern and democratic societies. In most of these countries, political representation is no longer structured by traditional class divisions. Everywhere, the winners of the meritocratic competition are pitted against those who feel forgotten by social transformations and despised by the elites. Everywhere, forces which, for want of a better term, are called populist, are trying to mobilise those who feel despised. Everywhere, identity-based emotions are superimposed on the old "class struggles". Everywhere, democratic institutions are threatened or, at the very least, weakened. Everywhere, we witness a competition of sufferings and discriminations: those subjected to discrimination feel despised because they are too visible, and those who are not subjected to discrimination feel invisible and despised in their turn.

Of course, contempt is not the only social emotion and there are less sombre and less sad ones, such as empathy, generosity, and attachment, which generate anger and moral crusades. But, as with contempt, these indignations often find it difficult to achieve political expression, and many individuals experience a kind of inner rupture between their indignations and their interests, between their values and their practices. How could it be otherwise when economy, culture and politics are no longer embedded, when the social is not society?

∙∙∙

The model of the embedded individual was born in societies which represented themselves as societies, as systems of integration between values, interests, and institutions. This model was born in modern, industrial, national, and democratic societies which referred other figures of the individual to history, tradition and radical cultural differences. Within this framework, emotions emerged when this integration appeared too powerful or too weak, in the same way that for Durkheim, individuals commit suicide when they are too integrated or not integrated enough.

This type of society, or rather this representation of itself, no longer functions and the figure of the individual falls apart. From now on, everyone is required to be both the actor and the author of his or her own life, and the feeling of contempt becomes the fundamental emotion of democratic societies among those who face an impossible to achieve trial. Thus, the question facing the social sciences is a political one. How can democratic societies represent individuals and not only social classes and interests? How can they give form and political content to emotions, especially feelings of contempt? How can individual trials and collective issues be understood together (Wright-Mills 1967)? Insofar as sociology's existence is bound to democracy, this question should be at the heart of its vocation. This "universal" vocation should be deployed in societies and cultures which do not hierarchise themselves throughout the course of a narrative of modernity. What are the trials and emotions of individuals in the Asian, Muslim, African, Latin American worlds?

Acknowledgment

I would like to thank warmly Senior Translator Nigel Briggs for his rigourous translation in English.

References

Archer, M. 2003. *Structure, Agency and the Internal Conversation*. Cambridge: Cambridge University Press.
Boudon, R. 1984. *La place du désordre*. Paris: PUF.
Bourdieu, P. 1972. *Esquisse d'une théorie de la pratique*. Geneva: Droz.
Coleman, J.S. 1990. *Foundations of social theory*. Cambridge: Harvard University Press.
Dubet, F. 1994. *Sociologie de l'expérience*. Paris: Seuil.
Dubet, F. 2002. *Le déclin de l'institution*. Paris: Seuil.
Dubet, F. 2019. *Le temps des passions tristes*. Paris: Seuil.
Elias, N. 1991. *La société des individus*. Paris: Fayard, [1939].
Honneth, A. 2000. *La lutte pour la reconnaissance*. Paris: Cerf.
Martuccelli, D. 2002. *Grammaires de l'individu*. Paris: Gallimard.
Nisbet, R.A. 1984. *La tradition sociologique*. Paris: PUF.
Parsons, T., and E. Shils, ed. 1959. *Toward a General Theory of Action*. Cambridge: Harvard University Press.
Riesman, D. 1964. *La foule solitaire*. Paris: Arthaud.
Wright-Mills, C. 1967. *L'imagination sociologique*. Paris: Maspéro.

CHAPTER 52

From the Deepest Dimension to Society

Yazawa Shujiro

1   Introduction: Self and Emotion Issues in Sociology

The Japanese word "*jiga* (自我)" means "self". This Chinese character means that you see yourself as a target. Therefore, one can imagine that the self means seeing ones and gradually seeing oneself in the context of what supports being oneself. It goes without saying that it is regulated by nature and by family, relatives, ethnic groups, communities, religions, etc. The scope of seeing oneself has not been expanded very much, but as those regulatory powers have weakened it has become clear that the self was clearly conscious of the environment surrounding the self. It was not until the modern age that the self was clearly established as a subject, a creative subject, and an imagination subject.

Sociology was established with one of the problems being to clarify the contradiction between society and the individual. The individual in this case is the self as seen as a member of a group or community. Therefore, sociology has made it a major issue in its history to elucidate how the individual self defined by it transforms as society develops. That is, how the social form (civil society, mass society, managed society) changes as modernization progresses, what kind of individual self is created by it, how to resolve contradictions, and how to transform society have been elucidated as major problems in sociology.

2   Toward a Sociology in the Making

It is Keiichi Sakuta who has consistently clarified the destiny of the individual from its birth to its future in Japan. In this study, he sees the future of the individual, which can no longer be divided. He distinguished three individuals: the super-individual, the independent individual, and the individual body (singularity) (Sakuta 1996: 99–108).

A transcendental individual is an extra-secular, transcendental, metaphysical individual. When an individual faces a new situation that he or she has already acquired, he or she can transcend his or her daily routine, or even stand outside the secular society to unravel the situation to try to get a new perspective and live. In this case, the biggest problem is how the super-individual returns to the secular society and daily life.

Individuals cannot be further divided. Therefore, the individual must increase individuality by independence. Or an individual can be decent to the roots of the individual, body, human nature, and so on.

Individual-body singularity is not a division of an individual. It means the organism and body of an individual who has been removed from the "structural linkage" that has made it possible to compose a unified human being and subject by restraining the individual. Therefore, in the case of a singularity, the impulses, desires, consciousness, and spirit inside the body and organism, which often act in the direction of dividing the subject and human beings, become a problem. For individuals, the most important issue is how to generate internal impulses and desires, how to create humans, and how to drive humans. Sakata's later years were devoted to solving this problem.

He tried to create a sociology of anthropology and a sociology of deep structure of society rather than a sociology of institution (Sakuta 1973). He continued to investigate the deep structure of the human being and society.

Then, he looked for the differences between these two relations. He thought that this difference was things sociology lost by taking a perspective of contradiction between society and the individual. He wanted to introduce Bergsonism into sociology. So, he called his sociology *sociology in the making* (Sakuta 1993: chapter 1). The first thing he did was find deeper drives (ascribed energy, libido) than instincts.

3 Materialist Theory of Self and Emotion

The self and emotional issues were particularly important to Japanese materialists as well. This is because Marxists have often criticized research that emphasizes consciousness and spirit as an idealism, with an understanding of materials limited to nature and economy. Appropriate elucidation of the problem of self and emotion was required.

The work of Yasunosuke Takizaki should be remembered as a starting point for the problem (Takizaki 1975). He sees humans as an intermediate between nature and the transcendental nature created by humans working on nature. So, of course, he starts with material metabolism between humans and nature, grasping objects and expressing correspondence. Object grasping is, in other words, self-objectification. Correspondence manifestation is the movement of materials, the interaction of materials and materials, which is helped by various tools to create something beyond nature. What should be noted here is that he pays attention to the consciousness and cognition (five senses, emotions, language) that are indispensable for self-objectification, and classifies the consciousness into a series of emotions and a series of modeling.

He further divided the areas of human activity into three areas: (1) economic-material life, (2) social-mental life, and (3) emotional life. He also divided the dimensions of human activity into three dimensions: (a) matter, (b) advanced consciousness, and (c) emotions (emotions, materials of beauty, etc.). Therefore, he understood emotions, tastes, and attitudes as solutions to simultaneous equations with six variables.

To briefly conclude Takizaki's argument, it is beautiful when there is an organic, integrated relationship in the three dimensions of human activity, and in addition to which there is an advantage in the level of emotion. It will be that there is a modeling subject of beauty.

From the latter half of the 20th century to the present day, Platonism and the Cartesian way of thinking, which pervaded human beings and society in Western Europe, have finally been fundamentally questioned. And sociology has been no exception.

A. Gouldner's criticism of Western sociology considers Parsons to be like Plato. (Gouldner 1970). He criticized Parsons and tried to solve the fundamental problems by using Heidegger and G. Marcel. It was a form of critical examination of Habermas's communication and rational social theory. First and foremost, rationalism, which supports capitalism, was criticized. In addition, Descartes's mind-body dualism and mind-material dualism were criticized. For example, we do not say that I am because I think of myself, but that I am one unit because I think of myself, and that is why I exist (Karatani 1992, 1994, 2004). The recognition axis, which was traditionally regarded as particular and the set regarded as general, becomes universal as the singular self, which is not collected by anyone, and the opposite (Yazawa 2015).

Psychologist Rom Harre divides self into three dimensions. Self 1 is rooted in one person's sense of self, with one and only one point of view. That is, it is aspatial self. This manifests itself in indexicality, the "empirical content of descriptive statements in local positions" (Rom 1998: 56) of body-rooted spatial self in individual situations. Self 2 is the whole attribute of one person. It includes his beliefs about himself, his self-reflective beliefs about who he is and what his strengths and weaknesses are, and his history up to that point. This does not appear anywhere other than its self-consciousness, its actions, and its history. Self 3 is the kind of self-acquired by others. This self-manifest itself in communication with others.

Rom made a distinction between these three selves. Distinguishing the three selves suggests that each self-considered the possibility of acting as an independent factor in forming human beings, consciousness, and society. And he insisted on taking it fully scientifically. He says psychology must be a dual science to do so. What that means is that psychology cannot fully capture human psychology unless it is not only conventional science but also psychology with ontology, like with Wundt. Self 1 is based on the body, the molecule, and requires many sciences, including molecular biology, neuroscience, and cognitive science, as well as anthropology and folklore.

Raising Rom's issue deserves attention. But one big problem remains. It is a question of how the three selves are related, the independence, autonomy. The active role of Self 3 may be erased in Self 2 and Self 1.

Although we cannot go deep into this issue, it is also being examined by the philosopher Kojin Karatani in Japan. According to him, when trying to grasp the problem of independence, it can no longer be grasped in the framework of modern subject–object-epistemology. Independent self 1 appears only in logic and definite description. So, he examined ontology, logic, linguistic theory, phenomenology, and so on. Finally, he found that this problem can be solved by investigating from Heidegger's ontology to the thought of Levinas. That is, formation of intersubjectivity could be possible by practice (Karatani 1992, 1994).

Regardless of the success or failure of his attempt, the implications of his attempt are clear. His attempt raises the question of whether communication with people with fundamentally different qualities and significant differences is possible, and if so, with what theory and method. More specifically, the question is whether the traditional communication theory represented by Habermas could solve this problem in a perfect way. It was for good reason that Gouldner's theory of crisis in Western sociology brought up Heidegger and took the direction of examining Habermas's theory of communication. Although Gouldner pointed out the coming crisis of Western sociology, he could not build a new theory of his reflexive sociology. Fifty years have passed since Gouldner's problem was raised. It is time to think about post-Western sociology extensively.

4 The Origin of Self and Various Dimensions of Subjectivity

At the age of seven, Munesuke Mita experienced the bombing of Tokyo by the US military, which caused human-made things to smolder overnight. As a result, he realized everything (Karatani, Mita and Osawa 2019: 127–130). Mita's sociology focuses on clarifying how humans (nature) build society and culture, and how they feel about their actions. He calls it the theory of value and value consciousness. His theory is always aware of the original sociological issues of what our society is, what the laws of its development are, what the ideal image of society is, and how we should live. However, sociology as a science cannot be established if the whole problem is taken from the front. So, he turned the original problem into a number of small problems that could be scientifically solved. He aimed to build various theories. The theory of value and value consciousness is the starting point and at the same time occupies a key position in bundling and mediating various theories.

Mita defines value as "the performance of an object that satisfies the desires of the subject" (Mita 1966) and value consciousness as the totality of explicit or implicit value judgments of individual subjects for many objects. Therefore, value is conscious. It serves as a criterion for choice in action (motivation, happiness, goodness, purpose of life), and an object whose value is judged by the subject constitutes social value. Mita then introduces a temporal perspective and a social perspective to clarify the structure, dimensions, and types of value. It is all about elucidating where values occupy and function in action, culture, personality, and society.

He applied this theory in trying to clarify the history of the beliefs of modern Japan after the Meiji Restoration. He picked up and analyzed popular songs as the best representation of the Japanese sentiment. This is probably one of the achievements of the human social theory that we have seen, which understands society as a conflict of various beliefs (Mita 1967, 1993, 2013). Mita says he has once again experienced a feeling like "all the blood in the body has been replaced" (Karatani et al. 2019: 116). This is because he traveled to Mexico and Latin America and experienced a society that was fundamentally different from the one he was thinking of. So, he understood the importance of a society that relies on wisdom broader than the intrinsic power and clarity of old people and children, rather than a society that relies primarily on clarity and power.

Mita mobilized the latest achievements in biology and discovered the origin of the ego and that it could create creative subjectivity from the inside, but he was followed by an inevitable solution. There was a problem he had to solve. It was a question of how to think about the idea that everything is empty and that all human beings are egoists. From his experience in India and Latin America, he considered these ideas to be a shadow created by modern times. This is because if you live in a non-modern nature = time, you will not have the feeling of being mobile in the context of nature, natural transitions, the body, and human life and death. Therefore, Mita returned to the origin and aimed at the full-scale development of the theory of time and social structure, as well as how and what kind of self is formed from nature and the body.

The above discussion is extremely interesting, but what is even more interesting and important is that the individual, which was thought to be independent, has nothing to do with anything else, but also is not a prokaryotic cell, but changes from the inside. It was clarified that it was made up of a large number of eukaryotic cells that could grow. In that sense, the individual is a complete compulsory system, and human symbiosis is already installed in life. From there, Mita explained that the way in which the self provides love and seduces the other self and forms a relationship and the way in which it is that underlies the life and death of living.

He showed us a sharp contrast between natural time and modern time in the comparative sociology of time. Of course, we will find different forms of time in modern time. So, our task is to figure out how to regain natural time and to get a spiral staircase type suggested by Merucci (1996) that integrates natural time, clock time, dot time, and all-time ideas so far clarified as time. In order for human beings to live better from the present to the future, we need a spiral staircase-shaped time as the future time. And the next issue of sociology is future sociology.

Recent Studies on Self and EmotionWithout mentioning Masataka Katagiri's theories of self, this article cannot come to an end. He investigated the self in its critical moments from discovery, establishment, and narrative formation (Katagiri 2000, 2011).

The history of sociology begins with É. Durkheim, G. Simmel, and M. Weber. They discovered the modern self. The history leads to the European and American theory of mass society and the counter-social movement theory (R.H. Turner) through the community theory (C.H. Cooley, G.H. Mead). The history comes to the discovery of reflexive self (A. Giddens and U. Beck). Finally, the history reaches the present, the discovery of liquid identity (Z. Bauman). In this historical narrative, Katagiri also discusses the individuation, privatization, personalization, psychologicalization, and subjectivity of the self in depth (Katagiri 2011). These attempts will be effective and will bring us many discoveries. Asano Tomohiko insists that the self is created and developed by telling the self and making a story. And in order to solve the problems that the self has, it is effective to combine this process with family therapy (Asano 1998).

Katagiri's book does not cover the history of Japanese sociology. What can we say about the history of Japanese sociology? The first thing to say is that Durkheim, Weber, and Simmel have consistently had a great influence on the postwar Bachelor of Arts in Japanese sociology. American pragmatism, psychology, sociology, and social psychology had a certain degree of influence before the war but became very influential early after it. Of course, that includes Cooley and Mead. In addition to them, William James and John Dewey must be named.

The first task of postwar sociology was to examine how social structure, social institution, people's self, and consciousness changed or did not change with the great social transition from prewar to postwar society. The main task of social psychology was to theorize the relationship between self, consciousness, and society and to clarify the structure of social consciousness. On top of that, sociology needed to present what humans are like to reshape society. Mead's self theory was considered to be able to meet this demand.

Since then, Mead's self-theory has continued to be a main theory in the field of self-theory as a theory that presents the ideal way of a self that can create a society. Various discussions have been held over the criticism that it may only be possible as microsociology, and the Marxist side has also raised discussions such as those on the union of Mead's and Marx's theories (Kawamura 2000).

In the late 1950s, Japanese social science was dominated by many mass society theories. Mass society theory considers mass society to be a transformation from civil society. In mass society people work like machines in organizations and are atomized outside the organization. They adapt to the system and are non-institutionalized by nonrational consciousness. The Japanese society at that time had not yet reached the construction of a mature civil society, and in that sense, the mass society theory seems to be a little premature, but the age of organization and the age of machinery were becoming reality. In that sense, the theory of mass society may have raised the problems of Western civil society and warned Japan of the future. But the extreme dichotomy between organizations and individuals was problematic and should be criticized. As Masao Maruyama showed in his examination of modernization theory, atomization and individuation are closely related to politics, economy, people's lives, etc., and the results of atomization must be considered very different in relation to them (Maruyama 1964).

In the late 1960s, understood by many researchers to be a turning point in history, E.H. Ericson's theory of identity was introduced to Japanese sociology by the political sociologist Akira Kurihara (Kurihara 1982). He translated identity into Japanese, the proof of historical existence, and presented the significance of Ericsson's theory of identity accurately. His introduction of the theory of identity would have introduced the theory of identity into Japan as a counter to, in a sense, corresponding to the change in social form, that is, the arrival of a managed society. However, the translated term "historical existence proof" did not take root in Japan, and it was accepted as an untranslatable one by using the original word "identity" as it was. It goes without saying that the importance of historical awareness has also been forgotten. As a result, the concept of identity was psychological zed and deeply penetrated into Japanese society.

Now, individuation and industrialization, which have been promoted in the name of modernization, have almost reached their peak in the United States and Europe since the latter half of the 1960s, and it has become difficult to see how society will change. Until the late 1960s, Japanese sociology was a state of trilemma sociological functionalism, Marxism, and other forms of sociology (such as critical theory). Therefore, many researchers emphasized the role of the reflective self, which reexamines the religious, metaphysical, philosophical, and ideological foundations of the individual, self, and society. They also emphasized a role of the reflexivity of self, organization, and society created by such a self. As a result, they called the future of society reflexive, recursive modernization, phenomenology, constructionism, symbolic interactionism, ethnomethodology, etc., created and supported these discoveries. It was Anthony Giddens and Ulrich Beck who formulated this trend (Giddens, Beck and Lash 1994).

After that, knowledge informalization and globalization progressed, the sources of wealth and power changed drastically, and the liquidation of human beings and society progressed. It is the theory of Baumann and Luhmann that captures this well.

As a result of the examination of the postwar history, Japanese sociology centered on discussions related to the self and emotion issues, and I would like to point out the following points.

5 Conclusion

First and foremost, it must be pointed out that there are surprisingly few references and analyses regarding psychology, emotions, and consciousness, except for mass society theory and counter-social movement theory. Is this the result of people's attention being focused on rationality, rational action, and rational societies? Only when the psychology and consciousness have a non-rational character will they be noticed.

All human actions and practices are supported by non-retinal enticement and emotion, which play active roles in these actions and practices. Furthermore, the relationship between structural linkage and consciousness cannot be a one-sided regulation of consciousness by structural linkage. We must reexamine the concept and function of rationality. We must pay more attention to not only negative functions of emotion but also positive roles of emotion.

Secondly, in many cases, it is possible to raise the question that there may be a problem with the way of thinking about psychology and consciousness. Psychology and consciousness are regarded as pure (Nishida 1920), and they are grasped as one system, and as a result of the unified development of it. Sentiments, emotions, wills, thoughts, intellectual sensations, religions, morals, good, etc., can be considered as parts of a system. Then, each consciousness indicates a part or one position of the system. The self's privatization and liquidation also can be understood not as change of self itself but as the stream of consciousness. They are the result of the unified development of consciousness caused by contradiction between consciousness and differentiation of consciousness.

The above theory of consciousness was brought about by Kitaro Nishida's philosophy based on the traditions of Taoism and Zen Buddhism. Nishida's philosophy, which considers consciousness as a system of one and rejects all dualism, is a philosophy that has taken on the oriental tradition and has similarities to the philosophy of pragmatism. On the surface, postwar sociology in Japan is the history of the introduction of Western European sociology. It is the history of the arrangement, so to speak. However, it may be thought that the consciousness theory of Nishida's philosophy was hidden in the foundation of Japanese sociology. If so, it may be said that the rise of American sociology in postwar Japan was possible based on Nishida's philosophy.[1]

Or we can think that Japanese sociology has been introducing Western sociology by using a unique way of accepting a different culture in cultural contact. Kazuko Tsurumi found that Japanese culture has been accepting a different culture, even if it was contradictory to Japanese culture by expanding on the cultural system and accumulating established culture. Kazuko Tsurumi named this *multi-layer structure theory* (Tsurumi 1980). In that sense, if you look closely, Japanese sociology has a character that can be called post-Western sociology. In the future, it will be necessary to consider this point further.

The current global information society is a society in which the source of wealth and power shifts from industry to knowledge, information, science, and technology, and at the same time, the mode of social relations changes from an economic mode to a sociological mode (Bell 1973). At the same time, society is becoming more fragmented and unequal (Castell 2001). As a result, people face many contradictions and experience contradictions and confusion in consciousness. Therefore, in today's society, sentiments and emotions erupt into various areas, and it is becoming extremely difficult to form good sense and common sense from them and to form new values. Sociology must study self and emotional issues even more deeply, especially in research areas such as communication, mass communication, and social movements, and much more is emerging.

---

1 Nishida's philosophy is one of the philosophical foundations of Japanese sociology. But his influence on sociology cannot be neglected.

References

Asano, Tomohiko. 2001. *The Narrative Approach to Self: From Family Therapy to Sociology* [jiko heno monogatari-teki sekkin: kazoku ryouhou kara shakaigaku he]. Tokyo: Keiso-Shobo.

Bell, Daniel. 1973. *The Coming of Post-Industrial Society: A Venture in Social Forecasting.* New York, NY: Basic Books.

Castell, Manuel. 2001. *The Internet Galaxy: Reflections on the Internet, Business, and Society.* Oxford: Oxford University Press.

Giddens, Anthony, Ulrich Beck, and Scott Lash. 1994. *Reflexive Modernization: Politics, Tradition and Aesthetics in Modern Social Order.* Cambridge: Polity Press.

Gouldner, Alvin W. 1970. *The Coming Crisis of Western Sociology.* New York, NY: Basic Books.

Karatani, Koujin. 1992. *Quest* [tankyu]. Tokyo: Kodanshia Gakujutsu Bunko.

Karatani, Koujin. 1994. *Quest II* [tankyu II]. Tokyo: Kodanshi Gakujutsu Bunko.

Karatani, Koujin. 2004. *History and Repetition*, edited by Seiji M. Lippit. New York, NY: Columbia University Press.

Karatani, Koujin. 2005. *Transcritique: On Kant and Marx.* Translated by Sabu Kohso. Cambridge, MA: MIT Press.

Karatani, Koujin. 2010. *The Structure of World History* [sekaish no kozou]. Tokyo: Iwanami Shoten.

Karatani, Koujin, and Munesuke Mita. 2019. *Reaching Point of Postwar Thoughts* [sen-goshisou no toutatsu-ten: Karatani Koujin, Mita Munesuke jishin wo kataru]. Tokyo: NHK Shuppan.

Katagiri, Masataka. 2000. *Sociology of Self and Narrative* [jiko to katari no shakaigaku]. Kyoto: Sekai Shisou-sha.

Katagiri, Masataka. 2011. *Discovery of Self: Frontier in the History of Sociology* [jiko no hakken: shakaigaku-shi no furontia]. Kyoto: Sekaishiso-sha.

Kawamura, Nozomu. 2000. *The Theory of Self and Communication* [jiga to comyunikeishon no riron]. Tokyo: Ningen no kagaku-shinsha.

Kuhn, Michael, and Shujiro Yazawa, eds. 2015. *Theories about and Strategies against Hegemonic Social Sciences: Beyond Social Sciences.* Stuttgart: Ibidem Verlag.

Kurihara, Akira. 1982. *History and Identity: Psycho-historical Study of Modern Japan* [rekishi to identity-kindai nihon no shinri rekishi kenkyu]. Tokyo: Shinyosha.

Maruyama, Masao. 1964. "Pattern of Individuation and the Case of Japan". In *Changing Japanese Attitudes toward Modernization*, edited by Marius B. Jansen. Princeton, NJ: Princeton University Press.

Melucci, Alberto. 1996. *The Playing Self.* Cambridge: Cambridge University Press.

Melucci, Alberto. 2000. "Individual Experience and Global Issues in a Planetary Society". *Social Science Information* 39 (4): 507–527.

Mita, Munesuke. 1966. *Theory of Value Consciousness: Sociology of Desire and Morality* [kachi ishiki no riron: yokubou to doutoku no shakaigaku]. Tokyo: Koubundo.

Mita, Munesuke. 1967. *History of Feelings in Modern Japan: Socio-psychological History of Popular Songs* [kindai nihon no shinjou no rekishi: ryuukouka no shakai shinri-shi]. Tokyo: Koudansha.

Mita, Munesuke. 1981. *Comparative Sociology of Time* [jikan no hikaku shakaigaku]. Tokyo: Iwanami-shoten.

Mita, Munesuke. 1993. *The Origin of Self: Animal Sociology of Love and Egoism* [jiga no kigen: ai to egoism no doubutsu shakaigaku]. Tokyo: Iwanami-shoten.

Mita, Munesuke. 2013. *Social Psychology of Modern Japan*. London: Routledge.

Nishida, Kitaro. 1954. *Inquiry into the God* [Zen no Kenkyu]. New Haven, CT: Yale University Press.

Rom, Harre. 1998. *The Singular Self: An Introduction to the Psychology of Personhood*. London: Sage Publications.

Sakuta, Kei'ichi. 1973. *Stippling Deep Society* [shinsoshakai no tenbyo]. Tokyo: Yuhikaku.

Sakuta, Kei'ichi. 1996. *Individual* [kojin]. Tokyo: Sanseido.

Sakuta, Kei'ichi. 1993. *Sociology in the Making* [seisei no shakaigaku]. Tokyo: Yuhikaku.

Takizaki, Yasunosuke. 1975. *The Dimension of Emotions and the Subject in Creation* [jokan no jigen to sozou no shutai]. Tokyo: Sobunsha.

Tsurumi, Kazuko. 1988. "A Road to Universalization of Endemic Culture" [dochaku bunka no fuhenka he no michi]. In *Dochaku Bunka to Gairai Bunka* [dochaku bunka to gairai bunka]. Tokyo: Koudansha.

Tsurumi, Kazuko. 1998. *Mandala Volume 4 Earth: Yanagita Kunio* [mandara dai 4 kann tsuchi no maki Yanagida Kunio ron]. Tokyo: Fujiwara Shoten.

Yazawa, Shujiro. 2013. "Transcendental Dimension of Constructing of Universal Social Science". In *Theories about and Strategies against Hegemonic Social Sciences*, edited by Michael Kuhn and Shujiro Yazawa. Tokyo: Seijo University.

CHAPTER 53

Emotions of Fear, Anger, and Disgust in Contemporary Korean Society

Kim Wang-Bae

1 Introduction

Since World War II, South Korea has become one of the world's most advanced countries through unprecedented "time-space compression growth". Korea, once one of the world's poorest countries, which underwent Japanese imperialism, division into South and North Koreas, and the Korean War, has grown (in the case of South Korea) into one of the world's top 10 economies today through state-led industrialization by authoritarian regimes since the 1960s. Some refer to this phenomenon as "the miracle on the Han River". State-led industrialization was achieved by thoroughly suppressing the human rights, freedoms, and the civil rights of citizens along with the ideology of extreme anti-communism. Despite such oppression, Korea has finally achieved status as a democratic nation through struggling for democracy. It is no exaggeration to say that Korea is almost the only country among the fledgling countries after World War II that has achieved both "industrialization" and "democratization".

However, the Korean Peninsula remains divided, and the legacy of the Korean War, the Cold War system, and the resulting ideological conflict and hostility are evident not only between the two Koreas but also between groups in the South. The Korean Peninsula is also the only place still shaped by the ideological conflict between liberal democracy (the United States) and communism (formerly the Soviet Union), which has almost disappeared nowadays, and by the Cold War. In addition, there are clear generational divisions in South Korea, which went together with rapid social changes. Emotional confrontation between the elderly, who experienced the trauma of war and poverty, and the younger generation, who are experiencing material abundance and consumption, is also very high. The older generation, tamed within collectivist culture, seek compensation and recognition for their patriotic blood and sweat, while the younger generation, who are more individualistic, find fault with the older generation for the complaints they have about their current situation. Despite living a life of material affluence driven by consumerism, the younger generation is racked with "anxiety" caused by unemployment and uncertainty in employment, economic polarization (inequality), and jobless development. They also express relative deprivation and anger, thinking that opportunities and goods are unfairly distributed.

Korean society today is characterized by feelings of mutual hostility, hatred, and anger that express themselves in conflicts marked by generational and ideological overlap. In particular, the recent hatred in Korean society has taken shape not only in political and ideological groups of progressives and conservatives but also in attitudes toward women, sexual minorities, and migrant workers among some groups. Undoubtedly, feelings of hatred in Korean society do not stem from the violent racism that is deeply rooted in Western society. There have been very few cases of hate crimes against particular races or religions similar to those observed in Europe or the United States. Korean citizens, who have emphasized ethnic identity, have recently encountered foreign groups through such phenomena as international marriage, migrant labor, and refugee migration, but their hatred toward them seems relatively low. However, feelings of hatred are rapidly spreading, driven by factors such as ideology, generational differences, resentment toward sexual minorities, and gender. In this paper, I will look at the emotions that amplify conflict and confrontation in modern Korean society, such as fear, anger, and hatred, while paying attention to ideological confrontation and intergenerational conflict.

2   Emotions and Self-Consciousness

Most thinkers, regardless of all ages in the East and the West, viewed emotions in contrast to reason, and as being lower than reason. While reason clearly recognized and regarded the nature of an object as a guide to moral practice, emotions tended to distort, prejudice, or incite contaminated notions of the object, and even served as a factor that would corrupt humans into nothing better than an embodiment of animal nature. Emotions were sometimes identified as instincts, desires, and the like that had to be "corrected, restrained and tamed". In Confucian ideology, emotions were to be controlled. Confucianism contends that in order to become someone who is intelligent, reasonable, and able to practice reason, one must cultivate proper emotional control.

Even in Western European philosophical traditions, emotions were treated as being far inferior to reason. Emotions were natural instincts that had to be controlled and restrained, as they posed a threat to reason and were the manifestation of impulsive, dangerous, non-intellectual, and primitive barbarism. Emotions are more private than public, and because of their basis in desire and selfish tendencies, they cannot lead to reasonable beliefs or judgments.

Moreover, in Christian religious tradition, emotions were regarded as a source of "sin" (Solomon 2008).[1] In short, in Eastern and Western philosophy, emotions were ranked lower than reason, or even became subject to moderation and control as a curtain that obscured the light of reason. Recently, however, scholars in the humanities and social sciences have taken more active and dynamic perspectives, perceiving emotions as part of the process of thinking, evaluation, and awareness. Emotions are not just reactions to senses or external stimuli but act as a force to recognize and judge the surrounding environment or other living beings through a very complicated cognitive process.[2] Emotions are the motivation behind action, or the power of practice, and the term "cognitive" means that they are engaged in social, political, and ethical evaluations or practical intentions of events or objects. In other words, emotions and morality are deeply related (Calhoun and Solomon 1984). A group of scholars trying to assign emotions a more active, dynamic, and complex status concluded that those emotions and reason are at times in a confrontational or tense, but complementary, relationship, and emotions engage in their own cognition, judgment, and moral practices.

Emotions are interpretations of the senses of the body. Lupton underscores the "physicalization of emotions" while emphasizing that the physical presence of emotions, expressions, physical movements, or physical signals of emotions are essential factors for emotional development (Lupton 2016). Mainstream sociology, which has pursued empirical theories or models, has tended to overlook "the body with blood and flesh" and "consciousness engraved in the body" by conceiving of humans and their behavior in the abstract. In other words, human bodies have been formed throughout humans' political, economic, and cultural lives, and their roles have been ignored. The body is important because emotional experience is connected to the body's senses, and self-conceptions are nourished in a body with blood and flesh. Of course, my raw and instinctive stance on emotions does not find support in my emphasis on the importance of my body. The body is not just a natural product but is also a subject that is constructed and mediated by socio-cultural processes:

> The ways in which our bodies are recognized, regulated, decorated, altered, and morally evaluated, and how we deal with things like birth,

---

1 Such an idea is strongly criticized by cognitive psychology and philosophy. A group of scholars who criticize the view of the body as inferior to the mind is, are mobilizing concepts such as the embodied mind or emotion, which will be discussed later.
2 "If there is no judgment, evaluation, or belief about the world, emotions such as fear and anger do not constitute the real anger or fear" (Solomon 2001: 10).

sexuality, and death, are all framed through the socio-cultural and historical situations in which we live. The way in which physical activity is understood and experienced as an emotional phenomenon depends on individual socialization and living experience.

LUPTON 2016: 63

We would also like to use the concept of habitus suggested by P. Bourdieu to resolve dichotomous discussions on whether emotions are instinctively present within the actors, socially present objects, products of individual and social interactions, or a medium for creating them. Bourdieu refers to the "constant propensity formed over a long period of time as a mediator in objective structure and subjective practice" as habitus and approaches the issue of class conflict based on the concept of the various and distinctive organizational principles that make up society.[3] Calhoun follows Bourdieu's genealogy and introduces the concept of "emotional habitus". People not only reveal unique emotions but also have unique ways to relate emotions to each other, and to relate emotions to cognition and perception, which include a sense of behavior and of gaming. It is by no means conscious and cannot be transformed purely by rule. Habitus is entirely owned by individuals and does not exist within them, but as a result of individuals being engraved onto social relationships (Goodwin, Jasper and Polletta 2009). Habitus can be said to be a physicalized feeling and thinking associated with class, gender, race, and the like. Bourdieu's concept of habitus allows the mental and physical emotional experience to be regarded as a product of internalization by social processes. Emotions are social habitus formed by time and space, history and culture, socialization, and something communicative and physical (Bourdieu 1990).

Physicalized emotions, or emotional habitus, exist in a type of habit that is passed down over a relatively long period of time for generations and are sometimes works in progress created by tense historical events or times. If the former are emotions internalized into a culture over a relatively long period of time, the latter is an emotion with a short-term or temporary tendency. If the former are relatively stable and difficult to change, the latter has a relatively variable and volatile nature. In other words, the level of emotion varies widely. Accumulated along an extensive historical time and space, both the content and expression of emotions are structured into one emotional framework (i.e., "habitus-ized" emotions), and many different emotions are structured

---

3   Bourdieu introduced the concept of a field and established diverse fields, including the political, the religious, the scholastic, and artistic fields. Each field is seen as consisting of its own competing goals and interests. See Bourdieu (2005).

2.1   Koreans' Emotional Habitus

What is a representative factor that acts as an emotional habitus to Koreans? The existence of a unique emotional framework called "*han*" (恨) has been traditionally noted. "Han" refers to the feelings of being "social underdogs" who are oppressed and exploited by established forces. Such groups include women, children, the elderly, and the lower class. It is a combination of various emotions, such as anger, remorse, compassion, patience, and self-criticism, and refers to the emotions of the so-called public of the lower class. It is also a depressed reaction to the impossibility of self-realization due to a lack of power, poverty, and scarcity. The emotion of *han* is anger derived from resignation that is clotted in the heart, but it also has the potential to explode strongly when met with certain conditions. In other words, *han* is expressed via passionate collective emotions that cause civil unrest or revolution, as they are conveyed by the power of strong resistance to the existing forces and order.

Korea has been constantly invaded by foreign powers; colonized by Japan during the imperial period; and historically traumatized by division, Cold War, and poverty. Among these historical events, many members of the "public" (*minjung*) who were particularly subject to oppression and exploitation had to endure the pain of life. Women suffered from double oppression, especially under the patriarchal order. However, they were unable to express their feelings easily and had to persevere. These emotions build up to become the emotional habitus of *han* and often appear as a physical pathogen (especially for women), which is diagnosed as a "*hwa-byung*". *Hwa-byung* is a typical type of depression that occurs in Koreans to the point that it is registered in the international medical community as a proper noun.

Patriarchy, which long dominated Korean society, made women especially prone to *han*. Patriarchy refers to hierarchical power relationships imposed on the physically and socially disadvantaged, through various forms of oppression, such as neglect and discrimination against women and children, domestic violence, crimes against minorities, and racism. Patriarchy has long operated as a norm in Korean society, along with the principles of Confucianism. The history of Confucianism and patriarchy is deeply rooted. Confucianism, which was the national ideology during the Joseon Dynasty, emphasized the principle of filial piety that was connected through paternal lineage centered on the state in supporting and respecting parents in various families. Loyalty to the nation also represented an expansion of filial piety, which served as a value system that maintained male-dominated family order and national order. Since liberation, authoritarian states have formed a very strong affinity for patriarchal traditions. Of course, Confucianism paternalism has lost its power along with the expansion of industrialization and democratization of Korean society and feminism today. Together with the abolition of the House Head System, which is a symbol of men's family lineage, and of discriminatory inheritance, the preference for girls, and the advancement of women in society, practices of gender discrimination are rapidly disappearing into history. However, Confucian patriarchal practices are still deeply embedded among the older generations. The ignorance and discrimination that cause shame and anger toward the socially disadvantaged, such as women, children, minorities, and the lower class, are observed everywhere. Women of the elderly generation, who have feelings of resentment due to discrimination, oppression, and neglect, still often appeal for such *han*.[4]

As noted, Korean society is undergoing rapid change, and emotions such as *han* structured by habitus are rapidly disappearing. Society is changing over and over again. There is little trace of *han*, which is imprinted on the body of the older generation, within the new generation equipped with material abundance, digital culture, and global sensibility. Emotions such as *han* are still observed among the older generation (especially those who have experienced colonialism, division, and the Korean War) and among those who have been deeply influenced by anti-communism, but for those who grew up in the neoliberal order, their emotional lives are structured around the types of emotions that arise in a new era, rather than emotions such as *han*.

However, if there is an "emotional habitus" that encompasses all generations in Korea, it is "anti-Japanese sentiment". The international order in East Asia, which had been shaped by Chinese influence, was characterized by tense confrontation during the Imjin War (1592) that broke out in the 16th century.

---

4 There also exists a worldview called "Han" (韓) thought, which sounds the same but means something different. It is an unconscious attitude towards the world rather than an emotion. Han is a unique worldview of the Korean people, which is a synthesis of the ideas of Confucianism, Buddhism, and Daoism. Unlike the Western dichotomous ways of thinking (i.e., human–nature, divine–human, body–spirit, etc.), there exist trichotomous (三數分) ways of thinking (for instance Woo 2012) among Koreans, which are commonly found in the Siberian descendants of East Asia. The trichotomous ways of thinking are a three-dimensional mental structure which transcends dichotomous thinking. It contrasts Levi-Strauss's binary view on the human mental structure. Following trichotomous thinking, the universe consists of sky–earth–human (天地人), not just of sky–earth. The contrast of emotions can be integrated with the trichotomy. That is, when the affection (情) is broken, it becomes Han (恨). The two do not stop at a confrontation. They are integrated into a harmony (和).

Following the war, the region entered into a period of peace for more than 300 years. Western imperialism caused the political order in East Asia to fluctuate in the 19th century, and Japan, whose imperialism was on par with Western imperialism, ruled Korea as a colony for more than 40 years. Politically, Koreans, who recognized their subordinate status but felt a national pride for their role in carrying on the legacies of Confucianism, to the extent that they considered China's Qing Dynasty as *orangkae*, became extremely disappointed by their colonized status. After liberation, South Korea and Japan established friendly relations under the international political order created by the United States, and South Korea pursued economic growth with capital and technological support from Japan, but the two countries have remained mentally at odds amid patterns of confrontation and competition. Such anti-Japanese sentiments have been passed on from generation to generation and are shared by young people. In particular, recent issues, such as the issue of "comfort women", "forced labor", and "disputes over Dokdo", have triggered and expanded anti-Japanese sentiments among younger generations. They also boycott Japanese goods.

2.2 *Ideological Conflict and Hatred*

Feelings of hatred that involve prejudice and discrimination, and at times violence, have recently been observed worldwide. Crimes against people of color, indiscriminate attacks on Muslims, and violence against refugees and migrants have been observed worldwide. Hatred and violence against Asians are taking place in broad daylight in the COVID-19 era. Far-right forces fueled by neo-nationalism, statism, and racism, and their spokespersons, with the support of some members of the public, have surged to the political forefront. In addition, as conservative right-wing governments have come to power, feelings of hatred toward certain races and religious groups have led to violence. Under a Neo-Darwinist world order, similar to the law of the jungle, shaped by the administration of former US President Donald Trump, who did not hesitate to make offensive remarks about other races, women, and minorities, along with China and Japan, which seek to regain hegemony in East Asia, hatred wanders around like a ghost, leaving the world peoples to discriminate against and antagonize each other.

Hate is basically an expression of rejecting the "different". Hate is a feeling of rejecting a particular object, which includes fear that a heterogeneous object will harm one's existence and a defensive stance against the heterogeneous. Hate is a different sentiment from simply disliking something. Something foreign is an object of repulsion, which implies the fear that it will pollute and eventually destroy one's group. The subject who encounters heterogeneity reacts passively to avoid heterogeneity but actively tries to "remove" the heterogeneity.[5] That is, it mobilizes violence. Such hatred has recently been found in much of Korean society. Political forces on the conservative right, such as the so-called *Taegukgi* troops in Gwanghwamun, are still calling for "the eradication of commies", while Protestants on the right have gone one step further and do not hesitate to criticize homosexuality and Islam.

If hatred in the United States or Europe is typically caused by racism and the confrontation between Christianity and Islam, as mentioned earlier in discussing Korea, the confrontation between left and right (liberal and communist) ideologies is closely related to generational differences. Equipped with anti-communist ideologies, right-wing conservatives in Korea define progressives as dangerous adversaries and spit out their hatred for them. Hate is reproduced through various linguistic expressions, such as gestures, discourse, terminology, songs, slogans, written works, etc. Hate is an expression of the free will to express one's opinion, but it is also an act of defamation that destroys human dignity. Hate is a propagandistic expression that threatens the physical and mental well-being of a particular individual or group and is highly likely to lead to personal injury and mass murder. Some conservative rightists with anti-communist beliefs do not hesitate to make hateful remarks, describing South Korea's progressives as "pro-North leftists" and "parasites". One right-winger describes the progressive camp as consisting of "parasites" and supporters of their group as "hosts" (Kim 2019).

Hate found in the older generation—the prewar generation that experienced the Korean War firsthand and their children's generation who were socialized to be anti-communist, or the baby boom generation—is based on national security fears and anger against leftist ideology and associated groups. In particular, the aftereffects of the tragedy of the left-right dog-eat-dog conflict that they experienced during the Korean War are precipitated by "trauma". The emotional dynamics of trauma are fear, terror, anger, and hatred. The scars of war remain in the form of a negatively entrenched memory that is directed against the left. The experience of fear and the memory of the entrenched trauma served as symbolic violence that led to ideological misunderstanding and legitimized anti-communist conservatism. The nation's anti-communist ideology has exercised the power to "control and call" its very subjects, forming a strong affinity with their entrenched memories.

The situation of the Korean Peninsula is still uniquely characterized by division and the Cold War. Small clashes continue to take place on the Military

---

5 Of course, heterogeneity does not necessarily provoke aversive responses. Heterogeneity sometimes evokes curiosity and awe of the oddity.

Demarcation Line, and the "dangers of North Korea's nuclear weapons" and "dangers of the possibility of war" remain. The memory of the Korean War remains vivid for the elderly. For the older generation, anxiety and fear about North Korea and its "group of people whom they believe to be in sync with the North" are internalized as emotional habitus. The ideological conflict and mutual hatred between conservatives and progressives, who are at odds with each other today, are inextricably linked to this historical context. The older generation, who experienced war directly, or the generation that was educated under Cold War ideology led by anti-communism, has strong anti-North Korea and anti-communist feelings.

Today, progressives in South Korea, as well as North Korea, are recognized by right-wing conservatives as a very dangerous group. Those conservatives regard the left-wing or progressive political and social activist groups in the South as followers of North Korea and communism, and these groups soon became objects of hate that need to be eliminated. Progressive groups are defined as dangerous groups that deny the liberal democratic system in which conservative right-wing groups have strong faith, incite anti-American sentiment, and confuse society. Just as white supremacists treat Blacks or people of color with discrimination, prejudice, and violence, Korean conservatives and right-wingers show strong hatred toward progressives, such as leftists and forces that drive social change.

2.3   *Hate among Right-Wing Conservative Protestants*

Korea's conservative and right-wing Protestant groups further encourage emotional confrontation, such as terror, fear, hate, and anger against left or progressive groups in Korean society. Conservative right-wing Protestant Koreans are becoming one of the most important forces in expanding and reproducing hatred within Korean society today. They have emerged as political players who enthusiastically support conservative and right-wing governments in the worlds of Korean politics, society, education, and culture. Conservative right-wing Christian forces in South Korea strongly advocate anti-communist and anti-North Korea ideology because of their historical experience of escaping to the South after past suppression by the North Korean regime. Early Protestant missions in the Korean Peninsula, established in the late 19th century, were mainly concentrated in North Korea and actively engaged in missionary work. However, after division and the communist seizure of power in North Korea, they were subject to persecution, and the church had to flee to South Korea. Since then, the Korean church has been influenced by American evangelism, giving absolute support to the United States, which has become a sponsor of the Korean government (many pastors studied theology in the

United States). Since liberation, Korean Protestant Christianity, which has been influenced by the United States, has grown into a political force that supports the US and South Korean governments under an anti-communist banner.

Protestantism on the conservative right in Korea argues that religion should take the lead in preserving the safety of the nation. Its adherents claim that the church should strive for national security because religion can exist only when it opposes communism and protects liberal democracy that does not allow for religious freedom. It also calls for resistance against materialism that claims that religion is based on fiction, socialist ideas that believe in this doctrine, and pro-North Korean forces that follow the DPRK. Therefore, friendly state power is part of a right-wing conservative regime that advocates anti-communism and security. Their common propensity is anti-North Korea ideologies (anti-communism), anti-leftism (anti-mutualism and anti-socialism), close industrial ties (building friendly relations with market capitalism), and the solidification of Korea–US relations (guardians of the gospel and the liberal democratic system). For conservative right-wing Protestant Christians, the state order of liberal democracy is mixed with religious salvation.[6] They believe that liberal democracy and capitalist industrialization are necessary conditions for the growth of the church. They refer to "the northern lands that abandoned God" as the last missionary site, showing a hostile and Cold War attitude toward the North's ruling forces.

In addition to anti-communism and anti-progressive government movements, they define "religious pluralism" and "acceptance of homosexuality" as heresies and explicitly discriminate against sexual minorities. They constantly condemn comprehensive anti-discrimination laws pursued by liberal governments and attempts to incorporate them into constitutional amendments. They completely reject the legislation of the Comprehensive Anti-Discrimination Act. They use strategies to portray homosexuality advocacy groups as pro-North Korean leftists, which threaten the general public. They claim that homosexuals are dangerous beings who threaten and destroy social order, and encourage feelings of fear, terror, hatred, and anger.

---

6 However, it does not make it a national religion, like the British or Russian Orthodox Church. And they do not have symmetrical power with the state. Religions in Korea are still subordinate to state power.

3 Intergenerational Struggle for Recognition and Emotional Confrontation

3.1 *From Collectivism to Individualism*

Korean society is described as being dominated by collectivist culture based on Confucian traditions or associationism. A collectivist culture based on associationism (family, school ties, cronyism, etc.) has somewhat suppressed the autonomy and worldview of "individuals". Of course, collectivism and individualism have coexisted in all societies, but scholars have tended to differentiate between the collectivist traditions of Eastern civilization and the individualistic traditions of Western civilization. In the Eastern tradition, loyalty toward the monarch or ruler has been emphasized, rather than individuals (people or citizens), and in Western cases, the rights and obligations of citizens have been emphasized under individual social contracts. In East Asian societies, where the central government developed early on, totalitarian collectivist relations developed along with hierarchical bureaucratic societies, whereas relations of individual autonomy have developed in the West, which experienced local autonomy and decentralized feudalism. In any society, collectivism and individualism have served as centripetal and centrifugal forces. However, as "individualism", which has been based on individual rights and obligations since modern times, has developed in Western society, individualistic lifestyles have definitely become dominant in Western society.

In the case of Korean society, the traditional model was one of family-based collectivism. Both the family as a physical group in the private sector and the state as a cultural group in the public sector were consistently structured according to the values of Confucian loyalty. The most important value of Confucianism was filial piety toward the head of the family, and the extended form of filial piety was the devotion to the head of state. The family managed organizational support, was arranged hierarchically, and served as a center for economic activities through family businesses, and as a venue for religious ceremonies through ancestral rites.[7] These principles extend to the state, and the state and family have mutually consistent types of principles. For a long time, Korean society has strongly maintained such family-oriented collectivism. The family-based collectivist culture created a society still present in the organizational culture of schools, administrative agencies, and companies, namely, a highly connected society.

---

7 Weber referred to such a Confucian-centered country as a patrimonial state (a private dynamic surely existed in the patriarchalism of such patrimonial states).

Today, of course, familyism is rapidly losing its force. The scope of the family is so reduced that nuclear families consisting of one or two children are dominant. It is difficult to find the culture of familyism, which was observed in cases in which people would gather as a unit of relatives during ancestral rites or holidays. In addition, the concept of lifelong work has become less prevalent due to the fragmented labor market and restructuring in the late industrial society, and the degree of family-based commitment (obsession) to the organization has rapidly diminished. Society becomes rapidly differentiated and individualized as citizens' interests diversify. Patriarchal culture, such as family and organization (company), is losing its relevance, and contract-based relationships are becoming dominant. In other words, the collectivist culture based on cronyism is rapidly diminishing. It is no exaggeration to say that the values and lifestyles of the younger generation are based on anonymous individualism. As U. Beck pointed out, the phenomenon of "personalization" is rapidly progressing, which refers to the emergence of a liberated individual who pursues his or her own choices, decisions, and anonymous freedom, and to the simultaneous emergence of a fragmented individual who has lost social solidarity.

In the transition from collectivism to individualism, generational conflicts and emotional confrontations have taken many forms. Intergenerational conflicts and confrontations are universal and ubiquitous phenomena that exist in any society or any era. However, the generational conflict in Korean society seems to have had very hostile and exhausting consequences. There is a pattern of struggle between generations over values and ideologies as well as over material distribution and the geography of the political system. Rather than acknowledging each other's generations, they often blame each other and engage in a conflict accompanied by feelings of hostility and hatred. Older generations, who have spared no effort to raise their children, want to be respected and recognized by their children's generation, while young people who want to enjoy the new values and lifestyles perceive the older generation's lifestyle as a tedious, clichéd obstacle, and they try to tear it down.

The younger generation mocks the older generation, who embody anti-communist ideology as a form of faith, by using various slang terms. The older generation also serve as objects of hatred, disparaged as "old man insects" (-*chung*) on subway free rides and mocked for the various benefits that they receive through welfare services for the elderly. The members of the older generation are characterized as unproductive, inefficient, and in need of quick liquidation as a stumbling block to social progress. On the other hand, today's young people are considered to be selfish individualists. The term "gnawing pathologies" is used to describe their influence on the family, ethnicity, and national foundation that the older generation built with passion and sacrifice.

They are thought to have no awareness of history and society. They are considered "weak, vulnerable and selfish individualists".

The older generation in Korea has lived by prioritizing groups over individuals and considering the value of the collective community of family, organization, ethnicity, and nation as more valuable than individuals. However, members of today's younger generation place a higher value on individualistic values. They tend to evaluate the validity and justification, wrongs or rights, and desirability and undesirability of collective behavior based on the new individualistic standard of life that was scarcely evident among older generations. The older generation in Korea is the generation that was nurtured and grew up under poverty, patriarchy, rapid industrialization, and dictatorship. Their "bodies" are at the heart of Confucian hierarchical traditions emphasizing the Confucian will and gender specificity (actually discrimination), the colonial heritage of authoritarian nationalism, and family-centered values. Above all, anti-communism, which was justified by the division of war, the fear of war, and fierce hatred and hostility toward North Korea, was implicated. Their bodies embody a sense of obedience to patriarchal order that is different from that of today's younger generation. They are a generation that has learned collectivism that puts family before the individual, and organizations and countries before the personal.[8] They are a generation with a moral view that regards the value of production and saving, rather than consumption, as virtue, neglects leisure, and respects labor ethics. They are also a generation in which individual rights have not been "respected", while universal values such as freedom and equality have been suppressed in the process of state industrialization.

However, the experience of the younger generation is quite different; in short, their experience is summed up by the terms "digital, global sensitization" and "hybridization of various cultures". As early as the 1980s, Western society moved on from the existing "large-scale production/consumption" to so-called "flexibility", "post-Fordism", and "postmodernism".[9] Similar phenomena have developed very rapidly since the 1990s in Korean society. As Korean society entered an era of consumerism and information science and technology, it was rapidly reorganized. As information is exchanged online in real time and the whole world is connected, the era of "cyberspace" has

---

8 "Bombshell", signifying the military order in an absolute hierarchical subordination to achieve goals of a public group rather than personal history, symbolizes strong masculinity and drive.
9 Western society, encountering consumer capitalism in the 1960s and 1970s, discussed not only the exchange of goods but also that of images and information, that is, the signifier. See also Jean Baudrillard (1998).

emerged. Twenty-something and thirty-something Koreans were born and raised in this context.

Unlike their parents, who grew up in a hierarchical and male-dominated patriarchal culture, the 2030 generation grew up in a relatively equal and free atmosphere. As mentioned earlier, if members of their parents' generation were socialized and raised according to the values of their families, groups, organizations (companies), ethnic groups, and nations (anti-unification), they grew up in a context of more individualistic relationships and values. Individualism is a lifestyle that reflects on one's true nature and values and prioritizes one's understanding, thinking, and lifestyle over those of the group, and is closely related to liberal thinking. An individual is not a person who is buried in a group and who is dedicated to and sacrifices for the group. The main tenets of individualism are that an individual is the basic unit of life and has a self-designed view of life, and that the lifestyle choices of an individual as an autonomous judge and responsible being should be respected. The essence of individualism is that enabling the individual to claim this personal preference and orientation should be a national or social priority.

It seems that everyday individualistic thinking in Korean society has emerged entirely since the 1990s, when industrialization progressed and democratization actually took place. People in their 20s and 30s today were born and nurtured or socialized into an individualistic worldview. For them, the individual has the upper hand over the group. Individuals' adherence to the state is also loosening. The idea that an individual wants to be a "citizen" rather than a "person" and that the state should exist to advance individual happiness has increased their sense of individual rights vis-à-vis the nation. This individual consciousness has nothing to do with democratization and the growth of civil society.

If civil society is a society supported by contractual relationships of individuals who are relatively free to move, the association of blood, cronyism, and school ties, which are the foundation of traditional society, tends to weaken or collapse as civil society develops. Of course, familyism, regionalism, academicism, and cronyism are still visible enough to be considered "social capital", and society is transforming into civil society, an anti-cronyism society, and an individualistic society centered on the state, nation, and community.

3.2   *Awareness of Fairness and Relative Deprivation*

For today's youth, a "fairness" judgment based on individualism is an important indicator of life. Members of the older generation tend to situate the criterion of fairness within collective interests. In other words, even if one's private interests are sacrificed, the older generation will evaluate the group's growth as fair if the group can develop. However, members of the younger generation tend to first evaluate the fairness of the group according to their interests. In other words, the situation in which one has to yield one's interests is not fair. No matter how important a group's interests, justifications, or causes are, they cannot be accepted if individual desires are undermined or thwarted by collective values. For example, the older generation takes it for granted for reasons of national unity and unification that the two Koreas participate in the International Olympic Games as one team. They say that individuals have no choice but to sacrifice themselves for the future of the group of people and countries. However, young people think differently. While conflict on the Korean Peninsula between the United States, North Korea, and South Korea was at its height in 2018, the two governments unified the women's ice hockey team during the PyeongChang Winter Olympics. The older generation welcomed this, but young people responded with aloofness. The prevailing opinion was that it was unfair and unacceptable that individual athletes who had endured hard training to participate in the Olympics should sacrifice themselves in the pursuit of the formation of a single national team. Young people with strong individualistic values find it difficult to accept someone receiving preferential treatment, unlike themselves. They are more sensitive to military service, employment, and educational opportunities in Korean society. Celebrities who avoided military service were immediately pushed into the abyss; aristocratic labor groups who were employed through succession received harsh criticism; and society showed strong opposition at the mere sign of special admission through family background.[10]

3.3 The Absence and Disregard of Intergenerational Recognition

Human beings realize the meaning of existence through mutual recognition in their relationships with others. Despite various problems and anxieties, Korea is also praised as a successful country that has achieved both industrialization and democratization in the shortest time among the so-called Third World countries. Through global domination of some high-tech industrial products, such as semiconductors and smartphones, the capacity of Korean society to industrialize has been recognized worldwide, and Korea has recently boasted a high level of democracy through peaceful candlelight vigils and the impeachment of incompetent and corrupt regimes. Moreover, the Korean Wave, including K-Pop, which is beloved by young people worldwide, is an unimaginable

---

10   Amid the vortex of industrialization, every Korean, who had a great desire for the upward social mobility, has embodied the desire to become equal through career advancement. Hogeun Song called this phenomenon "the habitus of equality" Song (2006).

phenomenon for the older generation of Koreans.[11] This series of images of Korea gives great pride to Koreans, especially the older generation, who have long been obsessed with the inferiority complex linked to their "weak status". Born in the poorest country after World War II, the older generation, who grew up in the soil of division, war, poverty, and dictatorship, wants to be recognized for their sweat and hard work. However, such aspirations lead them to express anger and remorse because of ignorance by the young generation.[12]

Meanwhile, it may be natural for the younger generation to see an "accomplished society" in its various aspects. The weary life of the older generation is only a page in fossilized history. The members of the younger generation were born and grew up in an era when Korea was already ranked as an advanced country, in an era when information and communication developed, when the Korean Wave dominated the world's pop culture, and when consumption and leisure-ism dominated the ethics of production and labor. Rather, they are anxious about the infinite competition in the neoliberal era; inequality that cracks the foundation of society; relative deprivation, polarization, unemployment, and frustration both with the reality of not being rewarded commensurately with their effort and with the reality of competition in comparison with others; and stress over having to achieve at least an average quality of life. For some young generations expressing cynical hostility, Korea is seen as "Hell Joseon". Young generation members with a developed individual consciousness regard collectivism and the patriarchal culture of the older generation as a legacy that must be liquidated.[13] The recent "feminism" phenomenon in

---

11   The enthusiasm of young people around the world, in Asia and South America, as well as in Western Europe, for Hallyu, especially K-Pop, is beyond comprehension.
12   Negative emotions, such as hostility, disgust, and anger, however, are not exclusively shared among young people. Members of older generations who think they are not socially recognized also express strong hostility and anger. Over the past decade, the suicide rate in Korean society has been marked by far as the highest among OECD countries, and suicide of the older generation is leading in the infamous high rank. In addition, as of 2017, the poverty rate for the elderly older than 65 years in Korea was 45.7%, implying that half of the elderly live in poverty. Korea also ranks at the top among OECD member countries. Korean society has been considered to have strong Confucianism of filial piety and the Confucian philosophical ideology of filial piety and "gentlemanship" (敬老思想). Foreign missionaries in the 19th century described Joseon as "a paradise for the elderly". The fact that the suicide of the elderly is rapidly increasing in this country reflects how quickly society is experiencing social disintegration.
13   The collective communality of the older generation engulfs individuals and is considered as having a strong patriarchal tendency in which the rights of social minorities, such as women, the disabled, and LGBT individuals are not respected. Furthermore, the mindset of the older generation, waving the *Taegeukgi* in front of the Seoul City Hall and shouting for anti-communism, is so heterogeneous that they cannot accept it.

Korean society, which is more powerful than in any other country in the world, is not irrelevant.

4 Moral Sentiment and Empathy

In Korean society, anxiety and fear are typical emotions that flow through generations.[14] Fear is sometimes used as a political tactic of a particular force. Some political groups use fear to gain the legitimacy of control and to control their citizens. Citizens who have embodied fears arising from historical events, such as war, slaughter, and terrorism, or from such a periodic situation as unemployment, dismissal, and competition, agree with the dominant strategy of these political groups of enabling hegemony.[15] In other words, the "politics of fear" is carried out. The fear of historical events is imprinted in the bodies of older generations who have experienced division and war. Meanwhile, members of the younger generation exposed to the infinitely competitive system of neoliberalism are fearful of their future, including going to school, employment, and unstable employment. These fears can also take the form of feelings of anger and hostility toward others.

Conflicts caused by ideological confrontation in a divided country and tensions between generations are deepening. Simply put, both social solidarity and trust between me and the other are necessary, and this requires mutual communication between groups of various interests. In Western society, thinkers such as Habermas and Rawls emphasized overlapping consensus and deliberate democracy through communication in civil society. Social solidarity is possible in a republican system based on civil morality, tolerance and consideration, respect and duty for the community, participation, and civic economy. Therefore, what are the feelings that make such solidarity possible? In brief, I would refer to the motivation to enable social solidarity as moral sentiment. Moral sentiments, in a word, enable reflection, and as an emotion composed through reflection, "sympathy" lies at the core. Sympathy acts as a

---

14 According to a survey, in the face of the COVID-19 outbreak, Koreans are surrounded by a higher level of fear than people in any other countries in the world. Korean society has a memory of authoritarian regime, but unlike other Asian countries, such as China and Singapore, where the state implemented totalitarian controls, the Korean government did not choose lockdown. The voluntary consent of civil society to the government's quarantine measures without lockdown is also related to that: due to the internalized fear.

15 Hegemony in this sense is a term coined by Antonio Gramsci to mean domination based on the consent of the ruled.

motive for action for the establishment of a "social solidarity" that can be considered the basis of reciprocal exchange or a net exchange.

Simply put, empathy is "an emotion to recognize and regenerate the feelings, attitudes, and situations that the other feels from the other's perspective through imagination or being in the others' shoes". Empathy has the methodological nature of social science (i.e., hermeneutics) as well as the ethical nature of the understanding of others and empathy. Moral sentiments can be seen as "a type of empathy that is recognized as appropriate after understanding the behavior of me and others from the standpoint of a third-party bystander". Such empathy is a moral criterion for judging right or wrong, or acceptance and non-acceptance. Adam Smith seems to be explaining the adequacy of empathy as a key element of moral sentiments. Moral feelings are ultimately emotions that arise from reflecting on others, which are based on "sympathy", including imagination and being in others' shoes.[16]

Such moral sentiments are a cognitive force that can achieve mutual "trust and solidarity" of humans in the form of "I–the other–I–the other", and they are a force that drives judgment and practice.[17] Morality is not only an understanding of the other through imaginative empathy for the other but also a conscience that rebukes the other and oneself for violating the standards of social justice and a feeling that incites public anger for contradiction, poverty, and irrational power. In other words, moral sentiments are feelings that make people feel angry at acts that are contrary to justice and shame at violations of justice.[18] This moral sentiment forms the basis of social solidarity.

The traditional Confucian principles of the East include the potential for sympathetic reflection today, in other words, the elements of moral sentiment necessary for social solidarity. The basis of Confucian consensus is Seo (恕), which is defined as "understanding the other based on their situation". Among Confucian ideologies, the greatest virtue is humanity, and one of the

---

16 Adam Smith seems to explain well the proper line of empathy as the core of moral emotion. See Smith (2009).

17 Here we need to pay special attention to solidarity. There are various types of solidarity, such as kinship-based ties based on intimacy, as in relationships with family and friends, community solidarity in regions or organizations, and national solidarity. I will leave the in-depth discussion of solidarity to be a future task, but here I would like to point out solidarity at the community level through anonymous relationships. See Kang (2012), Zoll (2008), Crow (2002), etc.

18 The emotion of introspection is the root of moral emotions. The values of Confucianism, "Seo" (恕) and "Shuoji Mind" (羞惡之心), are the basic emotions of moral emotion. I have already traced the genealogy to Adam Smith's moral sentiment theory and Durkheim's moral passion in the paper "Moral Emotions: The Solidarity of Debt, Gratitude, and Guilt" (2012).

key elements that makes up humanity is "*Seo*". *Seo* is used in conjunction with sincerity or loyalty, which also refer to universal moral norms.[19] Let us discuss this in more detail. In Confucianism's notion that everyone is imbued with the logic of the universe, or *do*, the position of emphasizing the other as the same person as myself is well expressed.[20] Human beings have four basic emotions, namely, compassion, shame, sympathy, and ignorance, which are clues to their humanity, and many of them considered benevolence as the best emotion. Benevolence consists of filial piety, brotherhood, loyalty, and forgiveness; among them, filial piety is considered the most important. Filial piety is known to look through the spirit of Confucianism, meaning that it looks through everything with one reason, which forms the basis of Confucianism (一以貫之). In short, the most basic emotion of understanding the other in Confucianism is filial piety. Filial piety, or *Chung*, refers to genuineness and sincerity in dealing with others with honesty and sincerity, rather than the unconditional obedience to the king or commitment to the state. The letter "*Chung*" means to "hold onto the center" (中), which refers to *do*, without change. Blind loyalty to the king, parents, and friends does not fall under this. Confucius says, "Always think of *chung* (忠) when you speak (言思忠)".

The idea of benevolence in Confucianism is that tolerance, imitation, and consideration for others is a good practice. Further, benevolence refers to the abandonment of self-interest. When asked what benevolence is, Confucius replied, "I give up my self-interest and pursue public purpose". Confucius says that if you cannot be moral, what is the use of examples, and what formal examples are needed without sincerity, namely, understanding and accepting the other as a priority of inner virtue (truth, faithfulness, and virtue)? The principle of *Neunggeunchibi* (能近取譬, learning from up close) is the practice of benevolence, which is to think of others (*chugigeupin*, 推己及人) and not make others do what they hate (己所不欲, 勿施於人). Benevolence is not far away, but near, and *chugigeupin* is the *do* of filial piety. The intent of *do* of filial piety is easier said than done. This is because humans have an ulterior motive and put their own interests first. When you say, "Don't let others do what you don't want to do", you say, "If you want to stand up, let others do what you want to do", and this communication is possible through suppressing self-interest (Confucius 2005: 122).

---

19   Various scholars discuss the relationship between the two (Hong 2016; Hwang 2014; Lee 2010; Lee and Kang 2004).
20   Buddhism also believes that the spirit of Buddha exists in everyone. Daoist thinkers claim that the Dao (道) exists everywhere.

Communication between groups of various values is essential to overcome negative emotions such as ideological conflicts or urgent social changes in Korean society caused by division and the Cold War, and the fear, anger, and hatred that cause or amplify this conflict. There is no need to reach a particular agreement (and it is almost impossible for everyone to reach a conclusion that is satisfactory), but at least through communication society can tentatively reach a "minimum co-distributive agreement". The process of trying to reach this agreement is the process of democracy and the establishment of mutual trust and solidarity in this society. It would be no exaggeration to say that the virtue of civil society is such a spirit of communication. Moral sentiments based on empathy for others will be an alternative for healing today's conflicted society. The traditional Confucian principles of Korean society contain many discussions on reflection and empathy. This is why a modern reinterpretation of Confucian principles has become more important.

References

Barbalet, Jack. 2009. *The Sociology of Emotion*. Translated into Korean by Hyungshin Park. Seoul: Ihak sa Co.

Baudrillard, Jean. 1998. *La societe de consummation*. Translated into Korean by Sangyul Lee. Seoul: Moonyea Co.

Bourdieu, P. 1990. *The Logic of Practice*. Palo Alto, CA: Stanford University Press.

Bourdieu, P. 2005. *Distinction*. Translated into Korean by Jongchul Choi. Saemulgeoul Co.

Calhoun, C., and R.C. Solomon. 1984. *What Is an Emotion? Classic Readings in Philosophical Psychology*. Oxford: Oxford University Press.

Confucius. 2005. *The Analects*. Seoul: Hongik Co. (In Korean.)

Crow, G. 2002. *Social Solidarities: Theories, Identities and Social Change*. Buckingham: Open University Press.

Goodwin, J., J.M. Jasper, and F. Polletta, eds. 2009. *Passionate Politics: Emotions and Social Movements*. Chicago, IL: University of Chicago Press.

Hong, Sungmin. 2016. *Emotion and Morality: The Moral and Emotional Theory of Neo-Confucianism*. Seoul: Somyung Co. (In Korean.)

Hwang, Taeyeon. 2014. *Hermeneutics of Emotions and Empathy*. Seoul: Cheongye Co. (In Korean.)

Kang, Sootaeck. 2012. *Solidarism: Overcoming the Monadism*. Paju: Hangilsa Co. (In Korean.)

Kim, Wang-Bae. 2019. *Emotion and Society: Korean Society Through the Lens of Emotion*. Paju: Hanul Academy Co. (In Korean.)

Lee, Hyangjoon. 2010. "Seo (恕), Moral Imagination". *Bumhan Philosophical Society* 57: 33–60. (In Korean.)
Lee, Sangik, and Jungin Kang. 2004. "Comparative Analysis of Eastern and Western Political Legitimacy". *The Korean Review of Political Thoughts* 9: 83–110. (In Korean.)
Lupton, Deborah. 2016. *The Emotional Self: A Sociocultural Exploration*. Translated into Korean by Hyunshin Park. Paju: Hanul Academy.
Park, Hyungshin, and Soonam Jeong. 2015. *How Does Emotion Drive Society?* Paju: Hangil Co. (In Korean.)
Smith, Adam. 2009. *Moral Sentiment*. Translated into Korean by Seil Park and Kyung-gook Min. Seoul: Bibong Co.
Solomon, R.C. 2008. "The Philosophy of Emotions". In *Handbook of Emotions*, edited by M. Lewis, Jannet M. Haviland-Jones and Lisa F. Barrett. New York: Guilford Press.
Song, Hogeun. 2006. *The Egalitarianism, Habits of Heart in Korea*. Seoul: Samsung Institute for Economy. (In Korean.)
Woo, Shilha. 2012. *The Worldview of Trichotomous*. Goyang: Sonamu Co. (In Korean.)
Zoll, Rainer. 2008. *Was ist Solidaritat heute?* Translated into Korean by Sunghwan Choi. Paju: Hanul Academy Co.

SECTION 13

Cities, Migration, and Work

∴

CHAPTER 54

Beyond "Post-Western" Urban Studies

Machimura Takashi

Since sociology was established as an academic discipline in the first half of the 19th century, it has been constructed as a system of knowledge that has tried to respond to the emergence of social problems and the transformation of social structure in modern society. In these historical processes, sociology first pursued an understanding of the wholeness of society, then, following an increasing division of society, it cut out more specific research subjects from a differentiated society. Focusing on each of them, sociology has developed subfields with relatively independent research themes. In addition, various research methods specific to each field have been developed and applied to other related fields.

1   Migrating Workers Made Modern Cities

The theme assigned to this chapter is cities, migration, and labor. At first glance, these may look different and disjointed. However, as modernization has progressed on a global scale, major changes, such as industrialization and/or urbanization, accompanied it in parallel. Capitalism has brought about a dramatic increase in productivity through the formation of world markets and imperialist colonial rule. More laborers were released from feudalism and other traditional status systems and began to move in search of new work opportunities. Then, a huge number of workers were rapidly concentrated into limited production sites.

In the advanced regions that achieved industrialization early, many large-scale metropolises that were unprecedented in history soon appeared. With the widespread use of relatively inexpensive mass transportation due to the energy revolution, a huge segment of the population began to migrate on a global scale. International migration across continents created agglomerations of workers around the world. The development of the capitalist economy had caused more severe inequality in economic conditions among different classes, especially in large cities. While the richest people in the world lived in these big cities, a huge amount of the disadvantaged population remained poor.

In addition, the international movement of labor gave rise to racial/ethnic, religious, and linguistic diversity in those cities. A large amount of the population came from lands under colonial rule or old imperial countries far from Europe or North America. The cultural variety of the population increased dramatically in cities with large numbers of migrants. Different classes, different racial and ethnic groups, and different religious factors intersected in an urban setting, and as a result, novel social structures were produced. It was the birth of the modern metropolis.

The accumulated changes in labor, cities, and migration, interlocking with each other, had formed a great transformation of modernization, which crossed over different spheres. Understanding and explaining both visible and invisible structures behind phenomena such as new forms of labor, cities, and migration became an important intellectual challenge in the coming era. Empirical methods for describing and recording people's lives and labor in the actual field of the city were developed by government officials, practical scientists, businesspeople, etc., who were interested in social issues. Collected quantitative data were accumulated in the form of statistics. From such tasks, various intellectual practices started to comprehensively elucidate the general mechanism of structural formation. The great pioneers such as Engels, Le Prey, Charles Booth, and others paved the way for numerous subsequent research attempts.

Sociology was one of the new intellectual disciplines thus born in the 19th century. Many of the major concepts and analytical frameworks in sociology to this day have also been created through the historical process of these intellectual challenges.

2   Unbalanced Structure in Knowledge-Making

However, social change since the 19th century has been extremely unbalanced on a global scale. Modern technological and economic innovations began in Western Europe and spread to North America. In the form of capitalism and imperialism, their influence spread further around the world. Huge amounts of wealth had been accumulated in Western Europe and North America, where highly developed industrial societies and huge cities soon emerged. Through imperialism and colonial rule, the world was overwhelmed by asymmetrical power structures. In this process, areas that were previously outside of the capitalist world system were incorporated into the periphery inside of that system, in which a society with a subordinate structure was gradually formed. Asia was also included in such a periphery of the capitalist world system.

Asymmetrical relationships were built not only in terms of economy and politics, but also in terms of cultural production. The knowledge that was used to describe and analyze the changes in modernization was often based on Western experiences. The concepts formed in the core countries of the West were propagated to other parts of the world through imported books, hired foreigners, and international students. In the peripheral areas, people were required to make difficult attempts to apply the concepts of Western origin to their vernacular world and translate those into the local native language.

Due to the large gaps that exist between different cultures, it was essentially impossible to accurately represent local phenomena with Western concepts. Therefore, the custom of observing and expressing one's own society with a foreign concept always included a sense of incongruity. Such intellectual experiences had been widely shared in the peripheral area since the 19th century. Japan is not an exception. However, the work of translating different ideas into the native language resulted in enriching the linguistic world of that region. In addition, the translation into the local vernacular language has made it possible for far more readers to encounter different ideas than if those ideas had remained in foreign European languages. Increasing local readership often produced an important basis for endogenous development. The transmission and acceptance of foreign knowledge were not necessarily just a one-sided process of intellectual subordination.

However, when viewed as a whole, it cannot be denied that an intellectually asymmetrical structure was reproduced between the central part and the peripheral part of the world. Being able to make full use of terms and ideas of Western origin became an important intellectual resource for the peripheral elite and contributed to supporting their dominant bargaining position. By being translated into the local language, many inhabitants could gain a wealth of knowledge, but on the other hand, people were voluntarily incorporated into asymmetric intellectual structures in the form of readership.

Such an asymmetrical structure was no exception in the case of sociology, which had developed in Western Europe and North America. Concepts and theories developed in Western countries, which experienced industrialization and urbanization earlier than other regions, were transplanted into non-Western countries and applied widely there.

3   Historical Changes in Structure and Knowledge: The Case of Urban Studies

By the end of the 20th century, major changes happened in this asymmetrical structure in which Western Europe and North America dominated. Factors that brought about such a transformation were varied, such as the rapid economic

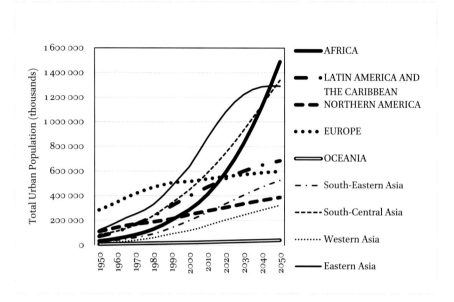

FIGURE 54.1　Urban population at mid-year, 1950–2050, by world region and Asian subregion (thousands)
Notes: The names and classifications of geographical areas follow those presented in the original data.
SOURCE: UNITED NATIONS, DEPARTMENT OF ECONOMIC AND SOCIAL AFFAIRS, POPULATION DIVISION (2018). WORLD URBANIZATION PROSPECTS: THE 2018 REVISION, ONLINE EDITION

growth of East Asia, the progress of globalization following the end of the Cold War, the rise of emerging economies in the world, the growing influence of the Islamic cultural sphere, and the continuing population growth in Global South. In the realm of economic activity, the Western-centric system has already disintegrated. However, asymmetrical structures still exist in terms of intellectual production and cognitive formation. Cultural lags in social change can be pointed out here. How should we deal with this cultural gap? Here is a great challenge which social sciences, including sociology, are facing.

Let's take a closer look at the history of the transformation of the relationship between structure and knowledge in urban studies. Figure 54.1 shows how the size of the world's urban population by region has changed since 1950. The trends from 2020 to 2050 are based on UN estimates. Asia is extremely vast, and the degree of urbanization varies greatly from area to area. Therefore, in the graph, the urban population of the Asian region is shown by dividing it into the subregions of Eastern Asia, Southeastern Asia, South-Central Asia, and Western Asia.

As this graph shows, from 1950 to 1980, Europe had the most populous region of urban residents. In addition, the urban population of North America was relatively high until the 1970s. Given the structure of the global distribution of the urban population, the modern urban experience certainly had major roots in Western Europe and North America. In that sense, it was not unreasonable for urban sociology to have made a full-scale appearance in Europe (e.g., G. Simmel et al.) and North America (e.g., Chicago School) in the early 20th century. Urbanization was one of the universal changes in modern times. However, at the same time, the modern urban phenomenon was also an event that emerged in a form strongly linked to the local characteristics of a specific limited area of Western Europe and North America.

Let's look at Figure 54.1 again. From the 1970s to the 1980s, changes began to occur in the global distribution of urban population. The urban population of South/Central Asia and Latin America surpassed that of North America. In East Asia, the urban population grew even more rapidly, surpassing that of Europe. During this period, Japan and countries such as the Four Asian Tigers (Korea, Taiwan, Hong Kong, Singapore) were entering an era of rapid urbanization with the progress of industrialization. In Latin America and South Asia, overpopulation was concentrated in the still underdeveloped primate cities, where huge slums formed.

The theory of dependent urbanization, which investigated the strong influences of former ruling nations and multinational corporations, widening disparities within the country, and the development of the informal economy, had gained a strong explanatory power about the experiences of those cities (Frank 1979). On the other hand, the leading metropolises of Western Europe and North America faced fierce competition with emerging countries and the overseas relocation of production bases, de-industrialization, and the decline of the city center, intensifying racial and ethnic conflicts, pollution, and environmental problems. Accumulated urban decline exacerbated the financial crisis of local governments aiming to solve these problems. In the developed countries of the West, urban crises became major policy issues.

The transformation of the subject matter of the city also influenced the academic institutions for studying the city as well. The Harvard–MIT Joint Center for Urban Studies was founded in 1959 jointly by Harvard University and the Massachusetts Institute of Technology. In the field of urban sociology, a political economy approach appeared in Western Europe and North America, influenced by critical thinkers such as H. Lefevbre, D. Harvey, and M. Castells. Soon it was to be called new urban sociology. The Research Committee 21 (RC21) on Sociology of Urban and Regional Development was established within the International Sociological Association in 1970. The *International Journal of*

Urban and Regional Research was first published in 1977 by researchers gathering at the RC21. Importantly, sociologists were not the only ones to gather in these groups and magazines. Members were interdisciplinary from the beginning, including representatives from sociology, geography, urban planning, political science, and economics. Researchers from Latin America, Asia, and Africa, albeit a minority then, also participated in these new challenges.

Fundamental changes had already occurred in Eurocentric urban studies. However, most researchers, beyond the differences between the core and the periphery, believed that they shared a universal subject of "city". Therefore, new intellectual challenges started from here, hoping for the creation of "global" urban studies.

4   The Urban Age of the Global East?

Global City, published by S. Sassen in 1991, looked at Tokyo as well as New York and London (Sassen 1991). The fact that Tokyo in the Far East is "lined up" in the metropolises of the old and new hegemons was regarded as the basis for the global structural transformation. In succession, many Chinese cities have achieved rapid growth. Megacities, whose main landscape is forested with skyscrapers, have emerged in East Asia, Southeast Asia, and South Asia. At the same time, the region with the largest urban population has moved from Europe to East Asia.

How should the experience of Asia be incorporated into urban studies that have for a long time been developed based on the experience of Europe and the United States? This task did not only mean expanding or shifting the scope of research from Europe/North America to Asia. There was historically an asymmetrical structure between Western and non-Western urban studies. Therefore, the shape of challenges to be overcome was not necessarily the same between the West and Asia.

For researchers doing work based on Asian experiences, the growing importance of Asian cities raised the dual challenges to be tackled. First, it meant that the Western concepts and theoretical frameworks on which they had long relied were no longer valid enough for the explanation of current situations. Thus, did they continue to use the same concept while modifying it, or did they explore a completely different concept? Second, however, the increasing importance of Asian cities does not simply lead to the need for Asia's own independent urban theory. With the progress of globalization at large, capitalism and culture of Western origin have already spread widely in Asia and are deeply incorporated into its domestic urban structures. The Asian elements that were once lost are closely connected again and articulated with the Western elements in a more complex way, rather than simply destroying or opposing each other (Hill and Kim 2000). Expressions such as *multilayered* and *coexistence* are not accurate enough for valid explanation, so various inventive words and works are being produced to overcome such limitations (for instance, Simone and Pieterse 2017).

Researchers at the core of the world system have also been required to change in other ways. If the Western-centric system has been distorted, transformations, including the redirection of "de-Westernization", cannot be avoided. For instance, the concepts of world cities and global cities were one of the leading forms of de-Westernization. Probably it is not a coincidence that J. Friedmann, M. Castells, and S. Sassen, who led this theory in North American universities, were all researchers with intellectual roots in Europe (especially its peripheral countries, not the United Kingdom, Germany, and France). Subsequently, postcolonial urban studies were developed by researchers, especially those with strong ties to the former colonies and diasporas. The "de-Western" reconstruction of knowledge is sought not only in the non-Western world but especially in the Western world (Molotch and Ponzini 2019).

Today, contemporary urban phenomena, such as megacities or skyscrapers, are more frequently seen in the Global East or Global South than in the West. Is it possible to use the concepts born in the Western context in cities outside the West? Neoliberalism (Doucette and Park 2019; Park, Hill and Saito 2011) and gentrification (Machimura 2021; Shin, Lees and López-Morales 2016; Waley 2016) became the focal concepts in such a controversy.

It is not appropriate to be caught up in dichotomized ideas such as the West or the East. Because first, Western elements have already been incorporated as an important part of the process of change in the non-Western world. Second, the non-Western world is diverse, and the simple contrast scheme of Western vs. non-Western has already collapsed.

However, not all Western wisdom that has been dominant until now has been abandoned as a thing of the past. In that sense, raising issues such as post-Westernism is not always an appropriate expression in that it still has a strong remnant of a naive dichotomy. At the same time, overemphasizing the significance of Asian cultural uniqueness and traditions is not only unrealistic, but rather leads to ideological fallacy. When exploring the themes of cities and labor, it is necessary, I think, that we respect basic human rights, equality and diversity, democratic governance, and a sustainable environment, while keeping both settlers and migrants in mind.

5 Conclusion: Beyond "Post-Western" Urban Studies

As Figure 54.1 shows, East Asia's top urban population position will soon be replaced by African cities. Now that the urban impact of the Global South has become so significant, it is not appropriate to limit "non-Western" to the context of Asia. Due to such global transformations, it is necessary to reconstruct the geographical frameworks of urban studies (for instance, McDonald 2008).

With the expansion of cyberspace represented by the Internet, the form of people's ordinary connections has changed significantly. A decade ago, the first stage of fashion and cutting-edge modes was in a crowded city. But now it's the world of the Internet. In a society where changes are accelerating along the "space of flows", cities are rather steadily starting to "delay".

However, even in a society that speeds any part of it up, not all factors are necessarily accelerated. Instead, a society emerges in which the elements that increase speed coexist with those that remain "slow". Virtual elements repeatedly collide with material elements that have a long tail. At the same time, the virtual element is still supported heavily by the material element.

Cities are beginning to have the characteristics of a dull "place" that remains rugged in a smooth "space". The modern city, which had been seen as having both robustness and functionality as a reasonably calculated built environment, was still not free of basic vulnerabilities. We have been reminded of this through events such as terrorism, disasters, and pandemics. Frustration and fear of risky cities can potentially increase the desire for full control and surveillance.

Today, we are reaching a stage where we can expect possible consequences of the first half of the 21st century. How do we capture the process of restructuring cities, labor, and mobility, starting from the difference between the West and the non-West, and then beyond that? At the end of the paper, let's summarize the characteristics that should be confirmed when proceeding with this work.

First, because of rapid urbanization progressing in China and the Global South, particularly Africa, urban studies are required to consider the planetary-scale environmental changes of the Earth (Brenner 2013; Lees, Shin and López-Morales 2016). The global trends surrounding the construction of megacities are accelerating changes in the environment on a global scale. Climate changes and other environmental issues are preparing a basic background for future city building.

Second, as the state's regulatory power declined relatively, various attempts by individuals, capital, and companies to search for alternative territory for activity erupted in the form of globalization. It is becoming more and more difficult to distinguish between those who migrate and those who settle. While various spatial scales are being generated in layers, the significance of the "city" as an activity unit that is relatively autonomous from the nation is reconsidered as a unit with resources, infrastructure, and historical identity.

Third, however, the rise of cyberspace has forced major changes in the functions and meanings of real cities. Cities are playing the role of an interface between real and virtual spaces. But at the same time, the city as a physical being has not lost its role as a final place of residence for human beings. Based on this duality, the re-creation of the "city" format itself has become a global common issue.

Fourth, cities around the world are full of poverty and disparities, old infrastructure and buildings, aging populations, and serious risk and destruction problems (environment, disasters, terrorism, wars, pandemics, etc.). These problems are becoming even more unevenly distributed than before. Disparity still exists between developed and underdeveloped countries, or Western and non-Western countries. However, for instance even in underdeveloped countries, there exists a wide disparity between the core group and the peripheral group inside of the city. More elaborate efforts in each location are required for sociological investigation.

And finally, in the face of historical and civilizational trials, cities are the setting a stage for new experiments and challenges to form democratic governance for better problem solving. The existence of a public space open to a wide range of people in a city becomes more essential for such a project (Hou and Knierbein 2017). Can 21st-century cities provide people with the conditions to resist narrow populism, exclusive nationalism, and growing authoritarianism? For current urban studies, this task has fundamental importance around the world and particularly in Asia (Daniere and Douglass 2009).

References

Brenner, N., ed. 2013. *Implosions/Explosions: Towards a Study of Planetary Urbanization*. Berlin: JOVIS Verlag.

Daniere, Amrita, and Mike Douglass, eds. 2009. *The Politics of Civic Space in Asia: Building Urban Communities*. Oxon: Routledge.

Doucette, Jamie, and Bae-Gyoon Park, eds. 2019. *Developmentalist Cities? Interrogating Urban Developmentalism in East Asia*. Leiden: Brill.

Frank, A.G. 1979. *Dependent Accumulation and Underdevelopment*. New York, NY: Monthly Review Press.

Friedmann, J. 1987. "The World City Hypothesis". *Development and Change* 17 (1): 69–83.

Hill, R.C., and J.W. Kim. 2000. "Global Cities and Developmental States: New York, Tokyo and Seoul". *Urban Studies* 37 (12): 2167–2196.

Hou, Jeffrey, and Sabine Knierbein, eds. 2017. *City Unsilenced: Urban Resistance and Public Space in the Age of Shrinking Democracy*. New York, NY: Routledge.

Lees, Loretta, Hyun Bang Shin, and Ernesto López-Morales. 2016. *Planetary Gentrification*. Cambridge: Polity Press.

Machimura, Takashi. 2021. "Gentrification Without Gentry in a Declining Global City? Vertical Expansion of Tokyo and Its Urban Meaning". *International Journal of Japanese Sociology* 30: 6–22.

McDonald, D.A. 2008. *World City Syndrome: Neoliberalism and Inequality in Cape Town*. New York, NY: Routledge.

Molotch, Harvey, and Davide Ponzini. 2019. *The New Arab Urban: Gulf Cities of Wealth, Ambition, and Distress*. New York, NY: New York University Press.

Ong, Aihwa. 2006. *Neoliberalism as Exception: Mutations in Citizenship and Sovereignty*. Durham, NC: Duke University Press.

Park, Bae-Gyoon, Richard Child Hill, and Asato Saito, eds. 2011. *Locating Neoliberalism in East Asia: Neoliberalizing Spaces in Developmental States*. Chichester: Wiley-Blackwell.

Sassen, Saskia. 1991. *The Global City: New York, London, Tokyo*. Princeton, NJ: Princeton University Press.

Shin, Hyun Bang, Loretta Lees, and Ernesto López-Morales. 2016. "Introduction: Locating Gentrification in the Global East". *Urban Studies* 53 (3): 455–470.

Simone, Abdou Maliq, and Edgar Pieterse. 2017. *New Urban Worlds: Inhabiting Dissonant Times*. Cambridge: Polity Press.

Waley, Paul. 2016. "Speaking Gentrification in the Languages of the Global East". *Urban Studies* 53 (3): 615–625.

CHAPTER 55

Sociology of Migration and Post-Western Knowledge

Laurence Roulleau-Berger

1   Introduction

For over 20 years, European and Chinese sociologists have unanimously recognized that the migration issue has become a major scientific and political challenge. Internal migrations stretch across all sector-specific sociologies in China and international migrations have gradually become of central importance in European sociological theories. Both internal and international migrations reveal the forces of social, political, and economic change at work in increasingly complex, plural, and diverse contemporary societies affected by a threefold acceleration, globalization and regionalization of migratory movements. Chinese and French sociologists have defined common ground on a theoretical and methodological level organized around the migration issue (Li Peilin and Roulleau-Berger 2013; Roulleau-Berger and Liu Yuzhao 2021).

2   Structural Processes, Individuals, and Interactions

Chinese and French sociologists produce a civilizational and historical narrative more than narratives of societies in which inflections are not placed in the same place to think about the relations between structural processes, spaces, individual and collective experiences, subjectivities. If Chinese sociologists have largely focused in recent years on the analysis of social/economic structures and the State, their modes of analysis signal a shift in understanding the structure of the experience of social life, subjectivity, and emotions. If, during the last 20 years, French sociologists have increasingly developed theoretical alternatives between structures, agency and individuation, Chinese sociologists have developed a theoretical posture that increasingly articulates social structures, State, and individual experiences. In a large and heterogeneous Sino-French constructivist space, a mosaic one, young migrants and children of immigrants has been defined by her/his capacity to be an autonomous and reflexive Subject and to construct his/her experience but also to have emotions and feelings. It is clear in European and Chinese societies how important individual experiences are in the understanding that migrants as actors have of them, and how social structures in process and individual experiences are constantly learning about differentiated modes in the two contexts. Individuals here are also seen as experiencing migration both in their concrete existence linked to collective life and in their most intimate subjectivity.

Between structural processes and agency, the status of interactions is introduced via family and interpersonal relationships, for example with peers. French and Chinese sociologists use the concept of interpersonal relationship networks and family networks to understand the educational, professional, urban, and religious socialization processes of young descendants of immigrants or second-generation migrants. The question of intergenerational solidarities is raised in both contexts. In Chinese sociology the concept of *guanxi* (interactions) has played and still plays a central role, one that is more important than it is in French sociology. Chinese sociologists considered social interactions and *guanxis* to be at the heart of material, symbolic, and emotional exchange (Luo 2008; Luo and Yeh 2012).

French and Chinese sociologists focus on the dilemmas and identity discrepancies between "not being from here" and "not being from there" which characterize "inside strangers" (Missaoui 2003). However, in China the tension between rural and urban belonging produces scrambled identities, especially for those "left-behind children" who became "follow-up children". In Europe, identity reconfigurations are the result of the interplay between the inherited cultural or ethnic identities and the present identities. The analyses of French and Chinese sociologists show how migrants and descendants of migrants construct their identities from a multiplicity of situations, interactions, and belongings linked to multi-situated socialization spaces. And the more this multiplicity increases, the more the unity and continuity of the self are threatened, the more the registers of inequality multiply and the less easily the individual can be someone.

In France we apprehend the social life experience of young migrants and young children of immigrants through turning points or biographical bifurcations produced by institutions—such as the educational establishment—and work markets (Tucci 2021; Roulleau-Berger 2010, 2019). Meanwhile, the professional mobility of young Chinese migrants is apprehended through "zig-zag journeys" (Chen Chen 2021). The objective and subjective dimensions of biographical bifurcations constantly interact in the French perspective; for instance, social disqualification and/or ethnic discrimination influence individual subjective identities, the relationship with oneself and one's dignity, and vice versa. On Chinese side, in their objective dimension, turning points do not seem to take a central position in the analysis of the individuation processes of young Chinese migrants (Li Chunling 2013). In their subjective dimension, the individual and collective biographies have become blurred, the struggle of places and the class struggle become embedded in each other. Rural–urban migration groups have been floating at the edge of the mainstream society of cities, confronted with situations of uncertainty about their individual and social identity (Zhao Yeqin 2021).

The issue of emotions exists in both French and Chinese sociology of the individual. As Abdelmalek Sayad put it, understanding the migratory challenge entails apprehending the tension between illusions and sufferings, although it is presented in slightly different terms. Both Chinese and French sociologists emphasize humiliation, depression, despair, loneliness but they also agree on insecurity, anxiety, disillusionment, and loss of individual and collective aspirations (Li Chunling 2019; Roulleau-Berger 2021).

Chinese and European sociologists converge in the way of thinking together, migration, social differentiation and discrimination. In the two contexts, the less endowed migrants in terms of social capital and economic and symbolic resources are defined as subjected to the forces of political and economic measures in a context of hyper-competition, uncertainty and globalization. But Chinese sociologists are using the concepts of *social structures, interactions and guanxis, and individual strategies* (Li Peilin and Li Wei 2013) to understand the migratory experience in Chinese cities; they consider available networks of trust and community solidarities, the strategies to find social and spatial anchorage in economic spaces. And French sociologists are using the concepts of *structural processes, individuation and subjectivation, agency and capabilities*; for example, we have noticed a proliferation of biographical bifurcations in trajectories structured in the conjunction of professional mobility and spatial mobility, where migrants are using individual and collective capabilities.

3 Migration, Integration, and Segregation

The process of urban integration in sociology is often related to the question of migration that we will introduce here. First, the assimilation approach characterizing the Chicago School's studies of immigration (Park, Burgess and McKenzie 1925) described how migrants could use adaptation strategies to be settled in urban enclaves, then they would usually leave these places, be involved in competition for space with other social groups and develop their own social trajectory. Park and Burgess dealt with the concept of urban integration and segregation. The question of upward social mobility among second-generation migrant communities was broached: the assimilation theory initially showed how the children and grandchildren of migrants gradually acceded to the social statuses of the host society and that this process had an element of irreversibility about it.

Today in European cities Chicago's School's theory still could be mobilized to analyze some ascendant social trajectories of migrants, for example new transnational entrepreneurs and traders. But about children of immigrants Chicago's School's theory is not adapted. In the neighborhoods of European cities, particularly in the working-class suburbs of French cities, spatial, social and economic segregation have increased over the last twenty years. In 2011, young people of North African origin took more than eleven months to get their first job, compared with six months or seven months for those of French descent, and twenty-four months on average to access a stable employment contract, compared with fifteen months for those of French descent. After three years of active life, youths of North African origin occupied more precarious jobs than those of French descent. For children of immigrants, intergenerational mobility seems to be clearly organized and may give rise to "segmented assimilation" (Zhou 1999) that reflects the irregular, reversible, unexpected, multidimensional, and differentiated aspects of urban and economic integration (Roulleau-Berger 1999).

The Chicago School's theory still makes sense in certain situations to understand the process of social mobility of Chinese migrant workers (Li Peilin 2012; Li Chunling 2013) and also of new international migrants in big cities, for example, successive waves of Arab and sub-Saharan traders in Guangzhou (Liu 2013) and Yiwu. But this theory cannot be used to analyze the process of social disqualification for the new, less-qualified, young, internal migrants, who form a new urban underclass and experience a new poverty in "urban villages", the "ant colonies" (Lian Si 2012), or new urban villages which appear on the outskirts of megalopolizes; some of them are constrained to leave big cities and go back to their *laojia*. Secondly, young internal migrants graduates gain access to skilled jobs in Chinese mega-cities as technicians, executives in private or public Chinese enterprises and in international enterprises, but most of them remain migrants and are in situations of job and housing insecurity; they designate themselves as *beipiao* (nomads in Beijing). These young people, the majority of whom do not have an urban *hukou*, are victims of employment discrimination by local authorities: for example, a young graduate with a rural *hukou* cannot easily get to an urban job; young graduates are forced into informal jobs or situations of unemployment (Roulleau-Berger and Yan Jun 2017).

We can understand the assimilation's theory in China still is influent in urban sociology to analyze the urban process of integration and segregation.

In France some sociologists have been more focused on the tension between mobility, captivity and sedentarity (Tarrius 2000; Roulleau-Berger 2010). But in the two academic contexts, through the figure of *young internal migrant in China* and the figure of *the descendant of immigrant* in Europe theoretical continuities are located around the challenge to understand the complex urban life constructed on the oscillation between isolation, segregation and partial integration in the City. In European cities, social, ethnic, and economic boundaries as well as new urban hierarchies are appearing and producing diffracted inequalities and situations of injustice. So, we have to consider the intersectionality between spatial integration/segregation, socio-economic integration/segregation and ethnic integration/segregation.

Now in French urban sociology we are talking more and more about the "cosmopolitan condition" (Agier 2013); it means for new migrants—asylum seekers and refugees—the circulations produced by globalization impose experiences—rather ordeals—of national, ethnic, religious, linguistic, social, and cultural borders, resulting in a cosmopolitan condition in European cities. Confronted with recurring risk situations, menaces and uncertainty, the most threatened and exposed new migrants are compelled to cross a succession of borders where, each time, lives are exposed, put in danger, after having fled wars, the Taliban ... The most at risk migrants are then obliged to stay, for a relatively long time, in liminal situations in European cities that do not necessarily evolve towards stable situations.

4 Migration, Time, and Space

Space and time constitute social and structural dimensions to understand migrants' and immigrants' experiences (Wang Chunguang 2017). It is clear that among young Chinese migrants and the descendants of immigrants in Europe, this tension is exacerbated by the mobility that follows, intertwines, and interweaves ... in a plurality of spaces and temporalities. Chinese and French sociologists unknowingly contribute to the production of a paradigm of mobility starting from different migratory situations which allow the analysis of the paths of young Chinese migrants and young French children of immigrants. They show how spatial segregation in French society produces first and foremost immobilism, social captivity, and perhaps professional mobilities which can lead to social mobility. On the Chinese field they pay attention to the sequences and entanglements of spatial mobilities which articulate with professional mobilities, to the multiple social positionings which could produce social immobility for migrants from a place, from a city to another.

Space appeared as a global determining factor of social inequalities and as a factor both influencing and influenced by the dynamics between activities and groups of migrants and descendants of immigrants. It was noted that its double status constituted a constraint, but it also produced value related to social habits and the effects of competition among individuals. Migrants and descendants of migrants do not have access to the same urban spaces and territories, which are subjects of different hierarchies, related to a diversity of activities and a heterogeneity of populations. Some spaces seem more "segregated" than others because of the local extent of entangled and cumulative relegation processes (Grafmeyer 1994), very clearly in French cities and much less so in Chinese cities. Urban villages known as "ant tribes" in China (Lian Si 2009) can be compared to "cousin hoods" (Boubeker 1999). Both are entrances to the city, at once segregated and sources of sociability. The close notions of community of experience and of belonging to communities of migrants are used to show their collective identities. However, research shows that in China the *hukou* takes an active part in tracing physical and moral barriers inside the cities, whereas no such equivalent can be found for the descendants of immigrants in France. The *hukou* is defined in different chapters as a major element in accessing citizenship and the production of spatial and social inequalities. But with the accelerated development of household registration in China in recent years, the *hukou*'s effect regarding urban integration has gradually declined.

In Chinese and European cities, mobility can be in conflict with sedentariness, how spaces recompose according to multiple temporalities. Chinese and French sociologists converge around the idea that geographic mobilities could produce social immobility in both contexts (Chen Chen 2018; Roulleau-Berger 1999). They also show how being in a subaltern condition does not necessarily entail spatial isolation, how a limited and constrained mobility in China can become a strategic resource. And vice versa, that spatial segmentations do not necessarily produce captivity but can produce professional and even social plurimobilities. The migratory experience can refer to a variety of spaces and activities which generate dynamics of social reconfiguration, spatial combinations that create circulations and appropriations of multi-situated places which react with one another. Chinese and French sociologists give a central position to space both as a constraint and as a resource, which an actor-migrant who is capable of enriching his repertory of social and economic resources at every new migratory stage can use.

However, in China, geographic mobility deeply subverts social interactions of individuals with their environment, which is challenged by their identities in a plurality of spaces and temporalities at the level of the Chinese continent, and even at the international level. The migratory circulations, experiences, and careers show how temporalities contract in exacerbated accelerations and a lack of limitations in urban and rural spaces located on different levels. The competences needed for mobility convey some "capabilities of aspiration" (in terms of power, dignity, and material resources) (Appadurai 2013) in given temporalities. Space is considered as a protection for migrants because they can move and escape social captivity; geographic and professional mobilities express some forms of resistance to the wage subordination of young workers, as does a refusal to consent to forced labor (Roulleau-Berger 2018). Chinese and French sociologists agree in considering spaces and activities together on different stages of times and spaces, seizing the games between mobilities and territorialities to link the spatial and economic dimensions of the migratory experience and account for entwined socialization processes which can generate economic integration, semi-disaffiliation, and social disaffiliation.

5 Uncertainty, Social Disqualification, and Work

Piore and Sabel's (1984) theories of the segmentation of labor markets or segmented assimilation theories (Zhou 1997; Silberman, Alba and Fournier 2006) are still used and revised by French and Chinese sociologists on Chinese and French fields. Flexibility and job insecurity are shared concepts, used to describe the de-skilling and disqualification process on labor markets. In China the labor markets are full of greater flexibility and uncertainty; a globalized neoliberal model has fostered employment systems which strengthen social inequalities and commonly exclude the less qualified, forcing them into disqualified and disqualifying jobs. Chinese and French sociologists have demonstrated that new generations of migrants and children of immigrants in the working classes are most likely to have to cope with uncertainty and disqualification; ethnic and class discriminations are distancing young people of foreign descent from labor markets. Precarious migrant populations are subjected to dominations, symbolic and identity-threatening violence, and discrimination, even racism, in their respective labor markets. Symbolic violence is constructed in professional relationships by means of phenomena of horizontal and vertical social disqualification, alienation of identities, contempt and humiliation in dirty jobs, low-income levels, no upward professional mobility, and low social protection in China; it is worth noting that Chinese and European sociologists converge in their analyses of disqualified or subaltern work (Pun Ngai 2016; Li Zhen 2021; Su Liang 2019; Roulleau-Berger 2021). Discrimination is a constraint on mobility in geographic, social, educational, and occupational domains.

In China and in Europe, sociologists have clearly shown that young migrants and descendants of immigrants are faced with social and moral risks: the less qualified may not find a "position", and those who are better qualified often have to make do with youth-labeled employment areas in which they cannot really start their professional socialization. Such systemic disqualification has been attenuated in the middle and upper classes, but it has greatly impacted the lower classes, especially young unqualified migrants in China and young people of foreign descent in France. Racism at work towards young migrants from Africa or the Maghreb is fueled by an internal colonialism, manifested by wariness and suspicion by employers and social inclusion stakeholders (Boubeker 2018; Giraudo-Baujeu 2018). It is clear that overqualified and overeducated young Chinese are indirectly discriminated against when the link between professional qualifications and the opportunity for professional mobility is severed. In this case, a university degree is no guarantee that one will secure positions that lead to vertical mobility in a company's hierarchy.

In China and Europe alike, sociologists have observed that young migrants and descendants of migrants refuse disqualification and loss of social status (Roulleau-Berger and Yan 2017). The main victims of the devaluation of academic diplomas have been—and still are—the academically less well endowed. The phenomenon of mass youth unemployment and loss of social status has created a sort of collective disillusionment resulting in a structural discrepancy between aspirations and chances, between the social identity which the teaching system seems to promise and the social identity offered by the labor market. The gulf separating the aspirations produced by the teaching system and the chances which it actually provides has been constantly widening, thus provoking the revolt and hatred among poorly qualified young people of working-class origin.

Young migrants of working-class origin and children of immigrants expressed a refusal of the "dirty work" inflicted upon their fathers: factory work, the production line and clocking in, specialized skilled work in the major industries, and the "donkey" work (packer, courier, salesperson, etc.), implying they thought of these jobs as having to be highly dependent on a small boss. The devaluing of the workers' conditions, the intensified pressure of work conditions, the increased precariousness of status, and the rise of unemployment transformed the factory into a repellent for the fathers working there and their children, who would do everything in their power to avoid working there. In China the children of migrants only accept the "dirty work" with great difficulty since they have seen their parents exhausted and even killed by work. The least qualified—often condemned to becoming unskilled workers—thus refuse to engage in work which disqualifies them, and they situate themselves in a distanced relationship to factory work. This disenchantment takes objectively and subjectively different shapes according to social class, with the phenomenon progressively affecting young people who are better endowed academically (Bourdieu 1978).

In both China and Europe, young migrants' aspirations have become progressively blurred and restricted, yet more firmly entrenched, while employment increasingly provokes the fear of never achieving stability in the labor market and never accessing a qualified and qualifying job. For these poorly qualified children of immigrants in Europe and of migrants in China—destitute, exploited, and revolted by their working conditions—work appears to be a cause of suffering and revolt. Today Chinese sociologists focus on the subjective experiences of second-generation migrants who bear the suffering and humiliation of the first generation. They are highly incensed and have developed competencies for resisting and combating situations of oppression and injustice. In France, the phenomenon of social disqualification first produced disillusionment before actively contributing to blurring the aspirations of young migrants and shaping situations of double constraints in the relationship to work. In China young migrants are developing new working-class cultures of resistance based on ties and solidarities brought from their home communities.

6 Migrants, *Compressed Individual* and Global Condition

In China, strong economic growth over the past four decades, accelerated urbanization and multiple inequalities between urban and rural worlds have driven the escalation of internal and international migrations. This has occurred in a context of *multi-compressed modernities* in the sense of Chang Kyung-Sup (2010, 2017). According to Li Peilin (2018, 2019) in the history of global modernization, the internal migration of workers represents a unique phenomenon in the history of Chinese modernization and the creation of "global factories" since the reform and opening of China. Young Chinese migrants have strongly internalized the idea of being the "heroes" of the new Chinese society, if not society in general, and are fascinated by the cult of success and excellence. Internal and international migrations intersect and intertwine to produce economic cosmopolitanisms. Young internal and international migrants from China invent new, local and global economic systems in a local and multi-ethnic society through discreet globalization, top-down and bottom-up globalization and intermediary globalization.

Internal multiple modernities in China restructured Chinese labor markets around manufacturing consent (Burawoy 1979). This occurred via the production of hierarchies based on domination, flexibility and symbolic violence that gave rise to an *enrichment economy* (Boltanski and Esquerre 2017). This economy replaced the planned socialist economy that provided workers with structure and protection through the *danwei* (labor unit), communist work organization systems. As a result, Chinese workers, in particular young migrants, were forced to commodify themselves, i.e., be both the trader and the commodity. The enrichment economy is part of a regime of high-order compressed modernity that causes extreme social inequality. It eliminates worker solidarity and obligates them to agree to violence and domination in labor markets. The process of widening inequality appears to be unpredictable and limitless under a global capitalism. These formations are assemblages of powerful economic agents, markets, technologies and governments as it constantly restructures itself under a regime of high-order compressed modernity. The hyper commodification of Chinese labor markets drives a perpetual conquest of new domestic and international sectors of economic activity.

For Chang Kyung-Sup (2018) time compression involves the phenomena of intense competition, collision, disjuncture and compounding between post-modern elements and traditional elements. On the one hand, the young Chinese migrant is a flexible complex traditional-modernized-post-modernized subject and, on the other, an indigenous-Westernized-cosmopolitan figure. This results in a local and global Individual. Young Chinese migrants must manage the effects of collisions between employment and work situations in traditional, "modern" and "postmodern" work cultures. Multi-compressed modernity also features the hyper commodification of emotions converted into *emodities* (Illouz 2019). This takes place in the hegemonic labor regimes created by authoritarian structures linked to *emotional capitalism* (Illouz 2006), and is experienced differently by young graduate and low-skilled migrants. Compressed modernity triggers strong emotions in young graduate migrants aspiring to become "heroes" of Chinese society. They are subjected to controlled personalization techniques as part of managerial strategies that produce maximum exploitation in labor markets.

Young Chinese migrants with more resources internalize to differing degrees the injunction to join the cult of excellence that affects their professional and personal lives in different ways. While the search for recognition and happiness at work becomes a key element in the production of emotional capitalism, a portion of young graduates respond "positively" to these injunctions. The most qualified perform emotional labor to conform to these social expectations and may overexert themselves by internalising norms of competition. The wide range of work situations slightly alters their relationship to labor founded on overinvestment and the search for excellence and self-realization. We can clearly see that the gap between emotions experienced and those imposed by a social order produce an intense emotional labor. Another category of young Chinese migrant graduates who are *tired of being themselves* (Ehrenberg 1998) distance themselves from work and criticize the injunction to internalize the norms of success and excellence, perceived as impeding their self-realization. Here the gap between emotions experienced and those imposed by a social order is reduced and less intense emotional work is produced.

As young Chinese migrants move to Europe, Africa or North America, they transition from a multi-compressed modernity where high-order compressed modernity regimes take precedence to spaces where *low or middle compressed modernity* is the dominant form. In the process of socialization attached to different regimes of modernity, they have internalized various ways of becoming Compressed Individuals. These are redefined in the context of the societies of arrival in transmigration. Young Chinese migrants apply the rules and norms of *high compressed modernity* to regimes of *low or middle compressed modernity*. For this reason, young Chinese migrants emerge as emblematic figureheads of the global condition of the Compressed Individual. During the international migration process, young graduates often encounter situations of social disqualification and racial discrimination that stymy their dream of becoming the "heroes of globalization". After being subjected to injunctions to become "heroes" under *emotional socialism*, they dream of becoming entrepreneurs in their own right within the framework of emotional capitalism. The least qualified rapidly become "those left behind by globalization" when confronting situations of economic, moral and social captivity in ethnic niches or enclaves in international cities.

The young Chinese Migrant as a *Compressed Individual* is also adept at developing strategies to distance, circumvent and resist the injunction to become an adherent of emotional capitalism (Roulleau-Berger 2021). Compressed *modernities* contains the effects of economic and social collisions where social, economic, moral processes, linked to regimes of premodernity, modernity and postmodernity, clash and hybridize. The resulting forms of individuation are both situational and, as they are active in Western societies, global. This individual has internalized the injunction to create a narrative of self-improvement and to become a "hero" of Chinese society and globalization.

Compressed *modernities* contains the effects of economic and social collisions where social, economic, moral processes, linked to regimes of premodernity, modernity and postmodernity, clash and hybridize. The resulting forms of individuation are both situational and, as they are active in Western societies, global. Young Chinese migrant incarnates the Global Individual, what I labeled as the *Compressed Individual*, a Homo Sentimentalis living in an environment of what Eva Illouz refers to as "emotional capitalism". This individual has internalized the injunction to create a narrative of self-improvement and to become a hero of Chinese society and globalization.

7 Conclusion

In order to further develop the paradigm of Post-Western theory, we created post-Western knowledge by crossing sociological perspectives on the topic of migration, by carrying out field research in Europe and in China, and by comparing our ways of carrying out qualitative research. We have analyzed the way in which sociological knowledge is built by observing the different forms of experiences on Chinese and European research fields. If Post-Western Sociology relies on different knowledge processes—"knowledge niches", intermediary epistemological processes, transnational epistemological spaces—in this chapter we have produced crossed analyses, allowing the production of more common knowledge than located knowledge; we have opened a clear Post-Western Space where we have drawn discontinuous and continuous continuities between Chinese and French sociologies.

References

Appaduraï, A. 2013. *Condition de l'homme global*. Paris: Payot.
Boubeker, A. 1999. *Familles de l'intégration, les ritournelles de l'ethnicité en pays jacobin*. Paris: Stock.
Boubeker, A. 2018. "Ethnicity and Individuation: The Victim, the Tricker and the Hero". In *Post-Western Sociology-From China to Europe*, edited by L. Roulleau-Berger and Peilin Li. London: Routledge.
Bourdieu, P. 1978. "Classement, déclassement, reclassement". *Actes de la recherche en sciences sociales* 24: 2–22.
Chang, Kuyng-Sup. 2010. "The Second Modern Condition? Compressed Modernity as Internalized Reflexive Cosmopolitization". *The British Journal of Sociology* 61 (3): 444–465.
Chen, Chen. 2021. "A second-generation Migrant Worker in China: geographical Mobility and Social Immobility". In *Sociology of Migration and Post-Western Theory*, edited by L. Roulleau-Berger and Liu Yuzhao. Lyon: ENS Editions.
Giraudo-Baujeu, G. 2018. "L'épreuve du racisme dans le travail: faire avec ou faire face?" *Les mondes du travail*, no. 21: 61–73.

Li, Chunling. 2013. "Institutional and Non-institutional Path: Different Processes of Socio-economic Status Attainment of Migrants and Non-migrants in China". In *China's Internal and International Migration*, edited by Peilin Li and L. Roulleau-Berger, 26–40. London/New York: Routledge Publishers.

Li, Chunling. 2019. "Gaige kaifang de haizimen: zhongguo xinsheng dai yu zhongguo fazhan xin shidai" [The new generation and new period of development]. *Shehuixue Yanjiu*, no. 3: 1–24.

Li, Peilin, ed. 2012. *Chinese Society-Change and Transformation*. London/New York: Routledge.

Li, Peilin, and Wei Li. 2013. "The Work Situation and Social Attitudes of Migrant Workers in China under the Crisis". In *China's Internal and International Migration*, edited by Peilin Li and L. Roulleau-Berger, 3–26. London/New York: Routledge Publishers.

Li, Peilin. 2018. "China's 40-year experience in managing the movement of migrant workers". *Chinese Journal of Sociology* (in Chinese version) 38 (6): 45–55.

Li, Peilin. 2019. "Changes, Problems and Countermeasures of Class Structure in China in the Past 40 years of Reform and Opening Up". *Journal of the Party School* 21 (06): 5–16.

Li, Peilin, and L. Roulleau-Berger, eds. 2013. *China's Internal and International Migration*. London/New York: Routledge.

Li, Zhen. 2021. "Education and Upward Socioeconomic Mobility of Children of Migrants in the Chinese Urban Labor Market: Institutional Barriers, Social Support and Personal Efforts". In *Sociology of Migration and Post-Western Theory*, edited by L. Roulleau-Berger and Liu Yuzhao. Lyon: ENS Editions.

Lian, Si. 2009. *Mazu* [Ants]. Cuilin: Guangxi Normal University Press.

Liu, Haifang. 2013. "Mapping the New Migrants between China and Africa: Theoretical and Methodological Challenges". In *China's internal and International Migration*, edited by Li Peilin and L. Roulleau-Berger, 234–245. Oxon and New York: Routledge Publishers.

Luo, Jarde. 2008. "Social Networks and Social Capital". *Sociology and Chinese Society*, edited by Li Peilin, Qiang Li, and Rong Ma, 341–363. Beijing: Social Sciences Academic Press.

Luo, Jarde, and K. Yeh. 2012. "Neither Collectivism nor Individualism. Trust in Chinese Guanxi Circles". *Journal of Trust Research* 2 (1): 53–70.

Missaoui, L. 2003. *Les étrangers de l'intérieur. Filières, trafics et xénophobie*. Paris: Payot.

Park, R. 1926. "The Urban Community as a Spatial Pattern and a Moral Order". In R. Park and E.W. Burgess, *The Urban Community*. Chicago: University of Chicago Press.

Piore, M., and C. Sabel. 1984. *The Second Industrial Divide: Possibilities for Prosperity*. New York: Basic Books.

Pun, Ngai. 2016. *Migrant Labor in China*. Cambridge: Polity Press.

Roulleau-Berger, L. 1999. *Le travail en friche. Les mondes de la petite production urbaine*. La Tour d'Aigues: Editions de l'Aube.

Roulleau-Berger, L. 2013. "Migration, plural economies and new stratification in Europe and in China". In *China: Internal and International Migration*, edited by Li Peilin and L. Roulleau-Berger, 259–275. London/New York: Routledge.

Roulleau-Berger, L., and Yan Jun. 2017. *Travail et migration. Jeunesses chinoises à Shanghai et Paris*. La Tour d'Aigues: L'Aube.

Roulleau-Berger, L., and Yan Jun. 2016. *Post-Western Revolution in Sociology. From China to Europe*. Leiden/Boston: Brill Publishers.

Roulleau-Berger, L., and Yan Jun. 2018. "Temporalités, espaces et 'Individu compressé' en Chine". *Temporalités: revue de sciences sociales et humaines* 26. https://doi.org/10.4000/temporalites.3819.

Roulleau-Berger, L. 2021. *Young Chinese Migrants, Compressed Individual and Global Condition*. Leiden/Boston: Brill Publishers.

Roulleau-Berger, L., and Liu Yuzhao. 2021. "Post Western Theory and Sociology of Migration". In *Sociology of Migration and Post-Western Theory*, edited by L. Roulleau-Berger and Liu Yuzhao. Lyon: ENS Editions.

Silberman, R., R. Alba, and I. Fournier. 2006. "Les secondes générations sur le marché du travail en France: une pénalité ethnique ancrée dans le temps". *Revue française de sociologie* 47 (2): 243–292.

Su, Liang. 2019. *Mobility and Deskilling Low-Educated Transnational Migrants' Decision—Making, Trajectory and Consequences in Multiple Migration*. Thesis in sociology, Shanghai University.

Tarrius, A., in collaboration with L. Missaoui. 2000. *Les nouveaux cosmopolitismes. Mobilités, identités*. La Tour d'Aigues: l'Aube.

Tucci, I. 2021. "Pathways in School and Biographical Turning Points". In *Sociology of Migration and Post-Western Theory*, edited by L. Roulleau-Berger and Liu Yuzhao, 67–73. Lyon: ENS Editions.

Wang, Chunguang. 2017. *Yimin Kongjian de jiangou* [*The Construction of Migratory Space*]. Peking: Shehui kexue wenxian chuban she [Press of social sciences].

Zhao, Yeqin. 2021. "Floating Between Cities and Rural Areas: the Second-Generation Immigrants". In *Sociology of Migration and Post-Western Theory*, edited by L. Roulleau-Berger and Liu Yuzhao, 181–188. Lyon: ENS Editions.

Zhou, Min. 1997. "Segmented Assimilation: Issues, Controversies, and Recent Research on the New Second Generation". *The International Migration Review* 31 (4): 975–1008.

CHAPTER 56

Social Integration of China's Floating Population

Wang Chunguang and Lu Wen

1 Introduction

Over the past four decades, the massive flows of people between rural and urban areas and across regions have been one of the most obvious phenomena in China's social change, which is also unprecedented in the history of mankind. The main problem arising from that is their social integration in the places to which they move. Although they do not suffer from the nationality and citizenship problems that international immigrants do, China's floating population runs into problems of social integration similar to those of international immigrants. To study this subject, Chinese researchers have drawn upon migration theories from other countries and made adjustments to enrich such theories.

Although it has been common to explain population mobility and social integration problems from the state, market and social perspectives, the effects of the three factors occur in different stages when it comes to the rural population's mobility to move to urban areas in China. The state system reforms play a decisive role in the massive flows of people from rural areas to urban areas. The policy of reform and opening up introduced in the late 1970s serves as a crucial watershed in China's modernization process. Before that, an urban-rural dualism where rural residents were restricted from flowing into cities or transferring to non-agricultural industries had dominated the country since the end of the 1950s. With the start of reform and opening up, thanks to the state system reforms and the market mechanism represented by industrialization, the rural population had the chance to flow outward, and dramatic changes in China's social structure began to take place. China had a floating population of 6.57 million in 1982 (National Health Commission of the People's Republic of China 2018), and up to 290.77 million in 2019 (National Bureau of Statistics 2019). The large rural floating population, leaving their native places for cities in search of work and starting a new life there, would inevitably encounter social inclusion and integration problems. Their mobility and social integration will be explained below in three dimensions in three stages.

2   Destination Cities

In the beginning of studies on the topic of rural population mobility, Chinese scholars tended to follow the classic push–pull theory. This theory has experienced a process of being complemented and improved. Traditional migration theories assume that individuals are the decision-makers, yet new economic migration theories believe that it's families that make migration decisions. Considering the heterogeneity among family members (differences in age, cultural literacy, and skill), to maximize the family welfare, some members would go to other places for jobs with higher pay, while the rest stayed at home and performed agricultural work.

Those going to other places and doing higher-paid jobs were responsible for sending most of their income back to their family, and they would be supported by the family in turn if they lost their job. This theory effectively explains that the migration of the rural population would still occur even if there was no income gap or expected income gap between two areas. This phenomenon does currently exist in many developing countries (including China). In other words, one or more members of a family would go to work in the city while the rest stayed at home in the countryside for agricultural work. Those working in the city would send most of their income (retaining a small part to cover their daily expenditure in the city) back to support their family.

However, it is not sufficiently forceful to explain the mass mobility in China with classic Western theories. So, some scholars started to seek theoretical explanations based on local experiences and phenomena in China. With regard to empirical facts, compared with population migration in Western society, the mass rural population mobility to urban areas in China has its unique aspects, which are mainly manifested as the special status of the migrant workers as both workers and farmers. In the rural population mobility problem in China, the household registration system is a key effect variable, which creates a dual structure: farmers in the countryside and citizens (residents) in the city. The "household registration system is the most prominent institutional obstacle affecting the rural–urban population flow in China. It not only has a general effect on the 'push–pull', but also invalidates the push–pull effect" (Li 2003: 125). In other words, the push–pull effect is mainly manifested at the economic level, yet under the limitation of the household registration system, the economic motivation fails.

3 Social Integration in Cities

Seen from the policy evolution, China's floating population management policies have evolved from being "open" to "regulatory" and then to "integrating" (Yin and Huang 2008). Along with this, the social integration developed step by step. Besides, when the social integration concept is further broken down to specific dimensions, we have the socioeconomic integration, cultural integration, psychological integration, etc. In addition, the floating population's social integration demonstrates intergenerational differences. To sum up, we could understand the social integration of the floating population from perspectives of factors affecting the floating population's social integration and their mechanism and effect, the process of floating population's social integration and its quantitative cognition, the intergenerational differences in floating population's social integration, and the social integration status of the floating population.

3.1 Factors Affecting Floating Population's Social Integration and Their Mechanism and Effect

The household registration system is believed to be a basic system restricting the floating population's social integration (Li and Ren 2011). Under the household registration system, it is a challenge for members of the floating population to settle in or assimilate into the city, and this is deemed an "institutional exclusion". As a public institutional arrangement, the household registration system not only concerns all the public welfare and guarantee for the floating population, but it also has profound effect on their occupational and economic status attainment. Some researchers examine how the household registration system, as an institutional segmentation mechanism, affects social mobility through comparing similarities and differences in the attainment of occupational and economic status between a migrant labor force and non-migrant labor force. They find that the triple institution segmentation (dual social, economic, and labor force market structures) confines the migrant labor force to a specific social and economic space, and formal institutions have weaker control over or effect on this space. As a result, the floating population has a really special socioeconomic stratification pattern and socioeconomic status attainment pattern, forcing them into special paths and informal rules if they want higher social status. These special paths and informal rules constitute a non-systematic pattern for acquiring socioeconomic status (Li 2006).

In addition to the basic household registration system, market economic factors, social capital, cultural identity, etc., also influence the floating population's social integration. As shown by an analysis based on data from a survey over the Pearl River Delta, economic adaptation, social interaction, cultural adaptation, and other factors are having increasingly significant effect on floating population's social integration. Among them, economic adaptation is the foundation of social integration, and cultural adaptation is the most important factor affecting social integration. And economic adaptation and social interaction have indirect effect on social integration (Lu and Wei 2011). When it comes to social integration in different dimensions, different factors have different effects on the integration of the floating population. Some other studies show that neither governments nor markets have an effect on the cultural integration of the floating population, and only societies have a marked effect on cultural integration. Social interaction between the floating population and local residents and longer time staying in the destination area are contributive to their acquisition of urban social culture, and accordingly to cultural integration. Governments, markets, and societies all have a marked influence on the socioeconomic integration and psychological integration of migrant workers, and governments have an indirect effect on social integration via markets and societies. Social interaction and social engagement could strongly facilitate social integration of floating population (Yue, Li and Li 2012).

Social capital or social networks are another important factor affecting the floating population's social integration. Social support for the rural floating population is mainly in the form of local relations or family relations. Governments, societies, and communities provide little of such support (Yang et al. 2006). How does this social network feature affect social integration? Studies have found that the local social network and internal homogeneity of the floating population do not constitute an obstacle to social inclusion as is believed by the assimilation theory. In particular, in the early days when the floating population come to the city, they would rely more on social capital based on blood and geographical relationships. Yet if they want to further assimilate into urban society, they need to expand their social capital, strengthen their own organizations, build more diverse social networks, and further interact and exchange with local residents. Besides, it has also been pointed out that human resources capital consisting of education, training, work experiences, etc., has a positive effect on social inclusion, meaning the stronger the human resources capital, the better the social integration (Ren and Wu 2006). Further studies classify social networks of the rural floating population as citizen relative relations, non-relative citizen relations, and non-citizen relations. They advocate that non-relative citizen relations have a remarkable and irreplaceable positive effect on the cultural integration and psychological integration of migrant workers, but have limited effect on socioeconomic integration, and that the unbalanced effects of citizen networks of migrant workers on different dimensions of social integration might keep migrant workers at the bottom of urban society for a long time (Yue et al. 2011).

3.2 Process of Floating Population's Social Integration and Its Quantitative Cognition

Some researchers summarize social integration as five sequential stages from the diachronic perspective: thorough segregation, initial structural integration, deeper structural integration and initial social engagement, deep cultural integration, and psychological identity (Yang 2016; Yue et al. 2012). Some researchers break social integration down into socioeconomic inclusion, cultural integration, psychological integration, etc., from a synchronic perspective. Some other researchers analyze social integration statuses of the floating population at the economic integration, social adaptation, cultural acquisition and psychological identity levels, and thus derive various quantitative indicators.

Some argue that "assimilation" is better than "integration" in describing the adaptation process and results of the rural–urban floating population in cities. Compared with "integration", "assimilation" is a dynamic, gradual, multi-dimensional, and interactive evolution process. Segregation is an inevitable problem facing new immigrants. During the process of integration, it is often the case that economic integration takes place first, followed by cultural acceptance, behavior adaptation, and then by self-identity (Yang 2009). Besides, 16 indicators have been sorted out in economic integration, behavior adaptation, cultural acceptance, and self-identity, to reveal the social inclusion of the floating population (Yang 2010). Analyses on quantitative data show that the floating population does not do well in social inclusion generally, and there is no significant difference among different dimensions. Among them, progress in economic and social inclusion lags behind in cultural and psychological integration due to institutional restraints and structural rejection. Good social services and an accepting environment are contributive to advancing the integration process, and connection between the places of origin and destination places and between the floating population and local residents has a direct effect on the integration process of the floating population (Yang 2015). By examining social integration indicators of EU society and the EU immigration integration index and considering the characteristics of China's population mobility, some researchers try to work out the indicator system of the floating population's social integration in China at both the city and individual levels. To be specific, social integration at the city level falls into policy integration and overall integration, which correspond to the "policy index of floating population's social integration" and the "overall index of floating population's social integration", respectively. At the individual level, they examine the subjective perception or evaluation of integration and the objective integration status, corresponding to the "individual index of floating population's social integration" (Huang 2011).

Social identity is a key variable to measure social integration status. From different standpoints, social identity could be classified into two concepts: individuals' self-identity and their city identity. Studies show that the choice of individuals' social identity is affected by multiple factors, both institutional and policy factors and the characteristic factors of individuals. Data analyses point out that the self-identity of the rural floating population is directly affected by factors like household registration systems, social rejection, social differences, and community involvement, apart from age, educational background, and time staying in local places (Cui 2012). Factors affecting individuals' city identity include variables in the four categories: cultural attitude, social interaction, economic success, and social environment. Among those variables, the degree of mastery of local languages, the willingness to make friends with local residents, the income and status levels of similar groups of people, the degree of perception of social discrimination, and the degree of insurance coverage are the decisive factors affecting individuals' city identity (Chu, Xiong and Zou 2014).

3.3 Intergenerational Differences in Floating Population's Social Integration

Domestic studies divide the rural floating population into the "older-generation rural floating population" and the "new-generation rural floating population" by the intergenerational variable. Chunguang Wang claims to have been the first to put forward the "new-generation rural floating population" concept (Wang 2000). He pointed out in 2001 that there had been intergenerational variation in the rural floating population, as marked differences had been witnessed between two generations of migrant workers in mobility motivation, community identity, native identity, and other social characteristics (Wang 2001). He explained the "new-generation rural floating population" on two levels in 2003: first, they are the rural floating population younger than age 25 years and leaving for other places in search of work or business in the 1990s. They're visibly different from the first-generation rural floating population in social and work experiences. Second, they are not the second-generation rural floating population, for they were not born to or raised by the first-generation rural migrants during the latter's working outside. Instead, they are the transitional rural floating population between the first and second generations of the rural floating population (Luo and Wang 2003). In addition, some hold that intergenerational distinction is essentially the distinction in sociocultural attributes. In the open modern society, the intergenerational distinction means the difference among different groups of people born in different ages, raised in different social environments and thus with different sociocultural attributes (Liao and Zeng 2004). In 2010, the "new-generation migrant workers" concept was mentioned in the No. 1 Central Document for the first time (National Council of the PRC 2009).

Compared with the older generation rural floating population, the new generation has new motivations to work outside, development expectations, institutional identity recognition, and native identity, so that some new-generation migrant workers endeavor to identify with and adapt to local societies (Wang 2001). However, some studies argue that from the perspectives of the will and result of identities, the new generation of migrant workers have a weaker adaptation to local places than the older generation of migrant workers. This has a common function as the objective household registration system distinguishing insiders from outsiders, and has the effect of fuzzy or lacking cognition caused by the specific subjective psychological cognition of the new-generation rural floating population (Yang, Wu and Zhang 2016). Generally, the new-generation rural floating population has a stronger will and ability to work in and adapt to cities. They are offered upward flow channels in the differentiated urban household registration reforms and the integrated urban-rural development wave. Against such a backdrop, they continue seeking their own ways to citizenship. Such ways are summarized by some people as the "succession-adaptation" way to citizenship (Pan 2013). Yet such an intergenerational characteristic difference does not explain the radical change in intergenerational social inclusion results. Peilin Li and Feng Tian (2012) describe the social inclusion statuses of the new and older generations of migrant workers from economic, social, psychological, and identity perspectives applying data from a comprehensive survey of social conditions in China, finding no radical difference between them in social inclusion. The key factor leading to such a result is policies and systems. With regard to this, Qiang Li (2011) also believes that what the rural floating population suffers from is not the "not adapting to" problem. In other words, it is not that the migrant workers do not want to adapt to the city, but that they are restricted by the city systems, making them unready to adapt to the city mentally and thus in a position "not adapting to" the city.

3.4   *Status of Floating Population's Social Integration*
From the standpoint of the citizenization of the rural floating population, Wang (2006) puts forward the peri-urbanization concept, believing that peri-urbanization is a status between back to the countryside and thorough

urbanization, manifested as disconnection among various systems, lack of integration in social life and behaviors, and involution in social identity. The mutually strengthening effect among the system, social life and behaviors, and social mentality, the peri-urbanization status of the rural floating population tends to exist for a long time, which hinders social integration and social change. Therefore, the peri-urbanization has three aspects: social institutional restrictions, internalization of social interaction, and suspension of social identity. The peri-urbanized population accounts for 17% of the total population of China.

In 2010 and beyond, the Chinese government further advanced the urban household registration system reform, and attained marked achievements in new rural construction and targeted poverty alleviation. In particular, after the "rural revitalization" program was launched in 2017, since super-large cities continued the strict citizenship restrictions, part of rural floating population started to move towards medium-sized and small cities near their hometowns. And accordingly, a group of people traveling between urban and rural areas emerged, meaning the rural floating population neither thoroughly urbanized nor back in the countryside (Wang 2019). A new transition trend of urban-rural social structure is likely to occur based on that.

To sum up, the social integration problem facing China's rural floating population is rooted in the structural institutional arrangement, but it is further complicated by markets and social forces. For one thing, progress in urbanization is guiding massive flows of the rural population into cities. In the background where national citizenship is highly concerned, the social inclusion of the rural floating population has been a key reference indicator to measure the fairness of national systems. To this end, the national floating population management policies have experienced an evolutionary process from "regulatory" to "integrating". Yet to solve this problem, the central government prefers to delegate specific responsibilities to local governments, thus transferring the civil rights to the rights of city residents (Chen 2005). For another thing, the ever-growing consumption levels in cities, especially the upsurging housing prices, have weakened the social integration of the rural floating population in turn. Compared with city residents, the rural floating population has generally lower education levels and obvious differences in cultural concept, behaviors, and habits. Such a divide at the social level has a strengthening effect on the social integration of the rural floating population. Therefore, over the course of history development, the rural floating population tends to be peri-urbanized and traveling between cities and the countryside in social integration.

4 Return of the Rural Floating Population

Since it is difficult to adapt to the city, the average member of the rural floating population chooses to return to the countryside. Presently, although such a return movement is on a small scale, studies on this trend are already in place. As part of the overall mobility process, the returning movement is worthy of explanation and organization.

Current studies on the return of the rural floating population to the countryside focus mainly on three aspects: analysis of the motivations and processes of the rural floating population in returning to the countryside, analysis on the intergenerational differences in the returning rural floating population, and analysis on the social effect of and re-participation in rural society by the returning rural floating population. Their re-participation in rural society varies based on their different motivations to return to the countryside. Researchers classify them into four groups by their primary consideration of returning (Liu and Lu 2020). First, there is the development-oriented returning group, mainly returning to pursue individual development. Second, there is the group of migrant workers returning the countryside when they were summoned back by their families. They return to the countryside mainly to perform family responsibilities. Third, there is the group of migrant workers returning the countryside because they found it difficult to settle in the city. They choose to return because they were limited in development or were rejected in the city. Fourth, there is the group of migrant workers returning to the countryside because of a strong attachment to their hometown. This group of people prefers the cultural values in their native places and has feelings for their homeland.

By contrast, the development-oriented returning group has significant advantages in social capital and development abilities. They are more active in participating in rural social, political and economic activities, which contributes to rural development and revitalization, but how big a role they play is yet to be seen.

In general, China's rural floating population members still face social inclusion problems in their destination areas (especially cities), for which the biggest cause is institutional rejection. Yet now there is a problem of the floating population being unwilling to integrate into cities, and some are in a status of traveling between cities and the countryside. Such a flow process and phenomenon are not unique to China but can be seen all over the world. However, what distinguishes China's rural floating population in social integration from those in other countries is the institutional restrictions and rejection, in spite of some effective reforms and changes. It is foreseeable that there will be free flows of people between rural and urban areas in the future, without restrictions from the urban–rural dualism.

References

Chen, Yingfang. 2005. "Migrant Workers: Institutional Arrangement and Self-Identity". *Sociological Studies* 3.

Chu, Rongwei, Yihan Xiong, and Yi Zou. 2014. "The Determinant Factors of Migrant Workers' Social Identity: An Empirical Study in Shanghai". *Chinese Journal of Sociology* 34 (4).

Cui, Yan. 2012. "A Study on Migrants' Psychological Integration and Self-identity". *Sociological Studies* 5.

Huang, Kuangshi. 2011. "The Indicators of Floating Population's Social Inclusion: European Union's Practice and China's Construction". *Journal of Nanjing College for Population Programme Management* 27 (1).

Li, Chunling. 2006. "Non-institutional Paths of Migrants' Status Attainment: Migrant Labors and Non-migrant Labors in Comparison". *Sociological Studies* 5.

Li, Peilin, and Feng Tian. 2012. "A Cross Generational Comparison of the Social Cohesion of Migrant Workers in China". *Chinese Journal of Sociology* 32 (5).

Li, Qiang. 2003. "Analysis on the Pushing and Pulling Factors Affecting Urban and Rural Floating Population in China". *Social Sciences in China* 1.

Li, Qiang. 2011. "'Semi-integration' and 'Non-integration' in the Process of Urbanization in China". *Hebei Academic Journal* 31 (5).

Li, Tao, and Yuan Ren. 2011. "Urban Household Registration System Reforms and Social Integration of Floating Population". *South China Population* 26 (3).

Liao, Xiaoping, and Xiangyun Zeng. 2004. "On 'Generation'". *Jianghai Academic Journal* 4.

Liu, Yuxia, and Wen Lu. 2020. *"Returning and Transcending: A Study on Social Roles of the Returning Migrant Workers"*. Peking: People's Publishing House.

Lu, Shuzhen, and Wanqing Wei. 2011. "The Structural Equation Model on Social Integration of Immigrants". *Population & Economics* 5.

Luo, Xia, and Chunguang Wang. 2003. "Motivations and Action Choice of the New-Generation Rural Mobile Population to Work Outside". *Zhejiang Social Sciences* 1.

National Bureau of Statistics. 2019. "Report on Migrant Worker Monitoring and Survey". http://www.stats.gov.cn/tjsj/zxfb/202004/t20200430_1742724.html.

National Council of the PRC. 2009. "Several Opinions on Improving the Balance Between Urban and Rural Development and Strengthening the Foundation for the Development of Agriculture and Rural Area". http://www.gov.cn/gongbao/content/2010/content_1528900.htm.

National Health Commission of the People's Republic of China. 2018. "Outlines of the 2018 Report on China's Floating Population Development". http://www.nhc.gov.cn/wjw/xwdt/201812/a32a43b225a740c4bff8f2168b0e9688.shtml.

Pan, Hua. 2013. "'Returning' Citizenization: A New Trend of Citizenization of the New-Generation Migrant Workers". *Theory Monthly* 3.

Ren, Yuan, and Minle Wu. 2006. "Social Integration of Floating Population in Urban China: A Literature Review". *Population Research* 30 (3).

Wang, Chunguang. 2000. "Desire of the New-generation Rural Mobile Population for Basic Civil Rights". *Democracy & Science* 1.

Wang, Chunguang. 2001. "Relationship Between Social Identity of the New-Generation Migrant Workers and Urban-Rural Integration". *Sociological Studies* 3.

Wang, Chunguang. 2006. "A Study of Rural Floating People's 'Semi-urbanization'". *Sociological Studies* 5.

Wang, Chunguang. 2019. "The Third Road to Urbanization: 'Traveling between Urban and Rural Areas'". *Journal of Sichuan University* (*Philosophy and Social Sciences*) 6.

Yang, Juhua. 2009. "From Isolation, Selective Integration to Integration: A Theoretical Reflection on Social Integration of the Mobile Population". *Population Research* 33 (1).

Yang, Juhua. 2010. "Indicator System for Social Integration of the Mobile Population in Destinations: A Further Study Based on the Theory of Social Integration". *Population & Economics* 2.

Yang, Juhua. 2015. "A Study on Social Integration of China's Mobile Population". *Social Sciences in China* 2.

Yang, Juhua. 2016. "On Social Integration". *The Journal of Jiangsu Administration Institute* 6.

Yang, Juhua, Min Wu, and Jiaojiao Zhang. 2016. "A Study on Intergenerational Differences in Self-Identity of Mobile Population". *Youth Studies* 4.

Yang, Xusong, Xiaoyi Jin, Qunying Xiao, and Meng Bai. 2006. "Situation and Policy Study on Rural Migrant Workers' Social Support and Social Integration". *China Soft Science* 12.

Yin, Deting, and Kuangshi Huang. 2008. "Changes and Prospects of China's Floating Population Policies in 30 Years of Reform and Opening-up". *Social Sciences in Xinjiang* 5.

Yue, Zhongshan, Shuzhuo Li, Xiaoyi Jin, and Marcus W. Feldman. 2011. "From Ascribed to Acquired: Migrant Workers' Social Networks and Migrant Integration in China". *Chinese Journal of Sociology* 31 (6).

Yue, Zhongshan, Weidong Li, and Yan Li. 2012. "Social Integration of Rural-Urban Migrants and Social Management: A Three Sectors Perspective including Government, Market, and Civil Society". *Journal of Public Management* 31 (4).

SECTION 14

Global Health and New Future

∴

CHAPTER 57

Global Health Challenges and a New Future

Zhao Yandong and Hong Yanbi

1 Health: Individual Issue or Government Responsibility?

The current health challenges show a globalized tendency. For example, during the 40 years of China's reform and opening up era, with the elimination of poverty and the improvement of national hygiene and levels of health, the main diseases causing death gradually changed from infectious diseases to chronic diseases. Various chronic diseases have become the primary cause of death for Chinese people. In 2017, hypertension, smoking, high-sodium diet, air pollution, hyperglycemia, hypercholesterolemia, obesity, and excessive drinking were the main risk factors responsible for the death of Chinese people (Zhou et al. 2019). This pattern is very similar to the transformation of Western diseases. At the same time, global health challenges and problems often break out suddenly and spread globally in a very short time period. With the rapid development of globalization processes and modern technology of communication and transportation, public health problems become one of the critical facets of modern risk society. Compared to the past, the current challenge from disasters and infectious diseases is much more globally threatening. However, the existing theories of health research are primarily based on the experiences of Western developed countries, and they relatively ignore the historical traditions and practices that non-Western countries have used to deal with health problems.

Affected by neo-liberalism since the 1970s, Western health theory usually deems that individuals are responsible for their own health. Moreover, the important influences of lifestyle on health are frequently misunderstood in that liberal individuals should be completely responsible for their own health problems (Druhle 2009: 3). This is not to say that the government ignores health issues in Western countries, but rather it is perceived that the individual and society are more accountable for individuals' health. For instance, Klinenberg's study on Chicago's heat wave points out that most officials and the public are more likely to consider that the severe weather fully accounted for Chicago's human catastrophe and high mortality, rather than the social and human dimensions (Klinenberg 2015). The resurgence of neo-liberalism in Western countries led to a resurgence in the 1990s of infectious diseases that were so lethal in the 19th century (White 2002: 59). One of the important implications of neoliberalism on public health is that clinical epidemiology primarily exclusively focuses on individual risk behaviors, rather than social and structural factors (White 2002: 61). Doubtlessly, the impact of neoliberalism on public health is likely to result in the burden of disease being placed on the poor, not the affluent. In sum, an individual-accountable health policy probably will increase health inequality.

However, this is not always the case in non-Western countries. In China, for example, health is not only an individual matter, it is also the essential responsibility of the government, which distinguishes it from the Western model. In 2009, the Chinese government launched a 850 billion yuan (USD $125 billion) reform plan as the first phase towards achieving comprehensive universal health coverage by 2020 (Yip et al. 2012). This universal health coverage project goes hand in hand with the elimination of poverty project. During the government-organized poverty elimination project, health improvement was identified as one of the key approaches for poor families to get out of poverty. At the same time, the elimination of poverty project helps to improve health conditions for those in previously poor families through a better living environment and better nutrition intake. Zhang and his colleagues found that a universal health coverage policy significantly benefits older people, poorer people, and those who have poorer health (Zhang, Xu and Chen 2019). Moreover, in 2019, the Chinese government issued *Healthy China Action (2019–2030)*, which proposes that people's health is a significant mark of national prosperity and that people's health is the important foundation of people's well-being, and emphasizes putting the issue of public health in the priority position of strategic development. Furthermore, it is required that the practical outcomes of *Healthy China Action* be an important indicator of evaluation of the healthy China construction. A supervision system is to be established and to perform special supervision each year. And an assessment and accounting system will be built to evaluate the outcomes of health policies for different areas and departments. These sorts of health-related policies are legacies from the traditional Chinese and communist cultures. Schwartz (1996: 114) argues that one of the most distinctive characters of Chinese civilization is the primacy and importance of political order, in other words, government always stands in the central place in Chinese history. After the foundation of the People's Republic of China, along with community-based health care, government-organized mass hygiene campaigns also have been a significant feature of post-1949 public health programs (Nakajima 2018: 240). Therefore, the Chinese government has been playing a critical and important role in improving the health of all Chinese people, which is also assumed to be an inescapable responsibility of the government.

The important role that the Chinese government plays especially emerges in major natural catastrophes and public health-related emergent events. These disaster and emergent public health events usually bring about serious health risks for society, which are amplified by the damage of normal social functions brought on by disasters. In the following parts, we will take the post-disaster reconstruction of Wenchuan Earthquake and the COVID-19 pandemic as examples to examine the Chinese–Western differences in governments' role facing large-scale emergent health risks.

2   Natural Disasters and Health Equity

In dealing with the health risks brought about by the natural hazards, compared to the Western coping system that was dominated by the market and society, the Chinese model, dominated by redistribution, could reduce health inequality more and improve the health of disadvantaged groups much better. In existing Western theories, the pressure and release (PAR) model and the access model are the two main frameworks for explaining the relationship between natural events and the social processes that generate unhealthy and unsafe outcomes (Wisner et al. 2004). Government plays a very limited and minor role in the two models. Studies on Hurricane Katrina in the United States show that the individual features—ethnicity and social status—have significant effects on post-disaster recovery (Elliott and Pais 2006; Masozera, Bailey and Kerchner 2007). The risk relief and management in free market and democracy institutions intend to cover structural inequality under the individual equity discourse, and ignore the process of how inequality in wealth and power affects the recovery and health outcomes of different individuals and groups. In contrast, the Chinese model of disaster relief and risk management is dominated by strong government intervention and related resource mobilization. Governments at various levels play a major role in resource collection and distribution, and the mobilization and organization of medical personnel. In consequence, the government could raise and collect a large amount of resources and organize medical personnel nationally in a short time, and then distribute these to the people in disaster areas.

During the post-disaster recovery of the 2008 Wenchuan Earthquake and other natural disasters, the Chinese central government proposed the *pairing-assistance model* in which one non-disaster area gave support and assistance to an oriented earthquake-affected area. In a very short time, a bulk of resources for recovery squeeze into disaster-affected areas, thus effectively relieving the shortage of material and medical resources. Using three waves of survey data, Hong and Zhao (2019) found that there were no significant educational and occupational differences on both self-rated health and mental health during the earthquake and first recovery stages. Because of the increase of redistributive resources and the distribution mainly followed the "relative need principle", disadvantaged groups' access to medical and hygiene resources and services was greatly improved, and thus the health inequality in disaster areas decreased accordingly (Hong and Zhao 2019). This "Government-led Nationwide System" seems to be very efficient and effective in coping with large natural disasters and hazards and emergent health risks (e.g., infectious diseases), because it could mobilize various resources very quickly for redistribution. This is especially important for disadvantaged groups' access to resources during and after a disaster. Efficiency of health care systems is always a troubling problem in both developed and developing countries. Asandului and colleagues examined 30 European countries and suggested that only a few are on the efficiency frontier, while the majority of the sample states are inefficient (Asandului, Roman and Fatulescu 2014). The efficiency of the redistributive system during disasters in China seems to be in the frontier. However, whether such efficiency could be maintained in routine health care systems is still an open question that needs more in-depth and comparative research.

3 COVID-19 and the Government-Led Nationwide System in Public Health: A Case Study

When facing large-scale emergent public health risk events, for example, SARS in 2003 and the COVID-19 pandemic in 2020, China's "Government-led Nationwide System" again showed its efficiency and effectiveness in controlling the dissemination of disease and ensuring public health, compared to some Western countries, where the government's roles were relatively weaker. Taking the example of the COVID-19 pandemic in early 2020, several experiences related to the government's role can be drawn.

A strong and capable central government could make rapid response policies and mobilize social resources with high efficiency. In the early phase of the COVID-19 pandemic, the central government resolutely took several major measures, including city lockdown, transport freezes, quarantine, and shutdown based on scientific evidence and suggestions, which effectively contained the spread of virus. Special hospitals and makeshift hospitals were constructed within a short time, which greatly relieved the problem of the hospitalization of patients. Following the successful experience of relief efforts during the 2008 Wenchuan Earthquake, the organizational pattern of "a province paired to a city" to aid prefectural-level cities of Hubei Province (the hardest hit area of COVID-19) was implemented. Professional medical workers from across the nation were dispatched to severely affected areas in Hubei Province. The central government's coordination and joint efforts ensured ample supplies of medical supplies and equipment, as well as supplies of major daily necessities for the affected population. The central and local governments also played a key role in releasing information and the dissemination of knowledge about disease prevention and control, which greatly eased the public panic and increased public confidence. According to a survey of Hubei Province dwellers conducted at the end of March 2020,[1] 87% of the respondents evaluated the central government's performance in coping with COVID-19 as "very good" or "good".

Under the guidance of the central government, local governments at various levels played active roles in fighting the virus. Especially at the community level, community-based management networks were built as the frontier of the joint prevention and control mechanism, a successful mechanism that was later summarized as "four early's"—early detection, early reporting, early isolation, and early treatment. Millions of community workers and volunteers were mobilized to participate in providing dragnet screening of potential virus carriers, communicating epidemic prevention knowledge, offering psychological counseling, and helping isolated households receive daily necessities, despite their extreme fatigue and the risk of infection. The local government's work was highly appreciated by the public. According to the Hubei dwellers survey from March 2020, 77% of the respondents said they were very satisfied or satisfied with community cadres. The Chinese model of a government-guided community joint prevention and control mechanism was also highly evaluated by international society (Yue and Hanser 2020).

4   Conclusion and Discussion

The success of China's "Government-led Nationwide System" in promoting public health is based on a series of social conditions, including a high level of social trust. Chinese people have a high level of trust in the government and

---

[1] The survey was conducted by the Chinese Academy of Science and Technology for Development, Renmin University of China, and the Institute of Sociology, Chinese Academy of Social Science in February 2020. An online sample of 30,000 people in Hubei Province was drawn, with 6949 questionnaires successfully completed. As a compensation for the possible bias of an online survey, 260 university students living in Hubei Province were mobilized to conduct a telephone survey for older and less educated people who seldom use the Internet. Finally, 10,478 questionnaires were completed.

science, especially in a disaster and risk context. For example, after the Sichuan Earthquake in 2008, public trust in the central government remained at a very high level, which constituted valuable social capital during the post-disaster reconstruction (Zhao and Shi 2016). For COVID-19 risk in 2020, it was also found that the high level of public trust in the government and science increased public willingness to accept suggested self-protection measures, such as wearing face masks, washing hands regularly, and ventilating rooms, and to accept more severe measures, like lockdowns and quarantines. In the Hubei dweller survey from March 2020, 84% and 85% of respondents said that they "highly trust" or "somewhat trust" the central government and scientists. Further analysis showed that those who trust the government and scientists have a higher chance of wearing face masks than those who do not trust. This constitutes a sharp comparison to cases in many Western countries.

Although the "Government-led Nationwide System" seemed to work efficiently, especially in a disaster and risk context, we also should note the sustainability problem of this model. It is doubtless that this "Government-led Nationwide System" with a strong state helps the people and society to live through the darkest moments during a disaster. However, it was also found that the investment of a large amount of resources might be unsustainable. Therefore, when the resource quantity falls back to the common level, the health inequality between different social classes will probably increase to the previous level (Hong and Zhao 2019). The cost and longer-term sustainability of the government-led system in COVID-19 in China also needs more reflections and discussions.

As Ulrich Beck (1996) pointed out, the world is stepping into a "risk society". Frequent risks and disasters will become the main health challenge for the global society in the future. Therefore, existing theories of public health based on the Western experience should be thoroughly reflected upon, and new theories and modes of public health systems that are oriented to the new global future should be explored. The "Government-led Nationwide System" model in promoting public health provided a case for further exploration and reflection.

References

Asandului, Laura, Monica Roman, and Puiu Fatulescu. 2014. "The Efficiency of Healthcare Systems in Europe: A Data Envelopment Analysis Approach". *Procedia Economics and Finance* 10: 261–268.

Beck, Ulrich. 1996. "World Risk Society as Cosmopolitan Society? Ecological Questions in a Framework of Manufactured Uncertainties". *Theory, Culture & Society* 13 (4): 1–32.

Brown-Jeffy, Shelly, and Steve Kroll-Smith. 2009. "Recovering Inequality: Democracy, the Market Economy, and the 1906 San Francisco Earthquake and Fire". In *The Political Economy of Hazards and Disasters*, edited by Eric C. Jones and Arthur D. Murphy, 83–106. Lanham: Altemira.

Druhle, Marcel. (1996) 2009. *Health and Society: The Social Formation of Health Problems*. Translated by Kun Wang. Nanjing: Yilin Press. (In Chinese.)

Elliott, James R., and Jeremy Pais. 2006. "Race, Class, and Hurricane Katrina: Social Differences in Human Responses to Disaster". *Social Science Research* 35: 295–321.

Hong, Yanbi, and Yandong Zhao. 2019. "Resource Redistribution and Health Inequality in Post-Disaster Recovery: On Three Surveys of Wenchuan Earthquake Recovery (2008–2011)". *Chinese Journal of Sociology* 6: 214–237. (In Chinese.)

Klinenberg, Eric. 2015. *Heat Wave: A Social Autopsy of Disaster in Chicago*. Chicago, IL: University of Chicago Press.

Masozera, Michel, Melissa Bailey, and Charles Kerchner. 2007. "Distribution of Impacts of Natural Disasters Across Income Groups: A Case Study of New Orleans". *Ecological Economics* 63: 299–306.

Nakajima, Chieko. 2018. *Body, Society, and Nation: The Creation of Public Health and Urban Culture in Shanghai*. Cambridge, MA: Harvard University Asia Center.

Schwartz, Benjamin I. 1996. *China and Other Matters*. Cambridge, MA: Harvard University Press.

White, Kevin. 2002. *An Introduction to the Sociology of Health and Illness*. London: Sage.

Wisner, Ben, Piers Blaikie, Terry Cannon, and Ian Davis. 2004. *At Risk: Natural Hazards, People's Vulnerability and Disasters*. New York, NY: Routledge.

Yip, Winnie Chi-Man, William C. Hsiao, Wen Chen, Shanlian Hu, Jin Ma, and Alan Maynard. 2012. "Early Appraisal of China's Huge and Complex Health-Care Reforms". *The Lancet* 379 (9818): 833–842.

Yue, Qian, and Amy Hanser. 2020. "How did Wuhan Residents Cope With a 76-Day Lockdown?" *Chinese Review of Sociology* 53 (1): 55–86.

Zhang, Dan, Zhigang Xu, and Pin Chen. 2019. "Does 'Basic Health Protection for All' Improve Farmers' Health? Reassessing the Effect of CNCMS on Medical Service Utilization, Health and Income of Inpatients". *The Chinese Journal of Sociology* 39 (2): 58–74. (In Chinese.)

Zhao, Yandong, and Changhui Shi. 2016. "The Structure and Change of Social Trust During Post-disaster Reconstruction: An Example of Wenchuan Earthquake-Affected Population". In *Ecological Risks and Disasters: New Experiences in China and Europe*, edited by Peilin Li and Laurence Roulleau-Berger. New York, NY: Routledge.

Zhou, M., H. Wang, X. Zeng, P. Yin, J. Zhu, et al. 2019. "Mortality, Morbidity, and Risk Factors in China and Its Provinces, 1990–2017: A Systematic Analysis for the Global Burden of Disease Study 2017". *The Lancet* 394(10204).

CHAPTER 58

East–West Dialogue for Global Health Care Challenges in the Era of COVID-19 and Beyond

Hosoda Miwako

1   Introduction: The Encounter of East and West in Medicine

We are now living in a transnational global society, where people and goods are constantly being exchanged, and cultures and lifestyles are becoming increasingly similar. The global outbreak of COVID-19 is one of the manifestations of this globalization of human mobility.

This chapter is an attempt to analyze how people deal with health and illness from a sociological perspective, focusing on the differences and similarities between the East and the West, including Japan, within the framework of dialogue. The medical care that was formed in the West (medical care based on medical experiments developed in Europe and North America) after the modern era, and the medical care in the East, such as traditional medicine, Kampo (medical care that was introduced from China and developed in Japan) and Ayurveda (traditional medicine of the Indian continent), have each had a history of development since their establishment and are present to this day. In the process, Western medicine and Eastern medicine have met, and while understanding and scientifically proving the characteristics of one another, they have tried to mix and create new forms of medical care.

In this long process of medical transition, medical sociology has developed theories such as the medicalization theory (Illich 1976), which criticizes the oppression of people's lives by medicine, and the concept of social determinants of health, which argues that in order to be healthy, it is important for people to be provided equally with not only medical care but also various social systems and mechanisms. This social determinant of health theory has recently gained popularity (Siegrist 2011). The former theory of medicalization criticizes the extremely bloated system of modern Western medicine and emphasizes that health can be achieved by people taking back their bodies from medical professionals, taking care of themselves, and building amicable relationships with others. This way of thinking can be seen as an argument with Eastern medical overtones. On the other hand, the latter social determinants of health consider it important for all people to have equal access to environments that protect their health, such as hygienic urban development and universal health insurance systems. This is the direction of global health, where Western countries that have achieved these goals can help countries in Asia and Africa that have not yet achieved them. This can be seen as a discussion with Western medical and public health implications.

In this way, our view of medicine and health in modern society is based on a multilayered intertwining of Eastern and Western ideas and practices. When we look again at the perceptions and practices of medicine and health in the East and the West from the perspective of sociology, which focuses on medicine and health, we can say that they are in a reciprocal position. If one becomes too strong, the other gains in importance as if to complement it.

In this paper, I will first outline the acceptance of Western medicine in Eastern countries, especially employing Japan as a case, and show how the current form of medicine has been shaped by the dialogue between Eastern and Western medicine. Next, I (1) will look at the response to the spread of COVID-19 infection in Japan, and (2) will show that the complementary structure of Western and Eastern medicine can be seen here as well. Through this process, (3) the state of medicine and health in the East will be analyzed. To go straight to the point, we can see the phenomenon in which Eastern and Western ways of thinking and practice, that is, Eastern methods that focus on lifestyle and Western methods that are experimental and based on biology, swing like a pendulum from time to time. Finally, in order to deal with the various problems that arise in a society that has experienced the COVID-19 pandemic, I will conclude the dialogue between East and West will become increasingly important, and I will propose the concept and practice of *kyosei* which roughly translates to co-existence, inclusion, and living together in Japanese, as the key to this.

2 A Genealogy of Medical Sociology

Before getting into the specifics, let me first attempt to review the genealogy of medical sociology from the perspective of Eastern and Western medicine.

There are two types of sociology in medical sociology: "Sociology of Medicine", which is a critical sociology that points out the power of medical professionals, and "Sociology in Medicine", which is an applied sociology that contributes to epidemiology and health promotion. These types were proposed in the 1950s and are considered as important frameworks (Straus 1957). Nowadays, rather than highlighting the differences between the two, there are many sociological studies on health that point out the social factors that impair health through concepts such as stigma and social disparity, and raise questions about social conditions. One of the central concepts is the "Social Determinant of Health" (Kawachi et al. 2001). The core of this concept is that various social factors, such as gender, age, race, genetics, lifestyle and living habits, family and community, educational level, employment status, housing environment, health care system and sanitation, politics, economy, and international situation, have a great impact on people's health. Therefore, people's health varies depending on their income, race, country, and location of residence, and the type of work they do. This is called "health disparity" and is an important issue in the sociology of health. This concept overlaps with the World Health Organization (WHO) concept of health, which defines health as a state of physical, mental, and social well-being, not merely the absence of disease. For people's health, it is important to have a well-balanced diet, good sleep, and moderate exercise, as well as to not be poor, not be unemployed, and have good relationships with others.

This idea that all social activities are connected to people's health has actually been an important concept underlying oriental medicine for a long time. Since human beings are also part of nature, the surrounding environment has a great influence on people's lives and the way they live. This concept, which originated in China and India more than 2,000 years ago, has a history of its own development in Japan and is still used in various fields today. Treatment methods based on this Eastern medical philosophy include acupuncture, moxibustion, *anma* (Japanese type of massage), Chinese herbal medicine, medicinal herbs, *qigong* (breathing exercise), and yoga. These are deeply related to beliefs, philosophy, and lifestyles. Since medical treatment is related to people's lives and deaths, it is not hard to imagine that it is also connected to religion and culture.

3 History of Medicine in Japan

Let's take a look at the history of the acceptance of Western medicine in the East, using Japan as a case study. In Japan, "oriental traditional medicine" in today's sense was established during the Edo period in the 18th century, when medical treatment was mainly based on Chinese medicine (Ministry of Health, Labor and Welfare 1976). In those days, there was no concept of hospitalizing patients for treatment, and there were no hospitals in Japan. However, in 1722, the 8th Shogun (General), Yoshimune Tokugawa, established the Koishikawa Training School in the Koishikawa Yakuen (medicinal herbal garden) in Tokyo to train doctors. It also had a hospital room that could accommodate 40 (later 117) patients. Yoshimune also implemented various medical reforms, including the full-scale cultivation of medicinal herbs at the Koishikawa Herbal Garden and the treatment of the poor and the sick with medicinal herbs. Later, in 1791, the medical school, the Igakukan, was opened. This medical school remained in existence until the end of the Edo period as a central educational institution for Chinese medicine. In this way, oriental medicine was developed.

In 1774, Genpaku Sugita and his colleagues translated Western medical texts, "Ontleedkundige Tafelen", written in Dutch, and published the book (which was called "Kaitai Shinsho", The New Book of Anatomy). This led to the rapid spread of Western medicine. In Nagasaki, Siebold, a German physician, taught Western medicine to Japanese physicians from all over the country. Dutch physicians became even more active when they effectively treated the patients with smallpox, an infectious disease prevalent at that time. A doctor of Japanese medicine (Kampo) originally, Seishu Hanaoka also studied Dutch medicine and successfully performed the world's first surgery under anesthesia. In this way, the fusion of Oriental medicine (Kampo) and Western medicine (Dutch medicine) progressed during this period.

The first Western-style hospital in Japan was established in 1861, in the middle of the 19th century. Pompe, a naval doctor dispatched from the Netherlands who had been allowed to visit Japan even under national seclusion, opened the Nagasaki Sanatorium in Nagasaki. At the Nagasaki Sanatorium, Pompe and his successor, Baldwin, ran the hospital and provided medical education to many Japanese doctors.

In Tokyo, the Otamagaike Vaccination Center was established in 1858 by a Japanese medicine doctor to provide Western medicine in the form of vaccines. The vaccination center also trained doctors, and it later became a medical center under the direct control of the government. In this way, the government came to have training facilities for both Kampo and Dutch doctors, together with the abovementioned medical center for Japanese medicine. These were fused together to form what later became the University of Tokyo Faculty of Medicine.

In the middle of the 19th century, the Boshin War, a war within Japan, broke out (1868–1869). It became clear that Kampo doctors could not cope with the emergency situation of treating those injured in war, and temporary war hospitals were set up in various places where doctors who had studied Western medicine performed surgical procedures. In this way, Western medicine spread throughout the country through the war.

In the 20th century, medical care was established to promote hygiene and health in Japan. Aiming to modernize medicine, the Meiji government implemented the "medical system" that established medical education based on Western medicine and a license system for practicing doctors (Shimazaki 2011). From this point on, only those who had studied Western medicine and passed the national medical examination could become doctors. Private hospitals that provided Western medicine also began to open around this time. However, for many people in those days, medical treatment meant taking Kampo, and it continued to take root in people's lives as a folk remedy.

As the Sino-Japanese War (1894–1895) and the Russo-Japanese War (1904–1905) broke out, medical care became even more important as a foundation to support a wealthy and strong military. In 1938, the Ministry of Health and Welfare was established, and the prototype of the National Health Insurance was introduced. At the same time, there was a discriminatory aspect to the system, as the sick and people with disabilities who were unable to recover were excluded from the national coverage.

After World War II, under the direction of the US occupation forces, Japan underwent a reform of its health care system modeled after that of the United States. Characteristic of this reform was the medical system as a social security system based on the spirit of democracy. Medical care was now provided under a national health insurance system, and people's access to medical care had rapidly improved. In recent years, the aging of the population has led to soaring medical costs that have put pressure on the government's finances, and medical care has shifted from treatment to prevention. As the number of patients with chronic diseases is on the rise, more emphasis is being placed on preventing lifestyle-related diseases and on the early detection of diseases. In this context, the concept and practice of lifestyle improvement and oriental treatment using medicinal herbs (Kampo) are being reevaluated.

This is a brief overview of the history of medicine in Japan. It cannot be denied that this is a view taken from the traditional self-definition of Japan as "the first Asian country to achieve modernization" and the frame of social science. In this frame, the comparison of "lagging Asia" and "advanced West" is the axis. In the field of medicine, modern Western medicine was introduced through Dutch medicine and recognized as legitimate by the state, changing the conventional way of dealing with medicine and people's health around the end of the 19th century. On the other hand, without the endorsement of the state, traditional Kampo medicine, which had been the mainstay of conventional medicine, lost its legitimacy as a folk remedy. A clear example of this can be seen in the education and medical systems. What is taught in formal higher education (university medical school) is Western medicine. On the other hand, Kampo medicine is taught in vocational schools and private training institutes. Also, in the health insurance system, Western medicine is covered by insurance. However, with certain exceptions, Kampo medicine, acupuncture, and moxibustion are not covered by insurance, but are paid for by the patient. Acupuncture and moxibustion are also used as private medical treatments, but those who wish to receive them at their own expense do so. In this way, the asymmetry between Eastern and Western medicine can be seen.

However, with the increase of chronic diseases in recent years and the advocacy of preventive medicine, the focus on Eastern elements is also considered important. It would be desirable for Eastern and Western medicine to be provided in an appropriate and accessible manner according to the symptoms and complaints of the patients.

4   Response to COVID-19: Eastern Cultural Aspects

Next, I would like to reconsider the response to COVID-19 in Japan from both Eastern and Western perspectives. As outlined above, Western medicine is considered to be legitimate in Japan, but there are many Eastern cultural elements in the way people think about and practice health and medicine in their daily lives. As an example, Japan's response to COVID-19 is interesting and will be introduced here.

In 2020, when COVID-19 spread, the Japanese Ministry of Health, Labor and Welfare (MHLW) used an illustration of a monster called *Amabie* for a poster to prevent the spread of COVID-19 (Fig. 58.1). *Amabie* is a half-human, half-fish creature that was believed to protect people from plague in the late Edo period (mid-19th century). There is a legend that *Amabie* said, "If there is a plague, copy my image on a piece of paper and show it to people so they won't get sick". The *Amabie* poster is aimed especially at young people, with the words, "Before you know it, it will spread" (Fig. 58.1).

Japanese temples and shrines are also offering prayers for the "dispersal of the plague" (Fig. 58.2). This is the main gate of Zojoji Temple in Tokyo. On the pillar is written, "New coronavirus and other epidemics dispelled".

FIGURE 58.1
Ministry of Health, Labor and Welfare's poster calling for prevention of the spread of the new coronavirus infection (April 2020)
SOURCE: HTTPS://WWW.MHLW.GO.JP/STF/COVID-19/KURASHIYASHIGOTO.HTML

FIGURE 58.2
The main gate of Zojoji Temple in Minato Ward, Tokyo

FIGURE 58.3
Gosyuin at Kokuryo Shrine in Chofu City, Tokyo

In some places, *Gosyuin* (red stamps) decorated with *Amabie* are distributed (Fig. 58.3). In the past, *Gosyuin* were used as a proof of payment of sutra copies to temples. In modern times, *Gosyuin* is not associated with the payment of sutras, but rather serves as a proof that one has paid a visit to a temple. The *Gosyuin* is a combination of the temple or mountain name stamped on the company's sacred seal, the name of the temple or shrine, the date of the visit, and other information, such as words of blessing.

Before the development of the vaccine, the way to prevent COVID-19 was to change one's behavior, such as taking social distance, washing hands, and wearing a mask. These are lifestyle alternations that people take in to be considerate of others. However, even if one person changes his or her behavior, this person can still get COVID-19. Once a person has COVID-19, he or she may be given intensive medical care with ventilators and ECMO, but still may not survive. Thus, COVID-19 is recognized as something that cannot be prevented by changing one's behavior or by medical care, and cannot be controlled by human hands. That is why people pray to God or Buddha to get rid of the plague of COVID-19 or to recover from COVID-19.

Here we can see the mutually complementary composition of Oriental medicine and Western medicine. It can be said that the Eastern and Western ways of thinking and practicing—the Eastern way of focusing on lifestyle and the Western way of being experimental and based on biology—swing like a pendulum from time to time and appear as phenomena in the world of daily life. In recent years, there has been a growing interest in alternative and holistic medicine from the side of Western medicine (Saks 2001). The efficacy of medicinal herbs has been evaluated on the basis of modern medicine, and cognitive behavioral therapy has been developed to empirically demonstrate the effects of Eastern medicine and attitudes toward health. In terms of dealing with infectious diseases, we can see that there is a dialogue between the East and the West.

5 Equality and Human Rights: Toward a Society That Recognizes Diversity and Coexists

In this section, I would like to conclude by stating that dialogue between the East and the West will become increasingly important in order to deal with the various problems that will arise in societies that have experienced the COVID-19 pandemic, and I would like to propose the concept and practice of *kyosei* (philosophy to live together) as the key to achieving this.

COVID-19 is a respiratory infection that has spread throughout the world and has had a major impact not only on physical and medical aspects of life but also on all societies and lifestyles on earth. In addition, in recent years, developed countries have been facing a (super-)aging society, and many people are living with illnesses and disabilities. It is predicted that this trend will soon be seen in middle and developing countries as well. In these modern societies, the health of socially vulnerable groups, such as the sick and people with disabilities, low-income people, indigenous peoples, and social minorities, is much worse, and the COVID-19 epidemic has only added to their suffering.

In this context, a vaccine has been developed, and the vaccination of the population is gradually spreading. However, there are issues of equality and human rights that need to be discussed sociologically. These include health disparities between rich and poor, inequality in vaccine supply, stigmas against those who have become ill, and discrimination against those who choose not to be vaccinated. These problems need to be solved on a global scale, not just in one region or country. That is why we need to continue the dialogue between East and West to protect health and life in the post-COVID-19 global society. It is hoped that not only medical providers, but also patients and citizens who are concerned will take the lead and participate in the dialogue (Hosoda 2020). This dialogue is very important for humanity to survive and overcome the various challenges that are occurring on a global scale.

Living with diverse people is an urgent challenge for all of us. The medical community, public health community, and others are advocating measures to eliminate health disparities from an institutional perspective based on Western medicine, such as establishing evidence-based medicine, improving access to health care services, and achieving socioeconomic equality. At the same time, it is also important to consider the Eastern aspects of eliminating social prejudice (stigma), recognizing diversity, and fostering the awareness and culture of "living together" with nature, including people. This concept of "living together" is called *kyosei* in Japanese, and it is a concept and practice similar to the English word "inclusion". It would be a sociological contribution to present the concept and practice of "inclusion" and *kyosei* as a clue to solve various problems of today. It is hoped that the dialogue between the East and the West toward a society where we can live together will continue.

References

Hosoda, M. 2013. "Living With a Misunderstood Disease: Myalgic Encephalomyelitis / Chronic Fatigue Syndrome in Japan". *Eubios Journal of Asian and International Bioethics (EJAIB)* 23 (3): 70–72.

Hosoda, M. 2020. "COVID-19 and the Metaphors of War". *Budhi* 24 (2): 131–140.

Hosoda, M. 2020. "The Role of Health Support Workers in the Aging Crisis". In *Support Workers and the Health Professions: The Invisible Providers of Health Care*, edited by M. Saks, 205–223. Bristol: Policy Press.

Illich, I. 1976. *Limits to Medicine, Medical Nemesis: The Expropriation of Health*. London: Marion Boyars Publishers.

Inogari, S. 2010. *Byoin no Seiki* [Theories of the Hospital Century]. Yuhikaku.

Kawachi, I., and Kennedy, B. 2001. *The Health of Nations: Why Inequality Is Harmful to Your Health*. New York: New Press.

Ministry of Health and Welfare, Bureau of Medical Affairs. 1976. *Isei Hyakunen Shi* [One Hundred Year History of Medical Service]. Tokyo: Gyosei.

Saks, M. 2001. "Alternative Medicine and the Health Care Division of Labour: Present Trends and Future Prospects". *Current Sociology* 49 (3): 119–134.

Shimazaki, K. 2011. *Nihon no Iryo: Seido to Seisaku* [Japan's Health Care System and Policy]. Tokyo: University of Tokyo Press.

Siegrist, J. 2011. "Social Determinants of Health: Contributions from European Health and Medical Sociology". *Politica y Sociedad* 48 (2): 249–258.

Straus, R. 1957. "The Nature and Status of Medical Sociology". *American Sociological Review* 22: 200–203.

CHAPTER 59

Expanding Epidemic Preparedness to Include Population Memory: A Key for Better Epidemic Management

Frédéric Le Marcis

1   Introduction

The African continent's response to the COVID-19 pandemic has surprised many. While the World Health Organization (WHO) declared the COVID-19 pandemic an International Health Emergency on January 30, 2020 (WHO 2020a), many African countries had already taken protective measures due to the news of the virus spreading in Asia and the West. Very quickly, within the major cities of different African countries, authorities controlled access to public spaces and installed systematic temperature-taking and hand-washing with soap, chlorinated water, or hydroalcoholic solution (Bonnet et al. 2021). In the Republic of Guinea, for example, already on January 25, 2020, an epidemiological surveillance and prevention system (taking temperatures, using alcoholic gel, and administering health questionnaires) was implemented at the airport and in the country's three most important ports (Conakry, Boffa and Boké).[1]

On February 14, a first COVID-19 case was notified in Egypt (WHO Africa 2020). At the time of writing, and despite predictions of the collapse of Africa under the assault of COVID-19, the surprising resistance of the continent had to be acknowledged. Against all odds and despite what is usually described as "failing health systems" (Gilbert et al. 2020), the official number of cases remains low and the spread of the pandemic limited, with significant epidemiological differences between African states (WHO 2020b). Although commentators generally agree on the good initial response of African states (Massinga et al. 2020), the future of the pandemic remains uncertain. Multiple questions remain (Mbow et al. 2020), especially in light of new COVID-19 strains in combination with scarce access to vaccines (Wouters et al. 2021) and a limited uptake when they are available (Afolabi and Ilesanmi 2021). As the pandemic continues, serological studies in the general population will be required to know the exact

---

1   For a detailed description of measures taken in West African countries, see Bonnet et al. 2021.

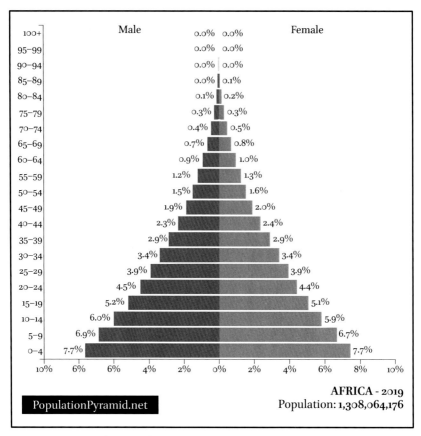

FIGURE 59.1 Gender-starred age pyramid, sub-Saharan Africa, 2019
RETRIEVED ON THE JUNE 10, 2021 FROM HTTPS://WWW.POPULATION
PYRAMID.NET/AFRICA/2019/

prevalence of infection. Currently, the lack of testing and its uneven distribution within countries and between capital cities make reliable estimates of the circulation of COVID-19 in Africa impossible. However, three factors allow us to understand the relatively low impact of the pandemic on the African continent. The first de facto relate to the age structure of the population on the African continent. The population is generally younger, which probably acts as a bulwark against the pandemic (Wayack-Pambè et al. 2020); although life expectancy is increasing, the elderly are still a minority (Rouamba 2015). In addition, the elderly are less "clustered" or grouped together in retirement homes compared with Europe and the United States, for example, leading to less collective exposure to the virus.

Finally, the lower population density, due to fact that the majority of the population is still rural, seems to be another protective factor (Mennechet and

Dzomo 2020).² In rural areas, households are more dispersed and situations of regular and important public gatherings are less frequent (absence of public transportation and large markets), limiting the spread of the virus. Conversely, the lack of a strong health network in rural areas, and the consequent lack of diagnostic capacity, might invisibilize the epidemic. Other hypotheses, such as a greater viral competition in West Africa or genetic specificity, that would have an impact on immune stimulation or resistance, or the current consumption of nivaquine, which would act as protection against the virus, have yet to be verified but are commonly held views in the West African general population. The legacy of Ebola, as well as the experience gained in managing epidemics, is also frequently mentioned but hardly demonstrated.

For now, COVID-19 cases in West Africa are limited. Rather than discussing the imaginary of an "Africa" that has learned the lessons of the Ebola epidemic, this comparative analysis of the COVID response offers an opportunity to discuss both the efficacy and the limits of preparedness programs. In focusing mainly on diagnostic and surveillance capacity, they tend to neglect general health system strengthening. They build on lessons learned during past epidemics as key components of preparedness but nevertheless tend to neglect epidemic embodied memory within communities. Some observers can be seen as afro-pessimists, promising the collapse of the continent due to the lack of a sufficiently strong health system. On the other side, afro-optimists claim this discourse conveys the return of the classical Western discourse condemning Africa to a never-ending catastrophe while downplaying both its capacity of reaction and its experience in epidemic management. I want to bypass this debate by developing an afro-realist perspective discussing the response of three African countries to COVID-19 on the basis of secondary quantitative and primary qualitative data. I compare the situations of Guinea, Burkina Faso, and Sierra Leone. Guinea and Sierra Leone have experienced an Ebola outbreak, while Burkina Faso has not. After providing a set of basic quantitative data comparing the three countries, I discuss the relationship between the Ebola and COVID-19 experience using first-hand ethnographic data collected in Guinea and a literature review on Sierra Leone and Burkina Faso. Preparedness is at the heart of many global health interventions (David and

---

2 See https://donnees.banquemondiale.org/indicator/SP.RUR.TOTL.ZS, accessed 30th of June 2021. It should be noted that African countries are not equal in this respect. The countries of the continent most affected are also the most urbanised countries: South Africa (1,973,972 cases, total population 60,051,644, rural population 33.4%), Egypt (281,282 cases, total population 104,248,863, rural population 57.27%) or Nigeria (167,618 cases, total population 211,198,870, rural population 48.84%). This situation is not comparable to Guinea (23,770 cases, total population 13,485,302, rural population 63.5%). See https://www.worldometers.info/coronavirus/, accessed on the 30th of June 2021).

Le Dévédec 2018; Lakoff 2017). It can be summarized as the recognition of the link between humans, non-humans, and the environment in terms of the risk of contamination, and the recognition of the need to put in place surveillance systems and diagnostic capacities to prevent the next pandemic (technics and stocks). It takes the form of exercises (online or onsite) to be ready for the next pending epidemic (Keck and Lachenal 2019). The discussion developed in this paper ends with an invitation to expand the meaning and practices of preparedness in paying attention to the way memories (institutional and popular) sustain the way population and states prepare for pandemic risk.

2   Methodology

Using the case of the Republic of Guinea, where I currently live and work in the health system, in combination with the literature on Sierra Leone and Burkina Faso, I qualitatively analyze the Ebola legacy in relation to the COVID-19 experience. Looking at the institutional and popular responses to the COVID-19 pandemic though the lens of the Ebola legacy questions the relevance of *preparedness* policies at the heart of global health (Caduff 2015; David and Le Dévédec 2018; King 2002; Lurie, Wasserman and Nelson 2006). These policies, which can be traced back to the 1990s in the field of health (Lakoff 2017), have been accentuated in sub-Saharan Africa and particularly in the Mano River countries after 2016 (Le Marcis and Gomez-Temesio 2021). Ethnographic data were collected in Guinea as part of the research projects "Ebola's shadow over the SARS-CoV-2 epidemic. Analysis of public policies, the practices of actors and popular representations relating to COVID-19 for a better Guinean response to the pandemic"[3] and "EBOVAC 3".[4] The first project consisted of the description and analysis of the measures taken by the health authorities and of the study of the evolution of the knowledge and behavior of the population in general and of health professionals in particular since the beginning of the COVID-19 epidemic. It is based on ethnographic research conducted among the population, consisting of daily observations of social interactions and

---

[3] Coordinated by Frederic Le Marcis, this project is run with Marie Yvonne Curtis (Cerfig), Moustapha Keïta Diop (Cerfig, U. Sonfonia), and Bienvenu Salim Camara (CEA, U. van Amsterdam, ITM). The author would like to thank the research assistants participating in this program: Fanny Attas, Amadou Tidiane Barry, Foromo Timothé Beavogui, Niouma Laurent Koniono, Sekou Kouyate†, Gassim Sylla, Paul Théa, and Christine Timbo Songbono. This program is financed by AFD (ARIACOV program led by IRD).

[4] "EBOVAC3 Bringing a prophylactic Ebola vaccine to licensure", funded by IMI (grant agreement number 800176) and run by LSTHM and INSERM.

formal and informal exchanges with individuals, and among health personnel (at the three levels of the health system: health post, medical center, and hospital levels in the cities of Conakry, Mamou, and Forecariah). The second study aimed at analyzing the question of preparedness in the context of a program aiming to make a prophylactic Ebola vaccine available. It consisted of a critical analysis of preparedness logics and practices in Guinea, focusing on a retro-ethnography of the past epidemic experience in population and virologic knowledge production in Guinea since the 1980s. Both studies received the approval of the National Ethics Committee for Health Research of the Republic of Guinea (nos. 068/CNERS/20 and 050/CNERS/21, respectively).

3 Three Countries with Specific Outbreak Experiences

The Infectious Disease Vulnerability Index, a quantitative tool aiming at providing a synthetic metric of vulnerability to infectious disease (Moore et al. 2017), ranks the three countries among the second-lowest prepared for the risk of epidemics (Gilbert et al. 2020: 873). The State Party Self-Assessment Annual Reporting database (WHO 2018), containing 24 indicator scores,[5] ranks Guinea in the middle of its worldwide list, with Burkina Faso and Sierra Leone situated just below. Beyond the predicted pandemic capacities, how did these countries concretely react to the COVID outbreak?

The COVID-19 epidemic took hold in all three countries in contexts characterized by a difference in population size, an equivalent socioeconomic situation, and a similar Ebola experience in the cases of Guinea and Sierra Leone but not in Burkina Faso. According to the World Bank, the Republic of Guinea (a former French colony) had a population of 11,883,516 inhabitants[6] in 2018, a GDP per capita of USD $926, and a literacy rate of 45% in 2015 (World Bank). Regarding Ebola, Guinea had a great deal of experience. The 2014–2016 outbreak officially killed 2412 people (3647 cases were reported), and the sanitary-humanitarian response was met with violence and fear (Le Marcis et al. 2019), leaving vivid memories within the population. These were felt

---

5 These indicators are "organised and grouped according to the following capacities (bracketed number shows indicators per capacity): legislation (three), International Health Regulation Coordination (two), zoonosis (one), food safety (one), laboratory (three), surveillance (two), human resource (one), national health emergency framework (three), health service provision (three), communication (one), points of entry (two), chemical events (one), and radiation emergency (one)" (Gilbert et al. 2020: 872).
6 https://www.populationdata.net/ (accessed June 25, 2020).

during the second, brief Ebola outbreak that happened between April and March 2021 in the forest region (Keïta et al. 2021).

Despite the late arrival of its first COVID case (on March 12, 2020) and a rapid implementation of preventive measures (borders were closed on March 26, 2020) (Bonnet et al. 2021), at the time of writing, Guinea was among the 5 West African countries worst hit by COVID-19 in terms of number of cases[7] (at the top of the COVID-19 list in sub-Saharan Africa). On July 30, the number of reported COVID cases was 7243.[8]

In neighboring Sierra Leone, 14,061 cases of Ebola and 3955 deaths were reported during the 2014–2016 outbreak. This country experienced, like Guinea, a violent reaction to the intervention from the population (Le Marcis et al. 2019). Sierra Leone has a smaller population than Guinea (7,794,974 inhabitants in 2018),[9] a literacy rate of 51% in 2015, and a GDP per capita of USD $523 in 2018 (World Bank). Contrary to Guinea and Burkina Faso, it collaborates in the public health field with English-speaking countries due to its colonial history. Regarding COVID-19, Sierra Leone closed its borders a day before Guinea (March 25, 2020) and reported its first case 15 days after Guinea (March 31, 2020). On July 30, Sierra Leone had 1823 COVID cases.[10] The lower numbers are probably linked to a weaker diagnostic capacity than in Guinea.

Lastly, Burkina Faso had a population of 29,870,060 inhabitants[11] in 2019, a literacy rate of 52% in 2015, and a GDP per capita of USD $744 in 2018 (World Bank). This country had no direct experience with Ebola. Among the three countries it was the first to report a COVID-19 case (March 9, 2020) and to close its borders (March 18, 2020). On July 30 it only had 1106 COVID cases[12] and presented a relatively slow evolution of COVID-19. This number is probably due to a weaker diagnostic capacity compared with the first two countries (Fig. 59.2). The capacity to perform polymerase chain reaction test (PCR) is directly related to the Ebola experience, as this technology was introduced in Guinea and Sierra Leone during the 2014–2016 pandemic. Despite presenting a lower incidence than Guinea and Sierra Leone (Fig. 59.3), Burkina Faso has a higher case fatality rate (Fig. 59.2).[13]

---

7   See https://coronavirus.jhu.edu/data/new-cases, accessed on July 10, 2021.
8   *Agence Nationale de Sécurité Sanitaire* (National Health Security Agency), ANSS official data, 30/07/2020.
9   https://www.populationdata.net/ (accessed June 25, 2020).
10 https://www.worldometers.info/coronavirus/ (accessed July 31, 2020).
11 https://www.worldometers.info/coronavirus/ (accessed July 31, 2020).
12 https://www.worldometers.info/coronavirus/ (accessed July 31, 2020).
13 Again, these figures should be read with caution. For example, only deaths occurring in COVID-specific care centres are counted. Thus, all so-called community deaths (deaths linked to COVID but not occurring in the hospital) remain invisible. In this context, the higher death rate may only reflect the difference in the amount of hospital care.

The comparison between the three countries highlights the impact of the epidemic of Ebola haemorrhagic fever only in terms of diagnostic capacity-building but not in the overall response to the pandemic. In deed the discrepancy in testing capacity between the three countries does not allow for a global comparison of the responses.

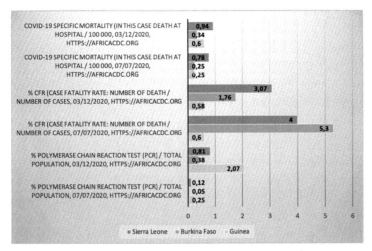

FIGURE 59.2   Mortality, fatality, PCR test: Guinea, Burkina Faso, Sierra Leone (December to July 2020)

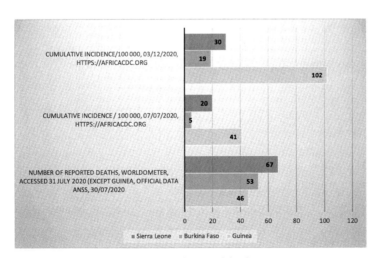

FIGURE 59.3   Incidence, number of reported deaths: Guinea, Sierra Leone, Burkina Faso (December to July 2020)

The impact of the diagnostic capacity in the aftermath of the 2014–2016 Ebola outbreak is evident, albeit unequal. Guinea has benefited more from these programs than Sierra Leone.[14] In Sierra Leone,

> Although the country has good experience of case finding, contact tracing, and quarantine from EVD, it lacks the localized testing capacity to monitor and crack down on local outbreaks of COVID-19.... The laboratory capacity for rapid turnaround of tests is not available. Little was done by aid donors after the epidemic of EVD to consolidate in-country laboratory testing capacities. Equipment was sometimes supplied, but training and payment of technicians, especially in provincial locations, was apparently beyond the capacity of governments hovering on the brink of post-Ebola bankruptcy to sustain.
>
> RICHARDS 2020: 497

Abu Bakarr Kamara, economist at the International Growth Centre at the London School of Economics, observes that in Sierra Leone: "Prior to the index case, the country implemented strategies that are largely regarded as proactive and innovative to prevent the pandemic from entering the country. This could be attributed to lessons learned from the Ebola epidemic in 2014/2015" (Kamara 2021). Nevertheless, the above comparison shows that Burkina Faso without Ebola experience reacted as quickly as Ebola-experienced countries did. The presence or absence of a direct Ebola outbreak experience had no direct impact on the rapidity of implementation of prevention measures at their borders.

The numbers regarding the follow-up of contacts are not considered in this comparison. Follow-up of contacts is a central activity of epidemic management, but these figures are highly sensitive and the subject of much controversy. In Guinea, they have been discussed between institutions mobilizing different sources (WHO, Agence Nationale de Sécurité Sanitaire), and actors in the field agree on their inaccuracy. Overall, in all three countries, communication on an extremely high rate of contact tracing was reported, but this says little about the reality. As we have seen, the number of cases does not avoid these criticisms too.

---

14   It should be stressed that these data say nothing about the unequal distribution of this capacity in the country, the laboratories with PCR being mainly concentrated in the capital city of Conakry.

4 The Ebola Experience: An Ambiguous Legacy

A recent scoping review acknowledges the impact of experience with Ebola (speed at which border crossing was subjected to sanitary checks, surveillance, and testing) but nevertheless highlights that a one-size-fits-all approach copied from European and Chinese contexts was uncritically adopted (such as confinement and social distancing) and appeared to be detrimental to the good management of COVID-19 in Africa (Alhassan et al. 2021, see also Sengeh et al. 2020 and Wallace et al. 2020). They conclude:

> Evidence from the reviewed literature suggests that countries, particularly in Africa, need to improve health infrastructure, human resources and medical technology using local resources to enable the continent respond adequately to public health emergencies. COVID-19 has taught the world, including Africa, that pandemic preparedness should be prioritised over response. A relatively less expensive yet effective investment should be community-level preparedness and response strategies long before pandemics strike.
> ALHASSAN et al. 2021: 11

The data presented above indeed show a relationship between Ebola experience and testing capacity but invalidate the idea that border closing is related to Ebola, as shown by the Burkina case. Rather, they testify about a classical and non-specific response to pandemics. Border closing was used in colonial times during yellow fever outbreaks, and it characterized the worldwide initial response to HIV/AIDS (see Farmer 1992 for a discussion of US policies regarding Haitian immigrants). The need to improve the capacity of the health system to detect early and to heal is patent. Instead of thinking epidemic preparedness in a technology-based dimension only aiming at surveillance and diagnostics (David and Le Dévédec 2018; Keck and Lachenal 2019), I concur with the authors that the community level should be seen as part and parcel of preparedness strategies. Nevertheless, they say little about how communities should be integrated. Here, I defend the idea that classical community mobilization strategies evoked for preparedness mechanisms would greatly benefit from a notion of preparedness conceived in terms of memory. This memory has a double dimension: one is institutional, the other popular. The first one refers to the experience collectively gained by states and fosters an institutional response to pandemic threats. The second one has to do with what Didier Fassin defined as embodiment of history (2007). It is the memory embodied following objective experience and subjective understanding of it, fostering the way people make sense of and engage with the present (Fassin 2007). This embodiment can have long roots in colonial history (Hayden 2008; White 2000) or in a more recent past, such as past Ebola outbreaks (Gomez-Temesio and Le Marcis 2017).

5 Ebola's Institutional Memory

The above comparison shows that the Ebola experience—and programs developed afterwards—had a positive impact on the development of testing capacity. In Guinea, their legacy is observable as well in the very existence of a National Health Security Agency (ANSS) and in the archipelago of CT-EPIs (*Centres de traitement des épidémies*) spread out in the country. CT-EPIs were built with World Bank funding after the Ebola outbreak and replaced former ETUs (Ebola Treatment Units). Nevertheless, what can be described as a success has its dark side.

The Ebola experience was used as a reference for institutional actors who, instead of taking the measure of the specificity of SARS-CoV-2, reproduced already known measures without paying attention to the specificity of the new pandemic. The specter of Ebola defined the first comments of public health actors (in the sense of "let's not relive the past, therefore we must learn from our past experience") and notions forged during the fight against Ebola (including quarantine). In Guinea, it went as far as adapting the title of a former Ebola control program ("zero Ebola in 60 days") to the current pandemic. The "Stop Covid in 60 days" (Stop COVID en 60 jours) strategy, aimed at tackling the pandemic and fostering community participation, was thus launched in June 2020.

At the beginning of the COVID-19 outbreak, the majority of the CT-EPIs were not functional. Some of them that were constructed within the premises of general hospitals had been dedicated to ordinary care and were not ready for pandemic management. They were understaffed, lacking in equipment and drugs. In those cases where they were functional, the specific status of their staff, and the relatively better equipment compared with their counterparts working in regular services, had the negative effect of sustaining the idea that infection risk was only the CT-EPIs' responsibility and not a matter of concern for other health professionals. As a consequence, biosecurity practices were difficult to integrate as routine activities within ordinary health centers. Moreover, the CT-EPI staff, initially recruited during the Ebola pandemic, had the tendency to deal with COVID-19 risk without questioning the specific nature of SARS-CoV-2 and thus organizing treatment centers as strict copies of former ETUS (CEA-PMCT 2020; Sow and Criel 2020). In Donka, Conakry General Hospital, a treatment center, was opened by the state, and its management was entrusted to the non-governmental organization (NGO) ALIMA. It took several weeks for this NGO to abandon systematic preventive measures directly stemming from their Ebola expertise and to reduce the biosecurity setting of their care center to better adjust to COVID-19. Symptomatic of this Ebola legacy at the beginning of the COVID-19 pandemic was the systematic use of full personal protective equipment similar to that used during Ebola by lab technicians and NGO workers alike. They were later abandoned. In the same vein, in Sierra Leone, according to a KAP survey, the "Ebola outbreak has likely exacerbated the perception of risk" (Sengeh et al. 2020, 5). Moreover, the capacity of CT-EPIs quickly appeared to be insufficient to host all patients. In Guinea, new places, such as part of the newly renovated University Hospital Donka in Conakry, former hotels were dedicated to isolation, initially with the aim of isolating all suspected cases, symptomatic or asymptomatic. Although this can be justified because health authorities assumed that the majority of the COVID-positive patients had no capacity to isolate themselves at home for lack of space, this policy strictly reproduced the way Ebola's risk was handled back in 2014.

Another legacy of Ebola was felt in the pandemic governance. The ANSS was created with the support of foreign donors in order to sustain a national agency able to react efficiently and more quickly than the Minister of Health to epidemic risk. Heavily funded, it became another vertical program in competition with other state actors (National Institute for Health, Ministry of Health), disputing funding and legitimacy. This de facto bicephalism fostered competition and tension detrimental to the COVID-19 pandemic response.

In Burkina Faso, it was not the Ebola legacy but structural health system inequalities that defined the Burkinabe response to the COVID-19 pandemic (Kobiane et al. 2020). In addition, fear of COVID-19 infection had an impact on health-seeking itineraries, at the level of both patients and health workers, who systematically preferred to redirect suspected cases to referral centers (Kobiane et al. 2020). This was also observed in Guinea during the 2014–2016 Ebola outbreak when, in order to avoid contamination, health centers located in the active zones of the epidemic, even if they had the necessary technical facilities, tended to refer individuals presenting with a suspicious sign, such as a simple fever or diarrhea, to dedicated centers without consulting them.

Preparedness had an impact in Guinea in terms of diagnostic capacity, but when it materialized as the reproduction of old recipes it had detrimental effects on the institutional capacity to analyze and act reflexively. This was pointed out at the beginning of the pandemic in Guinea, Liberia, and Sierra

Leone by health specialists comparing the trends of infection, and describing the rapid increase of cases in their country (Delamou et al. 2020).

6   Population Memory and Social Knowledge

Discussing preparedness in Mano River countries[15] without considering the Ebola trauma in the population and its effects on the way people react to a new epidemic would be misleading. "Epidemics are group-learning experiences. Responding to infection risks requires societal action as well as specialist medical intervention" (Richards 2020: 493). Social scientists have demonstrated how quick populations learn during a pandemic, developing means of avoiding risk. Paul Richards, based on his long commitment in Sierra Leone, argues that: "Evidence from the EVD epidemic in Sierra Leone in 2014–15 suggests that typically it took communities only about six to eight weeks to figure out the nature of the infection challenges they faced, and to mobilize against them" (ibid.: 503, see also Richards 2016). The meaning of social knowledge that he defines "as knowledge of the behavioural and organizational characteristics of the social group to which you belong" (Richards 2020: 498) can usefully encompass the memory of past events. Social knowledge is fuelled by experience and history; it is embodied knowledge, and this is exactly what global health institutions fail to recognize.

In Guinea, this memory translated into a quick and spontaneous reaction. Before any official declaration, as soon as the news of the COVID-19 pandemic was broadcast in the international media, the population of Conakry started wearing masks sold by street vendors, they started using hygiene kits dating back to Ebola, and plastic bottles with bleached water were seen at the entrance to shops and private houses (Sow and Criel 2020). These preventive measures were learned during the previous epidemic episode and were now part of the basic epidemic know-how embedded in popular practices.

But the Ebola trauma also led to a massive drop in the number of people attending health centers, resulting in a loss of opportunity for health care and vaccination campaigns, the effects of which have yet to be assessed. What is already known is that there was a significant drop in the income of health centers, as their activities are largely based on cost recovery. The fear of being locked down in dedicated treatment centers if they tested positive fostered test avoidance among people. Even if in Guinea the Ebola Treatment Centers were

---

15   Mano River countries refers to Guinea, Liberia, and Sierra Leone, which have the Mano River as a frontier.

now called CT-EPIs, they kept their sinister reputation (Gomez-Temesio and Le Marcis 2017; Le Marcis 2015).

The reactivation of mistrust logic—observed during the 2014–2016 Ebola outbreak—was also maintained, as a political reading of the epidemic shows. The COVID-19 outbreak happened in Guinea in the context of disputed presidential elections. At first, the population spontaneously started to wear masks, but soon after, when the government implemented other preventive measures (such as social distancing and a ban on public gathering), these were perceived by the opposition as a way to silence a contestation of Alpha Condé's project of running for a third mandate. Moreover, the population, facing an epidemic that was largely invisible—except in its socioeconomic consequences—was quick to consider the state an "epidemic sponsor" out of its own interest. This is coherent with observations made elsewhere on the continent, as in the case of Sierra Leone, where the use of chlorine in a health institution or the construction of a tent (two situations reminiscent of Ebola State response) results in the withdrawal of the public (Dubbink et al. 2020: 2). It is worth noting, however, that when in Rwanda, the "public trust of Rwanda's COVID-19 response is higher, this was attributed to Rwanda's efficient, effective, and transparent governance approach and success in combating Ebola from entering its borders in 2019" (Wallace et al. 2020). Another key point to consider with former population epidemic experience is the health systems' structural context in low- and middle-income countries characterized by chronic underfunding and a lack of human resources in quality and quantity. "As healthcare systems are obviously very different in LMIC compared to HIC, a one-size-fits-all approach does not work in the global fight against this pandemic" (Dubbink et al. 2020: 3; see also Ag Ahmed et al. 2020). Consequently, to be prepared for the next pandemic implies rebuilding the population's trust in the capacity of the health system to produce efficient care. This goes far beyond the technological capacity of performing PCR testing.

7 Expanding Epidemic Preparedness

The preparedness programs discussed here are mainly defined by a trust in technology (diagnostic capacity) and the idea that pandemics repeat themselves (Lakoff 2017). But empirical reality resists, and COVID-19 is not Ebola. Preparing oneself for the next pandemic by reproducing Ebola practices does not help develop the capacity to analyze the specificity of a virus, to understand it and to develop a response accordingly. The illusion of the technological fix downplays the need to situate interventions in specific contexts fueled with politics and histories. What is praised for its ability to anticipate the future (*preparedness*), however, produces its share of ignorance. It determines in advance what must be known and therefore what will be ignored: other pathologies, new viruses, health inequalities, the political and economic context in which epidemics unfold. By definition, the contextual and contingent part of interventions in epidemic contexts always escapes preparedness when understood in a narrow sense. Antoine de Bengy Puyvallée and Sonja Kittelsen rightly identify "some of the tensions inherent in this new global health security regime, particularly the resistance of national interest, the privileging of containment over prevention policy, and of short-term, technology-based responses over longer-term engagements in strengthening health systems" (Bengy Puyvallée and Kittelsen 2019: 61). The epidemic does not exist without its epidemic context, and viruses are not equal to each other. Each response to an epidemic calls for a reflexive response that learns from past experiences without making it the alpha and omega of the response to pandemics. Preparedness should not be thought of and implemented independently from the general health system. What is preparedness without tackling the geographic and socioeconomic inequalities of care?

This comparative and qualitative look at both the Ebola and COVID-19 epidemics in three West African countries constitutes a call to think about preparation in an articulated way with the health system, including one of its fundamental dimensions: the community dimension. Kamara, Mokuwa, and Richards suggest that rural people in Sierra Leone respond to infection risks in rational and calibrated ways. The benefits of this response were experienced in the Ebola epidemic of 2014–15. We see no evidence that the same will not also be the case with Covid-19. Communities should be trusted to play a fuller part in infection control (Kamara, Mokuwa and Richards 2020: 7).

Instead of working against the communities while "waging war on viruses", one would benefit from collaborating with them to collectively negotiate risk. We have seen that while memories embodied within communities can sometimes foster fears and logics of avoidance, they are also a powerful source of experience-based knowledge on which to build collective responses to a pandemic. Recognizing this knowledge could lead us to turn preparedness from a top-down program to a form of collectively owned prevention.

Acknowledgments

I thank Koen Peeters Grietens and Fanny Attas for their generous comments on a previous version of this text. I am grateful to Jean-François Etard for his input on quantitative data. All errors and inaccuracies remain mine.

References

Afolabi, Aanuoluwapo Adeyimika, and Olayinka Stephen Ilesanmi. 2021. "Dealing With Vaccine Hesitancy in Africa: The Prospective COVID-19 Vaccine Context". *Pan African Medical Journal* 38 (3). doi:10.11604/pamj.2021.38.3.27401.

Ag Ahmed, Mohamed Ali, Birama Apho Ly, Tamba Mino Millimouno, Hassane Alami, Christophe L. Faye, Sana Boukary, Kirsten Accoe, Wim Van Damme, Willem Van De Put, Bart Criel, and Seydou Doumbia. "Willingness to Comply With Physical Distancing Measures Against COVID-19 in Four African Countries". *BMJ Global Health* 5: e003632. doi:10.1136/bmjgh-2020-003632.

Alhassan, Robert Kaba, Jerry John Nutor, Aaron Asibi, Agani Afaya, Solomon Mohammed Salia, Maxwel Ayindenaba Dalaba, Mustapha Immurana, Alfred Kwesi Manyeh, Desmond Klu, Matilda Aberese-Ako, Phidelia Theresa Doegah, Evelyn Acquah, Edward Nketiah-Amponsah, John Tampouri, Samuel Kaba Akoriyea, Paul Amuna, Evelyn Kokor Ansah, Margaret Gyapong, Seth Owusu-Agyei, and John Owusu Gyapong. 2021. "Urban Health Nexus With Coronavirus Disease 2019 (COVID-19) Preparedness and Response in Africa: Rapid Scoping Review of the Early Evidence". *SAGE Open Medicine* 9:1–14. doi:10.1177/2050312121994360.

Bengy Puyvallée, Antoine de, and Sonja Kittelsen. 2019. "'Disease Knows No Borders': Pandemics and the Politics of Global Health Security". In *Pandemics, Publics, and Politics. Staging Responses to Public Health Crises*, edited by Krisitian Bjørkdahl and Benedicte Carlsen, 59–73. Singapore: Palgrave Macmillan. https://doi.org/10.1007/978-981-13-2802-2_5.

Birn, Anne-Emanuelle. 2020. "Perspectivizing Pandemics: (How) Do Epidemic Histories Criss-cross Contexts?" *Journal of Global History* 15 (3): 336–349. doi:10.1017/S1740022820000327.

Bonnet, Emmanuel, Oriane Bodson, Frederic Le Marcis, Adama Faye, Emmanuel Sambieni, Florence Fournet, Florence Boyer, Abdourahme Coulibaly, Kadidiatou Kadio, Fatoumata Binetou Diongue Lopes, and Valery Ridde. 2021. "The COVID-19 Pandemic in Francophone West Africa: From the First Cases to Responses in Seven Countries". *BMC Public Health* 21 (1490): 1–17.

Caduff, Carlo. 2015. *The Pandemic Perhaps: Dramatic Events in a Public Culture of Danger*. Berkeley: University of California Press.

CEA-PCMT (Centre d'Excellence Africain pour la Prévention et Contrôle des Maladies Transmissibles). 2020 (May). *De l'épidémie d'Ebola à la pandémie de coronavirus (Covid-19) : une analyse situationnelle rapide en Guinée. Rapport de recherche*. Conakry: ENABEL.

David, Pierre-Marie, and Nicolas Le Dévédec. 2018. "Preparedness for the Next Epidemic: Health and Political Issues of an Emerging Paradigm". *Critical Public Health* 29 (3): 363–369. doi:10.1080/09581596.2018.1447646.

Delamou, Alexandre, Sidikiba Sidibé, Alioune Camara, Mohamed Sahar Traoré, Abdoulaye Touré, and Wim Van Damme. 2020. "Correspondence: Tackling the COVID-19 Pandemic in West Africa: Have We Learned From Ebola in Guinea?" *Preventive Medicine Reports* 20: 101206. https://doi.org/10.1016/j.pmedr.2020.101206.

Dubbink, Jan H., Tiago Martins Branco, Kelfala B.B. Kamara; James S. Bangura, Erik Wehrens, Abdul M. Falama, Abraham Goorhuis, Peter B. Jørgensen, Stephen Sevalie, Thomas Hanscheid, and Martin Peter Grobusch. 2020. "COVID-19 Treatment in Sub-Saharan Africa: If the Best Is Not Available, the Available Becomes the Best". *Travel Medicine and Infectious Disease* 37: 101878. https://doi.org/10.1016/j.tmaid.2020.101878.

Etard, Jean-François, Abdoulaye Touré, Cheikh Tidiane Ndour, Leon Tshilolo, Philippe Katchunga Bianga, Samba Sow, and Yap Boum. 2020. "Covid-19 en Afrique: les chiffres reflètent-ils la réalité?" *The Conversation*. https://theconversation.com/covid-19-en-afrique-les-chiffres-refletent-ils-la-realite-141815.

Farmer, Paul. 1992. *AIDS and Accusation: Haiti and the Geography of Blame*. Berkeley: University of California Press.

Fassin, Didier. 2007. *When Bodies Remember: Experience and Politics of Aids in South Africa*. Berkeley: University of California Press.

Gilbert, Marius, Giulia Pullano, Francesco Pinotti, Eugenio Valdano, Chiara Poletto, Pierre-Yves Boëlle, Eric d'Ortenzio, Yazdan Yazdanpanah, Serge Paul Eholie, Mathias Altmann, Bernardo Gutierrez, Moritz U.G. Kraemer, and Vittoria Colizza. 2020. "Preparedness and Vulnerability of African Countries Against Importations of COVID-19: A Modelling Study". *Lancet* 395 (10227): 871–877. https://doi.org/10.1016/S0140-6736(20)30411-6.

Gomez-Temesio, Veronica, and Frederic Le Marcis. 2017. "La mise en camp de la Guinée. Ebola et l'expérience postcoloniale". *L'Homme* 222: 57–90.

Hayden, Christopher Ellis. 2008. *Of Medicine and Statecraft. Smallpox and Early Colonial Vaccination in French West Africa (Senegal-Guinea)*. PhD dissertation. Evanston, Northwestern University.

Kamara, Abou Bakarr. 2021. "Responding to Covid-19 in Fragile States. The Case of Sierra Leone". Accessed January 29, 2021. https://www.theigc.org/blog/responding-to-covid-19-in-fragile-states-the-case-of-sierra-leone/.

Kamara, Foday Mamoud, Esther Yei Mokuwa, and Paul Richards. 2020. "How Villagers in Central Sierra Leone Understand Infection Risks Under Threat of Covid-19". *PloS One* 15 (6): e0235108. https://doi.org/10.1371/journal.pone.0235108.

Keck, Frederic, and Guillaume Lachenal. 2019. "Simulations of Epidemics: Techniques of Global Health and Neo-liberal Government". In *The Anthropology of Epidemics*, edited by Ann H. Kelly, Frederic Keck, and Christos Lynteris, 25–42. London: Routledge.

Keïta, Alpha Kabinet, Fara R. Koundouno, Martin Faye, et al. 2021. "Resurgence of Ebola Virus in 2021 in Guinea Suggests a New Paradigm for Outbreaks". *Nature* 597: 539–543 https://doi.org/10.1038/s41586-021-03901-9.

King, Nicholas B. 2002. "Security, Disease, Commerce: Ideologies of Postcolonial Global Health". *Social Studies of Science* 32 (5/6): 763–789.

Kobiane, Jean-François, Bassiahi Abdramane Soura, Ali Sie, Idrissa Ouili, Idrissa Kaboré, and Sibi Guissou. 2020. *Les inégalités au Burkina Faso à l'aune de la pandémie de la COVID-19: quelques réflexions prospectives, Papiers de recherche, n°137, sous la coordination de Linda Zanfini* (unpublished report). Agence Française de Développement.

Lakoff, Andrew. 2017. *Unprepared: Global Health in a Time of Emergency*. Oakland: University of California Press.

Le Marcis, Frederic. 2015. "'Traiter les corps comme des fagots': Production sociale de l'indifférence en contexte Ebola (Guinée)". *Anthropologie & Santé* (11). http://anthropologiesante.revues.org/1907; doi:10.4000/anthropologiesante.1907.

Le Marcis, Frederic, Luisa Enria, Sharon Abramowitz, Almudena Mari-Saez, and Sylvain Faye. 2019. "Three Acts of Resistance During the 2014–2016 West Africa Ebola Epidemic: A Focus on Community Engagement". *Journal of Humanitarian Affairs* 1 (2): 23–31.

Le Marcis, Frédéric, and Veronica Gomez-Temesio. 2021. "Governing Lives in the Times of Global Health". In *The SAGE Handbook of Cultural Anthropology*, edited by Lene Pedersen and Lisa Cliggett, 554–578. Newbury Park, CA: SAGE Publications Ltd.

Lurie, Nicole, Jeffrey Wasserman, and Christopher D. Nelson. 2006. "Public Health Preparedness: Evolution or Revolution?" *Health Affairs* 25 (4): 935–945. doi:10.1377/hlthaff.25.4.935.

Massinga Loembé, Marguerite, Akhona Tshangela, Stéphanie J. Salyer, Jay K. Varma, Ahmed E. Ogwell Ouma, and John N. Nkengasong. 2020. "COVID-19 in Africa: The Spread and Response". *Nature Medicine* (26): 999–1003. https://doi.org/10.1038/s41591-020-0961-x.

Mbow, Moustapha, Bertrand Lell, Simon P. Jochems, Badara Cisse, Souleymane Mboup, Benjamin G. Dewals, Assan Jaye, Alioune Dieye, and Maria Yazdanbakhsh. 2020. "COVID-19 in Africa: Dampening the Storm?" *Science* 369 (6504): 624–626. doi: 10.1126/science.abd3902.

Mennechet, Franck J.D., and Guy R.T. Dzomo. 2020. "Coping with COVID-19 in Sub-Saharan Africa: What Might the Future Hold?" *Virologica Sinica* 35: 875–884. https://doi.org/10.1007/s12250-020-00279-2.

Moore, Melinda, Bill Gelfeld, Adeyimi Theophilus Okunogbe, and Paul Christopher. 2017. "Identifying Future Disease Hot Spots: Infectious Disease Vulnerability Index". *Rand Health Quarterly* 6 (3): 5. PMCID: PMC5568150, PMID: 28845357.

Richards, Paul. 2016. *Ebola: How a People's Science Helped End an Epidemic*. London: Zed Books.

Richards, Paul. 2020. "Ebola and COVID-19 in Sierra Leone: Comparative Lessons of Epidemics for Society". *Journal of Global History* 15 (3): 493–507. doi:10.1017/S1740022820000303.

Rouamba, George. 2015. *"Yaab-rãmba": une anthropologie du care des personnes vieillissantes à Ouagadougou (Burkina Faso)*. Anthropologie sociale et ethnologie. Bordeaux: University of Bordeaux, 2015. NNT: 2015BORD0397. tel-01299053.

Sengeh, Paul, Mohammad B. Jalloh, Nance Webber, Ibrahim Ngobeh, Thomas Samba, Harold Thomas, Helena Nordenstedt, and Mike Winters. 2020. "Community Knowledge, Perceptions and Practices Around COVID-19 in Sierra Leone: A Nationwide, Cross-sectional Survey". *BMJ Open* 10: e040328. doi:10.1136/bmjopen-2020-040328.

Sow, Abdoulaye, and Bart Criel. 2020. "First Line Response to COVID-19: Community Health Centres and Doctors' Offices in Guinea". Accessed June 28, 2021. https://blogs.bmj.com/bmjgh/2020/04/10/first-line-response-to-covid-19-community-health-centres-and-doctors-offices-in-guinea/?fbclid=IwAR1bwvbWyuC7r94bBc6LYfGHh0-9CBvrJ7E4sJNFTrbkOZzSZwe3xuvWrE8.

Wallace, Lauren J., et al. 2020. "COVID-19 in Sub-Saharan Africa: Impacts on Vulnerable Populations and Sustaining Home-Grown Solutions". *Canadian Journal of Public Health* 111: 649–653. https://doi.org/10.17269/s41997-020-00399-y.

Wayack-Pambè, Madeleine, Bruno Lankoande, and Seni Kouanda. 2020. "Comment la jeunesse de sa population peut expliquer le faible nombre de morts du Covid-19 en Afrique". *The Conversation*. https://theconversation.com/comment-la-jeunesse-de-sa-population-peut-expliquer-le-faible-nombre-de-morts-du-covid-19-en-afrique-139832 (accessed on January 31, 2022).

WHO. 2018. "International Health Regulations 2005 State Party Self-Assessment Annual Reporting Tool". https://apps.who.int/iris/handle/10665/272432 (accessed January 28, 2020).

WHO. 2020a. "Emergency Committee Statement on the Second Meeting of the International Health Regulations (2005) Emergency Committee Regarding the Outbreak of Novel Coronavirus (COVID-19)". https://www.who.int/news/item/30-01-2020-statement-on-the-second-meeting-of-the-international-health-regulations-(2005)-emergency-committee-regarding-the-outbreak-of-novel-coronavirus-(2019-ncov) (accessed June 10, 2021).

WHO. 2020b (June 8). "Weekly Epidemiological Update on COVID-19—8 June 2021, Edition 43". *Emergency Situational Updates*. https://www.who.int/publications/m/item/weekly-epidemiological-update-on-covid-19-8-june-2021 (accessed June 10, 2021).

WHO Africa. 2020 (April 7). "Covid-19 Cases Top 10000 in Africa". https://www.afro.who.int/news/covid-19-cases-top-10-000-africa#:~:text=Reaching%20the%20continent%20through%20travellers,countries%20have%20reported%20cases (accessed June 10, 2020).

White, Luise. 2000. *Speaking with Vampires: Rumor and History in Colonial Africa*. Studies on the History of Society and Culture. Berkeley: University of California Press.

Wouters, Olivier J., Kenneth C. Shadlen, Maximillian Salcher-Konrad, Andrew J. Pollard, Heidi J. Larson, Yot Teerawattananon, and Mark Jit. 2021. "Challenges in Ensuring Global Access to COVID-19 Vaccines: Production, Affordability, Allocation, and Deployment". *Lancet* 397 (10278): 1023–1034. https://doi.org/10.1016/S0140-6736(21)00306-8.

CHAPTER 60

South Korea Has Controlled the COVID-19 Outbreak But Failed to Prepare Accountable Hospitals and Doctors

Cho Byong-Hee

1   Success in Countering COVID-19

Since the outbreak of COVID-19, people around the world have been fearing death and experiencing hardships. Compared to other countries, South Korea succeeded in controlling COVID-19 and underwent a relatively minor economic shock from COVID-19. This was due to the effect of 3T's (test, trace, treat) which drew the world's attention. Specifically, the Korean government could trace people who had close contact with confirmed COVID-19 patients through an exhaustive epidemiologic investigation. They performed a rapid screening test, having the patients immediately be isolated and provided with a free essential medical treatment. The government could minimize the COVID-19-related deaths by increasing people's compliance with control measures. Several factors contributed to Korea's success in controlling the pandemic: conducting an exhaustive epidemiologic investigation; monitoring the patients' traveling routes and the people they had close contact with using information technology such as mobile phones, CCTV, and credit cards; developing and distributing polymerase chain reaction (PCR) testing kits in the early phase; making PCR testing available at most large hospitals nationwide; providing free treatment by using the national health insurance; people's compliance with social distancing and facemask wearing (Lee and Lee 2020; Kim et al. 2021; Son, Lee and Hwang 2021). Many countries have failed to control the pandemic in the early phases. By implementing a complete lockdown and strictly forbidding any traveling, they suppressed the freedom of individuals, causing economic activities to shrivel greatly. By contrast, Korea could control the pandemic successfully and impose comparatively flexible stipulations on people's social travel, which had a reduced impact on the economy.

As COVID-19 had a severe impact on economic, social, and psychological aspects, the global community began to reflect on the crisis of human civilization and the disturbed ecosystem, which is believed to have caused it and raised concerns that returning to the pre-pandemic lifestyle is not possible.

As for Korea, where COVID-19 was successfully controlled, it appears that such reflection did not become deeply saturated in people's minds. The assertion to make fundamental changes in lifestyles in preparation for future climate change is handled lightly by the press and politicians in Korea as if it is news from a foreign country. The issue regarding the system improvement for countering infectious diseases such as COVID-19 more effectively is interpreted politically by the interest groups and is put aside. The doctors' strike during the pandemic is an example. The number of doctors in Korea is significantly lower than the OECD average. Attempts to increase the number have failed due to resistance from doctors. When the Korean government introduced a policy to increase the number in preparation for future outbreaks of infectious diseases similar to COVID-19 based on a high probability, numerous doctors went on strike in protest. The doctors argued that Korea does not suffer from a small number of doctors, considering that not many occurrences of COVID-19 patients were observed due to successful pandemic control and the healthcare system was running smoothly. The doctors did not want an overly competitive medical job market because of the increased number. Under these circumstances, it was difficult for the government to secure the required hospital beds from private hospitals. Succeeding in controlling COVID-19 paradoxically made it difficult to reform the neo-liberalism structure of the healthcare system. A medical reformer criticized this as follows: "Korea was exemplary in preventing the spread of COVID-19, but the country was behind in establishing the healthcare system for COVID-19 patients" (Jung, D. 2020). In this article, we focus on an aspect different from the successful COVID-19 control story: the deep-seated marketization of Korean healthcare and the doctors trying to maintain their vested interests.

2   Governance for Countering COVID-19

The first outbreak of COVID-19 in Korea occurred in February 2020 in Daegu, a city with a population of over 2 million people. The second wave occurred in August 2020 in the Seoul metropolitan area, which is a densely populated area with 20 million residents. The third and fourth waves occurred in the capital area. There was a clear distinction in the response to COVID-19 between the first and second waves regarding the doctors' roles and governance. During the first wave, the local doctors in Daegu played a leading role, while during the second wave, the public health authority implemented a full range of governance to control it. This was influenced by the symptoms of COVID-19, regional characteristics, and the preparedness of the public health authorities.

When COVID-19 was first spread in Daegu in February 2020, there was a shortage of effective guidelines on how to respond to the novel epidemic. The epidemic response guidelines of the Korea Disease Control and Prevention Agency (KDCA) in 2015 reflected the experience of controlling the outbreak of Middle East Respiratory Syndrome (MERS), which affected a small number of patients. In many ways, the guidelines were not adequate for responding to COVID-19 because the number of patients was significantly higher. As a large-scale epidemiologic investigation was underway to track the transmission routes, thousands of confirmed patients were identified. At the local government level, there was a shortage of manpower and experience to conduct such a large-scale epidemiologic investigation. Moreover, securing hospital beds for thousands is a challenge. At this time, executive-level hospital staff from five university hospitals in Daegu convened at the city hall, put together a temporary response team, and began to solve problems one at a time. Under their leadership, almost all doctors in Daegu voluntarily participated in the consultation and treatment. The specialists in respiratory diseases developed a method to assess the severity of infected patients, and doctors practicing at private clinics voluntarily assessed the severity of thousands of infected patients. Based on this, they sorted out the priority for hospitalization and prevented chaos in the early phase (Kim, J.H. et al. 2020). They secured hospital beds for COVID-19 patients by discharging or transferring regular patients at Daegu Municipal Hospital, a government-funded hospital. Moreover, Keimyung University Hospital contributed significantly to securing the hospital beds during the early phase when they volunteered to take on the role of a medical facility for exclusively treating COVID-19 patients by using the vacant facility after they relocated to a new facility. Hospitals that still faced a shortage of beds were helped by the response team's allocation of hospital beds, in collaboration with other local hospitals. Some of the achievements of the response team include the drive-through testing method to quickly determine the infection status, opening a temporary medical facility (Residential Treatment Center) for mildly symptomatic patients. The doctors in the Daegu area voluntarily built a collaborative system between the government and private medical professionals contributed decisively to preventing the spread of COVID-19. Civic groups in Daegu also conducted a campaign to practice social distancing and personal hygiene, and the citizens quietly complied with social distancing. There was no panic buying of daily necessities in Daegu. A medical college professor collected the medical team's testimonials of that time and published a book entitled, "We Planted a Seed of Hope There" (Lee, J. 2020). This indicates that the city could overcome the crisis through the sacrificial participation of doctors and nurses who responded to the written appeal, "Let's save the city in crisis".

The COVID-19 outbreak revealed weaknesses in the healthcare system in Korea. The first problem they encountered during the first wave was the shortage of hospital beds. When the number of confirmed patients reached several thousand within a few days, they could not find sufficient hospital beds. Daegu had five university hospitals, with a total of 38,000 hospital beds throughout all hospitals in Daegu. When including hospital beds in nearby cities, there were over 50,000 beds. Nonetheless, there was a shortage of hospital beds for thousands of COVID-19 patients, and some died at their homes while waiting to be hospitalized. All COVID-19 patients could have been hospitalized by making one-tenths of the preexisting hospital beds available, which was practically impossible. The reasons for this were complicated. The biggest one is speculated to be that most hospitals are privately-owned and the government was not authorized to temporarily rearrange the beds for COVID patients. The hospital beds of private hospitals were either occupied with regular patients with other underlying diseases or had aversion to admitting respiratory patients with COVID-19 due to the fear of transmission. Eventually, the treatment of COVID-19 patients became the main responsibility of public hospitals, which could be controlled by the government.

Meanwhile, the shortage of hospital beds was worse regarding patients with severe symptoms. They had to be isolated in a negative-pressure room to prevent the spread of the disease. There were 62 negative-pressure isolation beds in Daegu, and only ten of them were managed by the government. COVID-19 patients with severe symptoms were divided and hospitalized in five university hospitals. On February 15, 2020, 92% of the negative-pressure isolation beds at these hospitals were utilized and by March 15, 2020, they were over-utilized by 151%. Many patients with severe symptoms could not receive in-hospital treatment, and by April 30, 2020, the number of deaths in Daegu and Gyeongbuk reached 181 (Cho, B. 2020). Another factor that contributed to the increase in deaths in Daegu was a shortage of experienced doctors and nurses who could treat COVID-19 patients with severe symptoms (Kim, J. 2020).

It was possible to manage COVID-19 patients more effectively by treating them exclusively at public hospitals and a large number of mildly symptomatic or asymptomatic patients at temporary hospitals. This division of COVID-19 treatment between public and private hospitals was applied throughout the country. Most were treated at a public hospital. However, they soon faced the risk of medical staff burnout because a small number of medical professionals had to treat a continually rising number of COVID-19 patients for a long period. To address the healthcare workforce shortage, the government publicly recruited doctors and nurses for dispatch. By contrast, privately-owned hospitals did not face this and could focus on treating regular patients. In the early stage of the COVID-19 outbreak, people were wary of transmission and avoided visiting private hospitals. However, when public hospitals took charge of treating COVID-19 patients, their traveling route was separate from that of general patients, and regular patients' visits were assured to be steady in privately-owned hospitals. Eventually, the division between public hospitals and privately-owned hospitals while responding to COVID-19 provided a buffer to protect private hospitals from its influence. Moreover, patients with respiratory symptoms were directed to go to the designated COVID-19 National Safe Hospitals in the region for screening tests and examinations, which created an environment for doctors in private hospitals to remain safe from transmission (Kang et al. 2020; Her 2020).

The structure of establishing and implementing health policies in Korea has strong centralized characteristics. The Ministry of Health and Welfare from the central government established most of them, and local government bodies implemented them. However, the COVID-19 outbreak temporarily crippled the centralized implementation of policies. COVID-19 was difficult to be controlled with bureaucratic rules. The unusual nature of COVID-19 empowered local governments and doctors, instead of the central government with bureaucratic control, to perform on-the-ground response work. As local governments were not equipped with human resources, organizations, or expertise to handle such an infectious novel virus, it provided the opportunity and justifiable cause for doctors outside the government organizations to actively participate in public health tasks. This was a rare achievement in local governance in Korea. Specifically, pandemic control was not separated from patient treatment; instead, both were handled simultaneously in collaboration between the local governments, doctors' associations and hospitals, and civil society. There were other contributing factors for the successful response to COVID-19: a well-established regional network among the residents of Daegu, a sense of We-group, and abundant healthcare resources such as five university hospitals, unlike other areas. As such, doctors' participation in Daegu was a good example of overcoming the central government's inadequate preparation and the local government's incompetency, with the expertise of medical professionals and their voluntary participation.

The spread of COVID-19 slowed after March 2020, but the second wave occurred in August in the Seoul area. On August 15th, tens of thousands of people rallied at an anti-government event at the center of Seoul by conservative Christians and social groups. The number of infected patients sharply increased after it. From the second wave onwards, the Korea Disease Control and Prevention Agency (KDCA) of the central government fully took charge of pandemic control. Unlike the first wave, there was no confusion at the start of the second wave because the central government had been preparing by taking the following measures after the first outbreak in Daegu: increasing the number of screening test sites and labs, epidemiologic investigators, hospital beds for treatment, promotion of social distancing. All activities regarding pandemic control were regulated by the KDCA and local government bodies and community health centers followed their pandemic control guidelines. Many public health experts in Seoul provided professional advice on task implementation to the KDCA and helped establish major policies on pandemic control.

Activities related to pandemic control were managed by the public health system of the country, separately from general patient care. When infected people were transferred to a public hospital exclusively treating COVID-19 patients. Patients with mild symptoms were treated in isolation at temporary hospitals, called the Residential Treatment Center. Among the patients, those with severe symptoms were transferred to an ICU designated for COVID-19 patients. Therefore, except for a few clinical doctors who were in charge of the ICUs at general hospitals or university hospitals, the doctors and specialists working at privately owned clinics and smaller hospitals were not treating COVID-19 patients. In contrast, doctors who worked at a public hospital that exclusively treated COVID-19 patients suffered from a heavy workload. Nonetheless, the number of doctors in the public sector is less than 10% of all. Due to the successful pandemic control, most privately owned hospitals and doctors could perform their regular medical care similar to before COVID-19. While COVID-19 was prevalent in 2020, the general public's visits to medical professionals significantly decreased regarding the number of emergency patients (−19.1%), inpatient (−10.7%), and outpatient (−2.2%) compared to the previous year (Byun and Cho 2021). Hence, doctors who did not treat COVID-19 patients had less workload.

A significant indicator for determining whether a country effectively responded to COVID-19 is examining if the government sufficiently secured the available resources. Specifically, a shortage of healthcare workers or a lack of facilities and competent political leadership were determinants of the success of a country's response. Germany successfully controlled the pandemic as it had sufficient hospital beds for patients with severe symptoms and people have strong confidence in their government (Song et al. 2021; Unruh et al. 2021; Looi 2020; Brunn et al. 2020; Kavanagh and Singh 2020; Sao and Hao 2020). Germany is an example of successfully overcoming the pandemic crisis through moderation and collaboration between various actors in the public and private sectors (Hattke and Martin 2020).

In Korea, the government did not have sufficient resources for healthcare. The central or local governments managed about 250 community health centers and 100 public hospitals, which were responsible for COVID-19 tests, contact tracing, and patient treatment. More than half of the workers at community health centers hold temporary positions and cannot be coerced to work night shifts; thus, a shortage of workforce is handled through the assistance of the general administrative workers of each district office. Meanwhile, most hospitals belong to the private sector. Over 90% of hospital beds belong to privately-owned hospitals. Similarly, the majority of doctors were employed by privately owned hospitals. Previously, the MERS outbreak in 2015 was not controlled successfully, even though there were only 186 infected patients. However, the two years COVID-19 has been successfully controlled using a small number of hospital beds and healthcare workers in the public sector, a stark contrast to the MERS epidemic. This was due to the reforming of the pandemic control response system by the government centering on the KDCA (Lim et al. 2021).

By ensuring the number of COVID-19 patients was not significantly high through successful pandemic control, the majority of private hospitals could focus on treating regular patients. Due to these outcomes, the contradicting issue of the medical system centering on privately owned hospitals could not be exposed. Korea has many hospital beds, but not for patients with severe symptoms. Regarding the number of hospital beds for patients who require intensive care, Germany has 33.9 hospital beds per 100,000 people, while Korea has only 10.6 hospital beds per 100,000 patients with severe symptoms (OECD 2020). As of September 2021, the case fatality rate of COVID-19 is 0.9%, which is very low (Johns Hopkins University 2021). If there had been a higher number of patients, the rate may have been higher due to the shortage of hospital beds for patients with severe symptoms. Although the central government can mobilize hospital beds from privately owned hospitals during the national health crisis, it can be difficult as it requires considerable compensation and persuading privately owned hospitals to refuse treatment of COVID-19 patients. The Korean government gave an executive order to mobilize hospital beds from privately owned hospitals due to the shortage of hospital beds when the fourth wave began, and the number of confirmed patients increased from hundreds per day to over 2,000 per day after July 2021. Despite the order to secure 765 ICU beds, the country could obtain only 103 hospital beds and suffered from a shortage (Gwak, S. 2021). However, even if hospital beds are secured, finding specialists to treat patients is more challenging. Moreover, ICU beds require more nurses, but the reinforcement of the workforce is also unfeasible. Specifically, as the supply of nursing staff is delayed, the workload for pre-existing nurses becomes extremely heavy, resulting in their resignation and worsening nurse shortage. The nursing workforce is sufficiently supplied by nursing school graduates every year, but the turnover rate is very high because the compensation is small. One out of two new nurses changed jobs within the first year of employment at a hospital (Baik 2020). Due to such a high turnover rate, it is difficult to train them to become skilled nurses, creating a vicious cycle with low quality and quantity of nursing service (Shin, K. 2021).

One of the adverse effects of the public hospitals exclusively treating COVID-19 patients is that it deprived low-income families of the opportunity to use the healthcare service. When the majority of the public hospitals discharged their regular patients and admitted COVID-19 patients, low-income patients who generally go to public hospitals lose their treatment opportunities. Specifically, vulnerable social groups such as HIV patients, low-income patients, and patients with disabilities often rely on public hospitals because of discrimination and high medical expenses at privately owned hospitals, but their way of receiving medical care was practically blocked when the public hospitals became the medical facility exclusively treating COVID-19 patients. (Human Rights Investigation 2020). With very few public hospitals present, the crisis made it difficult for regular patients to visit a public hospital.

Until the pandemic broke out, public healthcare in Korea did not draw people's attention politically or socially. As the medical market was led by large-scale private hospitals that boast highly effective treatment using the newest technology, declining public hospitals, and community health centers were neglected. The progressive and conservative governments did not have a strong interest in the public nature of healthcare. It has been regarded as the target of industrialization, while privately owned hospitals have focused on developing new medical technologies to increase the added value. Public hospitals had been treated as "chicken ribs (something that one hesitates to give up even though it is of little interest)" because they lacked capability and motivation for commercial success similar to that of privately owned hospitals. Specifically, when the Korean economy was managed by the IMF following the foreign currency crisis in 1997, the neo-liberalist reformation was promoted. Subsequently, public hospitals were forced to make profits as privately owned hospitals. As public hospitals were in red, nine out of 34 regional public hospitals became private or commissioned (Yeo, Lee and Kim 2016; Oh et al. 2011). In 2013, a provincial governor from a conservative party closed down the 103-year old Jinju Hospital.

Commercialization or neo-liberalism in medical care can be defined from different perspectives. Specifically, from the aspect of production, an important requirement is that the private sector, not the central government, should proactively own and operate medical facilities. From the consumption aspect, it is necessary to commercialize medical services and raise the value of medical commodities by meeting the patients' healthcare needs in the fastest and sufficient manner. Other characteristics of the neo-liberal system include the following: it encourages individuals rather than the government to take responsibility for health, and to use commercialized medical services; it gives private hospitals a guarantee for the opportunity to seek profits by loosening the restrictions on the activities of privately owned hospitals (McGregor 2001).

In the 1960s, about half of all hospital beds in Korean hospitals belonged to the public sector. The Korean government was one of the so-called developmental states in East Asia that systematically planned economic development on behalf of capitalists. The government mobilized most of the available resources in economic development, and social policy was underdeveloped (Kim 2007). Most of the investment necessary for providing medical care was made by the private sector, so private medical facilities grew rapidly. By 2017, the percentage of public medical providers declined: the number of hospitals and hospital beds dropped to 5.8% and 10.5%, respectively.

Nonetheless, COVID-19 greatly highlighted the significance of public medical care. The public hospitals, which used to be regarded as 'ugly ducklings', took full responsibility to treat COVID-19 patients and contributed to the success in overcoming the crisis, allowing privately owned hospitals to focus on treating regular patients steadily. Through the pandemic, we learned that infectious diseases can be effectively countered only with a sufficient number of public health centers and public hospitals, as well as a workforce with medical expertise and hospital beds with adequate medical equipment. Although a few health professionals addressed the need to ensure public healthcare, they could not influence the prevailing marketization. Under these circumstances, the central government's plan to increase the number of doctors and build more public hospitals was solely due to the COVID-19 outbreak. However, the extent of the expansion of public healthcare is unclear. As the medical circle has been dominated by market principles and neo-liberalism over the past few decades, it is difficult to predict if their acquired power will dwindle after COVID-19. For instance, the government established a plan to build seven nationwide hospitals specializing in infectious diseases after the MERS crisis in 2015, but the investment was not sufficient. Despite COVID-19, the construction of hospitals specializing in infectious diseases has been postponed.

Moreover, in circumstances where doctors are leading the healthcare market, the health policy that goes against the interests of doctors is difficult to implement. As health policies emphasizing public health have never been successfully implemented, doctors are opposing the new policy about strengthening public healthcare due to their conflicting interests, although they acknowledge the need for doctors to work in public healthcare.

3 Doctors' Strike

When pandemic control encountered a challenge due to the second wave of COVID-19 in August 2020, a conflict broke out between the government and the doctors' association. Tens of thousands of doctors went on a full-scale strike in protest against the government's new policy about building a new public medical school to counter future public health crises, such as newly emerging infectious diseases, and to secure additional doctors to work in public healthcare. The government initially handled the shortage of doctors during the pandemic by dispatching army surgeons or recruiting volunteer doctors and nurses. As the government perceived the probability of a recurring crisis similar to COVID-19, they recognized the need to reinforce public healthcare and formulated a proposal for expanding public hospitals and building a new public medical school. In response, doctors strongly opposed the proposal for building a new public medical school for several reasons. As the government desperately needed the doctors' cooperation during the COVID-19, they eventually put a hold on the policy implementation and agreed to discuss it in the future, which ended the doctors' strike (Kim 2020).

It is not uncommon to observe healthcare workers' walkouts during the pandemic. Medical professionals in Hong Kong went on strike in February 2020. The nurses in the US and the UK as well as doctors in Kenya, Spain, and Peru also did. However, these strikes were protests about working in a dangerous environment with thousands of healthcare workers dying of COVID-19 worldwide while treating patients because government policies failed to provide them with proper personal protective equipment (PPE) (Essex and Weldon 2021). In other words, healthcare workers in other countries went on strike either because they were exposed to hazards while performing their jobs or they were overworking due to a shortage of healthcare workers, or they were not compensated enough. In contrast, Korean doctors were given PPEs adequately, and there were almost no cases of healthcare workers dying from COVID-19 transmission. A small workforce or compensation did not become a major issue. The only reason for their strike was resistance to the increasing number of doctors in preparation for future disasters. Why do Korean doctors have such a strong aversion to future situations?

This incident symbolically shows a lopsided relationship between the Korean government and doctors. In the global community, the Korean government has commended to successfully controlling COVID-19. Domestically, however, it faced fierce attacks from political opponents during the early phase of the pandemic. The opposition party, the conservative press, and some Christian churches took an offensive anti-government stance over several agendas, such as restricting entry from China, mandating the use of facemasks, and holding unrestricted public assemblies. They demanded the impeachment of President Moon Jae-in by holding him accountable for the pandemic. The fact that the doctors in Daegu played a leading role in the early stage of COVID-19 served as the fuel for their pride as well as grounds for disapproving the government. Doctors felt the government was not acknowledging their hard work or great contribution in countering the crisis. The strikes were held mainly by medical students and residents. When they did not comply with the back-to-work order, the government filed criminal charges against the leaders. Medical college professors also joined the strike by defending their students (Lee, S. 2020). Regardless of participation, the entire healthcare community stood together in unison against the government.

Meanwhile, the government did not have any effective measures to call off the doctors' strike. Although the doctors' strike during the pandemic had no valid social justification, the doctors' associations went ahead with it. Eventually, the government appealed to end the strike. The government could have issued an order for them to return to work and could have taken legal action in case of failed compliance. If so, it could have created a bigger catastrophe by encouraging undecided doctors to join the strike. While the general public and civic groups were highly critical of the doctors' strike, the doctors maintained it by uniting internally, eventually achieving their goal of putting the brakes on the government policy.

The government's new policy measures against infectious diseases included establishing a public medical school to boost the number of doctors to resolve the long-lasting shortage of doctors working in rural areas and responding to infectious diseases. Doctors argued that, without lucrative incentives for doctors to work in the public sector or remote areas, the government's plan to increase the number will fail because doctors are likely to cluster in large cities, which will aggravate the imbalance in healthcare (Kim, D. 2020). The argument that it is necessary to increase medical school admissions because Korea has a smaller number of doctors than other countries and consequently worsening the phenomena of healthcare inequalities is as valid as the problem of unequal healthcare services is difficult to resolve without improving the work conditions for doctors. The government and experts in related fields could have sought a feasible solution through a policy decision meeting but the situation unfolded in a completely different direction. The government and the ruling party took the initiative to establish a public medical school without meticulous preparation, and the doctors' associations used it to start a full-scale strike against the government.

Such a confrontation between the government and doctors is political in nature. The necessity for increasing the number of doctors was an old agenda, which had been constantly raised by health policy experts long before the COVID-19 outbreak (Kim, Lee and Kwon 2020). As most healthcare providers are concentrated in large cities, small cities or rural areas suffer from a shortage of doctors. For instance, in Gangwon Province, which has many wooded and mountainous areas, women's clinics are located in only 7 out of 18 counties or cities, as of 2019, requiring expecting mothers to travel about over an hour for OB/GYN care (Jang, J. 2019). Previously, the government had not been able to establish effective measures to resolve the shortage of doctors, but as the shortage worsened during COVID-19 and became a major interest, the government pushed forward a plan to boost the number of doctors by establishing a public medical school. The government might have thought that doctors' resistance to the government's plan to increase the number of doctors would be subdued in the health crisis caused by COVID-19. Moreover, by building a public medical school desired by rural residents, the ruling party of the government could gain the additional benefit of political support from the locals.

Korean doctors were generally conservative and disinterested in social issues outside the scope of health policy. However, the president of the Korean Medical Association worked with conservative parties as an activist against the government. Ever since he was elected as the president of the doctors' association in 2018, he has confronted the government with regarding the healthcare policies that they were trying to implement (improving the health insurance coverage system so-called Moon Jae-in Care, installation of CCTV in operating rooms, strengthening the requirements for revocation of doctors' licenses, etc.). Regarding the policy about countering COVID-19, he also opposed the government's policy on forbidding Chinese people's arrival and mandating facemask wearing. He did not gain practical benefits from his fight against the government. However, amid the COVID-19 crisis, he won the first political victory from the strike in protest against the expansion of the medical workforce when the government paused the policy implementation. Many doctors have shown reservations about strikes during the pandemic. Their attitude was that of "Why can't they wait until it ends to recognize the doctors' hard work for pandemic control even if there is a need for medical workforce expansion?" The president of the doctors' association criticized the government's demeanor as a back-stabbing approach (Lim, S. 2020).

Meanwhile, medical residents fully supported the statement of doctors' associations. The medical residents and students throughout the country went on strike. Medical residents may have felt uneasy about their jobs because new graduates from a future public medical school are their potential competitors. The doctors' strike lasted approximately three weeks. It had a direct impact on patient care in hospitals. Doctors even refused to do vital jobs, such as working in emergency rooms. Such an extreme strike was unusual. It showed a huge contrast with a 'symbolic' strike by Malaysian doctors, which occurred due to the issue of employment contracts around the same time (Jamaluddin et al. 2021).

The Korean government did not have effective countermeasures against such doctors' strikes. As most doctors were employed at a privately owned hospital, the healthcare workforce that the government could mobilize was very limited, and practically there was no workforce to replace the doctors on strike. Even though the press and the public criticized the doctors' selfish interests, it did not have any impact. Despite the desperate need for the cooperation of doctors during the spread of COVID-19, the government had no choice but to accept their demand. For the past four years of the Moon Jae-in government, political opposition from the opposition party or the doctors' association did not produce any result because of the high rate of public support. However, the government unexpectedly faced a political defeat during the COVID-19 emergency despite the public's strong support for the current government.

The doctors' resistance and the incompetence of the government show the results of the marketization or neo-liberalism of the healthcare system, which has been established over the past few decades. Doctors have established themselves as the main actors of the healthcare providers on behalf of the government, while the government implemented the policy to industrialize healthcare and helped the doctors' efforts. The government avoided the policy on expansion of medical workforce and public healthcare. However, as the demand for public healthcare grew due to the unexpected pandemic, the government and doctors entered into temporary conflict. During COVID-19, the government newly recognized the necessity of public healthcare, but could not move forward for fundamental reformation of the healthcare system due to resistance from doctors and the difficulty of expanding the workforce for public healthcare.

4   Overworking Doctors

Several issues such as opposition to increasing the number of doctors, using the national health insurance for oriental medicine, and implementing tele-healthcare were raised as reasons for the doctors' strike. Nonetheless, the main reason was to object the expansion of the medical workforce. The Korean Medical Association claimed that the country was not suffering from a shortage of doctors. The OECD statistics are often cited to strengthen the argument for doctor increase. As of 2018, the average number of doctors in

OECD countries was 3.5 per 1,000 people, whereas that in Korea was only 2.4 per 1,000 people. Regarding physician density per population, Korea is only ⅔ of the OECD average. As of 2018, there were approximately 120,000 doctors in Korea. To reach the OECD average, Korea needs approximately 50,000 additional doctors. Moreover, the actual number of medical doctors is even smaller because the statistics include 20,000 doctors in traditional medicine without MD degree.

Nonetheless, the Korean Medical Association had a completely different rationale and argued that there was no shortage of doctors. They stated that Korean doctors see numerous patients, and there are almost no cases of patients not receiving healthcare, which is a sign of no shortage of doctors. According to the OECD statistics in 2018, the average number of visits to doctors per year was 6.6 in the OECD countries, whereas it was 16.9 in Korea. In other words, Korean people use healthcare services 2.5 times more than patients in other OECD countries. That is, doctors in Korea are meeting patients' needs by offering healthcare services more frequently than those in other countries. It is important to note that Korean doctors claim that there is no shortage of doctors because they work hard and increase their productivity, generally satisfying the desires of the patients.

In the meantime, doctors' heavy workload can lead to exhaustion and burnout. Doctors have been dying due to overwork. Two doctors died in early February 2019. They worked at a large hospital in Seoul and Gyeonggi Province, respectively, and the cause was presumed to be overwork (Song, S. 2019; Ock, H. 2919). According to a fact-finding survey by the Korean Medical Association, doctors work an average of 50 hours every week and medical residents work an average of 66.9 hours every week (KMA 2017). It is common for doctors at a university hospital to treat 100 patients a day (Song, S. 2021). Some doctors, specifically, medical residents, have been reported to work over 100 hours a week. Compared to regular employees' weekly 39 working hours, doctors are undoubtedly working overtime. Furthermore, considering that the tasks that doctors do require a high level of attention and care, working overtime increases the likelihood of burnout (Jang, E., et al. 2019).

Meanwhile, dying from overwork was not a current issue for the Korean Medical Association. As for Korean doctors, working overtime is regarded as working hard. For doctors, higher labor productivity mean higher earnings. As opposed to increasing the number of doctors to reduce the workload, Korean doctors seem to prefer keeping it a small number to earn more money. Korean doctors earn about five times more than regular workers (Shin 2018). Considering that the doctors in Europe earn about three times as much as other workers, Korean doctors' income is far from being small. The professional attitude of Korean doctors who highly value the improvement of labor productivity does not appear to be different from the mindset of entrepreneurs who pursue profits.

Traditionally, Korean doctors have become accustomed to entrepreneurism (Cho 1988). In the past, such professional culture was manifested in establishing a privately owned clinic or hospital. In the 1980s and the 1990s, large-scale private hospitals were established as the number of patients grew due to the increase in national income and the establishment of national health insurance. In the 1990s, the number of privately owned hospitals rose and prevailed over public hospitals, in the total number and the development of new healthcare technologies and production of added values. Due to the dense distribution of hospitals and the fully saturated healthcare market, it has become difficult to build new hospitals; however, the pursuit of industrialization through technology development has become more vitalized. Korean hospitals are now equipped with the newest medical machines at the world-class level, and patient care is organized and operated so intricately and meticulously resembling factory production. For example, the operating rooms of a mega-hospital are run for 24 h a day to treat cancer patients (Kim, C. 2012). Currently, Korean hospitals have a higher survival rate for cancer patients than other OECD countries. However, the number of doctors is not adequate for the smooth operation of such a gigantic healthcare industry. The shortage occurs not only in remote mountainous areas, but also in large hospitals. The increase in the number of physician assistant (PA) nurses and the death of medical residents from overwork is evidence of a doctor shortage.

PA nurses are nurses who perform the role of a physician's assistant. PA system can be found in other countries including the US. Although this system has not been legalized in Korea, doctors are temporarily delegating their jobs to nurses as an alternative to the shortage (Kim, E. 2021). Their jobs include more simple assistance to doctors; it is reported that PA nurses perform more difficult tasks such as abdominal incision and cardiac compression. As the PA nurse system is not legal in Korea, there is no guaranteed legal protection in case of medical accidents. The number of PA nurses throughout the country was estimated to be several thousand. It has been reported that 1,173 PA nurses work in national or public hospitals (Baik 2020). The PA nurse position was created because of a shortage of doctors. Korean hospitals hire a small number of fellows compared to the number of patients. Large hospitals have always made up for a shortage of doctors and medical residents. Medical residency is one of the toughest jobs that pay low wages and work long hours. However, the death of medical residents from overwork led the government to limit the work hours of medical residents to 80 hours per week starting in 2016. Eventually, it created a shortage of medical residents, and hospitals began to delegate the tasks performed by medical residents to nurses.

A reasonable solution for the shortage of doctors is to resolve the contradiction of the healthcare system by increasing the number or by legalizing the PA nurse system through training, maintaining the qualifications, and clarifying the job boundary. While large-scale hospitals that represent medical capital anticipate the legalization of the PA system (Yoon, W. 2020), the Korean Medical Association, representing the interest of doctors with their clinics, show strong resistance to the idea and refuse to share exclusive rights to treat patients with other professions (Hong 2018). The government is turning a blind eye to illegal practice in hospitals. Moreover, the Korean government issues doctors' licenses and superficially monitors them, although the management of licenses is a key responsibility of the central government. Consequently, doctors' licenses are rarely revoked, even when a serious crime is committed. Even if it is revoked, most are reinstated after a certain period. By contrast, the government is grudging about systemizing the alternative workforce for doctors' tasks. Korean doctors are enjoying exhaustive privilege regarding the licensure system.

In a situation where doctors' tasks are illegally delegated to nurses due to the shortage, why do doctors strongly oppose the expansion of the medical workforce? In Korea, healthcare services have developed based on hardware or equipment such as hospital beds, medical equipment, facilities, and medication rather than focusing on human services such as patient care and communication with patients. Unlike the small number of doctors, the number of hospital beds in Korea is much higher than the OECD average. In 2018, it was 4.5 per 1,000 people in the OECD countries, but Korea it was 2.8 times higher (12.4 per 1,000 people). The higher number of hospital beds per population indicates the full capability of producing healthcare services. This implies that Korea is producing and providing greater healthcare services compared to other countries. Moreover, Korean people utilize healthcare services 2.5 times more than people from other OECD countries. Doctors have no choice but to overwork to fill in hospital beds with more patients during the shortage of doctors. This is proof of a structural contradiction. Regardless of the reality, doctors insist that there is no shortage of doctors because they prioritize earning a greater profit. This demeanor of doctors is conflicting with that of nurses who demand a huge increase in the number of healthcare workers (Kim, E. 2021).

Doctors regard themselves as entrepreneurs in the healthcare industry and consider the government's intervention in healthcare as an oppression of the free market (Lee, E. 2021). Hence, they mock the government's intervention as 'medical socialism'. The director of the Ministry of Health and Welfare pushed for medical workforce expansion and justified the policy by saying, "Doctors are a public good compared with other professions". In response to this statement, the president of the Korean Medical Associations refuted, "How can doctors be public goods when the government did not provide anything regarding education, training, finding employment, and opening a private practice to become doctors?" (Choi, G. 2020). In other words, many doctors tend to think that the government is unduly interfering, using public healthcare as an excuse when privately owned hospitals are successfully operating the healthcare system as a result of their efforts and investments. Privately owned hospitals are not different from small business corporations as they both pursue profits. However, CEO doctors lack the intragroup mechanism, which is supposed to help transform professional value into group norms. Doctors developed a distinctive consciousness as business managers, as they became the main actors in establishing and operating healthcare facilities, while their professionalism was not mature.

5 Overcoming the Medicalization of Pandemic Control

Another factor for the doctors' strike during the COVID-19 crisis was the medicalization of most measures because the pandemic control system was not feasible apart from the doctors. Moreover, the policy advisor committee of the KDCA, the leader of pandemic control system mainly consisted of doctors and government officers. As a result, most measures countering the infectious diseases were medically implemented: the screening test for detecting any infected patients was emphasized; the number of confirmed patients and the number of deaths were reported daily; and people started their day by interpreting the number of confirmed patients for over a year. From the perspective of social determinants of health, the probability of COVID-19 transmission varies depending on occupation, social class, or place. Hence, it is necessary to preemptively inspect workplaces or facilities with a high risk of transmission and to take preventive measures. For example, call centers have a high risk of transmission because many employees work in crowded spaces. However, no preemptive measures were taken; instead, the workplace was repeatedly closed and tested for group infection. The risk of transmission can be lowered by changing the working environment only if social participation and economic considerations are considered beyond medical responses. However, pandemic control measures were mostly established exclusively by a committee of doctors and government officers. They centered on posterior COVID-19 tests and treatment led us to examine the risks from the perspective of medical management of diseases. The doctors performed the test and treatment, and the general public passively followed the instructions. Such a basic direction of government policy centering on medical governance provides a backdrop for doctors to increase their rights to speak out.

If COVID-19 is caused by socioeconomic factors associated with an ecological crisis, accountability or countermeasures cannot be approached from only a medical perspective. It can be a citizen's responsibility to reflect on what factors may pose a risk at work, school, home, and private gatherings, and how our lifestyles should change. Leaving out such a process, the Korean government only emphasized social distancing, hygienic practice of hand washing, and facemask wearing. Koreans, who have a comparatively deep fear of the disease, complied with the government's guidelines relatively. However, without fundamental reflection on COVID-19, being blindly compliant with the orders has a limitation. Korea is now facing a new dilemma, as the effectiveness of pandemic control is diminishing, and the number of infected patients is increasing even though the pandemic has persisted for over a year.

Through COVID-19, the importance of public health and public healthcare has been recognized again in Korea, and plans are being created to increase doctors and establish public hospitals nationwide. Even if public healthcare is expanded from the current condition, it is highly likely that it will only support the smooth operation of privately owned hospitals and offer public health services that private healthcare providers use to avoid. There is a lack of self-awareness or self-reflection that the current healthcare system, which is made up of neo-liberalism, needs a fundamental reform not only within the healthcare industry, but also in the socio-political circle. Despite the pandemic, it seems difficult to count on its effect on a radical change in the way of life before and after in Korea.

References

Baik, C. 2020. "1 of 2 newly employed nurses resigned within a year". *Nurse Times*, February, 24. http://www.fornurse.co.kr/news/articleView.html?idxno=980.

Baik, C. 2020. "There are 1,173 PA nurses in public hospitals, increasing annually and participating more in surgical operations". *Nurse Times*, October 22. http://www.fornurse.co.kr/news/articleView.html?idxno=5754.

Brunn, M., et al. 2020. "Why are there so many hospital beds in Germany?" http://dx.doi.org/10.13140/RG.2.2.28449.43363.

Byun, J., and B. Cho. 2021. "COVID-19's impacts on health care utilization". *Korean Social Trends 2021*.

Cho, B.H. 1988. "The State and Physicians in South Korea". PhD thesis of University of Wisconsin-Madison.

Cho, B.H. 2020. "The distribution of hospitals treating COVID-19 patients". *Korean Social Trends 2020*.

Choi, G. 2020. "Doctors who are crazy about the health bureaucrat's statement that doctors are public goods". *Young Doctors*, August 12. https://www.docdocdoc.co.kr/news/articleView.html?idxno=2001670.

Daegu Metropolitan City. 2020. "Overcoming COVID-19 in Daegu: The Path nobody taught us".

Essex, R., and Weldon, S.M. 2021. "Health care worker strikes and the COVID pandemic". *New England Journal of Medicine* 384: e93. https://doi.org/10.1056/NEJMp2103327.

Gwak, S. 2021. "After two weeks of government's administrative order for private hospitals, only 103 intensive care beds were mobilized". *Young Doctors*, August 28. https://www.docdocdoc.co.kr/news/articleView.html?idxno=2013955.

Hattke, F., and Martin, H. 2020. "Collective action during the COVID-19 pandemic: the case of Germany's fragmented authority". *Administrative Theory & Praxis* 42 (4): 614–632. https://doi.org/10.1080/10841806.2020.18052.

Her, M. 2020. "Repurposing and reshaping of hospitals during the COVID-19 outbreak in South Korea". *One Health* 10. https://doi.org/10.1016/j.onehlt.2020.100137.

Hong, M. 2018. "Doctors are outraged at PA legalization, "It is absurd"". *Doctor News*, November 5. http://www.doctorstimes.com/news/articleView.html?idxno=201854.

Human Right Investigation. 2020. "COVID-19 and the Exclusion of Health Care Opportunities". http://www.konkang21.or.kr/bbs/board.php?bo_table=pds1&wr_id=1053.

Jamaluddin, J., N.N. Baharum, S.N. Jamil, and M.A.M. Kamel. 2021. "Doctors strike during COVID-19 pandemic in Malaysia: between right and wrong". *Voices in Bioethics* 7. https://doi.org/10.52214/vib.v7i.8586.

Jang, E.S., S.M. Park, Y.S. Park, J.C. Lee, and N. Kim. 2019. "Work-life conflict and its health effects on Korean gastroenterologists according to age and sex". *Digestive Diseases and Sciences* 65: 86–95. https://doi.org/10.1007/s10620-019-05842-w.

Jang, J. 2019. "No place to have children—11 areas in Gangwon-do have no maternity clinics". *YTN News*, December 8. https://www.ytn.co.kr/_ln/0103_201912080136276649.

Johns Hopkins University Coronavirus Resource Center. 2021. "Mortality Analysis". https://coronavirus.jhu.edu/data/mortality.

Jung, D. 2020. "Korea succeeded in K-quarantine, but fail in K-medical care". *Oh My News*, July 20. http://www.ohmynews.com/NWS_Web/View/at_pg.aspx?CNTN_CD=A0002659066.

Kang, J.H., et al. 2020. "South Korea's response to stop the COVID-19 pandemic". *American Journal of Infection Control* 48: 1080–1086.

Kavanagh, M., and R. Singh. 2020. "Democracy, capacity, and coercion in pandemic response: COVID-19 in comparative political perspective". *Journal of Health Politics, Policy and Law* 45 (6): https://doi.org/10.1215/03616878-8641530.

Kim, A. 2020. "Why are Korean doctors striking? Row between doctors, government escalates amid pandemic". *The Korea Herald*, August 11. http://www.koreaherald.com/view.php?ud=20200811000941.

Kim, C. 2012. "Big 5 hospitals, full of patients, sent a text mail to a patient to come to hospital at 3 a.m. for cancer treatment". *Chosunilbo*, June 12. https://www.chosun.com/site/data/html_dir/2012/06/11/2012061102813.html.

Kim, D. 2020. "Four reasons why the government's plan for the increase of 4,000 doctors must fail". *Doctors' News*, July 23. https://www.doctorsnews.co.kr/news/articleView.html?idxno=135495.

Kim, E. 2021. "9 out of 10 PAS replace doctor's duty-PA resolves shortage of trainee doctors". *Young Doctors*, May 12. https://www.docdocdoc.co.kr/news/articleView.html?idxno=2010563.

Kim, E. 2021. "Coming of the biggest crisis of K-quarantine system? The Korean health care workers' union goes on general strike in September". *Young Doctors*, August 27. https://www.docdocdoc.co.kr/news/articleView.html?idxno=2013948.

Kim, J. 2020. "The experience of community responding to COVID-19". The paper presented at the annual conference of Korean Academy of Health Policy and Management.

Kim, J.H., J.A. An, P.K. Min, A. Bitton, and A.A. Gawande. 2020. "How South Korea responded to the COVID-19 outbreak in Daegu". *NEJM Catalyst Innovations in Care Delivery* 04. https://doi.org/10.1056/CAT.20.0159.

Kim, J.H., J.A. An, S.J. Oh, J. Oh, and J.K. Lee. 2021. "Emerging COVID-19 success story: South Korea learned the lessons of MERS". *Exemplars in Global Health*. https://ourworldindata.org/covid-exemplar-south-korea?country=.

Kim, J.H., S.M. Lee, and H.J. Kwon. 2020. "Physician shortage and policy alternative". *Korean Journal of Health Economics and Policy* 26 (3): 15–38. https://kmbase.medric.or.kr/KMID/1170320200260030015.

Kim, S.Y. 2007. "The east Asian developmental state and its economic and social policies: the case of Korea". *International Review of Public Administration* 12 (2): 69–87. https://doi.org/10.1080/12294659.2008.10805106.

Korean Medical Association. 2017. "2016 National Survey of Physicians".

Lee, E. 2021. *The Utopia of Public Health Care Named Bluebird—A Critic of Medical Socialism*. Seoul: Giparang Publication.

Lee, J.T. 2020. *People planted hope there*. Daegu: Hakisa.

Lee, S. 2020. "Are medical professors even participating in the strike against the government's accusation of doctors on strike?" *Whosaeng News*, August 30. http://www.whosaeng.com/120446.

Lee, S.M. and D.H. Lee. 2020. "Lessons learned from battling COVID-19: the Korean Experience". *International Journal of Environmental Research and Public Health* 17: 7548. https://doi:10.3390/ijerph17207548.

Lim, B., E.K. Hong, J. Mou, and I. Cheong. 2021. "COVID-19 in Korea: Success based on past failure". *Asian Economic Papers* 20 (2): 41–62. https://doi.org/10.1162/asep_a_00803.

Lim, S. 2020. "The government's self-righteousness to put a knife in the back of doctors. 130,000 doctors will fight to win". *Medigate News*, August 14. https://www.medigatenews.com/news/3261627698.

Looi, M.K. 2020. "The COVID-19 yearbook: world leaders edition". *BMJ* 371: m4728. https://doi.org/10.1136/bmj.m4728.

McGregor, S. 2001. "Neoliberalism and health care". *International Journal of Consumer Studies* 25 (2): 82–89.

Ock, H. 2019. "Koreans mourn overworked doctor's death—Emergency doctor's death sheds light on poor working conditions for emergency medical staff". *The Korea Herald*, February 10. http://www.koreaherald.com/view.php?ud=20190210000176.

OECD. 2020. "Intensive care beds capacity". https://www.oecd.org/coronavirus/en/data-insights/intensive-care-beds-capacity.

Oh, J., et al. 2011. "Struggle against privatization: a case history in the use of comparative performance evaluation of public hospitals". *International Journal of Health Services* 41 (2): 371–388. https://doi.org/10.2190/HS.41.2.j.

Shao, W., and F. Hao. 2020. "Confidence in political leaders can slant risk perception of COVID-19 in a highly polarized environment". *Social Science & Medicine* 261: 113235. https://doi.org/10.1016/j.socscimed.2020.113235.

Shin, K. 2021. "COVID-19 counter measures and action plan for improvement of nursing treatment". *Hira Research* 1 (1): 103–107. https://doi.org/10.52937/hira.21.1.1.103.

Shin, Y., et al. 2018. "National Health Care Personnel Survey". *Ministry of Health and Welfare and Korea Institute for Health and Social Affairs*.

Sohn, C. 2020. "The response of the Seoul Municipal hospitals against COVID-19 and its implications for public hospitals". *Korean Journal of Hospital Management* 25 (3): 38–52.

Son, K., T.J. Lee, and S.S. Hwang. 2021. "Does the health system's response matter to cope with the COVID-19 outbreak? Recent evidence from South Korea". *Bulletin of World Health Organization* 99: 62–66. http://dx.doi.org/10.2471/BLT.20.257758.

Song, E., J. Moon, et al. 2021. "Four European Countries COVID-19 Response". *Hira Research* 1 (1): 50–63. https://doi.org/10.13140/RG.2.2.28449.43363.

Song, E.S., J. Moon, J.H. Byun, J. Jun, and N.S. Kim. 2021. "A comparative analysis on four countries COVID-19 response: focused on the 1st wave". *Hira Research* 1 (1): 50–63. p-ISSN 2765-6764. https://doi.org/10.52937/hira.21.1.1.5.

Song, S. 2019. "Death of trainee doctor reveals 'repetitive overwork culture'". *Korea Biomedical Review*, August 20. https://www.koreabiomed.com/news/articleView.html?idxno=6304.

Song, S. 2021. "University hospital doctors who treat 100 outpatients a day". *Young Doctors*, September 4. https://www.docdocdoc.co.kr/news/articleView.html?idxno=2014223.

Unruh, L., et al. 2021. "A comparison of health policy response to the COVID-19 pandemic in Canada, Ireland, UK, and the USA". *Health Policy*. https://doi.org/10.1016/j.healthpol.2021.06.012.

Yeo, Y.H., K.H. Lee, and H.J. Kim. 2016. "Closure of a local public hospital in Korea: focusing on the organizational life cycle". *Journal of Health Care Leadership* 8: 95–105. https://doi.org/10.2147/JHL.S113070.

Yoon, W. 2020. "Can PA be legalized? 10 National University hospitals in favor of legalization". *Young Doctors*, October 26. https://www.docdocdoc.co.kr/news/articleView.html?idxno=2004150.

Conclusion

Laurence Roulleau-Berger, Li Peilin, Kim Seung Kuk and Yazawa Shujiro

1   Traveling in the Post-Western Space

At the end of this handbook, the co-production of post-Western sociology invites us to return to the traditions and histories of non-Western sociologies, to put them in motion and in dialogue with the Western thoughts that have ignored them.

In *A History of Sociology in China in the First Half of the Twentieth Century*, Li Peilin, Qu Jingdong and Yang Yabin (2009) demonstrated how Chinese sociology flourished in a context of intellectual blossoming comparable to that of the spring and autumn periods and to that of the warring states. In 19th-century China Yan Fu and Liang Qichao contributed the most to the emergence of Chinese sociology, the academic thought of gregariousness, transforming Western sociology with their indigenous knowledge; Liang Shuming deeply studied cultural differences between Eastern and Western cultures; Fei Xiaotong, in contributing to the world social sciences, has described the foundations of Chinese society in considering localized knowledge is not confined to local areas and in producing post-Western sociology (cf. Chapter 2 from Li Peilin). Fei Xiaotong used a traditional Confucianist perspective and modern social science theory to explore the way of modernization for traditional China's society; Liang Shuming believed that China's society and its culture have their own value and vitality, but he has suggested the introduction of Western science and democracy into Chinese society (cf. Chapter 21 from Sun Feiyu).

In Japan modern Western social science was introduced at the beginning of the Meiji period; many pre-modern Confucian scholars of the early modern period have produced thoughts comparable to those of Western sociology; for example, the Confucian concept of "Michi" means social order is produced in every human relationship (cf. Chapter 7 from Yama Yoshiyuki). The history of Japanese sociology gives important resources to Western-West sociologies from a reevaluation of the discipline in the Eastern-East world. For example, in prewar Japanese sociology Fukuzawa Yukichi played a major role in a theory of society and the individual, and Takada Yasuma produced a theory of social relations and of social establishment in distinguishing three types of *direct and indirect societies*: the first is a society in which kinship-based connections are predominant; the second is based on the territory; and the third is based on indirect connections (cf. Chapter 5 from Yazawa Shujiro).

The tense relationship between the West and postcolonial sociology cannot be found in the Chinese context. In contrast, Japan has a responsibility regarding the colonization of Taiwan and the Korean Peninsula, and tried to colonize China, so Japanese sociologists are thinking of the global society as a global civil society (cf. Chapter 9 from Shoji Kōkichi). For Korean sociologists, to understand the development of Korean society, they have to take into account Sinicism, Japanese occupation, imperialism, the Cold War, American influence, etc. Today, some Korean sociologists are adapting Western theories to understand Korean society and some others are looking for new ways to reappropriate traditional thoughts (cf. Chapter 10 from Lim Hyun-Chin); they are struggling to emphatically display the possibility of the balance of the body of knowledge developed and accumulated globally, with Korean society as a part of it, even though a hugely disproportionate contribution comes from Western contexts (cf. Chapter 31 from Kim Byoung-Kwan). We could consider the paradoxical characteristics of modernity, the limits and the crisis of "hegemonic modernity" in developing sociological imaginations (cf. Chapter 15 from Han Sang-Jin). Or if Western culture looks hegemonic in the process of globalization, glocal cultures—for example the Korean Wave—are an influential concept to demonstrate glocalization and refer to a hybridization of global and local culture that circulate through transnational spaces, even those of the hegemonic culture (cf. Chapter 19 from Jang Wonho).

The post-Western sociology is redefined and based on diverse theories, shared methods, and historical/political/civilizational context; conversations between Western and non-Western theory mean their mutual and reciprocal transformation, their non-reproduction. To deconstruct the universality of Western sociology, non-Western sociologists are invited to emphasize local experiences (cf. Chapter 6 of Li Youmei). From a post-sociology and *re-Easternized East* perspective, in his chapter Xie Lizhong developed a theory of discursive pluralism, distinct from geographic pluralism. While geographic pluralism favors the indigenization of sociological thought by producing a discourse in a specific time and space, discursive pluralism appears to be linked to a form of universalism containing a wide range of discourses that may be applied to any time and space. Post-Western sociology could enable us to view the intersection, overlap, and blending of sociologies constructed in the diversity of the Wests and the Easts which is producing localization or expanded localization (cf. Chapter 8 from Zhou Xiaohong and Feng Zhuqin). Furthermore, Max Weber's "fever" in China was particularly distinctive and has promoted fruitful academic exchanges between European and Chinese sociologists by giving to Weberian study a position of post-Western sociology (cf. Chapter 23 from He Rong). Japanese sociologists like Akira Kurihara highlighted the uniqueness of Japanese critical sociology that developed under the influence of German critical theory, especially under the influence of Erikson and Habermas; he demonstrated how the concept in Japanese sociology of tenderness (*yasashisa*) is *galapagozed—galapagosization* being used to refer to a Japanese product that is too local and unusual to be available outside Japan—and argued the sense of ego identity is closely related to change in historical society (cf. Chapter 20 from Deguchi Takeshi). Chinese sociologists also have analyzed the transformations of socialist countries like China, the Soviet Union, and those in Eastern Europe after the 1980s and they have been inspired by the "New Budapest School" created by Iván Szelényi and Gil Eyal. It is not appropriate to be caught up in dichotomized ideas such as the West or the East. Western elements have already been incorporated as an important part of the process of change in the non-Western world; secondly, the non-Western world is diverse, and the simple contrast scheme of Western versus non-Western has already collapsed (cf. Chapter 54 from Machimura Takashi).

Traveling through the post-Western space means the transgression of the boundaries dividing "the West" and the "rest of the world" in avoidance of consolidating the hegemony of existing modernization theory and not using Confucian or Islamic theories to overcome the limitations of Western centrism; if the cosmopolitan turn in sociology is a significant step, it could not be the final task for Post-Western sociology (cf. Chapter 11 from Kim Mun Cho). It also means to examine the instances of clashes between Western ethos and non-Western ethos based on unique experiences, for example, the developmental trajectory in post-war Japan and the production of a new collective memory; the question becomes how the voices of the citizens of Hiroshima influenced the sense of sociology and the fabric of a non-Western ethos in civil society and social sciences (cf. Chapter 14 from Nomiya Daishiro). There has been introduced the ontological state of the Oneness, which, in the general East Asian social theory based on the unity between the heaven, earth, and the human, this conception of the Oneness differs widely from the ways of thinking of the Oneness in the Western theories which do not include Sunism, Confucianism, Daoism, and Buddhism (cf. Chapter 4 from Kim Seung Kuk).

In China, Japan, and Korea, different forms of cosmopolitan imaginations are developing, translating differences and diversities of traditions and cultural influences. The political, historical, social, and economic contexts affect the production of intellectual epistemic autonomies that defend positions, sensibilities, and relationships to different worlds in the scientific field and depending on margins of action and liberty that vary from one country to another. Finally, the issue of producing a transnational public sociology is posed from the position of social science and knowledge in non-Western societies, the connections between common knowledge and scholarly knowledge, where the bearers of Post-Western sociology are located (cf. Chapter 16 from Okumura Takashi). Furthermore, in a post-Western space, the production of multiple narratives on contemporary societies depends on the individual and collective competencies of action, reflexivity, and subjectivity. To bridge time and space in sociology, the production of knowledge imposes, in a structural analysis, an exploration of all the transformation through narration and events in using multisited ethnographies, individual or collective biographies, or even the autobiography that could bear the nature of life course study (cf. Chapter 17 from Qu Jingdong). So, if sociology is a practice of creating society, if sociology could be a narrative of human life, in post-Western sociology we can come back to fundamental issues, for example how the social precedes or not what makes "Western" and "non-Western" societies (cf. Chapter 22 from Kikutani Kazuhiro).

In this handbook post-Western theory is produced in a pluridimensional and polycentric space. Post-Western sociology is constructed from connections between knowledge spaces in dialogue and mutual learning. The theoretical and epistemological polyphony is a way to develop a new non-hegemonic global sociology and to hear from new voices speaking together. Even Western-Wests are reimagined, and even the issue of Western hegemonies continues to be active; we are becoming able to produce a new geography of a plurality of epistemic autonomies and new assemblages of "Western" and "non-Western" knowledge, to improve a methodological cosmopolitanism (cf. Chapter 1 from Laurence Roulleau-Berger). From the non-Western traditions different approaches of post-Western sociology invite us to change the globalized hierarchies into social sciences, to come back to the issue of "what is sociology?"

2   Sociologies in Dialogue

We have shown in a constructed dialogue how "Western" and "non-Western" theories meet, how shared sociological knowledge and situated knowledge cohabit and become embedded. From the crossed perspectives, we have seen the emergence of continuous and discontinuous continuities between Chinese, Japanese, Korean, and French sociologies that open up a transnational space on central issues in the discipline:

- youth and education
- ethnicity and space
- migration and cosmopolitanism
- labor and economic uncertainty

2.1   *Youth and Education*

About the topic of "youth and education" the four essays focus on class-based inequality in educational attainment and how education, as an institution, shapes the life chances of youth in different social contexts. In the Chinese case we can see how educational expansion during the post-reform stage influenced the pattern of educational inequality and school-to-society transition for young people, and how it has important implications for the changes of gender and class structure (cf. Chapter 28 from Wu Yuxiao). In the French case, in using two ideal typical American models from Y. Hasenfeld and Ralph Turner, we discuss school socioeconomic segregation and its effects on class identity among students from lower-class or upper-class families, by reviewing empirical research on the sociology of education conducted in Western societies, such as the United States, the United Kingdom, and France; there are multiple societal effects of the internal dynamics of the French educational system (cf. Chapter 29 from Agnès van Zanten). In the Japanese case the question of who "youth" are may serve as a starting point for "East–West" dialogue; we analyze how the patterns of school-to-work transition in Japan changed in different historical stages and produced social and economic inequalities (cf. Chapter 30 from Asano Tomohiko). From the perspective of a non-Western sociology in the Korean context, we review sociological works on the topic of youth and education in Korea, focusing on the educational institutions, the characteristic features and practices in the production/reproduction of social and gender inequalities, and the strategic choice in the family (cf. Chapter 31 from Kim Byoung-Kwan).

It is common sense that different countries have their unique educational institutions and labor market structures. However, due to the trend of globalization, we also see quite a few things in common between Western societies and societies in East Asia on the issues of youth and education, such as increasing educational inequality, school socioeconomic segregation, and patterns of school-to-work transition. It is of great value to promote comparative studies that may shed light on the theoretical dialogue of post-Western sociology.

In the way of dealing with the issue of youth and education the question of the production and reproduction of social inequalities in the school space appears to be common to European, Chinese, Japanese, and Korean sociologies, more precisely with increasing school socioeconomic segregation in elementary and middle schools, the rising class gap in higher education (in particular in elite universities). Of course, contextual effects inform this process of production and reproduction of social inequalities, such as the urban–rural gaps in China and Japan. Furthermore, the issue of youth and education has been articulated in European, Chinese, Japanese, and Korean sociologies to the question of the relationship between training and employment in the transition from school to work. For French, Chinese, Korean, and Japanese sociologists, education in the age of globalization must produce and reproduce individuals who can get information and organize it into knowledge, individuals able/constrained to be autonomous in order to adapt to radically changing societies. That is why inequality, discrimination, and segregation matter.

The sociology of education clearly shows at the international level theoretical continuities between European, Chinese, Japanese, and Korean thinking and in this way could actively participate in post-Western sociology.

2.2   *Ethnicity and Space*

About the problematic "ethnicity and space" French sociologists provide a theoretical concept of ethnicity, the phenomenon of which is accordingly understood in a French context. The notion of "worlds of ethnicity" is articulating a view of "social worlds" specific to the symbolic interactionism of different regimes of historicity (cf. Chapter 35 from Ahmed Boubeker).

In Chinese sociology, just as in European sociology, the deconstruction of the ethnic entity should take societal and historical contexts into account, such as colonialism and nationalism, which produce classifications and fixed moral and social borders. This signifies the deconstruction of ethnic categorizations and classifications in a constructivist approach, interethnic relationships according to Fredrik Barth, as well as ethnic boundaries, globalized religions, and transnational spaces. Many scholars in China conceptualized the dynamic relationships between ethnicity and cultural identity to study ethnic interactions, the relationships between ethnic groups, and the state and the moral boundaries of ethnic groups (cf. Chapter 36 from Fan Ke). So, the constructivist approach appears to be a common heritage for European and Chinese sociologists. In Korean cases "the social", constructed with the building of the nation-state, is being deterritorialized through globalization. In another constructivist perspective, Korean sociologists are more focused on the theory of multiculturalism to overcome the reflection on the nation-states and territorialization of the social and to develop further the problematic on globalization and deterritorialization of the social. In post-Western sociology we could be able to articulate ethnicity and multiculturalism in a new Western/Eastern perspective.

2.3 Migration and Cosmopolitanism

Since the 1990s, the issue of migration has become a major scientific and political challenge, a global turning point in the social sciences. Although globalization continues to advance, the problem of the social integration of migrants is becoming more and more complicated and diversified. Within the West and the East, there are many obvious differences in the ways, paths, mechanisms, and policies of immigration integration in various countries. When migrant workers enter Korea or Japan, they appear "to be far too 'traditional', too 'backward', too community-oriented, too little educated, and unskilled"; they are not considered as future citizens or long-term residents; they are invited to work in menial dead-end jobs, not fellow humans who can construct a cosmopolitan society together (cf. Chapter 38 from Choi Jongryul). At same time, the social integration of the rural floating population also shows complexity in China and it is very difficult to generalize in one pattern. In other words, there are many patterns of social integration for the rural floating population, including the assimilation, segregation, interactions between them and original citizens, urban and rural "amphibious" actors, etc. (cf. Chapter 56 from Wang Chunguang and Lu Wen).

Intracontinental and international mobility has continued to accelerate, and circulation has intensified in recent years. More and more migrants move, circulate, return, and take different migratory routes; they work, live, and acquire plural experiences in a multiplicity of urban and rural spaces and temporalities, and are often challenged in their social, ethnic, and gender identities (cf. Chapter 54 from Machimura Takashi). Therefore, the existing paradigm of immigration sociology is increasingly lacking in explanatory power for such complexity. And the new migration research paradigm is in great demand. This may provide an important opportunity for the development of Western sociological theory. Migrants have been increasingly constructed as actors endowed with individual and collective capacities for action, their mobile skills, their reflexivity, their subjectivity; cosmopolitanisms show how "regimes of Otherness" become more complex and multiply, producing forms of unequally legitimized recognition of the place of migrants in different societies (cf. Chapter 55 from Laurence Roulleau-Berger).

We are today widely invited to rely on a new theory of transnationalism methodological cosmopolitanism to move towards a post-Western sociology that opens new perspectives on intracontinental and international migration, to grasp how accelerations and telescopes of intracontinental and international mobility inform the production of urban, social, economic, and ethnic inequalities; the construction of migratory careers; and the processes of subjectivation in European and Asian societies, in the world society. With reference to the Japanese experience, the Western theoretical concept of "super-diversity" has been proposed to create intercultural spaces for active dialogue between East Asian and Western sociologies and to contribute to an understanding of unprecedented social change and social transformation under globalized migration. Moreover, it must lead to the advancement of the intervals between East Asian and Western sociologies to create post-Western sociology (cf. Chapter 37 from Tarumoto Hideki).

2.4 Labor and Economic Uncertainty

Granovetter will appear as the main architect of the revival of economic sociology in the world. The revival of economic sociology is largely related to the development of network analysis that finds its main source in the work of Harrison White. In the course of this work, Granovetter in *Getting a Job* (1974) developed the famous thesis of "the strength of weak links" in access to employment—a thesis still very widely used in a lot of European empirical research—based on articulation between networks of sociability and social capital.

Economic sociology was born in the late 19th century and, after being forgotten, reappeared in the early 1980s, especially in Europe. Philippe Steiner and François Vatin (2009), authors of the *Traité de sociologie économique*, consider economic activity to be a dimension of social activity, the economic fact as a social fact. Chinese economic sociology has been directly affected by the renewal of economic sociology in Western sociology. There is a long and important tradition of studying economic phenomena in Chinese sociology, especially before the abolition of the discipline in the 1950s. The theory of transformation of social structure by Li Peilin, the theory of social capital and *guanxi* by Bian Yanjie (1997), and the theory of property rights, over the Western property rights theory, by Yang Dian and Liu Shiding have been produced in China (cf. Chapter 12 of Yang Dian) and do represent a trend in Chinese sociology. But besides these theories in labor sociology Shen Yuan (cf. Chapter 13 from Shen Yuan) has produced the concept of the production system of migrant workers and has demonstrated how the subjectivity of labor is one of the most important fields in labor sociology, how the concept of the "politics of production" put forward by Burawoy in the Chinese context has been transformed into the "politics of life".

These perspectives are opening a dialogue with French, Korean, and Japanese sociology about migrant workers. In different societies migrants are analyzed as subjects to dominations, symbolic and identity-threatening violence, and discrimination—even racism—in their respective labor markets; symbolic violence is constructed in professional relationships by means of phenomena of horizontal and vertical social disqualification, alienation of identities, and contempt and humiliation (cf. Chapter 55 from Laurence Roulleau-Berger). Here, sociologists converge in saying that the less endowed migrants in terms of social capital and economic and symbolic resources are subjected to the forces of political and economic measures; those who are well endowed in terms of social and economic resources have at their disposal networks of trust and can rely upon community solidarities and will also be able to develop strategies to divert these measures and find social and spatial anchorage in economic spaces.

If in the EU countries sociologists are conducting research on a double process of economic insecurity and ethnic discrimination, in Asian countries sociologists have in common the study of the proliferation of precarious forms of employment due to the plurality and flexibility of transitional employments. The rise of non-regular and precarious employment definitely contributes to the rise in wage inequality in the labor markets (cf. Chapter 27 by Sato Yoshimichi). For some two decades, intermittence and discontinuity of work have permeated all modes of production, thus signaling the weakening of the so-called Fordist salaried employment, and the institutionalization of the "precariat" (Castel 2009).

3   Distances, Dissonances, and Discontinuities

We have shown how "Western" and "non-Western" theories could coexist in relationships of distance and dissonance. From the crossed perspectives, we have seen the emergence of continuous and discontinuous discontinuities between Chinese, Japanese, Korean, and French sociologies that produce local knowledge on two central issues in the discipline:
- globalization and social stratification
- state, society, and collective action
- gender and inequalities
- individuation, self, and emotions
- environment and global health

3.1 Globalization and Social Stratification

No country in the contemporary world can be immune from the impact of globalization and also recent de-globalization. Economic globalization, as well as the global financial crisis of 2008, has led to the increase in income and wealth inequalities, the fluctuation of the middle class, and the flexibility of employment and work in many countries, which has brought about a challenge to the originally occupation-based class structure. However, globalization has also had different influences on social class and social stratification in various countries with different economic, political, cultural, and institutional contexts. While European and North American countries have suffered a shrinking of the middle class, China, as a major new emerging economy in the age of globalization, has achieved an extensive poverty reduction and fostered a growing middle class (cf. Chapter 24 from Li Chunling). Japan and South Korea also have demonstrated some differences in changes in class and social stratification from European and North American countries. These particularities displayed in China, Japan, and South Korea have prompted sociologists to rethink theories from Western sociology.

The relationship between globalization and societal singularities plays on the ways in which Western class theories are or are not adjusted to analyze non-Western configurations. If the phenomenon of the formation of the middle class and its multiple segmentations in China appears to be linked to the uniqueness of the Chinese experience, it is easy to understand why Chinese sociologists are elaborating on a located theory of social classes in a globalized context, but in which sense are they connected or not connected with Western theories? Similarly, the phenomenon of rewealthization as a major factor in class transformation could characterize many Western countries, while globalization has increased income inequality, wealth inequality, and inequalities between regular and non-regular workers in Europe and in Asia (cf. Chapter 25 from Louis Chauvel). The diversification of income and wealth in South Korea comes from the class formation trajectory that is different from that in other East Asian countries, such as Japan and China. Although South Korea has shown rapid industrialization, the occupation-based social stratification fails to capture the dynamics of the rising inequality (cf. Chapter 26 from Shin Kwang-Yeong). So, from a perspective of post-Western theory, the issue is how international sociologists could mix or not mix the Western and non-Western theories to explain quite similar processes about globalization and new social inequalities.

3.2 State, Society, and Collective Action

From a post-Western sociology perspective we are invited to enlarge the diversity considering the relationship between the state and individuals, touching upon different patterns of governance. The diversity could be expressed in two aspects. The first one is the intermediary agent between the state and the individual, shown as collective organizations on different scales, urban social movements, families, civil society organizations, etc. The second aspect leads to the boundary between the state and society during their interaction, which changes from a distinct and clear one to something more vague and permeated, caused by the inner tension between the legacy of authoritarian governance and the rising social participation driven by neoliberal globalization, especially in non-Western counties.

States and local governments produce differentiated models of participatory governance under political control that produce discrimination, marginalization, and exclusion. Some European sociologists are focusing on the issue of what really makes popular politics and local ties and resists the tyranny of urban renewal in the "South" and the "North" in taking distance with a Western theory of urban politics (cf. Chapter 32 from Agnès Deboulet). However, in the European, Chinese, Japanese, and Korean contexts intermediate actors and forms of citizen mobilization are pluralized and also develop "from below" from different forms of local solidarities. The individual and collective practices for distancing public policies are based on societal constraints and capabilities located in the different contexts. Discussing the relationships between the state, the society, and the local governance appears as an important theoretical perspective to introduce "citizen participation" (cf. Chapter 34 from Yamamoto Hidehiro). For example, in China, individuals still remain highly dependent on the authoritarian state and continue to think of themselves as part of the state even when they develop strategies for individual or collective emancipation (cf. Chapter 33 from Shi Yunqing). But neoliberal globalization, especially during the COVID-19 pandemic, reduced the function of the states on the one hand and maximized the role of non-state actors in the market on the other.

To develop post-Western theory on the relationships between state and society invites us to introduce the issue of the collective action that is constructed differently in France, China, Japan, and Korea. In his chapter Lilian Mathieu reminds us the United States approaches with the concepts of the "repertoire of collective action" by Tilly, of "political opportunity structure by Tilly and Tarrow", and "the frame analysis" by Goffman have become internationally dominant since the 1990s. In the French tradition, some research is on the side of the sociology of "new social movement" elaborated by Alain

Touraine or the dispositionalist sociology inspired by Pierre Bourdieu; others have been inspired by interactionist and pragmatist theories. French and Japanese sociologists focus on the diversity of protests and mobilizations by students, feminists, pacifists, and ecologists, bearing in mind that the sociology of social movements in Japan is mainly centered on ecological movements. In his chapter Hasegawa Koichi demonstrated Japanese environmental sociology has developed many original perspectives: (1) pollution, local development, the social mechanism of suffering victims; (2) intersections of daily life, culture, and ecology; (3) disaster effects and the recovery process; and (4) environmental justice, social discrimination, and social disparity. He proposed the sociology of environmental issues should be a "sociology of the downstream perspective" to develop a reinterpretation of the conception of a "risk society". In China the control of collective actions is really important in the technocratization of an authoritarian political regime; Chinese sociologists are using the American theories of collective action and the notion of "mass incident" (*quntixing shijian*) to analyze how the Chinese state perceives social movements and their politization in the past and in the present (cf. Chapter 41 from Feng Shizheng).

It is clear here that one can appreciate how the question of historical and political legacies deserves to be addressed in the production of a post-Western sociology. But the singularity of societal and political configurations favors the formation of niches of knowledge rather than the production of shared knowledge.

3.3 *Gender and Inequalities*

International sociology has been very much marked in the last decade by gender studies. About the problematic of "gender and inequalities" the French sociologists emphasize women's agency and keep a distance from the deterministic Western tradition evolving around structure and power where the male domination and the struggle for the place of men and women in the domestic and professional spheres are central (cf. Chapter 42 from Christine Détrez). While East Asian sociologists are cautious of the Western-centric, value-loaded terms of "modernization" and "modernity", they carefully investigate gender and family dynamics in the East Asian institutional configuration and local culture, in order to map out both similarities to and differences from the gender dynamics in the West. In China the theory of mosaic modernity has been developed to understand how tradition and modernity is interwoven (cf. Chapter 43 from Ji Yingchun). China and Japan follow different paths from Western societies, considering different economic institutions, welfare policies, and culture. Japanese family sociology now regards how to analyze the transformation of the traditional nuclear family into new types of family; and American positivistic family sociology has been influential on Japanese sociology (cf. Chapter 44 from Nemoto Kumiko). In Japanese and Korean sociologies gender inequalities are worked through family/intimacy-related conflicts based on the historical processes of modernization and democratization, and demographic transitions. With regard to women and the family in the situation of deepened inequality since the COVID-19 pandemic, Korean sociologists have described a *condensed radicalization of individualization*—about individualization, that is to say emancipation from tradition, with the other being emancipation from the group—and *family-oriented individualization or community orientation*—this theory indicates a post-Western trend in following the individuation trend of Western society on the one hand, and another one based on community orientation in East Asia (cf. Chapter 45 from Shim Young-Hee).

This reflection on and critique of Western-centric knowledge and modernization simultaneously comprise knowledge production in the West. This pluralistic and simultaneous way of interrogating gender inequality in different societies constitutes the essential logic of post-Western sociology.

3.4 *Individuation, Self, and Emotions*

In French, Chinese, Japanese, and Korean sociologies the issue of individuation, self, and emotions is embedded in the problematic of historical and structural processes, "new" inequalities, and social conflicts. So, we can clearly imagine how to produce a post-Western sociology of individuation.

From 1980 to 1995 strong controversies divided French sociologies. There was the Subject, which had been denied in the Marxist and Bourdieu school theories, according to the theory of the *habitus*. Then, Alain Touraine and Michel Wieviorka questioned the Subject, François Dubet produced a sociology of experience to help us better understand the "objective" social structures individuals find themselves trapped in and which they struggle against. After 1990, the Subject has been increasingly defined by her or his capacity to be an autonomous and reflexive actor and to construct his or her experience, but also possessing emotions and feelings. A sociology of ordeals has been produced around the concepts of respect, shame, and contempt (Martuccelli 2006); everyone is required to be both the actor and the author of his or her own life, and the feeling of contempt becomes the fundamental emotion of democratic societies among those who face an impossible-to-achieve trial (cf. Chapter 51 from François Dubet). Quite recently new propositions in sociology of emotions are appearing with the new generation of sociologists.

In Chinese sociology, Yang Yiyin (2012) shows how *we* implies "being one of us", which is characterized by the permeability of the boundaries of *we*, the elasticity of the boundaries of *we*, the precise borders of *me*. However, the boundaries of the *self* in Chinese sociology are also conceived in relation to the *guanxi*. We insist on the importance of the *guanxis* in the construction of individual and collective identities by recalling that it is inherent in Chinese civilization both past and present. Chinese sociologists considered that the status of emotions remains strong via the question of social interactions and *guanxis*. Cheng Boqing (2013) first combined social interaction, *guanxis*, and *Confucian self* to take into account the transformation of the *modern self*. Second he articulates the *ethical self*, which means the requirements, emotions, and limits in our relationship to others; *the aesthetical self*, which means affections and feelings; and the *transcendental self*. In his chapter according to Cheng Boqing and Wang Jiahui (2017), three emotional regimes have emerged correspondingly: *the managerial regime*; the *experiential regime* in consumption; and the *performative regime* in social interaction.

In Japanese sociology the issue of emotion and self has become one of the most important issues since 1980. In the Japanese tradition, the self means seeing one and gradually seeing oneself in an environment surrounding the self; in contemporary society, today's sociologists are invited to study the eruption of emotions and sentiments into various areas, and the production of a transcendental subject (see Chapter 52 from Yazawa Shujiro). In Korean sociology the relationship between the individual and community is a very important topic. Han and Shim purposed the concept of "postconventional networking individualization"; in his chapter Kim Wang-Bae shows how the emotions of fear, hatred, and anger are constructed and mixed into the emotionalized subjects and in polarized social conflicts; he is reinterpreting Bourdieu's conceptualization of *habitus* in the context of emotions.

So, the cultural variations of the definitions of the concepts of "individuation" and "subjectivation" in Western and non-Western sociologies allow us to see discontinuous continuities between local conceptual spaces and to understand how singular spaces are producing located knowledge and global knowledge.

3.5 *Environment and Global Heath*

New environmental and health risks are generating situations of uncertainty, new inequalities, new solidarities, and the production of new public spaces. In East Asia, social inequalities and natural inequalities merge into *compressed modernities* (Chang 2017) linked to spatial and historical processes of ecological and urban change.

Environmental sociology began in the 1980s and 1990s with the emergence of environmental problems. In Europe, the reflexive modernization theories of Anthony Giddens and Ulrich Beck inspired the notion of ecological modernization. Ecological modernization theory is one of the major environmental theories/discourses among scholars and policymakers in Japan. The concept of *environmental justice*, which emerged in the United States in the 1980s, referred to inequalities in the spatial distribution of risks. Since the 1990s, following various food and sanitary crises, food studies have been developed in sociology of risk. The sociology of food studies shows food anxiety is an anthropological invariant. More recently, in the face of unequal access to food, the *food justice* and *food sovereignty* concepts have emerged.

In China it was after the mid-1990s that the sociology of the environment was introduced as a discipline. A body of research has shown how rapid urbanization, industrialization, and economic liberalization has led to the emergence of environmental problems. Chinese sociologists also deal with environmental inequalities in emphasizing the issue of the reconstruction of trust and the issue of citizen participation in environmental protection. Mistrust, more fundamentally, is one of the great challenges in Chinese society (cf. Chapter 46 from Wang Xiaoyi and Anier). The origin of environmental sociology in Japan was the early 1970s. The pioneer was a female sociologist, Dr. Iijima, who majored in chemistry as an undergraduate and became a sociologist; she had recognized that the Japanese heavy metal and chemical industry destroyed the environment and produced serious pollution. The above process clearly shows us that ecology is not only a natural issue but also a social and cultural one. Environmental sociology must have wider spatial perspectives that extend beyond the damaged areas and peoples. Since the late 1970s environmental sociology has been developed by Funabashi, Kajita, and Hasegawa, and a theory of risk culture after the East Japan Great Earthquake and the tsunami disaster was developed to understand non-institutional, emergent sociation, horizontal orders, and reflexive community.

Concerning present-day East Asia, Ulrich Beck (2013) spoke of a cosmopolitan risk community (or "Cosmo-Climate"). He has distinguished "cosmopolitan empathy" and the subpolitics of "cosmopolitanism from below". Does this make sense for Chinese, Korean, and Japanese sociologists? In East Asia sociologists consider that we cannot conceive of the risk issue in the same terms in Europe and in Asia because different "compressed modernities" mean multiple modernizations, but also the complexities, diversities, and heterogeneities of risks that people face in East Asia today overtake those faced by the Western world (cf. Chapter 48 from Satoh Keiichi). If today Anthropocene theories appear to be very dominant in Western social sciences, a few Asian scholars have therefore deemed it necessary to redefine the concept from the angle of postcolonial criticism (cf. Chapter 47 from Paul Jobin). In environmental sociology "ecological crisis" is analyzed with the theory of the Anthropocene and the Capitalocene in a context of green capitalisms and de-growth (cf.

Chapter 49 from Hong Deokhwa and Ku Dowan). This question lies at the heart of post-Western sociology about the renewal of neocolonial domination in scientific sphere, and maybe we could deconstruct the Anthropocene from the postcolonial criticism elaborated by Asian scholars.

Existing theories in the sociology of health are mainly based on the experience of Western developed countries, which should be complemented by more studies on the traditions and patterns of non-Western countries in dealing with health problems (cf. Chapter 57 from Hong Yanbi and Zhao Yandong). In Europe as in Asia, although ecologies cover multiple and varied representations of the interface of nature-urban culture, these same ecologies produce environmental and health inequalities and injustices, regimes of action, and individual and collective mobilizations. In his chapter Yee Jaeyeol has reconstructed the concept of "publicness" based on the ideas of the socially embedded self, a hierarchically situated social order, and deeply contextualized social rules to propose, in the context of the COVID-19 pandemic, a theory of risk governance based on the different empirical realities of Western and East Asian countries.

In the context of the COVID-19 pandemic, in his chapter Hosoda Miwako considers the sociological issues of equality and human rights, health disparities between rich and poor, and stigmas and discrimination against those who choose not to be vaccinated; he proposed improving the dialogue between the East and the West in introducing the concept of "living together" with nature (*kyosei*). In a closed perspective in his chapter Frédéric Le Marcis invited us to expand the meaning and practices of epidemic preparedness in articulating the theories of health system and community, the concepts of institutional memory and popular memory to take into account the experience-based knowledge. According to Cho Byong-Hee in his chapter, if COVID-19 was caused by socioeconomic factors associated with an ecological crisis, sociologists are taking into account marketization or neo-liberalism of the health care system in many countries such as Korea, the medicalization of pandemic control, the dispositions of and resistance to overworking doctors, legal and illegal practices in hospitals, and the modes of cooperation between doctors and nurses; but we are invited to mobilize medical sociology and political sociology to understand the risks at work, school, home, etc., and the issue of what makes citizenship in a pandemic context and in a global community.

In a post-Western sociology we are invited to think about a new cosmopolis and how to rebuild the world. If health crises produce situations of great "uncertainty", multiply societal and international inequalities, and produce paroxysmal figures of dislocation, they also open spaces for the emergence of new figures of social restoration, new processes of reconstruction of Western and Eastern societies in a global world.

Post-Western sociology is a critical reflection on the imagined orthodoxy and purity of Western sociology. In its respect for Western sociology, post-Western sociology aims reinventing it. In its creative construction, however, post-Western sociology tries to explore new sociological horizon arising from non-Western and post-Modern context. This ambivalence inherent in post-Western sociology guides us to the world of hybridization, an undeniable nature of human and non-human society. Post-Western sociology must appreciate "purity in hybridity". Sociologists in the era of artificial intelligence must become new avant-garde full of imagination and self-fulfilling prophecy about cosmological freedom and liberation. Post-Western sociology then may start from a post-human awareness that will be led to "cosmological turn" for building new civilization of "everything-goes-together-peacefully".

References

Beck, U. 2013. "Risk, class, crisis, hazards and cosmopolitan solidarity/risk community—conceptual and methodological clarifications". *Working Papers Series*, no. 31 (April). FMSH.

Bian, Yanjie. 2010. "Guanxi shehui xue jiqi xueke diwei" [Network sociology and its position among other disciplines]. Xi'an Jiaotong Daxue Xuebao. *Shehui Kexue bao* 5: 1–6.

Castel, R. 2009. *La montée des incertitudes* [The rise of uncertainties]. Paris: Seuil.

Chang, Kyung-Sup. 2010. "The second modern condition? Compressed modernity as internalized reflexive cosmopolitization". *The British Journal of Sociology* 61 (3): 444–465.

Cheng, Boqing. 2013. 情感的社会学意 [The sociological signification of the emotion]. 山东社会科学 [Shandong Social Science] 2013 (03): 42–48. DOI:10.14112/j.cnki.37-1053/c.2013.03.031.

Granovetter, M. 1974. *Getting a job*. Chicago: Chicago University Press.

Li, Peilin, Qu Jingdong, and Yang Yabin. 2009. *An introduction to Chinese sociological classics*. Peking: Social Sciences Academic Press.

Martuccelli. 2006. *Forgé par l'épreuve. L'individu dans la France contemporaine* [Forged through ordeals. The individual in contemporary France]. Paris: Colin.

Yang, Yiyin. 2012. "Guanxilization and Categorization: Theoretical Considerations Based on Two Case Studies". In *European and Chinese Sociologies. A new dialogue*, edited by L. Roulleau-Berger and Peilin Li, 163–177. Leiden and Boston: Brill Publishers.

Postface

Sari Hanafi

Among relentless literature today questioning the imbalance in knowledge production between different regions in the world, the *Handbook of Post-Western Sociology: From East Asia to Europe* appears particularly innovative in its approach and the comparativism in theories and case studies. In this postface, I would like to show how this handbook is timely and resonates with my agenda as a president of the International Sociological Association (ISA) in connecting different traditions of sociology in order to forge a sort of a global sociology. A sociology that has three principles of *positionality*, *comparativism*, and *mild universalism*; a sociology that formulates criticism of some aspects of postcolonial discourse in some regions[1] and my call for *Sociologies in Dialogue* (Hanafi and Yi 2020) or dialogical sociology (Hanafi Forthcoming).

The handbook took us on a journey of crosscutting themes (social stratification, labor sociology, migration, gender, family, individualism, etc.) well thought out through research that carried out mostly by senior scholars who are capable of producing critical and epistemological reflection on paradigms that directed these themes. One will certainly enjoy reading them and particularly about Eastern Asia societies, research that is not always visible outside this region. The confrontation between theories coming from East Asia with western theories is the fruit of longstanding collaborations between French and Easter Asian scholars culminated in this wonderful edited volume of Laurence ROULLEAU-BERGER, LI Peilin, KIM Seung Kuk and YAZAWA Shujiro but with their previous works as well. This volume is not only theorizing Post-Western Sociology but providing many concrete contributions to how this sociology should be. As Laurence Roulleau-Berger clearly defines in this volume, Post-Western Sociology is several sociological systems constructed by Western and non-Western sociologists (not separately but together) and thus it should not be confused with non-Western, de-Western, and anti-Western sociology. This is why the handbook has two categories of authors thinking

---

1 While the importance of considering the impact of coloniality in the past is still salient today, the use of postcolonial studies is not without certain conceptual challenges. I will identify three of them before discussing them together: the way different contradictions within societies have been understood, the overemphasis on external factors with the simultaneous neglect of local ones, and the antagonistic logic of categories such as empire/colony, East/West, and universalism/contextualism (Hanafi 2019, 2020). Having said that, France academia needs to acknowledge the scars of the colonial era in knowledge production.

jointly and contrasting their reading to their society with the other societies: one located in the global North and the second located in the global South and particularly East Asia.

This is a substantive difference from postcolonial studies that are actually produced often by the global North even with the contribution of those who are originally from the global South. From South Asia, Latin America and the Middle East, often from well-to-do families with political connections, many migrated to metropolitan universities. They subscribed to, what Hussein Omar[2] called a "big bang" theory that no resistance had existed before them. In contrast, post-sociology is produced by scholars who are located in both the global South and North. Post-Western Sociology stood above the crude idea that ideas were dependent on the person delivering them. An equation between what one knows and what one is that even Edward Said had always opposed. Post-sociology's knowledge is thus evaluated based on its heuristic value and not the location of its emergence.

This volume accommodates theoretical hybridization but also some local theoretical orientations, as we see with the contribution of KIM Seung Kuk (from South Korea) (in this volume) who theorizes solipsist and spiritualist individualism and the middle way for love or with the contribution of Akira KURIHARA (from Japan), whose theory of identity of tenderness elucidates contradictions in the reproduction process of personal identity and society at large, namely how this dysfunction of identity formation generates the mentality of tenderness which is opposed to values of productivism. We are sufficiently surprised how convergent are the analysis of different societies on specific issues that rightly gathered under the same section. For instance, in Section 5, Louis CHAUVEL's sociology of social stratification, where "occupational classes" based on jobs cannot be understood without a context of wealth-based domination in the west, resonates with LI Chunling's analysis of the wealthization driven by housing wealth Inequality in China, despite the importance of rural population in this country compared to the western countries. Sometimes the contrast is more substantial like in the chapter of Kazuhiro KIKUTANI comparing the French Dreyfus Affair with a similar affair in Japan, the Taigyaku Affair. He labels sociology in Japan as without Society: "Unlike in Zola's France, in Nagai's Japan there was no awakening of an individual's creativity, no ordinary people in pursuit of liberty and art, and no people who confronted the state to win these. This means that Japan had been

---

2   https://thebaffler.com/salvos/unexamined-life-omar.

unable to produce the soil, namely, society". But more contemporarily, gender and family are two sites of the sharp contrast between western societies and other ones. Ji Yingchun's chapter on "Changing Gender Dynamics and Family Reinstitutionalization in Contemporary China" offers a great insight into China's mosaic modernity and how it has impacted gender and family relationships in an also mosaic way. While it is universal today to reduce gender inequality, gender boundaries have contrasting meanings depending on the society. For family, me too I find such strong contrast between the West and the Arab World today. Many Arab sociologists argue in favor of considering the family as a very salient social structure and are not ready to dilute it as this is the case in the West (Hanafi 2020).

Post-western sociology took its importance with the emergence of many works on the sociology of BRICS (Brazil, Russia, India, China and South Africa) where new East–South assemblages have been established outside the classical dichotomy of North–South. (See for instance, Li, Gorshkov and Scalon 2013 and Dwyer et al. 2018.)

Like the global sociology, Post-western sociology acknowledges the importance that a declaration of the *positionality* of its authors that must include everything related to their biographies and varying geographies that may affect their vision in relation to this sociology and to the "sociological tradition" into which one has been socialized during one's studies. I would praise how French scholarship in this volume whose authors add clearly positionality of their knowledge production by adding a geographical marker in the title of their contributions in this volume, something not often done in French sociology, as I studied empirically with a sample of journal articles and books produced in France (see Hanafi 2022).

Finally, in my scholarship, as someone who grow up in an authoritarian state (Syria), I am aware of how social knowledge production has been produced with many unspoken issues because of (self-)censorship. Where did knowledge production in a country like Syria go wrong? Did the problem really stem from using the tools and theories elaborated by sociologists such as Weber, Durkheim, and Parsons? Or was it a result of intellectual self-censorship, in an effort to manage the repressive state taboos? This is why sociological research omits any reflection of political economy and the nature of tyranny. The eternal question of "who writes history", which has long occupied postcolonial scholars, has been directed not only to the victorious colonialists but also to authoritarian regimes.

Let me finish by wishing long life to such conceptualization of post-Western sociology. I am sure it will find its paths in my academic fields worldwide.

References

Dwyer, Tom, Mikhail K. Gorshkov, Ishwar Modi, Li Chunling, and Mokong Simon Mapadimeng, eds. 2018. *Handbook of the Sociology of Youth in Brics Countries*. New Jersey: World Scientific Publishing Company.

Hanafi, Sari. 2019. "Global Sociology Revisited: Toward New Directions". *Current Sociology* 68 (1): 3–21.

Hanafi, Sari. 2020. "A Cognitive Arab Uprising?: Paradigm Shifts in Arab Social Sciences". In *The Oxford Handbook of the Sociology of the Middle East*, edited by Armando Salvatore, Sari Hanafi, and Kieko Obuse. Oxford University Press.

Hanafi, Sari. 2022. "Pour une « sociologie globale »". Translated by Pierre Bataille, Lucile Dumont, and Simeng Wang. *Socio-logos. Revue de l'association française de sociologie*, no. 17 (April). https://doi.org/10.4000/socio-logos.5724.

Hanafi, Sari. Forthcoming. *Ethics, Religion and Dialogical Sociology*.

Hanafi, Sari, and Chin-Chun Yi, eds. 2020. *Sociologies in Dialogue*. 1st edition. London: SAGE Publications Ltd.

Li, Peilin, M.K. Gorshkov, and Celi Scalon, eds. 2013. *Handbook on Social Stratification in the Bric Countries: Change and Perspective*. 1st edition. New Jersey: World Scientific Publishing Company.

Index

agency 15, 137, 206, 261, 368, 424, 426, 517, 597, 599, 603, 617, 721, 737, 893, 894, 895, 947, 989
altruism 55, 105, 198, 200, 201, 202, 214, 381, 712
Anier 13, 779, 992
anthropology 16, 39, 66, 125, 128, 144, 145, 146, 164, 166, 180, 183, 334, 351, 430, 602, 629, 644, 647, 650, 731, 849, 851
anxiety 284, 382, 392, 504, 653, 823, 859, 867, 875, 895, 992
Asano Tomohiko 9, 569, 853, 982
assimilation 15, 631, 895, 896, 899, 910, 911, 984
atomic bomb 6, 201, 293, 294, 295, 298, 299, 300
authenticity 143, 160, 612, 726, 833, 841, 844
autonomy 33, 137, 152, 225, 393, 563, 618, 621, 636, 716, 756, 757, 813, 828, 832, 840, 841, 844, 851, 869

Barraclough, Geoffrey 218, 219
Barth, Fredrik 38, 39, 629, 632, 636, 641, 643, 647, 660, 661, 983
Baudrillard, Jean 243, 573, 826, 871
Beck, Ulrich 2, 23, 28, 29, 92, 154, 235, 237, 293, 302, 379, 380, 577, 694, 703, 741, 742, 749, 762, 799, 800, 801, 853, 855, 870, 926, 991, 992
Bergson, Henri 462
Bhabha, Homi 108
Bhambra, Gurminder 23, 24
biographical bifurcations 894, 895
biosecurity 946, 947
Bonnet, Emmanuel 937, 942
Boubeker, Ahmed 10, 38, 629, 637, 898, 900, 983
Bourdieu, Pierre 14, 31, 32, 34, 37, 175, 496, 499, 563, 642, 714, 715, 732, 736, 841, 862, 901, 989, 990, 991
Briceno-Leon, Roberto 25, 26
BRICS 25, 997
Brinton, Mary 535, 539, 572, 575, 744, 745
Britain 1, 22, 52, 54, 292, 466, 503, 665, 666, 671, 672
Burawoy, Michael 26, 184, 264, 276, 277, 279, 280, 281, 366, 901, 985

Burkina Faso 939, 940, 941, 942, 943, 944, 947
Caduff, Carlo 940
Capra, Fritjof 95, 244
case study 6, 10, 167, 181, 349, 350, 351, 352, 353, 354, 356, 357, 359, 360, 361, 362, 363, 364, 366, 367, 368, 369, 370, 597, 693, 695, 817, 924, 930, 995
Chakrabarty, Dipesh 23, 218, 602, 787, 789, 790
Chang Kyung-Sup 39, 749, 901, 902
Chauvel, Louis 9, 37, 487, 495, 496, 502, 504, 987, 996
Cheng Boqing 13, 36, 823, 827, 833, 991
Chicago School 31, 66, 180, 691–692, 887, 895, 896
Chinese sociology 3, 4, 5, 26, 27, 28, 32, 35, 38, 39, 48, 49, 52, 55, 56, 58, 65, 77, 85, 86, 87, 88, 143, 151, 152, 154, 171, 172, 173n2, 174, 176, 177, 178, 182, 183, 184, 185, 187, 188, 190, 191, 251, 252, 274, 275, 307, 308, 309, 430, 464, 465, 466, 468, 471, 472, 474, 475, 476, 478, 480, 605, 737, 894, 895, 978, 983, 985, 990, 991
Cho Byong-Hee 16, 956, 959, 993
Choi Jongryul 11, 677, 984
citizenship 10, 36, 211, 238, 381, 394, 448, 456, 500, 597, 603, 608, 609, 613, 631, 638, 665, 898, 907, 913, 914, 993
city 207, 209, 263, 265, 267, 268, 269, 270, 277, 278, 297, 298, 299, 300, 316, 320, 324, 332, 423, 437, 438, 443, 492, 597, 600, 601, 602, 607, 608, 610, 635, 641, 648, 649, 651, 652, 654, 673, 746, 747, 748, 764, 765, 766, 767, 769, 772, 773n5, 790, 884, 887, 888, 890, 891, 897, 898, 908, 909, 910, 911, 912, 913, 914, 915, 924, 944n15, 957, 958
civil society 10, 137, 207, 210, 214, 215, 227, 260, 378, 435, 476, 503, 605, 616, 617, 619, 620, 622, 623, 756, 761, 807, 813, 848, 854, 872, 875, 878, 960, 979, 980, 988
civilization 1, 5, 16, 27, 33, 90, 91, 93, 96, 109, 115, 118, 119, 120, 126, 134, 135, 144, 145, 146, 151, 157, 184, 209, 218, 220n1, 241,

civilization (*cont.*)
    242, 244, 246, 309, 310, 316, 320, 321, 322, 356, 357, 359, 362, 363, 365, 369, 384, 432, 433, 464, 479, 581, 635, 779, 781, 782, 783, 784, 785, 869, 922, 956, 991, 994
climate change   603, 695, 702, 781, 790, 793, 799, 801, 803, 805, 808, 809, 812, 816, 890, 957
Cold War   202, 206, 207, 211, 214, 221, 222, 710, 794, 813, 814, 859, 863, 866, 867, 868, 878, 886, 979
collective action   12, 32, 36, 133, 265, 374, 392, 608, 610, 710, 711, 712, 714, 719, 721, 726, 986, 988, 989
collective memory   6, 292, 294, 295, 296, 297, 301, 302, 612, 980
commercialization   606, 607, 608, 609, 833, 963
communitarianism   224, 378, 635, 637
community   7, 10, 12, 15, 16, 29, 33, 39, 57, 66, 68, 131, 132, 146, 149, 150, 152, 165, 166, 167, 168, 169, 182, 204, 205, 208, 209, 210, 224, 227, 236, 252, 260, 265, 268, 269, 313, 314, 315, 322, 337, 338, 339, 340, 342, 343, 354, 355, 366, 374, 377, 378, 379, 384, 387, 388, 389, 390, 392, 394, 399, 401, 404, 406, 407, 408, 409, 410, 411, 417, 431, 432, 436, 437, 444, 468, 469n3, 471n4, 475, 476, 477, 479, 518, 572, 581, 584, 602, 606, 608, 610, 611, 612, 613, 616, 618, 619, 621, 630, 631, 635, 647, 648, 649, 652, 655, 659, 681, 685, 692, 694, 697, 698, 701, 704, 716, 734, 752, 753, 754, 761, 762, 768, 769, 770, 772, 773, 774, 784, 786, 791, 814, 824, 831, 841, 848, 853, 863, 871, 872, 875, 876n17, 895, 896, 898, 901, 910, 912, 922, 925, 930, 935, 939, 942n14, 945, 946, 948, 950, 956, 961, 962, 963, 965, 966, 984, 986, 990, 991, 992, 993
comparative studies   149, 230, 278, 316, 368, 432, 582, 583, 630, 712, 982
complexity   109, 242, 244, 245, 246, 278, 310, 314, 323, 353, 436, 496, 502, 565, 614, 665, 743, 758, 783, 835, 840, 842, 984, 992
Condé, Alpha   949

condensed radicalization of individualization   12, 761, 762, 763, 767, 768, 770, 774, 990
Confucius   112, 159, 160, 161, 163, 365, 385, 673, 877
connected sociologies   24, 26
Connell, Raewyn   1, 22, 23, 40, 189
consciousness   6, 33, 48, 57, 58, 81, 103, 130, 131, 133, 144, 147, 149, 151, 153, 157, 167, 178, 179, 200, 205, 209, 237, 241, 243, 265, 266, 267, 278, 280, 332, 342, 359, 363, 414, 415, 416, 418, 420, 445, 458, 459, 460, 461, 464, 475, 478, 479, 487, 501, 638n18, 658, 692, 737, 757, 825, 826, 841, 849, 850, 851, 852, 853, 854, 855, 856, 860, 861, 872, 874, 972
conservative modernization   754, 755, 756, 757
consumer society   573, 700, 825
consumption   14, 147, 398, 399, 409, 425, 477, 499, 505, 511, 574, 702, 733, 780, 782, 787, 790, 801, 803, 809, 814, 826, 827, 829, 831, 832, 833, 859, 871, 874, 914, 939, 963, 991
contest mobility   561, 562
cosmopolitan   2, 11, 23, 24, 28, 29, 32, 40, 135, 151, 153, 154, 191, 233, 235, 236, 237, 238, 239, 240, 246, 314, 683, 685, 741, 742, 800, 897, 901, 902, 980, 981, 982, 984, 992
cosmopolitan turn   2, 5, 236, 980
cultural tradition   30, 32, 66, 150, 153, 174, 176, 236, 252, 253, 313, 385, 836

danwei system   742, 743, 745, 746
David, Pierre-Marie   939, 940, 945, 951
De Sousa Santos, Boaventura   23, 716
Deboulet, Agnès   10, 154, 597, 598n2, 601, 988
decolonial   23, 25, 737
Deguchi Takeshi   7, 413, 414, 420, 980
democratic sociology   40
democratization   214, 376, 381, 383, 389, 537, 591, 800, 801, 806, 808, 812, 813, 814, 815, 816, 817, 818, 819, 859, 864, 872, 873, 990
dependency   1, 22, 25, 173, 175, 221, 223, 224, 227, 229, 234, 236, 583, 714, 813, 817

INDEX 1001

Détrez, Christine   12, 731, 734, 736, 989
developmental paths   184, 582, 583
developmental state   227, 799, 800, 801, 806, 807, 808, 812, 813, 814, 815, 816, 817, 818, 964
de-Westernization   1, 21, 28, 75, 76, 77, 81, 82, 85, 86, 87, 88, 218, 220, 308, 731, 889
diagnostic   939, 940, 942, 943, 944, 947, 949
Dirlik, Arif   23, 175, 189, 192
disciplinization   48, 75
discrimination   204, 336, 337, 338, 339, 342, 344, 358, 380, 381, 566, 589, 602, 631n7, 634, 638, 639, 681, 704, 711, 735, 757, 761, 842, 846, 863, 864, 865, 867, 868, 871, 894, 895, 896, 899, 903, 912, 935, 963, 983, 986, 988, 989, 993
disqualification   37, 38, 894, 896, 899, 900, 901, 903, 986
diversity   1, 2, 3, 11, 21, 22, 23, 25, 48, 92, 93, 110, 229, 239, 278, 309, 310, 465, 496, 506, 601, 613, 629, 635, 637, 638, 641, 643, 646, 647, 649, 650, 664, 665, 666, 668, 669, 670, 671, 672, 673, 674, 736, 737, 757, 794, 883, 889, 898, 935, 936, 979, 980, 985, 988, 989, 992
divorce   84, 162, 515, 566, 747, 762, 763, 764, 765, 772
Dreyfus Affair   7, 447, 448, 449, 450, 451, 453, 454, 456, 996
dual labor market   532, 533, 536, 539
Dubet, François   14, 840, 842, 844, 990
Durkheim, Émile   29, 31, 32, 33, 48, 69, 87, 129, 149, 162, 165, 166, 167, 179, 203, 204, 219, 220, 233, 241, 358, 367, 457, 458, 459, 461, 466, 499, 841, 846, 853, 876n18, 997

East Asian Sociological Association   26, 413n1
Ebola   939–950
ecological civilization   779, 781, 782, 783, 784, 785
ecological modernization   13, 694, 799, 800, 803, 812, 816, 817, 818, 819, 992
economic sociology   33, 251, 252, 253, 254, 263, 270, 271, 473, 985
education   9, 10, 25, 36, 131, 134, 137, 159, 172, 227, 280, 314, 329, 330, 331, 339, 381, 401, 421, 431, 432, 434, 435, 444, 490, 496, 498, 500, 503, 505, 511, 512, 520, 521, 522, 523, 524, 525, 545–557, 559, 561, 562, 564, 566, 567, 569, 570, 571, 573, 574, 577, 580, 582–592, 612, 621, 668, 682, 720, 733, 744, 757, 773n5, 806, 867, 910, 914, 931, 932, 972, 982, 983
educational attainment   9, 545, 548, 549, 550, 551, 553, 554, 556, 586, 587, 590, 982
educational expansion   9, 500, 545, 554, 556, 586, 587, 982
educational inequality   553, 557, 584, 589, 590, 982
educational opportunities   9, 545, 549, 552, 584, 587, 588, 589, 638, 873
Eisenstadt, Shmuel   23, 219, 235, 737
elite   327, 336, 384, 420, 436, 497, 498, 546, 561, 562, 563, 566, 601, 721, 752, 755, 885, 983
emotion(s)   13, 14, 36, 40, 282, 297, 301, 370, 379, 405, 434, 661, 713, 737, 823–835, 840, 841, 844–847, 848, 849, 850, 855, 856, 859–864, 874n12, 875, 876, 877, 878, 893, 895, 902, 903, 986, 990, 991
emotional habitus   862, 863, 864, 867
emotional regime   13, 14, 823, 824, 825, 826, 827, 831, 832, 835, 836, 991
empire   1, 21, 22, 24, 86, 157, 201, 207, 208, 210, 214, 237, 456, 501, 633, 646, 995n1
employment   9, 25, 176, 277, 279, 410, 493, 502, 503, 513, 523, 531, 532, 533, 534, 535, 536, 537, 538, 539, 540, 555, 557, 571, 572, 574, 576, 577, 598, 622, 634, 638, 639, 666, 679, 680, 681, 722, 743, 745, 752, 753, 754, 756, 783, 860, 873, 875, 896, 899, 900, 901, 902, 963, 968, 972, 983, 985, 986, 987
employment status   487, 512, 520, 521, 523, 525, 526, 536, 930
endogenous development   135, 341, 342, 343, 885
environmental conflict   782, 783, 815, 816
environmental disruption   204, 206, 207
environmental justice   696, 698, 704, 783, 816, 989, 992

environmental sociology   13, 691, 692, 694, 695, 697, 705, 706, 782, 783, 784, 785, 812, 815, 817, 819, 989, 991, 992
epidemic   15, 282, 925, 935, 937, 939, 940, 941, 943, 944, 945, 947, 948, 949, 950, 958, 962, 993
epistemic autonomy   3, 6, 21, 26, 27, 29, 30, 31, 32, 35, 664, 674, 980, 981
epistemic injustice   1, 11, 23, 40, 153, 664, 674
ethnic identification   39, 633, 641, 643, 644, 645, 649, 661
ethnicity   11, 38, 39, 132, 178, 204, 205, 380, 629, 630, 631, 632, 633, 634, 635, 636, 637, 638, 641, 642, 643, 644, 645, 646, 647, 649, 650, 660, 661, 686, 863, 870, 871, 923, 982, 983, 984
Eurocentric   1, 12, 21, 22, 23, 33, 218, 220, 310, 737, 790, 888
Eurocentrism   1, 33, 306, 308, 314
European sociology   25, 30, 34, 37, 38, 93, 188, 856, 893, 983
eventalization   359–369

familism   12, 375, 741, 742, 744, 745, 748, 749
family   12, 25, 36, 56, 57, 66, 68, 82, 111, 132, 137, 150, 158, 164, 165, 252, 312, 326, 327, 335, 337, 342, 352, 357, 363, 365, 379, 384, 388, 394, 417, 419, 429, 432, 433, 434, 438, 439, 440, 441, 442, 443, 444, 448, 451, 452, 456, 477, 487, 488, 489, 490, 502, 510, 511, 512, 514, 516, 520, 521, 522, 523, 525, 526, 534, 535, 538, 549, 551, 554, 563, 564, 565, 577, 586, 587, 588, 589, 590, 598, 612, 614, 633, 636, 645, 666, 696, 701, 715, 733, 741, 742, 743, 744, 745, 746, 747, 748, 749, 752, 753, 754, 755, 756, 757, 758, 761, 762, 766, 767, 768, 773, 774, 835, 842, 848, 853, 864, 869, 870, 871, 873, 876n17, 894, 908, 910, 915, 930, 982, 989, 990, 995, 997
Fan Ke   11, 39, 632, 633, 641, 983
Fassin, Didier   945, 946
Fei Xiaotong   4, 6, 35, 48, 57, 58, 66, 144, 145, 146, 147, 148, 149, 150, 151, 152, 153, 154, 172, 174, 177, 178, 179, 183, 187, 188, 190, 191, 251, 307, 343, 359, 363, 369, 430, 431, 445, 471, 499, 505, 978
female universalism   7, 399, 405, 406, 407, 408, 409, 410

Feng Shizheng   12, 719, 989
Feng Zhuqin   4, 171, 979
floating population   907, 909, 910, 911, 912, 913, 914, 915, 984
Foucault, Michel   32, 36, 207, 211, 352, 353, 631
Fukushima nuclear accident/disaster   29, 427, 691, 701, 803, 805, 807, 809
Fukuzawa Yukichi   126, 978
functionalism   66, 180, 181, 223, 233, 436, 855

gender dynamics   741, 742, 748, 749, 756, 989, 997
gender inequality   12, 36, 548, 549, 577, 590, 743, 752, 753, 757, 758, 761, 982, 990, 997
Giddens, Anthony   29, 175, 179, 235, 293, 302, 646, 659, 799, 801, 826, 853, 855, 991
Global East   888, 889
global sociology   3, 5, 6, 24, 26, 31, 190, 192, 198, 211, 323, 324, 981, 995, 997
global South   1, 22, 23, 28, 189, 311, 817, 886, 889, 890, 996
globalization   5, 9, 11, 15, 23, 39, 48, 59, 174, 175, 187, 189, 190, 206, 218, 221, 223, 235, 236, 237, 239, 246, 285, 286, 311, 314, 315, 398, 399, 410, 502, 530, 531, 532, 534, 536, 539, 540, 584, 620, 635, 638, 641, 657, 661, 697, 741, 745, 749, 781, 786, 800, 825, 855, 886, 888, 890, 893, 895, 897, 901, 903, 904, 921, 928, 979, 982, 983, 984, 986, 987, 988
glocalization   398, 399, 401, 408, 410, 979
governance   10, 55, 57, 178, 186n4, 258, 260, 261, 264, 277, 285, 312, 315, 316, 318, 320, 321, 352, 353, 364, 367, 374, 381, 383, 391, 429, 605, 606, 609, 610, 611, 613, 614, 616, 618, 619, 620, 623, 698, 781, 782, 783, 784, 788, 792, 793, 818, 889, 891, 947, 949, 957, 960, 973, 988, 993
Grande, Edgar   2, 23, 741, 801
Granovetter, Mark   255, 256, 985
green growth   812, 815, 817, 818, 819
guanxi   35, 36, 186n4, 252, 255, 257, 894, 895, 985, 991

Habermas, Jürgen   175, 237, 314, 315, 320, 323, 377, 379, 413, 414, 415, 416, 426, 850, 851, 875, 980

INDEX   1003

habitus   14, 655, 715, 841, 844, 862, 863, 864, 867, 873*n*10, 990, 991
Han Sang-Jin   5, 28, 29, 306, 979
Hanafi, Sari   1, 24, 995, 997
Hasegawa Koichi   11, 691, 989
He Rong   7, 33, 464, 466*n*2, 980
hedonism   120, 829, 831
hegemonic modernity   6, 306, 309, 310, 313, 314, 315, 320, 323, 324, 979
hibakusha   6, 292, 294, 295, 296, 297, 301, 302
Hiroshima   6, 201, 293, 294, 295, 296, 297, 298, 299, 300, 301, 980
Hochschild, Arlie   39, 40, 284, 762, 824, 827, 828
Holism   504
Honda Yuki   535, 575
Hong Deokhwa   13, 812, 993
Hong Yanbi   15, 921, 993
Hosoda Miwako   15, 928, 935, 993
Hsin-Huang, Michael Hsiao   22, 173
Hui Muslims   641, 648, 652, 656
hybridization   4, 5, 28, 29, 30, 32, 90, 92, 93, 94, 98, 99, 100, 101, 102, 104, 108, 109, 110, 111, 117, 118, 120, 239, 310, 496, 561, 635, 871, 979, 994, 996

identity   5, 7, 12, 25, 39, 40, 92, 110, 153, 164, 175, 179, 192, 221, 222, 224, 225, 226, 229, 238, 240, 275, 278, 307, 330, 377, 379, 386, 387, 409, 413, 415, 418, 422, 426, 434, 467, 475, 476, 493, 629, 631, 632, 635, 636, 637, 638, 643, 644, 647, 648, 649, 650, 654, 685, 712, 713, 716, 732, 831, 832, 843, 844, 845, 846, 853, 854, 860, 891, 894, 895, 899, 900, 909, 911, 912, 913, 914, 980, 982, 983, 986, 996
ideological conflict   859, 865, 867, 878
Illouz, Eva   39, 40, 902, 904
immigrant(s)   15, 330, 331, 565, 599, 602, 629, 631, 633, 634, 635, 637*n*18, 638*n*18, 665, 666, 667, 669, 671, 672, 673, 674, 692, 893, 894, 896, 897, 898, 899, 900, 901, 907, 911, 945
immigration   36, 38, 602, 632, 634, 635, 636, 637, 638, 664, 665, 666, 669, 671, 672, 673, 674, 895, 911, 984
imperialism   128, 134, 215, 210, 221, 224, 237, 306, 311, 716, 859, 865, 884, 979

inclusion   637, 645, 818, 911, 929, 936
income   9, 25, 228, 257, 278, 294, 391, 441, 488, 489, 490, 491, 496, 497, 499, 501, 502, 510–527, 530, 531, 533, 534, 535, 536, 637, 538, 552, 553, 554, 556, 589, 590, 622, 634, 696, 754, 761, 783, 899, 908, 912, 930, 935, 948, 949, 963, 970, 987
indigenization   5, 26, 27, 28, 32, 58, 65, 66, 67, 68, 69, 70, 71, 72, 74, 75, 77, 88, 175, 220, 226, 307, 308, 580, 792, 979
individual   7, 10, 12, 14, 32, 33, 35, 39, 40, 55, 56, 78, 79, 80, 81, 93, 94, 105, 111, 112, 113, 114, 115, 124*n*1, 125, 126, 133, 136, 137, 149, 150, 162, 163, 167, 199, 235, 240, 243, 244, 245, 260, 295, 296, 312, 313, 322, 335, 349, 355, 356, 366, 367, 369, 374, 378, 379, 384, 386, 388, 390, 391, 392, 393, 394, 415, 416, 418, 426, 432, 434, 436, 455, 456, 457, 458, 459, 460, 461, 462, 490, 499, 500, 505, 506, 510, 511, 512, 514, 515, 521, 522, 523, 524, 525, 526, 554, 556, 557, 559, 562, 573, 576, 587, 588, 591, 605, 609, 612, 613, 614, 617, 636, 637, 683, 699, 711, 713, 715, 735, 742, 743, 745, 756, 757, 762, 763, 769, 793, 815, 824, 825, 830, 833, 840, 841, 842, 843, 844, 846, 848, 849, 850, 852, 853, 855, 862, 866, 869, 870, 871, 872, 873, 874, 893, 894, 895, 901, 902, 903, 904, 911, 912, 915, 921, 922, 923, 978, 981, 984, 988, 991, 993, 994, 996
individualism   4, 54, 91, 104, 105, 110, 112, 113, 117, 118, 175, 176, 374, 377, 378, 384, 387, 388, 434, 495, 504, 506, 610, 757, 840, 842, 843, 869, 870, 872, 995, 996
individuation   15, 39, 433, 853, 854, 893, 895, 903, 986, 990, 991
industrial pollution   6, 619, 691, 695, 699
industrialization   13, 191, 228, 234, 251, 262, 263, 265, 268, 270, 277, 335, 344, 376, 381, 391, 587, 619, 620, 761*n*1, 779, 780, 781, 784, 799, 800, 801, 803, 806, 807, 813, 827, 829, 854, 859, 864, 868, 871, 872, 873, 883, 885, 887, 907, 963, 970, 987, 992
inequalities   14, 15, 29, 36, 37, 38, 189, 312, 392, 495, 496, 503, 540, 552, 562, 584, 589, 601, 682, 731, 733, 735, 749, 842,

inequalities (cont.)
    844, 845, 897, 898, 899, 901, 947, 950,
    966, 982, 983, 985, 986, 987, 989, 990,
    991, 992, 993
integration   15, 49, 51, 57, 95, 101, 151, 163, 164,
    173, 209, 234, 239, 270, 352, 359, 366,
    369, 380, 386, 499, 500, 553, 563, 598,
    599, 611, 630, 631, 635, 636, 638, 648,
    743, 842, 844, 846, 895, 896, 897, 898,
    899, 907, 909, 910, 911, 912, 914, 984
interactions   11, 39, 108, 167, 233, 242, 243,
    245, 362, 379, 416, 444, 560, 612, 632,
    636, 641, 642, 660, 726, 733, 830, 845,
    862, 893, 894, 895, 898, 941, 983, 984,
    991
interconnectedness   24, 95, 104, 106, 641
intergenerational difference   909, 912, 915
intermediate intellectual   167, 169
International Health Emergency   937
interpersonal relationships   14, 35, 241, 257,
    356, 357, 894
Inui Akio   573

Jang Wonho   7, 398, 979
Japanese sociology   4, 14, 29, 35, 124, 125, 128,
    129, 130, 132, 134, 135, 136, 137, 198, 414,
    420n5, 853, 854, 855, 856, 978, 980, 986,
    990, 991
Ji Yingchun   12, 36, 737, 741, 989, 997
Jia Chao   36
Jobin, Paul   13, 22, 786, 788, 790, 792, 992
Jung, Hwa Yol   28

Kampo   928, 931, 932
Keck, Frederic   940, 945
Kikutani Kazuhiro   7, 447, 981, 996
Kim Byoung-Kwan   10, 580, 982
Kim Mun Cho   5, 233, 980
Kim Seung Kuk   4, 22, 28, 90, 978, 980, 995,
    996
Kim Wang-Bae   14, 859, 991
Kobunjigaku   157, 160
Kogaku   157, 158, 163
Kokugaku   4, 158
Koleva Svetla   23, 25
Korean sociology   5, 10, 34, 40, 220, 221, 222,
    223, 224, 225, 227, 229, 580, 592, 982,
    983, 990, 991

Korean Wave (Hallyu)   7, 398, 399, 401, 405,
    406, 407, 408, 409, 410, 873, 874, 979
Ku Dowan   13, 812, 993
Kyosei   15, 929, 935, 936, 993

labor group   5, 265, 266, 267, 274, 275, 280,
    281, 282, 285, 286, 873
labor markets   9, 36, 228, 256, 265, 278, 502,
    503, 511, 513, 514, 522, 526, 532, 533, 534,
    535, 536, 538, 539, 540, 545, 554, 555,
    556, 573, 576, 577, 578, 588, 589, 590,
    591, 669, 670, 677, 679, 681, 682, 738,
    742, 743, 745, 752, 753, 754, 870, 899,
    900, 901, 902, 982, 986
labor sociology   5, 264, 266, 267, 274, 275,
    276, 277, 278, 280, 281, 283, 284, 285,
    286, 287, 985, 995
Lachenal, Guillaume   940, 945
Lakoff, George   940, 949
Lash, Scott   29, 235, 799, 855
Latin America   1, 25, 219, 234, 320, 322, 324,
    406, 408, 670, 710, 715, 716, 717, 847,
    852, 887, 888, 996
Le Dévédec, Nicolas   940, 945
Le Marcis, Frédéric   15, 937, 940, 941, 942,
    946, 949, 993
Li Chunling   8, 34, 37, 487, 895, 896, 987, 996
Li Fangying   32, 33
Li Lulu   34, 66
Li Peilin   3, 27, 48, 66, 190, 253, 254, 255, 275,
    893, 895, 896, 901, 978, 985, 995
Li Youmei   4, 143, 979
Liang Qichao   49, 50, 52, 54, 55, 56, 58, 68,
    978
liberalism   315, 756, 757, 758, 793
life environmentalism   29, 691, 692, 697
life-composition movement   327, 329, 332
Lim Hyun-Chin   5, 218, 979
Liu Neng   28
local institution   530, 532, 536, 538, 539, 540
local knowledge   5, 6, 8, 26, 40, 54, 153, 180,
    191, 363, 365, 593, 697, 986
localized knowledge   4, 143, 148, 154, 978
Lu Wen   15, 907, 984

Machimura Takashi   14, 883, 889, 980, 984
Malinowski Bronisław   66, 144, 145, 146, 150,
    430, 431, 499

INDEX 1005

market   6, 9, 12, 137, 175, 200, 205, 206, 210,
227, 228, 234, 252, 253, 254, 255, 256,
257, 258, 260, 261, 262, 263, 265, 266,
267, 271, 277, 278, 279, 315, 374, 376, 378,
383, 384, 388, 389, 390, 393, 407, 414,
426, 438, 440, 488, 489, 490, 491, 502,
503, 511,513, 514, 515, 518, 521, 522, 526,
532, 533, 534, 535, 536, 538, 539, 540,
545, 552, 554, 555, 556, 557, 573, 576,
577, 578, 588, 589, 590, 591, 605, 607,
608, 609, 610, 611, 613, 614, 616, 620,
653, 657, 669, 670, 677, 679, 681, 682,
697, 738, 741, 742, 745, 752, 753, 754, 755,
756, 758, 761, 793, 799, 800, 802, 805,
808, 809, 813, 814, 817, 818, 831, 842, 844,
845, 868, 870, 900, 907, 909, 923, 957,
963, 964, 970, 971, 982, 988
marketization   16, 184, 262, 265, 267, 270,
278, 279, 487, 490, 742, 743, 745, 827,
957, 964, 968, 993
marriage   25, 164, 165, 312, 337, 433, 434, 518,
538, 545, 553, 554, 555, 557, 589, 666,
671, 672, 744, 746, 748, 752, 754, 755, 762,
763, 764, 765, 768n3, 772, 860
Maruyama, Masao   124n1, 158, 161, 163, 854
Marx, Karl   29, 31, 32, 69, 191, 199, 204, 219,
220, 241, 264, 327, 414, 415, 436, 473,
823, 828, 854
Mathieu, Lilian   11, 710, 714, 988
McDonaldization   828, 830, 834
medicalization   928, 972, 993
memory   38, 62, 63, 168, 186, 295, 296, 297,
301, 302, 353, 449, 631, 632, 636, 637,
642, 866, 867, 875, 939, 945, 948, 993
merit   500, 505, 563, 565, 580
methodology   8, 10, 26, 30, 31, 32, 75, 111, 146,
148, 175, 180, 188, 225, 226, 257, 309, 310,
333, 334, 335, 349, 467, 469, 473, 480,
583, 585, 592, 823, 940
middle class   8, 9, 25, 37, 38, 93, 178, 358,
491, 492, 493, 495, 496, 497, 498, 499,
500, 501, 502, 503, 504, 505, 506, 513,
518, 524, 525, 531, 532, 601, 713, 716, 734,
758, 987
Mignolo, Walter   25
migrant workers   11, 178, 186n4, 255, 266,
267, 274, 275, 276, 277, 278, 279, 280,
281, 285, 286, 677, 678, 679, 680, 681,
682, 683, 684, 685, 860, 896, 908, 910,
911, 912, 913, 915, 984, 985, 986
migration   11, 14, 15, 178, 186, 238, 314, 439,
636, 640, 650, 664, 667, 672, 673, 674,
678, 681, 712, 744, 860, 883, 884, 893,
894, 895, 901, 903, 904, 906, 907, 908,
982, 984, 985, 995
Minamata disease   6, 327, 340, 341, 342, 343,
422n8, 691, 696
mind   2, 54, 98, 101, 102, 104, 105, 106, 108,
111, 112, 113, 114, 116, 118, 120, 130, 154, 180,
183, 191, 227, 229, 237, 241, 284, 286, 356,
373, 376, 387, 419, 420, 421, 423, 460,
599, 660, 722, 748, 792, 794, 850, 861,
889, 989
minjung   863
Mita Munesuke   29, 851
Miyadai Shinji   573, 574
mobilization(s)   11, 36, 37, 263, 267, 358, 362,
382, 442, 588, 609, 612, 617, 618, 710, 711,
712, 713, 714, 716, 717, 725, 756, 791, 792,
923, 945, 988, 989, 993
mobility   11, 14, 34, 37, 40, 209, 238, 255, 257,
275, 282, 352, 432, 480, 501, 504, 505,
510, 511, 520, 525, 530, 531, 532, 539,
540, 561, 562, 588, 632, 635, 641, 661,
682, 683, 685, 738, 753, 807, 833, 834,
873, 890, 894, 895, 896, 897, 898, 899,
900, 907, 908, 909, 911, 912, 915, 928,
984, 985
mobility channels   561
modernity   6, 12, 13, 23, 25, 28, 29, 36, 39, 40,
42, 90, 91, 93, 121, 136, 137, 176, 184, 185,
191, 219, 221, 224, 226, 227, 233, 235, 238,
241, 245, 293, 301, 302, 306, 309, 310, 311,
312, 313, 314, 315, 322, 323, 375, 400, 478,
479, 603, 615, 631, 741, 742, 745, 746, 747,
748, 749, 799, 800, 801, 808, 809, 829,
840, 841, 842, 847, 902, 903, 979, 989,
994, 997
modernization   5, 13, 25, 29, 55, 57, 96, 124,
127, 134, 135, 136, 137, 147, 162, 178, 179,
180, 184, 185, 186, 191, 219, 223, 224, 234,
235, 246, 254, 258, 268, 292, 293, 329,
333, 335, 336, 338, 375, 376, 400, 430,
433, 435, 445, 456, 469, 470, 478, 580,
586, 737, 741, 742, 743, 744, 745, 749, 755,
756, 758, 780, 789, 799, 800, 801, 806,

modernization (cont.)
    807, 808, 812, 817, 819, 825, 840, 848,
    854, 883, 884, 885, 901, 907, 932, 978,
    980, 989, 990, 991, 992
Moore Jr., Barrington   219, 755
moral sentiment   875, 876, 878
mosaic familialism   35, 36
Motoori Norinaga   29

Nagasaki   6, 201, 293, 294, 295, 296, 931
natural disasters   387, 392, 701, 923, 924
Nederveen Pieterse, Jan   28, 108n15, 239
Negri, Antonio   28, 207, 212, 244
neighborhood associations   618, 619, 621, 623
Nemoto Kumiko   12, 752, 990
neoliberalism   286, 532, 622, 741, 813, 875, 889, 921, 922, 957, 963, 964, 968, 973, 993
network(s)   22, 30, 57, 94, 104, 150, 167, 169, 202, 238, 243, 245, 246, 256, 257, 260, 283, 296, 314, 364, 368, 391, 392, 437, 461, 601, 620, 635, 658, 681, 704, 791, 813, 814, 833, 845, 894, 895, 910, 925, 939, 960, 985, 986
new social movements   12, 228, 340, 713, 716, 813, 988
Nomiya Daishiro   6, 29, 292, 980
non-profit organization   616, 618, 621, 622, 623, 784
non-regular worker   9, 533, 534, 535, 536, 537, 538, 539, 540, 574, 987

occupation(s)   131, 132, 221, 222, 275, 282, 312, 330, 339, 341, 375, 487, 488, 490, 510, 511, 512, 513, 514, 520, 521, 522, 523, 524, 526, 533, 537, 550, 551, 566, 618, 712, 714, 757, 758, 827, 828, 834, 932, 972, 979, 987
Ogyu Sorai   29, 157, 158, 160, 161, 163, 164, 167
Okumura Takashi   6, 326, 981
Oneness Logic   90, 91, 92, 93, 94, 95, 96, 97, 98, 99, 101, 102, 105, 107, 109, 111, 112, 113, 114, 115, 116, 117, 118, 119, 120, 309, 310
oneness   92, 93, 94, 95, 96, 98, 99, 100, 101, 102, 103, 104, 105, 106, 107, 108, 109, 110, 111, 112, 113, 114, 116, 117, 118, 119, 980
ontology   76, 98, 99, 103, 108n15, 851
orientalism   28, 211, 220, 385, 736

outbreak   16, 282, 342, 394, 696, 875n14, 928, 939, 941, 942, 944, 946, 947, 949, 956, 957, 958, 959, 960, 961, 962, 964, 967

pandemic   6, 12, 15, 16, 40, 306, 313, 314, 315, 316, 318, 320, 322, 323, 324, 374, 375, 381, 387, 392, 393, 394, 504, 601, 761, 762, 768, 769, 773n6, 774, 788, 890, 891, 923, 924, 929, 935, 937, 938, 940, 941, 942, 943, 944, 945, 946, 947, 948, 949, 950, 956, 957, 960, 961, 962, 963, 964, 965, 966, 967, 968, 972, 973, 988, 990, 993
participation   7, 283, 293, 294, 340, 374, 378, 379, 380, 381, 390, 394, 406, 409, 417, 465, 503, 504, 552, 556, 557, 562, 563, 602, 610, 611, 612, 616, 619, 620, 621, 623, 639, 683, 694, 742, 745, 783, 784, 807, 814, 816, 818, 832, 875, 915, 946, 958, 960, 966, 988, 992
particularism   179, 180, 181, 182, 233, 334
path dependency   583, 813, 817
Peeters Grietens, Koen   940n3, 950
periphery   11, 22, 24, 29, 143, 153, 189, 223, 234, 268, 311, 400, 534, 536, 538, 539, 540, 580, 599, 602, 664, 704, 884, 888
peri-urbanization   913, 914
phenomenology   66, 350, 359, 360, 361, 414, 851, 855
plurality   2, 3, 21, 23, 24, 25, 32, 243, 673, 897, 898, 981, 986
political opportunity   712, 818, 988
politicization   719, 724, 792, 794
politics of life   267, 279, 280, 985
pollution   204, 205, 340, 342, 422n8, 691, 692, 694, 696, 698, 699, 700, 701, 702, 703, 704, 705, 780, 781, 782, 783, 784, 791, 806, 813, 814, 818, 887, 921, 989, 992
post-war Japan   132, 295, 301, 302, 303, 537, 575, 754, 856, 980
pragmatism   49, 176, 327, 328, 329, 853, 856
public health   15, 381, 733, 921, 922, 923, 924, 925, 926, 929, 935, 942, 945, 946, 957, 960, 961, 963, 964, 965, 968, 972, 973
public sociology   26, 981
public space   35, 36, 381, 612, 635, 845, 891, 937, 991
publicness   6, 7, 374, 375, 377, 378, 379, 380, 381, 382, 383, 384, 387, 389, 391, 392, 393, 394, 993

qi   76, 100, 101, 102, 104, 105, 106, 107, 109, 118
Qu Jingdong   6, 27, 33, 67, 349, 978, 981
Quijano Anibal   22, 24, 45

recognition   3, 5, 7, 23, 24, 27, 117, 118, 129, 136, 161, 162, 163, 213, 245, 278, 301, 374, 426, 429, 445, 460, 461, 465, 581, 631, 638, 641, 710, 716, 829, 830, 844, 845, 850, 859, 869, 873, 902, 913, 940, 984
religion   33, 38, 39, 57, 86, 92, 96, 97, 118, 119, 209, 210, 228, 337, 358, 365, 390, 467, 473, 474, 480, 602, 635, 643, 653, 654, 657, 666, 668, 669, 672, 715, 735, 835, 848, 855, 860, 868, 930, 983
re-sinicization   75, 76, 77, 81, 82, 85, 87
resources   12, 34, 71, 73, 74, 96, 186, 206, 219, 222, 230, 234, 253, 255, 256, 257, 259, 262, 267, 279, 280, 365, 388, 391, 392, 438, 473, 476, 496, 515, 545, 553, 562, 563, 574, 582, 587, 589, 592, 602, 612, 617, 618, 621, 622, 623, 642, 648, 691, 694, 697, 698, 702, 704, 711, 712, 713, 714, 771, 779, 781, 782, 783, 784, 785, 787, 789, 806, 807, 808, 814, 817, 833, 843, 891, 895, 898, 899, 902, 910, 923, 924, 926, 945, 949, 960, 961, 964, 978, 986
Richards, Paul   944, 948, 950
Ricoeur, Paul   39
risk governance   374, 381, 391, 393, 993
risk society   29, 391, 694, 703, 704, 921, 926, 989
Roulleau-Berger, Laurence   1, 2, 3, 14, 21, 23, 24, 26, 27, 30, 31, 32, 40, 61, 92, 152, 188, 189, 190, 306, 309, 310, 313, 480, 499, 580, 603, 634, 635, 664, 737, 738, 742, 758, 762, 773, 774, 893, 894, 895, 896, 897, 898, 899, 900, 903, 978, 981, 984, 986, 995

Saburo Horikawa   29
sae   228
Saïd, Edward   147, 211, 221, 736, 996
Sassen, Saskia   39, 888, 889
Sakuta Keiichi   29, 420n5, 848, 849
Sato Yoshimichi   9, 530, 986
Satoh Keiichi   13, 799, 807, 992
school-to-work transition   570, 571, 575, 576, 584, 586, 589, 982
Schütz, Alfred   163, 181, 182, 360, 683

segregation   38, 511, 545, 553, 557, 598, 599, 601, 602, 638, 710, 752, 753, 895, 896, 897, 911, 983, 984
Shen Yuan   5, 66, 186n4, 266, 274, 985
Shi Yunqing   10, 39, 605, 988
Shim Young-Hee   12, 761, 990
Shin Kwang-Yeong   9, 28, 510, 987
Shoji Kōkichi   5, 198, 979
Sierra Leone   939, 940, 941, 942, 943, 944, 947, 948, 949, 950
Simmel, Georg   129, 180, 501, 682, 683, 829, 853, 887
singularity   243, 610, 638, 844, 845, 848, 849, 987, 989
sinicization   4, 27, 28, 75, 152, 171, 172, 173, 174, 175, 176, 177, 179, 183, 184, 186, 187, 190, 191
social capital   255, 257, 258, 387, 392, 586, 616, 655, 659, 684, 872, 895, 909, 910, 915, 926, 985, 986
social class   9, 37, 38, 182, 487, 492, 493, 500, 501, 510, 514, 533, 553, 735, 836, 840, 846, 901, 926, 972, 987
social construction   6, 253, 349, 357, 359, 361, 415
social governance   10, 186n4, 605, 606, 609, 610, 611, 614
social inclusion   900, 907, 910, 911, 913, 914, 915
social integration   15, 54, 55, 239, 417, 448, 840, 842, 844, 907, 909, 910, 911, 912, 913, 914, 915, 984
social knowledge   23, 143, 146, 180, 948, 997
social movements   11, 12, 135, 143, 211, 227, 228, 340, 344, 358, 413, 422, 574, 608, 616, 692, 705, 710, 711, 712, 713, 714, 715, 716, 719, 722, 792, 813, 814, 845, 856, 988, 989
social networks   149, 252, 255, 257, 355, 391, 602, 612, 652, 654, 658, 910
social participation   406, 605, 609, 610, 611, 612, 613, 614, 634, 972, 988
social quality   374, 378, 379, 381, 387, 391, 392, 393, 394
social reproduction   34, 38, 563, 584, 743
social science(s)   1, 2, 3, 5, 21, 22, 23, 24, 28, 35, 38, 40, 52, 65, 67, 75, 84, 85, 125, 126, 128, 129, 130, 131, 133, 144, 146, 148, 150, 171, 173, 174, 175, 179, 180, 181, 182, 183,

social science(s) (*cont.*)
184, 185, 186, 187, 189, 190, 192, 198, 199, 218, 219, 220, 221, 222, 226, 227, 229, 233, 234, 245, 246, 253, 333, 344, 349, 351, 370, 430, 464, 466, 469n3, 471, 472, 475, 477, 478, 479, 480, 512, 580, 644n1, 666, 691, 731, 732, 735, 736, 786n1, 787, 846, 854, 861, 876, 886, 932, 978, 980, 981, 984, 992
social stratification   8, 9, 25, 275, 487, 488, 491, 492, 493, 495, 510, 511, 512, 526, 530, 532, 533, 535, 538, 539, 986, 987, 995, 996
social structure   8, 13, 33, 51, 53, 66, 149, 176, 180, 181, 191, 251, 252, 253, 254, 255, 326, 331, 350, 352, 358, 364, 368, 369, 419, 424, 426, 470, 491, 492, 499, 505, 607, 611, 691, 692, 696, 701, 726, 823, 824, 825, 826, 842, 852, 853, 883, 884, 893, 894, 895, 907, 914, 985, 990, 997
social transformation   4, 175, 179, 183, 185, 186, 253, 254, 255, 265, 270, 271, 358, 434, 467, 674, 843, 846, 985
socialization   33, 331, 332, 416, 418, 500, 505, 560, 584, 631, 637, 715, 824, 841, 842, 843, 862, 894, 899, 900, 903
socioeconomic segregation   545, 553, 982, 983
space of social movements   714
space   1, 2, 3, 4, 14, 21, 24, 26, 28, 30, 31, 32, 34, 36, 37, 66, 71, 145, 152, 202, 205, 226, 242, 243, 247, 255, 267, 350, 351, 352, 355, 359, 366, 377, 436, 444, 458, 499, 605, 606, 607, 608, 609, 610, 612, 635, 637, 641, 642, 643, 646, 652, 657, 659, 660, 661, 666, 714, 732, 735, 764, 773, 789, 814, 840, 859, 862, 890, 893, 895, 898, 909, 947, 979, 980, 981, 982, 983
Spencer, Herbert   50, 51, 52, 53, 54, 58, 126, 127, 129, 172, 179, 241, 429, 457, 466n1
Spivak, Gayatri Chakravorty   211, 212, 602, 734
strong tie   256, 257, 406, 889
Sun Benwen   27, 65, 172, 174, 178, 466n1
Sun Feiyu   6, 429, 978
Sunism   91, 99n14, 108, 117, 118, 119, 980
super-diversity   11, 664, 665, 666, 671, 672, 673, 674, 985

surveillance   283, 315, 392, 393, 890, 937, 939, 940, 941n6, 945
Suzuki Kensuke   29
symbolic recovery   165, 166, 168, 169
Szelényi, Iván   175, 184, 980

Taigyaku Affair   7, 447, 450, 451, 453, 454, 996
Takada Yasuma   29, 130–132, 138, 978
Takebe, Tongo   128
Chen Tao   32, 33, 784
Tarumoto Hideki   11, 664, 985
Therborn, Göran   23, 495, 511
time   14, 28, 32, 34, 39, 50, 51, 52, 53, 54, 55, 56, 57, 58, 62, 63, 64, 65, 66, 71, 75, 84, 86, 93, 95, 101, 105, 119, 128, 130, 131, 134, 145, 154, 157, 159, 163, 164, 167, 171, 172, 173, 178, 186, 187, 200, 201, 202, 208, 213, 214, 215, 218, 226, 230, 234, 242, 251, 259, 262, 269, 274, 275, 276, 279, 284, 293, 294, 299, 312, 327, 328, 330, 331, 334, 335, 340, 341, 342, 343, 350, 353, 354, 355, 359, 360, 361, 366, 367, 371, 375, 379, 385, 391, 400, 405, 406, 420, 421, 423, 424, 425, 429, 430, 433, 434, 438, 442, 443, 447, 451, 454, 456, 457, 458, 459, 466, 468, 472, 473, 474, 476, 478, 479, 489, 492, 496, 501, 502, 503, 515, 528, 533, 539, 546, 549, 551, 552, 554, 555, 556, 557, 559, 571, 572, 573, 574, 575, 576, 577, 581, 582, 587, 588, 589, 590, 593, 598, 599, 600, 610, 612, 617, 618, 621, 622, 630, 637, 642, 644, 646, 647, 653, 654, 655, 656, 657, 658, 659, 666, 669, 670, 677, 683, 698, 700, 702, 711, 712, 714, 715, 722, 725, 733, 735, 742, 743, 744, 745, 746, 752, 754, 755, 761, 762, 765, 767, 771, 772, 773, 780, 786, 789, 805, 819, 825, 826, 827, 831, 832, 833, 834, 835, 841, 851, 852, 853, 854, 856, 859, 862, 863, 869, 871, 873, 887, 888, 889, 890, 891, 897, 902, 910, 911, 912, 913, 914, 921, 922, 923, 924, 929, 930, 931, 932, 934, 936, 937, 942, 958, 968, 979, 981, 984
Tiryakian, Edward A.   219
Torigoe Hiroyuki   29, 691, 692, 694, 697, 704

Touraine, Alain   12, 614, 713, 715, 716, 989, 990
trajectory   31, 48, 244, 293, 301, 313, 327, 357, 383, 560, 561, 565, 573, 602, 715, 735, 816, 895, 896, 980, 987
transition   10, 13, 57, 66, 145, 157, 164, 165, 175, 219, 227, 234, 239, 242, 244, 254, 257, 274, 275, 278, 279, 327, 350, 359, 368, 375, 376, 392, 429, 430, 431, 436, 437, 444, 445, 545, 569, 572, 573, 574, 575, 601, 603, 605, 606, 608, 609, 613, 614, 646, 692, 719, 720, 726, 742, 743, 748, 749, 800, 801, 803, 805, 812, 814, 816, 818, 819, 826, 854, 870, 903, 914, 928, 982, 983
transitional society   182, 185, 264, 266, 491, 741, 745, 749
translation(s)   29, 49, 50, 51, 52, 53, 57, 58, 65, 84, 97n8, 124, 125, 126, 127, 128, 143, 152, 157, 169, 220n1, 414, 435, 464, 465, 466, 467, 469, 470, 471, 472, 474n5, 475, 598n2, 639, 644n2, 645, 652, 735, 738, 847, 885
Tsurumi Kazuko   6, 135, 326–344, 856
two contradictory trends   12, 761, 762, 770, 774

underclass   38, 496, 896
universalism   2, 179, 180, 181, 182, 190, 233, 237, 238, 240, 241, 333, 334, 399, 405, 406, 408, 409, 480, 732, 735, 738, 979, 995
upward mobility   500, 561, 588, 600, 757
urban studies   14, 883, 885, 886, 888, 889, 890, 891
urbanization   14, 234, 252, 255, 261, 262, 263, 265, 267, 268, 269, 270, 437, 438, 439, 444, 492, 603, 605, 606, 607, 608, 610, 611, 613, 614, 620, 648, 692, 698, 780, 781, 784, 800, 883, 885, 886, 887, 890, 901, 913, 914, 992
urban–rural gap   9, 549, 557, 983

Van Zanten, Agnès   9, 559, 562, 563, 565, 982

wanderers   6, 326, 327, 333, 338, 339, 340, 341, 342, 343, 344, 682
Wang Chunguang   15, 897, 907, 912, 984
Wang Hejian   32, 33
Wang Jiahui   13, 823, 991
Wang Xiaoyi   13, 779, 992
wealth inequality   9, 487, 489, 490, 492, 493, 510, 511, 512, 515, 516, 517, 518, 522, 524, 525, 526, 527, 987
wealth   2, 9, 21, 54, 176, 210, 477, 487, 488, 489, 490, 491, 492, 493, 496, 497, 500, 503, 504, 505, 510–527, 635, 780, 789, 855, 856, 884, 885, 923, 987, 996
wealthization   487, 489, 490, 491, 492, 493, 996
Weber, Max   7, 31, 32, 33, 69, 180, 182, 203, 204, 219, 220, 223n4, 234, 241, 306, 313, 349, 350, 367, 369, 391, 431, 435, 445, 464–480, 636, 735, 830, 853, 869n7, 979, 997
Wei Jianwen   27
westernization   1, 21, 49, 75, 191, 224, 234, 246, 293, 294, 335
work   2, 3, 6, 11, 12, 14, 34, 38, 39, 40, 50, 52, 53, 61, 63, 80, 101, 144, 145, 160, 169, 172, 174, 177, 178, 184, 188, 191, 192, 237, 252, 265, 268, 274, 275, 276, 277, 279, 280, 281, 282, 283, 285, 286, 293, 303, 304, 307, 327, 332, 335, 337, 339, 343, 350, 351, 354, 355, 363, 383, 384, 387, 413, 416, 417, 424, 425, 430, 431, 437, 439, 440, 442, 444, 454, 457, 471, 475, 476, 477, 478, 479, 480, 490, 492, 499, 502, 510, 511, 513, 514, 518, 524, 526, 528, 529, 536, 538, 564, 570, 571, 572, 573, 574, 575, 576, 577, 584, 586, 589, 591, 602, 611, 623, 629, 631, 633, 634, 636, 639, 646, 649, 650, 660, 666, 669, 670, 677, 678, 680, 681, 682, 684, 685, 696, 704, 707, 713, 719, 720, 731, 732, 733, 734, 735, 737, 742, 743, 744, 745, 746, 747, 751, 752, 753, 754, 756, 757, 758, 762, 763, 764, 766, 767, 805, 814, 826, 827, 828, 829, 831, 832, 833, 834, 844, 849, 854, 867, 870, 874, 883, 885, 888, 890, 893, 894, 899, 900, 901, 902, 903, 907, 908, 910, 911, 912, 913, 925, 926, 930, 940, 947, 949, 960, 962, 964, 965, 966, 967, 969, 970, 972, 973, 982, 983, 984, 985, 986, 987, 993, 995

working class (*cont.*)
working class   25, 38, 57, 93, 264, 265, 266, 270, 283, 491, 492, 493, 500, 501, 502, 504, 518, 636, 637, 638, 710, 758, 896, 899, 900, 901
World Health Organization   930, 937, 944
world society   5, 132, 198, 204, 205, 206, 207, 236, 315, 985
Wu Chun   32
Wu Su   28
Wu Yuxiao   9, 545, 982

Xie Lizhong   3, 28, 32, 61, 188, 306, 307–309, 310, 979
Xie Yu   27, 171, 181, 183, 185, 186, 187, 191
Xunzi   51

Yama Yoshiyuki   4, 29, 157, 978
Yamamoto Hidehiro   10, 616, 988

Yan Fu   49–51, 52–55, 57–58, 68, 143, 152, 171–172, 429, 430, 978
Yanagita Kunio   6, 326–327, 333–339, 341, 344
Yang Dian   5, 251, 985
Yang Yiyin   35, 990
Yazawa Shujiro   4, 14, 29, 92, 124, 848, 978, 979, 991, 995
Yee Jaeyeol   6, 374, 993
Yi, Chin-Chun   24
youth   9, 10, 25, 37, 39, 146, 186n4, 300, 413, 420, 426, 518, 552, 553, 554, 555, 556, 557, 569, 570, 571, 573, 574, 575, 576, 577, 578, 586, 590, 621, 631n7, 711, 872, 896, 900, 982, 983

Zhang Jingting   36
Zhao Yandong   15, 921, 993
Zhou Xiaohong   4, 27, 171, 979
Zola, Émile   447, 449, 450, 451, 453, 454, 456, 457, 461, 463, 996

Printed in the United States
by Baker & Taylor Publisher Services